THE OXFORD HANDBOOK OF

FOOD, POLITICS, AND SOCIETY

THE OXFORD HANDBOOK OF

FOOD, POLITICS, AND SOCIETY

Edited by

RONALD J. HERRING

OXFORD
UNIVERSITY PRESS

OXFORD
UNIVERSITY PRESS

Oxford University Press is a department of the University of Oxford. It furthers the University's objective of excellence in research, scholarship, and education by publishing worldwide.

Oxford New York
Auckland Cape Town Dar es Salaam Hong Kong Karachi
Kuala Lumpur Madrid Melbourne Mexico City Nairobi
New Delhi Shanghai Taipei Toronto

With offices in
Argentina Austria Brazil Chile Czech Republic France Greece
Guatemala Hungary Italy Japan Poland Portugal Singapore
South Korea Switzerland Thailand Turkey Ukraine Vietnam

Published in the United States of America by
Oxford University Press
198 Madison Avenue, New York, NY 10016

The Oxford handbook of food, politics, and society / edited by Ronald J. Herring.
pages cm
Includes bibliographical references and index.
ISBN 978-0-19-539777-2 (hardback : alk. paper)
1. Food supply—Political aspects. 2. Food industry and trade. 3. Agricultural and politics.
I. Herring, Ronald J., 1947- editor of compilation. II. Title: Handbook of food, politics, and society.
HD9000.6.O94 2015
338.1′9—dc23
2014028700

1 3 5 7 9 8 6 4 2
Printed in the United States of America
on acid-free paper

Table of Contents

PART II NORMATIVE KNOWLEDGE: ETHICS, RIGHTS, AND DISTRIBUTIVE JUSTICE

PART III NATURE: FOOD, AGRICULTURE, AND THE ENVIRONMENT

PART IV FOOD VALUES: IDEAS, INTERESTS, AND CULTURE

PART V GLOBAL MEETS LOCAL: CONTESTATIONS, MOVEMENTS, AND EXPERTISE

List of Contributors

Bina Agarwal is Professor of Development Economics and Environment at the University of Manchester.

Kym Anderson is George Gollin Professor of Economics at the University of Adelaide and Professor of Economics at the Australian National University.

Zareen Pervez Bharucha is Senior Research Officer in the Department of Sociology at the University of Essex.

Saturnino M. Borras Jr. is Associate Professor at the International Institute of Social Studies in The Hague in The Netherlands.

Michael Burgess is Assistant Professor of Biological Science at the State University of New York, Plattsburgh.

M. Jahi Chappell is Director of Agroecology and Agriculture Policy at the Institute for Agriculture and Trade Policy, and Visiting Scientist at the School of the Environment at Washington State University.

Bruce M. Chassy is Professor Emeritus of Nutritional Sciences at the University of Illinois.

Emily Clough is a Doctoral Candidate in the Department of Government at Harvard University.

Richard Coe is Principle Scientist of Research Methods at the World Agroforestry Center (ICRAF) at the University of Reading.

Sarah Davidson Evanega is International Professor of Plant Breeding (adjunct) in the Department of Plant Breeding and Genetics, and Senior Associate Director of International Programs at the College of Agriculture and Life Sciences at Cornell University.

Pier Paolo Ficarelli is Knowledge Management Specialist at the International Livestock Research Institute.

Jennifer C. Franco is Coordinator of the Agrarian Justice Program at the Transnational Institute, Netherlands, and Adjunct Professor at China Agricultural University.

Raghav Gaiha is Professor of Public Policy in the Faculty of Management Studies at the University of Delhi, and Department of Urban Studies and Planning at the Massachusetts Institute of Technology.

Ann Grodzins Gold is Thomas J. Watson Professor of Religion and Professor of Anthropology at Syracuse University.

Gregory D. Graff is Associate Professor of Agricultural and Resource Economics at Colorado State University.

John Harriss is Professor in the School for International Studies at Simon Fraser University.

Ronald J. Herring is Professor of Government and International Professor of Agriculture and Rural Development at Cornell University.

Gal Hochman is Associate Professor of Agriculture, Food and Resource Economics at the Rutgers Energy Institute at Rutgers University.

Raghbendra Jha is Professor at the Australia South Asia Research Centre in the Arndt-Corden Department of Economics at the Australian National University.

Josée Johnston is Associate Professor of Sociology at the University of Toronto.

Nidhi Kaicker is Assistant Professor in the Faculty of Management Studies at the University of Delhi.

Michiel Korthals is Professor of Applied Philosophy at the University of Wageningen.

Ashok Kotwal is Professor of Economics at the University of British Columbia.

Vani S. Kulkarni is a Research Associate in the Department of Sociology at Yale University.

Tomas Larsson is a Fellow of St John's College and Lecturer in the Department of Politics and International Studies at the University of Cambridge.

Mark Lynas is a Visiting Fellow in International Programs in the College of Agriculture and Life Sciences at Cornell University.

Norah MacKendrick is Assistant Professor of Sociology at Rutgers University.

Alan McHughen is CE Plant Biotechnologist in the Department of Biological Sciences at the University of California, Riverside.

Purvi Mehta-Bhatt is Asia Head at the International Livestock Research Institute.

Rebecca Nelson is Professor of Plant Pathology, Plant Breeding, and International Agriculture at Cornell University.

Martina Newell-McGloughlin is Director of the UC Systemwide Biotechnology Research and Education Program, International Biotechnology Program, Department of Plant Sciences and Department of Plant Pathology at the University of California, Davis.

Robert L. Paarlberg is Professor of Political Science at Wellesley College.

David Pimentel is Professor Emeritus of Entomology and Ecology and Evolutionary Biology at Cornell University.

Jules Pretty, OBE, is Pro Vice-Chancellor (Sustainability & Resources) and Professor of Science and Engineering at the University of Essex.

Bharat Ramaswami is Professor in the Economics and Planning Unit at the Indian Statistical Institute.

Thomas Reardon is Professor of Agricultural Economics at Michigan State University and Renmin University of China.

David E. Sahn is International Professor of Economics in the Division of Nutritional Sciences and Department of Economics at Cornell University.

Kyoko Sato is Associate Director of the Program in Science, Technology, and Society at Stanford University.

Ian Scoones is Professorial Fellow at the STEPS Center in the Institute of Development Studies at the University of Sussex.

Siddhartha Shome is an engineer and currently a student in Liberal Arts at Stanford University.

Krishna Ravi Srinivas is Associate Fellow of the Research & Information System for Developing Countries.

Alexander J. Stein is a former Research Coordinator at the International Food Policy Research Institute.

Drew Stewart is a graduate of the Department for International Development at the London School of Economics.

Gregory Thaler is a Doctoral Candidate in the Department of Government at Cornell University.

Janice E. Thies is Associate Professor of Soil Biology, Crop and Soil Sciences and International Professor of Soil Ecology at Cornell University.

C. Peter Timmer is the Thomas D. Cabot Professor of Development Studies, Emeritus, at Harvard University.

Norman Uphoff is Professor of Government and International Agriculture and Acting Director of the Cornell Institute of Public Affairs at Cornell University.

Derrill D. Watson II is Assistant Professor in the Department of Accounting, Finance, and Economics at Tarleton State University.

Michael J. Watts is "Class of 1963" Professor of Geography and Development Studies at the University of California, Berkeley.

David Zilberman is the Robinson Chair of Agricultural and Resource Economics at the University of California, Berkeley.

THE OXFORD HANDBOOK OF

FOOD, POLITICS, AND SOCIETY

INTRODUCTION: FOOD, POLITICS, AND SOCIETY

CHAPTER 1

HOW IS FOOD POLITICAL? MARKET, STATE, AND KNOWLEDGE

RONALD J. HERRING

Food, Politics, and Society? The Hubris of a Title

Even in unlimited pages, coverage of the scope of this *Handbook* would be implausible. We focus on intersections of food, politics, and society: the dimensions of food that express both overt political action and deeper structural elements of political economy, in societies of different scale, from villages to an imagined global community. That conceptual narrowing is helpful in exploring intersecting analytical puzzles: Why should food be political? Why is food knowledge contested?

Michael Pollen tells us that society invariably has the right answers to food questions through a mechanism called "culture," which operationally reduces to "mom."

"Culture, when it comes to food, is of course a fancy word for your mom."

Mom knows what one needs to know about food in Pollan's world, whatever the machinations of the scientific-industrial complex built up around official nutritional recommendations from the state.[1] If your mom couldn't pronounce the ingredients, or if *you* can't pronounce the ingredients, whatever claims are made for some food product, it has strayed too far from society's evolutionary judgment of what constitutes "real food." Mom represents condensation of knowledge and norms of tradition.

Pollan's mom is a metaphor for evolutionary wisdom; ideas that persist and become embedded in cultures are selected in the same sense that natural selection works on species: fitness to conditions encountered over time. There is congealed wisdom in culture. The obvious inconvenience is that moms vary, but human physiology is fairly constant. Ethical and normative issues are also important to moms, and they have no easy consensus. Jewish and Muslim moms may agree about eating pigs, but Chinese moms will not. Politics matters as well: there is an activist Moms Against GMOs (http://momsagainstgmos.weebly.com). Modern claims from nutritional science may question all moms' wisdom on animal fat, or what it means to eat *enough* once all micronutrients are taken into account and the consequences of obesity are understood. Not all moms knew of global malnutrition that might or might not make a case for bio-fortification of cereals poor people can afford when pork is not an option. The FAO's publication *Edible Insects* (2013) advocated increased consumption of insects for food and feed security, reviving a tradition of some societies but quite discordant in others. Few moms predicted the challenges of global warming. Where mom's farmers had relied on cultural wisdom to tell them what to plant and when, extreme weather events and unpredictable variation make new demands on knowledge, innovation, and political response. As the knowledge base of food politics changes continually, new fissures deny the unitary notion of "society," exposing divergent interests, ethics, and knowledge claims (IAASTD 2009).

The metaphor of Mom as a stand-in for cultural wisdom does, however, define a critical element in food politics. The persistence of traditional values and valued ways of doing things has strong effects on production and consumption, and thus politics, but it is incomplete. Consider the persistent undernutrition of something like a billion humans on the planet. A global industry has grown up around research and policy analysis aimed at finding the means to right what most—but not all—would consider a self-evident ethical wrong. Those who work to feed the rest of us often cannot feed their own families adequately. That hunger of some people in some distant places constitutes a matter of altruistic concern and global policy is not, however, universally accepted, nor does it automatically evoke support for foreign assistance, agricultural research, or campaigns in global civil society. Nor is it clear which—if any—of these would make matters better. Obligations rest on a contested terrain of normative theory—notions of justice and right action; how to act depends as critically on systems of empirical knowledge—credible information about what is possible, about what will work. These two dimensions of knowledge—normative and empirical—define much of the political action and political contention around food locally and globally.

At the most elemental level, food has for most of our species-history been a game against nature; politics followed from divergent material interests facing scarcity: who gets to eat what, how often, through what means of acquisition or entitlement? The scale of polity has shifted over time, from very local divisions of the village grain pile in India's archetypal *jajmani* system to an imagined international community in the Millennium Development Goals of the United Nations. In the UN's aspirational and global vision, Goal 1 is elimination of poverty and hunger; Target 3 of Goal 1 is to halve by 2015 the proportion of people on the planet who suffer from hunger. That elusive target hovers around one billion people, though estimates of the extent and varieties of malnutrition vary widely.[2] In these grand developmental visions, conceptualizations of both the pile of grain and the array of legitimate claimants have shifted fundamentally.

Simultaneously, the numbers and causes of people asserting political interests in food and agriculture beyond their own grain pile have likewise shifted out and up. Europeans have used a variety of policy and social-movement tactics to influence what Africans can grow and eat (Paarlberg 2008, chap. 4). American diplomats apply pressure to alter European political choices about what not to grow and eat. An international organization of People for the Ethical Treatment of Animals (http://www.peta.org) challenges traditional practices confining and slaughtering animals—and thus livestock as livelihood and meat as market. Trade conflicts over whether or not phyto-safety regulations constitute another form of agricultural protectionism or an expression of democratic sovereignty cross powerful currents of science and culture: if Americans and Chinese can eat transgenic virus-resistant papayas, how can Japanese legally regulate them out of their markets? In theory, the *Codex Alimentarius* represents species-wide knowledge of standards for food safety,[3] which should allow deliberation within the World Trade Organization to set lines between agricultural protectionism and justifiable precaution in regulating novel foods. In practice, there are trade conflicts, ineffectual rulings, and intermittent rejection of WTO rulings. Bans on whale slaughter pit Japan against international political coalitions. Bans on eating companion animals such as horses and dogs, or intelligent animals such as dolphins, raise persistent politics in some places but not others, with consequences for international trade (Goodyear 2013). Shark fin is a valued and traditional food in some cultures, but restaurants are routinely raided for surreptitiously serving it in many jurisdictions. Demands for a ban on cow slaughter have raised intermittently powerful politics in India but not in Pakistan or Texas. Signs on bridges in Europe declare "GMOs Kill." If true (Ho 2000), such a claim would justify, perhaps morally compel, political mobilization to ban GMOs, create GMO-free zones, attack biotech research facilities, and restrict international trade in genetically engineered foods.[4]

Food politics thus depends fundamentally—and increasingly—on ideas, not simply the material interests that have dominated political economy as an approach (Blyth 2002). Conventional food politics was answerable in a context of classical political economy: the dynamic of interests within social systems. Major interests were fairly clear: control of surplus from the land. The landless fought for land that produced food, the landed resisted. Tenants mobilized around securing their interests; landlords mobilized around defending theirs. The hungry demanded food as traditional obligation or political right. Farmers demanded better deals from traders and moneylenders and state intervention to protect their livelihoods (Goodwyn 1991; Stinchcombe 1961). These demands on the state for protection from the market continue today, and have become globalized with international allies with less direct material interests in outcomes. The new world of food politics thus adds distinctly different dimensions. Contention exists not only around the expertise of agricultural and nutritional sciences, but also around what have been called, since the mid-20th century, alternative paths to "development."[5] Not only are distal populations recognizing a political imperative to alleviate hunger in societies our moms probably knew little about, but justifications differ, as do contending development theories advocating proper roles for states and markets.[6]

Michael Pollan adds to his evocation of tradition and culture the less obvious contention that eating itself "is a political act." Embedded in this claim is a link from individual behavior to food systems, in which there are good and bad preferences. Siddhartha Shome in his contribution to this volume uses that claim to motivate a critical look into the theory behind political acts promoted by the "alternative food movement" with which Pollan is associated. This movement is not just about food but about promoting a more sustainable, environmentally friendly, and just socioeconomic order—an alternative to current trajectories. Agreement on these valued outcomes should be easy, but a closer look uncovers deep political cleavages. Shome dissects the fault lines on both the social vision of end states and the means of obtaining them. Alan McHughen's chapter extends the critique of agrarian romanticism to "Mother Nature" itself: The natural, far from being a consensual good, is a world our species has tried to overcome with technology, beginning with agriculture—in the absence of which life would be nasty, brutish, and short. Yet there is perhaps no more powerful trope in the new food politics than "natural."

In Pollan's view of politicized eating, you not only are what you eat, but what you eat influences what others eat; choice has externalities. How this might happen concerns several subsequent chapters of this volume. Eating to reinforce specific values—organic, local, vegan, fair-wage and equal exchange, child-labor-free food, for example—creates market demand that could change the system of food production. Joseé Johnston and Norah MacKendrick entitled their chapter "The Politics of Grocery Shopping: Eating, Voting, and (Possibly) Transforming the Food System." The general phenomenon is called "political consumerism." This alternative politics is attractive when neither political parties nor social movements are available to make credible vehicles for change, but it depends heavily on knowledge. How are we to know that child labor applying pesticides is not promoted by our food choices? Or that our food is safe? In the case of safety, the common assumption is that the state is the appropriate mechanism for certification—though states vary greatly in what is relevant for safety standards and how to enforce them. In value-driven ethical consumerism, labels by non-state actors predominate. Emily Clough documents the considerable difficulty of knowing what reality labels reflect, or who actually benefits from normatively valued claims—it is often not the farmer. Moreover, there is a question of class and knowledge in political consumerism:

> critics view ethical food labeling as an elitist system plagued by problems of transparency, accountability, scalability, and consumer misinformation—ultimately an inadequate substitute for stronger state regulation.

Thus, the dilemma is: states are difficult to move to ethically principled positions, partly because of interests in the status quo and partly because of disagreements about the right thing to do. Livestock farmers prefer that vegans not rule. Markets offer an alternative to the state, via political consumerism, but market power is by no means distributed by any egalitarian or ethical principle. The fundamental political fault line is found here between market and state: which decides what, in production, technology, and distribution related to food? For market fundamentalists, bureaucrats and legislatures have no standing in food choices: the role of states is minimalist. Markets run on preferences, which decide outcomes.

But not all preferences are created equal. Some cross a threshold of intensity such that collective political mobilization to move issues from market and choice to the realm of state and law is successful. There are, for example, standards for "organic" food, standards for which are politically contested. There are laws about animal slaughter that are promoted by some social movements and rejected by others. Ideas that drive mobilization depend on convincing others that some preferences define moral imperatives worthy of political action and state authority (Elster 1993). Such preferences produce politics once a threshold is crossed; success of food politics is constrained by what ideas resonate sufficiently to drive collective action, in conjunction with structural conditions for political intervention in markets. Successful food politics involves making certain preferences binding on society, via state authority; traditional values and ethical principles provide ideational resources for mobilization. It is here that social movements and, increasingly, transnational advocacy networks impinge on food politics.[7]

Roadmap for the Chapter and the Volume:

Questions raised in this brief introduction suggest dimensions of the politics around food. Among the most contentious issues involve answers to three inescapable questions faced by all societies: First, *what* is to be produced? Second, *how* is it to be produced? Third, how is it to be *distributed*? These are normative questions: what ought to be the case? Their resolution is, however, inescapably political.

In the sections that follow, we explore first why these questions are both inevitable and political. No natural order settles matters. Across the answers, dimension by dimension, we find proponents of tradition, market, and state. Resolution typically involves some admixture of mechanisms. For example, we will look to a diagnostic example of the role of the state in nutritional choice: Mexico's attempts to rig consumer markets by state policy to promote national interests. The reason for the Mexican state to intervene in consumer choice was a looming nutritional crisis: deleterious effects of excess consumption of sugared drinks and "junk" food. The example shows how factors common to many dimensions of food politics interact: framing of a public interest, international and domestic mobilization of positions for action, a meditating role for technical expertise, and the centrality of knowledge in determining how actors understand their interests. Discouraging "junk" food in practice showed how market and state are commingled in practice: The mechanism used by the Mexican state to achieve public ends was the market. A second brief example introduces the most intense controversy in food politics at this point in history: the "GMO."

Opposition to biotechnology in agricultural production merged answers to the three questions to create a unique object of food politics: what is being produced, defined by how it is produced, with concerns for how distributive justice will be affected by production. The object is novel, but the strands of contention demonstrate continuity with the new food politics—knowledge intensive and transnational. We mean for this second brief example to illustrate how ideas and knowledge not only can be autonomous sources of politics, as commonly understood, but also can be conditioning factors of material interests: one's interest in biotechnology as consumer is mediated by what science one believes, how one constructs risk, what networks one trusts. Concluding the chapter scales up to the global question of "development" and the North-South divide. Food politics does not disappear with success in the historical struggle with scarcity, but does acquire new dimensions. If anything, new contentions have aroused more interest over time. Victor Magna (1991) began *Communities of Grain*:

> It is ironic that the late twentieth century has seen a renaissance of rural history. The march of industrial society continues to change the institutional fabric of every region on the globe; yet, intellectual interest in rural life has perhaps never been more pronounced.

Much of the reason for this renaissance is food politics. Separated so far from rural roots, modern populations beyond the biological crisis of getting enough to eat seem to crave an understanding of the food that we no longer produce ourselves, as well as a knowledge of the people who do.

The Three Unavoidable Questions:

Introductory texts in economics explain to students that every society must answer certain basic economic questions. This is true because of the inexorable economic problematic: wants are unlimited, but means to satisfy wants are limited. There is scarcity; there will be trade-offs. The questions generated by structured scarcity are unavoidable in any settled social order. These questions are traditionally stated as follows: First, *what* is to be produced—including a subset of *how much*? Second, *how* is it to be produced? Third, how is it to be *distributed*? Understanding the deeply structural bases of food politics requires taking a step back to political economy: We can think of choices around the place of economic decisions in society as meta-political questions.

All societies, of whatever scale, confront these meta-political choices. Answers may be roughly classified as tradition, markets, or regulatory authority—that is, the state. Karl Polanyi provided an influential account based on a rough historical logic of progression across these mechanisms (1944). In Polanyi's framework, the creation of markets for land, labor, and money disrupted traditional societal arrangements in destabilizing ways, producing outcomes that were socially unacceptable. Land and labor become mere commodities subject to market logic rather than traditional rights and restrictions.

> What we call land is an element of nature inextricably interwoven with man's institutions. To isolate it and form a market out of it was perhaps the weirdest of all undertakings of our ancestors. (1944, 178)

This dis-embedding of both land and the labor of people who worked the land from social institutions was the first half of Polanyi's "double movement"—the movement to encompass more and more social interactions in markets. He analyzed the second half of the "double movement" as a natural response of societies under stress as a defensive reaction against market dislocations.

> The protection of man, nature, and productive organization amounted to an interference with markets for labor and land as well as for the medium of exchange... [the] intervention was to rehabilitate the lives of men and their environment, to give them some security of status. (1944, 216)

"Society" defends itself, Polanyi argued, from unacceptable market determinations of life chances by re-embedding outcomes in proper social moorings, hemming in market dynamics according to a logic of preexisting societal values. There can then be a just price for food or for rent on farm land or for work in factories regardless of conditions of supply and demand. Societal responses put limits around market authority. Tradition then does not disappear as a means of determining outcomes; both reasons for and forms of public authority depend, in part, on tradition and their political mobilization. The modern welfare state is built on guarantees of security, brakes on extreme inequality, and de-commodification of that which should not be commoditized—contrary to determinations of unfettered markets.[8] Modern movements for agrarian reform and food security likewise begin with the premise that such market-driven outcomes as hunger and landlessness are unacceptable.[9] One sees a similar tension in diagnosis of the extreme state of hunger: famine. Michael Watts in this volume uses the lens of revisiting the Nigerian famine (1967–1970) to question and critique a common technocratic neo-Malthusian diagnosis:

> famine is a function of imperfect markets which are weak, unintegrated and possibly driven by speculative or hoarding behavior. Collectively these market pathologies drive up food prices beyond the capacity (of some) to buy. The International Food and Policy Research Institute's (IFPRI) synthetic work on African famines is a case in point.... Famine is largely seen in technocratic terms—a function of institutional, organizational and policy failures—which is to say famine is a poverty problem rooted in poor economic performance and failed or weak states.

This market failure diagnosis is contrasted by Watts with an alternative diagnosis rooted in Polanyi's view of traditional mechanisms of the "moral economy"[10]:

> At the same time, local protection systems rooted in the moral economy of the community were rapidly eroding, exposing peasants to the vicissitudes of the market.

These diagnoses of famine come from different knowledge traditions and produce divergent policy logics of what to do. This contingency of ethical reasoning on empirical analysis underlies much contention in food politics: No one advocates for unsustainable agriculture or the ruination of farmers, but prescriptions from that agreement diverge markedly.

If Polanyi is right, movements toward increased market determination of outcomes will produce counter-pressures to reinstate limits on markets; there is a dialectic. In the current era, politics are often framed around opposition to neoliberalism as *zeitgeist*—the retreat of state authority in favor of market hegemony. Demands for "food sovereignty," for example, challenge the power of markets and corporations and privilege instead civil society and "culturally appropriate" norms. This framing of countermarket objectives is promoted by Via Campesina, a transnational advocacy network that aspires—and often claims—to represent a global peasantry.[11] Because of boundary politics over time, all economies represent, and have long represented, some mix of mechanisms for answering economic questions. Markets are never fully hegemonic, cultural influences never fully disappear, and politics intermediates disputed terrain. Dogs will not be marketed as meat in the United States, whatever the market says; the question of beef in India is not so straightforward, but it is still charged politically in a way not true in Argentina. Regulating a market for "organic" produce is a political act rooted in a specific understanding of what constitutes good food and good farming—what makes agriculture sustainable and consumers healthy. Though consumer choices in markets determine success or failure of preference politics, states matter fundamentally. First, standards vary for the making and regulating of markets for "organic." Second, states may be convinced to support initiatives for organic farming materially, both domestically and through foreign aid projects. The global movement for organic agriculture reflects successful cultural mobilization, transnational advocacy, and responsive state authority to reset and regulate markets.[12]

Current food politics is everywhere entangled in prior framings of answers to these fundamental choices: is food treated as simply another commodity to be buffeted by market dynamics?[13] Or as an entitlement guaranteed as a basic right of citizenship?[14] Or as a cultural marker outside the provenance of the state but important to local identities and strategies?[15] Efforts to depoliticize food in favor of technical expertise founder on these societal divisions. So, for example, advocates of suppressing a market for beef in India evoke a cultural tradition of nonviolence, vegetarianism, and special respect for cows; the mechanism is to be a state-enforced ban on cow slaughter, decommodifying cow flesh and removing it from the market. Market forces have moved in the opposite direction. Ironically, India is close to being, or is already, the largest exporter of beef in the world.[16]

What is to be produced?

The physical surface of the planet is to some extent fungible, though transitions have costs. In the war between the trees and the grasses, humans have intervened decisively on the side of the grasses. Grasses, much modified by centuries of selection and breeding, are winning; the trees are losing out. In recent decades, societies have recognized that there are trade-offs in this choice. Recognition came late on the species learning curve: roughly the 1970s. The discovery of ecology—the interrelationship of all biophysical processes—as a science undermined the notion that either tradition or markets could be sole determinants of land and water use. Nature had a claim; in assessing that claim, both culture and science had political standing (Herring 2007d). A few decades after the global cognitive investment in ecology as science and sustainability as goal, climate change unsettled much of the technical and political wisdom around agriculture and its environment. Emissions of paddy fields and livestock turned out to matter, along with the burning of forests to enhance fertility, tractor fuel consumption, and long-distance transport of foodstuffs.[17] Not only are ecological services critical for robust agriculture, but also nature itself provides great variety and quantities of "wild foods," as Pretty and Bharucha document in this volume. Destruction of natural systems to grow more food destroys opportunities to gather existing food. Societies simultaneously recognized that it mattered in ways previously unrecognized whether answers to these questions were left to the market, to tradition, or to authority (Blaikie and Brookfield 1987; Shapiro 2001). Maximization of commercial production per unit of land yields one outcome, preservationist values written into law another, and traditional swidden cultivation another. Yet interdependencies are still not fully understood. Derrill Watson illustrates in his chapter of this volume the theoretical possibilities of "win-win" strategies of agricultural intensification without environmental damage, but future ecological challenges are difficult to anticipate.

Land-extensive, water-absorptive, energy-intensive technologies are increasingly challenged as unsustainable in the light of new understandings of species-interests, as mediated by science (The Royal Society 2009). Achieving sustainable balances in production and conservation raises the stakes in choosing mechanisms. It is clear that markets rarely accord sufficient value to either conservation or preservation; eco-system services are posited but difficult to measure or pay for. Use of the state as alternative mechanism to protect ecological services of natural systems foundered on the absence of a global Leviathan, on the one hand, and divergent interests of nation states, on the other (Herring 2002). Moreover, political coordination presupposed consensual knowledge, but political divisions within and between nations have often rendered ecological science impotent. Even if public goods in ecologies were politically obtainable, disagreements emerged on what they are and how to get there (Lomborg 2001; Specter 2009).

Though markets and states have demonstrated obvious limitations, tradition may be an unreliable mechanism as well, however popular a simpler agriculture remains in modern yearnings. Livestock provide a poignant example. The raising of animals has long been an integral part of agriculture and a prominent source of food, currently contributing about 40 percent of the global value of agricultural output. Livestock support the livelihoods and food security of almost a billion people, especially in poorer countries.[18] Yet a contemporary global debate now challenges these traditional patterns on multiple dimensions: the extravagant inefficiency of feeding grain to animals when people are malnourished; the ethical implications of confining animals fed only for slaughter; over-and undernutrition aggravated by rising meat consumption; contributions to greenhouse gases and thus global warming; opportunity costs in land that could be used for other purposes; externalities of animal wastes; environmental damage; and zoonotic diseases originating in farmed animals. Much of this critique emanates from richer countries, where subsistence problems have been solved and populations have moved up the Maslovian hierarchy of needs. Ethical preferences of relatively rich people—those of animal rights activists, for example—have implications for relatively poor people, both in markets and in politics. But more than ethical preferences are at stake: Material interests of the species depend on the science of global warming. If the livestock effect is as large as some critics claim, the material interests—whatever their ethical preferences—of both rich and poor human beings are affected by livestock choices driven both by food markets and cultural traditions.

What is to be produced entails an answer to how *much* is to be produced. Conversion of lands to the plow must at some point reach limits. Where are the limits? Paul Roberts wrote *The End of Food* in 2008 as an exploration of vulnerabilities around these limits at the level of a global food system; his conclusions sketch elements of doomsday scenarios. Will there be enough food to go around? Any answer immediately raises questions of distribution. This is the resilient Reverend Malthus: The race between production and production per capita as population increases exponentially.[19] Conclusions vary by ideology. Biotechnology firms argue that genetic engineering is necessary to "feed the world." Opponents counter on grounds of distribution: There is enough to go around, but it is unfairly distributed. The linkage is logically tight: How much needs to be produced surely depends on how it is distributed. Debates around distributive justice and technology then interact with political feasibility. Turning diets of the global rich from meat to grain and implementing redistribution across and within countries seem implausible; mechanisms are hard to conjure. "*How is it to be produced*" then energizes debates around choices of technology. Among the possible paths forward, which ones might be sustainable and more productive with fewest externalities? What path offers the best prospects? One path is "more of the same": could productivity increases in low-income country agricultures to levels equal to those of the Netherlands or Japan succeed with conventional technology? Or is the unsustainability of conventional approaches sufficient cause to concentrate research and incentives on agroecology?[20] Are agroecological approaches incompatible with, or complementary to, those of genetic engineering?[21] Given ecological imperatives, and the underlying crisis of extensive and crippling malnutrition, how do societies—of whatever scale—answer questions of *how* food is to be produced?

How is it to be produced?

How food is produced extends beyond narrow questions of technology. Contention around production techniques engages both political economy (who gets what and how? whose ox is gored?) and cultural framings of food—its symbolic place in society, what it represents, the value of meaningful landscapes of agriculture (McKibben 2008). Deep disputes exist as well over implications for the most vulnerable rural people engaged in agriculture: how do technologies affect income distribution and security?

The so-called Green Revolution of the 1960s generated fault lines across technologies that reverberate with the politics of the Gene Revolution decades later. Plant breeding for nitrogen response—widely called the Green Revolution by critics and supporters alike—required complementary inputs and made great demands on fresh water; it was variously constructed as necessary to feed the world or as an assault on the world's peasantry.[22] The answer for "*what is to be produced*" was predominately and urgently "more"; the mechanism was plant breeding for improved yields. International science and financial flows followed the path of plant breeding for increased global production, largely in international public-sector institutions. The political imperative for governments was clear: Regimes that cannot guarantee food supplies have historically proved ephemeral. One reading of new technologies for agriculture held that the Green Revolution would aggravate rural inequality; the fear that "the Green Revolution would turn red" was expressed by politicians and academics alike. The Green Revolution built on the best-endowed areas and first appealed to the best-endowed farmers. Moreover, environmental externalities from synthetic-chemical intensive agriculture were potentially harmful to the rural poor—eutrophication of village ponds meant unsafe drinking water and fewer fish to eat, for example. More fundamentally, critics charged that the new technology packages presaged the demise of peasant society, its cultural moorings and egalitarian ethos. These ideas, whether or not true, figured prominently in the building of political coalitions critical of new agricultural technology at local, national, and global sites. Alternatives varied in characterization, but largely they focused on agroecological approaches.[23]

In a fascinating replay of history, the Gene Revolution reproduces the cleavages and dynamics of the Green Revolution. Gordon Conway as president of the Rockefeller Foundation advocated a "doubly-green revolution" to avoid the environmental externalities of the Green Revolution while confronting new and urgent production imperatives (Conway 1998). This revolution would utilize biotechnology alongside improved agroecological knowledge and green practices. Africa became the reference point; bypassed by the Green Revolution, widespread poverty and poor agricultural performance in the continent seemed locked in a self-reinforcing spiral of low production leading to low investment leading to low production. Conway's vision suggested walking on two legs—agroecological practices and improvement of plant genetics. Opposition to biotechnology on a global scale—most effective in Africa—posed these two options not as complementary but as oppositional: One had to choose the agroecological path or the transgenic.[24] Transnational advocacy networks formed around a perception that "technological fixes" will not work; they will enrich only multinational firms and international consultants, with significant risks to the environment and the poor. In response, a "biotechnology for the poor" literature and policy stance emerged, with a sense of crisis and urgency similar to that of advocates of the Green Revolution. Although this position gained considerable acceptance in international organizations dealing with food, agriculture, and development in the early 2000s, global critics considered the juxtaposition ludicrous: by its very nature, biotechnology could be neither pro-poor nor environmentally friendly (Herring 2007a; Herring 2007c; Scoones 2002).

Genetic engineering thus teeters politically between framing as a powerful new instrument in the "toolkit" for responding to agricultural and nutritional challenges, on the one hand, to an eminent and unnecessary threat, on the other (McHughen 2000). The GMO was born. Mobilization of resistance to genetic engineering in agriculture turned state promotion of biotechnology in Europe into a moratorium on GMOs in the late 1990s (Tait 2001; Tiberghien 2007). Global mobilization produced the Cartagena Protocol on Biosafety under the framework Convention on Biological Diversity (CDB). This global soft law became important in the national regulation of "living modified organisms" in trade; in train, "bio-safety" regimes came to consume resources in both rich and poor nations, but they resolved few conflicts. Instead, new political conflicts arose over authoritative knowledge. Whose expertise counts? How is civil society represented in councils dominated by scientists? Are corporate-generated data trustworthy? How long is long enough to see if allergenicity results from novel proteins that North Americans consume readily but Europeans and Japanese shun? To borrow Donald Rumsfeld's awkward phraseology, does the absence of evidence of hazard constitute evidence of absence?

The United States and the European Union (EU) structured food markets after the Gene Revolution in different ways: either transgenic plants produce foods that are backed by science demonstrating "substantial equivalence"—and thus absence of additional risk—or evidence of safety is insufficient under logics of the "precautionary principle" to allow planting or consumption of the same plants. From the EU political position endorsing the precautionary principle, global segregation of food tradables followed logically, along with "traceability" requirements literally "from farm to fork," accompanied by labeling and separate regulatory treatment.[25] EU science is the same as American science, but the regulatory outcomes represent varying political organization and intensity of preferences among mobilized groups. The implications for friction in food trade and the ability of farmers to deal with the paperwork are daunting, but a hard interpretation of the precautionary principle mandated a whole new world of surveillance and control of farms, plants, and farmers based on how they produce food—a global proto-state restructuring markets. Like many "high-modernist" projects, one would predict that the Panopticon would not do well seeing into rural society (Scott 1998).

On the ground, in farming communities, diffusion of state regulation ironically contributed to diffusion of the technology itself; material interests proved stronger than distal edicts. Tight regulation by states and high prices of seeds from multinational firms drove farmers to illicit acquisition of transgenics—much like the illicit spread of pharmaceuticals, music, and software. Seeds followed a pattern indicated in the title of Moises Naim's (2005) treatment of the underground international economy: *Illicit*. There are few seed police in the villages or at international borders; "seeing like a state" encounters familiar limitations and ellipses. A global phenomenon of underground diffusion of "stealth seeds" reached unknown but clearly significant proportions (Herring 2007b). Seeds as genetic material resist surveillance and control, much as peasant history is one of resistance to the corvée, the tax collector, the record keeper. The spread of illicit seeds under the radar of firms and states offered new examples for James Scott's (1985) *Weapons of the Weak*. Despite an international control regime, actual diffusion of agricultural biotechnology departed radically from formal bio-safety regulations or patent regime dominance posited in international agreements and transnational advocacy. The reassuring political narrative of institutional bio-safety controls on an increasingly global food supply turned out to be more symbolic politics than meaningful regulation; as often, market logic and material interests competed with state preferences. A food Panopticon was conjured but proved astigmatic.

In both episodes of mobilizing against technological change in agriculture—the Green and the Gene Revolutions—much of the political heat came from transnational social movements, advocacy networks, and public intellectuals in urban areas. Food production technologies diffuse globally, along with techniques for processing, marketing, and retailing; political positions on what constitutes acceptable ways of growing food are now global as well. International flows of information enable ideational cross-hatching of micro-level farm production questions with broad critiques of science, risk, and corporate control of the world food system as integral to opposition to globalization.[26]

How is it to be distributed?

Politics of distribution within rural societies and between rural producers and the state have historically been contentious, sometimes cataclysmic. What Eric Wolf called "peasant wars" (1969) rocked the twentieth century far more than the anticipated proletarian revolutions predicted by nineteenth-century Marxist thought. Property institutions in agriculture have produced distinctive and often volatile politics, as classic works on variation across types of agrarian systems by Arthur Stinchcombe (1961) and Jeffrey Paige (1985) demonstrated. Residues of these conflicts fundamentally altered political economies: Barrington Moore Jr. subtitled his classic *Social Origins of Dictatorship and Democracy* "Lord and Peasant in the Making of the Modern World." Michael Lipton's theory of "urban bias" (1977) explained underdevelopment itself in terms of the superior power of urban political forces to skew taxes, prices, and public investments so as to milk the countryside of surplus for the benefit of cities.[27] In the monumental transition of peasants to farmers, both the place of rural producers in society and their political levers have undergone a great transformation.[28]

Once a distinct cultural, economic, and political tier in many societies, the peasantry was to produce the surplus on which better-born elites could develop themselves, and with which states could wage wars, expand territory, pay off debts, and reward loyal officials. Rejection of these distributive systems was both subterranean and overt (Scott 1985). Because nations have been intermittently convulsed by politics around food, states are pressured to placate the productive underbelly of society. Regimes reacted to uprisings, insurrections, famines, and tax revolts with such varied responses as land reforms, selective patronage, repressive war, abolition of slavery, make-work schemes, and, in more modern terms, development.[29] Some states, unable to respond, were swept away by rural revolutions.[30] Reciprocally, urban rioters held food to be governed by an inviolable moral economy of the kind Polanyi saw at risk from market commoditization: There is a "just price" for food. John Walton and David Seddon (1994) traced this tradition into modern times in *Free Markets and Food Riots*; the Brandt Commission called these uprisings "IMF riots" for the role of orthodox stabilization policies in raising prices in food-importing economies. Price rises of food globally in 2008 sparked riots in dozens of countries and renewed urgent debates on food security. Mobilization against the global "land grab" of recent years is a more global response to the exercise of power in land markets (Deininger 2011; Robertson and Pinstrup-Andersen 2010; Thaler, this volume).

Distributive contentions around food largely reject market logic, as Polanyi noted: There are some things markets should not decide. Of special importance to this volume will be the connecting of the historical themes of distributive politics to the impact of new technologies on security and well-being. Both the Green and the Gene Revolutions introduced technologies that opponents attacked as having adverse effects on income distribution. Distribution of gains from higher yields from new technologies in both cases depend on access to cash resources, credit, political connections, and, most of all, secure land holding.[31] The Gene Revolution raised new politics around both international distributive effects and intra-rural consequences: a rhetorically North-South global rift. The Green Revolution was driven by public-sector investment in plant breeding internationally; the Gene Revolution has been concentrated in private-sector research and development. Will multinational firms from relatively few wealthy nations capture the lion's share of benefits from technical change?[32] Or will public-sector investments in transgenic technology allow autonomous advances in those agricultural nations with strong science and technology capacity, such as China, India, and Brazil (Cohen 2005) or humanitarian organizations (Lybbert 2003)? Are the new seeds scale-neutral, and thus little differentiated between large and small farmers, or are they subject to economies of scale?[33] Intellectual property mediates the impact of technology on distribution. Ravi Srinivas notes in his contribution to this volume that global attempts to harmonize property in seeds have only notionally incorporated "farmers' rights," while buttressing claims of breeders and producers of seeds, though prospects for an open-access global commons for biotechnology knowledge continue to attract attention and some development.[34]

Intellectual-property disputes around seeds resonate with previous conflicts around distributive justice growing out of landed property, but they add significant new analytical and empirical puzzles.[35] In a perfect storm of objections to genetic engineering, a new question of *what* should be produced emerged from a social construction based entirely on *how* it is produced, with implications for concern about how acceptable distribution could be. We will return to these issues as a prelude to a discussion how ideas matter in food politics: The GMO is the anchor of the ideational continuum. Nevertheless, ideas figure prominently in framing other spheres of food politics in similar ways, though with less controversy around the normative and empirical dimensions of contested knowledge. "Junk" food offers an illustration.

Junk Food: State, Market, and Choice

Politics centered on the question of *what is to be produced*? are mediated by new, and less contested, knowledge interpolated by states and civil-society organizations. One example is helpful in illustrating the prominence of new knowledge and old interests is international convergence and disagreement around the proper roles of tradition, states, and markets.

Mexico in 2013 legislated new taxes on sugared beverages and "junk" food. The tax on sugar-sweetened beverages was set at 10 percent, with an additional 8 percent tax on "junk food" (defined as foods containing more than 275 calories per 100 grams). In response, Mark Bittman (2013) expressed in the *New York Times* an increasingly common consensus:

> ... with obesity-associated Type 2 diabetes at record levels, it's widely agreed that we have to moderate this diet. Which means that, despite corporate intransigence, we have to slow the marketing of profitable, toxic and addictive products masquerading as food.

What do we learn from this episode about broader food politics? First, knowledge mediation is critical. This view of threat and the framing—"addictive products masquerading as food"—are not *a priori* obvious or consensual; there is also conflict with at least some tradition. The triad of sugar-obesity-diabetes has not always been known, and is still not universally accepted; it is resisted, not surprisingly, by organized food-producer interests. Michael Pollan's Mom imaginary is not helpful; many mothers consume sugared beverages and "junk" food and reward kids with both. Tradition may not be so useful a guide as knowledge advances. Might the market provide better answers? Bittman attributes to junk food—along with "toxic and addictive"—the designation "profitable." Individual preferences drive markets to produce what consumers will buy—granted under the influence of propaganda from producers (Nestle 2002). Consumption is in a pure market world decided by market preferences of individuals: if one chooses badly, the harm is to the individual. *Caveat emptor*. Society—or its putative agent the state—has no standing. Or does it? Market outcomes in food turn out to have externalities, much like the externalities that drive state regulation of production decisions on the land, such as effluents of nitrogen and pesticides. But a necessary condition for action on those collective interests is, first, conceptualization of a community, and second, knowledge of collective consequences of individual behavior, and finally some means of protecting a putatively *public* interest.

What then gives the state an interest in how much sugar citizens eat? Legitimation for intervention depends on both framings of risk and institutional structures of governance. This is the classic boundary politics of markets and states: where does society draw the line between individual preferences and public interest? Characteristically, powerful beverage and food producers—national and global—argued for consumer choice over government interference in markets; they forcefully opposed regulations that would reduce demand for their products. Civil society organizations, nationally and internationally, campaigned for state action in the public interest (Bittman 2013).

Taxing sugary foods allowed Mexico to achieve what its richer neighbor to the north had not, despite local attempts: New York City mayor Michael Bloomberg's ban on big sugary drinks was ruled unconstitutional by an appeals court. The reasons for Mexico's success were both structural and conjunctural. First, Mexico recently surpassed the United States as being the most obese country in the world. Special shame was attached to being more obese than Americans; both America and NAFTA had been blamed for growing obesity in Mexico. In comparative terms, assuming nutritional knowledge—a matter disputed by industry—a clear and present danger to public health would seem to exist. This is the classic rationale for the very existence of state authority. The case for intervention was reinforced by political economy: Mexico had enacted a single-payer system of health insurance the previous year. Diabetes is a threat to fiscal sustainability of the program. Moreover, a constitutional addendum in 2011 guaranteed citizens "the right to nutritious, sufficient and quality food." Globally, a right to food has become an increasingly important component of political movements for social justice.[36] Moreover, new taxes—like all revenues—were attractive to the state itself. There was also an argument from the developmental state. Mexico's health minister, Mercedes Juan, stated publically that "obesity and diabetes are affecting school and work performances, and with it, the country's economic competitiveness." Mexico's health authorities estimated more than five million obese children and a 9.2 percent incidence of diabetes among children (BBC, October 31, 2013). The state, *in loco parentis*, moved where many moms would not go. President Enrique Peña Nieto also played an individual role, seeking an international model attributable to his leadership. His initiative was backed by a Nutritional Health Alliance of twenty-two NGOs and networks representing about 650 nonprofits and grass-roots organizations. Even members of opposition parties agreed.[37]

The argument for state over market in determining what Mexicans should be eating then has a structural base—a collective interest in a manageable health-care burden in which every citizen is implicated, fulfillment of a constitutional guarantee, and the state's appetite for more revenues. The sweetener for consumers was a promise to target new revenues for public goods—for example, safe drinking water in schools. Though authority to alter food practices is to come from the state, the *mechanism* is the market: assuming some elasticity of demand for junk food allows the state to alter consumption by raising taxes. Of course, disagreement exists about what these elasticities are—another mediation of knowledge, in this case micro-economic theory of consumer choice. The final lesson is that, predictably, market forces are obdurate and persistent; opponents quickly claimed that a black market was emerging in junk food, much like that in alcohol in areas of prohibition (Mallen 2014).

This sketch of a narrow food consumption issue illustrates elements of importance in understanding interactions among food, politics, and society that run through the *Handbook*. We noted that *interests* are mediated by both knowledge and institutional structure. We saw how consumer behavior in markets prompted state intervention; necessary conditions for intervention included settled nutritional knowledge and institutional commitment to a public interest. Yet the mechanism for alleviating a public bad turned out to be markets—raising prices of sugary things to damp consumption. The parallel to a carbon tax in the context of new knowledge about global warming is readily apparent. As with climate change, transnational advocacy networks increasingly impinge on national decisions of this kind; in Mexico, social movement interests coincided with the state's logic of public welfare. Convergence of this kind anchors one end of the food politics spectrum. At the other end of the spectrum are spheres of food politics where knowledge and interests diverge to polarized positions.[38] The perfect storm of global food politics illustrates with special clarity the importance of these factors merging the three fundamental questions into one conflict: GMOs.

The Perfect Storm: GMOs

The most intense controversies around food now center on genetic engineering. Conflicts extend beyond technology of plant breeding per se: i.e., the "*how*" of production. Genetic engineering in applications other than food and agriculture raises no special mobilizations or contentious politics. In pharmaceuticals, medicine, and industrial applications, recombinant DNA technology has been widely accepted as providing useful tools; in agriculture, products using these same tools have been coded as producing "GMOs," evoking almost universally an aura of unique risk and special regulation (Ho 2000; McHughen 2002). Agricultural biotechnology pivots on this framing to a degree matched by few other contentions. The most striking confirmation of this proposition is the fact that genetic engineering is controversial only in crop production and nowhere else (Herring 2008). Protagonists evoke alternative ideas of risk, uncertainty, and unsettled science. Richard Lewontin (2001) wrote in "Genes in the Food!":

> The introduction of methods of genetic engineering into agriculture has caused a public reaction in Europe and North America that is unequaled in the history of technology. Not even the disasters at Three Mile Island and Chernobyl were sufficient to produce such heavy and effective political pressure to prohibit or further regulate a technology, despite the evident fact that uncontained radioactivity has caused the sickness and death of very large numbers of people, while the dangers of genetically engineered food remain hypothetical.

Much of the food fight over biotechnology is indeed about technology: *how* is it produced? Who should decide what technologies are acceptable? The knowledge component is critical—what authoritative knowledge could establish the safety claimed by government agencies and scientific establishments for genetically engineered plants? But much more was at stake, since uncertainty is characteristic of many modern technologies—the common mobile phone among them. How uncertainty is constructed is itself an ideational question—where does acceptable uncertainty become unacceptable risk? *Science* is evoked and attacked as providing evidence for safety in use of GMOs; rival global networks have their own epistemologies, media and reference works. This is a puzzling outcome: genetic engineering is widely accepted in other life-and-death fields, such as pharmaceuticals, where risk is measured against benefit. Biotechnology in *food* became a lightening rod because food politics is suffused with questions of ethics, justice, and identity, with supporting visions of culturally validated livelihoods, landscapes, and techniques.[39] In mobilization framings, heirloom varieties confront Franken-Foods; organic confronts industrial; the global periphery confronts the core.

What is to be produced? Unlike dioxin or plutonium, the GMO does not exist unless one knows how it was produced. Regulatory provisions, politics, and the object itself define a *what* that is completely dependent on *how* it is produced.[40] Though it is difficult to find evidence of any consequential differences between plant breeding that is molecular and other ways of getting traits into plants, the GMO as an object of governmentality is widely subject to mobilization, special regulation, surveillance, and control.[41] The *how* of production evokes antithetical evocation of the *natural* that is normatively sanctioned. Criteria for the line between "natural" and "unnatural" are neither obvious nor consensual. For some, molecular plant breeding involves an unnatural act. Prince Charles famously proclaimed: "This kind of genetic engineering takes mankind into realms that belong to God, and to God alone. . . ." Not only is biotechnology here framed as crossing that nebulous line between the natural and the unnatural, but Prince Charles went on to endorse Vandana Shiva's claim that biotech seeds were responsible for mass suicides of farmers in India—"genocidal" in her words.[42]

The "GMO" had to be invented as an idea. It was created by framing—lumping and splitting of recombinant DNA techniques across uses, segregating food from other applications, such as pharmaceuticals; there are no Franken-Pills on posters. This framing was the work of intellectual activists in networks building on concerns first expressed by molecular biologists.[43] Material consequences of this ideational move were profound. Labels for organic products typically preclude molecular breeding of seeds, no matter what cultivation techniques are followed. There are spatial differentiations with legal standing—GMO-free zones and GMO-free countries. Markets are affected by trade restrictions, trade disputes, and a market premium niche for *GMO-free* food. The Cartagena Protocol on Biosafety deals only with international surveillance of genetically engineered plants. Labeling campaigns premised on a special status for GMO-food proliferate even in the United States, long considered the most biotechnology friendly of polities.

Both sides in the global rift over biotechnology contest "the Science." Though there are certainly controversies in science (Agin 2006; Waltz 2009), what has been politically potent is the concept of "risk." Science makes no pretense to address risk preferences. Risk in a strict scientific sense means probability of exposure to some hazard, usually expressed as *hazard X exposure = risk.*[44] Risk thus assumes a known probability distribution of some hazard—air travel and surgery are common examples of known risk distributions. This deceptively simple formulation is often irrelevant, however, because neither hazard nor probability is known, or cannot be measured. This condition is called "Knightian uncertainty."[45] This characterization obtains in regard to foods and plants produced with genetic engineering.

In a world of *uncertainty*, risk is of necessity a social construction. In everyday life, we think in terms of acceptable risk; some risks are taken even in the face of obvious hazard because the risk of doing nothing is higher—surgery, for example—or because of expected benefits—air travel, for example. Ideally, regulation of any technology would reach some threshold of acceptable risk—balanced with benefits—for a whole society. However, as Douglas and Wildavsky (1982) demonstrate in *Risk and Culture*, politics around risk are not influenced by the data alone, even when there are data. Given the plurality of values and knowledge in societies, consensus on how to weight caution, risk, and benefits will be difficult to attain. Resultant politics will prove contentious if much is at stake; different framings of the GMO debate refract different weightings of what is at stake. Consensual democratic procedures for weighting preferences prove elusive, and intensity of preference looms large. In assessing GMOs, globally, the "precautionary principle" is often evoked to justify opposition, but it is clearly difficult to know how much precaution is cautious enough (DeFrancesco 2013).

How is it to be distributed? Distributive questions are folded into biotechnology itself by arguments that the industry poses special threats to small farmers and poor nations. In this view, small farmers will be crushed by multinational control of seed property rights: "bio-feudalism" or "bio-serfdom."[46] The hoax of a "terminator gene" in genetically engineered crops generated a global movement to "Ban the Terminator"; the idea of sterile seeds proved remarkably persistent in politics despite widespread underground breeding of transgenic plants by farmers.[47] Thus an argument that *how* genetically engineered crops are produced raised questions of social justice: *How will fruits of production be distributed?* This critique based on inevitable corporate dominance has been persistent and powerful, though there are other sources of research and development (Cohen 2005). Public-sector crops such as Golden Rice or the ring-spot virus-resistant papaya come without property claims attached to the technology when used by small farmers (Evanega and Lynas, this volume). Stealth seeds that move in underground markets are likewise outside the orbit of exactions of property claims of firms (Herring and Kandlikar 2009). The difficult empirical questions are seldom significant in the heated political debates over income distribution: in which countries are there patents on plants? If there are patents, are they enforced? If enforced, is the marginal return on the technology fee larger than the marginal cost? How large a percentage of variable costs of production are seeds? The rapid diffusion of genetically engineered crops among farmers globally suggests that the net effects on income are on the whole positive, not negative—unless we assume farmers are incapable of choosing technologies that work for them.[48]

The North-South framing of biotechnology has proved politically important, but in fact the fault lines are not structured by geography or national income. After the United States, the leading producers include Argentina, India, Brazil, China, and Canada. Farmers growing biotech crops in the United States and Canada often operate large holdings as commercial businesses; biotech farmers in India and China operate holdings tiny by world standards. Though associated with wealthy economies historically, genetically engineered crops grown in "developing countries" exceeded total hectares grown in the so-called developed countries for the first time in 2012 (James, Annual).

The framing of GMO controversies illustrates the power of ideas to drive politics.[49] There is less and less a question of "do ideas matter," and more a question of "how ideas matter." In food politics, the ideational component is weighty in identifiable ways.

How Ideas Are Central to Food Politics

Ideas matter in all spheres of politics; John Maynard Keynes famously said that "the world is ruled by little else." Though political economy usefully centers interests, and thus structures from which interests are derived, Mark Blyth reminds us that "structures do not come with an instruction sheet" (2003). The relationship between one's position in a structure and political behavior is mediated in complicated ways. In some politics, even recognizing an interest requires cognitive processing: No one recognized interests in global warming prior to the science that connected future outcomes to present human behaviors. Ideas about other environmental risks define interests in controversies over legislation and practice (Lomborg 2001; Specter 2009). The financial crisis after 2007 induced consequential clashes over what policies would serve common and particular interests, opposing variants of Keynesian to neoliberal ideas (Blyth 2002, 2013). Likewise, many disagreements in food politics are rooted in different ideas about how best to answer the inescapable questions of political economy: whether through tradition, state, or market.

Some effects of ideas in food politics are apparent: Ethics drive politics around food entitlements, treatment of animals as livestock, and claims of future generations for sustainability, for example. To be sure, ethical agreement is only the beginning of food politics on any issue, as doing the right thing may or may not be politically possible—but it is a necessary condition (see Korthals, this volume). Ethical arguments are largely about end states—the way things ought to be. The ethicist observes that with sufficient food in the global production system, malnutrition afflicting something like a billion people should not exist. Agreement on first principles is much easier, however, than agreement on the means of attaining desired end states. It is thus important to distinguish between ideas we think of as *normative*—what ought to be the case—and ideas we think of as *empirical*—how things actually work. Normative ideas are often expressed as ethics or obligation; empirical ideas are expressed as claims about how the world works. Ideas about the empirical world—how things work—become necessary components of guides to policy and behavior in accord with normative preferences (Dryzek 2005).

How ideas matter in the chapters that follow fall into identifiable processes:

a) *Cognitive screening*: Ideas matter first because interests are not the stable stuff of neoclassical economics, nor are they unambiguously recognizable. Political economy begins with investigation of interests, then looks to their interaction. But knowing an interest depends not only on normative or ethical reasoning, but on information as well: The brute facts of the world do not come coded with implications for one's interests or means of attaining them. Cognitive screens are constructed of both science and culture.[50] The inchoate nature of interests, especially in distal spheres such as agriculture or new technology, creates a cognitive opportunity structure for framing by political entrepreneurs and social movements. Foundational components of these screens include such dichotomies as natural/unnatural and risky/safe and credible/biased. An individual's interests may or may not be served by organic or bio-fortified food, for example—deciding which it is requires information on outcomes.[51]
b) *Expertise and epistemic brokerage*: Interests are especially dependent on mediation by ideas and information in matters evoking risk, uncertainty, and the future (Elster 1993, chap. 4). Are there foods that cause or prevent cancer? High information costs and cognitive complexity necessitate epistemic brokerage—a trusted authority to sort the true from the false. Michael Pollan, for example, is a leading epistemic broker on matters of food: what we should believe, what is true, what are corporate talking points as opposed to facts on the ground. Epistemic brokerage will vary in importance with information costs and cognitive distance: We are almost all, for example, dependent on epistemic brokerage in atmospheric science on which the future of the species depends. Few of us read peer-reviewed atmospheric science. For climate change, global society has established internationally trusted sources. Global assessments for defining authoritative knowledge in food and agriculture, however, have proved controversial and inconclusive (IAASTD, 2009; Scoones, this volume). Information costs in food and agriculture for individuals are high for that large percentage of the world's population that has not ever grown crops for a livelihood. The information one gets is dependent on the networks one belongs to—and their associated media connections—and thus the epistemic brokerage dominant in that network (Herring 2010).
c) *Strategies and tactics*: Once interests are established, issues of collective action arise.[52] To act presupposes at least some sense that the action will be meaningful, and thus supported by others. Networks are critical intermediaries in this process of establishing a basis for collective action. If collective action is to be effective,

ideas about strategies and tactics become important. Schurman and Munro (2010) demonstrated that the success of anti-GMO movements in Europe, for example, resulted from focusing on food distributors, not producers: Monsanto failed to recognize that a focus on science and producer benefits was politically ineffectual and consequently lost the early contests in Europe. Ideas of labeling laws, global campaigns such as "Ban the Terminator," targets for mobilization such as GMO-free zones, and such creative framings as that presupposed by the "I AM NOT A LAB RAT" movement proved effective on the ground. The high degree of modularity in social movements builds on this imperative (Tarrow 2011). Likewise, the tactic of unsettling science by demonstrating lack of complete consensus has created anxiety and thus uncertainty that reinforces the narrative of special risk in agricultural biotechnology.[53] Industry has tried, but largely failed, to find comparably effective tactical ideas.

d) *Institutionalization*: Successful ideas create institutional niches. Institutionalized ideas also generate and define new interests, creating a path dependency for ideas. The existence of an official designation of "organic" agriculture and foods has proved internationally powerful. Certifications for other normatively driven labels have similar effects. Emily Clough in this volume analyzes how labels may function to safeguard environmental, labor, and health standards in food production that are unprotected by the state. The labels institutionalize an idea, such as "fair exchange," thereby enabling political consumerism, and potentially influencing production through market behavior of concerned individuals (Johnston and MacKendrick, this volume). Both voluntary, market-based regulation through networks and state-regulated labels have important effects on prices and opportunities for consumers and producers alike. Ideas about proper food handling and safety have strong effects when institutionalized. Thomas Reardon and Peter Timmer consider in their chapter the effect of legal standards on small and medium enterprises in the rapidly globalizing agrifood sector in the developing world:

> ... application of food safety and hygiene regulations to food businesses have been important examples imposing special burdens on small firms who lacked the investment surplus and access to bank loans to shift location, register their firm, and adopt all the measures (such as hygiene facilities and cement floors) needed to conform to new laws.

In this case, state regulation accelerates market forces—especially foreign direct investment—that have reshaped traditional organization of food processing and retailing in the "supermarket revolution" that began in the 1990s and accelerated thereafter:

> The accelerated penetration of retail clashes both with broadly shared self-perceptions in developing countries, as well as the pre-1990 retail literature (where often one heard that somehow the "traditional food culture," dense cities, low opportunity cost of labor, and "habit of frequent shopping" militated against modern

> retail). Why did it occur so quickly? Several factors explain it . . . especially where credence goods like food safety are involved.

The most power of institutionalized ideas of safety at the frontier of production technology comes from the Cartagena Protocol on Biosafety for regulating movement of biotechnology crops across national boundaries. By framing agricultural biotechnology as a matter of biosafety under an environmental treaty (Convention on Biodiversity), different political forces were empowered at the national level. Only by this institutionalized framing could ministers of environment have a stronger role than ministers of agriculture or health on matters of crop technology and food safety. That authoritative framing resulted from mobilization around an idea of special risk of some forms of plant breeding over others—a risk so far unconfirmed in scientific studies but pervasive in law, trade, and politics.[54]

Ethical reasoning, as suggested in the introduction to this section, is the most familiar and often powerful overt source of food politics, whether or not institutionalized. The ethics confronting social injustice, for example, may drive intervention in market distribution of food, for example in effective political demands for food subsidies for the poor—more powerful in some countries than others (Kotwal and Ramaswami, this volume). Ethical intent does not, however, invariably lead to ethical outcomes—a veil of knowledge intervenes. Interventions in food trade driven by ethically defensible political preferences, for example, often prove to be both "inefficient and inequitable," as explained by Kym Anderson's contribution to this volume. Subsidies to biofuel production show the same skew: Representation of farmers in the United States as worthy of public assistance reinforces the case for state spending that is neither equitable nor environmentally sound, as David Pimentel and Michael Burgess develop in their contribution to this volume. David Sahn's chapter in this volume questions whether the ethically plausible impulse to concentrate on food *per se* for combating malnutrition is the wisest policy for aiding infants and children in poor places.

Ethical preferences often fail to change state policy, but may remain consequential in individual efforts to effect change through markets (Johnston and MacKendrick, this volume). Ethical political consumerism, however, is fundamentally dependent on knowledge. Labels available to consumers are predominately provided by nonstate actors about whom little is verifiably known. Emily Clough points out in her chapter that there is considerable difficulty in knowing what reality labels reflect, or who actually benefits from normatively valued claims:

> There is also substantial debate about whether retailers capture too large a portion of the premium charged to consumers. Some point out that when retailers mark up ethically labeled food products, they often keep a large percentage of that margin for themselves, and the consumers are none the wiser. In one case, a retailer was criticized when it was found that 90% of the premium they charged for a cup of Fair Trade coffee went to the retailer, while only 10% was passed along to farmers.

Whether ethical preferences drive only individual behavior or institutionalize preferences through state regulation, ethical reasoning depends fundamentally on settled knowledge: The choice of what should be done depends on what will happen if we do one thing as opposed to another. If one begins with the normative premise that peasant farmers are to be protected and supported globally, and agricultural biotechnology is "suicidal, homicidal, and genocidal," opposition to genetic engineering in agriculture is normatively imperative.[55] If genetic engineering offers potential for drought-tolerant crops that could improve the prospects of poor farmers in ecologically stressed zones, the ethical case becomes inverted. One network's suicide seed is another's silver bullet. In both cases, political implications of the same ethical stance vary with divergent assessments of knowledge.[56]

The knowledge-intensive character of food politics then means that the effects of advocacy networks will be strong, whether in screening, framing, or institutionalizing ideas. Networks reinforce the already strong effect of "information cascades"—the "everyone knows..." phenomenon—even when what everyone knows is false (Heath and Heath 2007). Interaction in networks likewise strengthens ideological commitments and "biased assimilation" in a process dependent on cognitive consonance.[57] Networks reduce information costs and can lead to social polarization around identities that reinforce biased assimilation, confirmation bias, and information cascades. These effects are magnified by the observable fact that interests produce knowledge claims to further their interests—cigarette manufacturers find that smoking has no relation to cancer whatsoever, just as coal companies find that particulate matter has no discernible effect on health. Uncertainty is reinforced by the modern skepticism about facticity itself and the absence of consensual institutions for knowledge vetting.[58] Moreover, "information" that produces strong emotions—disgust, anger, outrage—is more likely to be noticed and to be disseminated. In her presidential address to the American Association for the Advancement of Science (AAAS) Nina Fedoroff said she was "scared to death" by the "anti-science movement" that was "driving science into a dark era" (McKie 2012). Federoff emphasized climate science, as well as attacks on the science of agricultural biotechnology, but the point is more general. Food politics lacks not only the honest broker that could provide a factual check on ethical reasoning, but also even agreement on methods for getting there. A major reason for this cognitive, and therefore political, divide in food politics involves pervasive cascade effects, biased assimilation, and group polarization enabled by modern networking capabilities with deep interests in generating authoritative narratives.

Development North-South?

Questions of food production and sufficiency in modern times have typically been relegated to studies of "development" as an intellectual enterprise and policy domain. Development was conceptualized as a problem for "underdeveloped" countries. Claims of authoritative knowledge concerning agricultural practices and policies in poor nations have long been the provenance of people in rich nations. Restriction of developmental problematics to relatively poor societies now seems quaint given current knowledge about malnutrition, food-related illnesses, and hunger in rich and rapidly growing nations. In truth, politics around appropriate technology, adequate nutrition, food safety, ecological impact of agriculture, and challenges of climate change know no income threshold. Nor are countries the obvious unit of analysis; rich individuals whether in India or the United States face risks of overconsumption, just as the poor in both countries face worse nutritional options than the rich. Nevertheless, "development" thinking still drives much food policy and politics.

The World Development Report 2008 of the World Bank, *Agriculture for Development*, specifically recommended greater investment in agriculture in "developing countries." The report warned that agriculture must be placed at the center of the development agenda "if the goals of halving extreme poverty and hunger by 2015 are to be realized." Food is a central element of recommended poverty reduction strategies; malnutrition is a first consequence of poverty. Globally, though roughly 75 percent of the world's poor live in rural areas in poor nations, only 4 percent of official development assistance is even targeted for agriculture; much less reaches food producers and hungry people. The report acknowledged the power of Michael Lipton's analysis of "urban bias."[59] Income growth originating in agriculture is "about four times more effective in raising incomes of extremely poor people than GDP growth originating outside the sector." In terms of regional poverty, sub-Saharan Africa illustrated the World Bank's point: "public spending for farming is also only 4 percent of total government spending and the sector is still taxed at relatively high levels." Subsequent chapters address where we are lacking knowledge, what we know about politics driving bad policies, and where knowledge at the frontier offers great hope for moving forward ethically.

For the richer countries, the production game against nature has declined in political significance—food is obtainable with money—and politics takes on issues characterized by luxury of choice: up the Maslovian hierarchy of needs toward treating food as a matter of identity and self-actualization.[60] Choosing between a local product that is not organic and an organic product that is not local would seem a frivolous anxiety for the majority of the world's food consumers. Nevertheless, genuine developmental dilemmas do not magically disappear at some level of per-capita income. As of early 2014, about 47 million Americans received benefits from the Supplemental Nutrition Assistance Program (SNAP)—the new name for "food stamps"—for those unable to afford an adequate diet.[61] Even in a society that has solved the aggregate food problem and claims high standards for science-based regulation, public trust in food wavers over time; anger at inadequate, politicized, or inept regulation erupts episodically. Americans have become accustomed to press reports of sporadic outbreaks of salmonella and *E coli*, often difficult to trace—some domestic, some with import histories. The Centers for Disease Control estimate that each year roughly 1 in 6 Americans (or 48 million people) become ill; 128,000 are hospitalized, and 3,000 die of foodborne illnesses (http://www.cdc.gov/foodborneburden/). Nor is the United States necessarily a laissez-faire outlier; the "mad-cow" crisis significantly affected European faith in government and science in regulating food. Insecurities of food supply in rich countries have largely been replaced by a new politics of food: controversies around safety, nutrition, ethics, regulation, subsidies, and trade.

What makes food political then has changed in recent decades. Issues of a classical political economy of interests have not disappeared—struggles for agrarian reform such that food producers can afford to eat, control of agricultural land to assure food security, state subsidies for those whose market power is insufficient for adequate nutrition. Mobilization around these issues is, however, more global and more complex, as the new food politics layers fresh issues onto the old. Biotechnology is supported and attacked by global networks, each claiming concern for the poor and for food security: suicide seeds and silver bullets.

The chapters that follow examine overt food politics of increasing importance: social movements, protests, subsidies, regulatory restrictions and certifications, ethical consumerism. We observe that these tensions frequently derive from deeper elements of the political economy: what kinds of questions ought be answered by state evocation of tradition or new knowledge or by markets responding to ethical or traditional preferences? Two aspects of the new food politics stand out: fundamental dependence on knowledge—both normative and empirical—and transnational advocacy bringing more and different voices to local grain piles. On the knowledge front, dispute abounds: Michael Pollan's Mom is fragmented, quarrelsome, and irresolute. Yet these knowledge claims operate both as political objectives in themselves—"sustainability"— and as mediation of interests—global warming and livestock, organic and conventional. Where the market-state boundaries in food are set reflects the interplay of both ideational interests, e.g., "GMO-free," and material interests mediated by knowledge, e.g., "free trade." The fundamental meta-choice continues to confront all societies: through what *mechanisms* will answers to the inescapable questions of production, distribution, and exchange of food be decided?

We have seen how these questions could be, and have been, answered by three mechanisms: *tradition*—established routines legitimated by long use—or *market*, or *state*—authoritative institutions at some level. No free-floating technical expertise exists to answer these questions; they are irreducibly political. Karl Polanyi's historical sequencing of dominant mechanisms provides a conceptual guide to resulting boundary politics between states and markets: The great transformation made food itself a commodity like any other object of production and exchange and, therefore, a sphere of insecurity for those at the bottom of national and international pyramids. That transformation is politically contested, across various arenas, along multiple dimensions. But we have also seen that "society," like "tradition," is more a political claim than coherent entity. Polanyi reified society as Pollan reified culture.

Food then generates distinct politics for interrelated reasons. First, the urgency of food provisioning, micro and macro, is biological, not merely preferential. Deep material interests in survival drive overt food politics contesting land and its products. Distributive questions in turn energize a politics of rights, security, and social justice, and thereby potential for collective action and contentious politics. Ethical concerns for justice over an imagined international community globalize these politics. Second, food engages deeply held cultural norms—"tradition"—that resist interest politics characteristic of less culturally embedded commodities. Lines are drawn thereby between the natural and the unnatural, the acceptable and the unacceptable. Finally, food is increasingly embedded in technical discourses that make outcomes dependent on knowledge and science; both are contested as components of larger ideational systems. A political economy of food outcomes is then especially dependent on politics of ideas, in which information costs, social networks, epistemic brokerage, and collective action loom large.

Agreement on how to settle disputed claims of knowledge, safety, and ethics has kept up with neither the pace of technological change nor the organization of contentious politics. Of special importance is the thread running through a number of chapters: the empirical contingency of normative claims. Coming together on desired end states is easier than reaching agreement on the empirically complex issue of means to ends, whether in sustainability or poverty alleviation. Given the increasingly transnational nature of contention, the knowledge dependence of food politics, and the asymmetric power relations in international networks, we return to Michael Lipton's critique of "urban bias": much of the international debate over food is driven more by consumers in cities than producers on farms.[62] Claimants for a legitimate voice in deciding how grain piles should be produced and how food should be distributed have multiplied, ever more distant from the grain pile itself. The class composition of claimants has changed as well; the skills that matter are not necessarily those honed on the farm. In evaluating the claims and counterclaims of global food knowledge politics, then, it is useful to recapture the humility of a president of the United States, Dwight Eisenhower, in a simpler time:

> You know, farming looks mighty easy when your plow is a pencil, and you're a thousand miles from the corn field.[63]

NOTES

1. Originally from Pollan 2008, the phrase has become pervasive in American food culture circles via numerous blogs, interviews, tweets, and postings. For example: www.omnivoracious.com/2008/02/table-talk-gues.html February 12, 2008; https://twitter.com/buckybox/status/194757709747326977 https://twitter.com/Zeppolis/status/357337877576826880 July 16, 2013. Nestle 2002 offers systematic evidence on industry power in setting official nutrition standards.
2. See Stein, this volume; Taubes 2001, 2007. David Sahn in this volume challenges the conventional emphasis on food in combating malnutrition's worst effects with a chapter entitled: "Is Food the Answer to Malnutrition?" Most estimates of hunger are snapshots in time; the more critical question is vulnerability over time—a family can be secure at one price level and acutely malnourished at another, or when unemployed, or following a crop failure, etc.
3. On international papaya politics, see Evanega and Lynas, this volume. Despite its nomothetic commitments to consensus, in practice science is disputed along ideological lines

congruent with other values; see chapters by McHughen, Newell-McGloughlin, and Chassy, this volume; Waltz (2009).

4. For a comparative analysis of mobilization, see Assayag (2005); Boal (2001): Herring (2006); Schurman and Munro (2008); Scoones (2008).
5. For a view of the larger debate around the macro political economy of development, emphasizing alternative paths and mechanisms, see Houtzager and Moore (2003); on privatization of nature as part of this politics, see Goldman (1998). Though technical elites often construct the term as apolitical and unproblematic, political realities diverge; see Ferguson (1994) and chapters by both Watts and Chappell, this volume.
6. See Korthals, this volume, on ethical traditions and logic from first principles; on implications of pro-poor normative commitments, see Kotwal and Ramaswami in this volume on politics of food subsidies. On the connection of ethics to policy more generally, see Pinstrup-Andersen (2007); on ethical challenges around technology, see Nuffield Council (1999, 2004).
7. On transnational advocacy politics generally, and social movement theory, see Tarrow (2005, 2011); Givan, Roberts, and Soule (2010); Smith and Johnston (2002).
8. Gøsta Esping-Andersen in *The Three Worlds of Welfare Capitalism* (1990) demonstrates essential dimensions and extent of variation among Western capitalist democracies along lines of decommoditization, security, and inequality.
9. See Borras, Edelman, and Kay (2008); Chappell, this volume. On possible outcomes and state logics of land reforms, see Herring (1983); Larsson (2012); Wolford (2010). For a grim contrary view of China, see Yang (2012); on markets in peasant revolt in China, see Thaxton (1983).
10. On the "moral economy" tradition of peasant studies, in contrast to rationalist approaches of methodological individualism, see Little (1992); contrast Hechter (1981); on ideational elements in the latter, see Lichbach (1994).
11. See Borras and Franco, this volume; Edelman (1999); Reitan (2007).
12. As Tomas Larsson explains in his chapter of this volume; see also Emily Clough's chapter on product differentiation that permits political consumerism via labeling. A critique of the cultural trope romanticizing traditional agriculture can be found in McHughen, this volume.
13. Chapters by both Reardon and Timmer in this volume, and Anderson, indicate the pervasive nature of these dynamic and divergent perceptions of legitimacy.
14. See the comparative treatment of this question in Kotwal and Ramaswami, this volume.
15. See Ann Grodzins Gold's treatment of farmer's production logics in North India in her contribution to this volume: the tension between market rationality of getting more and cultural logics of getting and sharing good food—logics very much rooted in the cultural authority of tradition.
16. Numbers vary but converge on dramatic growth of production and exports in India's "Pink Revolution." Pratiksha Ramkumar reported in the *Times of India* on April 1, 2013, that India became the world's largest exporter in 2012 ("Beef exports up 44% in 4 years, India is top seller"). The United States Department of Agriculture Foreign Agricultural Service reported (November 2013) that India is not quite there, but increasing rapidly.
17. On biofuels as a politically attractive, but dubious, use of agricultural land, see Pimental and Burgess, this volume; on the environmental Kuznets curve, see Watson, this volume.

18. See FAO 2006. Purvi Mehta-Bhatt and Pier Paolo Ficarelli explore the political controversies around livestock in their chapter of this volume. Global political forces both support and attack continued livestock rearing as livelihood.
19. On Malthus and the war against nature, see McHughen, this volume. On the notion of catastrophic visions of the food future, see Watson's essay on climate change and agriculture, appropriately subtitled "Countering Doomsday Scenarios," in this volume.
20. Uphoff (2002, 2012). In this volume, see chapters by Harriss and Stewart; Nelson and Coe; Uphoff. On the science, see Newell-McCloughlin, this volume, and National Research Council (2010a; 2010b) and The Royal Society (2009).
21. On the potential contributions of biotechnology to sustainability, see National Research Council of the National Academy of Sciences (2010a; 2010b). On the more general question of environmental effects of transgenic plants, see National Research Council (2002).
22. Vandana Shiva (e.g., 1997, 2000) is associated with the latter view, the international development community with the former (Paarlberg 2009, chap. 6). See also Lipton with Longhurst (1989); Harriss and Stewart, this volume. On the normative values of movements opposing globalization in agriculture, see Borras, Edelman, and Kay (2008); Reitan (2007).
23. In Norman Uphoff's view, expressed in his chapter for this volume, the goal should be maximizing yields of existing plants rather than investing in genetic improvements of plants that may never achieve their potential for want of optimal agroecological practices and conditions. See Nelson and Coe, this volume, on agroecological intensification in smallholder agriculture.
24. See the chapter by Robert Paarlberg in this volume on the special problems of African agriculture. His important 2008 book *Starved for Science* is subtitled "How Biotechnology Is Being Kept Out of Africa."
25. For national regulatory styles, Jasanoff (2007); on the conflict, Roberts (2008, 239–268); Herring (2008); on the science, National Research Council of the National Academy of Sciences (2004); on different cultural components of food safety generated by the GMO, see Kyoko Sato's chapter in this volume.
26. See Fukuda-Parr (2007) for national case studies; also Scoones (2008); Newell (2008); Herring (2009). On globalization and systems of food production and retailing, see Reardon and Timmer, this volume.
27. For discussion of theory and empirics, including Lipton's response, see the special issue of *Journal of Development Studies* 20:3 (1984) entitled *Development and the Rural-Urban Divide*. On Africa, see the influential work of Bates (1981).
28. The transformation itself is interpreted in quite different ways: see Brass (2000) and Shanin (1972). For an evocative case study emphasizing levers of power and development discourse, see Omvedt (2005).
29. Herring (1983). Though distribution *within* households was a powerful determinant of what accident of birth implied about life chances in agricultural societies, questions of gender distribution largely fell out of the discourse on land reforms and development generally, until recently, as Bina Agarwal has documented extensively (1994; and this volume). On the importance of class divisions, Alavi (1965).
30. For wide-ranging analytics and cases, see Lichbach (1994); Little (1992); Paige (1975); Popkin (1979); Skocpol (1979; 1982); Yang (2012).

31. See Borras and Franco, this volume; Herring (1983); Larsson (2012); Lipton and Longhurst (1989).
32. See Charles (2001); Kloppenburg (2004); Kloppenburg and Kleinman (1987); Shiva (2000).
33. See also Halewood, Norigea, and Louafi (2013); Herring (2007a, 2013); Lipton (2007); Nuffield Council (2004).
34. The political question that immediately arises from intellectual property in seeds is whether or not the claims of firms can be made actionable on the ground; patents are national and underground diffusion of transgenic seeds has been considerable.
35. On distributive questions and ideologies, see *Transgenics and the Poor* (Herring 2007c); Pinstrup-Andersen and Schioler (2000); Glover (2010).
36. See Kotwal and Ramaswami, this volume. In India, the Right to Food Act is buttressed by Article 21 (the fundamental "right to life") in the Constitution and Article 47 of the Directive Principles which privileges "raising of the level of nutrition and the standard of living of its people" as state obligations. The Supreme Court has issued several orders on enforcement of food entitlements. See Gaiha et al. in this volume on the nature and magnitude of the problem.
37. This section is based on contemporary press reports in the *Los Angeles Times, Huffington Post, Forbes, Bloomberg, Washington Post, Wall Street Journal, Guardian,* and other English-language media sources.
38. See Keck and Sikkink (1997); Reitan (2007); Tarrow (2005); on the knowledge question, Scoones in this volume.
39. Assayag (2005); McKibben (2008). See also chapters by Shome, McHughen, and Sato in this volume. On the ethics of agricultural biotechnology, see Nuffield Council (1999, 2004).
40. The distinction is not without consequence: global regulatory systems differ between whether a food product itself should be tested for safety or whether safety should depend on the process whereby the food was produced; see Chassy, this volume; National Research Council (2004). Trade disputes result from the distinction.
41. The European Commission Directorate-General for Research (2010) concluded from analysis of research funded by the European Union: "The main conclusion to be drawn from the efforts of more than 130 research projects, covering a period of more than 25 years of research, and involving more than 500 independent research groups, is that biotechnology, and in particular GMOs, are not per se more risky than e.g. conventional plant breeding technologies (p. 16)." See also the meta-analysis of A. E. Ricroch, J. B. Bergé, and M. Kuntz (2011) of forty-four "–omic" studies, as well as the extensive review by Italian scientists of the last decade of the global literature: Nicolia, Manzo, Veronesi, and Rosellini (2013). A sampling of national academies is provided by the Genetic Literacy Project: http://www.geneticliteracyproject.org/2013/08/27/glp-infographic-international-science-organizations-on-crop-biotechnology-safety/#.Uo_I4ihOS-J
42. Herring (2009). The claim of suicide seeds has spawned critically acclaimed films and has been dramatically influential internationally; it has no basis in fact, as the peer-reviewed literature indicates (Herring and Rao 2012; Herring 2013), as the government of India repeatedly states. See Kloor (2014) on how the hoax spread. Farmers have voted with their plows for Bt cotton.
43. Schurman and Kelso (2003); Schurman and Munro (2010, 1–13); on framing, see Benford and Snow (2000); on diffusion of social movements, Given, Roberts, and Soule (2008).

44. On transgenics and environmental risk specifically, Thies and Devare 2007. See also National Research Council of the National Academy of Sciences (2002).
45. After the work of the economist Frank Knight (1921). On the pervasiveness of risk in modern thought, and political consequences, see Giddens (1999).
46. For centering property in biotechnology on the seed, and the connection to multinational capital, see Charles 2001; Kloppenburg 2004; Kloppenburg and Kleinman 1987; Shiva 1997. For a contrary view on poverty effects, see Lipton 2007. Public-sector alternatives are discussed in Cohen (2005).
47. On framing of the "terminator," Gold (2003). The technology may not work and has not been deployed in any crop anywhere in the world, but it has succeeded as a social-movement target, generating a global campaign (Herring 2006).
48. The authoritative source on these questions is Clive James (Annual), though diffusion of biotechnology is understated in the aggregate data since illegal distribution of seeds underground is not counted, indeed cannot be counted. The questions in the text have been prominent in disputes around Bt cotton in India, where suicides have been attributed transgenic seeds. Though not a food crop, the distributive issues in the text are the same. See Herring (2007a) and Herring (2013) for a summary of issues and empirics.
49. For a moderating view, see Graff, Hochman, and Zilberman in this volume. They set out the political economy of regulation literature and explain why Europe has different interests in transgenics from those of the United States. On European regulatory contradictions and politics, see Wesseler and Kalaitzandonakes (2011).
50. John Dryzek (2005) deploys the concept of "environmental discourses" to explain the elements that cohere in different worldviews relevant to diagnosing and addressing problems. On the more general question of interplay of ideas and interests in political ecology, see Robbins (2004).
51. On framing effects, Benford and Snow 2000. Koopmans and Olzak (2004) discuss discursive opportunities that effect politics. On ethics as a source of interest that leads to action, see chapters by Clough, this volume, and Johnston and MacKendrick. On interests in biofortification, see Stein, this volume. Though the line dividing "organic" and "genetically modified" is ideational, very real interests are engaged for farmers, given market structuring effects of the organic premium. See the essay by Thies in this volume.
52. Few issues are more discussed with less resolution. For two different demonstrations that the methodological individualism approach needs reformation, consider Robert Wade's *Village Republics*, in which geophysical attributes of villages matter fundamentally, and Elizabeth Wood's *Insurgent Collective Action*, which makes a claim for moral outrage driving militant organization in peasant society, contrary to rational calculation of interests.
53. Oreskes and Conway (2010) in their book *Merchants of Doubt* demonstrate how a handful of scientists instrumentally unsettled the established science on linkages of tobacco smoke to cancer and carbon fuel emissions to global warming at the behest of corporate clients who stood to lose if the mainstream science became the basis of law and regulation.
54. Because science is widely contested by social networks opposed to genetic engineering as being American or corporate or both, and thus biased, it is useful to look to the meta-analysis of the European Union's Directorate-General for Research (2010) of decades of EU-funded studies; their conclusions confirm the global consensus in the text. A more recent meta-analysis of the last decade of global literature by Italian scientists confirms the EU findings (Nicolia, Manzo, Veronesi, and Rosellini 2013).

55. See Assayag (2005); Shiva et al. (2000).
56. *Seeds of Contention* lays out the structure of the argument (Pinstrup-Andersen and Schioler 2000). On the global assessment of knowledge on the question, see Scoones, this volume. Chapters by Shome and Chappell take contrasting positions on the incorporation of ethical objectives into social movements for sustainability and justice.
57. This section relies heavily on Sunstein's (2009) work on why false information spreads and becomes credible, as well as Specter's (2009) work on why denial of facts takes hold and persists in networks, and Heath and Heath (2007) findings on persistence of inaccurate information appropriately packaged: ideas need not be right to "stick."
58. Latour (2010); Oreskes and Conway (2010). On partisan attacks on science, Mooney (2006); in relation to food politics, Paarlberg (2009).
59. Lipton (1977); Professor Lipton has consistently raised the point, continuously confirmed, that investment in agricultural research yields very high returns but is underfunded. See World Bank (2007); Paarlberg (2008)
60. Chapters by both Clough on labels and Johnston and MacKendrick on grocery shopping provide examples of this behavior in relatively privileged classes and countries.
61. Numbers change with economic conditions and tweaking of eligibility requirements. See http://www.washingtonpost.com/blogs/wonkblog/wp/2013/09/23/why-are-47-million-americans-on-food-stamps-its-the-recession-mostly/; http://www.trivisonno.com/food-stamps-charts
62. On the competitive "scramble" for exposure, funds and recognition, recruitment of expertise and skills by transnational advocacy networks and NGOs, and their dependence on urban skill sets and media, see Cooley and Ron (2002), Heins (2008), Madsen (2001) and Bob (2005). For a less conventional version of the now-common critique of NGOs, see Petras (1999).
63. Address at Bradley University, Peoria, Illinois, September 25, 1956. http://www.eisenhower.archives.gov/all_about_ike/quotes.html

References

Agarwal, B. 1994. *A Field of One's Own: Gender and Land Rights in South Asia.* Cambridge, UK: Cambridge University Press.

Agin, D. 2006. *Junk Science: An Overdue Assessment of Government, Industry and Faith Groups That Twist Science for Their Own Gain.* New York: St Martin's Press.

Alavi, H. 1965. "Peasants and Revolution." *The Socialist Register.* London: Merlin.

Assayag, J. 2005. "Seeds of Wrath: Agriculture, Biotechnology and Globalization." In *Globalizing India: Perspectives from Below,* edited by Jackie Assayag and Chris Fuller, 65–88. London: Anthem Press.

Bates, R. H. 1981. *Markets and States in Tropical Africa: The Political Basis of Agricultural Policies.* Berkeley: University of California Press.

Benford, R. D., and D. A. Snow. 2000. "Framing Processes and Social Movements: An Overview and Assessment." *Annual Review of Sociology* 26: 611–639.

Bittman, M. 2013. ¡Viva México! *New York Times,* November 29.

Blaikie, P., and H. Brookfield. 1987. *Land Degradation and Society.* London: Methuen.

Blyth, M. 2002. *Great Transformations: Economic Ideas and Institutional Change in the Twentieth Century.* Cambridge, UK: Cambridge University Press.

Blyth, M. 2003. "Structures Do Not Come with an Instruction Sheet: Interests, Ideas, and Progress in Political Science." *Perspectives on Politics* 1(4): 695–706.

Blyth, M. 2013. *Austerity: The History of a Dangerous Idea*. Oxford: Oxford University Press.

Boal, I. A. 2001. "Damaging Crops: Sabotage, Social Memory, and the New Genetic Enclosures." In *Violent Environments*, edited by Nancy L. Peluso and Michael Watts, 146–154. Ithaca, NY: Cornell University Press.

Bob, C. 2005. *The Marketing of Rebellion: Insurgents, Media and Transnational Support*. Cambridge, UK: Cambridge University Press.

Borras, S., Jr., M. Edelman, and C. Kay, eds. 2008. *Transnational Agrarian Movements Confronting Globalization*. Chichester, UK: Wiley-Blackwell.

Brass, T. 2000. *Peasants and Populism: The Return of the Agrarian Myth*. London: Frank Cass.

Charles, D. 2001. *Lords of the Harvest: Biotech, Big Money, and the Future of Food*. Cambridge, MA: Perseus.

Cohen, J. I. 2005. "Poorer Nations Turn to Publicly Developed GM Crops." *Nature Biotechnology* 23(1): 27–33.

Conway, G. 1998. *The Doubly Green Revolution: Food for All in the 21st Century*. Ithaca, NY: Cornell University Press.

Cooley, A., and J. Ron. 2002. "The NGO Scramble: Organizational Insecurity and the Political Economy of Transnational Action." *International Security* 27 (1): 5–39.

DeFrancesco, L. 2013. "How Safe Does Transgenic Food Need to Be?" *Nature Biotechnology* 31 (9): 794–802.

Deininger, K. 2011. "Challenges Posed by the New Wave of Farmland Investment." *Journal of Peasant Studies* 38(2): 217–247.

Douglas, M., and A. Wildavsky. 1982. *Risk and Culture*. Berkeley: University of California Press.

Dryzek, J. S. 2005. *The Politics of the Earth: Environmental Discourses*. Oxford: Oxford University Press.

Edelman, M. 1999. *Peasants against Globalization: Rural Social Movements in Costa Rica*. Stanford, CA: Stanford University Press.

Elster, J. 1993. *Political Psychology*. Cambridge, UK: Cambridge University Press.

Esping-Andersen, G. 1990. *The Three Worlds of Welfare Capitalism*. Princeton, NJ: Princeton University Press.

European Commission. 2010. *A Decade of EU-Funded GMO Research, 2001–2010*. Luxembourg: Publications Office of the European Union.

Ferguson, J. 1994. *The Anti-politics Machine: "Development," Depoliticization, and Bureaucratic Power in Lesotho*. Minneapolis: University of Minnesota Press.

Food and Agriculture Organization of the United Nations (FAO). 2006. *Livestock's Long Shadow: Environmental Issues and Options*. Rome: FAO.

Food and Agriculture Organization of the United Nations (FAO). 2013. *Edible Insects: Future Prospects for Food and Feed Security*. FAO Forestry Paper 171. Rome: FAO.

Fukuda-Parr, S., ed. 2007. *The Gene Revolution: GM Crops and Unequal Development*. London: Earthscan.

Giddens, A. 1999. "Risk and Responsibility." *Modern Law Review* 62(1): 1–10.

Givan, R. K., K. M. Roberts, and S. A. Soule, eds. 2010. *The Diffusion of Social Movements*. New York: Cambridge University Press.

Glover, D. 2010. "The Corporate Shaping of GM Crops as a Technology for the Poor." *Journal of Peasant Studies* 37 (1): 67–90.

Gold, A, G. 2003. "Vanishing: Seeds' Cyclicality." *Journal of Material Culture* 8(3): 255–272.
Goldman, M., ed. 1998. *Privatizing Nature: Political Struggles for the Global Commons.* New Brunswick, NJ: Rutgers University Press.
Goodwyn, L. 1991. *The Populist Moment: A Short History of the Agrarian Revolt in America* Oxford: Oxford University Press.
Goodyear, D. 2013. "Beastly Appetites: The Animals We Love too Much to Eat." *The New Yorker.* November 4.
Halewood, M., I. L. Norigea, and S. Louafi, eds. 2013. *Crop Genetic Resources as Global Commons.* London: Routledge.
Heath, C., and D. Heath. 2007. *Made to Stick: Why Some Ideas Survive and Others Die.* New York: Random House.
Hechter, M. 1981. "Karl Polanyi's Social Theory: A Critique." *Politics and Society* 10 (4): 399–429.
Heins, V. 2008. *Nongovernmental Organizations in International Society: Struggles over Recognition.* New York: Palgrave.
Herring, R. J. 1983. *Land to the Tiller: The Political Economy of Agrarian Reform in South Asia.* New Haven, CT: Yale University Press.
Herring, R. J. 2002. "State Property Rights in Nature." In *Land, Property and the Environment,* edited by John F. Richards, Oakland, CA: Institute for Contemporary Studies 2002.
Herring, R. J. 2006. "Why Did 'Operation Cremate Monsanto' Fail? Science and Class in India's Great Terminator-Technology Hoax." *Critical Asian Studies* 38 (4): 467–493.
Herring, R. J. 2007a. "The Genomics Revolution and Development Studies: Science, Poverty and Politics." *Journal of Development Studies* 43 (1): 1–30.
Herring, R. J. 2007b. "Stealth Seeds: Biosafety, Bioproperty, Biopolitics." *Journal of Development Studies* 43 (1): 130–157.
Herring, R. J., ed. 2007c. *Transgenics and the Poor: Biotechnology in Development Studies.* London: Routledge.
Herring, R. J. 2007d. "Political Ecology from Landscapes to Genomes: Science and Interests." *The Sage Handbook on Environment and Society,* edited by Jules Pretty, Andrew S. Bael, Ted Benton, et al., 290–313. London: SAGE.
Herring, R. J. 2008. "Opposition to Transgenic Technologies: Ideology, Interests, and Collective Action Frames." *Nature Reviews Genetics* 9:458–463.
Herring, R. J. 2009. "Global Rifts over Biotechnology." V.T. Krishnamachari Memorial Lecture. New Delhi: Institute for Economic Growth, Delhi University, Distinguished Lecture Series.
Herring, R. J. 2010. "Framing the GMO: Epistemic Brokers, Authoritative Knowledge and Diffusion of Opposition to Biotechnology." In *The Diffusion of Social Movements,* edited by Rebecca Kolins Givan, Kenneth M. Roberts and Sarah A. Soule, 78–98. New York: Cambridge University Press.
Herring, R. J. 2013. "Re-constructing Facts in Bt Cotton." *Economic and Political Weekly* 48 (18): 63–66.
Herring, R. J., and M. Kandlikar. 2009. "Illicit Seeds: Intellectual Property and the Underground Proliferation of Agricultural Biotechnologies." In *The Politics of Intellectual Property: Contestation over the Ownership, Use, and Control of Knowledge and Information,* edited by Sebastian Haunss and Kenneth C. Shadlen, 56–79. Cheltenham, UK: Edward Elgar.
Herring, R. J., and N. Chandrasekhara Rao. 2012. "On the 'Failure of Bt Cotton': Analysing a Decade of Experience." *Economic and Political Weekly* 47 (18): 45–54.
Ho, M.-W. 2000. *Genetic Engineering: Dream or Nightmare? Turning the Tide on the Brave New World of Bad Science and Big Business.* New York: Continuum.

Houtzager, P. P., and M. Moore, eds. 2003. *Changing Paths: International Development and the New Politics of Inclusion*. Ann Arbor: University of Michigan Press.
IAASTD (International Assessment of Agricultural Knowledge, Science and Technology for Development). 2009. *Agriculture at a Crossroads: The Global Report International Assessment of Agricultural Knowledge, Science, and Technology*. Washington, DC: Island Press.
James, C. Annual. *Global Status of Commercialized Biotech/GM Crops*. Ithaca, NY: International Service for the Acquisition of Agri-Biotech Applications.
Jasanoff, S. 2007. *Designs on Nature: Science and Democracy in Europe and the United States*. Princeton, NJ: Princeton University Press.
Keck, M. E., and K. Sikkink. 1997. *Activists beyond Borders: Advocacy Networks in International Politics*. Ithaca, NY: Cornell University Press.
Kloppenburg, J. R. 2004. *First the Seed: The Political Economy of Plant Biotechnology*. Madison: University of Wisconsin Press 2004.
Kloor, K. 2014. The GMO-Suicide Myth. *Issues in Science and Technology* (Winter). Richardson: National Academy Press, pp. 65–70.
Kloppenburg, J. R., and D. L. Kleinman. 1987. "Seed Wars: Common Heritage, Private Property, and Political Strategy." *Socialist Review* 95 (September–October): 7–41.
Knight, F. H. 1921. *Risk, Uncertainty, and Profit*. Boston: Houghton Mifflin.
Koopmans, R., and S. Olzak. 2004. "Discursive Opportunities and the Evolution of Right-Wing Violence in Germany." *American Journal of Sociology* 110 (1): 198–230.
Larsson, T. 2012. *Land and Loyalty: Security and the Development of Property Rights in Thailand*. Ithaca, NY: Cornell University Press.
Latour, B. 2010. *On the Modern Cult of the Factish Gods*. Durham, NC: Duke University Press.
Lewontin, R. C. 2001. "Genes in the Food!" *New York Review of Books*, June 21.
Lichbach, M. I. 1994. "What Makes Rational Peasants Revolutionary? Dilemma, Paradox, and Irony in Peasant Collective Action." *World Politics* 46 (3): 383–418.
Lipton, M. 1977. *Why Poor People Stay Poor: Urban Bias in World Development*. Cambridge, MA: Harvard University Press.
Lipton, M. 2007. "Plant Breeding and Poverty: Can Transgenic Seeds Replicate the Green Revolution as a Source of Gains for the Poor?" *Journal of Development Studies* 43 (1): 31–62.
Lipton, M., and R. Longhurst. 1989. *New Seeds and Poor People*. Baltimore: Johns Hopkins University Press.
Little, D. 1992. *Understanding Peasant China: Case Studies in the Philosophy of Social Science* New Haven, CT: Yale University Press.
Lomborg, B. 2001. *The Skeptical Environmentalist: Measuring the Real State of the World*. London: Cambridge University Press.
Lybbert, T. J. 2003. "Humanitarian Use Technology Transfer: Issues and Approaches." *Journal of Food, Agriculture & Environment* 1(3–4): 95–99.
Madsen, S. T. 2001. "The View from Vevey." *Economic and Political Weekly*, September, 29, 3733–3742.
Mallén, P. R. 2014. Mexico May See Black Market for Soda, Junk Food after Tax Raises Prices. *International Business Times*, January 13.
McHughen, A. 2000. *Pandora's Picnic Basket: The Potential and Hazards of Genetically Modified Foods*. Oxford: Oxford University Press.
McKibben, B. 2008. *Deep Economy: The Wealth of Communities and the Durable Future*. New York: Henry Holt.

McKie, R. 2012. "Attacks Paid for by Big Business Are 'Driving Science into a Dark Era.'" *The Observer*, February 18.

Mooney, C. 2006. *The Republican War on Science.* New York: Basic Books.

Naim, M. 2005. *Illicit: How Smugglers, Traffickers and Copycats Are Hijacking the Global Economy.* New York: Doubleday.

National Research Council. 2002. *Environmental Effects of Transgenic Plants: The Scope and Adequacy of Regulation.* Washington, DC: The National Academies Press.

National Research Council. 2004. *Safety of Genetically Engineered Foods: Approaches to Assessing Unintended Health Effects.* Washington, DC: The National Academies Press.

National Research Council. 2004. *Safety of Genetically Engineered Foods: Approaches to Assessing Unintended Health Effects.* Washington, DC: The National Academies Press.

National Research Council. 2010a. *Impact of Genetically Engineered Crops on Farm Sustainability in the United States.* Washington, DC: The National Academies Press,.

National Research Council. 2010b. *Toward Sustainable Agricultural Systems in the 21st Century.* Washington, DC: The National Academies Press.

Nestle, M. 2002. *Food Politics: How the Food Industry Influences Nutrition and Health.* Berkeley: University of California Press.

Newell, P. 2008. "Trade and Biotechnology in Latin America: Democratization, Contestation and the Politics of Mobilization." *Journal of Agrarian Change* 8 (2–3): 345–376.

Nuffield Council on Bioethics. 1999. *Genetically Modified Crops: The Ethical and Social Issues.* London: Nuffield Council on Bioethics.

Nuffield Council on Bioethics. 2004. *The Use of Genetically Modified Crops in Developing Countries.* London: National Council on Bioethics.—http://www.nuffieldbioethics.org/

Omvedt, G. 2005. "Farmers' Movements and the Debate on Poverty and Economic Reforms in India." In *Social Movements in India: Poverty, Power, and Politics*, edited by Raka Ray and Mary F. Katzenstein, 179–202. New Delhi: Oxford University Press.

Oreskes, N., and E. M. Conway. 2010. *Merchants of Doubt: How a Handful of Scientists Obscured the Truth on Issues from Tobacco Smoke to Global Warming.* London: Bloomsbury Press.

Paarlberg, R. L. 2008. *Starved for Science: How Biotechnology is Being Kept Out of Africa.* Cambridge, MA: Harvard University Press.

Paarlberg, R. L. 2009. *Food Politics.* Oxford: Oxford University Press.

Paige, J. 1975. *Agrarian Revolution: Social Movements and Export Agriculture in the Underdeveloped World* New York: Free Press.

Petras, J. 1999. "NGOs: In the Service of Imperialism." *Journal of Contemporary Asia* 29 (4): 429–440.

Pinstrup-Andersen, P. 2007. *Ethics, Hunger and Globalization: In Search of Appropriate Policies.* Dordrecht, The Netherlands: Springer-Verlag.

Pinstrup-Anderson, P., and E. Schioler. 2000. *Seeds of Contention: World Hunger and the Global Controversy over GM Crops.* Baltimore: Johns Hopkins University Press.

Polanyi, K. 1944. *The Great Transformation.* Boston: Beacon Press: Boston.

Pollan, M. 2008. *In Defense of Food: An Eater's Manifesto.* New York: Penguin Press.

Popkin, S. L. 1979. *The Rational Peasant: The Political Economy of Rural Society in Vietnam.* Berkeley: University of California Press.

Reitan, R. 2007. *Global Activism.* New York: Routledge.

Robbins, P. 2004. *Political Ecology: A Critical Introduction.* Malden, MA: Blackwell.

Roberts, P. 2008. *The End of Food.* Boston: Houghton Mifflin.

Robertson, B., and P. Pinstrup-Andersen. 2010. "Global Land Acquisition: Neo-colonialism or Development Opportunity?" *Food Security* 2 (3): 271–283.

The Royal Society. 2009. *Reaping the Benefits: Science and the Sustainable Intensification of Global Agriculture.* London: The Royal Society.

Schurman, R. A., and D.T. Kelso. 2003. *Engineering Trouble: Biotechnology and Its Discontents.* London: University of California Press.

Schurman, R. A., and W. A. Munro. 2010. *Fighting for the Future of Food: Activists versus Agribusiness in the Struggle over Biotechnology.* Minneapolis: University of Minnesota Press.

Scoones, I. 2002. "Can Agricultural Biotechnology Be Pro-poor? A Sceptical Look at the Emerging 'Consensus.'" *IDS Bulletin* 33 (4): 114–119.

Scoones, I. 2008. "Mobilizing against GM Crops in India, South Africa and Brazil." *Journal of Agrarian Change* 8 (2–3): 315–344.

Scott, J. C. 1985. *Weapons of the Weak: Everyday Forms of Peasant Resistance.* New Haven, CT: Yale University Press.

Scott, J. C. 1998. *Seeing Like a State: How Certain Schemes to Improve the Human Condition Have Failed.* New Haven, CT: Yale University Press.

Shanin, T. 1972. *The Awkward Class.* Oxford: Clarendon.

Shapiro, J. 2001. *Mao's War against Nature: Politics and the Environment in Revolutionary China.* Cambridge, UK: Cambridge University Press.

Smith, J., and H. Johnston, eds. 2002. *Globalization and Resistance: Transnational Dimensions of Social Movements.* Lanham, MD: Rowman and Littlefield.

Shiva, V. 1997. *Biopiracy: The Plunder of Nature and Knowledge.* Cambridge, MA: South End Press.

Shiva, V. 2000. *Stolen Harvest: The Hijacking of the Global Food Supply.* Cambridge, MA: South End Press.

Shiva, V., A. H. Jafri, A. Emani, and M. Pande. 2000. *Seeds of Suicide: The Ecological and Human Costs of Globalization of Agriculture.* New Delhi, India: Research Foundation for Science, Technology and Ecology.

Skocpol, T. 1979. *States and Social Revolutions.* Cambridge, UK: Cambridge University Press.

Skocpol, T. 1982. "What Makes Peasants Revolutionary?" *Comparative Politics* 14 (3): 351–375

Specter, M. 2009. *Denialism.* New York: Penguin.

Stinchcombe, A. L. 1961. "Agricultural Enterprise and Rural Class Relations." *American Journal of Sociology* 67 (2): 165–176.

Sunstein, C. 2009. *On Rumors.* New York: Farrar, Straus, and Giroux.

Tait, Joyce. 2001. "More Faust than Frankenstein: The European Debate about the Precautionary Principle and Risk Regulation for Genetically Modified Crops." *Journal of Risk Research* 4(2): 175–189.

Tarrow, S. 2005. *The New Transnational Activism.* Cambridge, UK: Cambridge University Press.

Tarrow, S. 2011. *Power in Movement.* Cambridge, UK: Cambridge University Press.

Taubes, G. 2001. "The Soft Science of Dietary Fat." *Science* 30 291 (5513): 2536–2545.

Taubes, G. 2007. *Good Calories, Bad Calories: Challenging the Conventional Wisdom on Diet, Weight Control, and Disease.* New York: Knopf.

Thaxton, R. 1983. *China Turned Rightside Up.* New Haven, CT: Yale University Press.

Thies, J. E., and M. H. Devare. 2007. "An Ecological Assessment of Transgenic Crops." *Journal of Development Studies* 43(1): 97–129.

Tiberghien, Y. 2007. "Europe: Turning against Agricultural Biotechnology in the Late 1990s." In *The Gene Revolution: GM Crops and Unequal Development,* edited by Sakiko Fukuda-Parr, 51–68. London: Earthscan.
Uphoff, N. 2012. "Supporting Food Security in the 21st Century through Resource-Conserving Increases in Agricultural Production." *Agriculture & Food Security* 1:18. http://www.agricultureandfoodsecurity.com/content/1/1/18
Uphoff, N., ed. 2002. *Agroecological Innovations: Increasing Food Production with Participatory Development.* IUCN Policy and Global Change. London: Earthscan.
Wade, R. 1978. *Village Republics: Economic Conditions of Collective Action in South India.* Princeton, NJ: Princeton University Press.
Walton, J., and D. Seddon. 1994. *Free Markets and Food Riots: The Politics of Global Adjustment.* Oxford: Basil Blackwell.
Waltz, E. 2009. "Battlefield." *Nature* 461 (2009): 27–32.
Wesseler, J., and N. Kalaitzandonakes. 2011. "Present and Future EU GMO Policy." In *EU Policy for Agriculture, Food and Rural Areas,* edited by Arie Oskam, Gerrit Meesters, and Huib Silvis, 403–414. Wageningen, The Netherlands: Wageningen Academic.
Wolf, E. 1969. *Peasant Wars of the Twentieth Century.* New York: Harper and Row.
Wolford, W. 2010. *This Land Is Ours Now: Social Mobilization and the Meanings of Land in Brazil.* Durham, NC: Duke University Press.
Wood, E. J. 2003. *Insurgent Collective Action and Civil War in El Salvador.* New York: Cambridge University Press.
World Bank. 2007. *World Development Report 2008: Agriculture for Development.* Washington, DC: World Bank.
Yang, J. 2012. *Tombstone: The Untold Story of Mao's Great Famine.* London: Allen Lane.

PART I

PRODUCTION: TECHNOLOGY, KNOWLEDGE, AND POLITICS

CHAPTER 2

SCIENCE, POLITICS, AND THE FRAMING OF MODERN AGRICULTURAL TECHNOLOGIES

JOHN HARRISS AND DREW STEWART

> The tragedy of the Green Revolution lies precisely in its narrow technological focus that ignored the far more important social and structural underpinnings of hunger. The technology strengthened the very structures that enforce hunger. A new "gene revolution" will only exacerbate the worst errors of the Green Revolution.
>
> (Open Letter to M.Jacques Diouf, D-G, FAO 16 June 2004)

> The development of IR8 and its dissemination throughout Asia is . . . literally helping to fill hundreds of millions of rice bowls once only half full.
>
> (Lester Brown 1970)

Introduction

There have been two major developments in agricultural technology in the last half century, each of which continues to be the object of heated controversy. The first was the introduction of higher-yielding, or "modern" varieties (HYVs/MVs) of the major cereals. This process began in the 1940s, but it took off only in the 1960s (when the rice variety IR8, referred to by Lester Brown in our first epigraph, was introduced). This gave rise to what came to be known as the "Green Revolution" (GR). The second development involves the application of genetic engineering in agriculture, beginning in the 1980s. As a result of this innovation, what have been popularly labeled as "GMOs"—genetically modified organisms—began to be introduced into cultivation in the 1990s.

If there are good grounds for arguing that the introduction of MVs did bring about a "revolution," through their impacts on the modes of agricultural production, and on food supplies—and through these effects ultimately on economies and societies in Asia and Latin America—there is equally no doubt that, so far, there has been no comparable "gene revolution" in agriculture.

While there are reasons for believing that genetic engineering has the potential for bringing about even more dramatic changes in agriculture, rural livelihoods, and food supplies than those associated with the GR, its impacts have been felt, thus far, largely in North American agriculture, which accounts for the largest share of the current global acreage under genetically engineered varieties. While this is changing rapidly—developing countries are expected to exceed rich-country biotech agricultural production before 2015 (James 2010), and Brazil, Argentina, and India are already the principal followers of the United States—it is genetically modified cotton, grown by millions of small farmers in China and India, that has had the most significant effect upon the poor (though these effects are controversial; see Glover 2010 and Stone 2012 for an analysis of the difficulties that arise in resolving this problem). A "gene revolution" to compare with the "Green Revolution" hasn't yet come about because of the well-organized opposition to genetically engineered *staple food* crops, both in rich countries and in the major emerging economies—including, significantly, both democratic India and authoritarian China. Part of the reason for this, in some cases, is that popular opposition in rich countries makes governments in emerging economies nervous about their exports. The technology has been successfully framed in a negative way by critics, and this has caused politicians in many countries—often against what their farmers evidently want—to restrict its development. This negative framing has drawn in part on the earlier, though politically much less successful, critique of the Green Revolution. This chapter is about the ways in which these important agricultural technologies have been framed, and it offers an evaluation of evidence and arguments on both sides of the controversies surrounding them.

The Grounds for Critique: Concerns about "Nature" and about Capitalist "Imperialism"

In large measure, the critical opposition that the Green Revolution (GR) attracted—unsuccessful though it was in stopping that transformation of agriculture in many parts of the "developing" world—has spilled over directly into a much more successful campaign of resistance to the gene revolution, outside North America and some countries in South America (Herring 2010). Criticism of the GR brought together unlikely allies, including environmental populists who are critics of conventional science, and some from the political Left who have often been staunch advocates of the application of science and technology to social problems. The former attacked the technology on which the GR was based, because they saw it as depending on the "conquest of nature" rather than working both "with nature" and with the indigenous knowledge of farming people—and as imposing centralized capitalist control upon peasant farmers. The technology made peasants dependent upon externally manufactured inputs; it threatened the loss of genetic diversity and environmental devastation; and it would bring poverty and be the cause of violence in societies. A classic source for these views—which depend significantly on an idealized view of the "peasant" (see Shome, this volume)—is the Indian scientist Vandana Shiva's book *The Violence of the Green Revolution* (1991). For Shiva (who holds a PhD in the philosophy of science) and others, the people who would most benefit, in the end, from the technology would be the mainly American chemical and engineering companies that were seen as being the principal suppliers of the inputs that the GR required, and as having been able to prise open developing country markets as a result of the imposition of US power. It was this argument, having to do with the extent to which the GR could be seen as an imperialist, capitalist project, that would ultimately impoverish peasants of the former colonies (an important source for these arguments was an article by Harry Cleaver, published in 1972), that brought together the Left and the environmentalists.

How much more does the potential gene revolution open itself up to exactly the same criticisms, seeming as it does to involve even more profound "tinkering with nature," and depending as it has done to a great extent on the activities of a small number of mainly American corporations—and especially on one of them, Monsanto, which had already earned a terrible reputation for some of its products (Robin 2010; Monsanto Song). "Food sovereignty"—a term that the Left has used to express its resistance to corporate control of agriculture—is now believed to be imperiled, and "GMOs" are seen as playing a large role in such corporate control, in what McMichael (2005) calls the "corporate food regime" (see also Pechlaner and Otero 2008). The transnational farmers' organization La Vía Campesina brought the term "food sovereignty" to prominence at the World Food Summit in 1996, posing it as an alternative to neoliberal policies. Food sovereignty is taken to mean peoples' rights to define their own food and agriculture policy, and to protect and regulate domestic agricultural production and trade, outside the control of big capital and without fear of the dumping of cheap food by third countries (Patel 2009). The gene revolution, however, according to anti-GMO scholars and activists, means "enclosing of the commons"—in this case the private corporate ownership of genes that include the outcomes of millennia of collective human activity in cultivation, plant breeding, and selection. The legacy of the GR has disposed the Left to fight the "biopiracy" of GM technology—when corporations in rich countries with limited biodiversity go prospecting for genetic material in poor countries—and the threat that it poses to livelihoods and food sovereignty. For the 816 signatories in the open letter to M.Diouf cited in our second epigraph, the GR has already caused devastation, and the gene revolution threatens to wreak even more havoc with nature and societies.

Other scholars, however, strongly believe that the GR has had positive consequences for humanity as a whole, and that genetic engineering can realize similar, positive results for agriculture as those it has brought (without causing much controversy at all) in medicine. Some argue that it is morally wrong for small numbers of vociferous activists to attempt to deny societies, and especially poor people in poor countries, the possible—indeed, likely—benefits from the cultivation of genetically engineered food crops (see Nuffield Council on Bioethics 1999). Of course, we cannot be certain, they argue, that there will be no harmful effects in the future from the cultivation and the consumption of GMOs, even if the record so far—from the experience of the United States, where it is thought that 70 percent of all foods sold commercially have GMO content (Paarlberg 2010, 166)—seems positive. No amount of science can finally prove that there can *never* be harmful effects, for the environment or for the health of humans and of animals. This is to set the precautionary bar too high—at a height that would have prevented the development of air travel, for instance, or of cell phone technology. Therefore, the protagonists say, we must weigh this definite uncertainty against the known and measurable risks—to the environment, to health, and to the sustainability of livelihoods—of continuing cultivation on existing lines, and the definable benefits from genetically engineered cultivars.

We do not set out in this chapter to resolve the controversies over the GR and the gene revolution. That would be to invite hubris. But we do aim to explain the arguments on both sides, and the prior assumptions, value positions, and politics that frame them. We begin with an account of the characteristics of the technologies, before going on to explain the controversies over the Green Revolution and then over "GM." Though much of the criticism of the Green Revolution from the 1970s and 1980s has been fairly comprehensively refuted, elements of it remain influential, as they are amongst advocates of food sovereignty, who want to resist what they see as the strengthening of corporate control of agriculture. There are significant continuities with criticism of GM—shown in the open letter addressed to M. Diouf. As we have pointed out there is no "gene revolution," as yet, to compare with the Green Revolution, and we can trace its politics only tentatively. We do this through an examination of recent controversies over GM food crops in the two most important "emerging economies"—India and China.

The Technologies

The modern varieties (MVs), especially of wheat and rice, on which the GR was based, were the products of conventional plant breeding, the science—involving seed selection and selective breeding—that is essentially a refinement of the practical experimentation of farmers over millennia, and on which all agriculture has depended from its origins. The MVs were capable of much higher yields, if grown with adequate supplies of water and fertilizer. They were bred to be fertilizer-responsive, and the breeders succeeded in introducing a "dwarfing gene" that gave the plants much shorter and stiffer stalks (they were sometimes called "dwarf varieties"), so that more energy was put into producing grain. Some MVs reached maturity more quickly, making for increased cropping intensity. In practice some varieties, such as the IR20 variety of rice ("IR" refers to the fact that it had been bred at the International Rice Research Institute [IRRI] in the Philippines, which had been founded with Rockefeller support in 1962), turned out to be relatively tolerant of drought, and to produce comparatively good yields even in relatively unfavorable conditions. Varieties like this then came to be cultivated very extensively over large areas, giving rise, reasonably enough, to fears of the implications of monocropping, particularly because of the possibility of large scale pest and disease infestation. Indeed, cultivators of MVs very often found themselves on a "pesticide treadmill," having to invest more and more in plant-protection chemicals that proved to be less and less effective. At the same time, the moisture demands of MVs, particularly when they brought more intensive cultivation, could mean excessive use of water, and especially of groundwater. The varieties encouraged mechanized pumping of groundwater, and sometimes (though not invariably) this depended on government policiesthe mechanization of land preparation, harvesting, and threshing, whether or not this brought agronomic advantages (see, for example, Binswanger 1978).

MVs are actually GMOs, given that they involve genetic modification (such as the incorporation of the dwarfing genes), but they have not been genetically "engineered." In genetic engineering, desirable genes (and their inherent characteristics) are transferred, in a laboratory, between organisms (and usually across species) so as to create desirable traits that it would otherwise be impossible to bring about through conventional breeding. It may sound, to those who aren't scientists, to be a difficult process, but in fact such genetic engineering is regularly carried on by ordinary college students of biology. It is not, after all, so very "hi-tech"—and this is why, contrary to the arguments of anti-GMO campaigners, it has been possible for a veritable cottage industry to arise in parts of India, China, and Brazil, for the production of transgenics, often incorporating genetic material "pirated" from big corporations (very much like "pirated" film and music CDs, see Herring 2007b).

An important example of genetic engineering is that of the insertion of the gene Cry1Ac from the soil bacterium *Bacillus thuringiensis* (Bt) into plants to provide them with insecticidal qualities—the resulting Bt protein, when ingested by certain pests, causes the insects to die. This particular process has been widely approved with cotton and maize (used for fiber and feed respectively—though Bt enters the food chain from both sources), but it has, so far, been highly contested for use in food staples such as rice (as we discuss later, with particular reference to China). The labeling "GMOs," or just of "GM" in regard to the technology, which has acquired a powerful negative valence (Herring 2010), is used to refer to the products of genetic engineering—though this process is more accurately referred to as recombinant DNA (rDNA) technology, and the cultivars produced by it are better described as "transgenics" (Herring 2007a). These cultivars include both hybrids and open pollinated varieties. The distinction is important (see Swaminathan 2011). Hybrid plants, whether conventional ones or transgenics, typically yield 10-20 percent more than their parent plants, but they do not breed true if they are grown again. New seeds (the product of cross-pollination by hand—for the case of cotton, see Ramamurthy 2010) have to be purchased every season. In the case of open pollinated varieties—even if they are transgenics—seeds can be kept by farmers.

The transgenics (as we will now usually describe them) that have been widely cultivated hitherto—developed mainly, it is true, by a small number of US-based corporations, which have of course been interested primarily in profits and not in the welfare of poor people—have been engineered to incorporate two traits in particular, those of herbicide tolerance (the leading trait thus far), and of pest resistance (achieved through the insertion of Bt). Herbicide tolerance (HT) means that a weed-killing chemical, such as the broad spectrum glysophate of Monsanto's well-known RoundUp (though this has been off-patent for some time and is now available in India and elsewhere as a generic) can be applied without fear of killing the crop; Bt, as we have explained, is a natural pesticide. Thus far, four crops account for almost all the transgenics that have entered into production, though experimental work has gone on with many more: HT soy accounts for about 50 percent of the total area across the world under transgenics; HT and Bt maize for 31 percent of this area; Bt cotton for 14 percent; and HT canola for 5 percent (James 2010). It is striking that these are crops used for fiber (cotton), processed oils and starches (soy and canola), and animal feeds (yellow maize), rather than being staple food crops (though note our earlier qualification that Bt, certainly, has entered the food chain, while soy is contained in much that is eaten by people, especially in North America). The only transgenic staple to have received official state approval for commercialization and to be widely cultivated is white maize, grown in South Africa; a fact that reflects the considerable anxiety that surrounds the idea of "GM food" and the extent of popular resistance to it, in Europe in particular. But it is also important to note the rise in use of pirated or "stealth" seeds for producing transgenic staples—such as Bt rice in China and Vietnam—that small farmers find desirable despite the legal and economic risks associated with the contraband germplasm.

The most important trait that has been engineered—herbicide tolerance—is of value to large-scale commercial producers, who have been the main beneficiaries of the very limited portfolio of transgenic seed crop traits. HT may not be of value to small farmers in poor countries where labor is cheap (though, increasingly, not always available to farmers). Pest resistance, however, is certainly of value to such farmers, as the rapid spread of Bt cotton among small producers in China, India, and Pakistan has demonstrated. Protagonists of genetic engineering in agriculture point, however, to the potential of the technology for developing other traits that will be of considerable benefit to small farmers in poor countries, and ultimately to consumers as well—for whom they will mean lower food prices (see Lipton 2007, Pray and Naseem 2007). The most important trait that might be engineered is that of higher yield, not yet certainly realized in food staples, but clearly important in a context in which, for the first time since the Green Revolution, crop yields globally are growing more slowly than population, for even though population growth has slowed to around 1.4 percent per annum the yields of both wheat and rice are now almost flat ("The 9 Billion-People Question" 2011). Then there is a potential for enhancing nutrition and health—as has been claimed in regard to "Golden Rice," a transgenic variety of rice that can enhance intakes of vitamin A and protect children against blindness (Bouis 2007; Stein, this volume). Other important traits that might be developed include drought tolerance, making for water saving—a trait which is of great importance in the context of increasing water scarcity in much of the world—and resistance to salinity, which would have the effect of permitting cultivation again in the large areas of formerly cultivated land that have been subject to salinization.[1] Genetic engineering has the virtues—it is argued—by comparison with other types of plant breeding, both of speeding up development and of being more controlled

(Batista et al. 2008). Gressel (2008) has argued that the conventional plant breeding on which the GR was based has reached a yield and improvement plateau—a kind of a "glass ceiling," he calls it—because of the very limited set of traits with which it has worked. He argues indeed that genetic engineering has the potential actually to *recover* diversity in agricultural ecosystems.

Critics, on the other hand, including those who signed the letter to the Director-General of the Food and Agriculture Organization (FAO) from which we quoted in our second epigraph, fear that the cultivation of transgenics will enhance the damage that they see as having been brought about by the GR—through pauperization of people (because of what are believed to be the very high costs of the technology), loss of genetic diversity, environmental destruction, and by making nations dependent for their food security upon Western corporations. They fear it will bring new dangers as well, especially to human health. Thies and Devare (2007) list the major ecological concerns associated with transgenics as (1) the potential for "gene flow" from them to wild plant populations; (2) harmful effects on nontargeted organisms (including humans); (3) transgenic residue persisting in the environment with long-term negative effects; and (4) pests developing resistance to insecticidal crops. Gene flow to wild relatives has been demonstrated in field studies—as we shall see, this is an issue for GM rice—but as of yet it is claimed that "there are no known substantiated harmful effects of bioengineered crops on human health or the environment" (Gregory et al. 2008, 290). Thies and Devare (2007) suggested, however, that the development of resistance to insecticidal crops is "possible and eventually likely," and it seemed that they were proven prophetic when Monsanto claimed to have found resistance to its *Bt* cotton in India in late 2009 (Monsanto 2010). It should be noted, however, that the company has a financial interest in these claims, and Indian scientists working with cotton have not found resistance to the major bollworm species.

The Green Revolution Controversy

The new varieties of wheat, at first, and then of rice, began to be disseminated widely in the 1960s, at a time when there were widespread Malthusian fears about the consequences of the "population explosion," and the outstripping of agricultural growth by that of populations (e.g., Ehrlich 1968). Between 1960 and 1990, however, total cereal production and yields in developing countries doubled, outpacing population growth and bringing about an average increase of around 25 percent in the availability of calories (Davies 2003; and see Pingali 2012). Almost as important, from an environmental point of view, was that the increase in food production was achieved from about the same cultivated area. The GR saved the ploughing up of a great deal more land: it is estimated, for example, that for India to have produced the same quantities of grain by 2000 without MVs would have required at least a doubling of the cultivated area (Paarlberg 2010, 63). The aggregate picture seems a positive one. The weight of evidence from a range of studies across Asia also shows that the GR achieved the trick of increasing both farmers' and agricultural laborers' incomes, and of keeping down food prices for the poor—who are generally dependent upon purchased food, and whose expenditure on staples usually accounts for two-thirds or more of their incomes (Lipton with Longhurst 1989; Lipton 2007). Africa, however, was left out, at least until the 1980s. The varieties that were successful elsewhere in the world proved generally to be unsuited to African conditions, and the major food crops over most of Africa remained outside the GR until "improved varieties of sorghum, millet and cassava... started to emerge around the middle to late 1980s" (Pingali 2012, 12305).

Given the evidence of success, how can the GR be described—as in our second epigraph—as a "tragedy?" Remarkably, perhaps, it began to be described as such almost from the outset. The leading critics mostly identified themselves as being on the Left (for example, Frankel 1971; Cleaver 1972; Griffin 1972, 1979). They saw the new agricultural technology as supplying a technical "fix" for the social and political problems of poor countries, which have to do especially with inequalities in access to land and water, and which remained unaddressed, especially because of the failures of redistributive land reform (outside China, Taiwan, and South Korea). It was believed, with reason, that "the establishment of IRRI in 1962 was designed to prove that hunger could be solved by technology rather than by revolution" (Orr 2012); and the new technology was expected, by its advocates, to create a "Green Revolution" that would supplant the threat of "red revolution." The term "Green Revolution" seems to have been used for the first time by the chief administrator of USAID in 1968 with exactly this idea in mind. Rather than fixing these social problems, however, it was thought by critics that the introduction of the new technology would exacerbate them (as the letter addressed to M. Diouf argued). This, it was thought, was because although the new technology might be technically "scale neutral" (the necessary inputs being divisible into smaller packages for smaller farms), it was not "resource neutral." In other words, those farmers with more land, better access to water, and greater financial resources would be able to make more effective use of the technology. Smaller cultivators would make themselves dependent on purchased inputs and be driven into debt. The land holdings of some of them would be bought up by richer farmers. Not only would inequality be increased because of these changes, but poverty would increase as well. Environmental damage would be caused because of the excessive use of agrochemicals, both fertilizers and plant-protection chemicals, and by excessive use of water.

All of these things did happen, in some places at least, and in some periods—though whether they can be held to have been brought about by the new technology in itself remains a matter for debate. In India, for example, excessive use of inputs was encouraged by government subsidies (Harriss-White and Janakarajan 2004). Still, case studies with negative evidence lent credence to the way in which critics of the GR generalized an understanding of processes of agrarian social and economic change informed by a Marxist model which holds that there is a structurally determined process of polarization of rural classes in commercializing rural economies. It is pretty much inevitable, according to this model, that inequality will increase and that very many rural people will be pauperized. The influence of the model was reflected in the ways in which scholars viewed the facts (Harriss 1989; Orr 2012); while "the facts" themselves were derived initially especially from studies of particular villages. This was the method used, notably, in an influential research project conducted by the United Nations Research Institute on Social Development (Griffin 1972; Pearse 1980). The results of village studies were generalized, however, in a way that is unjustifiable. In Bangladesh, for instance, two-thirds of the 127 village studies included in one listing of them were conducted in just five of the (then) nineteen districts of the country—and their findings were shown to have been locally specific once large-scale nationally representative surveys were undertaken (Orr 2012; see also Harriss 1977 on bias in the perception of agrarian change in India). Return visits to villages and regions from which evidence had been obtained that supported the critique of the GR also showed that the early fears were sometimes unjustified, and that, for example, small farmers were able successfully to adopt MVs and to benefit from them—leading some of the critics to recant (Orr 2012). Different underlying concerns (reflecting different beliefs) influenced the design of research and the interpretation of empirical findings (Harriss-White and Harriss 2007; Orr 2012). All these problems of knowledge—the methodological problems that have to do with determining what "the facts" are, those that relate to the judgment of these facts (and their deployment as "evidence") in the light of preferred hypotheses or models, and the ways in which science is influenced by beliefs and values—are all also extremely important in the controversy over transgenics.

Reaching general conclusions about the economic, social, and environmental implications of the introduction of the GR technology is, then, fraught with difficulty. All "general" conclusions are liable to reflect fallacies of aggregation, and there is a sense in which only findings that are specific to place and time can possibly be valid. Yet much of the evidence calls the generalization of the "polarization model" into question, and it demonstrates that very many people, including very large numbers of very poor people in a country such as India, have benefited. Econometric studies generally "find high poverty reduction elasticities for agricultural productivity growth" (Pingali 2012, 12303; and see Lipton 2007), though nutritional gains have been uneven (Pingali 2012, 12304). It is difficult, however, as we have pointed out, to tease out the effects of changes in agricultural technology from those of other factors that have been in play at the same time (Harriss 1992). This affects assessments of both positive and negative outcomes. As Pingali writes,

> The GR also spurred its share of unintended negative consequences, often not because of the technology itself, but rather because of the policies that were used to promote rapid intensification of agricultural systems and increase food supplies. Some areas were left behind, and even where it successfully increased agricultural productivity, the GR was not always the panacea for solving the myriad of poverty, food security and nutrition problems facing poor societies.
>
> (Pingali 2012, 12304)

The fact that the GR can be described as a "tragedy," when there is strong evidence of its having had many positive outcomes, is due in large part to the pervasiveness of the early critiques in public consciousness, and these were given a new lease of life by the surge of environmentalism in the 1980s and into the 1990s. Environmentalism, internationally, gathered force in the 1970s and 1980s (for a history see Guha 2000), and it was in this context that concerns about the impact of the GR on genetic diversity; about the effects of intensive use of agrochemicals on water quality, on soils, and on the health of human beings and of animals; and over the mining of water resources were married to the old charge that the GR technology was the instrument of Western corporate capital (somewhat strangely, perhaps, given that the seeds were developed especially in the international *public* sector) and represented a threat to national food security or "sovereigny" (though, of course, ironically, India at least achieved "food sovereignty" through the GR). The whole was also tied, with especial force and effectiveness by Vandana Shiva (1991), to ideas about the value of "indigenous" farming knowledge, the merits of "traditional" agriculture (involving mixtures and rotations of crops, which were held often to be more productive than GR monocultures) and the virtues of a peasant way of life. There is substance to all these arguments (except perhaps, the last, which is a value judgment), but the presentation of them by writers like Shiva was stronger in terms of rhetoric than of fact, and dependent upon generalization from a few specific cases or sets of data in a way that was quite as ambitious as that of the early critics of the GR. The power of environmentalism has been such, however, that it trumped concerns about agricultural development and food supplies, especially in regard to Africa. Robert Paarlberg (2008, chapter 3), for example, thinks that populist environmentalism—through its influence on large numbers of western NGOs—has been a key factor in stalling efforts to bring a GR to Africa.

The controversies over the GR reflect different "framings" that have influenced the collection of evidence and the ways in which facts are viewed. The power of different framings is more cultural and political than it is dependent upon scientific understanding, as both Herring (2010) and Glover (2010) argue—though the former believes that transgenic varieties have been subject to particularly effective negative framing, whereas the latter claims they have received unduly positive constructions. Both refer to the effectiveness of particular individuals whose authority is accepted, who serve as "epistemic brokers" (Vandana Shiva has been one), successfully popularizing their particular readings of complex and contested scientific evidence. Different framings reflect differing values and worldviews that are not subject to empirical refutation (for a general discussion, see Thompson et al. 1990). But this is not a reason for refusing to test the propositions that follow from them as rigorously as possible—as has happened, for example, in the case of the "polarization thesis" in the context of the GR. The framing of evidence in regard to social questions- which is comparable with the "spin" that is now commonly put on events and problems by politicians and their speechwriters—is inevitable. So much the more important, therefore, that all "framings" be subjected to critical scrutiny.

The "GM" Controversy

Schurman and Munro (2010) argue that three factors underpin the "GM" controversy. First, there was the emergence of the "knowledge economy." In the 1950s, publicly funded research led most agricultural advances (notably the GR), but by the 1970s, and the first splicing of genes from one organism into another by American scientists in 1973, venture capital began to move into biotechnology. In America, the US Supreme Court decided in the case of *Diamond v. Chakrabarty* (1980) that "GMOs" were legally patentable, meaning that they are the subject of intellectual property rights and, thus, that profits from them can be protected (at least in the US—patents are national). By 1983, the Food and Drug Administration (FDA) of the United States had approved the first genetically engineered product for commercialization, human insulin; in the same year, Monsanto created the first genetically modified plant.

Second, Schurman and Munro (2010) show that this new domination of private players in scientific research didn't "just happen." The American government actively facilitated it through private research tax credits and regulatory cutbacks. In the international arena, foreign policy pushed developing countries to liberalize their agricultural markets. Finally, the new "knowledge economy" demanded internationally recognized international property rights (IPRs) in order that R&D investments in a global economy be protected. The 1994 Agreement on Trade-Related Aspects of Intellectual Property Rights (TRIPS) protected all technological products or processes that are new, involve an inventive step, and have an industrial application. These steps led to concentration of the seed industry globally into the hands of a few multinational corporations, with one prevailing leader: "If there was one company whose name became virtually synonymous around the world with the term GMO, that firm was unquestionably Monsanto" (Schurman and Munro 2010,18).

Third, in this same period, new transnational social movements sprang up in reaction to the new proficiencies of humanity to destroy itself—through nuclear power and weapons, chemical weapons, toxic waste, deforestation, and climate change. Two leading international environmental NGOs—Greenpeace and Friends of the Earth (FoE)—born in the mid-1970s, later became major anti-GMO forces. Chemical companies, including Monsanto, felt the backlash of the burgeoning environmental movement. Costs increased due to heightened regulation and new lawsuits. In this context the decision to make a transition from chemical production to agri-biotechnology was seen—ironically it seems, with hindsight—as exceptionally "green" (and see Shome, this volume). Scientists saw gene transfer as inherently "safe" when compared to conventional breeding methods:

> The act of splicing to generate a transgenic organism is a modest step when compared to the genomic changes induced by all the "crosses" and breeding events used in agriculture and husbandry. The molecular biology tools simply add a new precision, speed and reach to this indispensable process of species domestication.
>
> (European Commission 2010, 20)

As the European Commission went on to argue, however, in spite of these views on the part of many scientists, "public opinion did not 'buy into' this line of thought. . . . The fact that humans can "engineer" a gene from a species of one kingdom to produce a species of another has fuelled imaginations and frightened the public" (European

Commission 2010, 20). The archetypal image is that of "Frankenfoods." Thanks to the preceding decades of environmental activism, many people and organizations were predisposed to criticism of transgenics—labeled as "GMOs," and in this way very successfully separated in the public mind from other genetically engineered products, such as insulin, that have been widely accepted (Herring 2010). Multilateral organizations responded to these real or imagined fears at an early stage. The 1992 UN Conference on Environment and Development (popularly called the Earth Summit) launched the Cartagena Protocol on Biosafety, which, after its adoption in January 2000 (though it came into force only in 2003), created the beginnings of an international regime for regulating transnational trade in GMOs. Most significantly, the protocol followed a *precautionary approach* that gave developing countries the option of rejecting GMO imports in order to protect the environment or human health if it was felt that there was insufficient scientific evidence to prove a product safe. The critics of this precautionary approach—such as the Nuffield Council on Bioethics (1999)—argued, as we pointed out earlier, that it is impossible for science to predict or account for all the possible dangers of any new product, including transgenics. There will always be insufficient scientific evidence to prove the absolute safety of any product (GM or not), but disallowing its use negates any and all benefits that might be gained if the product is approved.

Anti-GMO activists' greatest success was Europe's turning away from transgenics, beginning in 1999, with a moratorium on approving more transgenic products for commercialization. Greenpeace blockaded Monsanto's first introduction of unlabeled GM crops into Europe, gaining instant press coverage. In the next three years, public opinion shifted dramatically in Europe. The European Parliament became increasingly anti-GMO, and the European public dismissed the potential benefits from cultivation of transgenics (while simultaneously reaping the benefits of pharmaceuticals produced by comparable genetic engineering). Europe's anti-GMO stance had ramifications for agriculturally dependent poor countries, which feared the economic effects of having their crops rejected or arable land "tainted" by transgenics. Many developing countries moved to stop GM seeds from passing their borders. And international development institutions, depending in part on European budgetary allocations, have not been big supporters of transgenics (Paarlberg and Pray 2007).

The Left has largely couched its resistance to corporately controlled agriculture—and the role of transgenics in that control through seed ownership—under the banner of "food sovereignty," as we noted earlier. The food price spikes of 2008, when staple prices increased by as much as 500 percent in many poor countries, lent force to the idea of limiting the "commodification" of food, by treating it as an exceptional product that shouldn't be allowed to be controlled by WTO rules. Such concerns about food sovereignty and about the destruction of the lifeways of rural people at the hands of a small number of capitalist corporations are enhanced by the history of aggressive tactics on the part of the corporations, and by knowledge of the intimate connections of these companies with state agencies that are responsible for food safety in the United States (see, e.g., Weis 2007, chapter 4). What are seen as aggressive tactics includes the development of the "terminator gene," which would create sterile seeds, and thus clearly be of enormous commercial advantage to seed companies, because it would mean that farmers would always have to buy new seeds. The patent for this, now owned by jointly by Monsanto and the US Department of Agriculture, does exist (though no one has ever actually applied for a license to use it, and, contrary to the claims of anti-GMO campaigners, the gene has not actually been incorporated into any seeds that have been put on the market).

These reasonable concerns are then married to fears about the possibly harmful ecological effects of the introduction of transgenics (see Thies and Devare 2007), and to fears about their implications for human health (e.g., Sahai 2011)—all in a context in which it is held that the regulatory capacities of states in regard to biosafety are woefully inadequate—and to claims about the impoverishment of rural people. The widely reported suicides of farmers in some parts of India that are held to have been because of indebtedness brought about by GM cultivation have provided a potent narrative in support of these claims. The whole has made for an extraordinarily powerful negative framing: "rDNA plants have been successfully constructed as *uniquely* risky plants" (Herring 2011a, emphasis added). One of the effects of this has been that in India and elsewhere, transgenics are being subjected to far more extensive testing than other products of agricultural biotechnology (such as those that have been developed through mutagenesis involving irradiation), even while the standards of biosafety that are required of them may be set impossibly high. The consequence has been that there is still no "gene revolution" in food crops.

But how justified are all these concerns? They cannot be finally disproved. That is certain. But just as certainly, there is contrary evidence. There is no doubt that Mahyco-Monsanto Biotech (MMB), a 50:50 joint venture between Mahyco and Monsanto, which markets Bollgard and Bollgard II Bt cotton technologies, has made massive profits from the Bt cotton hybrids that it was responsible for introducing into India (Damodaran 2010). Equally, there is no doubt at all that Indian cotton farmers have sought to cultivate Bt cotton hybrids on such a massive scale that they now account for 92 percent of the total cotton acreage of the country (Kranthi 2011). They have "voted with their ploughs" against the activists who sought to ban Bt cotton cultivation. Nor is there any doubt about the extensive pirating of genetic material from Mahyco-Monsanto, and of the development of a cottage industry that supplies pirated, "stealth seeds," the products of the back-crossing of MMB-derived plant material with local cultivars, and that are available much more cheaply and may be saved by farmers, even if their insecticidal properties are weaker than those of MMB hybrids (Herring 2007b). The evidence in support of the claim that it has been because of the cultivation of GMOs that large numbers of Indian farmers have been committing suicide is thin to say the least (see Nagaraj 2008 for a measured statement). With regard to the ecological and health hazards associated with transgenics, it is very striking, given the extent of hostility to them in Europe, that the European Commission Directorate-General for Research, in a publication titled *A Decade of EU-funded GMO Research (2001-2010)*, should draw the following conclusion:

> The main conclusion to be drawn from the efforts of more than 130 research projects, covering a period of more than 25 years of research, and involving more than 500

> independent research groups, is that biotechnology, and in particular GMOs, are not *per se* more risky than conventional plant-breeding technologies.
>
> (p.16; cited in Herring 2011a)

Herring (2011a) continues: "Bt proteins may present some hazard, but no biosafety testing anywhere has been able to find evidence," and the method employed in the research on which one negative claim was made "was dismissed by the GMO Panel of the European Food Safety Authority." There is evidence that mutagenic plants may well be more hazardous than transgenics, yet they have not generally been subjected to anything like as much stringent testing—because they have not been framed in the same way.

There are, of course, very strong reasons for exercising caution with regard to transgenics and biosafety (as Thies and Devare, among many other scientists, make very clear; see Thies and Devare 2007), and there is no doubt about the importance of strengthening mechanisms for ensuring biosafety (see Fukuda-Parr 2007b for various country studies; and see Andow 2011; Kranthi 2011; and Swaminathan 2011 in specific regard to India). Yet there is still reason, as we suggested above, for questioning whether the standards that are being set are not unreasonable. These standards reflect the fear that has so successfully been generated by the way the evidence is framed by the anti-GMO campaigners. Regulation of the cultivation of transgenics can also work in such a way as to favor larger, wealthier producers, who are able to comply with biosafety requirements when smaller, poorer producers are not. Getting the balance right is difficult (Fukuda-Parr 2007b).

Two case studies that enable us to elaborate upon this discussion are those of the stories of Bt brinjal (what is called "eggplant," or aubergine, in Britain and North America) in India, and of Bt rice in China—two food crops, neither of which has been officially released for cultivation in the countries in which they have been developed.

Bt Brinjal

Brinjal (aubergine) is a significant food crop in India, widely consumed by poor people and grown extensively by small farmers (who, unlike cotton farmers—producers of a highly important commercial crop, and who successfully won the battle to cultivate Bt cotton against stiff opposition from anti-GMO activists and from the Government of India—have little political clout).[2] It is highly susceptible to attack from the fruit and stem borer (FSB), which reduces the value of much of the crop, and against which pesticides are relatively ineffective—but which encourages their excessive use, to the detriment of the health both of farmers and of consumers. *Bt* brinjal, developed as a result of a USAID-funded project led by Cornell University (Agricultural Biotechnology Support Project [ABSP] II: see Gregory et al. 2008), has the potential, according to extensive trials, carried out over nearly a decade, greatly to reduce pesticide use, increase farmers' incomes, and improve the health of farmers and consumers. Under ABSP II, Cornell

University was successful in persuading the company Mahyco, partly owned—as mentioned above—by Monsanto, to sublicense its gene technology to three Indian public sector institutions—two universities and a government research institute—free of royalties. The idea was that these public sector institutions would then develop *open-pollinated varieties* (OPVs), on a cost-recovery basis, making them available easily and cheaply to farmers (one of the universities planned to distribute them through rural post offices), while Mahyco would be left with exclusive rights for supplying the market with its transgenic *hybrid* seeds (reckoned to account for about 30 percent of the total market). And this is indeed what happened. The universities did succeed in developing OPVs, and after very extensive trials the Government of India's Genetic Engineering Approval Committee approved Bt brinjal and recommended its cultivation, in October 2009. The Expert Committee that it set up reported "Bt brinjal is effective in controlling target pests, non-toxic as determined by toxicity and animal feeding tests, non-allergenic and has the potential to benefit the farmer."

The minister responsible, however, Jairam Ramesh, then the minister of environment and forests—in the light, no doubt, of earlier expressions of opposition to the Bt brinjal from anti-GMO campaigners—rejected this advice and embarked on extensive public consultation, through town-hall style meetings in seven cities. He has said, "I listened to everybody" (Ramesh 2011). Finally, in February 2010, he placed a moratorium on the release for cultivation of Bt brinjal. In reaching this decision, he was influenced significantly by India's most distinguished biological scientist, M. S. Swaminathan, a founder and original board member of the pro-GM think tank International Service for the Acquisition of Agri-biotech Applications (ISAAA), and whose own research foundation has a substantial biotechnology component, but who was concerned about the lack of independent evaluation of Bt brinjal. As he has said, "our official mechanisms are inadequate since they do not have their own testing facilities" (Swaminathan 2011) and rely too heavily on the work of those who have also been responsible for the development of transgenic cultivars. He was concerned, too, about what he perceived as a threat to brinjal biodiversity in the area of what is believed to be its origins. In this he apparently failed to recognize that the Bt brinjal varieties developed by the public sector institutions are open-pollinated, and not hybrids—which, in general, attract his criticism as threats to biodiversity. Indeed, he said, in the interview referred to above, "we should concentrate on the development of transgenic varieties rather than hybrids," and that "What is important... is to step up public-good research in the field of biotechnology." This is actually what was being done in ABSP II. The minister, too, seems not to have recognized this, for he spoke in an interview about there being issues of seed control in regard to Bt brinjal, "if 90 percent of the GM seed is going to be controlled by one company"—which is what ABSP II was designed precisely to avoid. But if there was some misunderstanding of the science involved in the Bt brinjal program, some scientists did the cause of science no good at all when they contributed to a subsequent report about Bt brinjal asked for by Minister Ramesh from six leading scientific establishments. It was discovered that the report had "lifted" at least six paragraphs from a December 2009 article in a pro-GM newsletter, *Biotech News* (published by the Department of Biotechnology), and that data from a report by the Monsanto-funded ISAAA went without references or citations (Bagla 2010; Sharma 2010). Despite the academies' apologies, Ramesh rejected the report, saying that it did not "appear to be the product of rigorous scientific evaluation" (Raj 2010), and he vowed not to lift the moratorium "anytime soon" (Bagla 2010).

The case shows the power of the framing of transgenics by anti-GMO campaigners—especially when one considers, as discussed above, that transgenic brinjal has been subjected to relatively more stringent testing than other products of agricultural biotechnology. It also points to the limitations of the idea that genetic engineering will be found more acceptable if it is carried on in public sector institutions, removed from corporate control. This didn't happen in this case, which also shows the possible misunderstandings (and misuse) of science, as well as its limits. It cannot be proved that there are *no* hazards associated with *Bt* brinjal. But the careful weighing of scientific evidence (and of the definable risks associated with the cultivation of conventional brinjal plants, and the measurable benefits of growing *Bt*) against the definite uncertainty associated with cultivation of the transgenic plant has been effectively prevented in this case by the way in which it has been politicized.[3]

Bt Rice

A variety of rice incorporating the *Bt* protein, with resistance to three major insect pests that attack the world's most important food crop, yield levels of which have been stagnating, was unveiled in China in 1997—but it has still not been released commercially for cultivation (though biosafety certificates for two strains were issued in 2009; see Jia 2010). China has invested substantially in agricultural biotechnology, both in public sector institutions and through funding private sector research for which the companies concerned have also received tax breaks (Stone 2008). At the same time, the state has proceeded cautiously in regard to food crops, being concerned, it seems, about the possible loss of export markets (Herring 2009). Thus far, in China as in India, transgenic cotton seeds are those that have spread most widely. By 2008, 68 percent of the cotton acreage of the world's biggest producer was believed to incorporate *Bt* (James 2009). But whereas in India it is *hybrid Bt* cotton that has spread widely, in China it has been GM varieties developed through back-crossing, most of them technically illegal. Though these varieties are not as productive as hybrids, they have often proven beneficial for poor cotton farmers—when their pesticide use has decreased and their incomes been increased (Huang et al. 2007).

The inability of the state to regulate the cultivation of *Bt* cotton fuels fears about *Bt* rice. Among mainstream scientists there is little concern about health implications, because of the fact that the *Bt* protein has been consumed so extensively with no evidence of ill effects (though see Qiu 2008). But there is concern both about gene flow and the possibility that *Bt* rice could pass on its pest-resistant properties to both weedy and wild relatives (Lu et al. 2003; Shivrain et al. 2007), and about the possibility that the pests will develop resistance to *Bt*. This is especially so given the likelihood—after the experience with *Bt* cotton—of the spread of pirated *Bt* varieties among large numbers of small farmers (Herring 2009). Such varieties are likely to be less potent against insect pests, and to give them a greater chance to build up resistance.

Greenpeace[4] has already very successfully built up fears about loss of food sovereignty, as well as about the rejection of *Bt* rice in export markets, and it has highlighted the possibility that scientists with financial interests in the spread of the technology are manipulating evidence. Even though *Bt* rice was developed in public sector institutions, it is still possible that scientists can have financial interests as shareholders in public companies that stand to profit from selling *Bt* rice (Greenpeace 2008; Pray et al. 2007). A Chinese organization called "Utopia" that styles itself as "New Left" but espouses nationalist sentiments, and which has been leading the criticism of genetically engineered rice, accuses the government of being beholden to big agribusiness (Stone et al. 2011). The Chinese government, still strongly committed to agricultural biotechnology, has been responding to this public criticism by putting considerable resources into science education and public communication about biotechnology (Jiao 2010; Jie 2010).

The story of *Bt* rice in China reflects problems that are very much like those that show up in the case of *Bt* brinjal in India, including the tension between expert scientific advice and public opinion as it can be mobilized by civil society organizations (even if the numbers of people involved are actually small), drawing upon the powers of modern social media and of consumer resistance (growing in countries like China and India, with their expanding middle classes), in a context in which governments, whether in a formally democratic regime or an authoritarian one, have to be concerned about their legitimacy. Both cases, too, demonstrate the limitations of science. It is one of the great ironies of the condition of modernity, as the sociologist Anthony Giddens has argued, that those living in modern societies look to science for truth when science actually advances through systematic doubt and the questioning of existing knowledge:

> Even philosophers who most staunchly defend the claims of science to certitude, such as Karl Popper, acknowledge that, as he expresses it, "all science rests upon shifting sand." In science *nothing* is certain, and nothing can be proved, even if scientific endeavour provides us with the most dependable information about the world to which we can aspire.
>
> (Giddens 1990, 39)

These fundamental limitations apply, of course, as much to public sector science as to corporate science, though Giddens's point also hints at the need always to be aware of the straightforward biases that can affect scientific research.

Conclusion

The foregoing discussion leads to the conclusion, unsatisfactory though it may seem, that there remains—and there will remain—uncertainty about the impacts of both the Green Revolution and of transgenics. In large part this is because of the complexity of agriculture as an economic activity, in which outcomes are dependent upon so many variables, all of them difficult to control for. It is extremely difficult, for example, to separate out the effects of technology from the social context in which it is introduced—and this can be used both in defense of technology ("It's not MVs but government subsidies that have caused these negative outcomes") and to critique it (as when it is argued that biotechnology is inherently supportive of the corporate control of agriculture). The methodologies employed in empirical research are subject to severe limitations (as Stone 2012 and Orr 2012 show), and much depends, in the case of social and economic research, upon the factors of time and space—when and where research has been carried out. These circumstances give great scope for epistemic brokers and the framings they offer of the "evidence." They also mean that is vital both for research results to be subjected to rigorous methodological scrutiny (not necessarily accomplished through the regular process of scientific peer reviewing; see Stone 2012), and for the ways in which evidence has been framed to be recognized. As Giddens says, even if "nothing is certain," science is still the source of "the most dependable information to which we can aspire."

At the same time, it must be recognized that although public policy should be informed by scientific "evidence," it cannot be dictated by "evidence." Policymakers have to exercise judgment. In doing so they should take account above all of what will contribute to human well-being. Would it have been right for policymakers in the 1960s to have opposed the introduction of MVs? While improved agricultural productivity and the well-being of masses of rural people in Asia and Latin America might well have been realized more effectively had there been thoroughgoing redistributive land reform—had the social and political problems that were sought to be "fixed" by technology been addressed, in other words—this was not practical politics at the time. It was surely right, in the circumstances they confronted, for policymakers to have encouraged the introduction of the new varieties—though they would have done well to have paid more attention than was usually the case to the negative implications of modern agriculture. They would have done well to have recognized that the MVs did not represent *the* (sole) answer to the problems they were addressing. In regard to transgenics, we have suggested that policymakers have to weigh the irreducible uncertainty about their possible impacts on human health and the environment against the definable risks associated with alternatives, or with the status quo (as in the case of brinjal cultivation in India). As they do so, they should recognize that transgenics have been very successfully framed as being uniquely risky plants (*pace* Glover's view that *Bt* cotton has been subject to unduly positive framing—2010), when the evidence for this is limited, as the GMO Panel of the European Food Safety Authority—not a protagonist of the technology—found. It should be recognized, too, as many of the critics of this technology have not, that there is an important difference between transgenic hybrids and open-pollinated varieties. Transgenics are, inherently, just like the Green Revolution, neither "good" nor "bad." But at present the way in which they have so effectively been subjected to negative framing by anti-GMO campaigners makes careful, critical judgment more difficult—and more than ever necessary.

Notes

1. We emphasize that the characteristics referred to here are still only possibilities, contrary to what has sometimes been claimed. See Glover 2010.
2. The following draws largely on Herring 2011b.
3. We have highlighted "risk" and "uncertainty" here in order to emphasize the fundamental difference between future hazards to which probabilities can be assigned (risk) and those to which they cannot (conditions of uncertainty).
4. The first public anti-GMO pressure on Chinese officials came from a paper jointly published by the Nanjing Institute of Environmental Studies (NIES), one of three research institutes under the auspices of the State Environmental Protection Authority (SEPA), and Greenpeace. Greenpeace International has had offices in Hong Kong since 1997, and more recently in Beijing and Guangzhou. Greenpeace collaborates on various issues with SEPA and is therefore allowed to operate in China (Pray and Huang 2007).

References

Andow, D. A. 2011. "Comment" in Symposium on "Transgenic Varieties and India's Agriculture." *Review of Agrarian Studies* 1(1). http://www.ras.org.in/transgenic_varieties_and_indias_agriculture_questions_for_Professor_m_s_swaminathan.

Batista, R., N. Saibo, T. Lourenço, and M. M. Oliveira. 2008. "Microarray Analyses Reveal that Plant Mutagenesis May Induce More Transcriptomic Changes Than Transgene Insertion." *Proceedings of the National Academy of Sciences* 105 (9): 3640–3645.

Binswanger, H. P. 1978. *The Economics of Tractors in South Asia: An Analytical Review*. New York: Agricultural Development Council; Hyderabad: ICRISAT. http://ec2-50-19-248-237.compute-1.amazonaws.com/630/1/RA_000005.pdf.

Bouis, H. E. 2007. "The Potential of Genetically Modified Food Crops to Improve Human Nutrition in Developing Countries." *Journal of Development Studies* 43 (1): 79–96.

Brown, L. 1970. *Seeds of Change: The Green Revolution and Development in the 1970s*. New York: Overseas Development Council.

Cleaver, H. 1972. "Contradictions of the Green Revolution." *American Economic Review* 62 (1–2):177–186.

Damodaran, H. 2010. "Monsanto to Earn Rs 340 Cr Tech Fee for Bt Cotton." *Business Line*, January 20. http://www.thehindubusinessline.in/bline/2010/01/19/stories/2010011951431600.htm.

Davies, W.P. 2003. "An Historical Perspective from the Green Revolution to the Gene Revolution." *Nutrition Reviews* 61 (6): S124.

Ehrlich, P. 1968. *The Population Bomb*. New York: Ballantine Books.

European Commission. 2010. *A Decade of EU-Funded GMO Research (2001–2010)*. EUR 24473. Luxembourg: Publications Office of the European Union.

Frankel, F. 1971. *India's Green Revolution: Economic Gains and Political Costs*. Princeton, NJ: Princeton University Press.

Fukuda-Parr, S. 2007a. "Emergence and Global Spread of GM Crops." In *The Gene Revolution: GM Crops and Unequal Development*, edited by S. Fukuda-Parr, 15–35. London: Earthscan.

Fukuda-Parr, S. 2007b. *The Gene Revolution: GM Crops and Unequal Development*. London: Earthscan.

Giddens, A. 1990. *The Consequences of Modernity*. Stanford, CA: Stanford University Press.
Glover, D. 2010. "Exploring the Resilience of Bt Cotton's 'Pro-Poor Success Story.'" *Development and Change* 41 (6): 955–981.
Greenpeace. 2008. *"Chinese" Genetically Engineered Rice in Foreign Patent Trap?* http://www.greenpeace.org/eastasia/Global/eastasia/publications/reports/food-agriculture/2008/chinese-genetically-engineered-rice-in-foreign-patent-trap.pdf.
Gregory, P., R. H. Potter, F. A. Shotkoski, D. Hautea, K. V. Raman, V. Vijayaraghavan, W. H. Lesser, G. Norton, and W. R. Coffman. 2008. "Bioengineered Crops as Tools for International Development: Opportunities and Strategic Considerations." *Experimental Agriculture* 44 (3): 277–299.
Gressel, J. 2008. *Genetic Glass Celings: Transgenics for Crop Diversity.* Baltimore: Johns Hopkins University Press.
Griffin, K. B. 1972. *The Green Revolution: An Economic Analysis*. Geneva, Switzerland: United Nations Research Institute for Social Development.
Griffin, K. B. 1979. *The Political Economy of Agrarian Change: An Essay on the Green Revolution*. 2nd ed. London: Macmillan.
Guha, R. 2000. *Environmentalism: A Global History*. New York: Longman.
Harriss, J. 1977. "Bias in the Perception of Agrarian Change in India." In *Green Revolution?: Technology and Change in Rice Growing Areas of Tamil Nadu and Sri Lanka*, edited by B. H. Farmer, 30–36. London: Macmillan.
Harriss, J. 1989. "Knowing about Rural Economic Change: Problems Arising from a Comparison of the Results of 'Macro' and 'Micro' Research in Tamil Nadu." In *Conversations between Economists and Anthropologists: Methodological Issues in Measuring Economic Change in rural India*, edited by Pranab Bardhan. Delhi: Oxford University Press.
Harriss, J. 1992. "Does the Depressor Still Work?: Agrarian Structure and Development in India." *Journal of Peasant Studies* 19 (2): 189–227.
Harriss-White, B., and S. Janakarajan. 2004. *Rural India Facing the 21st Century*. London: Anthem Press.
Harriss-White, B., and J. Harriss. 2007. "Green Revolution and After: The 'North Arcot Papers' and Long-Term Studies of the Political Economy of Rural Development in South India." Queen Elizabeth House Working Paper No.146. Oxford: Oxford University, Department of International Development. http://www3.qeh.ox.ac.uk/pdf/qehwp/qehwps146.pdf.
Herring, R. 2007a. "The Genomics Revolution and Development Studies: Science, Poverty and Politics." *Journal of Development Studies* 43 (1):1–30.
Herring, R. 2007b. "Stealth Seeds: Bioproperty, Bio-safety, Biopolitics. *Journal of Development Studies* 43 (1): 130–157.
Herring, R. 2009. "China, Rice, and GMOs: Navigating the Global Rift on Genetic Engineering." *Asia-Pacific Journal* 3(2). http://www.japanfocus.org/-ron-herring/3012.
Herring, R. 2010. "Framing the GMO: Epistemic Brokers, Authoritative Knowledge, and Diffusion of Opposition to Biotechnology." In *The Diffusion of Social Movements: Actors, Mechanisms, and Political Effects*, edited by Bebecca Kolins Givan, Kenneth M. Roberts, and Sarah A. Soule, 78–98. New York: Cambridge University Press.
Herring, R., 2011a. "Comment" in Symposium on "Transgenic Varieties and India's Agriculture." *Review of Agrarian Studies* 1 (1). http://www.ras.org.in/transgenic_varieties_and_indias_agriculture_questions_for_Professor_m_s_swaminathan.
Herring, R., 2011b. *State Science and Its Discontents: Why India's Second Transgenic Crop Did Not Follow the Path of Bt Cotton*. Paper presented at the Association of Asian Studies Annual Meetings, April 1–3, Honolulu, Hawaii.

Huang, J., R. Hu, S. Rozelle, and C. Pray. 2007. "China: Emerging Public Sector Model for GM Crop Development." In *The Gene Revolution: GM Crops and Unequal Development*, edited by Fukuda-Parr, 130–155. London: Earthscan.

James, C. 2009. *Global Status of Commercialized Biotech/GM Crops*. Brief No. 41. Ithaca, NY: International Service for the Acquisition of Agri-biotech Applications (ISAAA).

James, C. 2010. "A Global Overview of Biotech (GM) Crops: Adoption, Impact and Future Prospects." *Landes Bioscience* 1(1). http://www.landesbioscience.com/journals/gmcrops/03JamesGMC1-1.pdf.

Jia, H., 2010. "Chinese Green Light for GM Rice and Maize Prompts Outcry." *Nature Biotechnology* 28 (5): 390–391.

Jiao, L., 2010. "China's GM Debate Goes Public, Surprising Scientists." SCiDev.Net, December 21. http://www.scidev.net/en/news/china-s-gm-debate-goes-public-surprising-scientists.html.

Jie, D. 2010. "China to Double Science Communicators by 2020." SCiDev.Net, September 8. http://www.scidev.net/en/china/news/china-to-double-science-communicators-by-2020-1.html.

Kranthi, K. 2011. "Comment" in Symposium on "Transgenic Varieties and India's Agriculture." *Review of Agrarian Studies* 1 (1). http://www.ras.org.in/transgenic_varieties_and_indias_agriculture_questions_for_Professor_m_s_swaminathan.

Lipton, M. 2007. "Plant Breeding and Poverty: Can Transgenic Seeds Replicate the 'Green Revolution' as a Source of Gains for the Poor?" *Journal of Development Studies* 43 (1): 31–62.

Lipton, M., and R. Longhurst. 1989. *New Seeds and Poor People*. London and Boston: Unwin Hyman.

Lu, B. R., Z. P. Song, and J. K. Chen. 2003. "Can Transgenic Rice Cause Ecological Risks through Transgene Escape?" *Progress in Natural Science* 13:17–24.

McMichael, P. 2005. "Global Development and the Corporate Food Regime." *Research in Rural Sociology and Development* 11:269–303.

Monsanto. 2010. "Cotton in India." *Monsanto News and Views*, May 5. http://www.monsanto.com/newsviews/Pages/india-pink-bollworm.aspx.

Seize the Day. 2013. "Monsanto Song (Food 'n Health 'n Hope)." Accessed July 1. http://www.seizetheday.org/music.cfm?trackID=67&albumID=2&alphabet.

Nagaraj, K. 2008. "Farmers' Suicides in India: Magnitudes, Trends and Spatial Patterns." MacroScan, March 3. www.macroscan.org/anl/mar08/anl030308Farmers_Suicides.htm.

"The 9 Billion-People Question: A Special Report on Feeding the World." 2011. *The Economist*, February 26.

Nuffield Council on Bioethics. 1999. *Genetically Modified Crops: The Ethical and Social Issues*. London: Nuffield Council on Bioethics.

Orr, A. 2012. "Why Were So Many Social Scientists Wrong about the Green Revolution? Learning from Bangladesh." *Journal of Development Studies* 48 (11): 1565–1586.

Paarlberg, R., 2008. *Starved for Science: How Biotechnology is Being Kept Out of Africa*. Cambridge, MA: Harvard University Press.

Paarlberg, R. 2010. *Food Politics: What Everyone Needs To Know*. New York: Oxford University Press.

Paarlberg, R., and C. Pray. 2007. "Political Actors on the Landscape." *AgBioForum* 10 (3): 144–153. http://www.agbioforum.org/v10n3/v10n3a03-paarlberg.htm.

Patel, R. 2009. "What Does Food Sovereignty Look Like?" *Journal of Peasant Studies* 36 (3): 663–673.

Pearse, A. 1980. *Seeds of Plenty, Seeds of Want: Social and Economic Implications of the Green Revolution*. Oxford and New York: Oxford University Press.

Pearse, A., 1990. *Seeds of Plenty, Seeds of Want: Social and Economic Implications of the Green Revolution*. Oxford: Clarendon Press.
Pechlaner, G., and G. Otero. 2008. "The Third Food Regime: Neo-Liberal Globalization and Agricultural Biotechnology in Latin America." *Sociologia Ruralis* 48 (4): 351–371.
Pingali, P. L. 2012. "Green Revolution: Impacts, Limits and the Path Ahead." *Proceedings of the National Academy of Sciences* 109 (31): 12302–12308. http://www.pnas.org/content/109/31/12302.full.pdf.
Pray, C. and Huang, J., 2007. "Biofortification for China: Political Responses to Food Fortification and GM Technology, Interest Groups, and Possible Strategies." *AgBioForum* 10 (3): 161–169. http://www.agbioforum.org/v10n3/v10n3a05-pray.htm.
Pray, C.E. and Naseem, A., 2007. "Supplying Crop Biotechnology to the Poor: Opportunities and Constraints." *Journal of Development Studies* 43 (1): 192–217.
Pray, C., R. Paarlberg, and L. Unnevehr. 2007. "Patterns of Political Response to Biofortified Varieties of Crops Produced with Different Breeding Techniques and Agronomic Traits." *AgBioForum* 10 (3): 135–143. http://www.agbioforum.org/v10n3/v10n3a02-pray.htm.
Qiu, J., 2008. "Agriculture: Is China Ready for GM Rice?" *Nature* 455 (7215): 850–852.
Ramamurthy, P., 2010. "Why Are Men Doing Floral Sex Work? Gender, Cultural Reproduction, and the Feminization of Agriculture." *Signs: Journal of Women in Culture and Society* 35 (2): 397–424.
Ramesh, J., 2010. "In Conversation: Jairam Ramesh." *Current Science* 100 (11): 1610–1612.
Robin, M-M. 2010. *The World According to Monsanto: Pollution, Corruption and Control of the World's Food Supply*. New York: New Press.
Sahai, S., 2011. "Comment" in Symposium on "Transgenic Varieties and India's Agriculture," *Review of Agrarian Studies* 1(1). http://www.ras.org.in/transgenic_varieties_and_indias_agriculture_questions_for_Professor_m_s_swaminathan.
Schurman, R., and W. A. Munro. 2010. *Fighting for the Future of Food: Activists versus Agribusiness in the Struggle over Biotechnology*. Minneapolis, MN: University of Minnesota Press.
Shiva, V. 1991. *The Violence of the Green Revolution: Third World Agriculture, Ecology, and Politics*. London: Zed Books.
Shivrain, V. K., N. R. Burgos, M. M. Anders, S. N. Rajguru, J. Moore, and M. A. Sales. 2007. "Gene Flow between Clearfield(TM) Rice and Red Rice." *Crop Protection* 26 (3): 349.
Stone, G., 2012. "Constructing Facts: Bt Cotton Narratives in India." *Economic and Political Weekly* 47 (38): 62–70.
Stone, R., 2008. "China Plans $3.5 Billion GM Crops Initiative." *Science* 321 (5894): 1279–1279.
Stone, R., H. Xin, and L. Jiao. 2011. "Activists Go on Warpath Against Transgenic Crops—and Scientists." *Science* 331 (6020): 1000–1001.
Swaminathan, M. S. 2011. "Transgenic Varieties and India's Agriculture: Questions for M.S.Swaminathan." In Symposium on "Transgenic Varieties and India's Agriculture." *Review of Agrarian Studies* 1(1). http://www.ras.org.in/transgenic_varieties_and_indias_agriculture_questions_for_Professor_m_s_swaminathan.
Thies, J. E., and M. H. Devare. 2007. "An Ecological Assessment of Transgenic Crops." *Journal of Development Studies* 43 (1): 97–129.
Thompson, M., R. Ellis, and A. Wildavsky. 1990. *Cultural Theory*. Boulder, CO: Westview Press.
Weis, T. 2007. *The Global Food Economy: The Battle for the Future of Farming*. London: Zed Books.

CHAPTER 3

GENETICALLY IMPROVED CROPS

MARTINA NEWELL-MCGLOUGHLIN

OVER the coming decades, food and agricultural production systems must be significantly enhanced to respond to a number of transformative changes: global warming; growing world population; increasing international competition; globalization; shifts to increased meat consumption in low-income countries; and rising consumer demands for improved food quality, safety, nutritional enhancement, and convenience. New and innovative techniques will be required to ensure an ample supply of healthy food. To confound this challenge, the inequity between the affluent and developing countries will continue to grow, and only a handful of technologies is sufficiently scale neutral to help with redressing this imbalance. Of even greater concern is the very immediate need of global food security. In 2012 the United Nations issued an unprecedented warning about the state of global food supplies: global food reserves had reached their lowest level in almost forty years, and failing harvests in the United States, Ukraine, and other countries had eroded reserves to their lowest level since 1974, a period when the global population was much lower. The deputy secretary-general's remarks in New York warned of world grain reserves so dangerously low that another year of severe weather in the United States or other food-exporting countries could trigger a major hunger crisis. Unprecedented needs require effective solutions (Eliasson 2012).

Worldwide, plant-based products comprise the vast majority of human food intake, irrespective of location or financial status (Mathers 2006). In some cultures, either by design or default, plant-based nutrition makes up almost 100% of the diet. The world food crisis of 2006–2008 demonstrated that the vulnerability created by this dependence varied by country, with the poorest being most affected (FAO 2011). While some large countries were able to deal with the worst of the crisis, people in many small import-dependent countries experienced large price increases that, even when only temporary, can have permanent effects on their future earnings capacity and ability to escape poverty.

What could the nature of solutions to these complex dilemmas be? Over the millennia many technologies for plant breeding have been developed and used to enhance productivity of the original coterie of cultivated crops and to bring more into the domestic fold. Significant nutritional improvements have been achieved via modifications of staple crops (Stein, this volume). In the latter half of the twentieth century, major improvements in agricultural productivity were largely based on selective breeding programs for plants and animals, intensive use of chemical fertilizers, pesticides and herbicides, advanced equipment developments, and widespread irrigation programs. Though successful in raising productivity, these improvements have brought corresponding problems: a narrower genetic base of crop plants and domestic animals; pests that are resistant to chemical pesticides; adverse impacts on environmental quality; and capital-intensive production. From the food deserts of inner cities to actual barren wastelands of many world regions, access to a sufficient, healthy diet is a challenge.

Innovations in the future will necessarily involve new, science-based products and processes. This chapter focuses on the frontiers of plant breeding to meet these challenges, particularly through genetic engineering approaches. First, in the coming generations of crop plants the biotic-stress tolerance of the present generation is being supplemented by continuing improvement of agronomic traits such as yield and abiotic stress resistance. Sustainability is the critical issue for these traits; the environmental challenges of climate change are addressed in the subsequent section on green biotechnology. Green biotechnology's three major contributions toward mitigating the impact of climate change are greenhouse gas reduction, crop adaptation and protection, and yield increase in less desirable and marginal soils. Second, the future will see expansion of traits such as improved nutrition and food functionality. Functional food components are of increasing interest in the prevention and treatment of a number of the leading causes of death, including cancer, diabetes, cardiovascular disease, and hypertension. From a health perspective, dietary plant components can be broadly divided into four main categories, which can be further broken down into positive and negative attributions for human nutrition: macronutrients (proteins, carbohydrates, lipids [oils], and fiber); micronutrients (vitamins, minerals, phytochemicals); antinutrients (substances such as phytate that limit bioavailability of nutrients); and allergens, intolerances, and toxins. Modern molecular approaches can be employed to down-regulate or even eliminate the genes involved in the metabolic pathways for the production, accumulation, or activation of toxins in plants with positive food and environmental consequences. The conclusion returns to prospects for biotechnology in agriculture.

Developing and commercializing plants with these improved traits involves overcoming a variety of technical, regulatory, and political challenges. Most of the innovative technologies that have been applied to production agriculture historically have come into common usage without much controversy or even knowledge by the average consumer. Biotechnology has faced a different political and social response. Through social, cultural, and political processes, genetically engineered plants have been labeled as uniquely and uniformly risky in many parts of the world (Sato, this volume; Herring 2010). To separate the hype from the panic, it is necessary to disaggregate modern biotechnology and examine both potential on the horizon and obstacles to progress.

Agronomic Traits and Sustainability

The vast majority of biotech products approved to date involve agronomic traits that protect against biotic stress such as pests. The principal focus in the immediate future will remain on agronomic traits, especially the area of pest control, but with an increasing interest in abiotic stress tolerance, which is gaining prominence as external pressures from climate change to land use change.

The total area of biotech crops reached 170.3 million hectares or 420 million acres in 2012, an increase of 10 million hectares (25 million acres) from 2011. Comparing this level with 1.7 million hectares in 1996 highlights that biotech crops are the most rapidly adopted crop technology in the history of modern agriculture (James 2012). Developing countries in 2012 passed the 50% mark in share of global biotech crops, exceeding for the first time industrial countries' planted area. Of the twenty-eight countries planting biotech crops in 2012, nineteen were less developed. Of the 17.3 million farmers who grew biotech crops, over 90%, or 15 million, were small resource-poor farmers in developing countries. Adoption of existing biotech crops has demonstrated improved sustainability of farming in both wealthier and poorer countries as well as increased incomes for farmers (Elmegaard 2001; Trewavas 2001). No-till farming has reduced energy use in fields, for example. *Bacillus thuringiensis* (Bt) technology has reduced pesticide spraying and mycotoxin fungal fumonisins, both of which are known health risks, including risk of liver cancer in humans and animals.

While North America remains the epicenter for leading-edge research on genetically modified (GM) foods, other regions, such as China, are emerging as contenders on the global stage. Agricultural science is now China's fastest-growing research field with China's share of global publications in agricultural science: from 1.5% in 1999 to 5% in 2008 (James 2011). Indeed, China is emerging as a trendsetter in the adoption of novel traits with its approval of Bt rice and phytase maize on November 27, 2009. Rice is the principal staple for much of the world, and maize is the largest animal feed source. Bt rice has the potential to increase yields up to 8%, to decrease pesticide use by 80% (17 kg/ha), and to generate US$4 billion in benefits annually (James 2011). The phytase approval is a major step forward in approvals because it is the first transgenic since the FLAVR SAVR tomato focusing on a "quality" trait. However, it is far more than this both literally and figuratively since this single trait addresses issues from the nutritional to the environmental. Two additional quality traits are under consideration for deregulation: the Arctic apple and the reduced acrylamide potato.

Okanagan, the company that created the Arctic apple, modified it to resist oxidation when it is cut and the injured cells are exposed to oxygen, thus activating the polyphenol oxidase (PPO) gene. To achieve this effect, Okanagan co-expressed PPO genes and effectively achieved reduced oxidation by silencing the endogenous PPO gene (Carter 2012). The second improved quality product was a potato submitted by JR Simplot. Their potato with three specific modifications for quality improvement, was submitted for petition for determination of nonregulated status in 2013. It uses what it terms *innate technology*, basically utilizing RNA interference (RNAi) to silence genes related to black-spot bruising and to reduce asparagine and sugars in tubers.

One example of widespread success in the use of biotechnology to reduce the impact of biotic stress and enhance sustainability is India's experience with Bt cotton. The Maharashtra Seed Company (Mahyco) developed transgenic hybrids in partnership with Monsanto, utilizing a Cry1Ac transgene to produce hybrids expressing a protein lethal to the major pest of cotton: the bollworm. The number of approved cultivars expanded from three in 2002 to over a thousand by 2012. Farmer-bred illegal varieties have proliferated underground as well. Adoption has increased to over 90% of cotton acreage by 2012, with an increasing share of the market going to stacked gene technology (Herring and Rao 2012). Between 2002 and 2008, Bt cotton generated economic benefits for farmers valued at US$5.1 billion, halved insecticide requirements, contributed to the doubling of yield, and transformed India from a cotton importer to a major exporter (Choudhary and Gaur 2008, 2010). India has become the number one exporter of cotton globally as well as the second largest cotton producer in the world. A number of multi-institutional projects have been launched in India, including the development of transgenics for resistance to geminiviruses in cotton, mungbean, and tomato; resistance to rice tungro disease; development of a nutritionally enhanced potato with a balanced amino acid composition; and development of molecular methods for heterosis breeding. Other transgenic crops await approval for commercial cultivation, such as transgenic herbicide-tolerant mustard hybrids and nutritionally enhanced potato varieties. Despite the success of Bt cotton, further implementation of the Government of India's strategy for biotechnology has been restricted, however, by factors considered in the final section of this chapter (Bricknel 2010).

Work on biotic stress tolerance is expanding to multitiered control systems. This in theory serves a double advantage, primarily expanding the effectiveness of the broad based resistance events but also allowing more effective management of the resistance trait since there is less selective pressure when genes are stacked. Focus on biotic stress, especially in pest control, will continue, but interest in abiotic stress tolerance is gaining prominence as external pressures from climate change become manifest.

Climate Change and Agriculture: Green Biotechnology

The meta-issue of climate change overlays many of the emergent individual plant breeding efforts. It poses significant challenges in terms of available agricultural land and freshwater use. The Stern Report (2006) underlines the decline of crop yields, ocean acidification, poor plant nutrition and abiotic stress, population displacement, and threatened ecosystems as effects of climate change. In addition, broader, more systemic consequences of abiotic stresses such as drought beyond food insecurity are decreased household income, the loss of assets due to slaughter of livestock, health threats due to the lack of water for hygiene and household uses, environmental degradation, and less sustainable land management (Watson, this volume). These effects must be considered in the light of growing population levels. To feed the overall population the world will have to double its rate of agricultural production over the next twenty-five years, despite having already quadrupled it in the last fifty. It is estimated that only 10% of world's arable land may be categorized as free from stress. The rapid change in environmental conditions is likely to override the adaptive potential of plants. Such abnormal environmental parameters include drought, salinity, cold and freezing, high temperatures, waterlogging, high light intensity, ultraviolet radiation, nutrient imbalances, metal toxicities, nutrient deficiencies and are collectively termed *abiotic stress*. Severe drought accounts for half the world's food emergencies annually. In this context, solutions must be developed to adapt crops to existing but also evolving conditions such as marginal soils.

The agriculture sector is both a contributor to and provider of potential solutions to increased abiotic stresses. It impacts two of the principal components of climate change: greenhouse gases and water. Agriculture is a major source of greenhouse gas emissions. Practices such as deforestation, cattle feedlots, and fertilizer use currently account for about 25% of greenhouse gas emissions. When broken down, this amounts to 14% of carbon dioxide emission, 48% of methane, and 52% of nitrous oxide emissions (Stern Report 2006). In addition, agriculture uses a significant amount of fresh water; approximately 70% of the water currently consumed by humans is used in agriculture, and this is likely to increase as temperatures rise. The distributional impact will surely be asymmetrical globally, with much greater impact on resource-poor farmers in poorer nations.

Given the potential impacts of climate change on the range and extent of agricultural productivity and the impact of agriculture practice itself on global warming, effective technology should play a substantial part in mitigating climate change. This is especially relevant in emerging countries where producers and consumers are more subject to the vagaries of climate fluctuations than in the West, where there is greater capability of responding to the effects and managing resources. Green biotechnology offers a set of tools that can help producers limit greenhouse gas emissions as well as adapt their agricultural techniques to shifting climates. Green biotechnology's three major contributions toward mitigating the impact of climate change are greenhouse gas reduction, crop adaptation and protection, and yield increase in less desirable and marginal soils.

The first of these issues is greenhouse gas reduction. In addition to carbon dioxide, agriculture contributes two of the other major greenhouse gases; one of these, nitrous oxide, has a global warming potential of about three hundred times that of carbon dioxide. In addition, nitrous oxides stay in the atmosphere for a considerable period. Nitrous oxide is produced through bacterial degradation of applied nitrogen fertilizer.

Nitrogen fertilizer, through intemperate application, can also contribute to eutrophication at ground level, making its reduction desirable on several levels. However, nitrogen is essential for crop production since it is quantitatively the most essential nutrient for plants and a major limiter of crop productivity (Stewart et al. 2005, Erisman et al. 2008).

One of the critical factors limiting the efficient use of nitrogen is plants' ability to acquire it from applied fertilizer. Therefore, the development of crop plants that absorb and use nitrogen more efficiently can serve both the plant and the environment. Arcadia Biosciences of Davis, California, developed nitrogen-efficient crops by introducing a barley gene—AlaAT (alanine aminotransferase)—into both rice and canola. Arcadia's nitrogen use efficiency (NUE) technology produces plants with yields that are equivalent to conventional varieties but require significantly less nitrogen fertilizer because the AlaAT gene allows more efficient use. Compared with controls, transgenic plants also demonstrated significant changes in key metabolites and total nitrogen content, confirming increased nitrogen uptake efficiency. This technology has the potential to reduce the amount of nitrogen fertilizer lost by farmers annually due to leaching into the air, soil, and waterways. In addition to environmental pressures, nitrogen can represent a significant portion of a farmer's input costs and can significantly impact profitability. Farmers spend $60 billion annually for 150 million tons of fertilizer (Svoboda 2008). The technology has been licensed to Dupont for maize and to Monsanto for application in canola.

One of the first commercialized products to have included a "yield gene" was Monsanto's second-generation Roundup Ready 2 Yield Soybeans, which include both the glyphosate-tolerant trait and one that was developed using extensive gene mapping to identify specific DNA regions that segregated with yield increase (Monsanto 2010). First-generation Roundup Ready varieties had demonstrated yield drag due to the unfortunate insertion close to a gene that influenced seed size and co-segregated with the transgene. This is a perfect example of the power of combining recombinant DNA technology with genomics tools. The company claims that four years of field trials across six US states showed 7 to 11% higher yields compared with the first-generation of Roundup Ready soybeans, although there have been some problems with fungal (white mold) susceptibility in certain regions. In August 2010, the National Technical Biosafety Committee (CTNBio) in Brazil approved the Bt-enhanced version of this product for planting in Brazil.

The second area where green technology can help in a changing climate is crop adaptation to environmental stress and changing niches. Under stress, plants will divert energy into survival instead of producing biomass and reproduction; addressing this impact should have a substantial effect on yields. In addition, improved stress tolerance allows an expanded growing season—especially earlier planting—and further reduces yield variability and financial risk to the farmer. The most critical of these stresses is water. The physiological responses of plants to water stress and their relative importance for crop productivity vary with species, soil type, nutrients, and climate. On a global basis, about one-third of potential arable land suffers from inadequate water supply, and the yields of much of the remainder are periodically reduced by drought. One of the most effective methods of addressing water limitation problems—irrigation—unfortunately is also one of the major causes of arable land degradation. It is estimated that 24.7 million acres of farmland worldwide is lost each year due to salinity buildup resulting from over irrigation. In fact, salinity limits crops on 40% of the world's irrigated land (25% in the United States). To address the extreme end of irrigation impact, Eduardo Blumwald at the University of Calfornia at Davis (UC Davis) used AtNHX1, the most abundant vacuolar Na+/H+ antiporter in *Arabidopsis thaliana,* which mediates the transport of Na+ and K+ into the vacuole. By overexpressing this vacuolar Na+/H+ anti-porter transgenic tomatoes were able to grow, flower, and produce fruit in the presence of 200 mM sodium chloride (Sottosanto et al. 2007). Arcadia Biosciences has now introduced this gene into economically important crops.

It is estimated that water stress is the most important variable in determining crop yield and can explain approximately 80% variance in yields (Shin et al. 2009). Even at a more moderate level of water stress, it is estimated that about seventy to eighty million acres in the United States suffer yield losses annually (Kramer 1980). The most critical time for water stress is near pollination and flowering, where yields with or without irrigation can vary by up to 100%. In dry land, production yields can be cut in half in the absence of irrigation. At this time about 15% of US maize acres are irrigated; an estimated 20 million acres in the United States would benefit from a drought tolerance gene that gives a 10% yield increase. The trait would also allow shifting of high-value crops into production on more marginal land.

The physiological responses of plants to water stress and their relative importance for crop productivity vary with species, soil type, nutrients, and climate. On a global basis, about one-third of potential arable land suffers from inadequate water supply, and the yields of much of the remainder are periodically reduced by drought. Transcription factors are some of the most versatile tools being employed in developing stress-tolerant plants. One of the most versatile classes of transcription factors involved in environmental response is the DREB (dehydration-responsive element binding protein), which is involved in the biotic stress-signaling pathway. These transcription factors can activate as many as twelve resistant functional genes relying on DRE members of cis regulation under adverse conditions. For instance, rd29, cor15, and rd17 cause proline content to rise to enable plants to improve in many resistances, such as drought, freezing, and salt tolerance (Agarwal et al. 2006). It has been possible to engineer stress tolerance in transgenic plants by manipulating the expression of DREBs. One isolated from Arabidopsis has improved drought tolerance, increasing productivity by at least twofold during severe water stress. DroughtGard maize will be the first commercially available transgenic drought-tolerant crop. Hybrid seed sold under this trademark will combine a novel transgenic trait (based on the bacterial cspB gene, an RNA chaperone, which help to maintain normal physiological performance under stress by binding and unfolding RNA molecules so that they can function normally) with Monsanto's optimized conventional breeding program. In field trials using this approach, maize yields have increased under water stress by up to 30% (Castiglioni et al. 2008). The yield gain of this variety under drought appears to occur due to slowing of growth specifically under drought stress such that existing soil moisture is saved for the critical period surrounding flowering, resulting in less kernel abortion, higher harvest index, and greater yield (Castiglioni et al. 2008).

Other approaches include modification of individual genes involved in stress response and cell signaling. For example, drought-tolerant canola engineered to reduce the levels PARP [poly (ADP-ribose) polymerase], a key stress-related protein in many organisms, shows relative yield increases of up to 44% compared with control varieties. A subset of the transcription factors—homeodomain leucine zipper proteins (HDZip)—play a role in regulating adaptation responses including developmental adjustment to environmental cues such as water stress in plants (Deng 2006). One of these effectors is absisic acid (ABA), an important plant regulator controlling many environmental responses including stomata movement—which is itself modulated by the DREB elements. Some work is being done on modifying HDZip directly. Other work involves indirect mechanisms, for example, down-regulating farnesyltransferase, a signaling system in the production of absisic acid and stomata control, which results in stomata closure and water retention.

Eduardo Blumwald is also working on modifying basic acid to enhance the tolerance of plants to water deficit by delaying the drought-induced leaf senescence and abscission during the stress episode. This approach is now being introduced into rice, among other crops. The work is being done in conjunction with Arcadia Biosciences. Bayer CropScience, Pioneer Hi-Bred, BASF, and Dow, among others, are conducting research on maize, cotton, canola, and rice to develop a new generation of stress-tolerant, high-performance crop varieties. Clearly, stress-tolerant traits are of paramount importance in low-income countries, especially in sub-Saharan Africa and Asia. Major efforts are already under way on this front. The partnership, known as Water Efficient Maize for Africa (WEMA), was formed in response to a growing call by African farmers, leaders, and scientists to address the devastating effects of drought on small-scale farmers (Foundation 2007). Frequent drought leads to crop failure, hunger, and poverty. Climate change only aggravates this situation.

On the other end of the spectrum of climate change impact is flooding due to changing rain patterns and rising sea levels. This is already a major cause of rice crop loss. It is estimated that four million tons of rice are lost every year because of flooding; this loss is equal to the amount of rice sufficient to feed thirty million people. Rice is not grown in flooded fields through necessity but rather to control weeds. However, most rice varieties die after more than three days of complete submergence. Researchers know of at least one rice variety—accession number FR13A—that can tolerate flooding for longer periods, but conventional breeding failed to create a cultivar that was acceptable to farmers. The Ronald Laboratory at UC Davis cloned the submergence tolerance (Sub1) locus from this resistance variety using a map-based cloning approach (Jung 2010). The Sub1 locus encodes three putative transcription regulators, one of which (Sub1A-1) increases dramatically in response to oxygen deprivation in Sub1 seedlings while Sub1C levels decrease. Transgenic lines overexpressing the Sub1A-1 gene have been introgressed into a submergence-intolerant line and display enhanced submergence tolerance.

There is also some research in the final abiotic stress focus area: crops adaptable to less desirable and marginal soils and increased yields in those circumstances. For example, a gene that produces citric acid in roots can protect plants from soils contaminated with aluminum because it binds to the contaminant, preventing uptake by the root system (Lopez-Bucio et al. 2000). Genes such as these can allow crops to be cultivated in hostile soils and temperatures, increasing geographic range while reducing potential impact on fragile ecosystems.

The frontier should not divert attention from existing implications of existing contributions of biotechnologies in the context of climate change. Soil carbon sequestration will be an important part of any international strategy to mitigate the increase in atmospheric CO_2 concentrations. By adopting more sustainable management practices, agriculture may play a large part in enhancing soil carbon sequestration across the globe. One way is by reducing the amount of conventional tillage after long-term tillage soil carbon stocks are depleted. Glyphosate-tolerant transgenic crops have aided in this practice. Through reduced till production, this technology allowed significant reduction in the release of CO_2 emissions, which in 2010 was about 23.1 kg, equivalent to removing twelve million cars from the roads (Brookes and Barfoot 2012). In general, cultivation is not a sustainable practice. It is energy intensive and exposes soil to wind and water erosion. It allows rain to compact the soil and increases the oxygen content, thus allowing organic matter to oxidize away. In turn, lower organic matter in the soil allows more compaction and more nutrient loss. Additionally, in warmer and drier climates evaporative water loss may be reduced because residue remains on the soil surface, creating a wetter and cooler soil microclimate.

Nutritional Improvement

Both the panoply of traditional plant breeding tools and modern biotechnology-based techniques will be required to produce plants with desirable quality traits. Table 3.1 presents examples of crops that have already been genetically modified with macro- and micronutrient traits that may provide nutritional benefits (see also Stein, this volume).

While the correlative link between food and health, beyond meeting basic nutrition requirements, has been unequivocally proven only in a small number of cases, a growing body of evidence indicates that food components can influence physiological processes at all stages of life. Nutrition intervention from a functionality perspective has a personal dimension. Determining individual response is at least as complex a challenge as the task of increasing or decreasing the amount of a specific protein, fatty acid, or other component of the plant itself (Brigelius-Flohe and Joost 2006). Early food regimes can affect health in later life. For example, as some children who survived famine conditions in certain regions of Africa grew into adults, they battled obesity and related problems, presumably because the selective advantage of the thrifty gene in their early food-stressed environment became a hazard during more abundant times, especially if their adult diets were calorie dense.

Table 3.1 Examples of Crops in Research and Development with Nutritionally Improved Traits Intended to Provide Health Benefits for Consumers and Animals[1]

Trait	Crop (trait detail)	Reference
Protein and amino acids		
Protein quality and level	Bahiagrass (protein↑)	Luciani et al. 2005
	Canola (amino acid composition)	Roesler et al. 1997
	Maize (amino acid composition; protein↑)	Cromwell 1967, 1969; Yang et al. 2002; O'Quinn et al. 2000; Young et al. 2004
	Potato (amino acid composition; protein↑)	Chakraborty et al. 2000; Li et al. 2001; Yu and Ao 1997; Atanassov et al. 2004
	Rice (protein↑; amino acid)	Katsube et al. 1999
	Soybean (amino acid balance)	Rapp 2002; Dinkins et al. 2001
	Sweet Potato (protein↑)	Prakash et al. 2000
	Wheat (protein↑)	Uauy et al. 2006
Essential amino acids	Canola (lysine↑)	Falco et al. 1995
	Lupin (methionine↑)	White et al. 2001
	Maize (lysine↑; methionine↑)	CERA 2013; Lai and Messing 2002
	Potato (methionine↑)	Zeh et al. 2001
	Sorghum (lysine↑)	Zhao et al. 2003
	Soybean (lysine↑; tryptophan↑)	Falco et al. 1995; Galili et al. 2002
Oils and fatty acids		
	Canola (lauric acid↑; γ-linolenic acid↑; + ω-3 fatty acids; 8:0 and 10:0 fatty acids↑; lauric + myristic acid↑; oleic acid↑)	Del Vecchio 1996; Froman and Ursin 2002; James et al. 2003; Ursin 2003, Dehesh et al. 1996; CERA 2013; Roesler et al. 1997
	Cotton (oleic acid↑; oleic acid + stearic acid↑)	Chapman et al. 2001; Liu et al. 2002
	Linseed (+ ω-3 and–6 fatty acids)	Abbadi et al. 2004
	Maize (oil↑)	Young et al. 2004
	Oil Palm (oleic acid↑ or stearic acid↑; oleic acid↑ + palmitic acid↓)	Parveez 2003; Jalani et al. 1997
	Rice (α-linolenic acid↑)	Anai et al. 2003
	Soybean (oleic acid↑; γ-linolenic acid↑)	Kinney and Knowlton 1998; Reddy and Thomas 1996
	Safflower (γ Linoleic Acid GLA↑)	Arcadia, 2008

(Continued)

Table 3.1 Continued

Trait	Crop (trait detail)	Reference
Carbohydrates		
Fructans	Chicory (fructan↑; fructan modification)	Smeekens 1997; Sprenger et al. 1997 Sévenier et al (1998)
	Maize (fructan↑)	Caimi et al. 1996
	Potato (fructan↑)	Hellwege et al. 1997
	Sugar beet (fructan↑)	Smeekens 1997
frustose, raffinose, stachyose	Soybean	Hartwig et al 1997
inulin	Potato (inulin↑)	Hellwege et al. 2000
Starch	Rice (amylase ↑)	Chiang et al. 2005; Schwall, 2000
Micronutrients and functional Metabolites		
vitamins and carotenoids	Canola (vitamin E↑)	Shintani and DellaPenna 1998
	Maize (vitamin E↑; vitamin C↑; folate↑; lycopene) Cassava (+β-carotene)	Rocheford et al. 2002; Cahoon et al. 2003; Chen et al. 2003; Bekaert, 2008; Naqvi et al 2009; Harjes, 2010 Welsch R. et al. 2010
	Mustard (+β-carotene)	Shewmaker et al. 1999
	Potato (β-carotene and lutein↑)	Ducreux et al. 2005; Diretto et al 2010
	Rice (+ β-carotene, folate↑)	Ye et al. 2000; Storozhenko et al, 2007
	Strawberry (vitamin C↑)	Agius et al. 2003
	Tomato (folate↑; phytoene and β-carotene↑; lycopene↑; provitamin A↑)	Della Penna, 2007, Díaz de la Garza et al. 2004; Enfissi et al. 2005; Mehta et al. 2002; Fraser et al. 2001; Rosati 2000; Sun et al. 2012; Klee et al. 2011
Functional 2nd^{ry}metabolites	Apple (+stilbenes)	Szanowski et al. 2003
	Alfalfa (+resveratrol)	Hipskind and Paiva 2000
	Kiwi (+resveratrol)	Kobayashi et al. 2000
	Maize (flavonoids↑)	Yu et al. 2000
	Potato (anthocyanin and alkaloid glycoside↓; solanin↓)	Lukaszewicz et al. 2004
	Rice (flavonoids↑; +resveratrol)	Shin et al. 2006; Stark-Lorenzen 1997
	Soybean (flavonoids↑)	Yu et al. 2003

(Continued)

Table 3.1 Continued

Trait	Crop (trait detail)	Reference
	Tomato (+resveratrol; chlorogenic acid↑;flavonoids↑; stilbene↑anthocynanins↑)	Giovinazzo et al. 2005; Niggeweg et al. 2004; Muir et al. 2001; Rosati 2000, Gonzali et al. 2009
	Wheat (caffeic and ferulic acids↑; +resveratrol)	UPI 2002
Mineral availabilities	Alfalfa (phytase↑)	Austin-Phillips et al. 1999
	Lettuce (iron↑)	Goto et al. 2000
	Rice (iron↑)	Lucca et al. 2002
	Maize (phytase↑, ferritin↑)	Drakakaki 2005; Han 2009
	Soybean (phytase↑)	Denbow et al. 1998
	Wheat (phytase↑)	Brinch-Pedersen et al. 2000, 2006

[1] Excludes protein/starch functionality, shelf life, taste/aesthetics, fiber quality and allergen/toxin reduction traits. Modified from ILSI, 2004, 2008.

Functional food components are of increasing interest in the prevention and treatment of a number of the leading causes of death, including cancer, diabetes, cardiovascular disease, and hypertension. Many food components are known to influence the expression of both structural genes and transcription factors in humans (Go et al. 2005, Mazzatti et al. 2008). Examples of these phytochemicals are listed in Table 3.2. The large diversity of phytochemicals suggests that the potential impact of phytochemicals and functional foods on human and animal health is worth examining as targets of biotechnology efforts. From a health perspective, plant components of dietary interest can be broadly divided into four main categories, which can be further broken down into positive and negative attributions for human nutrition: macronutrients (proteins, carbohydrates, lipids [oils], and fiber); micronutrients (vitamins, minerals, phytochemicals); anti-nutrients (substances such as phytate that limit bioavailability of nutrients); and allergens, intolerances, and toxins.

Technological Challenges

Of the 200,000 or so metabolites (phytochemicals) produced by plants, approximately 25,000 of them have known effects in the human diet (Go et al. 2005). Analysis of these metabolites is a valuable tool in providing a better understanding of what has occurred during crop domestication, when traits are often lost or silenced, which can enable researchers to design new paradigms for more targeted crop improvement tailored to current needs (Hall et al. 2008). In addition, with modern techniques, we have the potential to seek out, analyze, and introgress traits of value that were limited in previous

Table 3.2 Examples of Plant Components with Suggested Functionality[1]

Class/Components	Source[2]	Potential Health Benefit
Carotenoids		
Alpha-carotene	Carrots	Neutralizes free radicals that may cause damage to cells
Beta-carotene	Various fruits, vegetables	Neutralizes free radicals
Lutein	Green vegetables	Contributes to maintenance of healthy vision
Lycopene	Tomatoes and tomato products (ketchup, sauces)	May reduce risk of prostate cancer
Zeaxanthin	Eggs, citrus, maize	Contributes to maintenance of healthy vision
Dietary Fiber		
Insoluble fiber	Wheat bran	May reduce risk of breast and/or colon cancer
Beta glucan[c]	Oats	May reduce risk of cardiovascular disease (CVD)
Soluble fiber[c]	Psyllium	May reduce risk of CVD
Whole Grains[c]	Cereal grains	May reduce risk of CVD
Collagen Hydrolysate	Gelatin	May help improve some symptoms associated with osteoarthritis
Fatty Acids		
Omega-3 fatty acids—DHA/EPA	Tuna; fish and marine oils	May reduce risk of CVD and improve mental, visual functions
Conjugated Linoleic acid (CLA)	Cheese, meat products	May improve body composition, may decrease risk of certain cancers
Gamma Linolenic Acid	Borage, evening primrose	May reduce inflammation risk of cancer, CVD disease, and improve body composition
Flavonoids		
Anthocyanidins: cyanidin	Berries	Neutralize free radicals; may reduce risk of cancer
Hydroxycinnamates	Wheat	Antioxidant-like activities; may reduce risk of degenerative diseases
Flavanols: Catechins, Tannins	Tea (green, catechins), (black, tannins)	Neutralize free radicals; may reduce risk of cancer

(Continued)

Table 3.2 Continued

Class/Components	Source[2]	Potential Health Benefit
Flavanones	Citrus	Neutralize free radicals; may reduce risk of cancer
Flavones: quercetin	Fruits/vegetables	Neutralize free radicals; may reduce risk of cancer
Glucosinolates, Indoles, Isothiocyanates		
Sulphoraphane	Cruciferous vegetables (broccoli, kale), horseradish	Neutralizes free radicals; may reduce risk of cancer
Phenolics		
Stilbenes—Resveratrol,	Grapes	May reduce risk of degenerative diseases; heart disease; cancer. May have longevity effect
Caffeic acid, Ferulic acid	Fruits, vegetables, citrus	Antioxidant-like activities; may reduce risk of degenerative diseases; heart disease, eye disease
Epicatechin	Cacao	Antioxidant-like activities; may reduce risk of degenerative diseases; heart disease
Plant Stanols/Sterols		
Stanol/Sterol ester[c]	Maize, soy, wheat, wood oils	May reduce risk of coronary heart disease (CHD) by lowering blood cholesterol levels
Prebiotic/Probiotics		
Fructans, Inulins, Fructo-oligosaccharides (FOS)	Jerusalem artichokes, shallots, onion powder	May improve gastrointestinal health
Lactobacillus	Yogurt, other dairy	May improve gastrointestinal health
Saponins	Soybeans, soy foods, soy protein-containing foods	May lower LDL cholesterol; contains anti-cancer enzymes
Soybean Protein	Soybeans and soy-based foods	25 g/day may reduce risk of heat disease
Phytoestrogens		
Isoflavones—Daidzein, Genistein	Soybeans and soy-based foods	May reduce menopause symptoms, such as hot flashes, reduce osteoporosis, CVD
Lignans	Flax, rye, vegetables	May protect against heart disease and some cancers; may lower LDL cholesterol, total cholesterol, and triglycerides

(Continued)

Table 3.2 Continued

Class/Components	Source[2]	Potential Health Benefit
Sulfides/Thiols		
Diallyl sulfide	Onions, garlic, olives, leeks, scallions	May lower LDL cholesterol; helps to maintain healthy immune system
Allyl methyl trisulfide, Dithiolthiones	Cruciferous vegetables	May lower LDL cholesterol; helps to maintain healthy immune system
Tannins		
Proanthocyanidins	Cranberries, cranberry products, cocoa, chocolate, black tea	May improve urinary tract health May reduce risk of CVD and high blood pressure

1 Examples are not an all-inclusive list.
2 U.S. Food and Drug Administration approved health claim established for component.
Modified from ILSI, 2004.

breeding strategies. Research to improve the nutritional quality of plants has historically been limited by a lack of basic knowledge of plant metabolism and the challenge of resolving complex interactions of thousands of metabolic pathways. A complementarity of techniques both traditional and novel is needed to metabolically engineer plants to produce desired quality traits. Metabolic engineering is generally defined as the redirection of one or more reactions (enzymatic and otherwise) to improve the production of existing compounds, to produce new compounds, or to mediate the degradation of undesirable compounds. It involves the redirection of cellular activities by the modification of the enzymatic, transport, or regulatory functions of the cell. Significant progress has been made in recent years in the molecular dissection of many plant pathways and in the use of cloned genes to engineer metabolism.

Although progress in dissecting metabolic pathways and our ability to manipulate gene expression in GM plants has progressed apace, attempts to use these tools to engineer plant metabolism have not quite kept pace. Since the success of this approach hinges on the ability to change host metabolism, its continued development will depend critically on a far more sophisticated knowledge of plant metabolism, especially the nuances of interconnected cellular networks, than currently exists. This complex interconnectivity is regularly demonstrated. Relatively minor genomic changes (point mutations, single-gene insertions) following metabolomic analysis are regularly observed to lead to significant changes in biochemical composition (Bino et al. 2005; Davidovich-Rikanati et al. 2007; Long et al. 2006). Giliberto et al. (2005) used a genetic modification approach to study the mechanism of light influence on antioxidant content (anthocyanin, lycopene) in the tomato cultivar Moneymaker. However, other genetic changes, which on the surface appear to be more significant, unexpectedly yield little phenotypical effect (Schauer and Fernie 2006).

Likewise, unexpected outcomes are often observed; for example, significant modifications made to primary Calvin cycle enzymes (fructose-1, 6-bisphosphatase, and phosphoribulokinase) have little impact, whereas modifications to minor enzymes (e.g., aldase, which catalyzes a reversible reaction) seemingly irrelevant to pathway flux, have major effects (Hajirezaei et al. 1994; Paul et al. 1995). These observations demonstrate that caution must be exercised when extrapolating individual enzyme kinetics to the control of flux in complex metabolic pathways. With evolving "omics" tools, a better understanding of global effects of metabolic engineering on metabolites, enzyme activities, and fluxes is beginning to be developed. Attempts to modify storage proteins or secondary metabolic pathways have also been more successful than have alterations of primary and intermediary metabolism (Della Penna 2006). While offering many opportunities, this plasticity in metabolism complicates potential routes to the design of new, improved crop varieties. Regulatory oversight of engineered products has been designed to detect such unexpected outcomes in biotech crops and, as demonstrated by Chassy et al. (ILSI 2004, 2008), existing analytical and regulatory systems are adequate to address novel metabolic modifications in nutritionally improved crops (Chassy, this volume).

A number of new approaches are being developed to counter some of the complex problems in metabolic engineering of pathways. Such approaches include use of RNA interference to modulate endogenous gene expression or the manipulation of transcription factors (Tfs) that control networks of metabolism (Bruce et al. 2000; Butelli et al. 2008; Gonzali et al. 2009; Kinney 1998). Such expression experiments hold promise as an effective tool for the determination of transcriptional regulatory networks for important biochemical pathways. Correctly choreographing the many variables is the factor that makes metabolic engineering in plants so challenging.

Several new technologies can overcome the limitation of single-gene transfers and facilitate the concomitant transfer of multiple components of metabolic pathways. One example is multiple-transgene direct DNA transfer, which simultaneously introduces all the components required for the expression of complex recombinant macromolecules into the plant genome. Nicholson et al. (2005) successfully demonstrated this by delivering four transgenes that represent the components of a secretory antibody into rice; Carlson et al. (2007) constructed a minichromosome vector that remains autonomous from the plant's chromosomes and stably replicates when introduced into maize cells. This work makes it possible to design minichromosomes that carry cassettes of genes, enhancing the ability to engineer plant processes such as the production of complex biochemicals. Naqvi et al. (2009) demonstrated that gene transfer using minimal cassettes is an efficient and rapid method for the production of transgenic plants stably expressing several different transgenes. Since no vector backbones are required, this prevents the integration of potentially recombinogenic sequences, which ensures stability across generations. They used combinatorial direct DNA transformation to introduce multicomplex metabolic pathways coding for beta carotene, vitamin C, and folate. They achieved this by transferring five constructs controlled by different endosperm-specific promoters into white maize. Different enzyme combinations show distinct metabolic phenotypes, resulting in 169-fold beta carotene increase, six times the amount of vitamin C, and doubling folate production, effectively creating a multivitamin maize cultivar (Naqvi et al. 2009). This system has an added advantage from a commercial perspective in that these methods circumvent problems with traditional approaches, which not only limit the amount of sequences transferred but also may disrupt native genes or lead to poor expression of the transgene. The result is thus to reduce both the numbers of transgenic plants that must be screened and the subsequent breeding and introgression steps required to select a suitable commercial candidate.

As demonstrated, "omics"-based strategies for gene and metabolite discovery, coupled with high-throughput transformation processes and automated analytical and functionality assays, have accelerated the identification of product candidates. Identifying rate-limiting steps in synthesis could provide targets for modifying pathways for novel or customized traits. Targeted expression will be used to channel metabolic flow into new pathways, while gene-silencing tools will reduce or eliminate undesirable compounds or traits or switch off genes to increase desirable products (Davies 2007; Herman 2003; Liu 2002). In addition, molecular marker-based breeding strategies have already been used to accelerate the process of introgressing trait genes into high-yielding germplasm for commercialization. Table 3.1 summaries the work being undertaken to date on specific applications in the previously listed categories. The following sections briefly review some examples under those categories.

Macronutrients: Protein

The FAO estimates that 850 million people worldwide suffer from undernutrition, of which insufficient protein in the diet is a significant contributing factor (FAO 2004, 2011). Protein-energy malnutrition (PEM) is the most lethal form of malnutrition and affects every fourth child worldwide according to the World Health Organization (2006). Most plants have a poor balance of essential amino acids relative to the needs of animals and humans. The cereals (e.g., maize, wheat, rice) tend to be low in lysine, whereas legumes (soybean, peas) are often deficient in the sulfur-rich amino acids methionine and cysteine. Successful examples of improving amino acid balance to date include high-lysine maize (Eggeling et al. 1998; O'Quinn et al. 2000), canola, and soybeans (Falco et al. 1995). Consumption of foods made from these crops potentially can help prevent malnutrition in developing countries, especially among children.

One method of modifying storage protein composition is to introduce heterologous or homologous genes that code for proteins containing elevated levels of the desired amino acid such as sulfur containing methionine and cysteine or lysine. An interesting solution is to create a completely artificial protein containing the optimum number of the essential amino acids methionine, threonine, lysine, and leucine in a stable, helical conformation designed to resist proteases to prevent degradation. A number of investigators achieved this using a sweet potato modified with an artificial storage protein (ASP-1) gene (Prakash et al. 2000). These transgenic plants exhibited a two- and fivefold increase in the total protein content in leaves and roots, respectively, over that of control plants. A significant increase in the level of essential amino acids such as methionine, threonine, tryptophan, isoleucine, and lysine was also observed (ILSI 2008; Prakash et al. 2000). A key issue is to ensure that total amount and composition of storage proteins is not altered to the detriment of the development of the crop plant when attempting to improve amino acid ratios (Rapp et al. 2002).

Some novel indirect approaches have also been taken to improve protein content. Uauy et al. (2006) "rescued" an ancestral wheat allele that encodes a transcription factor (NAM-B1) to accelerate senescence and increase nutrient remobilization from leaves to developing grains (modern wheat varieties carry a nonfunctional allele). Reduction in RNA levels of the multiple NAM homologs by RNA interference delayed senescence by more than three weeks and reduced wheat grain protein, zinc, and iron content by more than 30%. Young et al. (2004) used yet another approach to indirectly increase protein and oil content. With a bacterial cytokinin-synthesizing isopentenyl transferase (IPT) enzyme, under the control of a self-limiting senescence-inducible promoter, they were able to block the loss of the lower floret resulting in the production of just one kernel composed of a fused endosperm with two viable embryos. The presence of two embryos in a normal-sized kernel leads to displacement of endosperm growth, resulting in kernels with an increased ratio of embryo to endosperm content. The end result is maize with more protein and oil and less carbohydrate (ILSI 2008; Young et al. 2004).

Macronutrients: Fiber and Carbohydrates

Fiber is a group of substances chemically similar to carbohydrates that nonruminant animals including humans poorly metabolize for energy or other nutritional uses. Fiber provides bulk in the diet such that foods rich in fiber offer satiety without contributing significant calories. Current controversies aside, there is ample scientific evidence to show that prolonged intake of dietary fiber has various positive health benefits, especially the potential for reduced risk of colon and other types of cancer.

Recent microbiome twin studies by Jeff Gordon addressing the interrelationships between diet and gut microbial community structure/function indicated that differences in our gut microbial ecology affect our predisposition to obesity or malnutrition and that diet rather than applied probiotics was the single most important characterization of gut health (Turnbaugh 2009). These studies involved characterization of the gut microbiota and microbiome of twins who were concordant or discordant for malnutrition, were living in several developing countries, and were sampled just prior to, during, and after treatment with various dietry inputs.

When such colonic bacteria (especially *Bifidobacteria*) ferment dietary fiber or other unabsorbed carbohydrates, the products are short-chain saturated fatty acids. They may enhance absorption of minerals such as iron, calcium, and zinc; induce apoptosis, thus preventing colon cancer; and inhibit 3-hydroxy-3-methylglutaryl coenzyme-A reductase (HMG-CoAR), thus lowering low-density lipoprotein (LDL) production (German 2005). Plants are effective at making both polymeric carbohydrates (e.g., starches and fructans) and individual sugars (e.g, sucrose and fructose). The biosynthesis of these compounds is sufficiently understood to allow the bioengineering of their properties and to engineer crops to produce polysaccharides not normally present. Polymeric carbohydrates such as fructans have been produced in sugar beet and inulins and amylase (resistant starch) in potato (Hellwege et al. 2000) without adverse affects on growth or phenotype. A similar approach is being used to derive soybean varieties containing some oligofructan components that selectively increase the population of beneficial species of bacteria in the intestines of humans and certain animals and that inhibit growth of harmful ones (Bouhnik 1999).

Macronutrients: Novel Lipids

Genomics, specifically marker-assisted plant breeding, combined with recombinant DNA technology provide powerful means for modifying the composition of oilseeds to improve their nutritional value and provide the functional properties required for various food oil applications. Genetic modification of oilseed crops can provide an abundant, relatively inexpensive source of dietary fatty acids with wide-ranging health benefits. Production of such lipids in vegetable oil provides a convenient mechanism to deliver healthier products to consumers without requiring them to make significant dietary changes. Major alterations in the proportions of individual fatty acids have been achieved in a range of oilseeds using conventional selection, induced mutation, and, more recently, post-transcriptional gene silencing. Examples of such modified oils include low- and zero-saturated fat soybean and canola oils, canola oil containing medium-chain fatty acids (MCFA) whose ergogenic potential may have application in LDCs, high stearic acid canola oil (for trans fatty acid-free products), high oleic acid (PUFA), λ-linolenic (GLA; 18:3 n-6) stearidonic acids (SDA; C18:4 n-3), very-long-chain fatty acids (Zou, 1997), and omega-3 fatty acids (Yuan and Knauf 1997). These modified oils are being marketed, and many countries have a regulatory system in place for the premarket safety review of novel foods produced through conventional technology.

Edible oils rich in monounsaturated fatty acids provide improved oil stability, flavor, and nutrition for human and animal consumption. High-oleic soybean oil is naturally more resistant to degradation by heat and oxidation and thus requires little or no postrefining processing (hydrogenation), depending on the intended vegetable oil application. Oleic acid (18:1), a monounsaturate, can provide more stability than the polyunsaturates linoleic (18:2) and linolenic (18:3). Antisense inhibition of oleate desaturase expression in soybean resulted in oil that contained > 80% oleic acid (23% is normal) and had a significant decrease in PUFA (Kinney and Knowlton, 1998). Dupont has introduced soybean oil composed of at least 80% oleic acid and linolenic acid of about 3% and over 20% less saturated fatty acids than commodity soybean oil. Monsanto's Vistive contains less than 3% linolenic acid, compared with 8% for traditional soybeans. This results in more stable soybean oil and less need for hydrogenation. The genetically modified version Vistive gold (MON 87705) is engineered to reduce linolenic acid content by suppressing FATB and FAD2, endogenous enzymes that play a role in the biosynthesis of fatty acids. This alteration more than triples oleic acid content, raising it from approximately 20% to 70% of all fatty acids, and reduces the levels of linoleic acid, stearic acid, and palmitic acid present in seeds (Vistive Gold Soybeans 2011).

A key function of α-linolenic acid (ALA) is as a substrate for the synthesis of longer-chain ω-3 fatty acids found in fish, eicosapentaenoic acid (EPA; C20:5n-3) and docosahexaenoic acid (DHA; C22:6n-3) which play an important role in the regulation of inflammatory immune reactions and blood pressure, brain development in utero, and, in early postnatal life, the development of cognitive function. Stearidonic acid (SDA; C18:4n-3), EPA, and DHA also possess anti-cancer properties (Christensen et al. 1999; Reiffel and McDonald 2006; Smuts 2003). Research indicates that the ratio of n-3 to n-6 fatty acids may be as important to health and nutrition as the absolute amounts present in the diet or in body tissues. Current Western diets tend to be relatively high in n-6 fatty acids and relatively low in n-3 fatty acids. Production of a readily available source of long-chain-PUFA, specifically ω-3 fatty acids, delivered in widely consumed prepared foods could deliver much needed ω-3-fatty acids to large sectors of the population with skewed n-6:n-3 ratios. In plants, the microsomal ω-6 desaturase-catalyzed pathway is the primary route of production of polyunsaturated lipids. Ursin et al. (2000, 2003) has introduced the Δ-6 desaturase gene from a fungus *(Mortierella)* succeeding in producing ω-3 in canola. In subsequent work the same gene was added to soybean, and transgenic soybean oil was obtained containing greater than 23% SDA. It had an overall n-6:n-3 ratio of 0.5, which the body converts to heart-healthy EPA, one of three omega-3 fatty acids used by the body. This product is now being developed for commercialization by Monsanto (SDA 2011).

However, not all omega-6 fatty acids are created equal. Gamma linolenic acid (GLA, C18:3n-6) is an omega-6 fatty acid with health benefits similar and complementary to the benefits of omega-3 fatty acids including anti-inflammatory effects, improved skin health, and weight loss maintenance (Schirmer et al. 2007). Arcadia has engineered GLA safflower oil with up to 40% GLA, essentially quadrupling the levels obtained in source plants such as evening primrose and borage (Arcadia Biosciences, 2008). Structural lipids also have positive health benefits. For example, in addition to their effect in lowering cholesterol, membrane lipid phytosterols have been found to inhibit the proliferation of cancer cells by inducing apoptosis and G1/S cell cycle arrest through the HMG-CoAR as noted already (Awad 2000). In addition, specialty oils may also be developed with further pharmaceutical and chemical feedstock applications in mind.

Micronutrients: Vitamins and Minerals

Even mild levels of micronutrient malnutrition may damage cognitive development and lower disease resistance in children and increase incidences of childbirth mortality (UN SCN, 2004). The costs of these deficiencies, in terms of diminished quality of life and lives lost, are large (Pfeiffera and McClafferty 2007). Such deficiencies prevent children from reaching their full potential as adults; malnutrition, especially during the one thousand days between conception and age two, can lead to irreversible physical stunting and cognitive impairment. But children who are well nourished are able to grow, learn, and prosper. They achieve more in school, are better able to survive illnesses, and tend to earn more as adults (Kraemer 2012). The clinical and epidemiological evidence is clear: select minerals (iron, calcium, selenium, and iodine) and a limited number of vitamins (folate and vitamins E, B6, and A) play a significant role in maintenance of optimal health and are limiting in diets (Asensi-Fabado 2010).

As with macronutrients, one way to ensure an adequate dietary intake of nutritionally beneficial phytochemicals is to adjust their levels in plant foods. Using various approaches, including genomics, vitamin E levels are being increased in several crops, including soybean, maize, and canola. In addition, rice varieties are being developed with the enhanced vitamin A precursor β-carotene to address this vitamin deficiency that leads to macular degeneration and impacts development. Golden Rice II accumulates up to 37 μg β-carotene per gram of rice (23-fold more than the original). This β-carotene has been shown to be bioavailable in sufficient amounts that 100 to 200 g per day can provide adequate provitamin A to ameliorate against deficiency (Tang et al. 2009). A number of other staple crops on which many depend almost exclusively for calories have been produced enriched in β-carotene, including maize and cassava (Harjes et al. 2008; Welsch et al. 2010; Yan et al. 2010). The latter is being field tested in Nigeria.

Ameliorating another major deficiency common in LDCs—iron—has also been addressed. Iron is the most commonly deficient micronutrient in the human diet, and iron deficiency affects an estimated 1 to 2 billion people. Anemia, characterized by low hemoglobin, is the most widely recognized symptom of iron deficiency, but there are other serious problems such as impaired learning ability in children, increased susceptibility to infection, and reduced work capacity. Drakakaki et al. (2005) demonstrated endosperm-specific co-expression of recombinant soybean ferritin and Aspergillus phytase in maize, which resulted in significant increases in the levels of bioavailable iron. A similar end was achieved with lettuce (Goto et al. 2000).

A rather interesting approach was taken by Connolly et al. (2008) to increase the levels of calcium in crop plants by using a modified calcium/proton antiporter known as short cation exchanger 1 (sCAX1) to increase Ca transport into vacuoles. They also demonstrated that consumption of such Ca-fortified carrots results in enhanced Ca absorption. This demonstrates the potential of increasing plant nutrient content through expression of a high-capacity transporter and illustrates the importance of demonstrating that the fortified nutrient is bioavailable. Other targets include folate-enriched tomatoes and isoflavonoids (DellaPenna 2007; Yonekura-Sakakibara and Saito 2007).

Micronutrients: Phytochemicals

The primary evidence for the health-promoting roles of phytochemicals comes from epidemiological studies, and the exact chemical identity of many active compounds has yet to be determined. However, for select groups of phytochemicals, such as non-provitamin A carotenoids, glucosinolates, and phytoestrogens, the active compound or compounds have been identified and rigorously studied. Epidemiologic studies have suggested a potential benefit of the carotenoid lycopene in reducing the risk of prostate cancer, particularly the more lethal forms of this cancer. Five studies support a 30% to 40% reduction in risk associated with high tomato or lycopene consumption in the processed form in conjunction with lipid consumption, although other studies with raw tomatoes were not conclusive (Giovannucci 2002). Since carotenoids are lipid soluble and cooking breaks down carotenoid binding proteins, this is not an unexpected outcome. A study by Mehta et al. (2002) to modify polyamines to retard tomato ripening found an unanticipated enrichment in lycopene with levels up by 2 to 3.5-fold compared with conventional tomatoes. This approach may work in other fruits and vegetables. Flavonoids meanwhile are soluble in water, and foods containing both water-soluble and fat-dissolved antioxidants are considered to offer the best protection against disease. Anthocyanins offer protection against certain cancers, cardiovascular disease, and age-related degenerative diseases. There is evidence that anthocyanins also have anti-inflammatory activity, promote visual acuity, and hinder obesity and diabetes. Both Gonzali et al. (2009) and Butelli et al. (2008) used snapdragon transcription factors to achieve high-level expression of the reactive oygen scavengers, anthocyanins, in tomatoes. In a pilot test, the life span of cancer-susceptible mice (p53 mutants) was significantly extended when their diet was supplemented with the purple tomatoes compared to supplementation with normal red tomatoes.

Other phytochemicals of interest include related polyphenolics such as resveratrol, which has been demonstrated to inhibit platelet aggregation and eicosanoid synthesis in addition to protecting the sirtuins, genes implicated in DNA modification and life extension; flavonoids, such as tomatoes expressing chalcone isomerase that show increased contents of the flavanols rutin and kaempferol glycoside; glucosinolates and their related products such as indole-3 carbinol (I3C); catechin and catechol; isoflavones, such as genistein and daidzein; anthocyanins; and some phytoalexins. Table 3.1 summarizes activities in improving nutritional characteristics of various crops worldwide. A comprehensive list of phytochemicals is provided Table 3.2. To reiterate, although there is a growing knowledge base indicating that elevated intakes of specific phytochemicals may reduce the risk of diseases, such as certain cancers, cardiovascular diseases, and chronic degenerative diseases associated with aging, further research and epidemiological studies are still required to prove definitive relationships.

Fighting Plants Fighting Back

Plants deploy many defense strategies to protect themselves from predators. Many, such as resveratrol and glucosinate, which are primarily pathogen-protective chemicals, also have demonstrated beneficial effects for human and animal health. Many, however, have the opposite effect. For example, phytate, a plant phosphate storage compound, is considered an antinutrient as it strongly chelates iron, calcium, zinc, and other divalent mineral ions, making them unavailable for uptake. Nonruminant animals generally lack the phytase enzyme needed for digestion of phytate. Poultry and swine producers add processed phosphate to their feed rations to counter this. Excess phosphate is excreted into the environment resulting in water pollution. When low-phytate soybean meal is utilized along with low-phytate maize for animal feeds, the phosphate excretion in swine and poultry manure is halved. A number of groups have added heat- and acid-stable phytase from *Aspergillus fumigatus* inter alia to make the phosphate and liberated ions bioavailable in several crops (Potrykus 1999). To promote the reabsorption of iron, a gene for a metallothionein-like protein has also been engineered. Low-phytate maize was commercialized in the United States in 1999 (Wehrspann 1998).

In November 2009, the Chinese company Origin Agritech announced the final approval of the world's first genetically modified phytase-expressing maize (Han 2009). Research indicates that the protein in low-phytate soybeans is also slightly more digestible than the protein in traditional soybeans. In a poultry feeding trial, better results were obtained using transgenic plant material than with the commercially produced phytase supplement (Keshavarz, 2003). Poultry grew well on the engineered alfalfa diet without any inorganic phosphorus supplement, which shows that plants can be tailored to increase the bioavailability of this essential mineral. A Danish group achieved a similar effect, where temperature-tolerant phytase resisted boiling (Brinch-Pedersen 2006).

As noted previously, JR Simplot has created one of the first output products to be submitted for non-regulated status, a potato with three specific modification for quality improvement.

The three modified traits are important from a commercial perspective as they greatly improve the quality of the potato, making it more appealing to both producers and consumers. The first of those traits, reduced black spot from bruising and browning, is achieved through RNAi suppression of polyphenol oxidase (PPO), effectively limiting oxidation by silencing the endogenous PPO gene. Not only is this more appealing for the consumer, but it will also help reduce waste for growers since fewer potatoes will be discarded.

The second trait is a reduction in reducing sugars through down-regulation of phosphorylase and starch associated genes, slowing the conversion to sucrose and fructose, which provides potatoes with a consistent golden color that results in improved taste and texture qualities. The third trait is suppression of asparagine through expression of asparagine synthetase-1, which reduces the potential for the formation of acrylamide by 80%. The latter is created when potatoes are cooked at high temperatures. By reducing the levels of these sugars and asparagine in stored potatoes, they can significantly lower the levels of acrylamide in the food. Accordingly, this modification improves not just the quality but also the safety of the potato by reducing levels of this toxic chemical.

Other antinutrients that are being examined as possible targets for reduction are trypsin inhibitors, lectins, and several heat-stable components found in soybeans and other crops. Likewise, strategies are being employed to reduce or limit food allergens (e.g., albumins, globulins), malabsorption and food intolerances (gluten), and toxins (glycoalkaloids, cyanogenic glucosides, phytohemagglutinins) in crop plants and aesthetics undesirables such as caffeine (Ogita 2003). Examples include changing the levels of expression of the thioredoxin gene to reduce the intolerance effects of wheat and other cereals (Buchanan 1997) and using RNAi to silence the major allergen in soybeans (P34 a member of the papain superfamily of cysteine proteases) and rice (14-16 kDa allergenic proteins). Blood serum tests indicate that p34-specific IgE antibodies could not be detected after consumption of gene-silenced beans (Helm 2000; Herman 2003).

Modern biotech approaches can be employed to down-regulate or even eliminate the genes involved in the metabolic pathways for the production, accumulation, or activation of these toxins in plants. For example, the solanine content of potato has already been reduced substantially using an antisense approach, and efforts are under way to reduce the level of the other major potato glycoalkaloid, chaconine (McCue et al. 2003). Work has also been done to reduce cyanogenic glycosides in cassava through expression of the cassava enzyme hydroxynitrile lyase in the roots (Siritunga and Sayre 2003). When "disarming" plants natural defenses in this way one must be aware of potentially increased susceptibility to pests, diseases, and other stressors, so the recipient germplasm should have input traits to counter this outcome.

Prospects for Crop Biotechnology

Improvement of crop nutritional quality is a technical challenge hampered by a lack of basic knowledge of plant metabolism and the need to resolve the complexity of intersecting networks of thousands of metabolic pathways. With the tools now available through the field of genomics, proteomics, lipomics, glycobiomics, metabolmics, and bioinformatics, we have the potential to study and manipulate genes and pathways at the metalevel and simultaneously to study the expression and interaction of transgenes on tens of thousands of endogenous genes. With these newly evolving tools we are beginning to dissect the global effects of metabolic engineering on metabolites, enzyme activities, and fluxes. For essential macro- and micronutrients that are limiting in various regional diets, the strategies for improvement are clear, and the concerns such as pleiotropic effects and safe upper limits are easily addressed. However, for many putative health-promoting phytochemicals, clear links with health benefits are yet to be demonstrated. In addition, one must be careful when extrapolating attributes from an individual substance acting independently to that substance acting within a complex milieu. But if such links can be established, it will make it possible to identify the precise compound or compounds to target and which crops to modify to achieve the greatest nutritional impact and health benefit. With rapidly emerging technologies, the increase in our understanding of and ability to manipulate plant metabolism during the coming decades should place plant researchers in the position of being able to modify the nutritional content of major and minor crops to improve many aspects of human and animal health and well-being.

Barriers to Introduction

Commercialization of the first generation of products of recombinant DNA technology was another facet in a long history of human intervention in nature for agricultural and food production purposes (see McHughen, this volume). There is almost universal agreement that innovation is essential for sustaining and enhancing agricultural quality and productivity. There also would be general concurrence that this involves on some level new, science-based products and processes that contribute reliable methods for improving quality, productivity, and environmental sustainability. Most of the innovative technologies used in modern agriculture have created little controversy or even notice by consumers, with the partial exception of the Green Revolution in plant breeding for nitrogen response (Harriss and Stewart, this volume). To most producers and academic and industrial researchers, biotechnology is seen as offering a new dimension to innovation, providing efficient and cost-effective means to produce a diverse array of value-added products and tools. To others it represents an unnecessary, and for some unnatural, risk at a broad level to our food system and environment and at a very fundamental level a risk to our way of life or code of beliefs (see Shome, Chappell, this volume). Because of the globalization and democratization of knowledge afforded by the Internet, the cult of the amateur noted by Trewavas (2008) often accords in both society and politics equal weight to uninformed opinions as to established science.

Given the current regulatory climate for agricultural biotechnology, it is difficult to imagine many of the previously described traits ever reaching the marketplace. Most of the crops approved to date demonstrate that the deregulation process is prohibitive for everyone except well-financed companies whose focus is primarily the large commodity crops, as discussed previously. Just one trait from a public institution has successfully traversed the regulatory minefields and been translated into a commercially viable commodity: the viral coat protein protection system initially developed for the papaya ringspot virus pandemic in Hawaii. Papaya is a major tropical fruit crop in the Asian region. However, production in many countries is set back by the prevalence of the PRSV disease as well as postharvest losses. The PRSV-resistant papaya, based on RNAi suppression of the coat protein expression, literally saved the US$17 million papaya economy in Hawaii. Though the disease is of significant importance in Taiwan and other southeast Asian countries, the trait has yet to be approved (see Evanega and Lynas, this volume).

Rather interestingly it has been reported anecdotally that organic papaya growers now surround their plots with the transgenic rainbow variety as the PTGS system proves to be a most effective method to reduce the viral reservoir thus protecting susceptible varieties through a mechanism that is similar to herd immunity in mammalian systems.

The late blight resistant potatoes discussed above could feasibly provide the same cooperative resistance for organic potato farmers in Europe but, since BASF have pulled their production in the EU this cannot now be demonstrated. Research by Hutchison et al. (2010) interestingly demonstrates a variation of this halo effect for Bt maize. As noted, to mitigate against the evolution of resistance growers are required to maintain a 20% refugia of non-Bt maize. Despite predictions that this single gene protection may select for the development of resistant in corn borer larvae on maize or bollworm in cotton it has proven to be remarkably resilient. While some resistance has arisen most specifically in the latter where a mutation in the cadherin receptor has led to localized resistance, it is much lower than might be expected given the extent of usage of the Bt phenotype. Actually while mutations providing small decreases in susceptibility to Bt proteins are relatively common, those conferring sufficient resistance to enable survival on some types of Bt corn are exceedingly rare. Hutchison (2010) has demonstrated that this has led to cumulative benefits over 14 years of between $3.2 and $3.6 billion with $1.9 to $2.4 billion of this total accruing to non-Bt maize growers. They postulate that these results affirm theoretical predictions of pest population suppression and highlight economic incentives for growers to maintain non-Bt maize refugia for sustainable insect resistance management. While initially these refugia were required to be in specified plots it has been put forward that mixing Bt and non-Bt maize grain during planting may be an equally effective management strategy. However this effect is disputed by some entomologists. Again enforcement of these requirements had been relatively easy in the developed world; to do so in some regions may prove more challenging.

The obdurate attitude of the EU has consequences beyond the obvious economic. A case in point is the BASF's decision to pull the Fortuna potato as cited above. Now instead of adopting the GM Fortuna cultivar and the subsequent reduction of the use of harmful chemicals, European farmers must rely on the continued use of fungicides which are some of the least friendly biocontrol chemicals. Ironically, as noted, this choice obstructs further expansion of organically produced potatoes and tomatoes because adopting the GM Fortuna cultivar in "conventional" agriculture could have led to reduced disease pressures benefitting alternative farming systems (Dixelius et al. 2012). In addition, as a major consumer of potatoes the EU will now become increasingly dependent on import from other regions, as they inevitably lose the battle against P. infestans. Over time these imported potatoes are likely to be GM Fortuna so Europe is still left with the problem of tackling political resistance against it or any other GM crop.

While translation of biotech research into field crops is a challenge in the European Union (EU) and even the United States, it is more difficult in LDCs. A problem facing Africa in particular is the lack of a dynamic private sector to take technologies to the farmer. It has also been estimated that regulatory costs exceed the costs of research and experimentation needed to develop a given GM crop, which is a major problem in releasing such crops to farmers. A way to reduce the costs of generating food and environmental safety data is to develop regional "centers of excellence" with complementary facilities for biosecurity compliance. This can be done reliably and could help with reduction of regulatory costs. The economic gains from using genetically modified crop technology in sub-Saharan Africa are potentially large according to the World Bank Group (Anderson 2005). The results suggest that the welfare gains are potentially very large, especially from golden rice (beta carotene–enhanced rice) and nutritionally enhanced GM wheat and that those benefits are diminished only slightly by the presence of the European Union's current ban on imports of GM foods. Using the global economy-wide computable general equilibrium model known as the Global Trade Analysis Project, Anderson et al. (2005) specifically noted that if sub-Saharan African countries impose bans on GM crop imports in deference to EU market demand for non-GM products, the domestic consumer net loss from that protectionism would be more than the small gain derived from greater market access to the EU (see also Anderson, this volume).

In December 2012 FAO's Director-General, José Graziano da Silva, noted that food insecurity in Africa's Sahel region is closely linked to peace and stability, and he stressed that short-term humanitarian efforts in the Sahel needed to be replaced with longer-term development (Da Silva, 2012). Apart from the suggested implication of food and agricultural markets as being one of the trigger factors in catalyzing the "Arab Spring", the most recent global food crisis was in 2008 and as noted we may be facing an even greater one in 2013. During this crisis, which was erroneously laid disproportionately on the shoulders of biofuel production, most especially grain ethanol, the Gates Foundation announced $306 million in grants to boost agricultural yields in the developing world, with nearly $165 million to replenish depleted soils in Africa. As noted by *US News and World Report,* these efforts are not without controversy as they charge that critics consider that western philanthropists are violating African "food sovereignty" and promoting America at the expense of peasant farmers knowledgeable about local practices (Lavelle et al. 2008). But local practices have yielded scarcity. A farmer in India grows three to four times as much food on the same amount of land as a farmer in Africa; a farmer in China, roughly seven times as much.

Florence Wambugu (1999, 16) of Kenya states that the great potential of biotechnology to improve agriculture in Africa lies in its "packaged technology in the seed," which ensures technology benefits without changing local cultural practices. Golden rice is a seminal example of this contention. Incorporation of beta carotene into rice cultivars and widespread distribution of this packaged technology in the seed could prevent one to two million deaths each year. Wambugu observes that in the past many foreign donors funded high-input projects, which have not been sustainable because they have failed to address social and economic issues such as changes in cultural practice. Ismail Serageldin, former chair of the Consultative Group on International Agricultural Research, likewise notes that, a priori, biotechnology could contribute to food security by helping to promote sustainable agriculture centered on smallholder farmers in developing countries. Calestous Juma (2012) highlights that Africa's precautionary approaches to biotechnology are not only misguided but also expose the continent to long-term political risks. Juma maintains that biotechnology is not simply a matter of rhetorical debate guided by short-term interests but is also central to how African countries define their place in the global knowledge ecology.

Problems cited for the slow passage of GM crops from experimental to trial to commercial stage include the lack of capacity to negotiate licenses to use genes and research techniques patented by others, especially for crops with export potential. In addition, there are difficulties in meeting regulatory requirements and a lack of effective public commercialization modalities and working extension networks. Biosafety regulations still have to be enforced in many countries for an effective and purportedly safe use of genetically engineered crops, especially if their production is meant for the export market, whether or not there is evidence of hazard. Intellectual property rights continue to be a significant barrier in some regions and for some technologies. If the public sector is going to contribute in tangible ways to technological approaches for food security, the public research system needs to be optimized for translation in this arena.

Therefore, the actual commercialization of biotech products may have less to do with technical limitations and more to do with external constraints, primarily the process of regulatory approval. The flagship of improved nutritional varieties—namely, beta carotene–enhanced rice, commonly referred to as golden rice—despite being under consideration since the late 1990s and subject to a barrage of risk assessments will not be approved until 2014 at the earliest. Ingo Potrykus, the developer, claims that an unreasonable amount of testing has been required without scientific justification. In a 2010 *Nature* article he laid the blame solely at the door of the regulatory process: "I therefore hold the regulation of genetic engineering responsible for the death and blindness of thousands of children and young mothers."

Future Directions

As agriculture must adapt to rapidly changing needs and growing conditions, we must become more effective at producing more on less with limited resources. Only the tools of biotechnology will allow us to bypass physiological and environmental limitations to produce sufficient food, feed, fuels, and fiber on ever diminishing arable land to meet ever increasing demand. Some challenges going forward are technical, as we strive to modify qualitative (as opposed to quantitative) traits and intricate metabolic pathways and networks (as opposed to single genes), and the scientific hurdles are not trivial. However, with the tools now coming online in the fields of genomics, proteomics, metabolomics, and bioinformatics, there is genuinely new potential. For example, tools such as next-generation sequencing, RNAi, transcription factors, transcription activator-like effector nucleases, mini-chromosomes, combinatorial transformation, epigenetic modification, network engineering, and systems biology will allow us to apply both reductive and holistic approaches to identify, modify, introgress, and subsequently simultaneously study the expression and interaction of transgenes on tens of thousands of endogenous genes in elite germplasm backgrounds. With these newly evolving tools, we are beginning to dissect the global effects of metabolic engineering on metabolites, enzyme activities, and fluxes. With rapidly emerging technologies, the increase in our understanding of and ability to manipulate plant metabolism during the coming decades should enable plant researchers to modify crop traits to respond to the diversity of needs, from minimizing environmental impact to optimizing productivity and quality output.

Yet this potential is subject to constraints discussed in the previous section. Nontechnical limitations include the following: (1) intellectual property restrictions, which may limit translation of public research if not managed judiciously; (2) liability concerns over use, abuse, or misuse of constructs; (3) prohibitive and asymmetric biosafety regimes; and (4) public acceptance. The latter two in many ways are the most difficult to overcome, as they have little basis in rational process and thus—like much of politics—are difficult to redress. The two are interrelated: biosafety is a function of how the public perceives risk, reflecting in part how positions are presented by the opposing political factions (see Chassy, this volume). Emotion and fear often trump reasoned and judicious scientific rationale for risk analysis. Indeed, the actual commercialization of biotech products may have little to do with technical limitations and more to do with these external constraints. As a noted case in point, the flagship of improved nutritional varieties, namely, beta carotene–enhanced golden rice, despite being under consideration since the late 1990s still awaits appearance in the fields of farmers.

In the final analysis resources are finite, and true sustainability can come only from the development of resource-enhancing technologies. Yet many who profess sustainability as a political objective are, on occasion, the very ones who oppose the development and application of those tools that can help to ensure sustainability. The only sure way to confirm food security and protect the planet's resources is to refuse to settle into the complacency of maintaining the status quo and to engage in continual, constructive change based on scientific know-how.

References

Abbadi, A., F. Domergue, J. Bauer, J. A. Napier, R. Welti, U. Zahringer, P. Cirpus, and E. Heinz. 2004. "Biosynthesis of Very-Long-Chain Polyunsaturated Fatty Acids in Transgenic Oilseeds: Constraints on Their Accumulation." *Plant Cell* 16:2734–2748.

Agarwal, P. K., P. Agarwal, M. K. Reddy, and S. K. Sopory. 2006. "Role of DREB Transcription Factors in Abiotic and Biotic Stress Tolerance in Plants." *Plant Cell Reports* 25:1263–1274.

CERA 2013. "GM Crop Database. Accessed October 26, 2013. http://cera-gmc.org/index.php?action=gm_crop_database.

Agius, F., R. Gonzalez-Lamothe, J. L. Caballero, J. Munoz-Blanco, M. A. Botella, and V. Valpuesta. 2003. "Engineering Increased Vitamin C Levels in Plants by Overexpression of a D-Galacturonic Acid Reductase." *Nature Biotechnology* 21:177–181.

Anai, T., M. Koga, H. Tanaka, T. Kinoshita, S. M. Rahman, and Y. Takagi. 2003. "Improvement of Rice (Oryza sativa L.) Seed Oil Quality through Introduction of a Soybean Microsomal Omega-3 Fatty Acid Desaturase Gene." *Plant Cell Reports* 21:988–992.

Anderson, Kym, and Lee Ann Jackson. 2005. "Some Implications of GM Food Technology Policies for Sub-Saharan Africa." *Journal of African Economies* 14: 385–410.

Arcadia Biosciences and Bioriginal Food and Science Corp. 2008 "Enter Strategic Alliance to Market High GLA Safflower Oil." *Business Wire*, February 22.Accessed March, 2013 http://www.arcadiabio.com/news/press-release/arcadia-biosciences-and-bioriginal-food-and-science-corp-enter-strategic-alliance

Asensi-Fabado, M. A., and S. Munné-Bosch. 2010. "Vitamins in Plants: Occurrence, Biosynthesis and Antioxidant Function." *Trends in Plant Science* 15:582–592.

Atanassov, A., A. Bahieldin, J. Brink, M. Burachik, J. I. Cohen, V. Dhawan, R. V. Ebora, J. Falck-Zepeda, L. Herrera-Estrella, J. Komen, F. C. Low, E. Omaliko, B. Odhiambo, H. Quemada, Y. Peng, M. J. Sampaio, I. Sithole-Niang, A. Sittenfeld, M. Smale, Sutrisno, R. Valyasevi, Y. Zafar, and P. Zambrano. 2004. "To Reach the Poor—Results from the ISNAR-IFPRI Next Harvest Study on Genetically Modified Crops, Public Research, and Policy Implications." EPTD Discussion Paper—Environment and Production Technology Division, International Food Policy Research Institute.

Austin-Phillips, S., E. T. Bingham, R. G. Koegel, J. Rausch, R. J. Straub, J. Will, T. Zeigelhoffer, P. Zeigelhoffer, and R. R. Burgess. 1999. "Production of Industrial and Animal Feed Enzymes in Transgenic Alfalfa." Accessed June 16, 2006. http://www.molecularfarming.com/nonmedical.html.

Awad, Atif B., and Carol S. Fink. 2000. "Phytosterols as Anticancer Dietary Components: Evidence and Mechanism of Action." *Journal of Nutrition* 130:2127–2130.

BASF. 2011. "Business BASF Applies for Approval for Another Biotech Potato." http://www.research-in-germany.de/84190/2011-11-17-business-basf-applies-for-approval-for-another-biotech-potato.html.

Bekaert, S., S. Storozhenko, P. Mehrshahi, M. J. Bennett, W. Lambert, J. F. Gregory III, K. Schubert, J. Hugenholtz, D. Van Der Straeten, and A. D. Hanson. 2008. "Folate Biofortification in Food Plants." *Trends in Plant Science* 13:28–35.

Bino, R. J., C. H. R. de Vos, M. Lieberman, R. D. Hall, A. G. Bovy, H. H. Jonker, Y. Tikunov, A. Lommen, S. Moco, and I. Levin. 2005. "The Light-Hyperresponsive High Pigment-2dg Mutation of Tomato: Alterations in the Fruit Metabolome." *New Phytologist* 166:427–438.

Bouhnik Y, Vahedi K, Achour L, Attar A, Salfati J, Pochart P, Marteau P, Flourie Borne F, Rambaud JC (1999) Short-chain fructo-oligosaccharide administration dose-dependently. *J Nutr* 129: 113–116."

Bricknel, T. 2010. "India Delays BT Brinjal Decision." Accessed June 20, 2012. http://www.fruit-net.com/asiafruit/article/5731/india-delays-bt-brinjal-decision.

Brigelius-Flohe, R. and Joost, H. G. 2006. "Nutritional genomics: Impact on health and disease." Wiley-VCH Verlag GmbH & co, 3–17. ISBN 3-527-31294-3.

Brinch-Pedersen, H., A. Olesen, S. K. Rasmussen, and P. B. Holm. 2000. "Generation of Transgenic Wheat (Triticum aestivum L.) for Constitutive Accumulation of an Aspergillus Phytase." *Molecular Breeding* 6:195–206.

Brinch-Pedersen, H., F. Hatzack, E. Stoger, E. Arcalis, K. Pontopidan, and P. B. Holm. "Heat-Stable Phytases in Transgenic Wheat (Triticum aestivum L.): Deposition Pattern, Thermostability, and Phytate Hydrolysis." *Journal of Agricultural and Food Chemistry* 54(13):4624–4632.

Brookes G and Barfoot P (2012) Global Impact of Biotech Crops: Environmental Effects, 1996-2010, GM Crops 3: 2 April-June 2012, p 1–9. Acessed March 2013, www.landesbioscience.com/journal/gmcrops

Bruce, W., O. Folkerts, C. Garnaat, O. Crasta, B. Roth, and B. Bowen. 2000. "Expression Profiling of the Maize Flavonoid Pathway Genes Controlled by Estradiol-Inducible Transcription Factors CRC and P." *Plant Cell* 12:65–80.

Buchanan, B. B., C. Adamidi, R. M. Lozano, B. C. Yee, M. Momma, K. Kobrehel, R. Ermel, and O. L. Frick. 1997. "Thioredoxin-Linked Mitigation of Allergic Responses to Wheat." *Proceedings of the National Academy of Sciences USA* 94:5372–5377.

Butelli, E., Lucilla Titta, Marco Giorgio, Hans-Peter Mock, Andrea Matros, Silke Peterek, Elio G. W. M. Schijlen, Robert D. Hall, Arnaud G. Bovy, Jie Luo, and C. Martin. 2008. "Enrichment of Tomato Fruit with Health-Promoting Anthocyanins by Expression of Select Transcription Factors." *Nature Biotechnology* 26:1301–1308.

Cahoon, E. B., S. E. Hall, K. G. Ripp, T. S. Ganzke, W. D. Hitz, and S. J. Coughlan. 2003. "Metabolic Redesign of Vitamin E Biosynthesis in Plants for Tocotrienol Production and Increased Antioxidant Content." *Nature Biotechnology* 21:1082–1087.

Caimi, P. G., L. M. McCole, T. M. Klein, and P. S. Kerr. 1996. "Fructan Accumulation and Sucrose Metabolism in Transgenic Maize Endosperm Expressing a Bacillus Amyloliquefaciens SacB Gene." *Plant Physiology* 110:355–363.

Carlson, S. R., G. Rudgers, H. Zieler, J. Mach, S. Luo, E. Grunden, C. Krol, G. Copenhaver, and D. Preuss. 2007. "Meiotic Transmission of an In Vitro–Assembled Autonomous Maize Minichromosome." *PLOS Genetics* 3(10):e179.

Carter, N. 2012. "Petition for Determination of Nonregulated Status: Arctic™ Apple (Malus x domestica) Events GD743 and GS784." United States Department of Agriculture—Animal and Plant Health Inspection Service. Acessed March, 2012 http://www.aphis.usda.gov/brs/aphisdocs/10_16101p.pdf.

Castiglioni, P., D. Warner, R. J. Bensen, D. C. Anstrom, J. Harrison, M. Stoecker, M. Abad, G. Kumar, S. Salvador, and R. D'Ordine. 2008. "Bacterial RNA Chaperones Confer Abiotic Stress Tolerance in Plants and Improved Grain Yield in Maize under Water-Limited Conditions." *Plant Physiology* 147(2): 455.

Chakraborty, S., N. Chakraborty, and A. Datta. 2000. "Increased Nutritive Value of Transgenic Potato by Expressing a Nonallergenic Seed Albumin Gene from Amaranthus Hypochondriacus." *Proceedings of the National Academy of Science USA* 97:3724–3729.

Chapman, K. D., S. Austin-Brown, S. A. Sparace, A. J. Kinney, K. G. Ripp, I. L. Pirtle, and R. M. Pirtle. 2001. "Transgenic Cotton Plants with Increased Seed Oleic Acid Content." *Journal of the American Oil Chemists' Society* 78:941–947.

Chen, Z., T. E. Young, J. Ling, S. C. Chang, and D. R. Gallie. 2003. "Increasing Vitamin C Content of Plants through Enhanced Ascorbate Recycling." *Proceedings of the National Academy of Science USA* 100:3525–3530.

Chiang, C., F. Yeh, L. Huang, T. Tseng, M. Chung, C. Wang, H. Lur, J. Shaw, and S. Yu. 2005. "Expression of a Bi-functional and Thermostable Amylopullulanase in Transgenic Rice Seeds Leads to Autohydrolysis and Altered Composition of Starch." *Molecular Breeding* 15:125–143.

Choudhary, B. & Gaur, K. 2010. *Bt Cotton in India: A Country Profile.* ISAAA Series of Biotech Crop Profiles. ISAAA: Ithaca, NY. ISBN: 978-1-892456-46.

Choudhary, B., and K. Gaur. 2008. *The Development and Regulation of BT Brinjal in India (Eggplant/Aubergine).* ISAAA Brief No. 38, ISAAA: Ithaca, NY.

Christensen, J. H., M. S. Christensen, J. Dyerberg, and E. B. Schmidt. 1999. "Heart Rate Variability and Fatty Acid Content of Blood Cell Membranes: A Dose-Response Study with n-3 Fatty Acids." *American Journal of Clinical Nutrition* 70:331–337.

Connolly, E. L. 2008. "Raising the Bar for Biofortification: Enhanced Levels of Bioavailable Calcium in Carrots." *Trends in Biotechnology* 26(8):401–403.

Cromwell, G. L., R. A. Pickett, and W. M. Beeson. 1967. "Nutritional Value of Opaque-2 Corn for Swine." *Journal of Animal Science* 26(6):1325–1331.

da Silva, José Graziano. 2012. "Remarks by FAO's Director-General, Rome, UN Officials Stress Link between Food Security and Peace in Sahel UN News Centre." Accesed October 16, 2013 http://www.un.org/apps/news/story.asp?NewsID=43713&Cr=sahel&Cr1=#.UMl1mXfsLFo.

Davidovich-Rikanati, R., Y. Sitrit, Y. Tadmor, Y. Iijima, N. Bilenko, E. Bar, B. Carmona, E. Fallik, N. Dudai, J. E. Simon, E. Pichersky, and E. Lewinsohn. 2007. "Enrichment of Tomato Flavor by Diversion of the Early Plastidial Terpenoid Pathway." *Nature Biotechnology* 25:899–901.

Davies, K. M. 2007. "Genetic Modification of Plant Metabolism for Human Health Benefits." *Mutation Research* 622:122–137.

Deng, X., J. Phillips, A. Brautigam, P. Engstrom, H. Johannesson, P. B. Ouwerkerk, I. Ruberti, J. Salinas, P. Vera, R. Iannacone, A. H. Meijer, and D. Bartels. 2006. "A Homeodomain Leucine Zipper Gene from Craterostigma Plantagineum Regulates Abscisic Acid Responsive Gene Expression and Physiological Responses." *Plant Molecular Biology* l61:469–489.

Dehesh, K., A. Jones, D. S. Knutzon, and T. A. Voelker. 1996. "Production of High Levels of 8:0 and 10:0 Fatty Acids in Transgenic Canola by Overexpression of Ch FatB2, a Thioesterase cDNA from Cuphea Hookeriana." *Plant Journal* 9:167–172.

Del Vecchio, A. J. 1996. "High-Laurate Canola. How Calgene's Program Began, Where It's Headed." *INFORM—International News on Fats, Oils and Related Materials* 7:230–243.

DellaPenna, D. 2007. "Biofortification of Plant-Based Food: Enhancing Folate Levels by Metabolic Engineering." *Proceedings of the National Academy of Science USA* 104:3675–3676.

DellaPenna, D., and B. J. Pogson. 2006. "Vitamin Synthesis in Plants: Tocopherols and Carotenoids." *Annual Review of Plant Biology* 57:711–738.

Denbow, D. M., E. A. Grabau, G. H. Lacy, E. T. Kornegay, D. R. Russell, and P. F. Umbeck. 1998. "Soybeans Transformed with a Fungal Phytase Gene Improve Phosphorus Availability for Broilers." *Poultry Science* 77:878–881.

Diretto, G., S. Al-Babili, R. Tavazza, F. Scossa, V. Papacchioli, M. Migliore, P. Beyer, and G. Giuliano. 2010. "Transcriptional-Metabolic Networks in Beta-Carotene-Enriched Potato Tubers: The Long and Winding Road to the Golden Phenotype." *Plant Physiology* 154:899–912.

Dinkins, R. D., M. S. S. Reddy, C. A. Meurer, B. Yan, H. Trick, F. Thibaud-Nissen, J. J. Finer, W. A. Parrott, and G. B. Collins. 2001. "Increased Sulfur Amino Acids in Soybean Plants Overexpressing the Maize 15 kDa Zein Protein." *In Vitro Cell & Developmental Biology—Plant* 37:742–747.

Dixelius, C., T. Fagerström, and F. Sundström. 2012. "European Agricultural Policy Goes Down the Tubers." *Nature Biotechnology* 30:492–493 doi:10.1038/nbt.2255

Drakakaki, G., S. Marcel, R. P. Glahn, E. K. Lund, S. Pariagh, R. Fischer, P. Christou, and E. Stoger. 2005. "Endosperm-Specific Co-expression of Recombinant Soybean Ferritin and Aspergillus Phytase in Maize Results in Significant Increases in the Levels of Bioavailable Iron." *Plant Molecular Biology* 59:869–880.

Ducreux, L. J. M., W. L. Morris, P. E. Hedley, T. Shepherd, H. V. Davies, S. Millam, and M. A. Taylor. 2005. "Metabolic Engineering of High Carotenoid Potato Tubers Containing Enhanced Levels of b-Carotene and Lutein." *Journal of Experimental Botany* 56:81–89.

Eggeling, L., S. Oberle, and H. Sahm. 1998. "Improved L-Lysine Yield with Corynebacterium Glutamicum: Use of dapA Resulting in Increased Flux Combined with Growth Limitation." *Appl Microbiology and Biotechnology* 49:24–30.

Eliasson, Jan. 2012. "Deputy Secretary-General's Remarks to the State of the Planet 2012 Conference." Columbia University, New York City, October 11. http://www.un.org/News/Press/docs//2012/dsgsm646.doc.htm.

Elmegaard, N., and M. Bruus Pedersen. 2001. "Flora and Fauna in Roundup Tolerant Fodder Beet Fields." National Environmental Research Institute. 40 pp. Technical Report No. 349.

Enfissi, E. M. A., P. D. Fraser, L. M. Lois, A. Boronat, W. Schuch, and P. M. Bramley. 2005. "Metabolic Engineering of the Mevalonate and Non-mevalonate Isopentenyl

Diphosphate-Forming Pathways for the Production of Health-Promoting Isoprenoids in Tomato." *Plant Biotechnology* J3:17–27.

Erisman, Jan Willem, M. A. Sutton, J. Galloway, Z. Klimont, and W. Winiwarter. Oct. 2008. "How a Century of Ammonia Synthesis Changed the World." *Nature Geoscience* 1(10):636. doi:10.1038/ngeo325. Retrieved May 2013.

Falco, S. C., T. Guida, M. Locke, J. Mauvais, C. Sanders, R. T. Ward, and P. Webber. 1995. "Transgenic Canola and Soybean Seeds with Increased Lysine." *Biotechnology* 13:577–582.

Food and Agriculture Organization of the United Nations (FAO). 2004. "The State of Food and Agriculture 2003–2004, Agricultural Biotechnology, Meeting the Needs of the Poor?" *FAO Agricultural Series* 35:1–209.

Food and Agriculture Organization of the United Nations (FAO), 2011. *The State of Food Insecurity in the World—How does international price volatility affect domestic economies and food security.* Rome, Italy.

Foundation, A. A. T. 2007. "Combining Breeding and Biotechnology to Develop Water Efficient Maize for Africa (WEMA)." Concept Note, Afr Agric Technol Foundation.

Fraser, P. D., S. Romer, J. W. Kiano, C. A. Shipton, P. B. Mills, R. Drake, W. Schuch, and P. M. Bramley. 2001. "Elevation of Carotenoids in Tomato by Genetic Manipulation." *Journal of the Science of Food and Agriculture* 81:822–827.

Froman, B., and V. Ursin. 2002. "Genetic Modification of Oils for Improved Health Benefits: Production of Long Chain Omega-3 Fatty Acids in Plants." *Abstracts of Papers of the American Chemical Society* 223:U35–U35.

Galili, G., S. Galili, E. Lewinsohn, and Y. Tadmor. 2002. "Genetic, Molecular, and Genomic Approaches to Improve the Value of Plant Foods and Feeds." *Critical Reviews in Plant Sciences* 21:167–204.

German, J. B., S. M. Watkins, and L.-B. Fay. 2005. "Metabolomics in Practice: Emerging Knowledge to Guide Future Dietetic Advice toward Individualized Health." *Journal of the American Dietetic Association* 105:1425–1432.

Giliberto, L., G. Perrotta, P. Pallara, J. L. Weller, P. D. Fraser, P. M. Bramley, A. Fiore, M. Tavazza, and G. Giuliano. 2005. "Plant Manipulation of the Blue Light Photoreceptor Cryptochrome 2 in Tomato Affects Vegetative Development, Flowering Time, and Fruit Antioxidant Content." *Physiology* 137(1):199–208.

Giovannucci, E. 2002. "A Review of Epidemiologic Studies of Tomatoes, Lycopene, and Prostate Cancer." *Experimental Biology and Medicine* 227:852–859.

Giovinazzo, G., L. d'Amico, A. Paradiso, R. Bollini, F. Sparvoli, and L. DeGara. 2005. "Antioxidant Metabolite Profiles in Tomato Fruit Constitutively Expressing the Grapevine Stilbene Synthase Gene." *Plant Biotechnology Journal* 3:57–69.

Go, V. L. W., C. T. H. Nguyen, D. M. Harris, and W.-N.P. Lee. 2005. "Nutrient-Gene Interaction: Metabolic Genotype-Phenotype Relationship." *Journal of Nutrition* 135:3016S–3020S.

Gonzali, S., A. Mazzucato, and P. Perata. 2009. "Purple as a Tomato: Towards High Anthocyanin Tomatoes." *Trends in Plant Science* 5:237–241.

Goto, F., T. Yoshihara, and H. Saiki. 2000. "Iron Accumulation and Enhanced Growth in Transgenic Lettuce Plants Expressing the Iron-Binding Protein Ferritin." *Theoretical and Applied Genetics* 100:658–664.

Hajirezaei, M., U. Sonnewald, R. Viola, S. Carlisle, D. T. Dennis, and M. Stitt. 1994. "Transgenic Potato Plants with Strongly Decreased Expression of Pyrophosphate:Fructose-6-Phosphate Phosphotransferase Show No Visible Phenotype and Only Minor Changes in Metabolic Fluxes in Their Tubers." *Planta* 192:16–30.

Hall, R. D., I. D. Brouwer, and M. A. Fitzgerald. 2008. "Plant Metabolomics and Its Potential Application for Human Nutrition." *Plant Physiology* 132(2):162–175.
Han, G. 2009. "Origin Agritech Announces Final Approval of World's First Genetically Modified Phytase Corn." *Business Wire*. November 21. Accessed February 19, 2010. http://www.allbusiness.com/science-technology/biology-biotechnology-genetic/13453842-1.html.
Harjes, C. E., T. R. Rocheford, L. Bai, T. P. Brutnell, C. B. Kandianis, S. G. Sowinski, A. E. Stapleton, R. Vallabhaneni, M. Williams, E. T. Wurtzel, J. B. Yan, and E. S. Buckler. 2008. "Natural Genetic Variation in Lycopene Epsilon Cyclase Tapped for Maize Biofortification." *Science* 319:330–333.
Hartwig, E. E., T. M. Kuo, and M. M. Kenty. 1997. "Seed Protein and Its Relationship to Soluble Sugars in Soybeans." *Crop Science* 37:770–773.
Hellwege, E. M., S. Czapla, A. Jahnke, L. Willmitzer, and A. G. Heyer. 2000. "Transgenic Potato (Solanum tuberosum) Tubers Synthesize the Full Spectrum of Inulin Molecules Naturally Occurring in Globe Artichoke (Cynara scolymus) Roots." *Proceedings of the National Academy of Science USA* 97:8699–8704.
Hellwege, E. M., D. Gritscher, L. Willmitzer, and A. G. Heyer. 1997. "Transgenic Potato Tubers Accumulate High Levels of 1-Kestose and Nystose: Functional Identification of a Sucrose 1-Fructosyltransferase of Artichoke (Cynara scolymus) Blossom Discs." *Plant Journal* 12:1057–1065.
Helm, R. M., G. Cockrell, C. Connaughton, C. M. West, E. Herman, H. A. Sampson, G. A. Bannon, and A. W. Burks. 2000. "Mutational analysis of the IgE-Binding Epitopes of P34/Gly m Bd 30K." *Journal of Allergy and Clinical Immunology* 105:378–384.
Herman, E. M., R. M. Helm, R. Jung, and A. J. Kinney. 2003. "Genetic Modification Removes an Immunodominant Allergen from Soybean." *Plant Physiology* 132:36–43.
Herring, R. J. 2010. "Framing the GMO: Epistemic Brokers, Authoritative Knowledge and Diffusion of Opposition to Biotechnology." In *The Diffusion of Social Movements*, edited by Rebecca Kolins Givan, Kenneth M. Roberts and Sarah A. Soule, 78–96. New York: Cambridge University Press.
Herring, R. J., and N. Chandrasekhara Rao. 2012. "On the 'Failure of Bt Cotton': Analysing a Decade of Experience." *Economic and Political Weekly* 47(18):45–54.
Hipskind, J. D., and N. L. Paiva. 2000. "Constitutive Accumulation of a Resveratrol-Glucoside in Transgenic Alfalfa Increases Resistance to Phoma Medicaginis." *Molecular Plant-Microbe Interactions* 13:551–562.
Hutchison, W. D., E. C. Burkness, P. D. Mitchell, R. D. Moon, T. W. Leslie, S. J. Fleischer, M. Abrahamson, K. L. Hamilton, K. L. Steffey, M. E. Gray, R. L. Hellmich, L. V. Kaster, T. E. Hunt, R. J. Wright, K. Pecinovsky, T. L. Rabaey, B. R. Flood, and E. S. Raun. 2010. "Areawide Suppression of European Corn Borer with Bt Maize Reaps Savings to Non-Bt Maize Growers." *Science* 330:222–225.
International Life Sciences Institute (ILSI). 2004a. "Nutritional and Safety Assessments of Foods and Feeds Nutritionally Improved through Biotechnology." *Comprehensive Reviews in Food Science and Food Safety* 3:35–104. http://members.ift.org/NR/rdonlyres/27BE106D-B616-4348-AE3A-091D0E536F40/0/crfsfsv3n2p00350104ms20040106.pdf.
International Life Sciences Institute (ILSI). 2004b. "Nutritional and Safety Assessments of Foods and Feeds Nutritionally Improved through Biotechnology: An Executive Summary." *Journal of Food Science* 69:CRH62–CRH68.
International Life Sciences Institute (ILSI). 2008. "Nutritional and Safety Assessments of Foods and Feeds Nutritionally Improved through Biotechnology: Case Studies." *Comprehensive Reviews in Food Science and Food Safety* 7:50–99.

Jalani, B. S., S. C. Cheah, N. Rajanaidu, and A. Darus. 1997. "Improvement of Palm Oil through Breeding and Biotechnology." *Journal of American Oil Chemists' Society* 74:1451–1455.

James, C. 2011. *Global Status of Commercialized Biotech/GM Crops: 2010. ISAAA Briefs 42–2010.* Ithaca, NY: ISAAA. Accessed March 2013 http://www.isaaa.org/resources/publications/briefs/42/executivesummary/default.asp.

James, C. 2012. *Global Status of Commercialized Biotech/GM Crops: 2012 ISAAA, Brief No. 43.* Ithaca, NY: International Service for the Acquisition of Agri-biotech Applications. Accessed January 15, 2012. http://www.isaaa.org/.

James, M. J., V. M. Ursin, and L. G. Cleland. 2003. "Metabolism of Stearidonic Acid in Human Subjects: Comparison with the Metabolism of Other n-3 Fatty Acids." *American Journal of Clinical Nutrition* 77:1140–1145.

Juma, Calestous. 2012. "Biotechnology and Africa's Strategic Interests." Chicago Council on Global Affairs. Accessed December 2012. http://globalfoodforthought.typepad.com/global-food-for-thought/.

Jung, K. H., Y. S. Seo, H. Walia, P. Cao, T. Fukao, P. E. Canlas, F. Amonpant, J. Bailey-Serres, and P. C. Ronald. 2010. "The Submergence Tolerance Regulator Sub1A Mediates Stress-Responsive Expression of AP2/ERF Transcription Factors." *Plant Physiology* 152:1674–1692.

Katsube, T., N. Kurisaka, M. Ogawa, N. Maruyama, R. Ohtsuka, S. Utsumi, and F. Takaiwa. 1999. "Accumulation of Soybean Glycinin and Its Assembly with the Glutelins in Rice." *Plant Physiology* 120:1063–1074.

Keshavarz, K. 2003. "The Effect of Different Levels of Nonphytate Phosphorus with and without Phytase on the Performance of Four Strains of Laying Hens." *Poultry Science* 82:71–91.

Kinney, A. J., and S. Knowlton. 1998. "Designer Oils: The High Oleic Acid Soybean." In *Genetic Modification in the Food Industry*, edited by S. Roller and S. Harlander, 193–213. London: Blackie Academic and Professional.

Klee, H. J., and J. J. Giovannoni. 2011. "Genetics and Control of Tomato Fruit Ripening and Quality Attributes." *Annual Review of Genetics* 45:41–59.

Kobayashi, S., C. K. Ding, Y. Nakamura, I. Nakajima, and R. Matsumoto. 2000. "Kiwifruits (Actinidia deliciosa) Transformed with a Vitis Stilbene Synthase Gene Produce Piceid (Resveratrol-Glucoside)." *Plant Cell Reports* 19:904–910.

Kramer, P. J. 1980. "Drought, Stress, and the Origin of Adaptations." In *Adaptations of Plants to Water and High Temperature Stress*, edited by Neil C. Turner and Paul J. Kramer, 7–20. New York: John-Wiley & Sons.

Kraemer, Klaus. 2012. "Tackling Malnutrition and Micronutrient Deficiencies." Chicago Council on Global Affairs. Accessed December 2012. http://globalfoodforthought.typepad.com/global-food-for-thought/.

Lai, J. S., and J. Messing. 2002. "Increasing Maize Seed Methionine by mRNA Stability." *Plant Journal* 30:395–402.

Li, L., S. M. Liu, Y. L. Hu, W. P. Zhao, and Z. P. Lin. 2001. "Increase of Sulphur-Containing Amino Acids in Transgenic Potato with 10 ku Zein Gene from Maize." *Chinese Science Bulletin* 46:482–484.

Liang S, Bing Yuan, Mei Zhang, Ling Wang1, Mengmeng Cui1, Qi Wang1 and Ping Leng 2012. "Fruit-Specific RNAi-Mediated Suppression of SlNCED1 Increases both Lycopene and Beta-Carotene Contents in Tomato Fruit." *Journal of Experimental Botany*. 1:12

Liu, Q., S. Singh, and A. Green. 2002. "High-Oleic and High-Stearic Cottonseed Oils: Nutritionally Improved Cooking Oils Developed Using Gene Silencing." *Journal of the American College of Nutrition* 21:205S–211S.

Long, M., D. J. Millar, Y. Kimura, G. Donovan, J. Rees, P. D. Fraser, P. M. Bramley, and G. P. Bolwell. 2006. "Metabolite Profiling of Carotenoid and Phenolic Pathways in Mutant and Transgenic Lines Of Tomato: Identification of a High Antioxidant Fruit Line." *Phytochemistry* 67:1750–1757.

Lopez-Bucio, J., M. F. Nieto-Jacobo, V. V. Ramirez-Rodriguez, and L. Herrera-Estrella. 2000. "Organic Acid Metabolism in Plants: From Adaptive Physiology to Transgenic Varieties for Cultivation in Extreme Soils." *Plant Science* 160:1–13.

Lucca, P., R. Hurrell, and I. Potrykus. 2002. "Fighting Iron Deficiency Anemia with Iron-Rich Rice." *Journal of the American College of Nutrition* 21:184S–190S.

Luciani, G., F. Altpeter, and D. S. Wofford. 2005. "Over-expression of a Soybean Vegetative Storage Protein Gene in Bahiagrass (Paspalum notatum var. Flugge)." Poster presented at Florida Genetics, November 30–December 1, Gainesville, FL. Accessed June 14, 2006. http://www.ufgi.ufl.edu/Symposium/FG2005program_rev.pdf.

Lukaszewicz, M., I. Matysiak-Kata, J. Skala, I. Fecka, W. Cisowski, and J. Szopa. 2004. "Antioxidant Capacity Manipulation in Transgenic Potato Tuber by Changes in Phenolic Compounds Content." *Journal of Agriculture and Food Chemistry* 52:1526–1533.

Mathers, J. C. 2006. "Plant Foods for Human Health: Research Challenges." *Proceedings of the Nutrition Society* 65:198–203.

Mazzatti, D. J., E. Mocchegiani, and J. R. Powell. 2008. "Age-Specific Modulation of Genes Involved in Lipid and Cholesterol Homeostasis by Dietary Zinc." *Rejuvenation Research* 11(2):281–285.

McCue, K. F., P. V. Allen, D. R. Rockhold, M. M. Maccree, W. R. Belknap, L. V. T. Shepherd, H. Davies, P. Joyce, D. L. Corsini, and C. P. Moehs. 2003. "Reduction of Total Steroidal Glycoalkaloids in Potato Tubers Using Antisense Constructs of a Gene Encoding a Solanidine Glucosyl Transferase." *Acta Horticulturae* 619:77–86.

Mehta, R. A., T. Cassol, N. Li, N. Ali, A. K. Handa, and A. K. Mattoo. 2002. "Engineered Polyamine Accumulation in Tomato Enhances Phytonutrient Content, Juice Quality, and Vine Life." *Nature Biotechnology* 20:613–618.

Monsanto. 2010. "Insect Protected Roundup Ready 2 Yield Soybeans Achieve Important Milestone toward Commercialization in Brazill." Accessed March, 2013 http://news.monsanto.com/press-release/insect-protected-roundup-ready-2-yield-soybeans-achieve-important-milestone-toward-com

Monsanto, Stearidonic Acid (SDA) (2011). "Omega-3 Soybeans." March, 2013 http://www.monsanto.com/products/Pages/sda-omega-3-soybeans.aspx.

Muir, S. R., G. J. Collins, S. Robinson, S. Hughes, A. Bovy, C. H. Ric De Vos, A. J. van Tunen, and M. E. Verhoeyen. 2001. "Overexpression of Petunia Chalcone Isomerase in Tomato Results in Fruit Containing Increased Levels of Flavonols." *Nature Biotechnology* 19:470–474.

Naqvi, S., C. F. Zhu, G. Farre, K. Ramessar, L. Bassie, J. Breitenbach, D. Perez Conesa, G. Ros, G. Sandmann, T. Capell, and P. Christou. 2009. "Transgenic Multivitamin Corn through Biofortification of Endosperm with Three Vitamins Representing Three Distinct Metabolic Pathways." *Proceedings of the National Academy of Sciences USA* 106:7762–7767.

Nicholson, L., P. Gonzalez-Melendi, C. van Dolleweerd, H. Tuck, Y. Perrin, J. K. Ma, R. Fischer, P. Christou, and E. Stoger. 2005. "A Recombinant Multimeric Immunoglobulin Expressed in Rice Shows Assembly-Dependent Subcellular Localization in Endosperm Cells." *Plant Biotechnology Journal* 3:115–127.

Niggeweg, R., A. J. Michael, and C. Martin. 2004. "Engineering Plants with Increased Levels of the Antioxidant Chlorogenic Acid." *Nature Biotechnology* 22:746–754.

O'Quinn, P. R., J. L. Nelssen, R. D. Goodband, D. A. Knabe, J. C. Woodworth, M. D. Tokach, and T. T. Lohrmann. 2000. "Nutritional Value of a Genetically Improved High-Lysine, High-Oil Corn for Young Pigs." *Journal of Animal Science* 78:2144–2149.

Ogita, S., H. Uefuji, Y. Yamaguchi, N. Koizumi, and H. Sano. 2003. "Producing Decaffeinated Coffee Plants." *Nature* 423:823

Paul, M. J., J. S. Knight, D. Habash, M. A. J. Parry, D. W. Lawlor, S. A. Barnes, A. Loynes, and J. C. Gray, 1995. "Reduction in Phosphoribulokinase Activity by Antisense RNA in Transgenic Tobacco: Effect on CO2 Assimilation and Growth in Low Irradiance." *Plant Journal* 7:535–542.

Parveez, G. K. A. 2003. "Novel Products from Transgenic Oil Palm." *AgBiotechNet* 5:1–8.

Potrykus, I. 1999. "Vitamin-A and Iron-Enriched Rices May Hold Key to Combating Blindness and Malnutrition: A Biotechnology Advance." *Nature Biotechnology* 17:37.

Potrykus, I. 2010. "Regulation Must Be Revolutionized." *Nature*, 466 (7306):561.

Prakash, C. S., M. Egnin, and J. Jaynes. 2000. "Increasing the Protein Content in Sweet Potato Using a Synthetic Storage Protein Gene." *American Chemists' Society* 219:U36–U36.

Rapp, W. 2002. "Development of Soybeans with Improved Amino Acid Composition." In *Proceedings of the 93rd AOCS Annual Meeting & Expo, May 5–8, Montreal, Quebec, Canada*, 79–86. Champaign, IL: American Oil Chemists' Society Press.

Reddy, A. S., and T. L. Thomas. 1996. "Expression of a Cyanobacterial DELTA 6-Desaturase Gene Results in Gamma-Linolenic Acid Production in Transgenic Plants." *Nature Biotechnology* 14:639–642.

Reiffel, J. A., and A. McDonald. 2006. "Antiarrhythmic Effects of Omega-3 Fatty Acids." *American Journal of Cardiology* 98(4A):50i–60i.

Rocheford, T. R., J. C. Wong, C. O. Egesel, and R. J. Lambert. 2002. "Enhancement of Vitamin E Levels in Corn." *Journal of the American College of Nutrition* 21:191S–198S.

Roesler, K., D. Shintani, L. Savage, S. Boddupalli, and J. Ohlrogge. 1997. "Targeting of the Arabidopsis Homomeric Acetyl-Coenzyme A Carboxylase to Plastids of Rapeseeds." *Plant Physiology* 113:75–81.

Rosati, C., R. Aquilani, S. Dharmapuri, P. Pallara, C. Marusic, R. Tavazza, F. Bouvier, B. Camara, and G. Giuliano. 2000. "Metabolic Engineering of Beta-Carotene and Lycopene Content in Tomato Fruit." *Plant Journal* 24:413–419.

Schauer, N., and A. R. Fernie. 2006. "Plant Metabolomics: Towards Biological Function and Mechanism." *Trends in Plant Science* 11(10):508–516.

Schirmer, M. A., and S. D. Phinney. 2007. "Gamma-Linolenate Reduces Weight Regain in Formerly Obese Humans." *American Society for Nutrition, Journal of Nutrition* 137:1430–1435.

Schwall, G. P., R. Safford, R. J. Westcott, R. Jeffcoat, A. Tayal, Y. C. Shi, M. J. Gidley, and S. A. Jobling. 2000. "Production of Very-High-Amylose Potato Starch by Inhibition of SBE A and B." *Nature Biotechnology* 18:551–554.

Sévenier, R., R. D. Hall, I. M. van der Meer, H. J. C. Hakkert, A. J. van Tunen, and A. J. Koops. 1998. "High Level Fructan Accumulation in a Transgenic Sugar Beet." *Nature Biotechnology* 16:843–846.

Shewmaker, C. K., J. A. Sheehy, M. Daley, S. Colburn, and D. Y. Ke. 1999. "Seed-Specific Overexpression of Phytoene Synthase: Increase in Carotenoids and Other Metabolic Effects." *Plant Journal* 20:401–412.

Shin, Y., H. Park, S. Yim, N. Baek, C. Lee, G. An, and Y. Woo. 2006. "Transgenic Rice Lines Expressing Maize C1 and R-S Regulatory Genes Produce Various Flavonoids in the Endosperm." *Plant Biotechnology Journal* 4:303–315.

Shin, D. W., G. A. Baigorria, Y.-K. Lim, S. Cocke, T. E. LaRow, J. J. O'Brien, and J. W. Jones. 2009. "Assessing Crop Yield Simulations with Various Seasonal Climate Data." Science and Technology Infusion Climate Bulletin, Proceedings of 7th NOAA Annual Climate Prediction Application Science Workshop. Accessed November, 2013 http://www.nws.noaa.gov/ost/climate/STIP/RServices/dshin_032509.htm

Shintani, D., and D. DellaPenna. 1998. "Elevating the Vitamin E Content of Plants through Metabolic Engineering." *Science* 282:2098–2100.

Siritunga, D., and R. T. Sayre. 2003. "Generation of Cyanogen-Free Transgenic Cassava." *Planta* 217:367–373.

Smeekens, S. 1997. "Engineering Plant Metabolism." *Trends in Plant Science* 2:286–287.

Smuts, C. M., M. Huang, D. Mundy, T. Plasse, S. Major, and S. E. Carlson. 2003. "A Randomized Trial of Docosahexaenoic Acid Supplementation during the Third Trimester of Pregnancy." *Obstetrics and Gynecology* 101:469–479.

Sottosanto, J. B., Y. Saranga, and E. Blumwald. 2007. "Impact of AtNHX1, a Vacuolar Na+/H+ Antiporter, upon Gene Expression during Short and Long Term Salt Stress in Arabidopsis Thaliana." *BMC Plant Biology* 7:18.

Sprenger, N., L. Schellenbaum, K. van Dun, T. Boller, and A. Wiemken. 1997. "Fructan Synthesis in Transgenic Tobacco and Chicory Plants Expressing Barley Sucrose: Fructan 6-Fructosyltransferase." *FEBS Letters* 400:355–358.

Stark-Lorenzen, P., B. Nelke, G. Hanssler, H. P. Muhlbach, and J. E. Thomzik. 1997. "Transfer of a Grapevine Stilbene Synthase Gene to Rice (Oryza sativa L.)." *Plant Cell Reports* 16:668–673.

Stern, N. 2006. "Stern Review on The Economics of Climate Change (pre-publication edition). Executive Summary." HM Treasury, London.

Stewart, W. M., D. W. Dibb, A. E. Johnston, and T. J. Smyth. 2005. "The Contribution of Commercial Fertilizer Nutrients to Food Production." *Agronomy Journal* 97:1–6.

StorozhenkoS., V. De Brouwer, M. Volckaert, O. Navarrete, D. Blancquaert, G. F. Zhang, W. Lambert, and D. Van Der Straeten. 2007. "Folate Fortification of Rice by Metabolic Engineering." *Nature Biotechnology* 25:1277–1279.

Svoboda, Elizabeth. 2008. "The Future of Farming is in Nitrogen Efficiency." *Fastcompany*, October 1. http://www.fastcompany.com/magazine/129/seed-money.html.

Szankowski, I., K. Briviba, J. Fleschhut, J. Schonherr, H. J. Jacobsen, and H. Kiesecker. 2003. "Transformation of Apple (Malus domestica Borkh.) with the Stilbene Synthase Gene from Grapevine (Vitis vinifera L.) and a PGIP Gene from Kiwi (Actinidia deliciosa)." *Plant Cell Reports* 22:141–149.

Tang, G., J. Qin, G. G. Dolnikowski, R. M. Russell, and M. A. Grusak. 2009. "Golden Rice Is an Effective Source of Vitamin A." *American Journal of Clinical Nutrition* 89:1776–1783.

Times of India. 2012. "No Moratorium on GM Crop Trials till Stakeholders Heard: SC." Accessed October 2012. http://timesofindia.indiatimes.com/india/No-moratorium-on-GM-crop-trials-till-stakeholders-heard-SC/articleshow/17011950.cms.

Trewavas, A. 2001. "Urban myths of organic farming." *Nature* 410: 409–410.

Trewavas, A. 2008. "The Cult of the Amateur in Agriculture Threatens Food Security." *Trends in Biotechnology* 26(9):475–478.

Turnbaugh, P. J., M. Hamady, T. Yatsunenko, B. L. Cantarel, A. Duncan, R. E. Ley, M. L. Sogin, W. J. Jones, B. A. Roe, J. P. Affourtit, M. Egholm, B. Henrissat, A. C. Heath, R. Knight, and J. I. Gordon. 2009. "A Core Gut Microbiome in Obese and Lean Twins." *Nature* 457:480–484.

Uauy, C., A. Distelfeld, T. Fahima, A. Blechl, and J. Dubcovsky. 2006. "A NAC Gene Regulating Senescence Improves Grain Protein, Zinc, and Iron Content in Wheat." *Science* 314:1298–1301.

UN SCN. 2004. "5th Report on the World Nutrition Situation. Nutrition for Improved Development Outcomes." United Nations System Standing Committee on Nutrition, Geneva, Switzerland.

Ursin, V. 2000. "Genetic Modification of Oils for Improved Health Benefits." Presentation at conference, Dietary Fatty Acids and Cardiovascular Health: Dietary Recommendations for Fatty Acids: Is There Ample Evidence? American Heart Association, Reston VA.

Ursin, V. A. 2003. "Modification of Plant Lipids for Human Health: Development of Functional Land-Based Omega-3 Fatty Acids. Symposium: Improving Human Nutrition through Genomics, Proteomics and Biotechnologies." *American Society for Nutritional Sciences*: 4271–4274.

United Press International (UPI). 2002. "Wheat Inhibits Colon Cancer." Washington, DC: United Press International.

Vistive Gold Soybeans.2013 Currently in Phase IV of Monsanto's R&D Pipeline http://www.monsanto.com/products/Pages/vistive-gold-soybeans.aspx

Wambugu, F. 1999. "Why Africa Needs Agricultural Biotech." *Nature* 400:15–16.

Wehrspann, J. 1998. "New Traits of Seed Buying." *Farm Industry News* 31, p. 10.

White, C. L., L. M. Tabe, H. Dove, J. Hamblin, P. Young, N. Phillips, R. Taylor, G. Suresh, J. Ashes, and T. J. V. Higgins. 2001. "Increased Efficiency of Wool Growth and Live Weight Gain in Merino Sheep Fed Transgenic Lupin Seed Containing Sunflower Albumin." *Journal of Science and Food Agriculture* 81:147–154.

Welsch, R., J. Arango, C. Bär, B. Salazar, S. Al-Babili, J. Beltrán, P. Chavarriaga, H. Ceballos, J. Tohme, and P. Beyer. 2010. "Provitamin A Accumulation in Cassava (Manihot esculenta) Roots Driven by a Single Nucleotide Polymorphism in a Phytoene Synthase Gene." *Plant Cell* 22: 3348–3356.

Wolfgang P. and B. McClafferty. 2007. "Biofortification: Breeding Micronutrient-Dense Crops." In Breeding Major Food Staples, edited by M. S. Kang and P. M. Priyadarshan, 63–64. Blackwell.

World Health Organization (WHO). 2006. "Nutrition for Health and Development." Geneva, Switzerland: World Health Organization. Accessed March, 2013 http://www.who.int/nutrition/challenges/en/index.html.

World Bank. 2008. *The World Development Report, Agriculture for Development*. Washington, DC: World Bank.

Yang, S. H., D. L. Moran, H. W. Jia, E. H. Bicar, M. Lee, and M. P. Scott. 2002. "Expression of a Synthetic Porcine Alpha-Lactalbumin Gene in the Kernels of Transgenic Maize." *Transgenetic Research* 11:11–20.

Ye, X., S. Al-Babili, A. Kloti, J. Zhang, P. Lucca, P. Beyer, and I. Potrykus. 2000. "Engineering the Provitamin A (Beta-Carotene) Biosynthetic Pathway into (Carotenoid-Free) Rice Endosperm." *Science* 287:303–305.

Yonekura-Sakakibara, K., T. Tohge, R. Niida, and K. Saito. 2007. "Identification of a Flavonol 7-O-Rhamnosyltransferase Gene Determinig Flavonoid Pattern in Arabidopsis by Transcriptome Coexpression Analysis." *Journal of Biological Chemistry* 282:14932–14941.

Young, T. E., J. Giesler-Lee, and D. R. Gallie. 2004. "Senescence-Induced Expression of Cytokinin Reverses Pistil Abortion during Maize Flower Development." *Plant Journal* 38:910–922.

Yu J, Ao G. 1997. "Expression of 10 kDa Sulfur-Rich Prolamin Gene of Rice in Potato." *Acta Botanica Sinica* 39:329–334.

Yu, O., W. Jung, J. Shi, R. A. Croes, G. M. Fader, B. McGonigle, and J. T. Odell. 2000. "Production of the Isoflavones Genistein and Daidzein in Non-Legume Dicot and Monocot Tissues." *Plant Physiology* 124:781–794.

Yu, O., J. Shi, A. O. Hession, C. A. Maxwell, B. McGonigle, and J. T. Odell. 2003. "Metabolic Engineering to Increase Isoflavone Biosynthesis in Soybean Seed." *Phytochemistry* 63:753–763.

Yuan, L., and V. C. Knauf. 1997. "Modification of Plant Components." *Current Opinions in Biotechnology* 8:227–233.

Zeh, M., A. P. Casazza, O. Kreft, U. Roessner, K. Bieberich, L. Willmitzer, R. Hoefgen, and H. Hesse. 2001. "Antisense Inhibition of Threonine Synthase Leads to High Methionine Content in Transgenic Potato Plants." *Plant Physiology* 127:792–802.

Zhao, Z. Y., K. Glassman, V. Sewalt, N. Wang, M. Miller, S. Chang, T. Thompson, S. Catron, E. Wu, D. Bidney, Y. Kedebe, and R. Jung. 2003. "Nutritionally Improved Transgenic Sorghum." In: Plant biotechnology 2002 and beyond. Proceedings of the 10th IAPTC&B Congress, June 23–28, Orlando, FL.

Zou, J., V. Katavic, E. M. Giblin, D. L. Barton, S. L. MacKenzie, W. A. Keller, X. Hu, and D. C. Taylor. 1997. "Modification of Seed Oil Content and the Acyl Composition in the Brassicaceae by Expression of a Yeast sn-2 Acyltransferase Gene." *Plant Cell* 9:909–923.

CHAPTER 4

AGROECOLOGICAL INTENSIFICATION OF SMALLHOLDER FARMING

REBECCA NELSON AND RICHARD COE

Introduction

The food price crisis of 2007 focused the attention of scientists, policy bodies, activists, and corporations on the precarious state of global food production systems. Major journals have dedicated special issues to food security. *Science* magazine dedicated a special issue to the subject of food security on February 12, 2010, and *Nature*'s special issue of July 28, 2010 asked "Can Science Feed the World?" *The Economist* recently featured cover stories on food security several times, and in 2011 *Foreign Policy* had a first-ever "food issue" titled "Inside the Geopolitics of a Hungry Planet." The problems that threaten the productivity and stability of agriculture are hardly new, however; climate challenges, energy prices, and degrading agrobiological resources have long afflicted smallholder farmers.

Agricultural systems are required not only to produce food, but also to provide livelihoods for millions of resource-limited smallholder farmers. In most countries, the majority of people participate in agriculture (World Bank 2007). Most of the poorest billion people (70 percent) rely on agriculture for their livelihoods. Agriculture, as the major use of managed land globally, also has to contribute to the maintenance of ecosystems and the provision of ecosystem services. Agricultural systems are failing on a grand scale, however, and ecosystem services are in critical decline (Millenium Ecosystems Assessment 2005). In addition, nearly a billion people are currently undernourished, and the global population is expected to increase from seven to nine billion by 2050 (Bongaarts 2009).

While there is a general consensus that there is a need to increase food production and improve rural livelihoods without further undermining the earth's productive capacity, there is diversity of opinion on how this may be best achieved. Much of the increased productivity attained in Africa over recent decades has relied upon increasing the land area utilized, but there are few remaining opportunities to expand agricultural areas without conflict and excessive environmental damage (Young 1999; Balmford et al. 2012). Thus it is generally agreed that some sort of intensification is essential (Pretty et al. 2011). Increased production per unit area has historically been driven by technology change, much of it dependent on cheap fossil fuel inputs. The concept of intensification is often assumed to refer to the increased use of purchased inputs, such as improved seed, fertilizer, and irrigation to produce higher crop yields. It is, however, possible to intensify production based on an increased use of ecological knowledge and practices, or on a combination of ecological practices and purchased inputs. The outputs can be measured in terms of higher yields, but metrics can also include ecosystems services, nutrition, and livelihoods. Contemporary development discourse reflects these alternatives. In this chapter we examine what this means for smallholder farmers in developing countries, and for the systems that support them.

Alternative Trajectories and Strategies for Achieving Them

From the most simplistic point of view, three types of trajectories can be described for agricultural systems: those in which performance is being degraded (those following degenerative pathways), those in which performance is stable, and those in which performance is sustainably improving (those on regenerative pathways). How "performance" is defined is critical; that issue will be addressed below. The natural endowments, history, pressures, and constraints differ across systems, so in reality an infinite number of trajectories could be described. Research and development efforts aim to identify practical opportunities to nudge trajectories in a way that improves the performance of these systems.

Unfortunately, many of the world's farming systems are on degenerative trajectories, in which the basic agro-resources of soil, water, and genetic resources are being eroded. The Millennium Ecosystem Assessment determined that 40 percent of farmland is being critically degraded (Millenium Ecosystem Assessment 2005). Even many of the best-endowed African agroecosystems are under sufficient population pressure that their productivity has been compromised or is likely to be negatively affected in the near future (MacIntyre et al. 2009). Degradation of agricultural resources can be the consequence of intensification: irrigation can lead to groundwater depletion and to salinization; reduction in fallows can lead to reduced soil fertility; the overuse of chemical inputs can lead to pollution and to pest outbreaks; and tillage can lead to soil erosion. Degradation can also result from neglect. When inputs are not provided and fallows are shortened or eliminated, for example, soil fertility can be exhausted. When agriculture is extended to rainforests, hillsides, and other fragile environments, soil is typically eroded.

How can systems that are currently following degenerative trajectories be shifted to stable or regenerative ones? Reflecting on the need for transformative change to put the planet on the path to sustainability, Leach et al. (2012) point out the need for new technologies, new policies, and new modes of innovation. They define three dimensions requiring consideration: direction (where are we going?), diversity (how can we acknowledge and address the multiplicity of contexts and issues with correspondingly diverse approaches and forms of innovation?) and distribution (who are the winners and losers of any given approach?). Considering the direction to be taken implies being clear about the goals and principles to be applied. The goal of improving agricultural productivity alone would lead to a different direction than the goal of equitably improving food security. If the goal of protecting species diversity were also considered, that would again call for a different direction to be taken.

A focus on the goal of improving agricultural productivity could lead to a focus on the industrialization of large-scale agriculture. While this could succeed in producing greater surpluses that could benefit urban populations through lower prices, it could also lead to the marginalization and elimination of smallholders and the expansion of urban slums, as well as increasing the pressure on many ecosystem services. Half of the world's food insecure people are rural smallholder farmers (Cohen 2008); the goal of increasing their productivity might lead to a focus on improving input and output markets. While this would benefit those within reach of population centers, market-based approaches might increase ecological and market risks, and they would not inevitably improve food security. In sub-Saharan Africa, more than 30 percent of the rural population has poor access to markets (World Bank 2007). For this reason and others, substantial proportions of smallholder farmers consume the majority of what they produce. In 2004, for example, 80 percent of Nigerian farmers were classified as subsistence-oriented farmers (Davis et al. 2007, as cited in World Bank 2007). Helping these farmers to integrate into markets is a laudable goal, but market-based approaches are more likely to squeeze out resource-poor smallholders than to include them (Hartman 2012).

A focus on food security would have to acknowledge that increasing productivity is necessary but not sufficient to improve the food security of resource-poor people. The widely accepted definition of food security (USAID 1992) includes dimensions of availability, access, and utilization; some definitions also include aspects of risk and sustainability (FAO 2006). The access dimension implies financial as well as logistical access to food, and thus brings in elements of equity among and within households. The utilization dimension brings in nutritional considerations, as do qualitative aspects of the availability dimension. Thus, improving food security of the rural poor must entail improving market access for smallholders and increasing their employment options, but it must also improve the livelihoods of those engaged in subsistence or semi-subsistence farming.

The goals and principles of agricultural development strategies can and must go beyond concerns for food production and food security. Agriculture's multifunctionality is increasingly appreciated in wealthy countries, and accordingly a greater diversity of products and services are being demanded of agriculture (Van Acker 2008; Renting et al. 2009). Similarly, it is recognized that smallholder farming must also serve many needs for producers as well as the larger landscapes and populations (Amekawa et al. 2010). Agricultural policies will influence equity, dietary diversity, and environmental services such as water quantity and quality. Even a secondary focus on conservation of natural areas and biodiversity would require assessments at the landscape scale to assess impacts of agricultural strategies on forests and species (Leach et al. 2012).

Strategies for Improving the Performance of Smallholder Agriculture

Three main types of strategies are evident in debates about how to increase agricultural productivity. The first depends mostly on purchased inputs, the second on enhancing ecological processes, and the third on a combination of the two. The first envisages a market-driven pathway to prosperity that takes key lessons from agricultural successes that have been achieved elsewhere based on a "Green Revolution" (GR) model. Modern agriculture, in this view, is based on production systems in which the market supplies the inputs (e.g., fertilizers, pesticides, fuel for traction and transport) and receives the outputs; the main performance measures are yield and income. The Green Revolution took the input-based trajectory to Asia and Latin America, achieving widespread increases in cereal yields through the use of improved varieties, fertilizers, and irrigation between 1960 and 2000 (Evenson and Gollin 2003). While it did not have a major impact in Africa during this period, there are current efforts to achieve a Green Revolution in Africa through improved access to inputs and markets (Toenniessen et al. 2008).

In the first-world context, organic agriculture is often seen as the alternative to industrial agriculture (Seufert et al. 2012; Pollan 2006; Bennett and Franzel 2009). The debate on the future of food and agriculture is polarized, and those with a stake in "real" (industrialized) agriculture have seen "sustainable" or "organic" agriculture as an enemy camp. This unconstructive stand-off may be easing as concerns about the economic and environmental costs of reliance on purchased inputs becomes more mainstream in both industrialized and developing country contexts. The term "sustainable intensification" is increasingly widely used (Pretty 2008; Pretty et al. 2011; Godfray et al. 2010; Tilman et al. 2011; http://www.feedthefuture.gov/). This term suggests the aims of reducing the environmental costs of agriculture in the industrialized world and increasing production in poor countries with a minimum of damage to the environment (Balmford et al. 2012). The term does not imply much about how these aims will be achieved or assessed, and perhaps this ambiguity is the basis of its popularity.

The term "agroecological intensification" (AEI) also implies a concern for sustainability, but it suggests a further commitment to intensification strategies that emphasize the use of biological processes to achieve this. Other authors have used "eco-efficient agriculture" (Keating et al., 2010) and "ecological intensification" (Doré et al. 2011) to refer to the same or a similar concept. The concept of AEI can be loosely and flexibly defined as producing more of what is wanted based on the efficient use of biological interactions. AEI entails the integration of diverse components to produce heterogeneous, multifunctional systems that are locally adapted. The principles of AEI include improving productivity under resource limitations; improving water and nutrient capture and cycling efficiency within the system; improvement of components to support systems functions; development of local, context-specific options; and adapting social institutions to support the use of biological interactions. The research frontiers of AEI include systems diversification; soil and water management; pest, weed, and disease management; and social innovation (including value chains) to support diversification.

In some systems, such as much of Asia's irrigated ricelands, the major grain-producing areas of North America, and most intensive vegetable-production systems worldwide, productivity increases have been achieved through input intensification, with accompanying environmental costs and with declining returns on investment. In these systems, AEI would mean reducing the reliance on external inputs and increasing ecological efficiencies. Many other farming systems are on degenerative trajectories, with depletion and erosion of soil, water, and genetic resources. For these systems, AEI may require both ecological engineering and the selective use of purchased inputs. Ethiopia and Malawi, for example, have large rural poor populations that depend on agriculture. Agricultural productivity is constrained by degraded and unproductive soils. Government policy in both of these countries focuses on increasing fertilizer use, through subsidies and input supply. Detractors point out that the strategy is unsustainable, noting that alternative methods of maintaining soil fertility must be employed, such as the increased integration of leguminous crops. While the debate often seems polarized between voices advocating for one approach or the other, a hybrid approach could be regarded as the most pragmatic. The use of fertilizers can be critical for reversing a degenerative pathway. When soil fertility is too low, plant growth may not be sufficient to develop biomass for improving soil organic matter; such systems may require mineral fertilizers to allow legumes to thrive. That is, legumes can enrich the carbon and nitrogen content of soils and contribute to diets, but only if adequate P is supplied. At some point, the system may be on a sufficiently regenerative pathway so that lower input levels are effective.

There is mounting evidence to support the view that a combination of agroecological methods and judicious use of inputs is the most appropriate strategy for supporting the improved performance of smallholder agriculture. For instance, Snapp et al. (2010) found that the use of semi-perennial legumes together with modest quantities of mineral fertilizer was more effective and accessible for Malawian smallholders than the use of mineral fertilizers or legumes alone. Similarly, Vanek et al. (2010) found that phosphorous (P) fertilizer was required to support legume productivity in the Andes. Marenya and Barrett (2009) found that nitrogen fertilization was only cost-effective for Kenyan smallholders when soil carbon levels were adequate. When soil organic matter was too low, the increased maize yields associated with applied nitrogen fertilizer did not compensate for the cost of the fertilizer.

These examples illustrate the need to supply nutrients for many smallholder farming contexts, and they underline the point that maintaining healthy and productive soils involves more than supplying inorganic fertilizer. Soil organic matter must be maintained in order to support the efficient use of applied nutrients, as well as to hold water. Legumes can fix nitrogen and increase P availability, but only if their symbiotic relationships with microorganisms, as well as their pests and diseases, are effectively managed. In well-endowed farming contexts, organic agriculture often entails the massive import of nutrients into the system, typically in the form of high-quality manure, an asset not available to most resource-limited smallholder farmers. These issues are considered in greater detail below.

Examples and Evidence from AEI Frontiers

Managing Systems Diversity

Diversity has several potential functions within agroecosystems, including reducing risk (van Noordwijk et al. 1994), increasing productivity, and allowing for improved diets. In the context of well-endowed systems, these functions can be accomplished through the use of inputs and markets. Industrialized agricultural systems have favored monocultures, partly because these are easier to manage in mechanized systems, and partly because market efficiencies encourage specialization. Although the majority of calories produced through agriculture now come from just a few species, there is tremendous potential to diversify systems with the vast number of species and within-species diversity available. Crop and livestock diversity can be directly manipulated, with varying effects on systems productivity and stability. The diversity of farming systems includes the species intended by the farmer, as well as the associated diversity (life forms other than those planned by the farmer). Associated diversity can contribute to positive functions such as pollination and decomposition, or it can be harmful, as discussed in the section on pests below. The extent of associated diversity tends to correlate with the diversity that farmers implement (Vandermeer et al. 1998). Diversity can be handled in a range of ways, both temporally (simultaneous planting, overlapping life cycles, in series) and spatially (patch size, arrangements, segregation and integration at different scales). Options include intraspecific mixtures and multilines, intercrops, relay cropping (one crop goes in while the other is maturing), rotations, agroforestry and crop-livestock integration. A recent review summarized the various benefits and drawbacks of annual intercrops (Lithourgidis et al. 2011).

In studies of crop mixtures and intercrops, the more diverse systems typically outperform the corresponding monoculture systems. A range of mechanisms can contribute to the superior performance of polycultures. One mechanism is reduced competition, which leads to greater resource use efficiency, since interspecific or intervarietal competition is often lower than intraspecific competition. For example, there may be less root competition in mixtures, or less competition for light. Different crops or varieties may have different resource requirements, such as needing water at different times. The differing requirements of systems components can also mean that multiple components provide resilience. A given stress or shock may not affect all constituents equally, and those that survive can often compensate for those lost.

In addition to mechanisms related to competition and resource use efficiency, there is a set of mechanisms pertaining to facilitation, in which one species provides services to another through improved nutrient availability, water access, or pest protection. An obvious example of facilitation is nitrogen fixation by legumes, which can benefit associated cereal crops (Peoples et al. 2009). In countrywide assessments in Malawi, maize-legume rotations outperformed monoculture maize; pigeonpea (a semi-perennial legume) did particularly well (Snapp et al. 2010). Polycultures can contribute to improved nutrient use efficiency in other ways as well, for instance by contributing to increased P availability and to increased soil organic matter. More examples are noted below in the section on soil and water management. An additional set of mechanisms involves reduced losses due to insects, weeds, and pathogens (collectively considered "pests"). More on this range of mechanisms will be mentioned below, in the section on pest management.

Perennials can contribute special roles in polycultures. As illustrated by many successful examples of agroforestry systems, trees offer products and ecosystem services that other species cannot. Wood is obviously valued for fuel and construction material, and trees can provide fodder as well as protection from sun and wind. Trees and other perennials and semi-perennials have deeper roots that may be able to tap water and nutrients that are unavailable to other species (Cannell et al. 1996). This may smooth the impacts of weather variations, hence reducing risk. For example, enset ("false banana," the starchy staple in risk-prone southwestern Ethiopia) can survive drought periods that would kill a cereal crop. Trees can reduce runoff, transpiration, and erosion (Ong et al. 2002). They can generate islands of beneficial soil biological activity (Pauli et al. 2010). On the down side, trees may compete with crops for nutrients and water. Trees are long-lived and, as such, involve inflexibility. Investments in agroforestry can thus take a long time to pay off. Because of the superior rooting systems that can be attained by perennial crops, there is some effort being invested in developing perennial varieties of certain annual crops, including rice, wheat, and maize (Cox et al. 2002).

Diversity and functional diversity are different things. That is, the number of species is not as important as the number of distinct functional traits, and not all combinations are created equal. In one study, for instance, fava bean responded well to mixtures with maize, but not with wheat (Fan et al. 2006). Components may interact in positive ways, but also in negative or neutral ways. Some interactions can be predicted, but others may result from idiosyncratic features, such as the way that a secondary metabolite from one species influences another. Successful systems may be developed based on trial and error and/or the use of ecological and process understanding. Although a great deal of theoretical and empirical effort has been dedicated to plant breeding, the formal research sector has invested a relatively paltry effort in optimizing functional diversity. Concepts, tools, and models of relevance to mixing species in cropping systems were recently reviewed (Malezieux et al. 2009); some of these points are mentioned below.

"Mimic hypotheses" suggest that benefits derive from system designs that resemble the conditions of natural systems in a given region, or that maintain the levels of diversity found in natural systems (van Noordwijk and Ong 1999). A recent review (Malezieux et al. 2009) noted the following principles for cropping systems design based on natural ecosystems mimicry: the use of complementary traits to ensure production and resilience; maintenance of soil fertility through soil cover; ensuring complementarity and avoidance of competition; management of pests through multiple trophic levels, biopesticides, and botanical properties; and the emulation of ecological succession processes after disturbance.

Because of the multiple functions of intercrops, some of which are only realized in the longer term, it can be difficult to assess and compare the merits of different systems empirically. Carberry et al. (1996) found that simulation using APSIM (the Agricultural Production Systems Simulator) was useful for exploring the performance of different farming systems over time and space. APSIM was also used to explore the effect of different cowpea growth habits (morphological traits) and row spacing in intercrops with maize in low-input production systems (Carberry et al. 2002). That said, the tools of systems agronomy are poorly developed with regard to multispecies systems (Malezieux et al. 2009), and this deficit includes the modeling tools.

Lack of dietary diversity is a major issue for too many smallholders. While the Green Revolution succeeded in increasing the availability of carbohydrate-based calories to millions of people in Asia and elsewhere, the production of legumes decreased as cereal production increased. In parts of the world where the Green Revolution had little impact, including most of Africa, diets are typically based on starchy staples such as maize, sorghum, millets, banana, and cassava. Protein-energy malnutrition is an issue in many places, but micronutrient malnutrition is much more widespread.

A simple case of diversification that has the potential to increase nutrition is the diversification of maize-based system with legumes (e.g., adding beans or other legumes in intercrops, relay crops, or rotations). This approach has shown success in improving nutrition in Malawi when coupled with strategies to ensure that child feeding practices and gender relations support the use of the legumes for improving child care and feeding (Bezner Kerr et al. 2008). This sort of strategy can be extended by including other crops or sets of crops that can contribute to ensuring the availability of diverse foods throughout the year (or crops that can be sold to allow the purchase of diverse foods, if markets and gender relations support this). Another approach is the use of small patches to produce diverse foods for household consumption; intensive kitchen gardens have been successful on a large scale for improving diets in Bangladesh and elsewhere (Bushamuka et al. 2005). This is feasible because input requirements (labor, imported nutrients, water) can be managed at the small scale needed to feed an individual family. Fruit trees are often a component of such home gardens.

The ecological principles of diversification complementarity, facilitation, and selection are relevant to agricultural diversification (Malezieux et al. 2009). Plant breeding can enhance all three, in addition to directly affecting component productivity. To enhance complementarity, plant breeders can design and select polyculture components for distinct and noncompetitive niches. To enhance facilitation, breeders can select for traits such as nitrogen fixation and chemical traits that provide benefits to other systems components. In implementing participatory breeding strategies, formal-sector breeders can provide surplus diversity to farmers, who then select the most adapted germplasm for their local conditions (Ceccarelli et al. 2009).

Varietal performance of crops grown alone does not always predict performance in an intercrop. In many intercropping studies, significant genotype-by-cropping system interactions have been detected. This implies that varieties need to be evaluated in the system in which they will be used (Gebeyehu et al. 2006). This is not, however, commonly appreciated or practiced by plant breeders. For example, although 97 percent of teff fields were integrated with oilseed crops in a study in Ethiopia (Geleta et al. 2002), teff breeders do not test the performance of teff varieties in combination with other crops. In some cases, legumes have been bred for intercropping, for instance to avoid shading their companion crops (e.g., cowpea; Singh et al. 1997).

Breeding for AEI performance could mean not only breeding for compatibility with other crops in a system, but also better capacity for symbiotic relationships with microbes that fix nitrogen (Mpepereki et al. 2000), help plants access phosphorus (mycorrhizae), or protect them from pathogens (endophytes or epiphytes). More conventional traits that can be considered part of AEI breeding would include breeding for nutrient use efficiency and pest and disease resistance. These are broad fields that are largely outside the scope of this chapter. From a nutritional perspective, AEI breeding would entail selection for multiple production traits: leaf and grain, food and forage, grain and green manure quality (human, animal, and soil nutrition are among the ecosystem services to be considered). Increasing nutrient content and availability ("biofortification") is another active field of research.

Managing Pests and Diseases

Pests are major sources of systems inefficiencies in agriculture. Oerke (2005) estimated that ~40 percent of crops are lost to insects, diseases, and weeds (collectively known as pests) on a global basis. In East and West Africa, where little pesticide is used in most smallholder production, losses were estimated at >50 percent. These losses would be considerably higher if crop protection actions were not taken.

In the chemical boom-years that followed World War II, pesticides were considered the answer to pest problems. Since then, a number of problems have emerged, including health problems, environmental damage, and boom-and-bust cycles (Devine & Furlong 2007; Williamson et al. 2008). In spite of the well-known downsides of pesticide use, however, this remains the dominant method for pest management in agriculture.

Pesticide sales increased steadily between 1960 and 2004 (Oerke 2005). The concept of integrated pest management (IPM) arose in response to the widespread problems associated with chemical pesticides. IPM components include host plant resistance, cultural practices, repellent plants, natural enemies (natural and introduced), biopesticides, and the judicious use of synthetic pesticides. In some contexts, intensive IPM strategies can be successfully implemented in systems that inherently favor pests, such as monocultures of high-value horticultural crops or potato crops grown without rotation. In post–Green Revolution contexts in the developing world, successful IPM efforts have focused on integrating local farmer and research knowledge, knowledge transfer and learning, and collective action, often through the use of farmer field schools (Bentley 2009).

A focused IPM approach makes sense for highly destructive pests of high-value crops and main staples. Examples of the latter include Banana Xanthomonas wilt in East Africa, millet head miner in West Africa (Payne et al. 2011), rice blast in Asia, and late blight in potato in many regions of the world (Nelson et al. 2001). In many smallholder contexts, however, it is not feasible for farmers to deploy such intensive methods to deal with the diverse pest problems that afflict their systems (Orr 2003). Nor does conventional IPM make sense for various secondary pests of secondary crops. For such systems, it is more useful to implement diverse farming systems that are inherently more resilient with respect to pest population dynamics (Nelson 2010). For farmers with a range of crops and an assortment of constraints, it more often makes sense to focus on system health than on any particular problem.

Polycultures tend to have lower pest pressure than the corresponding pure stands. In a review of 209 studies involving crop mixtures, over half were found to have lower pest levels, while 15 percent had higher numbers of pests (Andow 1991). In a meta-analysis of plant diversification studies involving 552 experiments published in forty-five papers, diversity was found to reduce pests and damage overall, but also to incur a mean reduction in yield (Letourneau et al., 2011). Thus, while polycultures can outyield their corresponding monocultures, they do not inevitably do so, and some intercrops can actually increase pest pressure (B. Medvecky and J. Ojiem, personal communication). Polycultures can reduce pest pressures through a number of mechanisms, such as rotations, which can break pest cycles. For example, when *Striga* is a problem on cereals, rotations with nonhost legumes such as cowpea can cause "suicidal germination" (Oswald and Ransom 2001) of the parasitic weed, reducing the seed bank. In a mixture, there is a lower host density for a given pest. Nonhosts serve as barriers for pests looking for their hosts. Chemical ecology can be manipulated to disfavor pests in a variety of ways, attractant and repellent plants can be used to reduce pest damage, and plants can produce compounds that attract natural enemies of pests. Intraspecific diversity can be effective for pest management; varietal mixtures and multilines have been used extensively for management of crop diseases in particular (Wolfe 1985).

The push-pull system illustrates the potential of chemical ecology in pest management, as well as the potential of systems design to improve overall systems health and productivity. It also illustrates the vulnerability of a fixed-package approach. The stresses affecting maize yields in eastern and southern Africa include pests (principally the parasitic weed *Striga* and stemborers) as well as water and nutrient deficiencies. An intercropped legume (*Desmodium uncinatum*, which is considered a dangerous invasive weed in some countries) is dramatically antagonistic to *Striga*, while a border crop of Napier grass reduces the reproductive success of the stemborer. The economic viability of the approach is linked to the importance of the cut-and-carry livestock industry in the area, as well as to the importance of maize (De Groote et al. 2010; Khan et al. 2008). The value of the Napier grass component is high when (a) fodder is needed and (b) stemborers are a problem (De Groote et al. 2010). The value of *Desmodium* is high when *Striga* is a threat to maize production. In addition, *Desmodium* can also supplement Napier grass as a fodder. Local adaptation that maintains the key elements but varies detail is needed; this is already happening with extension to other cereals in western Kenya. The push-pull system's stability has been challenged by a disease of Napier grass that threatens not only the push-pull system, but also the viability of the crop-livestock system of the region. It might be anticipated that pests of *Desmondium* will become a problem if planting becomes more widespread. A greater diversity of fodder crops is clearly needed, and alternatives to provide the functions of *Desmodium* would be particularly useful.

According to Oerke (2005), weeds alone have the potential to cause 34 percent losses in major crops worldwide. IPM strategies for weeds include improving herbicide use efficiency (minimizing chemical use), developing biological and mechanical methods (alternative curatives), and developing cultural or ecological methods (Bastiaans et al. 2008). Crop competitiveness can be increased by transplanting, seed priming, targeting fertilizers to crop rows, and breeding for traits like early vigor and allelopathy. Systems approaches have shifted the work of weed ecologists from a focus on the effects of weed competition on crop growth to a focus on influencing weed population dynamics and the longer-term development of weed populations (Kropff 2001). Approaches to reducing weed seed production include the use of weed-suppressive crop varieties, particularly those that compete effectively for light through vigorous early growth or those with allelopathic properties (Belz 2007).

While much of the literature on polycultures considers plot-level issues, it is acknowledged that higher scales are important as well. The concept of "ecoagriculture" involves the importance of managing agricultural landscapes in such a way as to conserve biodiversity, including wild species (Scherr & McNeely 2008). The diversity of noncultivated crops can benefit farmers, including through the availability of harvestable foods. Noncultivated areas in agricultural landscapes can provide refugia for natural enemies of crop pests. Spatially explicit modeling revealed the importance of non-crop habitats surrounding agricultural plots and their spatial arrangements relative to crop fields (Bianchi et al. 2010), underlining the relevance of information about natural enemies' behavioral traits (e.g., ability to disperse, tendency to aggregate). Although aggregation of crop plots usually favors pest populations, the opposite was found for the Andean potato weevil: clustering potato fields is both traditional and effective in controlling this key pest (Parsa et al. 2011). A meta-analysis showed that the effects of landscape complexity on pest pressure were variable: in 45 percent of studies, landscape complexity reduced pest pressure, but no effect was seen in 40 percent of studies, and complexity increased pest pressure in 15 percent of studies.

Host genetic diversity can influence pathogen population structure, which can in turn affect disease epidemics. In an experimental study of the effect of landscape heterogeneity on the spread of wheat stripe rust, host frequency and the size of the initial epidemic focus were found to have significant effects on disease spread (Mundt et al. 2011). In a study involving joint analysis of three large, country-scale data sets on the wheat leaf rust epidemics in France, it was found that the extent to which specific varieties were cultivated affected the frequencies of the corresponding pathogen races, which in turn influenced the performance of varietal resistance. The results of both of these studies imply that greater varietal diversity will reduce epidemic pressure on a given host genotype, as expected.

Models can contribute to an understanding of plant disease epidemics and the roles of host resistance and diversity, pathogen population characteristics, and the environment (including farmers' management options as they affect any of these). Modeling can provide insights on trade-offs in pest management. For instance, simulation has been used to explore the utility of various innovations and how they interact with farm types. The costs and benefits were found to vary with the type of farm (Blazy et al. 2009). In the Collaborative Crop Research Program's (CCRP) Andean region, Rebaudo et al. (2011) are using agent-based, cellular automaton models to understand how decision making influences pest dynamics over time and space.

Plant breeding can make use of resistance at the gene, genotype, and population levels. Through the use of natural allelic diversity, conventional breeding can be effective at solving most pest and disease problems when well-resourced breeding programs apply well-designed strategies. Effective resistance breeding requires an understanding of the diversity of types of resistance genes and phenotypes available in crop biodiversity. Although breeding for forms of resistance governed by single dominant genes is relatively straightforward, it has often led to boom-and-bust cycles because insects and pathogens can rapidly evolve to overcome the resistance. For pest-disease systems with high evolutionary potential (McDonald and Linde 2002), breeding programs thus aim to accumulate multiple genes of small effect, which can be achieved by recurrent selection.

For some pests and diseases for which natural allelic variation for resistance is limited, it may be worthwhile and possible to seek genetically engineered forms of resistance. Many transgenic schemes have been designed for pest resistance, such as insect resistance through genes obtained from a bacterium (*Bacillus thuringiensis*, or Bt) and virus resistance (Marra et al. 2002). In sweetpotato, for example, weevils are a significant problem, and solutions have been sought in vain though conventional breeding, integrated management, and even pesticides. Given that sweetpotato is vegetatively propagated on small plots, it would be possible, in principle, to manage the pest through transgenic resistance provided by Bt genes without pollen contamination (through the use of nonflowering varieties) or excessive selection pressure for resistance build-up on pest populations (since sweetpotato is not grown in uniform monocultures).

Sweetpotato and other vegetatively propagated crops are plagued by virus diseases that might also be effectively managed through transgenic resistance, allowing farmers to maintain high-quality planting material for longer periods (e.g., Kreuze et al. 2008). Thus, while transgenic crops are associated with limiting farmers' seed-saving because of the notorious "terminator" technology, the technology can be utilized to support the opposite ends.

Many crops of importance in the developing world are not served by well-resourced breeding programs. Legumes have particular potential to improve soil fertility and human nutrition, but are they are particularly vulnerable to pests. Combining well-designed field-based breeding with participatory methods could go a long way to improving these programs. In addition, a strategic combination of molecular genetics and ecological genetics would enable more breeding programs to confront the specific pest challenges at hand (Salvaudon et al. 2008). Plants may be selected to attract pests' natural enemies. Populations can be designed to incorporate functional diversity for pest resistance while maintaining the degree of agronomic uniformity desired for production, harvest, and processing.

Managing Soil and Water

Integrated soil fertility management is an area that is well researched and documented. Successful cases have shown evidence of increased productivity, better resource use efficiency, and reduced risk, among other effects. There is a range of aspects that can be combined through a stepwise approach, including integration of improved crop germplasm.

The success and limitations of conservation agriculture provide an encouraging and illustrative example of a significant transformation in production technology that has been widely adopted (and sometimes oversold). Crop cultivation is traditionally considered to be synonymous with tilling of the soil (Hobbs et al. 2008). Since the 1930s, various practices have been developed to reduce or eliminate tillage, to cover the soil with a permanent or semipermanent layer of mulch, and to practice rotation. This set of practices has matured into a set of systems, collectively termed "conservation agriculture" (CA), that employ broad principles (cover, reduce tillage, rotation) that contribute to maintenance of soil fertility in different ways in different contexts (Ekboir 2001). The application of the principles is endlessly variable, depending on the context.

CA has been transformative on vast areas, reducing costs and reducing soil erosion. As of 2009, over 100 million hectares were estimated to be grown under CA practices (Kassam et al. 2009). There has been little ideological divide on this—where it works, it is widely accepted. Its relevance is not universal, however, and the principles can fail in specific contexts (Giller et al. 2009). For example, when there is not enough available biomass to provide soil cover, or where there are better uses for available organic matter, it cannot be applied. Kassie et al. (2009) compared plot-level data on the use of reduced tillage and chemical fertilizer in two areas of Ethiopia. They found that reduced tillage was superior in the low-rainfall area of Tigray, where it was associated with lower production costs, higher production, and environmental benefits. In the higher rainfall area in the Amhara region, however, chemical fertilizer was much more profitable. This variability has implications for the adoption of CA practices by farmers, which has been patchy. Synthesis studies have failed to find common factors that explain adoption, except the need for practices to be profitable (Knowler and Bradshaw 2007; de Graaff et al. 2008). Thus, efforts to adapt and promote uptake of CA practices must be location specific.

Many projects promote the composting of crop residues to maintain soil fertility. This may well be preferable to some alternatives, but in Africa, a continent of negative nutrient balances (Cobo et al. 2010), it cannot be the complete answer. Some reported effects are very small, and many are extremely variable (Sileshi et al. 2010; Bastiaans 2008). This variability can be interpreted as unreliability, or as a risk for farmers and others. Legumes and other crops are known as "green manures" when they are grown and incorporated into the soil as nutrient sources for subsequent crops. A meta-analysis of green manures for maize, analyzing the results of fifty-two studies, showed a significant positive contribution to maize yields from woody and herbaceous green manures (Sileshi et al. 2010), though with huge variation in the results. This huge variation has important consequences for strategies to use the findings. While green manures improve soil fertility, farmers prefer multifunctional legumes to straight green manures (Amede 2003; Kikafunda 2003).

Water is a limiting resource for agriculture in many environments. Water scarcity creates one set of problems, and the damage caused by rainfall creates another; in particular, soil erosion is an important threat to sustainability in many systems. An increase in the frequency of destructive rain events is predicted for some areas as a feature of climate change. AEI approaches must confront these challenges. At the plot level, options include the use of drought-tolerant species and varieties, building soil carbon levels to enhance water retention, and the construction of strips and terraces to increase water infiltration and reduce runoff. Many of the options for water management must occur at higher levels, such as the watershed level.

AEI and Markets

Most government and donor initiatives emphasize market-driven development, with little emphasis on system health, sustainability, or better meeting the nutritional needs of rural households. To meet their various objectives, smallholder farmers can generally benefit from improved market access and better performance of input and output markets. But insofar as initiatives neglect issues such as risks induced by pests and climate, they may subject households to potential ecological, nutritional, and financial hazards. Approaches that consider markets to the exclusion of self-provisioning, agroecology to the exclusion of inputs and markets, or markets without concern for stability and sustainability will subject people to unnecessary risk. In keeping with the needs of farm families, it is important to balance concerns for short-term profitability with long-term sustainability, and to balance support for market-oriented production with the fulfillment of dietary diversity.

The example of the quinoa boom in the Andes illustrates the idea that markets need AEI. The international market for organic quinoa has provided Andean farmers with a lucrative market (Kimble-Evans 2003). Because the quinoa price is high, farmers have reduced or abandoned their traditional fallows to maximize their quinoa production, which has in turn led to soil degradation (Medrano Echalar and Torrico 2009; Jacobsen et al. 2011). Local quinoa consumption has declined, and it is likely that farmers sell it and purchase less nourishing foods such as rice and wheat noodles. The reduced following has led to a loss of soil fertility and a build-up of pests attacking quinoa. In desperation, some farmers have applied pesticides, the residues of which have been detected by buyers. This has threatened the viability of the organic markets. The failure to base the value chain on sound AEI production principles has thus threatened the system with nutritional, ecological, and economic collapse. It should be noted that this narrative is contested (Winkel et al. 2012) and that further analysis of Andean agroecology is needed to fully understand the ecological and market dynamics involved in quinoa production.

Examples illustrating the ways in which AEI needs markets would include seed systems, diversified markets that support of crop diversification, and biological control agents. As described above, one of the AEI research frontiers is crop improvement aimed at providing germplasm with traits such as greater resilience (e.g., drought and pest resistance, local adaptation) and improved performance in diversified cropping systems. Ensuring that farmers have access to seeds of the species and varieties that are likely to enhance the performance of their production systems is one area of innovation (e.g., Dorward 2007). Another AEI input market would be for biological control agents and biopesticides. For example, the millet head miner is a pest of pearl millet. A very effective biological control agent has been identified and implemented by a team of national researchers (Payne et al. 2011). For this effective and environmentally friendly pest management agent to be made widely and sustainably available to farmers, it will need to be commercialized. The challenge of reaching millions of resource-limited smallholders with eco-inputs such as biological control agents and other improved component technologies is a frontier of AEI. Building effective output markets that support crop diversification is another critical area needed to support AEI (Shiferaw et al. 2008; Lenné and Ward 2010).

Getting from Here to There: Making AEI Happen

Because contexts vary widely, AEI requires that strategies for local agricultural development be tailored to local needs, objectives, capacities, and opportunities. In view of agroecological and cultural diversity, this is a demanding proposition that requires a flexible approach to research and development. Although there is widespread agreement on the needs for greater agricultural efficiency and sustainability, several opportunities and obstacles to the widespread implementation of AEI approaches should be noted.

The scientific basis of AEI, including both the theory and the evidence base, needs further development. This provides an enormous opportunity for the biophysical and social sciences to contribute to a process of agricultural transformation. Most recent agricultural research has focused on developing the theory and empirical basis for industrial agriculture, leaving substantial space for the development of the AEI research base. Doré et al. (2010) highlight a set of approaches that hold promise for enriching the scientific basis for AEI. These include taking advantage of advances in the plant sciences in breeding crops that are more resilient in terms of resource use efficiency and resistance to biotic and abiotic stresses; using knowledge of natural ecosystems in the design of more efficient agricultural systems; using more sophisticated statistical analyses to understand how options interact with contexts, such as meta-analysis and comparative systems studies; and taking more effective advantage of farmers' indigenous knowledge.

One set of constraints to AEI implementation has to do with the labor, time, and knowledge that may be required (Ruben 2001). The use of trees and legumes to build soil carbon, for instance, can take years. The input resource constraints may be absolute limitations, or they may be considered in relation to the risks entailed and the returns obtained (Ruben 2001). Measures aimed at reducing erosion can also be difficult and expensive to implement. Because such measures require investments of labor, time, and other resources, poverty and insecure land tenure can be obstacles to investments (Place 2009), such as those implied in AEI implementation.

A major challenge to the theory and practice of AEI is the inherent one of ecological diversity. African farming systems are, for example, notably diverse. Successful AEI will entail finding local "best fit" solutions to local problems and needs in a large number of environments. "Environment" here means not only the biophysical agricultural environment, but also the social, institutional, and economic context. For example, the viability of many options is known to depend on farmer resource endowment (e.g., Tittonell et al. 2010) and led to the development of the concept of socio-ecological niche for agricultural practices (Ojiem et al. 2006). Approaches based on the average performance across diverse environments and farmer resource endowments are not likely to perform particularly well in any given environment.

An important institutional constraint to identifying best-fit solutions to local production challenges and opportunities is that the policies and practices of national research systems that serve smallholder agricultural systems are oriented towards the production of sweeping prescriptions, such as blanket fertilizer recommendations made on a national scale. Farmers and researchers alike are aware of the enormous heterogeneity of soil conditions and the consequent absurdity of blanket recommendations. Even within a given farm, nutrient levels vary strongly among fields (Vanlauwe et al. 2006). An AEI approach would entail a change of strategy for national researchers, from a quest for "the mean" to an attempt to understand variability across environments and farmer types.

Although we stress the need for flexible strategies that respond to local conditions, most visible success stories related to AEI are more often presented as packages than as principles. There is a tendency for research and extension organizations to package, brand, and promote their technologies. Technology packages that utilize AEI principles include the push-pull (Khan et al. 2008) and conservation agriculture (Hobbs et al. 2008) systems mentioned above and the system of rice intensification discussed in "Alternative Paths to Food Security" by Norman Uphoff. While the these technologies are often seen and promoted as packages, they are also subject to centralized and local adaptation to respond to varying conditions and demands (e.g., integrating edible beans into the push-pull system, as described in Khan et al. 2009; tailoring of conservation agriculture to local contexts, as described in Ekboir 2001). It is important to develop strategies for technology promotion that support rather than suppress local innovation and adaptation.

Farm technology options must be suited to local conditions and adaptable to farmers' varying circumstances, and farm systems must have the resilience needed to cope with the variability that occurs from season to season and from year to year. It is unlikely that a centralized approach could deliver these results, particularly when national research and extension systems are strapped for resources. These requirements and conditions imply the need for a local innovation capacity. There is a need for approaches that build the social structures needed for group problem-solving and resource mobilization. Examples of such approaches include farmer field schools that allow farmer groups to learn about and experiment with agroecological methods (Pretty 2003). "Innovation platforms" bring together producers with other players along value chains to enhance smallholder market access and improve the efficiencies of input and output markets. Nontraditional market approaches can support diversification, local value addition and responsible input use. An example of such an approach is the "community basket" movement in Ecuador, which brings together Andean smallholder farmers and low-income urban markets for mutual benefits of fair pricing and valuing of culturally significant crops.

Research should be focused on understanding principles and processes underpinning agroecology and developing suites of component technologies, as well as concepts and models for their local integration (e.g., Whitbread et al. 2010). The underlying theory and principles of AEI should be the subject of aggressive international research, but the specifics of their implementation need to be worked out locally. Traditional research and extension approaches that are oriented to developing general prescriptions have little relevance in view of the diversity of farmers' conditions and requirements. There is a need to support local innovation processes through which communities and families can access, adapt, and integrate diverse options according to their particular objectives, problems, and opportunities.

We conclude with an endorsement of the call by Leach et al. (2012) for new technologies, new policies, and new modes of innovation. Smallholder farmers around the world need more ecologically efficient options that work under their resource constraints in their diverse social and biophysical contexts. We need policies and incentives that support researchers to work in new ways to support social and technical innovation at the local level.

ACKNOWLEDGEMENTS

This chapter is loosely based on a briefing paper commissioned by The McKnight Foundation and draws upon some experiences gained by the authors through their involvement with The McKnight Foundation Collaborative Crop Research Program (CCRP).

REFERENCES

Amede, T. 2003. "Pathways for Fitting Legumes into Farming Systems of East African Highlands: A Dual Approach." In *Grain Legumes and Green Manures for Soil Fertility in Southern Africa: Taking Stock of Progress*, edited by S. R. Waddington, 21–29. Harare, Zimbabwe: CIMMYT.

Amekawa, Y., H. Sseguya, S. Onzere, and I. Carranza. 2010. "Delineating the Multifunctional Role of Agroecological Practices: Toward Sustainable Livelihoods for Smallholder Farmers in Developing Countries." *Journal of Sustainable Agriculture* 34 (2): 202–228.

Andow, D. A. 1991. "Yield Loss to Arthropods in Vegetationally Diverse Agroecosystems." *Environmental Entomology* 20: 1228–1235.

Balmford, A., R. Green, and B. Phalan. 2012. "What Conservationists Need to Know about Farming." *Proceedings of the Royal Society B: Biological Sciences* 279 (1739): 2714–2724.

Barnett, B., C. Barrett, and J. Skees. 2008. "Poverty Traps and Index-Based Risk Transfer Products." *World Development* 36 (10): 1766–1785.

Bastiaans, L. et al. 2008. "Focus on Ecological Weed Management: What Is Hindering Adoption?" *Weed Research* 48 (6): 481–491.

Belz, R. G. 2007. "Allelopathy in Crop/Weed Interactions—An Update." *Pest Management Science* 63 (4): 308–326.

Bennett, M., and S. Franzel. 2009. *Can Organic and Resource-Conserving Agriculture Improve Livelihoods? A Meta-analysis and Conceptual Framework for Site-Specific Evaluation. World.* Nairobi: World Agroforestry Centre.

Bentley, J. W. 2009. "Impact of IPM Programs in Asian Agriculture." In *Integrated Pest Management*. Vol. 2, *Dissemination and Impact*, edited by R. Peshin and A. K. Dhawan, 333–346. Dordrecht, the Netherlands: Springer.

Bezner Kerr, R., L. Dakishoni, L. Shumba, R. Msachi, and M. Chirwa. 2008. "'We Grandmothers Know Plenty': Breastfeeding, Complementary Feeding and the Multifaceted Role of Grandmothers in Malawi." *Social Science & Medicine* 66 (5): 1095–1105.

Bianchi, F. J. J. A., N. A. Schellhorn, Y. M. Buckley, and H. P. Possingham. 2010. "Spatial Variability in Ecosystem Services: Simple Rules for Predator-Mediated Pest Suppression." *Ecological Applications: A Publication of the Ecological Society of America* 20 (8): 2322–2333.

Blazy, J.-M., M. Dorel, F. Salmon, H. Ozier-Lafontaine, J. Wery, and P. Tixier. 2009. "Model-Based Assessment of Technological Innovation in Banana Cropping Systems Contextualized by Farm Types in Guadeloupe." *European Journal of Agronomy* 31 (1): 10–19.

Bongaarts, J. 2009. "Human Population Growth and the Demographic Transition." *Philosophical Transactions of the Royal Society B: Biological Sciences* 364 (1532): 2985–2990.

Bushamuka, V. N., S. de Pee, A. Talukder, L. Kiess, D. Panagides, A. Taher, and M. Bloem. 2005. "Impact of a Homestead Gardening Program on Household Food Security and Empowerment of Women in Bangladesh." *Food and Nutrition Bulletin* 26 (1): 17–25.

Cannell, M. G. R., M. Noordwijk, and C. K. Ong. 1996. "The Central Agroforestry Hypothesis: The Trees Must Acquire Resources That the Crop Would Not Otherwise Acquire." *Agroforestry Systems* 34 (1): 27–31.

Carberry, P. S., R. I. McCown, R. C. Muchow, J. P. Dimes, M. E. Probert, P. L. Poulton, and N. P. Dalgliesh. 1996. "Simulation of a Legume Ley Farming System in Northern Australia Using the Agricultural Production Systems Simulator." *Australian Journal of Experimental Agriculture* 36 (8): 1037.

Carberry, P. S., M. Probert, J. P. Dimes, and B. Keating. 2002. "Role of Modelling in Improving Nutrient Efficiency in Cropping Systems." *Plant and Soil* 245: 193–203.

Ceccarelli, S., E. P. Guimaraes, and E. Weltzien, eds. 2009. Plant Breeding and Farmer Participation. Rome: Food and Agricultural Organization of the United Nations (FAO).

Cobo, J. G., G. Dercon, and G. Cadisch. 2010. "Nutrient Balances in African Land Use Systems across Different Spatial Scales: A Review of Approaches, Challenges and Progress." *Agriculture, Ecosystems & Environment* 136 (1–2): 1–15.

Cohen, M. J., C. Tirado, N.-L. Aberman, and B. Thompson, 2008. "Impact of Climate Change and Bioenergy on Nutrition." Rome: Food and Agricultural Organization of the United Nations (FAO).

Cox, T. S., M. Bender, C. Picone, D. L. van Tassel, J. B. Holland and E. C. Brummer, B. E. Zoeller, A. H. Paterson, and W. Jackson. 2002. "Breeding Perennial Grain Crops (Part 1 of 3)." *Critical Reviews in Plant Sciences* 21 (2): 59–91.

Davis, B., P. Winters, G. Carletto, K. Covarrubias, E. Quinones, A. Zezza, K. Stamoulis, G. Bonomi, and F. DiGuiseppe, 2007. "Rural Income Generating Activities: A Cross Country Comparison." Background paper for the WDR 2008.

De Graaff, J., A. Amsalu, F. Bodnár, A. Kessler, H. Posthumus, and A. Tenge. 2008. "Factors Influencing Adoption and Continued Use of long-term Soil and Water Conservation Measures in Five Developing Countries." *Applied Geography* 28 (4): 271–280.

De Groote, H., B. Vanlauwe, E. Rutto, G. D. Odhiambo, F. Kanampiu, and Z. R. Khan. 2010. "Economic Analysis of Different Options in Integrated Pest and Soil Fertility Management in Maize Systems of Western Kenya." *Agricultural Economics* 41: 1–12.

Devine, G. J., and Furlong, M. J. 2007. "Insecticide Use: Contexts and Ecological Consequences." *Agriculture and Human Values* 24 (3): 281–306.

Doré, T., D. Makowski, E. Malézieux, N. Munier-Jolain, M. Tchamitchian, and P. Tittonell. 2011. "Facing Up to the Paradigm of Ecological Intensification in Agronomy: Revisiting Methods, Concepts and Knowledge." *European Journal of Agronomy* 34 (4): 197–210.

Dorward, P., P. Craufurd, K. Marfo, W. Dogbe, and R. Bam. 2007. "Improving Participatory Varietal Selection Processes: Participatory Varietal Selection and the Role of Informal Seed Diffusion Mechanisms for Upland Rice in Ghana." *Euphytica* 155 (3): 315–327.

Ekboir, J., ed. 2001. *World Wheat Overview and Outlook 2000–2001: Developing No-Till Packages for Small Scale Farmers.* Mexico City: CIMMYT. http://apps.cimmyt.org/Research/Economics/map/facts_trends/wheat00-01/pdf/wheat0&000-01.pdf.

Evenson, R. E., and D. Gollin. 2003. "Assessing the Impact of the Green Revolution, 1960 to 2000." *Science* 300 (5620): 758–762.

Fan, F., F. Zhang, Y. Song, J. Sun, X. Bao, T. Guo, and L. Li. 2006. "Nitrogen Fixation of Faba Bean (Vicia faba L.) Interacting with a Non-legume in Two Contrasting Intercropping Systems." *Plant and Soil* 283 (1–2): 275–286.

FAO (Food and Agricultural Organization of the United Nations). 2006. "Food Security." Policy Brief 2. Geneva: FAO. ftp://ftp.fao.org/es/ESA/policybriefs/pb_02.pdf.

Gebeyehu, S., B. Simane, and R. Kirkby. 2006. "Genotype × Cropping System Interaction in Climbing Beans (Phaseolus vulgaris L.) Grown as Sole Crop and in Association with Maize (Zea mays L.)." *European Journal of Agronomy* 24: 396–403.

Geleta, M., Z. Asfaw, E. Bekele, and A. Teshome. 2002. "Edible Oil Crops and Their Integration with the Major Cereals in North Shewa and South Welo, Central Highlands of Ethiopia: An Ethnobotanical Perspective." *Hereditas* 137 (1): 29–40.

Giller, K. E., E. Witter, M. Corbeels, and P. Tittonell. 2009. "Conservation Agriculture and Smallholder Farming in Africa: The Heretics' View." *Field Crops Research* 114 (1): 1–12.

Godfray, H. C. J., J. R. Beddington, I. R. Crute, L. Haddad, D. Lawrence, J. F. Muir, J. Pretty, S. Robinson, S. M. Thomas, and C. Toulmin. 2010. "Food Security: The Challenge of Feeding 9 Billion People." *Science* 327 (5967): 812–818.

Hartman, A. 2012. Scaling Up Agricultural Value Chains for Pro-Poor Development. IFPRI Focus 19, Brief 7 (Scaling Up in Agriculture, Rural Development and Nutrition). Washington, DC: International Food Policy Research Institute. http://www.ifpri.org/sites/default/files/publications/focus19_07.pdf.

Hobbs, P. R., K. Sayre, and R. Gupta. 2008. "The Role of Conservation Agriculture in Sustainable Agriculture." *Philosophical Transactions of the Royal Society B: Biological Sciences* 363 (1491): 543–55.

IFPRI (International Food Policy Research Institute). 2011. *Leveraging Agriculture for Improving Nutirtion and Health: Highlights from an International Conference*. Washington, DC: IFPRI.

Jacobsen, S.-E. 2011. "The Situation for Quinoa and its Production in Southern Bolivia: From Economic Success to Environmental Disaster." *Journal of Agronomy and Crop Science* 197 (5): 390–399.

Kassam, A., T. Friedrich, F. Shaxson, and J. Pretty. 2009. "The Spread of Conservation Agriculture: Justification, Sustainability and Uptake." *International Journal of Agricultural Sustainability* 7 (4): 292–320.

Kassie, M., P. Zikhali, J. Pender, and G. Kohlin. 2009. "Sustainable Agricultural Practices and Agricultural Productivity in Ethiopia: Does Agroecology Matter?" Environment for Development Discussion Paper. Gothenburg, Sweden: Environment for Development. http://www.rff.org/rff/documents/EfD-DP-09-12.pdf.

Keating, B. A., P. S. Carberry, P. S. Bindraban, S. Asseng, H., Meinke, & J. Dixon. 2010. "Eco-efficient Agriculture: Concepts, Challenges, and Opportunities." *Crop Science* 50 (Suppl. 1): S109–S119.

Khan, Z., C. Midega, E. Njuguna, D. Amudavi, J. Wanyama, and J. Pickett. 2008. "Economic Performance of the 'Push–Pull' Technology for Stemborer and Striga Control in Smallholder Farming Systems in Western Kenya." *Crop Protection* 27 (7): 1084–1097.

Khan, Z. R., C. A. O. Midega, J. M. Wanyama, D. M. Amudavi, A. Hassanali, J. Pittchar, and J. A. Pickett. 2009. "Integration of Edible Beans (Phaseolus vulgaris L.) into the Push–Pull Technology Developed for Stemborer and Striga Control in Maize-Based Cropping Systems." *Crop Protection* 28 (11): 997–1006.

Kikafunda, J. T. T. Bogale, T. E. Mmbaga, and R. H. Assenga. 2003. "Legume Fallows for Maize-Based Cropping Systems in East Africa: Screening Legumes for Adaptability, Biomass and Nitrogen Production." In *Proceedings of the Seventh Eastern and Southern Africa Regional Maize Conference, 11th–15th February 2001*, 319–323. Mexico City: CIMMYT.

Kimble-Evans, A. 2003. "Quinoa, Lost Crop of the Incas, Finds New Life." Kutztown, PA: Rodale Institute. http://newfarm.rodaleinstitute.org/international/features/0803/quinoa/incaorganics.shtml.

Knowler, D., and B. Bradshaw. 2007. "Farmers' Adoption of Conservation Agriculture: A Review and Synthesis of Recent Research." *Food Policy* 32 (1): 25–48.

Kreuze, J. F., I. S. Klein, M. U. Lazaro, W. J. C. Chuquiyuri, G. L. Morgan, P. G. C. Mejia, M. Ghislain, and J. P. T. Valkonen. 2008. "RNA Silencing-Mediated Resistance to a Crinivirus (Closteroviridae) in Cultivated Sweetpotato (Ipomoea batatas L.) and Development of Sweetpotato Virus Disease Following Co-infection with a Potyvirus." *Molecular Plant Pathology* 9 (5): 589–598.

Kropff, M. 2001. "Systems Approaches for the Design of Sustainable Agro-Ecosystems." *Agricultural Systems* 70 (2–3): 369–393.

Leach, M., J. Rockström, P. Raskin, I. Scoones, A. C. Stirling, A. Smith, J. Thompson, et al. 2012. "Transforming Innovation for Sustainability." *Ecology and Society* 17 (2): 11.

Lenné, J. M., and A. F. Ward. 2010. "Improving the Efficiency of Domestic Vegetable East Africa: Constraints and Opportunities." *Outlook on Agriculture* 39 (1): 31–40.

Letourneau, D. K., I. Armbrecht, B. S. Rivera, J. M. Lerma, E. J. Carmona, M. C. Daza, S. Escobar, et al. 2011. Does Plant Diversity Benefit Agroecosystems? A Synthetic Review. *Ecological Applications: A Publication of the Ecological Society of America* 21 (1): 9–21.

Lithourgidis, A. S., C. A. Dordas, C. A. Damalas, and D. N. Vlachostergios. 2011. "Annual Intercrops: An Alternative Pathway for Sustainable Agriculture." *Australian Journal of Crop Science* 5 (4): 396–410.

MacIntyre, B., H. R. Herren, J. Wakhungu, and R. Watson. 2009. *International Assessment of Agricultural Knowledge, Science and Technology for Development (IAASTD): Global Report*. Washington, DC: Island Press.

Malezieux, E., Y. Crozat, C. Dupraz, M. Laurans, D. Makowski, H. Ozier-Lafontaine, B Rapidel, S. de Tourdonnet, M. Valantin-Morison. 2009. "Mixing Plant Species in Cropping Systems: Concepts, Tools and Models: A Review." *Agronomy for Sustainable Development* 29: 43–62.

Marenya, P. P., and C. B. Barrett. 2009. "State-Conditional Fertilizer Yield Response on Western Kenyan Farms." *American Journal of Agricultural Economics* 91 (4): 991–1006.

Marra, M. C., P. G. Pardey, and J. M. Alston. 2002. "The Payoffs to Transgenic Field Crops: An Assessment of the Evidence." *AgBioForum* 5 (2): 43–50.

McDonald, B. A., and C. Linde. 2002. "Pathogen Population Genetics, Evolutionary Potential, and Durable Resistance." *Annual Review of Phytopathology* 40: 349–379.

Medrano Echalar, A. M., and J. C. Torrico. 2009. "Consecuencias del incremento de la producción de quinua (Chenopodium quinoa Willd.) en el altiplano sur de Bolivia." *CinciAgro* 1 (4): 117–123.

Millenium Ecosystems Assessment. 2005. Ecosystems and Human Well-Being: *Health Synthesis*. Geneva, Switzerland: World Health Organization. http://www.who.int/entity/globalchange/ecosystems/ecosys.pdf.

Mpepereki, S., Javaheri, F., Davis, P., & Giller, K. E. 2000. "Soyabeans and Sustainable Agriculture Promiscuous Soyabeans in Southern Africa." *Field Crops Research* 65 (2–3): 137–149.

Mundt, C. C., K. E. Sackett, and L. D. Wallace. 2011. "Landscape Heterogeneity and Disease Spread: Experimental Approaches with a Plant Pathogen." *Ecological Applications* 21 (2): 321–328.

Nelson, R., R. Orrego, O. Ortiz, J. Tenorio, C. Mundt, M. Fredrix,, and N V. Vien. 2001. "Working with Resource-Poor Farmers to Manage Plant Diseases." *Plant Disease* 85 (7): 684–695. http://www.apsnet.org/publications/apsnetfeatures/Documents/2001/ResourcePoorFarmers.pdf.

Nelson, R. J. 2010. "Pest Management, Farmer Incomes and Health Risks in SSA: Pesticides, Host Plant Resistance and Other Measures." In *The African Food System and its Interaction with Human Health and Nutrition: Research and Policy Priorities*, edited by P. Pinstrup-Andersen, 109–127. Ithaca, NY: Cornell University Press.

Oerke, E.-C. 2005. "Crop Losses to Pests." *Journal of Agricultural Science* 144 (1): 31–43.

Ojiem, J. O., N. de Ridder, B. Vanlauwe, and K. E. Giller. 2006. "Socio-ecological Niche: A Conceptual Framework For Integrating Legumes in Smallholder Farming Systems." *Journal of Sustainable Agriculture* 4: 79–93.

Ong, C. K., J. Wilson, J. D. Deans, and J. Mulayta, 2002. "Tree–Crop Interactions: Manipulation of Water Use and Root Function." *Agricultural Water Management* 53 (1–3): 171–186.

Orr, A. 2003. "Integrated Pest Management for Resource-Poor African Farmers: Is the Emperor Naked?" *World Development* 31 (5): 831–845.

Oswald, A., and J. K. Ransom. 2001. "Striga Control and Improved Farm Productivity Using Crop Rotation." *Crop Protection* 20 (2): 113–120.

Parsa, S., R. Ccanto, and J. A. Rosenheim. 2011. "Resource Concentration Dilutes a Key Pest in Indigenous Potato Agriculture." *Ecological Applications: A Publication of the Ecological Society of America* 21 (2): 539–546.

Pauli, N., T. Oberthür, E. Barrios, and A. J. Conacher. 2010. "Fine-Scale Spatial and Temporal Variation in Earthworm Surface Casting Activity in Agroforestry Fields, Western Honduras." *Pedobiologia* 53 (2): 127–139.

Payne, W., H. Tapsoba, I. B. Baoua, B. N. Malick, M. N'Diaye, and C. Dabire-Binso. 2011. "On-Farm Biological Control of the Pearl Millet Head Miner: Realization of 35 Years of Unsteady Progress in Mali, Burkina Faso and Niger." *International Journal of Agricultural Sustainability* 9 (1): 186–193.

Peoples, M. B., J. Brockwell, D. F. Herridge, I. J. Rochester, B. J. R. Alves, S. Urquiaga, R. M. Boddey, et al. 2009. "The Contributions of Nitrogen-Fixing Crop Legumes to the Productivity of Agricultural Systems." *Symbiosis* 48 (1–3): 1–17.

Place, F. 2009. "Land Tenure and Agricultural Productivity in Africa: A Comparative Analysis of the Economics Literature and Recent Policy Strategies and Reforms." *World Development* 37 (8): 1326–1336.

Pollan, M. 2006. *The Omnivore's Dilemma: a Natural History of Four Meals*. New York: Penguin.

Pretty, J. 2003. "Social Capital and the Collective Management of Resources." *Science* 302 (5652): 1912–1914.

Pretty, J. 2008. "Agricultural Sustainability: Concepts, Principles and Evidence." *Philosophical Transactions of the Royal Society B: Biological Sciences* 363 (1491): 447–465.

Pretty, Jules, C. Toulmin, and S. Williams. 2011. "Sustainable Intensification in African Agriculture." *International Journal of Agricultural Sustainability* 9 (1): 5–24.

Rebaudo, F., V. Crespo-Perez, J.-F. Silvain, and O. Dangles. 2011. "Agent-Based Modeling of Human-Induced Spread of Invasive Species in Agricultural Landscapes: Insights from the Potato Moth in Ecuador." *Journal of Artificial Societies and Social Simulation* 14 (3): 7.

Renting, H., W. A. Rossing, J. C. Groot, J. D. Van der Ploeg, C. Laurent, D. Perraud, D. J. Stobbelaar, and M. K. Van Ittersum. 2009. "Exploring Multifunctional Agriculture: A Review of Conceptual Approaches and Prospects for an Integrative Transitional Framework." *Journal of Environmental Management* 90 (Suppl. 2): S112–S123. Elsevier Ltd.

Ruben, R. 2001. "Economic Conditions for Sustainable Agriculture." *LEISA Magazine* (October): 52–53.

Salvaudon, L., T. Giraud, and J. Shykoff. 2008. "Genetic Diversity in Natural Populations: A Fundamental Component of Plant-Microbe Interactions." *Current Opinion in Plant Biology* 11 (2): 135–143.

Scherr, S. J., and J. McNeely. 2008. "Biodiversity Conservation and Agricultural Sustainability: Towards a New Paradigm of 'Ecoagriculture' Landscapes." *Philosophical Transactions of the Royal Society B: Biological Sciences* 363 (1491): 477–494.

Seufert, V., N. Ramankutty, and J. A. Foley. 2012. "Comparing the Yields of Organic and Conventional Agriculture." *Nature* 485: 229–232.

Shiferaw, B., G. Obare, and G. Muricho, 2008. "Rural Market Imperfections and the Role of Institutions in Collective Action to Improve Markets for the Poor." *Natural Resources Forum* 32 (1): 25–38.

Sileshi, G., F. K. Akinnifesi, L. K. Debusho, T. Beedy, O. C. Ajayi, and S. Mong'omba. 2010. "Variation in Maize Yield Gaps with Plant Nutrient Inputs, Soil Type and Climate across Sub-Saharan Africa." *Field Crops Research* 116 (1–2): 1–13.

Singh, B., O. Chambliss, and B. Sharma. 1997. "Recent Advances in Cowpea Breeding." In *Advances in Cowpea Research*, edited by B. Singh, D. Mohan, K. Dashiell, and L. Jackai, 30–49. Ibadan, Nigeria: IITA.

Snapp, S. S., M. J. Blackie, R. A. Gilbert, R. Bezner-Kerr, and G. Y. Kanyama-Phiri. 2010. "Biodiversity Can Support a Greener Revolution in Africa." *Proceedings of the National Academy of Sciences of the United States of America* 107 (48): 20840–20845.

Tilman, D., C. Balzer, J. Hill, and B. L. Befort. 2011. "Global Food Demand and the Sustainable Intensification of Agriculture." *Proceedings of the National Academy of Sciences of the United States of America* 108 (50): 20260–20264.

Tilman, D., K. G. Cassman, P. A. Matson, R. Naylor, and S. Polasky. 2002. "Agricultural Sustainability and Intensive Production Practices." *Nature* 418 (6898): 671–677.

Tittonell, P., A. Muriuki, K. D. Shepherd, D. Mugendi, K. C. Kaizzi, J. Okeyo, L. Verchot, R. Coe, and B. Vanlauwe. 2010. "The Diversity of Rural Livelihoods and Their Influence on Soil Fertility in Agricultural Systems of East Africa—A Typology of Smallholder Farms." *Agricultural Systems* 103 (2): 83–97.

Toenniessen, G., A. Adesina, and J. DeVries. 2008. "Building an Alliance for a Green Revolution in Africa." *Annals of the New York Academy of Sciences* 1136, 233–242.

USAID. 1992. *USAID Policy Determination: Definition of Food Security*. Washington, DC: USAID. http://transition.usaid.gov/policy/ads/200/pd19.pdf.

Van Acker, R. C. 2008. "Commentary: Sustainable Agriculture Development Requires a Shift from an Industrial to a Multifunctional Model." *International Journal of Agricultural Sustainability* 6 (1): 1–2.

Vanlauwe, B., P. Tittonell, and J. Mukalama. 2006. "Within-Farm Soil Fertility Gradients Affect Response of Maize to Fertiliser Application in Western Kenya." *Nutrient Cycling in Agroecosystems* 76 (2–3): 171–182.

van Noordwijk, M., G. H. Dijksterhuis, and H. van Keulen. 1994. "Risk Management in Crop Production and Fertilizer Use with Uncertain Rainfall: How Many Eggs in Which Baskets?" *Netherlands Journal of Agricultural Science* 42 (4): 249–269.

van Noordwijk, M., and C K. Ong. 1999. "Can the Ecosystem Mimic Hypotheses Be Applied to Farms in African Savannahs?" *Agroforestry Systems* 45: 131–158.

Vandermeer, J., M. van Noordwijk, J. Anderson, C. Ong, and I. Perfecto. 1998. "Global Change and Multi-Species Agroecosystems: Concepts and Issues." *Agriculture, Ecosystems & Environment* 67 (1): 1–22.

Vanek, S. 2010. *Legume-Phosphorus Synergies in Mountain Agroecosystems: Field Nutrient Balances, Soil Fertility Gradients and Effects on Legume Attributes and Nutrient Cycling in the Bolivian Andes*. Ithaca, NY: Cornell University.

Whitbread, A. M., M. J. Robertson, P. S. Carberry, and J. P. Dimes. 2010. "How Farming Systems Simulation Can Aid the Development Of More Sustainable Smallholder Farming Systems in Southern Africa." *European Journal of Agronomy* 32 (1): 51–58.

Williamson, S., A. Ball, and J. Pretty. 2008. "Trends in Pesticide Use and Drivers for Safer Pest Management in Four African Countries." *Crop Protection* 27 (10): 1327–1334.

Winkel, T., H. D. Bertero, P. Bommel, J. Bourliaud, M. Chevarría Lazo, G. Cortes, P. Gasselin, et al. 2012. "The Sustainability of Quinoa Production in Southern Bolivia: From Misrepresentations to Questionable Solutions. Comments on Jacobsen (2011, J. Agron. Crop Sci. 197: 390–399)." *Journal of Agronomy and Crop Science* 198 (4): 314–319.

Wolfe, M. S. 1985. "The Current Status and Prospects for Multiline Cultivars and Variety Mixtures for Disease Resistance." *Annual Review of Phytopathology* 23: 251–273.

World Bank. 2007. *World Development Report* 2008: Agriculture for Development. Washington, DC: World Bank. http://web.worldbank.org/WBSITE/EXTERNAL/EXTDEC/EXTRESEARCH/EXTWDRS/0,,contentMDK:23062293~pagePK:478093~piPK:477627~theSitePK:477624,00.html.

Young A. 1999. "Is There Really Spare Land? A Critique of Estimates of Available Cultivable Land in Developing Countries." *Environment, Development and Sustainability* 1 (1): 3–18.

CHAPTER 5

THE HARDEST CASE

What Blocks Improvements in Agriculture in Africa?

ROBERT L. PAARLBERG

PROGRESS in ending hunger has been slower in Africa than in any other world region. Food consumption deficits in sub-Saharan Africa are large, and it is expected they will continue to grow. In 2010 the Economic Research Service (ERS) at the US Department of Agriculture (USDA) constructed estimates and projections of the numbers of food-insecure people in seventy different developing countries, with food insecurity defined as consumption of less than 2,100 calories per day per person (Shapouri et al. 2010). The ERS estimated that in 2010, approximately 390 million Africans, or nearly half the people in the region, were consuming less than this nutritional target. Under a baseline projection, without any significant increase in investment or any changes in historical trends for major indicators, this total number of food-insecure Africans was expected to increase to reach 513 million by 2020, which would be more than half of the region's projected population of 1 billion.

Under this baseline scenario, the region's food security position will also deteriorate relative to the other regions. In 2020, according to ERS projections, the region will account for only 27 percent of the population of the seventy countries, but it will hold 59 percent of all the food-insecure people in these countries. Africa, then, is the one part of the world where solutions to hunger have been most elusive. For those who study the politics of food and farming in search of attainable remedies to hunger, Africa remains the hardest case to solve.

What is the source of Africa's severe and still-worsening food crisis? A number of compounding factors must be considered, including difficult demographics, a disadvantageous geography for many countries on the continent, multiple damages done under colonial rule, and a continuing postcolonial indifference toward agricultural development in Africa from the international donor community. Still, the largest part of the problem today reflects a failure of governance within Africa itself. Too often since their independence, national governments in Africa have failed to provide public goods at the national level that are essential to agricultural development, including internal peace, rule of law, and adequate public investments in rural infrastructure and agriculture research. These goods are all critical to farm productivity growth, and in their absence incomes in the countryside have remained low, ensuring that food security will remain low as well. The problem expands numerically as the rural population continues to expand.

Tracing Africa's Hunger Problems to Low Farm Productivity

In sub-Saharan Africa, food production has struggled to keep pace with population growth in part because the productivity of farming in Africa has been growing so slowly. When economists measure the growth of "total factor productivity" in African agriculture (a ratio of the value of all outputs to all land, labor, and capital inputs) they find that between 1970 and 1990 it increased—from a low level—at an average annual rate of only .31 percent. Between 1991 and 2006 this rate of growth was a bit higher, at .86 percent, but this was still far behind the productivity growth rate for Latin American farming (2.44 percent) and for Asian farming (2.62 percent) (Fuglie 2008).

With farm productivity growth lagging, food production in Africa has actually been falling behind population growth for most of the past forty years. Between 1970 and 2000, food production per capita in Africa declined by 9 percent, even as it was increasing in the developing world as a whole by 51 percent (FAO 2001). Maize is Africa's most important food crop, yet between 1980 and 2006, per capita production of maize in sub-Saharan Africa declined by 14 percent (FAO 2006).

Because most Africans are still farmers, these lags in crop production per capita translate into little or no rural income growth, and hence into little or no increase in the capacity to purchase food. Decades of lagging farm productivity have resulted in a doubling of the number of Africans in deep poverty (those living on less than $1 per day), up from 150 million in 1980 to approximately 300 million in 2013. Low-productivity farmers fill the ranks of Africa's food insecure. A majority of Africa's farmers are women, and it is among pregnant and nursing women and their preschool children that calorie and micronutrient deficits are most acute.

Some analysts have tried to deny lagging food production is the source of Africa's persistent poverty and hunger, arguing instead that Africa's poverty problems stem from social inequality (Rosset 2000). This can be a powerful explanation for hunger in South Asia, and especially in Latin America, but not in Africa, where most rural dwellers have adequate access to land where social stratification is not so prominent. In Africa, where roughly 60 percent of all citizens are still farmers, poverty and hunger problems trace directly to the low productivity of labor in the growing of crops and the herding of livestock.

If you pay a visit to a rural community of smallholder farmers in sub-Saharan Africa, most of the farmers you meet will be women. In fact, three-quarters of all labor in African farming is performed by women. The men, after completing some heavy seasonal tasks such as plowing or repairing terraces, will often leave in search of work in urban areas, because labor on the farm pays such little reward. Most adult women in rural Africa are unable to read or write in any language. They are always busy, since the time they spend laboring to grow crops such as yams, maize, beans, sorghum, millet, or cassava must be fit in between numerous other tasks, such as preparing meals, caring for children, fetching water, and gathering fuel wood for the cooking fire. Typically, these farmers will have no improved seeds, no irrigation, no electrical power, and no access to chemical fertilizers or a veterinarian for the animals. These farmers are hardworking and highly resourceful, yet the returns on their labor are minimal given what little they have to work with. They are working within what economists call a "poverty trap." In the memorable phrase of T. W. Schultz, they are "efficient but poor" (Schultz 1964).

Innovations in agricultural science in the form of high-yielding "Green Revolution" seed varieties helped bring hundreds of millions of destitute farmers out of comparable poverty in Asia in the 1970s and 1980s, but these technologies had only limited application in Africa, because they required a substantial use of chemical fertilizers and irrigation, assets either not available or not affordable for most African smallholders. So as Asian farming surged forward near the end of the last century, African farming remained stuck behind. Today, more than four-fifths of all land in developing Asia is planted with scientifically improved crop varieties, compared to less than one third for Africa. Only 4 percent of cultivated land in sub-Saharan Africa is currently protected with irrigation, compared to roughly 40 percent in South and East Asia. In India, average fertilizer use is roughly 100 kilograms per hectare, compared to less than 10 kilograms per hectare in Africa (Paarlberg 2008). These deficits explain why cereal yields in Africa are less than one-third as high as in developing Asia, and why income from farming is so low. In Kenya, where farming is doing better than in most other countries on the continent, the average yearly income of a small farming household is just $553. In Zambia, it is just $122. In Mozambique, it is only $59 (Jayne, Mather, and Mghenyi 2005).

The inability of African farmers to access more productive technology has led them to use less sustainable methods to boost production in pace with population growth. One example is the shortening of fallow time, a practice that mines soil nutrients and can eventually lead to an actual decline in crop yield per hectare. The shortening of fallows is now removing nitrogen from the soil at an average annual rate of 22–26 kilograms per hectare in Africa, too much to be offset by current rates of fertilizer application, which average only 9 kilograms per hectare. The result of this "soil mining" is a deficit in soil nutrients that causes annual crop losses estimated at between $1 billion and $3 billion. And this is not the end of the problem. As cultivated soils become exhausted, farmers extend cropping onto new lands, cutting more trees and destroying more wildlife habitat.

Why Don't African Governments Act to Boost Farm Productivity?

Governments in Africa have opportunities to address these problems of agricultural stagnation. They could follow the lead of governments in Asia and invest more in rural public goods, such as roads, power, irrigation, schools, clinics, and agricultural research. This would gradually transform Africa's countryside from a poverty trap into a productivity and income center, yet governments in Africa have been slow to take this approach. Nearly all public investments needed for increased agricultural productivity have been underprovided in Africa. Rural road systems in Africa are primitive, with 70 percent of all rural citizens living more than a 30-minute walk from the nearest all-weather road (Sebastian 2007). There is virtually no rural electrical power, rural health clinics are sparse and poorly equipped, and rural education is rudimentary (a majority of farmers in Africa, who tend to be women, cannot read or write in any language). In addition, public investments in agricultural research are miniscule. Two-thirds or more of all citizens in Africa depend on farming for income and employment, yet governments continue to devote an average of just 5 or 6 percent of their annual budget spending on any kind of agricultural development. In many cases, this percentage has actually declined. Whereas the government of Uganda devoted 10 percent of its budget to agriculture in 1980, since 1991 agriculture has not received more than 3 percent of the budget in any year, and in some years the share has been below 2 percent (Oxford Policy Management 2007). The Government of India, during the early years of the Green Revolution, was devoting more than 20 percent of its budget to agricultural development (Hazell 2009).

Good governance in the area of agricultural development often comes down to an adequate allocation of budget resources for that purpose, and African political leaders know they are spending too little. In 2003, at an African Union meeting in Maputo, Africa's heads of government pledged to increase their share of the national public budget that went to the agricultural sector up to at least 10 percent by 2008. But a subsequent survey of forty-five countries in the region by the International Food Policy Research Institute (IFPRI) found that only eight of those countries had met the pledge (Fan, Omilola, and Lambert 2009).

Many governments in the developing world have a history of "urban bias" in the policy choices they make, for reasons originally pointed out by Michael Lipton in his classic study, *Why Poor People Stay Poor* (Lipton 1977). Rural populations in all developing countries find it harder to make effective political demands on the state because they are more difficult to organize for political action, being more isolated from each other, more distant from the capital city, less well educated, and typically unarmed. By contrast, urban populations are often already organized—into unions, a civil service workforce, and armed military or police units. Urban dwellers are also far better educated and politically informed. They may be fewer in number than rural dwellers, but they are physically proximate to the institutions of the state and to each other. They can threaten to block the streets, shut down commerce, or even take control of government ministries, radio stations, and airports, so the state must give priority to their concerns.

Yet the urban bias of government policy in Africa is so extreme as to require more than just these generic explanations, prompting a vigorous scholarly debate over why so many governments in Africa invest so little in the improvement of agriculture. The debate has not been resolved because so many of the alternative explanations are actually compatible with each other, suggesting that they all probably contribute to the adverse political outcome. In the sections that follow we shall consider three categories of such alternative but mutually reinforcing factors: demography and geography: ethnic diversity, conflict, and corruption; and colonial legacies plus various postcolonial effects.

Demography and Geography

One school of thinking attributes the unique neglect of agricultural investments by African governments to the unfortunate demographic and geographic destiny of the continent. Africa has a rural population that is growing rapidly and demanding new investments in farming, yet this population is not yet spatially dense enough to make the needed investments cost-effective.In addition, Africa's geography—its limited coastline, climate, topography, and soils—is often described as uniquely unpromising for productive farming, which further discourages government investment.

Population growth rates in Africa remain high (a dozen African countries still have overall growth rates of 3 percent or higher), yet population densities in most countries on the continent are quite low (less than half the global average) so relatively thin rural populations often remain dispersed over wide areas. The expense of providing adequate farming infrastructure—roads, power, and irrigation, and storage—to this highly dispersed rural population is more than most African governments can afford. One estimate from the Commission for Africa calculated that meeting Africa's infrastructure needs would require roughly a doubling of annual external assistance to the region, up to a level of $14 billion (World Bank 2006). Because donors have not provided these funds, and because the costs are so overwhelming, African governments have an excuse to not even try.

The fact that some past efforts to build rural infrastructure in Africa were not cost-effective provides another excuse. The large irrigation schemes constructed in the 1970s in the Volta Basin in West Africa cost an unaffordable $45,000 per hectare (Van de Giesen et al. 2005). In 2010 the International Food Policy Research Institute estimated the average internal rate of economic return in Africa on large-dam irrigation projects was only 7 percent. Because projected economic rates of return are so low, the average rate of expansion of irrigated area over the past thirty years in Africa was just 2.3 percent, actually slowing to just 1.1 percent per year during 2000–2003 period (You et al. 2010).

The same is true for rural roads. The high cost of rural transport due to poor rural road systems is one of the greatest constraints to agricultural productivity in Africa. Farmers have less incentive to intensify production because fertilizer is too expensive to bring to the farm, and because any surplus they might produce takes too much time and labor to bring to market. Population growth is making it impossible to replenish soil nutrients using the traditional system of shifting cultivation, since fallow times get shorter and shorter as population increases, yet populations are not yet dense enough to justify the cost of building (and maintaining) an adequate network of rural farm-to-market roads, and during rainy seasons all household transport must be on foot. Governments in Africa are also discouraged from investing in agriculture, some argue, because so many are in countries that are geographically landlocked, and thus unable to imagine building their farm sectors into a source of lucrative export revenues (Sachs 2001).

Arguments are also made that African governments invest little in agriculture because they know that topography, soils, and climate in the region are poorly suited to productive crop farming. Much of Africa is indeed burdened by the extremes of heat and drought, heavily weathered soils, and a tropical disease environment that reduces the productivity of both human and animal labor. Africa's high diversity of local ecosystems makes more difficult the region-wide uptake of simple mono-crop farming systems similar to the irrigated high-yield "Green Revolution" systems that worked for wheat and rice in Asia. Soils in Africa tend to be poor even by the standards of tropical countries, because they are highly weathered, acidic, and generally low in fertility. At the same time, rainfall tends to be either scarce and unreliable, or excessive. An estimated two-thirds of the continent is subject to high risk of drought, and some 46 percent has less than seventy-five days of rain a year, too little to grow even millet. Tree planting, normally an option for soil conservation, is problematic in the large parts of Africa that receive less than 1,000 millimeters of rainfall each year. Compared with other tropical regions, a much smaller part of Africa's land mass is moderated by proximity to oceans. Most of Africa lacks the monsoon effects that provide more abundant rainfall in much of Asia (Bloom and Sachs 1998). Local topography also tends to be highly irregular, complicating the engineering of irrigation systems while boosting road construction and other rural infrastructure costs. Irrigation costs in Africa are roughly double those of other continents.

The many pests and diseases in Africa that attack crops, livestock, and farmers are another natural impediment to higher productivity. As one example, stem borers are a major pest problem for Kenyan maize farmers, causing estimated losses of 15–45 percent of each maize crop, reducing Kenya's annual farm earnings by an average of 70 million dollars. In West Africa, cowpeas grown by women farmers on small plots are a major source of protein and cash income for 200 million people. Yet insect damage from pod borers and weevils can affect up to 95 percent of the crop, depending on the location and year (Murdock 1999). Farm size tends to be small in Africa partly because of the difficulty of keeping fields free from the invasive weeds that grow rampant. Parasitic weeds such as *Striga* attack cereals and food legumes in the arid savanna zones, while perennial grasses force farmers to abandon prime lands in the moist savanna (Akobundu 1991).

As much as a third of tropical Africa remains underexploited because of the presence of trypanosomiasis, a parasitic disease that affects both people and livestock.

All these difficult natural conditions might seem to give African governments ample excuse for not investing more public resources in agricultural development. Yet the constraints mentioned here do not have to block agricultural improvements in Africa. As global wealth has grown and the frontier of science has moved outward, the ability of human institutions to engineer an escape from natural constraint has expanded as well, so that geography and climate no longer have to be destiny. For example, many of the most productive lands in tropical Brazil today were considered unusable for crop farming two decades ago, before they were limed to correct soil acidity. Africa could be doing much better in working against natural constraints if governments in the region were willing to invest more in essential public goods such agricultural research and rural infrastructure. Public research and development expenditures can raise productivity in almost any environment (Masters and Wiebe 2000). Economic returns to agricultural research tend to be high, and even in Africa rates of return above 50 percent are not unusual. Yet most governments in the region have long skimped on public spending for agricultural science (Alston, Pardey, and Roseboom 1998). Investments in rural infrastructure can also increase farm productivity. Spending on rural roads in Uganda has better than a 9 to 1 ratio of benefits (in terms of agricultural growth and rural poverty reduction), yet once again Africa's governments have tended to put priorities elsewhere (World Bank 2007). Investments in agricultural biotechnology could bring to Africa crops more capable of withstanding abiotic stress, such as nitrogen deficits or drought.

Ethnic Diversity, Corruption, and Conflict

A second explanation for the tendency of African governments to invest so little in agricultural development is borrowed from critiques of the African state that go far beyond the farming sector. In every economic sector, it can be argued, African governments do a poor job of providing public goods. Public resources are used not for investment but for patronage to favored clans and ethnic groups, or to buy elections, or to equip and ensure the loyalty of armed forces, or simply to enrich the head of government, his party, and his extended family members. This tendency of African governments to shift, over time, from providing public goods that might sustain economic growth to providing private goods that only redistribute the growth, to finally becoming predatory and actually seizing private goods, has been described most systematically and most recently by Robert Bates of Harvard University (Bates 2008).

Democratic governance has been spreading in Africa since the early 1990s, and in that time the region has gone from almost no democracies to nearly half the continent under democratic rule. Significantly, there are no signs that this trend is reversing. Of the seventeen sub-Saharan African states that became democracies between 1990 and 1995, sixteen remain democracies today (Radelet 2010). Yet the governance failures that most damage farming are not quickly corrected by introducing multiparty elections, given the dominance of urban populations over election outcomes. Electoral competition can also have the unfortunate tendency of shortening the time horizon of governments, inspiring them to govern even more through short-term payoffs to supporters rather than through long-term investments in growth (Bates 2008).

Why does this pattern arise more often in Africa than in the rest of the developing world? Africa's extreme ethnic diversity is one candidate explanation. Many African countries feature dozens of distinct ethnic groups, each with its own separate language and regional homeland. Fourteen of the fifteen most ethnically diverse societies in the world are located in Africa. By one count, sub-Saharan Africa has seventy-four different ethnic minorities, compared to only forty-three in all of Asia, where the population is much larger overall (Gurr 1993). In sub-Saharan Africa, minorities comprise 42 percent of the population, versus the global average of 17 percent. In this environment of incomplete national integration, governance patterns of mistrust, patronage, and the formation of violent armed groups with distinct ethnic loyalties can displace nationwide investments in any kind of public good.

Once ethnic group competition becomes militarized, as it often does in Africa, a more extreme diversion of public resources away from public goods then becomes likely. If actual fighting takes place, the agricultural sector is often the first to suffer. Violent conflict reduces agricultural productivity and compromises secure access to food in multiple obvious ways. In rural farming communities, the recruitment of able-bodied young men into armies and militias takes labor away from food production, thereby reducing rural incomes. In areas of conflict, predatory activities by both militias and regular armies diminish food availability and access directly. These armed groups tend to subsist by eating whatever they can take from the unarmed rural population, and they then destroy any food they cannot use immediately in contested areas so as to deny it to their adversaries. Fearing theft and destruction of this kind, rural dwellers naturally chose to invest less energy in farming. They may abandon their land entirely and begin moving as internally displaced people toward cities or emergency feeding centers set up by relief agencies. For all these reasons, countries experiencing conflict in Africa also tend to experience significant drops in food production. They produce, on average, 12.4 percent less food per capita in war years than in peacetime. A comparison of actual historical food production in Africa after 1980 to a "peace adjusted trend" shows that peace would have added 2–5 percent to the continent's total food production per year (Messer, Cohen, and d'Costa 1998).

Because of frequent military conflict, many Africans are forced to cross national borders and become refugees, living in camps and depending for their survival on international food aid. At one point in the 1990s, while sub-Saharan Africa accounted for only 10 percent of the world's population, it was harboring 46 percent of the world's refugees and persons internally displaced by war (Haughton 1997). These urgent humanitarian needs suck resources away from productive investments in public goods.

The fundamental public good that goes missing first under these circumstances is the simple rule of law, including basic safeguards against loss of property or breeches of contract. Well-functioning national governments provide such safeguards by operating capable and noncorrupt civil and criminal justice systems. Without such systems, incentives to invest in wealth creation—including in the farming sector—tend to disappear. One indirect measure of how well African governments provide the rule of law can be found in the Index of Economic Freedom compiled yearly by the Heritage Foundation and the *Wall Street Journal*. One dimension this index measures is the protection of property rights, defined as security from government expropriation, the presence of an efficient court system to enforce contracts, and a justice system that punishes those who unlawfully confiscate private property. Of forty-two sub-Saharan African countries ranked in 2010 on a scale of 1 to 100, only three of the smallest (Botswana, Cape Verde, and Mauritius) scored higher than 50. Nigeria and Ethiopia scored only 30, the Democratic Republic of the Congo only 10, and Zimbabwe only 5. By contrast the United States scored 85, and Singapore scored 90 (Heritage Foundation 2013).

Weak property protection in Africa is particularly important as a key to understanding the persistence of slow economic growth across all sectors in the region, including agriculture. Economic growth in Africa would be higher if the level of investment were higher, but incentives to invest are weak because essential public goods such as property protection and contract enforcement are so often missing. It is significant that Africans as well as non-Africans are reluctant to invest in the region. A study by Collier and Gunning (1997) compared the portfolio choices of wealth holders across all regions, using data on capital flight and domestic capital stocks. They found that wealth owners in Africa relocated 37 percent of their wealth outside the continent. This compares to a 17 percent capital flight rate in Latin America and only 3 percent in East Asia. It led Collier and Gunning to conclude that if Africa reduced its own total capital flight to the level of Asia, its capital stock might increase by half.

Colonial Legacies and Postcolonial Influences

Low public investments in rural welfare and agricultural productivity in Africa can also be traced to colonial and postcolonial influences. Africa's early rural development was strongly shaped by the institutions that European colonizers introduced to support cash-crop export farming. While making no investments at all in the smallholder farming sector that produced staple food crops, European colonial authorities in the early twentieth century did make large investments in the production and export of tea, coffee, groundnuts (peanuts), cotton, and tobacco. To support this agricultural enterprise, the colonizers—French, British, Germans, Belgians, Portuguese—built infrastructures of road and rail designed to move products not to local population centers but to and from port facilities for international transport. Colonial capitals were often situated in port cities, looking outward rather than inward, and some of the most powerful institutions in these capitals were the monopoly export marketing boards that commandeered agricultural products from local growers at a low price, so as to maximize profit when the product was sold on the international market at a high price. Labor to operate the cash-cropping system was often locally commandeered as well, separating young men from their families and from traditional farming activities.

This institutional legacy did not disappear when the colonial period ended in the 1960s. The monopoly marketing boards continued to siphon wealth out of the farming sector, but now for the benefit of the newly independent African regimes, typically governed by a narrow European-trained urban professional class. The African political class that gained independence typically wanted nothing to do with farming. Eager to industrialize so as to catch up with the developed world, these new urban leaders of independent Africa continued to use the instruments of rural extraction they had inherited from the Europeans. In 1992, Maurice Schiff and Alberto Valdes, from the World Bank, calculated that between 1960 and 1985 the newly independent governments of Africa used direct and indirect policy measures to impose the equivalent of a 30 percent tax on their agricultural sectors, an extraction of resources from farming that was not matched or compensated by any offsetting public investments in the countryside (Schiff and Valdes 1992).

A second dimension of the colonial legacy is one that continues to the present day. Because the economies of Africa's young states did not prosper after independence, the governments of those states became dependent on international financial assistance, both from individual donor countries (often the former colonizer) and from international financial institutions (such as the World Bank and the International Monetary Fund [IMF]). On a per-capita basis, Africa receives three times as much foreign aid as any of the other developing regions. As a percentage of gross domestic product (GDP), Africa is even more dependent on aid (Devarajan, Rajkumar, and Swaroop 1999). Measures for 1970–1993 constructed by Burnside and Dollar (2000) show that a sampling of twenty-one nations in sub-Saharan Africa were, on average, more than four times as dependent on aid, relative to GDP, as a sampling of thirty-five developing countries outside of sub-Saharan Africa. The average sub-Saharan African country now derives roughly 13 percent of its entire GDP from foreign aid, which is five times the foreign-aid dependence experienced by the recovering nations of Western Europe after World War II at the height of the Marshall Plan. African governments today need a continuing stream of foreign assistance simply to service their accumulated external debts. Of the forty "heavily indebted poor countries" recently permitted to seek debt relief under a World Bank/IMF initiative, thirty-three were African countries. In these heavily indebted aid-dependent countries, new spending for development is seldom undertaken without some prior assurance of new donor support. Donor support for state investments in rural public goods went into an unfortunate decline beginning in the 1980s.

In the 1980s, aid donors to Africa noticed that the farm sector was underperforming, but the remedy prescribed was to get the state out of the business of running the economy, rather than to encourage more investment in public goods. The policy reform template advanced by the World Bank and the IMF in both Africa and Latin America was called "structural adjustment," and it included a number of worthy macroeconomic features designed to control inflation, free markets, and "get prices right." Lending money for policy change proved to be difficult, however, and the adjustments imposed in Africa were not always significant or long lasting. In 1994 the World Bank completed a study of 29 governments in sub-Saharan Africa that had undergone structural adjustment and found that 17 of those 29 had reduced the overall tax burden they placed on farming, while some, because of persistently overvalued exchange rates, had actually increased that burden. Only 4 of the 29 had eliminated parastatal marketing boards for major export crops, and none of the 29 had in place both agricultural and macroeconomic policies that measured up to World Bank standards (World Bank 1994). In addition, in their focus on "getting prices right" these international financial institutions had largely neglected the need for governments to make larger public goods investments in the rural sector. Public goods investments were actually discouraged under structural adjustment, because they could contribute to fiscal deficits condemned by World Bank and IMF economists as inflationary.

In its pursuit of structural adjustment in the 1980s and 1990s, the World Bank essentially withdrew from making loans in Africa for public sector investments in agriculture. Between 1978 and 1988, the share of lending from the World Bank that went to agricultural development fell from 30 percent to 16 percent, and by 2006 the lending share was only 8 percent. In 2005, World Bank president Paul Wolfowitz admitted in an offhand comment, "My institution's largely gotten out of the business of agriculture" (Hitt 2005). This withdrawal of international support for agricultural investment reinforced the existing tendency among African governments to underinvest in farming.

Bilateral donors also walked away from providing assistance to African agriculture beginning in the 1980s. The United States allowed its official development assistance to agriculture in Africa to fall from more than $400 million annually in the 1980s to only $60 million annually by 2006, a drop of 85 percent at a time when food grain production in Africa was declining on a per-capita basis and the numbers of hungry people on the continent were doubling (Chicago Council on Global Affairs 2009). This was a period during which donor countries were losing interest in agricultural development. They carelessly concluded from the success of Asia's Green Revolution and from low prices on the world market that food problems in the developing world had been solved. Between 1980 and 2003, the aggregate value of all bilateral agricultural development assistance from all rich countries to all poor countries fell by 64 percent. The fact that food and agricultural problems were still worsening in Africa did not seem to matter to donors during this period. Hence, among the donor-dependent governments of Africa, the pattern of underinvesting in rural public goods continued.

Pathways of Escape

The best policy path to escape Africa's current food and farming crisis is also a matter of considerable debate. The pathways of escape favored by the political Right differ dramatically from those advanced by the political Left. Scholars on the Right (led by neoclassical economists) predictably favor additional market-oriented economic reforms in Africa to attract private investment, political reforms to restore the rule of law, and a greater openness to international trade, including trade in agricultural products even when this means importing food staples while producing cash crops for export. Endorsements for this strategy can be found, for example, in the World Bank's (2007) study *World Development Report 2008: Agriculture for Development.* According to the Bank, "The private sector drives the organization of value chains that bring the market to smallholders and commercial farms." The subordinate role of the state is to "correct market failures, regulate competition, and engage in strategically in public-private partnerships" (9).

In the view of the World Bank, the structural adjustment efforts of the 1980s and 1990s were a considerable success: Between 1980 and 1984 and 2000 and 2004, net agricultural taxation was reduced in Africa from 28 percent down to 10 percent, and this is seen as one reason agricultural growth in Africa recovered slightly, from negative growth per capita in the 1980s to 1.5 percent per capita between 2000 and 2005. More growth will now be possible, according to the Bank, if markets—including international markets—are given more room to operate. This means an opening to more imports of food staples, despite the problems this could cause when world prices fluctuate. This recommendation for greater reliance on international food markets was inconveniently published in 2007, just before a sudden 2008 spike in international food prices punished those who had allowed themselves to rely on the world market. In 2008 the export price of maize doubled from two years earlier, the price of rice tripled in just three months, and wheat available for export reached its highest price in twenty-eight years. Street demonstrations and rioting broke out in Egypt, Cameroon, Ivory Coast, Senegal, and Ethiopia (Paarlberg 2010).

The World Bank vision included greater investment in smallholder agriculture, primarily in Africa's medium- and higher-potential areas. Subsistence farmers in lower-potential areas need food security and safety nets to ensure livelihoods. Some World Bank economists go farther than this, arguing that smallholder farmers in Africa will never be an adequate source of either food production or income growth. Paul Collier, Professor of Economics at Oxford and a former director of research at the Bank, concluded in 2008 that a better solution would be to move agriculture in Africa toward the "Brazilian model" built around larger-scale commercial farms. Smallholder peasant farmers, he argued, will never be able to keep up with the fast-evolving technologies seen in modern farming, and will never be able to connect to high value consumer food chains, given poor rural infrastructure. In the Brazilian model, private companies construct their own transportation infrastructure (Collier 2008). Smallholders can participate as subcontractors.

The limitations of the Brazilian model are nonetheless obvious. It is a proven method of generating more agricultural production and more commercial gains from farming, but not a fully proven method of using farming to bring adequate income or greater food security to the rural poor. Brazil has increased food security for the rural poor most recently through expensive public-sector conditional cash transfers, not through corporate investments. Defenders of the Brazilian approach argue that poor smallholders will be able to participate through contract farming, promising their crop to a large firm at a prearranged price in return for seeds, fertilizers, irrigation, and technical assistance. The authors of the World Bank's 2007 study insist that, even on their own, African smallholder farmers are capable producers: "Given the opportunity, smallholders in Africa have proved to be just as responsive to new technologies as their Asian counterparts. Witness the adoption of hybrid maize in much of southern Africa, the dairy revolution in East Africa, and the increased production of cocoa, cassava, and cotton in West Africa." The World Bank authors also warn that large-scale farming has a long record of disappointment in Africa, dating from colonial times (Byerlee and de Janvry 2009).

On the political Right, nearly all agree that Africa needs a technology upgrade in farming comparable to the Green Revolution that brought farm productivity and higher rural incomes to Asia in the 1960s and 1970s. In 2006, two pro-technology philanthropic foundations, the Rockefeller Foundation and the Bill and Melinda Gates Foundation, joined in a joint venture they called an Alliance for a Green Revolution in Africa (AGRA). Bill Gates himself explained the importance of introducing African smallholder farmers to modern agricultural science:

> In Africa today, the great majority of poor people, many of them women with young children, depend on agriculture for food and income and remain impoverished and even go hungry. Yet, Melinda and I have also seen reason for hope—African plant scientists developing higher-yielding crops, African entrepreneurs starting seed companies to reach small farmers, and agrodealers reaching more and more small farmers with improved farm inputs and farm management practices. These strategies have the potential to transform the lives and health of millions of families.
>
> (Bill and Melinda Gates Foundation 2006)

This Green Revolution vision for rural Africa, embraced uncritically by most on the Right, is firmly rejected by critics on the Left. When the AGRA initiative was announced in 2006, those who did not want a green revolution in Africa responded with reflexive hostility. Peter Rosset, from a US nongovernmental organization (NGO) named Food First, lampooned the Gates Foundation's "naïveté about the causes of hunger" and warned that the most likely result of the new initiative would be "higher profits for the seed and fertilizer industries, negligible impacts on total food production and worsening exclusion and marginalization in the countryside" (Rosset 2006).

The political Left is critical of trying to bring a Green Revolution to Africa in part because of what happened in Latin America when high-yielding seeds were introduced there in the 1960s and 1970s. Due to extreme social inequities in rural Latin America, ownership of productive farmland and access to credit for the purchase of essential

Green Revolution inputs such as fertilizer were restricted to a privileged rural elite, so the gains of the new technology were not equitably shared. Agricultural land was made more valuable by the new seeds, but this backfired on the poor who had previously been allowed to subsist on land they did not own. They were now pushed off this land by the landlords to make way for expanded commercial production. Some of the evicted peasants gained limited compensation in the form of seasonal employment as hired cotton pickers, but otherwise they were forced to move their farming efforts onto lands with irregular terrain, no access to irrigation, and less fertile soil, or become slum dwellers on the fringes of the urban economy (Williams 1986). This experience engendered a lasting hostility toward the Green Revolution among groups on the Left (including Food First) who saw the world primarily through a Latin American lens.

Asia had a much better experience with the new seeds because access to good land was less narrowly held (in this regard, Africa is more like Asia than Latin America), yet Green Revolution critics have even tried to depict Asia's experience with the new seeds as a social calamity. In 1992, despite growing evidence to the contrary, the celebrity activist Vandana Shiva published a polemic titled *The Violence of the Green Revolution*, which erroneously depicted the new seeds as a plot by multinational corporations (the seeds had actually been introduced by philanthropic foundations and governments) to lure farmers away from growing traditional crops, destroying their culture, and making them poor and dependent (Shiva 1992). In fact, the new seeds finally ended India's struggle with famine and helped cut rural poverty rates down from 60 percent in the 1960s to 39 percent by 1988 and an estimated 27 percent by 2000 (Deaton and Drèze 2002).

The alternatives to a Green Revolution for Africa offered by the political Left have both a technical side and an institutional side. Technically, the preference is for agroecology, a farming approach that favors traditional seeds over scientifically developed seeds, polycultures over monocultures, biological controls for pests rather than chemical controls, and crop rotations plus manuring rather than using synthetic nitrogen fertilizers. Many also favor organic farming, which eliminates synthetic chemicals entirely. On the institutional side, the political Left is mistrustful of private companies and private markets, so the preference is for something called "food sovereignty," where small peasant farmers avoid any dependence on inputs purchased from agribusiness firms or on the sale of their product into unreliable export markets. The call for food sovereignty is not so much a formal school of thinking as it is a social movement, launched in Belgium in 1992 by organization named La Vía Campesina, now nominally headquartered in Honduras (Tandon 2008).

Widely cited support for this alternative to the Green Revolution can be found in the 2008 International Assessment of Agricultural Knowledge, Science and Technology for Development (IAASTD), completed under the auspices of the World Bank and the United Nations. This assessment, authored by an international assembly of advocates that included representatives of national governments and NGOs as well as scientists, concluded that the Green Revolution had brought too many "unintended social and environmental consequences." The assessment calls for a greater emphasis on agroecological approaches and the incorporation of "traditional and local knowledge" (IAASTD

2008). The risk for Africa in following this assessment is that it can easily be used to endorse the status quo. Most smallholder farmers in African today practice something suspiciously close to pure agroecology: They use traditional seeds, plant their crops in polycultures, irrigate with collected rainfall, and purchase almost no inputs such as nitrogen fertilizers or pesticides from off the farm. They also work with great skill from dawn to dusk, yet the result is that their cereal crop yields are only 10–20 percent as high as in North America, they earn only $1 a day on average, and one-third are undernourished.

The best approach is usually to combine agroecological insights with Green Revolution seeds plus off-farm inputs. For example, integrated pest management (IPM) combines biological controls of pests with Green Revolution seeds, plus the limited use of chemical pesticides as a last resort. Integrated nutrient management would combine manuring and legumes with some nitrogen fertilizer, but not as much as currently used in the developed world. Yet the polarization of viewpoints between Green Revolution advocates and Green Revolution critics makes this sort of integrated approach extremely difficult.

One illustration is the current political battle over introducing genetically engineered crops (referred to as GMOs) into Africa. GMOs have enjoyed safe and widespread use over the past fifteen years in the United States, Canada, Argentina, Brazil, China, India, the Philippines, and elsewhere—but not in Europe, where consumer anxieties and regulatory restrictions have kept them out of farm fields. There is a strong scientific consensus in Europe that the use of genetic engineering in farming has not yet introduced any new risks to either human health or the environment, a view endorsed by Royal Society in London, the British Medical Association, the French Academy of Sciences, the German Academies of Science and Humanities, and the Research Directorate of the European Union (Paarlberg 2008). In 2010, in fact, the Research Directorate issued a new report that stated, "The main conclusion to be drawn from the efforts of more than 130 research projects, covering a period of more than 25 years of research, and involving more than 500 independent research groups, is that biotechnology, and in particular GMOs, are not per se more risky than e.g. conventional plant breeding technologies" (European Commission 2010). Government policies in Europe nonetheless remain strongly prejudiced against the technology, and because Europe continues to exercise a strong postcolonial influence over Africa, governments in sub-Saharan Africa have largely been persuaded to follow Europe in blocking the planting of agricultural GMOs. As of 2013, it was not yet legal for farmers to plant any genetically engineered seeds in forty-three out of forty-seven countries in Africa. In the majority of these countries it was not even legal for scientists to do research using these seeds.

Five channels of external influence from Europe help to explain this blockage of agricultural biotechnology in Africa. First, Africa's official development assistance (ODA) from Europe is three times as large as ODA from the United States, and governments in Europe have used their ODA influence to encourage African governments to draft and implement highly precautionary European-style regulatory systems for agricultural GMOs. European funding also shaped an important UNEP-GEF Global Project on the Development of National Biosafety Frameworks (NBFs) that coached African governments in parallel fashion to adopt highly precautionary European-style GMO regulations.

A second channel of external influence has been advocacy campaigns against GMOs from international nongovernmental organizations (INGOs), the most active of which are headquartered in Europe. Greenpeace International and Friends of the Earth International, both based in Amsterdam, have campaigned heavily in Africa against agricultural GMOs, telling stories of new medical and environmental risks, but never sharing with their African audience the fact of Europe's own scientific consensus regarding the absence of such risks so far. A third channel of external influence has been commercial agricultural trade. Africa's farm exports to Europe are six times as large as exports to the Untied States, so exporters must adjust to European consumer tastes and European regulatory requirements. In 2002, Zambia rejected GMO maize as food aid in part because an export company (Agriflora Ltd.) and the export-oriented national farmers union (ZNFU) were anxious that exports of organic baby corn to Europe not be compromised. The risks of export rejections from African countries that plant GMOs are actually quite small, as evidenced by the continued growth of food sales to Europe from the Republic of South Africa, which does plant GMOs, yet anxieties surrounding export loss continues to play a political role. A final channel of external influence is cultural. Most policymaking elites in Africa have closer cultural ties—based on history, language, schooling, media, and travel—to Europe than to the United States, so they are naturally inclined to view European practices as the best practices (Paarlberg 2008).

The Political Challenge for the Pragmatic Center

There is also a pragmatic center with its own favored remedy for Africa's agricultural challenges. Pragmatists know that Africa's agricultural sector will never become a source of productivity and income growth without larger investments in basic rural public goods: roads, power, schools, clinics, and agricultural research and technology extension. The political problem for the pragmatic center is how to stir Africa's governments to improve their performance in making these investments. The actions most needed for this task include revived external assistance for agricultural investments, external and peer pressure on governments in Africa to fulfill their 2003 Maputo pledge, and foundation-led projects designed to create partnerships between the African public sector and private international companies with access to technology and market outlets.

For most of the past three decades, the first pillar of this strategy—external assistance for agricultural investments—was largely missing in Africa, as noted above. Politically, at least three forces were pushing external donors away from the needed task of providing assistance to agricultural modernization in Africa. The first was a rejection of public-sector foreign assistance by those on the political Right who thought private markets should always be in the lead. Second was a rejection from the political Left of any attempt to extend a Green Revolution to Africa, on grounds that it would hurt the poor and not be environmentally sustainable. Third was Africa's growing need, beginning in the 1980s, for emergency food aid. Africa's food crisis was worsening to the point that efforts to rush food to hungry people in the short run were crowding out needed investments in agricultural development for the long run. Between 1980 and 2006, while US development assistance to African farming was falling by 85 percent, official spending for food assistance to Africa was more than doubling in real terms, up to $1.2 billion. By 2006 the United States was spending roughly twenty times as much giving away food in Africa as it was spending to help Africans do a better job of producing their own food (Chicago Council on Global Affairs 2009).

The shock of temporarily high world food prices in 2008, followed by the inauguration of Barack Obama as US president in 2009, led to a promising revival of donor support, and promised support, for agricultural development. Several months after taking office, President Obama pledged to ask Congress for a doubling of US agricultural development assistance, up to more than $1 billion by 2010, and at a summit meeting of the G8 countries in Italy in July 2009, Obama convinced the world's wealthy nations to make a collective pledge of $20 billion over three years to promote food security and agricultural development in poor countries. Not all of the money pledged was new money, not all would go for agricultural development, and not all would go to Africa (as the US assistance community faced more urgent nation-building problems in Iraq, Afghanistan, and Pakistan), but funding did increase, and for the moment a long period of official neglect for agricultural development assistance appeared to be ending.

By 2011, however, donor commitments to new agricultural development assistance had begun to falter. Donors backed off in Europe because of financial and sovereign debt crises, which had triggered budget austerity across the board. Appropriations became more difficult in the United States because a domestic "Tea Party" movement shaped the November 2010 congressional election, giving control of the House of Representatives to (newly) deficit-conscious Republicans. Appropriations for the Obama administration's new Feed the Future initiative—which focused on agricultural development in Africa—did increase through fiscal year 2012 but faced threats of cuts going forward (Bertini and Glickman 2012). The motive of donors to provide assistance to smallholder farmers in Africa rests primarily on a social and ethical foundation, rather than on commercial or national security advantage, making adequate efforts difficult to sustain.

References

Akobundu, O. 1991. "Weeds in Human Affairs in Sub-Saharan Africa: Implications for Sustainable Food Production." *Weed Technology* 5 (3): 680–690.

Alston, J. M., P. Pardey, and J. Roseboom. 1998. "Financing Agricultural Research: International Investment Patterns and Policy Perspectives." *World Development* 26 (6): 1057–1071.

Bates, R. 2008. *When Things Fell Apart: State Failure in Late-Century Africa*. New York: Cambridge University Press.

Bertini, C., and D. Glickman. 2012. *2012 Progress Report on U.S. Leadership in Global Agricultural Development*. Chicago: Chicago Council on Global Affairs.

Bill and Melinda Gates Foundation. 2006. "Bill & Melinda Gates, Rockefeller Foundations Form Alliance to Help Spur 'Green Revolution' in Africa." Press Release. Seattle: Bill and Melinda Gates Foundation. http://www.gatesfoundation.org/Media-Center/Press-Releases/2006/09/Foundations-Form-Alliance-to-Help-Spur-Green-Revolution-in-Africa.

Bloom, D. E., and J. D. Sachs. 1998. *Geography, Demography, and Economic Growth in Africa*. Cambridge, MA: Harvard Institute for International Development.

Burnside, C., and D. Dollar 2000. "Aid, Policies, and Growth." *The American Economic Review* 90 (September 4): 847–868.

Byerlee, D., A. de Janvry, J. VanWassenhove, and D. Barry. "Smallholders Unite." Letter to the Editor. *Foreign Affairs*, March/April 2009.

Chicago Council on Global Affairs. 2009. *Renewing American Leadership in the Fight Against Global Hunger and Poverty*. Chicago: Chicago Council on Global Affairs.

Collier, P. "The Politics of Hunger: How Illusion and Greed Fan the Food Crisis," *Foreign Affairs*, November/December 2008.

Collier, P., and J. W. Gunning. 1997. "Explaining African Economic Performance." Working Paper 97–2. Oxford: Centre for the Study of African Economies, Institute of Economics and Statistics, Oxford University.

Deaton, A., and J. Drèze. 2002. "Poverty and Inequality in India: A Re-examination." *Economic and Political Weekly*, September 7, 3729–3748.

Devarajan, S., A. S. Rajkumar, and V. Swaroop. 1999. *What Does Aid to Africa Finance?* Washington, DC: Development Research Group, World Bank.

European Commission. 2010. *A Decade of EU-funded GMO Research (2001–2010)*. Brussels: European Commission, Directorate-General for Research. ftp://ftp.cordis.europa.eu/pub/fp7/kbbe/docs/a-decade-of-eu-funded-gmo-research_en.pdf.

Fan, S., B. Omilola, and M. Lambert. 2009. "Public Spending for Agriculture in Africa: Trends and Composition." Working Paper No. 28. IFPRI. Cited in *Halving Hunger: Meeting the First Millennium Development Goal through Business as Unusual*, edited by Shenggen Fan. Washington, DC: International Food Policy Research Institute (IFPRI).

FAO (Food and Agriculture Organization of the United Nations). 2001. FAOSTAT (Food and Agriculture Organization Statistical data base). http://faostat.fao.org/site/339/default.aspx.

FAO (Food and Agriculture Organization of the United Nations). 2006. "World Agriculture: Towards 2030/2050." Interim report, Global Perspective Studies Unit. Rome: FAO.

Fuglie, K. 2008. "Is a Slowdown in Agricultural Productivity Growth Contributing to the Rise in Commodity Prices?" *Agricultural Economics* 39:431–441.

Gurr, T. R. 1993. *Minorities at Risk: A Global View of Ethnopolitical Conflict*. Washington, DC: US Institute for Peace.

Haughton, J. 1997. *The Reconstruction of War-Torn Economies*. Cambridge, MA: Harvard Institute for International Development.

Hazell, P. 2009. "The Asian Green Revolution." Discussion Paper 00911. Washington, DC: International Food Policy Research Institute (IFPRI).

Heritage Foundation. 2013. Index of Economic Freedom. http://www.heritage.org/index/.

Hitt, G. 2005. "A Kinder, Gentler Wolfowitz at World Bank?" *Wall Street Journal*, September 22, A4.

IAASTD (International Assessment of Agricultural Science, Technology, and Development). *Executive Summary of Synthesis Report 2008*. http://www.agassessment.org/docs/IAASTD_exec_summary_JAN_2008.pdf.

Jayne, T. S., D. Mather, and E. Mghenyi. 2005. "Smallholder Farming in Difficult Circumstances: Policy Issues in Africa." Paper presented at "The Future of Small Farms," International Food Policy Research Institute and Overseas Development Institute, and Imperial College, London, Wye, UK, June 26–29.

Lipton, M. 1977. *Why Poor People Stay Poor*. Cambridge, MA: Harvard University Press.

Masters, W. A., and K. Wiebe. 2000. "Climate and Agricultural Productivity." Paper prepared for presentation at the Conference on Raising Agricultural Productivity in the Tropics: Biophysical Challenges for Technology and Policy, Center for International Development, Harvard University, October 17.

Messer, E., M. J. Cohen, and J. d'Costa. 1998. "Food from Peace: Breaking the Links between Conflict and Hunger." 2020 Brief 50. Washington, DC: International Food Policy Research Institute (IFPRI).

Murdock, L. 1999. "Cowpea Biotechnology: Symposium/Workshop Draft Proposal." West Lafayette, IN. Department of Entomology, Purdue University.

Oxford Policy Management. 2007. *Uganda: Agriculture Sector Public Expenditure Review*. Oxford: Oxford Policy Management. http://www.opml.co.uk/news-publication/uganda-agriculture-public-expenditure-review-0.

Paarlberg, R. 2008. *Starved for Science: How Biotechnology Is Being Kept Out of Africa*. Cambridge, MA: Harvard University Press.

Paarlberg, R. 2010. *Food Politics: What Everyone Needs to Know*. New York: Oxford University Press.

Radelet, S. 2010. *Emerging Africa: How 17 Countries are Leading the Way*. Washington, DC: Center for Global Development.

Rosset, P. 2004. "Do We Need New Technology to End Hunger?" Oakland, CA: Food First/Institute for Food and Development Policy. http://www.foodfirst.org/media/opeds/2000/4-greenrev.html.

Rosset, P. 2006. "Bill Gates/Rockefeller Programs to Alleviate Hunger in Africa Via GMOs and Industrialized Farming Are Doomed," *Seattle Post-Intelligencer*, September 22.

Sachs, J. 2001. "New Approaches to International Donor Assistance." Speech to the International Development Research Centre, June 19, Ottawa, Canada.

Schiff, M., and A. Valdes. 1992. *The Plundering of Agriculture in Developing Countries*. Washington, DC: World Bank.

Schultz, T. W. 1964. *Transforming Traditional Agriculture*. New Haven, CT: Yale University Press.

Sebastian, K. 2007. "GIS/Spatial Analysis Contribution to 2008 WDR: Technical Notes on Data & Methodologies." Background paper for the *World Development Report 2008*. Washington, DC: World Bank.

Shapouri, S. S. Rosen, M. Peters, F. Baquedano, and S. Allen. *Food Security Assessment, 2010-20*. ERS Report Summary, July 2010. Washington, DC: USDA Economic Research Service. http://www.ers.usda.gov/Publications/GFA21/GFA21_ReportSummary.pdf.

Tandon, Y. 2008, "The Principle of Food Sovereignty." *Pambazuka News* 383 (June 18). http://www.pambazuka.org/en/category/features/48881.

Van de Giesen, N.C., T. Berger, W. Laube, C. Rodgers, and Paul L. G. Vlek. 2005. "Hydrological Potential, Economic Evaluation, and Institutional Constraints: Decision Support for

Irrigation Development in the Volta Basin." *Geophysical Research Abstracts* 7 (05179). European Geosciences Union.

Vandana S. 1992. *The Violence of the Green Revolution: Third World Agriculture, Ecology and Politics*. London: Zed.

Williams, R. G., 1986. *Export Agriculture and the Crisis in Central America*. Chapel Hill, NC: University of North Carolina Press.

World Bank. 1994. *Adjustment in Africa: Reforms, Results, and the Road Ahead*. http://econ.worldbank.org/external/default/main?pagePK=64165259&theSitePK=469372&piPK=64165421&menuPK=64166322&entityID=000178830_98101911304260.

World Bank. 2006. "World Bank Lending to Borrowers in Africa by Theme and Sector." In *World Bank Annual Report 2006*. Washington, DC: World Bank. http://web.worldbank.org/WBSITE/EXTERNAL/EXTABOUTUS/EXTANNREP/EXTANNREP2K6/0,,contentMDK:21048994~pagePK:64168445~piPK:64168309~theSitePK:2838572,00.html.

World Bank. 2007. *World Development Report 2008: Agriculture for Development*. Washington, DC: World Bank. http://web.worldbank.org/WBSITE/EXTERNAL/EXTDEC/EXTRESEARCH/EXTWDRS/0,,contentMDK:23062293~pagePK:478093~piPK:477627~theSitePK:477624,00.html.

You, L., C. Ringler, G. Nelson, U. Wood-Sichra, R. Robertson, S. Wood,, Z. Guo, T. Zhu, and Y. Sun. "What Is the Irrigation Potential for Africa? A Combined Biophysical and Socioeconomic Approach." IFPRI Discussion Paper 00993. Washington, DC: International Food Policy Research Institute. http://www.ifpri.org/sites/default/files/publications/ifpridp00993.pdf.

CHAPTER 6

THE POOR, MALNUTRITION, BIOFORTIFICATION, AND BIOTECHNOLOGY

ALEXANDER J. STEIN

Introduction

This chapter deals with agricultural approaches that are aimed at improving the nutritional status—and ultimately the health—of the poor in developing countries. Conventionally, nutrition problems in poor countries are first and foremost equated with outright hunger, meaning an insufficient consumption of dietary energy (see FAO 2010). Correspondingly, the discussion about how to solve the world food problem primarily revolves around the question of whether hunger is a (technical) problem of food production or a (social) problem of food distribution. This is an especially important question because agricultural biotechnology is being used for crop improvement (Chrispeels 2000). However, while the fact that there are about one billion hungry people in the world is an issue of serious concern, there is another nutrition problem that often goes unnoticed; namely, micronutrient malnutrition, which is also aptly dubbed "hidden hunger" (Kristof 2009; Hidden Hunger 2011; Micronutrient Initiative 2011a).

While undernourishment due to insufficient energy intakes is directly felt by those suffering from hunger, and is also easily recognized by others because it causes wasting and stunting, a lack of micronutrients in people's diets has less directly perceptible but nevertheless potentially serious consequences for the health and well-being of the affected individuals. Micronutrient deficiencies can cause, inter alia, lack of stamina, impaired physical and cognitive development, morbidity, blindness and—via increased susceptibility to infectious diseases—premature death.

Even if insufficient dietary intakes are recognized as the main cause of micronutrient deficiencies—that is, even if "hidden hunger" is identified as being a food-based problem—micronutrient deficiencies are nevertheless often regarded primarily as health problems. Indicative of this view is that the World Health Organization has a dedicated section on micronutrient deficiencies on its website (WHO 2011f). In this context, the most common approaches to control vitamin and mineral deficiencies are fortification or supplementation (e.g., WHO 2011f; UNICEF 2011; Micronutrient Initiative 2011b; GAIN 2011). In addition to these interventions, and as micronutrient malnutrition persists, a complementary approach has emerged: breeding staple food crops for higher micronutrient content. Given that micronutrient deficiencies are essentially a food-based problem, the idea of adding to people's food what is lacking in their diets is not new; this is already being done through fortification. However, using plants to fortify themselves with micronutrients had not been pursued as a coherent strategy to tackle vitamin and mineral deficiencies on a broader front until the late 1990s, when, inter alia, the "Micronutrients Project" of the Consultative Group on International Agricultural Research was initiated (Bouis et al. 2000).[1] Only a little later the term "biofortification" was coined to describe micronutrient fortification of plants through breeding approaches (CGIAR 2002), and the concept was introduced in the literature (e.g., Bouis et al. 2000; Welch and Graham 2000; Bouis 2002). Moreover, given that one of the first biofortified crops—Golden Rice—reached the headlines because it was genetically engineered (see Nash 2000), and given the political and social controversies surrounding this technology, it is pertinent to have a more detailed look at biofortification and how and where this concept overlaps with genetically modified crops.

Micronutrient Malnutrition

Each year the Food and Agriculture Organization of the United Nations publishes its estimates of the number of undernourished people in the world, which over the last forty years oscillated around 900 million people (FAO 2010). Over the same period the world population was continuously increasing, which means that the share of hungry people has fallen over the last four decades. Even so, about one in seven people still suffer from a lack of food, so that fighting hunger continues to be a challenge for humanity. On the other hand, the World Health Organization estimates that, worldwide, 1.5 billion people are overweight (WHO 2011g). Increasingly, these two forms of malnutrition, underweight and overweight, are occurring simultaneously within the same societies or even within the same households (Gillespie and Haddad 2003; FAO 2006).

Adding to this, estimates indicate that 2 billion people worldwide are anemic, many due to iron deficiency (WHO 2011c). A further 2 billion people likely have insufficient iodine intakes (de Benoist et al. 2008), and a similar number (1.2 to 2 billion people) are affected by zinc deficiency (Hotz and Brown 2004; WHO 2002). Moreover, at least half a billion people are estimated to suffer from selenium deficiency (Combs 2001), and an estimated 250 million preschool children alone are vitamin A deficient, with a substantial proportion of pregnant women in at-risk areas equally being suspected of suffering from vitamin A deficiency (WHO 2011d). For calcium, vitamin D, the B vitamins, and folate, low intakes can also be common (Allen et al. 2006). However, for many micronutrients, reliable prevalence data are not available, which makes substantiating the occurrence of vitamin and mineral deficiencies difficult (Borwankar et al. 2007).

Summing up these figures gives a total of at least 7 billion cases of people suffering from one form of malnutrition or another (Figure 6.1); in at least 5 billion cases this includes a micronutrient deficiency. Therefore, because not all of the entire human population is affected by malnutrition, many individuals must suffer from multiple nutrition problems. What these headcount figures do not show, though, is how severe the suffering is in each case—for instance, being iodine deficient is not necessarily comparable to being vitamin A deficient.

To address the issue of how different health outcomes can be quantified and compared, in the 1990s the World Bank and the World Health Organization introduced a summary measure for population health called "disability-adjusted life years," or DALYs (World Bank 1993; Murray and Lopez 1996). One DALY can be thought of as one "healthy" year of life that is lost due to mortality or morbidity. Each year of life lost due to premature death is counted as one DALY, and each year lived with a disease or injury is counted as a fraction of one DALY, depending on the severity of the condition.[2] The sum of DALYs across all health outcomes and across the entire population can be thought of as a measure of the overall gap between current health status and an ideal situation where everybody lives to an advanced age, free of disease and disability. This gap is also called the "burden of disease" (WHO 2011b).

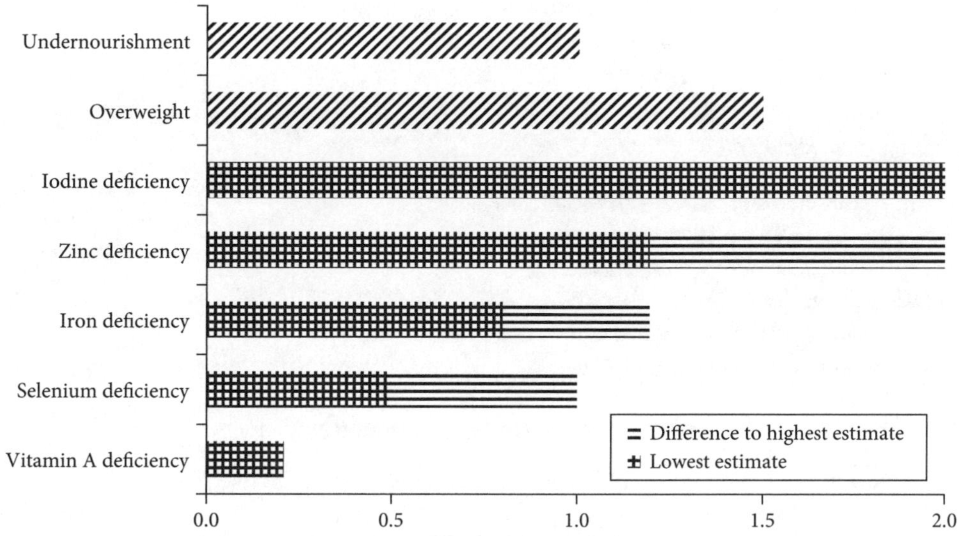

FIGURE 6.1 Billion people suffering from malnutrition worldwide.

Based on this concept, the WHO calculated the "global" burden of disease and attributed it to leading risk factors (WHO 2002). As can be seen from Figure 6.2, the biggest single risk factor contributing to the global burden of disease is underweight—almost one-tenth of the global potential for good health is lost due to this cause. However, adding up the three major micronutrient deficiencies represents the third most important risk factor. On the one hand, this shows that vitamin and mineral deficiencies are indeed a serious problem for public health, while on the other hand, it shows that not all forms of malnutrition are equally severe. For instance, many more people suffer from iodine deficiency than are undernourished, but the aggregated health consequences are more severe for underweight.

Apart from this quantification of the amount of ill health caused by micronutrient deficiencies, the economic loss these deficiencies impose on society has been estimated. In 1994 the World Bank suggested that iron, iodine, and vitamin A deficiencies could reduce the gross domestic product (GDP) in developing countries by as much as 5 percent. Subsequent estimates also placed the possible losses of GDP due to micronutrient deficiencies in different developing countries into the range of 2–4 percent (Horton and Ross 2003; Micronutrient Initiative 2004; Stein and Qaim 2007), with lower estimates still amounting to an annual loss of at least US$5 billion in China and India alone (Micronutrient Initiative 2009). On the other hand, in the long run, better nutrition can have a much larger impact; for instance, a historic analysis by Fogel (2004) shows that 30 percent of the growth of British per-capita income over the last 200 years can be attributed to improved nutrition.

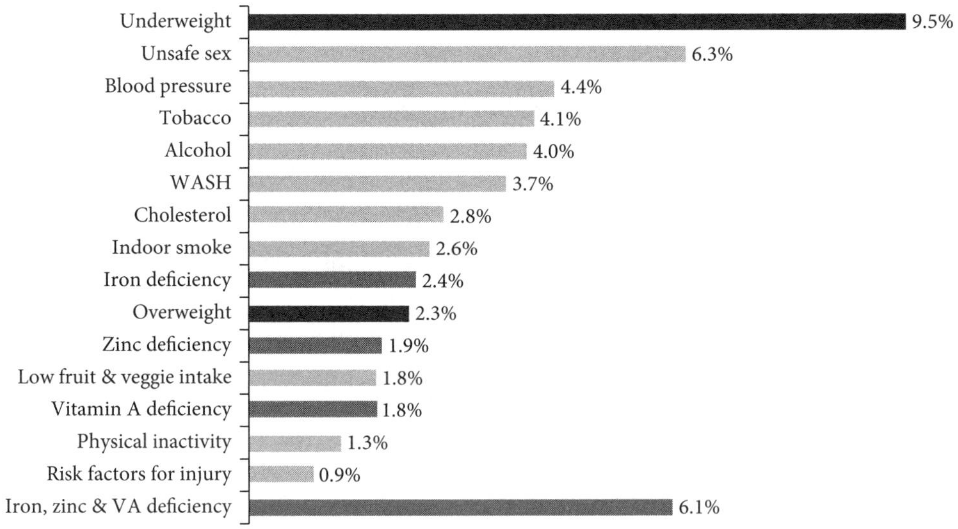

FIGURE 6.2 Global distribution of burden of disease of 15 leading risk factors.

Notes: WASH stands for "Unsafe water, sanitation & hygiene." Apart from the risk factors explicitly linked to malnutrition, "Cholesterol" and "Low fruit & vegetable intake" are also related to poor nutrition.

Source: WHO (2002).

Conventional Micronutrient Interventions

As explained in the previous section, micronutrient malnutrition is a serious nutrition problem with negative consequences for public health and overall economic growth. Consequently, different approaches have been pursued to control vitamin and mineral deficiencies. Apart from fortification or supplementation, this also includes dietary diversification and nutrition education. These are often considered preferable strategies to improve the micronutrient status of populations (Scrimshaw 2000; Müller and Krawinkel 2005; Thompson and Amoroso 2010).

Of these interventions, iodization of salt is considered to be a particular success, since the number of iodine-deficient countries has been reduced by almost half since 2000 (Micronutrient Initiative 2009; WHO 2011e; Speeckaert et al. 2011). In addition vitamin A supplementation has seen progress since the early 2000s (UNICEF 2007; Micronutrient Initiative 2009; Hellen Keller International 2011). Other major interventions are iron fortification and iron supplementation programs, and more recently the use of zinc supplements as part of diarrhea management (ILSI 1998; WHO 2001; Micronutrient Initiative 2009). Yet, not least because of poor health infrastructure, dispersed processing of foodstuffs that could otherwise be used for fortification, and limited financial resources, these strategies do not necessarily reach vulnerable populations to a sufficient extent (e.g. Hagenimana and Low 2000; Müller and Krawinkel 2005; Horton et al. 2011). Even for vitamin A supplementation, experience has shown that too many barriers exist to make this intervention the primary approach for achieving high coverage (Micronutrient Initiative 2009). On the other hand, dietary diversification efforts are deemed relatively expensive and difficult to sustain on a large scale (e.g. Unnevehr et al. 2007).

In other words, these measures are implemented with varying success and face hurdles such as low consumption of processed foodstuffs; difficulties with the supply, distribution, or acceptance of supplements; the need for behavior change; hidden opportunity costs for the beneficiaries; and a limited reach of projects. Moreover, most projects cause recurrent annual costs that are difficult to meet regularly for developing countries. Micronutrient interventions are nevertheless considered to be very cost-effective measures compared to other public health interventions, with supplementation and fortification costing around US$10–$100 per DALY saved (Fiedler et al. 2008; Micronutrient Initiative 2009; Meenakshi et al. 2010; Copenhagen Consensus 2011).

Rationale for Biofortifying Crops

Over the last years, biofortification has been added as a micronutrient intervention that should be considered by decision makers. While initially only referring to breeding for higher micronutrient concentrations, the term "biofortification" has been extended to encompass mineral fertilization of crops to increase their micronutrient content (e.g., White and Broadley 2009). In this case the crops are not bred to accumulate more micronutrients, but rather mineral fertilizer is applied to mineral-deficient soils to increase the availability of essential minerals to the crops. Other approaches that are sometimes also subsumed under "biofortification" include the improvement of the nutrient profiles of crops in general, such as quality-protein maize, crops with higher levels of omega-3 fatty acids, or a modified composition of starch or dietary fibers (Pray et al. 2007; de Groote et al. 2010; Nuss and Tanumihardjo 2011; Zhao and Shewry 2011).

Therefore, "biofortification" could be more widely understood as "the process of adding nutritional value to a crop" (Montagnac et al. 2009); this is in contrast to "fortification," where nutritional value is added to a processed food product. To differentiate the breeding approaches from the fertilizer approach, sometimes these concepts are referred to as *genetic* and *agronomic* biofortification, respectively (e.g., Cakmak 2008). In this chapter the main focus is on biofortification through plant breeding, which can be further differentiated into conventional breeding and the use of genetic engineering. While the rationale to do biofortification is the same in both cases, regulatory requirements and acceptance can be different for these two approaches, which will be discussed in more detail throughout this chapter.

Biofortification builds on the regular consumption of important amounts of a crop by all members of the respective target groups. For this reason biofortification is usually done with staple crops. Given that the poor often consume large quantities of these crops (but little else), and that it is primarily the poor who are malnourished, biofortification is also self-targeting. Moreover, in contrast to the other micronutrient interventions that are linked to (centralized) food processing facilities, health centers, or extension services, biofortification can take place on the farmers' fields; that is, biofortification can help reach the malnourished in remote rural areas. As these people usually have less access to other programs, biofortification complements these approaches (Nestel et al. 2006; Tanumihardjo et al. 2008; Mayer et al. 2008; Meenakshi et al. 2010; Bouis et al. 2011). Biofortification efforts are explicitly targeted at regions where at-risk populations live, also taking into account the major crops already grown and consumed in these areas. To this end, methods are developed to help set the regional focus of biofortification interventions by using spatial data on the risk of nutrient deficiency and on crop production, as well as socioeconomic and food consumption data (Zapata-Caldas et al. 2009; Rose et al. 2009).

Apart from this complementary focus of biofortification, another argument in favor of this approach is its expected sustainability. Other micronutrient programs impose recurrent costs at the individual or national level. With commercial fortification, consumers may decide to buy cheaper unfortified products when they come under economic hardship; in the case of mandatory fortification, food producers have an incentive to reduce the fortificant in their products; and supplementation programs are vulnerable to changing funding priorities of governments or donors. Once developed and disseminated, biofortified crops are not subject to such vagaries; rather, they can be grown and consumed year after year and provide a continuous benefit stream (Nestel et al. 2006; Pinstrup-Andersen 2006; Mayer et al. 2008; Bouis et al. 2011). Moreover, the germplasm of biofortified crops can be shared between countries to incorporate it into locally adapted varieties. Thus, after a largely one-time investment in the development of biofortified crops, their benefits can not only spread across time, they can also extend over space. The exploitation of such economies of scale can make genetic biofortification a very cost-effective intervention (Nestel et al. 2006; Tanumihardjo et al. 2008; Qaim 2009; Bouis et al. 2011). Biofortification can also be more economic for very practical reasons. For instance, breeding micronutrients into rice is less expensive than fortifying rice grains industrially (Horton 2006). A reason advanced for agronomic biofortification is the shorter time span needed to implement fertilizer programs (Broadley et al. 2006; Cakmak 2009).

While biofortified crops are developed to provide nutrition benefits for the poor, they may also offer agronomic benefits, since minerals help plants resist diseases and other stress factors. Consequently, at least on mineral-deficient soils, biofortified crops can even contribute to higher yields (Nestel et al. 2006; Pfeiffer and McClafferty 2007; Khoshgoftarmanesh et al. 2010). This is a crucial point because yields—and agronomic traits in general, such as drought tolerance, pest resistance, or ease of propagation—are important for the adoption of biofortified crops through farmers. Their preferences are specifically taken into account when farmers are, for example, given the possibility to test and select biofortified varieties during crop trials (Tanumihardjo 2010). Other factors that influence the adoption of biofortified crops by the farmers are seed prices, availability of appropriate varieties, and their marketability.[3]

Marketability requires the existence of markets as well as acceptance of the crops by consumers (whereby farmers themselves are also consumers). Mineral biofortification through conventional breeding represents an "invisible" trait that neither requires consumers to change their behavior nor induces sensory changes, so it is unlikely to cause acceptance problems. However, biofortification with carotenes may result in changes in crop color, taste, or dry matter content. In these cases, consumer acceptance hinges on consumers' awareness of the nutritional properties of the crops and on the degree to which they are affected by micronutrient deficiencies; that is, it depends on consumers' awareness of the benefits the crops have for themselves and their families.[4]

Feasibility of Biofortifying Crops

Targeting, economic feasibility, adoption by farmers, and consumer acceptance are all necessary conditions for the success of biofortification. However, the idea of putting more micronutrients into crops and improving the nutrition status of the beneficiaries also needs to work in reality (Bouis and Welch 2010; Bouis et al. 2011). For different micronutrients and various crops, studies have confirmed that biofortification is possible in principle: micronutrient-dense varieties can be bred, the micronutrient density remains stable across several plant generations and in different environments, fertilization can increase mineral accumulation in the crops, and increasing the micronutrient content in plants does not reduce yields.[5]

In the case of genetic biofortification, relying exclusively on conventional breeding is not always expedient. Some traits—like the accumulation of provitamin A in the endosperm of rice—cannot be achieved through conventional breeding; if desired traits are not present in any variety of the crop, cross-breeding is out of the question. Hence, in many cases, biofortification requires the use of genetic engineering. Using more advanced breeding technologies also facilitates the stacking of different traits in one plant, and it can speed up the overall development process.

For plant breeders and crop scientists, using the full array of breeding approaches is a matter of course, but genetically modified organisms have generated much discussion in the field of politics and society (e.g., Herring 2008). This debate will be covered in a subsequent section, but addressing micronutrient malnutrition is one of the fields where potential benefits of genetically engineered crops can unfold.[6]

The main crops and micronutrients that are targeted in biofortification research have been identified in a review of the literature on biofortification by Stein and Qaim (2009). They found that by far the most frequently named crop is rice, followed by maize and wheat, and then pulses, vegetables and fruits, cassava, sweet potato, sorghum, and model plants. Among the micronutrients, it is iron, vitamin A (including carotenes), and zinc that are referred to most often, followed by selenium, folic acid, calcium, iodine, magnesium, and copper.

For many of these crop-micronutrient combinations, promising results regarding their potential impact on people's nutrition status are reported, based on models, animal trials, or even studies with human subjects.[7] Moreover, first sensory analyses have shown that biofortification is possible without introducing a detectable difference in flavor or consistency (Park et al. 2009).

Impact and Cost-Effectiveness of Biofortification

So far the only biofortified crops that have been introduced on a larger scale are orange-fleshed sweet potatoes (OFSP) in sub-Saharan Africa (Low et al. 2007a, 2007b). However, for a number of other crops, ex ante impact assessments and cost-effectiveness analyses have been carried out.[8] These studies have shown that in many cases genetic biofortification promises to be a very cost-effective public health intervention, thus representing a sensible investment of the limited resources that are available for research into agriculture, nutrition, and public health in developing countries. To the author's best knowledge, no such studies have been done yet for biofortification through fertilization.

Most of these studies build on the DALY framework previously described, and more specifically on Stein et al. (2005), who adapted the methodology for the evaluation of iron, zinc, and vitamin A deficiencies. In short, the procedure is the following: First the burden of a deficiency in a given region is quantified and expressed in the number of DALYs lost, then the consumption of a biofortified crop is simulated (which leads to higher micronutrient intakes). Based on the new (higher) micronutrient intakes, the new (lower) prevalence of the deficiency is derived and used to calculate its new (lower) burden. The difference between the old and new burden, which is expressed in the number of DALYs that can be saved, represents the potential impact of the biofortified crop.

This step of the analyses demonstrates the potential effectiveness of the biofortified crops, which is a necessary condition for a positive evaluation. However, in a world of scarcity, costs also matter, so that superior cost-effectiveness is a sufficient condition. As the World Bank (1993, 61) explains, "Because interventions can differ so much in cost-effectiveness, making allocative decisions badly in either the public or the private sector costs lives.... Insisting on value for money is not only fully consistent with compassion for the victims of disease, it is the only way to avert needless suffering." Similarly, the World Health Organization confirms that "making best use of resources is vital in developing countries that are struggling to improve public health with limited funds" (Evans et al. 2005, 1133).

To determine the cost-effectiveness of a biofortified crop, its potential impact (measured in DALYs) is divided by the costs that need to be incurred for its development, dissemination, and use. Where appropriate, these costs are shared among several beneficiary regions. The metric that is thus generated is "Dollars per DALY," which indicates how much it would cost to save one "healthy" life year (DALY) if the given biofortified crop was consumed by the target population. Obviously, the less it costs to save one DALY, the more cost-effective the intervention, and with a given budget more DALYs can be saved. Moreover, because DALYs are not only used for the evaluation of micronutrient malnutrition but for a wide range of negative health outcomes (Figure 6.2), the results for biofortification can be compared with those for other interventions—to rank and prioritize different programs, for example.

An overview of the biofortification results from the different evaluations is given in Table 6.1. What can be seen is that results can vary by an order of magnitude between studies; across crops, micronutrients, and countries; and even between different scenarios within a study. One explanation is that these studies are ex ante analyses that rely on different data and assumptions (Figure 6.3) and are carried out at different levels of aggregation. In particular, the prevalence of the micronutrient deficiency, the size of the target population, the importance of the crop in their diet, the success of biofortification in terms of additional micronutrient content that can be bred into a crop, the expected coverage of the crop, and the current intake gap of the micronutrient all determine the ultimate success of biofortification. Consequently, the less that is known about these parameters, the wider the range of possible results. Filling such knowledge gaps and refining the parameters is part of the ongoing scientific and policy process. Moreover, such diverging results are not limited to analyses of biofortification. In a review of the

Table 6.1 Impact and cost-effectiveness of biofortified crops

	Reduction of burden of disease		Cost per DALY saved	
	Optimistic	Pessimistic	Optimistic	Pessimistic
Iron biofortification				
Wheat				
India[a]	39%	7%	$1	$10
India[b]	26%	7%	<$1	$9
Pakistan[a]	28%	6%	$3	$13
Rice				
India[a]	15%	5%	$3	$17
India[b]	38%	12%	<$1	$4
Bangladesh[a]	21%	8%	$5	$18
Philippines[a]	11%	4%	$55	$234
NE Brazil[e]	76%	39%	$2	$10
Beans				
NE Brazil[a]	36%	9%	$20	$134
NE Brazil[e]	99%	93%	$2	$3
Honduras[a]	22%	4%	$66	$402
Nicaragua[a]	16%	3%	$65	$439
Zinc biofortification				
Wheat				
India[a]	48%	9%	$1	$11
India[c]	12%	2%	$2	$39
Pakistan[a]	33%	5%	$2	$18
Rice				
India[a]	56%	20%	$1	$6
India[c]	41%	18%	<$1	$4
Bangladesh[a]	33%	17%	$2	$7
Philippines[a]	43%	13%	$12	$55
Honduras[e]	19%	10%	$35	$165
Nicaragua[e]	20%	10%	$73	$337
Beans				
NE Brazil[a]	20%	5%	$153	$1900

(Continued)

Table 6.1 Continued

	Reduction of burden of disease		Cost per DALY saved	
	Optimistic	Pessimistic	Optimistic	Pessimistic
Honduras[a]	15%	3%	$160	$1494
Honduras[e]	17%	13%	$46	$81
Nicaragua[a]	11%	2%	$576	$5940
Nicaragua[e]	14%	11%	$116	$225
Maize				
Honduras[e]	17%	2%	$32	$835
Nicaragua[e]	22%	6%	$55	$604
Provitamin A biofortification				
Rice				
India[d]	59%	9%	$3	$19
Philippines[f]	32%	6%	$18	$102
Bangladesh[g]	30%		$25	
Sweet potato				
Uganda[a]	64%	38%	$9	$30
Uganda[g]	38%		$2	
Cassava				
DR Congo[a]	32%	3%	$8	$124
Nigeria[a]	28%	3%	$8	$137
NE Brazil[a]	19%	4%	$127	$1006
Haitie	33%	8%	$10	$87
Maize				
Kenya[a]	32%	8%	$18	$113
Ethiopia[a]	17%	1%	$11	$289
Mexico[e]	81%	<1%	$18	$1408

Sources: [a]Meenakshi et al. (2010),
[b] Stein, Meenakshi, et al. (2008),
[c] Stein et al. (2007),
[d] Stein, Sachdev, and Qaim (2008),
[e] Stein (2010),
[f] Zimmermann and Qaim (2004),
[g] Sandler (2005).
Notes: NE = northeast, DR = Democratic Republic.

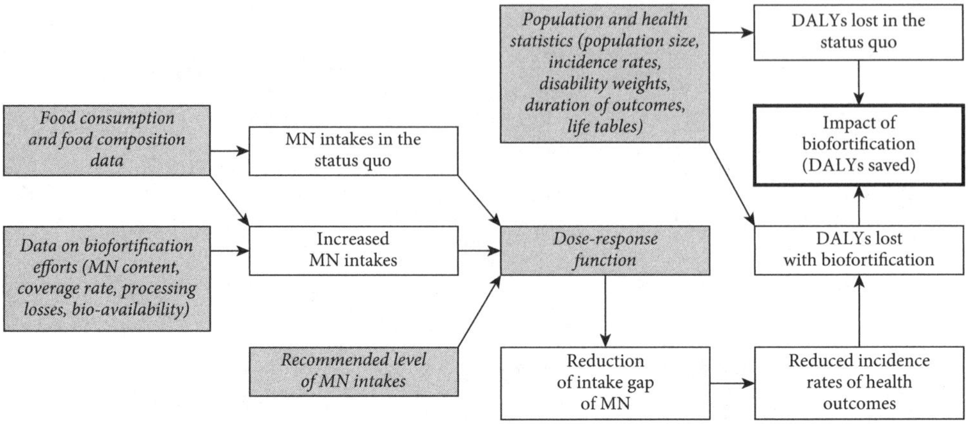

FIGURE 6.3 Parameters entering the DALY calculation for micronutrient deficiencies.

Notes: Gray shaded boxes with text in italics indicate where (potentially different) data or assumptions enter the DALYs calculation; MN = micronutrient.

Source: Stein (2006) and Meenakshi et al. (2010).

literature on general micronutrient interventions, Fiedler et al. (2008, 373) found "enormous variation in the estimated costs of these programs due to differences in program structure, delivery systems and a host of country-specific factors, differences in the studies' objectives, designs and costing methodologies."

Although sensitivity analyses in many of the biofortification case studies show that results are fairly robust to smaller variations of key parameters, what affects the success of biofortification most is the reach of the biofortified crops. This is probably intuitive: biofortification can have the biggest impact when the crops are consumed in greater quantities by deficient populations in many countries (or in countries with big populations like India or Brazil). In such cases, economies of scale can be exploited, making biofortification a cost-effective intervention. This is not to say that biofortified crops cannot also benefit smaller groups of beneficiaries who suffer from micronutrient malnutrition, but to offset the breeding and dissemination costs—and thus to make biofortification an economically viable intervention—achieving maximum coverage is paramount.

This points to several implications. First, only biofortification of crops that are eaten by a large number of deficient people is likely to be cost-effective, so that knowing the dietary patterns of the malnourished in target regions is important before biofortification efforts are started. Second, once elite lines with micronutrient-rich traits are developed, the germplasm should be disseminated widely across countries to facilitate further development and adaptive breeding into popular existing and promising new varieties. Finally, once biofortified varieties are adapted and introduced, their large-scale dissemination at national levels should be a top priority.

Where there are potential acceptance issues (e.g., because of a more intensive color of the crops due to a higher carotene content, or because the crops were developed through genetic engineering), dissemination efforts may require additional campaigns to increase consumer awareness and trust. For instance, in the projection of the cost-effectiveness of Golden Rice in India, in the high-impact scenario the costs for dissemination activities were assumed to be twice as high as those in the low-impact scenario. This reflected more costly dissemination efforts that were assumed to lead to higher coverage rates and ultimately to a much larger impact, thereby easily compensating the additional costs (Stein, Sachdev, and Qaim 2008). In this context it also becomes clear that political backing and the support of opinion leaders is crucial for the success of such crops. Especially when biofortification is done through genetic engineering, this may require supportive communication activities (see below).

In summary, what all studies show is that appropriately chosen target crops that reach a sufficient number of beneficiaries can have a substantial positive impact on micronutrient deficiencies and considerably reduce their burden of disease in the target countries. In general, biofortification promises to be a very cost-effective micronutrient intervention that in most cases is more efficient than other measures; in the other cases its cost-effectiveness is in about the same range as alternative interventions. What the studies discussed here have not considered, though, is the current impact of alternative interventions. Calculating the impact of biofortified crops in the presence of other micronutrient interventions may indicate only limited benefits, whereas the introduction of biofortified crops may in fact allow scaling back more costly programs.

Another approach to quantifying the potential impact of biofortification was taken by Anderson and colleagues) and (see Anderson 2010; Anderson and Jackson 2005; Anderson, Jackson, and Nielsen 2005), who used a global economic model to simulate the benefits of Golden Rice at a more aggregated level by assuming a productivity increase of unskilled labor of 0.5 percent. According to their calculations, Golden Rice could add the equivalent of over US$3 billion per year to the welfare of developing countries. Assuming the consumption of biofortified rice and wheat in sub-Saharan Africa and a related increase in the productivity of unskilled labor of 2 percent, they even project annual welfare gains of over US$3.5 billion.

Biofortification Programs

As noted above, so far the only biofortified crops that have been introduced on a larger scale are OFSP in sub-Saharan Africa, with cassava and maize rich in carotenes as well as high-iron pearl millet beans being set for release in 2012 in Nigeria, Zambia, India,and Rwanda (HarvestPlus 2011b, 2011c). All crops were developed in the context of the HarvestPlus Challenge Program of the Consultative Group for International Agricultural Research (HarvestPlus 2011a, 2011b). HarvestPlus has identified seven crops that are consumed by the poor and malnourished in Asia and Africa, namely beans, cassava, maize, pearl millet, rice, sweet potato, and wheat. These crops are bred for higher levels of iron, zinc, and provitamin A. In its biofortification efforts, HarvestPlus relies, for most of the work, on traditional plant breeding, mainly for reasons of consumer acceptance and to avoid regulatory problems (see next section); the work in Latin America is carried out in collaboration with AgroSalud (2011).

Another group of projects is funded by the Grand Challenges in Global Health program of the Bill & Melinda Gates Foundation. These projects rely on genetic engineering, not least because for some crop-micronutrient combinations, biofortification is not possible otherwise (see Bill & Melinda Gates Foundation 2011a, 2011b). The crops targeted in these projects are rice, cassava, sorghum, and bananas, which are bred for higher contents of iron, zinc, provitamin A, and vitamin E, but also protein. These projects are the Golden Rice Project (Golden Rice Project 2011, IRRI 2011a), the BioCassava Plus Project (Sayre et al. 2011, BioCassava 2011), the Africa Biofortified Sorghum Project (ABS 2010) and the Better Bananas for Africa Project (QUT 2011). It is foreseen that Golden Rice will be released to farmers for the first time in 2013 in the Philippines (IRRI 2011a). The BioCassava Plus Project received funding for its second Phase in April 2011 and will not be available to farmers before 2016 (BioCassava 2011); the other Grand Challenges crops are further away from dissemination.

In addition to these bigger projects there is also the INSTAPA (2011) project, which focuses, inter alia, on the potential of biofortified millet, sorghum, maize, and cassava in complementary food for young children in sub-Saharan Africa to prevent deficiencies of iron, zinc, and vitamin A. There are also two smaller projects on biofortification of cereals through fertilization (with zinc, selenium, and calcium) at the University of Nottingham and Sabanci University in Istanbul (Bagels 2008; HarvestZinc 2011).

Political Controversies

So far in this chapter, biofortified crops were differentiated into conventionally bred and genetically engineered ones. This was for a reason: While plant breeders tend to view genetic engineering and other approaches of modern biotechnology simply as one tool in their toolbox, and while the scientific consensus is that genetic engineering per se is not more risky than conventional breeding, in parts of society genetic engineering is much more of a controversial issue (e.g., *Economist* 2011; *New York Times* 2011; *Guardian* 2011).[9]

To what extent genetically modified (GM) crops are indeed a matter of concern for the greater public is not fully established, since consumer surveys are relatively scarce, and because they are methodologically so diverse as to preclude generalizations (Smale et al. 2009). In developed countries, consumer acceptance studies indicate that consumers have a greater willingness to pay for food products that are free of GM crops, but results vary between countries, consumers, their knowledge about genetic engineering, and the type of food or the GM crop (Qaim 2009). Yet, even in Europe, where acceptance of GM crops is usually considered to be low, only 8 percent of the respondents in the European Commission's "Eurobarometer" survey stated that they would be concerned about GM foods when asked an open question about food-related risks (European Commission

2010). Probing the real-life behavior of UK tourists to North America (where "GM food" is ubiquitous) showed that only 15 percent of respondents made attempts to avoid GM food (Moses 2008).

Still, even if large parts of society are probably indifferent about GM crops, there are vociferous opponents whose opinions are often given a disproportionate reception in the general media (e.g., Sample 2011; BBC 2011; Reville 2011). Generally, opposition to genetic engineering can be traced back to three broad groups of reasons: "risks," "social aspects," and "metaphysics" (Dürnberger 2011). Potential risks of new GM crops for human health or the environment are routinely assessed in the authorization process before the crops are commercialized. Hence using such alleged risks as justification for opposing safety-assessed and approved GM crops is more likely a sign of a deeper distrust of science or of government institutions and regulatory and political processes in general.

Often opposition to GM crops is also based on socioeconomic arguments regarding the alleged market power of agri-biotech companies, the patenting of GM crops, a feared control of the food chain through private corporations, or an expected structural change in rural areas due to technological change. Hence these arguments rather reflect political attitudes critical of market systems, "globalization," or technical progress, and GM crops are simply targeted as a convenient proxy. This view may also explain the inconsistencies in some arguments. For instance, conventional crops can also be patented, the market power of agri-biotech companies is probably much more limited than that of other players in the food chain (e.g., GM potatoes were taken off the market in the United States due to pressure from the downstream food industry), and GM crops are not exclusive to the private sector and industrial agriculture, since they can—and indeed are—also developed by public or humanitarian entities for use by small-scale farmers.

Finally, GM crops are also opposed because of metaphysical considerations, including respect for "nature." If these considerations take the form of categorical arguments, they generally preclude any compromise on the issue. For instance, if genetic engineering is seen as a violation of the sacredness of nature, potential benefits of GM crops can hardly compensate for what is perceived to be a fundamental mistake. Nevertheless, to be accepted as sensible arguments, these reasons need to be validated for consistency and rationality. This can be done by analyzing whether the arguments are also used to oppose biotechnology if used for other purposes, or if other technologies are opposed if used for the same purposes (Dürnberger 2011). In the case of GM crops, for instance, such metaphysical arguments are rarely used to oppose the application of modern biotechnology in the field of pharmaceutics and diagnostics, and neither are other breeding technologies opposed that are used to develop crops with novel traits. Hence, given this inconsistency, it is questionable whether such arguments are used out of genuine opposition to GM crops, or, again, whether they simply exploit GM crops to score points in a larger debate.

In this context biofortification has also come under fire, irrespective of any potential benefits it may bring, simply because—via Golden Rice—it can be linked to genetic engineering.[10] Most commonly Golden Rice is simply disparaged as a "Trojan horse" of the biotech lobby (Potrykus 2001), suggesting that the latter wants to use the social appeal of this project to make GM crops in general more acceptable. This ignores the fact that Golden Rice was conceived by public scientists and funded as a humanitarian project (Toenniessen 2009).

To further rationalize a rejection of Golden Rice, its effectiveness is often challenged by alleging that an impossible amount of rice would have to be consumed to prevent vitamin A deficiency. (Or the reverse, that too much vitamin A could be consumed and have a toxic effect.) Indeed, the first line of Golden Rice contained only limited amounts of carotene (provitamin A), but it merely represented a proof-of-concept study that showed that rice can be engineered to express carotenes in the endosperm (Enserink 2008). And while using data from such early R&D stages to discard a technology may be disingenuous in the first place, since peer-reviewed studies showed early on that even small amounts of carotene could have a beneficial effect and make Golden Rice an economic intervention (Zimmermann and Qaim 2004). Stein (2006) showed more explicitly that the activists' calculations were biased and unfounded. Moreover, subsequent research succeeded in increasing the levels of carotene in Golden Rice (Paine et al. 2005), and new, more detailed calculations confirmed the potential impact and cost-effectiveness of Golden Rice (Stein, Sachdev, and Qaim 2006). Over time new research also answered other questions, including those regarding the bioavailability of the carotenes in Golden Rice (Tang et al. 2009).

Further, detractors also claim that farmers will have to pay royalties on the seeds or cannot save them for resowing. Yet, also in this case, the issue had been solved early on, paving the way for the humanitarian use of Golden Rice and its dissemination to farmers in developing countries free of added charges (Potrykus 2001). Finally, the need for a new micronutrient intervention is often questioned by maintaining that current interventions can address micronutrient deficiencies. As discussed above, biofortification had been developed exactly to counter the shortcomings and weaknesses of existing interventions in eradicating micronutrient malnutrition.

As in the wider discussion of GM crops, in the case of Golden Rice it also seems that many opponents are not concerned with factual information or the validity and consistency of their arguments but, in opposing Golden Rice, rather follow another, wider agenda (Potrykus 2001). This is not to say that all conditions for the distribution of Golden Rice to farmers have already been fulfilled—not least, the food safety and biosafety of Golden Rice still need to be formally established, which is fully acknowledged by the developers (IRRI 2011b). Steps like the final safety assessment of a new product prior to its commercialization form part of any product development. Criticizing the lack of such an assessment while the rice is still in the R&D phase is not sincere.

Another facet of the controversy surrounding GM crops is that current regulations for their approval have become so demanding that only the biggest companies have the know-how and the financial standing to carry out the safety tests and compile the required dossiers—and that even for them doing so only pays off for major commercial crops. This clearly hampers the commercialization of humanitarian or other minor GM crops (Enserink 2008; Miller and Bradford 2010). Likewise, the time needed for these processes has led to delays in advancing the development of Golden Rice and other GM crops with product quality traits (Enserink 2008; Graff et al. 2009a; Potrykus 2010a, 2010b). This created a self-defeating situation: opponents of Golden Rice criticize that so far little has come out of the research, while, not least due to their opposition to GM crops, research on GM crops can only advance slowly.

In this context a main criticism of current regulation is the inconsistency with which GM crops are treated vis-à-vis crops produced through other breeding methods (Enserink 2008; Potrykus 2010a, 2010b; Fedoroff 2011). Whether this unequal treatment is likely to change any time soon is questionable, given that analyses of the underlying political economy indicate that "the sum of all interests involved ensures that subsistence farmers are systematically denied access to agricultural biotechnology" (Apel 2010, 635). For various reasons many stakeholders—whether the agri-biotech industry, agrochemical companies, the organic food industry, EU farmers, activist groups, Western consumers, or politicians in both developed and developing countries—have a self-interest in maintaining a strict regulatory framework even if the easier development of more and new GM crops would increase global welfare (Graff et al. 2009b).

Conclusions

Next to outright hunger and overweight, micronutrient deficiencies represent a third aspect of the global malnutrition problem. The lack of essential vitamins and minerals in people's diets may be less apparent at first sight, which is why it is also called "hidden hunger," but it is one of the leading contributors to the global burden of disease. While micronutrient malnutrition has been recognized as a public health problem, and interventions such as supplementation or fortification are being implemented with varying success in developing countries, progress has nevertheless been limited.

In this context a new approach has been developed that aims at complementing these existing interventions: staple crops are bred for higher contents of vitamins and minerals. This is called biofortification. The main advantage of this approach is its focus on rural areas, which are not as easily reached by conventional programs. Moreover, because these crops have to be developed only once, their widespread and continuous cultivation and consumption allows exploiting economies of scale in reaping the nutritional benefits. This makes biofortification potentially a very cost-effective intervention.

So far only very few biofortified crops have reached the stage of dissemination. Apart from orange-fleshed sweet potatoes (OFSP), their potential has not yet been confirmed in real-world settings. However, a substantial body of studies shows that increasing the micronutrient content in crops is possible, whether through breeding or agronomic approaches, and that the accumulated micronutrients have the potential to improve the micronutrient status of human subjects. Moreover, biofortifying crops does not affect relevant agronomic properties, which could reduce their acceptability to farmers. Perceptible changes to the crops, which may affect consumer acceptance, occur only when they are bred for higher carotene content, in which case the crops acquire a darker yellow or orange color. To ensure widespread acceptance of such crops, measures to raise awareness of micronutrient malnutrition and the related benefits of biofortification may be required.

Meanwhile, economic evaluations that simulated the consumption of biofortified crops have confirmed that if these crops can be targeted at large enough populations where vitamin and mineral deficiencies are prevalent, they can indeed represent very cost-effective public health interventions. However, in cases where biofortification is done through genetic engineering, the crops are bound to face resistance from activists that are opposed to the use of modern biotechnology in agriculture, even if it supports a humanitarian goal.

Notes

1. However, the idea as such, of making a plant produce an essential micronutrient, had been around at least since 1984, when the idea of developing provitamin A-rich "yellow endosperm" rice had been taken up by the Rockefeller Foundation (Toenniessen 2009), even if the actual proof of concept for such a genetically engineered "golden" rice, as it became known, could only be delivered in 2000 (Ye et al. 2000). And the idea of using plant breeding to improve the general nutrient content of staple crops has been around for decades, as evidenced by the first efforts to improve the protein content in maize in the latter part of the 19th century (Vasal 1999).
2. For each condition, "disability weights" are defined that range from close to 1 for health outcomes that limit functioning severely to weights close to 0 for outcomes that affect overall health only marginally. Multiplying the time spent with a condition with its disability weight then yields the corresponding number of DALYs that are lost.
3. For literature discussing the adoption of biofortified crops, see Hagenimana and Low (2000); Chong (2003); Mazuze (2007); Pray et al. (2007); Wolson (2007); Ortiz-Monasterio et al. (2007); and Muzhingi et al. (2008).
4. For literature discussing consumer acceptance of biofortified crops, see Nestel et al. (2006); Hagenimana and Low (2000); Low et al. (2007a); Stevens and Winter-Nelson (2008); González et al. (2009); Chowdhury et al. (2009); and De Steur et al. (2010).
5. For references to primary research supporting the possibility of biofortification, see Welch and Graham (2005); Welch et al. (2005); White and Broadley (2005); Lyons et al. (2005); Genc et al. (2005); Cichy et al. (2005); Broadley et al. (2006); Rébeillé et al. (2006); Dai et al. (2006); Ssemakula and Dixon (2007); White and Broadley (2007); Hawkesford und Zhao (2007); Shi et al. (2008); Harjes et al. (2008); Wissuwa (2008); Thavarajah et al. (2008); Cakmak (2008); Ríos et al. (2008); Jin (2008); White and Broadley (2009); Thavarajah et al. (2009); Salas et al. (2009); Cichy et al. (2009); Bóna et al. (2009); Šimić et al. (2009); Chen et al. (2009); Waters and Pedersen (2009); Khoshgoftarmanesh et al. (2009); Broadley et al. (2009a); Broadley et al. (2009b); Zhao et al. (2009); Phattarakul et al. (2009); Cakmak (2009); and Bai et al. (2011).

6. For literature discussing the role of biotechnology in biofortification, see Ye et al. (2000); Scott et al. (2000); Paine et al. (2005); Storozhenko et al. (2005); Basset et al. (2005); Stupak et al. (2006); Sautter et al. (2006); Storozhenko et al. (2007); Zhu et al. (2007); Mayer et al. (2008); Connolly (2008); Aluru et al. (2008); Bekaert et al. (2008); Naqvi et al. (2009); Wirth et al. (2009); and Hirschi (2009).
7. For references to primary research indicating an such impact, see Howe and Tanumihardjo (2006); Ariza-Nieto et al. (2006); Howe (2007); Nyhus et al. (2008); Tako et al. (2008); Denova-Gutiérrez et al. (2008); Mills et al. (2008); and Davis et al. (2008) for results from models and animal trials; see Haas et al. (2005); Low et al. (2007b); Tang et al. (2009); Rosado et al. (2009); and Wu et al. (2009) for studies with humans.
8. For such analyses, see Dawe et al. (2002); Zimmermann and Qaim (2004); Sandler (2005); Anderson and Jackson 2005; Anderson, Jackson, and Nielsen 2005); Stein (2006); Stein et al. (2006); Javelosa et al. (2006); Stein et al. (2007); Qaim et al. (2007); Ma et al. (2007); Stein, Meenakshi et al. (2008); Stein, Sachdev, and Qaim (2008); Meenakshi (2008); Anderson (2010); Meenakshi et al. (2010); Stein (2010).
9. Caveat: Given that this discussion is largely taking place outside the academic literature, this section is also more of a subjective presentation of the topic than a fully referenced review, thereby also drawing on the authors' personal experiences from years of work in the field of agricultural biotechnology. Factual information on genetic engineering can be obtained from various reviews and FAQs on GM crops or from scientific outreach websites (e.g. Lemaux 2008, 2009; WHO 2011a; Chassy and Tribe 2010; PRRI 2011; GMO Compass 2011); no links are provided to websites that disseminate nonfactual information to avoid implicit endorsement.
10. For instance, this categorical rejection of Golden Rice by some opponents became clear when the—then new and untried—executive director of Greenpeace, Kumi Naidoo, stated in an interview that he would like to have another look at the organization's position on Golden Rice to ensure that it is not passing up any new, good developments (Von Traufetter 2009). Within a day Greenpeace published a retraction in which Naidoo provided "guidance" on the interpretation of his statement, concluding that Golden Rice can never be an answer.

References

ABS (Africa Biofortified Sorghum). 2010. "The Africa Biofortified Sorghum (ABS) Project." http://biosorghum.org/abs_prj.php.

AgroSalud. 2011. "AgroSalud: The Development and Deployment of Biofortified Staple Crops to Reduce Nutrient Deficiencies and Improve Food Security in Latin America and the Caribbean." AgroSalud. Accessed August 14. http://www.agrosalud.org/.

Allen, L., B. de Benoist, O. Dary, R. Hurrell, eds. 2006. *Guidelines on Food Fortification with Micronutrients*. Geneva: World Health Organization. http://www.who.int/nutrition/publications/micronutrients/.

Aluru, M., Y. Xu, R. Guo, Z. Wang, S. Li, W. White, K. Wang, and S. Rodermel. 2008. "Generation of Transgenic Maize with Enhanced Provitamin A Content." *Journal of Experimental Botany* 59:3551–3562. http://dx.doi.org/10.1093/jxb/ern212.

Anderson, K. 2010. "Economic Impacts of Policies Affecting Crop Biotechnology and Trade." *New Biotechnology* 27:558–564. http://dx.doi.org/10.1016/j.nbt.2010.05.012.

Anderson, K,, and L.A. Jackson. 2005. "Some Implications of GM Food Technology Policies for Sub-Saharan Africa." *Journal of African Economies* 34:385–410. http://dx.doi.org/10.1093/jae/eji013.

Anderson, K., L. A. Jackson, and C. Pohl Nielsen. 2005. "Genetically Modified Rice Adoption: Implications for Welfare and Poverty Alleviation." *Journal of Economic Integration* 20:771–788. http://sejong.metapress.com/link.asp?id=4l7rnr94rktbbxq.

Apel, A. 2010. "The Costly Benefits of Opposing Agricultural Biotechnology." *New Biotechnology* 27:635–640. http://dx.doi.org/10.1016/j.nbt.2010.05.006.

Ariza-Nieto, M., M. T. Sanchez, L. I. Heller, Y. Hu, R. M. Welch, R. P. Glahn. 2006. "Cassava (*Manihot esculenta*) Has High Potential for Iron Biofortification." *FASEB Journal* 20:A624. http://www.fasebj.org/cgi/content/meeting_abstract/20/4/A624.

BAGELS (Biofortification through Agronomy and Genotypes to Elevate Levels of Selenium) Project. 2008. "Selenium, Bread and Man." Scottish Crop Research Institute, November 3. http://www.scri.ac.uk/research/epi/epihighlights/selenium.

Bai, C., R. M. Twyman, G. Farré, G. Sanahuja, P. Christou, T. Capell, and C. Zhu. 2011. "A Golden Era: Pro-Vitamin A Enhancement in Diverse Crops." *In Vitro Cellular & Developmental Biology—Plant* 47:205–221. http://dx.doi.org/10.1007/s11627-011-9363-6.

Basset, G. J. C., E. P. Quinlivan, J. F. Gregory III, and A. D. Hanson. 2005. "Folate Synthesis and Metabolism in Plants and Prospects for Biofortification." *Crop Science* 45:449–453. http://dx.doi.org/10.2135/cropsci2005.0449.

BBC (British Broadcasting Corporation). 2011. "BBC Trust Review of Impartiality and Accuracy of the BBC's Coverage of Science." London: BBC. http://www.bbc.co.uk/bbctrust/our_work/other/science_impartiality.shtml.

Bekaert, S., S. Storozhenko, P. Mehrshahi, M. J. Bennett, W. Lambert, J. F. Gregory III, K. Schubert, J. Hugenholtz, D. Van Der Straeten, and A. D. Hanson. 2008. "Folate Biofortification in Food Plants." *Trends in Plant Science* 13:28–35. http://dx.doi.org/10.1016/j.tplants.2007.11.001.

Bill & Melinda Gates Foundation. 2011a. "Challenge 9: Create a Full Range of Optimal, Bioavailable Nutrients in a Single Staple Plant Species." Grand Challenges in Global Health. Bill & Melinda Gates Foundation. Accessed August 14. http://www.grandchallenges.org/ImproveNutrition/Challenges/NutrientRichPlants/Pages/default.aspx.

Bill & Melinda Gates Foundation. 2011b. "Why the Foundation Funds Research in Crop Biotechnology." Bill & Melinda Gates Foundation. Accessed August 25. http://www.gatesfoundation.org/agriculturaldevelopment/Pages/why-we-fund-research-in-crop-biotechnology.aspx.

BioCassava. 2011. "BioCassava Plus." Accessed August 14. http://www.biocassavaplus.org/.

Bóna, L., N. Adányi, R. Farkas, E. Szanics, E. Szabó, G. Hajós, A. Pécsváradi, and E. Ács. 2009. "Variation in Crop Nutrient Accumulation: Selenium Content of Wheat and Triticale Grains." *Acta Alimentaria* 38:9–15. http://dx.doi.org/10.1556/AAlim.2008.0027.

Borwankar, R., T. Sanghvi, and R. Houston. 2007. "What Is the Extent of Vitamin and Mineral Deficiencies? Magnitude of the Problem." *Food and Nutrition Bulletin* 28:S174–S181. http://foodandnutritionbulletin.org/FNB/index.php/FNB/issue/view/138.

Bouis, H. E., R.D. Graham, and R.M. Welch. 2000. "The Consultative Group on International Agricultural Research (CGIAR) Micronutrients Project: Justification and Objectives." *Food and Nutrition Bulletin* 21:374–381. http://www.ifpri.org/sites/default/files/publications/bouis00_02.pdf.

Bouis, H. E. 2002. "Plant Breeding: A New Tool for Fighting Micronutrient Malnutrition." *Journal of Nutrition* 132:491S–494S. http://jn.nutrition.org/cgi/content/abstract/132/3/491S.

Bouis, H. E., and R. M. Welch. 2010. "Biofortification: a Sustainable Agricultural Strategy for Reducing Micronutrient Malnutrition in the Global South." *Crop Science* 50:S20–S32. http://hdl.handle.net/10113/41826.

Bouis, H.E., C. Hotz, B., McClafferty, J. V. Meenakshi, and W. H. Pfeiffer. 2011. "Biofortification: A New Tool to Reduce Micronutrient Malnutrition." *Food and Nutrition Bulletin* 32:S31–40S. http://www.ingentaconnect.com/content/nsinf/fnb/2011/00000032/A00101s1/art00005.

Broadley, M., M. Meacham, H. Bowen, J. Hammond, R. Hayden, A. Mead, G. Teakle, G. King, and P. White. 2009a. "Natural Genetic Variation in the Mineral Nutrient Composition of *Brassica oleracea*." *Comparative Biochemistry and Physiology, Part A* 146:S246. http://dx.doi.org/10.1016/j.cbpa.2007.01.573.

Broadley, M. R., J. P. Hammond, G. J. King. 2009b. "Biofortifying Brassica with Calcium (Ca) and Magnesium (Mg)." Paper presented at the International Plant Nutrition Colloquium XVI, Sacramento, August 26–30. http://repositories.cdlib.org/ipnc/xvi/1256.

Broadley, M. R., P. J. White, R. J. Bryson, M. C. Meacham, H. C. Bowen, S. E. Johnson, M. J. Hawkesford, et al. 2006. "Biofortification of UK Food Crops with Selenium." *Proceedings of the Nutrition Society* 65:169–181. http://dx.doi.org/10.1079/PNS2006490.

Cakmak, I. 2008. "Enrichment of Cereal Grains with Zinc: Agronomic or Genetic Biofortification?" *Plant and Soil* 301:1–17. http://dx.doi.org/10.1007/s11104-007-9466-3

Cakmak, I. 2009. "Enrichment of Fertilizers with Zinc: An Excellent Investment for Humanity and Crop Production in India." *Journal of Trace Elements in Medicine and Biology* 23:281–289. http://dx.doi.org/10.1016/j.jtemb.2009.05.002.

CGIAR (Consultative Group on International Agricultural Research). 2002. "Biofortified Crops for Improved Human Nutrition: a Challenge Programme Proposal." Washington, DC: CGIAR. http://www.cgiar.org/pdf/biofortification.pdf.

Chassy, B. M., and D. Tribe. 2010. "Academics Review." Accessed August 25. http://academics-review.org/reviewed-content/genetic-roulette/

Chen, J., G. Wang, and G. Lu. 2009. "Effects of Genotypes and Growing Locations on Iron and Zinc Contents in Sweetpotatoes." *Crop and Pasture Science* 60:684–690. http://dx.doi.org/10.1071/CP08291.

Chong, M. 2003. "Acceptance of Golden Rice in the Philippine 'Rice Bowl.'" *Nature Biotechnology* 21:971–972. http://dx.doi.org/10.1038/nbt0903-971.

Chowdhury, S., J. V. Meenakshi, K. Tomlins, and C. Owori. 2009. "Are Consumers in Developing Countries Willing-To-Pay More for Micronutrient-Dense Biofortified Foods? Evidence from a Field Experiment in Uganda." Paper presented at the 27th Conference of the International Association of Agricultural Economists, Beijing, August 16–22. http://purl.umn.edu/49945.

Chrispeels, M. J. 2000. "Biotechnology and the Poor." *Plant Physiology* 124:3–6. http://dx.doi.org/10.1104/pp.124.1.3

Cichy, K. A., G. V. Caldas, S. S. Snapp, and M. W. Blair. 2009. "QTL Analysis of Seed Iron, Zinc, and Phosphorus Levels in an Andean Bean Population." *Crop Science* 49:1742–1750. http://crop.scijournals.org/cgi/content/abstract/49/5/1742.

Cichy, K. A., S. Forster, K. F. Grafton, and G. L. Hosfield. 2005. "Inheritance of Seed Zinc Accumulation in Navy Bean." *Crop Science* 45:864–870. http://dx.doi.org/10.2135/cropsci2004.0104.

Combs, G. F. 2001. "Selenium in Global Food Systems." *British Journal of Nutrition* 85:517–547. http://dx.doi.org/10.1079/BJN2000280.

Connolly, E.L. 2008. "Raising the Bar for Biofortification: Enhanced Levels of Bioavailable Calcium in Carrots." *Trends in Biotechnology* 26:401–403. http://dx.doi.org/10.1016/j.tibtech.2008.04.007.

Copenhagen Consensus. 2011. "Copenhagen Consensus 2008: Outcome." Accessed July 28. http://www.copenhagenconsensus.com/projects/copenhagen-consensus-2008/outcome.

Dai, J. L., Y. G. Zhu, Y. Z. Huang, M. Zhang, and J. L. Song. 2006. "Availability of Iodide and Iodate to Spinach (*Spinacia oleracea L.*) in Relation to Total Iodine in Soil Solution." *Plant and Soil* 289:301–308. http://dx.doi.org/10.1007/s11104-006-9139-7.

Davis, C., H. Jing, J. A. Howe, T. Rocheford, and S. A. Tanumihardjo. 2008. "B-Cryptoxanthin from Supplements or Carotenoid-Enhanced Maize Maintains Liver Vitamin A in Mongolian Gerbils (*Meriones unguiculatus*) Better Than or Equal to B-Carotene Supplements." *British Journal of Nutrition* 100:786–793. http://dx.doi.org/10.1017/S0007114508944123.

Dawe, D., R. Robertson, and L. Unnevehr. 2002. "Golden Rice: What Role Could It Play in Alleviation of Vitamin A Deficiency?" *Food Policy* 27:541–560. http://dx.doi.org/10.1016/S0306-9192(02)00065-9.

de Benoist, B., E. McLean, M. Andersson, and L. Rogers. 2008. "Iodine Deficiency in 2007: Global Progress since 2003." *Food and Nutrition Bulletin* 29:195–202. http://www.who.int/vmnis/iodine/status/.

de Groote, H., N.S. Gunaratna, K. Ergano, and D. Friesen. 2010. "Extension and Adoption of Biofortified Crops: Quality Protein Maize in East Africa." Paper presented at the Third Conference of the African Association of Agricultural Economists, Cape Town, South Africa, September 19-23. http://purl.umn.edu/96429.

De Steur, H., X. Gellynck, S. Storozhenko, G. Liqun, W. Lambert, D. Van Der Straeten, and J. Viaene. 2010. "Willingness to Accept and Purchase Genetically Modified Rice with High Folate Content in Shanxi Province, China." *Appetite* 54: 118–125. http://dx.doi.org/10.1016/j.appet.2009.09.017.

Denova-Gutiérrez, E., A. García-Guerra, M. Flores-Aldana, S. Rodríguez-Ramírez, and C. Hotz. 2008. "Simulation Model of the Impact of Biofortification on the Absorption of Adequate Amounts of Zinc and Iron among Mexican Women and Preschool Children." *Food and Nutrition Bulletin* 29: 203–212. http://foodandnutritionbulletin.org/FNB/index.php/FNB/article/view/1994.

Dürnberger, C. 2011. *Konfliktwolke Grüne Gentechnik: Eine Rekonstruktion der kritischen Argumente in der Debatte um den Einsatz von Gentechnik in der Landwirtschaft*. Discussion Paper. Munich: Institut Technik-Theologie-Naturwissenschaften. http://www.ttn-institut.de/konflikt-gentechnik.

Economist. 2011. "Topic: Genetically Modified Organisms." *The Economist*. Accessed August 25. http://www.economist.com/topics/genetically-modified-organisms.

Enserink, M. 2008. "Tough Lessons from Golden Rice." *Science* 320:468–471. http://dx.doi.org/10.1126/science.320.5875.468

European Commission. 2010. *Food-Related Risks*. Special Eurobarometer 354. Brussels: European Commission. http://ec.europa.eu/public_opinion/archives/ebs/ebs_354_en.pdf.

Evans, D. B., T. Adam, T. Tan-Torres Edejer, S. S. Lim, A. Cassels, T. G. Evans. 2005. "Time to Reassess Strategies for Improving Health in Developing Countries." *British Medical Journal* 331:1133–1136. http://dx.doi.org/10.1136/bmj.331.7525.1133.

FAO (Food and Agriculture Organization of the United Nations). 2006. "The Double Burden of Malnutrition: Case Studies from Six Developing Countries." Rome: FAO. http://www.fao.org/docrep/009/a0442e/a0442e00.htm.

FAO (Food and Agriculture Organization of the United Nations). 2010. "The State of Food Insecurity in the World: Addressing Food Insecurity in Protracted Crises." Rome: FAO. http://www.fao.org/publications/sofi/.

Fedoroff, N. V. 2011. "Engineering Food for All." *New York Times*, August 18. http://www.nytimes.com/2011/08/19/opinion/genetically-engineered-food-for-all.html.

Fiedler, J. L., T. G. Sanghvi, and M. K. Saunders. 2008. "A Review of the Micronutrient Intervention Cost Literature: Program Design and Policy Lessons." *International Journal of Health Planning and Management* 23: 373–397. http://dx.doi.org/10.1002/hpm.928.

Fogel, R.W. 2004. *The Escape from Hunger and Premature Death, 1700–2100: Europe, America, and the Third World*. Cambridge: Cambridge University Press. http://www.cambridge.org/us/catalogue/catalogue.asp?isbn=9780511206979.

Global Alliance for Improved Nutrition. 2011. "GAIN's Nutrition Program." Accessed June 21. http://www.gainhealth.org/programs.

GMO Compass. 2011. "Agri-Biotechnology." GMO Compass. Accessed August 25. http://www.gmo-compass.org/eng/agri_biotechnology/breeding_aims/

Genc, Y., J. M. Humphries, G. H. Lyons, and R. D. Graham. 2005. "Exploiting Genotypic Variation in Plant Nutrient Accumulation to Alleviate Micronutrient Deficiency in Populations." *Journal of Trace Elements in Medicine and Biology* 18:319–324. http://dx.doi.org/10.1016/j.jtemb.2005.02.005.

Gillespie, S., and L. J. Haddad. 2003. *The Double Burden of Malnutrition in Asia: Causes, Consequences, and Solutions*. New Delhi: SAGE. http://www.uk.sagepub.com/books/Book226117

Golden Rice Project. 2011. "Golden Rice Is Part of the Solution." Accessed August 14. http://www.goldenrice.org/.

González, C., N. Johnson, M. Qaim. 2009. "Consumer Acceptance of Second-Generation GM Foods: The Case of Biofortified Cassava in the North-East of Brazil." *Journal of Agricultural Economics* 60:604–624. http://dx.doi.org/10.1111/j.1477-9552.2009.00219.x.

Graff, G. D., D. Zilberman, and A. B. Bennett. 2009a. "The Contraction of Agbiotech Product Quality Innovation." *Nature Biotechnology* 27:702–704. http://dx.doi.org/10.1038/nbt0809-702.

Graff, G. D., G. Hochman, and D. Zilberman. 2009b. "The Political Economy of Agricultural Biotechnology Policies." *AgBioForum* 12:34–46. http://agbioforum.org/v12n1/v12n1a04-graff.htm.

Guardian. 2011. "Environment: GM." *The Guardian*. Accessed August 25. http://www.guardian.co.uk/environment/gm.

Haas, J. D., J. L. Beard, L. E. Murray-Kolb, A. M. del Mundo, A. Felix, G. B. Gregorio. 2005. "Iron-Biofortified Rice Improves the Iron Stores of Nonanemic Filipino Women." *Journal of Nutrition* 135:2823–2830. http://jn.nutrition.org/cgi/content/abstract/135/12/2823.

Hagenimana, V., and J. Low. 2000. "Potential of Orange-Fleshed Sweet Potatoes for Raising Vitamin A Intake in Africa." *Food and Nutrition Bulletin* 21:414–418. http://foodandnutritionbulletin.org/FNB/index.php/FNB/article/view/291.

Harjes, C. E., T. R. Rocheford, L. Bai, T. P. Brutnell, C. Bermudez Kandianis, S. G. Sowinski, A.E. Stapleton, et al. 2008. "Natural Genetic Variation in Lycopene Epsilon Cyclase Tapped for Maize Biofortification." *Science* 319:330–333. http://dx.doi.org/10.1126/science.1150255.

HarvestPlus. 2011a. "About HarvestPlus." Washington, DC: HarvestPlus. Accessed July 5. http://www.harvestplus.org/content/about-harvestplus.

HarvestPlus. 2011b. "HarvestPlus Update 2010." HarvestPlus. http://www.harvestplus.org/content/harvestplus-update-2010.

HarvestPlus. 2011c. "Pearl Millet Set for Release in 2012." HarvestPlus, February 9. http://www.harvestplus.org/content/pearl-millet-set-release-2012.

HarvestZinc. 2011. "HarvestZinc Fertilizer Project." Accessed August 15. http://www.harvestzinc.org/index.php.

Hawkesford, M. J., and F.-J. Zhao. 2007. "Strategies for Increasing the Selenium Content of Wheat." *Journal of Cereal Science* 46:282–292. http://dx.doi.org/10.1016/j.jcs.2007.02.006.

Hirschi, K. 2009. "Nutrient Biofortification of Food Crops." *Annual Review of Nutrition* 29:401–421. http://dx.doi.org/10.1146/annurev-nutr-080508-141143.

Herring, R. J. 2008. "Opposition to Transgenic Technologies: Ideology, Interests and Collective Action Frames." *Nature Reviews Genetics* 9:458–463. http://dx.doi.org/10.1038/nrg2338.

"Hidden Hunger: How Much Can Farming Really Improve People's Health?" 2011. *The Economist*, May 24. http://www.economist.com/node/18438289.

Hellen Keller International. 2011. "Vitamin A Supplementation." Hellen Keller International. Accessed July 17. http://www.hki.org/reducing-malnutrition/vitamin-a-supplementation/.

Horton, S. 2006. "The Economics of Food Fortification." *Journal of Nutrition* 136:1068–1071. http://jn.nutrition.org/cgi/content/abstract/136/4/1068.

Horton, S., and J. Ross. 2003. "The Economics of Iron Deficiency." *Food Policy* 28:51–75. http://dx.doi.org/10.1016/S0306-9192(02)00070-2.

Horton, S., A. Wesley, and M. G. V. Mannar. 2011. "Double-Fortified Salt Reduces Anemia, Benefit:Cost Ratio Is Modestly Favorable." *Food Policy* 36 (5): 581–587. http://dx.doi.org/10.1016/j.foodpol.2011.06.002.

Hotz, C., and K. H. Brown, eds. 2004. "Assessment of the Risk of Zinc Deficiency in Populations and Options for Its Control." *Food and Nutrition Bulletin* 25:S91–S204. http://www.izincg.org/technical.php.

Howe, J. 2007. "Bioefficacy of Carotenoid-Biofortified Cassava." Paper presented at the ASA-CSSA-SSSA International Annual Meetings, New Orleans, November 4–8. http://a-c-s.confex.com/a-c-s/2007am/techprogram/P34086.HTM.

Howe, J. A., S. A. Tanumihardjo. 2006. "Carotenoid-Biofortified Maize Maintains Adequate Vitamin A Status In Mongolian Gerbils." *Journal of Nutrition* 136:2562–2567. http://jn.nutrition.org/cgi/content/abstract/136/10/2562.

ILSI (International Life Sciences Institute). 1998. *Guidelines for the Use of Iron Supplements to Prevent and Treat Iron Deficiency Anemia.* Washington, DC: International Life Sciences Institute. http://www.who.int/nutrition/publications/micronutrients/anaemia_iron_deficiency/1-57881-020-5/.

INSTAPA. 2011. "Improved Nutrition through Staple Foods in Africa." INSTAPA. Accessed August 14. http://www.instapa.org/.

IRRI (International Rice Research Institute). 2011a. "Golden Rice." Accessed 14 August. http://irri.org/goldenrice.

IRRI (International Rice Research Institute). 2011b. "Annual Report 2010." Los Baños: International Rice Research Institute. http://irri.org/about-irri/annual-reports/annual-report-2010/rice-with-a-vision.

Javelosa, J. C., C. B. Moss, A. Schmitz, J. L. and Seale Jr. 2006. "Derived Demand for Food Nutrients as Welfare Indicator of Biofortified Crops: High-Iron Rice in the Philippines." Paper presented at the Southern Agricultural Economics Association Annual Meeting, Orlando, February 5–8. http://purl.umn.edu/35405.

Jin, Z., W. Minyan, W. Lianghuan, W. Jiangguo, and S. Chunhai. 2008. "Impacts of Combination of Foliar Iron and Boron Application on Iron Biofortification and Nutritional Quality of Rice Grain." *Journal of Plant Nutrition* 31:1599–1611. http://dx.doi.org/10.1080/01904160802244803.

Khoshgoftarmanesh, A. H., R. Schulin, R. L. Chaney, B. Daneshbakhsh, and M. Afyuni. 2010. "Micronutrient-Efficient Genotypes for Crop Yield and Nutritional Quality in Sustainable Agriculture. A Review." *Agronomy for Sustainable Development* 30:83–107. http://dx.doi.org/10.1051/agro/2009017.

Kristof, N. D. 2009. "The Hidden Hunger." *New York Times*, May 23. http://www.nytimes.com/2009/05/24/opinion/24kristof.html.

Lemaux, P. G. 2008. "Genetically Engineered Plants and Foods: A Scientist's Analysis of the Issues (Part I)." *Annual Review of Plant Biology* 59:771–812. http://dx.doi.org/10.1146/annurev.arplant.58.032806.103840.

Lemaux, P. G. 2009. "Genetically Engineered Plants and Foods: A Scientist's Analysis of the Issues (Part II)." *Annual Review of Plant Biology* 60:511–559. http://dx.doi.org/10.1146/annurev.arplant.043008.092013

Low, J. W., M. Arimond, N. Osman, B. Cunguara, F. Zano, and D. Tschirley. 2007a. "Ensuring the Supply of and Creating Demand for a Biofortified Crop with a Visible Trait: Lessons Learned from the Introduction of Orange-Fleshed Sweet Potato in Drought-Prone Areas of Mozambique." *Food and Nutrition Bulletin* 28:S258–S270. http://foodandnutritionbulletin.org/FNB/index.php/FNB/article/view/1858

Low, J. W., M. Arimond, N. Osman, B. Cunguara, F. Zano, and D. Tschirley. 2007b. "A Food-Based Approach Introducing Orange-Fleshed Sweet Potatoes Increased Vitamin A Intake and Serum Retinol Concentrations in Young Children in Rural Mozambique." *Journal of Nutrition* 137:1320–1327. http://jn.nutrition.org/cgi/content/abstract/137/5/1320/.

Lyons, G. H., G. J. Judson, I. Ortiz-Monasterio, Y. Genc, J. C. R. Stangoulis, and R. D. Graham. 2005. "Selenium in Australia: Selenium Status and Biofortification of Wheat for Better Health." *Journal of Trace Elements in Medicine and Biology* 19:75–82. http://dx.doi.org/10.1016/j.jtemb.2005.04.005.

Ma, G., Y. Jin, Y. Li, F. Zhai, F. J. Kok, E. Jacobsen, and X. Yang. 2007. "Iron and Zinc Deficiencies in China: What is a Feasible and Cost-Effective Strategy?" *Public Health Nutrition* 11:632–638. http://dx.doi.org/10.1017/S1368980007001085.

Mayer, J. E., W. H. Pfeiffer, and P. Beyer. 2008. "Biofortified Crops to Alleviate Micronutrient Malnutrition." *Current Opinion in Plant Biology* 11:166–170. http://dx.doi.org/10.1016/j.pbi.2008.01.007.

Mazuze, F.M. 2007. *Analysis of Adoption of Orange-Fleshed Sweetpotatoes: the Case Study of Gaza Province in Mozambique*. Research Report 4E. East Lansing: Michigan State University. http://www.aec.msu.edu/fs2/mozambique/iiam/rr_4e.pdf.

Meenakshi, J. V. 2008. "Biofortification." Frederiksberg: Copenhagen Consensus. http://www.copenhagenconsensus.com/Default.aspx?ID=1306.

Meenakshi, J. V., N. L. Johnson, V. M. Manyong, H. DeGroote, J. Javelosa, D.R. Yanggen, F. Naher, C. Gonzalez, J. García, and E. Meng. 2010. "How Cost-Effective is Biofortification in Combating Micronutrient Malnutrition? An Ex Ante Assessment." *World Development* 38:64–75. http://dx.doi.org/10.1016/j.worlddev.2009.03.014.

Micronutrient Initiative. 2004. "Vitamin and Mineral Deficiency: A Global Progress Report." Ottawa: Micronutrient Initiative. http://www.micronutrient.org/english/view.asp?x=614.

Micronutrient Initiative. 2009. "Investing in the Future: A United Call to Action on Vitamin and Mineral Deficiencies." Ottawa: Micronutrient Initiative. http://www.micronutrient.org/english/view.asp?x=614.

Micronutrient Initiative. 2011a. "About Hidden Hunger." Ottawa: Micronutrient Initiative. Accessed July 17. http://www.micronutrient.org/english/view.asp?x=573.

Micronutrient Initiative. 2011b. "Our Programs." Ottawa: Micronutrient Initiative. Accessed June 21. http://www.micronutrient.org/english/view.asp?x=576.

Miller, J. K., and K. J. Bradford. 2010. "The Regulatory Bottleneck for Biotech Specialty Crops." *Nature Biotechnology* 28:1012–1014. http://dx.doi.org/10.1038/nbt1010-1012

Mills, J. P., P. W. Simon, S. A. Tanumihardjo. 2008. "Bioactive Compounds with High Antioxidant Potential in Biofortified Carrots Do Not Influence Provitamin A Carotenoid Bioefficacy in Gerbils." *FASEB Journal* 22:1105.5. http://www.fasebj.org/cgi/content/meeting_abstract/22/1_MeetingAbstracts/1105.5

Montagnac J. A., C. R. Davis, and S. A. Tanumihardjo. 2009. "Nutritional Value of Cassava for Use as a Staple Food and Recent Advances for Improvement." *Comprehensive Reviews in Food Science and Food Safety* 8:181–194. http://dx.doi.org/10.1038/nbt1010-1012

Moses, V. 2008. "Consumerchoice: Do European Consumers Buy GM Foods?" London: King's College. http://www.kcl.ac.uk/medicine/research/divisions/dns/projects/consumerchoice/index.aspx.

Müller, O., and M. Krawinkel. 2005. "Malnutrition and Health in Developing Countries." *CMAJ* 173:279–286. http://dx.doi.org/10.1503/cmaj.050342.

Murray, C. J. L., and A. D. Lopez, eds. 1996. *The Global Burden of Disease: A Comprehensive Assessment of Mortality and Disability from Diseases, Injuries, and Risk Factors in 1990 and Projected to 2020*. Global Burden of Disease and Injury Series, Vol. 1. Cambridge, MA: Harvard University Press.

Muzhingi, T., A. S. Langyintuo, L. C. Malaba, and M. Banziger. 2008. "Consumer Acceptability of Yellow Maize Products in Zimbabwe." *Food Policy* 33:352–361. http://dx.doi.org/10.1016/j.foodpol.2007.09.003.

Naqvi, S., C. Zhu, G. Farre, K. Ramessar, L. Bassie, J. Breitenbach, D. Perez Conesa, G. Ros, G. Sandmann, T. Capell, and P. Christou. 2009. "Transgenic Multivitamin Corn through Biofortification of Endosperm with Three Vitamins Representing Three Distinct Metabolic Pathways." *Proceedings of the National Academy of Sciences* 106:7762–7767. http://dx.doi.org/10.1073/pnas.0901412106.

Nash, J. M. 2000. "This Rice Could Save a Million Kids a Year." *Time*, July 31.. http://www.time.com/time/magazine/article/0,9171,997586,00.html.

Nestel, P., H. E. Bouis, J. V. Meenakshi, and W. Pfeiffer. 2006. "Biofortification of Staple Food Crops." *Journal of Nutrition* 136:1064–1067. http://jn.nutrition.org/cgi/content/abstract/136/4/1064.

Nuss, E. T., and S. A. Tanumihardjo. 2011. "Quality Protein Maize for Africa: Closing the Protein Inadequacy Gap in Vulnerable Populations." *Advances in Nutrition* 2:217–224. http://advances.nutrition.org/content/2/3/217.

Nyhus Dhillon, C. M., P. Pinstrup-Andersen, H. D. Haas, N. Balakrishna, and G. N. V. Brahmam. 2008. "The Effect of Biofortified Rice and Wheat in India's Food Supply on Dietary Bioavailable Iron." *FASEB Journal* 22:lb770. http://www.fasebj.org/cgi/content/meeting_abstract/22/2_MeetingAbstracts/770.

New York Times. 2011. "Topics: Genetically Modified Food." *New York Times*. Accessed August 25. http://topics.nytimes.com/top/reference/timestopics/subjects/g/genetically_modified_food/index.html.

Ortiz-Monasterio, J. I., N. Palacios-Rojas, E. Meng, K. Pixley, R. Trethowan, and R. J. Peña. 2007. "Enhancing the Mineral and Vitamin Content of Wheat and Maize through Plant Breeding." *Journal of Cereal Science* 46:293–307. http://dx.doi.org/10.1016/j.jcs.2007.06.005.

Paine, J. A., C. A. Shipton, S. Chaggar, R. M. Howells, M. J. Kennedy, G. Vernon, S. Y. Wright, et al. 2005. "Improving the Nutritional Value of Golden Rice through Increased Pro-Vitamin A Content." *Nature Biotechnology* 23:482–487. http://dx.doi.org/10.1038/nbt1082.

Park, S., M. P. Elless, J. Park, A. Jenkins, W. Lim, E. Chambers, K. D. Hirschi. 2009. "Sensory Analysis of Calcium-Biofortified Lettuce." *Plant Biotechnology Journal* 7:106–117. http://dx.doi.org/10.1111/j.1467-7652.2008.00379.x.

Pfeiffer, W. H., and B. McClafferty. 2007. "HarvestPlus: Breeding Crops for Better Nutrition." *Crop Science* 47:S88–S105. http://dx.doi.org/10.2135/cropsci2007.09.0020IPBS.

Phattarakul, N., I. Cakmak, P. Boonchuay, J. Wongmo, B. Rerkasem. 2009. "Role of Zinc Fertilizers in Increasing Grain Zinc Concentration and Improving Grain Yield of Rice." Paper presented at the International Plant Nutrition Colloquium XVI, Sacramento, August 26–30. http://repositories.cdlib.org/ipnc/xvi/1213.

Pinstrup-Andersen, P. 2006. "Agricultural Research and Policy to Achieve Nutrition Goal." In *Poverty, Inequality and Development*, edited by A. de Janvry, and R. Kanbur, 353–370. New York: Springer. http://dx.doi.org/10.1007/0-387-29748-0_17.

Potrykus, I. 2001. "Golden Rice and Beyond." *Plant Physiology* 125:1157–1161. http://dx.doi.org/10.1104/pp.125.3.1157.

Potrykus, I. 2010a. "Regulation Must Be Revolutionized." *Nature* 466:561. http://dx.doi.org/10.1038/466561a.

Potrykus, I. 2010b. "Lessons from the 'Humanitarian Golden Rice' Project." *New Biotechnology* 27:466–472. http://dx.doi.org/10.1016/j.nbt.2010.07.012.

Pray C., R. Paarlberg, and L. Unnevehr. 2007. "Patterns of Political Response to Biofortified Varieties of Crops Produced with Different Breeding Techniques and Agronomic Traits." *AgBioForum* 10:135–143. http://www.agbioforum.org/v10n3/v10n3a02-pray.htm.

PRRI (Public Research & Regulation Initiative). 2011. "GMO Questions and Interviews." PRRI. Accessed August 25. http://pubresreg.org/index.php?option=com_content&task=blogcategory&id=70&Itemid=71.

Qaim, M. 2009. "The Economics of Genetically Modified Crops." *Annual Review of Resource Economics* 1:665–693. http://dx.doi.org/10.1146/annurev.resource.050708.144203.

Qaim, M., A. J. Stein, J. V. Meenakshi. 2007. "Economics of Biofortification." *Agricultural Economics* 37:119–133. http://dx.doi.org/10.1111/j.1574-0862.2007.00239.x.

QUT (Queensland University of Technology). 2011. "Better Bananas for Africa." Accessed August 14. Queensland University of Technology. http://www.challengingboundaries.qut.edu.au/projects/bananas.jsp.

Rébeillé, F., S. Ravanel, S. Jabrin, R. Douce, S. Storozhenko, and D. Van Der Straeten. 2006. "Folates in Plants: Biosynthesis, Distribution, and Enhancement." *Physiologia Plantarum* 126:330–342. http://dx.doi.org/10.1111/j.1399-3054.2005.00587.x.

Reville, W. 2011. "Beware of Amateur Scientists." *Irish Times*, July 7. http://www.irishtimes.com/newspaper/sciencetoday/2011/0707/1224300202341.html.

Ríos, J. J., M. A. Rosales, B. Blasco, L. M. Cervilla, L. Romero, and J. M. Ruiz. 2008. "Biofortification of Se and Induction of the Antioxidant Capacity in Lettuce Plants." *Scientia Horticulturae* 116:248–255. http://dx.doi.org/10.1016/j.scienta.2008.01.008.

Rosado, J. L., K. M. Hambidge, L. V. Miller, O. P. Garcia, J. Westcott, K. Gonzalez, J. Conde, C. Hotz, W. Pfeiffer, I. Ortiz-Monasterio, and N. F. Krebs. 2009. "The Quantity of Zinc

Absorbed from Wheat in Adult Women Is Enhanced by Biofortification." *Journal of Nutrition* 139:1920–1925. http://dx.doi.org/10.3945/jn.109.107755.

Rose D., G. Burgos, M. Bonierbale, and G. Thiele. 2009. "Understanding the Role of Potatoes in the Peruvian Diet: An Approach That Combines Food Composition with Household Expenditure Data." *Journal of Food Composition and Analysis* 22:525–532. http://dx.doi.org/10.1016/j.jfca.2008.10.002.

Salas Fernandez, M. G., I. Kapran, S. Souley, M. Abdou, I. H. Maiga, C. B. Acharya, M. T. Hamblin, and S. Kresovich. 2009. "Collection and Characterization of Yellow Endosperm Sorghums from West Africa for Biofortification." *Genetic Resources and Crop Evolution* 56:991–1000. http://dx.doi.org/10.1007/s10722-009-9417-3

Sample, I. 2011. "BBC Gives Too Much Weight to Fringe Views on Issues Such as Climate Change." *The Guardian*, July 20. http://www.guardian.co.uk/science/2011/jul/20/bbc-climate-change-science-coverage

Sandler, B. J. 2005. "Biofortification to Reduce Vitamin A Deficiency: A Comparative Cost-Benefit Analysis of Golden Rice and Orange-Fleshed Sweet Potato." Master's thesis, Stanford University.

Sautter, C., S. Poletti, P. Zhang, W. Gruissem. 2006. "Biofortification of Essential Nutritional Compounds and Trace Elements in Rice and Cassava." *Proceedings of the Nutrition Society* 65:153–159. http://dx.doi.org/10.1079/PNS2006488.

Sayre, R., J. R. Beeching, E. B. Cahoon, C. Egesi, C. Fauquet, J. Fellman, M. Fregene, et al. 2011. "The BioCassava Plus Program: Biofortification of Cassava for Sub-Saharan Africa." *Annual Review of Plant Biology* 62:251–272. http://dx.doi.org/10.1146/annurev-arplant-042110-103751.

Scott, J., F. Rébeillé, and J. Fletcher. 2000. "Folic Acid and Folates: The Feasibility for Nutritional Enhancement in Plant Foods." *Journal of the Science of Food and Agriculture* 80:795–824. http://dx.doi.org/10.1002/(SICI)1097-0010(20000515)80:7<795::AID-JSFA599>3.0.CO;2-K.

Scrimshaw, N. S., ed. 2000. "Dietary Approaches to Vitamin A Deficiency." Special issue, *Food and Nutrition Bulletin* 21:115–247. http://archive.unu.edu/unupress/food/fnb21-2.pdf.

Shi, R., H. Li, Y. Tong, R. Jing, F. Zhang, and C. Zou. 2008. "Identification of Quantitative Trait Locus of Zinc and Phosphorus Density in Wheat (*Triticum aestivum L.*) Grain." *Plant and Soil* 306:95–104. http://dx.doi.org/10.1007/s11104-007-9483-2.

Šimić, D., R. Sudar, T. Ledenčan, A. Jambrović, Z. Zdunić, I. Brkić, and V. Kovačević. 2009. "Genetic Variation of Bioavailable Iron and Zinc in Grain of a Maize Population." *Journal of Cereal Science* 50:392–397. http://dx.doi.org/10.1016/j.jcs.2009.06.014.

Smale, M., P. Zambrano, G. Gruère, J. Falck-Zepeda, I. Matuschke, D. Horna, L. Nagarajan, I. Yerramareddy, and H. Jones. 2009. *Measuring the Economic Impacts of Transgenic Crops in Developing Agriculture during the First Decade.* Food Policy Review 10. Washington, DC: International Food Policy Research Institute. http://dx.doi.org/10.2499/0896295117FPRev10.

Speeckaert, M.M., R. Speeckaert, K. Wierckx, J.R. Delanghe, and J.-M. Kaufman. 2011. "Value and Pitfalls in Iodine Fortification and Supplementation in the 21st Century." *British Journal of Nutrition* 106 (7): 964–973. http://dx.doi.org/10.1017/S000711451100273X.

Ssemakula, G., and A. Dixon. 2007. "Genotype X Environment Interaction, Stability and Agronomic Performance of Carotenoid-Rich Cassava Clones." *Scientific Research and Essays* 2:390–399. http://www.academicjournals.org/SRE/abstracts/abstracts/abstracts2007/Sep/Ssemakula%20and%20Dixon.htm.

Stein, A. J. 2006. *Micronutrient Malnutrition and the Impact of Modern Plant Breeding on Public Health in India: How Cost-Effective is Biofortification?* Göttingen: Cuvillier. http://nbn-resolving.de/urn:nbn:de:bsz:100-opus-1574.

Stein, A. J. 2010. *The Potential of Biofortification of Rice, Beans, Cassava and Maize throughout Latin America*. Unpublished report for the International Food Policy Research Institute, Washington. http://www.ajstein.de/cv/Stein_IFPRI_biofortificationLatAm.pdf.

Stein, A. J., J. V. Meenakshi, M. Qaim, P. Nestel, H. P. S. Sachdev, Z. A. Bhutta. 2005. *Analyzing the Health Benefits of Biofortified Staple Crops by Means of the Disability-Adjusted Life Years Approach: A Handbook Focusing on Iron, Zinc and Vitamin A*. HarvestPlus Technical Monograph 4. Washington: International Food Policy Research Institute. http://www.harvestplus.org/content/analyzing-health-benefits-biofortified-staple-crops-means-disability-adjusted-life-years-app.

Stein, A. J., J. V. Meenakshi, M. Qaim, P. Nestel, H. P. S. Sachdev, Z. A. Bhutta. 2008. "Potential Impacts of Iron Biofortification in India." *Social Science & Medicine* 66:1797–1808. http://dx.doi.org/10.1016/j.socscimed.2008.01.006

Stein, A. J., P. Nestel, J. V. Meenakshi, M. Qaim, H. P. S. Sachdev, and Z. A. Bhutta. 2007. "Plant Breeding to Control Zinc Deficiency in India: How Cost-Effective Is Biofortification?" *Public Health Nutrition* 10:492–501. http://dx.doi.org/10.1017/S1368980007223857

Stein A. J., and M. Qaim. 2007. "The Human and Economic Cost of Hidden Hunger." *Food and Nutrition Bulletin* 28:125–134. http://foodandnutritionbulletin.org/FNB/index.php/FNB/article/view/1841.

Stein A. J., and M. Qaim. 2009. "Strategien zur Behebung von Mikronährstoffdefiziten" (Strategies to Remedy Micronutrient Deficiencies). Unpublished report for the Office of Technology Assessment at the German Parliament, Berlin.

Stein, A. J., H. P. S. Sachdev, and M. Qaim. 2006. "Potential Impact and Cost-Effectiveness of Golden Rice." *Nature Biotechnology* 24:1200–1201. http://dx.doi.org/10.1038/nbt1006-1200b.

Stein, A. J., H. P. S. Sachdev, and M. Qaim. 2008. "Genetic Engineering for the Poor: Golden Rice and Public Health in India." *World Development* 36:144–158. http://dx.doi.org/10.1016/j.worlddev.2007.02.013.

Stevens, R., and A. Winter-Nelson. 2008. "Consumer Acceptance of Provitamin A-Biofortified Maize in Maputo, Mozambique." *Food Policy* 33:341–351. http://dx.doi.org/10.1016/j.foodpol.2007.12.003.

Storozhenko, S., V. De Brouwer, M. Volckaert, O. Navarrete, D. Blancquaert, G.-F. Zhang,W. Lambert, and D. Van Der Straeten. 2007. "Folate Fortification of Rice by Metabolic Engineering." *Nature Biotechnology* 25:1277–1279. http://dx.doi.org/10.1038/nbt1351.

Storozhenko, S., S. Ravanel, G.-F. Zhang, F. Rébeillé, W. Lambert, and D. Van Der Straeten. 2005. "Folate Enhancement in Staple Crops by Metabolic Engineering." *Trends in Food Science & Technology* 16:271–281. http://dx.doi.org/10.1016/j.tifs.2005.03.007.

Stupak, M., H. Vanderschuren, W. Gruissem, and P. Zhang. 2006. "Biotechnological Approaches to Cassava Protein Improvement." *Trends in Food Science & Technology* 17:634–641. http://dx.doi.org/10.1016/j.tifs.2006.06.004.

Tako, E., J. M. Laparra, R. P. Glahn, R.M. Welch, X. Gen Lei, S. Beebe, and D.D. Miller. 2008. "Biofortified Black Beans in a Maize and Bean Diet Provide More Bioavailable Iron to Piglets Than Standard Black Beans." *Journal of Nutrition* 139:305–309. http://dx.doi.org/10.3945/jn.108.098657.

Tang, G., J. Qin, G. G. Dolnikowski, R. M. Russell, M. A. Grusak. 2009. "Golden Rice is an Effective Source of Vitamin A." *American Journal of Clinical Nutrition* 89:1176–1183. http://dx.doi.org/10.3945/ajcn.2008.27119.

Tanumihardjo, S. A. 2010. "In Defence of Biofortification." SciDev.Net, December 6. http://www.scidev.net/en/editor-letters/in-defence-of-biofortification.html.

Tanumihardjo, S. A., H. Bouis, C. Hotz, J. V. Meenakshi, and B. McClafferty. 2008. "Biofortification of Staple Crops: An Emerging Strategy to Combat Hidden Hunger."

Comprehensive Reviews in Food Science and Food Safety 7:329–373. http://dx.doi.org/10.1111/j.1541-4337.2008.00049.x.

Thavarajah, D., J. Ruszkowski, and A. Vandenberg. 2008. "High Potential for Selenium Biofortification of Lentils (*Lens culinaris L.*)." *Journal of Agricultural and Food Chemistry* 56:10747–10753. http://dx.doi.org/10.1021/jf802307h..

Thavarajah, D., P. Thavarajah, A. Sarker, and A. Vandenberg. 2009. "Lentils (*Lens culinaris* Medikus subspecies *culinaris*): A Whole Food for Increased Iron and Zinc Intake." *Journal of Agricultural and Food Chemistry* 57:5413–5419. http://dx.doi.org/10.1021/jf900786e.

Thompson B., and L. Amoroso, eds. 2010. *Combating Micronutrient Deficiencies: Food-Based Approaches*. Rome: Food and Agriculture Organization of the United Nations. http://www.fao.org/docrep/013/am027e/am027e00.pdf.

Toenniessen, G. 2009. "'Rock' and Rice: the Rockefeller-IRRI Biotechnology Saga." Transcript. *Rice Today* 8 (4): 36–38. http://archive.irri.org/publications/today/Toenniessen.asp.

UNICEF. 2007. "Vitamin A Supplementation: A Decade of Progress." New York: UNICEF. http://www.unicef.org/publications/index_39363.html.

UNICEF. 2011. "Micronutrients: Iodine, Iron and Vitamin A." New York: UNICEF. Accessed June 21. http://www.unicef.org/nutrition/index_iodine.html.

Unnevehr, L., C. Pray, and R. Paarlberg. 2007. "Addressing Micronutrient Deficiencies: Alternative Interventions and Technologies." *AgBioForum* 10:124–134. http://www.agbioforum.org/v10n3/v10n3a01-unnevehr.htm.

Von Traufetter, G. 2009. "Das eigene Leben riskieren." *Der Spiegel*, November 30. http://www.spiegel.de/spiegel/print/d-67963995.html

Vasal, S. K. 1999. "Quality Protein Maize Story." Paper presented at the IFPRI Workshop on Improving Human Nutrition through Agriculture: The Role of International Agricultural Research, Los Baños, October 5–7. http://www.ifpri.org/publication/quality-protein-maize-story.

Waters, B. M., and J. F. Pedersen. 2009. "Sorghum Germplasm Profiling to Assist Breeding and Gene Identification for Biofortification of Grain Mineral and Protein Concentrations." Paper presented at the International Plant Nutrition Colloquium XVI, Sacramento, August 26–30. http://repositories.cdlib.org/ipnc/xvi/1228.

Welch, R. M., and R. D. Graham. 2000. "A New Paradigm for World Agriculture: Productive, Sustainable, Nutritious, Healthful Food Systems." *Food and Nutrition Bulletin* 21:361–366. http://www.ingentaconnect.com/content/nsinf/fnb/2000/00000021/00000004/art00004.

Welch, R. M., and R. D. Graham. 2005. "Agriculture: The Real Nexus for Enhancing Bioavailable Micronutrients in Food Crops." *Journal of Trace Elements in Medicine and Biology* 18:299–307. http://dx.doi.org/10.1016/j.jtemb.2005.03.001.

Welch, R. M., W. A. House, I. Ortiz-Monasterio, and Z. Cheng. 2005. "Potential for Improving Bioavailable Zinc in Wheat Grain (Triticum species) through Plant Breeding." *Journal of Agricultural and Food Chemistry* 53:2176–2180. http://dx.doi.org/10.1021/jf040238x.

White, P. J., and M. R. Broadley. 2005. "Biofortifying Crops with Essential Mineral Elements." *Trends in Plant Science* 10:586–593. http://dx.doi.org/10.1016/j.tplants.2005.10.001.

White, P. J., and M. R. Broadley. 2007. "Genetic Aspects of Mineral Biofortification." *Comparative Biochemistry and Physiology, Part A* 146:S246. http://dx.doi.org/10.1016/j.cbpa.2007.01.572.

White, P. J., and M. R. Broadley. 2009. "Biofortification of Crops with Seven Mineral Elements often Lacking in Human Diets—Iron, Zinc, Copper, Calcium, Magnesium, Selenium and Iodine." *New Phytologist* 182:49–84. http://dx.doi.org/10.1111/j.1469-8137.2008.02738.x

WHO (World Health Organization). 2001. "Iron deficiency Anaemia: Assessment, Prevention, and Control." Geneva: WHO. http://www.who.int/nutrition/publications/micronutrients/anaemia_iron_deficiency/WHO_NHD_01.3/

WHO (World Health Organization). 2002. "The World Health Report 2002." Geneva: WHO. http://www.who.int/whr/2002/

WHO (World Health Organization). 2011a. "Food Safety: 20 Questions on Genetically Modified Foods." Geneva: WHO. Accessed August 25. http://www.who.int/foodsafety/publications/biotech/20questions/en/index.html

WHO (World Health Organization). 2011b. "Metrics: Disability-Adjusted Life Year (DALY)." Geneva: WHO. Accessed July 17. http://www.who.int/healthinfo/global_burden_disease/metrics_daly/

WHO (World Health Organization). 2011c. "Micronutrient Deficiencies: Iron Deficiency Anaemia." Geneva: WHO. Accessed June 19. http://www.who.int/nutrition/topics/ida/

WHO (World Health Organization). 2011d. "Micronutrient Deficiencies: Vitamin A Deficiency." Geneva: WHO.Accessed June 19. http://www.who.int/nutrition/topics/vad/

WHO (World Health Organization). 2011e. "Micronutrient Deficiencies: Iodine Deficiency Disorders." Geneva: WHO. Accessed June 21. http://www.who.int/nutrition/topics/idd/

WHO (World Health Organization). 2011f. "Micronutrients: Micronutrient Deficiencies." Geneva: WHO. Accessed June 21. http://www.who.int/nutrition/topics/micronutrients/

WHO (World Health Organization). 2011g. "Obesity and Overweight." Geneva: WHO. Accessed July 17. http://www.who.int/mediacentre/factsheets/fs311/

Wirth, J., S. Poletti, B. Aeschlimann, N. Yakandawala, B. Drosse, S. Osorio, T. Tohge, et al. 2009. "Rice Endosperm Iron Biofortification by Targeted and Synergistic Action of Nicotianamine Synthase and Ferritin." *Plant Biotechnology Journal* 7:631–644. http://dx.doi.org/10.1111/j.1467-7652.2009.00430.x.

Wissuwa, M., A. M. Ismail, R. D. Graham. 2008. "Rice Grain Zinc Concentrations as Affected by Genotype, Native Soil-Zinc Availability, and Zinc Fertilization." *Plant and Soil* 306:37–48. http://dx.doi.org/10.1007/s11104-007-9368-4.

Wolson R. 2007. "Assessing the Prospects for the Adoption of Biofortified Crops in South Africa." *AgBioForum* 10:184–191. http://www.agbioforum.org/v10n3/v10n3a08-wolson.htm.

World Bank. 1993. "World Development Report 1993." Washington, DC: World Bank. http://go.worldbank.org/6R5DC7G090.

World Bank. 1994. "Enriching Lives: Overcoming Vitamin and Mineral Malnutrition in Developing Countries." Washington, DC: World Bank. http://go.worldbank.org/N8BoYJMVBo.

Wu, J., C. Salisbury, R. Graham, G. Lyons, and M. Fenech. 2009. "Increased Consumption of Wheat Biofortified with Selenium Does Not Modify Biomarkers of Cancer Risk, Oxidative Stress, or Immune Function in Healthy Australian Males." *Environmental and Molecular Mutagenesis* 50:489–501. http://dx.doi.org/10.1002/em.20490.

Ye, X., S. Al-Babili, A. Klöti, J. Zhang, P. Lucca, P. Beyer, and I. Potrykus. 2000. "Engineering the Provitamin A (Beta-Carotene) Biosynthetic Pathway into (Carotenoid-Free) Rice Endosperm." *Science* 287:303–305. http://dx.doi.org/10.1126/science.287.5451.303.

Zapata-Caldas E., G. Hyman, H. Pachón, F.A. Monserrate, and L. Vesga Varela. 2009. "Identifying Candidate Sites for Crop Biofortification in Latin America: Case Studies in Colombia, Nicaragua and Bolivia." *International Journal of Health Geographics* 8:29. http://dx.doi.org/10.1186/1476-072X-8-29.

Zhao, F. J, and P. R. Shewry. 2011. "The Challenge of Global Food Sustainability." *Food Policy* 36:S94–S101. http://dx.doi.org/10.1016/j.foodpol.2010.11.011.
Zhao, F. J., Y. H. Su, S. J. Dunham, M. Rakszegi, Z. Bedo, S.P. McGrath, and P. R. Shewry. 2009. "Variation in Mineral Micronutrient Concentrations in Grain of Wheat Lines of Diverse Origin." *Journal of Cereal Science* 49:290–295. http://dx.doi.org/10.1016/j.jcs.2008.11.007.
Zhu, C., S. Naqvi, S. Gomez-Galera, A. M. Pelacho, T. Capell, and P. Christou. 2007. "Transgenic Strategies for the Nutritional Enhancement of Plants." *Trends in Plant Science* 12:548–555. http://dx.doi.org/10.1016/j.tplants.2007.09.007.
Zimmermann, R., and M. Qaim. 2004. "Potential Health Benefits of Golden Rice: A Philippine Case Study." *Food Policy* 29:147–168. http://dx.doi.org/10.1016/j.foodpol.2004.03.001.

CHAPTER 7

BIOFUELS

Competition for Cropland, Water, and Energy Resources

DAVID PIMENTEL AND MICHAEL BURGESS

Introduction

Malnutrition in the world today is incapacitating more people and causing more illness and deaths annually than any other disease affecting humans (Pimentel et al. 2007). The World Food Programme (2010) reports that 1.02 billion people, children plus adults, are protein/calorie malnourished. The WHO (2000) reported in 2000 that 3.7 billion people were micronutrient malnourished, while the World Food Programme (2010) reported the number of undernourished people reached 1.02 billion in 2009, increasing the number of malnourished and undernourished people to 4.7 billion, which means an estimated 66% of the world population suffers from malnourishment and undernourished due to a lack of one nutrient or another or multiple nutrients (See Gaiha et al. this volume; Stein this volume).

David Pimentel and Marcia Pimentel have identified stark contrasts between the availability of the Earth's resources and the billions of people who rely on them for their very survival (Pimentel and Pimentel 2008). Human survival, the food supply, and the vital environmental resources that make survival possible are being threatened by overpopulation. Each day about a quarter million people are added to the 7.0 billion who already exist on Earth (PRB 2012). While this rapid human population growth takes place, the supply of natural resources that supports human life—including food, fresh water, quality soil, energy, and biodiversity—is being polluted, degraded, and depleted (Pimentel et al. 2009).

The objective of this chapter is to analyze (1) the uses and interdependencies among land, water, and fossil energy resources in food versus biofuel production; and (2) the characteristics of the environmental impacts caused by food production and production of biofuels.

Food and Malnourishment

Considering the declining availability of natural resources that support agriculture and food production, it is evident that both the quality of human life and humanity's survival are being threatened. Many of these resources, especially those that are finite, such as fossil fuel, are being depleted by overexploitation. The ongoing rapid human population growth impacts all the life-supporting natural resources essential for agriculture and food production. Human population growth especially impacts cropland per capita worldwide, which has declined in just the past decade by more than 22% (Pimentel and Pimentel, 2008), and which continues to decline because of rapid population growth and ongoing soil erosion and soil salinization. Both soil erosion and soil salinization cause the loss of about 20 million hectares (ha) each year (Pimentel et al. 2009). Large forested areas are being cut down to replace some of the lost cropland.

Just before the Green Revolution in the 1950s, the average grain consumption per person in the world was about 250 kilograms (Earth Policy Institute 2008). After the Green Revolution started, world food production per person started to increase; by 1951, average grain consumption per capita had increased to 255 kilograms (kg) (Earth Policy Institute 2008), and 1960 it had increased to 272 kg. Then, from 1960 to 1984, per capita grain production usually increased each year through 1984 (FAO 2013). Starting in 1984–1985, grain production per capita started to decline, and continued to decline on average through 2007.

The reason that grains make a sound index of food production is that 80% of world food comes from grain and 50% of the world's agricultural lands are planted to grain (Pimentel and Pimentel, 2008). With continuing rapid human population growth, grain production per capita may continue to decline (Pimentel et al. 2009) if shortages of cropland and water resources are not dealt with. Increased natural gas supplies, as a result of the technology of high-pressure hydraulic fracturing of shale formations (fracking), may arrest the decline in nitrogen fertilizer use. Nitrogen fertilizer, the production of which is heavily dependent on methane, may remain relatively cheap and available for the foreseeable future.

Because fossil-fuel reserves are projected to continue their decline toward less accessible and less conventional reserves over the next hundred years, and because fossil energy use accounts for much of the increase in cereal grains and other foods, malnutrition will continue to be a serious problem. The estimated sustainable population for the world in the absence of fossil fuels is about 2 billion, well below the current 7.2 billion people (Pimentel et al. 2010; PRB 2012).

World Cropland and Water Resources

More than 99.7% of human food comes from the terrestrial environment, while less than 0.3% comes from the oceans and other aquatic ecosystems (FAO 2002). Worldwide, of the total 13 billion hectares of land area, the percentages according to use are: cropland,

11%; pastureland, 27%; forestland, 32%; urban, 9%; and other 21%. Most of the "other" land area (21%) is unsuitable for crops, pasture, and/or forests because the soil is too infertile or shallow to support plant growth, or the climate and region are too harsh, cold, dry, steep, stony, or wet (FAO 2013). Most of the land suitable for crops is already in use.

Because the human population has continued to increase rapidly, there has been an expansion of land area occupied by diverse human activities and human habitation, which has dramatically reduced cropland and pastureland. Much vital cropland and pastureland has been covered by transportation systems and urbanization. In the United States, about 0.4 hectares (1 acre) of land per person is covered with urbanization and roads (USCB 2008). In 1960, when the world population numbered only 3 billion, approximately 0.5 hectares (ha) was available per person for the production of a diverse, nutritious diet of plant and animal products (Giampietro and Pimentel 1994). Based on agricultural estimates for the United States in the 1960s, 0.5 ha includes land for human food and animal products essential for a healthy diet (Pimentel and Pimentel 2003). China's recent explosion in development provides an example of a rapid decline in the availability of per capita cropland (Pimentel and Wen 2004). The current available cropland in China is only 0.08 ha per capita. This relatively small amount of cropland provides most of the people in China with a predominantly (over 90%) vegetarian diet, which requires less energy, land, and biomass than the typical American diet.

In addition to land, water is a vital controlling factor in crop production (Gleick 1996; Homer-Dixon 2012). Enormous quantities of water are required for crop production. During the growing season for corn of a little over three months, a corn crop utilizes more than 6.5 million liters of water per hectare (Pimentel and Pimentel 2008). The production of nine tons per hectare (t/ha) of corn requires about 7 million liters of water (about 700,000 gallons of water per acre) (Pimentel et al. 2004). The production of rice requires even more water, or about 11 million liters of water per hectare.

Irrigation provides much of the water for world food production. The 17% of the cropland worldwide that is irrigated provides about 40% of total food produced each year (FAO 2003). Unfortunately, irrigated land is declining per capita at about 10% per decade (Pimentel and Pimentel 2008). Worldwide, about 70% of all freshwater consumed is consumed by irrigation, and in the United States about 80% of the water consumed is consumed by the 15% of the crops that are irrigated (Pimentel and Pimentel 2008). Global arid conditions are spreading and intensifying because of global warming (Aroca and Ruiz-Lozano 2009), and water use is increasing for activities other than agriculture, causing irrigation to decline. A major concern is that world irrigation water is projected to decline further because of global climate change (Cline 2007).

Energy Resources and Use

Since the industrial revolution of the 1850s, the rate of energy use from all sources has been growing even faster than world population. For example, from 1970 to 1995, energy use increased at a rate of 2.5% per year (doubling every 30 years) compared with the worldwide population growth of 1.7% per year (doubling every 40 to 60 years) (Pimentel and Pimentel 2008). Developed nations as of 2010 (roughly corresponding to the 34 country OECD membership), having 18% of the world population annually consume about 46% of the all energy used worldwide, while the developing nations (non OECD members), possessing about 82% of the world population, use only 52% of world fossil energy – the per capita energy use of people in the OECD countries is about four times that of people in non OECD nations (US Energy Information Agency 2013a; OECD 2013)!

Although about 50% of all the solar energy captured by worldwide photosynthesis is used by humans for food, fiber, forest products, and other systems, this solar energy is still inadequate to meet all human needs—namely, food production needs (Pimentel 2001). Although photosynthesis appears inefficient for current human needs, it has been effective for all human history and prehistory except for the past couple of hundred years.

Each year, the US population uses three times more fossil energy than the total solar energy captured by the total annual growth of all harvested US crops, forests, and grasses (Pimentel et al. 2009). Industry, transportation, home heating and cooling, and food production account for most of the fossil energy consumed in the United States (USCB 2009). Per capita use of fossil energy in the United States per year amounts to about 9,500 liters of oil equivalents—more than seven times the per capita use in China (Pimentel and Pimentel 2008). In China, most fossil energy is used by industry, although approximately 25% is now used for agriculture and in the food production system (Pimentel and Wen 2004).

The world supply of oil is projected to last 40 to 50 years if use continues at current production rates, and if unconventional sources such as oil shale and tar sands are not included (Campbell 1997; Duncan and Youngquist 1999; BP 2002; Conway 2004). Worldwide, the natural gas supply is considered adequate for about 100 years and coal supplies also will last for about 100 years (BP 2005; Youngquist 1997; Lunsford 2007; Konrad 2007; IEA 2007). Before fracking technology became widespread, US natural gas was in short supply, and projections indicated that the United States would deplete its natural gas resources in about 20 years (Youngquist and Duncan 2003). Current estimates suggest that fracking technology has increased natural gas production by 25%, and natural gas reserves are expected to last another 50 years (Bloomberg and Mitchell 2012). Many petroleum geologists agree that the world reached peak oil and natural gas in 2007; from this peak, these energy resources will decline slowly and continuously until exhaustion or the cost of extraction and processing exceeds the value of the fuel. "Peak oil" is not a theory but an observation that 50% of proved oil reserves have been extracted, refined, and consumed from large, easily exploitable, easily refined, and easily accessible deposits. Much of the unknown reserves left tend to be smaller deposits that are more remote and more difficult to extract, and of lower quality (more expensive to refine) (Youngquist and Duncan 2003; Campbell 2006; Heinberg 2003; Lunsford 2007; Konrad 2007; IEA 2007). Just as the world leadership has paid little more than lip service to climate change, "peak oil" doesn't seem to have been paid any lip service. Both climate change and "peak oil" are based on observations and data. The increased production of natural gas through fracking technology is lowering the price of natural gas relative to coal and older coal-fired power plants that cannot meet new, more stringent EPA standards for carbon dioxide and other toxic emissions. These plants are being replaced by power plants using natural gas (Leek 2012; Lydersen 2012; *New York Times* 2012).

Biomass Resources

The previous section concludes that fossil fuels cannot be assumed to be readily available forever, even if changes in technology such as hydraulic fracturing create short-term disturbances of the trend line. Given these forecasts, attention turns to biomass as an alternative energy source. Our analysis now has to consider how much biomass—of what kinds, and used in what ways—might address the interdependent needs of energy and agriculture.

Of particular significance is the fact that fuels from biomass are liquid fuels, either ethanol or biodiesel. Why liquid fuels? Other than some trains and the occasional electric car, the industrialized world's transport systems run on liquid fuels, and virtually all motorized or jet-propelled vehicles are powered by liquid fuels. Alternative power sources other than biomass produce electricity, not a liquid fuel. Clearly, the decision has been made by the political and corporate systems in the developed world that rather than retooling and adapting the transport system, attempts should be made to exploit biomass as a possible new source of liquid fuels.

One of the first questions asked should be how much cellulosic biomass resource is available for energy production? The two rough estimates of how much cellulosic biomass should be used to produce ethanol are from a study by Perlack et al. (2005), which reported that 1.3 billion tons of biomass could be collected in the United States to produce 30 billion gallons (11 kg of biomass per liter) of ethanol per year, and by President George W. Bush, who in 2007 estimated there was about 1.6 billion tons of biomass available, and that by 2020 the United States could be producing 36 billion gallons of ethanol per year. Neither Perlack et al. nor President Bush reported on the total biomass produced in the United States annually, nor what proportion could be harvested each year as biofuel.[1] The amount of biomass produced annually in the United States, including all agricultural crops, all forests, and all grasses, is about 1.8 billion tons, according to the best data available (Pimentel et al. 2010), and the same value as calculated by Perlack et al., but the data for the different sources are quite different. Note that this net annual primary productivity of about 1.8 billion tons per year for the United States includes *all* the human food consumed each year. The total food consumed annually in the United States is about 400 million tons (USDA 2008). This means that the net primary productivity minus food is only 1.4 billion tons of cellulosic biomass per year. After harvest of the food crops and nonfood crops, about 500 million tons of crop residues remain on the land (Lal et al. 1999). Worldwide, the amount of biomass produced is significantly greater: our estimate totals 1,764 x 10^9 tons of biomass produced per year (Pimentel et al. 2010), almost a thousand times greater than the US biomass production.

In developing countries, about 2 kcal (kilocalories) of wood are utilized in cooking 1 kcal of food (Fujino et al. 1999). Thus, more biomass, land, and water are needed to produce the biofuel for cooking than are needed to produce the food to be cooked (Pimentel and Pimentel 2008). Worldwide, most biomass is burned for cooking and heating, but biomass can also be converted into electricity. Assuming an optimal yield globally of three dry metric tons per hectare per year of woody biomass, harvested sustainably (Ferguson 2001, 2003), a gross energy yield of 13.5 million kcal/ha results. Harvesting this wood biomass requires an energy expenditure of approximately thirty liters of diesel fuel per hectare, plus the embodied energy for cutting and collecting wood for transport to an electric power plant. Thus, the energy input per output ratio for such a system is calculated to be 1:25 (Hendrickson and Galland 1993).

Per capita consumption of woody biomass for heat in the United States amounts to 625 kilograms (kg) per year (Kitani 1999). The diverse biomass resources (wood, crop residues, and dung) used in developing nations averages about 630 kg per capita per year (Kitani 1999). Woody biomass has the capacity to supply the United States with about 5 quads (1.5 x 10^{12} kWh thermal) of its total gross energy supply by the year 2050, provided that the amount of forestland stays constant (Pimentel 2008). A city of 100,000 people using the biomass from a sustainable forest (3 t/ha per year) for electricity requires approximately 200,000 ha of forest area, based on an average electrical demand of slightly more than 1 billion kilowatt hours (kWh) (860 kcal = 1 kWh) (Pimentel 2008).

Air quality impacts from burning biomass are less harmful than those associated with coal, but more harmful than those associated with natural gas (Pimentel 2001). Biomass combustion releases more than two hundred different chemical pollutants, including fourteen carcinogens and four cocarcinogens, into the atmosphere (Burning Issues 2006). As a result, approximately 4 billion people globally suffer from continuous exposure to smoke (Smith 2006). In the United States, wood smoke kills 30,000 people each year (Burning Issues 2011), although many of the pollutants from electrical power plants that use wood and other biomass can be mitigated. These controls include the same scrubbers that are frequently installed on coal-fired plants.

The estimated 1.8 billion tons of biomass produced per year on US land area translates into about thirty-two quads of energy, which means that the solar energy captured by all plants in the United States per year equates to only 32% of the energy currently consumed as fossil energy (Pimentel et al. 2008). The United States lacks the volume of biomass to produce the ethanol and biodiesel fuel to make the United States oil independent (Pimentel et al. 2012).

Of the total world land area in cropland, pasture, and forest, about 38% is cropland and pasture and about 30% is forests (FAO 2013). Devoting a portion of this cropland and forestland to biofuels will stress both managed and unmanaged ecosystems and would not, in any event, be sufficient to solve the world fuel problem.

Photosynthetic efficiency (the percentage of visible light energy used for carbon fixation by plants) for intensively managed plants can average as high as 3%, while most crops range from 1 to 4% (Moore et al. 1998), but this efficiency only holds true while the plants are actively growing. Corn in temperate climates such as the US Corn Belt only grow for 120 days or so, leaving 240 days of no corn productivity, which lowers photosynthetic efficiency from perhaps 3% during the growing season to about 1% for the whole year. If not for the fact that almost the entire transport system of the industrialized world depends on liquid fuel, no one would consider using cellulosic biomass or crops such as sugarcane or corn as raw material for making liquid fuel.

Corn Ethanol

Having considered the aggregate biomass resources available for conversion to biofuels, we now turn to consideration of specific biofuels in use. Each has a particular profile of ecological and energy costs, and thus different implications for the political and ethical questions of sustainable development.

In the United States, ethanol constitutes 99% of all biofuels (Farrell et al. 2006). For capital expenditures, new plant construction costs from $1.05 to $3.00 per gallon of ethanol (Shapouri and Gallagher 2005). Fermenting and distilling corn ethanol requires large amounts of water. The corn is finely ground and approximately 15 liters of water are added per 2.69 kg of ground corn. After fermentation, to obtain a liter of 95% pure ethanol from the 10% ethanol and 90% water mixture, 1 liter of ethanol must be extracted from the approximately 10 liters of the ethanol/water mixture. To be mixed with gasoline, the 95% ethanol must be further processed and more water must be removed, requiring additional fossil energy inputs to achieve 99.5% pure ethanol (Pimentel et al. 2009). Thus, a total of about 12 liters of wastewater must be removed per liter of ethanol produced, and this relatively large volume of sewage effluent has to be disposed of, at an energy, economic, and environmental cost. Manufacture of a liter of 99.5% ethanol uses 45% more fossil energy than it produces and costs $1.05 per liter ($3.97 per gallon) (Pimentel et al. 2012). The corn feedstock alone requires more than 33% of the total energy input.

The largest energy inputs in corn ethanol production are for producing the corn feedstock plus the steam energy and electricity used in the fermentation/distillation process. The total energy input to produce a liter of ethanol is 7,438 kcal (Pimentel et al. 2009). However, a liter of ethanol has an energy value of only 5,130 kcal. Based on a net energy loss of 2,344 kcal of ethanol produced, 45% more fossil energy is expended than is produced as ethanol. The total cost, including the energy inputs for the fermentation/distillation process and the apportioned energy costs of the stainless steel tanks and other industrial materials, is $1,045 per 1,000 liters of ethanol produced (Pimentel et al. 2009).

All differences in ethanol production processes from biomass and genetic manipulation of crop plants to biofuel plants are peripheral to the point that only from 1–4% of visible light is captured by photosynthesis. Over the course of a year (except in tropical regions), this percentage is actually under 1%. Plants are relatively inefficient in converting solar energy. Photovoltaic cells, even inefficient cells, can capture 10% or more of visible light and convert this light into electricity for a full year whenever there is sunlight, regardless of the growing season (Patzek 2012).

The subsidies for corn ethanol totaled more than $12 billion per year in 2008 (Koplow and Steenblik 2008). This means that the subsidies per liter of ethanol are 60 times greater than the subsidies per liter of gasoline. In 2006, nearly 19 billion liters of ethanol were produced on 20% of US corn acreage (USCB 2008). This 19 billion liters represents only 1% of total US petroleum use (USCB 2008). However, 45% more fossil energy is required to produce a liter of ethanol than the energy yield of that liter of ethanol. Only subsidies from the political system sustained so inefficient a process. However, the $6 billion per year federal tax credit which is equivalent to an outright subsidy (Friedman 2011) for corn ethanol was allowed to expire by Congress after three decades in 2011 but replaced by the Renewable Fuel Standard mandate enacted in 2005 which for 2011–2012 mandated that at least 37% of the US corn crop be converted to ethanol. A Congressional Budget Office report states, "In the future, the scheduled increase in mandated volumes [of corn ethanol] would require biofuels to be produced in amounts that are probably beyond what the market would produce if the effects of the tax credits were included" (Pear 2012; Drum 2012; Congressional Budget Office 2010, p. 16).

However, even if we completely ignore corn ethanol's negative energy balance and high economic cost, we still find that it is absolutely not feasible to use ethanol to replace US oil. Indeed, virtually wherever ethanol is used as a fuel, it supplements and does not replace fossil liquid fuel, even in Brazil. Sugarcane ethanol has been referred to as a "transitional fuel" by one researcher (Claudinei Andreoli, personal communication, 2010) and has a positive energy return on energy invested when the effects on agricultural land and non-agricultural land and water and wildlife are discounted. If all 341 billion kg of corn produced in the United States (USDA 2007) were converted into ethanol at the current rate of 2.69 kg corn per liter of ethanol, then 129 billion liters of ethanol could be produced, replacing only 7% of total oil consumption in the United States. Of course, in this situation there would be no corn available for livestock feed, human food, and other needs.

In addition, the environmental impacts of corn ethanol are enormous:

1. Corn production causes more soil erosion than any other crop grown (NAS 2003).
2. Corn production uses more nitrogen fertilizer than any other crop grown, and the runoff from the Corn Belt is the prime cause of the "dead zone" in the Gulf of Mexico (NAS 2003). In 2006, approximately 4.7 million tons of nitrogen was used in US corn production (USDA 2007). Natural gas is required to produce nitrogen fertilizer, and the United States imports more than half (54%) of its nitrogen fertilizer (Huang 2004; USDA, Economic Research Service 2013). However, the greater availability of cheap natural gas due to fracking technology may extend the availability of relatively cheap nitrogen fertilizer. In addition, about 1.7 million tons of phosphorus was used in the United States (USDA 2007).

3. Corn production uses more insecticides than any other crop grown (McLaughlin and Walsh 1998).
4. Corn production uses more herbicides than any other crop grown (Patzek 2004).
5. More than 1,700 gallons of water are required to produce 1 gallon of corn ethanol (Pimentel and Patzek 2008).
6. Enormous quantities of carbon dioxide are produced due to the large quantity of fossil energy used in production and to the immense amounts of carbon dioxide released during corn fermentation and soil tillage. All this speeds global warming (Socolow et al. 2004).
7. Air pollution is a significant problem (Hodge 2003; Jacobson 2007; Pimentel and Patzek 2007). Burning ethanol emits pollutants into the air, including peroxyacetyl nitrate (PAN), acetaldehydes, alkylates, and nitrous oxide (Davis and Thomas 2006). These chemicals can have significant human health effects, as well as impacting other organisms and ecosystems.

In addition to corn ethanol's intensive environmental degradation and the inefficient use of food-related resources, the production of corn ethanol also has a great effect on world food prices. For instance, the use of corn for ethanol production has increased the prices of US beef, chicken, pork, eggs, breads, cereals, and milk by 10% to 20% (Brown 2008).

Grass and Cellulosic Ethanol

Tilman et al. (2006) suggest that all 235 million ha of grassland plus crop residues can be converted into cellulosic ethanol. Tilman et al. recommend that crop residues, such as corn stover (leaves and stalks), can be harvested and utilized as a fuel source. This would be disastrous for the agricultural ecosystem, however, because crop residues such as corn stover are vital for protecting topsoil. Leaving the soil unprotected would intensify soil erosion by a factor of ten or more (Rasnake, 1983), and it may increase soil loss as much as by a factor of one hundred (Fryrear and Bilbro 1994). Furthermore, even a partial removal of the stover can result in increased CO_2 emissions and intensify acidification and eutrophication in fresh water and coastal marine water bodies due to increased runoff (Lal, 2004; Kim and Dale, 2005). Already, the US crop system is losing soil ten times faster than the sustainable rate (NAS, 2003). Soil formation rates are extremely slow—less than 1 t/ha/yr (NAS 2003; Troeh et al. 2004). Increased soil erosion caused by the removal of crop residues for use as biofuels facilitates soil-carbon oxidation and contributes to the greenhouse emissions problem (Lal 2004).

Tilman et al. (2006) assume about 1,032 liters of ethanol can be produced through the conversion of the 4 t/ha/yr of grasses harvested. However, Pimentel and Patzek (2007) report a negative 50% return in ethanol produced compared with the fossil energy inputs in switchgrass conversion (Pimentel et al. 2009). Converting all 235 million ha of US grassland into ethanol at the optimistic rate given by Tilman et al. would provide only 12% of annual consumption of US oil, and it of course assumes that there is food to burn (USDA 2006; USCB 2008). Verified data, however, confirm that the output in ethanol would require 1.5 liters of oil equivalents to produce 1 liter of ethanol (Pimentel et al. 2009). The amount of electricity produced by the ethanol from 1 ha of switchgrass can be matched by 30 square meters of 10% efficient (considered inefficient) photovoltaic cells, and photovoltaic cells are designed to run for 30 years with very little maintenance (Patzek 2012).

To achieve the production of this much ethanol, US farmers would have to displace the 100 million cattle, 7 million sheep, and 4 million horses that are now grazing on 324 million ha of US grassland and rangeland (USDA 2006). Overgrazing is already a serious problem on US grassland, and an overgrazing problem exists worldwide (Brown 2002). Thus, the assessment of the quantity of ethanol that can be produced on US and world grasslands by Tilman et al. (2006) appears to be unduly optimistic.

Converting switchgrass into ethanol results in a negative energy return (Pimentel et al., 2009). The negative energy return is 57%, or a slightly more negative energy return than corn ethanol production (Pimentel et al. 2009). The cost of producing a liter of ethanol using switchgrass was 93¢ in 2009 (Pimentel et al. 2009).

Several problems occur in the conversion of cellulosic biomass into ethanol. First, from two to five times more cellulosic biomass is required to achieve the same quantity of starches and sugars as are found in a given quantity of corn grain, since no energetically efficient or economically viable method exists to break the cellulose down into simple sugars (Pimentel et al. 2012). Thus, two to five times more cellulosic material must be produced and handled, compared with corn grain (Pimentel and Patzek 2007). In addition, the starches and sugars in cellulosic biomass are tightly held in lignin. These starches and sugars can be released using a strong acid to dissolve the lignin. Once the lignin is dissolved, the acid action is stopped with an alkali. The solution of lignin, starches, and sugars can be fermented. Some claim that the lignin can be used as a fuel, but not when dissolved in water. The lignin in the water mixture can be extracted using various energy-intensive technologies. Usually less than 25% of the lignin can be extracted from the water mixture (Pimentel and Patzek 2007).

Soybean Biodiesel

Processed vegetable oils from soybean, sunflower, rapeseed, oil palm, and other oil plants can be used as fuel in diesel engines. Unfortunately, producing vegetable oils for use in diesel engines is costly in terms of economics and energy. Comparative analysis concludes that these sources should be exploited only in situations where accumulations of waste or by-product vegetable oil already exist (Ozaktas 2000; Pimentel and Patzek 2007; Pimentel et al. 2009). A slight net return on energy from soybean oil is possible only if the soybeans are grown without commercial nitrogen fertilizer. Under favorable conditions, the soybean, a legume, will produce its own nitrogen. Still, soy biodiesel has a 63% net fossil energy loss (Pimentel et al. 2009). Not surprisingly, subsidies provided the conditions for expansion of production. The US federal government had provided $500 million annually in subsidies for the production of 3.6 billion liters of biodiesel (Koplow 2006; US Energy Information Administration 2013b)—which is 74 times greater than the subsidies per liter of diesel fuel—before Congress allowed biodiesel tax incentives to expire in 2011 (Yacobucci 2012).

The environmental impacts of producing soybean biodiesel are second only to that of corn ethanol:

1. Soybean production causes significant soil erosion, second only to corn production (NAS. 2003).
2. Soybean production uses large quantities of herbicides, second only to corn production (USDA 2007). These herbicides cause major pollution problems with natural biota in the soybean production areas (Artuzi and Contiero 2006; Pimentel 2006).
3. The USDA (2005) reports a soybean yield worldwide of 2.2 tons per hectare.

With an average oil extraction efficiency of 18% (USDA 1975, 2005), the average oil yield per year would be approximately 0.4 tons per hectare. This converts into 454 liters of oil per hectare. Based on current US diesel consumption of 227 billion liters/year (Tickell, 2006), this would require more than 500 million ha of land in soybeans, or more than half the total US land planted set aside just for soybeans. In addition, all 71 billion tons of soybeans produced in the United States (USDA 2006) could only supply less than 3% of total US oil consumption.

Rapeseed and Canola Biodiesel

The European Biodiesel Board estimates a total biodiesel production of 4.89 million tons for the year 2006 (EBB 2007). Well suited to the colder climates, rapeseed is the dominant crop used in European biodiesel production. Often confused with canola, rapeseed is an inedible crop of the Brassica family, yielding oil seeds high in erucic acid. Canola is in the same family, but it is a hybrid created to lower saturated fat content and erucic acid content for human consumption in cooking oil and margarine (Tickell 2006).

Rapeseed-based biodiesel yields in Europe averaged 1,390 liters per hectare in 2005 (Frondel and Peters 2007). Using the density of biodiesel defined as 0.88 kg/l (Frondel and Peters 2007), it can be estimated that the average annual production of rapeseed biodiesel in Europe is 1.1 million tons total. Because of its high oil content (30%), rapeseed is preferred as a biodiesel feedstock source (Tickell 2006). While Europe currently dominates the rapeseed production in the world, as the market for high-yield oilseed feedstock for biodiesel grows, interest in canola and rapeseed oil is likely to increase in many northern states of the United States, and in Canada (Tickell 2006).

Rapeseed and canola require the application of fertilizers and pesticides in production. The energy required to make these pesticides and fertilizers detracts from the overall net energy produced (Frondel and Peters 2007); conventional production of corn requires energy inputs totaling 32 x 10^6 kcal per hectare, while production of a hectare of corn using an organic system only requires a 3.5 x 10^6 kcal, though it requires 40% more human labor. Organically grown corn reduces energy inputs almost enough to balance energy inputs to the ethanol energy output, in addition to greatly decreasing the environmental impacts of corn cultivation (Pimentel et al. 2008). Although soybeans contain less oil than canola—about 18% soy oil compared with 30% oil for canola oil—soybeans can be produced with nearly zero nitrogen inputs (Pimentel et al. 2008).

The biomass yield of rapeseed/canola per hectare is also lower than that of soybeans—about 1,600 kg/ha for rapeseed/canola compared with 2,890 kg/ha for soybeans (Pimentel et al. 2008; USDA 2004). The production of 1,568 kg/ha rapeseed/canola requires an input of about 4.4 million kcal per hectare and costs about $669/ha (Pimentel et al. 2008). About 3,333 kg of rapeseed/canola oil is required to produce 1,000 kg of biodiesel (Pimentel et al. 2008). Therefore, all 333 million tons of rapeseed and canola produced in the United States in 2006 (USDA 2007) could be used to make 100 million liters of biodiesel, or 0.005% of the total oil used in the United States. The total energy input to produce the 1,000 liters of rapeseed/canola oil is 13 million kcal. This suggests a net loss of 58% of energy inputs (Pimentel et al. 2008). The cost per kilogram of biodiesel is also high, at $1.52. Rapeseed and canola are energy-intensive and economically inefficient biodiesel crops.

Oil Palm

There is a major effort to plant and harvest oil palms for biofuels in some tropical developing countries, especially Indonesia, Malaysia, Thailand, Colombia, and some in West Africa (Thoenes 2007). From 1997–98 to 2012–13 the production of palm oil has more than tripled, from 17 x 10^6 metric tons to 55 x 10^6 metric tons with production by Indonesia and Malaysia accounting for about 85% of total world production (USDA Foreign Agricultural Service 2001; USDA Foreign Agricultural Service 2013). Palm oil makes up over 34% of vegetable oils produced worldwide (USDA, Foreign Agricultural Service 2013a). The oil palm, once established after four years, will produce about 4,000 kg of oil per hectare per year (Carter et al. 2007). The energy inputs for maintaining the hectare of oil palm are indicated in Pimentel et al. (2008). The data suggest that about 7.4 million kcal are required to produce 26,000 kg of oil palm bunches. This 26,000 kg is sufficient palm nuts to produce 4,000 kg of palm oil. A total of 6.9 million kcal are required to process 6,500 kg of palm nuts to produce one ton of palm oil (Pimentel et al. 2008). Thus, the net return on fossil energy invested in production and processing totals 30%. This is clearly a better return than corn ethanol or soybean biodiesel. However, an estimated 200 milliliters (ml) (2,080 kcal) of methanol is a required addition to the

1,000 kg of palm oil, for transesterification (a reversible reaction in which one ester is converted into another as by interchange of ester groups with an alcohol in the presence of a base). This results in a negative 8% net energy output for palm oil.

There are several negative environmental and social issues associated with oil palm plantations. First, the removal of tropical rainforests to plant the oil palm results in an increase in CO_2 emissions (Thoenes 2007). Secondly, the removal of tropical rain forests and the planting of oil palms reduce the biodiversity of ecosystems. Finally, using oil palm for fuel reduces the availability of palm oil for human use and increases the price of palm oil. Although palm oil is not important nutritionally, it is the oil used by many in the developing world to cook their food (Thoenes 2007).

Algae for Oil Production

Some cultures of algae consist of 30% to 50% oil (Dimitrov 2007) which has sparked interest in using algae to increase the US oil supply, based on the theoretical claims that 47,000 to 308,000 liters/hectare/year (5,000 to 33,000 gallons/acre) of oil could be produced using algae (Briggs 2004; Valcent Products Inc. 2007). Based on these theoretical claims, the calculated cost per barrel would be $15 (Green Car 2006). The average commodity price for a barrel of crude oil in 2012 was $105 (World Bank 2013). If the above estimated production and price of oil produced from algae were correct, US annual oil needs could theoretically be met if 100% of all US land were in algal culture.

Despite all the algae-related research and claims dating back to 1970s, none of the projected algae and oil yields have been achieved (Dimitrov 2007). To the contrary, one calculated estimate, based on all the included costs of using algae, put the cost at $800 per barrel, not $15 per barrel. Still, estimates vary widely, in part because algae biodiesel has largely failed to get beyond the laboratory or the pilot plant stage. Algae, like all plants, require large quantities of nitrogen and water in addition to significant fossil energy inputs for the production system (Goldman and Ryther 1977). The absolute maximum visible light energy fixation rate for photosynthesis for *any* plant is 8%, whereas 1–3% is common for crop plants, but only while they are growing, since a portion of the year in the temperate zone nothing grows, and any photosynthetic efficiency has to take this nonactive period into account (Moore et al. 1998).

Conclusion

Recent policy decisions have mandated increased production of biofuels in the United States and worldwide. For instance, in the Energy Independence and Security Act of 2007 (US Energy Information Agency 2008), President Bush set "a mandatory Renewable Fuel Standard (RFS) requiring fuel producers to use at least 36 billion gallons of biofuel in 2022." This mandate would require 1.6 billion tons of biomass harvested per year as well as harvesting 80% of all biomass in the United States, including all agricultural crops, grasses, and forests (Pimentel et al. 2009). With nearly total biomass harvested, biodiversity and food supplies in the United States would be decimated; there is no evidence either in Perlack et al. (2005) or in the legislation (which is based largely on Perlack et al.'s assumptions) that this eventuality was ever considered.

Most conversions of biomass into ethanol and biodiesel result in a negative energy return, based on careful up-to-date analysis of all the fossil energy inputs. Four of the negative energy returns are as follows: corn ethanol at minus 46%; switchgrass at minus 50%; soybean biodiesel at minus 63%; and rapeseed at minus 58%. Even palm oil production in Thailand results in a minus 8% net energy return, when the methanol requirement for transesterification is considered in the equation.

Increased biofuel production also has the capability to impact the quality of food plants in crop systems. The release of large quantities of carbon dioxide associated with the planting and processing of plant materials for biofuels is reported to reduce the nutritional quality of major world foods, including wheat, rice, barley, potatoes, and soybeans (Taub et al. 2008). Carbon dioxide levels are already over 30% higher than preindustrial levels, and they may double or even triple over the course of the 21st century (Loladze 2002). When crops are grown under twice the ambient atmospheric concentration of carbon dioxide, the mean protein levels in the crops may be reduced as much as 14%, and other micronutrients, such as phosphorus, sulfur, iron, calcium, zinc and copper, decline significantly as well (Loladze 2002; Taub et al. 2008).

There are additional problems associated with biofuels that have been ignored by some scientists and policymakers. The biofuels being created in order to diminish the dependence on fossil fuels actually depend on fossil fuels. In most cases, more fossil energy is required to produce a unit of biofuel compared with the energy that is produced (Pimentel et al. 2009). Furthermore, the United States is importing oil and natural gas to produce biofuels, which is further increasing the US dependence on foreign fossil fuels. Publications promoting biofuels have used incomplete or insufficient data to support their claims. For instance, claims that cellulosic ethanol provides net energy (Tilman et al. 2006) have not been experimentally verified because most of their calculations are theoretical—not a single commercial cellulosic ethanol production plant exists. Finally, environmental problems including water pollution from fertilizers and pesticides, global warming, soil erosion, and air pollution are intensifying with biofuel production. There is simply not enough land, water, and energy to produce biofuels at acceptable cost in terms of the externalities already apparent. Increased use of biofuels would therefore further damage the global environment and, especially, the world food system.

Are there alternatives to the current trend of increasing production of biofuels? One alternative that has not even been suggested in the United States since the Carter administration is energy conservation. Conservation would probably involve the federal government having a say in how products are produced and how efficiently these products utilize energy. For example, the Obama administration has worked to set targets for miles/gallon for vehicles produced by the automotive industry; a more expansive energy conservation policy would extend beyond vehicles to virtually all manufactured products—especially products used widely and that consume significant energy. Another possibility would be for the federal government to end *all* subsidies offered to the fossil fuel sector of the economy and give these subsidies to companies and universities to support research and development of alternative energy technologies (other than biofuels), such as wind power, solar thermal, solar voltaic, hydroelectric, infrastructure technologies necessary for integrating alternative electricity generation into the national power grid, and energy storage technologies.

In the case of the United States, such policies have been discussed under broad initiatives to build a national electric high-speed railway transport system for both goods and passengers, as well as local commuter transport powered by electricity. The focus on biofuels reflects the almost total dependence of the world transport system on liquid fuels, but chemical researchers are discovering different catalysts that would synthesize methanol and possibly allow the synthesis of other chemicals and fuels from water and carbon dioxide (Barton et al. 2008; Riduan et al. 2009; Huang et al. 2010; Wesselbaum et al. 2012). Production of methanol and other chemicals from a catalyst-mediated reaction between carbon dioxide and water, powered by electricity from either the sun or wind, can recycle carbon dioxide from major emission sources back into fuel and other chemicals, and no fossil energy would be needed (Zandonella 2012). These avenues of research suggest that there is nothing inevitable about the displacement of agricultural cropland currently used for food production, or about the energy extensive and ecologically disruptive effects of a global push for biofuels.

ACKNOWLEDGEMENT

This research was supported in part by the Podell Emeriti Award at Cornell University.

NOTE

1. Dr. David Pimentel was at a meeting in Washington, D.C., with Perlack after the publication of his report (Perlack et al. 2005) and told him that his 1.3 billion tons of biomass to be collected was much too high; Perlack did not agree.

REFERENCES

Artuzi, J. P., and R. L. Contiero. 2006. "Herbicides Applied in Soybean and the Productivity of Corn in Succession." *Pesquisa Agronpecuaria Brasilera* 41:1119–1123.

Aroca, R., and J. M. Ruiz-Lozano. 2009. "Introduction of Plant Tolerance to Semi-arid Environments by Beneficial Soil Microorganisms—A Review." In *Sustainable Agricultural Reviews*. Vol. 2, *Climate Change, Intercropping, Pest Control and Beneficial Microorganisms*, edited by E. Lichtfouse, 121–135. Dordrecht, The Netherlands: Springer.

Barton, E. E., D. M. Rampulla, and A. B. Bocarsly. 2008. "Selective Solar-Driven Reduction of CO2 to Methanol Using a Catalyzed p-GaP Based Photoelectrochemical Cell." *Journal of the American Chemical Society* 130:6342–6344.

Bloomberg, M. R., and G.P. Mitchell. 2012. "Fracking is Too Important to Foul Up." *Washington Post*, August 23. http://www.washingtonpost.com/opinions/fracking-is-too-important-to-foul-up/2012/08/23/d320e6ee-ea0e-11e1-a80b-9f898562d010_story.html.

BP (British Petroleum). 2002. *BP Statistical Review of World Energy 2001*. London: BP.

——. 2005. *BP Statistical Review of World Energy*. London: BP.

Briggs, M. 2004. "Widescale Biodiesel Production from Algae." *Energy Bulletin*, October 3. http://www.energybulletin.net/node/2364.

Brown, L. R. 2002. *World's Rangelands Deteriorating under Mounting Pressure*. Washington, DC: Earth Policy Institute. http://www.earth-policy.org/plan_b_updates/2002/update6.

Brown, L. R. 2008. *Why Ethanol Production Will Drive World Food Prices Even Higher in 2008*. Washington, DC: Earth Policy Institute. http://www.earth-policy.org/plan_b_updates/2008/update69.

Burning Issues. 2006. *What Are the Medical Effects of Exposure to Smoke Particles?* Point Arena, CA: Burning Issues. http://burningissues.org/health-effects.html.

——. 2011. *The 150 Billion Dollar per Year Problem*. Point Arena, CA: Burning Issues. http://www.burningissues.org/150-billion-dollar-problem.html.

Campbell, C. J. 1997. *The Coming Oil Crisis*. Brentwood, Essex, England: Multi-Science Publishing & Petroconsultants.

Campbell, C. J. 2006. "The Coming Global Oil Crisis: Regular Conventional Oil Production to 2100 and Resource Based Production Forecast." Revised August 15, 2006. http://www.hubbertpeak.com/campbell/.

Carter, C., W. Finley, J. Fry, D. Jackson, and L. Willis. 2007. "Palm Oil Markets and Future Supply." *European Journal of Lipid Science and Technology* 109:307–314.

Cline, W. R. 2007. *Global Warming and Agriculture: Impact Estimates by Country*. Washington, DC: Peterson Institute for International Economics. http://www.petersoninstitute.org/publications/briefs/cline4037.pdf.

Conway, E. 2004. "There is Enough Oil to Last 40 Years, Says BP." *Energy Bulletin*, January 13. http://www.energybulletin.net/node/659.

Davis, J. M., and V. M. Thomas. 2006. "Systematic Approach to Evaluating Trade-offs among Fuel Options: The Lessons of MTBE." *Annals of the New York Academy of Sciences* 1076:498–515.

Dimitrov, K. 2007. *Green Fuel Technologies: A Case Study for Industrial Photosynthetic Energy Capture*. Brisbane, Australia. http://my-co2.net/documents/documents_in_english/biofuels-Algae-CaseStudy-09.pdf.

Drum, K. 2012. Ethanol Subsidies: Not Gone, Just Hidden a Little Better. *Mother Jones*, January 5, 2012.http://www.motherjones.com/kevin-drum/2012/01/ethanol-subsidies-not-gone-just-hidden-little-better.

Duncan, R. C., and W. Youngquist. 1999. "Encircling the Peak of World Oil Production." *Natural Resources Research* 8 (3): 219–232.

EBB (European Biodiesel Board). 2007. *European Biodiesel Production Doubles in 2 Years; EBB Warns on Need to Eliminate "Legislative and Standards Desert."* Brussells: EBB. http://www.greencarcongress.com/2007/07/european-biodie.html.

Earth Policy Institute. 2008. *World Grain Consumption and Stocks, 1960–2007*. Washington, DC: Earth Policy Institute. http://www.earthpolicy.org/index.php?/plan_b_updates/2008/update72.

FAO (Food and Agriculture Organization of the United Nations). 2002. *Food Balance Sheets*. Food and Agriculture Organization of the United Nations. Rome: FAO.

——. 2003. *Food Balance Sheets*. Rome: FAO. http://faostat.fao.org/site/368/default.aspx#ancor.

——. 2013. FAOSTAT. Rome: FAO. Accessed July 1. http://faostat.fao.org/.

Farrell, A. E., R. J. Plevin, B. T. Turner, A. D. Jones, M. O. O'Hare, and D. M. Kammen. 2006. "Ethanol Can Contribute to Energy and Environmental Goals." *Science* 311:506–508.

Ferguson, A. R. B. 2001. *Biomass and Energy*. Manchester, England: Optimum Population Trust.

——. 2003. "Implications of the USDA 2002 Update on Ethanol from Corn." *Optimum Population Trust Journal*. http://www.populationmatters.org/journal/j31.pdf?phpMyAdmin=e11a8a687c20198d9ad050fba1aa7f2f

Friedman, D. 2011. "What the Tea Party Gets Wrong." In: IDEAS (Blog), August 10, 2011. http://daviddfriedman.blogspot.com/2011/08/what-tea-party-gets-wrong.html

Frondel, M., and J. Peters. 2007. "Biodiesel: A New Oildorado?" *Energy Policy* 35:1675–1684.

Fryrear, D. W., and J. D. Bilbro. 1994. "Wind Erosion Control with Residues and Related Practices." In *Managing Agricultural Residues*, edited by P. W. Unger, 7–17. Boca Raton, FL: Lewis Publishers.

Fujino, J., K. Yamaji, and H. Yamamoto. 1999. "Biomass-Balance Table for Evaluating Bioenergy Resources." *Applied Energy* 62:375–389.

Giampietro, M., and D. Pimentel. 1994. "Energy Utilization." In *Encyclopedia of Agricultural Science*. Vol. 2, edited by C.J. Arntzen and E.M. Ritter, 63–76. San Diego, CA: Academic Press.

Gleick, P. H. 1996. "Basic Water Requirements for Human Activities: Meeting Basic Needs." *Water International* 21:83–92.

Goldman, J. C., and J. H. Ryther. 1977. "Mass Production of Algae: Engineering Aspects." In *Biological Solar Energy Conversion*, edited by A. Mitsui, 367–378. New York: Academic Press.

Green Car. 2006. "Malaysia and Indonesia Set Aside 40% of Palm Oil Crop for Biodiesel Production." *Green Car Congress*, July 21. http://www.greencarcongress.com/2006/07/malaysia_and_in.html.

Heinberg, R. 2003. *The Party's Over: Oil, War and the Fate of Industrial Societies*. Gabriola, BC: New Society Publishers.

Hendrickson, O. Q. and J. Galland. 1993. "Residential Wood Heating: Forest, the Atmosphere and Public Consciousness." Paper written for the 1993 Air and Waste Management Association Conference. http://www.woodheat.org/index.php?option=com_content&view=article&id=77&Itemid=84.

Hodge, C. 2003. "More Evidence Mounts for Banning, Not Expanding, Use of Ethanol in Gasoline." *Oil and Gas Journal* 101 (38): 20–25. http://www.calgasoline.com/CalHodge/a20%20on%20ethanol%20ban%20do%20not%20expand%20update%20100603.pdf.

Homer-Dixon, T. 2012. "Climate Change's Costs Hit the Plate." *Globe and Mail*, July 24. http://www.theglobeandmail.com/commentary/climate-changes-costs-hit-the-plate/article4436775/.

Huang, W. 2004. "U.S. Increasingly Imports Nitrogen Fertilizer." *Amber Waves*. February: 9. Washington, DC: U.S. Department of Agriculture, Economic Research Service. http://ageconsearch.umn.edu/bitstream/131799/2/findings_scienceandtechnology.pdf.

Huang, F., G. Lu, L. Zhao, H. Li, and Z.-X. Wang. 2010. "The Catalytic Role of N-heterocyclic Carbene in a Metal-Free Conversion of Carbon Dioxide into Methanol: a Computational Mechanism Study. *Journal of the American Chemical Society* 132:12388–12396.

Jacobson, M. Z. 2007. "Effects of Ethanol (E85) versus Gasoline Vehicles on Cancer and Mortality in the United States." *Environmental Science and Technology* 41:4150–5157.

Kim, S. and B. E. Dale. 2005. "Life Cycle Assessment of Various Cropping Systems Utilized for Producing Biofuels: Bioethanol and Biodiesel." *Biomass Engineering* 29:426–439.

Kitani, O. 1999. "Biomass Resources." In *CIGR Handbook of Agricultural Engineering.* Vol. 5, edited by O. Kitani, T. Jungbluth, R. M. Pearth, and A. Ramdani, 6–11. St. Joseph, MI: American Society of Agricultural Engineering. http://www.cigr.org/documents/CIGRHandbookVol5.pdf

Konrad, T. 2007. "International Energy Agency Wakes Up and Smells the Peak Oil." Seeking Alpha. http://seekingalpha.com/article/40617-international-energy-agency-wakes-up-and-smellsthe-peak-oil.

Koplow, D. 2006. *Biofuels—At What Cost?: Government Support for Ethanol and Biodiesel in the United States.* Geneva, Switzerland: The Global Studies Initiative (GSI) of the International Institute for Sustainable Development (IISD). http://www.globalsubsidies.org/files/assets/Brochure_-_US_Update.pdf.

Koplow, D. and Steenblik, R. 2008. "Subsidies to Ethanol in the United States." In *Biofuels, Solar and Wind as Renewable Energy Systems: Benefits and Risks,* edited by D. Pimentel, 79–108. Dordrecht, The Netherlands: Springer.

Lal, R. 2004. "Soil Carbon Sequestration Impacts on Global Climate Change and Food Security." *Science* 34:1623–1627.

Lal, R., R. F. Follett, J. M. Kimble, and C. V. Cole. 1999. "Managing U.S. Cropland to Sequester Carbon in Soil." *Journal of Soil and Water Conservation* 54:374–381.

Leek, L. 2012. "Obama's Riskiest Jobs-Killer." *New York Post,* June 11. http://www.nypost.com/p/news/opinion/opedcolumnists/obama_riskiest_jobs_killer_jcCc1GTNgDfeOPAx40JlVN.

Loladze, I. 2002. "Rising Atmospheric CO2 and Human Nutrition: Toward Globally Imbalanced Plant Stoichiometry?" *Trends in Ecology & Evolution* 17 (10): 457–461.

Lunsford, P. 2007. "Is the IEA Admitting the Peak Has Been Reached?" Relocalization Network. http://old.relocalize.net/is_the_iea_admitting_the_peak_has_been_reached.

Lydersen, K. 2012. "Is Natural Gas Killing Coal?" *Midwest Energy News,* April 17. http://www.midwestenergynews.com/2012/04/17/is-natural-gas-killing-coal/.

McLaughlin, S. B., and M. E. Walsh. 1998. "Evaluating Environmental Consequences of Producing Herbaceous Crops for Bioenergy." *Biomass and Bioenergy* 14:4317–4324

Moore, R., W. D. Clark, D. S. Vodopich, K. R. Stern, and R. Lewis. 1998. *Botany.* 2nd ed. New York: WCB/McGraw-Hill.

NAS (National Academy of Sciences). 2003. *Frontiers in Agricultural Research: Food, Health, Environment, and Communities.,* Washington, DC: NAS. Briefs from the book at the following website: http://dels.nas.edu/Report/Frontiers-Agricultural-Research-Food-Health/10585.

NGO. 2013. "Negative Population Growth: Facts and Figures—Total Midyear World Population: 1950–2040." Negative Population Growth. http://www.npg.org/facts/world_pop_year.htm

New York Times. 2012. "Coal." Accessed August 2. http://topics.nytimes.com/top/news/business/energy-environment/coal/index.html.

OECD. 2013. OECD: *Membership and Partners.* Organization for Economic Co-operation and Development. http://www.oecd.org/about/membersandpartners/

Ozaktas, T. 2000. "Compression Ignition Engine Fuel Properties of a Used Sunflower Oil-Diesel Fuel Blend." *Energy Sources* 22:4377–4382.

Patzek, T. W. 2004. "Thermodynamics of the Corn-Ethanol Biofuel Cycle." *Critical Review in Plant Sciences* 23:6519–6567.

Patzek, T.W. 2012. "Can Switchgrass Deliver the Ethanol Needed to Power U.S. Transportation?" In *Global Economic and Environmental Aspects of Biofuels*, edited by D. Pimentel, 97–146. Boca Raton, FL: CRC Press.

PRB (Population Reference Bureau). 2012. *2012 World Population Data Sheet*. Washington, DC: PRB. http://www.prb.org/Publications/Datasheets/2012/world-population-data-sheet.aspx.

Pear, R. 2012. "After Three Decades, Tax Credit for Ethanol Expires." *New York Times*, January 1. http://www.nytimes.com/2012/01/02/business/energy-environment/after-three-decades-federal-tax-credit-for-ethanol-expires.html.

Perlack, R. D., L. L. Wright, A. Turhollow, R. L. Graham, B. Stokes, and D. C. Erbach. 2005. *BIOMASS as Feedstock for a Bioenergy and Bioproducts Industry: The Technical Feasibility of a Billion-Ton Annual Supply*. ORNL/TM-2005/66. Washington DC: US Department of Energy; US Department of Agriculture, Forest Service. http://www1.eere.energy.gov/biomass/pdfs/final_billionton_vision_report2.pdf.

Pimentel, D. 2001. "Biomass Utilization, Limits of." In *Encyclopedia of Physical Science and Technology*. Vol 2, edited by R. A. Meyers, 159–171. 3rd ed. San Diego: Academic Press.

Pimentel, D. 2006. "Soil Erosion: A Food and Environmental Threat." *Environment, Development and Sustainability* 8:119–137.

Pimentel, D. 2008. "Renewable and Solar Energy Technologies: Energy and Environmental Issues." In *Biofuels, Solar and Wind as Renewable Energy Systems: Benefits and Risks*, edited by D. Pimentel, 1–17. Dordrecht, The Netherlands: Springer.

Pimentel, D., B. Berger, D. Filiberto, M. Newton, B. Wolfe, E. Karabinakis, S. Clark, E. Poon, E. Abbett, and S. Nandagopal. 2004. "Water Resources: Current and Future Issues." *BioScience* 54:909–918.

Pimentel, D., S. Cooperstein, H. Randell, D. Filiberto, S. Sorrentino, B. Kaye, C. Nicklin, et al. 2007. "Ecology of Increasing Diseases: Population Growth and Environmental Degradation." *Human Ecology* 35:653–668.

Pimentel, D., A. Marklein, M. A. Toth, M. Karpoff, G. S. Paul, R. McCormack, J. Kyriazis, and T. Krueger. 2008. "Biofuel Impacts on World Food Supply: Use of Fossil Fuel, Land and Water Resources." *Energies* 1:41–78. DOI: 10.3390/en1010041. http://www.mdpi.org/energies/papers/en1020041.pdf.

——. 2009. "Food versus Biofuels: Environmental and Economic Costs." *Human Ecology* 37:1–12.

Pimentel, D., and T. W. Patzek. 2007. "Ethanol Production: Energy and Economic Issues Related to U.S. and Brazilian Sugarcane." *Natural Resources Research* 16:3235–3242.

——. 2008. "Ethanol Production Using Corn, Switchgrass and Wood; Biodiesel Production Using Soybean." In *Biofuels, Solar and Wind as Renewable Energy Systems: Benefits and Risks*, edited by D. Pimentel, 375–396. Dordrecht, The Netherlands: Springer.

Pimentel, D., and M. Pimentel. 2003. "Sustainability of Meat-Based and Plant-Based Diets and the Environment." *American Journal of Clinical Nutrition* 78 (Suppl.): 660S–663S.

——. 2008. *Food, Energy and Society*, 3rd ed. Boca Raton, FL: CRC Press.

Pimentel, D., J. Trager, S. Palmer, J. Zhang, B. Greenfield, E. Nash, K. Hartman, D. Kirshenblatt, and A. Kroeger, 2012. "Energy Production from Corn, Cellulosic Biomass and Algae." In *Global Economic and Environmental Aspects of Biofuels*, edited by D. Pimentel, 321–355. Boca Raton, FL: Taylor & Francis.

Pimentel, D., and D. Wen. 2004. "China and the World: Population, Food and Resource Scarcity." In *Dare to Dream: Vision of 2050 Agriculture in China*, edited by T. C. Tso and K. He, 103–116. Beijing: China Agricultural University Press.

Pimentel, D., M. Whitecraft, Z. R. Scott, L. Zhao, P. Satkiewicz, T.J. Scott, J. Phillips, et al. 2010. "Will Limited Land, Water, and Energy Control Human Population Number in the Future?" *Human Ecology* 38 (5): 599–611.

Pimentel, D., S. Williamson, C. E. Alexander, O. Gonzalez-Pagan, C. Kontak, and S. E. Mulkey, 2008. "Reducing Energy Inputs in the U.S. Food System." *Human Ecology* 36 (4): 459–471.

Rasnake, M. 1983. "Tillage and Crop Residue Management." Lexington: University of Kentucky College of Agriculture. Food and Environment, AGR-99. http://www.ca.uky.edu/agc/pubs/agr/agr99/agr99.htm.

Riduan, S. N., Y. Zhang, and J.Y. Ying. 2009. "Conversion of Carbon Dioxide into Methanol with Silanes over N-heterocyclic Carbene Catalysts." *Angewandte Chemie, International Edition* 48:3322–3325.

Shapouri, H., and P. Gallagher. 2005. *USDA's 2002 Ethanol Cost-of-Production Survey*. Agricultural Economic Report 841. Washington, DC: US Department of Agriculture. http://ethanolrfa.3cdn.net/6dfd76a7273de6109c_uwm6bh2wy.pdf.

Smith, K. R. 2006. "Health Impacts of Household Fuelwood Use in Developing Countries." *Unasylva* 224. http://www.fao.org/docrep/009/a0789e/a0789e09.html.

Socolow, R., R. Hotinski, J. B. Greenblatt, and S. Pacala, 2004. "Solving the Climate Problem." *Environment* 46:108–119.

Taub, D. R., B. Miller, and H. Allen. 2008. "Effects of Elevated CO2 on the Protein Concentration of Food Crops: a Meta-Analysis." *Global Change Biology* 14 (3): 565–575.

Thoenes, P. 2007. *Biofuels and Commodity Markets—Palm Oil Focus*. Rome: Food and Agriculture Organization of the United Nations, Commodities and Trade Division. http://www.rlc.fao.org/es/prioridades/bioenergia/pdf/commodity.pdf.

Tickell, J. 2006. *Biodiesel America: How to Achieve Energy Security, Free America from Middle-east Oil Dependence, and Make Money Growing Fuel*. Yorkshire Press. Published in association with the Biodiesel America Organization and the National Biodiesel Board.

Tilman, D., J. Hill, and C. Lehman. 2006. "Carbon-Negative Biofuels from Low-Input High-Diversity Grassland Biomass." *Science* 314:1598–1600.

Troeh, F. R., A. H. Hobbs, and R. L. Donahue. 2004. *Soil and Water Conservation*. Upper Saddle River, NJ: Prentice Hall.

USCB (US Census Bureau). 2008. *Statistical Abstract of the United States: 2009*. 128th ed. Washington, DC: USCB.

——. 2009. *Statistical Abstract of the United States: 2010*. 129th ed. Washington, DC: USCB.

US Congressional Budget Office. 2010. Using Biofuel Tax Credits to Achieve Energy and Environmental Policy Goals. A CBO Study. Congress of the United States, Congressional Budget Office. http://www.cbo.gov/sites/default/files/cbofiles/ftpdocs/114xx/doc11477/07-14-biofuels.pdf.

USDA (US Department of Agriculture). 1975. *Nutritive Value of American Foods*. Agriculture Handbook No. 456. Washington, DC: USDA, Agricultural Research Service.

——. 2004. *Agricultural Statistics, 2004*. CD-ROM. A1.47/2:2004.Washington, DC: USDA, National Agriculture Statistics Service.

——. 2005. *Statistics of Oilseeds, Fats, and Oils*. Chapter III. Washington, DC: USDA-NASS Agricultural Statistics. http://www.nass.usda.gov/Publications/Ag_Statistics/2010/Chapter03.pdf.

——. 2006. *Agricultural Statistics 2006*. Washington, DC: US Government Printing Office.

——. 2007. *Agricultural Statistics 2007*. Washington, DC: US Government Printing Office.

——. 2008. *Amber Waves: The Economics of Food, Farming, Natural Resources and Rural America*. Washington, DC: USDA. http://www.ers.usda.gov/amberwaves/allissues/ShowIssue.asp?Issue=February08.

USDA, Economic Research Service. 2013. Farm Practices and Management: Chemical Inputs—Overview. http://www.ers.usda.gov/topics/farm-practices-management/chemical-inputs.aspx

USDA, Foreign Agricultural Service. 2001. Oilseeds: Palm Oil: World Supply and Distribution. http://www.fas.usda.gov/oilseeds/circular/2001/01-07/palm.pdf.

USDA, Foreign Agricultural Service. 2013a. Oilseeds: Table 3: Major Vegetable Oils: World Supply and Distribution (Commodity View). In: Production, Supply and Distribution Online, Reports (Listed by Category), Oilseeds. http://www.fas.usda.gov/psdonline/psdHome.aspx.

USDA, Foreign Agricultural Service. 2013. Oilseeds: Table 11: Palm Oil: World Supply and Distribution. In: Production, Supply and Distribution Online, Reports (Listed by Category), Oilseeds (see Table 11: Palm Oil). http://www.fas.usda.gov/psdonline/psdHome.aspx.

US Energy Information Administration. 2008. *Energy Independence and Security Act of 2007: Summary of Provisions*. Washington, DC: US Energy Information Administration. http://www.eia.doe.gov/oiaf/aeo/otheranalysis/aeo_2008analysispapers/eisa.html.

US Energy Information Administration. 2013a. *International Energy Outlook 2013*. US Department of Energy, US Energy Information Administration. http://www.eia.gov/forecasts/ieo/pdf/0484(2013).pdf

US Energy Information Administration. 2013b. Petroleum & Other Liquids: Monthly Biodiesel Production Report. Table 2. U.S. Biodiesel Production, Sales, and Stocks. http://www.eia.gov/biofuels/biodiesel/production/table2.pdf

Valcent Products Inc. 2007. "Initial Data from the Vertigro Field Test Bed Plant Reports Average Production of 276 Tons of Algae Bio Mass on a Per Acre/per Year Basis." Press Release. http://www.marketwire.com/press-release/Valcent-Products-Inc-Initial-Data-From-Vertigro-Field-Test-Bed-Plant-Reports-Average-OTC-Bulletin-Board-VCTPF-802275.htm.

WHO (World Health Organization). 2000. *Nutrition for Health and Development: A Global Agenda for Combating Malnutrition*. Geneva, Switzerland: WHO. http://whqlibdoc.who.int/hq/2000/WHO_NHD_00.6.pdf.

Wesselbaum, S., T. vom Stein, J. Klankermayer, and W. Leitner. 2012. "Hydrogenation of Carbon Dioxide to Methanol by Using a Homogeneous Ruthenium-Phosphine Catalyst." *Angewandte Chemie, International Edition* 51:7499–7502.

World Bank. 2013. Commodity Price Forcast Update (Released: January 15, 2013). Table 1: Commodity Prices and Price Forcast in Nominal US Dollars. http://siteresources.worldbank.org/INTPROSPECTS/Resources/334934-1304428586133/Price_Forecast.pdf

World Food Programme. 2010. *Annual Performance Report for 2009*. WFP/EB.A/2010/4. Rome: World Food Programme. http://one.wfp.org/eb/docs/2010/wfp218692~1.pdf.

Yacobucci, B. D. 2012. *Biofuels Incentives: A Summary of Federal Programs*. Washington, DC: Congressional Research Service. http://www.fas.org/sgp/crs/misc/R40110.pdf.

Youngquist, W. 1997. *GeoDestinies: The Inevitable Control of Earth Resources over Nations and Individuals*. Portland, OR: National Book Company.

Youngquist, W., and R. C. Duncan. 2003. "North American Gas: Data Show Supply Problems." *Natural Resources Research* 12:4229–4240.

Zandonella, C. 2012. "Startup Born in Princeton Lab Turns Carbon Dioxide into Fuels." *News at Princeton*, June 14. http://www.princeton.edu/main/news/archive/S33/95/96G16/index.xml?section=featured.

CHAPTER 8

ALTERNATIVE PATHS TO FOOD SECURITY

NORMAN UPHOFF

INTRODUCTION

EVER since the successes of the Green Revolution in Asia in the 1970s and 1980s, the primary strategy for raising agricultural production has been what is commonly referred to as "modern agriculture." This is based upon (i) making varietal improvements in targeted crops, achieved through either conventional plant breeding or, more recently, through genetic engineering (GE), together with (ii) increased utilization of purchased inputs, such as inorganic fertilizers, agrochemical crop protection, and usually petroleum-derived energy to support larger-scale production with extensive mechanization. Also part of the "modern agriculture" package has been increased irrigation which provides more applications of water than previously. This "seeds-and-fertilizer" strategy has shaped most research and extension programs for promoting food production, and, not surprisingly, it has become buttressed over time by significant commercial and political interests.

In this chapter an approach to agricultural development is considered that depends neither on making changes in crop varieties nor on greater expenditure on external inputs. While the focus here is on plant crops, we note that the same agroecological principles are being used to improve livestock production (Savory and Butterfield 1999). As seen below, it is possible to increase the productivity of currently available crop varieties very substantially just by modifying the management of plants, soil, water, and nutrients in certain ways that improve their environment for growth. There is no requirement of new seeds, although new varieties can be used beneficially with improved practices. An added benefit is that altered management results in crops that are more robust and better able to resist threats to crop production that are now increasing as a consequence of climate change, particularly losses due to pests and diseases, as well as stresses from extremes in rainfall (drought or flooding) and in temperature. Alternative management practices, as discussed below, mobilize biological processes that elicit beneficial interspecies interactions and enhance plants' expression of their existing genetic potentials.

This approach, broadly characterized as "agroecological," can be undertaken either as an alternative or as a complement to what is called "modern agriculture." From an ecosystem perspective, crops are not regarded as isolated species, with other organisms seen mostly as competitors or adversaries (weeds, pests, or pathogens). Nor is the soil treated as an essentially inert medium, in which the plants being grown are primarily dependent upon farmers' inputs. Rather, agroecological approaches aim to capitalize on symbiotic relationships among the huge number of complementary species, both flora and fauna, that cohabit agroecosystems. This strategy is not some kind of backward or atavistic version of agriculture. In fact, it derives support from contemporary knowledge in disciplines such as microbiology, soil ecology, plant genomics and proteomics, and epigenetics.

Most agricultural research and practice in the latter half of the twentieth century paid little attention to the effects of the soil biota, for example. Closer connections between soil science and crop science are now emerging, however, with the realization that soil microorganisms that reside in plants "above-ground canopies can enhance crops" expression of their genetic potentials (Uphoff et al. 2012). In this century, much is being learned about the contributions and management of soil organisms in their symbiotic relationships with plants (e.g., Selosse and Rousset 2011; Kiers et al. 2011). Possibly this will enable us to improve world agricultural production in the next several decades as much as (or possibly even more than) was achieved with the Green Revolution in preceding decades. Even though this chapter focuses primarily on rice, the single most important food crop worldwide, it is about more than rice cropping. It considers a paradigm shift taking shape within agriculture that is already improving the productivity of a wide variety of crops, from millet and mustard to turmeric and teff.

This shift could enable farmers in the future to meet society's food needs with reduced economic costs and with fewer adverse environmental impacts than now result from the practices of "modern agriculture." Whether this will occur, and how fast, will be determined in the decades ahead. However, even the prospect of many desirable benefits will not assure that the changes are easy, or welcomed by all. Technical and paradigmatic changes get introduced and advanced within a context of contending political interests and of institutional leverages and resistance. The experience reported here from recent innovation in the rice sector shows how technical change is connected with and sometimes impeded by the processes and frictions of politics and society.

Agroecological Approaches

Agroecology is based on understanding and engaging with the genetic potentials that already exist in plants (and animals) and within the soil and its resident biota (Altieri 1995, 2002; Gliessman 2007; Uphoff 2002). Agroecological applications seek to raise production by optimizing the growing environments for crops (and livestock), rather than by making modifications in their genes or by utilizing more synthetic or inorganic materials in agricultural production. It is true that further improvements made in crop genetic potentials can contribute to better results from the agroecological management of plants and animals. And some use of inorganic fertilizers may help farmers optimize their yield levels, provided there are no adverse effects on the microbiome, the communities of microbes that inhabit all plant and animal organisms, interacting with each other and with their host organisms. Agroecology is not necessarily "organic," although it generally favors organic nutrient amendments as a matter of pragmatics and economics.

The potentials of agroecological management to meet food needs—particularly for households with the most limited resources and with the greatest food insecurity—are considered here with reference to improvements being made in rice production. The System of Rice Intensification (SRI), developed some twenty-five years ago by a French priest during three decades of grassroots work with farmers in Madagascar (Laulanié 1993; Uphoff 2006), can raise paddy yields by 50 to 100 percent, or more, with less inputs of seed, water, fertilizer (although with more provision of compost), and often with less labor once the methods are mastered or mechanization is introduced. Producing "more with less" is, however, a challenge to the currently prevailing scientific paradigm, which is based on introducing external inputs, as well as to many commercial interests that benefit from providing these inputs.

One might expect that an opportunity to produce more output with less input would be seized upon quickly and widely. However, getting SRI accepted and utilized has been a slow and difficult process, although it is now finally gaining speed as the merits of SRI ideas and methods are demonstrated in Asia, Africa and Latin America (http://sri.ciifad.cornell.edu/countries/index.html). This case study on SRI does not suggest that making further genetic improvements is not desirable; only that these may be less necessary and less urgent than argued by proponents of "modern agriculture," and especially by those who promote transgenic plant breeding. Creating new varieties with certain genetically determined traits has been presented as a *sine qua non* for "feeding the world." However, this may not be correct.

Whether (or to what extent) food production can be improved without requiring development of new varieties and without increasing the use of external inputs is of considerable significance for this chapter, looking ahead as well as to the past and present. Given the adverse effects of climate change on crop performance anticipated in the decades ahead, crops' resilience to biotic and abiotic stresses, to pests and diseases, and to climatic hazards will become ever more important to meet world food needs.

This case gives evidence of the ways in which political and institutional interests can impinge upon making changes in agricultural theory and practice. Even getting SRI methods *evaluated* has been resisted by some scientists who work within the established paradigm for crop improvement (Sinclair 2004; Sinclair and Cassman 2004). Conservation agriculture, an agroecological strategy that eliminates tillage (plowing) in conjunction with maintaining vegetative cover on the soil and rotating the crops grown, countervailing the powerful trend toward monoculture (Friedrich et al. 2009; www.fao.org/ag/ca), has met with some similar resistance (Giller et al. 2009; Andersson and Giller 2012). So SRI should not be considered as an isolated case.

In analytical terms, agroecologically informed methods aim to optimize the environmental conditions (*E*) that affect the expression and realization of the genetic endowments for a particular plant (or animal). The latter is referred to as a phenotype (***P***), the actual biological phenomenon. This will diverge from the initial genetic potential (the genotype, **G**) according to the organism's history of development. Plant and animal breeders summarize the relationship among ***E*, *G*** and ***P*** in this notional equation:

$$P = (f)\ G + E + [G \times E],$$

where any crop (or animal) being produced (***P***) is seen as a result of its genotype (***G***) and its environment (***E***), and of *continuous interaction* between the genotype and all relevant environmental factors [***G x E***].

Paradigms for agricultural development can be distinguished analytically as follows. Biotechnology and genetic engineering focus on how to change and improve the ***G*** factor in this equation, seeking to achieve greater productivity of crops (or livestock) in a specific environment or for many environments by making changes in the genome. The environments (***E***) in which a crop (or an animal) is grown are expected to be managed to suit the given **G**, by providing inorganic nutrients from fertilizer, agrochemical means of protection, water inputs through irrigation, or other mechanisms. Everything pivots around **G**. With agroecology, in contrast, the primary concern is with making modifications in ***E*** so as to achieve, by promoting more productive and sustainable ***G x E*** interactions, the greatest productivity from any given **G** in the present and/or over time.

This equation makes clear that *both* **G** and **E** are important, indeed essential. Genetic potentials are the starting point for all organisms, from microbes to mammals. All living organisms (phenotypes) are the outcome of myriad environmental inputs and influences that affect the expression of their genetic endowment (genotype). In agroecological practice, there is particular concern with engaging the services of beneficial microbes (bacteria and fungi), other soil organisms, and the ubiquitous earthworms and other soil-system enrichers that function both above- and belowground (Wardle 2002; Wolfe 2001). To the extent that modifying management can produce cost-effective and more profitable results, a breeding strategy for agricultural improvement that focuses primarily on **G** and gives short shrift to ***G x E*** interactions will become less attractive. This observation could have significant implications for the future of what is now called "modern agriculture."

The chapter reviews, first, the opportunities that SRI methods are opening up compared to current agricultural practices, even "best management practices" now recommended by crop scientists. SRI is presented here as an example of agroecological management that is convergent with other production strategies, such as agroforestry, conservation tillage, and integrated pest management. These have been grouped under the broad heading of "low-input intensification" in a study commissioned by the European Parliament (Meyer 2009), and as "sustainable intensification" in a report for the British Royal Society (Royal Society 2009). SRI is thus not an isolated example, but rather an exemplification of the "agroecological intensification" discussed by Nelson and Coe in their chapter "Agroecological Intensification of Smallholder Farming, Chapter 4 of this volume."

The chapter also reports on recent research that documents beneficial symbiotic associations between plants and microbes (section 4). These could help explain the phenotypical results achieved with SRI management practices. We will consider also how other crops, such as wheat, sugarcane, finger millet, teff, mustard (rapeseed), and even some pulses and vegetables, are benefiting from extensions or extrapolations of SRI ideas and practices (section 5). What is being learned from SRI experience is not relevant only for rice. Agroecological methods represent a departure from genocentric strategies for raising agricultural production that rely heavily on agrochemical inputs (section 6), although this departure has not been without controversy (section 7). Broader implications for politics and society are discussed in the concluding section. The sources for this article are more varied and more contemporary than for most academic presentations because the SRI phenomenon is "a work in progress."

The System of Rice Intensification

This methodology for agroecological crop management resulted from three decades of observation and experimentation in Madagascar by a French Jesuit, Fr. Henri de Laulanié. Working closely with Malagasy farmers from 1961 to 1995, he studied carefully what conditions could best support their rice plants. Modifying age-old practices such as dense planting and continuous flooding led to rice phenotypes that were not only more productive, but also had more resistance to various stresses, from pests and diseases to adverse climatic events like drought or storms.

With SRI, what is "intensified" is not farmers' use of purchased inputs (new seeds, chemical fertilizers, crop protectants, and more water). That is how intensification is usually understood (Reichardt et al. 1998). What are in fact intensified with SRI practice are knowledge, skill, and management. Although initially SRI can be more labor-intensive while the methods are being learned, once these are mastered, labor inputs can generally be reduced. In many countries a major selling point for SRI is its *reduction* in farmers' labor expenditure, while requiring also less seed, water, fertilizer, and other inputs (Xu et al. 2005). Intensification with SRI is more mental than material.

Evidence of these effects continues to accumulate, some getting published in the peer-reviewed agronomic literature after earlier resistance (e.g., Ceesay et al. 2006; Chapagain and Yamaji 2010; Lin et al. 2009; Mishra and Salokhe 2008, 2010; Thakur 2010; Thakur, Rath, et al. 2010, Thakur, Uphoff, and Antony 2010; Zhao et al. 2009, 2010). Most evidence thus far has come from field reports from nongovernmental organizations (NGOs) such as the Aga Khan Foundation, which introduced SRI methods in the mountains of northeastern Afghanistan, an environment not very favorable for growing rice (Thomas and Ramzi 2011), or from Africare, working in the Timbuktu region of Mali on the edge of the Sahara Desert (Styger et al. 2011).

While SRI is often considered as a *recipe*, it is better understood as a *menu* of practices. SRI is more a matter of *degree* than of *kind*, and part of SRI methodology is farmer experimentation and evaluations, with adaptation of general principles to specific local conditions. There is an "ideal type" of SRI that has been validated in large-scale factorial trials under contrasting soil and climatic conditions (Randriamiharisoa and Uphoff 2002; Uphoff and Randriamiharisoa 2002). However, various combinations and extents of SRI practice can improve crop production, provided that soil conditions are made and kept mostly aerobic, or well oxygenated, so that plant roots and aerobic soil organisms can thrive there. Crop performance will be better to the extent that more of the recommended SRI practices are used together, and the more they are used as recommended; however, not all need to be used, and used perfectly, to get better yields.

The SRI innovation is presented concretely in terms of certain recommendations that change the methods commonly used for irrigated rice production. These changes usually, if not always, result in more productive and robust phenotypes:

- **Transplant younger seedlings**, usually less than fifteen days after the seeds have been sown in a garden-like nursery, not inundated—rather than using larger, older seedlings that look more impressive but have less potential for growth (Mishra and Salokhe 2008, 2010).
- **Reduce the plant density in the field by 80 to 90 percent**—plants should be spaced widely and in a square pattern, 25x25 cm (or even wider if the soil is very fertile), putting only 1 seedling in each hill, or at most 2, instead of planting 3–6 plants together with the hills set out in rows or randomly spaced.
- **Transplant quickly and carefully**, to minimize trauma to the roots of young seedlings—not pulling them up roughly from crowded nurseries, and not leaving them exposed to the sun and air for hours before plunging them into flooded soil; seedlings treated this way take 7–10 days to recover from what is called "transplant shock" and begin growing again.
- **Keep the soil moist but with no standing water**, or alternately **flood and drain** the paddy fields—continuous flooding of deprives the soil of oxygen and leads to root degeneration (Kar et al. 1974).
- **Control weeds in a soil-aerating way** by passing a mechanical weeder up and down between the hills in perpendicular directions to churn up the top layer of the soil. This is preferable to pulling up weeds by hand or using herbicides. Soil-aerating weeding should start early and be done several times during plants' vegetative growth. This practice enhances crop yield, as seen in Figure 4 of a report from Afghanistan (Thomas and Ramzi 2011).
- **Enrich the soil's stock of organic matter as much as possible,** providing compost, manure, or other biomass, rather than rely primarily on chemical fertilizer.

Fertilizer can be used beneficially with the other SRI practices, but it does little to improve the structure and functioning of soil systems (Uphoff et al. 2006). SRI is not necessarily an "organic" production methodology, but enhancing the soil's organic matter is essential for it and its resident organisms to function most productively.

A number of variations have derived from these original insights of Fr. Laulanié. There are, for example, rainfed, unirrigated versions of SRI in India, Cambodia, and Myanmar, with similar good results (e.g., Kabir and Uphoff 2007). Some farmers do direct-seeding rather than transplanting, using wide spacing, soil aeration, enhanced soil organic matter, and so on, and getting comparable yields with less labor inputs. Conservation agriculture with no tillage is being combined with SRI: transplanting young seedlings into permanent raised beds; maintaining mulch or other ground cover on the soil; and rotating crops. SRI operations can be almost fully mechanized to save labor as well as water (Sharif 2011). Also, SRI concepts and methods are being adapted to other crops, as reviewed in section 5.

Such changes underscore that SRI is not a *technology* so much as a different *paradigm* for optimizing the expression of crops' genetic potentials, changing their growing environment rather than their genes. The recommended practices can look risky to farmers at first. In Cambodia and Sri Lanka, however, it has been found that they reduce farmers' risks of crop failure and economic loss (Anthofer 2004; Namara et al. 2008). SRI practices are found to reduce rice plants' susceptibility to damage from insects and pathogens and to lodging from wind and rain, as well as to the effects of drought (Adhikari et al. 2010; Chapagain and Yamaji 2010; Uphoff 2011). Phenotypical improvements associated with SRI crop management have been documented in Barison and Uphoff (2011), Lin et al. (2009), Mishra and Salokhe (2010), Thakur, Uphoff, and Antony (2010), and Zhao et al. (2009). Fully explaining all this still requires further study, however.

Contributions of Microbes to Agricultural Success

Beneficial Effects of Microbes in the Roots and Rhizosphere

Positive relationships have been observed with SRI practices among crop management, populations of soil microorganisms, and rice plant performance (Uphoff et al. 2009). An association between higher yields and soil bacteria living within rice plant roots was first seen in factorial trials done in 2001 in Madagascar evaluating different combinations of SRI and non-SRI practices, using random block design and with replications of each treatment (Randriamiharisoa and Uphoff 2002; Uphoff and Randriamiharisoa 2002). With all-standard practices (20-day-old seedlings, 3 per hill, continuous flooding, and chemical fertilizer), paddy yield was 3.0 tons per hectare (ha), somewhat better than the 2.0 ton national average yield. With contrasting SRI practices (8-day-old seedlings, 1 plant per hill, intermittent irrigation, and compost application), average yield achieved was 10.35 tons per hectare.

How could there be more than a three-fold increase on the same soil with the same rice variety and the same climate? The research design included an evaluation of the populations of *Azospirillum*, a nitrogen-fixing bacterium, counted in tissue samples taken from the roots of the rice plants growing in the plots receiving different treatments. There turned out to be a very strong correlation between crop performance and the concentrations of this microorganism, considered as a proxy for the many communities of beneficial soil organisms. When there were no nutrient additions to the soil, *Azospirillum* populations were more than ten times greater with SRI practices than with conventional management. When compost was used with SRI practices, their numbers were three times higher than when chemical (NPK) fertilizer was applied (Uphoff et al. 2012).

Subsequent studies in India and Indonesia examined the populations and activity of beneficial soil organisms in the root zones (rhizospheres) of rice plants, using the same variety on the same soil but grown with either conventional or SRI practices. These evaluations showed that the number and the biochemical activity of beneficial microbes in rice plant root zones were usually increased with SRI methods (Uphoff et al. 2009; Anas et al. 2011). It remains to be determined why beneficial organisms should be more abundant in the rhizospheres around roots, and also in the roots themselves as endophytes, when rice plants are grown with SRI practices. That changes in microbiological density and activity would accompany these practices should not be surprising, however, because SRI management makes the soil better aerated and more endowed with organic matter.

Beneficial Effects of Microbes in Plant Leaves and Seeds

Symbiotic relationships in the root zone are reasonably well known to soil biologists and plant physiologists (Pinton et al. 2007; Waisel et al. 2002). However, recent research on the *phyllosphere* (the leaf zone, where microorganisms live in, on and around the leaves) has produced some unexpected findings. These indicate that associations between plants and microorganisms, like those between microoganisms and animals, are more significant, intimate, and beneficial than previously understood. This adds another ecological dimension to the concept of agroecology as we look more closely at the interactions between and among species, rather than focusing on just one species at a time. The positive relationships between plants and microorganisms now being discovered parallel those that medical researchers are identifying between human bodies and what is called the "human microbiome" (Turnbaugh et al. 2007).

Research on rice plants by Chi and associates (2005) found that certain soil microorganisms (rhizobia) migrated up from the soil through plants' roots and stems and into the plants' leaves, where they had significant effects on the plants' growth, physiology, and productivity. Compared to rice plants that had no soil rhizobia living in their leaves, rice plants inoculated with rhizobia exhibited a greater volume of roots and a greater weight of the aboveground parts of the plant. Inoculated plants also had higher rates of photosynthesis and greater water utilization efficiency, with twice as much photosynthate produced per unit of water transpired. Rice plants with microbial inoculation had grain yields 20 to 68 percent higher than the control plants' yield, with "crop per drop" substantially increased.

The only difference associated with these changes in crop phenotype and productivity was whether the plants' *leaves* had become inhabited by *soil* organisms. In further research, Chi et al. (2010) found that the presence of soil rhizobia in rice plants' leaf tissues was correlated with the up-regulation of certain genes' expression in the leaves' cells, producing more proteins that supported photosynthesis. Further, their presence in root tissues and cells was found to correlate with producing more proteins that helped protect rice plants against soil pathogens that can cause disease.

That soil bacteria infecting rice plants' leaves as well as their roots can raise grain yield significantly suggests some shifting in the paradigm that we employ for understanding and improving crop productivity (Uphoff et al. 2012). Crops' genetic potentials of course are important; but the interactions between and among organisms within an ecosystem, at both micro and macro scales, appear to be also important, even very influential.

Even more unexpected have been research results documenting beneficial effects for the root growth of rice plant seedlings from "infecting" rice seeds with a certain fungus (*Fusarium culmorum*) before planting and germination (Rodriguez et al. 2009). This fungus is known as a plant pathogen that causes a number of diseases in cereals, grasses, and other plants. However, rice seeds inoculated with this fungus produced seedlings with five times more early root growth, and root hairs emerged two days sooner, compared to seedlings of same rice variety whose seeds were not inoculated with the fungus. At ten days, the average weight of inoculated seedlings was 68 percent higher than for seedlings from sterilized seeds with no microorganisms.

These studies open up an area for investigation rather than giving conclusive answers. But they indicate that microbial endophytes, organisms living within plants in beneficial or mutualistic associations rather than in parasitic relationships, can make significant contributions to plant performance, which warrant more study (Uphoff et al. 2012). Appreciation for what microorganisms contribute to plant growth and performance parallels what is being learned in recent years about their contribution to animals, including our own species *Homo sapiens* (Turnbaugh et al. 2007).

These and other findings suggest the importance of understanding plants as *systems*, rather than as discrete organisms. Plants depend, to an extent still inadequately understood, on their associations with microorganisms in, on, and around their roots and their shoots. Plants are not carbon-based, machine-like entities that are primarily dependent upon *our* inputs, and whose genotypes need to be redesigned to become more responsive to inputs that *we* provide them. Such a strategy forfeits some or many of the benefits that can be reaped from providing plants with more conducive environments in which they can function in ecologically interactive ways that yield higher productivity and greater sustainability.

Effects of Agroecological Management with Other Crops

Although the insights and methods that constitute SRI were developed for irrigated rice production, they have been extended to unirrigated (i.e., rainfed or upland) rice cultivation with similar success. In the last five years, SRI ideas and practices have been extrapolated to a variety of other crops such as wheat (Bhalla 2010; Prasad 2008; Styger et al. 2011) and sugarcane (ICRISAT-WWF 2009). Other crops for which higher production is reported from making adaptations of SRI ideas and methods include sugarcane; red, green, and black gram; mustard; and eggplant. In Ethiopia, yields of teff, the nationally preferred staple grain, are being increased three-fold with appropriate adaptations of SRI ideas (Berhe et al. 2013). SRI experience is thus becoming relevant for agroecological innovation beyond rice, within the broader agricultural sector (Abraham et al. 2013).

Reviewing the Dynamics of an Agroecological Innovation

That the performance of many crops, not just rice, can be improved by making changes in the management of plants, soil, water, and nutrients, thereby enhancing yield and also conferring resilience to the hazards of climate change, is extending our understanding of agroecological practices and their effects. There are still gaps in the scientific understanding of agricultural strategies that focus more on the improvement of *E* than on *G*. But this should not be surprising, since the resources devoted to explicating and refining the newer paradigm have been, at most, a few percent of what has been invested in developing and promoting "mainstream" methods. What may be surprising is the opposition that SRI has encountered, with some scientists arguing that SRI should not even be evaluated, and characterizing any evaluation as a waste of resources.

Gains from Conventional Improvement Methods Compared with Agroecological Management

Scientific findings in the realm of plant-microbial interaction, as seen in section 4, are making the logic of agroecology increasingly persuasive as a complement or alternative to the current crop improvement strategy based on genetic modification and applications of inorganic nutrients. In fact, the gains from these gene-centered and input strategies have produced less yield improvement in recent years than are now being seen with agroecological theory and practice.

Genetic Improvement

The gains in yield achievable through hybridization (heterosis), compared to those attainable from inbred varieties, are theoretically 30 percent, and more practically about 15 percent (Yuan 1994; Zhong et al. 2005). Moreover, some part of the yield increases reported for hybrid rice varieties should be attributed to the use of management practices that are part of SRI: transplanting single, young (13-day) seedlings, spaced 30x30 cm in a square pattern, with reduced water application, and with increases in organic fertilization; however, inorganic fertilizers and herbicides are still heavily relied upon (personal communication from the originator of hybrid rice, Prof. Yuan Long-ping, September 13, 2004).

On-farm comparison trials done in Bali, Indonesia, in 2006 found that SRI management methods added 50 percent to the yields of Chinese hybrid varieties grown with standard practices (13.3 tons per ha vs. 8.4 tons per ha; Sato and Uphoff 2007). That the gains reported from hybridization are in part a consequence of changes in ***E***, not just in ***G***, is clearer from a new world record for paddy yield set in Bihar State, India, in 2011 (Diwakar et al. 2012). One farmer using SRI methods got a paddy yield of 22.4 tons per hectare, measured by state officials and accepted by the Indian Ministry of Agriculture; four other farmers in the same village, also first-time SRI users, got yields or 19 or 20 tons per hectare. These "super-yields" were reached with modern hybrid varieties and with integrated nutrient management, using a combination of organic and inorganic fertilization). Relevant here is that these farmers, when using the same hybrid varieties on their farms with conventional crop management methods, the same soil, and same climate, had paddy yields of 7 tons per hectare, which is very good, but much less than attained with SRI management (data from Dr. M.S. Diwakar, director of Directorate of Rice Development, Govt. of India).

In the 1990s, scientists at the International Rice Research Institute (IRRI) reported that they had developed a "new plant type" (NPT) that could give, on average, 25 percent higher yields (Khush and Peng 1996). The NPT would have many fewer tillers (stalks), but all would have large grain-bearing panicles. Some part of the claimed increase should have been credited, however, to researchers' different management practices, ones associated with SRI: 14-day-old seedlings planted singly in a square pattern 25x25 cm apart. NPT plants were grown under standard flooded-field conditions, however, with heavy applications of chemical fertilizer and herbicides. Despite heavy investment in developing the NPT, this strategy for raising rice yields ostensibly through plant-breeding improvements in ***G*** has remained little used, and is no longer mentioned in IRRI's annual reports.[1] The recent history of making improvements in rice production by focusing on modifications of ***G*** with suboptimum ***E*** has thus not been very successful.

Input Strategies

A large international research program on site-specific nutrient management (SSNM), which sought to optimize and balance chemical fertilizer inputs, has reported average rice yield increases of 7 to 11 percent with its interventions, raising profitability, on average, by 12 percent (Dobermann et al. 2002). In 25 percent of the cases, however, farmers experienced declines in net income with SSNM because of the cost involved in application or a decline in yield. The program focused almost entirely on soil chemistry, with little attention paid to the endogenous mobilization and cycling of nutrients within soil systems by soil organisms. It thus regarded soils as more passive than active, with soil chemistry emphasized over soil biology.

The percentage increases in rice yield achieved already with agroecological management have been several times greater than those obtained recently by making genetic improvements or by optimizing external inputs in soil-chemistry terms. Over the last two decades there has been a slowing of the rates of yield increase with the gene-centered approach, possibly indicating that the genocentric research paradigm, like so many phenomena, may be encountering diminishing returns. World production of cereal grains per capita peaked in 1984 (Dyson 1999), and the overall rates of yield growth have been declining ever since. Total global grain production peaked in the mid-1990s.

The alternative approach, which emphasizes management, can benefit farmers by generally reducing costs of production, while natural environments are better off with reduced extractions of water from surface flows or groundwater reserves, and with less application of agrochemicals that affect soil and hydrological ecosystems. The management approach may also run into diminishing returns in the future; indeed, it would be surprising if it were immune to this relationship, which is so ubiquitous. But for the foreseeable future, agroecological management appears worth investigating, and worth utilizing to the extent that its results warrant application. Openness to alternative approaches has not been generally evident, however, as seen not only for SRI but also for conservation agriculture, as noted below.

Resistance to Paradigm Change within the International Scientific Community

What are referred to as "modern" agricultural technologies, and the knowledge base and practices upon which they rest, have come to represent a dominant paradigm for agricultural development. This paradigm is well entrenched in government, academic, and private-sector institutions, as well as in policy circles. Some researchers who work within that paradigm have found it difficult to accept the results of and explanations for SRI's agroecological methods.

- Dobermann (2004), for example, concluded, with very limited evidence, that SRI is at best "a niche innovation." His argument relied mostly on a crop model with coefficients based on the performance of conventional rice phenotypes, not necessarily applicable for SRI phenotypes, which have larger root systems that do not degenerate from hypoxia induced by flooding (Kar et al. 1974). Farmers using SRI methods have achieved yields double the world average in environments as contrasting as mountainous northeastern Afghanistan (Thomas and Ramzi 2011) and the arid Timbuktu region of Mali (Styger et al. 2011), and in many kinds of agroecosystems in between.

- Sheehy et al. (2004) concluded that "SRI has no major role in improving rice production generally," based on Dobermann's modeling and on the results of three small test plots in China, which did not follow a proper protocol for SRI. The authors' conclusion did not consider the substantial body of research by Chinese rice scientists that had already confirmed SRI effectiveness (http://sri.ciifad.cornell.edu/research/chinaSRIpubs09.pdf).
- Some other rice scientists argued that SRI should not even be evaluated (Sinclair 2004; Sinclair and Cassman 2004). They contended that reported outstanding results from SRI practices were not possible because they conflicted with "known principles"—so any resources invested in assessing SRI would be a waste of funds. The principles that were referred to, however, have been empirically contradicted by research of Chinese and Indian scientists (Lin et al. 2009; Zhao et al. 2009; Thakur, Uphoff, and Antony 2010; this controversy is discussed in Uphoff 2012).
- Skeptics' rejection of SRI was based in part on their insistence that "super-yields" with SRI methods reported from Madagascar were beyond a "biological maximum" calculated from computerized crop modeling (Sheehy et al. 2004). As noted above, however, such yields have been achieved also in India, confirmed by district, state, and national officials using standard methods of measurement. In any case, attention should have been focused on differences in *average* yield, which were clearly significant; the controversy engendered over highest yields was a diversion.
- Reasons for objecting to even evaluating SRI can only be clarified by those scientists who have rejected even investigating alternative methods for rice production. While there was controversy about SRI within the scientific community (Surridge 2004), demonstrations and in-field assessments of the new crop management methods proceeded and expanded during the 2000s. Even without the approval or acceptance of SRI in theory or practice by scientists, who influenced decisions by donor agencies and foundations not to fund SRI evaluation or extension, the new methodology nevertheless began to spread, country to country and within countries.

Expansion of SRI Methods within National Production Systems

Scientific resistance to SRI has ebbed in recent years, even if it has not been withdrawn. Negative journal articles attempting to "debunk" SRI have ceased, perhaps because governments and rice researchers in countries where two-thirds of the world's rice is grown—China, India, Indonesia, Vietnam, and Cambodia—now support SRI methods based on their own evaluations. National rice programs are becoming somewhat delinked from international scientific advice, since they rely increasingly on their own expertise and experience.

- ***China.*** The Sichuan Provincial Department of Agriculture (PDA) started popularizing SRI in 2004, with 1,133 hectares (ha) in that year. By 2010 the area on which SRI methods were used reached 301,000 ha, totaling 941,068 ha over seven years. The additional production, which the PDA attributed to farmers' use of most if not all of the SRI methods during this period, was 1.66 million tons of paddy rice. Its total value was over $300 million, produced with less 24 percent less water (Zheng et al. 2011). Similar gains have been achieved in Zhejiang province, where rice scientists at the China National Rice Research Institute (CNRRI) worked closely with the Zhejiang PDA and with farmers. According to a senior CNRRI scientist, SRI is becoming the main cultivation system in southern China (IRIN 2012).
- ***Indonesia.*** The president of this country has strongly endorsed SRI (http://ciifad.cornell.edu/sri/countries/indonesia/indopresident073007.pdf; video at http://www.srivideo.zoomshare.com/), but only part of the Ministry of Agriculture has welcomed SRI, its Land and Water Resources Management Directorate. The Food Crops Directorate has continued to emphasize varietal improvement and fertilizer use for raising rice production. However, the Ministry has announced a target of 1.5 million hectares of SRI use by 2015 (IRIN 2012). SRI is also supported by the Irrigation Department (PU) and various NGOs, universities, and the private sector (Sato and Uphoff 2007).
- ***India.*** NGOs, universities, and other parts of civil society have given leadership on SRI extension here, assisted by the World Wide Fund for Nature (WWF), the Sir Dorabji Tata Trust, and the National Bank for Agriculture and Rural Development (NABARD). The government's Directorate of Rice Development has been supportive, along with its National Food Security Mission, and rice scientists of the Indian Council for Agricultural Research are now also agreed on SRI merits. The prime minister and head of the Planning Commission have endorsed SRI, particularly for its water-saving potentials. The Bihar State government set a target of 1.4 million hectares of SRI extension in 2012, while the state of Tamil Nadu reports over 1 million farmers using SRI methods on 850,000 hectares; other state governments are similarly gearing up to spread the new methods.
- ***Vietnam.*** When the Ministry of Agriculture and Rural Development endorsed SRI as a "technical advance" in 2007, there were fewer than 10,000 farmers using SRI methods. Four years later, the Ministry reported that this number had risen to over 1 million, with a tripling in just three years' time (http://qdnd.vn/qdndsite/en-US/75/72/182/156/189/164012/Default.aspx).
- ***Cambodia.*** SRI got started here with twenty-eight farmers in 2000. By 2006 the government had decided to include SRI in its national development plan for agriculture, and the SRI Secretariat in the Ministry of Agriculture, Forestry and Fisheries now

> reports that over 200,000 farmers are using the methods. Yield increases for smallholder rainfed farms have been as much as four-fold (http://sri.ciifad.cornell.edu/countries/cambodia/camldsrpt07.pdf), but usually SRI methods are adding only 1.0 to 1.5 tons per hectare, because most Cambodian farmers have no irrigation facilities.

What has been seen in these countries is that after some initial resistance from farmers and rice experts, the merits of agroecological management are increasingly understood and supported. The scientific controversy has slowed acceptance to some extent; but the new ideas are buoyed by productivity gains.

Considerations Affecting the Dynamics of a Paradigm Shift for Agricultural Improvement

That the national acceptance and promotion of SRI reported above has not been widely publicized could reflect preferences and perceptions that favor Green Revolution strategies, with a fixation on continuing to make changes in genetic potential and to increase external inputs. Such approaches, perhaps not coincidentally, are ones that can be controlled for privatized profit in ways that management-based technologies cannot. It is hard to establish intellectual property rights (IPRs) over practices like wider spacing or reduced age of transplanted seedlings. Few commercial interests stand to profit from SRI promotion, and producers and sellers of seed, fertilizer, and agrochemicals are, indeed, adversely affected. That SRI management reduces the need for irrigation water is something that policymakers can readily appreciate, since water scarcity and conflicts are increasingly becoming a public concern rather than only a private or individual matter.

Resistance to management-oriented innovations can have various sources, as discussed below. Because the scientific issues are not yet fully resolved, there is no reason or need here to try to draw any firm or final conclusions about agroecological alternatives. However, considering possible explanations for the resistance that has been encountered with SRI introduction raises social and political issues that researchers and policymakers should reflect on. Thinking about the SRI experience illuminates certain aspects of the workings of current systems, institutions, and cultures for agricultural improvement.

The lack of enthusiasm for SRI in high-level circles for research and policy is anomalous, because two of the world's most eminent rice scientists, based on their own evaluations, early on expressed approval of SRI; namely, Prof. Yuan Long-ping in China, known widely as "the father of hybrid rice," and Dr. M. S. Swaminathan in India, often referred to as "the father of the Indian Green Revolution" and a former director-general of IRRI (Yuan 2001, 2002; MWR 2006; see Uphoff 2012). However, even endorsements by such prominent leaders in agricultural innovation did not carry much weight within the international rice science community (Dobermann 2004; Sheehy et al. 2004; Sinclair and Cassman 2004).

Resistance to acceptance of SRI, and of agroecology more generally, can be attributed to *contending interests* or *cognitive factors*. The latter often correlate with the first set of influences, but each is distinguishable and worth considering in its own right. Commitment to ideas can be a powerful motivation that shapes behavior as much as material interests do. Often the two can be enmeshed, of course. Yet they should not be conflated where their respective influences can be delineated.

Individual Considerations

Scientists in all domains, not just in agriculture, are known to have personal ambitions and competitive drives that contribute to the acceptance or rejection of new theories or inventions. The "not invented here" syndrome, an unwillingness to adopt an idea or product because it originates elsewhere, is a common phenomenon. This can derive simply from pride, but financial interests can also be involved. Several rice scientists who dismissed SRI as based on "unconfirmed field observations" (UFOs), and who argued that SRI should not be investigated, expressed concern about possible competition for the funding of rice research (Sinclair 2004; Sinclair and Cassman 2004). A reasonable inference is that the disparagement and dismissal of SRI was prompted at least in part by perceived financial stakes.

These could be just individual concerns, however. At a higher level, the emergence of SRI has been a challenge to the professions and institutions of rice research, and for agricultural research in general, because the ideas and methods of SRI were developed by an amateur, not a professional, someone working on his own without sponsorship or funding (Laulanié 1993).[2] That a priest could develop insights that eluded thousands of well-funded researchers could be taken as an affront by some scientists.

There have been, to be sure, a number of agronomists who welcomed this contribution from outside their institutional domain, and who proceeded to contribute to a scientific understanding of SRI (e.g., Lin et al. 2009; Mishra and Salokhe 2008; Stoop and Kassam 2005; Tao et al. 2002; Thakur, Uphoff, and Antony 2010; Wang et al. 2002; Zhao et al. 2009; Zhu et al. 2002). Given the focuses of this article, we should not dwell on explanations at the personal level, even if they have some plausibility and merit. There are some higher-level systemic implications for the food and agriculture sector from considering an agroecological innovation such as SRI. Cognitive and political influences at the societal level usually operate more pervasively, beyond the lower-level intersections of personal and institutional interests.

Higher-Level Considerations

The term "paradigm" is used often in the humanities and social sciences, as well as in the physical sciences (Kuhn 1962), but not so often in the agricultural sciences. Yet it is very relevant for an understanding of changes that occur in agriculture and food production in broader social and political terms. The concepts, criteria, methods, and objectives of "modern agriculture" are regarded by their proponents and practitioners as something scientifically established, and thus as fundamentally and ontologically true. The challenge of SRI and other agroecological applications makes clear that there can be more than one intellectual framework for organizing and evaluating technological choices. The emergence of an agroecological paradigm as an alternative to the paradigm of genetic engineering has been examined at some length by Vanloqueren and Baret (2009). The issue of paradigmatic influences shaping the SRI debate has been considered also by Glover (2011), with elaboration by Uphoff (2012).

The language of "engineering" reflects a vision of agricultural production that equates this with an industrial process. Much of our agricultural research, even before genetic engineering was conceived of, considered plants as something like biological machines, operating in standardized ways, with their genetic endowments (**G**) considered like blueprints. Initially, through conventional plant breeding, and now increasingly through transgenic operations, plants were expected to become ever more efficient processors of inputs, particularly exogenous agrochemical materials manipulated by farmers. These inputs were to be converted into crop outputs that could receive a premium for becoming ever more homogeneous for mass-marketing purposes. Monoculture in agricultural was developed in parallel with the assembly line for manufacturing, with corresponding mechanization of production processes and similar labor displacement. Economies of scale are a dominant attraction in "modern" agriculture, with "externalities" such as environmental impacts largely ignored.

An agroecological perspective values diversity of biological forms and appreciates the many interactions and synergies among them. This view was never incorporated into the dominant paradigm, even when its application in farmers' fields exhibited significant vulnerabilities to pests, diseases, and climatic and other stresses. A statistic that is emblematic of "modern agriculture" is the parallel increase in pesticide use in the United States and crop losses to pests. Between 1944 and 1989, the use of pesticides in the United States increased fourteen-fold; in this same period, crop losses due to insects rose rather than declined, from 7 percent to 13 percent (Pimentel et al. 1991). Pesticides do indeed kill insect pests, but they also alter the populations of predator species, as well as induce resistance to pesticides; so the "treadmill" of chemical crop protection may not only continue, but accelerate.

Such statistics are seldom publicized, but this perverse relationship between pesticide use and pest incidence, explainable by Chaboussou's theory of trophobiosis (2004), has given impetus to the now widely accepted agroecological strategy known as integrated pest management (IPM). By utilizing ecosystem dynamics, IPM aims to reverse the chemical dependence that became a key part of "modern agriculture." IPM initially encountered scientific resistance, much like SRI. However, it has now gained scientific and policy respectability, and the UN Food and Agriculture Organization (FAO) presently refers to IPM as "the preferred method" for crop protection (http://www.fao.org/agriculture/crops/core-themes/theme/pests/ipm/en/).

Similarly, minimum or zero tillage—once regarded as primitive and atavistic, as backward as the dibble stick—is now the basis for the worldwide "conservation agriculture"

(CA) movement. CA farming systems, which minimize or give up plowing while maintaining organic mulch on the soil and rotating crops, are increasingly being used around the world (http://www.fao.org/ag/ca/). Depending upon the criteria used to classify what constitutes minimal soil disturbance and/or zero tillage, numbers vary. But around one-third of US cropland is now under CA systems, as well as over 125 million hectares worldwide (Kassam et al. 2009). All three approaches—IPM, CA, and SRI—draw upon the same agroecological principles outlined by Altieri (1995) and Gliessman (2007). However, note that these innovations have their origins and roots more in rural civil society than in the scientific research community.

Apart from the resistance that can be attributed to shifting paradigms, there has also been a shift in the institutional stakes in agricultural research. In the first two-thirds of the 20th century, most agricultural research around the world was done in the public sector, by government agencies like the US Department of Agriculture and by publicly supported universities. The scientific and technological knowledge produced was made freely available in the public domain, because agriculture was thought to be a sector that differed from manufacturing. Widespread access to and use of new technologies for agricultural production was considered to be in the public interest. Public resources could justifiably be invested in improving and extending new technologies, because keeping food supplies abundant and low-cost was considered important for the economy, and for society as a whole.

In the last two decades of the past century, private-sector investments in agricultural research grew as public-sector fiscal capabilities contracted, and as public funding of agricultural research receded. These were separate trends, but not entirely independent of each other. Agricultural research agendas in recent decades have favored innovations that can be protected by patents to recoup private investments. Intellectual property rights have become a major issue in the agricultural sector, where for many decades this was only a marginal concern.

It is no accident that research investments in recent decades have focused on improved varieties (seeds), on a succession of agrochemicals (the so-called chemical treadmill), and on sophisticated machinery—all amenable to private patents, ownership, and profitability. This has paralleled investment priorities in the health sector, where research funding has been more abundant for marketable medications and costly procedures than for preventive practices such as a healthful diet and exercise. As the paradigm of "modern agriculture" has become well established and shaped research priorities, the arguments for devolving research to the private sector have become more dominant. The goals of research have been increasingly framed in terms of producing more and better private goods with appropriable benefit streams, rather than for promoting public goods and public welfare.

By achieving its productivity gains by making changes in the management of resources that farmers have in hand, SRI shifts the locus of control and benefit back to the public realm and to individual users. Rather than requiring the purchase of patentable inputs, SRI involves the dissemination of knowledge as a public good. Knowledge is itself a positive-sum commodity, not diminished by its being shared with others.

Once farmers understand SRI principles and methods, they can raise their outputs with reduced inputs, while also gaining other benefits such as quicker crop maturity and not needing to take out loans. They can also freely share their knowledge and experience with others. This does not mean that with agroecology there is no need for institution-based research or for research products that can be patented and sold. But the balance between privatized and publicly accessible research, which has been shifting to the private sector, has to some extent shifted back to the public domain by agroecological innovations like SRI. Such a rebalancing is unlikely to be welcomed in commercial and administrative circles, however.

The SRI experience raises some interesting questions about the ways in which scientific research is evaluated. For statistical testing of hypotheses or evaluating claims about scientific facts, we learn the difference between Type I and Type II errors, that is, between false positives and false negatives. The first category includes things that are claimed to be true but which are not; whereas the second refers to rejecting something as being false when it is actually true.

It is curious that these two kinds of errors, ostensibly symmetrical, are treated so differently within the scientific community and in public policy. Persons making false-positive claims are subject to scientific attack and possibly to legal or other penalties. Yet false-negative conclusions do not receive similar disapproval or suffer serious sanctions. Persons who have, by their criticisms, impeded funding for the evaluation of SRI methods, let alone their dissemination, have no liability under present institutional arrangements, including biases in the peer-review processes of scientific journals. Although this can result in the withholding of benefits to millions of farmers (and consumers), there is no responsibility or accountability for Type II errors, whatever the motives, innocent or ignoble. There is, however, penalization of Type I errors, which can deter the timid from venturing into contested terrain.

This observation does not confirm a view that large institutions conspire to maintain the status quo, presenting an impregnable front against innovation. While some government agencies have been slow to respond to SRI opportunities, as noted above, in the major rice-producing countries there is now acceptance and promotion of SRI methods. The president of the World Bank has publicly endorsed SRI (*Hindustani Times*, December 2, 2009), and the World Bank Institute has produced a "toolkit" to promote SRI (http://info.worldbank.org/etools/docs/library/245848/index.html). The Worldwide Fund for Nature (WWF), in conjunction with the International Crop Research Institute for the Semi-Arid Tropics (ICRISAT), supported evaluation and expansion of SRI in India, and also the extension of SRI methods to sugarcane production (ICRISAT-WWF 2009). The WWF has cooperated with other major NGOs in publicizing the benefits of SRI achieved in Africa and Asia (Africare, Oxfam America, and WWF-ICRISAT Project 2010).

It is not that large institutions, through their normal processes of decision making, make commitments to embarking in significantly new directions. Rather, the impetus to support innovation has come mostly from certain individuals within institutions who have a greater commitment to the institutions' expressed goals and a higher propensity for risk taking and for activation of others. They can and do use institutions as platforms for pursuing reforms and changes that fall within the institutions' purview, and they work to bring about a convergence of institutional and individual values and objectives. That a large majority of persons are disinclined to deviate from predominant paradigms does not prevent institutions from being prodded or induced to move in new directions by certain individuals within them, albeit often lurchingly, and sometimes stealthily.

Looking Ahead

Agroecological alternatives are gaining acceptance at an opportune time. "Modern agriculture" evolved in the latter half of the twentieth century under very different conditions from those foreseeable for the decades ahead. Something like "postmodern" agriculture (Uphoff 2007) will probably become more economically efficient and environmentally tenable in the decades ahead. Modern agriculture, with its high degree of mechanization to reduce labor inputs, has followed an extensive rather than an intensive trajectory, being land-extensive and seeking economies of scale from ever-larger units of production. By 2050, however, arable land per capita will be one-third what it was in 1950, due to population growth as well as land degradation. This will make intensive strategies more productive agronomically and relatively more profitable in economic terms.

Energy costs in the years ahead will be considerably higher than they were over the past fifty years. This will make mechanized production processes as well as the long-distance transportation of food to foreign markets more costly. More localized and more labor-intensive production will become economically more competitive. Harnessing biological processes, which ultimately are processing and providing solar energy as a "free" input rather than depending heavily on petrochemical inputs for agriculture, will become more attractive, especially if the full costs of negative environmental externalities are calculated, and if those who create the costs must pay or reimburse them.[3]

Further, current agricultural production methods were developed within a fairly stable set of water supplies and constraints, and for relatively predictable climates. In the decades ahead, the parameters of water availability—and reliability—are going to change considerably. Most of the expected changes will be adverse for agriculture—droughts, storms, floods, hot spells, cold snaps, and other "extreme events." These climatic stresses are more debilitating for agricultural production than is gradual global warming. Crops grown with agroecological practices, the most evident example being SRI, are better able to tolerate a wider ranges of adverse climates because of larger and deeper root growth, and because they promote greater abundance, diversity, and activity of the soil biota. Both roots and soil biology have been, at least until recently, marginal concerns in contemporary crop and soil science, receiving only a small fraction of scientists' attention and agencies' funding.

There is considerable agreement that the twenty-first century will be "the century of biology," but there is less consensus on what kind of biology will be preeminent.

The vision of Venter and Cohen (2004) and others focuses on the genome (**G**). But already we see that epigenetics, which explicates how genetic potentials get *expressed*, is becoming more promising for both scientific insight and for practical application. Both genetic engineering and the agronomic sciences will do well to move beyond the genetic-deterministic paradigm of the preceding century, in which the DNA of the double helix is regarded as a blueprint for manufacturing organisms, to comprehend in broader and deeper detail the dynamics of ecological systems. The latter include the complexities of highly diverse and contingent expression of genetic potentials, with microorganisms functioning as intimate, essential parts of plant and animal organisms. Moving research and development efforts in this direction will have political and political-economic dimensions, not just scientific ones, just as all scientific transitions proceed with institutional constraints and the influences of power and privilege, along with the need for cognitive reformulations and doctrinal restatements.

Notes

1. Comparisons of NPTs with inbred high-yielding varieties found that while NPTs had good "sink" capacity—i.e., more spikelets (flowers) per plant that could receive carbohydrates and convert these into grains—their "source" capacity is insufficient, meaning they do not have enough roots to support the production of sufficient carbohydrates for complete grain-filling (Makarim and Suhartatik 2006). The computer modeling that guided NPT development apparently overlooked the fact that rice plants with fewer tillers will also have fewer roots, since tillers and roots originate concurrently from the same meristematic plant tissues. An understanding of agroecology and plant physiology would have made this limitation for the NPT more obvious from the start.
2. While Laulanié was not a professional agronomist, he was not without scientific training. Before entering a Jesuit seminary, he completed a degree in agriculture at an eminent French college of agriculture; and before going to Madagascar, he had been a lecturer at the Ecole Supérieure d'Agriculture in Angers, France. Following the precedent of Gregor Mendel, who established the intellectual foundations for the modern science of genetics, Laulanié developed systematic knowledge through careful and discerning observations, checking them out and validating them through several decades of his own monitoring and experimentation.
3. A recent study in Europe has estimated the economic costs of inorganic/reactive nitrogen pollution there at between 70 and 320 billion euros, considerably greater than the marginal value of N fertilizer applications (Sutton et al. 2011). In China, the relative costs of use/overuse of N fertilizers may be even greater, since groundwater supplies there are being heavily polluted (Gong et al. 2011).

References

Abraham, B., H. Araya, T. Berhe, S. Edwards, B. Gujja, R.B. Khadka, Y.S. Koma, D. Sen, E. Styger, N. Uphoff, and A. Verma. 2013. "The System of Crop Intensification (SCI_): Agroecological

Innovations to Improve Agricultural Production, Food Security, and Resilience to Climate Change." Monograph posted on SRI-Rice website: http://sri.ciifad.cornell.edu [this reference may be replaced by an article we expect to be published in Agriculture & Food Systems, 2013, if accepted before this gets published]

Adhikari, P., D. Sen, and N. Uphoff. 2010. "System of Rice Intensification as a Resource-Conserving Methodology: Contributing to Food Security in an Era of Climate Change." *SATSA Mukhapatra* 14 (Annual Technical Issue): 1–17. http://www.satsawb.org/New_Arrivals/SRI_as_a_Resource.pdf.

Africare, Oxfam America, and WWF-ICRISAT Project. 2010. *More Rice for People, More Water for the Planet.* Hyderabad, India: WWF-ICRISAT Project. http://www.oxfamamerica.org/files/more-rice-for-people-more-water-for-the-planet-sri.pdf.

Altieri, M. 1995. *Agroecology: The Science of Sustainable Agriculture.* Boulder, CO: Westview.

Altieri, M. 2002. "Agroecological Principles or Sustainable Agriculture." In *Agroecological Innovations: Increasing Food Production with Participatory Development*, edited by N. Uphoff, 40–46. London: Earthscan.

Anas, I., O. P. Rupela, T. M. Thiyagarajan, and N. Uphoff 2011. "A Review of Studies on SRI Effects on Beneficial Organisms in Rice Soil Rhizospheres." *Paddy and Water Environment* 9:53–66.

Andersson, J. A., and K. E. Giller. 2012. "On Heretics and God's Blanket Salesmen: Contested Claims for Conservation Agriculture and the Politics of Its Promotion in African Smallholder Farming." In *Contested Agronomy: Agricultural Research in a Changing World*, edited by J. Sumberg and J. Thompson. London: Earthscan.

Anthofer. J. 2004. "The Potential of the System of Rice Intensification (SRI) for Poverty Reduction in Cambodia." Paper presented at the Conference on International Agricultural Research for Development, Berlin, October 5–7, 2004. http://www.tropentag.de/2004/abstracts/full/399.pdf.

Barison, J., and N. Uphoff. 2011. "Rice Yield and Its Relation to Root Growth and Nutrient-Use Efficiency under SRI and Conventional Cultivation: An Evaluation in Madagascar." *Paddy and Water Environment* 9:65–78.

Berhe, T., Z. Gebretsadik, S. Edwards, and H. Araya. 2013. "Boosting Tef Productivity Using Improved Agronomic Practices and Appropriate Fertilizer." In *Achievements and Prospects of Tef Improvement*, edited by H. Assefa, S. Chanyalew, and Z. Tadele, 133–140. Addis Ababa: Ethiopian Institute of Agricultural Research, and Bern: Institute of Plant Sciences.

Bhalla, N. 2010. "New Farming Method Boosts Food Output for India's Rural Poor." Reuters, March 30. http://in.reuters.com/article/2010/03/30/idINIndia-47328120100330.

Ceesay, M., W. S. Reid, E. C. M. Fernandes, and N. Uphoff. 2006. "Effects of Repeated Soil Wetting and Drying on Lowland Rice Yield with System of Rice Intensification (SRI) Methods." *International Journal of Agricultural Sustainability* 4:5–14.

Chaboussou, F. 2004. *Healthy Crops: A New Agricultural Revolution.* Charnley, UK: Jon Anderson Press.

Chapagain, T., and E. Yamaji. 2010. "The Effects of Irrigation Method, Age of Seedling and Spacing on Crop Performance Productivity and Water-Wise Rice Production in Japan." *Paddy and Water Environment* 8:81–90.

Chi, F., S. H. Shen, H. P. Cheng, Y. X. Jing, Y. G. Yanni and F. B. Dazzo. 2005. "Ascending Migration of Endophytic Rhizobia, from Roots to Leaves, inside Rice Plants and Assessment of Benefits to Rice Growth Physiology." *Journal of Applied and Environmental Microbiology* 71:7271–7278.

Chi, F., P. F. Yang, F. Han, Y. X. Jing, and S. H. Shen. 2010. "Proteomic Analysis of Rice Seedlings Infected by Sinorhizobium meliloti 1021." *Proteomics* 10:1861–1874.

Diwakar, M. C., A. Kumar, A. Verma, and N. Uphoff. 2012. "Report on the World-Record SRI Yields in Kharif Season 2011 in Nalanda District, Bihar State, India." *Agriculture Today* (New Delhi) 15:54–56.

Dobermann, A. 2004. "A Critical Assessment of the System of Rice Intensification (SRI)." *Agricultural Systems* 79:261–281.

Dobermann, A., C. Witt, D. Dawe, et al. 2002. "Site-Specific Nutrient Management for Intensive Rice Cropping Systems in Asia." *Field Crops Research* 74:37–66.

Dyson, T. 1999. "World Food Trends and Prospects to 2025." *Proceedings of the National Academy of Sciences of the United States of America* 9 (11): 5929–5936.

Friedrich, T., A.H. Kassam, and T. F. Shaxson. 2009. "Conservation Agriculture." In *Agricultural Technologies in Developing Countries*, edited by R. Meyer. STOA Project. Brussels: European Parliament.

Giller, K. E., E. Witter, M. Corbeels, and P. Tittonell. 2009. "Conservation Agriculture and Smallholder Farming in Africa: A Heretic's View." *Field Crops Research* 114:23–34.

Gliessman, S. R. 2007. *Agroecology: The Ecology of Sustainable Food Systems*. Boca Raton, FL: CRC Press.

Glover, D. 2011. "The System of Rice Intensification: Time for an Empirical Turn." *NJAS-Wageningen Journal of Life Sciences* 57:217–224.

Gong, P., L. Liang, and Q. Zhang. 2011. "China Must Reduce Fertilizer Use Too." *Nature* 473:284–285.

ICRISAT-WWF Project. 2009. *Sustainable Sugarcane Initiative: Improving Sugarcane Cultivation in India*. Andhra P-radesh, India: ICRISAT-WWF Project. http://assets.panda.org/downloads/ssi_manual.pdf.

IRIN. 2012. "Analysis: Why Rice Intensification Matters in Asia." Bangkok: UN Office for Coordination of Humanitarian Affairs. http://www.irinnews.org/Report/95342/Analysis-Why-rice-intensification-matters-in-Asia.

Kabir, H., and N. Uphoff. 2007. "Results of Disseminating the System of Rice Intensification with Farmer Field School Methods in Northern Myanmar." *Experimental Agriculture* 43:463–476.

Kar, S., S. B. Varade, T. K. Subramanyam, and B. P. Ghildyal. 1974 "Nature and Growth Pattern of Rice Root System under Submerged and Unsaturated Conditions." *Il Riso* 23:173–179.

Kassam, A.H., T. Friedrich, F. Shaxson, and J. Pretty. 2009. "The Spread of Conservation Agriculture: Justification, Sustainability and Uptake." *International Journal of Agricultural Sustainability* 7:292–320.

Khush, G. S., and S. Peng. 1996. "Breaking the Yield Frontier of Rice." In *Increasing Yield Potential in Wheat: Breaking the Barriers; Proceedings of a workshop held in Ciudad Obregon, Sonora, Mexico*, edited by M. P. Reynolds, S. Rajaram, and A. McNab, 36–51. Mexico City: CIMMYT.

Kiers, E.T., M. Duhamel, Y. Beesetty, J. A. Mensah, O. Franken, E. Verbruggen, C.R. Feilbaum, et al. 2011. "Reciprocal Rewards Stabilize Cooperation in the Mycorrhizal Symbiosis." *Science* 333:880–882.

Kuhn, T. 1962. *The Structure of Scientific Revolutions*. Chicago: University of Chicago Press.

Laulanié, H. 1993 "Le système de riziculture intensive malgache." *Tropicultura* 11:110–114.

Lin, X. Q., D. F. Zhu, H. X. Chen, S. H. Cheng, and N. Uphoff. 2009. "Effect of Plant Density and Nitrogen Fertilizer Rates on Grain Yield and Nitrogen Uptake of Hybrid Rice (*Oryza sativa* L.)." *Journal of Agricultural Biotechnology and Sustainable Development* 1:44–53.

Makarim, A. K., and E. Suhartatik. 2006. "Partial Efficiency Concept in New Rice Plant Type as Indicated by N Uptake." In: *Rice Industry, Culture, and Environment*, edited by Sumarno, Suparyono, A.M. Fagi and M.O. Adnyana, 185–191. Sukamandi: Indonesian Center for Rice Research.

Meyer, R. 2009. *Agricultural Technologies for Developing Countries*. Brussels: European Parliament. http://www.europarl.europa.eu/stoa/default_en.htm.

Mishra, A., and V. M. Salokhe. 2008. "Seedling Characteristics and Early Growth of Transplanted Rice under Different Water Regimes." *Experimental Agriculture* 44:1–19.

Mishra, A., and V. M. Salokhe. 2010. "The Effects of Planting Pattern and Water Regime on Root Morphology, Physiology and Grain Yield of Rice." *Journal of Agronomy and Crop Science* 196:368–378.

MWR (Ministry of Water Resources). 2006. *Report of Sub-committee on More Crop and Income per Drop of Water*. New Delhi: MWR. http://wrmin.nic.in/newdetails.asp?langid=1&newscode=15—section III.

Namara, R., D. Bossio, P. Weligamage, and I. Herath. 2008. "The Practice and Effects of the System of Rice Intensification (SRI) in Sri Lanka." *Quarterly Journal of International Agriculture* 47:5–24.

Pimentel, D. 1997. *Techniques for Reducing Pesticides: Environmental and Economic Benefits*. Chichester, UK: John Wiley.

Pinton, R., Z. Varanini, and P. Nannipieri, eds. 2007. *The Rhizosphere: Biochemistry and Organic Substances at the Soil-Plant Interface*. 2nd ed. Boca Raton, FL: CRC Press.

Prasad, A. 2008. "Going against the Grain: The System of Rice Intensification is Now Being Adapted to Wheat—With Similar Good Results." *Outlook Business* (New Delhi), Oct. 18.

Randriamiharisoa, R. P., and N. Uphoff. 2002. "Factorial Trials Evaluating the Separate and Combined Effects of SRI Practices." In *Assessments of the System of Rice Intensification*, edited by N. Uphoff, E. C. M. Fernandes, L. P. Yuan, J. M. Peng, S. Rafaralahy, and J. Rabenandrasana, 40–46. Ithaca, NY: Cornell International Institute for Food, Agriculture and Development (CIIFAD). http://ciifad.cornell.edu/sri/proc1/sri_10.pdf.

Reichardt, W., A. Dobermann, and T. George. 1998. "Intensification of Rice Production Systems: Opportunities and Limits." In *Sustainability of Rice in the Global Food System*, edited by N. G. Dowling, S. M. Greenfield, and K.S. Fischer. Los Baños, Philippines: International Rice Research Institute.

Rodriguez, R. J., D. C. Freeman, E. D. McArthur, Y. O. Kim, and R. S. Redman. 2009. "Symbiotic Regulation of Plant Growth, Development and Reproduction." *Communicative and Integrative Biology* 2:1–3.

Royal Society. 2009. *Reaping the Benefits: Science and the Sustainable Intensification of Global Agriculture*. London: TheRoyal Society.

Sato, S., and N. Uphoff (2007). "A Review of On-farm Evaluations of System of Rice Intensification Methods in Eastern Indonesia." *CAB Reviews: Perspectives in Agriculture, Veterinary Science, Nutrition and Natural Resources*, 2:54.

Savory, A., with J. Butterfield. 1999. *Holistic Management: A New Framework for Decision-Making*. Washington, DC: Island Press.

Selosse, A., and F. Rousset. 2011. "The Plant-Fungal Marketplace." *Science* 333:828–829.

Sharif, A. 2011. "Technical Adaptations for Mechanized SRI Production to Achieve Water Saving and Increased Profitability in Punjab, Pakistan." *Paddy and Water Environment* 9:111–119.

Sheehy, J. E., S. B. Peng, A. Dobermann, P. L. Mitchell, A. Ferrer, J. C. Yang, Y. B. Zou, X. H. Zhong, and J. L. Huang. 2004 "Fantastic Yields in the System of Rice Intensification: Fact or Fallacy?" *Field Crops Research* 88:1–8.

Sinclair, T. R. 2004. "Agronomic UFOs Waste Valuable Scientific Resources." *Rice Today*, July 23. Los Baños, Philippines: International Rice Research Institute. http://irri.org/index.php?option=com_k2&view=item&id=10053:agronomic-ufos-waste-valuable-scientific-resources&lang=en.

Sinclair, T. R., and K. G. Cassman. 2004. "Agronomic UFOs?" *Field Crops Research* 88:9–10.

Sinha, S. K., and J. Talati. 2007. "Productivity Impacts of the System of Rice Intensification (SRI): A Case Study in West Bengal, India." *Agriculture Water Management* 87:55–60.

Stoop, W.A. and A.H. Kassam 2005. "The SRI Controversy: A Response." *Field Crops Research* 91:357–360.

Styger, E., M. A. Attaher, H. Guindo, H. Ibrahim, M. Diaty, I. Aba, and M. Traore. 2011. "Application of System of Rice Intensification Practices in the Arid Environment of the Timbuktu Region of Mali." *Paddy and Water Environment* 9:137–144.

Surridge, N. 2004. "Rice Cultivation: Feast or Famine?" *Nature* 428:360–361.

Sutton, M. A., O. Oenema, J. W. Erisman, A. Leip, H. van Grinsven, and W. Winiwart. 2011. "Too Much of a Good Thing." *Nature* 472:1159–1161.

Tao, L.X., X. Wang, and S.K. Min. 2002. "Physiological Effects of SRI Methods in the Rice Plant." In *Assessments of the System of Rice Intensification*, edited by N. Uphoff, E.C.M. Fernandes, L.P. Yuan, J.M. Peng, S. Rafaralahy, and J. Rabenandrasana, 132–136. Ithaca, NY: Cornell International Institute for Food, Agriculture and Development (CIIFAD).http://sri.ciifad.cornell.edu/proc1/sri_29.pdf.

Thakur, A. K. 2010. "Critiquing SRI Criticism: Beyond Skepticism with Empiricism. *Current Science* 98:1294–1299.

Thakur, A.K., S. Rath, S. Roychowdhury, and N. Uphoff. 2010. "Comparative Performance of Rice with System of Rice Intensification (SRI) and Conventional Management Using Different Plant Spacings." *Journal of Agronomy and Crop Sciences* 196:146–159.

Thakur, A. K., N. Uphoff, and E. Antony. 2010. "An Assessment of Physiological Effects of System of Rice Intensification (SRI) Practices Compared to Recommended Rice Cultivation Practices in India." *Experimental Agriculture* 46:77–98.

Thomas, V., and A. M. Ramzi. 2011. "SRI Contributions to Rice Production in Water Management Constraints in Northern Afghanistan." *Paddy and Water Environment* 9:101–109.

Turnbaugh, P. J., R. E. Ley, M. Mahady, C. M. Fraser-Liggett, R. Knight, and J. I. Gordon. 2007. "The Human Microbiome Project." *Nature* 449:804–810.

Uphoff, N., ed. 2002. *Agroecological Innovations: Increasing Food Production with Participatory Development*. London: Earthscan.

——. 2006 "The Development of the System of Rice Intensification." In *Participatory Research and Development for Sustainable Agriculture and Rural Development*. Vol. 3, edited by J. Gonsalves, et al., 119–125. Ottawa: International Development Research Centre.

——. 2007. "Agricultural Futures: What Lies Beyond 'Modern Agriculture'?" *Tropical Agriculture Association Newsletter*, September 13–19.

——. 2011. "Agroecological Approaches to Help 'Climate-Proof' Agriculture While Raising Productivity in the Twenty-First Century." In *Sustaining Soil Productivity in Response to Global Climate Change*, edited by T. Sauer, J. Norman and M. Sivakumar. Hoboken, NJ: Wiley-Blackwell.

——. 2012. "Comment to 'The System of Rice Intensification: Time for an Empirical Turn' [*NJAS—Wageningen Journal of Life Sciences* 57 (2011) 217–224]." *NJAS—Wageningen Journal of Life Sciences* 59 (1–2): 53–60. doi:10.1016/j.njas.2012.02.001

Uphoff, N., I. Anas, O. P. Rupela, A. K. Thakur, and T. M. Thiyagarajan. 2009. "Learning About Positive Plant-Microbial Interactions from the System of Rice Intensification (SRI)." *Aspects of Applied Biology* 98:29–54.

Uphoff, N., A. Ball, E. C. M. Fernandes, H. Herren, O. Hussain, M. Laing, C.A. Palm, et al., eds. 2006. *Biological Approaches to Sustainable Soil Systems*. Boca Raton, FL: CRC Press.

Uphoff, N., F. Chi, F. B. Dazzo, and R. J. Rodriguez. 2013. "Soil Fertility as a Contingent Rather Than Inherent Characteristic: Considering the Contributions of Crop-Symbiotic Soil Microbiota." In *Principles of Sustainable Soil Management in Agrosystems*, edited by R. Lal and B. Stewart, 141–166. *Advances in Soil Science*. Boca Raton, FL: CRC Press.

Uphoff, N., and R. P. Randriamiharisoa. 2002. "Reducing Water Use in Irrigated Rice Production with the Madagascar System of Rice Intensification (SRI)." In *Water-Wise Rice Production: Proceedings of an International Workshop, April 8–11, 2002*, edited by B. A. M. Bouman, H. Hengsdijk, B. Hardy, P. S. Bindraban, T. P. Tuong, and J. K. Ladha, 71–87. Los Baños, Philippines: International Rice Research Institute.

Vanloqueren, G., and P. V. Baret. 2009. "How Agricultural Research Systems Shape a Technological Regime That Develops Genetic Engineering but Locks Out Agroecological Innovations." *Research Policy* 38:971–983.

Waisel, Y., A. Eschel, and U. Kafkaf, eds. 2002. *Plant Roots: The Hidden Half*. 3rd ed. Boca Raton, FL: CRC Press.

Wang, S. H., W. X. Cao, J. Dong, T. B. Dai, and Z. Yan. 2002. "Physiological Characteristics of High-Yield Techniques with SRI Rice." In *Assessments of the System of Rice Intensification*, edited by N. Uphoff, E. C. M. Fernandes, L.-P. Yuan, J.-M. Peng, S. Rafaralahy, and J. Rabenandrasana, 116–124. Ithaca, NY: Cornell International Institute for Food, Agriculture and Development (CIIFAD). http://sri.ciifad.cornell.edu/proc1/sri_27.pdf.

Wardle, D. A. 2002. *Communities and Ecosystems: Linking the Aboveground and Belowground Components*. Princeton, NJ: Princeton University Press.

Wolfe, D. W. 2001. *Tales from the Underground: A Natural History of Subterranean Life*. Cambridge, MA: Perseus.

Xu, X. L., X. Y. Li, and H. Li. 2005. "Socio-economic Impact of the SRI in China." *China Rural Economics*, March. In Chinese; English version at http://ciifad.cornell.edu/sri/countries/china/cnciadeng.pdf.

Yuan, L. P. 1994. "Increasing Yield Potential in Rice by Exploiting Heterosis." In *Hybrid Rice Technology: New Developments and Future Prospects*, edited by S.S. Virmani, 1–6. Los Baños, Philippines: International Rice Research Institute.

——. 2001. "The System of Rice Intensification." In Chinese. *Hybrid Rice* 16:1–3.

——. 2002. "A Scientist's Perspective on Experience with SRI in China for Raising Yields of Super-Hybrid Rice." In *Assessments of the System of Rice Intensification*, edited by N. Uphoff, E. C. M. Fernandes, L. P. Yuan, J. M. Peng, S. Rafaralahy, and J. Rabenandrasana, 23–25. Ithaca, NY: Cornell International Institute for Food, Agriculture and Development (CIIFAD).http://sri.ciifad.cornell.edu/proc1/sri_06.pdf.

Zhao L. M., L. H. Wu, Y. S. Li, X. H. Lu, D. F. Zhu, and N. Uphoff. 2009. "Influence of the System of Rice Intensification on Rice Yield and Nitrogen and Water Use Efficiency with Different N Application Rates." *Experimental Agriculture* 45:275–286.

Zhao L. M., L. H. Wu, Y. S. Li, S. Animesh, D. F. Zhu and N. Uphoff. 2010. "Comparisons of Yield, Water Use Efficiency, and Soil Microbial Biomass as Affected by the System of Rice Intensification." *Communications in Soil Science and Plant Analysis* 41:1–12.

Zheng, J. G., L. Zhou, Z. Z. Chi, and X. L. Jiang. 2011. "Agricultural Water Savings Possible through SRI for Future Water Management in China." Paper prepared for international water management conference in Vietnam, October. Chengdu: Sichuan Academy of Agricultural Sciences. http://sri.ciifad.cornell.edu/countries/china/ChSichuan_AgricWaterSavings_Zheng11.pdf.

Zhong, X. H., S. B. Peng, F. Wang, and H. G. Huang. 2005. "Using Heterosis and Hybrid Rice to Increase Yield Potential in China." In *Rice Is Life: Scientific Perspectives for the 21st Century; Proceedings of the World Rice Conference*, Tsukuba, Japan, edited by K. Toriyama, K. L. Heong, and B. Hardy, 138–140. Los Baños, Philippines: International Rice Research Institute.

Zhu, D. F., S. H. Cheng, Y. P. Zhang, and X. Q. Lin. 2002. "Tillering Patterns and the Contributions of Tillers to Grain Yield with Hybrid Rice and Wide Spacing." In *Assessments of the System of Rice Intensification*, edited by N. Uphoff, E. C. M. Fernandes, L. P. Yuan, J. M. Peng, S. Rafaralahy, and J. Rabenandrasana, 125–131. Ithaca, NY: Cornell International Institute for Food, Agriculture and Development (CIIFAD). http://sri.ciifad.cornell.edu/proc1/sri_28.pdf.

PART II

NORMATIVE KNOWLEDGE: ETHICS, RIGHTS, AND DISTRIBUTIVE JUSTICE

CHAPTER 9

ETHICS OF FOOD PRODUCTION AND CONSUMPTION

MICHIEL KORTHALS

Introduction of Food Ethics: What Ethics Is and Is Not

"You *should* eat this healthy fruit salad!"; "*Don't* eat this piece of pork!"; "A farmer *should* take care of her cows!"; "It is *unethical* to confront children with junk food advertisements." With respect to eating and producing food, one is faced several times a day with ethical expressions such as these. Everyday language on food is permeated with prohibitions, refutations, exhortations, recommendations, and even less explicit ethical notions such as "this is a natural product." But people are confronted not only with these personal ethical issues; worldwide hunger, animal abuse, fair and unfair trade, and the role of competition between biofuels and food crops are recurrent topics in newspapers and other media if not a daily reality for many. Food and production of food are continuing and disturbing themes in the past, the present, and the future; although nowadays they have more urgency than ever due to the increasing gap between producers and consumers which produces a lot of uncertainty on both sides (see the next two sections).

Academic food ethics starts with these ethical issues to develop a critical analysis, and in the end, to assist citizens in dealing with them. As a critical discipline, it takes into account various standpoints with respect to agriculture and food, including less dominant ones. However, although academic (food) ethics cannot always avoid moral expressions, it tries to stay away from prescribing a set of answers. Instead, it develops, sometimes provocatively, tools (concepts, strategies, approaches) required to reflect clearly and effectively on the questions themselves. Moreover, in developing these tools, it has to take into account basic empirical issues related to food production, distribution, consumption, and disposal.

Food ethics as a critical academic discipline is preceded by movements like vegetarianism, reform movements and farmers' movements and gets at least partial inspiration from those movements. However, as an academic discipline (which doesn't exclude that it also has a societal role!), it strives for debate and reflection on the basis of arguments and rational exchange of views in search for the (ethical) Holy Grail: what is good food?

There are many difficulties in tackling this question: Food (and food production) is a bit of everything. Food and agriculture belong to nature and to culture; they include manual labor and high technology; they are dirty and edible; they are material and symbolic, work and leisure, profit and care; they are seen as fuel to fill the stomach and have a social function; they imply health and pleasure, they sustain life and killings. It is seductive to be selective regarding one of these aspects; therefore, one of the main tasks of food ethics is to uphold the broad view and to reduce the gap between production and consumption. The citizen concerned with local and global production has to make concrete choices, a process that is sometimes incredibly difficult due to empirical ambiguities and controversies that the citizen often cannot understand. Moreover, there are conflicting values and obligations of an ethical or broadly normative character. Sometimes, one can only try out a certain decision, in the hope that one can later on make a wiser decision.

This chapter first presents a very introductory history of food, to give a context to the themes of this rather new philosophical discipline. The discipline got a serious start with a number of quite pressing social concerns that citizen-consumers, policymakers, and other involved people expressed about the present-day food production system; in the next section, the most urgent of these concerns will be discussed. The core of food ethics comprises the development of concepts and approaches, to be outlined in the section about Approaches and Concepts. Next, these concepts and approaches will be used in discussing two urgent food ethical problems: malnutrition and producing and eating meat. The ethical concerns of citizens and the critical analysis of food ethics have a relationship with politics, and we will deal with these in the section on Ethics and Politics. Finally, in the last section we will discuss the future of food and food ethics.

The Context: The Evolving Gap between Food Production and Consumption

One of the most salient features of human evolution is the continuing reduction of time needed to produce and to digest food, which presently forms the background for many food ethical issues. The first humans, approximately a million years ago, started among other things to differ from other animals not by hunting and collecting foodstuffs but by cooking and reducing the number of raw foods. Raw food always takes more time to digest and to get feelings of satiety and the necessary nutrients; cooking requires less time for chewing and digesting food. The second phase in human evolution was the slow development of collecting and cooking more and more sophisticated types of grasses, leaves, herbs and other plants. This gradual transformation of humans' diet started approximately 50,000 years BC, by pastoralists, who also succeeded in living together with animals, later domesticated animals, moving from one fertile area to another. Great transformations happened in the Neolithic era with the transformation of pastoral into agricultural life, the third phase. These transformations implied that still more time could be spent on other activities than searching for and digesting food. Wrangham writes: "thanks to cooking, we save ourselves around four hours of chewing time per day" (2009, 142). The last transformation coincided with the rise of the industrialization of agriculture and the huge reduction of the number of peasants, which started in industrializing England in the eighteenth century. This reduction meant that the majority of the working population could do work other than farming—indeed was forced to do so.

This evolution reveals one of the main ethical paradoxes of food: Humans have become humans due to the continuing reduction of food processing time (time-saving cooking mechanisms), and this enables them to be severed from food (production), to forget about food (production) and to degrade food (production). The evolutionary advantages to reduction of food collecting, producing, and digesting time, produce also the risk that people became alienated from food and become subordinated to corporate production of food. In the end, people no longer know what to buy and what they eat—but of course they must eat. Alienation is the core word here; it derives from the gap between food production and food consumption; this gap is the starting point of most ethical approaches. This gap is illustrated by the predominance and diffusion of the "fast-food" system, in which profits are high and costs increasingly focus on production efficiency—here not meaning sustainability, but profitability—along with food advertisements and marketing strategies. Fast-food chains require continual expansion of production, which in turn means that consumers have to eat for companies to make a profit—at least, that is their idea. Higher yields, more intensive use of nature and more consumption is the logic of the system.

There is a second level to this paradox: due to the easy digestibility of cooked food, we think that we can eat without limit. Humans are constantly cheated by both their bodies (senses) and the sciences. Senses do not signal the number of calories that are digested—for example, they suggest that in drinking we do not digest many calories—and the food sciences are, until recently, misleading in measuring uniform units of calories, independent of what form the food is eaten (digested). The consequences are overweight and obesity, which imply higher risks of diseases and a shorter lifespan (Patel 2008) [On nutrition generally, see Sahn, this volume; Gaiha et al, this volume; Kotwal and Ramaswami, this volume].

This evolution from nomads to pastoralists to peasants to farmers to consumers-citizens severed from the land—in the wealthy parts of the globe—results not from a natural law (McHughen, this volume). Rather, the path can be changed or transformed again in another direction. Food ethics suggests alternative paths—for example, in the direction of more concern with food production and with the context of production and consumption. It is with this assumption about the open future and the necessity to think about the ethical issues such as sustainability, malnutrition, and obesity with which humankind is confronted that food ethics starts its analysis.

Ethical Issues of Food Production

Ethicists are confronted with numerous hot ethical issues involving current food and agricultural systems, partly due to this long, continuing process of alienation of humans from food and partly because of the experiences and work of food practioners, consumers, and ethicists. This section considers seven issues; it does not pretend to present an exhaustive list, but is indicative of the range and scope of ethical issues that are potentially relevant to food and its politics.

First, although there is enough food to feed 8 billion people, more than one billion people on earth suffer from hunger and even more from malnutrition (FAO 2010). This is often an issue of people not having enough to buy food (no jobs, not in possession of their own plots anymore, etc.). Nevertheless, the increases of population and of demand make the problem of food security the more urgent. Harvest catastrophes, more mouths to feed, and speculation cause not only the rise of prices but also the increase in demand of animal products and, therefore, crops for animal feed and of biofuels (which has as a side effect a higher pressure on food crops). Rising food prices play a role in food riots in countries in which people have to spend a lot of their household budget on food (Pinstrup-Andersen 2007). Do well-fed people have an obligation to help the hungry? What should be the role and responsibilities of states and international bodies? Can food aid help? Are any types of biofuels ethically acceptable (Pimentel and Burgess, this volume)? Is more production necessary or should the existing food stocks be more justly distributed (Sen 2010; Tansey 2008)? These questions will be treated in Case Studies in Food Ethical Issues.

Second, connected with the first issue is that of malnutrition. Many people in the poorer areas having often enough to eat suffer from severe diseases due to lack of necessary micronutrients (vitamins, minerals), such as stunted growth, blindness, and concentration problems (Stein, this volume). In the richer areas, there are also problems of malnutrition due to long-term unhealthy effects of the current food system, including obesity (Critser 2003), cardiovascular diseases, type 2 diabetes, and various types of cancer (Lang and Heasman 2004; Korthals 2011). What can be done about malnutrition and who has responsibility to tackle this problem? This question will be treated in Case Studies in Food Ethical Issues as well.

Third, the current food and agricultural system is not sustainable. Consider the question of consumption of animals as food, though it constitutes only one of many effects of agriculture as a whole. Animal husbandry, for example, contributes disproportionally to climate change, approximately 18% due to its methane emissions (Steinfeld 2006); this issue will be discussed more extensively in Case Studies in Food Ethical Issues. It also depletes finite resources; it is responsible for degradation of the soil by over intensification and for deforestation (in particular in Latin America and Southeast Asia); it pollutes water by manure and chemicals and increases antibiotic resistance in humans by abuse of antibiotics in intensive animal factories. Fishery and aquaculture empty the seas quickly. All these material and immaterial costs are externalized and the burden is put on the shoulders of taxpayers and nature (Tansey 2008).

Fourth, human use of animals raises other ethical issues, in particular in intense systems; the animals, not having a voice, endure pain and suffering by being confined in very small pens, inhumane forms of slaughtering, and degrading treatment as mere objects; approximately 55 billion land animals are slaughtered every year. In the western countries, there is a growing concern and sensibility for the abuse of animals, which gives rise to strong NGOs and sometimes governmental measures, and increasing intensification will not make these concerns disappear (Palmer 2011; see also Case Studies in Food Ethical Issues). At the same time, livestock remain the mainstay of some of the poorest people on earth, a vital component of mixed farming systems for small landholders (Mehta-Bhatt and Ficarelli, this volume).

Fifth, in terms of economic impacts, the current food system with its food and agro-monopolies is an important part of the global trend of the establishment of monopolies that standardize production and decrease the number of organisms used for agriculture, reducing agrobiodiversity and increasing the risk of outbreaks of diseases and pests. These companies and monopolistic networks operating on a global free market are more powerful than individual states; large shareholders speculate with food and make the food trade a casino, with all the risks for food security and price stability (Nestle 2002; De Schutter 2010). For many it has unacceptable consequences that food is treated as a mere commodity, just like cars and computers. First, the commodification of food has unfair distributive consequences: it increases the gap between rich and poor by suppressing poor farmers and even chasing them from their land in exchange for large plantations that are managed mechanically. Prices show huge fluctuations, which makes it difficult for a farmer producing for the market to plan ahead. Moreover, high prices, for the most part, do not translate into high revenues for farmers, but low prices paid to farmers do not necessarily mean low prices for consumers. Sometimes, the worst situation happens: The few rich farmers get the highest prices, and consumers in poor areas, when they are living in towns, have to pay much more. The large farmers get richer, the smaller get poorer, and in the end, the small farmers have to give up and become jobless slum inhabitants. The fluctuations also stir up speculation which often has disastrous consequences. Second, commodification degrades and humiliates farmers and their communities, harvests, animals, and land; these commodities are only there for use and profit, which is, for producers and consumers, often the principal motive in engaging with food: Can I make a profit from it? Respectively, where can I buy the cheapest food? (Shiva 2008). This system degrades everything connected with food: It makes it grades of food lower compared with the grades it could get according to a normative view on the good life that respects agriculture and food. A third criticism is also that commodification in the form of a huge reduction of labor in agriculture and time spent for cooking and eating, implies outsourcing skills and capacities to maybe 1% of the labor force and large processing industries (as is the case in one of the most intensive agricultural countries, the Netherlands). These capacities are essential to bring humans into contact with nature and the world. This lack of engagement with the living environment is a common trait of radical commodification: It allows only passive consumption (Sunder 2012). A consequence is the enormous waste of food, because producers and consumers don't respect food.

Economic policies premised on free global markets are held in some ethical systems to run the risk that commodification of nature becomes a universal dogma. When, for example, ecosystem services, like fresh water or carbon sequestration are monetized, this imposes, first, that the biosphere is sliced into components or itemized, and then these items get a price tag. Rich groups or nations can afford these prizes and, therefore, deplete these services. The ensuing disaggregating of nature's functions in the end destroys them (O'Neill, Holland, and Light 2008). A last socioeconomic issue is the drive of powerful nations and companies to buy arable land from governments, often neglecting informal local rights, with the consequence that poor farmers have to live elsewhere (Thaler, this volume). "Land grabbing," as this is called by critics, implies producing biofuel or animal feed for meat supply (farmlandgrab.org).

Sixth, food risks, zoonosis, or technological risks developing with new biotechnologies (like nanotechnology or genetic modification) are also often mentioned (Kaplan 2012). Food safety is a problem for many, although probably behind the fear of contamination, residues, and pollution lurks the often unspoken distrust of the public toward a food system that exercises immense but not controllable power. Governments, mostly guardians of risk management, are often not trusted.

The relationship between science, technology, and society confronts consumers with a seventh ethical problem. Many talk about the distorted relation between scientists and consumers: Consumers fear that technologists go too far in denaturalizing food items and in the use of recombinant DNA technology in transforming agricultural plants and animals (Gaskell 2010). Science-based health claims connected with functional foods are encountered with criticisms. Scientists bring in the so-called advantages of lower farm cost determined by genetic modification, but they are replied with the arguments about environmental costs of genetic pollution, food safety, and hazards (Thompson 2007). Moreover, according to many, the extension of intellectual property rights over organisms both hinders bottom-up innovation and stimulates monopolies (Drahos 2010; Krikorian and Kapczynski 2010). Many politicians and scientists perceive consumers' opinions, in particular with respect to genetically modified organisms (GM) and additives as irrational and emotional. Alternatively, marketers and nutritional scientists construct, in their textbooks, the consumer into a convenience shopper who no longer wants to spend time in the kitchen; in leaving food preparation to the food industry, she or he, in fact, entrusts the food industry to develop and sell ready-made foodstuffs with additives and other chemicals. These different constructions of the consumer as either irrational or lazy are often barriers for a fruitful understanding of the motives of consumers. As a consequence, differentiation of food purchasing through labeling and certification allows at least some consumers to express ethical concerns through their purchasing choices (Clough, this volume).

With respect to the issues mentioned, science and technology can work in both ways, either reducing the labor force by focusing on monocultural plantations or encouraging social and biological biodiversity by enlightening the labor force by making the farm work more pleasant, more productive, and less tiresome. There are good examples of how "external science," indigenous technological development, and cash-crop orientation integrate to increase harvest quality and quantity, partly for the market and partly for the subsistence of farmers. For example in the Kilombero Valley, Tanzania, rice is a cash crop as well as a subsistence crop; the subsistence crop serves as an income generator for technological investments in the cash crop.

Many ethicists argue that, because of these concerns, business as usual, in the sense of continuing the current agricultural and food system, is not possible anymore. The socioeconomic issues are very urgent because they threaten peaceful cooperation. For many, it is not acceptable that approximately 2% of the global population produces food and more than 12% is jobless, living in slums.

Approaches and Concepts

Principles, values, and practices

In food ethics, the foregoing issues are analyzed via various approaches and concepts that are either taken from general academic ethics (due to the fact that most food ethicists have an academic background or come from other disciplines, such as philosophy of technology and social philosophy), or inspired by the actions and thoughts of people caring for animals, nature, or farming.

In academic ethics one can distinguish between foundational or principalist positions, value-oriented positions, and pragmatist positions. In the first approach, the idea is that ethics should start by identifying and justifying fundamental *principles* and obligations that can claim universal respect and agreement. On the basis of these principles (foundations), people can than try to tackle more practical problems by paying attention to local circumstances and stakeholders. The ideal principles function as a foundation but also as criteria that identify the main bones of contention and best solutions. Utilitarians like Peter Singer and Mason (2006) or deontologists like Tom Regan (1983) argue in this way. Singer favors a calculation of costs and benefits of the consequences of an action; Regan, stressing rights, argues for not interfering with animals ("abolitionism") on the basis of the right or principle of animal integrity. The approach called "ethical matrix" synthesizes deontological *principles* such as autonomy and justice with *utilitarian* values of doing no harm and doing well in mapping approaches to a problem (Mepham 1996). The ethical matrix spells out the different ethical possibilities over all stakeholders. This approach is helpful in delineating various possibilities but does not assist in procedural questions; moreover it leaves out value-oriented ethics and long-term processes.

The *value*-oriented approach resembles the two top-down approaches, but begins by positing right values, and then delineating what a valuable agriculture could be (Sandler 2007). A kind of ideal picture is sketched, and concrete reality is measured against that standard. A last approach, the *pluralist democratic* approach, starts with the *practices* that people are involved in, and then tries to find their standards of excellence and their aims; on the basis of these operative values and norms, it searches for problems, inconsistencies, and failures, and then develops ideas for improvements (O'Neill et al. 2008; Keulartz et al. 2004). Although the pluralist approach uses the other approaches as searchlights in these processes, they are not used as principles. For example, in the case of animals, this approach would mean that the a priori abolitionist position of a theorist such as Regan is rejected; one looks instead to practices in which human-animal relationships can flourish, and attempts to expand these (Donaldson and Kymlicka 2011; Haraway 2008). This approach has a clear connection with the capabilities approach of Amartya Sen (2010), who stresses that the concept of justice can be given shape, step by step, in comparing different practices that let people's capabilities flourish.

Food ethicists try to give a broad view of all the important aspects of food and food production—nutritional, social, ethical, esthetical, cultural, religious, and personal aspects of food. Concepts from neighboring scientific disciplines are also incorporated, such as "ecosystem services;" sustainability becomes one additional principle, as agriculture is embedded in natural systems of necessity. One definition of sustainable agriculture is:

> agriculture that conserves and enhances natural resources. It uses an ecosystem approach that draws on nature's contribution to crop growth... and applies appropriate external inputs at the right time and in the right amount to improved crop varieties
>
> (www.fao.org/ag/save-and-grow)

In defining and elucidating food ethical problems, food ethics, as a branch of philosophy, is bound up with other nonethical philosophical disciplines like social philosophy, epistemology, and philosophy of science and technology. For example, from animal ethics, the concept of animal integrity is deployed in discussions about genetic modification of domesticated animals, although the concept originally was used for an abolitionist' purpose with an emphasis on the superior value of wild animals. One can, on the basis of these connections, discern at least four types of perspectives on agriculture that all have some answers to the issues listed earlier. They, respectively, put special emphasis on industry, science, farmers, or civil society. The *industrial* perspective views good agriculture as a kind of industry, to be steered by global markets in which producers and consumers determine food streams in market interactions. The second perspective considers *scientific and technological* approaches to sustainable agriculture as offering the best outlook for solving our current problems (McGloughlin, this volume; McHughen, this volume). The agrarian vision puts all emphasis on *farmers and rural* considerations, and not on consumers ("consumer economy last" is a watchword). Finally, *pluralism* respects the various perspectives of all citizens and tries to locate them according to best practices, differentiated by circumstance. For example, with respect to one food item (like grain or soybeans), global agriculture can play a role and, with respect to another, for instance fresh produce, local systems would have special consideration.

In the first approach, "industrial" or "productionist" perspective, agribusiness, global markets, and "efficiency" figure prominently; high yields are seen as crucial to producing safe, sufficient, and affordable food (Borlaug 2000). In this first approach, the first ethical issue—that of hunger and malnutrition—is seen as the most decisive ethical principle. Specific values and behaviors can be derived in a utilitarian way or a deontological way. Usually, however, a utilitarian calculation is made, and the best outcome for food security is framed as concentration and vertical integration of the links of a food chain like seed supply, agrichemicals, food processing, machinery, storage, transport, distribution, marketing, advertising, and retail sales. If monopolies result, that outcome is incidental, unless it interferes with foundational values of maximizing production to meet global food requirements. Contract farming and "comparative advantage" ought to take precedence over self-provisioning on the basis of family farms and local food sovereignty. Harm to nonmonetary, important values like biodiversity and local communities are seen as external costs to be paid by others. This ethical reasoning is consistent with the claims of large corporations such as Monsanto, Cargill, Nestle, and Unilever, which exercise great power in determining current world food chains and networks.

The second approach stresses scientific knowledge and its application to agriculture through technological innovation. Its claims are quite broad. Technological innovations might offer improved production and efficiency, alleviation of pressure on nature, more ethical treatment of animals and better prospects for long-term health effects on the current system (Sachs 2005). Advances in science and technology might, for example, give us animals that do not suffer (because of genetic modification of their nervous system), or provide sustainable energy systems and functional foods where unhealthy "fatmaking" molecules are replaced by better lipids. This perspective on agriculture is also often sustained by a mix of utilitarian and deontological approaches. However, social-economic arrangements will probably not be that easy to change; they are not like molecules. Moreover, moving food production into large companies and laboratories runs the risks of losing the trust of consumers.

In the third perspective, *agrarianism*, connection with place, actual plants and animals, and family farming, are seen as having the most value. Often this approach is antitechnological; Berry (2010), one of the most outspoken propagators of this view, considers a farmer who uses a computer a bad farmer. Consumers' preferences are not the main driver of ethical considerations in this approach; it derives from a sense of virtue as the source of good and bad farming. According to Berry, consumers have wrongly put their trust in the hand of large corporations and technological regimes; it is time to take our responsibilities and to entrust small farmers and craftsmen (Thompson 2010). Agrarianism is quite a normal practice in peasant societies and can be very sophisticated with respect to food security and sustainability, as in China (Bray 1984) and Japan (Fukuoka 1978). In more global-oriented variants, agro-ecology and agro-forestry are seen as crucial, which implies not the reductionist approach to harvests, but a broad orientation to what the soil and its interaction with various crops and tree species can give to a farmer (for example, through rotation and intercropping). Farming, according to this view, will make farmers less vulnerable to market trends (price fluctuations, concentration and up-scaling), but the total share of this type of farming may well decline globally, despite counterpolitics (Larsson, this volume; Chappell, this volume).

In the fourth perspective, a pluralist approach to ethics, all kinds of farming, from urban gardening, to intensive farming, can be acceptable, so long as they meet ethical criteria of *respect*—for land, people, animals, and nature. This position agrees on some dimensions with agrarianism, but emphasizes the capacities of individuals to flourish with different life and food styles (Crocker 2008; Pretty 2002). A mixed system could also be of great benefit to (agro-) biodiversity and make its practitioners less vulnerable to global market fluctuations. This type of pragmatist pluralism is also part of a larger democratic perspective, in which consumers' ethical preferences are taken into account seriously. Pluralist values in a democratic context with regard for scientific and technological innovations are seen as the most important ethical drivers for a global and local fair agro-food sector. This perspective goes against the dogma of one-size-fits-all; depending on the varieties of the soil, culture, social context, and technologies, agriculture has to find its own shape (Norton 2005; Korthals 2004).

Concepts

Food ethics not only tackles the ethical issues discussed above, but also develops its own concepts. The endeavor of food ethics starts as a matter of fact with a critical analysis of the fundamental question: what is food? Is it culture or nature, is it only fuel, or a bunch of nutrients, or purely symbolic? Food ethics assumes, contrary to the more usual perspectives of technologists and marketers, that consumers in one way or another are willing to spend some time to think about the food system.

Food ethics has a short history, and its overlaps with other systems of ethics and applied philosophy. When food production is seen as nothing other than a typical human destruction of the environment or wild nature (which is often the opinion of many environmentalists), there is little place for an ethics of food production; however, when food production is considered to be an important human-nature relationship, there is room for an independent discipline of food ethics. There is, therefore, an uneasy relationship between food ethics and environmental ethics. Nevertheless, in the short history of food ethics, several interdependent and particular concepts and approaches have emerged in trying to understand and evaluate the problems discussed earlier.

These concepts are: food choice, consumer concerns, informed (food) choice and labeling, ethical traceability, food sovereignty, co-existence of different agro-food systems, and animal welfare and integrity.

Food choice may not be, in itself, an ethical concept, but many ethical issues are connected with this concept. Social scientists have identified multiple factors involved in food choice: costs, availability, sensory aspects like taste, social and cultural aspects, convenience, cognitive restraint, and familiarity. However, ethical aspects may play a significant role, not only in the obvious case of vegetarianism or religious dietary laws, but also in the range of products that one finds acceptable or even desirable to eat. The most important ethical issues regarding food choice are that choice should be the right of consumers and is recognized as an expression of their autonomy. In fact, however, consumers often are compelled to buy certain foods; food choices can often be placed somewhere between the poles of autonomy and dependency. Moreover, there are good ethical arguments that it is not necessary to make food choices continuously in an explicit and reasoned way. The concept of an autonomous life cannot mean a life in which every choice is argued about; an autonomous life means being connected with routines and habits and building new routines when necessary. Moreover, the choice context is always structured by past decisions of others, and sometimes it is ethically acceptable to change that context, as is argued in the theory of nudging (Thaler and Sunstein, 2009). However, from a deontological, principalist view, real-world barriers that act autonomously cannot be accepted as moral arguments against the right to choose your own food per se.

Consumer concerns: Respect for consumers' concerns is mostly motivated by deontological considerations on the right of consumers to make their own food choices. These concerns can be divided into two categories. First, consumers have *substantive concerns* about the seven ethical issues like animal welfare or fair trade. These are issues that relate directly to the consequences of production practices or to the consequences or impacts of food consumption, for instance human health and food quality. They are substantive in that they are a matter of substance rather than a matter of procedure; one could also term them vertical (up the chain from farm to fork) or specific concerns. The issues of these concerns can be inspired by the kinds of ethical approaches mentioned earlier. The second category, the *procedural concerns*, includes matters of access to information, transparency, and trust. Procedural refers in this context to the communicative aspects of information sharing, feedback and listening procedures, participatory methods, and co-production. They are procedural in the sense that they are not matters of substance but, rather, are horizontal and cut across the various substantive or vertical concerns. They are about access to, and availability of, information, the reliability of information, and the opportunity for consumers to have a voice on substantive concerns. The two categories are of a different nature and, therefore, they raise different problems and demand different solutions. Consumers differ in the emphasis and the weighing of these concerns, and it is impossible to make a uniform system that covers all the concerns equally; information, labeling, and certification are, therefore, necessary implications of taking these concerns seriously (Coff et al. 2008; Clough, this volume).

Informed food choice and labeling are important concepts for ethical approaches (Clough, this volume). On the basis of either a deontological (like that of Kant) or a utilitarian (like that of Mill) approach, it can be argued that consumers have a right to be informed about the food they want to buy and a right to make their own decision (the right to food autonomy). Food choice is seen as something for which consumers rightly require autonomy, and honest and relevant information about composition and origin, for instance, are considered to be important items. In the United States many producers and others are against giving this type of information; however, in the European Union there are strict rules about what to put in the labeling of foodstuffs. Labeling and types of certification on content and production are helpful for consumers, because they enable them to make a reasonable food choice in accordance with his or her life and food style. What should be put on the label and what should be certified and how are ethical issues.

Ethical traceability is developed in the context of extending consumer control over large networks of food chains; producers already use traceability schemes to find where potential risks in those chains can occur. However, many consumers, conscious of the fact that in those chains ethical decision are also made, for example, on animal welfare (are the pigs penned or allowed to forage?) and fair treatment of farmers, want to develop their own systems of information, with the aim that they get information on the basis of which they can choose the products that satisfy their often differing values. Consumers also want information about environmental footprints and climate-changing gas emission during the production process. Some experiments are being done with this approach. New social media can assist in making the information available to those consumers who are interested (Coff 2008).

Food sovereignty is a concept that originated with small and medium farmers in Latin America (Chappell, this volume). It posits as foundational:

> the right of peoples to define their own food and agriculture; to protect and regulate domestic agricultural production and trade in order to achieve sustainable development objectives; to determine the extent to which they want to be self-reliant; to restrict the dumping of products in their markets; and to provide local fisheries-based communities the priority in managing the use of and the rights to aquatic resources.
>
> (Desmarais, Wiebe, and Witman 2010

However, the concept is now often used by movements in the developed world, such as those promoting urban gardening and urban community farming, which do not always produce all their food, but do seek control of many of the fresh food produced locally or elsewhere. Food sovereignty in this shift is then changed into values more consistent with *consumer sovereignty* (which takes on here a quite different meaning than the doctrine in market economics).

Co-existence of different food and agro systems takes into account that both producers and consumers can differ in their appreciation of different agricultural systems; for example genetically modified crops and organic crops are connected with very different values about what good food is and what the value of nature is. Nevertheless, it is possible that these different types of agriculture co-exist, and, perhaps, even can learn from each other. Co-existence is typically a concept that originated from the pragmatist approach, but can also have a function in the other ones. Co-existence does not try to overcome the differences in values and appreciations by making one food system dominant but, rather, looks for voluntary recognition of these differences. In the EU, co-existence is the main strategy for living with genetically modified (GM) and non-GM crops; as long as both areas are separated from each other, interference between the two is assumed to be prevented; the same holds with respect to organic and nonorganic ways of farming (Thies, this volume).

Animal welfare and animal integrity are concepts that play a pivotal role not only in animal ethics but also in food ethics, since most animals nowadays are managed in animal husbandry systems. One can distinguish here among utilitarian, deontological, care or virtue ethical and pragmatist positions (Palmer 2011). For the utilitarian positions, like that of Singer (2006), the main question is: "Can they suffer?" Calculation of suffering of all sensitive animals gives the solution to what harms to prevent and what goods to accept in this line of ethical reasoning. A deontologist—for example, like Regan (1983)—considers every animal as an autonomous being that requires respect. For the care or virtue theory, like that of Sandler (2007), virtues are important, which are character traits that stimulate human and nonhuman flourishing. In the ethics of pragmatists, like that of Norton (2005) or Korthals (2004), the various practices of human animal interactions (like farming and zoos), have their own standards of excellence and ideals that practioners uphold.

Case Studies in Food Ethical Issues: Malnutrition and Eating Meat

Malnutrition

Hunger and malnutrition are among the most fundamental issues in food ethics and a pressing concern for many citizens in the wealthy world. For reasons of space, only micronutrient and not caloric malnutrition will be discussed here (Stein, this volume). This is a severe problem because more than half the world's hungry people are hungry not due to lack of energy (calories and proteins) but due to lack of essential minerals and vitamins, resulting in severe diseases and malfunctioning. One example is that almost one-third of the world's people do not get enough iodine from food and water. The result is dwarfism, cretinism, and mental slowness. Some national and international governmental bodies, NGOs, and companies feel responsibility for this issue, but the history of preventing micronutrient deficiencies has no foreseeable end yet. International efforts to reduce these deficiencies started in the 1970s. In 1992, the *International Conference for Nutrition* declared:

we pledge to make all efforts to eliminate before the end of this decade:

- famine and famine-related deaths;
- starvation and nutritional deficiency diseases in communities affected by natural and man-made disasters; iodine and vitamin A deficiencies.

International initiatives of supplementation and biofortification emerged in many parts of the globe for tackling nutritional deficiencies. Supplementation mostly means providing micronutrients to victims of malnutrition as supplements either in pill form or in form of cooking oil, sauces, or drinks. Another strategy is biofortification, which means that nutrients are incorporated in seeds of crops either via breeding or via genetic modification. Four arguments are mostly given: it is cheap, it attacks the cause of the problem directly, it is easy to give, and it has presumably huge effects (Johns and Eyzaguirre 2007). Currently, there are several large technology networks sponsored either by public organizations or by private funding agencies active in the field of biofortification, focusing on increasing the density of particular micronutrients in crops, to produce the effective reduction of malnutrition (Stein, this volume).

There are several food ethical issues: first, who has responsibility to take the lead and to reduce malnutrition? A simple example is mostly used to argue that, in fact, the rich, well fed world has the main responsibility here. It goes like this: if you are able to save a child who is nearly drowning in the pond near your house, you have the duty to assist; international relations do not make a difference compared with personal relations; and because for both utilitarians and deontologists, space and time should not play a role in identifying someone as a suffering moral subject. The ethical conclusion from both lines of reasoning is that research should be promoted and aid delivered in recognition of the obligation to assist.

However, besides the issue of responsibility there is another, even trickier one: What is the ethically desirable strategy of assistance? The answer to this question will frame the proposed solution. The current strategies of supplementation and biofortification define the problem of malnutrition as a health problem, and use health strategies: they target one particular deficiency (e.g., iodine deficiency), propose a specific micronutrient, and try to increase its presence in crops without looking for longer term and wider effects such as sustainability. One could compare this kind of solution to a drug solution—like medical researchers look to when a health problem is diagnosed. Although these strategies have already been in use for more than 30 years and give relief during short periods of food shortages, they do not seem to provide sustainable solutions to micronutrient malnutrition and, therefore, the problem of malnutrition still persists. The absolute number of malnourished people is growing globally.

An example of a biofortified crop is "golden rice," designed to alleviate vitamin A deficiency in households dependent on rice and too poor to diversify diets. Support for this research derives from a notion of sustainability: farmers can continually produce these crops with better micronutrient content from saved seeds. This approach, however, is itself subject to criticism as an "end of pipe" or "top down" solution (IAASTD 2008).

Enhancement brought about through genetic modification is seen as the most important task and the steps toward the actual deployment of the seeds by the farmers and the digestion of the seed product as porridge or bread by the consumers are secondary considerations (Brooks 2010). That is, biofortification is one-sided in that it neglects the role of farmers and consumption. Farmers have to deal with scarce resources and food preferences of consumers. Are biofortified crops in their interest, if more water is needed, but not available, or are markets available?

Malnutrition is a multifaceted problem: physiological, agricultural, social, and cultural; all these views should be taken together. The overall orientation of framing malnutrition as a health problem has several severe disadvantages that express themselves in the continuation of micronutrient malnutrition. Because both strategies frame malnutrition in terms of health disentangled from food (production), they risk underestimating the complexity of the problem. The issue is not an intentional or nonintentional mistake from the side of the scientists. The whole landscape of treatment of malnutrition is torn between the two large boxes that are used in classifying complex human body issues by national and international administrations: they are either health (belonging to World Health Organization, WHO) or food problems (FAO). Mostly, the health side has more power and wins, because it looks so much more urgent to care for health problems.

The current solutions seem not to be very effective so long as they concentrate only on the seeds and not on farmers and consumers, who have their own interests; the solutions are not favorable toward local farmers (mostly women; see Agarwal, this volume). From a deontological position, such a solution is not acceptable. Utilitarianism, on the other hand, will perhaps make a calculation with a different outcome because rights are just calculable items. The pragmatists' solution would be to bring together all the stakeholders from the beginning and find out where the root causes of malnutrition lie; perhaps, rather than more production, there is a need for prevention of leakage of nutrients in particular in the postharvest period and during food preparation and cooking. Education may be important as well as health improvements with the result that available nutrients are actually and effectively used in the body (Sahn, this volume).

Eating meat

Meat eating is an enduring bone of contention: when a vegetarian says, "You eat a piece of a corpse and feed for a cow is stolen from hungry people," the meat eater replies: "don't be so sour, it's so tasty and healthy." Meat eating or not and moralizing are closely related.

Originally, vegetarianism was inspired by respect for animals and their abuse in animal husbandry. The (vegetarian) animal-rights movement is an abolitionist movement that wants to get rid of domesticated animals. However, the battle between meat-eaters and vegetarians got more ammunition since the FAO report, directed by Henning Steinfeld and called *Livestock's Long Shadow* published in 2006. That report powerfully inserted meat eating and vegetarianism into the debate on climate change and sustainability. The report showed that production of meat for consumption produces more global warming than driving. Although transport is responsible for 13% of climate gases, livestock is responsible for 18%. In the wake of this finding, studies on the pros and cons of meat production multiplied; moreover, research on various alternatives to meat (like insects, and in-vitro meat) got a boost in both the Netherlands and the rest of the world. The FAO report, especially through the film of the Dutch Party for the Animals, *Meat the Truth*, got a lot of public attention. The movie is an attempt to correct Al Gore's film, *An Inconvenient Truth*, with regard to the environmental costs of meat production. In a book with the same title (Koffeman 2009), the arguments are put forward: In addition to greenhouse gas emissions by cows and the cultivation of corn and soy and their transport, the water use of ruminants is very high (some say 200,000 liters per cow); add to this the erosion by intensive land use and the destruction of fertile land and of species, which lead to further loss of biodiversity, and finally the grain used to feed animals instead of starving people. Intensive, non-land-based farming has the greatest adverse environmental impacts through overuse of fertilizers and pesticides. Other consequences include the increase of animal diseases of grazers (increased by feed such as wheat and soy their stomachs are not built for), and of zoonosis due to the large-scale housing of livestock. In non-land-based farming there is no match between input and output streams, manure is not or insufficiently used for fertilization of land, and due to the centralization of production, the search for the cheapest concentrates and fattening and slaughter companies leads to a huge increase in transport of feed and livestock. Cattle fed with concentrates produce more methane emissions than grass-fed cattle.

However, the environmental problems of animal husbandry are not compelling justifications for vegetarianism; they could also lead to confining farm animals in the smallest possible space and to controling their output. Animal welfare is in trouble then. The dilemma is: Do you really want to reduce greenhouse gases, when the risk of doing this comes at the expense of animal welfare, or do you want to respect animal welfare (and let animals graze freely) with the risk of not reducing greenhouse gases. Here the animal rights and welfarist people clash with the environmentalists. Vegetarianism evades this dilemma by recommending that everyone refrains from eating meat out of the deontological reason that all mammals have the right to be respected; however, a vegetarian world is today clearly not a reality. What to do in the meantime?

There is another approach that comes to mind when one distances oneself from vegetarianism and the abolitionist and animal-rights program. In a report launched by the Royal Society of Protection of Birds (RSPB), the story is told of Tarnhouse farm, on Geltsdale reserve in the North Pennines of UK, a piece of marginal land, where grazing of cattle and sheep is combined with organic management of the soil and water supply. Here, one can see some environmental advantages of extensive animal farming; recently, Fairlie (2010) has analyzed these benefits. He asks himself: Could it not be the case that if we reconstruct the current system the result can be sustainable and animal friendly? Do we not lose an important aspect of human–animal relationship, and livestock, when we reduce the use of meat to zero? He wonders why we feed our cows, pigs, and chickens with such strange foods as wheat, maize, and soya and don't let them eat grass, waste, and other stuff we throw away? Are pigs not just the animals par excellence to devour waste in a sustainable way? When cows eat grass, which no man can eat, will that not change the conversion?

Fairlie knocks down the stories about the environmentally negative conversion at 10 kg of grain to 1 kg of beef. Considering all the things a cow's body can offer, Fairlie calculates animal husbandry restricted to the land a conversion of 2 to 1. In addition, some crops lead, through the stomachs of cows, to higher nutritional value than directly through our stomachs (the nutritional value of animal protein is higher than that of vegetables). Do not forget the fertilizing role of manure but also the value of good fodder as peas, beans, and legumes for soil enrichment in the form of nitrogen and phosphates. On top of this, when our meat eating reduces to zero, the environmental impact becomes negative because food residues cannot anymore be eaten by animals and there would be no organic fertilizer, so farmers would have to use more chemical fertilizers (and produce more greenhouse gasses). Fairlie is equally harsh on the bio-industry (factory farming), that refuses to give cows grass, and lets them live, like the pigs, on an inappropriate diet. Factory farming assumes an increase in meat production and does not review the resources available. Extensive farming would imply more employment for grazing cattle ranchers in the South and less influx of jobless people into overcrowded cities.

Eating meat from this ethical perspective is a "benign" luxury, and meat production can happen in an environmentally sound way that could imply the reintegration of farm animals in our society. Such a re-integration enriches the relationship between city and countryside, and it is consistent with the ethical position of agrarianism and pragmatism. Farm animals play an important role in the distribution of forest and meadow, dark and light, and also, seen from this consideration, they deserve a positive place in the production system. Moreover, one should not forget the role of livestock in poor countries as a form of capital and as an extremely efficient form of transport and energy (Mehta-Bhatt and Picarelli, this volume).

This discussion illustrates the problem with a deontological approach to ethical questions of consuming meat. The ethical conclusion from this position is absolutist—killing animals for food violates an ethical premise of the rights of animals to life as fellow creatures sharing the earth. Yet the premise of the vision—of vegetarians, and of abolitionists like Regan and defenders of meat substitutes—is that farm animals are unnecessary. These visions suggest an all-or-nothing solution in a complex field of cultural and social relationships in which such a simple approach is not without drawbacks. It will lead to a reduction in partners compared to the wealth of relationships we might have with animals like pigs, cows, sheep, and chickens. Farm animals need not be mistreated or even be slain for humane and enriching animal-human relationships. There are many forms of animal and people friendly livestock management styles, one is exemplified in the book of Fairlie, and another one by Mahatma Gandhi, who is the initiator of an alternative livestock system, in which animals are only kept for their products and not for their lives; it is not necessary to chase your own wild animal in providing your own food.

Food Ethics and Politics

The rise of consumer concerns in the developed countries is accompanied by activism, by writing on fair food, by organizing boycotts and buycotts, by initiating local food areas (urban gardening), by participating in social media, and by political action. Moreover, there is "ethical consumerism" taking action in the supermarket by urging for more and relevant information about where the products come from, how they are made, and what ethical decisions are made in production and rewards to producers. Political action can be so strong that governments are compelled to issue stricter regulation or better oversight of existing regulations; some companies are playing a key role, and some businesses claim the position of a "green avant-garde." As is clear from the list of concerns (see Ethical Issues of Food Production), many ethically conscious consumers find it frustrating that positions on food and food production are mostly not expressed by political parties. Voting according to one's food preferences is seldom an option. Some consumers express their agency via traditional media, new social media, or directly via the marketplace. Although food prices are rising and sustainable, animal welfare friendly and fair food is, for many, a preference, food is still not a big issue in election campaigns.

Therefore, many ethical consumers become member of NGOs and other organizations while they contribute to "other regarding" political and ethical action. They contribute to these joint actions, although it is often not in their own direct interest but, rather, in the interest of others, often people abroad, transcending the borders of national states. Ethical consumerism is often "subpolitical" and superpolitical, that is, oriented beneath or beyond the nation state, either toward issues not publicly thematized by national politics or toward transnational corporations and agencies, indirectly to nations. Many activists act out a new kind of obligation, and, in particular, in acting together they develop a first-person plural perspective of a group that acts "vicariously," as advocates for other groups like small farmers, next generations, or nearly extinct animals that do not have substantial political voice.

For (academic) ethicists engaged in often-controversial issues like animal welfare or environmental degradation, it is not always easy to meet standards of scholarly integrity and to take the relevant aspects fairly into account. Neutrality in this field is impossible; however, the rules and values of good scholarship are, for many, clear, and upholding them can have a purifying and idea-generating effect. One of these values is the concrete involvement with practioners in animal and crop husbandry and with consumer groups; it can at least neutralize the idea that farmers are mostly not caring for their animals or make it understandable why profit is an important driving force. The problem of animal welfare is not always caused by farmers but lies somewhere else in the chains. Consumers addicted to cheap meat and retailers putting high profit margins on fresh and animal food then come into the picture as important factors determining the way farmers conduct their farms.

Task of Food Ethics

The discussion of the cases shows that food ethics has a difficult task. It is not an easy job of simply applying certain ethical principles, but a deep going analysis has to be done, in which technical (empirical) details are to be taken seriously and through which often no clear answers can be found, just as in daily life consumers sometimes can get no clear answer to challenging food dilemmas. During this process it can be that cherished notions of fundamental, nonapplied branches of philosophy are proven to be insufficient; food ethics can play a fundamental role in philosophy. Food ethics often provokes, just as other branches of philosophy sometimes do.

The main tasks of food ethics are first to give a coherent overview of all the ethical problems that potentially confront people involved in the current food production system and second to overcome the gap between producers and consumers (as sketched in The Context: The Evolving Gap Between Food Production and Consumption). The assumption here is that ethical reasoning is embedded in communities—for many, the community of the human species. In this respect, food ethics is, first, intensely collaborating with the other agro-food disciplines, but it tries to do more than these particular regimes to integrate aspects and levels of consideration. Second, food ethics focuses on the most relevant and burning ethical issues in the food production and consumption processes (discussed in Ethical Issues of Food Production), by explicating, analyzing and critically evaluating them in conjunction with one another. Again, together with other disciplines, but also in close contact with stakeholders, ethical examination can contribute to acceptable solutions. Third, food ethics can delve deeper by explicating and putting forward ethical principles, norms, and values that are important in food-production processes. The analysis of cases in Case Studies in Food Ethical Issues is one example. Finally, food ethics can contribute to important questions: How should one study food production and consumption in ways that contribute to the nutritional and food sciences. Food constitutes multiple ethically contested sites. It can be studied in an objective way, although not neutrally, and ethics can help in working through that apparent contradiction.

As in any other philosophical discipline, nothing is outside debate and unquestionable. Controversies abound. Nevertheless, one value seems to be a fundamental assumption: Food and food production are essential elements of human life. Beyond this indisputable fact, many food ethicists argue for more—for example, that food has meanings for self, identities, and societies and can be neglected only at great costs. Food and food production cover relationships that one cannot fully outsource. They require maintenance, exercise, and cultivation with respect to the various aspects of food production and consumption. When humans distance themselves too much from these relations—for example, when food is condensed in a pill or food production is totally delegated to a tiny proportion of the labor force—they are degrading these relations and themselves.

The meanings of food and food production are culturally and socially differently shaped, but humans have to continuously learn to deal with those differences and to be sensitive to the relevant problems. Furthermore, the bodily and social features of food imply that even in a mobilized society a sense of place is important in connecting with landscapes and people we trust. This anthropological insight can contribute to a better dealing with satiety and possibly reduce overweight as well as waste. Many food ethicists would argue that people, therefore, need to pay more respect to food, more attention to knowledge of food and food portions, and need to spend more time with food preparation and eating, producing less waste and more seasonally appropriate (and sustainable) eating.

Conclusion: the Future of Food and Food Ethics

Similar to other philosophical disciplines, it is normal for the discipline of food ethics to spend a lot of time analyzing the current strategies to feed the world. Some would say that food ethics, in questioning and critically analyzing, makes the task of feeding the world unnecessarily difficult. The difference that food ethics can make is either superfluous or a nuisance. However, serious mistakes were made in the past, and it is better to be critical with respect to established routines than to aim at giving immediate relief for very complex and fundamental problems that, on reflection, do not allow for quick and easy solutions. Taking the history of food production and food consumption into account, one sees that one cannot continue with the current strategies of improving production without looking at the quality of food (production) and its embedding in human practices. The past does not dictate the future; citizens have to ask themselves how far one should redirect efforts to feed the world toward a food system in which humans are ethically responsible for food production and consumption. Food ethics will have to do more to make it clear that farming is not only a respectable job but also a livelihood that is essential for basic human capacities. Reciprocally, respect for food and the meal is an essential complement. Food can only a have role in the good life as good food.

References

Berry, W. 2010. *What Matters? Economics for a Renewed Commonwealth.* Berkeley: Counterpoint Press.

Bray, F. 1984. *Agriculture*, Science and Civilization in China. In, *Biology and Biological Technology*, Vol. 6. Part II. edited by J. Needham. Cambridge: Cambridge University Press, p. 726.

Borlaug, N. E. 2000. Ending world hunger: The promise of biotechnology and the threat of antiscience zealotry. *Plant Physiology*, 124, 487–490.

Brooks, S., 2010. *Rice Biofortification: Lessons for Global Science and Development*. London: Earthscan.

Coff, C., David Barling, Michiel Korthals, Thorkild Nielsen. 2008. *Ethical Traceability and Communicating Food*. Dordrecht: Springer.

Critser, G. (2003). *Fat Land: How Americans Became the Fattest People in the World* Boston: Mariner Books.

Crocker, D. A. 2008. *Ethics of Global Development: Agency, Capability, and Deliberative Democracy*. Cambridge, UK: Cambridge University Press.

De Schutter, O., 2010, Special Rapporteur on Food. http://www.unhchr.ch/tbs/doc.nsf/0/3d02758c707031d58025677f003b73b9 (accessed 27/08/2012).

Desmarais, A., Nettie Wiebe, and Hannah Wittman. 2010. *Food Sovereignty: Reconnecting Food, Nature and Community*. London: Food First Books.

Donaldson, S., Will Kymlicka. 2011. *Zoopolis: A Political Theory of Animal Rights*. Oxford, UK: Oxford University Press.

Drahos, P. 2010. *The Global Governance of Knowledge: Patent Offices and Their Clients*. Cambridge, UK: Cambridge University Press.

Fairlie, S. 2010. *Meat. A Benign Extravagance*. HempShire: Permanent Publications.

Food and Agriculture Organization (FAO). 2010. The State of Food Insecurity in the World. Addressing Food Insecurity in Protracted Crises. http://www.fao.org/docrep/013/i1683e/i1683e.pdf (accessed 27/08/2012)

Fukuoka, M. 1978. *The One-Straw Revolution: The Natural Way of Farming*. Emmaus, PA: Rodale Press.

Gaskell, G., Sally Stares, Agnes Allansdottir, Nick Allum, Paula Castro, Yilmaz Esmer, Claude Fischler, Jonathan Jackson, Nicole Kronberger, Jürgen Hampel, Niels Mejlgaard, Alex Quintanilha, Andu Rammer, Gemma Revuelta, Paul Stoneman, Helge Torgersen and Wolfgang Wagner 2010. "Europeans and Biotechnology in 2010: Winds of Change?" *Eurobarometer 73.1 on the Life Sciences and Biotechnology*. Brussels: European Commission. http://ec.europa.eu/public_opinion/.

Haraway, D. 2008. *When Species Meet*. Minneapolis, MN: University of Minnesota Press.

International Assessment of Agricultural Knowledge, Science and Technology for Development (IAASTD). 2008. http://www.unep.org/dewa/agassessment/reports/IAASTD/EN/Agriculture%20at%20a%20Crossroads_Synthesis%20Report%20%28English%29.pdf (accessed 27/08/2012).

Johns, T. and Pablo B. Eyzaguirre, 2007. "Biofortification, Biodiversity and Diet: A Search for Complementary Applications against Poverty and Malnutrition." *Food Policy* 32 (1): 1–24.

Kaplan, D. (ed.). 2012. *Philosophy of Food*. Berkeley: University of California Press.

Keulartz, J., M. Schermer, M. Korthals, and T. Swierstra. 2004. "Ethics in a Technological Culture. A Programmatic Proposal for a Pragmatist Approach." *Science, Technology and Human Values* 29(1): 3–30.

Koffeman, N. (ed.). 2009. *Meat the Truth. Essays on Life Stock Production, Sustainability and Climate Change*. Amsterdam: Nicolaas Pierson Foundation.

Korthals, M. 2004. *Before Dinner*. Dordrecht: Springer.

Korthals, M. (ed.). 2011 *Genomics and the Battle of Responsibilities*. Dordrecht: Springer.

Krikorian, G., A. Kapczynski. 2010. *Access to Knowledge in the Age of Intellectual Property*. New York: Zone Books.

Lang, T., and M. Heasman. 2004. *Food Wars*. London: Earthscan Books.
Mepham, B. (ed.). 1996. *Food Ethics*. London: Routledge.
Nestle, M. 2002. *Food Politics: How Food Industry Influences Nutrition and Health*. Berkeley: University of California Press.
Norton, B. 2005. *Sustainability: A Philosophy of Adaptive Ecosystem Management*. Chicago: University of Chicago Press.
O'Neill, J., A. Holland, and A. Light. 2008. *Environmental Values*. London: Routledge.
Palmer, C. 2011. *Animal Ethics in Context*. New York: Columbia University Press.
Pattel, R. 2008. *Stuffed and Starved*. London: Melville House.
Pinstrup-Andersen, P. and P. Sandoe (eds.). 2007. *Ethics, Hunger and Globalization*. Dordrecht: Springer.
Pollan, M. 2006. *The Omnivore's Dilemma: A Natural History of Four Meals*. New York: Penguin Press.
Pretty, J. 2002. *Agri-Culture: Reconnecting People, Land and Nature*. London: Earthscan.
Regan, T. 1983. *The Case for Animal Rights*. Berkeley: University of California Press.
Sachs, J. 2005. *The End of Poverty: Economic Possibilities of Our Time*. New York: Penguin.
Sandler, R. 2007. *Character and Environment: A Virtue-Oriented Approach to Environmental Ethics*. New York: Columbia University Press.
Sen, A. 2010. *The Idea of Justice*. London: Penguin.
Shiva, V. 2008, *Soil Not Oil*. Cambridge, MA: South End Press.
Singer, P. and J. Mason. 2006. *The Way We Eat*. New York: Rodale.
Steinfeld, H., Pierre Gerber, Tom Wassenaar, Vincent Castel, Mauricio Rosales, Cees de Haan, 2006, Livestock's long shadow. Environmental issues and options. Rome: UN/FAO.
Sunder, M. 2012. *From Goods to the Good Life: Intellectual Property and Global Justice*. New Haven, CT: Yale University Press.
Tansey, G. 2008. *The Future Control of Food: A Guide to International Negotiations and Rules on Intellectual Property, Biodiversity and Food Security*. London: Earthscan.
Thaler, R. and C. Sunstein. 2009. *Nudge: Improving Decisions about Health, Wealth and Happiness*. London: Penguin.
Thompson, P. B. 2007. *Food Biotechnology in Ethical Perspective*. Dordrecht: Springer.
Thompson, P. B. 2010. *The Agrarian Vision*, Lexington: University Press of Kentucky.
Wrangham, R. 2009. *Catching Fire. How Cooking Made Us Human*. London: Profile.

Websites

http://www.campaignforrealfarming.org/
http://grist.org
http://www.fairfoodnetwork.org/
http://fao.org
http://www.ciwf.org.uk/
http://www.nrdc.org/about/
http://www.foodethicscouncil.org/
http://www.eursafe.org
http://grain.org
http://farmlandgrab.org
http://www.fastcoexist.com/1678651/people-are-starving-but-theres-enough-food

CHAPTER 10

FOOD, JUSTICE, AND LAND

SATURNINO M. BORRAS JR. AND
JENNIFER C. FRANCO

Introduction: Revisiting the Food-land Nexus

Food politics is closely linked to land politics: "who controls what land, how and for how long, and for what purposes"? One of the brutal realities brought to light by the 2007–2008 global food price spike is the existence of one billion people living in hunger (Sahn, this volume; Stein, this volume). They were, they are, hungry not because there is not enough food in the world, but because they do not have access to enough food, primarily because they cannot afford to buy. The productivist narrative on food scarcity—that we need to double food production by 2050 if we are to "feed the world"—is one of the most important contemporary global questions, as political positions precipitate around it. But whatever aggregate questions confront an imagined global community, the persistent food-politics questions are inescapable: "what is to be produced, where, how much and how, by whom, and with what patterns of distribution and consumption"? Answers to these questions differentially privilege state or market, but inevitably raise issues of politics, power and social justice.

The countryside is where the bulk of the world's food is produced, but, ironically, it is also where the bulk of hungry people live: Up to 75% of those who suffer hunger live in the rural areas of developing countries (IFAD 2011). Though more people now live and work in urban spaces than in the countryside, the absolute number of those who live in the countryside remains staggering: more than 3 billion people a majority of whom depend on land for their livelihood. They depend on a wide-range of livelihoods: farming, forest product gathering, pastoralism, small-scale fishing, animal husbandry, and related activities. For those directly dependent on land-based production, food vulnerability is obvious. Their dependence on land for their livelihood does not only mean being able to cultivate land for agricultural purposes. For some plantation workers, they needed to nominally own or control land so that they can enter into a range of contracts with companies whether as laborers or as contracted small farmers. Indigenous peoples need access to land to allow them to gather forest products. Pastoralists need to control relatively extensive land for their animals (Mehta-Bhatt and Ficarelli, this volume).

Though much of the political and policy discourse centers on farmers or peasants, and aggregate production, the most pressing human questions concern security. Hunger and food insecurity in rural areas afflict many farming families whose access to and control over land remain insecure. Poor households who do not produce food, or do not produce enough, are vulnerable to food price spikes, which is especially true in the case of urban working classes. However, this is the same situation for net food-buying rural households, such as landless rural laborers and land-poor producers. Included in this category of net food-buying households are poor peasants who have to sell most of their farm produce to buy other subsistence needs. The quantity of food produced that is retained for household consumption, and/or the disposable net income that can be used to buy food and other basic subsistence needs, largely depends on existing social relations of land property.

Among these social relations are dimensions of *autonomy* and *capacity* (Fox 1993). In situations in which producers own the land—and let us assume that appropriate public infrastructure support and policy environment were in place—they may have a higher degree of autonomy and capacity to produce what they want to produce, and do whatever they want to do with it (to consume, trade, or both) (see Nelson and Coe, this volume). The situation is significantly different if a producer does not own the land. Even if appropriate public infrastructure support and policy environment were in place, they still have to pay the landlord (or other " land brokers" in some settings where other forms of land control other than private ownership prevail) ground rent or crop share. Indeed, even with an appropriate support environment, land-based class differentiates capacity and autonomy: it is the owners of the land and other well-to-do classes that tend to benefit more from state supports than the landless laborers or sharecroppers.

In whatever situation, a plot-owning producer has inherently greater potential to deal with food price spike: a ready and available plot of land to produce food in times of food scarcity and price spike. This is not the case for landless and land-poor households: their degree of autonomy is relatively lower: If their landlords want them to produce coconut and prevent them from intercropping it with corn for consumption and to raise some pigs, they tend to be powerless not to comply; their degree of capacity to generate food for consumption and/or marketable surplus and disposable income is relatively constrained compared to households that own the land they work.

This land-food nexus has been a prominent legitimation for land reform globally: to give security and opportunity to direct producers and prevent their exploitation by more powerful actors and institutions (Lipton 2009). Land reform in its classical formulation would address not only injustice, but also disincentives to production—improving security of land rights could "turn sand to gold" (Herring 1983, chapter 9). Traditional land reform assumed a peasant society—smallholders could survive as they had traditionally, so long as a secure foothold could be secured (Chappell, this volume). In the contemporary world, that view is challenged by very powerful market forces that put ever more land into play and changes in the challenges of agriculture generated by both stresses and pathogens endemic to global warming (Watson, this volume).

One of the reasons that classic land reform—redistribution of land from large private landowners to landless and land-poor peasants and laborers—was carried out in many parts of the world, historically, was in part to address rural poverty and inequality, and the political threat of an impoverished peasantry. In places where it was carried out radically and successfully, we have witnessed its positive correlation with the state's ability to feed the local population and significant degree of social improvement in the lives and livelihoods of the rural poor: China, South Korea, Vietnam, and Kerala, as some of the examples (Griffin, Khan, and Ickowitz 2003; Herring 1983). That land reform is correlated with improvement in the degree of autonomy and capacity of rural poor producers to produce and secure means of subsistence and livelihoods is a likely—but not automatic—scenario. The original Bolivian and Ethiopian land reforms are some of the older examples in which extensive land reforms did not translate to significant improvements in the lives and livelihoods of the rural poor (Kay and Urioste 2007). Moreover, land reform contributes to the broader process of national development (seen from conventional industrial-, urban-oriented development), as in the context of China, South Korea, Taiwan, and Japan (Putzel 1992). But again, this is not an automatic relationship, as shown in the Latin American experience (Kay 2001), and more recently, in the post-1988 land-redistribution experience in the Philippines (Borras 2007). For land reform to have a positive connection with the rural poor people's degree of autonomy and capacity to feed themselves, improve their well-being, and contribute to national development more broadly depends on a host of factors, including the infrastructure support for small-scale farmers and a policy environment friendly to newly created small-scale farmers. In the end, however, it seems almost impossible to find justice in situations in which those who produce the food cannot avoid hunger and insecurity (see Korthals, this volume). Land policy addresses this burning issue.

New Contexts of Pro-Poor Land Policy: The Global Land Rush

Land reform is no longer a dominant policy perspective globally, but the fundamental questions underlying land policy that have always confronted societies remain: What food is to be produced? Where? How? By whom? How is food to be distributed in a context of insecurity of price regimes and supply? This is the set of questions accentuated by the contemporary global land rush (Thaler, this volume). Answers have overlapped—not accidentally—with the questions of social structure and political power: Who controls and uses what land and for what purposes?

The current global land rush is not only motivated by the food scarcity narrative but also by responses to converging crises confronting humanity and the planet: food, fuel/energy, climate change, and finance. The land grab is not entirely about food. Fairhead, Leach, and Scoones (2012) write of "green grabbing" (land grabbing in the name of the environment) that includes production for biofuels—see the chapter by Pimentel and Burgess in this volume—and climate change mitigation strategies such as REDD+. Mehta, Velwisch, and Franco (2012) write of water grabbing. McMichael (2012) talk about increasing financialization of agricultural commodity production partly as reaction to the financial crisis. Land has recently become a highly visible object of conflict again, and not only for its food-producing potential.

One of the overarching narratives that accompanies this global land rush is a simple but fundamental mainstream assumption: There is enough land, but it is distributed in ways that result in suboptimal efficiency, and, thus, there is unnecessary global insecurity of food supply. The solution to the aggregate supply question lies in the existence of marginal, underutilized, empty, and available lands. Deininger and others (2011) have estimated this land in the aggregate to be 445 million hectares at a minimum, and, depending on other factors, could be stretched up to 1.7 billion hectares of land worldwide. It is concentrated in the poorer countries of the globe. Conventional notions of land reform applied within national borders and addressed redistribution of large private land property. Contemporary land policy debates confront a new global context. Nevertheless, despite the political decline of conventional land reform that had such important historical consequences, redistributive land policy requires rethinking, with many of the same evaluative strands in place.

Not all urgent land issues today have to do with global land grabbing, despite its global importance. As Borras, Gomez, Kay, and Wilkinson (2012) highlighted in their study of current land grabbing in Latin America, generic "land concentration"—not land grabbing *per se*—is resurging in the region (alongside more straightforward "land grabbing" cases). The dynamics partly involve "foreignization" of space that continues to animate controversial and heated debates in the region, highlighting some controversies especially around the rise of Brazilian acquisitions of land in Bolivia and Paraguay. This creeping land concentration—in the midst of universal revaluation of land as a scarce resource in response to converging multiple crises and the industrial-commercial-financial rise of BRICS countries (Brazil, Russia, India, China, and South Africa)—is also felt in the North. Yet, aside from weak voices for conventional land reform, as in Bolivia and Paraguay, one does not see significant political support in the form of policy. This political absence does not mean there is no popular demand and call for some form of "redistributive land policies." There is, and, as they did historically, social movements continue to raise the issue of land and justice. The general response of La Vía Campesina to global land grabbing is to call for "land reform." But the very fact that the call seems to have not gained traction in different parts of the world, even among those struggling against current global corporate enclosures, indicates the need to re-cast analysis of pro-poor land policy.

This chapter proceeds on the premise that the changed global agrarian context has revived the relevance of land reform—but has, at the same time, exposed its narrow parameters. That land reform is a relevant policy linked to food politics is beyond question. In settings marked by unequal distribution of private lands, the conventional land reform remains as urgent and necessary as ever before. But it is not the only relevant and urgent redistributive land policy, or even the most important one. One reason is that the current global enclosures target lands that are not under full-scale private property systems. A broader and inclusive concept of "pro-poor redistributive land policy" captures more fully the nexus between food politics and land politics in contemporary era of global land rush. Hence, there is a need to rethink land reform in the current era.

Dominant Land-Policy Currents

During the past three decades, there has been a move away from conventional land reform in development-policy thinking—but not as a response to the changing context explained earlier. Rather, it has been part of the neoliberal resurgence. It is important to explain this phenomenon because it is casually passed on as a good thing that land has been revived in mainstream development discourse, and, at times, insinuated to be what and how "land reform" ought to be in contemporary context.

The meaning of land and land policies is diverse across, and contested within, local and international settings. The diversity of the policy questions required to address diverse land issues is perhaps one of the key reasons why "land policy" is the popular phrase used to refer to all policies that have something to do with land. Conventional phrases that are quite specific in terms of what they actually mean are used increasingly less, such as "land reform." These and other land-related policies are gathered together under one catch-all label, *land policy*. Instead of value-laden terms such as *land reform,* the term *land policy* (often with the prefix *pro-poor*) portrays an almost "neutral" message (see, e.g., World Bank 2003).

The contemporary interest in land and land policies in the context of development has been triggered by a combination of factors. The persistence of poverty and inequality has encouraged mainstream economists to problematize access to productive assets by the rural poor. Perhaps the most important mainstream policy position that links land and poverty is the one that is promoted by Hernando de Soto. De Soto (2000) believes that land without clear private individual property rights is "dead capital," because it cannot be used as a basis for guaranteeing financial transactions. Without financial inflow, the rural economy will not get activated and grow. And the reality is that the majority of land in developing countries does not have clear private individual property titles (World Bank 2003). In order to transform this sleeping capital into active, financially tradable instruments, nonprivate lands should be privately titled. Formalization of land rights is deemed necessary and is thus widely promoted today. This is generally aimed at instigating vibrant land markets. The resurging importance of land in the context of commodity booms (food, biofuels, and so on) and the prior and ongoing advocacy for privatization of land resources that are still public or state-controlled are becoming a powerful development-policy combination that may contribute to profound agrarian transformations worldwide in the near future.

Against the backdrop of these promarket land policies, "governance" around land policies has emerged to become an important issue. However, the dominant thinking is firmly located within the issues of economically efficient (re)allocation of resources, administrative efficiency ("corruption-free") and fiscal prudence ("cheap"), the latter almost always meaning a cutback in public expenditures. Many land policy campaigns today involve support to "one-stop-shop" types of land privatization, registration, and titling programs in developing countries, commonly labeled as "land administration and management" projects (World Bank 2003). The general effect of this kind of treatment is to embrace and promote technicist, de-politicized administrative functions of the state around land-policy questions (see Borras and Franco 2010).

Therefore, the dominant advocacy for the market-oriented land policy prescriptions within some international development agencies is concerned with how many "clean" land *titles* are produced. It is, in essence, concerned about the physical land title, a tradable good, *a thing*. The concomitant "governance" issue is generally about administering an efficient production of private land titles. It is engaged in and part of what James Scott (1998) called "state simplification."

This line of contemporary—and dominant—thinking on land policies is problematic on two grounds. On the one hand, landed property rights are not "things"; they are *social relations* between people (Tsing 2002). These social relations are linked to the dynamic process of land-based wealth creation. On the other hand, governance cannot be reduced to technical administration or "management" of land markets or land policy reforms, and it cannot be confined to the sole issue of land taken in isolation of other state and societal issues related to wealth and political power distribution. Governance is about political relations between (groups of) people and the institutions (rules and regulations, both formal and informal) that "govern" them. It is linked to how, and how well, decision-making power is aggregated and (re)distributed in a polity over time, and how decisions become authoritative, or not, in society. For our purposes, land governance shapes and is (re)shaped by the ongoing interaction of various diverse groups and classes (and competing interests) in society and the state, in endless contestation to gain effective control of, among other things, land-based wealth. This classic contest is usually among national state actors, regional political and economic elites, and the rural poor. It is from this dynamic political-economic, historical-institutional and multilevel perspective that one should explore the links between "pro-poor land policies."

It is important to clarify a few interrelated concepts and issues about property rights and land policies. First, by "ownership and/or control over land resources" we mean here the *effective control* over the nature, pace, extent, and direction of surplus production, distribution, and disposition (Borras 2007). This framing will enable us to detect actually existing land-based social relations regardless of what official documents claim. This framing also provides us with a disaggregated view of the various competing social classes linked to each other by their varying relationships to land (Herring 2003). Second, a land policy does not emerge from or is not carried out in a vacuum. When carried out in the real world, a land policy causes a change in the actually existing land-based social relations. Some changes favor the landed classes, other elites, or the state, whereas others may favor the poor. Third, land laws and land policies are not self-interpreting and not self-implementing. It is during the interaction between various, often conflicting, actors within the state and in society that land policies are actually interpreted, activated, and implemented (or not) in a variety of ways from one place to another over time (Franco 2008). Fourth, land-based social relations are varied and diverse from one setting to the next shaped by socio-economic, political, cultural, and historical factors. Fifth, land-based social relations are dynamic and not static. These are not like development projects that can be contained within a timeline. Land-based social relations remain in a continuum and are ever-changing long after a land-titling project or a land-reform program has officially ended, for example. Land-based social relations are not automatically changed when official documents are changed, as. for example, granting formal titles without instigating reforms on actually existing tenure. Conversely, actually existing land-based social relations may dynamically change, whereas official documents remain unchanged (Herring 1983). Finally, property rights and land policies are often the focus of contestation and struggle between different social actors and interest groups.

Therefore, *multiple* land policies have become necessary, even in one national setting, in order to address the varying land-based social relations existing in society. These policies can be in the form of land reform, land restitution, land-tenure reform, land stewardship, and so on. The critical consideration is reforming land-based social relations, meaning reform of the *terms* under which land-based wealth is created, appropriated, disposed, and consumed. Inevitably implicated in this process will be the ways and means by which such processes are effectively controlled by different groups, which entails political power relations—or governance. Hence, the meaning of land reform should not be restricted to its conventional narrow definition of redistributing large private estates to landless and near-landless rural poor, but should envision a political process that recasts land-based social relations by redistributing land-based wealth and power from propertied classes and the state to various classes of labor, such as peasants, landless laborers, pastoralists, forest product gatherers, small-scale fisher folks. This way of looking at land reform requires some clarification of basic normative features. We now turn to this discussion.

Key Themes in Pro-Poor Land Policy

Land policies are not technical-neutral devices. When implemented, land policies impact different social classes and groups of people differently, favorably or otherwise. Not all nominally pro-poor land policies are meant to favor the poor. Not all pro-poor land policies automatically result in pro-poor outcomes, even if well intentioned. There are unintended and unexpected land policy outcomes, both positive and negative. Therefore, it is important to specify normative features of a categorically pro-poor land policy—the "redefined" land reform discussed above. In this context, we identify eight interlinked key themes (Borras and Franco 2010).

1. *Protection or transfer of land-based wealth in favor of the poor.* A pro-poor land policy transfers wealth to, or protects existing land-based wealth of, the rural poor (as broadly defined earlier). Land-based wealth means the land itself, water, and minerals therein, other products and resources linked to it such as crops and forest, as well as the farm surplus created from this land. Any pro-poor land policies must involve protection or transfer of land-based wealth *in favor of* the working poor people. It is only by specifying the direction of the flow of land-based wealth transfers that we will be able to assess whether and to what extent a land policy is truly pro-poor. This criterion is in contrast to the mainstream economic doctrine that is concerned mainly with the most efficient allocation and use of (scarce) land resources, oftentimes agnostic to the direction of change in property relations

2. *Transfer of land-based political power.* A pro-poor land policy transfers (or protects) political power to control land resources to the landless or near-landless rural poor. It is a policy that confronts, and does not back away from, political conflicts that are inherently associated with land-based social relations and any serious attempts at recasting the latter. By political power transfer we mean here the actual transfer of real or effective control over land resources. This means control over the nature, pace, extent, and direction of wealth creation from the land, as well as the distribution and disposition of such wealth. It is important to specify the issue of "real and effective control" because there are numerous official and legal transactions that occur only on paper, but not in the real world. There are various types of land transactions that are part of what Herring (1983, 269) calls "apparent but not real" reforms where land records are altered, but not the actually existing land-based social relations. This perspective follows the framework of the "theory of access" to land resources developed by Ribot and Peluso (2003) that argued for the concept of "bundle of powers" rather than "bundle of rights" as more useful in understanding current struggles over (land) resources.

3. *Class-conscious.* A pro-poor land policy is class-conscious. It ensures that the policy benefits the landless and near-landless working classes. Land policies should be informed by the notion of heterogeneous agrarian societies or communities, by the notion of "social differentiation of the peasantry" (Bernstein 2010; see also Bernstein 2002). Communities are usually made up of various classes, which are, in turn, defined by their relationship to the means of production, especially, but not solely, land. The subject of (re)distribution, or the original entities that controlled wealth and power may be the landed classes or the state. When implementing a land policy, land-based wealth transfers may occur, but these transfers may or may not

benefit the working class poor. For example, mainstream land titling and land rights formalization initiatives carried out in settings marked by high degree of inequality and power imbalances between social classes are likely to benefit local elites, not the rural poor. But even some radical conventional redistributive land reforms that are blind to social class differentiation may, at best, benefit only a small section of the rural poor, usually the better-off section of the rural dwellers.

For our purposes, a pro-poor land policy is one that recognizes that the interests of landless and near-landless rural poor are *plural*: these are the diverging and, at times, competing interests of landless peasants, rural laborers, indigenous communities, artisanal fisherfolk-cum-rural laborers, male and female, and so on. By specifying the *plurality* of subgroups among the rural poor, we will be able to *disaggregate the outcomes* of a land policy and see its *differentiated impact* upon the socially differentiated rural poor. A land policy may benefit one section of the poor, but not another; or benefit one section of the poor, but harm another. Making land policies more inclusive is a difficult challenge; the resolution may lie in resolving the land question *and beyond*, to include other reforms within the agrarian structure and rural livelihood complex of the poor, especially labor reforms. "*Too land-centered agrarian reform* advocacy" may overlook critical *labor reforms*, with strategic negative implications. Bringing class back in land policy studies (see Bernstein 2010; Herring and Agarwala 2006) and political struggles will be critical for categorically pro-poor land policies to emerge and get promoted.

4. *Historical.* A pro-poor land policy is historical in its perspective. This means, the policy should understand the issue of land-based wealth creation, political power transfers and recipients from longer historical perspectives. This allows for a "social justice" framework to be fully developed. By embedding a land policy view from deep historical circumstances, it is able to detect and prevent possible pitfalls in land policy frameworks that may undermine some sections of the poor. Problems of social conflict and political instability may occur when ahistorical land policy is carried out, based solely on the "here and now" calculation which are often guided by monetary considerations, e.g., market value of the land, "legitimate legal" claimant of the land. Straightforward ahistorical land policies—or ahistorical interpretations of land policies—are likely to result in antipoor outcomes. Ahistorical land policies are likely to undermine the legitimate claims of other poor people and unable to contribute to inclusive development or political stability. For example, under the contemporary Philippine land reform, potential beneficiaries have to be prioritized because there are more claimants than there are available lands for redistribution. In commercial plantation sectors (rubber, pineapple, banana), actually employed workers are the priority beneficiaries. It is only when there are excess lands after satisfying the demand by actually employed workers that other poor people near the plantation can be considered as possible beneficiaries. Many plantations in the Southern Philippines were originally part of Muslim territories. Several decades ago, when the commercial plantation belt was being established, many Muslim communities were

violently evicted from their lands by transnational companies supported by the central state's police and military apparatus. The dispossessed people continue to live around the commercial plantations. They employed non-Muslin workers coming from other parts of the country. The latter became the beneficiaries of contemporary land reform. Hence, although the land-reform policy was radically pro-poor in the context of the latter, it has at the same time legitimized the injustice to the original occupants of the land.

5. *Gender-sensitive.* A pro-poor land policy is one that, in the minimum, does not undermine, and in the maximum, promotes the distinct right of women for their own land rights—as peasants or rural laborers and as women. In many instances, women have access to land resources distinct to men within their households, such as by being a farmworker, a (part-time) farmer, firewood gatherer, and so on. These links to land entitle them to their distinct land rights (Agarwal 1994, Kabeer 1999), both as peasants and as women. However, it is well known now that previous land policies, especially land reform policies, excluded women. This is shown in the studies by, among others, Deere (1985) and Deere and León (2001) in the context of Latin America, Agarwal (1994) in the context of South Asia, Whitehead and Tsikata (2003) for a general discussion in African context, and Razavi (2003, 2009) for a general overview worldwide. Recent land policies started to incorporate women into the agenda. Where it has been done, implementation is a major challenge, as in the case of South Africa (Walker 2003).

6. *Ethnic-sensitive.* Similar to that of the issue of gender, a pro-poor land policy is one that, in the minimum, does not undermine, and in the maximum, promotes the distinct right of ethnic groups (and other race- and caste-related groupings) to their territorial claims, often as peasants and as a people. Previous land policies, especially land reforms, have been generally ethnic-blind. Land policies of colonization or public land resettlements as well as extractive industry policies have, in varying extents, encroached into the territories of indigenous peoples, undermining the access to and control over land resources and territories by indigenous peoples (Scott 1998, 49). Many contemporary land-oriented violent conflicts have some degrees of ethnic or indigenous peoples dimension to them. It is important to be conscious of this social fault-line.

7. *Productivity-increasing.* A pro-poor land policy contributes to increasing land and labor productivity. This means, land policy leads to more intensive land and labor use after implementation. One of the arguments for or against land reform is the question of land and labor productivity in the context of scale and productivity. The debate goes on, without a decisive conclusion, with one position maintaining that small-scale farms are more efficient and productive than large-scale farms, whereas the other camp argues that large farms are more efficient and productive than small family farms (see, Griffin, et al. 2002, as well as Byres 2004 and Sender and Johnston 2004). These two competing perspectives largely shape the debates about whether to carry out land reform, how and with what development orientation. The debate is not limited to land reform. Our point regarding this matter is

that potential for productivity increases—or decreases—after policy implementation is not inherently associated with any particular type of land policy. In different places and in varying conditions, we have seen that productivity increases through conventional land reform, in others via leasehold or rental arrangement, still in others through group stewardship contracts. The conditions of existing agrarian structures play as much role in shaping the impact of policy upon land and labor productivity as the land policy itself.

8. *Livelihood-enhancing.* A pro-poor land policy contributes to building diverse and sustainable complex of livelihoods. Land policies are usually thought of as something that has to do with agricultural or forestry development. Although to a large extent this is correct, greater understanding of the complex of livelihoods of the rural poor demonstrate the extent to which farm, on-farm, and off-farm sources of livelihood are, to varying extents, mixed from one household to the next, from one country to the next (Scoones 2009). Hence, it is important to view land as part of this diverse portfolio of livelihood strategies of the rural poor. "*Too farm-centered agrarian reform*" may prove to be problematic, counterproductive and nonviable in many cotemporary rural settings today.

These eight aspects of pro-poor land policy are necessarily complementary to each other. In the real world, however, it may not always be straightforward to achieve this set, especially in places where there are contradictions between two or more aspects. Take, for example, a case in which a contested land is limited in quantity and the land claim makers—all legitimate on the bases of the key aspects discussed here—exceed the available land for redistribution. In the face of conflicting normative principles, which dominates? Would it be class-based, ethnicity-based, gender-based social justice, or some productivity consideration? These are not easy choices at the level of normative theory. Governments and international development agencies have made choices that, in retrospect, seem contrary to pro-poor interests, but the same can be said of many progressive, even left-wing, rural social movements.

Dynamics of Reform

As a critical conversation with the conventional land reform (restricted to redistribution of large private estates) and the dominant mainstream discourse around so-called "pro-poor land policy" today—and equipped by the normative features of a truly pro-poor land policy discussed earlier— discussion of trajectories of resultant social change is warranted.[1] Historically, based on various country experiences, there are at least four broad trajectories of agrarian change resulting from implementation of land policies: redistribution, distribution, non(re)distribution, and (re)concentration (Borras and Franco 2010).

Redistribution

The first is redistribution. The defining principle for this type is that the land-based wealth and power are transferred from the monopoly control of either private landed classes or the state to landless and near-landless working poor (poor peasants and rural laborers). It changes the relative shares of groups in society. It is a "zero-sum" reform process (Fox 1993, 10). Here, redistributed wealth and power is a matter of degree, depending on the net loss of the landed entities and on the net gain of the landless and near-landless poor. And so, policies that expropriate lands without compensation and distribute these to peasants are redistributive reforms. The revolutionary land reform in China *in the early 1950s* is an example. Arguably lands that are expropriated can, in turn, be appropriated by the state to create state farms to benefit the landless poor by giving them employment in these large-scale farms, as in the case of Cuba. A classic redistributive land policy acquires land at slightly below the commercial market value, and re-sells the same to peasants at slightly below the full market value. This is the more common type of land reform, as in the case of Taiwan (Tai 1974). Arguably, the former is more redistributive than the latter, as illustrated empirically in the cases of Chinese and Taiwanese processes of the early 1950s, respectively (Borras 2007).

The conventional notion of redistributive land reform, that is, applied only in (relatively) large private lands, is the most commonly understood example of land-based redistributive reform. These are explained in important works such as Tuma (1965) and Griffin et al (2002). However, we argue that there are a variety of policy expressions beyond the conventional notion that can result in changing the relative shares of groups in society. These include redistributive land reform, land restitution, share tenancy, or land-tenure reform, land stewardship, indigenous land-rights recognition, labor reform, and so on. This variety exists regardless of whether a policy is applied to a private or public land. The key is the degree and directionality of redistributed wealth and power.

Distribution

The second type of reform is *distribution*. The defining character of this type of reform is that the landless and near-landless working poor are the recipients of land-based wealth and power. However the original source of wealth and power can either be the state or community (or a private entity that has been fully compensated by the state). In many settings, this type of reform would mean affirming and protecting preexisting land access and occupancy by poor peasants whose tenures are insecure, as in many countries in Africa (Cousins 2007). It is a "positive sum" reform process. It does not take resources from one group in society to redistribute to another. In fact, often such a policy is passed precisely to avoid having to resort to redistributive policies (Fox 1993, 10). For example, a piece of land that is officially categorized as public or state forest is actually an agroforest land tended and tilled by poor peasants or forest dwellers. A long-term forest- land use-rights allocation was issued to the poor peasants or forest dwellers in order to make their preexisting access to the forest land more formal and secure. This is a distributive reform.

A handful of successful forest-land allocation experiences in Vietnam in recent years can qualify in this category, whereas the more widespread (re)allocation of agricultural land in Vietnam is also an example of this type of reform (see, e.g., Kerkvliet 2006). These types of land can be alienated in favor of the peasant tillers, with a similar distributive effect as in the case of some formalization of land rights initiatives that actually benefited the poor. Meanwhile, a government may purchase at market price a piece of private land and then distribute this to the landless for free or for a minimal cost. This type of transaction can, under certain conditions, qualify as distributive reform. The postapartheid South African land reform is, arguably, an example, by the fact that beneficiaries receive cash transfers from the government in order to purchase land (Lahiff 2007). Some past and present public-land resettlement programs, in theory and under certain conditions, may qualify in this category.

Similar to the discussion under the redistributive type of reform, the landed property rights that are distributed can be private, state, or community owned. The forms of organizations of distributed landed property rights can be individual, group, or cooperative. The distributive type of reform, in general, is perhaps not as controversial or conflictual as the redistributive type. This is because the key question here is more "who gets what" and avoids taking lands from the landed classes (Fox 1993, 10). However, it would be a serious mistake to assume that all reforms involving such lands are free of conflict. Many so-called public lands are sites of persistent and heated struggles between various social groups and classes to gain access to and control over the land resource (Franco 2008).[2] This is especially so when there is a perception by some elites that such distributive reforms may actually erode some of their economic privileges, prestige, and opportunities, whether real or perceived losses, as in some cases of commercial farmers in southern Africa.

Non-(re)distribution

The third category is *non-(re)distribution*. The defining nature of this category is the maintenance of the status quo, where the latter is a condition that is marked by inequity and exclusion in land-based social relations. Here, the most typical land policy is "no land policy." In settings where there are vast inequities and exclusion in land-based social relations, a "no land policy policy" effectively means nonredistribution of land-based wealth and power. In many other settings, a similar effect is created by having a land policy, even a pro-poor land policy such as land reform, but then leaving the policy dormant. Another example is the forcible evictions done by landlords, agribusiness or real estate companies in potentially or actually contested landholdings to avoid any forms of land and labor reforms. The post-apartheid farm dweller evictions in South Africa are provide one example. However, there are also active land policies that are categorically non-(re)distributive. We now turn our discussion to these types.

Formalization of inequality occurs when in agrarian societies marked by socio-economic inequality and lopsided power relations, an apolitical, ahistorical, gender-blind, ethnic-blind and class-blind "formalization" of land rights campaign is carried out. Formalizing land rights of legal claimants in settings marked by high degree of inequality is likely to cement land claims by the non-poor, mostly elite, claimants. In such cases, formalization policies have only formalized inequality and institutionalized historical injustice. Many private land-titling programs carried out by former colonial powers thus dispossessed the local population and facilitated land-grabbing by colonizers. Today, some cases of technical formalization of land rights initiatives under certain conditions may have effects similar to the earlier waves of enclosures in the context of contemporary Africa (Nyamu Musembi 2007). In some settings marked by inequality, carrying out market-led agrarian reform is also tantamount to formalizing inequality, as in several actual cases in the Philippines (Borras, Carranza, and Franco 2007).

Restitution without redistribution happens when large-scale land-based wealth and power transfers were carried out in the name of the poor, but in reality the latter have no significant effective access to or control over land resources having transferred. Land restitution policy is supposed to simply restore the control over land resources of previously dispossessed people, for example, South African blacks due to apartheid or Colombian internally displaced people due to rural violence (*la violencia*) and land grabbing. In places where land restitution has been attempted, previously expelled people do not automatically regain their land rights. Examples include some (post-)conflict situations in which land restitutions were carried out via large tracts of lands or territories were awarded to communities without any process of democratizing access to and control over these land resources and territories. One example of a particular kind, arguably, is the way in which many of the land-restitution claims have been handled in postapartheid South Africa that were devoid of any significant redistributive content, where, in some cases, it became a transaction similar to "disturbance compensation" paid to affected people; people were not given back their lands, they were being compensated for their earlier displacement.

Many civil wars were partly caused by or have complicated struggles to control land resources or territories. Therefore, almost always, peace settlements included land policies. However, seldom do redistributive reforms in land figure in the political settlements, partly because forces opposed to redistributive land policies are located in all warring factions, as in the case of the political conflict and peace-building efforts in the Southern Philippines (Gutierrez and Borras 2004). In cases in which land was inserted into the terms of peace settlement in recent times, the kinds of land policies adopted were too market-oriented to guarantee actual land restitution to those who were previously displaced by civil wars for various reasons, including the fact that they are much weaker actors in the (land) market. As a result, most of these settlements were less effective, benefiting the elite more than the poor. We see these dynamics in the many country cases involved in the Central American peace accords from 1996 onward, in which land policy was indeed inserted into the peace settlement process—but was based on "willing seller, willing buyer" land market transaction principle that is far from a social-justice-oriented concept of land restitution (Gauster and Isakson 2007, De Bremond 2007).

Finally, there is also a trajectory that can be termed *counter-reform*. The conventional use of resettling potential and actual land claimants to empty public lands may, under certain conditions, have potential for redistribution, although historically resettlement has negatively affected preexisting settlements of local populations (Scott 1998, 69). However, where such a resettlement policy is done precisely *to avoid and undermine political agitation for redistributive reforms* in the larger agrarian society, then, in effect, it constitutes a counter-reform. Feder (1970) once called the policy of land reform in public lands "counter-reform" (see also Thiesenhusen 1971, 210; Tai 1974, 234). The counter-reform in this context is still practiced in some places today, such as in Brazil. João Pedro Stedile (2007, 203–204), leader of the Movement of the Landless Workers (MST), explains that in recent years under the Lula administration the government settled 380,000 families, but that 64 percent of these families were sent to the Amazon, which avoided any expropriation of private land owners. "The families are now completely out of the class struggle... Our people are stranded in the Amazon, lost in a hostile environment. Not even a small market for their produce is available there."

(Re)concentration

The fourth type is *(re)concentration*. The defining character of this type is that, although land-based wealth and power transfers do occur, access to and control over the land resource actually gets (re)concentrated in the hands of the non-poor: private landed classes, corporate entities, state or other elite community groups. This kind of change can occur in private or public lands. The organization of control over land resources can be through individual, corporate, state, or community group institutional arrangements in property rights. The transfer may involve full land ownership or not. Different variations are possible, but the bottom line is the same: the recipients of land-based wealth and power transfers are landed classes and other non-poor entities or the state. For example, White commercial farms transferred to emerging elite entrepreneurs from previously (racially) disadvantaged groups, such as those in Southern Africa, qualify to be in the broad category of "(re)concentration." There are at least two broad trajectories within the (re)concentration category.

First, *reverse redistribution* occurs when previously redistributed land-based wealth and power (from the landed classes or from the state to the working poor) was later redistributed back again to the landed classes, other elites, or the state. This kind of reversal was seen in Chile after the 1973 coup by Pinochet, who returned a significant portion of land redistributed by the Allende government to its previous owners and other elite entities Arguably, many of the (peri-urban) land conflicts in China today exemplify this type: landholdings expropriated from landlords and redistributed in the 1950s were later collectivized; then, years after, the land would be de-collectivized through a household-responsibility scheme. Since the 1980s, many of these became the object of competing land use. On many occasions, local government units have taken over such lands from the villagers without sufficient or fair compensation to the affected communities. This process has underpinned recent escalating rural conflict and violence. In addition to such large-scale reversals, there are also "micro" reversals involving specific landholdings that were previously redistributed to peasants. This type of reversal can be seen today in settings that have significant land redistribution or have had land tenure reform in the past, such as in the Philippines (Borras 2007).

Second, *perverse redistribution* is a trajectory in which land-based wealth and power are transferred *from the working poor people* to the landed classes, other elites, or the state or elite community groups. This can happen under a variety of policies, including land-reform policy, forest-land allocation or management devolution, formalization and privatization of land rights, a variety of land-based joint venture agreements and land lease arrangements. This kind of redistribution has occurred in many guises and in many places historically. These include the many private land titling initiatives past and present that were captured by elites, in which the poor lost access to and control over land resources, as shown in the vast critical literature on the subject. A recent example comes from the Philippines, where a market-led agrarian reform experiment, in some instances, facilitated the formalization of land-grabbing of indigenous communities' lands, leading to poor people losing their actual occupancy and formal claim over land rights that were in turn given formally to elite claimants (Borras, Carranza and Franco 2007).

In sum, land policies, when implemented, have intended and unintended outcomes; historically, there have been four broad categories of such outcomes. These four categories offer analytical signposts for observers to understand land policies in terms of their impact on the rural poor.

Conclusion

The land-and-food nexus has been a persistent political question in human history. Land reform—the conventional variant of it—is one policy and political device to address the question of social justice and production through redistribution of large estates to landless and near-landless rural poor (Tai 1974). There are other dimensions of land reform (e.g., political democratization), but the land-food nexus tends to be a central one. That land reform remains a critical issue today—especially in relation to the politics of food and hunger—is beyond question (Lipton 1993; 2009). This importance has been re-emphasized by the current global land rush.

However, to argue that land reform is a sufficient umbrella conceptual, political, and policy framework to tackle the land-food nexus in the context of current dynamics is incomplete. The advocacy of La Vía Campesina for land reform in confronting the current situation of global land rush, for example, is only partly correct, and is largely misplaced. Much of the lands targeted in contemporary global enclosure are not relatively large private landholdings, but the vast nonprivate lands, many of which are perceived to be underutilized and are under various forms of occupancy by a variety of people, often with rights poorly institutionalized in formal state practice. A more inclusive and relevant position in the current context is a comprehsive pro-poor land policy, along the lines developed earlier.

There are two ways in which a pro-poor land policy—conceptually and politically—has relevance to the land-food-poverty nexus today. The narrow conventional meaning of land reform—framed within the redistribution of large private landholdings to landless and land-poor rural poor—may be situationally relevant, but needs expansion in order to address the range of issues that connect land and hunger. We need to recast policies addressing land-based social relations by redistributing land-based wealth and power regardless of the preexisting land-property-rights regime, on both private and public lands. This is easily done conceptually—but difficult politically. The other option is to move beyond traditional land reform to include policies such as restitution, forest management programs, leasehold reform, water rights reform, policies on "peasant land reserves," price policies and terms of trade, etc. This is easy conceptually and politically feasible. The concept of redistributive *land* policy is also to be embedded, analytically and politically, within emerging contemporary (re)distributive social policies that are gaining traction worldwide, moving beyond the land to address the needs of the land poor. The land-food nexus need not be determinative of life chances. One specific example is the rise of state-sponsored conditional cash transfer schemes that improve food security for the poor, such as India's MGNREGA (Mahatma Gandhi National Rural Employment Guarantee Act) and Brazil's Bolsa Familia—whether seen as a substitute for or a complement to conventional land-oriented policies.[3]

Notes

1. This section draws on Borras and Franco (2010).
2. We just have to think of land conflicts in Central and Northern Highlands as well as lowland agricultural farms in Vietnam (Kerkvliet 2006), Indonesia (Tsing 2002, Li 1996, Peluso 1992), Bolivia (Kay and Urioste 2007) and China that all involve public—not private—lands.
3. See, for example, the chapters in this volume by Sahn, Gaiha et al., and Kotwal and Ramaswami.

References

Agarwal, Bina. 1994. *A Field of One's Own: Gender and Land Rights in South Asia*. Cambridge, UK: Cambridge University Press.

Bernstein, Henry, 2002. "Land Reform: Taking a Long(er) View." *Journal of Agrarian Change* 2(4):433–463.

Bernstein, H. 2010. *Class Dynamics of Agrarian Change*, Halifax: Fernwood.

Borras, Saturnino Jr. 2007. *Pro-Poor Land Reform: A Critique*. Ottawa: University of Ottawa Press.

Borras, Saturnino, Danilo Carranza, and Jennifer Franco, 2007. "Anti-Poverty or Anti-Poor? The World Bank's Market-Led Agrarian Reform Experiment in the Philippines." *Third World Quarterly* 28(8): 1557–1576.

Borras, S. Gomez, C. Kay, and J. Wilkinson. 2012. "Land grabbing and global capitalist accumulation: key features in Latin America." *Canadian Journal of Development Studies*, 33(4).

Borras, S. and J. Franco. 2010. "Contemporary Discourses and Political Contestations around Pro-poor Land Policies and Land Governance." *Journal of Agrarian Change*, 10(1): 1–32.

Byres, Terence. 2004. "Neo-Classical Neo-Populism 25 Years On: Déjà vu and Deja Passe: Towards a Critique." *Journal of Agrarian Change* 4(1/2):17–44.

Cousins, Ben. 2007. "More Than Socially Embedded: The Distinctive Character of 'Communal Tenure' Regimes in South Africa and Its Implications for Land Polic." *Journal of Agrarian Change* 7(3):281–423.

Deere, Carmen Diana. 1985. "Rural Women and State Policy: The Latin American Agrarian Reform Experience." *World Development* 13(9):1037–1053.

Deere, Carmen Diana, and Magdalena León. 2001. "Who Owns the Land: Gender and Land-Titling Programmes in Latin America." *Journal of Agrarian Change* 1(3): 440–467.

De Bremond, Ariane. 2007. "The Politics of Peace and Resettlement through El Salvador's Land Transfer Programme: Caught between the State and the Market." *Third World Quarterly* 28(8): 1537–1556.

Deininger, K., D. Byerlee, J. Lindsay, A. Norton, H. Selod and M. Stickler. 2011. *Rising Global Interest in Farmland: Can it Yield Sustainable and Equitable Benefits?*, Washington DC: World Bank.

De Soto, Hernando. 2000. *The Mystery of Capital: Why Capitalism Triumphs in the West and Fails Everywhere Else*. New York: Basic Books.

Fairhead, J., M. Leach and I. Scoones. 2012. 'Green grabbing: a new appropriation of nature?', *Journal of Peasant Studies*, 39(2): pp. 237–261.

Feder, Ernest. 1970. "Counterreform." In *Agrarian Problems and Peasant Movements in Latin America*, edited R. Stavenhagen, pp. 173–224. New York: Anchor Books.

Fox, Jonathan. 1993. *The Politics of Food in Mexico: State Power and Social Mobilization*. Ithaca: Cornell University Press.

Franco, Jennifer. 2008. "Peripheral Justice?: Rethinking 'Non-State Justice' Systems in the Philippine Countryside." *World Development* 36(1):1858–1873.

Gauster, Susana, and Ryan Isakson. 2007. "Eliminating Market Distortions, Perpetuating Rural Inequality: an Evaluation of Market-Assisted Land Reform in Guatemala." *Third World Quarterly* 28(8): 1519–1536.

Griffin, Keith, Azizur Rahman Khan, and Amy Ickowitz. 2002. "Poverty and Distribution of Land." *Journal of Agrarian Change* 2(3):279–330.

Gutierrez, Eric and Saturnino Borras Jr. 2004. "The Moro Conflict: Landlessness and Misdirected State Policies," East-West Center—Washington. *Policy Studies Series 8*, pp. 1–89 (for PDF version, see www.eastwestcenterwashington.org).

Herring, Ronald. 1983. *Land to the Tiller: The Political Economy of Agrarian Reform in South Asia*. New Haven, CT: Yale University Press.

Herring, Ronald. 2003. "Beyond the Political Impossibility Theorem of Agrarian Reform." In *Changing Paths: International Development and the New Politics of Inclusion*, edited by P. Houtzager and M. Moore, pp. 58–87. Ann Arbor, MI: University of Michigan Press.

Herring, Ronald, and Rina Agarwala. 2006. "Restoring Agency to Class: Puzzles from the Subcontinent." *Critical Asian Studies* 38(4).

IFAD. 2011. *Rural Poverty Report 2011*. Rome: International Fund for Agricultural Development.

Kabeer, Naila. 1999. "Resources, Agency, Achievement: Reflections on the Measurement of Women's Empowerment." *Development and Change* 30(3): 435–464.

Kay, Cristóbal. 2001. "Reflections on Rural Violence in Latin America." *Third World Quarterly* 22(5):741–775.

Kay, Cristóbal, and Miguel Urioste. 2007. "Bolivia's Unfinished Reform: Rural Poverty and Development Policies": In H. Akram-Lodhi, S. Borras and C. Kay, eds., *Land, Poverty and Livelihoods in an Era of Neoliberal Globalization: Perspectives from Developing and Transition Countries*. London: Routledge.

Kerkvliet, Benedict, 2006. "Agricultural Land in Vietnam: Markets Tempered by Family, Community and Socialist Practices." *Journal of Agrarian Change* 6(3):285–305.

Lahiff, Edward. 2007. "Willing Buyer, Willing Seller: South Africa's Failed Experiment in Market-Led Agrarian Reform." *Third World Quarterly* 28(8):1577–1598.

Li, Tania Murray. 1996. "Images of Community: Discourse and Strategy in Property Relations." *Development and Change* 27(3):501–527.

Lipton, Michael. 2009. *Land Reform in Developing Countries: Property Rights and Property Wrongs*. London and New York: Routledge.

Lipton, Michael. 1993. "Land Reform as Commenced Business: The Evidence Against Stopping." *World Development* 21(4):641–657.

McMichael, Philip. 2012. "The Land Grab and Corporate Food Regime Restructuring." *Journal of Peasant Studies*, 39(3&4):681–701.

Mehta, L., G. J. Veldwisch and J. Franco. 2012. "Water Grabbing: Editorial Introduction." *Water Alternatives*, 5(2):193–207.

Nyamu-Musembi, Celestine. 2007. "De Soto and Land Relations in Rural Africa: Breathing Life into Dead Theories about Property Rights." *Third World Quarterly* 28(8):1457–1478.

Peluso, Nancy. 1992. *Rich Forests, Poor People: Resource Control and Resistance in Java*. Berkeley: University of California Press.

Putzel, James. 1992. *A Captive Land: The Politics of Agrarian Reform in the Philippines*. New York: Monthly Review Press; Quezon City: Ateneo de Manila University Press.

Razavi, Shahra, ed. 2003. "Agrarian Change, Gender and Land Rights," *Journal of Agrarian Change* 3(1/2): 2–32.

Razavi, Shahra. 2009. "Engendering the Political Economy of Agrarian Change." *Journal of Peasant Studies* 36(1):197–226.

Ribot, Jesse, and Nancy Peluso. 2003. "A Theory of Access." *Rural Sociology* 68(2): 153–181.

Scott, James. 1998. *Seeing Like a State: How Certain Schemes to Improve the Human Condition Have Failed*. New Haven, CT: Yale University Press.

Scoones, Ian. 2009. "Livelihoods Perspectives and Rural Development." *Journal of Peasant Studies* 36(1):171–197.

Sender, John, and Deborah Johnston. 2004. "Searching for a Weapon of Mass Production in Rural Africa: Unconvincing Arguments for Land Reform." *Journal of Agrarian Change* 4(1&2):142–164.

Stedile, João Pedro, 2007. "The Class Struggles in Brazil: The Perspective of the MST." In *Global Flashpoints: Reactions to Imperialism and Neoliberalism*, edited by L. Panitch and C. Leys, *Socialist Register 2008*. Wales: Merlin Press.

Tai, Hung-Chao. 1974. *Land Reform and Politics: A Comparative Analysis*. Berkeley: University of California Press.

Thiesenhusen, William. 1971. "Colonization: Alternative or Supplement to Agrarian Reform." In *Land Reform in Latin America*, edited by P. Dorner, pp. 209–226. Madison: Land Economics, University of Wisconsin.

Tsing, Anna. 2002. "Land as Law: Negotiating the Meaning of Property in Indonesia." In *Land, Property, and the Environment*, edited by F. Richards, pp. 94–137. Oakland: Institute for Contemporary Studies.

Tuma, Elias. 1965. *Twenty-Six Centuries of Agrarian Reform: A Comparative Analysis*. Berkeley: University of California Press.

Walker, Cherryl. 2003. "Piety in the Sky? Gender Policy and Land Reform in South Africa." *Journal of Agrarian Change* 3(1/2):113–148.

Whitehead, Anne, and Dzodzi Tsikata. 2003. "Policy Discourse on Women's Land Rights in Sub-Saharan Africa: The Implications of the Re-turn to the Customary." *Journal of Agrarian Change* 3(1/2): 67–112.

World Bank. 2003. *Land Policies for Growth and Poverty Reduction*. Washington D.C., Oxford, UK: World Bank; Washington D.C., UK: Oxford University Press.

CHAPTER 11

FOOD SECURITY, PRODUCTIVITY, AND GENDER INEQUALITY[1]

BINA AGARWAL

Introduction

Of the many global challenges we face today, perhaps the most significant and of the longest duration is that of providing food security and eliminating hunger. This challenge is compounded by developments such as the rise and volatility of food prices; the shift from foodcrops to biofuels in major food-exporting countries; the neglect of agriculture in many developing countries, especially in terms of investment in infrastructure; and the looming threat of climate change with its predicted adverse effects on food production.

These developments are both cause for serious concern and an opportunity for change, since there is now a renewed global interest in agriculture to reduce the constraints to economic growth and improve food security. There is also a growing recognition of the need to tap the potential of small farmers, a vast number of whom are women. For sustainability, we need long-term efforts to increase production, stabilize food availability, and improve distribution. Here the role of women as farmers, as consumers, and as family food managers, can prove pivotal.

Food security requires both the availability of adequate food and economic and physical access to what is available. The quality of food (e.g., adequate micronutrients) is also important. In each respect, women play a critical role. They are major food producers and hence significant contributors to food availability. Their access to food has an important bearing on their own and their family's food security. And nutritional quality is of particular importance for women, given their special needs during pregnancy and lactation.

This chapter examines the relationship between gender inequality and food security with a particular focus on the following dimensions: (i) women as food producers, the production constraints they face as farmers, and the potential for increasing agricultural output globally if the constraints are overcome; (ii) women as consumers and key managers of food in the home, and the implications of their unequal access to food; and (iii) the mechanisms, especially institutional, for overcoming the constraints and inequalities women face as producers, consumers, and family food managers. Before focusing on the gender dimensions, however, I outline some general factors that impinge on the question of food security today.

Some General Factors

A key factor that has an important bearing on long-term prospects of global food security is the regional concentration of foodgrain production and exports. In 2008, Asian farmers produced 90% of the world's rice and around 40% of its wheat and total cereals. Most Asian countries, however, consume what they produce, and the exports come from only a few. Sixty-five per cent of all cereal exports came from North America and Europe in 2008 (Figure 11.1).

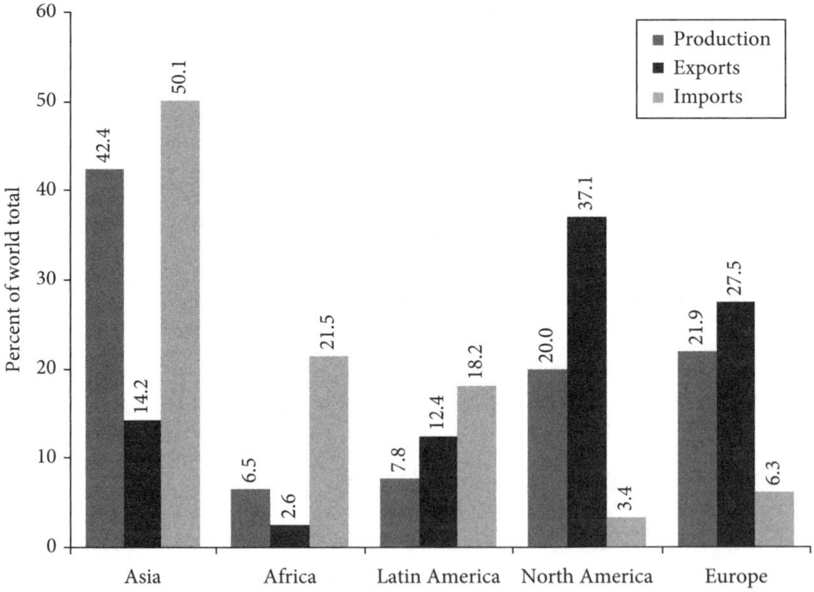

FIGURE 11.1 Production, exports, and imports of total cereals by the world's regions, 2008 (percentages).

Source: Based on FAO Statistics (http:/faostat.fao.org).

This regional concentration makes food deficit regions overdependent on certain countries. It also leaves food-importing countries vulnerable to policies in the exporting countries. For instance, if the latter shift large areas from food grains to biofuels, or manage their agriculture inefficiently, or cut exports to deal with their own needs, or do little to control speculative hoarding, the impact would be felt by the importing countries. Adverse weather conditions can compound these other effects. In fact, these are exactly the kinds of factors that underlay the 2007–2008 price rise, when the food price index rose by nearly 40% relative to 9% in 2006 (von Braun 2008). The adverse effects of this price rise fell on food-grain importing countries and on net buyers of foodgrains within countries (Quisumbing, et al. 2008, see also von Braun 2008–2009). The worst affected were the poor, especially women and children. By World Bank estimates, the price rise added 105 million to the poor, mostly in South Asia and sub-Saharan Africa (Ivanic and Will 2008). Although the 2007–2008 price spike was especially dramatic, the overall upward trend in prices continues and is cause for major concern globally, as is the prospect of price volatility.

To these short-term factors, we need to add long-term ones such as (i) dietary shifts toward meat and milk with rising incomes in developing countries, leading to a higher demand for grain to feed livestock and the land to grow it[2]; (ii) rising world population, which is predicted to be 9 billion by 2050; and (iii) neglect of agriculture in developing countries over a long period, reflected especially (as mentioned) in falling public investment in agricultural infrastructure and services.

In addition, we have the predicted averse effects of climate change on foodgrain production. The impact is expected to be especially negative in South Asia and sub-Saharan Africa. Assessments by the International Food Policy Research Institute (IFPRI) in Washington DC, for instance, show that in 2050, climate change relative to the no-climate-change scenario, could lower production of rice, wheat, and maize by around 14%, 49%, and 9%, respectively, in South Asia, and by 15%, 36%, and 7%, respectively, in sub-Saharan Africa (IFPRI 2009).[3] Indeed, climate change, coupled with a growing demand for food as populations and incomes grow, is also expected to trigger price rise in the major staples, namely rice, wheat, and maize. These price increases need not translate into increased production, given supply-side constraints faced by small producers, who constitute a vast proportion of farmers in developing countries. Also, higher feed prices will raise meat prices.

Extraordinary efforts will thus be needed to meet the food security demands of the estimated 9 billion people by 2050, even without climate change. With climate change, this is even more of an imperative. If food output lags behind population, the availability of per capita calories in the developing world in 2050 will be lower than in 2000. By some estimates, this could result in a 20% higher child malnutrition than would be the case with no climate change (IFPRI 2009). Indeed, even with the best efforts at mitigating climate change, the poor, and especially women and children, are likely to suffer disproportionately. The gender factor is, in fact, a critical one as we look toward the future, given women's multiple roles in ensuring food security.

Women as Food Producers

Agriculture today contributes less than 10% of the GDP of most countries, but continues to be a major source of employment and livelihoods in many. This is especially so in Asia and Africa, where close to 60% of workers are in agriculture (figure 11.2). This divergence in major developing regions, between agriculture's GDP contribution and the population it supports, means that many are trapped in low-productivity livelihoods. And this trap is gendered, given women's disproportionate dependence on agriculture for a living.

Women workers depend much more on agriculture for survival than male workers, due to their lesser access to nonfarm jobs. In Africa, for instance, in 2008, 63% of female workers relative to 48% of male workers depended on agriculture-based livelihoods. For Asia, the figures were 57% for females and 48% for males (figures 11.3 and 11.4). Women also constitute a substantial proportion of the *total* agricultural labor force (figure 11.5). In Asia, for instance, 43% of all farm workers in 2008 were female, with figures as high as 52% in Cambodia and the Lao People's Democratic Republic, 50% in Bangladesh, 49% in Vietnam, and 48% in China. In the world's major rice producing and exporting regions, therefore, almost half the agricultural work force is female. In Africa, again, women form almost 50% of agricultural workers. Moreover, based on time use data for parts of sub-Saharan Africa, India, and China, Doss (2010: 9) finds that women contribute 60–70% of the total labor needed to bring food to the table in

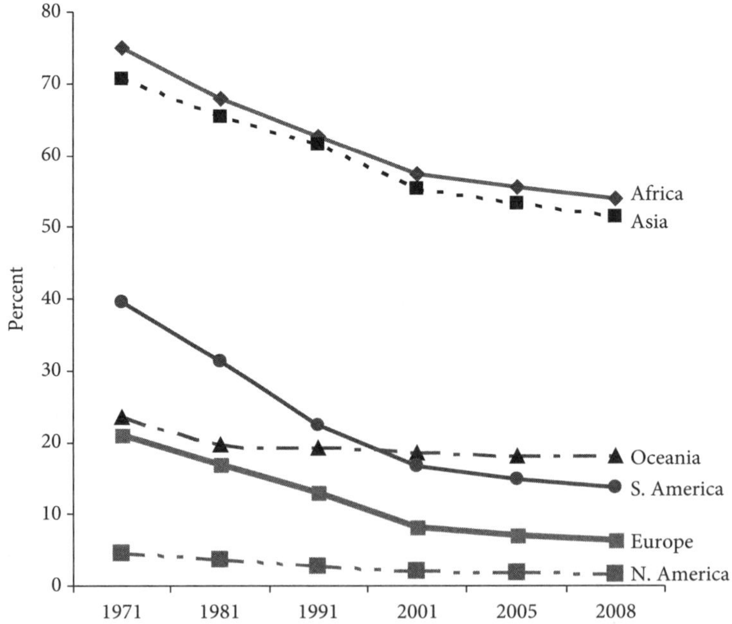

FIGURE 11.2 Percent of total labor force in agriculture: world's regions.

Source: Based on FAO Statistics (http:/faostat.fao.org).

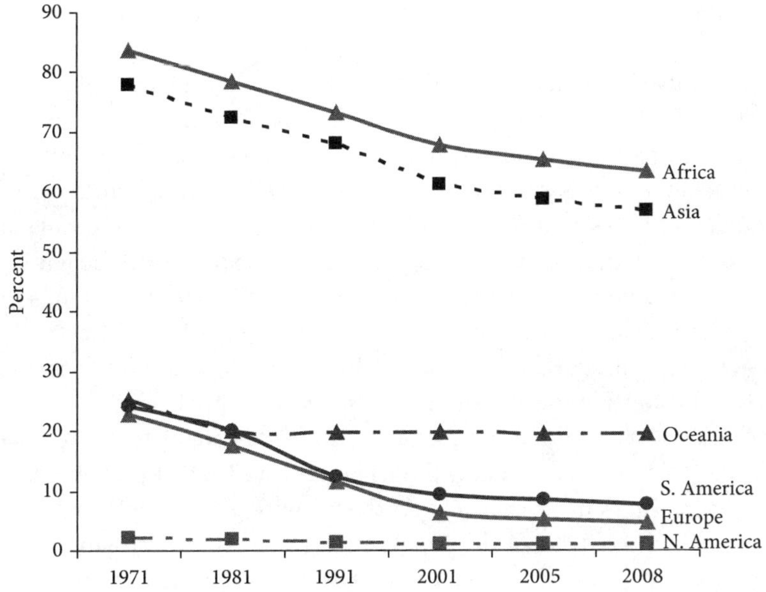

FIGURE 11.3 Female labor force in agriculture as a percent of economically active female population: world's regions.

Source: Based on FAO Statistics (http:/faostat.fao.org).

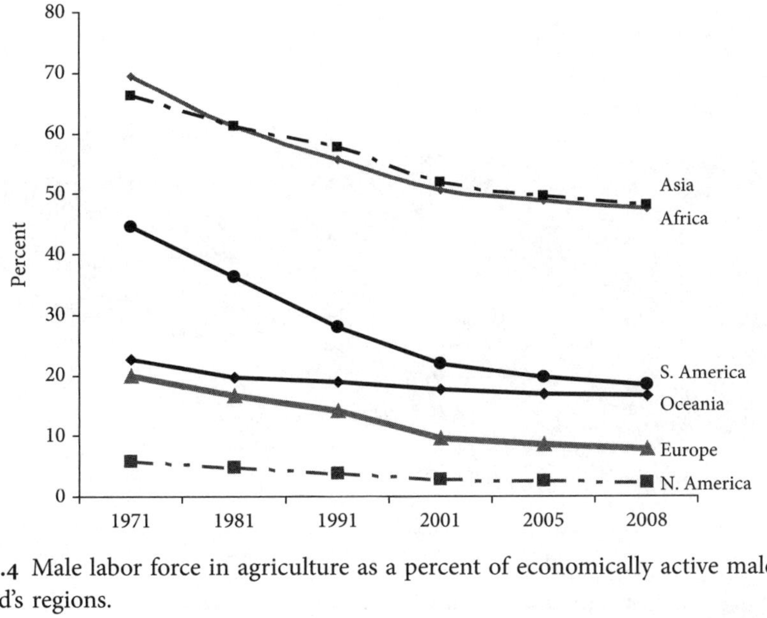

FIGURE 11.4 Male labor force in agriculture as a percent of economically active male population: world's regions.

Source: Based on FAO Statistics (http:/faostat.fao.org).

developing countries, if we aggregate the time spent on food production, processing and preparation.

Indeed, not only is dependence on women's work in agriculture high, but it is growing, since men have been moving to nonfarm jobs to a much greater extent than women. Over the past four decades, in all parts of the world except Europe, women workers have been rising as a proportion of the total agricultural work force—in some cases gradually, as in Asia, and in other cases substantially, as in Oceania and South America (figure 11.5). In other words, we are seeing a move toward the feminization of agriculture (defined here as a rise in the proportion of women in the total agricultural work force, even if the absolute proportion remains half or below). Clearly, the agrarian transition—the shift of workers from agriculture to industry and services, and from rural to urban areas—that is expected with development, has been notably gendered.

To revive and sustain agricultural growth, as well as adapt to or mitigate climate change, the role of women farmers will thus be central. How effectively they can contribute, however, will depend crucially on their having secure rights in the land they cultivate, as well as access to credit; inputs such as fertilizers, irrigation, technology; information on new agricultural practices; and marketing infrastructure.

Gendered Production Constraints

Women farmers face a wide range of gender-specific constraints that affect their productive potential as agricultural workers. First, like the majority of male farmers in

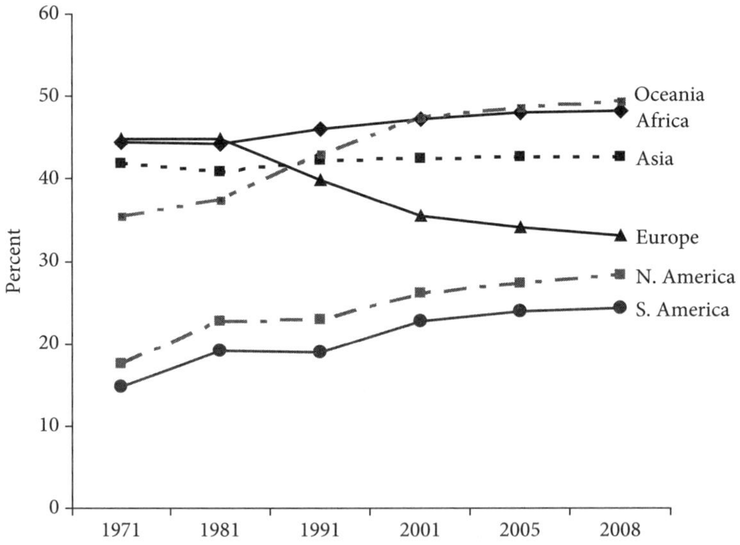

FIGURE 11.5 Percent females in total agricultural labor force: world's regions.

Source: Based on FAO Statistics (http:/faostat.fao.org).

developing countries, women operate small farms (in most of South Asia, 80% of farmers cultivate under two hectares). Landlessness has also been growing. Women, in any case, have historically been largely landless, in that most own little or no land themselves, even if their families own some. A vast proportion of them works as unpaid labor on family farms, or as laborers on the fields of others, or under insecure tenure arrangements on land obtained through the family or markets (World Bank 2007, 80). In most regions, the "self-employed" women are typically those working on family farms where the land is owned by spouses or male relatives, rather than by the women themselves.

Although few countries collect country-level gender-disaggregated data on land or asset ownership, information gleaned from those that do, and from small-scale studies in others, shows a substantial gender inequality. In most of South Asia, except Sri Lanka, for instance, few women own land (Agarwal 1994). In Nepal—a rare country that collected information on landownership by gender in its 2001 census—women were found to own land in only 14% of landowning rural households (Allendorf 2007). In India, although there are no comprehensive data for ownership holdings, the Agricultural Census of 2010–2011 shows that women held only 12.8% of all operational (i.e., cultivated) land holdings covering 10.4% of the operated area (GoI 2010–2011). In rural China, women constitute an estimated 70% of the landless since they are not alloted use rights in community land under the household responsibility system, when they relocate on getting married or divorced (Li 2003: 4).

Within Asia as a whole, the gender gap in access to land is much larger in South Asia than in Southeast Asia; and within South Asia the gap is larger in the northern belt (northwest India, Bangladesh, and Pakistan) than in south India and Sri Lanka (Agarwal 1994). Underlying these regional variations are differences in laws, culture (especially postmarital residence: distant marriages reduce access), ecology-linked cropping patterns (e.g., women's work contribution is more visible in rice than in wheat cultivation), ethnic and religious diversity, political freedoms, and overall development. In Africa, again, we see substantial gender gaps. In Ghana, women hold land in only 10% of the households relative to 16–23% among men (Deere and Doss 2006). In Kenya, women are 5% of registered landholders. In Latin America, too, there are notable gender inequalities in land ownership (Deere and de Leon 2001; Lastarria-Cornhiel and Manji 2010). But even when women have access to land, their control over it (in terms of rights to lease, mortgage, or sell it, or use it as collateral) tends to be more restricted than men's.[4]

A comparison of land held by male and female headed households is also revealing.[5] Household surveys, compiled by the Food and Agricultural Organisation (FAO) for 20 countries, show that male-headed households (MHHs) operate much larger farms on average than female-headed households (FHHs). In Bangladesh, Ecuador, and Pakistan, for instance, the farm size of male household heads is twice that of female household heads.[6] Moreover, Anriquez (2010) finds that rural FHHs have a higher share of elderly dependents (over 64 years of age), whereas rural MHHs have a higher share of child dependents. Female-headed households are therefore likely to be more labor constrained than MHHs which would have access to youth labor as the children grow to adulthood.

Second, there are well-documented gender inequalities and male biases in women farmers' access to technical information, credit, extension services, critical inputs such as fertilizers and water, and marketing (World Bank 2009, FAO 2011, Peterman, Behrman, and Quisumbing 2009). Membership in rural cooperatives, which provide inputs, is also predominantly male in most countries (see Saito, et al 1994, among others). In addition, there are significant gender differences in the tools owned by male and female farmers. In Kenya, for instance, the value of farm equipment owned by FHHs was found to be half that owned by MHHs (Saito, et al. 1994, 23). In Gambia, under 1% of women farmers are found to own a weeder, seeder, or multiuse agricultural implement, compared with 12%, 27%, and 18%, respectively, of male farmers (cited in Peterman et al. 2009, 28).

Third, women face social restrictions in public participation and mobility in many regions (such as in northern South Asia, the Middle East, and North Africa). This adversely affects their ability to freely procure inputs, or sell their produce, or hire labor. In other words, it restricts their ability to function fully as farmers (Agarwal 1994, FAO 2011, World Bank 2009).

Fourth, these constraints, in turn, restrict women's ability to take advantage of opportunities for higher-value production. Lack of secure land rights and other resources can exclude women farmers from contract farming arrangements, as research in Kenya and Senegal shows (Dolan 2001, Maertens and Swinnen 2009). And in family farms, where men hold the contracts, women tend to face heavier workloads, while men control the cash generated (Collins 1993, FAO 2011). Women are also less able to adopt high-yielding crop varieties and improved management systems due to poorer access to extension services (see Doss 2001, for Africa).

What impact do these constraints have on farm productivity?

Gender Differences in Farm Productivity

A substantial body of available evidence indicates that gender inequalities in access to land, other production inputs, and agricultural support systems, can significantly affect farm productivity. The effects are especially revealing in contexts in which men and women cultivate both separate and joint plots, as is common in sub-Saharan Africa. For this region, a fair number of studies have measured productivity differences between male and female farmers (Table 11.1). The studies vary in their methodologies and in what they measure (individual crop yields, all farm output, or farm incomes), but all of them are based on medium to large samples and statistical analysis. Typically the comparison is between FHHs and MHHs, but a few studies measure differences between plots managed by men and women within the same extended household.

Table 11.1 Gender differences in agricultural productivity/efficiency: A summary of existing studies

Country	Author and Year	Sample	Crop(s)	Productivity/ efficiency differences	Differences attributable to constraints faced by women farmers
AFRICA RELATED STUDIES					
Benin (Central)	Kinkingninhoun-Mêdagbé et al. (2008)	50 farmers from an irrigated rice scheme (and 145 farmers in total)	Rice	Women's yields are 27% below those of male farmers in one season.	Women lack timely access to ploughing, planting and transportation services
Burkina Faso (Subnational)	Udry et al (1995)	ICRISAT sample survey covering 150 households and 4,655 plots over four years	All crops, sorghum and vegetables	Women's yield is 18% lower than that of men for all crops, 40% less for sorghum and 20% less for vegetables.	Women use less inputs, especially fertilizers. Overall output could be increased by 10–20% with a reallocation of inputs between male and female plots
Burkina Faso (Subnational and National)	Akresh (2008)	ICRISAT sample survey used by Udry et al (1995) and a nationally representative survey of 2,406 farms in 1990/91	Millet-Sorghum and Cotton-Rice-Fonio	Women are 32% less efficient in ICRISAT areas, just under 7% less efficient in near-ICRISAT areas, and equally efficient in other areas.	No information
Burkina Faso (National)	Bindlish, Evenson, & Gbetibouo (1993)	Nationally representative survey of 2406 farms in 1990/1991	All crops	15% lower value of total output on female headed farms.	No information
Cameroon (Southern)	Kumase, Bisseleua, & Klasen (2008)	Survey covering 1030 cocoa farmers in 2007	Cocoa	Similar productivity of male and female farmers. *With equal access to inputs and extension women would be slightly more productive.*	Women have less access to inputs and extension services.

(Continued)

Table 11.1 Continued

Country	Author and Year	Sample	Crop(s)	Productivity/ efficiency differences	Differences attributable to constraints faced by women farmers
Côte d'Ivoire (Northern)	Adesina and Djato (1997)	Survey of 410 farmers in three districts, 1993/1994.	Rice	Dummy for gender of farmer is statistically insignificant. Relative economic efficiency is the same for male and female farmers.	No information
Ethiopia (Central Highlands)	Tiruneh et al. (2001)	180 Heads of households	All farm output	Value of gross output per hectare: FHHs obtain 35 per cent less than MHHs.	Women use less inputs and have lower access to extension services.
Ethiopia (Highlands)	Holden, Shiferaw, & Pender (2001)	1998 survey of 102 heads of households (and 606 farm plots) in 7 villages	Barley and other cereals	Land productivity was 49–67% higher on plots operated by MHHs than by FHHs.	FHHs have lesser access to male labor and oxen.
Ghana (Akwapim)	Goldstein and Udry (2008)	–	Maize-cassava	Wives achieve lower profits than their husbands.	Women have insecure land tenure leading to less investment in land fertility.
Ghana (Subnational)	Hill and Vigneri (2009)	Panel for 428 farmers covering 2002 and 2004	Cocoa	No statistically significant difference. Women are as productive as men.	No information
Ghana (Western)	Quisumbing et al (2001)	281 heads of households in 10 villages. 1996/1997 survey	Cocoa	No differences observed based on gender of parcel manager.	No information

(Continued)

Table 11.1 Continued

Country	Author and Year	Sample	Crop(s)	Productivity/ efficiency differences	Differences attributable to constraints faced by women farmers
Kenya (Subnational)	Saito et al (1994)	750 Heads of households with plot specific information. Regression for 494 plots. Three districts covered in 1989/90.	Maize, beans and cowpeas	Men's mean gross value of output per hectare is 8.4% higher than that of women. The gender dummy is statistically insignificant.	Gender differences in productivity are attributable to gender difference in input use.
Kenya (Western)	Moock (1976)	152 farmers	Maize	Yields on female plots are lower, but the difference is not statistically significant. *Women would produce 6.6% more output than men, everything else being equal.*	Productivity differences due to lower inputs by women, in particular of chemical fertilizer.
Kenya (Western)	Alene et al. (2008)	800 heads of households	Maize	FHHs obtain yields that are 23% lower than those of MHHs (not indicated whether the difference is statistically significant).	Yield differences largely due to women's lower access to land and education. After controlling for these factors, women and men are equally efficient, technically and allocatively.
Kenya (Western)	Ongaro (1990)	257 smallholder farmers	Maize	Women obtain about 16% lower yields than male farmers.	Women use substantially lower amounts of fertilizer.
Kenya	Bindlish & Evenson (1993)	675 farm heads of households in 7 representative districts	All farm output	Dummy for gender of head is not statistically significant.	No information

(Continued)

Table 11.1 Continued

Country	Author and Year	Sample	Crop(s)	Productivity/ efficiency differences	Differences attributable to constraints faced by women farmers
Malawi (National)	Gilbert et al. (2002)	1,385 farmers	Maize	Male plots have 12-19% higher maize yields.	Women's plots have lower input use, notably fertilizer and labor.
Nigeria (Oyo State)	Adeleke et al. (2008)	70 smallholder farmers	Maize, yam, cassava, vegetables, legumes	No significant difference in value of production (gross margin) for male and female farmers.	No information
Nigeria (Ondo&Ogun States)	Timothy and Adeoti (2006)	287 small-scale cassava farmers; data for 2004.	Cassava output	Women are slightly more technically efficient but less allocatively efficient.	Women underutilize inputs, and/or purchase inputs of different quality or prices than men.
Nigeria (Osun State)	Oladeebo & Fajuyigbe (2007)	100 farmers; data for 2002/2003.	Rice	Female farmers have 66% lower rice yields than male farmers.	Gender differences are attributable to differences in input levels.
Nigeria (Oyo State)	Saito et al (1994)	720 heads of households and plot specific data for 1989/1990. Regression analysis for 226 heads of households & 1,175 plots.	Food	Dummy for gender of plot user is statistically insignificant for household level analysis. However, dummy for the gender of plot manager is 0.56 and statistically significant for plot level regressions.	No information

(Continued)

Table 11.1 Continued

Country	Author and Year	Sample	Crop(s)	Productivity/ efficiency differences	Differences attributable to constraints faced by women farmers
Senegal (Upper Senegal River Valley)	Lilja, Randolph, & Diallo (1998)	135 rice farmers in the Upper Senegal River Valley in 1998.	Rice	Female farmer's rice yields are 20% below those of male farmers.	Women are constrained in terms of their lower access to inputs, the intensity and timing of input use, timely weeding and guarding the fields against birds.
Zimbabwe (3 rural areas)	Horrell and Krishnan (2007)	300 heads of households; data for 2001.	Maize, Groundnuts, Roundnuts, & Cotton	Dummy for FHHs is significant only for cotton. Large differences in yields obtained by MHHs and FHHs	FHHs are disadvantaged in input quality, timely access to inputs and differences in experience.
	ASIA RELATED STUDIES				
China (Six rural provinces)	Zhang et al (2004)	1,199 heads of households; data for 2000.	All crops, rice, wheat and maize	Women-run farms are as efficient as those run by men.	No information
Korea, Republic of	Jamison & Lau (1982)	1,363 mechanized farms.	Rice	Dummy for male HH head is statistically significant and positive.	No information
Korea, Republic of	Jamison & Lau (1982)	541 non-mechanized farms.	Rice	Insignificant coefficient for dummy for gender of HH head.	No information

Source: Compiled by author from information provided by the SOFA Gender equity team, in particular Teri Raney and Andre Croppenstedt, FAO, Rome, 2011.

The findings are notable. Several studies find no statistically significant difference in managerial efficiency by the gender of the farmer, in terms of crop yields or production.[7] Some show mixed effects, with no significant impact at the household level but a significant impact by the gender of the plot manager (see, e.g., Saito et al. 1994 for Nigeria). The majority of studies, however, find lower yields on women's plots/farms. This is not attributable, however, to women's lesser capability as farmers but to one or more of the following constraints: women's lower access to inputs, especially fertilizers; insecure land rights; lower access to male labor, oxen, and extension services; and difficulties in ensuring timely ploughing, weeding, or transportation. A few studies also demonstrate that if women had access to the same inputs and extension services as men, they would have higher outputs than male farmers.[8] In Kenya, Dey (1992) found maize yields to be almost 7% more on female-managed farms than on male-managed ones, when they had the same access to extension. In Burkina Faso, Udry et al. (1995) estimated that output could be increased by 10–15% if factors of production (such as manure and fertilizers) were reallocated from men's plots to women's plots in the same household. Quisumbing (1996) concludes that if Kenyan women farmers had had the same access as male farmers to agricultural inputs and experience, their crop yields could have been raised by up to 23%. This could have led to a doubling of Kenya's GDP growth rate from 4.3% to 8.3% in 2004, according to World Bank estimates (World Bank 2009, 16).

There can also be an intrahousehold incentive effect if women control the products of their labor. In Kenya, for instance, the introduction of weeding technology in maize production raised yields on women's plots by 56%, where women controlled the output, and only by 15% on the men's plots, where too women weeded but men got the proceeds (Elson 1995). Since men tend to use more inputs and should, therefore, produce more output, this substantial difference may be seen as a disincentive effect when women do not receive compensation for their efforts within the family.

Studies in Asia are more sparse, but existing ones show that women farmers are as productive as male farmers (Table 11.1), or would be as productive with the same access to inputs and services (see Thapa 2008 for Nepal). Also illustrative is a rare study from rural India, which examined the productive efficiency of men and women in using potato-digging equipment. It found women to be several times more productive, by all the measures used: women and men took 69 and 185 hours, respectively, for the same job, and women's potato digging yield rate was 23.9 kg per 20 meters, whereas men's was 18.2 (Agarwal 1983: 56). Moreover, in South Asia, groups of women, farming collectively, have helped to bring large tracts of fallow land under cultivation and enhanced household and community food security (see Agarwal 2003, and Section 7 of this chapter).

The overwhelming conclusion derived from the existing body of work is, therefore, two fold. On the one hand, if women had the same access to inputs as men, production would increase substantially on their farms. According to FAO's 2011 *State of Food and Agriculture Report*, reducing the constraints faced by women farmers could raise yields on their farms by 20–30% and raise total agricultural output in developing countries by 2.5–4%, thus making a significant impact on food availability (FAO 2011).[9] On the other hand, if we fail to bridge the gender gaps in access to production inputs and services, the growing proportion of women in farming is likely to remain confined to low productivity agriculture. Infrastructure development and other measures taken to revive agriculture would fail to reach them. In turn, this would undercut world potential for increasing agricultural output and ensuring food security. The situation would be exacerbated further by the predicted effects of climate change, which will impinge negatively on the incomes and nutrition of millions of poor farmers, and specially on women and children.

Women as Food Consumers and Household Food Managers

The second face of food insecurity is the lack of *access* to food, despite aggregate availability. There are high inequalities in food access across countries, within countries, and within households. By FAO's calculations for 2007–2010, there are an estimated 868 million undernourished persons across the world, of which 852 million are in developing countries, largely due to poverty (FAO 2012).

An increase in small-farm productivity can reduce poverty and increase food access among such households. However, ensuring food security for agricultural laborers and nonfarm workers who do not grow their own food will require enhancing their economic resources and employment, so that they can buy adequate food; improving delivery systems, including rural roads, for transporting food where it is needed most; reducing storage losses; and establishing public distribution systems that work. Moreover, simply increasing household-level access is not enough, since there are undernourished women and female children even within nonpoor families, due to well-known *intra*household distributional inequalities in access to food and health care.

In addition, in many developing countries, nonmarketed foods gathered from forests and commons provide an important supplement to diets and, hence, to food security.[10] The degradation and decline of forests and commons, coupled with women's reduced access to common pool resources, means a fall in such supplements, especially in the diets of poor women (Agarwal 2010a). Food price spikes and climate change can further exacerbate these gender inequalities.

All these factors point strongly to the need to reduce gendered inequalities in direct access to the means to acquire food. This is important in itself, but, additionally, women's enhanced access can bring intergenerational benefits. Mothers who are well nourished during pregnancy and lactation enhance the life chances and growth abilities of their children. Assets and incomes in mothers' hands are also found to have substantially greater positive effects on the nutrition, health, and survival of children, than assets and incomes in fathers' hands.[11] Moreover, women owning land face significantly lower risk of domestic violence, which, in turn, would reduce their own and their children's health and nutrition risks linked with such violence (Agarwal and Panda 2007).

Increasing women's direct access to food would, however, require a range of measures, such as raising the productivity of women farmers, improving the capacity of nonfarm women to buy food by enhancing their incomes and assets, formulating policies to increase women's access to food gathered from common pool resources, and initiating schemes that directly raise food availability for women in poor households.

Increasing Women's Farm Productivity

Increasing the productivity of women farmers is likely to need a range of measures, such as the following:

- Recognizing women as farmers and not simply as farm helpers.
- Improving women's direct access to land and tenure security.
- Increasing women's direct access to production credit, agricultural inputs, technology, information on improved agricultural practices, storage and marketing outlets.
- Directing more agricultural research and development to crops that women cultivate, based on a better understanding of women's farming systems.
- Promoting institutional innovations, such as promoting a group approach to farm investment and cultivation.

Let us consider each aspect in turn.

First, the dominant perception of women as farm wives/helpers rather than farmers can seriously affect the way in which assets, information, and productive inputs are directed to farming families. Based on this perception, farm-related services tend to be directed to household men rather than to women farmers themselves. Perception changes could be facilitated by gender-sensitization in the training of government officials who deliver the services. In such sensitization, NGOs and the media could also play a role.

Second, improving women's direct access to land and assets will require acting on three major sources of land: the family (via gift, inheritance, or transfer of usufruct rights), the state (via land transfers), and the market (via purchase or lease). Access via families depends especially on inheritance laws and their effective implementation. Such laws are gender equal or moving in that direction in many countries, especially in Asia and Latin America,[12] but they remain unequal in others. In India, for instance, where inheritance laws vary by religion, the 2005 amendment of the Hindu Succession Act made inheritance laws relating to all property, including agricultural land, gender equal, for over 80% of Indian women who are Hindus (Agarwal 2005a). Laws relating to Christians and Parsis had already been amended to make them gender equal, but inequalities remain for Muslims and tribal communities (Agarwal 2005b). There are also substantial gaps between de jure and de facto rights in most countries, due to poor implementation of laws and social barriers, including male bias in bequeathing property within families.[13] Exceptions include countries such as Bhutan, where women own an estimated 70% of the land (FAO n.d.-b.), and Sri Lanka where most women from landed families inherit some land, even if unequal to men (Agarwal 1994). The effective implementation of laws will require not only transforming social norms and attitudes, but also spreading legal literacy, providing legal aid, and gender-sensitizing land registration officials and the judiciary.

In countries in which land access is dependent on customary practices and mediated via clans or families, as is common in many communities of sub-Saharan Africa, and where women (as noted) are among the main food producers, increasing security of tenure on an individual basis is likely to prove more difficult (see also Saito, et al. 1994). Here efforts at creating group rights for women (as discussed later) may be more effective.

The state and the market are important additional sources of immovable assets for women. At present, agricultural land distributed by governments under their anti-poverty, land reform, or resettlement schemes goes largely to men, and only limitedly to women, either individually or jointly with husbands. Land titles transferred solely to women could go some way toward compensating for male bias in inheritance. Governments can also facilitate women's market access to land through subsidized grant-cum-credit schemes for purchasing or leasing in land. In particular, facilitating land leasing for women who are still dependent on agriculture is important, as men move to nonfarm jobs and educated children want to leave farming. For this, innovative institutional arrangements will be needed, since formal land leasing is often difficult, especially due to laws that bar such leasing (as in many states of India), or due to fears by landlords that tenants, if formally recognized, will acquire rights over their land. Typically, small tenants, therefore, depend on informal leasing of small plots, for short periods, on exploitative terms. Here alternative types of institutions would help.

For instance, a Public Land Bank (PLB) could be established at the level of a village council, as recommended in India by the Twelfth Five Year Plan "Working Group on Disadvantaged Farmers, including Women" which I chaired. Under this proposal (see, Agarwal and Sharma 2012), owners wanting to lease out their land would "deposit" it in the PLB for a specified period (say, a year or more), on a voluntary basis, with the freedom to withdraw the land with due notice. They would get a small payment on deposit (varying by period of deposit), and a share of the rent if the land got leased out. The PLB could lease out the land to designated categories of vulnerable farmers, such as marginal farmers and women (but not to large farmers or the corporate sector). It would provide a guaranteed lease for a defined period, and (where possible) in a consolidated plot of reasonable size; a calibration of rent with land quality; and a reduction of the uncertainty faced by poor farmers in negotiating leases, sometimes from several owners, to get a viable area. The PLB would, thus, reduce individual transactions costs for both lessors and lessees, help match land demand and supply, and especially benefit women who tend to get exploited in an unregulated lease market. In could also facilitate land development.

Third, women farmers' access to credit, production inputs, technical information, and marketing outlets needs substantial improvement. A range of measures could help, such as enhancing women's membership in existing credit and service cooperatives, and, where needed, creating new all-women service cooperatives that provide inputs and marketing support; gender-sensitizing the providers of technical information to farmers, with a clear emphasis on reaching women farmers; directly training women in new farm practices; and creating special service stations with designated officers to cover groups of villages, whom women could request to provide training, crop information, and support for input purchase and marketing (for elaboration, see GoI 2011).

Fourth, agricultural research and development (R&D) efforts would be more effective if R&D institutions, as well as extension services, worked with a better understanding of women's farming systems, including practices of multicropping. This is especially needed in parts of Africa, where there are notable differences in the crops grown mainly by women and those grown mainly by men. Doss (2001), for instance, after reviewing an extensive literature on African women farmers, covering 25 years, emphasizes the need for developing technologies and crop varieties that take account of the constraints women farmers face. Devising effective ways of delivering extension advice on new agricultural practices is also important (Gilbert, Salaka, & Benson 2002), as are efforts to design technology dissemination programs that recognize women's constraints and local contexts. Five agencies in sub-Saharan Africa, for instance, helped large numbers of women adopt improved technology by using existing women's networks to identify women's needs and reach them quickly; consulting potential beneficiaries to identify their constraints; developing and selecting appropriate technology to overcome those constraints; and paying special attention to poorer women (Saito, et al. 1994: 69).

Fifth, the effectiveness of all these measures could be enhanced by institutional innovations in the form of group approaches to farming. There are many potential advantages of women working together in small groups. At a minimum, across a village or ecological zone, women could benefit through cooperation in crop planning and pooling their finances to buy inputs, machinery, and crop insurance. Groups can also improve women's clout with government agencies and thereby increase their access to formal credit, inputs and information (Braverman, et al. 1991). Most important, groups can substantially raise women's chances of accessing land by enlarging their financial pool as well as their bargaining power in land purchase and lease markets. This process could be furthered by state-subsidized credit to groups of women for land purchase or lease.

However, it is with group farming, based on pooling owned or leased in land, that we would expect the most gains in productivity and social empowerment, compared with single family units. Potentially, it could help small holders take advantage of economies of scale;[14] spread the risks of farming among a larger number; facilitate experimentation with higher value, more risk-prone crops with larger payoffs; enlarge scope for crop diversification; allow labor sharing; and bring together a greater diversity of talents, knowledge, and managerial skills. Labor shortages during peak seasons could also be overcome more effectively, both because more labor would be available within the group and because labor could be saved (Foster and Rosenzweig 2010). Moreover, a group would be better placed to enter into nonexploitative contract farming arrangements that (as noted) typically exclude small farmers and women, or include them under exploitative conditions.[15] Within a group, it would also be easier to transfer knowledge about improved farming techniques to a second generation, especially to adolescent girls who could be future farmers and farm managers. In addition, groups would deal better with short-term shocks, such as rising input prices, and the long-term effects of climate change. Collective effort is necessary, for instance, for conserving soils, water, and forests. Potentially, these benefits of joint investment and cultivation can extend to both land owners and land lessees. Socially, working in a group can help women overcome disabling social norms that restrict their public interactions in conservative cultures, by drawing on the support of other women. In community forest management, for instance, women are found more likely to attend meetings, speak up for their interests, and take on leadership roles when they constitute a critical mass of 25–30% of the group members (Agarwal 2010a, 2010b).

Overall, therefore, we would expect the poor to be better protected, both as producers and as consumers, if they form groups. As producers, they would have better prospects of overcoming their production constraints and moving from being deficit to surplus farmers. As consumers, they could more effectively undertake income smoothing and enjoy welfare benefits. Can this potential be fulfilled in practice? Known examples of group farming suggest so.

There are diverse examples of small farmers cooperating successfully, including in terms of joint planning and investment in farm inputs; collective marketing of produce via cooperatives and producer companies; joint investment in irrigation and other lumpy inputs; and most particularly, farming collectively by pooling resources, including land (owned, purchased, or leased in). Successful group farming with land pooling can be found especially in the transition economies and in parts of South Asia. The groups are constituted of families in the former and of poor rural women in the latter (see Agarwal 2010c for details).

Countries in Central Asia and Eastern Europe that undertook large-scale collectivization during the 1950s to 1970s, de-collectivized in the 1980s and 1990s, thus enabling farmers to revert to individual family farming. However, many families in countries such as Kyrgyzstan, Romania, and East Germany, voluntarily chose to form new group enterprises (with friends, relatives, or neighbours), by pooling their land and other resources to farm collectively on the restituted land, or by continuing in much downsized former collectives. The productivity in these group enterprises is found to be significantly higher than in individual family farms, since, as a group, they could overcome constraints arising from small land size, labor scarcity, a lack of access to machinery, and so on.[16]

In the second type of example, drawn mainly from India, the groups consist only of women. The earliest initiative relates to Andhra Pradesh in south India and dates from the 1980s. With the support of the Deccan Development Society (DDS, an NGO), poor, low-caste women in the drought-prone Medak district have been leasing in or purchasing land in groups of 5 to 15 women, through various government schemes that provide subsidized credit and/or grants (Agarwal 2003, 2010c). The land is then cultivated collectively. The aim is to ensure food security in an environmentally friendly way, through organic farming and multiple cropping. In 2008, the group leasing program covered 26 villages, cultivating around 85 hectares. In addition, 25 women's groups were cultivating about 225 hectares of purchased land in 21 villages. This land had been bought through a grant-cum-credit scheme of the state government, meant to help poor women purchase land as a group. The land is registered in equal portions in individual women's names but cultivated jointly. These women would not have been able to buy this land or use it as productively, on an individual basis. The groups are voluntary in nature, socioeconomically homogenous, constituted of women who know each other, small in size, participatory in decision making, and equitable in task sharing and distribution of produce. Standard collective action problems are solved by peer review at weekly meetings. Some groups grow up to 24 crop varieties a year (the seeds of which they preserve), thus reducing the risk of total crop failure and providing a balanced diet. Group members report that working together has enhanced their ability to overcome production constraints, meet government officials, and enjoy flexibility in the use of their labor time. They also report an improvement in family diets and healthcare, among other benefits.

Other examples of group farming can also be found in South Asia. In Andhra Pradesh, India, for instance, through a different initiative from that of DDS, around 7,500 women farmers are farming in groups of anything between 15 to 30 women in each group, covering a total of about 425 hectares of dryland in 250 villages.[17] The land is typically obtained on lease, but some women also pool their own land that was uncultivated due to input constraints. The initial impetus for group formation was provided by a five-year project begun in 2000 by the United Nations Development Programme and the Government of India, involving 42,000 women living in around 1,000 villages in three states (Burra 2004). Even after the project ended, however, the groups have continued in many villages under other arrangements. Another notable example is the Kudumbashree program launched by the government of Kerala (south India) for supporting landless and land-poor women to lease in land for group farming. Additionally, since 2010, the Joint Liability Group (JLG) scheme of the National Bank for Agriculture and Rural Development (NABARD), has helped link the groups with subsidized credit. There are reported to be several thousand women leasing land for group farming in all districts of the state. The community has also gained, since the women's groups have brought substantial fallow land into cultivation.[18] In Bangladesh, too, we can find examples of women's groups leasing in land for joint cultivation. These are found to have notable growth potential, if provided access to credit and technical support.[19]

The preceding examples demonstrate in different ways the potential of small-scale farmers voluntarily working together in groups for the output and food security gains they bring, and the resource constraints they help overcome. In sub-Saharan Africa, where communal systems of land ownership are still widespread, the possibility of women farming collectively warrants similar exploration. We need to know much more, however, about the factors that are most conducive to sustainable group formation; the productivity benefits (carefully measured) of these groups; and the potential for their geographic growth, say, by encouraging existing women's groups, such as India's Self-Help Groups (SHGs)—of which there are over 2.5 million—to take up joint ventures.

Women as Consumers and Food Managers: Improving Access

Women's role in mitigating hunger for themselves and their families will be served to an important extent by increasing their access to assets and land, and enhancing their farm productivity and control over incomes. However, there are also large numbers of women (rural and urban) who depend for their food security on wage employment and nonfarm self-employment. Here, food security is linked directly to how many jobs go to women, and whether the schemes that provide work are directed at women.

In recognition of the special role women play in mitigating family hunger, some countries have initiated measures that directly increase women's resources, such as making conditional cash transfers to women in Latin America (World Bank 2001), or the Mahatma Gandhi National Rural Employment Guarantee Act (MNREGA) in India, which guarantees 100 days of employment for one person per household. Although not specifically directed at women, MNREGA has attracted a large number of women; a study of six states found that women constituted 32% of the MNREGA workers on average (Khera and Nayak 2009: 52).

Many of the general schemes being discussed by governments and international agencies for enhancing food security could also gain by the greater involvement of women. In Andhra Pradesh, for example, federations of women's Self-Help Groups (SHGs) have been buying foodgrain in bulk and selling them to poor members at a nominal price or on short-term credit, thus contributing to income smoothing (Nair and Shah 2007). Recent studies show that 55–60% of SHG members are poor and socially disadvantaged (EDA 2006, NCAER 2008), but even when the SHGs do not consist mainly of the poor, they can reach the poor. The DDS women's groups, described earlier, have also set up community grain banks (Agarwal 2003). All this suggests that, women's groups could prove effective in creating local buffer stocks and regional food banks, and in improving public distribution systems, if they had access to infrastructure for food storage and distribution. Women-inclusive forest governance can also bring substantial gains, both in terms of improved conservation outcomes and women's greater access to gathered food items (Agarwal 2010a).

Essentially, viewing agriculture and related sectors through the lens of gender will reveal the many ways in which women farmers are contributing to food systems globally, and it helps pinpoint mechanisms for making their efforts more effective. This would also improve the chances of achieving several millennium development goals, such as ending poverty and hunger, increasing gender equality, and improving child health and maternal health.

An additional challenge lies in improving the statistical data base for assessing and monitoring gender-differentiated access to land, farm credit, inputs, technical information, and marketing, as well as monitoring nutrition and health indicators for women and children in both poor and nonpoor households.

Concluding Comments

Ensuring food security is both the most basic of development issues and the most complex. Gender inequalities are a significant part of the problem and reducing those inequalities will be a critical part of the solution. The inequalities women face as producers reduces the potential productivity of agriculture and hence of overall food availability in countries, regions, and worldwide. It does so both by failing to take into account the specific constraints that women farmers face, even as dependence on women farmers is growing; and by failing to recognize that in particular contexts the productivity gains would be higher if existing inputs were directed at women. Estimates indicate the potential of substantial productivity gains from bridging gender gaps in land security and access to inputs and services. However, this will need not only technical and financial support but also institutional innovation, including more group approaches to farm investment and management.

Similarly, the inequalities women face as consumers adversely affects both their own well-being as well as that of future generations of children who inherit the disabilities arising from poor maternal health. Reducing inequalities embedded in women's access to income-earning opportunities and productive assets would thus benefit not only the women themselves but also their children, by enhancing women's bargaining power within the home and so their ability to direct more household resources to children's well-being.

Reducing gender inequalities faced by women as farmers and workers is, therefore, an imperative, both for its intrinsic importance and for its wider implications. Doing so would prove to be a wise strategy for tackling the food crises and creating a more food-secure world.

Notes

1. This is an updated and revised version of a working paper, Agarwal (2011). I am grateful to Ronald Herring for his comments on an earlier draft. I also thank Frances Stewart, Ana Cortez, Hiroshi Kawamura, Raghav Gaiha, Ramesh Chand, Joachim von Braun, Sara Ahmed, and Sudipto Mundle for their helpful comments on a draft of the working paper;

Ram Ashish Yadav and Swati Virmani for their research assistance; and Teri Raney and Andre Croppenstedt for sharing background material on women farmers and agricultural productivity.

2. Halving meat consumption in the OECD countries, Brazil and China by 2030, could free an estimated 200 million hectares or more of livestock-raising land globally, which, if used for non-meat food production, could substantially improve food and nutrition security in developing countries. (Presentation by Mark Rosegrant, Agriculture-Nutrition-Health Linkages conference, New Delhi, February 2011).
3. IFPRI gives various scenarios for (spatially disaggregated) temperature rise, precipitation, and so on. The illustrative estimates, cited here, are based on data from the National Centre for Atmospheric Research (which uses IPCC information), and do not adjust for "carbon dioxide fertilization." Adjusted estimates still give adverse predictions (albeit less so) for yields of major crops in developing countries.
4. See e.g. Agarwal (1994) for South Asia, and Saito et al. (1994) for Nigeria and Kenya. When household heads were excluded from the sample, Saito et al. (1994: 48) found that a substantially lower percentage of female than male farmers had rights to even improve the land, with implications for their relative productivity.
5. However, this does not tell us how much of all land is held by women, or what percentage of all women hold land. To access this, we also need data on the intra-household distribution of land holdings, and not just distribution by head of household.
6. See FAO (2011: 23–4) and also studies for developing countries summarized in Anriquez (2010).
7. See e.g. Adesina and Djato (1997), Adeleke, et al. (2008), Quisumbing, *et al.* (2001), Moock (1976), Kumase, et al. (2008), Bindlish & Evenson (1993), and Hill and Vigneri (2009).
8. See, Udry et al. (1995), Kumase, *et al.* (2008), Moock (1976), and Dey (1992).
9. I have focused on crops, but the argument that improving women's resource access could increase output could be extended to other types of food, such as fish.
10. See e.g. Jodha (1986), Agarwal (1990, 2010a), and Mazhar et al. (2007). Mazhar, et al. (2007) found that in Andhra Pradesh (south India), village women could identify seventy-nine species of uncultivated leafy greens gathered for food, in addition to roots, tubers, and fruits. In Bangladesh's Tangail district, such uncultivated plants provided, on average, 65% of the food weight of poor landless households and 34% of the food weight of better-off landed households.
11. See Strauss and Beegle (1996) for India; Thomas (1990, 1994) for Brazil; and Quisumbing and Maluccio (2000) for Bangladesh, Indonesia, Ethiopia, and South Africa.
12. For instance, in Asia, Bhutan, Vietnam, Sri Lanka and most communities in the Philippines have gender equal laws. For Latin America, see Deere and de Leon (2001) and Lastarria-Cornhiel and Manji (2010).
13. See Agarwal (1994) for India, Pakistan, Bangladesh, Nepal, and Sri Lanka; Estudillo, Quisumbing, & Keijiro (2001) for the Philippines; and various CEDAW reports for several other countries.
14. Foster and Rosenzweig's (2010) analysis of panel data for 17 Indian states, for the period 1999 to 2008, shows that even consolidating marginal farms to reach 5 acres can significantly increase profits per acre (1 acre = 0.4047 ha).
15. For Mexico, see specially, Runsten and Key (1996); for India, see Singh (2000) and Kumar (2006); and for Africa, see Dolan (2001) and Maertens and Swinnen (2009).

16. See, e.g. Sabates-Wheeler (2002); Sabates-Wheeler and Childress (2004), and Mathijs and Swinnen (2001). See also Agarwal (2010c) for a detailed discussion.
17. These are the latest figures provided by the Director of the Andhra Pradesh Mahila Samakya program.
18. The author is currently researching both the Andhra Pradesh and Kerala examples of women's group farming in depth.
19. IFAD 2009 Evaluation Bangladesh. [http://www.ifad.org/evaluation/public_html/eksyst/doc/country/pi/bangladesh/cesba94e_3.htm]. Last accessed on 14 September 2009.

References

Adeleke, O. A., O. I. Adesiyan, O. A. Olaniyi, K. O. Adelalu, and H. M. Matanmi. 2008. "Gender Differentials in the Productivity of Cereal cereal Crop Farmers: A Case Study of Maize Farmers in Oluyole Local Government Area of Oyo State." Agricultural Journal 3(3):193–198.

Adesina, A. A. and K. K. Djato. 1997. "Relative Efficiency of Women as Farm Managers: Profit Function Analysis in Côte d'Ivoire." Agricultural Economics 16(1):47–53.

Agarwal, B. 1983. Mechanization in Indian Agriculture New Delhi, India: Allied Publishers.

Agarwal, B. 1990. "Social Security and the Family: Coping with Seasonality and Calamity in Rural India." The Journal of Peasant Studies 17(3):341–412.

Agarwal, B. 1994. A Field of One's Own: Gender and Land Rights in South Asia. Cambridge University Press, Cambridge.

Agarwal, B. 2003. "Gender and Land Rights Revisited: Exploring New Prospects via the State, Family and Market." Journal of Agrarian Change, 3(1-2):184–224.

Agarwal, B. 2005a. "A Landmark Step to Gender Equality." The Hindu, Sunday Magazine, September 25, pp. 1–2.

Agarwal, B. 2005b. "Women's Inheritance: Next Steps." Indian Express, editorial page, October 17.

Agarwal, B. 2010a. Gender and Green Governance: The Political Economy of Women's Presence Within and Beyond Community Forestry Oxford, UK: Oxford University Press.

Agarwal, B. 2010b. "Does Women's Proportional Strength Affect Their Participation? Governing Local Forests in South Asia." World Development 38(1): 98–112.

Agarwal, B. 2010c. "Rethinking Agricultural Production Collectivities." Economic and Political Weekly, February 27, 55(9):64–78.

Agarwal, B. 2011. "Food Crises and Gender Inequality," Working Paper No 107, United Nations Department of Economic and Social Affairs, New York.

Agarwal, B. and P. Sharma. 2012. "An Idea to Bank On," Times of India, editorial page, January 12.

Agarwal, B., and P. Panda. 2007. "Toward Freedom from Domestic Violence: The Neglected Obvious." Journal of Human Development 8(3):359–388.

Akresh, R. 2008. "(In)Efficiency in Intrahousehold Allocations." Working Paper, Dept. of Economics, University of Illinois at Urbana Champaign.

Alene, A. D., V. M. Manyong, G. O. Omanya, H. D. Mignouna, M. Bokanga, and G. D. Odhiambo. 2008. "Economic Efficiency and Supply Response of Women as Farm Managers: Comparative Evidence from Western Kenya." World Development 36(7): 1247–1260.

Allendorf, K. 2007. "Do Women's Land Rights Promote Empowerment and Child Health in Nepal?" World Development 35(11):1975–1988.

Anriquez, G. À. Paraître. 2010. "Rural Feminization and the Gender Burden: A Cross-Country Examination." Background paper, 2011 *State of Food and Agriculture Report* (SOFA Report), FAO, Rome.

Bindlish,V., R. Evenson, and M. Gbetibouo. 1993. "Evaluation of T and V-based extension in Burkina Faso." World Bank Technical Paper No. 226, Africa Technical Department Series, World Bank, Washington, DC.

Braverman, A., J. L. Guasch, M. Huppi, and L. Pohlmeier. 1991. "Promoting Rural Cooperatives in Developing Countries." Discussion Paper No. 121, World Bank, Washington DC.

Burra, N. 2004. "Empowering Women for Household Food Security: UNDP's Experience." United Nations Development Programme, Delhi.

Collins, J. L. 1993. "Gender, Contracts and Wage Work—Agricultural Restructuring in Brazil's Sao Francisco Valley." Development and Change 24(1):53–82.

Deere, C. D., and Magdalena de Leon. 2001. Empowering Women: Land and Property Rights in Latin America Pittsburgh, PA: University of Pittsburgh Press.

Deere, C. D. and C. R. Doss. 2006. "The Gender Asset Gap: What Do We Know and Why Does it Matter?" Feminist Economics 12(1-2):1–50.

Dey, J. 1992. "Gender Asymmetries in Intra-Household Resource Allocation in Sub-Saharan Africa: Some Policy Implications for Land and Labor Productivity." Paper presented at IFPRI workshop on Intra-Household Resource Allocation.

Dolan, C. S. 2001. "The "Good Wife": Struggles over Resources in the Kenyan Horticultural Sector." Journal of Development Studies 37(3):39–10.

Doss. C. R. 2001. "Designing Agricultural Technology for African Women Farmers: Lessons from 25 Years of Experience." World Development 29(12):2075–2092.

Doss, C. R. 2010. "If Women Hold Up Half the Sky, How Much of the World's Food Do They Produce?" Background paper, 2011 *State of Food and Agriculture Report* (*SOFA Report*), FAO, Rome.

EDA. 2006. Self-Help Groups in India: A Study of Lights and Shades. EDA Rural Systems Private Ltd. Gurgaon, and the Andhra Pradesh Mahila Abhivruddhi Society, Hyderabad.

Elson, D. 1995. "Gender Awareness in Modelling Structural Adjustment." World Development 23(11):1851–1868.

Estudillo, J. P., A. R. Quisumbing, and O. Keijiro. 2001. "Gender Differences in Land Inheritance and Schooling Investments in the Rural Philippines." Land Economics 77(1):130–143.

Food and Agricultural Organisation (FAO). n.d.-g. "Asia's Women in Agriculture, Environment and Rural Production—Bhutan." SDdimensions. Sustainable Development Department. Rome: FAO. [http://www.fao.org/sd/WPDirect/WPre0105.htm]. Last accessed on July 9, 2009.

Food and Agricultural Organisation (FAO). 2011. The State of Food and Agriculture Rome: FAO.

Food and Agricultural Organisation (FAO). 2012. The State of Food Insecurity in the World Rome: FAO.

Foster, A. D., and M. R. Rosenzweig. 2010. "Is There Surplus Labour in Rural India?" Discussion Paper No. 991, Economic Growth Centre, Yale University, New Haven.

Gilbert, R. A., W. D. Sakala, and T. D. Benson. 2002. Gender Analysis of a Nationwide Cropping System Trial Survey in Malawi. African Studies Quarterly 6(1-2):223–243.

Goldstein, M., and C. Udry (2008). "The Profits of Power: Land Rights and Agricultural Investment in Ghana." Journal of the Political Economy, 116(6):981–1022.

Government of India (GoI). 2010-2011. Agricultural Census 2010-11: All India Report on Number and Area of Operational Holdings. New Delhi, India: Agriculture Census Division, Department of Agriculture and Co-Operation, Ministry of Agriculture, GoI,.

Government of India (GoI). (2011). *Report of the Twelfth Plan Working Group on Disadvantaged Farmers, Including Women*, Chaired by Bina Agarwal. New Delhi, India: Planning Commission, GoI,.

Hill, R. V. and M. Vigneri. 2009. "Mainstreaming Gender Sensitivity in Cash Crop Market Supply Chains." Background paper, 2011 *SOFA Report*. Rome: FAO.

Holden, S., B. Shiferaw, and J. Pender. 2001. "Market Imperfections and Land Productivity in the Ethiopian Highlands." Journal of Agricultural Economics 52(3):53–70.

Horrell, S. and P. Krishnan. 2007. "Poverty and Productivity in Female-Headed Households in Zimbabwe." Journal of Development Studies 43(8):1351–1380.

IFAD (2009). Evaluation: Bangladesh. [http://www.ifad.org/evaluation/public_html/eksyst/doc/country/pi/bangladesh/cesba94e_3.htm]. Accessed September 14 2009.

International Food Policy Research Institute (IFPRI). 2009. Climate Change: Impact on Agriculture and Costs of Adaptation. Washington DC: IFPRI.

Ivanic, M. and W. Martin. 2008. "Implications of Higher Global Food Prices for Poverty in Low-Income Countries." Policy Research Working Paper Series 4594. Washington DC: World Bank.

Jamison, D. T. and C. J. Lau. 1982. Farmer Education and Farm Efficiency. Baltimore: Johns Hopkins University Press.

Jodha, N. S. 1986. "Common Property Resources and the Rural Poor." Economic and Political Weekly 21(27):1169–1181.

Khera, R. and N. Nayak. 2009. "Women Workers and Their Perceptions of National Rural Employment Guarantee Act." Economic and Political Weekly 44(43):49–57.

Kinkingninhoun-Mêdagbé, F. M., A. Diagne, F. Simtowe, A. R. Agboh-Noameshie, and P. Y. Adegbola. 2008. "Gender Discrimination and Its Impact on Income, Productivity and Technical Efficiency: Evidence from Benin." Agriculture and Human Values 27(1):57–69.

Kumar, P. 2006. "Contract farming in India: Options and Implications for Small and Large Farmers." Institute of Economic Growth Working Paper No. E/267/2006.

Kumase, W. N., H. Bisseleua, and S. Klasen. 2008. "Opportunities and Constraints in Agriculture: A Gendered Analysis of Cocoa Production in Southern Cameroon." Discussion Paper No. 27. Courant Research Centre, University of Göttingen.

Lastarria-Cornhiel, S. and A. Manji. 2010. "Land Tenure, Land Policy, and Gender in Rural Areas." Background paper, 2011 *SOFA Report*, Rome: FAO.

Li, Z. 2003. "Women's Land Tenure Rights in Rural China: A Synthesis." Mimeo, Ford Foundation, Beijing.

Lilja, N. K., T. F. Randolph, and A. Diallo. 1998. "Estimating Gender Differences in Agricultural Productivity: Biases Due to Omission of Gender-Influenced Variables and Endogeneity of Regressors." Paper submitted to the American Agricultural Economics Association meeting, Salt Lake City, Utah, August 2–5.

Maertens, M. and J. F. M. Swinnen. 2009. "Are Modern Supply Chains Bearers of Gender Inequality?" Paper presented at the ILO-FAO workshop, Gender Dimension of Rural Employment, Rome, March 30–April 3.

Mathijs, E. and J. F. M. Swinnen. 2001. "Production Organization and Efficiency during Transition: An Empirical Analysis of East German Agriculture," Review of Economics and Statistics 83(1):100–107.

Mazhar, F., D. Buckles, P. V. Satheesh, and F. Akhter. 2007. Food Sovereignty and Uncultivated Biodiversity in South Asia Ottawa, Canada: IDRC.

Moock, P. R. 1976. "The Efficiency of Women Farm Managers Kenya." American Journal of Agricultural Economics 58(5):831–835.

Nair, A. and P. Shah. 2007. "Self-Help Works." Times of India, December 27.

National Council of Applied Economic Reseaarch (NCAER). 2008. Impact and Sustainability of SHG Bank Linkage Programme. New Delhi: National Council of Applied Economic Research.

Oladeebo, J. O., and A. A. Fajuyigbe. 2007. "Technical Efficiency of Men and Women Upland Rice Farmers in Osun State, Nigeria." Journal of Human Ecology 22(2):93–100.

Ongaro, W. A. (1990). "Modern Maize Technology, Yield Variations and Efficiency Differentials: A Case of Small Farms in Western Kenya." Eastern Africa Economic Review 6(1):11–29.

Peterman, A., J. Behrman, and A. R. Quisumbing. 2009. "A Review of Empirical Evidence on Gender Differences in Non-Land Agricultural Inputs, Technology and Services in Developing Countries." Background paper, 2011 *SOFA Report*. Rome: FAO.

Quisumbing, A. R. 1996. "Male-Female Differences in Agricultural Productivity: Methodological Issues and Empirical Evidence." World Development 24(10):1579–1595.

Quisumbing, A. R. and J. A. Maluccio. 2000. "Intrahousehold Allocation and Gender Relations: New Empirical Evidence." Discussion Paper. Washington DC: IFPRI.

Quisumbing, A. R., Ellen Payongayong, J. B. Aidoo, and Keijiro Otsuka. 2001. "Women's Land Rights in the Transition to Individualized Ownership: Implications for the Management of Tree Resources in Western Ghana." Economic Development and Cultural Change 50(1):157–182.

Quisumbing, A. R., R. S. Meinzen-Dick, L. Bassett, M. Usnick, L. Pandolfelli, C. Morden, and H. Alderman. 2008. "Helping Women Respond to the Global Food Price Crises." Policy Brief 7. Washington DC: IFPRI.

Runsten, D. and N. Key. 1996. "Contract Farming in Developing Countries: Theoretical Aspects Analysis of some Mexican Cases." Economic Commission for Latin America and the Caribbean, RLC/96/14-RLCP-01.

Saito, K. A., H. Mekonnen, and D. Spurling. 1994. "Raising the Productivity of Women Farmers in Sub-Saharan Africa." World Bank Discussion Papers, Africa Technical Department Series No. 230. Washington DC: World Bank.

Sabates-Wheeler, R. 2002. "Farm Strategy, Self-Selection and Productivity: Can Small Farming Groups Offer Production Benefits to Farmers in Post-Socialist Romania." World Development 30(10):1737–1753.

Sabates-Wheeler, R. and M. D. Childress. 2004. "Asset-Pooling in Uncertain Times: Implications of Small-Group Farming for Agricultural Restructuring in the Kyrgyz Republic." Working Paper 239. Sussex, UK: Institute of Development Studies.

Singh, S. 2000. "Theory and Practice of Contract Farming: A Review." Journal of Social and Economic Development 3(2):228–246.

Strauss, J., and K. Beegle. 1996. "Intrahousehold Allocations: A Review of Theories, Empirical Evidence and Policy Issues." MSU International Development Working Paper No. 62, Dept. of Agricultural Economics, Michigan State University, East Lansing.

Thapa, S. 2008. "Gender Differentials in Agricultural Productivity: Evidence from Nepalese Households Data." Munich Personal ReREC Archive, MRPA Paper No. 13722.

Thomas, D. 1990. "Intra-household Resource Allocation: An Inferential Approach." Journal of Human Resources 25(4):635–663.

Thomas, D. 1994. "Like Father Like Son, or, Like Mother Like Daughter: Parental Education and Child Health." Journal of Human Resources 29(4):950–988.

Timothy, A. T. and A. I. Adeoti. 2006. "Gender Inequalities and Economic Efficiency: New Evidence from Cassava-Based Farm Holdings in Rural Southwestern Nigeria." African Development Review 18(3):428–443.

Tiruneh, A., T. Tesfaye, W. Mwangi, and H. Verkuijl. 2001. "Gender Differentials in Agricultural Production and Decision-Making Among Smallholders in Ada, Lume and Gimbichu Woredas of the Central Highlands of Ethiopia." International Maize and Wheat Improvement Center, Mexico, and Ethiopian Research Organization, Addis Ababa.

Udry, C., J. Hoddinott, H. Alderman, and L. Haddad. 1995. "Gender Differentials in Farm Productivity: Implications for Household Efficiency and Agricultural Policy." Food Policy 20(5):407–423.

von Braun, J. 2008. "Rising Food Prices: What Should be Done?" Eurochoices 7(2):30–35.

von Braun, J. 2008–2009. "Food-Security Risks Must Be Comprehensively Addressed." Annual Report Essay 2008-09. Washington DC: IFPRI.

World Bank. 2001. "Brazil: An Assessment of the Bolsa Escula Programs." Report No. 20208-BR. World Bank, Latin America and the Caribbean Regional Office.

World Bank. 2007. World Development Report 2008: Agriculture for Development. Washington DC: World Bank.

World Bank. 2009. Gender in Agriculture Sourcebook Vols 1 and 2. Washington DC: World Bank.

Zhang, L., A. de Brauw, and S. Rozelle. 2004. "China's Rural Labor Market Development and Its Gender Implications." China Economic Review 15 (2):230–247.

CHAPTER 12

DELIVERING FOOD SUBSIDY

The State and the Market

ASHOK KOTWAL AND BHARAT RAMASWAMI

Introduction

For the 3 billion people in the world who live under $2 a day, no question is more important than where their next meal will come from. Undoubtedly, over the long run it is difficult to address the problem of food security without eradicating poverty or, in other words, without economic development. However, development is a long and uncertain process, and leaving generations of the poor to an uncertain future is neither morally defensible nor politically acceptable. Moreover, there is growing awareness that a crucial determinant of economic progress is the development of human capital, which in turn implies availability of food for all. Developing countries therefore have no alternative but to act now by devising schemes of subsidizing food for the poor. Given the enormous number of competing claims on the meager fiscal resources that a developing country can command, the issues of food subsidy become inevitably contentious.

The debate is especially intense in a country where a sizable proportion of the population is poor enough to need food subsidy. On one hand, a vast majority needs the subsidy, and on the other hand, a subsidy to so many puts a big dent in the national budget of a poor country. It creates two camps: "Can we afford to let the poor starve?" versus "Can we afford the subsidy bill?" It matters how this question is answered—it will dictate whether the subsidy ought to be universal (with minimal exclusion of only the obviously affluent) or narrowly targeted.

In this context, the issues of waste and corruption become paramount. Any delivery system that is prone to a sustained leakage of the government resources through inefficiency, fraud, and corruption becomes a liability. In a country where a vast majority is poor, it becomes difficult to argue openly against food subsidy on the grounds of fiscal priorities. Those who rank other priorities ahead of food subsidy find it convenient to point at the waste and corruption of a delivery system and argue for limiting the coverage much below what is needed. There is thus pressure on those advocating food subsidies to come up with an effective delivery system—a system that would cover most of the needy at an affordable cost to the public.

In a statist model, the government puts in mechanisms to procure, store, and distribute food to defined target populations at prices below market cost. In some sense, this is a natural intervention. After all, in the absence of an intervention the market in free play leads to outcomes that are deemed undesirable. The response is to displace (and in some cases suppress) food markets by direct state interventions. However, this is not the only possible response. The alternative is to use markets to deliver subsidies. In this market model, subsidies are monetary or cash transfers, compared with in-kind transfers of the statist model.

Inevitably, a search for a more efficient system leads to a debate over whether a system that uses market for the delivery of the subsidy should be preferred over a system where all the activities from procurement to distribution are handled by the government. The purpose of this chapter is to examine various issues that invariably come up in a discussion over how to deliver food subsidy. While our focus is on the cash versus in-kind transfers debate, we also comment on the implications for the targeting debate.

Neither of these debates is unique to developing countries. The size of welfare programs and whether the targeting criteria expand or contract their reach is a live issue in rich countries. However, as argued in this chapter, the administration of targeting is a much bigger issue and therefore an important component of the debate in developing countries. Similarly, rich countries also debate the choice between cash and in-kind transfers. In fact, despite the ideological dominance of the market as an economic institution in these countries, in-kind transfers are much more important than cash transfers—thanks to the subsidies on health, education, and housing (Currie and Gahvari 2008). However, rich-country debates do not stress the corruption and poor governance that are commonly associated with statist models in poor countries.

As always, context matters, and this chapter is firmly anchored to the issues relevant in poor-country debates. The debate often has an ideological subtext, and no analysis of the political economy of food security policy would be satisfactory without taking stock of the ideological divide among those with a voice in policymaking. Economists typically attach value only to economic outcomes. The state and the market are economic institutions, and, a priori, neither is privileged. Other social scientists and civil society participants may, however, mark either of these institutions as special for their effect on democratic politics and community institutions.

Though many of the arguments discussed herein are not country specific, the focus is on India for several reasons—besides the fact that we know India the best. First, India has more than a quarter of the world's poor (i.e., those who live on less than $2 a day). This means that it is home to more of the world's poor and to more malnourished people than any other country. One-third of the population and over 40% of the children under the age of three are underweight. More than half the women are anemic. In short, India is a test case for policies related to malnourishment. Second, India has one of the world's largest food subsidy programs. It is likely to become larger, too, because of a great deal of political activity related to the issues of food security, which will possibly lead to legislation called the National Food Security Act. The impending passage of such a law has led to a sizable public debate about the coverage and means of delivering food subsidies that are appropriate to a poor country. These arguments are relevant beyond the context (of India) in which they were made.

In this chapter, we first trace the evolution of the Indian model of food distribution. We then discuss the distribution system's outcomes and performance as well as the rights approach to food security and the move to bind the government legally toward food subsidies. The key issues introduced by this debate, which are generic to the design of food subsidies, are addressed in subsequent sections. The attempt is to evaluate the merits of various arguments in terms of their intrinsic logic as well as the available evidence from the experiments tried around the world. Last, we reflect on the ideological divide and the political economy of self-interest that together shape the course of food politics in a developing country such as India.

Subsidy Transfers in Kind: The Indian Model

Food subsidies in India are delivered through the public distribution system (PDS). This system consists of a network of retail outlets (popularly known as ration shops) through which the government sells grain (principally, rice and wheat). Grain sales occur at a fixed price called the issue price, which is typically lower than the market price. Two conditions govern the sale of subsidized grain: the buyer of grain must possess a ration card; and grain purchases are subject to a quota. The PDS is supported by a procurement operation that procures and funnels supplies to it. Through the Food Corporation of India (FCI), the government procures grain at the procurement price and then stores and transports it to the various consuming locations.

The Indian model is not unique. Comprehensive rationing schemes, where the state is the single intermediary between consumers and producers and has monopoly over all domestic and foreign trade, was prevalent in the erstwhile socialist states. In developing countries, it is usual for subsidy transfers in kind to operate along with private food markets. Supplies may come from imports, foreign aid, or domestic procurement. Food subsidies may cover all or some consumers. Common institutional arrangements are a parastatal to procure the commodity and a retail network for distribution.

In India, the origins of government intervention lie in the Second World War when the colonial British government used its powers to promulgate orders on price control, movement, and requisition of foodgrains. The government decided that it would procure the basic staples and distribute them to select urban populations. However, there was still room for debate on the best means by which government should procure foodgrains.[1] Should the government purchase grain at market prices, or should it enforce a monopoly of grain trade and obtain supplies at a low cost? After debating these alternatives, the government opted for a "compromise" middle path. There would be no monopoly, and a private trading structure would be allowed to function. However, the government would operate a parallel marketing chain from procurement to distribution. Thus, private markets would be excluded from the marketed surplus procured and distributed by the government. In addition, there would be curbs on market activity so that the government could obtain its supplies relatively cheaply. In effect, through market suppression farmers would be taxed to part finance the subsidy to urban consumers.

These policies continued even after the end of the colonial government in 1947. Ironically, though, till the mid-1960s, domestic procurement (compared with commercial imports and food aid) was neither an important nor reliable source of supply to the PDS. The lack of success of the procurement machinery is repeatedly acknowledged in government reports of the time and is ascribed to the existence of a free market where traders compete away supplies. The Foodgrains Policy Committee of 1966 stated the desired policy direction as follows:

> In order to achieve the basic objectives of food policy, it is necessary for Government to acquire a large share of the foodgrains produced in the country. It is in the light of this requirement that systems of procurement and regulations affecting private trade have to be formulated and appraised. Government has to strengthen its own machinery for the procurement, transport and distribution for foodgrains for the surplus as well as deficit areas.
>
> (quoted in Chopra 1981)

These views reached their logical end with the state takeover of wholesale wheat trade in 1974. However, the move was unsuccessful and the policy had to be rescinded.

The reshaping of food price policies began in 1965 when the government formed the Food Corporation of India, which became the principal central agency responsible for purchase and storage of foodgrains. The other important event in the same year was the formation of the Agricultural Prices Commission to advise on price policies for wheat, rice, sorghum, millet, and other field crops. The state would offer a support price to mitigate the uncertainties of the market. The intent was to provide incentives to producers to adopt the new high-yielding varieties of wheat and rice that reached India in the mid-1960s.

The success of the Green Revolution meant that the harsher aspects of the earlier food policy directed at maximizing procurement could be moderated. At the same time, the food surplus states now had clout in national politics that could be used to lobby for prices favorable to farmers. Even by 1970, B. M. Bhatia (p 125,127) noted:

> The concern of the Government in the matter of agricultural prices for the first twenty years of independence was to keep down the prices of foodgrains through controls, imports and rationing. The beginning of the Green Revolution has

> coincided with a marked shift in the price policy of the State Governments, from the desire to protect the interests of the urban consumer to promoting the interests of the agricultural producer. The new policy solves the procurement problem of the State governments.... Such a policy is necessary to provide the much needed incentives to the farmer to use costly but highly productive inputs, thus increasing food production in the country. Behind these economic arguments, however, lie powerful political considerations. In most of the states, strong agricultural lobbies have emerged.... In such a situation prices fixed are bound to be what are politically feasible and not what are economically fair, as determined by an expert body like the Agricultural Prices Commission. (pp. 125, 127)

However, not all elements of food price suppression were discarded. Anti-hoarding laws still remain on the books to restrain competition to government procurement from private trade. Further, till India reformed its trade policies to comply with treaty obligations at World Trade Organization, farmers' access to world markets were tightly regulated by the government. Indeed, the situation did not materially change even in the 2000s when the government was supposed to have given up on quantitative restrictions on trade. For instance, wheat and rice exports were banned in the latter half of the 2000s during the boom in world commodity prices.

Notwithstanding these qualifiers, the government achieved a greater balance between producer and consumer interests starting from the 1970s, when the food policy context changed because of the Green Revolution's technological breakthroughs. Earlier concerns about movements in intersectoral terms of trade adverse to industry faded away. With the decline of food aid, the growth of domestic food surpluses, declining real prices of foodgrains, and greater political clout of farmers, the emphasis of food distribution shifted to support of farmgate prices, stabilization, and subsidy for lower income groups. The policies of procurement and buffer stocks dovetailed neatly into the public distribution system (Mooij 1998; Varshney 1993).

Targeting

The public distribution system was converted from a general entitlement to a targeted scheme in 1997. Subsidies now depend on whether the household is classified as above poverty line (APL), below poverty line (BPL), or poorest of the poor (POP). APL households are charged the highest prices, whereas the POP households pay the least. The administration of targeting has brought into focus India's federal structure. While the federal government is largely responsible for funding, procurement, and transport of grain, the implementation and delivery of food subsidies is in the hands of the states.

A similar division of responsibilities underlies the implementation of targeting. On the basis of household expenditure sample surveys and other means, the federal government determines the aggregate number of BPL and POP households within a state that are deserving of subsidy. It uses this figure to allocate and distribute the grains (and subsidy) to the state governments. It is the job of the state government to identify deserving households and to distribute grain accordingly.

Identification is supposed to be done on the basis of some observable correlates of households (e.g., type of housing, type of employment, land holdings, caste characteristics). Even if done honestly, it cannot be expected that such a process would yield totals that match the figures determined by the federal government. When identified households exceed the estimate of the federal government, the state government either has to trim its list or must dig into its own resources to bridge the gap.

This has led to some discord between the federal and state governments. The federal government is accused of using targeting to limit its subsidy bill while burdening the state government with the unwelcome task of implementation. On the other hand, if the federal government were to offer subsidies to all households identified as deserving by state governments, the latter would have no incentive to observe discipline in the identification process.

One response of state governments has been to depart from the targeting parameters that govern federal policy. The federal government allocates subsidies to states on the basis of an entitlement of 35 kg of grain to BPL and POP households. By offering only 20 kg of grain, the southern state of Tamil Nadu has stretched the federal subsidy to operate a near-universal subsidy scheme (with some resources from its coffers as well). The willingness of some of the state governments to use the central subsidy together with its own resources has been increasingly seen in the 2000s.

The Shadow of Procurement

Grain procurement has had several impacts on the wider agricultural economy of India (Landes and Gulati 2004; Saxena 2004). Land and other resources have shifted to the state-supported crops of rice and wheat. While this was understandably the original intent of state policies formulated in the period of acute food shortage of the 1960s, it is not clear this is appropriate today when the demand for nonstaple foods such as dairy, fats, fruits, and vegetables are growing faster than the demand for grains. Second, the cost-effective strategy for procurement is for the buying agencies to focus attention on the "surplus" regions of North India, namely, Punjab, Haryana, and Uttar Pradesh. This has led to complaints of lack of price support operations in other parts of India, notably the eastern region. These are regions with conditions favorable to agricultural growth, yet it is claimed that they have not emerged as effective food exporters because of the concentration of resources in North India. More generally, because of the availability of subsidized grain, the "deficit" states have neglected price support to their own farmers and continue to have a food shortage. Third, procurement may be adverse to the long-term interests of even the favored regions. The summer rice–winter wheat rotation has environmentally degraded the lands in these regions. Fourth, procurement has nothing to offer to the farmers growing the so-called coarse cereals (principally sorghum and millet). These are hardy low-productivity crops typically grown in semi-arid regions with no irrigation. They have suffered from policy neglect because of the focus on rice and wheat.

The exigencies of procurement have also cast a shadow on policies elsewhere in the agricultural economy. In the early 2000s, the government (at the federal and state level) undertook several reforms to transform agricultural marketing—a sector that serves both producers and consumers poorly.[2] The goal was to lighten the regulation that deterred private-sector entry and investment in areas of marketing such as processing, transport, and storage.[3] Yet these reforms have not been irreversible. The contingent nature of these policy changes was illustrated in the commodity boom of 2006 to 2008. The run-up in world commodity prices till the first quarter of 2008 led the government to impose bans (official and unannounced) of various kinds—on procurement of grain by private players, on exports of rice and wheat, and on futures contracts in many agricultural commodities. The ban on private players and on grain exports bought the government some stability and enabled it to procure grain cheaper than what would have been possible otherwise.[4]

Thus, reforms in agricultural marketing do not sit well with the necessities of procurement. In flush periods with low prices and abundant supplies, the competition with private trade is not an issue. But when supplies are tight, procurement operations will not allow free activity by private trade. Such backtracking by the government is not without cost. Clearly, private players will be wary of investing in the marketing chain when their activities can be curtailed at will. For this reason, progress toward transforming the marketing sector will remain slow.

Outcomes: The Delivery of Food Subsidy

In one of the first studies of its kind, Parikh (1994) showed that in 1986–87 the poor received negligible subsidies in all but two states of India. Despite this, however, the program itself was costly. A transfer of one rupee to the bottom 20% cost the government at least five times as much.

It turned out that most of the poor did not use the PDS. Even when they did, their PDS purchases were a small fraction of their total grain consumption. The early studies showed (1) that the PDS was not targeted toward the poor; in fact the nonpoor received a significant fraction of the income transfer; (2) the subsidy amounts itself were very small because of low subsidy rates as well as limited entitlements; and (3) there was considerable fraud in terms of illegal diversion of subsidized foodgrains to the open market (Ahluwalia 1993; Dev and Suryanarayana 1991; Dutta and Ramaswami 2001; Howes and Jha 1992; Radhakrishna et al. 1997; World Bank 2001).

Besides these quantitative assessments, some case studies also documented the difficulties of access to the PDS. Even when the poor possessed the ration cards, they faced problems with respect to the low quality of grain, cheating on weights by the PDS dealer, and irregular hours of operation of the PDS shops.

The timing, availability, and quantity of grain supplies at the PDS shops were not predictable, and often it took repeated trips to complete the purchase. Customers were not permitted to split their entitlement into multiple purchases. This discouraged the poor, who did not always have the cash when supplies were available.

On paper, the program was run with various safeguards including government inspectors and monitoring teams from the community. The aggregate evidence showed that these measures failed.[5] The studies also showed that legitimate commissions earned by PDS dealers were too low to offset costs. Illegal diversions and limiting store hours were ways by which the dealers compensated for the costs of legal operations.[6]

The major policy response to the problems of PDS was the introduction of targeting (described in the earlier section). But could a targeted program successfully reform the PDS? First, there are the difficulties of targeting. Most of India's workforce is either self-employed as farmers, traders, vendors, and craftsmen or are wage workers in the informal sector of trade and manufacturing. Such employment is characterized by the absence of formal contracts, salary records, and tax payments. Means testing as it is practiced in developed countries is impossible. Identification of poverty status depends on proxy indicators of land ownership, habitation, type of housing, and social characteristics. It cannot be expected that these would perfectly correlate with poverty status defined by the official poverty line. Second, even if adequate targeting mechanisms would be devised, it does not address the issues of illegal diversions and the unviability of PDS retail outlets.

More recent data from 2004–05 confirm these apprehensions and show that only about 40% of the poor (by the official definition) were correctly classified as either BPL or POP. Most of the poor do not receive the subsidies meant for them. Even among the poor that are correctly classified, only about 60% reported using the PDS in the reference period of a month. The difficulties of access mentioned earlier continue to be relevant.

Figure 12.1 displays a decomposition of food subsidy expenditures (in 2004–05) into various constituent elements. Only about 30% are accounted by income transfer to households whether poor or nonpoor. The remainder of expenditures are absorbed by the costs of illegal diversion (43%) and the excess costs of state agencies (28%). Illegal diversions happen as agents in the government marketing chain sell the subsidized grain in the open market and profit from the difference between the market price and the subsidy price. Jha and Ramaswami (2012) show that, in 2004–05, 55% of the subsidized grain was illegally diverted. Excess costs occur when the price of procuring and distributing grain is higher for the state agencies than for the private sector.

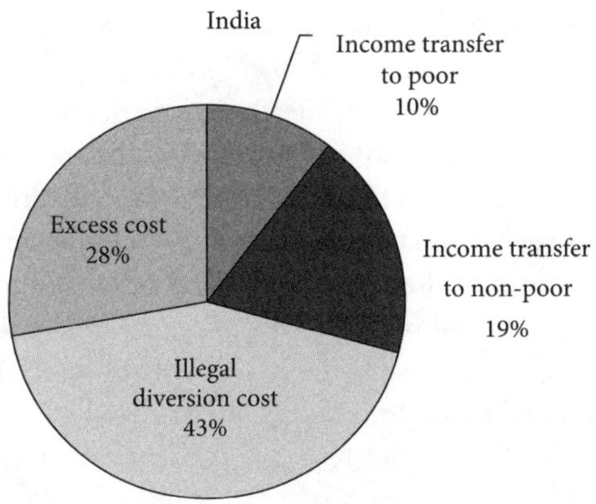

FIGURE 12.1 Decomposition of Food Subsidy Expenditures: India

Source: Jha and Ramaswami (2012)

The Rights Approach to Food Security

Agitated by the poor performance of the public distribution system and the lack of political interest, some civil society organizations have pushed to embed food security in the legal framework and secure some degree of state commitment. In 2001, the People's Union of Civil Liberties filed a public interest petition in the Supreme Court of India demanding judicial oversight of the state's food intervention. They argued that the right to food derives from the right to life that is guaranteed by the Constitution.

The case is still ongoing. However, the court has been sympathetic to the petition and has passed a wide range of "interim" orders. It has appointed commissioners to monitor the compliance of these orders, most of which relate to legal enforcement of existing government programs. Some court orders have also expanded the scope of government programs. A prominent instance of it is when the court made it mandatory for all government primary schools to have a school feeding program.

A network of individuals and organizations has organized around the public interest litigation to campaign for a right to food. The campaign has pressed for a range of interventions beyond just food programs such as public works programs, public services of nutrition, health and education to young children, and securing equitable land and forest rights. The willingness of the judiciary to adjudicate on these issues has provided sustenance to this movement.

The rights approach received political validation with the promise of a "right to food" by the United Party Alliance that returned to power in India's general elections of 2009. This campaign promise has now seen the approval of a National Food Security Bill by the Parliament. Some of the individuals associated with the campaign of civil society organizations were also involved in the drafting of this legislation.[7]

The National Food Security Bill commits the government to reach food subsidies to 75% of the rural population and 50% of urban population. The coverage has been extended from existing levels to what has been called near-universal coverage. However, the near-universal coverage has not put an end to the debate about targeting as the government still has the task of excluding 25% of the rural population and 50% of the urban population..The PDS with its in-kind transfers is seen as the principal instrument of subsidy delivery in the bill. However, some of the clauses seem to also leave open the possibility of cash transfers. The run-up to this bill has been contentious as the government advisors, media, and the independent experts debated alternatives that can effectively deliver the right to food.

The Food Subsidy Debates

Two issues have been prominent in the debates about the food security legislation. The first issue is about the scale of the food subsidy program. Should it continue as a targeted program, or should it have universal access? The second issue is about the form of the subsidy program. Should the subsidy program be modeled on the public distribution system, or are there alternative and more efficient forms of delivery? In particular, should cash transfers replace in-kind transfers?

Neither of these issues is unique to the Indian context. Hence, the debate is of wider significance and has relevance to the delivery of welfare programs in low-income countries.

Coverage

The massive exclusion errors of PDS targeting, noted in the previous section, question the continuance of targeted programs. Until a reliable way of identifying the poor is found, might near-universal coverage be necessary to avoid exclusion errors?

A great deal depends on the specific context of a country. Consider India, for example, with 92% of its labor force in the informal sector. Many are self-employed.

Some days they earn some income. Some days they don't. How do we even measure their incomes? How do we identify the poor? Any process that we use is likely to leave out many from the list. If we leave the job of identifying the poor to the local community—presumably because they have local knowledge—we would be leaving the job to the local elite, who cannot always be trusted to make an objective identification of the poor.[8]

Even if it were possible to identify the poor, clearly the poor are defined as those under an arbitrarily defined line. In India, the official poverty line is close to $1.25 a day at PPP. In 2005, according to the World Bank calculations, about 41.6% of the population was estimated to be under this extremely low poverty line. These people are destitute, not just poor. The basic arguments invoked to provide food subsidies for the poor are valid even for the people with the level of consumption at twice the official poverty line. Over three-quarters of India's population has an expenditure level under $2 a day. Moreover, it is difficult to claim that someone just under $2 a day is in need of food subsidy and someone just above it is not. The harm done by excluding the truly needy far outweighs the gains of wasting the subsidy on those who do not need it. In addition, there is likely to be some self-selection due to the inconvenience of collecting the subsidy that would make the rich stay away. Clearly, there are few arguments against universal coverage in a country like India. Of course, in a rich country like the United States where the poor are a much smaller group and where they have well-developed formal institutions such as the Internal Revenue Service, it makes sense to have a targeted program. Even Latin America is a lot richer than South Asia or sub-Saharan Africa, and the poor that need subsidies constitute a minority. Also, institutional development is further along in Latin America, so identifying the poor through means testing or other methods is not an insurmountable problem. For all these reasons, it makes much more sense to have targeted programs in Latin America than in South Asia or sub-Saharan Africa.

The available evidence on the exclusion error in the present targeted public distribution system in India strengthens the theoretical arguments in favor of universal coverage. In fact, the clamor for universal coverage is growing is in part because of increasing awareness that more than half of the poor as defined by the Government of India's official criterion are left out of the official list of those classified as BPL (Jha and Ramaswami 2012).

While the logic of near-universal coverage in reducing targeting exclusion errors has not been challenged, some economists—and especially those in government—fear that it will lead to unaffordable subsidy expenditures. Another concern is that near-universal coverage with substantial entitlements will mean a substantial expansion of the PDS and hence of grain procurement by the government. The worry is that this will accentuate the adverse effects of procurement discussed earlier. The domination of grain trade by parastatals is not comforting either for those who worry about costs and efficiency in grain marketing.

The disquiet about what the food security bill implies for procurement and grain markets could be easily settled if the food subsidy is given in cash. Under such systems, the food subsidy is directly transferred to the beneficiaries. Households use this transfer to buy grain from designated retail outlets. As the grain would move through the usual market channels, procurement is not necessary.

The coverage question is therefore connected with the mechanism of subsidy delivery. Near-universal coverage with in-kind transfers is likely to be costly. The move would also increase the market price of food, for which reason the farm states would favor in-kind transfers. This is discussed later in the paper.

Why Cash Transfer

Countries other than India have also had to face up to the corruption in in-kind food transfers. Olken (2006) estimates that minimum leakages in Indonesia are of the order of 18% of the supply of subsidized rice. More realistic assumptions lead to estimates of around 30%. For the Philippines, Mehta and Jha (2009) report a 54% gap between the NFA rice supply and reported consumption. While they acknowledge that some of the discrepancy could be because of timing issues in sample survey data, the gap is too large to be due to these errors alone. They conclude that the figure "indicates possibly significant pilferage."

Similarly, Jha and Ramaswami (2012) show that excess costs comprise about 8% of the government costs in supplying rice in the Philippines. Figure 12.2 is a decomposition of food subsidy expenditures in the Philippines. The pie chart is not very different from the similar chart for India (Figure 12.1). Most of the subsidy is lost to illegal diversions and excess costs.

By their very design, a direct cash transfer eliminates the corruption and excess costs of the PDS. As the food subsidy is transferred as cash to households, there is no separate marketing channel for government grain. The dual price system of in-kind transfers that offers possibilities of illegal arbitrage and profit does not exist anymore. Grain moves through the usual market channels of the private sector, so subsidy is not lost to excess costs either.

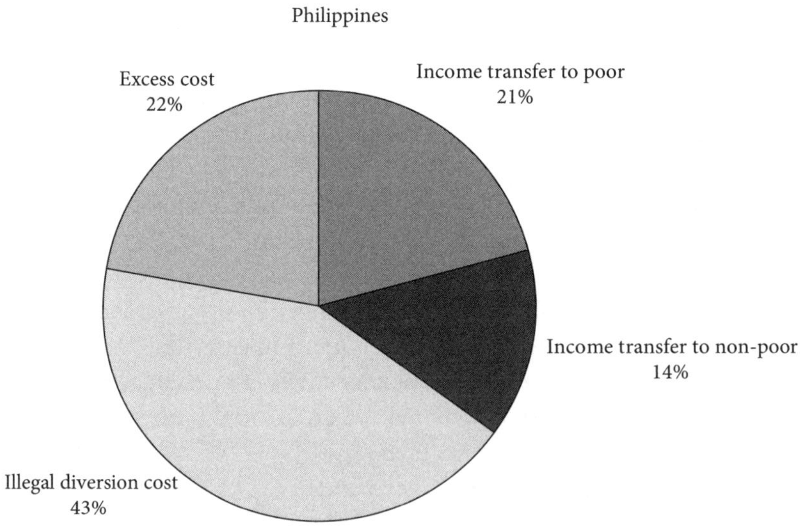

FIGURE 12.2 Decomposition of Subsidy—Philippines

Source: Jha and Ramaswami (2012)

Direct cash transfer has other advantages as well. Because of limited volumes, the viability of the government marketing channel (the PDS retailers) is an endemic issue. This is not a problem with direct transfers because it eliminates the dual marketing system (of private and government). Second, there would be greater economic access, as consumers are restricted not just to particular outlets. Further, poor consumers need not worry about timing their purchases with wage payments.

Third, direct transfers allow consumers to choose foods according to their needs and preferences. In parts of India, poor consume grains such as sorghum and pearl millet that are not subsidized by the current regime. Local grains and varieties are not supported by the PDS. Cash transfers could allow consumers to spend their budget on their preferred commodities and would therefore be less distortionary in consumption. This is the textbook economics case for the superiority of cash transfers over in-kind transfers. It also has implications for reducing regional inequalities.

In a system with in-kind transfers, the government needs to engage in procurement, storage and distribution. Naturally, it finds it logistically convenient to procure grain in two or three large surplus states and then distribute it. The farmers in these surplus states are generally well to do, and they receive the benefit of government-assured support prices. These benefits are not received by the poor growers of local grains. A local grain that is not included in the subsidized basket clearly suffers from the disadvantage of having to compete with a subsidized substitute. Growers of local grains like sorghum and millet are typically located in arid and semi-arid areas, and they do not have the option of switching cultivation to rice and wheat because of lack of complementary inputs (particularly water). The rationing system of in-kind transfers thus invariably generates inequality between the farmers of the surplus states and those in arid and semi-arid areas. It is easy to see that cash transfers would do the opposite, as the consumers in the poorer areas would choose to spend their cash on local grains and thus boost their demand and hence their prices.

Despite these potential advantages, cash transfers have been vigorously opposed by civil society organizations. A leading advisor to the Right to Food campaign referred to a proposal on cash transfers as "ill conceived, not thought through… fraught with grave risks" and as a result "is a solution that is worse than the problem it seeks to address" (Patnaik 2010). The Right to Food campaign has organized protest rallies in states that have wished to pilot programs of cash transfers. If the public distribution system is so dysfunctional, why is there so much resistance to replacing it with direct cash transfers?

Challenges to Cash Transfers: Feasibility

An immediate objection is infeasibility. How can cash be transferred? Does a poor country have the systems to implement it? A cash transfer system is constructed on two pillars: a payments system to distribute the cash; and an authentication system to verify that the transaction is with the intended beneficiary. Conventional payment systems are brick-and-mortar banks and post offices. By definition, such infrastructure is not well developed in the poor remote areas of low-income countries. This has been a barrier to the use of cash transfers.

Computerization of financial systems and the use of the Internet and mobile devices have broken through this impasse. Africa leads the world in the use of mobile phones to transfer cash. It has allowed urban migrants to remit money to their families still living in rural areas. Effectively, any retailer is potentially a point for banking transactions.

In India, post offices have typically delivered cash payments in welfare programs (such as those arising from pension and public works), but this process is vulnerable to capture by the intermediaries, which results in both delay and loss. Policy now emphasizes the direct transfer to savings accounts of beneficiaries in banks and post offices. This is possibly only because of computerization of financial systems. This still does not address the issue of "last-mile" connectivity. An emerging model here is the use of intermediaries between the banks (situated in towns and larger habitations) and the beneficiaries (resident in villages). These intermediaries, called banking correspondents, provide services of withdrawal and deposit with the help of Internet-enabled portable devices that record these transactions in real time. Internet connectivity is provided through the usual mobile phone networks.

Authentication systems require verification of the identity of the beneficiary. In a digital system, this can be done through a user-supplied numeric code or password. More secure systems rely on biometric identification. India has a nationwide project to store biometric data about its residents. In applications to the delivery of public services, the service provider can use it to verify the identity of the recipient. This does require biometric scanners. However, they are easily built into the portable Internet-enabled devices used for recording transactions.

Until a decade ago, cash transfer feasibility was restricted to areas with a high density of payments systems, such as the big cities. This is not so anymore.

Challenges to Cash Transfers: The Paternalism Argument

The economics case for cash transfer is that it allows people to make their own spending decisions. However, this is exactly what bothers cash transfer opponents. To them, it is not self-evident that individual decisions are made wisely. The goal of food subsidy is to increase food intake and improve nutrition. This is furthered only by the supply of food and not cash, which can be dissipated in various ways.

Paternalistic arguments are particularly appealing when men receive cash transfers and use it for their own and not their families' self-interest. The argument is that men will use the cash for alcohol and cigarettes. There is anecdotal evidence that some money from cash transfers is diverted to undesirables such as alcohol. One of the problems in coming up with empirical evidence regarding this phenomenon is that in surveys people are very unlikely to report alcohol purchases from cash transfers. However, certain studies have tried to get indirect evidence. In Somalia, for example, a post-transfer monitoring team conducted interviews with qaat (a kind of drug) traders to see if there had been any increase in sales following the cash distribution. The team found that "there were no reports at the household level of cash use for qaat purchase. Focus group and key informant interviews showed that although there did appear to be a short-lived increase in business for qaat dealers, this reflected the circulation of cash among the business community rather than a usage among drought-affected vulnerable pastoralists" (Narbeth 2004).

The overwhelming evidence has been that cash transfer programs work and recipients do spend the cash received on necessary goods. Table 12.1 (reproduced from Harvey 2005) summarizes the findings for a range of cash transfers done in different countries. The observations do not give a great cause for alarm over the misuse of cash transfers. Note that the underreporting bias that applies to alcohol, cigarettes, and drugs does not apply to the surveys in Table 12.1, which look at the change in only expenditures on food and other essentials.

Most recently, Cunha (2010) used a randomized controlled trial in rural Mexico to compare the benefits of in-kind transfers with those of cash transfers and found that in-kind transfers did not result in better outcomes than cash transfers though they entailed 20% more administrative costs. Cunha concludes:

> Importantly, households do not indulge in the consumption of vices when handed cash. Furthermore, there is little evidence that the in-kind food transfer induced more food to be consumed than did an equal-valued cash transfer.... There were few differences in child nutritional intakes, and no differences in child height, weight, sickness, or anemia prevalence. While other justifications for in-kind transfers may certainly apply, there is minimal evidence supporting the paternalistic one in this context.

The Fungibility of Transfers

Cunha's (2010) findings point to the fact that different ways of directly transferring food subsidy (in-kind of cash) have one thing in common—the subsidy transferred ends up becoming fungible. This contests the assumption of paternalistic arguments that in-kind transfers make people consume more food than they would with an equivalent value of cash transfer.

In economic theory, the paternalistic assumption is valid only if (1) the in-kind transfer cannot be resold and (2) the transfer (i.e., the provision of food) is larger than what the household would voluntarily consume in its absence. If either of these is violated, the in-kind transfer is equivalent to a cash transfer in terms of impacts on consumption choices. The first condition is obvious: without it, the in-kind transfer would be freely transacted and would be equivalent to a cash transfer.

To see the force of the second condition, consider Figure 12.3. It shows for India the monthly per capital consumption of rice and wheat for different expenditure deciles of the

Table 12.1 Spending of the cash received in cash transfers

Project	Spending
A 2003–2004 emergency cash grant in Sool/Sanaag, Somalia by Horn Relief and NPA	Debt, food, water, medicine, soap and transport
A cash-for-work project in Meket and Wallo, Ethiopia, by Save the Children (2001)	food, secondhand clothes, basic necessities, farm tools, seed, chickens, and repaying loans
Cash-for-work project by Ethiopian Red Cross Society/International Federation of Red Cross in Ethiopia in 2000–01	Cheap food grains, petty trade, and debt repayment
Cash payments as part of an agricultural rehabilitation package implemented by the Red Cross in Guatemala and Nicaragua after Hurricane Mitch in 1998	Mainly food, medicines, agricultural inputs, chickens, pigs and tools
Cash as part of a repatriation package in Cambodia in1992–93	Mainly building materials, land, or housing plots to establish small businesses, assist relatives in income-generating activities, and find family members.
Cash-for-work programs by Oxfam in Kitgum, Uganda, 2001	Food, livestock, basic household utensils, school fees
Oxfam, cash-for-work, Turkana, 2000–03	Food not in the relief ration, debts, school fees; lump-sum payments tended to be used to buy productive assets such as livestock, stock for shops, and donkey carting
Oxfam in Bangladesh, 2001	Food, debts, school expenses, clothes, livestock, and fertilizer
Cash grant program in response to the 1999–00 floods in Mozambique	Household goods, food, clothes, seeds, construction materials, and livestock
Cash grants following1999–00 floods in Mozambique	Household goods, clothes, livestock, food, seed, and construction materials
Cash-for-work in Zambia, 2002, by HODI (a Zambian nongovernmental organization)	Maize, grain grinding, basic essentials (salt, sugar, soap, matches), vegetable seeds, investment in small businesses
Save the Children cash-for-work in Democratic Republic of Congo	Women reported that men spent cash on gifts, debt repayments, and beer. Women spent the money on food,school fees and household items
Swiss Agency for Development and Cooperation cash grants in Mongolia, 2002	The money was spent mostly on animals (50%) and on food, clothes, housing repair, and debt repayment
Swiss Agency for Development and Cooperation cash grants in Moldova,2003	Food, medicine, clothing, heating, land tilling, seeds, paying land tax, and debt repayments

Source: Harvey (2005)

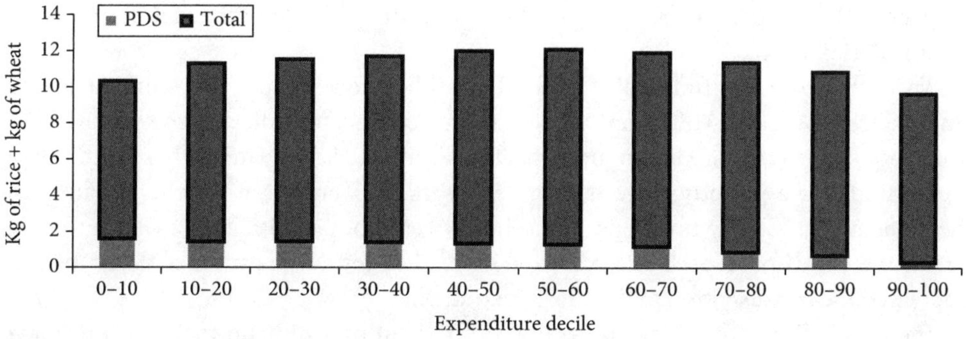

FIGURE 12.3 Per capita grain consumption, PDS and total, 2004–05

Source: Roy Chaudhuri and Somanathan (2011)

population. In this figure, 0–10 is the bottom-most decile of the population when ranked by expenditure. The average consumption of rice and wheat for every person in this decile is a about 10 kg per month, of which the PDS supplied a little less than 2 kg. Similar interpretation attaches to the other bars. It is clear that the second condition is violated.[9]

Even if the subsidy transfer were to increase 5 kg per person (as proposed in the food security act), it would still fall short of what households purchase anyway. So even though it is an in-kind transfer, households save the money that would have been used to buy food to purchase other commodities. The point is not that in-kind transfers will not increase food intake but that the impact may well be no different from that of a cash transfer.

In fact, it is likely that whatever the form of subsidy, the effect on grain purchases will be small. Figure 12.4 shows the average total consumption expenditure per person within each of these deciles. From both these figures, it is clear that despite wide differences in total consumption expenditure the amounts of wheat and rice purchases do not differ that much between the rich and the poor. As the poor become better off, the major

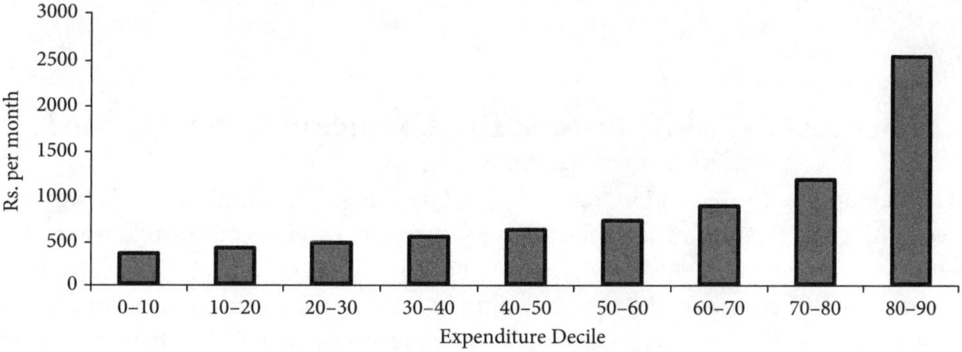

FIGURE 12.4 Per capita consumption expenditure by expenditure decile, 2004–05

Source: Roy Chaudhuri and Somanathan (2011)

impact of their expenditures will be not on grain intake but on other foods and other commodities.

An example of the fungibility of food subsidies comes from the work of Jensen and Miller (2011). In two regions of China, they offered subsidies on the purchases of the basic staple (rice in Hunan and wheat flour in Gansu) to randomly selected poor households for a period of five months. Households were given vouchers that could be redeemed at local grain shops. Households were not permitted to resell the vouchers or the goods purchased with the vouchers. They found no evidence that subsidies increased the consumption of the subsidized staple.

The fungibility of transfers means that it is exceedingly difficult for society to make sure that the poor utilize the aid they receive for the intended purpose of nutrition. Every household has its own priorities, and if a particular household decides to buy a cell phone instead of improving their food basket it may very well be that they feel a stronger need for that phone than for more calories. In short, there is a limit to the control that a society can exercise over individual lives (Banerjee and Duflo 2007, 2011).

The implication is that both in-kind transfers and cash transfers are essentially means of income support. When that is the case, the task of policy is to find the best mechanism for income support. Paternalism goals are irrelevant because they cannot be achieved anyway.

Between the extremes of in-kind transfers through government procurement and direct cash transfers are other intermediate models. A well-known model is the food stamps system of the United States. Here, beneficiaries are given stamps or coupons of fixed monetary value, which are then redeemed in stores.[10]

The stamps can be redeemed for only permitted foods. The resale of stamps and their use as general currency is prohibited. The supposed virtue of such "restricted" cash transfer systems is the paternalism goal of boosting food consumption. However, if such effects are negligible or absent, then the appeal of hybrid models is not clear. Compared with a cash transfer system, a food stamp/coupon model is more demanding. The additional requirements are systems of redemption at stores and the reimbursement of stamps by the government. In addition, it would also be necessary to audit and enforce the legitimate use of stamps.

Challenges to Cash Transfers: The Absence of Self-Selection?

Another justification of in-kind transfers is that it leads to self-selection of only the truly needy. The effectiveness of self-selection unfortunately depends on the relative inconvenience of buying in a ration shop or even having a lower quality of food available in ration shops. The inconvenience of standing in a queue for buying something from a ration shop could be perhaps enough to deter the rich from taking advantage of it except for the fact that they can send their domestic help for such chores. A cash transfer with biometric identification would make the self-selection work more effectively, thus making even universal coverage affordable.

Challenges to Cash Transfers: Inflation

An infusion of cash in a local area could give rise to a sudden increase in prices. In an environment where the markets are not well developed, the rise in prices may not trigger imports from other areas to bring down the prices in a short time. In-kind transfers of food may induce an increase in demand for nonfood items but will not cause food price inflation. Clearly, this is a real concern about cash transfers, and it suggests that cash transfers are more appropriate for the areas where the markets are well developed.

Challenges to Cash Transfers: Price Fluctuations

The most serious objection to any sort of cash transfer is that food prices fluctuate and that a commitment to the poor in terms of a certain quantity of food per person cannot be maintained very easily. Consider the logistics of the problem. Suppose it is decided to give each household 25 kg of grain each month at a subsidized price and the subsidy amount required for a recipient to purchase that much grain is deposited into her account at the beginning of the month. If the market price has risen by 10% by the time the recipient goes to buy the grain, the subsidy amount would fall short of what is required. The subsidy amount should therefore be adjusted as the market price changes. It is, of course, expensive to adjust the subsidy amount too frequently, and the cost of not adjusting it frequently enough will be borne by the poor.[11] This can be an objection against any cash transfer scheme.

In-Kind Transfers and the Market Price of Food

What happens to the market price of grain under cash and in-kind transfers, respectively? The question is important because, in practice, it is difficult to devise a perfect safety net. Some of the poor could be left out even if the coverage was meant to be universal. Moreover, if a policy intervention causes a rise in the market price of grain, the nonpoor who are not entitled to a food subsidy would be adversely affected, and this would make the scheme politically difficult to implement.

Grain markets have a well-defined seasonal pattern. Price levels are at their lowest at harvest time and then rise through the year to cover the costs of carrying stocks. Grain prices can be higher either because of a higher harvest price or because of greater margins of storage and distribution.

When governments procure, the initial harvest price is determined not by the forces of supply and demand but by the support price set by the government. For politicians, the demand for a higher support price affords an opportunity to mobilize a constituency. In India most of the grain is procured from two states—Punjab and Haryana. These two surplus states have a powerful farmers' lobby that the local governments must placate. As a result, the support price, and hence the harvest price, is typically determined through bilateral bargaining between the central government and the state governments. Given the nature of parliamentary democracy in India, the ruling party cannot ignore the votes in these surplus states, and consequently the outcome of the bargaining game is a price that is higher than it would otherwise be (i.e., cash transfers). Hence, there could be a great deal of opposition to a cash transfer system from the procurement granaries of Punjab and Haryana. Though what we have described is specific to India, such a situation may occur wherever price is determined through the political process.

The power of the farm lobby to dictate prices does vary with circumstances. Shortage in the world market reduces the threat of imports and increases their power, but their power diminishes if government stocks are far in excess of need.

Government intervention could also impact storage and distribution margins. Near-universal food subsidies could leave the government as the overwhelming dominant player in grain trade. The monopoly of government agencies could leave their costs unchecked by competition.

Lessons from Social Assistance Programs across the World

The accumulated record of social assistance programs across the world over the last four decades offers some clues on what works and what does not in developing countries. Some of these programs were designed explicitly to enhance the access of the poor to food. Others were designed broadly as social assistance programs for the poor but were assessed in terms of their impact on the access of the poor to food. It is safe to say that many of these programs did have a beneficial impact on the nutritional intake of the poor. What is missing is a careful comparative assessment of their effectiveness in terms of their costs, and this is what would give us a better idea of whether they are worth emulating. All the same, some of these programs earned a reputation as successful and others not so. In either case, we would like to probe why that might be so.

Some of the earlier programs that have been subjected to academic analysis date to the 1970s and 1980s. An interesting case study is Sri Lanka, a country that gained a reputation for being able to raise its human development index despite having a relatively low per capita income (Edirisinghe 1987). During Sri Lanka's post-Independence period through 1979, they had a system of ration shops through which subsidized rice was distributed to about half the population. The price subsidy to rice was extremely beneficial to the Sri Lankan poor. Sri Lanka had, however, maintained an overvalued exchange rate, and that, along with other macro policies, generated severe balance of payments difficulties, which brought on International Monetary Fund (IMF) intervention. The IMF sponsored structural adjustments, as was common under the circumstances, and had as their first priority a severe cut in the government expenditure. The structural adjustment included a replacement of the rationing system with food stamps. The food subsidy share in total government expenditure fell from 15% during the mid-1970s to 3% in 1984. The benefits of food subsidy fell immediately to 83% of what they were before the structural adjustments. Food prices rose under the restructuring, and since the food stamps scheme was nonindexed real benefits were reduced to 43% by 1981–82 of what they were in 1979. Food price subsidies formed 18% of the budget of an average household; under the food stamp scheme it dropped to 9.6%. However, targeting improved under the food stamp scheme. Under the rationing system, only 50% of the total outlays in subsidy went to the bottom 40% of the households that included most of the households consuming less than the recommended energy allowance; under the food stamps scheme this number went up to 66%. But since there was a net reduction in the total real subsidy, the nutritional status of the poor worsened. Per capita calorie consumption of the bottom 20% declined about 8% from an already low 1490 calories during 1978–79 to 1368 calories during 1981–82.

It is clear from the previous account that the change from an in-kind transfer system to a restricted cash transfer system (food stamps) took place during a period when the overriding consideration of the government was budget cutting. The change in the system was undertaken with perhaps an explicit intention of reducing the net subsidy as evidenced by the issuance of nonindexed food stamps in an environment where price rises were inevitable. The Sri Lankan experience raises a red flag in the minds of skeptics that a proposal to change a food transfer system to a cash transfer system may be a Trojan horse to reduce the level of support to the poor.

Jamaica is another example of a country where a general price subsidy program was replaced by a food stamp program. In the aftermath of the worldwide financial turmoil in 1980, the Jamaican government was compelled to undertake austerity measures. One consequence was the total elimination of general price subsidy and its replacement by a targeted food stamp program and an expanded school-feeding program. Grosh (1992) gives an appraisal of the food stamps program. Food stamps were issued to 142,000 beneficiaries out of a population of 2.2 million within seven months of the announcements of the program. The administrative costs were just 9% of the total cost of the program. The gains in targeting were impressive. With food stamps, 57% of the benefits accrued to the bottom 40%, while only 8% accrued to the wealthiest quintile. With a general price subsidy, these numbers were 34% and 26%, respectively. What about the impact on nutrition? No systematic study that we know of exists that could quantify what part of the nutritional impact over the next few years could be attributed to the change from general price subsidy to the food stamps in Jamaica. All we have is circumstantial evidence. For example, according to Grosh, malnutrition among children below an age of five years declined from 14.6% in 1985 to 7.3% in 1989, and the food stamp program was launched in 1984.

A poster child for a cash transfer program of recent vintage is Mexico's PROGRESA program, launched in 1998. It provided cash transfers to families conditional on the regular attendance of their children in schools and health clinics. The idea was to provide a safety net while ensuring human capital formation. According to a study by Hoddinott and Skoufias (2003) of 24,000 households from 506 communities, the households receiving PROGRESA benefits had a caloric intake that was 7.1% higher than those that were not. More importantly, the quality of their nutrition, as measured by the caloric value coming from vegetables and animal products, was higher. The program now covers 25% of Mexican population. The success of the program in achieving the desirable impact at a reasonable cost has made 30 other countries emulate it.

Another very successful conditional (on regular school attendance by children) cash transfer program that is being copied everywhere is Brazil's Bolsa Familia. It is similar in structure to Mexico's PROGRESA. A debit card is issued preferably to a female head of a family whose income is below poverty level. The program has been found to be successful in many dimensions. It is well targeted: 80% of the benefits go to the poor. In 2006, it cost only 0.5 % of the Brazilian gross domestic product (GDP) and covered 11.2 million families. It is credited to have had significant impact on poverty as well as income inequality in one of the most unequal countries (Ravallion 2011).

We have discussed only a few country studies. Unfortunately, we have no systematic comparative studies that would allow us to pass a definitive verdict on the relative merit of cash and in-kind transfers of food subsidy. However, it would not be unfair to claim that cash transfers tried across the world are administratively cheaper to implement and are used by the recipients mostly for legitimate uses. Several countries have used them successfully, and more and more countries are following suit.

Opposition to Cash Transfers: Interests and Ideology

Despite the available evidence and a persuasive case for cash transfers, there seems to be a strong reluctance among politicians as well as civil society activists to move away from in-kind transfers. Why? As far as the politicians are concerned, we cannot discount vested interests. In India, this is best illustrated by the power of the grain procurement lobby.[12] It also consists of the local politically connected interests that run the ration shops and make huge profits by diverting subsidized grain to the open market. Indeed, it is the prospect of such profit that leads the bulk of ration shops to be cornered by local politicians or their cronies.

We believe that there may also be subtler factors influencing the motivations of politicians. For example, subsidizing the essentials of subsistence is powerfully symbolic in keeping alive the conscience of an otherwise unjust society. After all, food subsidies were not constructed as technocratic solutions to malnutrition and hunger but as one of the important means to pacify the poor multitudes. Their historical origins explain why paternalism sits so well with food subsidies. It may also explain why politicians long accustomed to being arbiters of food prices may be reluctant to embrace the unknown political potential of cash transfers.

Civil society activists and especially those groups advocating and working to expand the rights of the poor—for food, health, education, and other public services—have opposed cash transfers for the most part. Their steadfast commitment to in-kind transfers is deeply ironical. A tool of social pacification is held up as a radical means of affirming the rights of the poor. Although they are deeply distrustful of the state, the enlargement of subsidies via in-kind transfers expands state powers and intervention to unprecedented levels. Their preferred method for controlling the incentives for cheating and fraud built into the design of in-kind transfers is an elaborate policing system stretching upward from the community to the bureaucrats and to the judiciary. Although they live and work among the poor, activists are more reluctant to grant agency to the poor than the cash transfer advocates (often economists) who have little contact with the lives of the poor and analyze poverty only in terms of statistical aggregates.

The activists do not all speak with one voice, but many of them are driven by idealism of a sort that compels them to evaluate economic policies not just by the outcomes but also by the perceived purity of the means employed to attain those outcomes. Cash transfers are tinged with their association with markets, the World Bank, and neoliberal economics. Although the case for cash transfers is just that it gets rid of the incentives for corruption, it smacks of a market-based solution and therefore seems distasteful. Electronic transfers of cash and the use of biometric identification seem like technical fixes that rely too much on the profit-seeking banking and corporate sector.

But the government too is not to be trusted. It has also lost its credibility. It is corrupt and incompetent and does not really work for the poor. The role of keeping the governments accountable has therefore been taken up by the civil society activists. Indeed, this arrangement has worked to some extent in India, so far typically by getting progressive legislation passed by the parliament that requires government action. However, since the government is corrupt, the legislation is monitored using the muscle of collective action at the local level. For example, organize the local community to monitor, to make grievances, and to picket. A vigilant and alert local community is therefore the favored solution of the supporters of PDS to the corruption in the system.

While the notion of a local community has been criticized elsewhere, the concept of a village community capable of collective action toward a common goal has immense appeal to those who value democratic politics.[13] The mobilization of communities around their right to food and getting them to collectively police the distribution of government grain supplies builds local organizations and community solidarity that could be transferred to other causes as well: the right to health, education, and especially the right to their land and water resources (against depredation by the government and corporations). Therefore, in this narrative, the "democratic struggle" is a value in itself. In this larger conception of rights and politics, the "narrow" pragmatism of an economist does not stand a chance.

A hard-headed look at food subsidies might have, however, convinced some of the advocacy groups among the poor that subsidies (in-kind or cash) are primarily distributive measures, and hence no particular value ought to attach to the means of delivery. Only the outcomes ought to be valued. Such a statement would be dismissed, though, as deeply ideological by the advocates of in-kind transfers. In their conception, cash transfer marks the retreat of the state from its commitment to the inclusion of the poor and the deprived in the democratic process.

Concluding Comments

The only sorts of arguments that can become compelling against cash transfers are whether they are feasible and whether they will indeed reduce corruption. On feasibility, one can ask whether cash transfers are possible in the Indian setting where the banking network is not widespread in rural areas and most people do not have bank accounts. On corruption, one can ask whether cash cannot be siphoned off just as easily as grain. Indeed, these two questions are related, since for cash transfers to be able to reduce corruption they need to be a part of a well-functioning system.

As discussed earlier, new technologies that allow secure biometric identification and permit access to bank accounts through cell phone networks hold great promise. Any potential beneficiary will then be able to have a bank account in which the due amount can be directly deposited bypassing the local bureaucracy that is often responsible for siphoning off the money. Notice that new technologies also can be applied to reform in-kind transfers. Real-time policing of the supply chain and secure biometric id can reduce corruption losses. However, these reforms will not address the potential adverse impacts of expanded government involvement in procurement.

But is it conceivable that a system can create and maintain a databank for over 1.2 billion people and use it without significant errors? This is a reasonable doubt, and all we can hope for is that there will be many pilot projects and experiments so that we get to examine whether the system works. The best possible scenario is where states are allowed to experiment with different systems including cash transfers, reformed in-kind transfers, or hybrid models (e.g., cash transfers in cities and in-kind transfers in financially underdeveloped regions). We will learn a lot about the strengths and weaknesses of various ways to deliver food subsidy, and the most effective ways will sought to be emulated across the country.

Notes

1. For accounts of India's early food policy, see Bhatia (1970) and Chopra (1981).
2. This is acknowledged officially. The latest such statement is from the Planning Commission (2011, p. 77), which stresses that unless the supply chain is modernized and private investment encouraged, "the intermediation process for farm products, especially perishable products, will remain antiquated with considerable wastage, low net realization to the farmers and high consumer prices."
3. There are many such regulations intended for the protection of either producers or consumers. For instance, private players can buy produce only from the so-called regulated markets. In particular, they are not permitted to directly buy from farmers or to set up their own markets. The reforms of the 2000s aimed to dilute the monopoly of these regulated markets.

4. The government did incur the displeasure of farmers and pressure by farm lobby states and threats of procurement boycott led to substantial hikes in procurement prices in the 2008 season.
5. As might be expected, the aggregate picture masks the variation across states. In general, the southern states have a better record in delivering food subsidies.
6. The local-level politics that accommodate and encourage rent seeking in the PDS is described by Mooij (1999, 2001).
7. Their formal involvement was restricted to the first draft.
8. This is not to say that identification by local bodies will always fail. Indeed, it could well be the preferred option in a set of none too promising alternatives.
9. That is, if the subsidy was discontinued, per capita grain consumption will not drop below 2 kg per month.
10. Paper stamps have now been replaced by debit cards.
11. Of course, the shortfall this month can be added to the amount sent to the consumer next month. In addition, the market prices can go down as frequently as they go up, so over a long time it can be a wash.
12. This includes the farm surplus states as well as the oversized government agencies in charge of procurement.
13. Kotwal, Murugkar, and Ramaswami (2011) cast a critical eye on whether local communities can discipline the PDS.

References

Ahluwalia Deepak. 1993. "Public Distribution of Food in India." *Food Policy* 18: 33–54.

Banerjee, A., and E. Duflo. 2007. "The Economic Lives of the Poor." *Journal of Economic Perspectives* 21 (1): 141–167.

Banerjee, A., and E. Duflo. 2011. *Poor Economics*. New York: Public Affairs.

Bhatia, B. M. 1970. *India's Food Problem and Policy since Independence*. Bombay: Somaiya Publications.

Chopra, R. N. 1981. *Evolution of Food Policy in India*. Delhi: Macmillan India.

Cunha, M. 2010. "Testing Paternalism: Cash vs. In-Kind Transfers in Rural Mexico." Working Paper, Naval Postgraduate School, *Monterey, California*.

Currie, J., and F. Gahvari. 2008. "Transfers in Cash and In-Kind: Theory Meets the Data." *Journal of Economic Literature* 46 (2): 333–383.

Dev, S. Mahendra, and M. H. Suryanarayana. 1991. "Is PDS Urban Biased and Pro-Rich?" *Economic and Political Weekly* 26 (4): 2357–2366.

Dutta, B., and B. Ramaswami. 2001. "Targeting and Efficiency in the Public Distribution System: Case of Andhra Pradesh and Maharashtra." *Economic and Political Weekly* 36 (18): 1524–1532.

Edirisinghe, N. 1987. "The Food Stamp Scheme in Sri Lanka: Costs, Benefits and Options for Modification." International Food Policy Research Institute, Research Report 58.

Grosh, M. 1992. "The Jamaican Food Stamps Programme: A Case Study in Targeting." *Food Policy* 17 (1):23–40.

Harvey, P. 2005. "Cash and Vouchers in Emergencies." Discussion Paper, Overseas Development Institute, Humanitarian Policy Group, London, United Kingdom.

Hoddinott, J., and E. Skoufias. 2003. "The Impact of PROGRSA on Food Consumption." International Food Policy Research Institute, Discussion Paper 150.
Howes, S., and S. Jha. 1992. "Urban Bias in Indian Public Distribution System." *Economic and Political Weekly* 27 (19): 1020–1030.
Jensen, R. T., and N. H. Miller. 2011. "Do Consumer Price Subsidies Really Improve Nutrition." *Review of Economics and Statistics* 93 (4): 1205–1223.
Jha, S., and B. Ramaswami. 2012. "The Percolation of Public Expenditures: Food Subsidies in India and the Philippines." *India Policy Forum* 8: 95–138.
Kotwal, A., M., Murugkar & B. Ramaswami, 2011. "PDS Forever?" *Economic and Political Weekly* 46 (21): 72–76.
Landes, R., and A. Gulati. 2004. "Farm Sector Performance and Reform Agenda." *Economic and Political Weekly*, August 7, 3611–3619.
Mehta, A., and S. Jha. 2009. "Governance and Hunger: A Case Study from the Philippines. University of California–Santa Barbara Center of Global Studies." Working Paper 7.
Mooij, J. 1998. "Food Policy and Politics: The Political Economy of the Public Distribution System in India." *Journal of Peasant Studies* 25 (2): 77–101.
Mooij, J. 1999. "Dilemmas in Food Policy: About Institutional Contradictions and Vested Interests." *Economic and Political Weekly*, December 25, A114–A120.
Mooij, J. 2001. "Food and Power in Bihar and Jharkhand: PDS and Its Functioning." *Economic and Political Weekly*, August 25, 3289–3299.
Narbeth, S. 2004. "Emergency Cash Relief to Drought Affected Families of Sool Plateau: Post Distribution Survey Findings." United Nations Office for the Coordination of Humanitarian Affairs Somalia.
Olken, B. 2006. "Corruption and the Costs of Redistribution: Micro Evidence from Indonesia." *Journal of Public Economics* 90: 853–870.
Parikh, K. 1994. "Who Gets How Much from PDS—How Effectively Does It Reach the Poor?" *Sarvekshana*, 17 (3) 1–34
Patnaik, B. 2010. "Devil Is in the Delivery: Why Cash, Stamps for Food Will Never Work." *Times of India*, November 26.
Planning Commission. 2011. "Faster, Sustainable and More Inclusive Growth: An Approach to the Twelfth Five Year Plan." http://planningcommission.nic.in/plans/planrel/12appdrft/appraoch_12plan.pdf
Radhakrishna, R., K. Subbarao, S. Indrakant, and C. Ravi. 1997. "India's Public Distribution System: A National and International Perspective." World Bank Discussion Paper 380, Washington, DC.
Ravallion, M. 2011. "A Comparative Perspective on Poverty Reduction in Brazil, China and India." *World Bank Research Observer* 26 (1): 71–104.
Roy Chaudhuri, A., and E. Somanathan. 2011. "Impact of Biometric Identification-Based Transfers." *Economic and Political Weekly* 56 (21): 77–79.
Saxena, N. C. 2004. "Agricultural Policy and Rural Poverty Reduction in India." In *Integrating the Rural Poor into Markets*, ed. B. Debroy and A. U. Khan. Academic Foundation.
Varshney, A. 1993. "Self-Limited Empowerment: Democracy, Economic Development and Rural India." *Journal of Development Studies* 29 (4): 177–215.
World Bank. 2001. "India Improving Household Food and Nutrition Security." Report 20300-IN, Rural Development Sector Unit, South Asia Region, Washington DC

CHAPTER 13

DIETS, NUTRITION, AND POVERTY

Lessons from India

RAGHAV GAIHA[1], RAGHBENDRA JHA, VANI S. KULKARNI, AND NIDHI KAICKER

Introduction

India is currently undergoing a rapid economic and demographic transformation characterized by a sustained and rapid rise in average living standards—increase in GDP per capita growth rates, decline in poverty, rising urbanization, and improvements in health outcomes. A key feature of this transformation has been the change in the nature of the Indian diet, driven partly by the integration of global markets and improvements in communication.

According to FAOSTAT, dietary changes in the 1980s included a sharp rise in consumption of both animal and vegetable products, with milk having the largest proportional increase among animal products, and, rice, pulses (dried peas, beans, lentils, chickpeas, etc.), wheat, spices, and oils constituting the largest increase among vegetable products.[2] During the 1990s, significant changes in the pattern of food consumption included a marked increase in the consumption of animal products (especially animal fats), and a relatively modest increase in consumption of vegetable products. Although the consumption of wheat, starchy roots, vegetable oils, sugar and sweeteners, and fruits increased, that of rice, pulses and other cereals declined. There was also a sharp increase in potato consumption, given its predominance in energy-dense food products (e.g., fries and potato chips). A significant change was in the consumption of wheat due to a move away from the traditional *chapatti* to more commercialized and westernized bread products.[3]

Thus, dietary transition was characterized by a substitution of traditional staples by primary food products that are more prevalent in western diets. These shifts are reflected in higher consumption of proteins, sugars, fats, and vegetables.

Some of the underlying factors behind this dietary transition are expansion of the middle class, higher female participation in labor markets, emergence of nuclear two-income families, a sharp age divide in food preferences (with younger age groups more susceptible to new foods advertised in the media), and rapid growth of supermarkets and fast-food outlets.[4]

The health implications of the dietary transition are unclear. A more varied and nutritionally balanced diet and higher levels of food hygiene are associated with better health. But there is a trade-off as more energy-dense foods are linked to higher incidence of diet-related noncommunicable diseases (NCDs) such as diabetes, coronary heart disease, and certain types of cancer. Although India lags behind other developing countries in the epidemiological transition—decline in infectious disease mortality compensated for increasingly by higher mortality from chronic degenerative NCDs—there is some evidence of this transition taking place. Estimated deaths from NCDs are projected to rise from 3.78 million in 1990 (40.46% of all deaths) to 7.63 million in 2020 (66.70% of all deaths)

The scheme of this chapter is as follows: The second and third sections review the evidence on nutrient intake and dietary changes, focusing particularly on the downward shift in calorie, protein, and other nutrient intakes over the period 1993–2004. In the fourth section, recent evidence on eating out as an aspect of dietary transition in India is reviewed. The fifth section undertakes a demand-theory based explanation of the factors driving the downward shifts. In the sixth section, we use a different measure of undernutrition, based on the calorie share of staples. The seventh, eighth, and ninth sections, respectively, focus on poverty nutrition traps, an assessment of whether child undernutrition is underestimated; and the links among aging, obesity, affluence, expansion of the middle class, urbanization, and noncommunicable diseases (NCDs). The tenth section examines the (potential) contribution of National Rural Employment Guarantee Scheme (NREG) and Public Distribution System (PDS) toward mitigating the extent and severity of undernutrition (including micronutrient deficiency). As current debates on food security have veered toward a right to food, a new perspective is delineated in the eleventh section, to suggest that food security involves a right to policies (or a "right to a right") designed to ensure fulfillment of food entitlements. The final section makes some concluding observations from a broad policy perspective.

Nutrient Intake

Various sources—including detailed household consumption expenditure surveys conducted by the National Sample Survey Organisation (NSSO) every five years in India (the so-called thick samples)—point to a puzzle. Despite rising incomes, there has been sustained decline in per capita nutrient intake. In an important contribution, Deaton and Dreze (2009) (henceforth DD) offer an analysis of the decline in nutrient intake over the period 1983 to 2004. Their principal findings are that the average calorie consumption was about 10% lower in rural areas in 2004–2005 than in 1983. The proportionate decline was larger among the more affluent sections of the population, and negligible for the population in the bottom quartile of the per capita expenditure scale. In urban areas, there was a slight change in average calorie intake over this period. Proteins and other nutrients also experienced a drop in per capita consumption, whereas the intake of fat increased in both rural and urban areas. Because incomes rose over this period, these declines are puzzling.

A contentious view offered by DD is that the declines are not attributable to changes in relative prices because an aggregate measure of the price of food—treated synonymously with the price of calories—changed little during this period. So the puzzle boils down to this: Per capita calorie consumption is lower at every given level of per capita household expenditure, across the expenditure scale, at low levels of per capita expenditure as well as high, that is, there is a steady downward shift of the calorie Engel curve.[5]

DD are emphatic that the downward shift of the calorie Engel curve is due to lower calorie "requirements," associated mainly with better health and lower activity levels. Specifically, they draw attention to major expansions in availability of safe drinking water, vaccination rates, transport facilities, and ownership of various effort-saving durables, relying on evidence furnished by the Indian Council of Medical Research (1990).

This section throws more light on the declines in calorie, protein, and fat intake over the period 1993–2004, and the explanations offered of this decline. The analysis is based mostly on unit record data collected for the 50th and 61st rounds of the NSS (corresponding to 1993–94 and 2004–05, respectively).

Changes in Calorie, Protein, and Fat Intake

Calories

Until recently, a calorie intake of 2400 per day was considered adequate for a typical adult engaged in physically strenuous work of a certain duration in rural India. More recent assessments have used lower calorie "requirements" (1800 calories).[6]

As can be seen from Table 13.1, using the higher calorie requirement of 2,400, over 71% of the rural households were calorie deprived or more generally undernourished in 1993.[7] With the lower norm of 1,800, this proportion falls sharply to about 31%, implying a large concentration of households in the calorie intake range of 1,800–2,400. The proportion of undernourished rises from 71% to nearly 80% in 2004, and the proportion below the lower cut-off from about 31% in 1993 to close to 37% in 2004, indicating high levels of calorie deprivation. Although the mean calorie intake of those below 1,800 rose slightly (from 1,491 to 1,516), the mean intake (overall) reduced from 2,156 in 1993 to 2,047 in 2004.

In urban India, assuming lower calorie norms of 1700 and 2100 (given less strenuous physical activity in urban areas), about 28% consumed less than 1700 calories in

Table 13.1 Calorie Intake Distributions in Rural India, 1993 and 2004

	Range of Calorie Intake Per Capita Per Day				
Year	<1800	1801-2400	2401-3000	>3000	Total
1993	31.09 (1491)	40.07 (2084)	19.42 (2650)	9.42 (3636)	100 (2156)
2004	36.68 (1516)	43.11 (2071)	15.07 (2629)	5.14 (3925)	100 (2047)

Source: Authors' calculations based on the 50th and 61st rounds of the NSS.

Table 13.2 Calorie Intake Distributions in Urban India, 1993 and 2004

	Range of Calorie Intake Per Capita Per Day				
Year	<1700	1701-2100	2101-2600	>2600	Total
1993	28.12 (1426)	29.62 (1900)	25.76 (2320)	16.49 (3107)	100 (2074)
2004	29.40 (1440)	34.52 (1900)	24.67 (2313)	11.41 (3252)	100 (2021)

Source: Authors' calculations based on the the 50th and 61st rounds of the NSS

1993 (Table 13.2). About 58% were below the higher calorie norm of 2100. Worse, this proportion rose to about 64% in 2004. The proportion of people below the lower cut-off changed only slightly. Although less alarming than the calorie deprivation increase in rural India, it is nevertheless worrying.

Protein

A cut-off of 60gm of protein intake is used.[8] Although protein deficiency is in large measure linked to calorie deficiency, we note that well over 57% of rural households consumed fewer than the required protein intake in 1993. Just under a quarter of the households consumed <45gm of protein. Within both ranges of protein intake, the proportions rose more than moderately (e.g., in the lower range, the proportion of households rose from about 24% in 1993 to about 29% in 2004). Although the mean intakes of protein reduced from 60gm in 1993 to 56gm in 2004, the intake for households in the lower range remained unchanged (Refer to Table 13.3).

The share of protein-deficient households in urban India (considering the 60 gm cut-off) remained unchanged between 1993 and 2004. Overall mean protein intakes, however, reduced (Refer to Table 13.4).

Fats

Although a precise range for fat requirements cannot be specified, a range of 40–60gm of fat intake is desirable.[9] Even considering the first three ranges of fat intake, an astonishingly high estimate of fat deficient households for rural India (over 85%) is obtained

Table 13.3 Protein Intake Distributions in Rural India, 1993 and 2004

	Range of Protein Intake Per Capita Per Day (gms)				
Year	<45	46–60	61–75	>75	Total
1993	23.81 (37.1)	33.79 (52.4)	22.79 (66.8)	19.61 (94.4)	100 (60.3)
2004	28.81 (37.4)	38.05 (52.2)	21.46 (66.3)	11.68 (93.9)	100 (55.8)

Source: Authors' calculations based on the the 50th and 61st rounds of the NSS

Table 13.4 Protein Intake Distributions in Urban India, 1993 and 2004

	Range of Protein Intake Per Capita Per Day (gms)				
Year	<45	46–60	61–75	>75	Total
1993	24.90 (37.1)	37.77 (52.4)	23.11 (66.5)	14.23 (90.7)	100 (57.3)
2004	29.40 (37.8)	34.50 (52.3)	24.69 (66.2)	11.40 (94.9)	100 (55.4)

Source: Authors' calculations based on the the 50th and 61st rounds of the NSS

Table 13.5 Fat Intake Distributions in Rural India, 1993 and 2004

	Range of Fat Intake Per Capita Per Day (gms)				
Year	<20	21–30	31–50	>50	Total
1993	34.30 (14.0)	25.08 (24.7)	26.09 (38.3)	14.54 (72.1)	100 (31.5)
2004	22.59 (15.0)	27.21 (24.9)	33.58 (38.3)	16.62 (74.6)	100 (35.4)

Source: Authors' calculations based on the the 50th and 61st rounds of the NSS

for 1993. As can be seen from Table 13.5, well over one-third of households are under the lowest range of <20gm. The corresponding household share with fat intakes <50gm fell to over 83% in 2004. The share of households consuming <20gm of fat fell sharply (from over 34% to well over 22%). Mean fat intakes increased over the period 1993 to 2004.

Using higher ranges of fat intake for urban areas (Table 13.6), fat deprivation was pervasive (about 81% of the households consumed <60gm of fats in 1993). About a quarter consumed <25gm. Over the period 1993–2004, the reduction in the proportion of fat-deprived was slight (from 81% in 1993 to 78% in 2004). However, as in rural India, the proportion consuming fats <25gm fell sharply. Mean fat intakes increased.

Thus, taking the nutritional norms as valid, the overall picture of nutritional deprivation worsened considerably over the period 1993–2004, despite significantly enhanced economic growth in per capita income.

Table 13.6 Fat Intake Distributions in Urban India, 1993 and 2004

	Range of Fat Intake Per Capita Per Day (gms)				
Year	<25	26–40	41–60	>60	Total
1993	25.04 (18.2)	29.84 (32.3)	26.15 (48.6)	18.97 (80.2)	100 (42.1)
2004	15.39 (19.4)	31.02 (32.6)	31.56 (48.9)	22.04 (85.8)	100 (47.4)

Source: Authors' calculations based on the the 50th and 61st rounds of the NSS

Changes in Diets and Nutrition

Food composition and diet changed considerably in both rural and urban areas over the period 1993–2004.[10] Although there was some reduction in cereal intake, there were large reductions in the intake of pulses/nuts/dry fruits too. In contrast, intakes of Vanaspati-oil, eggs, and fruits rose. Because these are linked to intakes of calories, proteins, and fats with varying importance, an investigation of how food consumption patterns changed in response to changes in income and relative prices is necessary. We build on the DD analysis (2009) of food commodities that contributed to reduction in calories, protein, and fats.

Calories

In rural India in 1993, cereals accounted for about 71% of total calorie intake, which reduced to 68% in 2004. Calories from cereals recorded a significant reduction (from 1,530 calories to 1,383 calories). The contribution of vanaspati-oil rose moderately. Altogether, calorie intake declined from 2,156 to 2,047 between 1993 and 2004.

In urban India, calorie intake declined from 2,074 in 1993 to 2,021 in 2004, a reduction of about 3%, much of it due to reduction in cereal calories—from 1,213 to 1,133—a reduction of 7%. Among other calorie sources, milk/milk products/ghee/butter, Vanaspati-oil and pulses/nuts/dryfruits/others contributed a slight increase.[11] By contrast, the contribution of sugar decreased.

Protein

In rural India, protein intake declined—from 60.3gm in 1993 to 55.8gm in 2004— that is, by about 7%. Much of it is reflected in a reduction in protein intake from cereals. Intake from other sources remained largely unchanged between 1993 and 2004. Similarly, average protein intake in urban India fell from 57.3gm in 1993 to 55.4gm in 2004, that is, by about 3%, most of it due to a reduction in protein intake from cereals.

Fats

Between 1993 and 2004, fat intake rose from 31.5 gm to 35.4 gm in rural India, that is, by 12%. There was a slight reduction in fat intake from cereals and milk/milk products/ghee/butter, and the main contributor to the higher intake was vanaspati-oil. Pulses/nuts/dry fruits also contributed a slightly higher amount.

Urban India also recorded increased intake of fats—from 42.1gm in 1993 to 47.5gm in 2004, that is, by 13%. As in rural India, much of the increase came from Vanaspati-oil. Contribution of pulses/nuts/dry fruits also rose by a small amount.

Changes in Diets

Underlying these changes in nutrient intakes from different food commodities are the changes in their consumption. In rural India, there was a sharp reduction in cereal consumption—10% between 1993 and 2004. The intake of sugar decreased by 6% between 1993 and 2004. Pulses/nuts/dry fruits/others recorded a sharp drop of 44% between 1993 and 2004. By contrast, intakes of Vanaspati-oil and eggs rose more than moderately, as did meat/fish/poultry, fruits and vegetables in 2004. Reduction in cereal intake was lower in urban India (7%). Pulses/nuts/dry fruits recorded a sharp reduction of 37%, whereas sugar recorded a moderate decline. Milk/ghee/butter, meat/fish/poultry, and fruits and vegetables recorded small increases in 2004, and eggs and Vanaspati-oil recorded moderately higher intakes.

Dietary patterns of Indian households changed over this period; relative prices are of course important, and elasticities of demand varied across food categories. An increase in the price of milk, for example, leads to a negligible reduction in its demand—a case of highly inelastic demand. The demand for cereals, meat, and vegetables is highly responsive to price changes; the responsiveness of demand for fruits and pulses is moderate; and that of Vanaspati oil and eggs is small. The expenditure elasticity is the smallest for cereals. Our analysis is based on the 1993 and 2004 household surveys conducted by the NSS.[12] The demand for each of the commodities analyzed is inversely related to its own price, consistent with demand theory, with varying elasticities.[13] These variations reflect changing food preferences over time—preferences for taste and variety.

Household characteristics, such as size, proportion of adults, and caste affiliation have significant impacts on the demand for various food commodities. The links between caste affiliation and demand for food commodities are interesting. In comparison to Scheduled Castes, Others (a residual caste group) demanded larger amounts of milk, Vanaspati oil, fruits and vegetables, and lower amounts of meat and cereals. This may in part reflect cultural differences among these categories. There are also significant differences between urban–rural samples, pointing to urban lifestyles driving dietary changes (fatty and starchy convenience foods).

How do we measure *diversity* in the diet? One approach is to count the number of different food items consumed. Because this does not allow for their relative importance in food expenditure, we have followed a different approach, which relies on their shares in

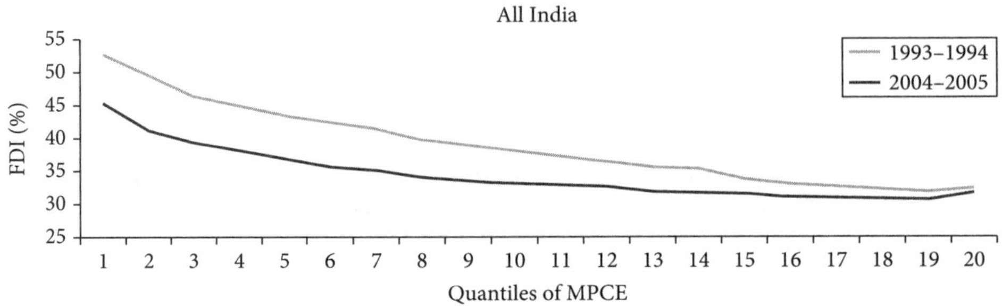

FIGURE 13.1 Food Diversity Index at Various Levels of MPCE

food expenditure. A Food Diversity Index (FDI) is computed.[14] In percentages, this lies between 0 and 100. *The higher the ratio, the lower is the food diversity.*[15] We use five food groups to construct the FDI: (1) cereals and pulses; (2) milk, milk products, eggs, and meats; (3) oil; (4) sugar; and (5) fruits and vegetables. We consider a less disaggregated classification of food commodities than used before, but there is no more than a slight loss of information.

A graphical representation of variation in FDI by per capita expenditure quantiles is given in figure 13.1. Diets are more diversified at higher expenditure levels; moreover, diet diversification was greater in 2004 than in 1993.

The FDI and its effect on calorie intake are analyzed in two-stages: The first stage focuses on the determinants of FDI and the second on the effects of FDI on calorie intake.[16] Cereal and relative food prices (ratio of cereal price to that of animal products including milk, poultry, and meat price, cereal price to that of Vanaspati oil) influence FDI. Specifically, for example, the higher the cereal price, the lower is FDI, and the greater is food diversification. On the other hand, given the cereal price, the lower is the price of animal products, the greater is the demand for these products and consequently the greater is food diversification. Higher expenditure lowers FDI and enhances food diversification. Those belonging to the middle class (identified on the basis of consumer durables such as TVs) also have more diversified diets, as do those located in urban areas.

In the second stage, controlling for the effects of all these variables (except for that of the middle class), dietary diversification reduces calorie intake.[17] Although this link has been hinted at or simply glossed over in recent studies, this is the first robust confirmation.[18]

How Pervasive is Eating Out in a Transitional Economy?

How extensive is the dietary transition in terms of eating outside the household? The nationwide household survey, *India Human Development Survey 2005* (IHDS), conducted jointly by the University of Maryland and the National Council of Applied Economic Research permits analysis and answers. Eating out refers to meals or snacks served in restaurants, roadside eating places, tea and snack shops, and street vendors. Our focus is on the socioeconomic status of households eating out, and their spatial distribution.[19]

Eating out was more common among the metro residents, as one would expect; they also spent larger amounts. Yet eating out is pervasive; about 30% of the households did so. A large proportion of those eating out (about 42%) spent under rupees (Rs) 99 per month, and about a quarter spent over Rs 200 per month (at 2004–2005 prices). Eating out is a feature not just of the metros or urban areas, but also of urban slums and rural areas, though it is less pervasive in the last two areas. In the six largest metros (Mumbai, Delhi, Kolkata, Chennai, Bangalore, and Hyderabad), about 34% of the households ate out, as compared to about 27% elsewhere. Over 47% of the former spent Rs 200 or more per month on eating out, and less than one-quarter of the latter did so. There are also differences by caste. About 25% of the Scheduled Castes (SCs), about 27% of the Scheduled Tribes (STs), and about 31% of the Other Backward Castes (OBCs), and Others ate out. Even some of the most deprived and socially excluded groups—especially the SCs and STs—have switched from traditional staples to fast foods and opted for greater variety in food consumption. When the sample is split into the poor and nonpoor households using the official poverty line, we find that a much larger proportion of the nonpoor households (about 32%) ate out, but about 12.5% of the poor ate out as well.[20] A more disaggregated classification of the households into four Monthly Per Capita Expenditure (MPCE) classes (less than Rs 300, between Rs 300–500, between Rs 500–1000, and greater than Rs 1000) further qualifies the common perception that eating out as a manifestation of dietary transition is mostly a middle-class phenomenon.

Using an econometric model, we obtain additional insights into the *marginal* contribution of household traits, their (relative) affluence, and locational characteristics.[21] The results show that location of households, their demographic and caste characteristics, and, above all, their relative affluence determine both the decision to eat out, and, conditional on it, the amount spent. Further details are omitted to focus better on the latter.

Amounts spent on eating out vary with location. Households located in both metros and nonmetro urban locations are likely to spend larger amounts on eating out, relative to rural areas. Between the metros and nonmetros, households in the former are likely to spend much larger amounts. SCs, STs, and OBCs are likely to spend lower amounts relative to Others. The higher the number of adult males in paid employment in the age-group 25–45, and of females in the older age-group, >45 years, the greater is the amount spent. The effect of higher per capita expenditure relative to the poverty line is large and significant, confirming that the more affluent are not just more likely to eat out but also likely to spend larger amounts. The higher the share of salary in household income, the lower is the amount spent. By contrast, the higher the share of business income, the larger is the amount spent.

Our analysis thus broadly confirms the important role of urbanization, demographic changes, expansion of middle class and its growing affluence in eating out, or, more generally, consumption of snacks, beverages, and precooked meals. Nevertheless, even more deprived sections of the society are not immune to these evolving dietary patterns.

DEMAND-THEORY BASED EXPLANATION OF SHIFT IN NUTRIENT INTAKE

One explanation of a downward shift in the calorie Engel curve relies on lower "requirements" due to health improvements, less strenuous activity levels, and more sedentary lifestyles (Deaton–Dreze 2009). There is an alternative explanation provided by a standard demand-theory framework, with food prices[22] and expenditure (as a proxy for income) cast in a pivotal role. Demand functions are estimated for each of three nutrients, namely calories, protein, and fats. We find -consistently robust food price and expenditure effects. We will discuss the results for rural and urban samples separately.[23]

Rural India

Calories

Our results confirm significant food price effects on calorie demand—negative for prices of cereals, and fruits and vegetables, and positive for inferior cereals, milk/milk products/ghee/butter, Vanaspati oil, sugar, eggs and pulses/nuts-dry fruits/others. The expenditure/income effect on calorie demand is positive and large.[24] Household size and composition matter too. The larger the number of adult males and females, the greater is the calorie demand. Controlling for the number of adults, variation in household size reflects variation in number of children. So it is not surprising that household size has a significant negative effect on calorie demand.[25] Both SC and Others (as a residual caste group) demand more calories than the omitted group of STs. Education level matters too. Other things being equal, households in which adult males and females have more than middle level of schooling demand fewer calories than those with lower educational attainments. Over and above these effects, it is found that calorie demand was lower in 2004 as compared to 1993. This could be in part the combined effect of epidemiological improvements, less strenuous activity patterns, and more sedentary life-styles.[26]

Protein

There are significant food price effects on protein demand too—negative for prices of cereals, Vanaspati oil, fruits, and vegetables, and positive for those of milk/milk products/ghee/butter, sugar, eggs, and pulses/nuts-dry fruits/others. Expenditure has a significant positive effect. Turning to household characteristics, the larger the numbers of adult males and females, the higher is the protein demand, whereas household size has a significantly negative effect. In all these cases, however, the effects are negligibly small.

The caste affiliations (SCs and Others relative to STs) have significant positive effects, but the coefficients are negligibly small. Households with adult males and females possessing above middle schooling have lower protein demands than those with lower educational attainments. Of some significance is the fact that the effect of adult males with above middle schooling is much lower than that of adult females. There is a positive shift of the protein demand curve over the period 1993–2004, implying a residual positive effect.[27]

Fats

Beginning with the food-price effects, cereal, milk/milk products/ghee/butter, Vanaspati oil prices have negative effects; whereas prices of sugar, eggs, meat/poultry/fish, pulses/nuts/dryfruits, vegetables and fruits have positive effects. The elasticity of expenditure is significantly positive and large. Most household characteristics other than the number of adult females have significant effects, but the magnitudes are negligible. Over and above these effects, there is a downward shift of the fat demand curve, due to factors other than those specified in the demand function over time.[28]

Urban India

Calories

Prices of cereals, pulses/nuts/others, inferior cereals and fruits and vegetables have negative but small effects (in absolute value), whereas prices of milk/milk products/ghee/butter, Vanaspati-oil, sugar and eggs have positive effects. The expenditure elasticity is positive. Excluding the caste variables, all other household characteristics have significant but negligible effects. As in rural India, the demand function shifted downward over time, presumably because of less strenuous activity patterns and more sedentary life-styles, among other time-related factors.

Protein

Prices of cereals, inferior cereals, meat/fish/poultry, fruits and vegetables have negative coefficients, whereas prices for milk/milk products/ghee/butter, sugar, eggs, and pulses have positive coefficients. The expenditure elasticity is positive and high. Except for SCs (with a small positive coefficient), all other household variables have significant coefficients but negligible in value. As in the case of rural India, there is a positive shift in the demand curve.

Fats

Cereal, inferior cereal, milk/milk product/ghee/butter prices have negative coefficients whereas those of Vanaspati oil, sugar, eggs, meat/fish/poultry, pulses, and vegetables have positive coefficients. The expenditure elasticity is high. All household variables, with the exception of SCs, have significant effects but negligible in value. SCs demand more fats relative to STs. As in rural India, the demand function shifted downward over 1993–2004.

We developed an alternative explanation of changes in the consumption of calories, protein, and fats over the more recent period, 1993–2004. Our results show consistently robust food price and expenditure effects. Besides, shifts in food price elasticities over time are significant, indicating changes in price responsiveness of demand. Over and above these effects, there are shifts in demands due to factors other than those specified in the demand equations. In the context of calories, for example, it is plausible that part of the reduction in their consumption was due to health improvements and less strenuous activity levels. In conclusion, although the Deaton–Dreze (2009) explanation is not rejected, it is arguable that it is complementary to the demand-theory based explanations.[29]

Calorie Thresholds and Undernutrition

There are important conceptual and measurement issues in undernutrition. If the proportions of undernourished people are measured using fixed calorie norms, there is an increase in the prevalence of undernutrition (synonymous with calorie-deprivation). Even if the calorie norms are taken to be lower, a grim picture emerges. Using fixed calorie norms to measure undernutrition is suspect for familiar reasons.[30] A recent study (Jensen and Miller, 2011) proposes an alternative measure that relies on consumption behavior, as opposed to calorie norms. The basic argument is that individuals tend to switch away from the cheapest source of calories (staple food), after surpassing subsistence, and move toward more expensive sources of calories. If this switch occurs at a certain share of calories from staples, all those above the threshold are counted as undernourished.

Our analysis with the National Sample Survey data for 1993 and 2004 shows that such a measure is potentially misleading as it confines variation in the calorie share to a measure of wealth, ignoring the role of relative prices. We first experimented with "Lowess" in which the dependent variable is share of calories from cereals (cheapest and largest source of calories) and the explanatory variable, wealth of a household per capita, is approximated by monthly per capita expenditure (MPCE).[31]

In rural areas, in 1993, counting those above the calorie share threshold (below and above the corresponding expenditure cut-off point), the proportion of undernourished works out to about a quarter of the rural population, which is below that under the calorie cut-off of 1,800 per capita per day. In striking contrast to our analysis with fixed calorie norms, which shows a sharp rise in the proportion of undernourished in rural India during 1993–2004, the Lowess results show a substantial reduction. In urban areas too, there is a reduction in the proportion of undernourished (from 15% to 9%), due to a sharp reduction in the proportion of those above the calorie threshold and above the expenditure cut-off. This contrasts with the sharp increase in the proportion of undernourished with the calorie cut-off of 2,100 (the proportion rises from about 58% to about 64%).

Following the extant literature establishing the important role of food prices in inducing substitutions between different sources of calories, we explore with the NSS data how sensitive calorie shares are to food prices and whether a calorie threshold exists and, in case it does, whether estimates of undernourished change substantially.[32] For an assessment of relative importance of expenditure and price effects, their elasticities were computed. To avoid repetition, our comments are selective and brief. Expenditure elasticities for the poor in rural India remained stable at −0.14 over the period 1993–2004. By contrast, the elasticity (in absolute value) reduced in urban India (from over −0.20 to −0.17). Among the affluent, their (absolute) values fell more in urban India than in rural India. In both rural and urban India and in both 1993 and 2004, the (absolute) expenditure elasticities were lower for the poor.

Confining to food-price elasticities, an important finding is that although they vary between food commodities, across different subsamples, and over time, they are substantially lower (in absolute value) than expenditure elasticities, implying that expenditure has a much larger influence on calorie shares. This, of course, does not negate the effects of food prices.

The calorie thresholds obtained from Lowess are lower than those obtained from robust regressions, whereas expenditure cut-offs are considerably higher. As a result, the estimates of undernourished vary greatly. Consider, for example, the estimates for rural India. In 1993, the Lowess estimate of the undernourished is 27% of the population, whereas the robust regression estimate is 0.3%.[33] In 2004, the Lowess estimate was about three times greater than the regression estimate. Besides, although the rate of reduction with regression is negligible, it contrasts with a sharp reduction in Lowess estimates. Similarly, for urban India, the estimate of undernourished from Lowess was about twice that obtained from robust regression for 1993 and even greater for 2004.

In sum, our analysis confirms that calorie and associated income thresholds are influenced by several other factors—especially food prices—that are omitted. Since even the poor substitute in response to changes in food prices, the thresholds change. Thus, purely notional adjustments to estimate the extent of undernutrition will not do, because their bases are uncertain.

Poverty–Nutrition Trap (PNT)

An assertion by Deaton and Dreze (2009) that poverty and undernutrition are unrelated is contentious.

The efficiency-wage hypothesis postulates that, in developing countries, particularly at low levels of nutrition, workers are physically incapable of doing hard manual labor. Hence their productivity is low, which then implies that they get low wages, have low purchasing power and, therefore, low levels of nutrition, completing a vicious cycle of deprivation. These workers are unable to save very much so their assets—both physical and human—are minimal. This outcome reduces their chances of escaping the poverty–nutrition trap (PNT).[34]

Our analysis is based on a nation-wide household survey conducted by the National Council of Applied Economic Research in 1994.[35] We test for the existence of a PNT in the case of calories and four key micronutrients—carotene, iron, riboflavin, and thiamine—for three categories of wages (sowing, harvesting, and other) and for male and female workers separately.

PNT exists in one-third (i.e., 10) of the 30 cases analyzed. It exists for female harvest wage and female sowing wage for calories. In the case of carotene, male workers engaged in harvesting are subject to the PNT, whereas both male and female workers engaged in harvesting are subject to PNT in the case of iron. In the case of riboflavin female workers engaged in harvesting and sowing and male workers engaged in harvesting are subject to PNT. In the case of thiamine, female workers engaged in harvesting and sowing are subject to PNT. Since harvesting is physically more demanding than sowing, there is a higher incidence of PNT in harvesting.

This analysis shifts the focus to nutritional adequacy as a precondition for participation in labor market activities. Even if some succeed in participating, their wage earnings will not allow them to escape the poverty–nutrition trap. Indeed, a mild labor shock (e.g., associated with a crop shortfall) would worsen their plight, because the risk of loss of employment would be considerably higher. In particular, female workers are more prone to PNT than male workers, and there is a persistent gender inequality in rural India. We find that improving nutrient intakes can have significant effects on rural wages and, therefore, on the possibility of breaking PNT as well as reducing poverty.

Is Child Undernutrition Underestimated?

Since poverty is multidimensional, money-metric indicators such as minimum income or expenditure are not reliable, as these cannot adequately capture all the dimensions. Attention has, therefore, shifted to other indicators that are more closely related to basic capabilities of individuals, such as health outcomes. In fact, welfare indicators including income/expenditure, health, and education reflect a diverse pattern in India. Although most indicators have continued to improve, social progress has followed diverse patterns, ranging from accelerated progress in some fields to slowdown and even regression in others (Sen, 1985, 1999; Deaton and Dreze, 2009).

The most commonly used anthropometric measures of child malnutrition are stunting (low height for age), wasting (low weight for height) and underweight (low weight for age). Stunting is an indicator of chronic undernutrition, attributable to prolonged food deprivation, and/or disease or illness; wasting is an indicator of acute undernutrition, caused by more recent food deprivation or illness; underweight is an indicator of both acute and chronic undernutrition. Children whose measurements fall below a certain threshold of the reference population, based on recent WHO standards, are considered undernourished: stunted, wasted or underweight (WHO, 2004; WHO, 2006 a, b).

An important feature of these indicators is the overlap among them, indicating a need for a more comprehensive measure of child undernutrition. Following the important work of Svedberg (2000, 2007), and application by Nandy et al. (2005), we construct a new aggregate indicator that encompasses all undernourished children, based on IHDS (Gaiha, Jha, and Kulkarni 2010b). This is the *composite index of anthropometric failure* (CIAF). The details are given in Table 13.7.

The results point to more pervasive anthropometric failure relative to conventional indicators of being underweight, stunted, or wasted. The CIAF is about 59%.

Among the subcategories, stunting and underweight and stunting alone account for well over half of the CIAF. Children who fail in all three dimensions (simultaneously wasted, stunted, and underweight) account for a non-negligible share (13.5%).

The contrast between the poor and nonpoor children is striking. The CIAF is considerably higher among poor children than among the nonpoor. However, the number of poor children suffering from any of the anthropometric failures is considerably lower than that of nonpoor.

Thus, the CIAF and its disaggregation into subcategories of undernourished 5-year-old children reveal a grimmer story of child undernutrition than conventional anthropometric indicators do. Not only is the prevalence of undernutrition in its diverse forms higher but also simultaneous occurrence of anthropometric failures (e.g., stunting and underweight, and stunting, wasting, and underweight) varies from moderate to high. Although poor children in general are more vulnerable to these failures, it is nonpoor or (relatively) affluent children who account for significantly larger shares of total undernourished children.

Table 13.7 Subgroups of Child Undernutrition and CIAF in 2004–05

Groups	Share of under 5 children (%)
1. No Failure	41.36
2. Wasting Only	6.86
3. Wasting and Underweight	9.41
4. Wasting, Stunting and Underweight	7.92
5. Stunting and Underweight	19.80
6. Stunting Only	11.08
7. Underweight Only	3.57
CIAF (=2+3+4+5+6+7)	58.64

Source: Authors' calculations based on IHDS, 2004–05.

Our findings on determinants of CIAF yield new insights. The higher the age of the household head, the lower is the composite index. Surprisingly, there is no relationship between CIAF and caste of the household, gender of the household head, or the marital status of the household head. Maternal education reduces it, because it is linked to better child care and healthier diets. Quality of kitchen—whether it has a vent—contributes to more hygienic living conditions and thus reduces CIAF. Rural areas and metros had higher undernutrition than nonmetro urban areas. Above all, the higher the income, the lower is child undernutrition. Food prices affect child undernutrition significantly as changes in relative prices induce substitutions between food commodities and in nutrient intake. Although prices of cereals and pulses have a negative effect, those of sugar and eggs have a positive effect.

Following Svedberg (2000, 2007) and Nandy et al. (2005), our analysis with the IHDS focuses on the links between susceptibility to infectious diseases (diarrhoea, acute respiratory infection (ARI)) and CIAF but the results are mixed, as discussed later. Except for wasted and underweight, and stunted only, in all other groups the prevalence of diarrhea was higher than in the reference group of no failure. The highest prevalence rate was among those children who were *simultaneously* stunted and underweight, and those who were wasted, underweight, and stunted. These differences are statistically significant.[36]

The differences in the prevalence of ARI are less striking. The highest prevalence occurs among stunted and underweight, followed by wasted and underweight children. Somewhat surprisingly, children with the triple failure of wasting, stunting, and underweight had a lower prevalence rate than that of no failure. However, only the difference between stunted and underweight and no-failure children was statistically significant.

Thus, there is support for the disaggregated classification of undernourished children for understanding better the prevalence of infectious diseases. *Specifically, those with more than one failure were worse-off in this respect than children with no failure.* The policy implications seem clear: There is a strong case for income growth acceleration along with food price stabilization. Careful attention must be given also to the overhaul of supplementary child feeding programs such as the Integrated Child Development Services (ICDS). Another priority is awareness building for hygienic living while female literacy grows.

Affluence, Obesity, and Noncommunicable Diseases

Dietary transition involves not just a more varied and nutritionally balanced diet and higher levels of food hygiene but also consumption of energy-dense foods—high in salts, fats, and sugars— that are linked to higher prevalence of diet-related noncommunicable diseases (NCDs).[37] The excess energy from these foods may affect children and adults *within* the same household differently. Children may use up the excess energy and still remain underweight whereas adults are more likely to gain weight. Intrahousehold food-allocation biases between adults and children, on the one hand, and, between males and females, on the other, compound these effects.

Over half the disease burden (55% including injuries) in India is now attributable to NCDs, a larger share than communicable diseases and maternal- and child-health (MCH) issues. Ischemic heart disease is the leading cause of both deaths and forgone disability adjusted life years (DALYs) in working age adults (15–69 years).[38] But communicable diseases (e.g., tuberculosis, respiratory infections, and water- and vector-borne disease) are still prominent in the total population, reflecting a "double disease burden."

Although India lags behind other developing countries in the epidemiological transition—decline in infectious disease mortality compensated for increasingly by higher mortality from chronic degenerative NCDs—there is some evidence of this transition taking place. The estimated deaths from NCDs are projected to rise from 3.78 million in 1990 (40.46% of all deaths) to 7.63 million in 2020 (66.70% of all deaths).[39]

NCDs constitute a major economic burden in India, entailing high levels of out-of-pocket spending by households with members suffering from NCDs, the limited levels of insurance coverage (including subsidised public services), and the income losses that befall affected households. Associated with these costs are risks of catastrophic spending and impoverishment, and, of course, macro impacts in terms of lower GDP (Mahal, Karan, and Engelan 2009).

Analysis of the prevalence of NCDs can throw new light on the underlying causes, including socioeconomic, demographic, and locational characteristics of households. Of particular importance are the links among aging, obesity, growing affluence, expansion of the middle class, urbanization, and NCDs.[40] We present here a summary of the findings on the prevalence of overweight and obesity among the adults (older than 22 years), based on body mass index (BMI).[41]

About 9.5% of the adult males were overweight and about 2.5% were obese. The corresponding rates among adult females—12.65% and 3.18%, respectively—were higher. Although overweight and obesity are largely a core urban phenomenon—about 22% of the urban adults were overweight and about 7% were obese—these disorders are observed in urban slums and rural areas too. Specifically, the proportion of overweight in urban slums (about 15%) was lower but not markedly so. In the rural areas, however, the proportion of overweight (above 9%) was a little less than half that in the urban areas, and that of obese (about 2%) was just over one-fourth of the figure in urban areas. Overweight and obesity are not confined to relatively affluent households. Although lower among the poor, their proportions are non-negligible. Our analysis shows that, among the nonpoor, the proportions of overweight and obese were about 14% and just under 4%, respectively. Among the poor, the shares were 7% and about 1.25%, respectively.

Disaggregation of the overweight and the obese by caste and tribe further suggests that even socially and economically deprived sections are not immune to such disorders. Among the Scheduled Castes, the proportions of overweight and obese were about

9% and a little less than 2%, respectively; among the Scheduled Tribes, the proportions were slightly lower—about 6% and above 1%, respectively; among the Other Backward Castes (OBCs), the corresponding estimates were above 12% and about 3%, respectively; and among the remaining, the estimates were the highest—above 17% and about 5%, respectively. Finally, there was a sharp increase in the proportions of the overweight and obese over the period from 1998 to 2005. The proportion of the overweight more than tripled, whereas that of the obese rose at least six times.

Let us briefly consider the *subset* of households that contain *both* underweight children (< age 5) and obese adults—or the double burden of malnutrition. Although their share was low—about 3.3% in the aggregate sample—it varied slightly between the poor and nonpoor (2.35% and 3.75%, respectively). In a more disaggregated monthly per capita expenditure classification (<Rs 300, Rs 300–500, Rs 500–1000, and >Rs 1000), there was, however, a clear progression, with the obesity rate rising from 2.85% to 6.5%. In the urban areas and urban slums, the rate (about 4.86%) was almost twice as high as in the rural areas (2.75%).

As a recent article in *The Economist* (2012) observes, India has an obesity epidemic in cities, as people eat more processed food and adopt more sedentary lifestyles. And with obesity, the risk of NCDs (diabetes and heart diseases) rises. Our findings on the correlates of NCDs are summarized next.

In all four cases—prevalence of high blood pressure, heart disease, diabetes, and cancer—the majority suffering from these diseases were in the older age group (i.e., above 45 years). Among those reported to be suffering from high BP and heart diseases, the majority were females. In the case of diabetes and cancer, the majority were males. A vast majority of those suffering from high blood pressure (90%), heart diseases (90%), diabetes (93%) and cancer (83%) were nonpoor. What further corroborates the role of affluence is that, in the more detailed expenditure classification, the proportion suffering from NCDs rises with expenditure interval. For example, the proportion of those suffering from high blood pressure rises from 11% in the lowest expenditure interval (<Rs 300 per capita per month) to over 36% in the highest interval (>Rs 1000 per capita per month). In the case of heart disease, the prevalence rate was considerably higher in the highest expenditure interval (over four times that in the lowest). Although a majority of those suffering from high blood pressure (39%) were in urban areas, a majority of those suffering from heart diseases (51%), diabetes (54%), and cancer (75%) were in rural areas. About 43% of the obese reported to be suffering from high BP. The corresponding numbers for heart disease and diabetes are 13% and 25%, respectively.

Our econometric analysis focuses on determinants of *average* prevalence of NCDs (i.e., number of household members suffering from high blood pressure or heart disease or diabetes or cancer/household size). The highest elasticity is associated with age; the next highest with respect to per capita expenditure; and much lower is the elasticity with respect to overweight/obese adults[42]; metros display slightly higher prevalence, compared to the remaining urban areas.

One obvious policy imperative is to avert the specter of growing disabilities and deaths due to NCDs, through awareness building of healthy food choices and physically active lifestyles.[43]

State Responses to Nutritional Deprivation

With spiraling food-price inflation and sluggish employment growth in both rural and urban areas, the specter of hunger and nutritional deprivation looms large for millions of households.

The government of India redesigned the Public Distribution System (PDS) in 1997 in the form of a new Targeted Public Distribution System (TPDS), aimed to reduce subsidies to the nonpoor and enhance those to the poor. Its salient features are summarized in the following list, based on Bhalotra (2004), Kochar (2005), Svedberg (2010), Jha and Ramaswami (2010), and Planning Commission (2008).

1. It distinguishes between households that fall below the poverty line (BPL households) and those above the official state-specific poverty lines (APL).
2. Food grains are purchased by the central government, through the Food Corporation of India (FCI), at predetermined minimum support prices (MSP). The government also determines a uniform central issue price at which food grains are sold by FCI to state governments for distribution through the PDS.
3. The TPDS initially fixed the BPL household entitlements at 10 kg of food grains per month and gradually raised them to 35 kg. Since 2000–2001, BPL households are entitled to purchase rice from fair-price shops (FPS) for Rs 5.65 per kg and wheat for Rs 4.15.
4. APL allocations varied across states and were calculated as the difference between the state's allocation of food grains and BPL allotments.
5. As market prices rose more than subsidized prices, there were substantial increases in BPL subsidies.
6. As of 2002, a new TPDS window was opened, the *Antyodaya Anna Yojana* (AAY), under which the poorest of the poor are given the option to buy food at even more subsidized prices. The prices for AAY households are Rs 3 per kg of rice and Rs 2 per kg of wheat, respectively (Svedberg, 2010).

(a) Real Income Transfers

The intent and normative underpinnings of public food distribution to the poor are clear; but what are the effects on the ground? By far the most comprehensive analysis is Svedberg (2010). His findings are summarized next.

Although the BPL and AAY cardholders are allowed to buy 35 kg of subsidized grains per month, the actual purchase is just 14.7 kg in rural areas and 17.4 kg in urban areas. According to the NSSO 2004–2005 survey, only 37.6% of the rural households below the poverty line have BPL cards; the corresponding figure is 25.7% for urban areas.

The reasons include long distances to a fair-price shop, irregular availability of grains in these shops, participants not being allowed to buy grains in small installments, low quality of grains offered, and small difference between TPDS and market prices. As a result, the actual subsidy received by the poor is extremely low—less than Rs 4 per person. The income boosts are 1.4% in rural areas and 0.9% in urban areas.

The poverty impacts were also low. Confining to the income gap measure, based on the NSS data for 2004–2005, the estimated gap was 20.2% in both rural and urban areas, implying that the monthly per capita expenditure (MPCE) for the average poor household fell short of the poverty line by 20.2%. The reduction in income gap is about 1% as a result of the TPDS subsidy.

The extent of leakages is substantial. More than one-third (36.7%) of the subsidized grain intended for poor households ends up as sales to nonpoor households. About 10% of all grains are spoiled during storage and transportation. The Planning Commission (2008) reports that 58% of the subsidized food grains do not reach BPL families because of identification errors, nontransparent operations, and unethical practices in the implementation of TDPS. Add to it the high cost of handling food grains, and the government ends up spending Rs 8.5 to transfer one rupee to the poor.

Khera (2011) offers a detailed analysis of profitability of FPS, forms of corruption at different stages and diversion of PDS supplies to open markets. Although restricted to a sample of 388 households in 8 villages in Rajasthan in 2002–2003, many of the findings are new and insightful, whereas some corroborate the findings of others. The important contribution of this study is to highlight low profitability of FPS, corruption at different levels, and extent of diversion of PDS supplies to open markets.

Estimates of diversion of PDS supplies, based on comparison of off-take data from the Ministry of Food and Consumer Affairs, Government of India, and consumption data from NSS (round 61), are alarmingly high. Taking these estimates at face value, two-fifths of the official PDS off-take was diverted. Less than one-fifth of rice was diverted compared with more than two-thirds of wheat. There is also a clear north–south divide in these diversions. In mainly rice-eating southern states, the proportion of food grains diverted ranged from 11–48%. Wheat eating states concentrated in the north had diversions ranging from 43–88% (Khera, 2011).

Wheat diversions for FPS are very profitable. The shopkeeper gets a paltry margin of 7 *paise* per kg of wheat sold to a BPL household, as compared with a margin of Rs 1.97 for selling this amount in the open market and a much higher margin of Rs 4.50 per kg of *Antyodaya* wheat. An honest FPS earns no more than Rs 100 per month, whereas, on certain assumptions of amounts diverted, the profit is Rs 7972 (net of transportation costs). Hence, the incentive to cheat is irresistible.

Corruption is rampant in obtaining a license; commissions are paid to FCI officials for expediting supplies; and amounts supplied are frequently lower than recorded. BPL consumers are often turned away on grounds of inadequate supplies, quality sold is abysmal, and buying quotas in installments is discouraged. Under TPDS, low margins are compounded by shrinkage of sales volume.

Real income transfers (RIT) through the TPDS in three Indian states (Andhra Pradesh, Maharashtra, and Rajasthan), based on primary data collected by the authors, and building on extant literature provides underscores this rather discouraging assessment (Jha et al. 2013).[44] Table 13.8 provides definitions of acute poverty, moderate poverty, moderate nonpoverty and affluence for the three states.

The mean RIT among participating households per month from wheat is the highest in Rajasthan (Rs 93) and lowest in Maharashtra (Rs 60). In Rajasthan, RIT from TPDS for wheat to half of the participating households is Rs 100 or less (in fact, about 48% of the households have no real income transfer from TPDS), about 28% have between Rs 100 Rs 200, and 19% have more than Rs 200. By contrast, in Maharashtra, about 34% of the households had no real-income transfer, and about 20% had real-income transfers of greater than Rs 100—around $2 in 2013 exchange rates.

As an explicitly propoor food policy, the targeted food-distribution system had indifferent results. For wheat, the mean RIT among the acutely poor households (Rs 56) is lower than that among moderately poor (Rs 121) and nonpoor (Rs 71 for moderately nonpoor and Rs 128 for the relatively affluent) in Rajasthan; and, in Maharashtra, the RIT among the acutely poor (Rs 65) is slightly higher than those among other categories (Rs 55 among moderately poor and Rs 58 among moderately nonpoor).[45]

Table 13.8 Definitions of Different Levels of Poverty

Levels of poverty	Rajasthan	Andhra Pradesh	Maharashtra
Acute poverty	If per capita monthly consumption expenditure <Rs.383	If per capita monthly consumption expenditure <Rs.299	If per capita monthly consumption expenditure < Rs 371
Moderate poverty	If per capita monthly consumption expenditure >=383 but < Rs.450	If per capita monthly consumption expenditure >=Rs.299 but <Rs.352	If per capita monthly consumption expenditure >=Rs.371 but <Rs.436
Moderate Nonpoverty	If per capita monthly consumption expenditure >=Rs.450 but < Rs.585	If per capita monthly consumption expenditure >=Rs.352 but < Rs.458	If per capita monthly consumption expenditure >=Rs. 436 but <Rs.567
Affluent	If per capita monthly consumption expenditure >= Rs.585	If per capita monthly consumption expenditure >=Rs.458	If per capita monthly consumption expenditure >=Rs.567

Turning to RIT from TPDS rice consumption, we observe that mean RIT for participating households is highest in Andhra Pradesh (Rs 142), followed by Maharashtra (Rs 54), and then Rajasthan (Rs 25). In Rajasthan, about 63% of the participating households have no RIT, and about 32% have mean RIT of Rs 100 or less. In Andhra Pradesh, about 80% of participating households got mean RIT of more than Rs 100. In Maharashtra, only 16% households obtained mean RIT of more than Rs 100 from rice consumption; 33% obtained no real-income transfer and 50% had real-income transfers less than Rs 100.

Our analysis points to several factors determining real-income transfers through subsidized wheat and rice, and variation in these transfers across the three states. Land as a proximate indicator of economic status has mixed effects varying by commodity and state. Specifically, among households with owned land, real-income transfers are lower for rice in Andhra Pradesh, and higher for wheat and rice in Maharashtra, and for wheat in Rajasthan, suggesting that those better endowed benefited more in some cases. Inequality in land distribution takes different forms (concentrations of landless and near landless or of the well-endowed) and influences real incomes in complex ways (leakages and larger supply or just leakages). As a result, the effects vary by commodity and state (negative for rice in Andhra Pradesh, positive for wheat in Rajasthan, and rice in Maharashtra). The extent of price subsidy, in most cases, results in larger real income transfers. There is some evidence of transaction cost (e.g., distance to FPS) limiting income gains (wheat in Rajasthan and Maharashtra). There is overwhelming support for supply inadequacy limiting income gains, given proximate indicators.

(b) Nutritional Deprivation

In November 2005, the Indian government embarked on an ambitious workfare scheme, the National Rural Employment Guarantee Scheme (NREGS), which guarantees a hundred days of employment in unskilled manual labor at a minimum wage to every rural household each year.[46] Some of its features include a time-bound employment guarantee and wage payment within 15 days (otherwise the government is penalized), prohibition of the use of contractors and machinery (to enhance direct benefits of the program to the participants), a 60:40 wage and materials cost ratio, and a mandatory 33% participation for women. The scheme devolves considerable powers in planning and allocating resources to the local village councils (*panchayats*) and through social audits allows the community to monitor the progress.[47]

Do real income transfers through TPDS and NREGS mitigate undernutrition? Our analysis using IHDS[48] produces some relevant findings. NREG and TPDS significantly increase the intake of protein, carbohydrates, calories, phosphorous, iron, thiamine, and niacin in Andhra Pradesh, Maharashtra, and Rajasthan. In Andhra Pradesh, in most cases, TPDS had a larger effect than NREG. By contrast, in Maharashtra, NREG had larger effects in most cases. Rajasthan presents a more complex picture. For some nutrients (e.g., calories, iron and niacin) TPDS has larger effects than NREG, whereas for others (e.g., protein, riboflavin) the latter has larger effects. So a general inference about the greater effectiveness of TPDS or NREG is ruled out. Further, the effects of NREG wages on nutrient intake in many cases (e.g., protein, calories, niacin) are larger than those of non-NREG income. An implication of these findings is, however, worth emphasizing. Cash transfers touted to avoid administrative costs and corruption involved in NREG and TPDS are likely to be much less effective if the objective is to enable large segments of the rural population to break out of NPT.[49]

Does a Right to Food Matter?

Prior to the 2009 general elections, the Indian National Congress promised 25 kg of foodgrains per month, at Rs 3 per kg, to every poor family in India (Khera, 2010). The proposed National Food Security Bill (NFSB) seeks to deliver on this promise.

There are strong advocates of a Right to Food (RTF) Act, given pervasive hunger and child malnutrition. Besides, there are legal compulsions. Article 21 (the fundamental "right to life") of the Indian Constitution encompasses the right to food, whereas Article 47 of the Directive Principles directs the state to "regard the raising of the level of nutrition and the standard of living of its people... as among its primary duties." Finally, the Supreme Court has issued several orders on fulfilment of food entitlements (Khera, 2010).

We offer a perspective on the RTF that differs from the vast literature that has emerged around it in recent years.[50]

The RTF, as an enforceable claim to a minimum quantity of food of a certain quality, carries with it correlated duties, particularly of the state.[51] These include the duty to avoid loss of the means of subsistence, and to provide for the subsistence of those unable to provide for their own (Shue, 1980). Much, of course, will depend on the specific form of the right to food, the corresponding duties/obligations, and the implementation mechanisms. In practical terms, RTF translates into food entitlements, that is, enforceable claims on the delivery of food. These entitlements could be based on trade, production and employment.

Since RTF does not involve state provision of food except under special circumstances of failures of duties to avoid and protect against emergencies, in an important sense it could be viewed as a right to policies (or, as "a right to a right") that enables individuals to produce or acquire minimum food requirements (Osmani, 1999). This may yield useful insights into whether nonfulfilment of the right to food is due to insufficiency of public resources or due to policies followed or both.

Recent debates on the National Food Security Bill (NFSB/NFSA) have concentrated on a rigid interpretation of the RTF as being confined mostly to state provision of food.[52] A selective summary of that debate is given below to identify analytical and policy issues addressed by this chapter.[53]

The National Advisory Council (NAC) proposed subsidized food grains to 75% of the total population of the country covering 90% of the rural and 50% of the urban population.[54] These groups are subdivided into (a) a "priority" group (BPL), comprising 46% of the rural and 28% of the urban population, to get 7 kg of food grains per person at Re 1 per kg for millets, Rs 2 per kg for wheat and Rs 3 per kg for rice. (b) The second group is "general" (APL), covering 44% of the rural and 22% of the urban population, with an entitlement of 4 kg per person at 50% of the minimum support price.

There is significant controversy around such proposals. Himanshu and Sen (2011) insist that a universal PDS is the only option consistent with RTF and, more contentiously, that feasible alternatives that are more universal and less targeted are more likely to be effective in benefiting the poor.[55] Second, between 1993–1994 (a universal PDS) and 2004–2005 (TPDS), the leakages grew enormously—that of rice from 19% to 40%, and that of wheat from 41% to 73%. Per capita per month, consumption of PDS rice and wheat remained unchanged although PDS off-take doubled and subsidy rose even more. There was, however, a slight improvement in access by the poorest 50% of the population—from 28% to 30%. But this must be judged a colossal failure, given the massive cost of leakages. A recent analysis (Svedberg, 2010) shows that the cost of transferring Re 1 to the poor is Rs 8.5. A considerable chunk of budgeted food subsidies (81% in 2008–2009) goes to the Food Corporation of India (FCI) to cover its expenses for procurement, transportation, distribution, and for carrying over huge stocks. The high costs reflect inclusion errors, as well as corruption and leakages of grains at all stages in the supply chain (Svedberg, 2010).

Cost and leakage are major issues in this debate. Himanshu and Sen (2011) are emphatic that the more universal the food subsidy—as in Tamil Nadu, among a few other states—the lower would be the leakage. Two issues are conflated in this proposition: one is the huge diversion of PDS food grains to the market, and the second is losses during storage in open *go-downs*. Whether a universal subsidy would reduce leakages to the market has little to do with how universal the food subsidy is and more to do with the wedge between the market price and PDS price. If procurements are higher, market price is likely to rise relative to the PDS price, and the market diversions would be larger. Our analysis corroborates this. As far as wastage is concerned, with larger procurements and given storage facilities, wastage is also likely to be larger under a universal scheme. Fourth, only a fraction of entitlements is bought by BPL households, thus limiting real income subsidy to them. Only 30% of total TPDS purchases of subsidized food grains (rice and wheat) are made by poor households with AAY or BPL ration cards.[56] Almost two-thirds of the poor (62.4%), however, do not possess these cards, limiting their purchases to miniscule amounts. Add to this difficulty high transaction costs (long distances to FPS and waiting periods) and perceptions of poor quality and underweighing, to get a clearer picture of why the poor, on average, tend to buy amounts considerably lower than their entitlements. As a result, the food subsidy per person among BPL households is abysmally low in both rural and urban areas (Svedberg, 2010). So even with existing budget outlays there is considerable scope for better targeting the poor.[57]

One alternative is to think of integration of development, poverty, and food subsidies as these interact. If, for example, a revamped PDS on a much smaller scale were to be combined with more sensible policies that aim to augment low productivity in agriculture, avoid market imperfections that come in the way of remunerative farm gate food prices, and expand livelihood options, fulfillment of food entitlements could be far less costly. In fact, an analysis of round 61 of the NSS yields two useful insights: The higher the agricultural wage rate, the lower is the demand for rural public works; and the lower the food price, the lower is the demand for subsidised food (Gaiha et al., 2009). A crucial requirement is a clear enunciation of time-bound objectives and a coherent policy framework. Although not specific to the right to food, what really matters is the effective use of resources in enforcement. As experience accumulates—both juridical and policy related—these costs may decline substantially (Gaiha, 2003).

Finally, Himanshu and Sen (2011) are dismissive of the macroconstraints of food availability and fiscal food subsidy under the universal scheme, emphasized by the Rangarajan Committee (RC). Their alternative requirements, based on the assumptions that 60% of the households access the full 7 kg per person per month under the universal scheme, are 60 million tons. If the off-take is lower, about 4–5 kg per person per month, the total requirements are about 43 million tons, as compared with the actual TPDS off-take of 42.4 million tons and the RC's projected off-take of 41.9 million tons if PDS entitlements are restricted to only 40% of the population. On the face of it, the Himanshu–Sen endorsement seems persuasive, except that it does not guarantee that the benefit to the poor would be substantially greater. In any case, the food subsidy (estimated to be Rs 560 billion in 2009–2010 or about 1% of GDP and 3.3% of government expenditure) arguably diverts resources from more productive use.[58] The long and short of it is that the TPDS cries out for reforms without which more ambitious interventions are just as likely to fail.

Hence, contrary to the assertions that "right to food" is both "undefinable" and "undeliverable," we find that the right is evolving slowly into an enforceable right. Its potential for enabling governments to do what they should by providing a strong foundation for their poverty alleviation programs and policies, and for sharpening the focus of civil society organizations as active agents in such programs is substantial. Although realization of this right is likely to be slow, difficult, and uncertain, and not synonymous with a universal food subsidy, it would be a mistake to discard it on the ground that "too many rights may well make a wrong" (*The Economist*, 2001, p. 20).

Concluding Observations

This chapter focused on dietary changes, their nutritional implications, and policy responses to alleviate nutritional deprivation in a rapidly changing economy that retains a high degree of poverty. India provides a valuable laboratory for examining complicated relationships too often oversimplified in discussions of food and food security. There is a rich database with great variation over time and space, and vigorous debate in civil society and the political system over best practices in alleviating malnutrition.

One important insight is that dietary diversification reduces calorie intake. Downward shifts in the calorie and protein intakes over the period 1993–2004 in India were associated with *both* food prices and near stagnant expenditure/income in rural India *and* simultaneous changes in diets. There is then room for compatibility between a view of caloric intake exclusively focused on demand, and one allowing for lower calorie "requirements" due to less strenuous activity patterns, life-style changes and improvements in the epidemiological environment. Dietary changes are associated with food prices, their time-varying effects, income/expenditure changes, rural–urban location, household characteristics, and environmental changes reflected in life-style and activity patterns. Although some of these changes (for example, urbanization and growing prosperity) in both rural and urban areas are *irreversible*, a policy insight from the analysis in this chapter is that prices and income also shape dietary patterns in important ways. Recent evidence on eating out, for example, shows it to be more pervasive than a middle-class urban phenomenon. More people in metropolitan areas eat out and spend larger amounts, as do the relatively affluent. But others—especially the socially disadvantaged—are also prone to eating out and spending moderate amounts.

The most important food questions concerns those at greatest risk of insufficiency. Undernutrition has serious welfare implications, not just in the present but also in the longer-term. The poverty-nutrition trap (PNT), for example, is a vicious circle in which at low levels of nutrition, productivity is low, wages are low, purchasing power is low and, consequently, there is low nutrition. This chapter introduced a new measure of child undernutrition, more comprehensive than conventional ones, that indicated much higher levels of undernutrition (6 out of 10 are undernourished) and higher risks of infectious diseases. The double burden of undernutrition and obesity exacerbates the gravity of malnutrition. Aging is a *key* factor in the growing burden of NCDs. Affluence also has a significant role through life-style changes and dietary composition. Because the share of NCDs in the disease burden is likely to rise and will increase demand on the health-care system and highly scarce resources of those least likely to afford the costs of health care, cost-effective interventions that address tobacco use, alcohol abuse, consumption of unhealthful fats, and excessive salt intake are well understood but need careful implementation.

Though noncommunicable diseases represent a major societal problem induced by malnutrition, policy imperatives are more readily recognized in cases in which individuals face deprivation from structural pressures rather than choice. A range of interventions to lessen the vulnerability of those who cannot easily choose their diets for want of resources is on the global agenda. This chapter has analyzed two poles of intervention: public works in the form of an employment guarantee (NREGA) and Targeted Public Distribution System (TDPS) of food. A choice between these mechanisms is difficult because their effects varied across states and by nutrient in our analysis. Any general inference about the greater effectiveness of TPDS or NREG is ruled out. More importantly, the question is not really one of larger allocations to the TPDS and NREG, but how to make sure that the transfers intended for the poor reach them. Because current debates on food security have veered toward a right to food as a major policy initiative, this chapter offers a new perspective: The food adequacy imperative should be articulated as a right to policies (or, as a right to a right) designed to ensure fulfillment of food entitlements. Whether it will make a difference to the lives of the poor will depend largely on how it is conceptualized and implemented.

APPENDIX A: ENGEL CURVES

Calories

DD drew attention to the downward shift in the calorie Engel curve over the period 1983–2004. We find that, for the period 1993–2004, the calorie Engel curves for rural India (Figure A1) display a downward shift—especially above extremely low levels of monthly per capita expenditure (MPCE) at 2004 prices. The proportionate reduction in calorie intake is much higher at higher MPCE.

The calorie Engel curve in urban India for 2004 lies above that of 1993 at lower levels of MPCE (Figure A2). At MPCE >Rs 500, calorie intake was higher in 1993 than in 2004. Thus, there is evidence of a downward shift of the calorie Engel curve in both rural and urban India, especially at higher levels of MPCE.

Protein

Figures A3 and A4 show protein Engel curves for rural and urban India during the period 1993–2004. The rural–urban contrast in protein intake is striking. In the rural areas, protein intake was consistently lower across expenditure classes in 2004 than in 1993. The gap between 1993 and 2004 intakes widens considerably at higher MPCE. In urban areas, the 2004 curve was above the 1993 curve at low levels of MPCE and, after the cross-over expenditure of about Rs 500, the former lies below the 1993 curve.

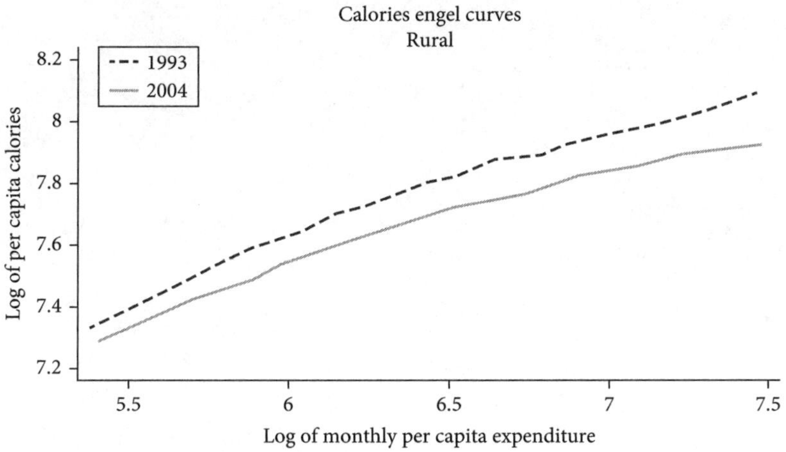

FIGURE A1 Calorie Engel Curves, Rural India, 1993–2004

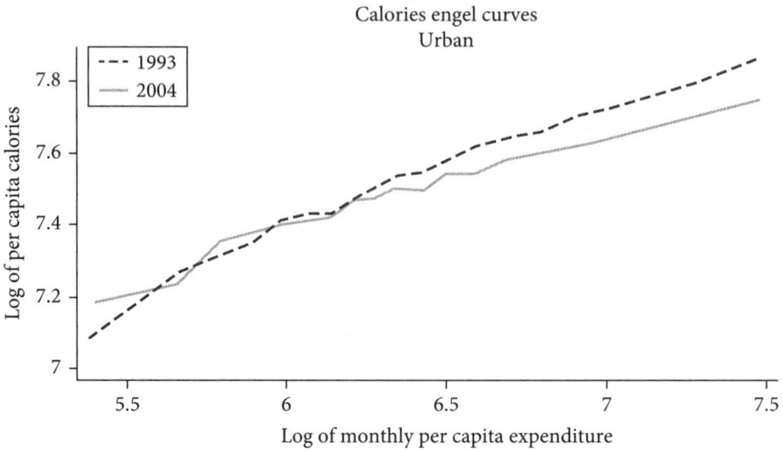

FIGURE A2 Calorie Engel Curves, Urban India, 1993–2004

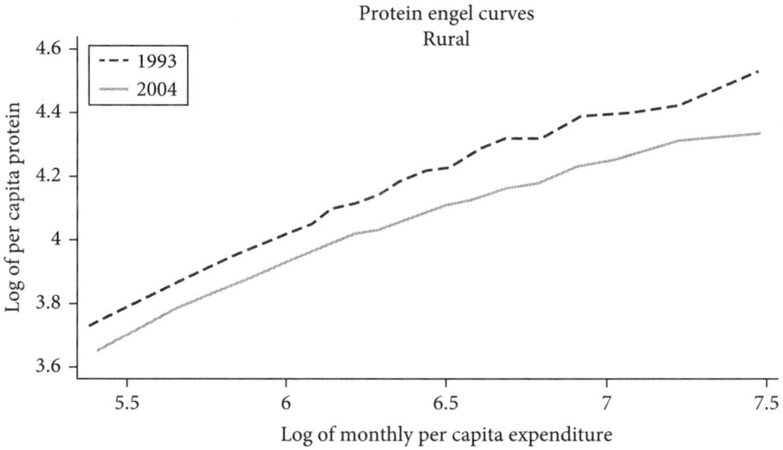

FIGURE A3 Protein Engel Curves, Rural India, 1993–2004

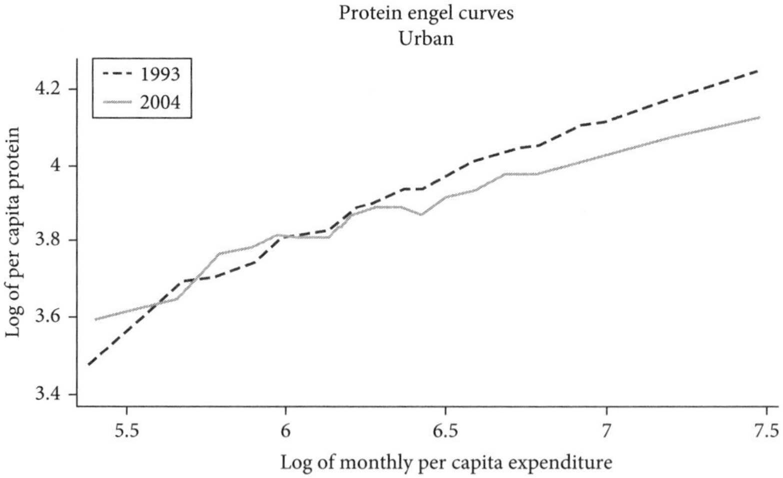

FIGURE A4 Protein Engel Curves, Urban India, 1993–2004

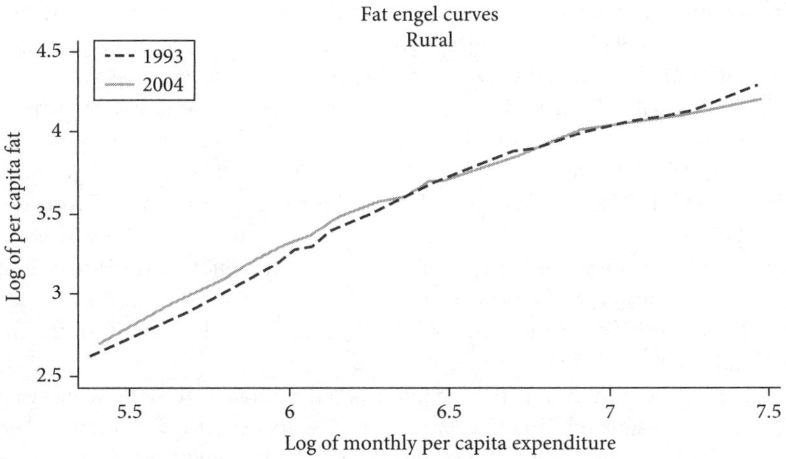

FIGURE A5 Fats Engel Curves, Rural India, 1993–2004

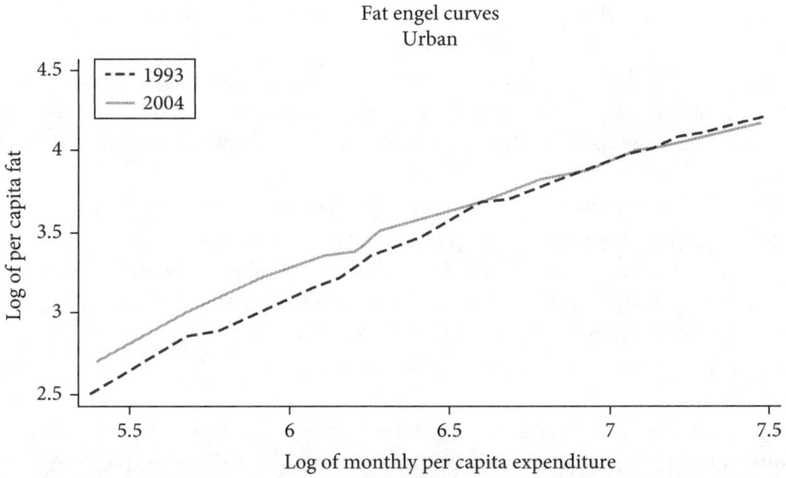

FIGURE A6 Fats Engel Curves, Urban India, 1993–2004

Fats

In rural areas, the fats Engel curves for 1993 lies below that for 2004 at lower levels of MPCE (Figure A5). The crossover is at approximately Rs650. In urban areas, the crossover is at Rs1000 (Figure A6). The curves converge beyond this.

NOTES

1. Much of the research summarized here was conducted by the first author during his stay at the Department of Urban Studies, MIT, and subsequently at Harvard School of Public Health, in close collaboration with the co-authors. He would like to thank Bish Sanyal,

David Bloom, and Peter Timmer for their support, encouragement, and advice. We are grateful to Anil Deolalikar for valuable advice throughout this study, and to P. Svedberg, L. Haddad, and Kenneth Hill for useful discussions. Sonal Desai was most helpful in acquainting us with the use of the India Human Development Survey, which she had designed and conducted jointly with the National Council of Applied Economic Research. Raj Bhatia carried out the statistical analysis with great efficiency. Last but not the least, we are grateful to Ron Herring for his meticulous suggestions. Any errors are our sole responsibility.

2. We follow a more disaggregated classification of vegetables in our analysis with NSS household data for 1993 and 2004.
3. FAO follows a classification different from that used by us. For details of the former, see Pingali and Khwaja (2004).
4. As observed by Popkin, Adair, and Ng (2012), on the global level, new access to technologies (e.g., cheap edible oils, foods with excessive "empty calories," modern supermarkets, and food distribution and marketing), and. the regulatory environments (the World Trade Organization and freer flow of goods, services, and technologies) are changing diets.
5. This curve denotes a relationship between calorie intake and income proxied by expenditure.
6. Srinivasan (1992) is deeply sceptical of such requirements on the ground that energy expenditure adjusts to intake within a range.
7. Although calorie deprivation is an aspect of undernutrition, we sometimes use them interchangeably for expositional convenience, as also undernutrition and malnutrition.
8. For details, see Gopalan (1992), Gopalan, Sastri, and Balasubramanian (1971), and ICMR (1990).
9. Gopalan et al. (1971) observe: "The quantity of fat that should be included in a well balanced diet is not known with any degree of certainty. However, it appears desirable in the present state of knowledge that the daily intake of fat should be such that it contributes no more than 15 to 20% of the calories in the diet. A total of about 40 to 60 gms of fat can therefore be safely consumed daily, and in order to obtain the necessary amounts of essential fatty acids, the fat intake should include at least 15 gms of vegetable oils" (p. 8). Also see ICMR (1990).
10. For a rich and insightful analysis of dietary changes in India—specifically, the higher fat consumption by the bottom six per capita expenditure deciles over the period 1993–2004—see Deolalikar (2010).
11. Often, some of these commodity groups are referred to by their main components (e.g., pulses, milk).
12. A reduced form demand relation (Gaiha, Jha, and Kulkarni 2010 a, 2012) is used in which the dependent variable is consumption of a food commodity, and the right side/explanatory variables include own and other food prices, income, household characteristics, and the general environment. We have pooled the rural and urban samples and over time (1993 and 2004). To avoid cluttering the text, our remarks are confined to own price effects and income. For details, see Kaicker and Gaiha (2012).
13. Price elasticity of demand refers to proportionate change in quantity demanded divided by proportionate change in price.
14. This builds on Kulkarni and Gaiha (2010), and Nidhi Kaicker et al. (2011).
15. The FDI is calculated as the sum of the squares of the shares of various food commodities in the food consumption basket or food expenditure. This is akin to the Herfindahl index which is used to measure the competitiveness of an industry. In particular, given the 0–100

range for this index, a high value implies a monopolistic industry (or, in our case, a more concentrated diet) and a low value implies a nearly perfectly competitive industry (or, a more diversified diet).

16. An instrumental variable (IV) robust regression is used.
17. As the middle class is an instrument in the first stage IV regression, it is not used in the second stage.
18. For further confirmation of dietary diversification reducing calorie intake over the period 1993–2009, see Gaiha, Kaicker, Imai, and Thapa (2013).
19. For details, see Gaiha, Kaicker, Imai, Kulkarni, et al. (2013).
20. We use Rs 300 monthly per capita expenditure as the cut-off point.
21. We use a Heckman model in which two steps are involved: first, the probability of eating out is determined and then, conditional on it, the amounts spent on eating out. For details, see Gaiha, Jha and Kulkarni, et al. (2013).
22. The analysis is based on unit record data collected for the 50th and 61st rounds of the NSS (corresponding to the years 1993–1994 and 2004–2005, respectively). Price effects capture both own and cross-price effects through substitutions between food commodities. Briefly, as prices change, demands for commodities change and consequently calorie (and other nutrients') intakes. Underlying this is a presumption that food choices are informed by their nutritional content. As Deaton and Dreze (2009) emphasize, people do not buy calories and other nutrients but food commodities. However, if food choices are informed by their nutritional values, it is meaningful to talk about demands for calories and other nutrients
23. For details, see Gaiha et al. (2012).
24. Comparisons of effects of different variables are based on (absolute) elasticities.
25. Note that a significant effect is one that is statistically different from 0.
26. Note that this is a residual time effect. What the graphical representations reflect is the combined effect of all factors that varied over time whereas the regressions results relate to the residual time effect.
27. This is not inconsistent with the segments of the protein Engel curve for 2004 lying above that for 1993 in figure: 13.3.
28. This is not inconsistent with segments of the fat Engel curve lying above those of the 1993 curve.
29. Our explanation is corroborated (with varying food price and expenditure effects) over the longer period, 1993–2009 (Gaiha, Kaicker, Imai, and Thapa (2013).
30. For example, there is lack of a consensus on what the correct minimum calorie threshold is, how it should be computed or even whether such a threshold exists (Dasgupta, 1993, Srinivasan, 1992, 1994, and Svedberg, 2000). On the related issue of a taste for variety, see Behrman and Deolalikar (1989).
31. Briefly, Lowess is used for locally weighted scatter plot smoothing. For an intuitive exposition, see Deaton (1995).
32. For details, see Kaicker and Gaiha (2012).
33. Recall that Lowess estimates allow for calorie share variation due to expenditure variation alone, while our robust regression estimates include the additional effects of food prices.
34. See Dasgupta and Ray (1986, 1987). Srinivasan (1994) offers a cogent critique.
35. For details of the survey and methodology for estimating PNT, see Jha, Gaiha, and Sharma (2009).
36. This is confirmed by a t-test of mean differences.
37. Noncommunicable diseases include cardio-vascular diseases (CVD), cancers, diabetes, chronic obstructive pulmonary disease (COPD), asthma, neuro-psychiatric conditions

(e.g., mental disorders), eye conditions, skin diseases, diseases of the digestive system and genitourinary conditions (prostate disorders), among others (Mahal et al. 2009).

38. Age-standardized undiscounted DALYs have been widely used to measure the burden of disease. These measure the number of years a person would lose due to disability and premature mortality. An advantage of using DALYs is that it considers years with disability and thus includes conditions that, although not fatal, can be a large social and economic burden (World Bank, 2011).
39. For details, see Popkin et al. (2012).
40. For details, see Gaiha, Jha, and Kulkarni (2010c).
41. BMI= (weight in kg/height in metres^2). Those with BMI in the range 25–30 kg/m^2 are classified as overweight, whereas those exceeding 30 are classified as obese. An expert consultation organized by WHO in 2002 concluded that current WHO cut-off points do not provide an adequate basis for taking action on risks related to overweight and obesity in many Asian populations.
42. The relatively small effect of overweight/obesity should not be accepted at face value as it is vitiated by selective reporting of BMI by adults.
43. On the latter, see Ruhm (2012) and Lee et al. (2012).
44. Real income transfer is measured as the difference between market and TPDS prices multiplied by the amount bought. For details, see Jha et al. (2013).
45. For definitions of acute and moderately poor, and moderately non-poor and relatively affluent, see Table 13.A.1 at the end of this chapter.
46. Renamed recently as Mahatama Gandhi National Rural Employment Guarantee Scheme (MNREGS).
47. For a recent assessment, see Shankar and Gaiha (2013).
48. These are obtained by estimating an equation in which the dependent variable is nutrient intake (including micronutrients) and the explanatory variables comprise TPDS participation and NREG wage, nonwage income (all three appropriately instrumented) and other household characteristics. To compare the effect of a change in TPDS participation with that of a change in NREG wage on nutrient intake, we use one standard deviation increase in these variables. For details, see Jha, Bhattacharya, and Gaiha (2011).
49. The presumption that Unique Identification *or Aadhar will* help target these transfers better is not just naïve but mistaken (Khera, 2013).
50. This draws upon Gaiha (2003) and our more recent research on related issues. See also, Kotwal and Ramaswami, this volume.
51. For an elaboration, see Gaiha (2003).
52. National Food Security Act implies ratification of NFSB by parliament. As the debate continues unabated and the Bill's passage without major modifications is not unlikely, we prefer NFSB to NFSA. For amendments proposed to NFSB, see Lok Sabha Secretariat (2013), and for a comment on these amendments, see Dreze (2013).
53. This summary relies largely on Himanshu and Sen (2011) but the critique draws on our own research.
54. There are three different versions of the NFSB: one by the National Advisory Council (NAC); another by the Department of Food and Public Distribution; and the third by the Prime Minister's Advisory Council headed by C. Rangarajan (RC). For details, see Kumar and Ghosh (2012).
55. See Kochar (2005) who argues in favor of a universal food subsidy on the ground that under TPDS targeting of BPL has suffered as amounts bought are a lower fraction of their

entitlements simply because Fair Price Shops (FPS) are forced to carry lower stocks, as the number of customers is lower than under the universal PDS.

56. Under the AAY scheme, the poorest of the poor are given the option to buy food at even more subsidized prices than BPL households.
57. The case for cash transfers as an alternative to a universal food subsidy is not persuasive, as it does not confront the difficulties of identifying the poor and risks of collusion among functionaries at different levels. A case in point is Svedberg (2010).
58. A recent estimate of the cost of the NFSB by Kumar and Ghosh (2012) in the first three years, taking into account the costs of covering BPL and APL households in rural and urban areas, storage costs for the additional food procurement, leakages, provision of free nutritious meals during pregnancy and six months thereafter and an additional maternity benefit of Rs 1000 per month, nutritional food to children—especially the malnourished and midday meals to those in lower and upper classes—and transportation costs to FPS works out to be a staggering Rs 500,000 crore.

References

Behrman, J., and A. Deolalikar. 1989. "Is Variety the Spice of Life? Implications for Calorie Intake." *Review of Economics and Statistic*, 71: 666–672.

Bhalotra, S. 2004. "Welfare Implications of Fiscal Reform: The Case of Food Subsidies in India." In *Fiscal Policy for Development: Poverty, Reconstruction and Growth*, edited by T. Addison and A. Roe, 237–259. Palgrave Macmillan, Houndmills, Basingstoke, UK.

Dasgupta, P. 1993. *An Inquiry into Well-Being Destitution*. Oxford, UK: Oxford University Press.

Dasgupta, P., and D. Ray. 1986. "Inequality as a Determinant of Malnutrition and Unemployment: Theory." *Economic Journal* 96: 1011–1034.

Dasgupta, P., and D. Ray. 1987. "Inequality as a Determinant of Malnutrition and Unemployment: Policy." *Economic Journal*, 97: 177–188.

Deaton, A. 1995. *The Analysis of Household Surveys: A Microeconometric Approach in Development Policy*. Baltimore: Johns Hopkins University Press.

Deaton, A., and J. Dreze. 2009. "Food and Nutrition in India: Facts and Interpretations." *Economic and Political Weekly* XLIV (7): 42–65.

Deolalikar, A. 2010. "The Middle Class in Asia: Emerging Trends and Patterns and Their Implications." Paper presented at a Workshop on the Asian Middle Class, Asian Development Bank, May 27–28.

Dreze, J. 2013. "Fix Food Bill for Millions of People Facing insecurity." *The Economic Times*, 15 February, p. 5.

The Economist. 2001. "Righting Wrongs." August 18.

The Economist. 2012. "Poverty and Food: The Nutrition Puzzle." February 18.

Gaiha, R. 2003. "Does the Right to Food Matter?" *Economic and Political Weekly*, October 4, 38(40): 4269–4276.

Gaiha, R., R. Jha, and Vani S. Kulkarni. 2010a. "Prices, Expenditure and Nutrition in India." Australia South Asia Research Centre (ASARC), Australian National University, Working Paper No. 2010/15.

Gaiha, R., R. Jha, and Vani S. Kulkarni. 2010 b. "Child Undernutrition in India." ASARC, Australian National University, Working Paper No. 2010/11.

Gaiha, R., R. Jha, and Vani S. Kulkarni. 2010c. "Obesity, Affluence and Urbanisation in India." ASARC Working Paper 2010/10, Canberra: ANU.

Gaiha, R., R. Jha, and Vani S. Kulkarni. 2012. "Demand for Nutrients in India, 1993–2004." *Applied Economics*, Available online on February 1, 2012., http://www.tandfonline.com/doi/abs/10.1080/00036846.2011.639744#tabModule

Gaiha, R., R. Jha, and Vani S. Kulkarni. 2013. "How Pervasive Is Eating Out in India?" Available on line *Journal of Asian and African Studies*. http://jas.sagepub.com/content/early/2013/01/01/0021909612472040

Gaiha, R., N. Kaicker, K. S. Imai, Vani S. Kulkarni, and G. Thapa. 2013. "Has Dietary Transition Slowed Down in India: An Analysis Based on 50th, 61st and 66thRounds of NSS." Occasional Paper 16, Rome: IFAD.

Gaiha, R., N. Kaicker, K. S. Imai, and G. Thapa. 2013. "Demand for Nutrients in India: An Analysis Based on the 50th, 61st and 66th Rounds of the NSS." Rome: IFAD, mimeo.

Gaiha, R., Vani. S. Kulkarni, G. Thapa, and K. Imai. 2009. "Wages, Prices and Anti-Poverty Interventions in Rural India." Mimeo. [School of Economics Discussion Papers, University of Manchester]

Gopalan, C. 1992. "Undernutrition: Measurement and Implications." In S. Osmani (ed.) *Nutrition and Poverty*. New Delhi: Oxford University Press.

Gopalan, C., B. Sastri, and S. Balasubramanian. 1971. *Nutritive Value of Indian Foods*. National Institute of Nutrition: Indian Council of Medical Research: Hyderabad.

Himanshu, and A. Sen (2011) "Why Not a Universal Food Security Legislation?." *Economic and Political Weekly* XXXVI(12):. PP 38–47.

Indian Council of Medical Research. 1990. *Nutrient Requirements and Recommended Dietary Allowances for Indians*. New Delhi: ICMR.

Jensen, R. T., and N. H. Miller. 2011. "A Revealed Preference Approach to Measuring Hunger and Undernutrition." Mimeo., NBER Working Paper No. 16555.

Jha, R., S. Bhattacharya and R. Gaiha. 2011. "Social Safety Nets and Nutrient Deprivation: An Analysis of the National Rural Employment Guarantee Programme and the Public Distribution System in India." *Journal of Asian Economics* 22:189–201.

Jha, R., R. Gaiha, M. K. Pandey, and N. Kaicker. 2013. "Food Subsidy, Income Transfer and the Poor: A Comparative Analysis of the Public Distribution System in India's States." *Journal of Policy Modeling*, 35(6): 887–908.

Jha, R., R. Gaiha and A. Sharma (2009), "Calorie and Micronutrient and Poverty Nutrition Traps in Rural India." *World Development*, 37(5): 982–91.

Jha, S., and B. Ramaswami. 2010. "How Can Food Subsidies Work Better? Answers from India and the Philippines." Asian Development Bank, Working Paper No 221.

Kaicker, N. and R. Gaiha (2013), "Calorie Thresholds and Undernutrition in India, 1993–2004." *Journal of Policy Modeling*, 35: 271–288 forthcoming.

Kaicker, N., Vani S. Kulkarni and R. Gaiha. 2011. "Dietary Transition in India: An Analysis Based on NSS Data for 1993 and 2004." Paper presented at the World Congress of the International Economic Association, Beijing, July.

Khera, R. 2010. "India's Right to Food Act: Beyond the Rhetoric." *India in Transition* July 7., Centre for the Advanced Study of India, University of Pennsylvania

Khera, R. 2011. "India's Public Distribution System: Utilisation and Impact." *Journal of Development Studies* 47(3):1–23.

Khera, R. 2013. "A Cost-Benefit Analysis of UID." *Economic and Political Weekly*, XLVIII(5):13–15.

Kochar, A. 2005. "Can Targeted Food Programmes Improve Nutrition? An Empirical Analysis of India's Public Distribution System." *Economic Development and Cultural Change*, 54(1): 203–35.

Kulkarni, Vani. S. and R. Gaiha. 2010. "Dietary Transition in India." Philadelphia: *India in Transition*, CASI, University of Pennsylvania, March. http://casi.sas.upenn.edu/iit

Kumar, R. and S. K. Ghosh. 2012. "It Will Not Stop at Rs 60,000 Crore." *The Indian Express*, February 15.

Lee, I-Min, E. J. Shiroma, F. Lobelo, P. Puska, S. N. Blair, and P. T. Katzmarzyk. 2012. "Effect of Physical Activity on Major Non-Communicable Diseases Worldwide: An Analysis of Burden of Disease and Life Expectancy." *The Lancet* 380:219–229.

Lok Sabha Secretariat. 2013. National Food Security Bill, 2011, presented by Standing Committee On Food, Consumer Affairs And Public Distribution, Ministry of Consumer Affairs, Food And Public Distribution, Government of India.

Mahal, A., A. Karan and M. Engelan. 2009. *The Economic Implications of Non-Communicable Diseases for India*, Washington DC: World Bank.

Nandy, S., M. Irving, D. Gordon, S. V. Subramanian and G. D. Smith. 2005. "Poverty, Child Undernutrition and Morbidity: New Evidence." *Bulletin of the World Health Organisation*, 83(3):210–216.

Osmani, S. 2000. "Human Rights to Food, Health and Education." *Journal of Human Development*, 1(2): 273–298.

Pingali, P. and Y. Khwaja. 2004. "Globalisation of Indian Diets and the Transformation of Food Supply Systems." ESA Working Paper No. 04–05, Rome: FAO.

Planning Commission. 2008. *Eleventh Five-Year Plan*, New Delhi: Planning Commission.

Popkin, B. M., L. S. Adair, and S. W. Ng. 2012. "Global Nutrition Transition and the Pandemic of Obesity in Developing Countries." *Nutrition Reviews* 70(1): 3–21.

Ruhm, C. J. 2012. "Understanding Overeating and Obesity." *Journal of Health Economics*, 31:781–796.

Sen, Amartya. 1985. *Commodities and Capabilities*. Amsterdam: North Holland.

Sen, Amartya. 1999. *Development as Freedom*. New York: Knopf.

Shankar, S., and R. Gaiha. 2013. *Battling Corruption: Has NREGA Reached India's Rural Poor?* New Delhi: Oxford University Press.

Shue, H. 1980. *Basic Rights*. NJ: Princeton University Press.

Srinivasan, T. N. 1992. "Undernutrition: Concepts, Measurements and Policy Implications." In S. R. Osmani (ed.), *Nutrition and Poverty*. Clarendon Press, UK.

Srinivasan, T. N. 1994. "Destitution: A Discourse." *Journal of Economic Literature* 32: 1842–1855.

Svedberg, P. 2000. *Poverty and Undernutrition: Theory, Measurement, and Policy*, Oxford: Oxford University Press.

Svedberg, P. 2007. "Taking Action for the World"s Poor and Hungry People." Speaker Summary Note, Beijing, China, October 17–19 (mimeo).

Svedberg, P. 2010. "Poverty in India Can be Halved in Five Years. . . ." (mimeo) Institute for International Economic Studies, Stockholm University, Sweden.

WHO. 2004. "Appropriate Body-Mass Index for Asian Populations and Its Implications for Policy." *The Lancet* 363:157–63.

WHO. 2006. "Obesity and Overweight." *Fact Sheet no. 311*, September.

WHO. 2006. "WHO Child Growth Standards: Length/Height for Age, Weight for Age, Weight for Length, Weight for Height." Available at http://www.ncbi.nlm.nih.gov/pubmed/16817681.

World Bank. 2011. *Capitalising on the Demographic Transition: Tackling Non-Communicable Diseases in South Asia*. Washington DC: World Bank.

CHAPTER 14

FOOD PRICE AND TRADE POLICY BIASES

Inefficient, Inequitable, Yet Not Inevitable

KYM ANDERSON

Introduction

Farm subsidies have been prevalent on both sides of the North Atlantic for decades. Despite their high budgetary cost, society seems willing to tolerate them. Some think of it as justice for those left behind in rural areas by modern urban-based economic growth. Others (most notably in France) see it as a way of preserving the quaint peasant lifestyle they or their forebears left when they moved to the city. It is also argued that such policies help farmers preserve the natural environment in rural areas, provide food security for the nation, and (in countries such as Norway) help to populate and retain social vitality in remote areas.

Laudable though these societal objectives may be, they could be achieved far more effectively and efficiently by direct measures than by farm subsidies. This has been demonstrated by many economists (including this one, see Anderson 2000), so the arguments won't be repeated here. Instead, this article seeks to show that farm subsidies are just the tip of a huge iceberg of governmental distortions to food markets in high-income countries. These distortions are predominantly the result of trade policies that, even more than direct subsidies, are not only ineffective and inefficient but are also adding to global inequality and poverty.

Moreover, these policies of high-income countries are only half the problem. The other half comes from governmental distortions to markets for food and other farm products in developing countries. For many decades the latter policies have taxed rather than supported farmers, but an anti-agricultural policy bias can be just as inefficient and inequitable as a pro-farmer policy bias.

Pervasive though these policy biases seem to have been, they are not unchanging. On the contrary, new data reveal that they have evolved in fairly systematic ways as national economies have developed over the past half century. The challenge is to harness that capacity for change and direct it toward growth-inducing policy reforms and institutional innovations that also reduce inequality and poverty and thereby enhance global food security.

The chapter begins by briefly summarizing the history of thought on the role of agriculture in economic development. It then presents evidence from a new study of the evolution of price-distorting policies in both high-income and developing countries. That new empirical study covers seventy-five countries that account for more than 90 percent of world's population and agricultural output. It reveals that, among the high-income countries, some have been able to rid themselves of farm subsidies, and some have at least changed their key policy measures to less inefficient and less inequitable forms of support. Among developing countries, much of the earlier anti-agricultural bias has been phased out over the past quarter century. A worrying sign, however, is that agricultural protection has begun to emerge as the more advanced of those emerging economies industrialize. The third section reports on the contribution of agriculture to the current global welfare cost of distortions to farm and nonfarm goods markets, and on the impact of those distortionary policies on income inequality and poverty. The chapter concludes with an assessment of what might evolve in the coming decades, of the alternative measures available for dealing with the perceived problems associated with agriculture's changing role in economic development, and of their potential for reducing inequality and poverty and enhancing global food security.

Agriculture's Perceived Role in Development

Post–World War II development economists had a dim view of the contribution that farmers made to modern economic growth. In contrast to the perceived advantages of manufacturing, agriculture was seen as a low-productivity, constant-returns-to-scale activity whose producers were not very responsive to incentives. In addition, the real international prices of farm products were known to be volatile and thought to be in permanent long-term decline (Singer 1950; Prebisch 1950). This led Prebisch and others to argue that developing countries should strive to diversify their economies and reduce their dependence on a small number of primary commodity exports. To do this, they encouraged developing countries to develop their manufacturing sectors through import-substituting industrialization aided by manufacturing protection policies (Prebisch 1959). A corollary to this was the taxation of agricultural exports that, like import tariffs on manufactures, had the perceived additional benefit of raising government revenue in settings where there were still very high costs associated with collecting income or consumption taxes.

Agricultural production also was effectively taxed through requiring farmers to deliver some of their crop to parastatal agencies that paid them below-market prices. Meanwhile, agricultural development economists such as Johnston and Mellor (1961) saw the farm sector's contributions mainly as a market for manufactures and as a supplier of low-wage labor to nonfarm sectors. This view drew on Arthur Lewis's (1954) closed-economy model, which assumed unlimited supplies of agricultural labor.

An assumption implicit in much of this early thinking was that farmers were not very responsive to price incentives. This assumption was first challenged by T. W. Schultz (1964), who argued that farmers in developing countries were "poor but efficient." Schultz believed that farm output would respond positively to improved incentives, and he suggested there would be high returns from removing price distortions and boosting public investment in rural public goods, both physical (e.g., transport and communications infrastructure) and human (e.g., rural health and education, agricultural R&D).

Over time this Schultzian view was embraced, especially as and when economists and then policymakers came to understand the high cost of an anti-agricultural, anti-trade, import-substituting industrialization strategy. By the late 1960s, comprehensive empirical evidence of the huge extent of the distortions to incentives associated with manufacturing protectionism in developing countries had emerged (Little, Scitovsky, and Scott 1970; Balassa and Associates 1971). It was already clear that much faster industrial and overall economic growth was occurring in the few cases where import-substituting industrialization had been replaced by a more open-economy strategy, notably in East Asia. Development economists gradually abandoned their former support for intervention in favor of freer trade and flexible exchange rates, but it took other developing countries a decade or more to heed those policy lessons—prodded from the early 1980s on by loans from international financial institutions that were conditional on the adoption of structural adjustment programs.

Meanwhile, the densely populated East Asian economies, like Europe before them, worried that industrialization was eroding their former agricultural comparative advantages and causing farm household incomes to lag behind incomes in the rapidly growing cities. Their policy responses did not focus on ways of boosting farmer productivity; instead, they focused on increasingly protecting farmers from import competition (Anderson, Hayami, et al. 1986). This occurred despite the clear arguments and evidence presented by D. Gale Johnson in his seminal 1973 book, *World Agriculture in Disarray*, on the costly national economic folly and the international public "bads"—in the form of lower and more volatile international agricultural prices—that such a policy development entails.

Evidence of Evolving Distortions to Agricultural Incentives

To gauge how changes in farmer incentives have evolved over time, a recent World Bank study compiled evidence from seventy-five countries and five decades of policy experience (Anderson and Valenzuela 2008, summarized in Anderson 2009). That study reports a nominal rate of assistance (NRA), defined as the percentage by which government policies have raised producer returns above what they would be without the government's intervention (or the percentage by which government policies have lowered returns, if the NRA is less than zero). Since farmers are affected by the prices of not just their own outputs but also those of nonagricultural producers who compete with them in the common national markets for mobile labor and capital, the World Bank study also estimates a relative rate of assistance (RRA). The RRA is defined as the percentage by which government policies have raised prices of tradable farm products *relative to* prices received by producers of nonfarm tradable products (most of which are manufactures—see Anderson et al. 2008).

Historically, national nominal rates of assistance to agriculture (and relative rates of assistance even more so) have tended to be higher when a country's per capita income is higher, and RRAs have tended to be negative for developing countries and positive for high-income countries (Anderson 1995). However, since the 1980s the anti-agricultural policy bias in developing countries and the pro-agricultural bias in high-income countries have diminished, so that the two groups' average RRAs have converged toward zero since the mid-1980s (Figures 14.1 and 14.2). The extent and speed of that movement toward zero varies across regions, however: among developing countries it has been greatest for Asia and least for Africa, and among high-income countries it has been greatest for the European Union and not at all for other Western European countries, apart from the dip in the most recent period (2005–2007), when international food prices rose steeply (Figure 14.3). Australia and New Zealand are

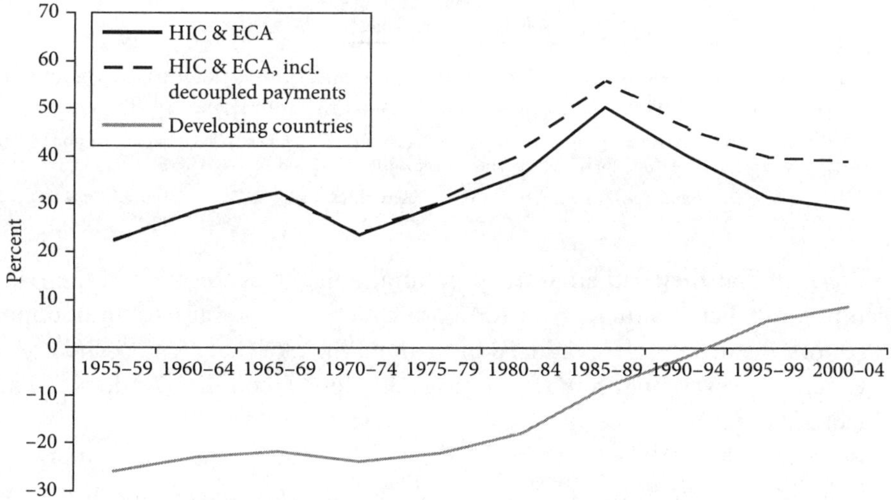

FIGURE 14.1 Nominal rates of assistance to agriculture in high-income, transition[a] and developing countries, 1955 to 2004

[a] Denoted by the World Bank as ECA, for (Central and Eastern) Europe and Central Asia.

Source: Anderson (2009, Ch. 1), based on estimates in Anderson and Valenzuela (2008).

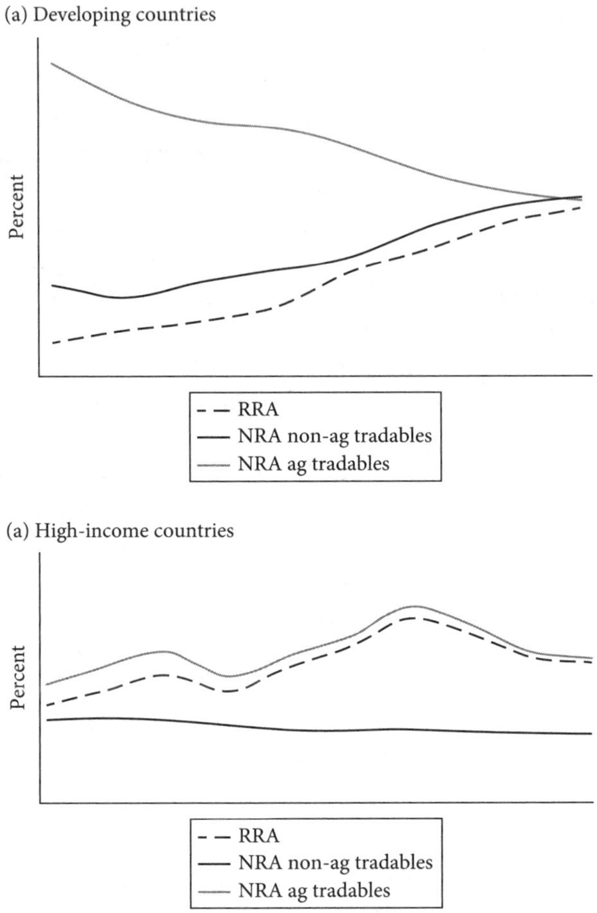

FIGURE 14.2 Nominal rates of assistance to agricultural and non-agricultural tradable sectors and relative rate of assistance,[a] developing and high-income countries, 1955 to 2004

[a] The RRA is defined as $100*[(100+NRAag^t)/(100+NRAnonag^t)-1]$, where $NRAag^t$ and $NRAnonag^t$ are the percentage NRAs for the tradables parts of the agricultural and non-agricultural sectors, respectively.

Source: Anderson (2009, Ch. 1), based on estimates in Anderson and Valenzuela (2008).

exceptional in that they had an anti-agricultural policy bias for most of the twentieth century, and their manufacturing tariff protection exceeded agricultural supports. Both sectors' distortions were reduced in the final third of that century and are now close to zero, however, not unlike the average developing country (Anderson, Lloyd, and MacLaren 2007).

Those averages hide the fact that there is still much variation across developing countries in both the level and rate of change in distortion indicators. National RRA estimates for 2000–2004 varied from around -50 percent for several African countries to nearly 150 percent for a few high-income countries (Figure 14.4).

Within the agricultural sector of each country, whether developed or developing, there is a wide range of product NRAs (Figure 14.5). Some product NRAs are positive

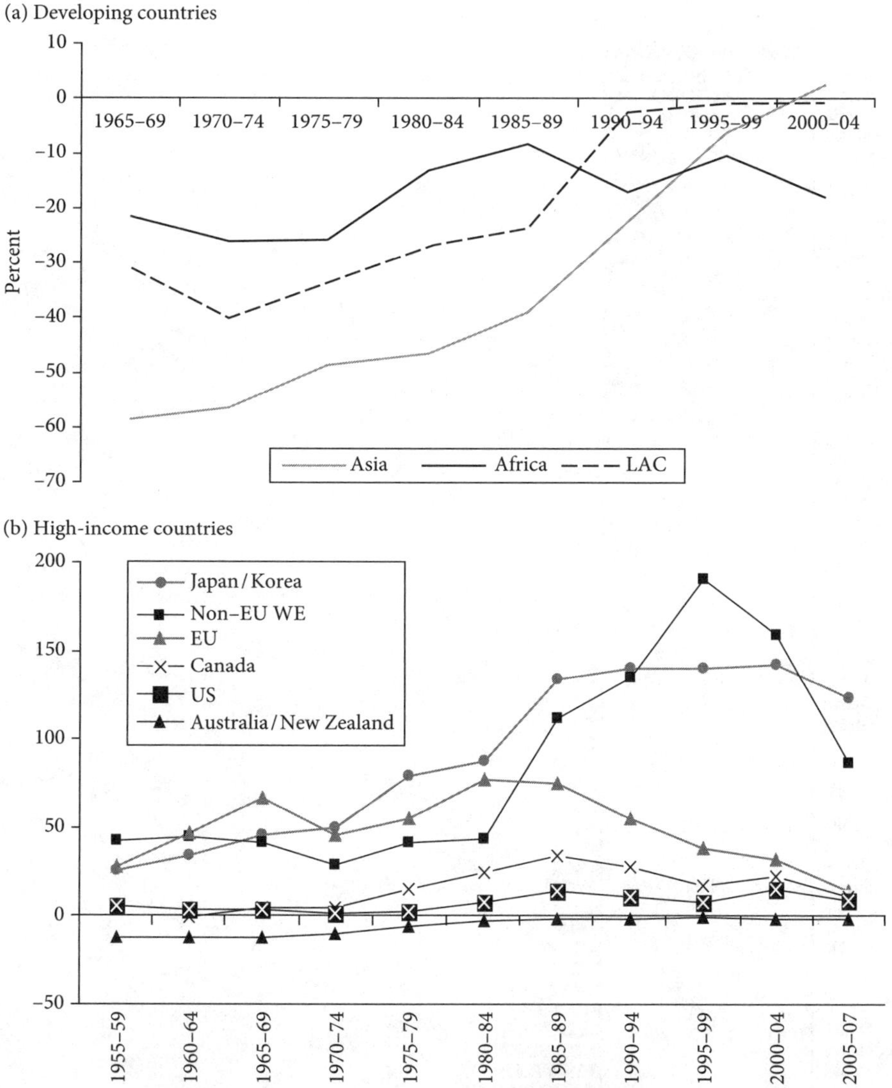

FIGURE 14.3 Relative rates of assistance to agriculture, by region, 1955 to 2007

Source: Anderson (2009, Ch. 1), based on estimates in Anderson and Valenzuela (2008).

and high in almost all countries (sugar, rice, milk), others are positive and high in developed economies but highly negative in developing countries (most noticeably, cotton), and yet others are relatively low in all countries (feedgrains, soybean, pork, poultry). An important aspect of this dispersion of NRAs is that the agricultural policy regime of each country still tends to have an anti-trade bias. This bias has declined over time for the developing country group, mainly because of cuts in agricultural export taxation and in spite of growth in agricultural import protection. For the high-income group, the anti-agricultural trade bias has shown a lesser decline over time (Figure 14.6), mainly

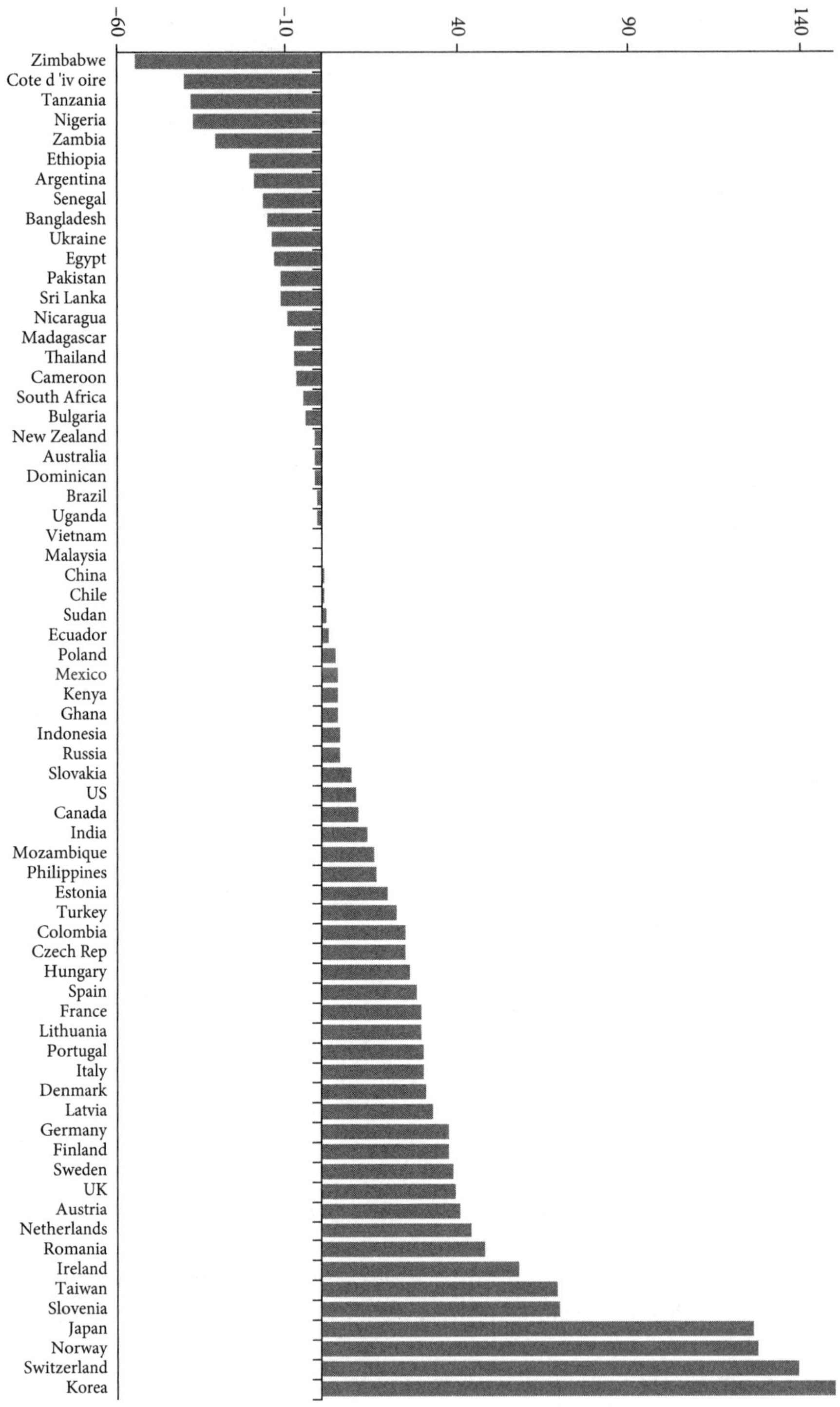

FIGURE 14.4 Cross-country dispersion in RRAs, 2000–04

Source: Anderson (2009, Ch. 1), based on estimates in Anderson and Valenzuela (2008).

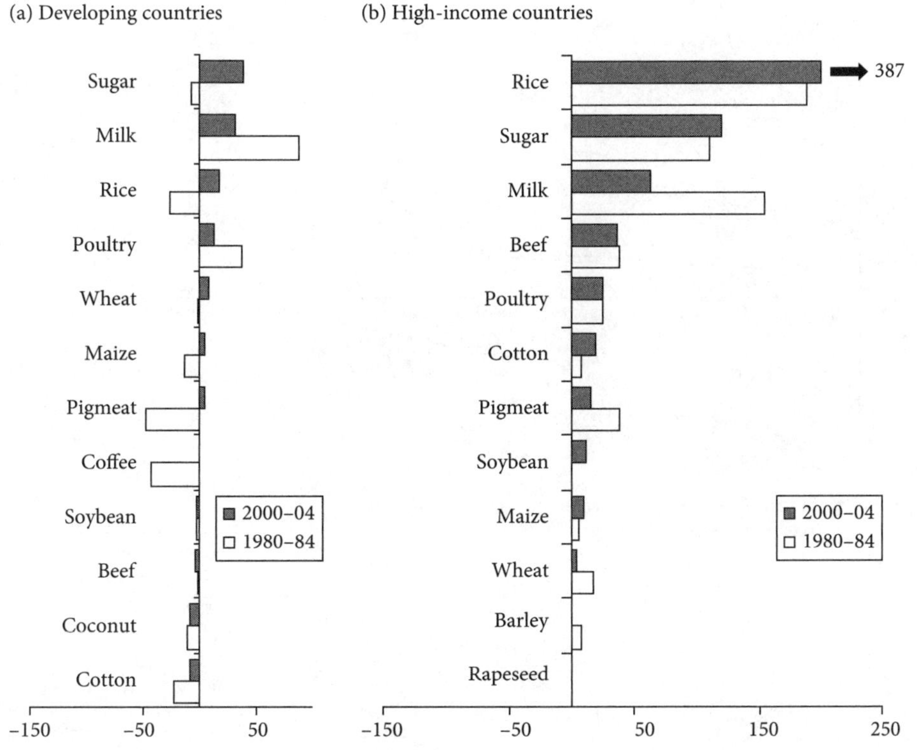

FIGURE 14.5 NRAs by product, developing and high-income countries, 1980–84 and 2000–04 (percent)

Source: Anderson (2010, Figure 2.6), based on estimates in Anderson and Valenzuela (2008).

because the rise and then decline in agricultural export subsidies has been matched by a similar trajectory for import protection.

The fall in assistance to producers of nonfarm tradable goods has contributed to just over half the rise in the RRA for developing countries between 1960–1984 and 2000–2004.

Up to the 1980s, and in some cases into the early 1990s, it was not uncommon for government interventions in the market for foreign exchange in developing countries to add to the overall anti-trade bias in policy regimes. Those interventions had all but disappeared by the mid-1990s, however, as part of overall macroeconomic policy reform initiatives.

The phasing out of export taxes by most developing countries, shown in Figure 14.6(a), is particularly striking. There have been some reversals of that policy reform in a few developing countries, though, with Argentina being the most important example. Meanwhile, with the growth in assistance to the agricultural import-competing subsector of developing countries (upper line in Figure 14.6(a)), the relative importance of import taxes has increased substantially (Figure 14.7).

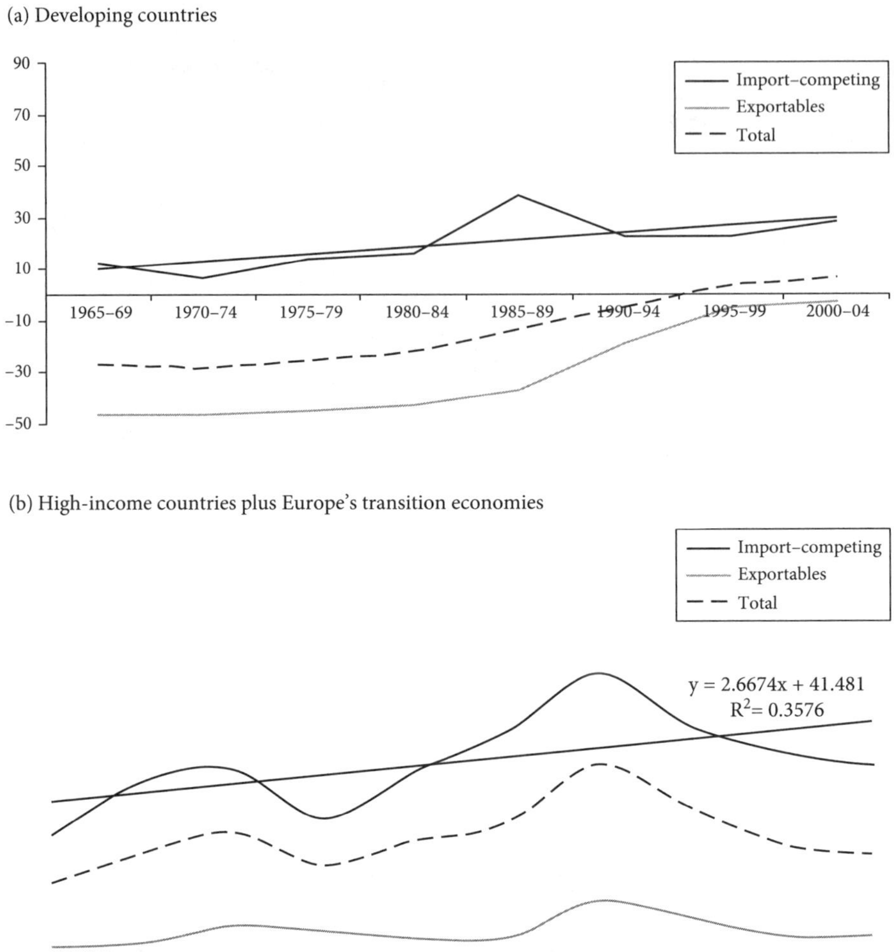

FIGURE 14.6 Nominal rates of assistance to exportable, import-competing and all covered agricultural products,[a] high-income, transition and developing countries, 1955 to 2004

[a] Covered products only. The total also includes nontradables. The straight line in the upper segment of each graph is from an ordinary-least-squares regression based on annual NRA estimates.

Source: Anderson (2009, Ch. 1), based on estimates in Anderson and Valenzuela (2008).

In high-income countries, the growing use of somewhat decoupled, more direct income support measures by some high-income countries, and the virtual abolition of all support measures in Australia and New Zealand, contrast with the continuing dominance of border measures of support in East Asia's high-income countries (Figure 14.8).

Yet even when decoupled payments are included in total support estimates, trade policy instruments (export and import taxes, subsidies or quantitative restrictions, plus dual exchange rates) account for no less than three-fifths of agricultural NRAs globally. Hence they account for an even larger share of their global welfare cost, since trade measures also tax consumers, and welfare costs are proportional to the square of a trade

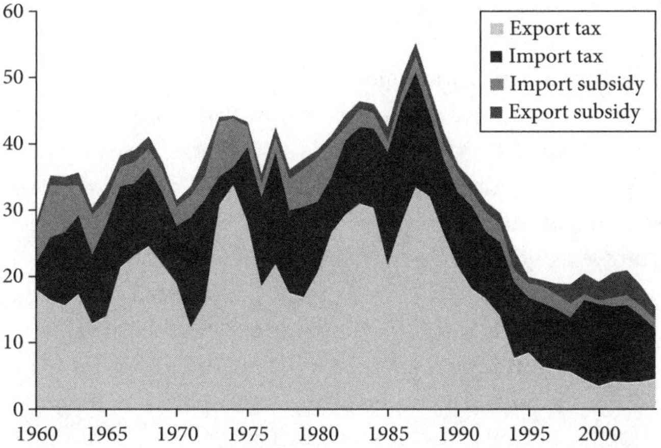

FIGURE 14.7 Contributions of different instruments to the border component of the welfare reduction index[a] for developing countries, 1960 to 2004

[a] The welfare reduction index is the percentage trade tax equivalent which, if applied uniformly to all goods, would generate the same welfare cost as the actual intra-sectoral structure of trade distortions.

Source: Derived from estimates reported in Croser and Anderson (2011), based on data in Anderson and Croser (2009).

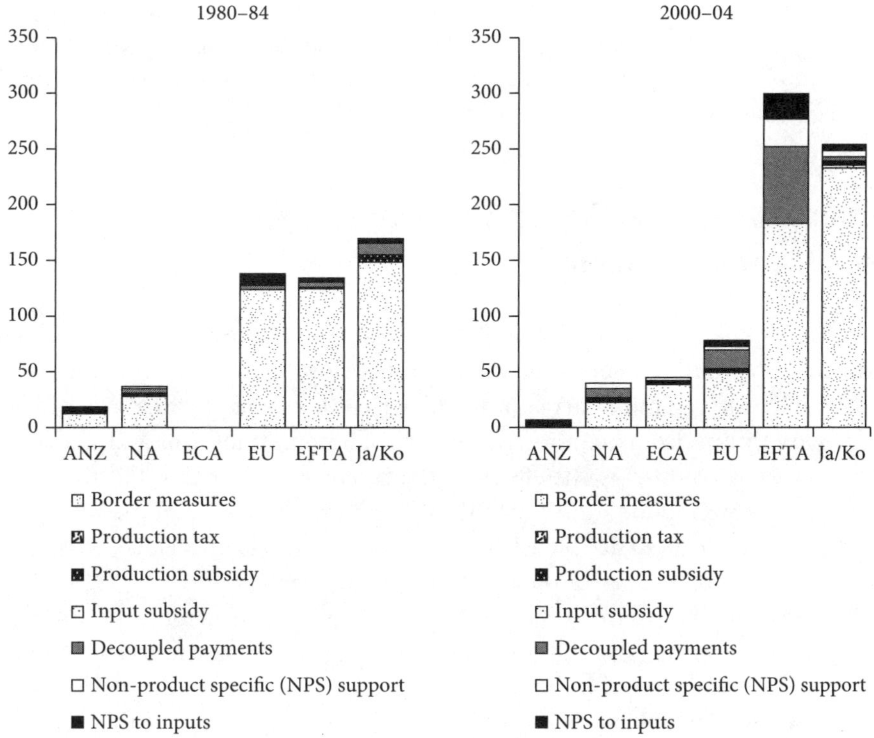

FIGURE 14.8 Contributions of different instruments to the producer component of the welfare reduction index[a] for various high-income and transition countries, 1980–84 and 2000–04

[a] The welfare reduction index is the percentage trade tax equivalent which, if applied uniformly to all goods, would generate the same welfare cost as the actual intra-sectoral structure of trade distortions.

Source: Croser and Anderson (2011), based on data in Anderson and Croser (2009).

tax (see also Anderson, Martin, and Valenzuela 2006). That is, domestic subsidies to or taxes on agricultural outputs and inputs make only minor contributions. In particular, subsidies to farm inputs and support for public agricultural research have added little to overall farmer assistance in high-income countries, and they have done relatively very little in the past to offset the effective taxation of agriculture in developing countries, with the important exception of India (Anderson 2009, Ch. 10). Public agricultural research investments in 2000–2004, for example, amounted to less than 2 percent of the gross value of agricultural output at undistorted prices in high-income countries, and to only 1 percent in developing countries (Anderson 2009, Table 1.11), with similar percentages in earlier decades. That is very minor compared with the percentage NRAs delivered through national governments' product price distortions.

Impacts of Distortions on Economic Welfare, Inequality, and Poverty

Using the above estimates of price distortions, recent estimates have been made of the impacts of past reforms and remaining policies on their global welfare cost, and of the impact of the current distortion pattern on income inequality and poverty. Consider first the aggregate economic welfare effects.

National and Global Economic Welfare Effects of Price-Distorting Policies

Valenzuela, van der Mensbrugghe, and Anderson (2009) provide a combined retrospective and prospective assessment of how far the world has come, and how far it still has to go, in rectifying the disarray in world agriculture. That is, their economy-wide modeling exercise seeks to quantify the impacts of both past reforms and current policies. It does so by comparing the effects of the recent World Bank project's distortion estimates for the period 1980–1984 with those of 2004, making use of the World Bank's global Linkage model (van der Mensbrugghe 2005) to estimate the effects on individual countries as well as on country groups and the world as a whole.

Several key findings from that modeling study are worth emphasizing. First, the policy reforms from the early 1980s to the mid-2000s are estimated to have improved global economic welfare by $233 billion per year, and removing the distortions remaining as of 2004 would add another $168 billion per year. This suggests that, in a global welfare sense, the world moved three-fifths of the way toward global free trade in goods over that quarter century.

Second, developing countries benefited proportionately more than high-income economies (1.0 percent compared with 0.7 percent of national income) from those past policy reforms, and would gain nearly twice as much as high-income countries by completing that reform process (an average increase of 0.9 percent compared with 0.5 percent for high-income countries). Of those prospective welfare gains from global liberalization, 70 percent would come from agricultural and food policy reform. This is a striking result given that the shares of agriculture and food in global GDP and global merchandise trade are only 3 and 6 percent, respectively. The contribution of global farm and food policy reform to the prospective welfare gain for just developing countries is even slightly greater, at 72 percent.

Third, the share of global farm production exported (excluding intra-European Union trade) in 2004 was slightly smaller as a result of those reforms since 1980–1984, because of less farm export subsidies: the 8 percent share of production exported for agriculture in 2004 contrasts with the 31 percent share for other primary products and the 25 percent for all other goods. If the policies distorting goods trade in 2004 were removed, the share of global production of farm products that is exported would rise from 8 to 13 percent, thereby "thickening" international food markets and thus reducing the instability of international prices and the quantities of those products traded.

Fourth, the developing countries' share of the world's primary agricultural exports rose from 43 to 55 percent between 1980–1984 and 2004, and its farm output share rose from 58 to 62 percent, because of those reforms, with rises in virtually all agricultural industries except rice and sugar. Removing remaining goods market distortions would boost their export and output shares to 64 and 65 percent, respectively. That is, the past and current pattern of price distortions means there has been far more farm production in high-income countries, and less in developing countries, than would have been the case without those distortionary policies in both sets of countries.

Fifth, for developing countries as a group, net farm income (value added in agriculture) is estimated to be 4.9 percent higher than it would be without the reforms of the past quarter century, which is more than ten times the proportional output gain for nonagriculture.

Consequences for Income Inequality and Poverty

To assess the effects of the world's agricultural and trade policies as of 2004 on income inequality and poverty within and between individual countries and country groups, Anderson, Valenzuela, and van der Mensbrugghe (2010) also used the World Bank's global Linkage model. Their results suggest that developing countries would gain nearly twice as much as high-income countries in welfare terms if 2004 agricultural and other trade policies were removed globally. In this broad conception of the world as just two large country groups, global trade reform would reduce international inequality. The results also indicate that net farm incomes in developing countries would rise by 5.6 percent, compared with 1.9 percent for nonagricultural value added, if those policies were eliminated. This suggests that inequality between farm and nonfarm households in developing countries would fall. By contrast, in high-income countries, net farm incomes would fall by 15 percent on average, compared with a slight rise for real nonfarm value added. That means inequality between farm households in developing countries and those in high-income countries would fall substantially. If only agricultural policies were removed, these results do not change much, which underscores the large magnitude of the distortions from agricultural, as compared with nonagricultural, trade-related policies. True, agricultural protection policies may lower the gap between average urban and rural household incomes, but the gains tend to get capitalized into the value of land, and thus they benefit farm households in proportion to their farm output and land holding—a highly inequitable outcome within rural areas (Johnson 1973, Ch. 9).

That study also reports that unskilled workers in developing countries—the majority of whom work on farms—would benefit most from reform (followed by skilled workers and then capital owners). The average change in the real unskilled wage across developing countries would rise by 3.5 percent. However, the most relevant consumer prices for poor people relate to food and clothing. This includes those many poor farm and other rural households who earn most of their income from their labor and are net buyers of food. Hence deflating by a food and clothing price index rather than the aggregate CPI provides a better indication of the welfare change for those workers. The real unskilled wage across developing countries would rise by 5.9 percent with that deflator. That is, inequality between unskilled wage earners and the much wealthier owners of capital (human or physical) within developing countries would fall with full trade reform. So too would the incidence of poverty: under the full merchandise trade reform scenario, there would be 2.7 percent fewer people living on less than US$1 a day in developing countries. Using the more moderate definition of poverty—people living on no more than US$2 per day—the number of poor in developing countries would fall by nearly 90 million compared to an aggregate baseline level of just under 2.5 billion in 2004, or by 3.4 percent.

Anderson, Cockburn, and Martin (2010, 2011) report results from ten more-detailed individual country case studies and compare these with the above results from a global model. As with the global modeling, these individual country case studies focus on price-distorting policies as of 2004, but they include more sectoral and product disaggregation than the global models, and they are able to consider multiple types of households and types of labor. The national results for real GDP and household consumption suggest that GDP would increase from full global trade reform in all ten countries, but only by 1 or 2 percent. Given falling consumer prices, real household consumption would increase by considerably more in most cases. Generally, these numbers are somewhat larger than those generated by the global Linkage model. When all merchandise trade is liberalized, the poverty reduction ranges from close to zero to about 3.5 percentage points, except for Pakistan, where it is more than 6 points. On average, nearly two-thirds of the alleviation is due to nonfarm trade reform, and the contribution of own-country reforms to the reduction in poverty appears to be equally important as rest-of-world reform.

The estimated poverty alleviation is also subdivided into rural and urban sources. In every case, rural poverty is reduced much more than urban poverty. This is true for both farm and nonfarm trade reform, and for own-country as well as rest-of-world reform. Since the rural poor are much poorer on average than the urban poor, this would lead one to expect trade reform to also reduce inequality. That is indeed what the results show for this sample of countries: inequality declines in all three developing country regions following full trade liberalization of either all goods or just agricultural products, and for both own-country and rest-of-world reforms. The effect of nonfarm trade reform on its own is more mixed, providing another reason to urge trade negotiators not to neglect agricultural reform in trade negotiations. Inequality within rural or urban household groupings are not altered very much by trade reform compared with overall national inequality, which underlines the point that trade reform would tend to mainly reduce urban-rural inequality rather than inequality within regions.

In summary, the benefits for the world's poor from the full liberalization of global merchandise trade would come more from agricultural than nonagricultural reform; and, within agriculture, more from the removal of substantial support provided to farmers in developed countries than from developing country policy reform. According to the economy-wide model used in Anderson, Cockburn, and Martin (2010, 2011), such reform would raise the real earnings of unskilled workers in developing countries, most of whom work in agriculture. Their earnings would rise relative to both unskilled workers in developed countries and other income earners in developing countries. This would thus reduce inequality both within developing countries and between developing and developed countries, in addition to reducing poverty. The studies all find global trade liberalization to be poverty alleviating, regardless of whether the reform involves only agricultural goods or all goods, with the benefit to developing countries coming roughly equally from reform at home and abroad. They also find that rural poverty would be cut much more than urban poverty in all cases.

Policy Implications

These empirical findings have a number of important policy implications. First and foremost, the attractive poverty- and inequality-alleviating effects of unilateral and multilateral trade policy reforms provide yet another argument for countries to seek further liberalization of national and world markets. The potential benefits are generally much greater for global reform than from just own-country reform. The results of this set of studies also show that the winners from trade reform would overwhelmingly be found among the poorer countries and the poorest individuals within these countries. However, even among the extreme poor, some will lose out. Hence the merit of compensatory policies, ideally ones that focus not on private goods but rather on public goods that reduce underinvestment in pro-growth areas such as rural human capital formation.

Second, the strongest prospective benefits come from agricultural reform. This underscores the economic and social importance of securing reforms for the agricultural sector in particular, notwithstanding the political sensitivities involved. There are more direct, and hence more efficient, domestic policy instruments than trade policies for meeting governments' Millennium Development Goals of poverty, malnutrition, and hunger, but generally they are more of a net drain on treasury finances. This is particularly true for governments of low-income countries, which still rely heavily on trade tax revenue. One solution for this is to expand aid-for-trade funding as part of official development assistance programs (Hoekman and Wilson 2010). Another is to make (more) use of value added or consumption taxation measures.

Third, most of the national case studies show that domestic reform on its own can be a way of reducing poverty and inequality. This suggests that developing countries should not hold back on domestic reforms while negotiations in the World Trade Organization's Doha Round and other international forums continue. It also suggests that from a poverty alleviating perspective, developing countries have little to gain, and potentially much to lose, from negotiating exemptions or delays in national reforms in the framework of WTO multilateral agreements.

Most commentators believe that Asia's developing economies will keep growing rapidly in the foreseeable future, provided they remain open and continue to practice good macroeconomic governance. Their growth is expected to be more rapid in manufacturing and service activities than in agriculture. In the more densely populated economies of the region, the growth in labor-intensive and manufactured component exports will be accompanied by rapid increases in the per capita incomes of low-skilled workers (Baldwin 2011). Agricultural comparative advantage is thus likely to decline in these economies (Anderson and Strutt 2012). Whether these economies become more dependent on imports of farm products, however, depends on what happens to their RRAs. The first wave of Asian industrializers (Japan, and then Korea and Taiwan) chose to slow the growth of food import dependence by raising their NRA for agriculture even as they were bringing down their NRA for nonfarm tradables, so that their RRA became increasingly above the neutral zero level. A key question is: Will later industrializers follow suit, given the past close association of RRAs with rising per capita income and falling agricultural comparative advantage?

The progress of lower-income countries relative to first industrializers can be found by mapping the RRAs for Japan, Korea, and Taiwan against real per capita income, and superimposing a graph of the RRAs for lower-income economies onto this. Figure 14.9 does this, and it shows that the RRA trends for China and India (and ASEAN countries to a lesser extent) over the past three decades are similar to those of richer Northeast Asian countries. True, the earlier industrializers were not bound under GATT to not raise their agricultural protection, but the WTO legal bindings on China, India, and ASEAN also are unlikely to constrain the governments very much in the next decade or two. One can only hope that China and South and Southeast Asia will not make use of the legal wiggle room they have allowed themselves in their WTO bindings and follow Japan, Korea, and Taiwan into high agricultural protection. If they do, Anderson and Nelgen (2011) estimate that the future cost of agricultural protection policies will rise substantially.

A much more efficient and equitable strategy would be to instead treat agriculture in the same way many developing countries have been treating nonfarm tradable sectors in recent decades. That would involve opening the sector to international competition

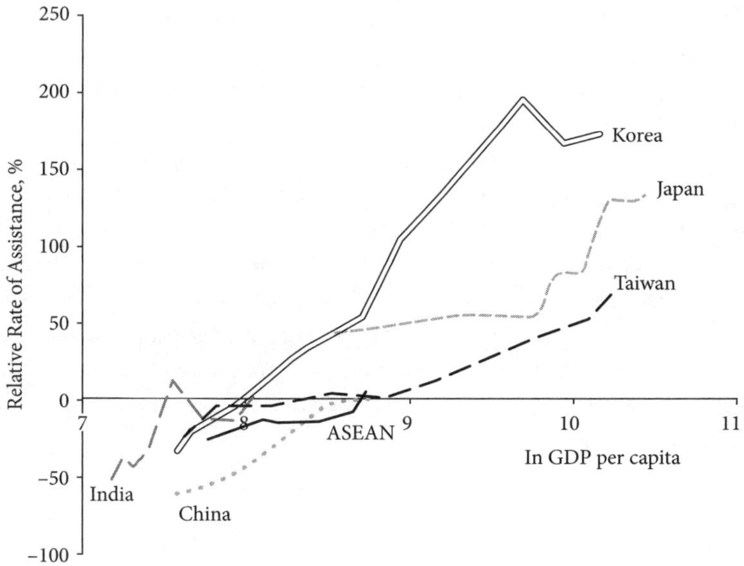

FIGURE 14.9 Relative rate of assistance to agriculture and log of real per capita GDP, large Asian economies, 1955[a] to 2004

[a] The starting dates are 1965 for India, 1970 for ASEAN and 1981 for China, due to lack of RRA estimates for earlier years for those countries. The GDP per capita data are in 1990 international Geary-Khamis dollars, from Maddison (2003).

Source: Author's derivation from data in Anderson and Valenzuela (2008).

and relying on more efficient domestic policy measures to raise government revenue (e.g., income and consumption or value-added taxes) and to assist farm families (e.g., public investment in rural education and health, rural infrastructure, and agricultural research—see Fan 2008). Even if just one-twentieth of the current NRA provided to Asian farmers via farm price-support policies was replaced by agricultural R&D expenditure, that would more than double their current public spending on R&D—and the latter would increase economic welfare, whereas price-distortionary policies reduce it. Such a boost to Asian R&D could generate another green revolution of the same order of magnitude of the one in the 1960s, especially if it took full advantage of the new developments in biotechnology (as shown for rice, for example, in Anderson, Jackson, and Nielsen 2005). The example of Brazil's R&D-led agricultural revolution over the past two decades also points the way for others to follow, not only in Latin America but also in sub-Saharan Africa—where again the potential for yield and food-quality improvements via transgenic crop development is enormous (Anderson and Jackson 2005).

In short, the world's food price and trade policy biases are still very wasteful of resources. They lead to food production occurring in higher-cost settings than is necessary, and they contribute to global poverty, to income inequality between countries, and to income and wealth inequality within rural areas of protective countries. Yet the historical data summarized above indicates that these policy biases have declined somewhat over the past quarter century. Thus, even though it may seem like farm subsidies and import protection are fixtures too politically difficult to move, this evidence suggests those measures—like export taxes on farm products in developing countries—are not inevitable.

Unfortunately, the same cannot yet be said for policies that insulate domestic food markets from international price fluctuations. While not discussed above (but see Anderson and Nelgen 2012), both high-income and developing countries alter their trade barriers in an attempt to protect consumers from food price spikes. It turns out, though, that both food-surplus and food-deficit countries tend to so respond, and to a similar extent. Hence they tend to cancel out each other's ability to stabilize their home markets—but at the same time they exacerbate the instability in international food prices (Martin and Anderson 2012). Beggar-thy-neighbor food policy actions are thus a long way from being a thing of the past, and they are likely to continue until enough countries get together and agree multilaterally to desist from protecting and insulating their domestic food markets.

References

Anderson, K. 1995. "Lobbying Incentives and the Pattern of Protection in Rich and Poor Countries." *Economic Development and Cultural Change* 43 (2): 401–423.

——. 2000. "Agriculture's 'Multifunctionality' and the WTO." *Australian Journal of Agricultural and Resource Economics* 44 (3): 475–494.

——, ed. 2009. *Distortions to Agricultural Incentives: A Global Perspective, 1955–2007*. Washington DC: World Bank. http://siteresources.worldbank.org/INTTRADERESEARCH/Resources/544824-1272467194981/DAI_Global_Perspective.pdf.

——, ed. 2010. *The Political Economy of Agricultural Price Distortions*. Cambridge and New York: Cambridge University Press.

Anderson, K., J. Cockburn, and W. Martin, eds. 2010. *Agricultural Price Distortions, Inequality, and Poverty*. Washington, DC: World Bank. http://econ.worldbank.org/external/default/main?pagePK=64165259&theSitePK=469382&piPK=64165421&menuPK=64166322&entityID=000333037_20100407012231.

——, 2011. "Would Freeing Up World Trade Reduce Poverty and Inequality? The Vexed Role of Agricultural Distortions." *The World Economy* 34 (4): 487–515.

Anderson, K., and J. L. Croser. 2009. *National and Global Agricultural Trade and Welfare Reduction Indexes, 1955 to 2007*. Washington, DC: World Bank. Spreadsheet at www.worldbank.org/agdistortions.

Anderson, K., Y. Hayami, et al. 1986. *The Political Economy of Agricultural Protection: East Asia in International Perspective*, London: Allen and Unwin.

Anderson, K., and L. A. Jackson. 2005. "Some Implications of GM Food Technology Policies for Sub-Saharan Africa." *Journal of African Economies* 14 (3): 385–410, September.

Anderson, K., L. A. Jackson, and C. P. Nielsen. 2005. "GM Rice Adoption: Implications for Welfare and Poverty Alleviation." *Journal of Economic Integration* 20 (4): 771–788.

Anderson, K., M. Kurzweil, W. Martin, D. Sandri, and E. Valenzuela. 2008. "Measuring Distortions to Agricultural Incentives, Revisited." *World Trade Review* 7 (4): 675–704.

Anderson, K., P. J. Lloyd, and D. MacLaren. 2007. "Distortions to Agricultural Incentives in Australia Since World War II." *The Economic Record* 83 (263): 461–482.

Anderson, K., W. Martin, and E. Valenzuela. 2006. "The Relative Importance of Global Agricultural Subsidies and Market Access." *World Trade Review* 5 (3): 357–376.

Anderson, K., and S. Nelgen. 2011. "What's the Appropriate Agricultural Protection Counterfactual for Trade Analysis?" In *Unfinished Business? The WTO's Doha Agenda*, edited by W. Martin and A. Mattoo, 325–354. London: Centre for Economic Policy Research for the World Bank.

——. 2012. "Trade Barrier Volatility and Agricultural Price Stabilization." *World Development* 40 (1): 36–48.

Anderson, K., and A. Strutt. 2012. "Agriculture and Food Security in Asia by 2030." Background Paper 7 for a forthcoming book, *ASEAN, China and India: A Balanced, Sustainable, Resilient Growth Pole*, Tokyo: Asian Development Bank Institute.

Anderson, K., and E. Valenzuela. 2008. *Global Estimates of Distortions to Agricultural Incentives, 1955 to 2005*. Data spreadsheets available at www.worldbank.org/agdistortions.

Anderson, K., E. Valenzuela, and D. van der Mensbrugghe. 2010. "Global Welfare and Poverty Effects: Linkage Model Results." In *Agricultural Price Distortions, Inequality and Poverty*, edited by K. Anderson, J. Cockburn, and W. Martin, 49–86. Washington, DC: World Bank. http://econ.worldbank.org/external/default/main?pagePK=64165259&theSitePK=469382&piPK=64165421&menuPK=64166322&entityID=000333037_20100407012231.

Balassa, B., and Associates. 1971. *The Structure of Protection in Developing Countries*. Baltimore: Johns Hopkins University Press.

Baldwin, R. E. 2011. "Trade and Industrialization after Globalization's 2nd Unbundling: How Building and Joining a Supply Chain are Different and Why It Matters." NBER Working Paper 17716. Cambridge, MA: National Bureau of Economic Research.

Croser, J. L., and K. Anderson. 2011. "Changing Contributions of Different Agricultural Policy Instruments to Global Reductions in Trade and Welfare." *World Trade Review* 10 (3): 297–323.

Fan, S. 2008. *Public Expenditures, Growth and Poverty in Developing Countries: Issues, Methods and Findings*. Baltimore: Johns Hopkins University Press.

Hoekman, B., and J. S. Wilson. 2010. "Aid for Trade: Building on Progress Today for Tomorrow's Future." Chap. 7 in *Postcrisis Growth and Development: A Development Agenda for the G-20*, edited by S. Fardoust, Y. Kim and C. Sepúlveda. Washington, DC: World Bank.

Johnson, D. G. 1973. *World Agriculture in Disarray*. (Revised edition 1991.) London: St. Martin's Press.

Johnston, B. F., and J. W. Mellor. 1961. "The Role of Agriculture in Economic Development." *American Economic Review* 51 (4): 566–593.

Lewis, W. A. 1954. "Economic Development with Unlimited Supplies of Labour." *Manchester School* 22:139–191.

Little, I. M. D., T. Scitovsky, and M. Scott. 1970. *Industry and Trade in Some Developing Countries: A Comparative Study*. Oxford: Oxford University Press.

Maddison, A. 2003. *The World Economy: Historical Statistics*. Paris: OECD Development Centre. Updated data available at www.ggdc.net/maddison/content.shtml.

Martin, W., and K. Anderson. 2012. "Export Restrictions and Price Insulation during Commodity Price Booms." *American Journal of Agricultural Economics* 94 (2): 422–427.

Prebisch, R. 1950. *The Economic Development of Latin America and its Principal Problems*. Lake Success, NY: United Nations Department of Economic Affairs.

——. 1959. "Commercial Policy in Underdeveloped Countries." *American Economic Review* 49 (2): 251–273.

Schultz, T. W. 1964. *Transforming Traditional Agriculture*. New Haven, CT: Yale University Press.

Singer, H. W. 1950. "The Distribution of Gains between Investing and Borrowing Countries." *American Economic Review* 40 (2): 473–485.

Valenzuela, E., D. van der Mensbrugghe, and K. Anderson. 2009. "General Equilibrium Effects of Price Distortions on Global Markets, Farm Incomes and Welfare." Chap. 13 in *Distortions to Agricultural Incentives: A Global Perspective, 1955–2007*, edited by K. Anderson. Washington, DC: World Bank. http://siteresources.worldbank.org/INTTRADERESEARCH/Resources/544824-1272467194981/DAI_Global_Perspective.pdf.

van der Mensbrugghe, D. 2005. *Linkage Technical Reference Document: Version 6.0*. Washington DC, World Bank. http://siteresources.worldbank.org/INTPROSPECTS/Resources/334934-1100792545130/LinkageTechNote.pdf.

CHAPTER 15

INTELLECTUAL PROPERTY RIGHTS AND THE POLITICS OF FOOD

KRISHNA RAVI SRINIVAS

INTRODUCTION

THE linkage between food and plant genetic resources needs no great elaboration; plants provide genetic material that has been modified over millennia to meet human food needs by creation of specialized cultivars suited to particular human needs (see McHughen, this volume). But the linkage between intellectual property rights and food is not obvious; intellectual property rights are typically not considered either as an important issue in the politics of food or as an issue of ethical concern. Intellectual property rights are state-granted monopolies for a limited number of years for incentivizing inventions and creation of works of art and to promote innovation and technology transfer. The FAO Panel of Eminent Experts on Ethics in Food and Agriculture observed that most innovation in food and agriculture does not depend upon intellectual property rights, yet acquisition and exercise of intellectual property rights raises a variety of ethical concerns. It expressed concern, for example, about patenting of merely isolated genes that are essentially part of nature and not inventions. It is not clear what constitutes an invention or what can become property. Something like a global intellectual property rights regime is provided by the Trade Related Intellectual Property Rights (TRIPS) agreement. Under the TRIPS agreement, intellectual property (IP) refers to seven categories, including patents and plant varieties rights as well as copyright and related rights. An exhaustive analysis of the relationship between intellectual property and politics of food would include issues relating to copyrights and intellectual property protection for cuisines and geographical indication.[1] Such an analysis is beyond the scope of this entry.

The Evolution of Global Regimes of Plant Genetic Resources

A good portion of the food we consume is derived from plants, directly or indirectly. Crop plants are estimated to contribute more than 80 percent of our calories and the edible dry weight. Most of the food humans consume is based on less than twenty species and just three staple crops— rice, wheat, and maize—account for about 60 percent of the calories and about 56 percent of the proteins (Lenné and Wood 2011, 9). Plant genetic resources[2] constitute the core of this agricultural biodiversity and agricultural biodiversity itself is the outcome of continuous interaction among humans, nature, and evolution. Humans took to farming and, since doing so, they have developed and derived many thousands of varieties of plants. Domestication of food crops started about 11,000 years ago, first with rice, then maize, and later wheat. Crop improvement is a cumulative process and the plant genetic resources found in nature are modified by humans into germplasm, which can be used for further improvement and/ or for cultivation. Germplasm

> refers to the sum total of all hereditary material in a plant, as coded in its DNA. For a crop, it reflects the compounding nature of sequential improvements carried out by breeders over a long period of time, all of which, of course, is encapsulated in the seed. (Moschini 2010, 5)

The origin and distribution of crops is a fascinating story; the introduction of crops played an important role in spreading access to new plant varieties and thereby enabling their use in the development of new varieties for crops and other purposes. Migration, trade, interaction among communities, colonial expansion, and other factors ensured that varieties bred and domesticated in one region spread to other regions.[3] Newly introduced plant varieties had significant advantages that went beyond enhancing diversity. According to Kloppenburg, the crops that now dominate the agricultural economies of the advanced industrial nations are not, for the most part, indigenous species. They have been introduced from elsewhere, principally from what is now the Third World.

> ... If the United States now has a food weapon, as former Secretary of Agriculture Earl Butz so bluntly put it, it is because nations such as Nicaragua, Ethiopia, Iran, and China have supplied, respectively, the corn, wheat, alfalfa, and soybean for its arsenal.[4]

In many countries botanical gardens were established to receive, classify, and transfer the species received from elsewhere. Scientific breeding emerged after the rediscovery of Mendel's law in the early twentieth century, and this helped in searching for material on the basis of genetic features. Public-sector breeders developed pools of germplasm based on these collections, and the relatively open system of exchange made available germplasm for varietal development without many restrictions among breeders (Byerlee and Dubin 2010). In the early decades of the twentieth century Russian botanist

Nicolay Vavilov identified major centers of crop diversity and collected thousands of samples for genetic study. His efforts helped in mapping the geographical origins of crops and their diversity.

While germplasm pools were created, they were often ad hoc efforts and for short-term purposes. In the post–World War II period, exchange of plant genetic resources received a boost with advances in genetics and the realization of the need for a systematic global approach for exchanging and storing materials. In 1948 the Food and Agricultural Organization (FAO) set up a global clearinghouse to advance the sharing, and the cataloging, of resources to facilitate their use in breeding programs. FAO delivered samples often through plant introduction stations that were based mostly in Europe, Australia, the Soviet Union, and the United States.

The advent of the Green Revolution and the development of plant breeding programs in many parts of the world resulted in more demand for accessing the genetic diversity among the stored plant genetic resources. At the same time, concerns grew about erosion and loss of genetic diversity because of the spread of modern varieties (Fowler and Mooney 1990). FAO convened the first technical conference on plant genetic resources in 1967, with collective conservation emerging as an important theme. At the same time, many centers for agricultural research in different parts of the work were contributing to, and working for, the Green Revolution with support from governments, the World Bank, and private foundations (see Harriss and Stewart, this volume). In 1971 the Consultative Group on International Agricultural Research (CGIAR) was established; many of the research centers were brought under CGIAR, which operated officially outside the UN system. CGIAR gave more importance to *ex situ* conservation, that is, storing samples under controlled conditions, than to *in situ* conservation, that is, conservation through their use on the farm as practiced by farmers and farming communities historically. The centers under CGIAR were dedicated to a single crop or to a limited number of crops and had access to germplasm collections held at universities. They have engaged in exchanging collections and, thus, over the years they have succeeded in building up a huge, diversified collection of germplasm of crops that are important for global food security. The varieties they developed were based on this collection and from germplasm received from elsewhere.

The establishment of the International Board on Plant Genetic Resources (IBPGR) marked a step forward in global efforts to collect, classify, exchange, and conserve plant genetic resources. By the early 1980s, a global pool of plant genetic resources housed in different centers and repositories had emerged. The exchange and use of materials available under this pool was based on the Common Heritage of Mankind (CHM) approach. This approach was grounded in the notion that plant genetic resources constitute a commons that should be accessible to all with very few or no restrictions on collection, exchange, use, and classification. Plant genetic resources were considered a global resource not subject to restrictions under national sovereignty. This enabled CGIAR centers and the FAO to freely collect, exchange, store, and share materials with many stakeholders, including plant breeders, researchers, and private-sector breeders.

At the 1981 FAO biennial conference, developing nations called for drafting a legal convention on plant genetic resources; this was opposed by developed countries. In 1983 FAO established a Commission on Plant Genetic Resources for Food and Agriculture (CPGR). The CPGR adopted the International Undertaking on Plant Genetic Resources (IUPGR) that same year. IUPGR is a nonbinding agreement that dealt with rules and standards for conservation and exchange of plant genetic resources. It was based on the position that plant genetic resources are the "common heritage of mankind." Plant genetic resources subject to the IUPGR included plant varieties and elite breeding lines; it treated traditional landraces, wild plants, and commercial plant varieties protected by plant breeders' rights to be on the same footing.

This position was contested by the United States and some European governments, which argued that this position conflicted with the International Union for the Protection of New Varieties of Plants (UPOV) Convention and national patent laws. IUPGR was a nonbinding undertaking; nevertheless, its position was considered controversial because it did not differentiate between "raw" germplasm and "modified/improved" germplasm. While the former was considered to be a product of nature and, hence, could not be subject to the grant of intellectual property rights, the latter could be subject to intellectual property protection through patents and/or plant breeders' rights. The controversial position of treating plant genetic resources as the "common heritage of mankind" was based on the principles of open access and reciprocity, which had governed the international transfer, exchange, and storage of plant genetic resources. A useful summary is provided by Brush (2004, 221–222):

> Common heritage refers to the treatment of genetic resources as belonging to the public domain and not owned or otherwise monopolized by a single group or interest. Common heritage is similar to common property regimes that anthropologists and other social scientists have described for nonmarket economies. Neither common heritage nor common property implies lack of rules (*res nullius*).... Rather they imply community management (*res communes*) that involves regulated access to common resources and reciprocity among them.

Critics of this approach pointed out that developed nations had used this open-access model throughout history to justify free transfer of plant genetic resources for development, and they had simultaneously granted plant breeders' rights and patents on "improved/modified" germplasm—in effect, privatizing open-access genetic commons. This put developing nations in a doubly disadvantageous position as they benefited neither from the Common Heritage approach nor from the grant of intellectual property rights on plant varieties and seeds.

As developing nations were also the centers of origin for many crops, it was claimed that the "gene rich" South contributed to the development of agriculture and industry in the North through transfer of plant genetic resources, but they did not gain anything in return. Most of the gene banks were in developed nations, and the North benefited greatly from the transfer of germplasm. But interdependency among the regions of the world in plant genetic resources was an undisputed fact; both North and South benefited from the transfer and exchange of plant genetic resources. Moreover, as improved varieties were genetically uniform and were vulnerable to new pests and blights, the need for accessing germplasm, which could help in developing new varieties with better traits, underscored the need for transfer and exchange among countries.

But the Common Heritage approach was not acceptable to South and North alike; the status of plant genetic resources, particularly those stored in CGIAR centers, became a contentious issue. The United States refused to participate in the IUPGR. Developed nations were generally unwilling to accept the Common Heritage principle as applicable to all plant genetic resources, especially those protected under plant breeders' rights. After negotiations, it was agreed that the Common Heritage concept would not be applicable to plants protected by plant variety or under the UPOV convention. It was also agreed that applying Common Heritage or the open-access principle to landraces and wild and weedy crop relatives did not mean that access would be free of obligation or that access was free of charge. Plant breeders or collectors could be asked to pay for what was collected in a country's territory.

Negotiations through subsequent years weakened the Common Heritage approach, which was then abandoned. In 1989 FAO adopted a new interpretation of IUPGR that formally recognized "farmers' rights." Given the contributions made by farmers in conserving plant genetic resources and domesticating crops and varieties over thousands of years, farmers' rights should be recognized. Although farmers' rights were indicated as a normative principle, no rights in the legal sense of the term were established. These compromises in FAO dealt a blow to the Common Heritage approach; in the early 1990s two important developments changed global norms. At the 1992 United Nations Conference on Environment and Development (also known as the "Rio Conference 1992" or the "Earth Summit") the Convention on Biological Diversity (CDB) was adopted. It subsequently became the single most important international convention on conservation and sustainable use of biodiversity. CBD's coverage of genetic resources broadened the field of coverage to agricultural biodiversity in emphasizing both sustainable use and conservation of biodiversity.

In the negotiations on CBD, the North-South divide in the debates in FAO on IUPGR resurfaced. In the final document, the CBD rejected the Common Heritage approach and recognized *national* sovereignty over biological resources occurring within national boundaries, though biodiversity was recognized as a common concern (Jaeckel 2013). CBD provided for regulated access and state control. Moreover, CBD included provisions that facilitated access and benefit sharing (ABD) based on the principles of prior informed consent (PIC) and equitable benefit sharing. It contained provisions that emphasized transfer of technology and it recognized availability of intellectual property protection. The erosion of the Common Heritage of Mankind approach culminated in the TRIPS agreement of 1994. That agreement sought to harmonize intellectual property rights globally; it included intellectual property protection for plant varieties. Regarding collections held by centers under the CGIAR, as per the agreement between CGIAR and FAO, designated germplasm is held in trust, and CGIAR is required to ensure that their dealings do not undermine the interests of stakeholders. According to article 3(a) and (b) of the agreement:

(a) The Center shall hold the designated germplasm in trust for the benefit of the international community, in particular the developing countries in accordance with the International Undertaking on Plant Genetic Resources and the terms and conditions set out in this Agreement.

(b) The Center shall not claim legal ownership over the designated germplasm, nor shall it seek any intellectual property over that germplasm or related information.

In 1994 FAO launched intergovernmental negotiations for revision of IUPGR so that it could be made a legally binding treaty and its provisions could be harmonized with CBD. After many rounds of negotiations, in 2001 the International Treaty on Plant Genetic Resources for Food and Agriculture (ITPGR) was signed. ITPGR affirmed farmers' rights; one of its objectives was to create a multilateral system (MLS) for facilitating access to, and sharing of, plant genetic resources. ITPGR came into effect in 2004 and established a "multilateral system of access and benefit sharing" for sixty-four specifically identified crops and forages. ITPGR has a long way to go to fulfill its objectives as there are many unresolved issues, but it is considered an important step in global efforts to conserve and share plant genetic resources.[5]

Thus in the course of two decades the status of plant genetic resources changed dramatically. Negotiations and treaty-making have resulted in plant genetic resources that are today subject to the provisions of more than one agreement or treaty, and they are dealt with by overlapping regimes (CBD, UPOV, TRIPS, and ITPGR). As a result, inconsistencies and tensions have emerged even as attempts are made to achieve global harmonization. The picture gets more complex when nations implement the provisions of CBD and TRIPS in many different ways. The legal status of plant genetic resources has undergone major changes since the 1980s, resulting in the demise of the Common Heritage approach and the increasing use of intellectual property rights. As a result, the North- South divide on access to, and utilization of, genetic resources continues to be a contentious issue in many international for a, including the WTO, CBD, and ITPGR.

Though the Common Heritage approach is no longer in favor, open-source opportunities and conceptualization of plant genetic resources as a global commons, as well as sharing under licenses based on copy left principles, are now discussed as options that could strike a balance between the free for all that characterizes the Common Heritage approach and the proprietary norm of intellectual property rights. In fact, ITPGR itself creates a sort of commons in plant genetic resources with regulated access and benefit-sharing principles.[6] This does not mean free for all access. Rather, it calls for appropriate institutional mechanisms to develop, protect, and promote commons in PGR. The development of licenses is one important issue; the extent to which the general public license (GPL) or its core principles could be applied for developing relevant licenses in the case of plant genetic resources has yet to be addressed. This approach uses intellectual property rights not to enclose or to monopolize but to share, exchange, and facilitate further innovation.[7] Development of commons in plant genetic resources can be useful for public-sector institutions to work together; they can use the open innovation model to develop new plant varieties and release these varieties under licenses that respect both breeders' rights and farmers' rights. But as of now these models and approaches are yet to be tested and validated.

Farmers' Rights

The term *farmers' rights* was a term coined by Pat Mooney and Cary Fowler of Rural Advancement Fund International (RAFI) to highlight the contributions of farmers and farming communities for global plant genetic resources and food diversity. In one sense it served as a term to counter the argument that promoted plant breeders' rights and other intellectual property rights that disregarded the contributions of farmers. The 1989 FAO conference adopted Resolution 5/89, which defined farmers' rights as "rights originating from past, present and future contributions of farmers to conservation, development and availability of plant genetic resources, particularly from centers of origin/diversity"; these rights were nominally vested with the international community. In 1991, Resolution 3/91 proposed that farmers' rights would be implemented by establishing an international fund to support conservation in developing countries. But this never took off. While CBD did not mention farmers' rights, Article 8(j) dealt with local communities and indigenous populations.

Although many international instruments mention farmers' rights, no consensus exists on its meaning and on the ways to implement it. In the negotiations over ITPGR, farmers' rights became a hotly contested topic, finally affirmed in its preamble. Article 9.2 states: "The contracting parties agree that the responsibility for realizing farmers' rights, as they relate to plant genetic resources for food and agriculture, rests with national governments." It specifies what rights could be protected and promoted as farmers' rights. But this is not a mandatory provision and ITPGR did not provide a comprehensive list of rights. As a result, while farmers' rights are mentioned in many international legal instruments, no binding treaty or convention has been enacted. While consensus exists on rights, leaving enactment at the national level has resulted in divergent interpretations and implementations. Farmers' rights can be construed as a set of narrow rights pertaining to the rights of farmers and farming communities to access plant genetic resources or it could be construed as a set of broad rights that go beyond the role of these actors in conservation of genetic resources so as to promote their participation in decision making and development of new varieties.

One important aspect of farmers' rights is the right to save and reuse seeds and to exchange and sell farm-saved seeds. As developed later in this entry, this right has been circumscribed by intellectual property claims on plant varieties. Rights granted to plant breeders and patent holders often limit or eliminate farmers' rights to sell, reuse, and exchange seeds. On the ground, however, it often proves difficult to enforce such claims, or enforcement is prohibitively expensive or cumbersome. This is especially true in large developing countries, such as Brazil, India, and China, where farmers cultivate unauthorized varieties and "stealth" seeds are widely exchanged (Herring 2007; Herring and Kandilkar 2009).

Internationally ITPGR is the only treaty that has resulted in some form of benefit sharing for farmers, but its scope and funding are limited. An important question is how to harmonize intellectual property laws with farmers' rights and the right to food. Haugen (2014) points out that states can adopt a number of measures on public health and nutrition in such a way that they are compatible with TRIPS and still promote benefit sharing and provide exceptions in provisions relating to intellectual property rights. It has been suggested that ITPGR is not sufficient to realize farmers' rights internationally and that a global coalition of stakeholders should take efforts to alter the situation (Winter 2010).

Commitment to farmers' rights is often reduced to providing a few exemptions and rights over seed use rather than a comprehensive approach that recognizes farmers as innovators and promotes their involvement in participatory plant breeding. Agreements have also failed to create a policy space that promotes farmers' empowerment. The absence of an international treaty and the weak provisions in ITPGR ensured that while farmers' rights are widely discussed, little is done to promote and protect them. The irony is that while the rights of plant breeders and the private seed industry are well protected, the rights of farmers and farming communities who have nurtured diversity in plant genetic resources, developed countless varieties of crops with different traits, and contributed to exchange and conservation of plant genetic resources are left to the discretion of the states without any binding global commitment.

Plant Variety Protection and Intellectual Property Rights

Plant varieties and seeds were once considered outside the purview of the industrial mode of production. They were considered to be products of nature and, hence, not eligible for intellectual property protection.[8] Farmers had all the rights over seeds, including the right to reuse, sale, and exchange; today the very right of farmers to save seeds and reuse them is under dispute. Traditionally, plants could be multiplied and a handful of seeds were enough to (re)create plantations or fields filled with plants. This reproducibility is a feature that resisted commodification through the grant of intellectual property rights on germplasm/plant genetic resources. Colonial expansion, the transfer of exotic germplasm, and the introduction of new crops and varieties in distant lands went hand in hand. Colonial expansion also resulted in establishing botanical gardens in many places and the use of germplasm brought from elsewhere for varietal development or for use as new crops. The biological limitation of reproducibility was overcome by both scientific discoveries and legal regimes that gave intellectual property rights over seeds and plant varieties.

With the rediscovery of Mendel's work in genetics in the first decades of the twentieth century, plant breeders acquired a better understanding of the transmission of traits across generations. Thus it was possible to improve existing varieties by back crossing with germplasm from other countries' varieties that possessed the desired traits. In the 1930s, hybridization was established as a new technique to develop new plant varieties. The hybrids produced high yields when first employed; however, in subsequent seasons the farmer had to buy seeds again to get the same or higher yield.[9] In the United States, based on demands from the private-sector plant-breeding and seed industry, the Plant Patent Act was passed. The key feature of this legislation was the grant of patent-like protection to asexually propagating species.

A historic decision given by the U.S. Supreme Court in 1980 gave a new understanding about what could be patented. In *Diamond v. Chakrabarty*, the products-of-nature bar on patenting living products was overturned. The Court ruled that a human-made microorganism is patentable subject matter as a "manufacture" or "composition of nature." The majority opinion held that the genetically modified microorganism was "not nature's handiwork, but his own; accordingly it is patentable subject matter." This radical concept of human agency as enunciated in *Diamond* raised many questions and the decision was widely debated. The reverberations are heard even today, particularly in the context of patenting genes. Although the judgment was very clear about patenting criteria, the PVPA office rejected applications for nonhybrid plants based on the reasoning, or the understanding, of the separate protection regimes for plants. But a ruling given in 1985 clarified the matter, one that was further affirmed in another ruling given in 1987. In *Ex parte Hibberd* the issue was whether a patent could be issued covering the tissue culture, seeds, and whole plant of a maize line selected from that tissue culture, as applied by Kenneth Hibberd. The Appeals Board gave the opinion that as long as the criteria for patents (i.e., novelty, utility, and non-obviousness) were met, there was no bar in granting patents, and PVPA and PPA do not limit such claims [*Ex parte Hibberd*, 227 USPQ 443 (Bd. Pat. App. & Inter. 1985)]. Thus the board concluded that patents could be issued for all plants, including open-pollinated seeds. The utility patent offers a very strong protection when compared to plant breeders' rights. The breadth of the patent claim could include plants, modified genes, and seeds; thus, the former differentiation between sexually reproducing and asexually reproducing was irrelevant. If the technology could produce anything that could meet the criteria for patentability, there was no bar in patenting inventions relating to plants. Patent rights are extensive. Without the permission of the patent holder, no one can make, sell, or use a product covered by a utility patent. Thus, farmers would be violating the law if they were to engage in selling or exchanging seeds for consideration if the seeds were the outcome of a plant covered by a utility patent. The PVPA provided for what is known as a "farmers exemption," under which farmers are permitted to sell or exchange seeds; such sales are known as brown bag sales. But when plant varieties are covered by patents *and* PVPA, dual protection is available to the developer. The farmers' right to sell or reuse the seeds is not permissible, as that would amount to an infringement of the patent right.

In *J.E.M. Ag Supply, Inc. v. Pioneer Hi-Bred Int'l, Inc.*, the U.S. Supreme Court affirmed that dual protection—i.e., patent protection and plant variety—was permissible for plant varieties. As germplasm could be protected under trade secrets for plant genetic resources, three modes of protection are available in the United States. In 2013, in *Bowman v. Monsanto Co.*, the Supreme Court held that the patent exhaustion doctrine was not applicable to patented seeds, meaning that the farmer did not have the right to reproduce patented seeds through planting and harvesting without the permission of patent holders. Thus, farmers in the United States, under this ruling, do not have the right to replant or sell the produce as seeds to others unless those activities are done with the permission of the patent holder.

As we see from the cases discussed above, the strongest position on intellectual property rights in plants has evolved in the United States. The position is summarized as below:

Plant Variety Protection Act—Applicable for species that undergo sexual reproduction and for tuber propagated plants and first generation (F1) hybrids

Patent Act—Protection for inventions that meet the requirements of utility, novelty, and inventive step is available. This facilitates patenting of biotechnological inventions and genetically modified organisms (GMOs).

Plant Patent Act—Applicable for species of vegetative and asexual propagation excluding edible tubers. This is used widely in the case of ornamentals, fruit, and forest trees.

In Europe, the Union for the Protection of New Varieties (UPOV) was established in 1961.[10] In 1970 the Plant Variety Protection Act (PVPA) was enacted in the United States. Under this act, protection is given if it is proved that the three criteria ("novelty," "uniformity," and "stability") are met.[11] If the conditions are met, a certificate of protection is given and this gives the holder the exclusive right to use the variety for seventeen years from the date of issue. Significantly, PVPA also provides for exemptions to farmers and for research purposes. Similarly, the UPOV Convention defines norms for protection and exemptions. Both the PVPA and UPOV Convention were amended later, resulting in strengthening the rights of plant breeders with restrictions on both the farmers' rights to reuse seeds and the plant breeders' exemption, thus enabling use of germplasm for varietal development.

According to the 1991 UPOV Convention, the right to save seed is classified as a farmers' privilege, and it is an option for members to consider "within reasonable limits and subject to the safeguarding of the legitimate interests of the breeder" (Article 15(2)).[12] The rights granted the plant breeder for a protected variety, generally, are the exclusive rights to do or to permit (normally by licensing) the following acts in relation to the propagating material of the protected variety:

1. Produce or reproduce the material
2. Condition the material for propagation
3. Offer the material for sale
4. Import/export the material, and
5. Stock the material for the above-mentioned purposes.

Thus, the rights available are extensive while exceptions are limited for two purposes—if permitted by law. That is, a country can frame its laws under the framework provided by the 1991 UPOV Convention and specify the limits of exemptions to plant breeders' rights. It can restrict the so-called farmers' exemption or eliminate it altogether.

Article 53(b) of the European Patent Convention excludes plant varieties from patent protection. Article 4(1), Paragraph 2 of the European Biotechnology Directive allows patenting of plants where "the technical feasibility is not confined to a particular plant variety." The Enlarged Boards of Appeal of the European Patent Office in the *Novartis* case held that GM plants can be granted patent protection when the invention is not limited to a single variety. This exception to patentability is narrow, as inventions are not limited to any single plant variety per se.[13] Plant variety protection in the United States and in Europe differs, partly due to the issue of differentiating plants and plant variety/varieties in the intellectual property laws. In addition, variations are found among countries within Europe in implementing plant variety protection.

In the Uruguay Round negotiations, intellectual property rights became a matter for vigorous debate. Developed nations were determined to push for a global agreement that would expand the subject matter of intellectual property rights. The resulting TRIPS agreement mandated intellectual property protection for plant varieties. With the advent of the TRIPS agreement, a global shift in plant variety protection occurred as countries had to adhere to the norms specified in TRIPS. Article 27.3(b) states that members may exclude from patentability

> plants and animals other than micro-organisms, and essentially biological processes for the production of plants and animals other than non-biological, and microbiological processes. However, Members shall provide for the protection of plant varieties either by patents or by an effective sui generis system or by any combination thereof.

The rules of the UPOV Convention have served as the basis for plant variety protection in many countries. But some countries opted for stronger protection even before the revision of the UPOV Convention in 1991. Since only a small percentage of the population is engaged in farming as the primary occupation, the expanding scope of intellectual property rights did not provoke a very intense response, although some opposition was registered. Farmers were used to hybrids and they have been fully integrated into the industrial mode of production, in which seeds are just another input. In contrast, many developing nations had no laws to offer protection to plants, nor very well defined intellectual property regimes. They had no option but to change their intellectual property regime to make it compatible with TRIPS. So the choice before them was not one of whether or not to provide protection for plant varieties; rather, it was which option to choose. More important is that member states cannot establish legal concepts of invention that exclude any living or non-living material from intellectual property protection as novelty, non-obviousness, and usefulness, i.e., the relevant requirements for patentability can be met by inventions relating to living material as well.

The obligation under 27.3(b) is for granting protection to plant varieties only. Hence, defining plant variety is essential. But TRIPS does not elaborate on this. One can define plant variety in a scientific sense, based on taxonomy, or in a legal sense, based on specific criteria to be met for protection. A plant variety can also be defined as a combination of both. It can be argued that the term *plant varieties* is more a legal construct than a scientific fact. With the advent of biotechnology the legal construct has also undergone changes as claims have been made for protection of genes and hybrid plants. Thus, although a wide scope appears to exist both for flexibility in defining plant varieties and for intellectual property, protection has to be balanced with other objectives, such as farmers' rights and promoting research in plant breeding.

TRIPS does not define what is meant by "effective protection" under Article 27.3(b). Countries have responded in many ways, so much so that many types of varieties are defined by the laws differently. For example the Plant Variety Protection and Farmers Rights (PVPFR) Act of India defines four types (new variety, extant variety, farmers' variety, and essentially derived variety) with different criteria, rights, and durations.[14] Many countries, particularly developing countries, have opted for a sui generis system of protection for plant varieties.[15]

A TRIPS compatible system of protection can be one of the following:

1. Exclude plants and plant varieties and set up a sui generis system, which can be under patent law or a separate system;
2. Cover plants and plant varieties under patentability;

Table 15.1 Comparison of TRIPS Compatible Patent Law, UPOV 1978, UPOV 1991 and "Sui Generis"

Feature	TRIPS Compatible Patent Law	UPOV 1978	UPOV 1991	"Sui Generis"
Eligibility for Protection	Novelty, Inventive Step and utility	Novel, Distinctive, Uniform and Stable	Novel, Distinctive, Uniform and Stable	Novel, Distinctive, Uniform and Stable but other criteria also for some types of varieties
Exclusive Rights	Patent like protection	Plant Breeders' Rights with exemptions	Plant Breeders' Rights and Patents, exemptions optional	Plant Breeders' Rights with exemptions for Breeders and Farmers
Minimum Term of Protection	20 years	18 years for trees and grapevine, 15 years for all other plants	25 years for trees and grapevines, 20 years for all other plants	Varies—no uniformity

3. Provide for dual protection under patent law and under another system or law, as in the United States;
4. Exclude plant varieties only from patentability and establish a sui generis system.

The UPOV convention is the relevant convention on plant varieties but TRIPS does not mandate joining UPOV and it did not specify the UPOV Convention as the model to be followed. Whether countries should join the UPOV Convention or not depends on many factors. The major advantage is that countries can readily use its rules and provisions and need not extend protection to all varieties.

In TRIPS Plus agreements, which are negotiated under bilateral trade agreements, countries are to provide stronger protection for plant varieties by providing patent protection or adhere to the 1991 UPOV convention norms, with very few exceptions.[16] This provides "effective" protection for plant varieties from the perspective of the United States and the European Union. However, in the changing intellectual property landscape, patents are preferred to mere plant breeders' rights or a combination of both is sought. The UPOV Convention also allows dual protection. Hence, in the United States and Europe, effective protection means dual protection with virtually no exemption or little exemption for farmers and plant breeders. Countries that are joining UPOV now, although they may start with a sui generis system in applying protection to a limited number of varieties, may have little option later. But whether they can retain a farmers' exemption is an important question as the UPOV Convention is being revised and countries have to adhere to the 1991 UPOV Convention if they join now.

Large developing countries, such as India, China, and Brazil, have taken different approaches in plant variety protection. While China has adopted the UPOV Convention as the model, India opted for a sui generis system that gives effect to plant breeders' rights and farmers' rights through a separate law. In developed nations, patent protection is emerging as the de facto standard for protecting plant varieties, while in many developing countries a balance is struck between plant breeders' rights and farmers' rights to use the variety for varietal development without permission of the intellectual property right holder.

Legally the patent holder can deny access to plant genetic resources necessary to develop new varieties and this can become a constraint in developing varieties using biotechnology. The European Community Directive 98/44 on the Legal Protection for Biotechnological Inventions enables breeders to apply for a compulsory license for nonexclusive use of the patented invention; the patent holder is entitled to royalties. In implementing this provision, France and Germany have provided for a flexibility that enables exemption for scientific research and breeders (Santilli 2012, 98–99).

Irrespective of the 1991 UPOV Convention and the TRIPS agreement, some European countries have enacted laws to safeguard and promote the use of local varieties and to provide farmers with the opportunity to choose varieties. Norway has adhered to the 1978 UPOV Convention. In some countries, including Brazil, many types of varieties, such as local varieties and conservation varieties, are recognized by law, and the provisions on seed saving and use and exemptions from registration and other provisions enable them to strike a balance between TRIPS/UPOV norms and the rights of farmers and breeders.

What constitutes a "balanced" plant variety protection regime and how to develop a "sui generis" system that is "balanced" and still is TRIPS compliant is an important issue.[17] Seed industry development and providing incentives for innovation in plant breeding cannot be separated from intellectual property rights concerning plant variety. Striking a balance to safeguard different interests of various stakeholders is not an easy task. The sheer diversity in implementing the provisions of the TRIPS agreement and the UPOV Convention indicates that intellectual property protection for plant varieties is contested terrain, and it will remain so for years to come.

Plant Biotechnology and Intellectual Property Rights

Since the 1990s transgenic technology has transformed the development of new varieties with desired traits. Areas under genetically modified (GM) crops have expanded dramatically. Patenting of plant biotechnology innovations has increased rapidly; it is estimated that more than a thousand patents have been granted for transgenic plants in the United States alone. In agricultural biotechnology, different components, such as vectors, genes of interest, selectable marker genes, and methods of gene transfer, are deployed. Many of these have been patented; as a result, the patenting of seeds, plant varieties, and processes and components used in plant transformation technology has resulted in a proliferation of patents related to plant biotechnology.[18]

In the case of Golden Rice—transgenic rice developed to overcome Vitamin A deficiency—commercialization necessitated access to seventy-two patents held by forty different organizations (see Stein, this volume). This constraint was overcome by agreement by patent holders to the use of technology for humanitarian purpose with some conditions; the Golden Rice Humanitarian Board was formed for this purpose. Otherwise the technology would have encountered difficulty in gaining access to patented technologies or would have become expensive as patent holders are entitled to royalties.[19] But Golden Rice should be considered an exception; in most cases, the technology is commercialized by the private sector or licenses are provided to seed companies for using the technology. Seed companies can then incorporate the patented genes in the varieties developed and released by them.

In contrast, when the Green Revolution was launched, plant breeding and seed production were mostly done by public-sector institutions, including International Agricultural Research Centers (IARCs). The private sector provided agrochemical inputs. Public-sector institutions developed and provided open pollinated varieties (OPVs) that could be replanted without any reduction in the yield in subsequent generations. While hybrids were also developed, public-sector institutions did not behave as a monopolist seeking control by using intellectual property rights. In the case of agricultural biotechnology—or the "gene revolution" in agriculture—the private sector is the dominant player with the public sector paying more attention to basic research and provision of germplasm (see Pray and Naseem, 2007; Harriss and Stewart, this volume). Moreover, the private sector has built a strong patent portfolio covering many technologies; the public sector's share in such patents is much less than that of the private sector. For example, in the case of patents related to Bt cotton in India, it was found that the private sector had a major share while the public sector had a limited share.[20] But the availability of seeds of unapproved varieties containing patented genes and their rapid diffusion among farmers demonstrate the difficulty in enforcing intellectual property rights and in regulating genetically modified crops. In India, this has been the case with Bt cotton, which has been a favorite with farmers for more than a decade (Herring and Rao 2012).

India does not allow patents on plant varieties and explicitly allows farmers to replant seeds or exchange seeds saved by them. But the bar on patenting plant varieties does not prevent the patenting of genes, DNA fragments, research tools, processes, and other technologies required for creating genetically modified plant with desired traits. Under TRIPS, patents should be available for all technologies; interpreting exceptions is a contentious issue. Technically, genetically modified plant varieties with desired traits can be sold as hybrids and farmers will have to buy seeds for second and later generations if they want to get good yields. Thus, patenting of technologies, materials, and processes and selling the cultivars as hybrids make the bar on patenting plant varieties irrelevant to a great extent.

Globally, public-sector involvement in the seed sector has also diminished. In China, the public sector competed with the private sector (Monsanto) in Bt cotton; it developed and delivered Bt cotton varieties, resulting in lower seed prices for farmers.[21] In India, the public sector failed to produce Bt cotton, but private firms developed over a thousand legal hybrids, which now dominate cotton farming in India. Monsanto became the dominant player by licensing technology to different seed companies for incorporating it in many hybrids. In Latin America, Monsanto's efforts to seek royalties on GM crops became a contentious issue. Monsanto failed to get patents for transgenic soy in Argentina, but the company had obtained patents in Europe. Monsanto argued that it was entitled to receive royalties from Argentinean exports of soya meal to Europe as it had patents on GM soya in Europe, but this claim was rejected. In *Monsanto Technology LLC vs. Cefetra BV* (2010), the European Court of Justice ruled that Monsanto could not bar the imports of the soya meal from Argentina. Since 1996 Monsanto has held a European patent relating to a DNA sequence, which, when inserted into the DNA of a soya bean plant, confers resistant to the herbicide glyphosate. This herbicide is widely used in agriculture. But the DNA in the soya meal was not performing this function, i.e., providing resistance to herbicide glyphosate. The European court ruled that the patent could be enforced only in cases where DNA was performing the function that was covered by the patent.[22]

The TRIPS agreement has provisions that include compulsory licensing to promote competition, protect public interest and prevent anti-competitive measures. But their scope is limited and any policy has to be compatible with the provisions of the TRIPS agreement. Compulsory licensing has hardly been used in agricultural biotechnology, although it has been used by many countries to facilitate access to intellectual property in pharmaceuticals. Vitamin A deficiency among the poor has not been considered a health emergency that would compel compulsory licensing, but that option is legally available to governments, as is the case with all technologies.

Since the 1980s the agrochemical and seed industries have undergone a massive transformation, including horizontal and vertical integration. The result is increased market power in the hands of a few players. It is estimated that the top four pesticide firms control about 60 percent of the global market, and the top four seed firms control 56 percent of the global seed market (based on sales of the branded seeds). Global expansion of private seed companies has been facilitated by globalization of intellectual property regimes through TRIPS and other agreements and by the decline of public-sector activity. In the United States, it is estimated that 85 percent of transgenic cotton patents and 70 percent of non-corn transgenic plant patents are held by the top three companies. Cross-licensing of transgenic technology and acquisition of seed companies have helped the dominant players to consolidate and expand their hold.[23]

This trend was predicted by Jack Kloppenburg in *First the Seed,* which traces the history of commodification of germplasm and chronicles the rise of the agricultural biotechnology sector. According to Moschini (2010, 9):

> For some of the main US crops, the consolidation that has occurred in the seed industry over the last 15 years has been accompanied by remarkable changes driven by the advent, and strong adoption, of GM crops and by the increased role of IPRs.

This consolidation has raised concerns about abuse of monopoly position and development of cartels in the agriculture input industry (Matson, Tang, and Wynn 2012). In many developed countries today, farmers are more dependent on external inputs than they were a century ago; seeds are no exception.[24] The quantum of saved and reused seed is likely to decline further with continued consolidation in the seed industry and the farm sector. For some this is a welcome trend; farm sector output has grown many times over even with fewer farmers and farms. The story is different in developing and least developed countries, where the farm sector is still a major sector in terms of employment and livelihood and serves as an important contributor to GDP.

The impact of intellectual property rights on food security and small and medium farmers is a much debated issue. Linkages to questions of human rights and food security, the right to food, and the right to enjoy the benefits of science have been prominent (De Schutter 2011, 2014; Helfer and Austin 2011). This debate should be seen in the broad context of debates over the role of intellectual property rights in fulfilling developmental needs and providing access to technologies and germplasm that are vital for food security. The major positions can be summed up below:

1. Intellectual property rights have an impact on food security and the right to food but are not the determining forces. Countries have many options to address the negative impacts and thereby can balance their obligations under the TRIPS agreement and public policy objectives on food security and the right to food.
2. Intellectual property rights adversely affect access to seeds and the right to reuse seeds, and they make food more expensive; the spread of commercial seeds adversely affects crop diversity. To address these and other issues many corrective measures, such as making agricultural research more responsive to the needs of the poor, protecting farmers' rights, and protecting innovation through alternative approaches, have to be undertaken by governments.
3. Intellectual property rights do not adversely affect food security or human rights. Protecting intellectual property rights is essential for promoting innovations and for technology transfer. Addressing issues in food security calls for better application of science and technology; advances in biotechnology and other technologies are necessary to meet the challenges in food security and to increase food output.

Suggestions have been made, including reorienting the agricultural research system, encouraging more involvement of the public sector in agricultural biotechnology research, and developing and using the flexibilities in TRIPS—particularly the provisions that enable promotion of competition and restricting anticompetitive behavior (De Schutter 2009, 2011).

Using open source models as an alternative has been suggested, although this has not been tested widely so far.[25] CAMBIA—based in Australia—has used the open-source approach to license some technologies in agricultural biotechnology and has used Biological Open Source (BiOS) license to ensure that any improvements made will be shared. Public Intellectual Property Resource for Agriculture (PIPRA), an alliance of more than forty public institutions in twelve countries, has been formed with the objective to facilitate technology transfer, reduce barriers created by intellectual property rights, and develop mechanisms such as clearing houses for providing access. PIPRA helps in capacity building and provides intellectual property- related services. In recent years, initiatives under Public-Private Partnerships (PPP) have been formed for specific research and development purposes (e.g., African Orphan Crops Consortium). As public-sector institutions have access to, or have collected, vast quantities of valuable germplasm, getting access to them is an incentive for the private sector, although such access raises questions of commodification.

Using intellectual property rights in agricultural biotechnology has been an especially contentious issue, particularly regarding the effects on small farmers and restriction on further research. Nevertheless, enforcement of intellectual property rights has not been easy in developing countries, as farmers have found ways to evade formal regulations (Herring 2007).

New Technological Options, Climate Change, Intellectual Property Rights

Traditional plant breeding combined with new technologies can hasten the development of new varieties or can result in the development of transgenic plants with desired traits.[26] For example, marker assisted selection (MAS) in breeding has reduced the number of generations needed to evaluate breeding materials. But MAS has not been used effectively by public crop improvement projects due to high costs and restrictions imposed by intellectual property rights. Patents on many selectable markers used in transgenics have been granted (e.g., genetic markers associated with drought tolerance in maize). New techniques like reverse breeding, cisgenesis and intragenesis, and synthetic genomics are useful in introducing traits such as male sterility, modified starch content, and bacterial resistance, but there are many patents on these techniques. What is important is not just the number, but also the scope of patent claims. Obtaining multiple related patents could effectively block access to newer techniques.[27] When many related patents are granted to many parties with none of them able to use the technologies without the consent or license from others, a situation known as anti-commons can emerge: fragmented ownership can result in increased transaction costs and restricted access to patented technologies. The proliferation of patents on techniques, parts of DNA, and biological materials may then hamper access to technologies or raise costs prohibitively.

Climate change is likely to affect agriculture adversely, particularly in developing countries, and result in significant reductions in food output. The need for developing varieties that could be useful in climate change mitigation and adaptation is clear (see Watson, this volume). Varieties have to be developed and deployed within the next few decades. These varieties are needed most in countries in Africa, Asia, and Latin America that are less likely to have the capacity to develop and deploy them. Brazil, India, and China have strong national agricultural research innovation systems, and they are giving importance to this problem. Research centers under CGIAR (Consultative Group on International Agricultural Research) are likewise developing such varieties. While many traditional varieties have the desired traits such as drought, flood, and salinity tolerance, developing modern varieties with such multi-gene traits and good yields is a daunting challenge, requiring access to germplasm and state-of-the-art techniques (Newell-McGloughlin, this volume).

Patenting of genes relating to plant varieties relevant for climate change adaptation and mitigation has become a contentious issue. In 2008 the ETC Group released a study that claimed that multinationals such as BASF, DuPont, and Monsanto have sought many patents related to "climate ready" genetically modified crops. Another study in 2008 identified thirty patents related to drought tolerant genes. In an update in 2010, the ETC Group claimed that it has identified 262 patent families. Claims related to abiotic stress tolerance such as drought, salinity, heat, and cold have increased within a short period. Furthermore, the group claimed that while public-sector institutions owned 9 percent of the patent families, three companies accounted for about 66 percent of the total.[28] While these claims have been contested and the number of patents granted might turn out to be much smaller with changes in the scope of the claims, this trend indicates that the private sector will be an important player in developing genetically modified varieties that are useful in meeting the climate change challenge.

A study done for the Organisation for Economic Co-operation and Development (OECD) pointed out that, while patent applications in adaptation related biotechnology have increased substantially from 1995 to 2007, more than 80 percent of the patent applications were related to inventions in OECD member countries. Moreover, researchers observed that the private-sector plays a key role in adaptation-related biotechnology innovation as four of the five most active patenting organizations, which together account for 23 percent of all patent applications, are from the private sector, although in some countries, such as Japan, China, and Korea, the public sector has had a significant role (Agarwala et al. 2012).

In 2013 Monsanto's patent application for a method of "enhancing stress tolerance in plants and methods thereof" was rejected by India's Intellectual Property Appellate Board (IPAB), which stated that the technology was merely a discovery of a new property of known substance and, hence, could not be considered as an invention under Section 3(d) of the Indian Patent Act. The IPAB cited Section 3(d) and for the first time this section has been invoked in the case of plant patents; under Section 3(j) patents and animals could not be patented. While Monsanto was successful in obtaining patents in Europe and the United States, the rejection in India raises questions both about the validity of such claims as inventions and about the possibility for any single system of intellectual property rights applying across the globe.

While studies based on patent data cannot predict application of technologies, the increase in patenting activities in agricultural biotechnology has implications for the transfer and application of technology. Whether the private sector and the public sector will work together to meet the challenges of climate change in agriculture or whether intellectual property rights will become barriers to the transfer of technology is not yet known. The Public-Private Partnership (PPP) model can be used to balance the interests of the private and public sectors and governments should provide more incentives for the public sector to develop relevant technologies (Kolady and Lesser 2008). The Green Revolution constituted a successful example of the application of science and technology through international partnerships to avert famines and enhance food security (Harriss and Stewart, this volume). Many models exist in theory. Much discussion is ongoing concerning how CGIAR centers and public-sector institutions in developing countries might work together and develop varieties that could be licensed under agreements that promote further innovation without restricting research through the exercise of rights conferred by intellectual property. To the extent new traits and varieties involve genetic engineering, a significant political obstacle constrains development and deployment of climate resilient crops (Newell-McGloughlin, this volume). Intellectual property rights are typically justified as an incentive for innovation; it is also possible that governments can explore options such as prizes and advance marketing commitments.[29] Strong intellectual property rights do have externalities: primarily the anti-commons that restricts access for use and research. The AIDS crisis in Africa demonstrated this point in regard to pharmaceuticals; in the context of climate change, strong and enforceable intellectual property claims in plant germplasm could become significant barriers in technology development, transfer, and diffusion.

Conclusion: The Regime Complex in Plant Genetic Resources and the Role of Intellectual Property Rights

The increasing importance of intellectual property rights in accessing, sharing, and exchanging plant genetic resources—and the politics of challenge and contestation of these claims—constitutes a salient feature of the global politics of food. Contestation over intellectual property claims and efforts to minimize their impacts are continuous and they apply across various forums. One reason is that the global regime for plant genetic resources has become more complex and less coherent since the early 1980s, in the processes analyzed in this entry. The idea of *regime complex* has been developed by scholars working on international relations and global environmental governance. The idea is to capture the dynamic overlay and interplay among institutions and actors (including states) interacting in different forums (Raustiala and Victor 2004). Evolution of the regime complex in plant genetic resources has introduced more complexity with overlapping treaties, conventions, and agreements. This institutional and legal outcome offers scope for both developing nations and developed nations for forum shopping, coalition building, and use of various multilateral settings to press their agenda. Who has gained most in the negotiations, how effective have been efforts by developing nations to safeguard their interests in the context of the growing importance of intellectual property, and how effective has been agricultural biodiversity governance in developing nations given the evolving global regime complex and commitments made under different treaties and conventions is a matter of debate. There are no easy answers to these questions.

Bièvre and Thomann (2010) argue that while developing nations have been able to secure the adoption of agreements favorable to them in global arenas, these agreements do not have effective enforcement. In WTO/TRIPS, the enforcement mechanism is strong, but developed nations have managed to prevent issues that are of importance to developing nations from being negotiated in these forums. Although developing nations achieved some success in forums other than the WTO, developed nations registered gains as many new members joined the 1991 UPOV Convention. Baumgartner's (2011) study of regime complexity and fluidity found that weak actors had more influence and power in biodiversity-related intellectual property rights than plant genetic resources used in agriculture. The elements that make up the regime complex consist of residues of multiple agreements, treaties, and conventions with different objectives; harmonizing these protocols at different levels (national and global) remains a distant dream. The Nagoya Protocol on Access to Genetic Resources and the Fair and Equitable Sharing of Benefits Arising from their Utilization was negotiated in 2010 under the framework convention of the Convention on Biological Diversity; what "fair and equitable" means in practice and how enforcement of provisions will harmonize with other elements of the regime complex governing intellectual property remain unclear. Moreover, the challenges of climate change and the impact of synthetic biology both present conceptual and political challenges for the Nagoya Protocol, which remains only one part of the complex. The fragmented and unstable nature of the regime complex renders more difficult any search for solutions to global food security and farmer welfare.

A certain irony is evident in the long-term evolution of this regime complex. In the progression from a property framework of "Common Heritage" to one of "Common Concern of Human Kind," rights over plant genetic resources were settled on sovereign states, but without creating noticeably better governance or more effective coordination at the global level. The decades to come will almost certainly make cooperation more consequential than ever before, as the challenges—both political and technical—facing food security and sustainability of agriculture are daunting.[30] What role intellectual property rights per se will play, and how property claims will affect the politics of food in the years to come, are open questions. Extension of intellectual property rights to plant genetic resources is not an unmixed blessing. While strong property rights have spurred innovation and incentivized development of agricultural biotechnology, there is strong political opposition to extending rights down the genomic chain. If plant genetic resources are treated as a public good with no restrictions on access and use, sharing is facilitated, but the effect has not always been beneficial for those developing countries that are significant centers of origin for many crops. Commodification of genetic resources through intellectual property rights, then, does promote innovation, but simultaneously it raises questions of access and use of these rights to restrict further innovation—the problem of the anti-commons. Striking a balance between these two poles is a challenging task facing international agencies, national governments, and relevant organizations.

Notes

1. See Raustiala and Sprigman (2012) on copyrights and cuisines; see Barham and Sylvander (2012) on geographical indications.

2. There is no universal definition for genetic resources. Article 2 of the Convention on Biological Diversity defines them as "genetic material of actual or potential value"; genetic material, in turn, is defined as "any material of plant, animal, microbial or other origin containing functional units of heredity." Although "biological material" is often used as a synonym for "genetic resources," the EU Directive on Legal Protection of Biotechnological Inventions defines biological material as "material containing genetic information and capable of reproducing itself or being reproduced in a biological system." Article 2 of the FAO International Treaty on Plant Genetic Resources for Food and Agriculture defines plant genetic resources as "any material of plant origin including reproductive and vegetative propagating material, containing functional units of heredity." Article 2.1(a) of the FAO International Undertaking on Plant Genetic Resources (1983) provides an expansive definition that includes wild and weed species (Blakeney 2011).
3. See Kloppenburg and Kleinman (1988), Crosby (1972), and Wood (2011) for details.
4. Kloppenburg (1988, 49).
5. See Halewood, Norigea, and Louafi (2013) and Frisoon, Lopez, and Esquinas (2011) for extensive analysis of the treaty and its implementation.
6. Oguamanam (2014) and Aoki (2008) have examined this in detail.
7. See Srinivas (2006S) and Marden and Godrefy (2012) for details.
8. See Kloppenburg (2004) for an extensive analysis.
9. Lewontin and Berlan (1986) and Ramey (2010) provide a Marxist analysis of the development of hybrids and the expansion of the seed industry. See also Fitzgerald (1993).
10. See Dutfield (2008) for details on the origins of UPOV and its growth.
11. Under UPOV 1991 the criteria are distinctness, uniformity, and stability (DUS), which are defined as:

    Distinctness (Article 7): The variety must be "clearly distinguishable from any other variety whose existence is a matter of common knowledge" at the time when protection is applied for; Uniformity (Article 8): The variety must be sufficiently uniform in its distinguishing characteristics, such that different individuals of the same variety are reasonably similar; and Stability (Article 9): The variety must be stable in its distinguishing characteristics, that is, it remains "unchanged after repeated propagation or, in the case of a particular cycle of propagation, at the end of each such cycle."
12. http://www.upov.int/upovlex/en/conventions/1991/act1991.html.
13. For an in-depth analysis of plant variety protection and in Europe, see Llewelyn and Adcock (2006).
14. See Rangnekar (2013) for an analysis of the Indian PVP system.
15. See Santilli (2012) for details.
16. See Maskus (2012) and Drexl, Ruse-Khan, and Nadde-Phlix (2014) for details.
17. See Narasimhan (2008) for an analysis. To what extent countries have been able to implement such systems is an important question; for a case study on Thailand, see Lertdhamtewe (2012).
18. See Dunwell (2010) for details with examples.
19. http://www.wipo.int/edocs/mdocs/mdocs/en/wipo_ip_rio_13/wipo_ip_rio_13_www_247930.pdf
20. See Sastry, Rashmi and Badri (2011) for details. See also Ramasundaram, Kurup, and Chand (2011).
21. See Linton and Torsekar (2010) for details and a comparative study of the role of the public sector in China and India, and Spielman et al. (2011) for an analysis of the private sector and public sector in the seed sector in India.

22. The European Directive on the Legal Protection of Biotechnological Inventions (Directive 98/44/EC of 6 July, 1998 in Article 9) states that the protection conferred by a patent on a product containing or consisting of genetic information shall extend to all material in which "the genetic information is contained and performs its function." See http://europa.eu/rapid/press-release_CJE-10-73_en.htm?locale=en and http://www.ippt.eu/files/2010/IPPT20100706_ECJ_Monsanto_v_Cefetra.pdf for details of the ruling. See Hansson (2011) for an analysis of this ruling.
23. See Howard (2009) for details.
24. See Parday et al. (2013) and Janis and Smith (2007).
25. See Adenle et al. (2012), Kloppenburg, (2013) Oldham, Hall, and Forero (2013), Deibel (2012), and Srinivas (2006) for details.
26. See Tuberosa, Graner, and Frison (2014) [Vol. 1 and Vol. 2]; Newell-McGloughlin, this volume.
27. See Yadav et al. (2014) for examples of patents on various plant genetic transformation technologies, selectable markers, and innovations in plant biotechnology.
28. See Blakeney (2013) for an analysis.
29. See Srinivas (2013) for an analysis of the use of these options and various "push" and "pull" mechanisms for creating incentives to innovate and share.
30. See entries in this volume by Watson, Herring, McHughen, and Newell-McGloughin in particular.

    According to Raustila and Victor (2004)

    "Rather than a single, discrete regime governing PGR, the relevant rules are found in at least five clusters of international legal agreements—what we call *elemental regimes*—as well as in national rules within key states, especially the United States and the European Union (EU.) These elemental regimes overlap in scope, subject, and time; events in one affect those in others. We term the collective of these elements a *regime complex*: an array of partially overlapping and nonhierarchical institutions governing a particular issue-area."

    Brand et.al. (2008) provide an excellent overview of the responses of the states to developments on plant genetic resources at various international fora. See also the recent literature on the analysis of regime complex in plant genetic resources, e.g., Morin and Orsini (2014) and literature on global environmental regimes e.g., Orsini, Morin, and Young (2013) to understand how scholars analyze the regime complexity

References

Adenle, A. A., S. K. Sowe, G. Parayil, and O. Aginam. 2012. "Analysis of Open Source Biotechnology in Developing Countries." *Technology in Society* 34:256–269.

Agarwala, S., C. Bordier, V. Schreitter, et al. 2012. *Adaptation and Innovation: An Analysis of Crop Biotechnology Patent Data*. Paris: Organisation for Economic Co-operation and Development.

Aoki, K. 2008. *Seed Wars: Controversies and Cases in Plant Genetic Resources and Intellectual Property*. Durham, NC: Carolina Academic Press.

Barham, E., and B. Sylvander, eds. 2012. *Labels of Origin for Food*. Cambridge, MA: CABI.

Baumgartner, H. 2011. *Patents, Power and Rhetoric: Intellectual Property Rights and Politics of Regime Complexity*. Lucerne, Switzerland: Institute of Political Science, University of Lucerne.

Bièvre, D. B., and L. Thomann. 2010. *Forum Shopping in the Global Intellectual Property Rights Regime*. Mannheim: MannheimerZentrumfürEuropäischeSozialforschung.

Blakeney, M. 2011. *Trends in Intellectual Property Rights Relating to Genetic Resources for Food and Agriculture*. Rome: CGRFA, FAO.

Blakeney, M. 2013. "Climate Change and Intellectual Property." In *Genomics and Breeding for Climate Resilient Crops*, edited by C. Kole, 433–460. Berlin: Springer.

Brand, U., C. Görg, J. Hirsch, and M. Wissen. 2008. *Conflicts in Environmental Regulation and Internationalisation of the State*. London: Routledge.

Brush, S. 2004. *Farmers' Bounty: Locating Crop Diversity in the Contemporary World*. New Haven, CT: Yale University Press.

Byerlee, D., and H. J. Dubin. 2010. "Crop Improvement in the CGIAR as a Global Success Story of Open Access and International Collaboration." *International Journal of the Commons* 4 (1):1–19.

Crosby, A.W. 1972. *The Colombian Exchange*. Westport, CT: Greenwood Press.

Deibel, E. 2012. "Open Variety Rights." *Journal of Agrarian Change* 13 (2): 282–309.

De Schutter, O. 2009. *Report of the Special Rapporteur on the Right to Food: Seed Policies and the Right to Food*. Geneva, Switzerland: United Nations High Commissioner for Refugees.

——. 2011. "The Right of Everyone to Enjoy the Benefits of Scientific Progress and the Right to Food." *Human Rights Quarterly* 33:304–350.

——. 2014. *The Transformative Potential of the Right to Food*. Geneva, Switzerland: UN Human Rights Council.

Drexl, J., H. G. Ruse-Khan, and S. Nadde-Phlix, eds. 2014. *EU Bilateral Trade Agreements and Intellectual Property*. Berlin: Springer.

Dunwell, J. M. 2010. "Patents and Intellectual Property Rights Issues." In *Transgenic Crop Plants*. Vol. 2, *Utilization and Biosafety*. edited by C. Kole, C. H. Michler, A. G. Abbott, and T. C. Hall, 411–434. Berlin: Springer.

Dutfield, G. 2008. "Turning Plant Varieties into Intellectual Property: The UPOV Convention." In *The Future Control of Food*, edited by G. Tansey and T. Rajotte, 27–47. London: Earthscan.

Fitzgerald, D. 1993. "Farmers Deskilled: Hybrid Corn and Farmers' Work." *Technology and Culture* 34:324–343.

Fowler, C., and P. Mooney. 1990. *Shattering: Food Politics, and the Loss of Genetic Diversity*. Tucson: University of Arizona Press.

Frisoon, C., L. Lopez, and J. T. Esquinas, eds. 2011. *Stakeholder Perspective on International Treaty on Plant Genetic Resources for Food and Agriculture*. London: Earthscan.

Halewood, M., I. L. Norigea, and S. Louafi, eds. 2013. *Crop Genetic Resources as Global Commons*. London: Routledge.

Hansson, S. 2011. "Reaping More Than You Sow?" LLM Thesis, Department of Law, University of Gothenburg, Sweden.

Haugen, H. M. 2014. "The Right to Food, Farmers' Rights and Intellectual Property Rights." In *Rethinking Food Systems*, edited by E. A. Lambek, 195–218. Berlin: Springer.

Helfer, L. R., and G. W. Austin. 2011. "The Human Right to Food, Plant Genetic Resources and Intellectual Property." In *Human Rights and Intellectual Property*, by L. R. Helfer and G. W. Austin, 364–431. Cambridge, UK: Cambridge University Press.

Herring, R. J. 2007. "Stealth Seeds: Biosafety, Bioproperty, Biopolitics." *Journal of Development Studies* 43 (1): 130–157.

Herring, R. J., and M. Kandilkar. 2009. "Illicit Seeds: Intellectual Property and the Underground Proliferation of Agricultural Biotechnologies." In *Politics of Intellectual Property*, edited by S. Haunss and K. C. Shadlen, 56–79. Cheltenham, UK: Edward Elgar.

Howard, P. 2009. "Visualizing Consolidation in the Global Seed Industry, 1996–2008." *Sustainability* 1:1266–1287.
Jaeckel, A. 2013. "Intellectual Property Rights and the Conservation of Plant Biodiversity: A Common Concern of Human Kind." *Transnational Environmental Law* 2 (1):167–189.
Janis, M., and S. Smith. 2007. "Technological Change and the Design of Plant Variety Protection Regimes." *Chicago-Kent Law Review* 82 (3): 1557–1615.
Kloppenburg, J. R. 1988. *First the Seed: The Political Economy of Plant Biotechnology, 1492–2000*. Cambridge, UK: Cambridge University Press.
Kloppenburg, J. R. 2004. *First the Seed: The Political Economy of Plant Biotechnology 1492–2000*. Madison: University of Wisconsin Press.
Kloppenburg, J. R. 2013. "Re-purposing the Master's Tools: The Open Source Seed Initiative and the Struggle for Seed Sovereignty." Food Sovereignty: A Critical Dialogue, International Conference, Yale University, September 14–15, 2013. Conference Paper 56. www.yale.edu/agrarianstudies/foodsovereignty/pprs/56_Kloppenburg_2013.pdf.
Kloppenburg, J., and D. L. Kleinman. 1988. "Plant Genetic Resources: The Common Bowl." In *Seeds and Sovereignty*, edited by J. Kloppenburg, 1–15. Durham, NC: Duke University Press.
Lenné, J. M., and D. Wood. 2011. "Agrobiodiversity Revisited." In *Agrobiodiversity Management for Food Security*, edited by J. M. Lenné and D. Wood, 1–11. Cambridge, MA: CABI.
Lertdhamtewe, P. 2012. "Thailand's Plant Protection Regime: A Case Study in Implementing TRIPS." *Journal of Intellectual Property Law & Practice* 7 (3): 186–193.
Lewontin, R. C., and J. P. Berlan. 1986. "The Political Economy of Hybrid Corn." *Monthly Review* 38 (7): 35–47.
Linton, K., and M. Torsekar. 2010. "Innovation in Biotechnology Seeds: Public and Private Initiatives in India and China." *Journal of International Commerce and Economics* 3:1–34.
Llewelyn, M., and M. Adcock. 2006. *European Plant Intellectual Property*. Oxford: Hart Publishing.
Marden, E., and R. N. Godfrey. 2012. "Intellectual Property and Sharing Regimes in Agricultural Genomics." *Drake Journal of Agricultural Law* 17:369–411.
Maskus, K. 2012. *Private Rights and Public Problems: The Global Economics of Intellectual Property in the 21st Century*. Washington, DC: Peterson Institute of International Economics.
Matson, J., M. Tang, and S. Wynn. 2012. "Intellectual Property and Market Power in the Seed Industry." Madison: University of Wisconsin Law School, Government and Legislative Clinic.
Morin, J.-F., and A. Orsini. 2014. "Policy Coherence and Regime Complexes: The Case of Genetic Resources." *Review of International Studies* 40 (2): 302–324.
Moschini, G. C. 2010. "Competition Issues in the Seed Industry and the Role of Intellectual Property." Working Paper No. 10015. Ames: Department of Economics, Iowa State University.
Narasimhan, S. M. 2008. *Towards a Balanced "Sui Generis" Plant Variety Regime*. New York: United Nations Development Programme.
Oguamanam, C. 2014. "Open Innovation in Plant Genetic Resources for Food and Agriculture." *Chicago-Kent Journal of Intellectual Property* 13 (1): 11–50.
Oldham, P., S. Hall, and O. Forero. 2013. "Biological Diversity in Patent System." *PLoS One* 8 (11): e78737 1–16.

Orsini, A., J.-F. Morin, and O. Young. 2013. "Regime Complexes: A Buzz, a Boom, or a Boost for Global Governance." *Global Governance* 19 (1): 27–39.

Pardey, P., B. Koo, J. Drew, J. Horwich, and C. Nottenburg. 2013. "The Evolving Landscape of Plant Varietal Rights in the United States, 1930–2008." *Nature Biotechnology* 31 (1): 25–29.

Pray, C. E., and A. Naseem. 2007. "Supplying Crop Biotechnology to the Poor." *Journal of Development Studies* 43 (1): 192–217.

Ramasundaram, P., S. A. Kurup, and R. Chand. 2011. "Maneuvering Technology for Surplus Extraction: The Case of Bt Cotton in India." Policy Brief 37. New Delhi: National Centre for Agricultural Economics and Policy Research.

Ramey, E. A. 2010. "Seeds of Change: Hybrid Corn, Monopoly, and the Hunt for Superprofit." *Review of Radical Political Economics* 42 (3): 381–387.

Rangnekar, D. 2013. "The Cunning State of Farmers' Rights in India: Aligning with Global Law or Emancipating Farmers?" Food Sovereignty: A Critical Dialogue, International Conference, Yale University, September 14–15, 2013. Conference Paper 73. www.yale.edu/agrarianstudies/foodsovereignty/pprs/73_Rangnekar_2013.pdf.

Raustiala, K., and C. J. Sprigman. 2012. *The Knockoff Economy*. New York: Oxford University Press.

Raustiala, K., and D. G. Victor. 2004. "The Regime Complex for Plant Genetic Resources." *International Organization* 58 (Spring): 277–309.

Santilli, J. 2012. *Agbiodiversity and the Law*. London: Routledge.

Sastry, K. R., H. B. Rashmi, and J. Badri. 2011. "Research and Development Perspectives of Transgenic Cotton." *Journal of Intellectual Property Rights* 16 (March): 139–153.

Spielman, D., D. Kolady, A. Cavalieri, and N. C. Rao. 2011. "The Seed and Agricultural Biotechnology Industries in India." IFPRI Discussion Paper 01103. Washington, DC: International Food Policy Research Institute. www.ifpri.org/sites/default/files/publications/ifpridp01103,pdf.

Srinivas, K. R. 2006. "Intellectual Property Rights and Bio Commons." *International Social Science Journal* 58 (188): 319–334.

——. 2013. "Climate Change, Technology Development and Transfer: An Exercise in Thinking outside the Box." In *Environmental Technologies, Intellectual Property and Climate Change: Accessing, Obtaining and Protecting*, edited by A. Brown, 152–180. Cheltenham, UK: Edward Elgar.

Tuberosa, R., A. Graner, and E. Frison, eds. 2014. *Genomics of Plant Genetic Resources*. Vol. 1, *Managing, Sequencing and Mining Genetic Resources*. Amsterdam: Springer.

——, eds. 2014. *Genomics of Plant Genetic Resources*. Vol. 2, *Crop Productivity, Food Security and Nutritional Quality*. Amsterdam: Springer.

Winter, L. 2010. "Cultivating Farmers' Rights: Reconciling Food Security, Indigenous Agriculture, and TRIPS." *Vanderbilt Journal of Transnational Law* 43:223–254.

Wood, D. 2011. "Crop Introduction and Agbiodiversity Management." In *Agrobiodiversity Management for Food Security*, edited by J. M. Lanné and D. Wood, 53–63. Cambridge, MA: CABI.

Yadav, D., G. Anand, and S. Yadav. 2014. "Intellectual Property Rights in Plant Biotechnology: Relevance, Present Status, and Future Prospects." In *OMICS Applications in Crop Science*, edited by D. Barh, 621–670. Boca Raton, FL: CRC Press.

CHAPTER 16

IS FOOD THE ANSWER TO MALNUTRITION?

DAVID E. SAHN

Introduction

WIDESPREAD hunger and malnutrition are perhaps the most egregious manifestation of deprivation. The fact that approximately one billion people, primarily children, suffer from undernutrition is not only an affront to notions of social justice, but also represents an entitlement failure with large economic and social costs (Behrman, Alderman, and Hoddinott 2004). These costs are not just contemporaneous, in terms of compromising productivities of those currently affected by the ravages of malnutrition, but inevitably persist across the entire life course of individuals and from one generation to the next.

Although there is little disagreement on the magnitude and importance of the global malnutrition problem, its causation and control continue to be the subjects of debate and research. Part of the search for solutions to alleviate malnutrition emanates from confusion over terminology, for example, incorrectly defining malnutrition as synonymous with the problems of food shortages and food insecurity. There has also been a general failure in terms of response by governments, international organizations, and a range of stakeholders; their efforts to purportedly reduce malnutrition have often been inconsistent with existing evidence on what is really required in terms of policy and programs. In this chapter, I will argue that the persistence of the global reach of malnutrition results, in part, from the distorted response to this enormous challenge; and even worse, the growth of institutions and programs that have failed to address the root causes of the problem. This misallocation of resources may have indirectly contributed to the perpetuation of malnutrition, especially among the most vulnerable groups—women and children.

Malnutrition and Undernourishment: Some Terminology

This chapter focuses on the problems of malnutrition, as distinct from other terms such as poverty, food insecurity, and food shortages. Of paramount concern is the widespread undernutrition, primarily found in developing countries. Undernutrition is generally assessed by examining anthropometric indicators, which are the most general indicators of health and nutritional status, especially among young children (Beaton et al. 1990; de Onis, Frogillo, and Blossner 2000). For infants and children, there are three widely used anthropometric indicators. The first, stunting, or below normal height-for-age, is a failure to reach an expected level of stature at a given age. It is generally associated with long-term undernutrition that results from chronic episodes of illness and inadequate nutrient intake, and feeding and care practices. The second is wasting, below normal weight-for-height, which is a measure of acute malnutrition that usually results from dramatic deficits in intake and/or serious illness. This is often associated with acute inadequacies in nutrient intakes from events such as famines and severe economic shocks, as well as ravages associated with diseases such as measles, HIV/AIDS, and diarrheal disease. The third is underweight or below normal weight-for-age. This is a composite indicator of undernutrition that can be caused by any combination of stunting and wasting. In all three cases, the individual's anthropometric outcomes are compared with norms used to define a healthy population, where the norms are developed based on readily available and widely adapted international reference standards (WHO 1983).

Among adults who have achieved their full stature, the primary anthropometric indicator of general nutritional status is the body mass index (BMI), defined as weight in kilograms (kg) divided by height in meters (m) squared (kg/m^2). A BMI of less than 18.5 is considered an indicator of wasting or being too thin for good health. Low BMI can be caused by deficits in any of a range of nutrients, but also by infection that contributes to poor absorption of consumed nutrients. For example, undernutrition or wasting among adults is widely observed among adults with AIDS or acute episodes of diarrheal disease and respiratory infections in high-risk populations.

Beyond using anthropometric indicators to assess nutritional status, there is also a wide range of more specific mineral and vitamin deficiencies that have various clinical and functional consequences. Among these are vitamin A deficiency that contributes to stunting, disease and death, and blindness, as well as reproductive health problems; iodine deficiency that results in a range of deleterious outcomes that range from goiter to impaired neurological and mental function to stillbirths and unwanted abortion; and anemia, often caused by iron deficiency or related absorption problems that can contribute to impaired cognitive development, reduced ability to work, and increased risk of maternal and child mortality.

To make matters a bit more complicated, we must also consider that the broader concept of malnutrition includes an abnormal physiological condition caused by imbalances, not just deficiencies in energy, protein, and/or other micronutrients. Malnutrition thus applies to intake that is greater than physiological needs for good health and performance, not just deficiencies. The most obvious manifestation of these excesses is the global epidemic of overweight and obesity. The same anthropometric indicators such as weight-for-height and body mass index that are used to define wasting and acute undernutrition are employed as indicators of overweight and obesity. Specifically, a BMI in excess of 25 is an indicator of overweight, and a BMI over 30 defines obesity.

Although the focus of this chapter is on malnutrition, this should be distinguished from another concept, that of food security. Although there are myriad definitions found in the literature, one that perhaps comes closest to a consensus is from the Food and Agriculture Organization, which states, "Food security [is] a situation that exists when all people, at all times, have physical, social and economic access to sufficient, safe and nutritious food that meets their dietary needs and food preferences for an active and healthy life" (FAO 2002). As will be discussed next, the use of these terms synonymously with malnutrition can indeed be misleading, as the underlying notion of access to food is only one input into the production of good nutritional outcomes.

Dimensions of Malnutrition

The stark reality of the global scale of undernutrition is illustrated in Table 16.1. The prevalence of underweight remains at around 40% in the most affected region, South Asia, despite the success in reducing these levels over the past three decades. Africa's prevalence of underweight children, 30%, although lower than in South Asia, has, in fact, not declined over the same period. Owing to population growth, the number of undernourished children in Africa is on the rise.

The figures on the prevalence of micronutrient deficiencies are equally staggering. For example, nearly 25% of the general population suffers from anemia, which corresponds to over 1.6 billion people. The highest rates are found among preschool age children where the share of those with anemia are 47.4%, a number that is nearly as high for pregnant women globally. In fact, the prevalence rate is 57.1% among pregnant women in Africa and nearly 50% in Southeast Asia. There are additionally 468 million nonpregnant women globally who suffer from anemia (de Benoist et al. 2008). The number of individuals in the general population who are estimated to have insufficient iodine intake is two billion. And over one-third of school age children suffer from low iodine intake. The hardest hit region is South East Asia where around 100 million children have iodine intakes below what is required (de Benoist et al. 2004). In the case of vitamin A, the World Health Organization indicates that deficiencies are a significant health problem in 60 countries, with one-third of the preschool-aged population at risk of vitamin A deficiency. Among the serious manifestations of vitamin A deficiency is night blindness, which affects 5.2 million preschool-aged children and 9.8 million pregnant women.[1]

Table 16.1 Percent Prevalence of Underweight Preschool Children (0–60 Months) in Developing Countries, 1975–2005

Region	1975	1980	1985	1990	1995	2000	2005
Sub-Saharan Africa	31.4	26.2	26.7	27.3	27.9	28.5	29.1
Middle East/North Africa	19.8	17.5	16.4	15.6	14.8	14.0	13.2
Latin America and the Caribbean	19.3	14.2	12.2	10.2	8.3	6.3	4.3
South Asia	67.7	58.1	54.5	50.9	47.3	43.6	40.0
East Asia	43.6	43.5	39.9	36.2	32.6	28.9	25.3

Source: The Fourth Nutrition Situation Report, SCN
(http://www.unsystem.org/SCN/archives/rwns04/index.htm)
The 1975 data is from the First Nutrition Situation Report, SCN

The preceding figures illustrate the enormity of the global problem of undernutrition. They also illustrate that malnutrition is multidimensional. As will be discussed further later, the causation and control of these various dimensions of malnutrition differ; this has important implications in terms of how we think about the role of, and scope for, agriculture and food policy in addressing these problems. Furthermore, the choice of indicators to assess the degree of undernutrition are age and gender specific, which again adds complexity to describing the problem, understanding its causation, and seeking solutions and opportunities to alleviate the burden of undernutrition.

Beyond the problems of undernutrition, recent estimates indicate that 1.6 billion adults are overweight and 400 million are obese. Additionally, 150 million school-aged children are overweight, with nearly one-third of this group being clinically obese, and 20 million children under age 5 are also overweight.

The high prevalence of obesity is traditionally considered to be synonymous with the affluence and excesses of the wealthier countries in North America and Europe. However, this is no longer the case. Obesity and overweight has emerged as a major public health challenge on all continents and in low- and middle-income countries as well. The latest World Health Organization figures indicate that well over one-quarter of all women in low-income countries are overweight. And the situation is far worse in many countries. For example, more than two-thirds of the adults in Egypt and Panama are overweight, with the comparable number being 48% in Malaysia and 38% in Zimbabwe.[2] Projections are that there will be a continued and rather dramatic increase over the next decade in the share of the population who are overweight and obese in developing countries, contributing to large increases in deaths from chronic diseases such as heart and cardiovascular disease, hypertension and stroke, diabetes, and some forms of cancer. Recent estimates, for example, indicate that globally more than 17.5 million people will die of cardiovascular disease in 2005, making it the main cause of death on a global scale. As a point of comparison, 2.8 million people will die from HIV/AIDS during the same period. Estimates are that overweight and noncommunicable diseases comprise approximately 60% of the global burden of deaths, and out of this, 79% occur in developing countries (WHO https://apps.who.int/infobase/).

One further paradox is the coexistence of undernutrition and overnutrition in the same countries, communities, and even households, making clear that affluence is not the direct or even primary cause of overconsumption leading to overweight; conversely, poverty and the inability to command adequate access to food (i.e., food security) is not necessarily the direct or primary cause of undernutrition. This phenomenon, often referred to as the "dual burden" of overnutrition and undernutrition, is presented by displaying the high share of stunted children that exists alongside the large numbers of overweight women. For example, in Cameroon, 29% of the women are overweight, and 35% of the preschool-aged children are undernourished. In Bolivia, where nearly one-half of the women are overweight, nearly one in four children are stunted.[3]

This phenomenon of undernutrition and overnutrition is not merely a story of inequality in distribution across households—that is, the wealthier food secure, overconsuming households residing in the same country or communities as the food insecure poor households where undernutrition is present. Indeed, undernutrition and overnutrition exist simultaneously within the same households. For example, in the case of Malawi, among households where mothers were underweight, 47% of the children were stunted; but 35% of the children were stunted in households in which the children's mothers were overweight. In Burkina Faso, in 2003, in a household in which the mother was overweight, nearly one in five of her children were stunted. Although the share of stunted children was higher when the mother was of normal weight or underweight, it is not unusual to find households in which children are suffering from long-term and chronic malnutrition, despite the fact that their mothers are overweight or obese. Again, this pattern illustrates the multidimensionality of malnutrition and the complex etiology that contributes to these deleterious outcomes. This, in turn, has important implications for thinking about the role of food and food policy in the production of, and as a solution to, the problem of malnutrition. It also suggests the need to consider a more formal conceptual model for understanding these relationships.

The Nutrition Production Function

A simple model of malnutrition is useful for understanding its causation and possible pathways to improving nutritional outcomes. Following Grossman's (1972) model of health as a stock variable, and the discussion of the nutrition production function by Strauss and Thomas (1995), assume that nutritional status is both produced and maintained by investments made in the current period, which, when combined with the previous period's nutrition stock, generates current nutritional status:

$$N_{it} = N(N_{it-1}, Z_{it}^{f}, Z_{it}^{nf}, C_{it}, T_{it}^{H}, E_{it}, M_{it}, BF_{it}, HB_{it}, S_{t}) \tag{1}$$

The time subscripts are intended to demonstrate the dynamic nature of nutrition outcomes. In addition to the previous period's nutrition stock or status, an individual's current nutrition is a function of the vector nutrient consumption from foods, Z_{it}^{f}; nutrient consumption from nonfood, for example, in the form of micronutrient supplementation programs such as the distribution of vitamin A capsules, Z_{it}^{nf}; other consumption goods, such as shelter and the general living/housing environment, C_{it}; time devoted to the maintenance of health, T_{it}^{H}; the education of person, E_{it} (or her/his caregivers); consumption of medical and related preventative health services, M_{it}; the duration/intensity of breastfeeding (for children under 36 months) BF_{it}; a range of other health behaviors such as smoking, alcohol consumption, and sex (generally for adults) HB_{it}; and the sanitary environment, including water quality and access to latrine and toilets, S_t. Through backward recursion, current nutrition is, therefore, a function of all previous values of these inputs as well as the genetically determined initial endowment of health and other physical attributes, η_i.

Closely related to the production of nutrition, as represented in Equation (1), is the production of the vector of nutrients, a key input into the nutrition production function:

$$Z_{i}^{f} = Z(C_{i}, E_{m}, T_{m}^{P}, S, \eta_{i}) \tag{2}$$

In Equation (2), T_{M}^{P} denotes the caregiver's time spent in home production, including the preparation of food. Although nutrient production is primarily a function of food consumption, the mother's skill or education level, time spent processing and preparing food, and food storage and sanitation facilities, captured by S, all affect her ability to extract nutrients from raw food inputs. The food preparer's skills and time also enter into nutrient production functions of other household members.[4]

As elaborated by Meyerhoefer and Sahn (2006), nutrition of household members is, thus, the outcome of a series of behaviors and decisions that the household makes, given a set of prices, assets, and community and individual endowments. These decisions affect the range of inputs that affect nutrition, such as nutrients consumed from food, as shown in Equation (2), or participation in programs such as vitamin A supplementation as represented by Z^{nf}. Although not shown, a series of other input demand functions, as in Equation (2), apply to other parameters in the nutrition production function. Thus, inputs such as the use of curative and preventative health care; levels of activity from work and leisure; time inputs in terms of child care; health-related behaviors such as decisions regarding smoking, alcohol consumption, and breastfeeding; and household public goods such as shelter characteristics, water, and sanitary facilities are a function of community-level factors affecting the nutritional environment, ranging from public investments in schools and latrines to the efforts to control communicable disease to public information campaigns regarding healthy food choices. Education also enters the model, both directly and through its impact on how inputs are used to affect nutritional outcomes. Likewise, individual characteristics, such as gender and age, are also represented in the model. There are also "unobservables," such as genetic makeup or innate healthfulness that influence nutritional outcomes. Some of these unobservables are random. Others, however, may be correlated with observed factors that represent a major challenge for modeling this production function.

There are several salient features of this production function that merit closer consideration. First, the vector of nutrients is one of a long list of inputs that affect nutritional outcomes. Too often, consumption of food, and even nutrients, is confused with nutritional status. This is a serious mistake that has contributed to considerable confusion in terms of the relationship between food security and intake, on the one hand, and nutritional outcomes, on the other. In fact, as expanded on below, the conflating of food consumption, or nutrient inputs, as described earlier in the production function, with nutritional outcomes has often led to distortions and inefficiencies in policies that are purportedly designed to reduce malnutrition. It is not uncommon for policymakers to talk about improving nutrition, when they really are focused on food consumption, or even worse, food availability or production. Thus, the concept of food security is two steps removed from nutritional outcomes: (1) food security is about access, not actual consumption of food. Behaviors at the household or individual level may contribute to inadequate nutrient intake in a food secure household; and (2) as pointed out, even if food security translates into increased or adequate nutrient consumption, it is just one of many inputs that determine nutritional outcomes.

Second, although the nutrition production function can be estimated at any specific point in time, as noted earlier, it is a dynamic construct and characterized by considerable path dependency. That is, this production function is not fixed, and changes over the life course. And similarly, a properly specified nutrition dynamic production function incorporates the fact that current nutritional status depends on all current and prior inputs.

The reason that I emphasize this point is illustrated by appreciating the role of prenatal events in terms of nutritional health across the life course and generations. In the short-term, the impact of prenatal health and, thus, nutrition of the fetus is critical in determining the nutritional status of the newborn and during its first couple of years of life. The fact that stunted mothers, for example, are far more likely to have stunted children suggests that far greater attention be accorded to the provision of prenatal care and the prevention of maternal morbidity. However, the problem of malnourished mothers giving birth to underweight children who are more susceptible to the ravages of undernutrition is not the entire story. There is now a great deal of evidence that chronic nutrition-related diseases such as obesity, diabetes, and cardiovascular diseases that appear late in life are, in part, a consequence of nutritional deficits *in utero* and early in life. More specifically, increasing attention has been given to the Barker hypothesis, which basically describes the association between health *in utero* and the first weeks of life with health outcomes during adulthood (see Barker (1994), and Godfrey and Barker (2000)). The epidemiological evidence in this regard is explained by what is often referred to as the thrifty phenotype concept (Hales and Barker 2001). It posits that poor nutritional status *in utero* will contribute to impaired development and function of β -cells and insulin-sensitive tissues. In combination, this will result in increased insulin resistance later in life and subsequent deleterious outcomes such as diabetes and cardiovascular disease.

A number of recent studies have elucidated this relationship, including the work of Almond (2006), Almond and Chay (2006), Barker (2006), and Godfrey and Barker (2000). It is a challenge to disentangle the mechanisms or causal components of these correlations, because issues such as genetic endowment and unobservables may partly explain these relationships. But what is quite clear is that there are intergenerational determinants of health status, and that fetal malnutrition is an important factor determining health deficits later in life. Although food intake, and specifically, diseases of affluence associated with a diet high in calories, refined sugars, and saturated fats, may affect the probability of nutrition-related chronic disease of adults, it is the interaction of the diet in the more immediate term with health inputs that go back to the prenatal period that will be critical in determining nutritional outcomes later in life. Again, failure to appreciate this has potentially serious implications for our understanding of the relationship between food consumption and nutritional outcomes.

An important implication of taking this life-course perspective is that it highlights the particular importance of nutritional outcomes early in childhood. This point has been forcefully made in a number of recent academic and policy documents, including a recent series of papers in *The Lancet* that emphasizes that the period of greatest vulnerability to becoming malnourished and suffering short- and long-term functional consequences, is just before birth and during the first two years of life (Black et al. 2008). This has led to a rethinking of nutritional strategies by a range of international organizations, such as the World Bank who has refocused their nutrition initiatives on the period from *in utero* through the child's first 24 to 36 months of life. Consequently, and consistent with the nutrition production function presented earlier, the design of programs and interventions gives primacy to inputs such as breastfeeding behavior, the quality of child care and nurturing behaviors, the sanitary and home environment, and provision of micronutrients through supplementation programs, all of which are of critical importance in determining nutritional outcomes of this most vulnerable group. This contrasts with the reduction in efforts such as school feeding programs, that might be effective incentives for getting children to enroll and remain in school, but which are unlikely to be effective in combating malnutrition and its short- and long-term consequences.

Another lesson that can be gleaned from the production function is that the inputs in the production of nutrition are substitutes. Likewise, changes in prices, such as for health care and food, will affect the household choices regarding the availability of inputs, operating through the input demand functions such as those for nutrients in Equation (2). One price, which is of particular importance and often not fully appreciated in terms of how it affects nutrition, is the shadow cost of time. Thus, labor market conditions, particularly employment opportunities, will affect the demand for nutrients, the demand for health care, the demand for leisure, and the time allocated to child care and other "home-produced" inputs that affect the health and nutrition of children. Thus, there will be important nutritional consequences of a range of public policies that go beyond the impact of the more obvious ones such as interventions in food prices or food availability, including instead a range of investments that will raise the shadow wage of women. We, therefore, need to be cognizant of the cross-price elasticities or patterns of substitution between the consumption of food, nonfood goods, leisure, and health care.

To amplify, the production function framework emphasized the importance of health services, time inputs of mothers, and nutrient consumption on health and nutrition outcomes. Government involvement in the health care sector has traditionally been high in developing countries, with public expenditures financing large portions of health care networks. Similarly, there is no shortage of examples in which government intervenes in the food sector, particularly using food price policy as a means to maintaining low and stable food prices. And, of course, active labor market policies are a hallmark of government intervention in their economies. In practice, there are the obvious trade-offs in terms of government spending on health versus food subsidies, which will, in turn, have differential impact on nutrition. Likewise, money spent on food subsidies may displace resources to sustain government spending on jobs. The direct comparisons of the impact of spending on health inputs or food subsidies or labor market policies are difficult enough to make. However, there is the additional complication that involves substitution effects in the production function: food price policy that affects food consumption decisions will also affect demand for other goods, labor supply, and the demand for health care through substitution. A similar story can be told for the impact of spending on health services. The implication is that there are a series of potential complementarities and trade-off policies that affect the price of food, health care, and other nonfood goods, as well as the price of labor that will affect nutritional outcomes.

There is a serious paucity of research that addresses the joint demand for health care, leisure, food, and nonfood goods. One of the few examples of which I am aware is the work by Meyerhoefer, Sahn, and Younger (2007), using data from Vietnam, where the conventional commodity demand framework is expanded to incorporate the demand for health through an empirical model derived from a flexible representation of preferences. Subsequent estimation of a mixed continuous/discrete choice commodity demand and provider choice model allows the derivation of own and cross-price elasticities for health care, leisure, foods, and nonfood goods, quantifying the substitution patterns between health and other goods at various income levels. The results provide interesting insights into the potential impact of various health care financing mechanisms, as well as allowing for the calculation of substitution effects that can be used to forecast the impact of commodity (including food) taxes and subsidies and/or labor market policies on health care utilization. Among their interesting results is that the demand for health care is found to be responsive to changes in the price of nonfood goods, rice, and wages. The strong cross-substitution effect between health care and leisure is indicative of significant trade-offs between the treatment of illness and household labor supply, and suggests the opportunity cost of travel to treatment centers plays an important role in establishing visitation patterns. The fact that nonfood goods emerge as a substitute for health care leads to the consideration of a tax on these goods as an alternative health care financing mechanism. Such a tax could be used to cross-subsidize the public provision of health services and reduce regressive user fees without providing a disincentive to health-seeking behavior. Although the findings in this study provide important baseline estimates of substitution effects existing between health care provider choice, food, nonfood goods, and leisure, more research is necessary to characterize these substitution patterns under varying socioeconomic conditions and to generate consensus on the observed magnitudes of cross-price elasticities. This is particularly important in considering the impact of a range of intervention programs that have dual objectives, one of which is improving food and nutritional outcomes. One such example is food for work schemes that have objectives including employment generation, infrastructure creation and nutritional improvement (see Kotwal and Ramaswami, this volume). There are myriad complexities in terms of behavior responses to such programs that will have uncertain and conflicting impacts on the health of particularly vulnerable children and women. These range from potential changes in intrahousehold allocation, because bargaining power may be altered in ways that depend on which members participate in the scheme, to changes in allocative choices as a result of changes in labor supply-altering energy output and, thus, relative needs of family members, to shifts in time use and the price of leisure that may affect demand for health care and the nature of infant care practices. A similar set of complexities apply to other interventions such as conditional cash transfer programs, in which food is provided as a condition for activities ranging from girls attending school to receiving prenatal care.

Yet another related issue that emerges from the production function is that income itself is not included; rather, the model includes consumption goods that are purchased with earned and nonearned income. Nonetheless, reduced form results using household-level data sets show a relatively modest short-term impact of income on nutritional outcomes (Alderman, Hoogeveen, and Rossi 2006). This finding is mirrored in the literature that finds that the impact of income on calorie consumption is quite modest, as measured by the low-income elasticities of demand. For example, Bouis and Haddad (1992) estimate that, in the Philippines, the elasticity is around 0.1, whereas Behrman and Deolalikar (1990) suggest that it may be close to zero among poor villages in South India. Subramanian and Deaton's (1996) estimates for India are at the high end of the spectrum, being 0.5. In all cases, the food expenditure elasticities are much higher—perhaps on the order of two times higher—because consumers alter the composition of their food purchases as incomes increase. This latter process is, in part, a consequence of households valuing dietary diversity, both for reasons of taste and variety. Thus, as incomes rise, even when overall dietary requirements are not met, households switch into "higher quality" foods and food groups, such as meat instead of cereals, or rice instead of cassava. Likewise, there is a pattern of purchasing higher quality foods within relatively homogenous commodities, such as rice or meats. Indeed, this search for diversity and quality (measured in terms of appearance, palatability, and other nonnutrient characteristics) in combination contribute to a higher unit cost per calories as incomes rise. This increased diversity may also help address nutrient deficits other than calories, such as proteins, although the evidence about income elasticities of nutrients other than calories is much less clear. The important point we can glean from this discussion is that at least at the household level, even the poorest households in the most underdeveloped economies will spend most of any increment in income in ways other than increasing the quantity of food and calories consumed. This reinforces the importance of targeted nutrition programs, beyond efforts to raise income and reduce poverty, to reduce levels of malnutrition at a pace that is consistent with achieving the Millennium Development Goals for 2015.

It is noteworthy that this household level data is consistent with the macro story of relatively modest short-term impact of GDP growth and poverty reduction on alleviating malnutrition. Although there is strong evidence that health improves with income (see, for example, Pritchett and Summers (1996) and Sala-i-Maartin (2005)), the accumulated evidence over the past nearly 40 years suggests that even if there is rapid GDP growth, malnutrition in developing countries will persist (Berg 1981; Reutlinger and Selowsky 1976; Alderman et al. 2003).

At the same time, there are other important global implications of the move to "higher quality" of food as incomes rise. Most obvious is the spectacular rise in global demand for meat and dairy products, as well as processed food. The implications of these changes are profound. They range from the more proximal effects on food prices for staple grains and the supply chain that affects both the earnings of, and prices paid by, small and subsistence farmers as well as net consumers of their products, to the implications for the demand for fossil fuels and thus the potential for climate change. In addition, as I discuss later, the dietary shifts that are occurring, as populations in India, China, and elsewhere adapt western diets and are integrated into the global food marketing chain of large retailers and restaurateurs, will have direct health implications as a result of dietary change, which will lead to increased burden associated with chronic disease.

In sum, the short-term efforts to raise incomes and promote improved food security are not likely to be effective means of reducing malnutrition. Indeed, over the long-term, broad-based economic growth that reduces poverty and food insecurity is crucial. But, as illustrated by the figures on the dual burden of disease, the reality is that malnutrition is widespread in environments with high levels of food security and even where poverty is relatively low. This reflects problems such as failure of mothers to get appropriate care and take appropriate measures to ensure their health during pregnancy; failure to exclusively breastfeed for children under six months of age; the late introduction of complementary solid foods; high prevalence of infectious disease; inappropriate care for children suffering from diarrheal disease and other infections; poor hygiene and lack of access to clean water; mothers being too busy to provide for the proper care of their newborns and young children, and so forth. Thus, the micro and macro story also suggests the paramount importance of nonfood-related direct measures to alleviate malnutrition, ranging from immunizations and micronutrient supplementation and fortification to other targeted health and nutrition services.

Food: A Resource in Search of a Cause

The first thing that governments and international organizations think of in their efforts to combat undernutrition is food. Quite simply, the history of public action to combat malnutrition, in developed and developing countries, has frequently conflated the problem with issues of food security and access to food, and more generally the performance of the agricultural sector and related issues such as food delivery, distribution, and subsidy programs. This is not entirely irrational since food, as noted earlier, is a potentially important constraining input in the nutrition production function. But, certainly, food is not always the answer. Nonetheless, consider the institutions that are primarily responsible for raising nutritional standards: the United States Department of Agriculture in the United States, and the Food and Agricultural Organization and the World Food Programme of the United Nations among the U.N. agencies in the developing world. Or, historically, the Office of Food for Peace in the United States Agency for International Development was an agency purportedly motivated by the objective of better nutrition among the most needy populations. Programmatically, these institutions have one thing in common: the imperative of responding to the needs of their primary constituents: farmers, those engaged in the marketing of food, and agribusiness, as well as achieving the humanitarian goal of promoting access to food and improving food security. The reality is that the "need" that food aid donors and food distribution and subsidy programs are responding to is not reducing malnutrition, and their primary constituents are not the malnourished; instead, food surpluses was a resource in search of a "cause," and fighting malnutrition has proven quite convenient in that regard.

A first case to consider is the U.S. Food Stamp Program.[5] The modern Food Stamp Program has its genesis in the Food Stamp Act of 1964, although earlier iterations of the program date back to the period of the Depression in the 1930s. Much of the political rhetoric that justified and sustained this program revolved about improving nutrition. Even in its enabling legislation and earliest years of application, however, there was an understanding that the objectives of supporting agriculture and agribusiness were given primacy over the needs of improving nutrition among the poor. Thus, the initial Food Stamp legislation and the political support necessary for its passage was garnered from U.S. farmers and the agribusiness lobby primarily concerned with supporting the agricultural sector (Paarlberg 1963).

Regardless of its origins, the question has been and remains whether the Food Stamp Act and subsequent modifications of the legislation constitute an effective nutrition program, consistent with the stated objective of the program. Economists, nutritionists, and other social scientists have searched for the answer for decades. The preponderance of the evidence seems to point to the stark reality that the Food Stamp Program has not been a cost-effective modality for combating malnutrition. This is not something that has been realized only in recent years. Among the seminal studies was the early work of Kenneth W. Clarkson (1975), who concluded that, "the failure of the food stamp program comes generally from the inability of a single policy instrument to solve two or more potentially competing objectives..." and that "if problems of malnutrition are to be reduced, an alternative solution appears to be necessary" (67).

This early sentiment has been echoed time and again in years since. Again, to illustrate, a recent review by Townsend (2006) argues that there is a need for a "redesign of the existing Food Stamp Program to a health and nutrition intervention" (35). In large measure, this call is not based only on the potential inefficiency of the program in meeting nutritional objectives, but also on the potential that there are deleterious consequences of participation. In particular, the concern in recent years is that food stamps contribute to obesity. This possibility revolves around two contested questions: first, whether the marginal propensity to consume food purchased with food stamps is any different than it would be from cash or an income transfer. Among the most comprehensive reviews of the subject, studies by Fraker (1990) and Levedahl (1991) suggest that food stamps will increase food consumption more than an equivalent value of cash. Although these results still remain the subject of considerable debate, and, at least initially, a larger marginal propensity was considered evidence that food-related transfers are more efficient than cash transfers in meeting nutritional objectives. With the rise in obesity, however, the potential that food stamps will contribute to overconsumption, especially of foods that are high in calories and fat, has been given new urgency. Since there have not been any randomized control trials or even opportunities for quasi-experimental designs to address this question, there is certainly still some debate and a paucity of rigorous studies. Nonetheless, recent studies tell a somewhat consistent picture. Gibson (2003), for example, finds a correlation between receipt of food stamps and obesity among low-income women. This finding is also reported by Meyerhoefer and Pylypchuk (2008), who, using more sophisticated econometric techniques to try to get at the issue of causality, find that the use of food stamps contributes to obesity among low-income women but not men. The review by Ver Ploeg and Ralston (2008) suggests that although there is little evidence that most demographic groups in households receiving food stamps witness an increase in body mass index as a result of program participation, nonelderly women are the exception. They comprise 28% of the Food Stamp Program caseload. Other less direct evidence suggests that food stamps may worsen the obesity epidemic. For example, Wilde, McNamara, and Ranney (1999) find that households receiving food stamps consume significantly more sugar and fat than a comparison group of nonrecipients who nonetheless meet the eligibility criteria. Townsend et al. (2001) find that there may be a form of binge or excessive consumption at the beginning of the food stamp cycle that contributes to obesity.

The consensus is that a major redesign would be required to transform the Food Stamp Program from a food intervention, where the interests of the agricultural and food processing industry are given primary emphasis, to a health and nutrition program where concerns over improving diet quality and even reducing the number of calories consumed is considered paramount (Townsend 2006). Indeed, this is not a new challenge, but rather one that dates back to the program's inception during the period of the 1930s.

One important caveat is worth highlighting in considering the calls for overhauling the Food Stamp Program to make it an effective nutrition program. There is evidence that the use of food stamps is an effective antipoverty measure (Winicki, Gundersen, and Joliffe 2002; Rank and Hirschl 2009). In fact, the recession that began in 2008 served to highlight the importance of food stamps as a safety net. Therefore, I want to be clear that any critique of the Food Stamp Program in reference to achieving nutritional objectives must be considered in the context of how well it achieves other goals, such as protecting the poor during periods of economic downturn.

The story of the Food Stamp Program having conflicting objectives wherein nutrition has been accorded secondary importance is, in fact, quite similar to comparable initiatives in the international arena. Perhaps, the most egregious example is the much heralded and sometimes vilified U.S. PL 480 Food for Peace Program. Like the Food Stamp Program, Food for Peace was an outgrowth of the food surpluses that resulted in part from the distortions in agricultural markets and incentives that arose from generous subsidies to producers in the United States and Europe. A broad constituency that consisted of farmers, corporations who owned the shipping lines that transported the grain under federal regulations that stipulated the use of U.S. vessels, and nongovernmental agencies charged with programming and distributing the food represented a powerful lobby. The original motivation of the food aid program was unambiguously to facilitate surplus disposal and market development, not to improve the nutrition of the poor. Additionally, food aid programming has a long, and some would argue, sordid history of being driven by foreign policy objectives that rewarded our friends and punished our adversaries (Gustafsson 1976; Wallensteen 1976; Wallerstein 1980).

Over the past few decades, changes in the legislation governing food aid has resulted in some needed reforms, including eliminating some of the more overt mention of political goals, such as prohibitions against food aid going to communist countries. Likewise, the diminution of global surpluses over the past decade has reduced the importance of the food aid program's surplus disposal objectives (Uvin 1992; Hopkins 1992). Food aid shipments have also declined dramatically, and the role of, and advantages of relying on, multilateral aid agencies, such as the World Food Programme of the United Nations has reduced markedly the size of the Food for Peace Program and bilateral U.S. food aid programming.

Beyond the fascinating story of the politics and evolution of food aid policy, the most essential point is that origins of food aid were tied to the extensive interference of government in food markets, market failures that led to enormous surpluses in developed countries, and the pursuit of food and agricultural policies in the United States which contributed to policies that discriminated against agriculture and farmers in developing countries where crippling distortions in food markets were endemic. Indeed, hunger and the humanitarian crises were side effects of the very policy distortions that food aid encouraged and helped perpetuate; and ironically, these market failures were used to advocate for the legitimacy of food aid to address the malnutrition, which, in part, resulted from the same policy failures to which food aid had contributed. The vicious circle arose wherein food aid only exacerbated bad policies and delayed needed reforms in the food and agricultural sectors that discriminated against producers.

Over the decades, food aid programs have continued to evolve from their origins to place greater emphasis on humanitarian relief and development programs. In fact, as expected in light of the enormity of the resource, there are examples of positive impact of food aid programs, particularly in response to drought, on nutritional outcomes (See, for example, Yamano, Alderman, and Christiaensen (2005), and Quisumbing (2003)). Nonetheless, the fact remains that there rarely is a compelling rationale to rely on food aid rather than financial aid. The common perception that malnourished people need food aid, not cash aid, is an idea no longer in good currency. Nonetheless, many non-governmental organizations and food distribution organizations continue to perpetuate such myths, even if well intended. Indeed, a range of actors involved in food aid programming espouses the imperative of feeding the hungry and reducing malnutrition through food distribution programs. But there is little evidence that they have done so in a cost-effective manner that avoids deleterious unintended consequences, such as disincentives to local producers and discouraging needed policy reforms and investments in the agricultural sector. Indeed, a range of stakeholders are reliant on food aid as a resource to sustain their programs, and, thus, have been complicit in promoting food aid and food-based assistance programs as the answer to the hunger problem. This will not change until many misconceptions that underlie food aid programs are dispelled. These include that poor people are less likely to waste food than money, and that food aid, instead of financial aid, will help households avoid making bad consumption choices; that food aid is a way of avoiding market inefficiencies that arise from greedy monopsonist traders; and that when you give people food aid, they eat it instead of selling it to get cash that they need for a range of other purposes, such as schooling, health care, and investment in small enterprises.

The lack of consistency between rhetoric and reality is not limited to the institutional behavior of the U.S. government and aid agencies, where food programs have conflicting objectives and are often promoted as nutrition programs despite that not being their primary purpose. The United Nations Food and Agricultural Organization (FAO) serves as another example of what could be characterized as an organization that espouses a primary focus on nutrition to motivate its work but, instead, has a number of other overriding objectives. According to its mission statement, "FAO's mandate is to raise levels of nutrition, improve agricultural productivity, better the lives of rural populations and contribute to the growth of the world economy."[6] Despite this laudable statement, by all indications, FAO falls far short of one of its central organizing themes of prioritizing improved human nutrition.

Organizationally, the concern with human nutrition is primarily the domain of the Nutrition and Consumer Protection Division (NCPD), which is organized into three major groups. The first is Human Nutrition, whose mandate revolves around promoting sustainable improvements in nutritional status, particularly of poor households, through "actions to address local causes of malnutrition, improvements in national and sectoral policies and programmes; support to civil society institutions... and enhancement of education and public information." The second is Food Safety and Quality, which is charged with maintaining and improving food safety by establishing regulatory frameworks. And the third is the related role of Codex Alimentarius, which is focused on protecting consumers and ensuring fair trade practices in food trade and developing and promoting food standards (http://www.fao.org/ag/agn/index_en.stm). Although the latter two roles are certainly of great importance, the focus of the work on human nutrition is the domain of the Human Nutrition group. The question is how much priority FAO accords to direct measures to improve nutritional status is indeed a difficult question to address. It is possible to gain some insights from looking at staffing and the organization's budget. In 2006, the most recent year for which I could get reliable data, the NCPD consisted of a staff of 21 members and 10 consultants. The overall budget for the unit was less than $2.5 million. This number needs to be put into perspective, given that FAO's budget exceeds $1 billion. Thus, only a couple of tenths of 1% of the total budget is allocated to the nutrition division.

Of course, this does not mean that other units throughout the organization ignore nutrition-focused programming and research. For example, there is the Special Program on Food Security (SPFS) that was started in 1994/1995. The motivation for setting up this special unit, however, was to address problems of food insecurity by assisting farmers to increase the intensity of production and raise productivity. Similarly, there are research units within FAO, such as the Agricultural and Development Economics Division, which have an interest in issues related to nutritional improvement but whose main focus tends toward issues of food production and food security. Perhaps the unit that has paid most attention to nutrition at FAO is the small Global Perspective Studies Unit which has been tracking dietary changes and examining the implications, especially in terms of the emerging epidemics, obesity, and chronic disease. Although this is, again, a rare example of a unit that has gone beyond a focus on the supply side of the food and agricultural system and related issues of marketing and the supply chain, it is a very small group that does not reflect the mainstream programming and research efforts of FAO.

The fact that improving nutritional status is not the core mission of FAO does not in any way denigrate the institution's possible contribution to promoting a more robust agricultural sector and achieving food security. This is similar to the story of programs like the Food Stamp Program, which may indeed be very effective in improving the economic well-being of the poor, an objective that is of paramount importance. My highlighting of examples such as food stamps and the activities of FAO is intended to underscore the general point that although raising incomes and promoting food security are instrumentally valuable in the longer-term efforts to alleviate malnutrition, including overnutrition that is often the result of poor food choices, these activities are not synonymous with cost-effective strategies to reduce malnutrition over the near-term horizon. Instead, there is a shorter and more direct path to improving nutrition, which is often neglected at the expense of other initiatives that have captured the attention and resources of a range of governmental institutions and stakeholders in international and nongovernmental organizations. Instead of a continued focus on meeting the needs of producers, agribusiness, and the farm lobby first, we need to understand that the fight against malnutrition begins with a set of principles that have, in fact, been recently enunciated by the World Bank (2006) in their new strategy to fight hunger and undernutrition in the developing world. More specifically, there is a need to dispel some myths that have underscored the inadequate and inappropriate global efforts to reducing malnutrition. These include, first, the myth that malnutrition is primarily a matter of inadequate food supply. Second, the myth that improved nutrition is a by-product of other measures of poverty reduction and economic advance. Instead, the focus is correctly put on the need to invest in the youngest children who are most likely to become malnourished and suffer the ravages across their entire life course, including dramatic losses in cognitive ability and productivity. Food security is indeed an input into achieving the vision of nutritional improvement. And, a food and agricultural system that is consistent with both providing employment opportunities and low costs wage goods is a necessity for economic growth and development. However, a large share of the activities required to reach the Millennium Development Goals for nutrition are to be found in realms outside of the food sector.

A final point that I would like to highlight in considering the future prospects for food-related intervention programs, regardless of whether their espoused or real objectives are to reduce malnutrition, is that the architecture of the world food system is changing rapidly. The paradigm of food being a resource in search of a cause is rapidly receding into the annals of history. Instead, the prospects of food shortages and increased global demand driven by China, India, and other growing economies is an emerging challenge. Likewise, the increased emphasis of organizations such as the World Food Programme on local procurement and combining cash with, or as a substitute for, direct distribution of food, will undoubtedly change the face of food-related transfers in the future in developing countries. Although these changes may be positive in terms of agricultural incentives, in and of themselves, they will not necessarily contribute to reducing the dual burden of undermalnutrition and the emerging crisis of overmalnutrition.

Conclusions

As global institutions, including governments, nongovernmental organizations, and bilateral and multilateral international aid agencies consider how to most effectively combat the burden of global malnutrition, perhaps the most intractable misperception is that food insecurity and inadequate access to food are the exclusive, or even primary, causes of malnutrition. Likewise, national and regional food self-sufficiencies are often incorrectly viewed as critical to the fight against malnutrition, especially insofar as they ignore the role of trade and the importance of well-developed food markets.

Instead, it seems quite clear that with the exception of situations such as famines and acute crises, which contribute to what Amartya Sen (1983) has characterized as dramatic entitlement failures, far too little attention has been given to the inappropriate or insufficient care behaviors during pregnancy and early childhood. More specifically, the long-term functional and human consequences of malnutrition *in utero* and in the first months of life are particularly devastating. The damage from undernutrition at these critical periods will persist across the entire life course, as manifested in deficits in cognitive abilities, physical work productivity, as well as susceptibility to disease later in life, including chronic diseases such as diabetes and cardiovascular disease.

The question then becomes how to address undernutrition in these most critical periods. Although the answer is not simple, one clear reality is that women too often do not follow best practices in terms of breastfeeding, and families do not take appropriate measures to prevent infection and disease. This may be either due to ignorance of the importance of behaviors such as boiling water and washing hands and ensuring a more hygienic and healthier environment for infants and young children, or a lack of material resources to purchase critical inputs such as clean water, soap, and primary health care. Similarly, food consumption choices are often inappropriate and fail to recognize, for example, the importance of dietary diversity to achieve adequate intake of micronutrients. There is also an overall lack of knowledge or attention to the preventative and primary health care needs of pregnant women, infants, and children. By implication, these factors can be viewed as a market failure, not of food markets, but instead of health care markets, and more generally, the market for information and knowledge.

The focus on promoting health services and related behavioral change is not to diminish the paramount importance of building on the amazing success of the green revolution and the new technologies that are to be credited with preventing widespread famine. Complacency, in terms of continued research and investment in agriculture, food markets, supply chains, and so forth would be a tragic mistake. This is especially so, since a robust agricultural sector is often a critical pathway for countries and households to rise out of poverty. However, when we think about combating the global malnutrition problem, we must be equally cognizant that many traditional strategies, such as food aid distribution programs, school feeding programs, and food stamps, as well as interference in food markets through food subsidies and ration programs, are likely not to directly address the most direct and immediate causes of undernutrition and micronutrient deficiencies.

Why such programs have been sold as cost-effective nutrition interventions and are widely accepted as such, in developed and developing countries is an interesting question. The answer is likely to be found in the fact that food was a resource looking for a purpose, and nutrition seemed to be a cause that the food and agricultural lobby, as well as institutions such as the United Nations and volunteer agencies from developed countries, were eager to embrace. Similarly, governments seem all too eager to showcase feeding programs and other food-based initiatives as a sign of commitment to nutrition problems. In practice, such externally financed projects may be easy on the budget of poor countries, but they are also short on results, which, in part, explains the seeming intractability of providing for what is arguably the most basic human right—the right to health and adequate nutrition.

Another underlying theme of this chapter is the potential for unintended deleterious health consequences of food-related interventions that are purportedly designed to improve nutrition. I have discussed the emerging obesity epidemic and emphasized that it is no longer confined to the wealthy countries of North America and Europe. Although there is worrisome evidence that programs like food stamps may contribute to increased obesity in the United States, there is far more limited evidence of studies suggesting that feeding programs and the like may have similar consequences in developing countries. It is certainly advisable, however, to remain vigilant to this possibility. Similarly, other negative consequences of food-based nutrition programs, particularly those based on the use of food aid, are also well documented. These include the negative impact on the policy environment where aid contributes to a complacency on the part of policymakers, the potentially deleterious consequences on farmers and producer incentives, and the changing of consumers' patterns of demand for commodities, some of which are less healthy or that are less likely to be produced locally, increasing the reliance on procurement on international markets. The potential that food aid would be used as a weapon of foreign policy with the consequent harmful effects on recipients seems to have declined in recent years, but such policy certainly was a widespread practice for several decades. Indeed, careful programming of food aid and its propitious deployment can avoid or mitigate these potential negative consequences.

As we consider the way forward, I am intrigued by a question that was posed by Ian Darton-Hill, Senior Adviser, Child Survival and Nutrition at UNICEF; Martin W. Bloem Chief, Nutrition, World Food Programme; and Mickey Chopra, Director, Health Systems Research Unit, Medical Research Council of South Africa: "*When will nutrition stop being the Cinderella of health interventions when it comes to global funding priorities?*" (Darton-Hill, Bloem, and Chopra 2006). Why, for example, is there no Global Fund for broad-based nutrition programming (as there is for HIV/AIDS, tuberculosis, and malaria)? Part of the answer may lie in a lack of understanding of the complexity of the causes of malnutrition as well as the appropriate interventions to alleviate the problem. Nevertheless, there is an emerging evidence base that points the way forward, in terms of promoting the types of actions discussed here for investing in the health of women, infants, and children.

Notes

1. See http://www.who.int/vmnis/vitamina/prevalence/report/en/index.html.
2. http://apps.who.int/bmi/index.jsp
3. Author's calculations from the Demographic Health Surveys.
4. In the developed country context where markets are more complete and nutrient availability is less constrained, the framework just given would likely be considered sufficient to model health production, nutrition, and fertility with the household's other consumption decisions. Such separability between consumption and production, or factor markets, may not apply in certain African contexts for two main reasons: (a) many rural households in Africa engage in both own-account agriculture and the cultivation of cash crops, so their food consumption and production decisions are jointly determined; and (b) nutrient availability is more variable and often reaches levels at which health and labor market

productivity are adversely affected. In these circumstances, labor market productivity and agricultural production will ideally be modeled jointly with household consumption decisions.

5. In 2012, the Food Stamp Program was given a new name: the Supplemental Nutrition Assistance Program (SNAP). It gives recipients an electronic benefit card, similar to a bank debit card or credit card that can be used like cash to purchase food at authorized retail food stores. In the remainder of this paper, the use of Food Stamps should be taken to include SNAP as well.
6. See http://www.fao.org/about/mission-gov/en/

References

Alderman, Harold, Simon Appleton, Lawrence Haddad, Lina Song, and Yisehac Yohannes. 2003. "Reducing Child Malnutrition: How Far Does Income Growth Take Us?" *World Bank Economic Review* 17(1):107–131.

Alderman, Harold, Hans Hoogeveen, and Mariacristina Rossi. 2006. "Reducing Child Malnutrition in Tanzania: Combined Effects of Income Growth and Program Interventions." *Economics of Human Biology* 4(1):1–23.

Almond, Douglas. 2006. "Is the 1918 Influenza Pandemic Over? Long-term Effects of In Utero Exposure in the Post-1940 U.S. Population." *Journal of Political Economy* 114(4):672–712.

Almond, Douglas, and Kenneth Chay. 2006. "The Long-run Intergenerational Impact of Poor Infant Health: Evidence from Cohorts Born during the Civil Rights Era." Mimeo, Department of Economics, University of California, Berkeley.

Barker, D. J. P. 1994. *Mothers, Babies and Health in Later Life*. London: BMJ Publishing Group.

Barker, David J. P. 2006. The Developmental Origins of Ageing. Esther and Isadore Kesten Memorial Lecture, Leonard Davis School of Gerontology, University of Southern California, November 2.

Beaton, G. H., A. Kelly, J. Kevany, R. Martorell, and J. Mason. 1990. "Appropriate Uses of Anthropometric Indices in Children: A Report Based on an ACC/SCN Workshop." Nutrition Policy Discussion Paper 7. United Nations Administrative Committee on Coordination/Subcommittee on Nutrition (ACC/SCN) State-of-the-Art Series. New York.

Behrman, Jere R., Harold Alderman, and John Hoddinott. 2004. "Malnutrition and Hunger." In *Global Crises, Global Solutions*, edited by Lomborg, Bjørn, 363–420. Cambridge, UK: Cambridge University Press.

Behrman, J. R., and A. B. Deolalikar. 1990. "The Intrahousehold Demand for Nutrients in Rural South India: Individual Estimates, Fixed Effects, and Permanent Income." *Journal of Human Resources* 25(4): 665–696.

Berg, Alan. 1981. *Malnourished People: A Policy View*. Washington DC: World Bank.

Black, Robert E., Lindsay H. Allen, Zulfiqar A. Bhutta, Laura E. Caulfield, Mercedes de Onis, Majid Ezzati, Colin Mathers, Juan Rivera, and Maternal and Child Undernutrition Study Group. 2008. "Maternal and Child Undernutrition: Global and Regional Exposures and Health Consequences." *The Lancet* 371(9608): 243–260.

Bouis, H., and L. J. Haddad. 1992. "Are Estimates of Calorie-Income Elasticities Too High? A Recalibration of the Plausible Range." *Journal of Development Economics* 39(2):333–364.

Clarkson, Kenneth W. 1975. *Food Stamps and Nutrition*. Washington, DC: American Enterprise Institute for Public Policy.

Darton-Hill, Ian, Martin W, Bloem, and Mickey Chopra. 2006. "Achieving the Millennium Development Goals through Mainstreaming Nutrition: Speaking with One Voice." *Public Health Nutrition* 9(5):537–539.

de Benoist, Bruno, Erin McLean, Ines Eglis, and Mary Cogswell (eds.). 2004. *Iodine Status Worldwide: WHO Global Database on Iodine Deficiency*. Geneva: WHO.

de Benoist, Bruno, Erin McLean, Ines Egli, and Mary Cogswell (eds.). 2008. *Worldwide Prevalence of Anaemia 1993–2005: WHO Global Database on Anaemia*. Geneva: WHO.

de Onis, M., E. A. Frongillo, and M. Blossner. 2000. "Is Malnutrition Declining? An Analysis of Changes in Levels of Child Malnutrition Since 1980." *Bulletin of the World Health Organization* 78(10): 1222–1233.

Food and Agriculture Organization (FAO). 2002. *The State of Food Insecurity in the World 2001*. Rome: FAO.

Fraker, Thomas M. 1990. *The Effects of Food Stamps on Food Consumption: A Review of the Literature*. Alexandria, VA: Food and Nutrition Service.

Gibson, Diane. 2003. "Food Stamp Program Participation is Positively Related to Obesity in Low Income Women." *Journal of Nutrition* 133: 2225–2231.

Godfrey, Keith, and David Barker. 2000. "Fetal Nutrition and Adult Disease." *American Journal of Clinical Nutrition* 71(5):1344S–1352S.

Grossman, M. 1972. *The Demand for Health: A Theoretical and Empirical Investigation*. New York: Columbia University Press for the National Bureau of Economic Research.

Gustafsson, M. 1976. "US Food Aid Policy." In *Political Economy of Food*, edited by V. Harle. Research Report No. 12. Tampere, Finland: Tampere Peace Research Institute.

Hales, C. N., and D. J. Barker. 2001. "The Thrifty Phenotype Hypothesis." *British Medical Bulletin* 60:5–20.

Hopkins, Raymond. 1992. "Reform in the International Food Aid Regime: The Role of Consensual Knowledge." *International Organization* 46(1):225–264.

Levedahl, W. 1991. "The Effect of Food Stamps and Income on Household Food Expenditures." Washington DC: Economic Research Service, USDA.

Meyerhoefer, Chad D., and Yuriy Pylypchuk. 2008. "Does Participation in the Food Stamp Program Increase the Prevalence of Obesity and Health Care Spending? *American Journal of Agricultural Economics* 90(2):287–305.

Meyerhoefer, Chad D., and David E. Sahn. 2006. The Relationship between Poverty and Marternal Morbidity and Mortality in Sub-Saharan Africa. Presented at the AERC/Hewlett Foundation Workshop, "Poverty and Economic Growth: The Impact of Population Dynamics and Reproductive Health Outcomes in Africa" in Brussels, Belgium, November 5–6.

Meyerhoefer, Chad D., David E. Sahn, and Stephen D. Younger. 2007. "The Joint Demand for Health Care, Leisure, and Commodities: Implications for Health Care Finance and Access in Vietnam." *Journal of Development Studies* 43(8):1475–1500.

Paarlberg, Don. 1963. *Subsidized Food Consumption*. Washington, DC: American Enterprise Institute for Public Policy Research.

Pritchett, L., and L. H. Summers. 1996. "Wealthier Is Healthier." *Journal of Human Resources* 31(4): 841–868.

Quisumbing, Agnes R. 2003. "Food Aid and Child Nutrition in Rural Ethiopia." *World Development*. 31(7):1309–1324.

Rank, Mark R., and Thomas A. Hirschl. 2009. "Estimating the Risk of Food Stamp Use and Impoverishment During Childhood." *Archives of Pediatric & Adolescent Medicine* 163(11):994–999.

Reutlinger, Shlomo, and Marcelo Selowsky. 1976. *Malnutrition and Poverty: Magnitude and Policy Options*. Baltimore, MD: Johns Hopkins University Press.

Sala-i-Martin, X. 2005. "On the Health-Poverty Trap." In *Health and Economic—Findings and Policy Implications*, edited by López-Casasnovas, G., B. Rivera, and L. Currais, 95–114. Cambridge, MA, and London: MIT Press.

Sen, Amartya. 1983. "Poor, Relatively Speaking." *Oxford Economic Papers* 35(2): 153–169.

Strauss, John, and Duncan Thomas. 1995. "Human Resources: Empirical Modeling of Household and Family Decisions." In *Handbook of Development Economics*, Vol. 3A, edited by Jere Behrman and T. N. Srinivasan. Amsterdam: North Holland Publishing Company. 1885–2023.

Subramanian, S., and Angus Deaton. 1996. "The Demand for Food and Calories." *Journal of Political Economy* 104(1):133–162.

Townsend, Marilyn S. 2006. "Obesity in Low-income Communities: Prevalence, Effects, a Place to Begin." *Journal of the American Dietetic Association* 106(1):34–37.

Townsend, Marilyn S., Janet Peerson, Bradley Love, Cheryl Achterberg, and Suzanne P. Murphy. 2001. "Food Insecurity Is Positively Related to Overweight in Women." *Journal of Nutrition* 131:1738–1745.

Uvin, Peter. 1992. "Regime, Surplus and Self-Interest: The International Politics of Food Aid." *International Studies Quarterly* 36(3):293–312.

Ver Ploeg, Michele, and Katherine Ralston. 2008. "Food Stamps and Obesity: What Do We Know?" *Economic Information Bulletin* No. 34, March 2008. United States Department of Agriculture, Economic Research Service, Washington, DC.

Wallensteen, Peter. 1976. "Scarce Goods as Political Weapons: The Case of Food." *Journal of Peace Research* 13(4):277–298.

Wallerstein, Mitchell. 1980. *Food for War-Food for Peace: U.S. Food Aid in a Global Context*. Cambridge: MIT Press.

World Bank. 2006. *Repositioning Nutrition as Central to Development: A Strategy for Large-Scale Action*. Washington, DC: World Bank.

World Health Organization (WHO). 1983. *Measuring Change in Nutritional Status: Guidelines for Assessing the Nutritional Impact of Supplementary Feeding Programmes for Vulnerable Groups*. Geneva: WHO.

Wilde, Parke E., Paul E. McNamara, and Christine K. Ranney. 1999. "The Effect of Income and Food Programs on Dietary Quality: A Seemingly Unrelated Regression Analysis with Error Components." *American Journal of Agricultural Economics* 81(4):959–971.

Winicki, Joshua, Craig Gundersen, and Dean Jolliffe. 2002. Issues in Food Assistance—How Do Food Assistance Programs Improve the Well-Being of Low-Income Families? Food Assistance and Nutrition Research Report No. (FANRR26-9), October.

Yamano, Takashi, Harold Alderman, and Luc Christiaensen. 2005. "Child Growth, Shocks and Food Aid in Rural Ethiopia." *American Journal of Agricultural Economics* 87(2):273–288.

PART III

NATURE: FOOD, AGRICULTURE, AND THE ENVIRONMENT

CHAPTER 17

FIGHTING MOTHER NATURE WITH BIOTECHNOLOGY

ALAN MCHUGHEN

INTRODUCTION

SOME two hundred years ago, Thomas Malthus (1766–1834), in thinking about the growth of the global human population and the various restraints on such population growth, predicted that humans would sooner or later run out of food and other resources and then suffer a catastrophic population crash (Malthus 1798). He may have predicted "sooner" due to ravages of disease, pestilence, and war, but humanity's creative capacity for innovation drove such technological advances as irrigation, fertilizers, plant breeding and animal husbandry, food preservation storage and transport, along with contaminant control technologies, modern medical interventions, and other subsequent human manipulations to tweak the food/feed/fiber and fisheries supply to push the "sooner" into "later." Nevertheless, Malthus's fundamental argument is sound. We humans inhabit a physically limited planet with finite resources constraining and denying our fervent desire for or—at least history of—continued human population growth. The "later" is nigh.

More than 6.8 billion living humans currently occupy Earth. The natural carrying capacity of the planet—that is, Earth's ability to sustain a human population without human technical intervention and without depletion of sustaining resources—is vigorously debated, but most experts cite 3 to 4 billion or so (see, e.g., Cohen 1995; Ehrlich and Ehrlich 1990; Ehrlich and Holdren 1971; Pulliam and Haddad 1994) with the techno-optimists saying we could sustain perhaps 10 billion humans, but only with massive technological intervention combined with global dietary belt tightening (Smil 2001). The human population and eating habits are, therefore, already unsustainable. More than a billion humans are chronically malnourished; more than 1,000 humans die every hour attributable to lack of sustenance (http://www.afaceaface.org/blog/2011/01/facts-on-world-hunger/). And yet the human population continues to rise, with an expected peak of more than 9 billion before leveling off around 2050.

In addition to the immense and increasing pressure on the food supply, one of six humans now lacks reliable regular access to clean water. We'll also have to contend with climate change altering our environment, usually to the detriment of food production by making arable farmland too hot or dry for efficient productivity. Creeping urbanization displaces our most productive farmland with homes, roads, factories, and shopping centers, none of which converts sunlight to food. Pollution worldwide degrades soil, water, and air, all negatively impacting the productivity of farms. So we have an increasing human population, many demanding high maintenance nutriments (a simple bowl of rice doesn't cut it anymore, as increasing affluence—especially in China and India—drives increasing demand for animal protein and perturbing the entire dietary source framework [Braun 2007]) at the same time dealing with diminishing resources. Similarly, in the technologically advanced countries, while the current "eat local" locavore food fad resonates loudly, actions do not seem to indicate consumers are willing to give up imports of distantly grown fruits and veggies, nor other highly traveled comestibles as Kobe beef, Belgian chocolate, or Canadian maple syrup. Yet a return to natural lifestyles necessitates living off the local land, much as pre-contact Native Americans or Australian Aborigines. And, within twenty years, we need to somehow generate 50 percent more food than we do currently.

Clearly, doing what we've been doing got us into the mess we're now in, and doing nothing is certainly not sustainable. So what do we do?

Some argue that we should use our human ingenuity and whatever technologies are available to exploit the remaining resources and feed as many people as possible for as long as possible. Such technologies would not exclude genetic engineering and other biotechnologies along with whatever else may arise from the fertile minds of motivated (albeit malnourished, perhaps) men and women.

Others argue that our mistake was in adopting human technologies that interfere with natural processes in the first place, thus rejecting Mother Nature, and so we should now eschew industrial agriculture, especially biotechnology, and return to her benevolent succor.

We have some tough decisions. We can either return to Mother Nature and follow her rules or continue to use human ingenuity and innovation to fight her desire to keep our human population within the limits of the Earth's carrying capacity.

Let's follow each path to its logical conclusion, starting with the "return to nature" route.

Humans in Harmony with Mother Nature

Mother Nature's Replacement Rule

Mother Nature is usually portrayed as a benevolent and kindly overseer, ensuring a nurturing, healthy, and sustainable environment for us all to thrive, cradle to grave.

But these come at a price; Mother Nature demands strict adherence to some tough rules. According to one such rule, from the realm of biology, every individual of every species gets to reproduce, on average, just one progeny surviving long enough to also generate progeny. Nature's 1:1 replacement ratio ensures relatively stable populations of each species. Obviously, any population generating less than 1 reproductively successful progeny per individual will eventually succumb to extinction. Indeed, species extinction has occurred many times over the period of life on Earth. Conversely, any species successfully reproducing to generate a replacement ratio higher than 1 will eventually inundate the planet. Unlike extinction, such inundation has not happened—yet.

A popular high school thought experiment to illustrate this inundation through exponential reproductive growth shows how a pair of fertile cockroaches (sometimes the hypothetical species will be flies, other insects, or even bacteria), given unlimited resources and assuming a stated gestation period, number of fertile eggs per litter, and breeding lifespan, will quickly smother the Earth (for a fascinating look at insects and how they've influenced human society over the years, see Berenbaum 1996). Fortunately, Mother Nature ensures cockroaches—and all other species—do not enjoy unlimited resources, and she keeps the cockroach population in check with numerous constraints, including food and water scarcity, diseases, insectivorous predators, and even cockroachphobic humans with thick soled shoes. Taken as a whole, Mother Nature's replacement rule holds that in spite of the potential to take over the Earth, each cockroach will, on average and calculated over the course of many generations, leave behind exactly one reproductively successful progeny. All other progeny will succumb to starvation, disease, predators, or, in at least some cases, shoes.

Mother Nature metes out harsh punishment for violating her replacement rule. The punishment for those populations falling below the 1:1 replacement—for other than short periods—is extinction. All extinct species, from dinosaurs in ancient times to dodos more recently, had a replacement ratio of less than 1:1 during their downfall, and they paid the ultimate price for their lack of fecundity. If the species dies out due to lack of food, or water, and those resources later replenish, well, by then it's too late. The resources might return, but extinct species do not.

Certainly, many species diverge from the replacement ratio trajectory for short periods, and some do it with almost predictable frequency. Consider the population dance of predators and their prey, such as hares and lynx or lions and gazelles, fluctuating together almost in lockstep (the relationship is close but not perfect as other factors can also influence either or both species). But averaged over several generations, the ultimate ratio remains the same: 1:1 replacement for each species.

Species also exist that enjoy temporary reproductive capacity above 1:1, enjoying a population boom giving rise to a sustained, long-term total population increase. We see this in what population biologists call a sweepstakes route, such as when mammals first discovered Australia. Plenty of food, no predators, and few limits to growth prevailed, so the population expanded above the 1:1 replacement ratio until food and other resources became limiting and the population leveled off at the 1:1 replacement ratio. Another example of divergence is in ordinary ecological successions, such as seen along the shoreline of an aging lake, where a sequence of successive species invades, expands to dominate the area, and then gradually dies off, giving way to the next order of species until eventually the area that was once lake becomes forest. But again, over the period of several generations, the number of individuals of any given species in the planetary ecosystem remains remarkably stable.

Species have been identified with a long-term replacement ratio below 1:1 (i.e., all species that are now extinct) and many with fluctuations around the 1:1 ratio. But no species has sustained a long-term ratio above replacement, so we're not sure how Mother Nature will punish such impudence. But we're about to find out. One arrogant species has been increasing at above replacement ratio for many generations. If left unchecked, that presumptuous species will ultimately cover the planet, thus destroying itself and everything else still here. That species is, of course, *Homo sapiens*.

Humans as Unnatural Species

Ordinarily, Mother Nature restricts population growth of any species by any of several limiting factors, such as food availability, predators and diseases (e.g., myxomatosis in rabbits, bubonic plague in humans), famine, and pestilence and other plagues. But human ingenuity and technology has effectively overcome many of these strictures. Modern humans rarely succumb to large-scale famine, to predators, or to tuberculosis, diphtheria, smallpox, measles, malaria, or even cancer (curiously, wars and other human conflicts do not effectively reduce long-term human population growth as the victims are primarily males. In human reproductive biology, males are readily substituted, with one fecund (lucky?) male able to compensate for many males lost in battle. If, instead, young females were the primary casualties of war, human populations would suffer much more. And in any case, war is a human construct, not a "natural" population control mechanism). So far, we are the only species to maintain a reproductive replacement ratio above 1:1 for a substantial number of generations.

Mother Nature also uses physical and geographical measures to limit species distribution. The natural niche for humans is tropical and temperate subtropical parts of the globe in nondesert areas where water and nutriments are plentiful. But human ingenuity has overcome these conditions, too, with innovations ranging from warm clothing (starting with animal furs involuntarily donated by other creatures of Mother Nature) and central heating (starting with fire, one of the first technologies adapted by human ingenuity to serve humanity) that allow us to live in cold climates. Irrigation, a human innovation to divert the natural flow of water, and agriculture, a human artifice to replace those natural species inhabiting a given plot of land with those few species important as foodstocks for humans, allowed us to thrive in arid and barren areas.

Again, we're the only species to use unnatural, artificial means to expand our geographical range.

As well, we're the only species to have literally changed the face of the Earth, as our human activities have altered the physical appearance of the planet. A quick look at Google Earth or other satellite views show man-made features, such as cities, farms, and open pit mines, all of which are unnatural and none of which would exist if our early ancestors had remained in their natural niche. Although *Homo sapiens* are natural as biological and physical entities, human behavior consistently repudiates Mother Nature and her attempts to keep us in line with other of her species.

In a very real sense, we humans have not just rejected Mother Nature, we're constantly fighting against her efforts to reign in our burgeoning population. We're exploiting natural resources to our exclusive benefit and at the expense of other species. If we don't like human domination of the planet's resources, the option is to reject human technology and return to Mother Nature.

Consequences of Returning to Mother Nature's Fold

Having Mother Nature look after us in a sustainable way may be a warm and comforting thought, but the cold reality is decidedly discomforting, and it carries some frightening consequences.

First, Mother Nature has no answer to the expanding human population, not unless we revert to her ways and shun human interference in natural processes altogether. Humanity is already so far removed from Mother Nature that she might not recognize us. After all, we spent 10,000 years defacing and polluting her planet and enslaving her species to the benefit of only ourselves. Assuming she was merciful enough to take us back, it would be on the condition, of course, that we follow her rules to keep all species in balance and harmony.

Second, we'd have to say good bye to our grandparents and grandchildren. As with other species, our natural role is fulfilled when we raise our children to reproductive independence. After our biological replacements are capable of looking after themselves, somewhere around the mid to late teen years, we proud parents become not only expendable but also an actual drain on resources. Every additional day beyond—let's be generous—our fortieth birthday, we eat food, drink water, and breathe air that is rightfully due to someone else, someone not yet completing their natural, biological duty. Mother Nature is kicking us out of the nest. But don't worry, we're still useful to her, as our corpses provide nutrients for other of her hungry creatures—unless, of course, we render our cold carcasses useless through embalming or cremation. And during our forty years or so of natural lifespan, we have to accommodate yet other natural inhabitants. Various parasites, bacteria, fungi, and vermin have long been denied their natural due, their pound of human flesh, or at least their domicile inside or alongside humans, all because of our interference with their doing what comes naturally. We'll just have to get over our arrogant repugnance to germs, bugs, and vermin and get used to living with creepy-crawlies, as there are no synthetic antibiotics, miticides, dewormers, or even mechanical rat traps in Mother Nature's dwelling place that we call "Earth."

Third, in returning to Mother Nature's fold, we humans, having abandoned such human technologies as irrigation, plant breeding, animal husbandry, central heating, air conditioning, long distance transport, refrigeration, and other means of preservation of foodstuffs, would have to relocate to our natural geographical regions and reoccupy our "natural" niches. Naked humans are not naturally adapted to survive in high latitudes or deserts, so we'd have to pack ourselves into those few temperate areas with mild winters and sufficient fresh water. Say goodbye to Canada and Chicago as well as most of California, China, and Europe. The ones remaining behind perish.

Fourth, far more humans would have to return to basic agrarian lifestyles. Not that there's anything wrong with a more simple existence; farming can be a highly satisfying and rewarding vocation. But too many urbanites have a dreamy romantic vision of farming; they are often the ones espousing a return to "traditional" or natural farming. But the reality is more sanguine—just ask any of the farmers surviving the dust bowl of the "dirty thirties" just how romantic pre-industrial agriculture actually is. Even with modern technologies, farming is invariably hard work and often financially unrewarding and frustrating. As Dwight Eisenhower noted, "Farming looks mighty easy when your plow is a pencil, and you're a thousand miles from the corn field."

There's also a difference between making a conscious decision to practice to work the land and an involuntary directive forcing people to become farm laborers. During China's cultural revolution of the late twentieth century, now invariably considered a resounding failure, millions of urban Chinese were forced out of the cities and back to the farm, where they were largely unhappy and unenthusiastic, unmotivated, and unproductive workers. But that was predictable and even expected. Traditional, nonindustrial agriculture is labor intensive, and a return to traditional farming will necessitate more human labor. A hundred years ago, about one-third of the US population labored on US farms (http://www.agclassroom.org/gan/timeline/farmers_land.htm). Today, only 2 percent of the US population lives on a farm and only about half of those claim farming as their occupation (http://www.epa.gov/agriculture/ag101/demographics.html). A return to "traditional" farming in the USA means roughly three out of ten humans currently working elsewhere will be required to move to a farm and labor there. Volunteers are preferable, of course, as they are more motivated and more efficient workers. But those who voluntarily choose farming are already doing it; they are accounted within the 2 percent of the American population now farming. Who gets to choose and send the three out of ten unwilling workers?

Fifth, those espousing a return to natural or traditional lifestyles presume those lifestyles to be natural, stable, sustainable, and equitable. They are not. They may have been at one time, many years ago, but again the reality of the current human population dashes the illusion. Farming, even as practiced by our ancestors 10,000 years ago, is not natural. Our human ancestors tilled—that is, plowed—the soil, disturbing the land in a manner disruptive to the species living there in order to plant seeds of a single or few species to serve the needs and wishes of the humans alone and without regard for the other species thus displaced. Tillage also results in loss of a nonrenewable resource, topsoil, by exposing the valuable sand, silt, and clay particles to erosion by wind and water.

Some naïve Europeans may talk with a straight face about the "natural agricultural environment," but I consider that expression an oxymoron. Certainly, Europe encourages farmers to serve two masters—one being agricultural production and the other preservation of biodiversity and, by implication, "Nature." But the biodiversity being nurtured on European farms is a far cry from the plant, animal, and microbial species occupying the same land prior to early European humans tilling the soil. Human stewardship of the environment, even for sublime goals, does not accurately reflect Mother Nature's plan. Our human biases ensure certain species would get preferential treatment, usually by interfering with a natural dynamic that would favor a different set of species, ones less interesting (or more threatening) to humans.

All kinds of "natural" farming destroys biodiversity; whenever soil is tilled, the rich native biodiversity is disrupted and replaced with a small number of species, especially, in recent history, non–native plants grown as crops. Where is Mother Nature's "balance and harmony" respecting the multitude of species previously resident in that soil? In actuality, because of the massive loss of biodiversity and erosion of soil, tillage remains the cause of the greatest environmental degradation the planet and biosphere has ever suffered (Sparrow 1984). And it's 100 percent the fault of human activity engaged in "traditional" farming.

The concept described as the Red Queen hypothesis assures that a technologically unchanging regime, as under the traditional or natural lifestyle, will deteriorate to eventual extinction of the population refusing to adapt. The Red Queen, Lewis Carroll's character in *Alice in Wonderland*, was constantly running but found herself going nowhere. The analogy is that one must continue moving just to stay in place, relative to others, because the others are moving. In biological terms, stability means, paradoxically, constant evolution. For example, in the dance of host and disease, the host is constantly changing, trying new genes and gene combinations to thwart the pathogen, while the pathogen, in turn, is constantly modifying its own genes in trying to overcome the host's new defenses, like a biological version of our arms race. After a period of many generations, both host and pathogen remain locked in the dance but both are genetically different from their respective ancestors. After all these generations and genetic changes, the net result, relative to one another, is stasis (to appreciate the added titillation of sex appeal to the Red Queen, see Ridley 1993).

Applying the Red Queen hypothesis to farming and human sustenance, farmers and farming must similarly continue to improve just to maintain relative productivity. We know, for example, that farmers can control certain weeds using certain herbicides, but that eventually the weeds will evolve a resistance to that herbicide. The farmer then must replace the no-longer-useful herbicide with a new one or productivity will decline from the increasing presence of the weeds competing with the crop plants for nutrients, water, sunshine, etc. Of course, management techniques are available to delay the onset of such weed populations with resistance to the old herbicide, but those weed management strategies may themselves be innovations violating the "traditional" practice. In any case, those strategies are merely stopgap measures to delay the inevitable. Sooner or later, the weeds will change sufficiently to overcome any management strategy. New strategies must constantly be developed and implemented.

For another example, consider traditional farmers growing "heritage" plant varieties. Although even these varieties are invariably of modern breeding provenance, some consumers believe growing these older varieties under traditional farming methods promotes sustainability in agriculture. Unfortunately, reality shows that the older varieties, perhaps elite and productive when first bred, are not particularly productive now as they have not evolved to keep up with the genetic changes in their natural pest and disease species. In actuality, the foods eaten by our pre-industrial agriculture ancestors are much more limited and are of poorer quality than many consumers believe. The human-derived innovations in plant breeding during the era of industrial agriculture include seedless watermelons and other fruits, exotics such as kiwifruit, and even entire new artificial species, such as triticale, now grown across millions of acres worldwide as animal feed. Triticale was developed by humans combining genes from different species by forcing wide crosses in the 1950s (for more on the history and development of this synthetic, artificial, unnatural man-made species, triticale, see Mergoum and Gomez-Macpherson 2004).

Popular Misconceptions: "Species Barrier" and Proprietary Genes

A popular misconception holds a natural "species barrier" prohibits genes moving from one species to another. This misconception is built upon another misconception, that genes are somehow proprietary to their respective species. No doubt, these misunderstandings arose due to an apparent human desire to categorize or pigeonhole things into discrete boxes, as we humans seem uncomfortable conceptualizing blended continua; however, Mother Nature prefers ranging across spectra. For example, humans like to talk about colors as separate entities—orange, blue, red, etc. Mother Nature, in contrast, provides a rainbow where each color gradually blends into the next. Undoubtedly, if humans designed a rainbow, each color would be separate, discrete, and delineated with a distinct border. The same is true in biology, as many species (itself, a human-derived discrete categorization concept that we seem to find comforting) are so similar that human taxonomists and systematists have difficulty keeping them separate. Genomic analyses often support the view that such distinctions that split close relatives are artificial contrivances. To illustrate, consider two clearly distinct species, corn and wheat. They cannot successfully cross pollinate to produce hybrid progeny so some people fabricate an artifice—"species barrier"—to explain why corn genes don't mix with wheat genes. But molecular analyses show that the genetic makeup of the two species is actually very close. And not only is there a high degree of similarity between individual genes (aka "homology," see discussion below) but also the arrangement of the genes along chromosomes is similar. This phenomenon, called "synteny," is true for several cereal species: The chromosomes of rice, millet, sugar cane, wheat, sorghum, and corn can be lined up in parallel, and the specific genes will (with some exceptions) follow the same order in all. Skeptics will, of course, argue that this is no big deal; after all, the species are all related grassy cereals, so seeing an alignment of genes along chromosomes should come as no surprise. But what about genetic synteny shared between humans and fish? Yes, genetic similarity is sufficient to arrange chromosomes of humans and fugu fish such that genes will appear in the same order (for details, see http://www.ncbi.nlm.nih.gov/pubmed/15141032).

Perhaps more convincing, let's consider chromosome architecture, comparing human chromosome 21 with a fellow mammal, the mouse. Observation of the respective chromosomes shows hundreds of shared genes between man and mouse, and the ordered sequence of the genes is also preserved along the chromosome. For example, segments of three mouse chromosomes could be snapped together to reconstruct the long arm of human chromosome 21 without significant loss of genetic information or even the order of gene arrangement (http://www.nature.com/scitable/content/regions-of-synteny-between-human-chromosome-21-5849). Clearly, the chromosome blueprint/plans for mice and men were laid down long before Steinbeck or even Burns, but that reality still may leave us nothing but grief and pain if we fail to recognize and exploit—for the sake of human and planetary sustainability—such natural phenomena. The synteny is not as complete as with the cereals, but these examples of genetic similarity and chromosomal structure across species should suffice to make the point that DNA, genes, and chromosomes are not unique or proprietary to the species that contain them.

Sloppy language by scientists certainly contributes to the "species barrier" popular misconception, as scientists often speak of "fish genes" or "tomato genes" or "human genes" as if each species owned a set of unique genes. In fact, most genes are common across many species, a phenomenon called genetic homology. They may differ slightly in their DNA base sequence; consequently, the protein may have slightly different amino acid sequence, and so the resulting protein may show slight differences in performance. For example, all mammals (including humans) carry an insulin gene, and they do so for the same reason—to regulate blood sugar content. The DNA sequence of the human insulin gene—and the consequent amino acid sequence of the insulin protein—differs from the bovine or porcine insulin genes only slightly, which is why human diabetics were able to use insulin extracted from farm animals to treat their own diabetes. Today, diabetics use insulin produced by microbes genetically engineered to carry and express the human insulin gene. Although microbes do not ordinarily produce insulin (they have no blood, thus no need for blood sugar regulation), they are able to read the human origin DNA and from that genetic recipe make the same protein as is made in humans. This ability shows the universality of the genetic code, disproving the uniqueness or species proprietary aspect of genes. Without the commonality of the genetic code across all species, genetic engineering simply wouldn't work.

This common language of the genetic code, the homology of genes, and synteny in the order of genes in chromosomes should bury the arrogant concept of proprietary genes belonging to a given species. The human insulin gene can be read and insulin synthesized by bacteria. Mice and other mammals carry insulin genes as well, and they produce insulin sufficiently similar to human insulin as to satisfactorily treat diabetics. In humans, the insulin gene recipe is located on the short arm of chromosome 11. In mice, the insulin recipe is located on chromosome 7. And the DNA sequence is very similar. But this is not unexpected, as mice, unlike bacteria, do have blood and do need to regulate blood sugar. As the functions are so similar, it's not surprising to find the DNA base sequence is also similar. But let's take a different approach. Genes are arranged in a linear fashion along a chromosome, so consider the nearest neighbors to the human insulin gene on chromosome 11: on one side, upstream—in the parlance of genomics—of the insulin gene in humans is a tumor suppressor gene called TSPAN 32. On the other side, downstream, is TNNT, a gene for a protein facilitating fast muscle contraction. These three genes are functionally unrelated, they just happen to be geographical neighbors. What about our vermin relative? The closest gene upstream of the mouse insulin gene is TSPAN32. On the other side is—you guessed it—TNNT. (These genetic comparisons are available online at: http://www.ncbi.nlm.nih.gov/IEB/Research/Acembly/.)

At what point is a human gene no longer "human"? If we take the human insulin gene, for example, and change one or two bases in the DNA, which are so insignificant that the resulting insulin is identical to the original insulin, is the modified gene still "human"? Let's go a step further. Let's change a few bases in the DNA, such that the resulting insulin molecule shows two or three amino acids changed but still fully functional in regulating blood sugar. Is the modified gene still human or is it synthetic? Finally, what if it turns out that the human insulin gene with a few base changes is identical to the insulin gene of a musk ox? Have we violated the proprietary genetic rights of the big beast?

To finally refute the concept of the "species barrier," consider that transfer of genetic material from one species to another is actually not unusual in nature. While fish do not pass their DNA to tomatoes directly, that's due only to physical barriers, not genetic, as a gene copied from a fish and transferred to a tomato could settle amid the tomato genome and be treated by the tomato as any other segment of

DNA in its genome. And many examples of gene transfer from one species to others can be cited. Different bacterial species do it regularly without any human help, and *Agrobacterium* species transfer DNA to higher plants, inserting bacterial DNA into the plant genome, where it is read and expressed by the plant machinery. Closer to home, recent research shows that even the human species, *Homo sapiens*, carries DNA originally from other species, from viruses to a now extinct relative, *Homo Neanderthalis*.

On this latter point, it seems our genetic ancestors, *H. sapiens* and *H. Neanderthalis* met and carried out some early cross species gene transfer experiments shortly after the great migration out of Africa (Green et al. 2010; Yotova et al. 2011)) some fifty to eighty thousand years ago. Unfortunately, we have no contemporaneous sociological data on the social mores or propriety of such early interspecies fraternizations from either of the species involved. However, some of these early mating experiments not only disproved the "species barrier" concept (by successfully producing fertile and fecund progeny) but also they were so successful that virtually all subsequent human populations still carry genetic remnants—as much as 4 percent—of those early interspecies trysts. Perhaps even more interesting, the DNA of humans remaining in Africa was not thusly contaminated with nonhuman Neanderthal genes, so their descendants, modern Africans, are, scientifically, the genetically "purest" of the human races, a fact undoubtedly disputed by those humans carrying a larger than normal proportion of Neanderthal features.

Many other species analyzed also show the presence of DNA originating in foreign species. This "horizontal gene transfer," while not all that common in higher species, is also not all that rare. Wheat, the "staff of life" and source of "our daily bread," is itself a complex hybrid of genes from at least three distinct species. Both Mother Nature and human plant breeders, even those using "traditional" breeding methods, regularly transfer genes across the mythical species barrier.

Paradoxically, "sustainable agriculture" cannot succeed if based on pre-industrial farming practices but must continually change, adapt, and evolve to match the correspondingly evolving challenges. This doesn't mean we should continue the current practice of industrial agriculture, as that trajectory is clearly nonsustainable as well, with its reliance on nonrenewable petroleum supplies for so many aspects of modern farming, from tractor fuel to raw material for synthetic fertilizers. Instead, it means recognizing current challenges (such as diminishing petroleum reserves) and adopting appropriate innovations. It means more judicious application of technological innovations, with the goal not to maximize food production but to optimize food production. Optimizing production integrates efficiency and sustainability into the calculus, as opposed to maximizing production, where there is no consideration of any factors beyond volume. Optimizing food production means deliberative analysis of differing options and judicious selection of adopting the options giving the best balance of food quality, food quantity, and preservation of input resources along with minimal environmental and ecological degradation.

Nowhere is optimizing of food production more apparent than in plant breeding. Humans have been genetically modifying plants to generate new improved genetically novel varieties of various crops for thousands of years. Apart from occasional or regional crop failures, famines, and civil unrest, the food supply has been generally adequate to sustain the human population— that is, up until the twentieth century.

Plant breeding includes not only traditional crossing (what most people think of exclusively as "plant breeding") but also a spectrum of other methods to alter the genetic makeup of a plant to generate improved varieties (see discussion below).

These innovations in breeding and animal husbandry, combined with more powerful fertilizers (especially those from Haber Bosch processes invented in the early twentieth century to produce synthetic nitrogen-based fertilizers), extensive irrigation systems, and food storage, preservation, and transportation methods led to dramatic increases in food availability and security, both in quantity and in quality.

However, these advances were matched by dramatic increases in human demand for food—both quantity and quality—from increased numbers of humans (the population explosion of the twentieth century, burgeoning from 1.6 billion humans to the current 6.8 billion), increased longevity of humans already present (average world human lifespan doubling from about 30 in 1900 to over 64 years today) and expanding dietary demand for more animal protein and less grain, driven by increases in economic affluence and social stability (Braun 2007).

Borlaug's Green revolution of the mid-twentieth-century illustrates the power of judiciously adopting and adapting selected technologies. Combining modern mutated wheat varieties with irrigation and careful farm management, previously poor countries of Asia suddenly became better able to feed their populations of hungry humans.

Advocates for a return to pre-industrial agriculture, when a third of the US population was required to work on a farm to generate enough food for 76 million Americans, will have to explain how the current 300 million Americans will be fed with farms staffed by just 2 percent of the population, all in the absence of modern crop varieties, fertilizers, pesticides, and machinery. In a very real and literal sense, stasis in agriculture means starvation for humans.

Thomas Hobbes in *Leviathan* recognized this natural state of mankind, describing human life under "natural" conditions as "... nasty, brutish and short." Those who advocate a return to Mother Nature's bosom will have a hard time garnering sufficient political support once people realize what it actually entails. If this difficulty is not evident from a scientific perspective, consider the political angle: Human intervention is required to control the population, and politically mandated human population control is feasible only in totalitarian states. The same problem exists with resource management: Capitalist democracies will have to agree to have a centrally controlled economy to dole out dwindling global resources in what the central committee (or dictator) determines to be a fair and equitable manner. In my opinion, long before that eventuality, we'll see genetically engineered flying pigs.

Let's turn to investigate the alternate path, namely, dependence on judicious application of human ingenuity.

History of Agriculture

Homo sapiens are, under Mother Nature, nomadic hunter-gatherer omnivores. About 10,000 years ago, our ancestors first threw down Mother Nature's gauntlet by putting down roots, both figuratively, by settling on one spot, and literally, by sowing seeds of local plants chosen as having "desirable" (in the eyes of our ancestors) attributes.

In the intervening millennia, human ingenuity developed additional technologies to increase agricultural productivity, many of which continue in use today. For example, irrigation—the diversion of rivers and streams from their natural courses to provide water to otherwise naturally arid farmlands—was a very early human interference that is still being exploited and expanded today.

Techniques of plant breeding and animal husbandry were explored, adapted, expanded, and honed long before Mendel described genetics, and they involve far more unnatural and intrusive technologies than simple mating between male and female of the same species. The result is an ever-increasing "tool box" of breeding technologies offering a spectrum of options that breeders continue to use and adapt today. Grafting, for example, was recorded as early as 7,000 years ago in China when courtier Feng Li took scions (small branches) from various fruit trees and attached them to rootstocks of others (Wheeler 2011). Today, grafting is standard practice for many fruit, nut, and other crops to gain, for example, better disease resistance or water and nutrient delivery than is available naturally.

Hybrid crops can increase yields substantially via the robust vigor known as heterosis. Hybrid seed technology, less than one hundred years old, now claims the majority of corn and many other crop acreages, even though the technology requires farmers to purchase fresh seeds each year, a sea change from traditional seed-saving practice in which farmers set aside a portion of the harvested grain to use as seed the following season.

A more recent innovation, mutation breeding with irradiation or chemical mutagens, arose out of the atomic "Atoms for Peace" program following World War II. What mutation breeding does is disrupt the natural DNA of a plant sufficiently to result in nonlethal heritable changes, some of which are useful to human consumers (if not to the plant species itself). More than 2,700 registered crop varieties were developed using mutation breeding in the last half century, including many major crops used by conventional and even traditional and organic farmers (Ahloowalia et al. 2004 and website at http://mvgs.iaea.org/default.aspx).

Curiously, mutation breeding is known to cause disruptions to the DNA, from minor changes, such as single base "point" mutations, through more substantial physical cytogenetic mutations, inversions, and translocations to massive destructions, deletions of chromosomes, etc. The latter are almost invariably lethal, as the plant cannot survive such gross genetic disruptions. Of the crop cultivars developed using mutation methods, none are characterized at a genetic level, apart from the new trait, so we have no idea what additional mutations may have occurred.

Like all other non-GMO forms of plant breeding, not only are the features of new mutated cultivars not investigated or described at a molecular level but also they undergo no safety testing. Instead, new cultivars need be described only as *D*istinctive from other cultivars, *U*niform, meaning a field full of plants of the new cultivar must appear similar, and *S*table, meaning the genetic features must pass from one generation to subsequent generations. This "DUS" system is a worldwide requirement of all new plant cultivars under the International Union for the Protection of New Varieties of Plants (UPOV), including genetically modified cultivars. In the USA, new crop cultivars are administered by the USDA under the Plant Variety Protection Act (PVPA); details are available online at http://ams.usda.gov/science/PVPO/PVPO_Act/PVPA2005.pdf. Perhaps surprisingly, in most jurisdictions—including the USA—the new crop cultivars undergo no food or environmental safety assessments prior to commercial release; only the GM cultivars additionally undergo food and environmental safety assessments.

The question of when "traditional" agriculture gave way to "industrial" agriculture is thus not a simple or trivial one, as the historical agricultural enterprise is a temporal sequence of innovation upon innovation; there is no obvious starting point for "modern" farming. Most of our fruits and veggies were not known to our ancestors. What we know today as corn was developed by early plant breeders from the grass-like teosinte several thousand years ago. Broccoli and cauliflower were derived from cabbage (itself only about 2,000 years old) in the fifteenth and sixteenth Centuries, with Brussels sprouts coming in the 1700s. Carrots were developed around the same time, with the now familiar ubiquitous orange color bred, according to legend, by human plant breeders in Holland in honor of the reigning House of Orange, although the veracity of this latter colorful story is now being challenged (http://www.carrotmuseum.co.uk/history.html). Kiwifruit, hybrid plants, and seedless fruits were all developed in the twentieth century. Plant breeding, enhancing plants by changing their genetic makeup, is an uninterrupted stream of innovations that dates back 10,000 years, so no clear temporal point exists to serve as a division between "traditional" and "industrial" agriculture, at least not using breeding as the sole criterion.

However, the transition is often arbitrarily pegged with the development of synthetic fertilizer, the Haber Bosch process of 1909, that made nitrogen fertilizer available on a large scale at affordable prices (Smil 2004). Subsequent innovations accelerated after this development, especially in farm mechanization, breeding, and agronomy (including soil and farm management).

In the last one hundred years, we've dramatically improved the production of crops and domesticated animals to provide more food—more nutritious and safer food—than that supplied by Mother Nature alone. In spite of some popular misconceptions that modern agriculture produces food that is inferior, less safe, or devoid of nutrients (see, e.g., Pawlick 2006) food produced using modern technologies is the safest and most nutritious ever. Most pathogens and vermin are almost eradicated, the nutritional quality of today's produce is at least equivalent to traditional or heritage varieties, and increased quantities mean nutritional consumption is enhanced.

Modern Technologies to Sustain Humans

We humans will likely continue this approach, using both traditional and modern technologies, including genetic engineering (GE or rDNA technologies) to further push back the time of human demise to perhaps long enough for clever humans to devise a true long-term sustainable solution.

Genetic engineering arose in the early 1970s and generated considerable anxiety, even among the scientific community developing the application of the technology. The Asilomar conference of 1975 was a gathering called by scientists themselves, who publicized the potential risks in applying GE (Berg et al. 1975). The meeting and subsequent discussions led to a code of conduct and regulatory scheme to oversee GE research and researchers. In the USA, applications of GE to agriculture came under the watchful eye of the White House Office of Science and Technology Policy (OSTP) coordinating the regulatory offices of the FDA, EPA, and USDA in evaluating the safety of new foods and feeds bred using GE technologies. The first government regulated field trials in the US were conducted in 1988, with the number of such trials, the crop species developers, and traits all expanding rapidly in the following years.

The first GE food on the commercial market was cheese made with chymosin, produced by GE microbes. The first whole food was the now defunct FlavrSavr tomato, from Calgene, in 1994, followed soon after by approved GE cultivars of corn, soy, cotton, canola, papaya, squash, flax, and others.

Over the years, various groups and individuals have expressed their fears concerning the safety of GE-derived foods. The US National Academy of Science conducted a series of studies into the basis of the fears (see, e.g., National Academy of Science 1987, 1989, 2002, 2004, 2010) as did similar scientific authorities in other countries, such as the UK's Royal Society (2002, 2009) and the French Academy of Sciences (ADSF 2002). In addition to these august national bodies, other professional medical and scientific bodies undertook investigations into the charges of potential hazards associated with genetically modified organisms. In these studies by professional scientific and medical groups such as the American Medical Association (American Medical Association Council on Scientific Affairs 1991), the Organisation for Economic Cooperation and Development (OECD, 1986) and the American Dietetic Association (2006), the basic conclusions were the same: GE is not inherently risky, and the risks associated with specific applications are the same as those risks seen with conventional technologies. Worthwhile noting here is the fact that conventional technologies are not without risk. Several examples exist where potentially hazardous crop varieties had to be recalled at various stages in the breeding process, including after commercial release, due to the presence of toxins. Among the best known are celery, with excessive amounts of psoralen, and potato, with novel glycoalkaloid content (see National Academy of Sciences 2004 for additional information on problems from new varieties from traditional breeding methods).

In the intervening years, more and more commercial farmers began growing GE crops on a large scale, and consumers began eating foods derived from genetic engineering. By 2009, GE crops were being grown in twenty-nine countries and consumed by billions of humans (James 2010). Not one case of harm to either humans or environments caused by GE crops or foods has yet been documented.

Notwithstanding the relative safety of GE, or, to put it colloquially, "so far, so good," an argument has been made that GE has not, in spite of its successful invasion of worldwide acreage, increased food production (see, e.g., Gurian-Sherman 2009). That is, the traits in current GE crops are fairly simple, offering improved insect resistance or weed control, but, Gurian-Sherman argues that GE has not enhanced overall yield, a highly complex trait, so there's no "real" food production benefit from the technology.

It is true that the current GE crops were not directly engineered for yield increases, and it's true that yield is a highly complex combination of traits; there's no such thing as a "yield" gene. There are GE plants in various stages of development that have been modified to enhance yield directly, by increasing, for example, the efficiency of photosynthesis. However, those plants are still in testing stages and not yet commercialized. But to say the current GE crops have not improved yield or increased food production is misleading if not disingenuous. While the GE crops do not directly increase yield, they *indirectly* increase yield by reducing the constraints to yield potential. That is, in ordinary farm systems, crop yields are reduced, sometimes substantially, by the ravages of disease, depredation by insects, or the competition from weeds. Current GE crops, protected from those constraints, are better able to perform up to their natural yield potential. This is most readily illustrated in poorer countries, as US farmers ensure high-yield potential in conventional cropping by using sufficient pesticides to limit the pests causing the yield reduction. In poorer countries, farmers often cannot afford sufficient chemical to give this high degree of control so they end up harvesting whatever the diseases, insects, and weeds leave behind. In the Philippines, for example, when Bt corn was first introduced, the reported corn yields increased from about 4 tons per hectare to 12 tons per hectare (Deshpande 2009). In South Africa, the introduction of GE Bt corn since 2000 is resulting in yield increases ranging from 5 percent to 32 percent (Brookes and Barfoot 2011).

And in the United States, a more recent study on the impacts of genetic engineering on sustainability of US agriculture from the National Academy of Sciences concluded that in the United States alone, farmers, society, and the environment were all beneficiaries of agricultural biotechnology (National Academy of Sciences 2010).

In considering issues related to sustainability, current targets of agricultural biotechnology include such traits as drought tolerance or water use efficiency, nutritional enhancements (such as provitamin A enriched "Golden" rice), and removal of allergens or other toxic substances from various foods. And, with the current specter of climate change, genetic engineering is the only tool able to respond to such rapidly changing environments by quickly breeding and releasing new crop cultivars able to produce efficiently in the new conditions. That is, traditional breeding requires twelve or more years of breeding effort to bring a new variety to market (depending on species, trait sought, etc.), but genetic engineering can shave several years off the overall process. New GE crop cultivars with enhanced water use efficiency genes are nearing commercial readiness and will undoubtedly be watched closely for possible expansion to other crop species and regions where water is an increasingly expensive resource. The same gene constructs developed to help corn farmers in Texas or California remain productive in spite of diminished water availability will be attractive to farmers of other crops in drought-prone regions worldwide. Similarly, genes offering improved heat protection, transient flooding protection, or other rapid climate change–related traits will be highly sought as traditional sources of such genes are either already exploited or unavailable.

Hunger and Poverty

An oft-stated argument against using biotechnology to help a growing population is that we don't need any more food, that current world food production is sufficient to feed everyone, but that the problem is, instead, one of food distribution. If we properly manage food distribution, hunger would be eradicated. Therefore, if we focus attention on food distribution, we could obviate the need for industrial agriculture, especially agricultural biotechnology, altogether. While this position carries some emotional appeal, we must set aside emotion and instead invoke rational, critical thinking to challenge the underlying assumption that we already produce enough food globally to feed everyone. While this was a truism historically, when the human population was within the Earth's carrying capacity, it is less obvious today. And it is ironic that those arguing that biotechnology is unnecessary because we already produce sufficient food fail to recognize that current food production is largely due to human manipulation of nature through technical innovations such as irrigation, artificial fertilizers, genetic manipulation via modern, unnatural—but non rDNA—breeding methods, crop rotations, etc.

Distribution

But even if we accept, for argument's sake, that sufficient food is produced to feed everyone today, the glossed-over problem of "distribution" remains today as it has been throughout human history, when we've always had to contend with local or regional famines or other natural disasters resulting in mass starvation. If simple redistribution was the answer to feeding everyone, why haven't we humans simply redistributed surplus food whenever a need to do so arose? A moment's thought will illustrate the fatal flaw. The redistribution of food as a solution to world hunger requires an assumption that food is grown and delivered to the hungry free of charge. It is not. Think of a farmer in the US Midwest who grows corn and soybeans to sell to the market. The farmer is not going to grow the crops in the first place if he or she must hand it over (after keeping just enough to satiate the family), gratis, to the hungry. This is especially true if the farmer must deliver it to hungry populations who inconveniently happen to live overseas. The simplistic redistribution argument fails to account for the cost of transport, among other things.

Hunger is, in essence, an economic problem. Access to food is a function of wealth. If hungry people had enough money, they would not be hungry. I doubt anyone would challenge my assertion that, of the billion hungry humans on the planet today, not one of them is financially wealthy. Hungry people, invariably, have insufficient financial resources to purchase food; the cost of food is beyond their financial resources. Penury and hunger are proxies for each other; they are so inextricably linked that we could eradicate starvation by providing the hungry with either food or money. Given food, the hungry would eat it directly; given sufficient cash, they'd be able to buy food to satiate their hunger.

This brings us to a more compelling illustrative analogy. There is plenty of wealth in the world, so we can eradicate poverty simply by redistributing wealth from the rich to the poor. Poverty has also been with us throughout recorded human history, as has hunger, and the apparently simple solution to both problems has always been available: redistribution. But never in our human history has this solution been adopted, at least not on a large scale. This is another example of a relatively straightforward technical solution, but one that is politically impracticable.

So until someone figures out a way to get the rich to hand over their excess money, and farmers to produce food without getting paid to do so, we will have to contend with hunger and poverty, fighting them as best we can. This is unlikely to include waiting around for someone else to figure out how to redistribute the wealth and food.

An alternative to solving the hunger problem by redistributing either money or food, which—as we've seen—may be a technical solution but politically impossible, could instead involve approaching the problem economically and in a politically palatable manner: reducing the cost of food. An axiom of a functional free market economy holds that supply and demand dictate price. The price rises when demand exceeds supply, the price drops in times of plenty. In a given market, hungry people cannot buy food because the relationship between food supply and consumer demand sets a price too high for the impoverished hungry to afford. We can reduce the price, without political intervention, by either reducing the demand for food or increasing the supply of food. Reducing the demand is impracticable wherever there is poverty, as the penurious cannot simply ignore their hunger as easily as they might suppress their wish for a new yacht.

The more pragmatic and realistic option is to increase the food supply. Increasing the amount of food in this market will quench demand and the price will drop, allowing more people to buy more food and satiating the hunger of at least some of the impoverished.

Taking action to reduce hunger and poverty means using every available tool until that tool is shown unequivocally to cause more harm than good. Biotechnology has not (yet) been shown to cause more harm than good, in spite of considerable effort to identify actual harms to food or environment (see, e.g., European Commission 2010; Stein 2009). And biotechnology has been shown to increase food, both in quantity and in quality (National Academy of Sciences 2010). In basic economics, increasing the supply of any given commodity will lead to a decrease in price. So using biotechnology to increase food production will lead to reduced cost to consumers. And, as impoverished people by definition lack wealth, a reduction in food cost will enable them to purchase more and better food with their limited money. And we can achieve this without taking excess wealth away from rich people or forcing farmers to hand over their crops.

Conclusion

In the final analysis, genetic engineering is no more than an additional tool added to the plant breeder's toolbox. The biotechnology tool has no intrinsic value; the tool itself is neither "good" nor "bad." Those values are placed on the specific application of the tool. Indeed, the biotech tool when used to produce pharmaceuticals, e.g., insulin for diabetics, attracts almost no controversy whatsoever; the same technology to develop a crop that delivers lifesaving nutrients, e.g., vitamin A in rice, is used by some activist groups to incite unwarranted public fear and anxiety. Using the biotech tool wisely can provide more food, healthier food, and more nutritious food in a more sustainable manner. Alternatively, of course, we humans might use the tool irresponsibly to create crops that merely drain resources more quickly, accelerating the rate of diminution of water, soil, and other resources without offering offsetting compensation to humanity. Perhaps humans will reject the biotech tool entirely and, instead, continue with what we're currently doing, the status quo, until we exhaust the planetary resources entirely, accelerating the inevitable mass human starvations. Or we could eschew all of the "unnatural" tools of industrial agriculture and reclaim our natural niche as nomadic hunter-gatherers under Mother Nature's guidance.

All of these options are open. But before we reject biotechnology or choose to return to our "natural" ecological niche, we should contemplate the Malthusian consequences. The status quo is not a viable, let alone sustainable, option; the historical disorganized and injudicious application of technology has brought us to where we are, on a fast track to catastrophic planetary collapse. The awareness of our trajectory has led some to call for a rejection of human technology altogether, with a return to "natural" systems and our place in the biosphere, one species among many others, all with an equal right of access to resources.

But that option is politically impossible when people realize what that choice entails in terms of abandoning almost all "modern" comforts and conveniences. And Mother Nature may not welcome us back. The costs certainly are high—the loss of at least half the current human population and abandonment of most of the technologies that have allowed us to slip the natural constraints on our species and expand our rather limited niche and geographic territory. This route, too, may not work because the damage already done may continue apace, even without additional human interference. For example, in the current debate over anthropogenic climate change, the suggested remedies (mainly that we humans cease carbon release in various forms) do not address the likelihood that rapid climate change is now self-perpetuating. If that is the case, the deterioration in climate will continue in the absence of major human intervention to reverse it. That approach is, of course, anathema to those campaigning for a return to Mother Nature's fold.

But reverting to Mother Nature's plan, in which humans are merely one species among many, means catastrophic collapse of the human population sooner rather than later. Judicious human management of global resources provides the only option for a sustainable future.

Judicious application of biotechnology, integrating food production with environmental sustainability, is the only option offering a long-term human future. Critics of using technology to overcome natural limits to population growth argue that doing so just delays the inevitable crash by some years. But careful and deliberative application of technology does not mean supporting human population growth indefinitely but only to the point where human population naturally levels off, as it is expected to do in the mid-twenty-first century. At that point, the resources depleted in sustaining the then-stable human population will be balanced by resources replenished. However, the future planet Earth will not look as pristine and natural as she did in times past. The evidence of human activities will be evident everywhere since humans will have to manage planetary resources on a global scale to optimize efficiency and sustainability. Fortunately, it will not require politically impracticable policies, such as mandated reproductive control or mass euthanasia, but rather benign policy encouragement based on principles of agronomically, environmentally, socially, and economically sustainable development.

Barring some unforeseen catastrophic event such as a wayward giant asteroid attack, the Earth should remain intact until the Sun expands in its old age and engulfs our planet in some five billion years. Whether humans will be around to experience that will depend on the policy decisions we make now.

References

ADSF (Académie des Sciences Françaises). 2002. *Les plantes génétiquement modifiées*. Rapport sur la science et la technologie nr. 13. Paris: Académie des Sciences Françaises.

Ahloowalia, B. S, M. Maluszynski, and K. Nichterlein. 2004. "Global Impact of Mutation Derived Varieties." *Euphytica* 135: 187–204.

American Dietetic Association. 2006. "Position of the American Dietetic Association: Agricultural and Food Biotechnology." *Journal of the American Dietetic Association* 106 (2): 285–293.

American Medical Association Council on Scientific Affairs. 1991. "Biotechnology and the American Agricultural Industry." Policy Nr. H-480.985. *Journal of the American Medical Association* 265.11 (March 20): 1429–1436. doi: 10.1001/jama.1991.03460110095032

Berg P., D. Baltimore, S. Brenner, R. O. Roblin III, and M. F. Singer. 1975. "Summary Statement of the Asilomar Conference on Recombinant DNA Molecules." *Proceedings of the National Academy of Sciences* 72: 1981–1984. Also available in *Science* 188 (1975): 991.

Berenbaum, M. R. 1996. *Bugs in the System: Insects and Their Impact on Human Affairs*. New York: Basic Books.

von Braun, Joachim. 2007. *The World Food Situation: New Driving Forces and Required Actions*. Washington, DC: International Food Policy Research Institute. Accessed 4/21/2014. http://www.ifpri.org/sites/default/files/pubs/pubs/fpr/pr18.pdf/

Brookes G., and P. Barfoot. 2011. "The Income and Production Effects of Biotech Crops Globally, 1996–2009." *International Journal of Biotechnology* 12: 1–49.

Cohen, Joel. 1995. *How Many People Can the Earth Support?* New York: W. W. Norton.

Deshpande, V. 2009. "How Philippines Mountain Slopes Were Converted into Rich Bt Corn Fields." *Indian Express* (India), October 23.

Ehrlich, P. R., and A. H. Ehrlich. 1990. *The Population Explosion*. New York: Simon and Schuster.

Ehrlich, P. R., and J. P. Holdren. 1971. "Impact of Population Growth." *Science* 171: 1212–1217.

European Commission. 2010. *A Decade of EU-Funded GMO Research, 2001–2010*. Luxembourg: Publications Office of the European Union.

FAO (Food and Agriculture Organization of the United Nations). 2009. *Global Agriculture towards 2050. High Level Expert Forum: How to Feed the World in 2050*. Accessed4/21/2014 http://www.fao.org/fileadmin/templates/wsfs/docs/Issues_papers/HLEF2050_Global_Agriculture.pdf.

Green, R. E., J. Krause, A. W. Briggs, et al. 2010. "A Draft Sequence of the Neanderthal Genome." *Science* 328: 710–722.

Gurian-Sherman, D. 2009. "Failure to Yield: Evaluating the Performance of Genetically Engineered Crops." Cambridge, MA: Union of Concerned Scientists. Accessed 4/21/2014. http://www.ucsusa.org/food_and_agriculture/our-failing-food-system/genetic-engineering/failure-to-yield.html

James, C. 2010. *Global Status of Commercialized Biotech/GM Crops: 2009. The First Fourteen Years, 1996 to 2009*. ISAAA Brief 41–2009. Ithaca, NY: International Service for the Acquisition of Agric-biotech Applications. Accessed 4/21/2014 http://www.isaaa.org/resources/publications/briefs/41/executivesummary/default.asp.

Malthus, Thomas. 1798. *An Essay on the Principle of Population*. London. Accessed 4/21/2014 http://www.esp.org/books/malthus/population/malthus.pdf.

Mergoum M., and H. Gómez Macpherson, eds. 2004. *Triticale Improvement and Production*. FAO Plant Production and Protection Paper 174. Rome: Food and Agriculture Organization of the United Nations.

National Academy of Sciences. 1987. *Introduction of Recombinant DNA-Engineered Organisms into the Environment: Key Issues*. Washington, DC: National Academies Press.

National Academy of Sciences. 1989. *Field Testing of Genetically Modified Organisms: Framework for Decisions*. Washington, DC: National Academies Press.

National Academy of Sciences. 2002. *Environmental Effects of Transgenic Plants*. Washington, DC: National Academies Press.

National Academy of Sciences. 2004. *Safety of Genetically Engineered Foods*. Washington, DC: National Academies Press.

National Academy of Sciences. 2010. *Impact of Genetically Engineered Crops of Farm Sustainability in the United States*. Washington, DC: National Academies Press.

OECD. (Organisation for Economic Cooperation and Development). 1986. *Recombinant DNA Safety Considerations: Safety Considerations for Industrial, Agricultural and Environmental Applications of Organisms Derived by Recombinant DNA Techniques*. Paris: OECD.

Pawlick, T. 2006. *The End of Food: How the Food Industry Is Destroying Our Food Supply: And What We Can Do about It*. Fort Lee, NJ: Barricade Books.

Pulliam, H. R., and N. M. Haddad. 1994. "Human Population Growth and the Carrying Capacity Concept." *Bulletin of the Ecological Society of America* 75: 141–157.

Ridley, M. 1993. *The Red Queen: Sex and the Evolution of Human Nature*. New York: Penguin.

Royal Society. 2002. *Genetically Modified Plants for Food Use and Human Health: An Update*. London: Royal Society.

Royal Society. 2009. *Reaping the Benefits: Science and the Sustainable Intensification of Global Agriculture*. London: Royal Society.

Smil, V. 2001. *Feeding the World: A Challenge for the Twenty-First Century*. Cambridge, MA: MIT Press.

Smil, V. 2004. *Enriching the Earth: Fritz Haber, Carl Bosch, and the Transformation of World Food Production*. Cambridge, MA: MIT Press.

Sparrow, H. 1984. Soil at risk: a report on soil conservation by the Senate Standing Committee on Agriculture, Fisheries, and Forestry to the Senate of Canada. Government of Canada. Senate Reports.

Stein, A. J., and E. Rodríguez-Cerezo. 2009. *The Global Pipeline of New GM Crops: Implications of Asynchronous Approval for International Trade*. Brussels: European Commission Joint Research Centre.

Wheeler, Adam R. 2011. "The Art and Science of Grafting." Accessed4/21/2014 http://www.slideserve.com/presentation/123073/Adam-R-Wheeler

Yotova, V., J. F. Lefebvre, C. Moreau, et al. 2011. "An X-Linked Haplotype of Neandertal Origin Is Present among All Non-African Populations." *Molecular Biology and Evolution* 28 (7): 1957–1962.

CHAPTER 18

CLIMATE CHANGE AND AGRICULTURE

Countering Doomsday Scenarios

DERRILL D. WATSON II

INTRODUCTION

CLIMATE change threatens agriculture on multiple levels; agriculture in turn has a significant role to play in mitigating climate change and helping humans adapt to its impacts.[1] Food systems will not be sustainable or fulfill their primary mission of providing human health and nutrition without an adaptive agriculture in tune with its natural resource base and resilient to climate changes. The worst impacts of climate change are expected to fall on the poorest, who are the least well-equipped to adapt to it. Most climate-change literature focuses on difficult trade-offs generated by these interdependences. For example, environmental preservation depresses economic growth and, thus, reproduces or exacerbates poverty. At the extreme, these fateful trade-offs converge on doomsday scenarios.

This chapter posits that significant positive complementarities between improving agricultural production, mitigating and adapting to climate change, and reducing poverty. This is a slightly different claim from the classical argument that there are synergies between them. The idea of synergies between the three posits, for instance, that reductions in poverty can help mitigate some forms of environmental degradation. Synergies imply that improvements in one sector can provide additional spillover benefits to other sectors, creating multiple-win policy options. The evidence for such synergistic multiple-wins was reviewed in Lee and Barrett (2001) and found to be incomplete.

Complementarity claims that these multiple-win synergies increase with the estimated impacts of climate change. Thus, the worse you believe the effects of climate change will be, the more valuable it will be for governments and nongovernmental actors to invest in sustainable agricultural growth and poverty reduction. Sassi and Cardaci (2012) are among the few to explicitly take into account the fact that the triple burden of poverty, food insecurity, and climate change interact nonlinearly. They conclude that policy coordination between poverty, food, and climate will be essential in dealing with any of them. Ongoing investment in agriculture and poverty reduction are essential to mitigate and adapt to climate change, whereas policies to mitigate and adapt to climate change can themselves be tools to improve food security and reduce poverty.

This approach differs from much of the current thinking in taking an integrated, holistic, systems approach to dealing with the nexus of climate, agriculture, and poverty. Failure to consider the entire system—as, for example, by crop scientists focusing on increasing yield without regard for environmental constraints and changes, or by natural and environmental scientists ignoring hunger and nutrition in their quest to reduce agriculture's environmental damage—will lead to ineffective research, ill-informed policies, and less than optimal outcomes.

Agriculture will better support climate goals to the extent that positive and negative externalities are internalized by market participants. That is, producers and consumers should reap the benefits or bear the costs, respectively, that they impose on others who are not party to the transaction. This is essential not only as part of meeting current obligations toward improving countries' environmental standards, but also to ensure that agriculture can sustainably meet the food security needs of current and future generations. The "polluter pays" principle (PPP) imposes a cost on those doing something contrary to public interest as determined by government policy. Providing "payments for environmental services" (PES) rewards those whose actions promote a larger public good. Together PPP and PES form a continuum we refer to as full-costing. Although government is the only organization likely to be involved in PPP, nongovernmental organizations have also established networks to facilitate PES. There are different approaches to internalization, such as taxes and subsidies, creating markets for environmental services, and assigning Coasian property rights.

This approach has deliberate conceptual biases. It takes an explicitly anthropocentric viewpoint: climate change matters only insofar as human welfare is affected, either today or in the future. It follows the Brundtland Commission's definition of sustainability: Processes are sustainable if they meet the needs of current generations without weakening the ability of future generations to meet their needs. Substitution between natural and human-made resources is also permitted in order to achieve this. After this brief introduction of the issues, the second section explores these complementarities between climate change, agriculture, and poverty in detail. The third section examines the relationship between economic growth and the environment. The fourth section discusses the practical application of full costing and considers how it may be used to generate multiple wins. The fifth concludes the chapter.

Exploring Complementarities

Climate Change Impacts Food Security and Poverty

How does climate change impact agriculture? The effects of climate change on agriculture, food security, poverty, and indeed all of humanity may work subtly and gradually until their combined weight reaches a tipping point, releasing a torrent of irreversible change. That is one possible scenario. However, in less apocalyptic scenarios, climate effects grow much more linearly and with increasing obviousness, as better data on temperature shifts and the frequency of extreme weather shocks become available. The cumulative impacts of climate change could occur in gradual proportionality, meet up against unexpected, irreversible thresholds, scale up geometrically, or follow even more chaotic patterns (Brown 2009; Pinstrup-Andersen and Watson 2011).

The larger and more dramatic we expect climate change to be, the more important it will be to invest in improving agricultural productivity and reducing poverty. Consider the food price spikes in 2006–2008. Did changes in weather, soil, and air lead directly to the sudden increase in food price volatility starting in 2006, spiking as the climate and planet passed a critical threshold? Or did its effects come much more indirectly, as anticipations of climate change encouraged legislatures to mandate the pursuit of biofuels, just as speculators and investors alike turned their attention to food crops at a time of low stocks? In some ways, it is very difficult to separate these intertwined stories, yet they have profoundly different implications for the kind of policy that should be pursued going forward. If the former is more accurate, then these biofuel policies may be an essential ingredient in mitigating global warming; if the latter, the policies should be abandoned before greater harm is done (see Pimentel and Burgess, this volume). In either case, investments in long-term agricultural productivity would ameliorate local price fluctuations, and reductions in poverty would enable more people to cope with (direct and indirect) climate shocks.

The uncertainties surrounding how much climate will change and what its effects will be have led to many varying estimates of what to expect from climate change in the twenty-first century, ranging from doomsday scenarios to the relatively benign. Schwartz and Randall (2003) predict climate change will lead to nuclear war and Roberts (2008) foresees "The End of Food" with climate change playing a participatory role. Ereaut and Segnit (2006) show that alarmism is the most frequent rhetorical device used to discuss climate change. More measured reports that predict severe climate-induced outcomes include Willenbockel's (2012) estimations of extreme weather events leading to a doubling and trebling of food prices from their 2006–2008 food crisis levels and World Bank (2012) that warns that even moderate warming could lead to irreparable harm, mass exodus, further deforestation, and famine. The prominent Stern Report[2] (Stern 2007) estimated that it would cost roughly 1 percent of global production to make the investments necessary to avoid significant damage.

One thing each of those studies shares is a deliberate selection of unlikely negative outcomes. IPCC (2007 and 2012) has, in part, justified this by highlighting that past estimates of how much some variables would change (e.g., arctic temperatures) have consistently underestimated reality by significant margins. There is evidence, however, that newer models designed to address this are instead becoming more precise and less accurate in measuring global mean temperatures and the frequency of extreme temperatures (Swanson 2013).

Studies that examine the full range of possible climate outcomes tend to support the notion that negative outcomes for sub-Saharan African agricultural productivity before

2050 are highly probable. However, the impacts are fairly small in most countries and over most specifications. It is generally only in the worst predictions that climate change has dire consequences before 2050 (e.g., Lobell, et al., 2008; Schlenker and Lobell, 2010; Chinowsky, et al. 2012, IFPRI 2013). Such a generalization glosses over a great deal of variance and uncertainty, particularly for crops that are more reliant on historic rainfall patterns (Lobell et al. 2008). As only one example, IFPRI's (2013) two models of rainfall in West Africa disagree on whether Liberia will see an increase in annual rainfall of 200–400 ml or a decrease of over 400 ml; the Sahel might see only a small change (+/– 50 ml) or rainfall might increase by 100-200ml. One of the most important areas for future climate research as far as sub-Saharan agriculture is concerned is improving our estimates of future rainfall patterns.

Although this chapter emphasizes our current uncertainties, we can claim to understand which aspects of climate change will matter most for agricultural production going forward. Rising temperatures change crop growing periods, relative performance of different varieties of the same crop, and in extreme cases even what crops can be grown at all (IFPRI, 2009). Rainfall patterns matter most in the rain-fed agricultural regions of the world. Because climate change alters where the rains will come and when, how predictably, how much on average, and how intensely they fall, it can destroy crops and lead to large-scale food insecurity and malnutrition (IPCC, 2012; IFPRI, 2009). Increasingly frequent extreme weather events grab the attention of policymakers better than slowly developing and observationally doubtful global warming and increase the likelihood of extreme food price shocks recurring (Willenbockel 2012). Whether sea levels rise by one meter or by only one-half and whether that occurs by 2050 or 2100 is of vital importance to island nations and those whose most fertile or populated lands lie near the coast (UNU-WIDER, 2012). Increasing atmospheric CO_2 levels will help many plants, but some will benefit more than others, altering ecosystems around the world (Taub, 2010). Increased soil degradation caused by soil-nutrient mining and erosion, deforestation and desertification, water logging, falling water tables, oversalinization, and, potentially, climate change render barren the marginal cropland the poor had counted on for survival (Davidson and Janssens, 2006; Pinstrup-Andersen and Watson, 2011).

As investments in agriculture (e.g., research, roads, human capital, fertilizer, irrigation) reduce other capacity constraints, the climate and weather constraints will become increasingly important. This is an example of how the concept of complementarities differs from that of synergies. Weather plays the largest role where productivity is already high, as in Zimbabwe and South Africa (Schlenker and Lobell 2010). In other countries—where fertilizer, infrastructure, or other, structural constrains matter most—variations in weather are less of a determining factor. At the same time, the worse climate change impacts are expected to be, the more complementary investment is needed in agriculture and poverty. Butt et al. (2005) expect higher temperatures and soil degradation alone to result in reduced supply, leading to vastly higher prices by 2030. They expect net producers to be slightly better off, but consumers would be significantly worse off as the incidence of hunger increases by 20 percentage points. Multiple estimates reviewed by de la Fuente and Villarooel (2013) for Mexico predict an increase in poverty by roughly two percentage points from climate shifts and another two percent from climate shocks. In all cases, larger changes are associated with more poverty.

Ultimately, the impacts of climate change on food security and poverty depend on how households respond. The food system is a dynamic, behavioral system (Pinstrup-Andersen and Watson, 2011). As the external environment changes, food system actors are certain to change their actions in order to pursue their various goals. These goals include meeting income and dietary needs and wants both now and in the future, fulfilling social obligations, and producing environmental services that are valued by the household.

Climate change poses at least two types of challenges to which households must respond. One is the gradual change of environmental factors such as shifts in average rainfall and average temperature; the other is the increasing variance of those factors (e.g., rainfall), increasing the chance of large shocks (e.g., drought and natural disasters). Households are likely to adapt differently to these "shifts" and "shocks" of climate change (Baez, Kronick, and Mason 2012). Increased shocks will make agricultural conditions in the coming season more uncertain, reducing farmers' ability to recognize, evaluate, and respond to weather signals. This is likely to increase precautionary savings, but not in forms that would lead to increased investment (Meza, Hansen, and Osgood 2008; Ackerman, et al., 2009;). Yet it is investment that could potentially increase capacity to adapt to future changes in climate. Linear projections, and many academic treatments, do not account for agent responsiveness or social learning. To the extent climate change leads farmers to adopt techniques that successfully mitigate its impacts, this adaptation will lead researchers to overestimate its impact on agriculture. On the other hand, as will be argued in more detail later, to the extent that increasing climate stress and extreme weather events lead farmers to adopt more myopic strategies in order to survive today's challenges, despite the costs they realize those events will impose on them in the future—if they survive—they may be underestimates.

Agricultural Activities Impact the Environment and Poverty

It is obvious that agricultural activities impact the natural resources involved in production. Agricultural activities also impact their external environment. The most important impacts of agricultural activities on the environment include carbon sequestration, deforestation, soil degradation, water usage, and methane production. Carbon sequestration refers to capturing atmospheric carbon in plants and soils. Some agricultural practices naturally increase carbon sequestration (e.g., growing crops), whereas others release that stored carbon (e.g., harvesting crops). Since soils contain twice as much carbon as the atmosphere or vegetation, agriculture is an essential part of humanity's impact on greenhouse gasses. Deforestation releases the carbon sequestered in forests into the atmosphere. Nearby, poor people who depend on forests for their livelihoods and the women and children who must travel further in search of firewood are likely to suffer, whereas farmers and developers who gain access to the newly cleared land benefit.

Soil degradation reduces potential production. Removing more nutrients from the soil than are returned through fertilization is called soil mining. High levels of soil mining can lead to desertification and can be very expensive to reverse. In sub-Saharan Africa, 85 percent of agricultural land loses at least 30 kg/ha in nutrients annually, and half of that land loses more than 60, varying from 9 kg/ha in Egypt to 179 kg/ha in Uganda (Henao and Baanante 2001; Nkonya et al. 2008). In addition to the problems of soil mining, overuse or poor fertilizer-application technique can result in burnt soils and water pollution. Because of the high organic matter content of top soils, even low levels of soil erosion lead to large yield losses. Poor irrigation practices lead to waterlogging or salinization. These problems plus overgrazing and deforestation have caused more than two-thirds of global soil degradation since 1945 (de Haen 1997). Pinstrup-Andersen (2002) argues that soil degradation is caused or worsened by a variety of factors, many of which are beyond farmers' control: poor property rights and land tenure issues; population pressure; government policies; poor market access; and technologies and techniques that are not sustainable. Fifteen percent of manmade greenhouse gas emissions come from agriculture, with methane from livestock a leading contributor (Popp, Lotze-Campen, and Bodirsky, 2010).

The Green Revolution provided a mixed bag of positive and negative externalities for environmental quality (Harriss and Stewart, this volume). On the negative side was the greater reliance on monoculture cropping (which decreased farmer interest in preserving biodiversity on their lands) poor water management, and improper pesticide and fertilizer-application practices. These were not necessary features of the Green Revolution per se, but certainly accompanied the increased reliance on irrigation, fertilizer, and pesticides. Most of these negative effects could have been prevented by incorporating social costs into private prices. On the positive side, however, the increased productivity made possible by improved seed varieties and agricultural intensification reduced demands on human expansion onto marginal lands. Goklany (1998) estimates it would have required 80 percent more land to provide the increased food produced between 1961 and 1993 without the spread of Green Revolution technologies. Preserving the marginal lands that would have otherwise been cleared and plowed simultaneously preserved biodiversity, reduced soil erosion and deforestation, and preserved environmental services to the nearby communities. Costanza, et al. (1997) estimate that global environmental services are worth between \$16 and \$54 trillion, which, at the time of the study, was one to three times the value of all human production.

Improving agricultural productivity is essential for both preservation of environmental services and for poverty reduction. Schlenker and Lobell (2010, p. 7) agree with World Bank (2007): "There is arguably little scope for substantial poverty reductions in SSA [sub-Saharan Africa] without large improvements in agricultural productivity." Making land, water, and labor more productive is essential for poverty reduction and feeding a growing global population while preserving marginal lands and biodiversity. Current practices fall well short of those that would simultaneously ensure sufficient food production and environmental sustainability. Rice production in China leads to soil erosion, damage of forest ecosystems, and degradation of grassland, causing between $9.8 and $21.2 billion of damage in 1990 alone (Smil, 1997). Two-thirds of tropical deforestation is done to prepare land for agriculture, nearly half of which degrades to only half its initial quality within three years (Pinstrup-Andersen and Pandya-Lorch, 1994). That land then quickly moves from forest to farm to livestock pasture. However, agricultural intensification does not necessarily, as often claimed, reduce environmental quality (Pinstrup-Andersen and Pandya-Lorch 1994; Lee and Barrett 2001; Bouwman, et al. 2011). Rather, input mismanagement both harms the environment and reduces farming efficiency; overgrazing, erosion, poor irrigation processes, and excessive, insufficient, or poorly timed fertilizer and pesticide applications are the problem, not these resources' proper usage.

Steady, reliable, clean sources of water are essential for the food system. Ground and surface water depletion (partially caused by agricultural mismanagement) and changing rainfall patterns discussed earlier are significant binding constraints, particularly where irrigation has not been properly developed. IPCC (2007) predicts that nearly half the world's current population could face a shortage of clean water by 2080, whereas the Bonn Declaration (GWSP, 2013) warns that more than half will face a severe water shortage within a generation. Most fresh water is consumed by agriculture. However, use efficiency is generally low and significant amounts evaporate or leak from poorly maintained irrigation channels. Obtaining more food from less water is essential to feed growing global and local populations without depleting or harming water resources. This challenge is exacerbated by the growth of demand for livestock, which consumed 8 percent of all fresh water in 2000 and is expected to reach 16 percent by 2050 (Steinfeld et al. 2006; see also Mehta-Bhatt and Ficarelli, this volume). The uncertainties about how climate change will affect future rainfall patterns make this challenge even greater.

These inefficiencies stem in large measure from a failure to internalize the social value of water in private costs and large public water subsidies. When farmers are forced to pay the same market prices for irrigation water as industry and housing, they invest in techniques that increase water-use efficiency. These include drip irrigation, consistent irrigation channel maintenance, and mulch layers or zero tillage that reduce evaporation and soil erosion while improving water saturation and carbon sequestration. Brown (2009) discusses successful initiatives in India and Mexico that devolved control of water resources to local farmers associations. Although local farmers bore the costs of their own water use, the gains from greater control and management of those resources were greater.

Each of these impacts from agriculture to poverty and climate change is more amenable to public policies of specific national governments than is mitigation of global climate change. Responding to these pressures through smart investments in agriculture will be part of a package of responses to help poor farmers adapt to climate change and escape poverty (ILO, 2005; World Bank, 2007; IPCC 2012; Pinstrup-Andersen and Watson 2011). With most poor people in rural areas, increasing food access, farm incomes, and labor productivity can have a significant impact on people's livelihoods and well-being. Numerous studies have found significant multipliers from agricultural growth to other sectors of the economy as well (summarized in Pinstrup-Andersen and Watson, 2011). Drought and heat resistant crops are particularly well positioned to help farmers adapt to climate change (Butt et al. 2005; Kamara et al. 2006; La Rovere et al. 2010). Increasing labor productivity in rural areas spills over to the landless as well in increased wages and work opportunities. India's policy initiatives to introduce high-yielding varieties with complementary investments in irrigation and transportation networks during the Green Revolution increased the real incomes of smallholders by 90 percent and of the landless by 125 percent (ILO, 2005). Further, increased agricultural productivity lowers food prices, which will benefit the landless poor. Although investments in labor-using technology increase wages for the landless, investment in labor-saving technologies can be used to free up women's time for other activities, promoting greater gender equality and empowerment.

Among the proposals to make agriculture more sustainable is the organic movement (see Larsson, this volume). There are several areas, however, where organic production is not synonymous with sustainable production. In practice organic farming focuses farmers' attention on restoring soil fertility better than traditional methods in developing countries, leading to a lessening of soil mining and improvements in crop productivity. This is not, however, a complete restoration. Gosling and Shepherd (2005) find that organic management has benefitted from previous investments in soil fertility on modern systems, drawing down phosphorous and potassium from the soil. By disallowing chemical fertilizers it becomes more costly in time and land to properly fertilize crops and replace the nutrients used in farming. This can lead to—and in Gosling and Shepherd's (2005) opinion has led to—soil mining. Any removal of nutrients from the soil that is not replaced—either naturally or by substitutable manmade capital—is, by definition, unsustainable. Hole, et al. (2005) show that organic production has been no better at preserving biodiversity than modern agriculture with targeted land set-asides. Though there is great political support for organic agriculture, it is not clear that sustainability is enhanced by ideological approaches (Edwards-Jones and Howell 2001; Milestad and Darnhofer 2003).

The definitions of organic agriculture currently used by the United States and EU governments reflect ideology and politics. Sustainability, on the other hand, requires pragmatic approaches, which may well include technical change that protects the environment, reduces risks, and increases yields. There is no reason in principle that a sustainable approach cannot blend the best of practices to improve nutrient cycling, nitrogen fixing, soil regeneration, and protecting the natural predators of unwanted pests as developed by today's organic farming. Sustainable approaches would likely incorporate nutrient additives that include both green fertilizer and limited inorganic fertilizers, limited and timely pesticide applications, and scientific plant breeding advances that are safe for human consumption and biodiversity (Dima and Odero 1997; Pretty and Hine 2001; Pinstrup-Andersen and Watson 2011; Newell-McGloughlin, this volume).

Expanding the Environmental Kuznets Curve

The most controversial of the links in the argument for synergies between desirable outcomes in environmental protection, agricultural improvements, and poverty reduction is from reduction of poverty to improved environmental outcomes. Early empirical evidence identified a decidedly nonlinear relationship between economic growth and a number of pollutants in the early 1990s (reviewed in Grossman and Krueger 1995). Graphing pollution or damage against income produced an inverted U-shaped curve: For poorer countries, economic growth appears to lead to increases in some forms of environmental damage. As growth continues, however, the damage begins to reverse itself so that increased income is associated with better environmental outcomes. Because of its similarity with Kuznets' hypothesized relationship between inequality and income—in which inequality increases at lower levels of national income but improves with higher levels of income—this relationship has been called the Environmental Kuznets Curve (EKC).

The EKC generated considerable controversy. Even as this relationship was being introduced, Grossman and Krueger (1995) were quick to emphasize that this is not an automatic relationship. Although greener technology has a clear role to play and is connected with economic growth, they argue, policy changes are the more important factor. A number of other hypotheses will generate similar dynamics. It may be that environmental quality is a luxury good that people invest in through consumer and political advocacy, being willing to pay higher prices for goods and service delivered in eco-friendly ways, and accepting higher direct and indirect taxes to reduce environmental externalities (Jaeger, 1998). Andreoni and Levinson (2001) demonstrate that the inverted U-shaped curve can be generated by increasing returns to abatement technology; that is, it is cheaper to abate one unit of pollution the more pollution there is. A hypothesis that the phenomenon is caused by exporting polluting industries to developing countries was discounted by Cole's (2004) evidence. Yet another possibility is that people's discount rates depend on their income and particularly chances of survival; the more likely it is that I will not live to see the future, the less concern I give for long-run concerns like environmental sustainability. Improvements in income lead to improvements in survival and, therefore, lower discount rates.

Since the early work, numerous papers have tested the EKC. Some, such as Fodha and Zaghdoud (2010) in Tunisia, find support for the EKC in some pollutants but not others. Others support the EKC in some geographic areas but not others, such as Culas (2012) who finds an inverted U-shaped relationship between deforestation and growth in Latina America and Africa, but a U-shaped relationship in Asia. Most do not find a turning point for carbon dioxide (e.g., Fodha and Zaghdoud 2010, He and Richard 2010). Webber and Allen (2010) conclude that the relationship between income and pollution differs by pollutant and process. Consequently, this section of the chapter focuses on soil degradation and deforestation among the poorest subpopulations within a country. Most of the existing literature on the EKC focuses on national average incomes rather than activities among the poorest citizens. Activities among the poorest are likely to differ from the population average because of marginalization from markets, lack of public safety nets that effectively reach them, and fewer chances to invest in human and physical capital. Although most research that focuses on national average incomes finds that higher incomes generate more deforestation, one study dealing with regions within Costa Rica found faster deforestation in lower income areas than higher from 1963 to 2000 (Prates and Bacha 2012).

We have argued elsewhere that the poorest—predominantly subsistence farmers in rural areas of developing countries -seek to avoid downside risk rather than to maximize profit (Pinstrup-Andersen and Watson 2011). They are also more likely to face negative shocks with fewer coping mechanisms. Facing these constraints, the poorest will likely prioritize current survival over long-term environmental sustainability. They recognize that by removing more nutrients from the soil they are reducing their land's future productivity, and that by clearing more marginal lands or harvesting unsustainably many fish or trees, they similarly reduce their livelihoods options for the future. However, they view unsustainable natural resource management as sacrifices that are necessary in the present. Severe poverty can thereby cause environmental degradation. They may also face technical and market constraints because of their poverty, which prevents them from choosing more efficient and sustainable production processes.

The complementarities between climate change, agriculture, and poverty are, thus, likely to create environmental poverty traps: farmers will be unwilling to borrow to invest in better technologies such as high-yielding seeds and proper fertilizer use because of the risk of being unable to pay the loan back; that risk increases as climate change reduces the certainty of rainfall coming in good time; the lack of investment in fertilizer reduces the productivity of the land, sinking farmers deeper into poverty and increasing their withdrawals from the soil nutrients. Reducing poverty would arguably reduce such environmental degradation (Pinstrup-Andersen and Pandya-Lorch, 1994; Nkonya et al., 2008). As discussed earlier, soil mining is endemic in marginal rural areas with unreliable rainfall patterns. Reductions in poverty and improvements in agricultural productivity would presumably enable farmers to invest more in fertilizers and thus reduce the necessity of withdrawals from the natural resource base. This dynamic would produce a sideways-S relationship between soil mining and income (Pinstrup-Andersen and Watson, 2011). Figure 18.1 depicts this relationship.

During Stage 1, technologies that are inefficient both from a production and environmentalist perspective, poverty, and negative shocks from climate change or idiosyncratic factors leave farmers few options other than degrading their natural resource base. In Stage 1 there are very strong synergies between poverty, agricultural production, and the environment. Policies, investments, or interventions that reduce poverty will enable farmers to purchase more fertilizer and avoid the necessity of harvesting more from the land than is sustainable. Safety nets that reassure farmers of their survival will similarly reduce the pressures on farmers and can produce multiple wins (Barrett 2008).

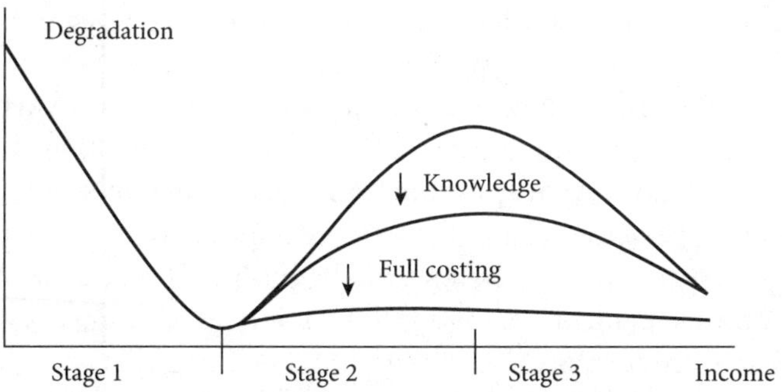

FIGURE 18.1 Hypothetical Relationships between Farmer Income and Soil Degradation
Source: Pinstrup-Andersen and Watson (2011)

Investments in agricultural productivity, particularly investments that improve soil quality or require less water (e.g., crop rotation and mulching), will increase farmer incomes and reduce environmental pressures. Improving soil fertility, increasing forest cover, and improving access to other environmental goods will increasingly relax the constraints farmers face, increasing agricultural productivity and reduce poverty. The Nkonya et al (2008) meta-analysis and study in Uganda provides empirical evidence that this is not merely wishful theorizing, but an empirical reality. They conclude that modernizing African agriculture can produce these triple wins. Additional evidence suggests that public goods such as education and social capital assets may also succeed in accomplishing multiple goals simultaneously (Granja e Barros, Mendonça, and Nogueira 2002).

The top line in Stages 2 and 3 follow the typical EKC stories. Greater market access reduces the costs of deforestation; increased incomes encourage farmers to overuse or misuse chemical inputs resulting in soil and water degradation. Eventually higher income levels reach the point that policy changes, consumer demand, or increasing returns to scale lead to reducing environmental impacts. However, there is no reason to expect that the current EKC in a country for a particular pollutant is fixed permanently. As technology processes improve in developed countries, better technologies become cheaper for developing countries to acquire, lowering the peak of the EKC (as in the middle line of Figure 18.1 labeled "Knowledge"). Increased international public goods and political pressure from developed countries may also succeed in lowering the peak or shifting it to the left. Lomborg (2001) demonstrates that these factors are already at play: environmental degradation is peaking out at a lower level in today's developing countries than in developed countries' past.

The trade-off between growth and the environment can be reduced by investment in agricultural productivity. There are numerous technocratic fixes that would produce considerable and consistent triple wins. Water quality can be improved and water use lowered by improving irrigation systems that reduce in-transit evaporation and leakage, installing sprinkler and drip systems, and introducing mulch to reduce on-farm evaporation (Bruns and Meinzen-Dick 2000; Knox, Meinzen-Dick, and Hazell 2002).

SRI, the System of Rice Intensification introduced in the 1980s, can reduce the water needs by over half while increasing production (Mishra and Salokhe 2011; see Uphoff, this volume). Organic production methods, such as integrated pest management and green manure, significantly reduce water run-off, potentially doubling land productivity and halving soil erosion (Wani et al. 2003). Nitrogen-fixing trees and other crops that lower chemical fertilizer demand and increase food production can be planted (Pretty and Hine 2001). Pesticide use can be lowered by push-pull pest control systems[3] and integrated pest management, providing additional sources of income as well as lowering costs and increasing productivity (Cook, Khan, and Pickett 2007).

Biogas plants are an increasingly attractive option to reduce greenhouse gas emissions from livestock by harnessing energy from animal waste. Xu, Xiang, and Higano (2012) show that investing in biogas plants in Jiaxing, China, would significantly reduce the economic damage (measured in gross regional product) from tougher environmental regulations. The authors further argue that "it is impossible to achieve the dual targets of economic development and environment conservation when we don't treat the pig farming waste properly" (p. 12). Without such investment, limiting water pollution levels significantly lowers economic growth and stifles the region's pig farms; with a biogas plant, even pig farming can grow while improving water quality. Other possible investments not considered by Xu, Xiang, and Higano (2012) include improved feed grains that reduce the ecological damage from animal waste (Chen, et al. 2008) and animals bred to emit fewer harmful chemicals (e.g., Forsberg, et al. 2003 and Yang, et al. 2008). Popp, Lotze-Campen, and Bodirsky's (2010) model indicates that although improvements in technology can reduce livestock's production of methane, changing consumer diets can have a far larger impact on total methane production.

Full-Costing

Even improvements in technology and knowledge will likely be insufficient to completely remove the trade-off between growth and environmental outcomes in Stage 2. This is because the fundamental negative/positive externalities have not been addressed: Firms that produce and consumers that purchase goods and services that damage or improve the environment affect other people who are not party to the transaction. This imbalance between "private costs" (what the firm and consumer pay) and "social costs" (which include the costs to others) leads to overprovision of products that harm the environment. The other side of the same coin is that there are positive externalities in the production of environmental services, which benefit others who are not party to the transaction and those who bear the cost of producing them receive no benefit. This leads to the underprovision of environmental services (Kumar and Managi 2009; Mankiw 2011). Degradation and lack of environmental services are liable to continue until social and private costs are aligned in some way.

One of the primary solutions that economists have long proposed to this conundrum is to ensure that social costs and benefits are internalized into economic actors' decision making. Equalizing social and private costs is generally referred to as the polluter pays principal (PPP). Doing the same for benefits is providing payments for environmental services (PES). The distinction between PPP and PES is a small one, however, because governments could punish for not doing approved things (e.g., a fine for failing to set aside land for forestry) and reward for not doing disapproved actions (e.g., a payment for reducing deforestation) (see also Engel, Pagiola, and Wunder 2008). Game theory suggests in this regard that PPP will serve better to prevent an action and PES to incite action (Dixit and Skeath, 2004). We thus regard both principles as part of the same continuum, which we term *full-costing*. The usefulness of considering both can be seen in the case of the Green Revolution. Although it succeeded in protecting marginal lands, biodiversity, and forests, the subsidies for fertilizer use in Asia led to their overuse and misapplication. Overuse, in turn, harmed water resources, a harm that was never directly compensated. Full-costing policies would have encouraged further land preservation and either prevented the overuse of fertilizer or provided funds to repair the damages it created.

There are three primary classes of policy action put forward by economists to effect full costing: imposing Pigouvian taxes and subsidies, creating a market where limited permits to pollute are traded, and establishing Coasian property rights (see additional readings for more information). Each of these options encounters technical, practical, and political challenges in implementation. Even Pigou (1954), the father of the PPP, argued toward the end of his career that governments will rarely have the information necessary to identify the optimal level of tax (or subsidy) that would ensure perfect full-costing. The practical challenges deal with implementation, assuming we knew the right target. As with Pigou, Coase (1991) likewise argued that the point of his theorem was to highlight how central the transaction costs are that prevent the mutually beneficial trades it envisions. Even if we know the right target and how to get there, obtaining political permission to do so may be a stumbling block.

On the other hand, understanding the weaknesses of each method can help policy analysts identify which will be most conducive to solving different problems. For instance, consider the shape of the relationship between human action and environmental quality discussed earlier. To the extent that human activities impact the environment approximately linearly, fixed per-unit taxes/subsidies or cap and trade with a fixed price will be sufficient. If the price of environmental harm/benefit is fixed and impacts are nonlinear, however, any price will sometimes underincentivize and sometimes overincentivize adjustment inefficiently. In such a case, policies that reduce Coasian transaction costs in order to encourage private deals will be most beneficial. If there are significant threshold effects, such as the extinction of a species, cap and trade will be far more appropriate than a simple tax. Programs are more likely to be enacted in situations in which it is most favorable, both politically and environmentally, so it is likely that new programs will have smaller impacts *ceteris paribus* and a lower chance of being enacted than those currently in place.

Without strong enforcement of international agreements, full-costing is unlikely to occur on a global scale. Lack of agreement at environmental conferences and lack of compliance when agreements are made severely limit what the current global governance structures can accomplish. Cramton and Stoft (2012) propose one very noteworthy solution: Have each country "vote" for the level of commitment it would like to establish universally, with the lowest vote becoming international law. They continue:

> While accepting the least-strict commitment may sound weak, the result is the globally-optimal price for carbon. Voting succeeds because each country realizes that, if its vote is accepted, its vote will determine abatement in every country. So, unlike with global cap and trade, adopting a stronger policy does not just impose a national burden that mainly benefits others. Instead, adopting a stronger policy causes all others to abate more, which benefits the voting country. Hence voting for a collective commitment succeeds, where choosing individual commitments fails.

They also demonstrate how the Green Climate Fund (established in 2010 and with funding expected in late 2013) could further increase participation and make bids higher and more binding.

Even if full-costing is not adopted in entirety, it is still possible for national and local governments to move in a direction that is closer to full-costing without causing significant harm to domestic industries. Current subsidies that lead to the overuse of water, fertilizer, and pesticides could be removed and replaced with environmentally neutral income support. Deforestation could be slowed or halted by appropriately penalizing overlogging or rewarding deforestation abatement. Decentralized PES schemes in which users pay for the services tend to be more efficient than when government pays, because the latter schemes are poorly targeted, often include other goals that lower environmental efficiency, and feature less enforcement of conditions (Wunder, Engel, and Pagiola, 2008). Water scarcity in southern Australia and the southwestern US led to experiments with limited trading of water entitlements since the 1980s. Between 5 and 20 percent of the total water flow in each area was traded in 2007–08. Grafton et al. (2011) indicate that schemes are more successful where water rights are decoupled from land rights, water storage capacity is large and able to facilitate both upstream and downstream trade, and there is significant institutional support. Indeed, they cite institutional support and third-party concerns as the primary constraints in current systems. Porras (2013) argues that Costa Rica's reforestation PES encouraged NGOs proliferation around environmental issues, often creating additional PES schemes. Cassin, et al. (2011) catalogue a growing number of NGO-sponsored PES programs throughout sub-Saharan Africa that are successfully reducing deforestation, improving soil and quality, and conserving biodiversity.

Alix-Garcia, et al. (2009) give a detailed description of the political processes involved in Mexico's forestry and hydrology PES, which give a cautionary tale about neglecting the political economy. The program was plagued from beginning to end by intra- and interdepartmental conflict. Its funding rules, terms, and goals were changed multiple times as it moved between organizations and met with resistance from other government factions. After moving to another group, the program had to be sold to higher and higher levels of government in order to overcome obstacles from lower levels. Even after the National Congress approved it, conflict during the budgeting process cost the program more than one-third of potential revenues. The delays and changes severely hampered project efficiency and equity. Policymakers will have to be aware of and attempt to prevent leakages—for example, instances in which the regulation protects one forest and the logging activity only moves to another forest (Wunder, Wertz-Kanounnikoff, and Ferraro 2010).

Putting these factors together, it is likely that perfect full-costing will not be an attainable reality in the near future. However, it is possible to take steps in that direction to bring private and social costs/benefits into greater alignment. Doing so will take advantage of the synergies between climate change, agriculture, and poverty and has the potential to increase system resiliency, improve market efficiency, and enhance food system sustainability. Regardless of what the final impacts of climate change are, these are investments worth making. The worse we believe climate change will be, the greater is the urgency to do them and the potential benefits to be derived from them.

Conclusions

Much of the literature on climate change, poverty, and the environment is quite depressing for anyone hopeful about the human condition. Difficult trade-offs seem inevitable. In these choices among poor options, most research recognizes that the most deleterious impacts of climate change are expected to fall on the poorest, who are least well-equipped to adapt to it. There is, however, an alternative conceptual lens for looking at the intersections. This chapter has explored significant complementarities and synergies between agricultural production, climate change, and poverty. These synergies imply that multiple wins exist and that complementary investments will be increasingly necessary as the estimated impacts of climate change rise. This leads to the conclusion that ongoing investment in agriculture and poverty reduction are essential parts of efforts to mitigate and adapt to climate change, whereas policies to mitigate and adapt to climate change are themselves tools to improve food security and reduce poverty.

Food systems cannot be sustainable without proper natural-resource management. Agriculture has a significant role to play in preventing climate change and helping humans adapt to its impacts. Adaptations will inevitably involve some mix of individual learning and change, technological progress and the incentive structures produced by public policy. On the latter, this chapter examined as an example an expansion of the Environmental Kuznets Curve to explain the dynamics that produce soil mining and deforestation at very low-income levels when farmers make difficult choices in order to survive in the face of negative shocks.

Individual farmers and land managers operate in systems over which they individually have no control. It is cheaper and more effective for individuals and governments to anticipate the impacts of climate change and prepare for them than to wait for the problems to develop and respond after the fact. Incentives that now produce perverse consequences will have to change if the multiple-wins that are theoretically available are to be achieved. Changing incentive structures is, in turn, largely a matter of government policy. We have demonstrated how a shift toward greater internalization of positive and negative externalities would alter behavior on the part of the most important actors. This change is called "full-costing." Without shifts of the nature explored here, it is difficult to see how current obligations toward improving environmental standards can be met. Nor is it clear that without these changes agriculture can sustainably meet the food security needs of current and future generations.

Even though complete full costing at a global level may be out of reach for technical, practical, and political reasons, exploring the possibilities illustrates that numerous options exist to bring current policies and market prices closer to socially optimal values. Socially optimal values in turn are those that are consistent with reducing the impact of agriculture on the environment and climate change's impact on agriculture and poverty. To the extent that full-costing generates additional revenues, the repairing of environmental damage and constructing of new productive possibilities becomes more feasible. This is the meaning of sustainability: meeting the needs of today's generations in ways that do not impair the ability of future generations to meet their needs. Full-costing is one way toward incentivizing significant structural and behavioral change in dynamic food systems, moving them closer to long-run sustainability.

Notes

1. This paper owes a great debt to Per Pinstrup-Andersen who worked with me in the development of the sideways-S curve concept for Pinstrup-Andrsen and Watson (2011). I gratefully acknowledge comments from Charles Reith and Ron Herring that improved the chapter, as well as the outstanding research assistance of Omorogbe Omorogiuwa.
2. Noteworthy criticisms of the Stern Report include: Nordhaus, William (2007). "A Review of the Stern Review on the Economics of Climate Change. *Journal of Economic Literature* XLV, 686–702; Lomborg, Bjørn (November 2, 2006). "Stern Review, The Dodgy Numbers behind the Latest Warming Scare." *Wall Street Journal*; and Varian, Hal. (December 14, 2006). "Recalculating the Costs of Global Climate Change." *New York Times*.
3. Push-pull systems mix the main crop with two other plants, one designed to push pests away from the main crop and the other to pull the pests toward it instead of the main crop.

Additional Readings on Pigovian Taxes, Cap and Trade, and the Coase Theorem

Ackerman, Frank, Stephen J. DeCanio, Richard B. Howarth, and Kristen Sheeran. 2009. "Limitations of Integrated Assessment Models of Climate Change." *Climatic Change* 95:297–315.

Baumol, William. 1972. "On Taxation and the Control of Externalities," *The American Economic Review* 62(3): 307–322.
Buchanan, James. 1973. "The Coase Theorem and the Theory of the State." *Natural Resources Journal*, 13, 579–594.
Coase, Ronald H. 1960. "The Problem of Social Cost." *Journal of Law and Economics* 3(1): 1–44.
Colby, Bonnie G. 2000. "Cap-and-Trade Policy Challenges: A Tale of Three Markets." *Land Economics*, 76: 638–658.
Cook, Samantha, Zeyaur Khan, and John Pickett. 2007. "The Use of Push-Pull Strategies in Integrated Pest Management." *Annual Review of Entomology* 52:375–400.
Medema, Steven G., and Richard O. Zerbe Jr. 1995. *The Coase Theorem*. CRESP, Center for Research on Economic and Social Policy, University of Colorado at Denver.
Pigou, A. C. 1920. *The Economics of Welfare*. London: Macmillan. (available online at the Library of Economics and Liberty: http://www.econlib.org/library/NPDBooks/Pigou/pgEW.html)
Stavins, Robert. 2008. "A Meaningful U.S. Cap-and-Trade System to Address Climate Change," FEEM Working Paper No. 82.2008. Available at SSRN: http://ssrn.com/abstract=1281518 or http://dx.doi.org/10.2139/ssrn.1281518.

Works Cited

Ackerman, Frank, Stephen J. DeCanio, Richard B. Howarth, and Kristen Sheeran. 2009. "Limitations of Integrated Assessment Models of Climate Change." *Climatic Change* 95:297–315.
Alix-Garcia, Jennifer, Alain de Janvry, Elisabeth Sadoulet, and Juan Manuel Torres. 2009. "Lessons Learned from Mexico's Payment for Environmental Services Program." In *Payment for Environmental Services in Agricultural Landscapes*, edited by Leslie Lipper, Takumi Sakuyama, Randy Stringer, and David Zilberman, 163–188. Rome: FAO and Springer.
Andreoni, James, and Arik Levinson. 2001. "The Simple Analytics of the Environmental Kuznets Curve." *Journal of Public Economics* 80: 269–286.
Baez, Javier E., Dorothy Kronick, and Andrew D. Mason. 2012. "Rural Households in a Changing Climate" IZA Discussion Paper No. 6872, September.
Barrett, Christopher. 2008. "Poverty Traps and Resource Dynamics in Smallholder Agrarian Systems." In *Economics of Poverty, Environment and Natural-Resource Use*, edited by R. Dellink and A. Ruijs. Dordrecht: Springer.
Bouwman, Lex, Kees Klein Goldewijk, Klaas Van Der Hoek, Arthur Beusen, Detlef Van Vuuren, Jaap Willems, Mariana Rufino, and Elke Stehfest. 2011. "Exploring Global Changes in Nitrogen and Phosphorus Cycles in Agriculture Induced by Livestock Production over the 1990–2050 Period." *Proceedings of the National Academy of Sciences*. doi:10.1073/pnas.1012878108
Brown, Lester. 2009. *Plan B 4.0: Mobilising to Save Civilization*. New York: Norton.
Bruns, B. R., and R. S. Meinzen-Dick (eds.). 2000. *Negotiating Water Rights*. New Delhi: Vistaar, and London: Intermediate Technology Press. www.capri.cgiar.org/negwaterrights.asp
Butt, T. A., B. A. McCarl, J. Angerer, P. T. Dyke, and J. W. Stuth. 2005. "The Economic and Food Security Implications of Climate Change in Mali." *Climate Change* 68:355–378.

Cassin, Jan, Slayde Hawkins, Alice Kenny, Michael Richards, and Amrei von Hase. 2011. *Creating New Values for Africa: Emerging Ecosystem Service Markets*. The Ecosystem Marketplace, www.forest-trends.org/documents/files/doc_3015.pdf, accessed June 14, 2013.

Chen, Rumei, Guangxing Xue, Ping Chen, Bin Yao, Wenzhu Yang, Qianli Ma, Yunliu Fan, Zuoyu Zhao, Mitchell C. Tarczynski, Jinrui Shi. 2008. "Transgenic Maize Plants Expressing a Fungal Phytase Gene." *Transgenic Research* 17:633–643.

Chinowsky, Paul, Amy Schweikert, Niko Strzepek, and Kenneth Strzepek. 2012. "Road Infrastructure and Climate Change in Vietnam," UNU-WIDER Working Paper 2012/80.

Coase, Ronald. 1991. "Prize Lecture—The Institutional Structure of Production," Nobelprize.org. Nobel Media AB 2013, www.nobelprize.org/nobel_prizes/economic-sciences/laureates/1991/coase-lecture.html, accessed June 14, 2013.

Cole, Matthew A. 2004. "Trade, the Pollution Haven Hypothesis and the Environmental Kuznets Curve: Examining the Linkages." *Ecological Economics* 48(1): 71–81.

Cook, Samantha, Zeyaur Khan, and John Pickett. 2007. "The Use of Push-Pull Strategies in Integrated Pest Management." *Annual Review of Entomology* 52:375–400.

Costanza, Robert, Ralph d'Argo, Rudolf de Groot, Stephen Farber, Monica Grasso, Bruce Hannon, Karin Limburg, Shahid Naeem, Robert V. O'Neill, Jose Paruelo, Robert G. Raskin, Paul Sutton, and Marjan van den Belt. 1997. "The Value of the World's Ecosystem Services and Natural Capital." *Nature* 376(6630): 253–260.

Cramton, Peter and Steven Stoft. 2012. "How to Fix the Inefficiency of Global Cap and Trade." *The Economist's Voice*, 9, April.

Culas, Richard. 2012. "REDD and Forest Transition: Tunneling through the Environmental Kuznets Curve," *Ecological Economics* 79: 44–51.

Davidson, Eric, and Ivan Janssens. 2006. "Temperature Sensitivity of Soil Carbon Decomposition and Feedbacks to Climate Change." *Nature* 440:165–173.

de Haen, Hartwig. 1997. "Environmental Consequences of Agricultural Growth in Developing Countries," in *Sustainability, Growth, and Poverty Alleviation*, ed. S. Vosti and T. Reardon. Baltimore: IFPRI, Johns Hopkins University Press.

Dima, S. J. and A. N. Odero. 1997. "Organic Farming for Sustainable Agricultural Production." *Environmental and Resource Economics*, 10:177–188.

Dixit, Avinash, and Susan Skeath. 2004. *Games of Strategy* (2nd ed.). New York: Norton.

Edwards-Jones, G., and O. Howells. 2001. "The Origin and Hazard of Inputs to Crop Protection in Organic Farming Systems: Are They Sustainable?" *Agricultural Systems* 61(1):31–47.

Engel, Stephanie, Stephano Pagiola, and Sven Wunder. 2008. "Designing Payments for Environmental Services in Theory and Practice: An Overview of the Issues." *Ecological Economics*, 65(4): 663–674.

Ereut, Gill, and Nat Segnit. 2006. "Warm Words: How Are We Telling the Climate Story and Can We Tell It Better?" *Institute for Public Policy Research*, www.ippr.org/images/media/files/publication/2011/05/warm_words_1529.pdf, accessed June 8, 2013.

Fodha, Mouez, and Oussama Zaghdoud. 2010. "Economic Growth and Pollutant Emissions in Tunisia: An Empirical Analysis of the Environmental Kuznets Curve." *Energy Policy* 38(2):1150–1156.

Forsberg, C. W., J. P. Phillips, S. P. Golovan, M. Z. Fan, R. G. Meidinger, A. Ajakaiye, D. Hilborn, and R. R. Hacker. 2003. "The Enviropig Physiology, Performance, and Contribution to Nutrient Management Advances in a Regulated Environment: The Leading Edge of Change in the Pork Industry." *Journal of Animal Science* 81(14):68–77.

De la Fuente, Alejandro, and Marcelo Villarroel. 2013. "The Poverty Impact of Climate Change in Mexico." World Bank Policy Research Working Paper 6461.

Goklany, I. M. 1998. "Saving Habitat and Conserving Biodiversity on a Crowded Planet," *BioScience* 48:941–953.

Gosling, P., and M. Shepherd. 2005. "Long-Term Changes in Soil Fertility in Organic Arable Farming Systems in England, with Particular Reference to Phosphorus and Potassium." *Agriculture, Ecosystems & Environment* 105(1–2):425–432.

Grafton, R.Q., G.D. Libecap, E.C. Edwards, R.J. O'Brien, and C. Landry. 2011. "A Comparative Assessment of Water Markets: Insights from the Murray-Darling Basin of Australia and the Western US," International Centre for Economic Research Working Paper 8/2011.

Granja e Barros, Fabio, Augusta Mendonça, and Jorge Nogueira. 2002. "Poverty and Environmental Degradation: The Kuznets Environmental Curve for the Brazilian Case." University of Brasilia Working Paper 267.

Grossman, Gene, and Alan Krueger. 1995. "Economic Growth and the Environment." *Quarterly Journal of Economics* 110(2):353–377.

GWSP—The Global Water System Project. 2013. *The Bonn Declaration on Global Water Scarcity*. Bonn, Germany: Global Water System Project.

He, Jie, and Patrick Richard. 2010. "Environmental Kuznets Curve for C)2 in Canada." *Ecological Economics* 69(5):1083–1093.

Henao, Julio, and Carlos Baanante. 2001. "Nutrient Depletion in the Agricultural Soils of Africa." In *The Unfinished Agenda: Perspectives on Overcoming Hunger, Poverty, and Environmental Degradation*, edited by P. Pinstrup-Andersen and R. Pandya-Lorch. Washington, DC: International Food Policy Research Institute.

Hole, D. G., A. J. Perkins, J. D. Wilson, I. H. Alexander, P. V. Grice, and A. D. Evans. 2005. "Does Organic Farming Benefit Biodiversity?" *Biological Convservation* 122(1):113–130.

IFPRI (International Food Policy Research Institute). 2009. *Climate Change: Impact on Agriculture and Costs of Adaptation*, Washington, DC: IFPRI.

IFPRI. 2013. *West African Agriculture and Climate Change: A Comprehensive Analysis*, Washington, DC: IFPRI.

ILO (International Labour Organization). 2005. World Employment Report 2004–05: Employment, Productivity and Poverty Reduction. Geneva.

IPCC AR4 SYR. 2007. Core Writing Team; R. K. Pachauri and Reisinger, A., eds. *Climate Change 2007: Synthesis Report*, Contribution of Working Groups I, II, and III to the Fourth Assessment Report of the Intergovernmental Panel on Climate Change, Cambridge University Press.

IPCC. 2012. *Managing the Risks of Extreme Events and Disasters to Advance Climate Change Adaptation*. New York: Cambridge University Press.

Jaeger, W. 1998. "A theoretical basis for the environmental inverted-U curve and implications for international trade." Williams College, Working Paper.

Kamara, Alpha, Ibrahim Kureh, Abebe Menkir, Peter Kartung, Bitrus Tarfa, and Paul Amaza. 2006. "Participatory On-Farm Evaluation of the Performance of Drought-Tolerant Maize Varieties in the Guinea Savannas of Nigeria," *International Journal of Food, Agriculture and Environment* 4(1):192–196.

Knox, A., R. Meinzen-Dick, and P. Hazell. 2002. "Property Rights, Collective Action, and Technologies for Natural Resource Management: A Conceptual Framework." In *Innovation in Natural Resource Management: The Role of Property Rights and Collective Action in Developing Countries*, pp. 12–44, edited by R. S. Meinzen-Dick, A. Knox, F. Place, and B.

M. Swallow. Baltimore, MD: Johns Hopkins University Press and International Food Policy Research Institute.

Kumar, Surender, and Shunsuke Managi. 2009. "Compensation for Environmental Services and Intergovernmental Fiscal Transfers: The Case of India." *Ecological Economics* 68(12): 3052–3059.

La Rovere, Roberto, Genti Kostandini, Tahirou Abdoulaye, John Dixon, Wilfred Mwangi, Zhe Guo, and Marianne Banziger. 2010. *Potential Impact of Investments in Drought Tolerant Maize in Africa*. Addis Ababa, Ethiopia: CIMMYT.

Lee, David, and Christopher Barrett. 2001. *Tradeoffs or Synergies? Agricultural Intensification, Economic Development and the Environment*. New York: CABI Publishing.

Lobell, David B., Marshall B. Burke, Claudia Tebaldi, Michael D. Mastrandrea, Walter P. Falcon, and Rosamond L. Naylor. 2008. "Prioritizing Climate Change Adaptation Needs for Food Security in 2030," *Science* 319(February 1):607–610.

Lomborg, Bjørn. 2001. *The Skeptical Environmentalist: Measuring the Real State of the World*. Cambridge: Cambridge University Press.

Mankiw, Greg. 2011. *Principles of Microeconomics* (6th ed.). Mason, Ohio: Cengage Learning. (See Chapters 10–11 in particular.)

Meza, Francisco, James Hansen, and Daniel Osgood. 2008. "Economic Value of Seasonal Climate Forecasts for Agriculture: Review of Ex-Ante Assessments and Recommendations for Future Research." *Journal of Applied Meteorology and Climatology* 47: 1269–1286.

Milestad, Rebecka, and Ika Darnhofer. 2003. "Building Farm Resilience: The Prospects and Challenges of Organic Farming." *Journal of Sustainable Agriculture* 22(3):81–97.

Mishra, Abha, and Vilas M. Salokhe. 2011. "Rice Root Growth and Physiological Responses to SRI Water Management and Implications for Crop Productivity." *Paddy and Water Environment* 9(1):41–52.

Nkonya, E., J. Pender, K. C. Kaizzi, E. Kato, S. Mugarura, H. Ssali, and J. Muwonge. 2008. "Linkages between Land Management, Land Degradation, and Poverty in Sub-Saharan Africa." IFPRI Research Report 159. Washington, DC: IFPRI.

O'Brian, Bob. 2010. "Water Licences Valued at A$2.8 Billion Traded in Australia's Emerging Water Markets." www.voxeu.org/article/price-precious-commodity-water-trading-australia, accessed March 28, 2012

Pigou, Arthur. 1954. "Some Aspects of the Welfare State." *Diogenes* June 2:1–11.

Pinstrup-Andersen, Per, and Derrill D. Watson II. 2011. *Food Policy for Developing Countries: The Role of Government in Global, National, and Local Food Systems*. Ithaca, NY: Cornell University Press.

Pinstrup-Andersen, Per, and Rajul Pandya-Lorch, 1994. "Alleviating Poverty, Intensifying Agriculture, and Effectively Managing Natural Resources," IFPRI Food, Agriculture, and the Environment Discussion Paper 1. www.ifpri.org/sites/default/files/publications/vp1.pdf

Pinstrup-Andersen, Per. 2002. "Food and Agricultural Policy for a Globalizing World: Preparing for the Future." *American Journal of Agricultural Economics* 84(5):1201–1214.

Popp, Alexander, Hermann Lotze-Campen, and Benjamin Bodirsky. 2010. "Food Consumption, Diet Shifts and Associated non-Co2 Greenhouse Gases from Agricultural Production." *Global Environmental Change* 20(3):451–462.

Porras, Ina. 2013. "Payments for Environmental Services: Lessons from the Costa Rican PES Programme," Munich Personal RePEc Archive Paper No. 47186.

Prates, Rodolfo and Carlos Bacha. 2012. "An Econometric Study of Deforestation in the Brazil's Amazonian Principalities," Paper submitted to the 52nd European Congress of the Regional

Science Association International (ERSA 2012) to be held at Bratislava, Slovakia, August 21st to 25th, 2012. http://www-sre.wu.ac.at/ersa/ersaconfs/ersa12/e120821aFinal00653.pdf

Pretty, Jules, and Rachel Hine. 2001. "Reducing Food Poverty with Sustainable Agriculture: A Summary of New Evidence." Final report from the "SAFE-World" Research Project, University of Essex.

Roberts, Paul. 2008. The End of Food. New York: Houghton Mifflin.

Sassi, Mario, and Alberto Cardaci. 2012. "Impact of Climate Change on Cereal Market and Food Security in Sudan: Stochastic Approach and CGE Model," Agricultural Economics Society 86th Annual Conference, April 16–18, 2012, Warwick University, Coventry, UK. http://purl.umn.edu/134779

Schlenker, Wolfram, and David B. Lobell. 2010. "Robust Negative Impacts of Climate Change on African Agriculture." *Environmental Research Letters* 5: 1–8 doi:10.1088/1748-9326/5/1/014010.

Schwartz, Peter, and Doug Randall. 2003. "An Abrupt Climate Change Scenario and Its Implications for United States National Security." http://www.fas.org/irp/agency/dod/schwartz.pdf, accessed June 7, 2013.

Smil, V. 1997. "China Shoulders the Cost of Environmental Change" *Environment* 39(6):6–9, 33–37.

Steinfeld, H., P. Gerber, T. Wassenaar, V. Castel, M. Rosales, and C. de Haan. 2006. *Livestock's Long Shadow: Environmental Issues and Options*. Rome: Food and Agriculture Organization.

Stern, Nicholas. 2007. *The Economics of Climate Change: The Stern Review*. Cambridge University Press.

Swanson, Kyle. 2013. "Emerging Selection Bias in Large-Scale Climate Change Simulations." *Geophysical Research Letters*. doi:10.1002/grl.50562

Taub, D. 2010. Effects of Rising Atmospheric Concentrations of Carbon Dioxide on Plants. *Nature Education Knowledge* 3(10):2.

UNU-WIDER—United Nations University—World Institute for Development Economics Research. 2012. *Report: Implications of Climate Change for Economic Growth and Development in Vietnam to 2050*, Hanoi, Vietnam: UNU-WIDER.

Wani, S. P., H. P. Singh, T. K. Sreedevi, P. Pathak, T. J. Rego, B. Shiferaw, and S. R. Iyer. 2003. "Farmer-Participator Integrated Watershed Management: Adarsha Watershed, Kothapally India." In *Research towards Integrated Natural Resource Management*. Rome: CGIAR.

Webber, D.J. and D. O. Allen. 2010. "Environmental Kuznets Curves: Mess or Meaning?" *International Journal of Sustainable Development & World Ecology*, 17(3), 198–207.

Willenbockel, Dirk. 2012. "Extreme Weather Events and Crop Price Spikes in a Changing Climate: Illustrative Global Simulation Scenarios." OXFAM Research Report, September 2012. http://www.oxfam.org/sites/www.oxfam.org/files/rr-extreme-weather-events-crop-price-spikes-05092012-en.pdf, accessed June 8, 2013.

World Bank. 2007. *World Development Report 2008: Agriculture for Development*. Washington, DC: World Bank.

World Bank. 2012. "Turn Down the Heat: Why a 4°C Warmer World Must be Avoided." Washington DC: The World Bank.

Wunder, S., S. Engel, and S. Pagiola. 2008. "Taking Stock: A Comparative Analysis of Payments for Environmental Services Programs in Developed and Developing Countries." *Ecological Economics*, 65(4): 834–852.

Wunder, S., S. Wertz-Kanounnikoff, and P. Ferraro. 2010. "Payments for Environmental Services and the Global Environment Facility: A STAP Advisory Document." Nairobi, Kenya: Scientific and Technical Advisory Panel.

Xu, Feng, Nan Xiang, and Yoshiro Higano. 2012. "Comprehensive Evaluation of Environmental Policy for Water Pollutants Reduction in Jiaxing City, China." European Regional Science Association conference paper. http://www-sre.wu.ac.at/ersa/ersaconfs/ersa12/e120821aFinal00608.pdf

Yang, X. M, C. F. Drury, T. Q. Zhang, A. Ajakaiye, C.W. Forsberg, M. Z. Fan, J. P. Philip. 2008. "Short-Term Carbon Dioxide Emissions and Denitrification Losses from Soils Amended with Low-P Manure from Genetically Modified Pigs." Nutrient Cycling in Agroecosystems 80(2):153–160.

CHAPTER 19

WILD FOODS

JULES PRETTY AND ZAREEN PERVEZ BHARUCHA

Introduction

Wild foods lie at the nexus between biodiversity conservation, food security, and poverty alleviation. The evidence reviewed in this chapter shows that for agricultural communities worldwide, and particularly those most vulnerable to hunger and poverty, wild biodiversity on and near farms provides a vital source of food security and income.

In parallel with the much-publicized global food crisis, the year 2010 marked the UN's International Year of Biodiversity. Biodiversity contributes to food security via the thousands of uncultivated, wild edible species that still form a part of the diets of roughly a billion people (Aberoumand 2009). It also contributes to poverty reduction through improvements to public health, income generation, and adaptive capacity. In this way, species conservation is linked with wider development goals (Emerton 2009).

The global discourse on food security is overwhelmingly concerned with increasing agricultural productivity. However, despite considerable progress over several decades, a large number of people remain undernourished. By recent estimates (Foresight 2011), the global undernourished population currently numbers about one billion. In addition, some two billion people are estimated to suffer from micronutrient malnutrition (Bouis and Welch 2010, Tulchinsky 2010). The nutritional status of children is a particular concern—those from the poorest households are twice as likely to be underweight as those from the richest, and rural children are more likely to be underweight than urban (UN 2013). Globally, 26 percent of children under five in the developing world are underweight (UN 2009). This is of special concern, since the effects of micronutrient deficiencies, particularly in early life, ultimately "foster persistent poverty, reinforcing the consequences of food insecurity" (Barrett 2010, 827). Globally, the provision of fortified foods and nutrient supplements has been the foremost strategy for the alleviation of micronutrient malnutrition. Several nutritional analyses of wild foods have documented their current and potential role in providing valuable nutritional supplements to those who depend on them.

Recent food and economic crises made matters substantially worse (FAO 2009; UN 2009). Especially hard-hit have been countries of sub-Saharan Africa and East Asia (excluding China).

Of those who have inadequate access to food, many are primarily involved in the production of food. It is partly for this reason that the literature on vulnerability, food security, and ecosystem services has tended to emphasize the value of food production from agriculture (MEA 2005; Ericksen et al. 2009), and tends to neglect the contribution of wild foods. At the regional and national level, food balances (calculated from data on household-level food production and consumption) guide policies on food trade, the declaration of food crises, and food aid. Notably absent from such balances is the contribution made by the on- and off-farm collection of wild foods for either consumption or sale. Yet, for some communities and social groups, wild products constitute a vital resource, especially during times of food shortage. It is clear from these studies and previous assessments (Scoones et al. 1992; Etkin 1994; Pretty 1995; Heywood 1999; MEA 2005; Kuhnlein et al. 2009; Bharucha and Pretty 2010) that nonfarmed and apparently wild biodiversity deserves inclusion in food security assessments and policy.

Around one billion people use wild foods in their diets (Aberoumand 2009). Forests provide livelihoods and food for some 300 million people in the form of non-timber forest products (NTFPs). In general, food security and NTFPs are strongly interlinked in rural communities, especially for the most vulnerable groups (Belcher et al. 2005), even among agricultural communities (Vincetti et al. 2008). Urban communities also rely on wild foods. For instance, affluent urban households are willing to pay 43 to 157 percent more for bushmeat in Zambia and Mozambique (Barnett, 2000). In Rajasthan, India, wild foods benefit both urban and rural children (Rathore 2009). Titus et al. (2009) explored the importance of wild game in Alaska, where 80 percent of the population is urban, and found urban households routinely consuming significant amounts of wild game. Jaarsveld et al. (2005) cite estimates on the largely underreported role of wild foods in food and nutritional security across the southern African region. These range from 0.1 percent in South Africa to 8.5 percent in the Democratic Republic of the Congo. Ninety percent of all African off-take occurs through subsistence hunting and gathering.

The reliance on forest products for food or income is greatest for those most at risk of malnutrition and hunger, even among agricultural communities (Vincetti et al. 2008). In general, the rural poor are found to have a "disproportionately high" dependence on NTFPs under certain conditions (Belcher et al. 2005). Within the sixty-one cases of NTFP use examined by Belcher et al., "even commercial NTFP producers tend to be poor or very poor compared to national averages" (2005, 1443).

With the routine underestimation of the role of wild edible plants in diets comes the danger of not recognizing the importance of provisioning ecosystems and supportive local knowledge systems that sustain these food chains (Grivetti and Ogle, 2000; Mazhar et al. 2007; Pilgrim et al. 2007, 2008). A more comprehensive understanding of the combined use of cultivated and uncultivated species has led some to call for a revision of the current understandings of terms such as "agriculture," "food security" and "common property resources" (Mazhar et al. 2007).

The role and importance of wild foods requires the development of explicit linkages between policies for species conservation and food security. For communities dependent on wild species, conservation policies result in trade-offs with food security. The combined success of conservation agendas and development policy requires that these trade-offs be confronted and minimized.

The Continuum between "Wild" and Domesticated Food

A key insight from the literature on wild foods is that there are no easy distinctions between farmed and nonfarmed species, nor between farmers, foragers, and hunter-gatherers. Wild and cultivated species exist along a continuum, with varying levels of domestication and management, rather than as a simple dichotomy. Since "domestication grew out of food gathering, which almost imperceptibly led to cultivation," many wild edible species can be considered to be "in various stages of domestication as a result of human selection, however slight" (Heywood 1999). Thus, wild food species exist along a continuum, with no management interventions on one extreme, progressing to various degrees of transplanting, propagation and other management practices designed to support their use (Harris and Hillman 1989; Thomas and Van Damme 2010).

Similarly, the livelihoods of those who depend on wild foods might be more properly thought of as variants of cultivator-hunters or farmer-foragers, in recognition of the fact that foraging and farming can be viewed as "overlapping, interdependent, contemporaneous, coequal and complementary" (Sponsel 1989, 37).

It was long supposed that cultures progressed, in distinct phases, from hunter-gatherer to agricultural to industrial. Each of these was viewed as superior to the one that preceded it. Beginning with Hobbes's 1651 observation that the life of "natural man" was "solitary, poore, nasty, brutish and short," cultural evolutionary views—distinguishing between "natural" and "civilized" peoples—persisted from the eighteenth to the late twentieth centuries (Meggers 1954; Lathrap, 1968).

However, evidence from across the world shows that communities are more complex and varied. Some horticulturalists move, some hunter-gatherers are sedentary (Vickers 1989; Kelly 1995). Some groups maintain gardens for cultivated food as well as to attract antelopes, monkeys, and birds for hunting (Posey 1985). Many apparently hunter-gatherer and forager cultures farm; many agricultural communities use large numbers of nondomesticated resources. The Hohokam are well-known as sophisticated canal irrigators and desert farmers of the American Southwest, yet they were hunters, gatherers, and foragers, too. Szuter and Bayham (1989) thus observed that the labels of hunter-gatherer and farmer are not valuable, as the two activities are in fact complementary. Hypotheses generated in the 1980s questioned the assumption that hunter-gatherers could ever subsist in tropical forest environments without access to domesticated food species (Headland 1987; Bailey et al. 1989). The "wild yam question" led to debate and assorted studies within ecological anthropology. Some of these have indicated that some tropical forest sites support hunter-gatherer communities without recourse to any cultivated food. In others, communities rely on both entirely "wild" as well as semidomesticated food species (Headland 2002).

With no easy distinctions between the cultivated and the wild, or between farmers and hunter-gatherers, it becomes clear that there is a huge variety of subsistence strategies that vary spatially as well as over time (Kelly 1995). These strategies allow for the management of nonfarm landscapes in order to increase the productivity and stability of useful plants and animals.

The Management of Nonagricultural Environments

What is also clear is that farmers, hunters, gatherers, fishers, and foragers do not simply take resources from a compliant environment. They manage and amend resources in much the same way as is standard practice on a farm (Table 19.1). Foragers maintain resources by intentional sowing of wild seeds, irrigation of stands of grasses, burning to stimulate plant growth, selective culling of game animals and fish, replanting of portions of roots, enrichment planting of trees, and extraction of only parts of honeycombs so sites are not deserted by bees (Steward 1938; Lawton et al. 1976; Woodburn 1980; Kelly 1995).

Many cultures and groups directly manage trees on and off the farm. The forest islands of Amazonia were found by Posey (1985) to have emerged as a result of Kayapo directly planting-up mounds. In the lower Amazon, smallholder farmers enrich the forests with desirable fruit, timber, and medicinal trees, often broadcasting seeds when cutting timber (Brookfield and Padoch 2007). In dryland Kenya, *Acacia tortilis* tree recruitment occurs on the sites of abandoned pastoralist corrals that are high in organic matter and nutrients from the penned livestock. Acacia seedpods are a favored fodder, and some pass through the animals to then germinate in the next season. The result is circular woodlands of dense Acacia (Reid and Ellis 1995; Berkes 1999). In China there is widespread use of wild trees in integrated systems of land management, and wild plants and animals are gathered from a variety of microenvironments, such as dykes, woods, ponds, and irrigation ditches (Li 2001).

Farmers also widely transplant species from the wild. In northern Nigeria, they plant *Hibiscus* on field boundaries; in South Africa, wild fruit trees and edible herbs are grown on farms; and in northeastern Thailand, a quarter of all the 159 wild food species gathered from field boundaries, irrigation canals, swamps, and roadsides are transplanted and propagated by rice farmers (Price 1997; High and Shackleton 2000; Harris and Mohammed 2003). Home gardens are particularly important for many rural smallholders, and are

Table 19.1 The management of nonagricultural ecosystems by farmers, hunter–gatherers and foragers

Practice	Detail	Agricultural equivalent	Examples
Harvesting and hunting	Hunting of particular species or individuals, at particular times Sparing young animals and fish Rotational hunting and no-take zones Closed fishing areas and closed season Allowing portion of fish catch to escape Taboos and rituals for certain people and animals Nomination of stewards to regulate hunting	Crop harvesting Livestock raising	Muttonbird (sooty shearwater) gathering by Māori Aboriginal caretakers Beaver bosses of Cree, rested hunting and trapping areas Sparing lead caribou individuals (as have knowledge of migration routes) Pacific island closed fishing areas and seasons
Planting	Enrichment planting of fruit and medicinal trees in forests and home gardens Scattering seeds and roots Replacing portions of roots Replanting of propagules Selectively tended wild gardens Agroforestry on- and off-farms	Planting of domesticated seeds	Tree, palm and bamboo enrichment by Amazonian cultures Aboriginal wild gardens Distribution and reproduction of mongongo nut trees by San Transplanting willow for basketry by Shoshone
Raising animals	Selective culling and sparing Transplanting eggs and young Feeding young animals	Raising domesticated animals	Managing wild pigs in Papua New Guinea
Nutrient additions	Human and animal wastes near settlements Mulching and charcoal as soil amendments Feed for fish and wild pigs	Fertilizer, compost, animal manure	Pastoralist corrals in sub-Saharan Africa leading to Acacia woodlands Wild pig management in Papua New Guinea

(Continued)

Table 19.1 Continued

Practice	Detail	Agricultural equivalent	Examples
Pest management	Protection by removal of weeds, pests, or predators	Pest management	Management of oyster beds in UK
Habitat amendment and creation	Coppicing and thinning of trees to increase yields and biodiversity Creation of ponds and fleets Creation of maize and sorghum game cover Clearing of forest glades Creation of rock cairns to attract lizards Creation of hunting gardens	Habitat amendment for agriculture	Swidden agriculturalists Farmers creating ponds for fishing or wildfowling in UK Farmers maintaining woodland and game cover for shooting
Water management	Diversion of streams to irrigate wild strands of grasses Channel diversion for fish trapping Clearing of streambeds for fish spawning	Irrigation Drainage	Irrigation by Hohokam in USA
Fire use	Burning to increase grass yields to encourage game, reveal burrows and tracks Broadcasting seeds of annuals and perennials after burning	Burning crop stubbles and straw Clearing swiddens Burning heather moors	Firestick farming by Australian Aborigines Creation of parklands by Native Americans (Yosemite and Vancouver Island) Burning of prairies by Blackfoot to improve grasses for wild herds

Sources: Bharucha and Pretty (2010); Kent (1989); Rosman and Rubel (1989); Kelly (1995); Bird Rose (1996); Balée (1998); Fowler and Turner (1999); Kehoe (1999); Pretty (2002, 2007); Harris and Mohammed (2003); Anderson and Nuttall (2004); Berkes (1999, 2009); Brookfield and Padoch (2007); Stephenson and Möller (2009); Heckenberger (2009)

notably diverse, sometimes containing more than two hundred useful species (Eyzaguirre and Linares 2004). In northeast Thailand, 88 percent of home gardens contain wild species. Home gardens are often a refuge for wild species threatened by deforestation and urbanization, and in periods of drought when the wild relatives suffer, those surviving in the home gardens provide considerable additional value to farm households.

Burning is a widespread management practice. Australian Aborigines call it "firestick farming," and they used fire to make the "country happy," to keep it "clean" (Bird Rose 1996). Burning allowed people to walk without fear of snakes and the nuisance of grass seeds; it created new food for kangaroos and wallabies; and it made it easy to see animal tracks and burrows. The observation of smoke is still taken to be a sign that the country is healthy. Burning was also common in North America, helping to create the "parkland" type environments of Yosemite and Vancouver Island, and it was used by plains groups to increase herd size on the prairies (Berkes 1999; Lee and Daly 1999).

To many cultures, the ideas of wild, wildlife, and wilderness remain problematic. The term *wild* is commonly used today to refer to ecosystems and situations where people have not interfered, yet we now know that people influence, interfere with, and manage most if not all ecosystems and their plants and animals. In Papua New Guinea, wild and domesticated pigs are central to many subsistence strategies (Rosman and Rubel 1989). Wild pigs are hunted and managed in various ways: boars and sows are brought together to breed, females are followed to their nests, litters and piglets removed for raising, and wild pigs are fed with sago and roots. Some groups raise extra gardens of sweet potatoes just for pigs. Forest-dwelling cassowaries are never bred, but their chicks are captured, tamed, and raised. Similar merging of the wild and raised occurs in reindeer (caribou) herding and hunting communities of Siberia (e.g.Anderson 1999).

What is common in all cases is that people pay close attention to what the land is telling them. Such knowledge and understanding is then encoded into norms, rules, institutions, and stories, and thus forms the basis for continued adaptive management over generations (Basso 1996; Pretty 2007; Berkes 2009). This knowledge is an important capital resource.

Many farmers continue to blur distinctions between cultivated and uncultivated foods (Mazhar et al. 2007), reinforcing the lack of a simple dichotomy between agricultural and hunter-gatherer livelihoods, or wild and cultivated species. Food research and policy, in contrast, do not take account of these linkages. Yet wild food species are also actively managed. Farmers transplant species onto or near fields. In northeastern Thailand, a quarter of the 159 wild food species gathered are deliberately propagated (Price 1997; High and Shackleton 2000; Harris and Mohammed 2003). Smallholders' home gardens are another example of wild food interactions—these are notably diverse, sometimes containing more than 200 useful species (Eyzaguirre and Linares 2004).

Farming communities have long benefited from a "hidden harvest," using co-evolved species and other wild biodiversity in and around their farms to supplement their foods and earnings (Harris and Hillman 1989; Scoones et al. 1992; Heywood 1999; Grivetti and Ogle 2000). Many species are found within the fields themselves. The harvesting of wild species from paddy fields is an excellent example. In Thailand, farmers harvest wild herbs, insects, trees, and vines (Price 1997; Halwart 2008); in Bangladesh, 102 species of greens and 69 of fish (Mazhar et al. 2007) are collected. In Svay Rieng, Cambodia, wild fish from in and around paddies contribute up to 70 percent of total protein intake as well as being a source of income. Their relevance as a buffer against hunger is considerable in this area, since rice yields here are amongst the lowest in Southeast Asia (Guttman 1999). Table 19.2 summarizes the range of species used by rice-based

Table 19.2. The diversity of aquatic wild food species within rice agroecosystems in four Asian contexts (from Halwart 2008)

	Cambodia	China	Laos	Vietnam
Plants	13	20	20	15
Amphibians	2	3	10	3
Crustaceans	6	4	5	3
Fish	70	54	26	14
Molluscs	1	5	8	7
Reptiles	8	1	7	3
Insects	2	-	16	6
Total	102	87	92	51

agricultural communities in four Asian countries, with total use varying from 51 to 102 species (overall mean, 83; plants, 17; animals, 66). Boxes 1 and 2 summaries the importance and use of wild foods in two particularly vulnerable agricultural systems: tropical swidden cultivation, and dryland agriculture.

Evidence suggests that wild food species are declining in many agricultural landscapes (MEA 2005). The spread of agriculture and the homogenization of agricultural landscapes increasingly limit the availability and use of wild foods of nutritional importance to agricultural communities, but most of all to the landless poor and other vulnerable groups (Scoones et al. 1992; Pretty 2002). Their continued availability depends on the maintenance of synergies between farming and wild biodiversity (Pretty 2007; Royal Society 2009).

The Diversity of Wild Foods Used

Food security has come to depend on a small handful of widely cultivated species. Over 50 percent of the world's daily requirement of proteins and calories comes from just 3 crops—wheat, maize, and rice (Jaenicke et al., 2006), and 12 species contribute to 80 percent of total dietary intake. Of 200,000 seed plant species, just 30 provide 90 percent of the world's food products (Hammer 2004), and only 150 crops are widely commercialized. Yet, ethnobotanical surveys of wild plants indicate that more than 7,000 species have been used for human food at some stage in human history (Grivetti and Ogle 2000; MEA 2005) and at present, wild foods continue to provide great dietary diversity to those who rely on them. Some communities use 200 or more wild species for food (Kuhnlein et al., 2009); in India, 600 plant species are known to have food value (Rathore, 2009); DeFoliart (1992) records 1,000 species of insects used for food worldwide, with 600 of these in Africa; 80 have been reported in Thailand alone (Morris 2008). Wild edible fungi are important sources of food and income for some rural communities (Boa 2004). A total of 1,069 species of wild edible fungi are used as food worldwide (820 of them for food alone; 249 for food and medicine combined).

Edible non-timber forest products (NTFPs) are a particularly important food resource in tropical and subtropical regions (MEA 2005). Bushmeat and fish, for example, provide 20 percent of protein in at least sixty developing countries (Bennet and Robinson, 2000), and in rural areas there is a significant relationship between food security and the contribution of NTFPs to households.

Ethnobotanical surveys of even relatively small samples of respondents can yield surprisingly high numbers of species used. In addition, researchers also note that wild species have diverse uses: 80 percent of 62 wild food plants consumed in Nepal have multiple uses (Shrestha and Dhillon 2006). Johns et al. (1996) found that the 44 edible species reported by the Batemi, a group of agro-pastoralists in Tanzania, are used variously as food (31 species), as thirst quenchers (6 species), for chewing (7 species), as flavorants (2 species) and for the preparation of honey beer (1 species). A further 35 wild food and beverage plants are cultivated. In the Mekong Delta and central Vietnamese Highlands, several wild food species are also used as medicine and livestock feed—a fifth of them are used for all three purposes (Ogle et al., 2003). Within a group of five wild plants traditionally used by tribal communities in India's Satpura hills, Jagtap et al. (2010) identify six different uses: medicine for a variety of ailments, food, tonics, aphrodisiacs, fodder, and green manure.

Estimates of numbers of species used should be subject to two caveats. First, averages do not reflect differences in wild food use between social groups, between individuals of different ages, or seasonal differences in availability. Second, numerical estimates of diversity do not fully capture the social and cultural value that such diversity entails. Jain (2000, 459) states, "Faith, tradition, taboos and several such associations with forests and particular plant species have helped in conservation of plant diversity. The richness of plant diversity in any area is not evaluated merely by the number of species occurring there, but by the intensity of associations and dependence of the indigenous communities on that plant wealth."

We summarize evidence on the use of wild species in Tables 19.3 to 19.5. From 31 studies in 20 countries of Asia and Africa (Tables 19.3 and 19.4), the mean use of wild foods (discounting country- or continent-wide aggregates) is 92 species per place and community group. Individual country estimates can reach 300–800 species (India,

Table 19.3 The diversity of species of wild foods used in selected countries of Asia

Country	Area characteristics	Number of species	References
Bangladesh	Floodplain rice farming communities	**171**	Mazhar et al. 2007
Cambodia	Rice field agroecosystem, lower Mekong basin	**20**	Shams et al. (n.d.)
Cambodia	Rice field agroecosystem, Tonle Sap, Mekong basin	**102**	Balzer et al. 2002

(Continued)

Table 19.3 Continued

Country	Area characteristics	Number of species	References
China	Rice field agroecosystem in Xishuangbanna, Yunan Province	**92**	Halwart 2008
India	General countrywide estimate	**600**	Rathore 2009
India	Tribal/nontribal; cultivation & livestock, deciduous forest	**73**	Kala 2009
India	Tribal and nontribal, transhumance and rainfed agriculture, temperate forests	**21**	Misra et al. 2008
India	Mornaula Reserve Forest in western Himalaya	**114**	Pant and Samant 2006
India	Sikkim Himalaya	**190**	Sundriyal and Sundriyal 2001
India	Rainfed agricultural community of Deccan Plateau; 79 species of plants used, plus hunting of monitor lizards, wild pigs, rabbits and fish	**79**	Mazhar et al. 2007
Jordan	Arid, countrywide estimate	**56**	Tukan et al. 1998
Lebanon	Dry Mediterranean, rural	**6**	Jeambey et al. 2009
Mongolia	Steppe, nomadic pastoralists	**77**	Huai and Pei 2000
Nepal	Rural, forest dwelling	**62**	Shrestha and Dhillon 2006
Nepal	Chepang community, shifting cultivation	**85**	Aryal et al. 2009
Palestinian Authority	Rural agricultural communities (irrigated and rainfed) on West Bank	**100**	Ali-Shtayeh et al. 2008
Thailand	Irrigated rice in NE and tropical/sub-tropical forest	**159**	Price 1997
Thailand	Pwo Karen community; swidden cultivation in dry mixed deciduous forest	**134**	Delang 2006
Turkey	Western and central Anatolia	**121**	Dogan et al. 2004
Vietnam	Cultivation & livestock, Mekong Delta and Central Highlands	**90**	Ogle et al. 2003

* Only plant species listed.
Source: Bharucha and Pretty (2010)

Table 19.4 The diversity of species of wild foods used in selected countries of Africa

Country /Region	Summarized area characteristics	Number of species	References
Africa	Continent-wide estimate (insects only)	**600**	DeFoliart 1992
Africa	Sub-Saharan Africa (insects only)	**250**	van Huis 2003
Africa	Central and West Africa (plants only)	**1500**	Chege 1994
Botswana	Tyua grow crops and use wild plants, animals, birds, fish and insects	**171**	Hitchcock 1999
Congo	Mbuti Pygmies of forest: cultivators of cassava and plantain plus users of 230 animal and 100 plant species	**330**	Ishikawa 1999
Ethiopia	Subsistence agriculture, animal husbandry, semi-arid to humid	**44**	Fentahun and Hager 2009
Ethiopia	Countrywide estimate	**203**	Asfaw and Tadesse 2001
Ethiopia	Countrywide estimate	**300**	Asfaw 2009
Ethiopia	Agricultural, arid, open woodland (50% of plants in region edible)	**25**	Becker 1983
Ethiopia	Humid to semi-arid; forest to savannah, 3 ethnic groups in south Ethiopia	**66**	Balemie and Kebebew 2006
Kenya	Countrywide estimate for agricultural communities (plants only)	**800**	Maundu 1996
Kenya	Turkana agro-pastoralists and rural fishing communities, arid and semi-arid	**14**	Levine and Crosskey 2006
Madagascar	Forest-dwelling, swidden cultivation in tropical forest	**150**	Styger et al. 1999
Namibia	Agriculture and livestock; tropical wetland, swamp and woodland in Caprivi	**21**	Mulonga 2003
Nigeria	Agricultural, savanna, semi-arid	**121**	Harris and Mohammed, 2003
Tanzania	Agricultural, tropical forest, East Usambara mountains	**28**	Kessey, 1998

(Continued)

Table 19.4 Continued

Country /Region	Summarized area characteristics	Number of species	References
Tanzania	Agricultural, tropical forest, East Usambara mountains	**46**	Hårkönen and Vainio-Mattila 1998
Tanzania	Batemi agropastoralists, semi-arid (with 35 wild species cultivated)	**44**	Johns et al. 1996
Uganda	Agricultural households in SW Uganda (some wild species cultivated and gathered from the wild)	**94**	Musinguzi et al. 2006.
Zambia	Countrywide estimate	**15–25**	Pegler and Pearce 1980

Source: Bharucha and Pretty (2010)

Table 19.5. The diversity of species of wild foods used by 12 indigenous communities (adapted from Kuhnlein et al. 2009)[1]

	Study area					Total
No.	Cultural Group	Region	Ecosystem	Flora	Fauna	species used
1	**Awajan**	Peruvian Amazon	Tropical forest	93	113	206
2	**Bhil**	Gujarat, India	Tropical forest	68	23	91
3	**Dalit**	Andhra Pradesh, India	Semi-arid	179	40	212
4	**Karen**	Thungyai Naresuan National Wildlife Sanctuary, Thailand	Tropical; paddy cultivation	252	63	315
5	**Mand (Pohnpei)**	Pacific Ocean, Federated States of Micronesia	Tropical	67	162	229
6	**Igbo**	Southern Nigeria	Tropical	171	45	216
7	**Ingano**	Colombian Amazon	Tropical forest	NA [2]	92	(92 + NA)
8	**Ainu**	Saru River Valley, Japan	Riverine	10	3	13
9	**Maasai**	Kajiado District, Kenya	Semi-arid	33	21	54
10	**Inuit**	Canadian Territory of Nunavut	Polar	15	64	79
11	**Nuxalk**	Bella Coola, British Columbia	Polar	42	25	67
12	**Tetlit Gwich'in**	Canadian Arctic	Polar	15	35	50

[1] Communities 1–7 are formally seen as farming communities.

[2] NA = total cannot be accurately ascertained from original text as named traditional species are a mix of wild and cultivated.

Ethiopia, Kenya). Among indigenous communities (Table 19.5) the mean use of wild species is 120 per community, rising to 194 for those 7 communities formally designated as agricultural.

The Nutritional Value of Wild Foods

Malnutrition is a major health burden in developing countries, and the recognition that nutritional security and biodiversity are linked is fundamental for enlisting policy support to secure wild food use and preserve habitats for wild edible species, which make significant contributions to dietary diversity and nutritional security (Ogle et al. 2001; Smith and Longvah 2009). This might be especially important for some groups; for example, women are at high risk of micronutrient malnutrition in regions that depend on a small number of dietary staples (Arimond et al. 2010).

Understanding the micro- and macronutritional properties of wild foods currently lags behind that of cultivated species (Vincetti et al. 2008). Comprehensive food composition data and information on the bioavailability of nutrients for commonly used wild food species is a critical first step (Flyman and Afolayan 2006; Frison et al. 2006), and is of especial importance for communities most vulnerable to malnutrition (Misra et al. 2008; Afolayan and Jimoh 2009). Also important is spreading awareness among farmers and policymakers of the potential nutritional importance of "weeds." For example, negative perceptions of plants as "weeds" could entail reduced consumption, as in the case of farmers' perceptions of the nutritive *Corchorus spp.* in fields of Ethiopia (Benor et al. 2010).

Though the energy density of wild foods is generally low (with the exception of honey and high-fat organs or in-season fat deposits) (McMichael et al. 2007; Samson and Pretty 2006), some wild species can still contribute significantly to total dietary energy in certain communities. Kuhnlein et al. (2009) find that it can range from 30–93 percent in twelve indigenous communities spread across the world.

In the Sahel, several edible desert plants are sources of essential fatty acids, iron, zinc, and calcium (Glew et al. 1997). In the arid Ferlo region of Senegal, some 50 percent of all plants have edible parts, and those that are commonly consumed are critical suppliers of vitamins A, B2, and C, especially during seasonal lean periods (Becker 1983). Lockett et al. (2000) found that among the plants used by the Fulani in Nigeria, those available during the dry season (and thus important for ensuring nutritional security during potential food shortages) were superior in energy and micronutrient content to those from the wet season.

For many indigenous communities, traditional wild foods outweigh modern store-bought items in terms of nutrient content. Their gradual replacement by store-bought produce causes discernable and significantly negative impacts on nutritional security at household and community levels (Samson and Pretty 2006; Raschke and Cheema 2008).

The Economic Value of Wild Foods

There is no comprehensive global estimate of the economic value of wild foods. Quantitative analyses face two methodological difficulties. First, case studies using different valuation methods and diverse scales are rarely comparable. Second, sales may be missed by conventional accounting mechanisms when it is informal, occurring at local markets, or underreported because it is illegal (Jaarsveld et al., 2005). What is not in dispute is that trade in and use of wild foods provide an important supplement to general incomes and are especially critical during economic hardship.

Households reliant on the mangroves of the Bhitarkanika Conservation Area in India derive 14.5 percent of their total household income from resources extracted from the mangroves. Goods sold in the market (forestry products and fish) are estimated to have a market price of $107 per household per year (Hussain and Badola 2010). Among the Tsimane' of Bolivia, only 3 percent of goods consumed in the household come from the market; a significant proportion comes from freshwater and forest (Reyes-García et al. 2008). In the Democratic Republic of the Congo, almost 90 percent of harvested bushmeat and fish is sold rather than consumed (de Merode et al. 2003).

Bharucha and Pretty (2010) summarize estimates of direct use values for wild foods in selected African countries. From the limited data available, it is clear that wild plants and animals can provide between $170 to $900 worth of value to rural households in South Africa and Tanzania. In Ghana, the bushmeat market is worth $275 million annually.

A central aspect of wild food use is its relative importance poorer households. The conventional understanding is that poorer households depend more on wild foods. However, detailed analyses do not show simple correlations between wealth and use of harvested resources (de Merode et al. 2003; Allebone-Web 2009; Kamanga et al. 2009). A range of context-specific social and economic factors (e.g., price, individual or cultural preference, and wealth) are also relevant. Consumption is also influenced by household wealth (Roe et al. 2002; de Merode 2003; McSweeny 2003).

Drivers of Change in Wild Food Availability and Use

There are a number of important drivers for wild food availability and use. While some clearly increase or decrease the use of wild foods, the impact of others is ambiguous and context-dependent. The importance of understanding current trends for wild foods is underscored by the recognition that food insecurity is a particular problem among indigenous populations (Ford and Berrang-Ford 2009). For some of these communities, problems of species loss, hunger, and poverty overlap.

Wild Foods in a Changing Climate

Forecasting the precise impacts of the changing climate on the availability of wild foods is difficult (MEA 2005; Woodruff et al. 2006). Studying resilience and vulnerability in two communities in Tanzania and Niger, Strauch et al. (2009) concluded that there was insufficient evidence to predict the impacts that climate change would have on both human foraging and the interlinked processes of local ecological knowledge transmission, cultural continuity, and land-based subsistence livelihood.

At a regional level, White et al.'s (2007) study of the effects of a changing climate on wild food supplies in the Arctic described multiple impacts as a result of hydrological changes. These stresses are compounded by rapid sociocultural change in the region (Samson and Pretty 2006; Loring and Gerlach 2009). Although wild food use is potentially affected by these changes, wild species might also play a critical role in buffering against food stress caused by climate change. "The innate resilience of wild species to rapid climate change, which is often lacking in exotic species," means that they could play an increasingly important role during periods of low agricultural productivity associated with climate events (Fentahun and Hager 2009, 208).

Land Use Change and Degradation

Current trends in land use, including expansion of intensive agriculture, limit the capacity of ecosystems to sustain food production and maintain the habitats of wild food species (Foley et al. 2005). The commercialization of agriculture potentially implies decreased reliance on wild foods (Treweek et al. 2006). Agricultural and land use policy, infrastructure development, and widened access to markets all drive land use change, and are implicated in declines of wild species in Thailand (Padoch et al. 2007; Schmidt-Vogt 2001) and China (Xu et al. 2009).

Biodiversity in intensely managed swidden (shifting) fallows has traditionally provided communities with the means to increase incomes, improve diets, and increase labor productivity. Most of the wild food species utilized by swiddeners come from fallows, rather than mature forests. With the replacement of swidden farming by annual or perennial crops (Bruun et al. 2009), wild foods that accompanied fallows are being lost, leading to decreased diversity, and with it downgraded nutritional status, health and income, and the removal of a vital "safety net" for the rural poor (Rerkasem et al. 2009). Somnasang et al. (1998) report that in twenty villages surveyed in Thailand, deforestation had led to a decline in wild food species. Efforts by the local community to stem this loss by domesticating important species were unsuccessful, since many species do not survive outside their natural forested habitat.

Overall, the challenge of feeding a growing world population, if it does not focus on sustainable intensification (Royal Society 2009), will further threaten naturally biodiverse landscapes. These landscapes host species that are important for ensuring dietary diversity and associated nutritional security. This calls for a biodiversity-focused strategy in food, public health, and poverty alleviation policies (Johns and Sthapit 2004).

Unsustainable Harvesting

Sixteen of the world's biodiversity hotspots correspond with areas of malnutrition and hunger, placing pressure on biodiversity for food provision (Treweek et al. 2006). In these locations, unsustainable harvests have led to declines in wild food species.

The illegal use of and trade in bushmeat is well documented. In the long-term, overharvesting will have a negative impact on wild food availability, and thus on nutritional security for those communities who rely on bushmeat for protein. An important driver is the widespread availability of firearms (Jaarsveld et al. 2005). Nevertheless, despite the threat to wildlife, Cowlishaw et al. (2005) found some evidence of sustainable harvesting after the extinction (through historical hunting) of key species. After vulnerable species had been depleted, robust species (fast reproducers) were then harvested and traded at sustainable levels. Management policies might therefore benefit from according stricter protection to key species but allowing robust ones to continue being traded sustainably.

Where species have traditionally been harvested sustainably, the commercialization of species can result in overharvesting (Kala 2009). Brashares et al. (2004) found links between unsustainable harvesting of bushmeat and fish stocks in Africa: years of poor fish catches coincided with increased hunting over a thirty-year period. Policies to restrict unsustainable exploitation of landscapes have often sought to restrict local users. Yet those who dwell on the land depend vitally on access to the resources it provides. Restricting access may therefore have negative implications for food security and livelihoods, and can worsen income inequalities (Kamanga et al. 2009).

Deepening Poverty, HIV/AIDS and Conflict

In Africa, climate-induced vulnerabilities combined with HIV/AIDS have produced such significant declines in food security that they have spurred new thinking on the origins of famine (e.g., new variant famine (NVF) hypothesis; de Waal and Whiteside 2003). A Hlanze et al. (2005) state, "increasingly it is becoming difficult to separate the food security impact of drought from that of HIV/AIDS. The two work in tandem to cause poor harvests and reduced incomes." For households afflicted by HIV/AIDS, wild foods offer nutritious dietary supplements at low labor and financial costs. This is important when considering the negative impact of a household's HIV/AIDS status on income and food security (Kaschula 2008), together with the fact that deficiencies of micronutrients (in which many wild foods are rich) critical to immune-system function are "commonly observed in people living with HIV in all settings" (Piwoz and Bentley 2005, 934). Food stress associated with HIV/AIDS can drive households to intensify wild food use, putting unsustainable pressure on local resources, especially when combined with deepening poverty or indeed conflict (Dudley et al. 2002). In South Africa, Kaschula (2008) found that wild food use was significantly more likely in households afflicted by HIV.

However, use of wild foods could also decline due to HIV/AIDS. For example, at one site, it was found that "households suffering the loss of a head of household were actually less likely to gather from the bush" (Hunter et al. 2009, 29). Further relevant drivers include the loss of ecological knowledge as adults die (Ansell et al. 2009), declines in household labor (de Waal and Whiteside 2003; Kaschula 2008), and the stigma attached to HIV/AIDS (Kaschula 2008).

Armed conflict and associated internal displacement are associated with heavy subsistence use of wild foods by refugees, combatants, and resident noncombatants, and with the sale or barter of wildlife for food (Loucks et al. 2009) or other goods. Conflict—often positively correlated with areas of high biodiversity—is generally associated with landscape degradation (Loucks et al. 2009). It is conceivable that this could lead to a decline in the long-term use of wild food species. Climate change is also predicted to increase armed conflict in some developing countries (Buhaug et al. 2008).

Loss of Local Ecological Knowledge (LEK)

Local ecological knowledge is required for the identification, collection, and preparation of wild foods (Pilgrim et al. 2008). The distribution of LEK between individuals in a community is usually differentiated by gender, age, or social role. Several studies show women score higher on food-related knowledge (Price 1997; Somnasang 1998; Styger et al. 1999). In one Nepalese site, women above thirty-five years of age were able to describe the uses of 65 percent of all edible species, whereas young men could only describe 23 percent (Shrestha and Dhillon 2006). Somnasang et al. (1998) found that while men had more knowledge of hunting and fishing, women had more knowledge of wild food plants, insects, and shrimp. In Ethiopia, children gather fruit for consumption by the whole community, and unsurprisingly, those under thirty had the most knowledge of wild fruits (Fentahun and Hager 2009).

Research has pointed to declines in LEK (Pilgrim et al. 2008) as communities rely increasingly on store-bought foods and move away from land-based livelihoods.

Somnasang et al. (1998) found that young people working outside the village did not have the chance, and in some cases the desire, to acquire food-relevant LEK. It is thus possible that as young adults leave land-based livelihoods, knowledge transmission to younger generations will be diminished. In Zambia, the intergenerational transfer of LEK related to wild foods and famine coping strategies is disrupted by HIV/AIDS (Mason et al. 2010), providing an example of how the drivers and impacts of changed wild food use interact. In other cases, individuals' preferences change as they grow, and thus their stock of LEK changes, even if they remain within their community. In Ethiopia, Fentahun and Hager (2009, 215) found that "grown-ups succumb to the culture of the society which regards the consumption of wild fruits [commonly consumed by children] as a source of shame" (insert added). As climate change alters habitats, so knock-on effects are expected on LEK (Strauch et al. 2009).

Socioeconomic Change and the Expansion of Markets

The replacement of wild foods with store-bought products is linked to reduced dietary diversity, rising rates of chronic lifestyle-related conditions such as obesity and type II diabetes, poor intake of micronutrients (Batal and Hunter 2007; Hawkes et al. 2009) and malnutrition (Erikson et al. 2008). Food advertising and promotion are associated with the globalization and simplification of diets (Hawkes et al. 2009). As exotic species and new processed products become available, traditional species are undervalued and underutilized, as has been found in India (Rathore 2009) and the Amazon (Byron 2003). Yet the importance of wild foods to *nutritional* security means that they are not necessarily replaced by store-bought foods that provide the same amount of calories, and their replacement has been associated with concomitant rises in the incidence of diabetes and obesity (Hawkes et al. 2009). Global trends indicate that more people will, however, come to depend solely on store-bought, cultivated foods (Johns and Maundu 2006), thus marginalizing wild foods. With the disappearance of traditional foods from diets comes the gradual loosening of people's bonds with landscape, rituals, and elements of their culture.

In regions isolated from sweeping transformations, traditional food systems can persist. Pieroni (1999) suggests that the geographical isolation of the upper Serchio valley in northwestern Tuscany has enabled popular knowledge of wild foods to be maintained. Here, over 120 wild species continue to provide food and medicine. Likewise, 123 edible species are still used in Spain (Tardío et al. 2003); and in many Mediterranean countries, wild foods are still prevalent enough to be considered an important part of local diets (Leonti et al. 2006).

In the Arctic, changing climatic and sociocultural conditions have resulted in the increased dependence on store-bought foods, with significant negative effects to physical and mental health at the community level (Samson and Pretty 2006; Loring and Gerlach 2009). In the Canadian Artic, children now obtain more than 40 percent of their total energy from store-bought processed foods ("sweet" and "fat" foods). In adults, however, the benefits of continuing to consume traditional wild foods are clear, as "even a single portion of local animal or fish food resulted in increased ($p < 0.05$) levels of energy, protein, vitamin D, vitamin E, riboflavin, vitamin B-6, iron, zinc, copper, magnesium, manganese, phosphorus, and potassium" (Kuhnlein and Receveur 2007, 1110). Although wild foods have always played a critical role in circumpolar communities (Ford 2009a, 2009b; Ford et al. 2009; Titus et al. 2009), public health policy across many countries tends to operate within a model of food security that discounts the traditional food practices of these communities (Power, 2008).

Securing the Future for Wild Foods

The Millenium Ecosystem Assessment (MEA 2005) lists 250 mammalian, 262 avian, and 79 amphibian species as threatened from overexploitation for food. Mechanisms such as CITES regulate cross-border trade in wild species, but they require international cooperation. At national level, however, trade is generally poorly regulated and monitored, and lack of sufficient data and inadequate management regimes pose challenges to sustainable harvesting (Schippman et al. 2006).

Policy support for wild foods contributes to both nutritional security and biodiversity conservation, and it is crucial for both. Lack of policy support has been implicated in the continued overharvesting of African bushmeat (Scholes and Biggs 2005). By contrast, support for agroforestry systems has potentially ensured sustainable harvests from indigenous tree species in areas otherwise prone to deforestation (Sileshi et al 2007).

Management of common forests has become successful with the emergence of joint forest management and community-managed forest groups (Molnar et al. 2007). Worldwide, some 370 million hectares (m ha) of various habitats are estimated to be under community conservation, including 14 million hectares managed by 65,000 community groups in India and 900,000 hectares managed by 12,000 groups in Nepal. A recent report by an ad-hoc working group for the UN's convention on biological diversity referred to the fact that the FAO has "estimated that the total area of planted forest has increased from 209 million ha in 1990 to 271 million in 2005, equivalent to 7 percent of the total forest area. Furthermore, "trees outside forests" (e.g. open woodlands and agroforestry systems) also provide tree products and services that support the livelihoods of more than one billion smallholders" (Koskela et al. 2010, 2).

Such cases provide the basis for the inclusion of food security provisions within regimes aimed at conservation. Overall, a concern for preserving the habitats and land uses that yield wild food species could be of immense value to the effort to "reduce poverty while increasing food supplies and maintaining functional ecosystems" (Herrero et al. 2010, 824). In Italy, Vitalini et al. (2009) linked the continued use of wild food and plants with a sites' EU designation of "Site of Community Interest." The preservation of habitats bodes well for species conservation, but there are also concerns that protected area status might exclude local people from access and use.

However, the clear importance of wild foods implies potential conflict with two streams of policy: the conservation of landscapes by restricting local use and habitation, and the conversion of land to farmland to raise agricultural productivity. Kamanga et al. (2009) comment on the possible implications of both these initiatives in Malawi, where some 21 percent of land is designated as protected, and therefore unavailable for use by local people. On the other hand, there is a trend across Africa to raise agricultural productivity by converting landscapes to farmland, which implies a potentially significant loss of availability of wild foods and other provisioning services. There is, so far, a lack of proper evaluation on how these different policies interact to produce particular outcomes for the well-being of both landscapes and the people who depend upon them (but see, for example, McElwee 2009 2010).

The extent to which habitats are converted to farmland and the intensification of cultivation have clear implications for the continued availability of wild food species. Encouragingly, it is also increasingly recognized that while agricultural productivity will need to rise, "sustainable intensification" is needed (Royal Society 2009; Foresight, 2011). There is also recognition of the importance of smallholders to current and future food security, especially for the world's poor (Herrero et al 2010). The vulnerability of small crop-livestock systems and their centrality to food security means that more attention must be paid to the wild species that farmers in these systems are already using as staples, supplements, and famine foods. In environments where LEK is being lost, it is important that it be recorded. Local communities might themselves desire to preserve wild food species through, for example, the establishment of community enterprises based on wild food resources, as in Nepal (Shrestha and Dhillon 2006), or through strengthening traditional community sanctions against overuse and enlisting the support of state law, as in northeastern Thailand (Price 1997).

Conclusions

Wild food species form a significant portion of the total food basket for households from agricultural, hunter, gatherer, and forager systems. However, the focus on the contribution of cultivated species to food security has resulted in the routine undervaluation of wild food species. The continued contribution of wild species to food and nutritional security is threatened by some of the very processes that seek to increase agricultural production and enhance economic development.

Although wild foods cannot entirely bridge existing supply and demand gaps, without them these gaps would be much wider. Edible species provide more than just food and income. Important stakeholder groups depending on wild foods include some of the most vulnerable groups in terms of poverty and hunger: women, children, subsistence farmers, and those in areas prone to conflict, drought, and famine. In communities with a tradition of wild food use, it is part of a living link with the land, a keystone of culture (Pretty 2007; Pilgrim and Pretty 2010). The decline of traditional ways of life and decreased wild food use are interlinked. Recent initiatives to revitalize traditional foods aim to reverse both declines, and the are being used to provide health and cultural benefits to traditional communities otherwise subject to the nutrition transition (Pilgrim et al. 2009).

Research needs are twofold: There is a need for (1) standardized, accessible, and comparable studies on the nutritional and toxicological properties of currently underutilized wild species on a broad scale; and (2) the identification of priority areas for conservation of wild food species and the recording of food-relevant local ecological knowledge.

While policies to conserve habitats and increase agricultural productivity can themselves act as drivers for decreased wild food use, the crucial need is for integrated policies that deliver conservation, food security, and sustainable intensification. The FAO recognizes that "nutrition and biodiversity converge to a common path leading to food security and sustainable development," and that "wild species and intraspecies biodiversity have key roles in global nutrition security" (FAO, 2009). Effective biodiversity conservation, too, depends on a recognition that wild species contribute to food security, are actively managed for food provision, and are therefore affected by policies (or lack thereof) to protect habitats and species.

References

Aberoumand, A. 2009. "Nutritional Evaluation of Edible *Portulaca oleracia* as Plant Food." *Food Analytical Methods* 2 (3): 204–207

Afolayan, A. J., and Jimoh, F. O. 2009. "Nutritional Quality of Some Wild Leafy Vegetables in South Africa." *International Journal of Food Sciences and Nutrition* 60 (5): 424–431

Ali-Shtayeh, M., R. M. Jamous, J. H. Al-Shafie, W. A. Elgharabah, F. A. Kherfan, K. Qarariah, H. Khdair, et al. 2008. "Traditional Knowledge of Wild Edible Plants Used in Palestine (Northern West Bank): A Comparative Study." *Journal of Ethnobiology and Ethnomedicine* 4 (13). http://www.ethnobiomed.com/content/4/1/13.

Allebone-Webb, S. M. 2009. "Evaluating Dependence on Wildlife Products in Rural Equatorial Guinea." PhD diss., Imperial College, London, and Institute of Zoology, London.

Anderson, D. G. 1999. Evenki. *In* Lee, R.B. and Daly, R. (eds.) *Cambridge encyclopedia of hunters and gatherers*.pp. 142–146. Cambridge, UK: Cambridge University Press.

Ansell, N., E. Robson, F. Hajdu, L. van Blerk, and L. Chipeta. 2009. "The New Variant Famine Hypothesis: Moving beyond the Household in Exploring Links between AIDS and Food Insecurity in Southern Africa." *Progress in Development Studies* 9 (3): 187–207

Arimond, M., D. Wiesman, E. Becquey, A. Carriquiry, M.C. Daniels, M. Deitchler Fanou, N. Fogny, et al. 2010. "Simple Food Group Diversity Indicators Predict Micronutrient

Adequacy of Women's Diets in 5 Diverse, Resource-Poor Settings." *Journal ofNutrition* 140 (11): 2059S–2069S. doi:10.3945/jn.110.123414

Aryal, K. P., Å. Berg, and B. Ogle. 2009. "Uncultivated Plants and Livelihood Support: A Case Study from the Chepang People of Nepal." *Ethnobotany Research and Applications* 7:409–422.

Asfaw, Z. 2009. "The Future of Wild Food Plants in Southern Ethiopia: Ecosystem Conservation Coupled with Enhancement of the Roles of Key Social Groups." *Acta Horticulturae* 806:701–708. http://www.actahort.org/books/806/806_87.htm.

Asfaw, Z., and M. Tadesse. 2001. "Prospects for Sustainable Use and Development of Wild Food Plants in Ethiopia." *Economic Botany* 55 (1): 47–62

Bailey, R.C., H. Genevieve, M. Jenike, R. Rechtman, and E. Zechenter. 1989. "Hunting and Gathering in the Tropical Rain Forest: Is It Possible?" *American Anthropologist* 91 (1): 59–82

Balemie, K., and F. Kebebew. 2006. "Ethnobotanical Study of Wild Edible Plants in Derashe and Kucha Districts, South Ethiopia." *Journal of Ethnobiology and Ethnomedicine* 2:53 http://www.ethnobiomed.com/content/2/1/53.

Balzer, P., T. Balzer, and S. Pon. 2002. "Traditional Use and Availability of Aquatic Biodiversity in Rice-Based Ecosystems." In *Aquatic Biodiversity in Rice-based Ecosystems: Studies and Reports from Cambodia, China, Lao People's Democratic Republic, and Viet Nam*, edited by M. Halwart, D. Bartley, and S. Funge-Smith. Rome: Food and Agricultural Organization of the United Nations. ftp://ftp.fao.org/fi/cdrom/awarnessagrbiodiv/Kampong%20thom%20reportA.pdf.

Barnett, R. 2000. *Food for Thought: The Utilization of Wild Meat in Eastern and Southern Africa*. Nairobi, Kenya: TRAFFIC East/Southern Africa.

Barrett, C. B. 2010. "Measuring Food Insecurity." *Science* 327 (5967): 825–828.

Basso, K. 1996. *Wisdom Sits in places*. Albuquerque, NM: University of New Mexico Press.

Batal, M., and E. Hunter. 2007. "Traditional Lebanese Recipes Based on Wild Plants: An Answer to Diet Simplification?" *Food Nutrition Bulletin*. 28 (Suppl. 2): 303S–311S. (Supplement).

Becker, B. 1983. "The Contribution of Wild Plants to Human Nutrition in the Ferlo (Northern Senegal)." *Economic Botany* 1 (3): 257–267.

Belcher, B., M. Ruíz-Pérez, and R. Achidiawan. 2005. "Global Patterns and Trends in the Use and Management of Commercial NTFPs: Implications for Livelihoods and Conservation." *World Development* 33 (9): 1435–1452

Bennet, E. L., and J. G. Robinson. 2000. *Hunting of Wildlife in Tropical Forests, Implications for Biodiversity and Forest Peoples*. Environment Department Paper 76. Washington, DC: World Bank.

Benor S., F. R. Blattner, S. Demissew, and K. Hammer. 2010. "Collection and Ethnobotanial Investigation of *Corchorus* Species in Ethiopia: Potential Leafy Vegetables for Dry Regions." *Genetic Resources and Crop Evolution* 57 (2): 293–306.

Berkes, F. 1999. *Sacred Ecology*. Philadelphia, PA: Taylor and Francis.

Bharucha, Z., and J. Pretty. 2010. "The Role and Value of Wild Foods in Agricultural Systems." *Philosophical Transactions of the Royal Society B: Biological Sciences*. 365 (1554): 2913–2926.

Boa, E. 2004. *Wild Edible Fungi: A Global Overview of Their Use and Importance to People*. Series on Non-Wood Forest Products, No. 17. FAO Technical Papers, FAO Forestry Department. Rome: Food and Agricultural Organization of the United Nations (FAO).

Bouis, H. E., and Welch, R. M. 2010. "Biofortification: A Sustainable Agricultural Strategy for Reducing Micronutrient Malnutrition in the Global South." *Crop Science* 50:S20–S32.

Brashares, J. S., Arcese, P., Sam, M. K., Coppolillo, P. B., Sinclair, A. R. E. and Balmford, A. 2004. Bushmeat hunting, wildlife declines and fish supply in West Africa. *Science* 306: 1180–1183.

Brookfield, H., and C. Padoch. 2007. "Managing Biodiversity in Spatially and Temporally Complex Agricultural Landscapes." In *Managing Biodiversity in Agricultural Systems*, edited by D. I. Jarvis, C. Padoch, and H. D. Cooper, 338–361. New York: Columbia University Press.

Bruun, T. B., A. de Neergaard, D. Lawrence, and A. D. Ziegler. 2009. "Environmental Consequences of the Demise in Swidden Cultivation in Southeast Asia: Carbon Storage and Soil Quality." *Human Ecology* 37:375–388.

Buhaug, H., N. P. Gleditsch, and O. M. Theisen. 2008. "Implications of Climate Change for Armed Conflict." Paper for the World Bank Workshop on the Social Dimensions of Climate Change, March 5–6, 2008. Washington, DC: World Bank. http://siteresources.worldbank.org/INTRANETSOCIALDEVELOPMENT/Resources/SDCCWorkingPaper_Conflict.pdf.

Byron, E. 2003. "Market Integration and Health: The Impact of Markets and Acculturation on the Self-Perceived Morbidity, Diet, and Nutritional Status on the Tsimane' Ameridians of Lowland Bolivia." PhD diss., University of Florida, Gainesville.

Chege, N. 1994. "Africa's Non-timber Forest Economy." *World Watch* 7 (4): 19–24.

Cowlishaw, G., S. Mendelson, and J. M. Rowcliffe. 2005. "Evidence for Post-depletion Sustainability in a Mature Bushmeat Market." *Journal of Applied Ecology* 42 (3): 460–468.

DeFoliart, G. R. 1992. "Insects as Human Food." *Crop Protection* 11 (5): 395–399.

Delang C. 2006. "Not Just Minor Forest Products: The Economic Rationale for the Consumption of Wild Food Plants by Subsistence Farmers." *Ecological Economics* 59 (1), 64–73.

de Merode, E., K. Homewood, and G. Cowlishaw. 2003. "The Value of Bushmeat and Other Wild Foods to Rural Households Living in Extreme Poverty in Democratic Republic of Congo." *Biological Conservation* 118 (5): 573–581.

de Waal, A., and A. Whiteside. 2003. "New Variant Famine: AIDS and the Food Crisis in Southern Africa." *Lancet* 362: 1234–1237.

Dogan, Y., S. Baslar, G. Ay, and H. H. Mert. 2004. "The Use of Wild Edible Food Plants in Western and Central Anatolia." *Economic Botany* 58 (4): 684–690.

Dudley, J. P., J. R. Ginsberg, A. J. Plumptre, J. A. Hart, and L. C. Campos. 2002. "Effects of War and Civil Strife on Wildlife and Wildlife Habitats." *Conservation Biology* 16 (2): 319–329.

Egal, F., A. Ngom, and P. D. Ndione. 2000. "Integration of Food Security and Nutrition in Forestry Planning: the Role of Participatory Approaches." *Unsylva* 51 (3): 19–23.

Emerton, L. 2009. "Making the Case for Investing in Natural Ecosystems as Development Infrastructure: The Economic Value of Biodiversity in Lao PDR." In Ninan, K.N. (ed.) *Conserving and Valuing Ecosystem Services and Biodiversity: Economic, Institutional and Social Challenges*. p. 85–98. London: Earthscan.

Erikson, M., J. Fang, and J. Dekens. 2008. "How Does Climate Change Affect Human Health in the Hindu Kush-Himalaya Region?" *Regional Health Forum* 12 (1): 11–15.

Ericksen, P. J., J. S. I. Ingram, and D. M. Liverman. 2009. "Food Security and Global Environmental Change: Emerging Challenges." *Environmental Science and Policy* 12 (4): 373–377.

Etkin, N. L. 1994. *Eating on the Wild Side: the Pharmacologic, Ecologic and Social Implications of using Noncultigens*. Arizona Series in Human Ecology. Tuscon: University of Arizona Press.

Eyzaguirre, P. B. and Linares, O. F. (eds.) 2004. *Home Gardens and Agrobiodiversity*. Washington, DC: Smithsonian

FAO (Food and Agriculture Organization of the United Nations). 2009. *The State of Food Insecurity in the World 2009: Economic Crises—Impacts and Lessons Learned*. Rome: Food and Agricultural Organization of the United Nations. http://www.fao.org/docrep/012/i0876e/i0876e00.htm.

Fentahun, M. T., and H. Hager. 2009. "Exploiting Locally Available Resources for Food and Nutritional Security Enhancement: Wild Fruits Diversity, Potential and State of Exploitation in the Amhara Region of Ethiopia." *Food Security* 1 (2): 207–219.

Flyman, M. V., and A. J. Afolayan. 2006. "The Suitability of Wild Vegetables for Alleviating Human Dietary Deficiencies." *South African Journal of Botany* 72 (4): 492–497.

Foley, J. A., R. DeFries, G. P. Asner, C. Barford, G. Bonan, S. R. Carpenter, S. Chapin, et al. 2005. "Global Consequences of Land Use." *Science* 309: 570–574.

Foresight. 2011. *The Future of Food and Farming. Final Project Report*. The Government Office for Science, London, UK. http://www.bis.gov.uk/assets/foresight/docs/food-and-farming/11-546-future-of-food-and-farming-report.pdf.

Ford, J. D. 2009b. "Dangerous Climate Change and the Importance of Adaptation for the Arctic's Inuit Population. *Environmental Research Letters* 4:1–9.

——. 2009a. "Vulnerability of Inuit Food Systems to Food Insecurity as a Consequence of Climate Change: A Case Study." *Regional Environmental Change* 9:83–100.

Ford, J. D., and L. Berrang-Ford. 2009. "Food Insecurity in Igloolik, Nunavut: An Exploratory Study." *Polar Record* 45:225–236.

Ford, J. D., W. A. Gough, G. J. Laidler, J. MacDonald, C. Irngaut, and K. Qrunnut. 2009. "Sea Ice, Climate Change, and Community Vulnerability in Northern Foxe Basin, Canada." *Climate Research* 38:137–154.

Frison, E. A., I. F. Smith, T. Johns, J. Cherfas, and P. B. Eyzaguirre. 2006. "Agricultural Biodiversity, Nutrition and Health: Making a Difference to Hunger and Nutrition in the Developing World." *Food and Nutrition Bulletin* 27: 167–179.

Glew, R. H., D. J. VanderJagt, C. Lockett, L. E. Grivetti, G. C. Smith, A. Pastuszyn, and M. Millson. 1997. "Amino-Acid, Fatty Acid and Mineral Composition of 24 Indigenous Plants of Burkina Faso." *Journal of Food Composition and Analysis* 10: 205–217.

Grivetti, L. E., and B. M. Ogle. 2000. "Value of Traditional Foods in Meeting Macro- and Micronutrient Needs: The Wild Plant Connection." *Nutrition Research Reviews* 13:31–46.

Guttman, H. 1999. "Rice Field Fisheries: A Resource for Cambodia." *Naga, the ICLARM Quarterly* 22 (2):11–15. http://www.worldfishcenter.org/Naga/na_2194.pdf.

Halwart, M. 2008. "Biodiversity, Nutrition and Livelihoods in Aquatic Rice-Based Ecosystems." *Biodiversity* 9 (1–2): 36–40.

Hammer K. 2004. *Resolving the Challenge Posed by Agrobiodiversity and Plant Genetic Resources: An Attempt*. Kassell, Germany: Kassel University Press. http://www.upress.uni-kassel.de/online/frei/978-3-89958-056-3.volltext.frei.pdf.

Hårkönen, M., and K. Vainio-Mattila. 1998. "Some Examples of Natural Products in the Eastern Arc Mountains." *Journal of East African Natural History* 87 (1): 265–278.

Harris, D. R., and G. C. Hillman, eds. 1989. *Foraging and Farming: The Evolution of Plant Exploitation*. London: Unwin Hyman.

Harris, F. M. A., and S. Mohammed. 2003. "Relying on Nature: Wild Foods in Northern Nigeria." *Ambio* 32 (1): 24–29.

Hawkes, C., M. Chopra, and S. Friel. 2009. "Globalization, Trade, and the Nutrition Transition." In *Globalization and Health: Pathways, Evidence, and Policy*, edited by R. Labonté, T. Schrecker, C. Packer, and V. Runnels, 235–264. New York: Routledge.

Headland, T. 1987. "The Wild Yam Question: How Well Could Independent Hunter-Gatherers Live in a Tropical Rain Forest Ecosystem?" *Human Ecology* 15 (4): 463–491.

Headland, T. N. 2002. "Could 'Pure' Hunter-Gatherers Live in a Rain Forest?: A 1999 Review of the Current Status of the Wild Yam Question." http://www.sil.org/~headlandt/wildyam.htm

Herrero, M., P. K. Thornton, A.M. Notenbaert, S. Wood, S. Msangi, H.A. Freeman, D. Bossio, et al. 2010. "Smart Investments in Sustainable Food Production: Revisting Mixed Crop-Livestock Systems." *Science* 327:822–825.

Heywood, V. 1999. *Use and Potential of Wild Plants in Farm Households*. FAO Farm Systems Management Series. Rome: Food and Agricultural Organization of the United Nations (FAO). http://www.fao.org/DOCREP/003/W8801E/w8801e02.htm.

High, C., and C.M. Shackleton. 2000. "The Comparative Value of Wild and Domestic Plants in Home Gardens of a South African Rural Village." *Agroforestry Systems* 48 (2): 141–156.

Hitchcock, R. 1999. Introduction: Africa. In Lee, R.B. and Daly R. (eds.) *Cambridge Encyclopedia of Hunters and Gatherers*. pp. 175–184. Cambridge, UK: Cambridge University Press.

Hlanze, Z., T. Gama, and S. Mondlane. 2005. *Impact of HIV/AIDS and Drought on Local Knowledge Systems for Agrobiodiversity and Food Security*. FAO-LinKS Project, Report No. 50. Rome: Food and Agricultural Organization of the United Nations. http://www.fao.org/docrep/009/ag251e/ag251e00.htm.

Huai, H., and S. Pei. 2000. "Wild Plants in the Diet of Arhorchin Mongol Herdsmen in Inner Mongolia." *Economic Botany* 54 (4): 528–536.

Hunter, L. M., L. Patterson, and W. Twine. 2009. "HIV/AIDS, Food Security and the Role of the Natural Environment: Evidence from the Agincourt Health and Demographic Surveillance Site in Rural South Africa." IBS Population Program Working Paper. Boulder: University of Colorado at Boulder, Institute of Behavioral Science. http://www.colorado.edu/IBS/pubs/pop/pop2009-0001.pdf.

Hussain, S. A., and R. Badola. 2010. "Valuing Mangrove Benefits: Contribution of Mangrove Forests to Local Livelihoods in Bhitarkanika Conservation Area, East Coast of India." *Wetlands Ecology and Management* 18 (3): 321–331.

Ishikawa, M. 1999 Mbuti. In Lee, R.B. and Daly, R. (eds.) *Cambridge Encyclopedia of Hunters and Gatherers*. pp. 210–214. Cambridge, UK: Cambridge University Press.

Jaarsveld, A.S. van, R. Biggs, R. J. Scholes, E. Bohensky, B. Reyers, T. Lynam, C. Musvoto, and C. Fabricius. 2005. "Measuring Conditions and Trends in Ecosystem Services at Multiple Scales: The Southern African Millenium Ecosystem Assessment (SAfMA) Experience." *Philosophical Transactions of the Royal Society B: Biological Sciences* 360: 425–441.

Jaenicke, H., and I. Höschle-Zeledon, eds. 2006. *Strategic Framework for Underutilized Plant Species Research and Development, with Special Reference to Asia and the Pacific, and to Sub-Saharan Africa*. Colombo, Sri Lanka: International Centre for Underutilised Crops; Rome: Global Facilitation Unit for Underutilized Species.

Jagtap, S., S. Deokule, S. Mukherjee, A. Kuvalekar, S. Devkar, A. Harsulkar, and P. Pawar. 2010. "Assessment of Nutritional Value of Some Wild Edible Plants from Satpura Hills of Maharashtra." *India Journal of Herbal Medicine and Toxicology* 4 (1): 77–82.

Jain, S. K. 2000. "Human Aspects of Plant Diversity." *Economic Botany* 54 (4): 459–470.

Jeambey, Z. T. Johns, S. Talhouk, and M. Batal. 2009. "Perceived Health and Medicinal Properties of Six Species of Wild Edible Plants in North-East Lebanon." *Public Health Nutrition* 12 (10): 1902–1911.

Johns, T., and P. Maundu. 2006. "Forest Biodiversity, Nutrition and Population Health in Market-Oriented Food Systems." *Unasylva* 224 (57): 34–40.

Johns, T., E. B. Mohoro, and P. Sanaya. 1996. "Food Plants and Masticants of the Batemi of Ngorongoro District, Tanzania." *Economic Botany* 50 (1): 115–121.

Johns, T., and B. R. Sthapit. 2004. "Biocultural Diversity in the Sustainability of Developing-Country Food Systems." *Food and Nutrition Bulletin* 25 (2): 143–155.

Kala, C. P. 2009. "Aboriginal Uses and Management of Ethnobotanical Species in Deciduous Forests of Chhattisgarh State in India." *Journal of Ethnobiology and Ethnomedicine* 5:20. URL: http://www.ethnobiomed.com/content/5/1/20.

Kamanga, P., P. Vedeld, and E. Sjaastad. 2009. "Forest Incomes and Rural Livelihoods in Chiradzulu District, Malawi." *Ecological Economics* 68 (3): 613–624.

Kaschula, S. A. 2008. "Wild Foods and Household Food Security Responses to AIDS: Evidence from South Africa." *Population and Environment* 29 (3–5): 162–185.

Kelly, R. L. 1995. *The foraging spectrum: diversity in hunter-gatherer lifeways*. Washington, DC: Smithsonian.

Kessey, J. F. 1998. "Conservation and Utilization of Natural Resources in the East Usambara Forest Reserves: Conventional Views and Local Perspectives." WAU Dissertation No. 2396. Wageningen, the Netherlands: Wageningen Agricultural University. http://www.library.wur.nl/WebQuery/wda/lang?dissertatie/nummer=2396.

Koskela, K., B. Vincetti, W. Dvorak, D. Bush, I. Dawson, J. Loo, E. D. Kjaer, et al. 2010."The Use and Exchange of Forest Genetic Resources for Food and Agriculture." Rome: United Nations Commission on Genetic Resources for Food and Agriculture.http://69.90.183.227/doc/meetings/abs/abswg-09-3rd/information/abswg-09-3rd-inf-11-en.pdf.

Kuhnlein, H., B. Erasmus, and D. Spigelski. 2009. *Indigenous Peoples' Food Systems: The Many Dimensions of Culture, Diversity and Environment for Nutrition and Health*. Rome: FAO Centre for Indigenous People's Nutrition and Environment.

Kuhnlein, H.V., and O. Receveur. 2007. "Local Cultural Animal Food Contributes High Levels of Nutrients for Arctic Canadian Indigenous Adults and Children." *Journal of Nutrition* 137:1110–1114.

Lathrap, D. W. 1968. The hunting economics of the tropical forest zone of South America. *In* Lee, R.B. and DeVore, I. (eds). *Man the hunter*. pp. 23–29. Chicago, IL: Aldine.

Lawton, H., Wilkie, P., Decker, M. & Mason, W. 1976 Agriculture among the Paiute of Owens Valley. *Journal of California Anthropology* 3(1): 13–50.

Lee, R. B. and Daly, R. (eds.) 1999. *Cambridge encyclopedia of hunters and gatherers*. Cambridge, UK: Cambridge University Press.

Leonti, M., S. Nebel, D. Rivera, and M. Heinrich. 2006. "Wild Gathered Food Plants in the European Mediterranean: A Comparative Analysis." *Economic Botany* 60 (2): 130–142.

Levine, S., and A. Crosskey. 2006. *Household Economy Assessment of North East Turkana*. Nairobi: Oxfam.

Li, W. 2001. *Agro-ecological farming systems in China*. Paris, France: UNESCO.

Lockett, C. T., C. C. Calvert, and L. E. Grivetti. 2000. "Energy and Micronutrient Composition of Dietary and Medicinal Wild Plants Consumed During Drought: Study of Rural Fulani, Northeastern Nigeria." *International Journal of Food Sciences and Nutrition* 51 (3): 195–208.

Loring, P. A., and S. C. Gerlach. 2009. "Food, Culture and Human Health in Alaska: An Integrative Health Approach to Food Security." *Environmental Science and Policy* 12 (4): 466–478.

Loucks, C., M. B. Mascia, A. Maxwell, K. Huy, K. Duong, N. Chea, B. Long, N. Cox, and T. Seng. 2009. "Wildlife Decline in Cambodia, 1953–2005: Exploring the Legacy of Armed Conflict." *Conservation Letters* 2:82–92.

Mason N. M., T. S. Jayne, C. Antony, and R. J. Myers. 2010. "A Test of the New Variant Famine Hypothesis: Panel Survey Evidence from Zambia." *World Development* 38 (3): 356–368.
Maundu, P. M. 1996. "Utilization and Conservation Status of Wild Food Plants in Kenya." *In The Biodiversity of African Plants*, edited by L. J. G. van der Maesen, X. M. van der Burgt, and J. M. van Medenbach de Rooy, 678–683. Dordrecht, the Netherlands: Kluwer.
Mazhar, F., D. Buckles, P.V. Satheesh, and F. Akhter. 2007. *Food Sovereignty and Uncultivated Biodiversity in South Asia: Essays on the Poverty of Food Policy and the Wealth of the Social Landscape*. New Delhi: Academic Foundation, IDRC.
McElwee, P. D. 2009. "Reforesting 'Bare Hills' in Vietnam: Social and Environmental Consequences of the 5 Million Hectare Reforestation Program." *AMBIO: A Journal of the Human Environment* 38 (6): 325–333.
McElwee, P. D. 2010. "Resource-Use among Rural Agricultural Households Near Protected Areas in Vietnam: The Social Costs of Conservation and Implications for Enforcement." *Environmental Management* 45:113–131.
McMichael, A. J., J. W. Powles, C. D. Butler, and R. Uauy. 2007. "Food, Livestock Production, Energy, Climate Change, and Health." *The Lancet* 370:1253–1263. http://www.thelancet-globalhealthnetwork.com/wp-content/uploads/2008/04/energy_health5.pdf.
McSweeny K. 2003. "Tropical Forests as Safety Nets? The Relative Importance of Forest Product Sale as Smallholder Insurance, Eastern Honduras." Paper presented at The International Conference on Rural Livelihoods, Forests and Biodiversity, May 19–23, 2003, Bonn, Germany. http://www.cifor.cgiar.org/publications/corporate/cd-roms/bonn-proc/pdfs/papers/T1_FINAL_McSweeney.pdf
MEA (Millenium Ecosystem Assessment). 2005. "Biodiversity." Chap. 4 in Current State and Trends Assessment Vol.1. p. 77–122. Washington, DC: MEA. http://www.unep.org/maweb/en/condition.aspx.
Meggers, B. J. 1954 Environmental limitations on the development of culture. *American Anthropologist* 56: 801–824.
Misra, S., R. K. Maikhuri, C. P. Kala, K. S. Rao, and K. G. Saxena. 2008. "Wild Leafy Vegetables: A Study of Their Subsistence Dietetic Support to the Inhabitants of Nanda Devi Biosphere Reserve, India." *Journal of Ethnobiology and Ethnomedicine* 4:15. URL: http://www.ethnobiomed.com/content/4/1/15
Molnar, A., M. Liddle, C. Bracer, A. Khare, A. White, and A. Bull. 2007. *Community-Based Forest Enterprises in Tropical Forest Countries: Status and Potential.* Washington, DC: Rights and Resources Initiative. http://www.rightsandresources.org/publication_details.php?publicationID=109.
Morris, B. 2008. "Insects as Food amongst Hunter-Gatherers." *Anthropology Today* 24 (1): 6–8.
Mulonga, S. 2003. "Wild Food: Use of Natural Resources for Food in Eastern Caprivi." DEA Research Discussion Paper 62. Windhoek, Namibia: Directorate of Environmental Affairs, Ministry of Environment and Tourism.
Musinguzi, E., J. K. Kikafunda, and B. T. Kiremire. 2006. "Utilization of Indigenous Food Plants in Uganda: A Case Study of South-Western Uganda." *African Journal of Food Agriculture and Development* 6 (2). http://www.bioline.org.br/request?nd06012.
Ogle, B. M., P. H. Hung, and H. T. Tuyet. 2001. "Significance of Wild Vegetables in Micronutrient Intakes of Women in Vietnam: An Analysis of Food Variety." *Asia Pacific Journal of Clinical Nutrition* 10 (1): 21–30.
Ogle, B. M., H. T. Tuyet, H. N. Duyet, and N. X. Dung. 2003. "Food, Feed or Medicine: The Multiple Functions of Edible Wild Plants in Vietnam." *Economic Botany* 57 (1): 103–117.

Padoch C, K. Coffey, O. Mertz, S. J. Leisz, J. Fox, and R. L. Wadley. 2007. "The Demise of Swidden in Southeast Asia? Local Realities and Regional Ambiguities." *Danish Journal of Geography* 107 (1): 29–41.

Pant, S., and S. S. Samant. 2006. "Diversity, Distribution, Uses and Conservation Status of Plant Species of the Mornaula Reserve Forests, West Himalaya, India." *International Journal of Biodiversity Science and Management* 2 (2): 97–104.

Pegler, D. N., and G. D. Pearce. 1980. "The Edible Mushrooms of Zambia." *Kew Bulletin* 35 (3): 475–489.

Pieroni, A. 1999. "Gathered Wild Foods in the Upper Valley of the Serchio River (Garfagnana), Central Italy." *Economic Botany* 53 (3): 327–341.

Pilgrim, S., L. Cullen, D. J. Smith, and J. Pretty. 2008. "Ecological Knowledge is Lost in Wealthier Communities and Countries." *Environmental Science and Technology* 42 (4): 1004–1009.

Pilgrim, S. and Pretty, J. 2010. *Nature and Culture*. London,UK: Earthscan.

Pilgrim, S., C. Samson, and J. Pretty. 2009. "Rebuilding Lost Connections: How Revitalisation Projects Contribute to Cultural Continuity and Improve the Environment." ICES Occassional Paper 2009-01. Colchester, UK: Interdisciplinary Center for Environment and Safety, University of Essex. http://www.essex.ac.uk/ces/occasionalpapers/CES%20OP%2009-1%20Pilgrim%20et%20al%20%E2%80%93%20Revitalisation%20projects.pdf

Pilgrim, S, D. J. Smith, and J. Pretty. 2007. "A Cross-Regional Assessment of the Factors Affecting Ecoliteracy: Implications for Policy and Practice." *Ecological Applications* 17 (6): 1742–1751.

Piwoz, E. G., and M. E. Bentley. 2005. "Women's Voices, Women's Choices: The Challenge of Nutrition and HIV/AIDS." *Journal of Nutrition* 135:933–937.

Posey, D. 1985. "Indigenous Management of Tropical Forest Ecosystems." *Agroforestry Syst.* 3, 139–158.

Power, E. 2008. "Conceptualising Food Security for Aboriginal People in Canada." *Canadian Journal of Public Health* 99 (2): 95–97.

Pretty, J. 1995. *Regenerating Agriculture*. London: Earthscan.

——. 2007. *The Earth Only Endures*. London: Earthscan.

Price, L. L. 1997. "Wild Plant Food in Agricultural Environments: A Study of Occurrence, Management, and Gathering Rights in Northeastern Thailand." *Human Organization* 56 (2): 209–221.

Raschke, V., and B. Cheema. 2008. "Colonisation, the New World Order, and the Eradication of Traditional Food Habits in East Africa: Historical Perspectives on the Nutritional Transition." *Public Health Nutrition* 11 (7): 662–674.

Rathore, M. 2009. "Nutrient Content of Important Fruit Trees from Arid Zone of Rajasthan." *Journal of Horticulture and Forestry* 1 (7): 103–108.

Reid, R. S. and Ellis, J. E. 1995. Impacts of pastoralists in South Turkanba, Kenya. *Ecological Applications* 5(4): 978–992.

Rerkasem, K., D. Lawrence, C. Padoch, D. Schmidt-Vogt, A. D. Ziegler, and T. B. Bruun. 2009. "Consequences of Swidden Transitions for Crop and Fallow Biodiversity in Southeast Asia." *Human Ecology* 37:347–360.

Reyes-García, V., V. Vadez, N. Marti, T. Huanca, W. R. Leonard, and S. Tanner. 2008. "Ethnobotanical Knowledge and Crop Diversity in Swidden Fields: A Study in a Native Amazonian Society." *Human Ecology* 36: 569–580.

Roe, D., T. Mulliken, S. Milledge, J. Mremi, S. Misha, and M Grieg-Gran. 2002. *Making a Killing or Making a Living? Wildlife Trade, Trade Controls and Rural Livelihoods*. Biodiversity and

Livelihood Issues No. 6. London: International Institute for Environment and Development; Cambridge: TRAFFIC. www.traffic.org/general-reports/traffic_pub_trade4.pdf.
Rosman, A. and Rubel, P. G. 1989. Stalking the wild pig. In Kent, S. (ed.) *Farmers as hunters: the implications of sedentism*. pp. 27–36. Cambridge, UK: Cambridge University Press.
Royal Society. 2009. *Reaping the Benefits: Science and the Sustainable Intensification of Global Agriculture*. London: The Royal Society. http://royalsociety.org/policy/publications/2009/reaping-benefits/.
Samson, C. and J. Pretty. 2006. "Environmental and Health Benefits of Hunting Lifestyles and Diets for the Innu of Labrador." *Food Policy* 31:528–553.
Schmidt-Vogt, D. 2001. "Secondary Forests in Swidden Agriculture in the Highlands of Thailand." *Journal of Tropical Forest Science* 13 (4): 748–767.
Scholes, R. J. and R. Biggs. 2005. "A Biodiversity Intactness Index." *Nature* 434:45–49.
Scoones, I., M. Melnyk, and J. Pretty. 1992. *Hidden Harvest: Wild Foods and Agricultural Systems; A Literature Review and Annotated Bibliography*. London: International Institute for Environment and Development.
Shams, N., T. Samran, D. Gutierrez, M. Phanny, and N. Sameoun. n.d. *Much More Than Rice: Rice Field Biodiversity and Food Security in Southeastern Cambodia; Report on Study and Workshop by Catholic Relief Services*. Phnom Penh, Cambodia: Catholic Relief Services.
Shrestha, P. M., and S. S. Dhillon. 2006. "Diversity and Traditional Knowledge Concerning Wild Food Species in a Locally Managed Forest in Nepal." *Agroforestry Systems* 66 (1): 55–63.
Sileshi, G., F. K. Akinnifesi, O. C. Ajayi, S. Chakeredza, M. Kaonga, and P. W. Matakala. 2007. "Contributions of Agroforestry to Ecosystem Services in the Miombo Eco-Region of Eastern and Southern Africa." *African Journal of Environmental Science & Technology* 1 (4): 68–60.
Smith, I. F., and T. Longvah. 2009. "Mainstreaming the Use of Nutrient-Rich Underutilized Plant Food Resources in Diets Can Positively Impact on Family Food and Nutrition Security—Data from Northeast India and West Africa." *Acta Horticulturae* 806:375–384.
Somnasang, P., G. Moreno, and K. Chusil. 1998. "Indigenous Knowledge of Wild Food Hunting and Gathering in North-East Thailand." *Food and Nutrition Bulletin* 19 (4): 359–365.
Sponsel, L.E. 1989. Farming and Forage: A Necessary Complementarity in Amazonia? p. 37–46 In Kent, S. (ed.) *Farmers as Hunters: The Implication of Sedentism*. Cambridge University Press: Cambridge
Strauch, A. M., J. M. Muller, and A. M. Almedom. 2009. "Exploring the Dynamics of Social-Ecological Resilience in East and West Africa: Preliminary Evidence from Tanzania and Niger." *African Health Sciences* 8 (1): 28–35. http://www.bioline.org.br/request?hs08061.
Steward, J. H. 1938. Basin plateau aboriginal socio-political groups. *Bureau of American Ethnology Bulletin 120*. Washington, DC.
Styger, E., J. E. M. Rakotoarimanana, R. Rabevohitra, and E. C. M. Fernandes. 1999. "Indigenous Fruit Trees of Madagascar: Potential Components of Agroforestry Systems to Improve Human Nutrition and Restore Biological Diversity." *Agroforestry Systems* 46 (3): 289–310.
Sundriyal, M., and R. C. Sundriyal. 2001. "Wild Edible Plants of the Sikkim Himalaya: Nutritive Values of Selected Species." *Economic Botany* 55 (3): 377–390.
Szuter, C. R. & Bayham, F. E. 1989. Sedentism and prehistoric animal procurement among desert horticulturalists of the North American Southwest. In Kent, S. (ed.)*Farmers as hunters: the implications of sedentism*. pp. 80–95. Cambridge, UK: Cambridge University Press.
Tardío, J., H. Pascual, and R. Morales. 2003. "Wild Food Plants Traditionally Used in the Province of Madrid, Central Spain." *Economic Botany* 59 (2): 122–136.

Thomas, E., and P. Van Damme. 2010. "Plant Use and Management in Homegardens and Swiddens: Evidence from the Bolivian Amazon." *Agroforestry Systems* 80:131–152.

Titus, K., T. L. Haynes, and T. F. Paragi. 2009. "The Importance of Moose, Caribou, Deer and Small Game in the Diets of Alaskans." In *Ingestion of Lead from Spent Ammunition: Implications for Wildlife and Humans*, edited by R. Watson, M. Fuller, M. Pokras, and G. Hunt, 137–143. Boise, ID: The Peregrine Fund. http://www.peregrinefund.org/Lead_conference/2008PbConf_Proceedings.htm.

Treweek, J. R., C. Brown, and P. Bubb. 2006. "Assessing Biodiversity Impacts of Trade: A Review of Challenges in the Agriculture Sector." *Impact Assessment & Project Appraisal* 2 (4): 299–309.

Tukan, S. K., H. R. Takruri, and D. M. Al-Eisawi. 1998. "The Use of Wild Edible Plants in the Jordanian Diet." *International Journal of Food Sciences and Nutrition* 49 (3): 225–235.

Tulchinsky, T. H. 2010. "Micronutrient Deficiency Conditions: Global Health Issues." *Public Health Reviews* 32 (1): 243–255.

United Nations. 2009. *The Millennium Development Goals Report: 2009*. New York: United Nations. http://mdgs.un.org/unsd/mdg/Resources/Static/Products/Progress2009/MDG_Report_2009_En.pdf.

———. 2013. *Millennium Development Goals*. New York: United Nations.

van Huis, A. 2003. "Insects as Food in Sub-Saharan Africa." *Insect Science and Its Application* 23 (3): 163–185.

Vickers, W. T. 1989 Patterns of foraging and gardening in a semi-sedentary Amazonian community. *In* Kent, S. (ed.) *Farmers as hunters: the implications of sedentism*. pp.46–59. Cambridge, UK: Cambridge University Press.

Vincetti, B., P. Eyzaguirre, and T. Johns. 2008. "The Nutritional Role of Forest Plant Foods for Rural Communities." In *Human Health and Forests: A Global Overview of Issues, Practice and Policy*, edited by C. J. P. Coler, 63–96. London: Earthscan.

Vitalini S., Tome F., Fico G. 2009. Traditional uses of medicinal plants in Valvestino (Italy). *Journal of Ethnopharmacology* 121:106–116.

White, D. M., S. C. Gerlach, P. Loring, A. C. Tidwell, and M, C. Chambers. 2007. "Food and Water Security in a Changing Arctic Climate." *Environmental Research Letters* 2 (4). http://www.iop.org/EJ/abstract/1748-9326/2/4/045018/.

Woodburn, J. 1980. Hunters and gatherers today and reconstruction of the past. In Gellner, A. (ed.) *Soviet and western anthropology*. pp. 95–117. London, UK: Duckworth.

Woodruff, R. E., T. McMicheal, and C. Butler. 2006. "Action on Climate Change: The Health Risks of Procrastinating." *Australian and New Zealand Journal of Public Health* 30 (6): 567–571.

Xu, J., L. Lebel, and J. Sturgeon. 2009. "Functional Links between Biodiversity, Livelihoods, and Culture in a Hani Swidden Landscape in Southwest China." *Ecology and Society* 14 (2): 20.

CHAPTER 20

LIVESTOCK IN THE FOOD DEBATE

PURVI MEHTA-BHATT AND PIER PAOLO FICARELLI

Introduction

Spikes in world food prices since 2007–2008, combined with the global financial crisis generated deep concern, as well as social and political unrest, in both the Global South and in the North (Torero 2011). Anxiety concerning 2012 was significant in this context, and unlikely to go away. The World Bank's Food Price Index, which tracks the price of internationally traded food commodities, estimated a 7% leap in global food prices in comparison to the previous year, consolidating the threat of increased hunger for the planet's poorest (Wroughton 2012). Food prices hit international headlines again and again.

Food, climatic and economic turbulences have signalled the beginning of a seemingly irreversible trend of global instability, which will affect livelihoods of the weakest members of many societies. The most affected by this turmoil are the 1.3 billion poor, living in fragile nations, developing economies, and in remote areas of Africa and Asia. Ensuring global food security is not only a political priority for the public sector, but above all the most basic human right.

The means to these universally endorsed ends, however, are subjects of considerable controversy. Despite the importance of livestock to mixed farming strategies of smallholders and to pastoralists who are among the most vulnerable of the world's poor, political conflict and policy indifference threaten this vital sector. Pressing questions posed by politicians, stirred by the public concerns on food safety and animal welfare in the last 10 years challenge the raising of animals for human use. More recently, climate scientists have demonstrated concern for livestock emissions as one of the major drivers of global warming. These political, ethical, and policy concerns are influencing and often limiting support to the global livestock sector by development agencies. The vocal concerns of the overfed are silencing the feebler voices of the undernourished. We seek in this chapter to explain the role of livestock in supporting and supplementing agriculture in sustaining nutritional security and sustainable development, while explaining the basis for trenchant critiques in current politics.

Livestock "Agriculture"

Agriculture remains the primary source of food production. Mechanization of agriculture and optimization of the production factors (labor, land, and capital) have been able to respond to the food demands of the burgeoning world population. Increases in grain and farm animal productivity have contributed to a net increase of global food availability per person. According to the World Resources Institute's data and the FAO (2006), the average food production per capita index 1961–2005 had been steadily rising worldwide, and, with the exception of Africa, food production growth had been greater than population growth. Agriculture will continue to play this role for the foreseeable future and feed the increasing world population, which is expected to peak at 9.3 billion in 2050 (Evans 2009). Yet, systemic turbulences have shown to increase barriers to access and distribution of food for the hundreds of millions of vulnerable households in the South and an increasing number of urban poor in the North, falling victims of recurrent national economic crisis. Access to food of animal origin is undergoing changes, presenting different challenges in terms of agricultural development policies and practices. Projections based on the continuation of current policies and practices indicate that global demographic changes and income distribution over the next 50 years will lead to different patterns of food consumption and increased demand of livestock products. Most of this increase will take place in the middle-income countries: Brazil, Russia, India, and China, the so-called BRIC countries (World Bank 2008; Smith 2008; Dijkman 2013).

Through the millennia, livestock rearing and food of animal origin have played a crucial role in agriculture. Farm animals, despite their relevance for the survival of almost 2 billion people in the developing world, often miss a key position in the agricultural development debate, whereas the contribution of livestock to global food security remains underestimated. Livestock as a sector is also often targeted in the climate-change debate, together with fossil fuel power plants. Although the latter enjoy government and industry support, farm animals are often scapegoated as a cause of the ecological collapse generated by dominant models of economic growth.

Livestock is an integral part of agriculture and a prominent source of food. Livestock contributes 40% of the global value of agricultural output and supports the livelihoods and food security of almost two billion people (Delgado 2008). Animal products provide one-third of human protein intake and are a critical component of a balanced diet. Mainly, liver, egg, and dairy products provide, on average, 61% of Vitamin A (USDA 2008). In the 2000s, in an average Western diet, 63% of the total protein intake, and 27% of the calories come from animal based sources (meat, eggs, and animal fats) Looking back at the 1960s, there have been relatively small decreases of these values—3% and 8%, respectively.[1]

Farm animals are part of the culture and *world life* of all rural societies and have co-evolved for the past 11,000 years (FAO 2007a, b; Smith 2013; Ficarelli 2009). Cows are a symbol of wealth and prosperity the world over. In India, since the ancient Vedic period (1500–900 BCE), the cow has been an important religious symbol in Hinduism, as the lamb is in Christianity (Patton, 2004).

Although pigs and poultry have been reared for their ability to provide a large array of products by scavenging around rural homesteads, cattle, sheep, and goats, transform inedible fibres of green grasses and standing hays of grasslands into milk and meat. Organic manures produced with their excreta maintain soil fertility, supplying, in a natural way, organic matter and nutrients to the soil. Buffaloes and oxen have been providing essential power for tilling soils and preparing land for crop production all along. Livestock *agriCulture* has a consistent share in achieving the Millennium Development Goals (Smith 2008; 2013). Livestock provides a vital, and often the only, source of income for the poorest and most marginal of the rural poor, such as pastoralists, sharecroppers, female-headed households, and the landless in rural and urban areas.

A Wealthy-driven Livestock Revolution

Thomas Malthus famously warned that the growth of human population would outstrip its ability to produce food. The extraordinary increase of agricultural yields and efficiency of agricultural value chains (from field to fork) remains one of the greatest achievements of humankind, averting the Malthusian scenario (Martin 2006). This has been achieved primarily through technological innovations and off-farm inputs provided by agro-industry and publicly funded research, enabling food supply to match increasing demand.

Food consumption has risen, of course, but with significant differences across countries and food types. Average yearly growth rates for global animal products in the last 25 years have been more than double those of cereals. Production of fruits and vegetables has grown more than cereals but not at the same pace as pork and poultry (6% and 7% per year, respectively; Delgado 2008).

Global meat production has reached 302 million tons by the end of 2012, according to new research published by the World Watch Institute. Between 1995 and 2012, per capita meat consumption has increased 15% especially in developing countries. Economic growth in developing countries led to increased consumption of 25% during the same period, whereas in industrialized countries it increased just 2%. Over the last decade (2000–2011), meat production grew nearly 26% in Asia, 28% in Africa, and 32% in South America. These changes reflect a dramatic shift in production from industrialized to developing countries over the last decade. In 2000, for example, North America led the world in beef production, at 13 million tons, whereas South America produced

12 million tons, and Asia 10 million tons. By 2011, North America had lowered its beef output by 200,000 tons and was overtaken by both South America and Asia, which produced 15 million and 17 million tons, respectively.

Even though the disparity between meat consumption in developing and industrialized countries is shrinking, differences remain large: the average person in a developing country ate 32.3 kg of meat in 2011, whereas in industrialized countries people ate 78.9 kg on average. Pork was the world's most popular meat in 2011. At 110 million tons, it accounted for 37% of both production and consumption. 50% of the total production occurred in China, 10% in the United States, and 5% Germany. Vietnam, the largest producer in South East Asia and the sixth largest in the world, accounted for only 1% of the world pork market (Best, 2013). Pork was followed closely by poultry meat, with 101 million tons produced. Yet, pork production decreased 0.8% from 2010, whereas poultry meat production rose 3%. About 40% of the poultry meat comes from the Asia-Pacific area (Watt 2010). The average daily 36 calorie rise in Western diets due to animal food sources has to be attributed to an increased consumption of poultry meat and not red meat, eggs, and butter, which have decreased or remained the same in the past 40 years.[2] Poultry is expected to become the most-produced meat in the next few years (Nierenberg & Reynolds 2012) and the most consumed the world over. World milk-consumption patterns have been somewhat different in the same period. The developed world still had the largest share of the world consumption with EU-27 countries having the absolute highest milk volumes produced in 2012 (150 million tons of milk, from 22.7 million cows). (http://www.euromilk.org) High-income countries, thus, continue to consume disproportionate amounts of milk, with very high yields, but milk consumption has doubled in developing countries, where consumption is also rising. India had the biggest relative production and consumption share (127 million tons produced in the year 2011–2012 from 72 million cows and 54 million female buffaloes) (NDDB 2013).

Global egg production in 2012 was of almost 1.1 billion eggs. Since 1990, there has been a tenfold increase in egg production in developing countries. At the end of 2012 there were approximately 6.4 billion egg-laying hens in the world, each capable of producing up to 300 eggs per year. People in industrial countries eat about twice as many eggs as people in developing countries, approximately 226 eggs per person per year. Egg consumption generally is either stable or falling in most countries. Notable exceptions are China, India, and Mexico, where the highest increase has been registered. China has the lion share in world egg consumption and production. In 2011 China alone produced nearly 36% of the world eggs—23.6 million tons—more than four times as many as the next largest producer, the United States and more than seven times the number in India, the third largest; FAO 2012).

The Price of the Plenty

The opportunities offered by the livestock revolution have not been equally distributed among agricultural producers. Only a small number of better-off farmers have seized the economic advantages of a growing industry, driven by market forces and consumer demand. Large numbers of smallholder farmers, both in the developed and developing world have been left out from the food revolution (Catley 2008). Especially in developing countries, livestock production remains a small-scale, low input-low output production system. The transition from agrarian to industrial society in developing and many emerging economies has been markedly uneven, with consequences for nutritional insecurity and health. The gap between rich and poor has assumed a new dimension. Because of the plenty, the global number of overweight people has surpassed the number of the undernourished. Global nutritional inequality is rising; the world—including poor nations—is increasingly faced with a double burden of malnutrition co-existing with obesity (FAO, 2012a). The industrialization of food production fills granaries and stomachs of the wealthy but leaves those of the poor empty (Sahn, this volume).

The livestock sector has undergone radical structural changes in the last 30 years, especially in developed nations. Animal rearing practices have been shaped by consumers` demands not only for quantities but also affordability and quality, such as lean and safe meat. Intensive animal production has been divorced from its natural environment and concentrated in industrial animal farms, in order to increase land use efficiency, and leave space for expanding cities and crop fields. This is the industrialization of the livestock sector.

Some of the slighting of the sector in developing countries and development planning result from the inefficiency of the preindustrial ways of managing livestock. Production of animal products and draft power is a very inefficient process (Trivedi 2008). Given the attention increasingly being paid to a global food crisis, inefficient use of scarce agricultural lands is harder to defend. Even if the average price at a United States supermarket of 1L of high quality pasteurized whole milk (0.62–0.75/pint) does not differ from the one of a 1kg of carrots (0.66–0.75/lb.) or yellow onions (0.75/lb.), there is a basic difference between vegetables and animals. Based on a purely input-output ratio, a field of cows produces fewer nutrients than a field of vegetables—or, more importantly, grain, such as that used to feed animals. Animal breeding offers partial answers. Like car manufacturers, animal breeding keeps making engines more efficient. But certain engines are more efficient than others. For instance, chickens are more efficient than pigs and pigs are more efficient than beef and dairy cattle. Animals farmed intensively are subject to the same efficiency limitations posed by the second law of thermodynamics. Only part of the energy contained in feeds is converted into a useful produce, the rest is wasted as heat, much like an incandescent light bulb.

Biological inefficiency, market prices, consumers′ demand for lean meat, quality milk and safe food have forced animal keepers first in the North, and now increasingly in middle-income economies of countries such as Brazil, Russia, and China to: (1) intensify production to benefit from economies of scale along the value chains, (2) concentrate animals in large units, to reduce land costs and space, and energy-using animal movements, and to improve disease control, (3) move close to urban centers to save on transport for input supply and marketing of the produce, (4) focus on a few highly efficient breeds of animals to maximize the food conversion into meat, milk, and eggs. This strategy has created an "animal-based" food industry that has little in common with traditional animal-rearing practices used in smallholder farming on mixed farms or by pastoralists grazing on grasslands in Africa and Asia. With the only exception of West Africa and North Africa, where grazing provides half of the meat produced in these regions, it is through industrial systems that animal food is produced in the rest of the world, driven by consumer demand and cost considerations (Smith 2008).

Livestock Rearing: the Pros and the Cons

Livestock industrialization creates an efficient sector, vertically integrated—from the breeding of dairy cows to the different milk packages and types found on the shelves. This is true for all farm animals, independently from their characteristics, including fish farming. This way of doing business with animal food is very successful, but it is more capital and technology intensive than modern precision farming. Despite increasing pressure from civil society and dwindling farm gate prices in Europe, this model is spreading quickly to developing countries with silent or overt support of political powers who are under pressure to fast-track economic growth. Developing economies simply need more and safer animal-based food for their growing urban populations with growing buying power. They have to respond to the same efficiency and economic imperatives that have shaped the industry in developed countries. The annual urban growth rates of developing economies are expected to double the levels of the 2000s in the next 20 years (World Bank 2012). The animal business goes hand in hand with the supermarket and fast-food revolution, spreading rapidly in several parts of the world. The supermarkets and fast-food outlets bombard consumers with the most appetizing animal-based food products, with an extremely wide choice of brands, prices, and quality originating from global agribusinesses. Yet, it also clear that the underlying commercial logic behind the industrial animal production and related food industry is not different from the one followed by the car industry, clogging cities' traffic arteries.

The industrialization of animal production has other critical consequences. There are consequences of public interest in economic, social, and environmental dimensions of sustainability. A first consideration is the gradual transfer of ownership of animals from a large number of dispersed smallholders caring for and grazing their animals in pastures to a few companies driven by economic efficiency and quality standards along a chain that conforms to the food safety requirements of supermarkets. Rising market demand for animal products pushes for larger-scale operations for the production of beef, and bigger proportions of pork, poultry, milk, and eggs. For smallholders to stay involved with this fast-growing segment of the markets, they need to meet evolving food safety standards to establish credibility with market outlets. Present trends indicate that prospects for smallholder livestock producers may not be good. For example, Delgado

(2008) reports that in Brazil, the chilling and milking technologies required on farms in recent years to meet food-safety requirements have made the participation of producers with less than 100 litres of milk/day per day impossible. About 65% of pigs in China are still produced by small farms selling between 50 and 500 pigs annually (representing more than 90% of all existing pig farms). But environmental, health, and safety concerns have resulted in plans to have 65% of the pigs be raised in large-scale operations producing up to 50,000 pigs per year by 2015 (Baowen 2008). Similarly, nearly 60% of China's egg production in 2005 was done on farms with not more than 500 layers. One could project that small producers of pigs and poultry in rural areas will become consumers in urban areas, keeping internal demand for pork high.

Despite these pressures, small-scale livestock producers are unlikely to disappear in the foreseeable future; but they face new challenges, as does the political system. Milk production in India offers an alternative model. The "white revolution" was orchestrated by the public sector setup, the National Dairy Development Board (NDDB), in a large-scale scheme known as "Operation Flood." This model has created, starting from the 1960s, a national milk-collection grid linking smallholders owning one to three heads of cattle fed on straws and crop residues throughout the country. This unique smallholder movement has been founded on the capillary establishment of village milk producers' co-operatives. These grassroots dairy societies procure milk and provide inputs and services to 80 million members, of which 71% are women. Landless laborers and small farmers are able to derive a small income from the sale of a few litres of milk a day (FAO 2007a). In 2011–2012, the dairy unions affiliated with Amul, the iconic Gujarat Cooperative Milk Marketing Federation, procured an average of 970,000 litres of milk daily from nearly 320,000 producer-members. Assuming only three-fourths to be active suppliers, contribution would work out to just 4 litres of milk each. Even though subtle changes in system intensification are taking place because of labor and feed scarcity, the legacy of village-level cooperative societies will remain the bedrock of the Indian dairy industry for the foreseeable future (Damodaran 2012).

There is a political argument for the protection of small livestock producers as a dominant part of the sector, even as contrary pressures mount. They clearly take better care of their animals and feed them with agricultural by-products with less food grains than large-scale feedlots. They pollute less and make more efficient use of natural resources. They make use of family labor and create job opportunities for the younger generations in rural areas. Yet, we often observe that only the top 10–15% of these small farms have enough resources and technical skills to get the necessary services and take the risks involved in intensification of animal production (Kitali et al. 2005). Perishable commodities such as milk and meat have fluctuating prices, exacerbated by the costly health and hygiene standards required.

Intensification and specialization of farming can integrate the relatively small number of "top smallholders" in market-driven value chains. This can be achieved through contract farming with supermarkets or ad-hoc arrangements with the private sector, which already have process-based food safety and branding systems (IFAD 2004). The biggest ethical concern should be what to do to support the billions of dispersed and marginal farmers growing hardly enough food to feed their families (Sachs 2005). This majority of "bottom smallholders" have a very fragile and dynamic resource endowment with little capacity to secure credit, access to subsidies and information to be able to produce the quality and quantity required by formal markets. What will remain of them and what their families will do around high-tech commercial farms, supplying, as efficiently as possible, the growing rural towns and the ever-expanding mega-cities? South Africa has artificially fast-tracked urban and industrial development based on migrant labour from rural "black reserves." Could this social buffer function be an example for the future of the small farms in the rural space of the other middle-income economies?

Other challenges threaten the future existence of small producers in other types of agro-ecologies. For example, we might consider areas where only extensive livestock production systems are possible, as in the vast grasslands of South America and Africa, the cold steppes and mountains of central Asia, the remote semidesert of the Sahel. These areas have low agricultural potential either because of environmental fragility or underexploitation because of their remoteness or socioeconomic marginalization because of politics (Kerven, 2003). Grazing animals in nomadic pastoral systems are well attuned with nature and adapted to difficult environmental conditions, such as the domesticated yak grazing thorny shrubs in the treeless highlands of Asia or the *muturu* West African dwarf shorthorn cattle in Nigeria tolerant of sleeping sickness (Blench 1999).

The reality of the incredibly vast areas of low productivity and limited use poses other urgent questions. About 26% of global land area is grassland (Dijkman 2013). Rangelands in Africa, Asia, and Latin America represent the last reserves of land that are available on earth to expand agriculture for food production and terrestrial carbon sink (Tennigkeit & Wilkes 2008; Herrero & Thornton 2009). Large parts of these areas are suitable only for extensive livestock production for grazing animals, sheep, goats, and cattle, capable of making use of the fodder sources, in very harsh environments. Decisions made for the sustainable use of grazing commons will be critical for the future sustainable management of these vast land resources. Grasslands have a function in ensuring environmental services, food production, and livelihood opportunities for their nomadic populations (Mueller 2008).

Extensive animal production systems and pastoralism have great potential for producing animal food, supporting local economies, and sustaining livelihoods in sensitive and unique environments, where land is scarce or unproductive. However, radically changing political and economic frameworks in various countries (e.g., the former Soviet Union) have threatened livelihoods and herd mobility. Without support for appropriate pasture monitoring measures, investments in infrastructures or access to alternative forms of livelihoods, livestock keeping by pastoralists pressed by poverty and food insecurity has led to degradation of natural grazing resources and contributed to deforestation. Yet, this important food system has been largely ignored by mainstream development cooperation in the last 20 years (Tarawali 2012).

A second critical consequence of the industrialization of livestock production has been loss of genetic biodiversity, similar to what has happened to crops. The need of increasing efficiency in feed conversion of farm animals and poultry has led to highly specialized breeding companies providing commercial farmers with the best-performing stock. These animals are the result of complex breeding programs based on crossing different pure-line breeds, artificially created on the basis of the natural genetic pool of the many domesticated herbivores and birds. More than 7,000 domestic breeds of animals and birds have been developed by farmers and pastoralists in diverse environments in the 8,000 years since the first livestock species were domesticated. These breeds now represent the unique gene combinations and heritage for the future of humanity (FAO 2007a, b). All animal and crop genetic resources for food production are the result of human intervention: They have been consciously selected and improved by pastoralists and farmers since the origins of agriculture. They have co-evolved with economies, cultures, and societies, passed down from one generation to the next through knowledge networks and social learning. Loss of the unique features and genetic diversity of domestic animals are a factor of importance when considering how to ensure fair and equitable sharing of benefits deriving from them, and in tailoring future policy and regulatory measures.

Super Flues and Mad Cows

Similar to humans, farm animals are subject to diseases that are picked up from their fellows and/or their wild cousins (e.g., Foot and Mouth Disease) or from the physical environment (e.g., Anthrax, a soil-borne disease). Over 60% of human diseases have a biological reservoir in the wild. Normally, diseases are species-specific and rarely cross species barriers. Because of the long evolutionary association between people and animals, microorganisms and parasites have evolved to take advantage of this proximity to jump from one species to another. Such diseases that are transmitted between humans and animals are called *zoonoses*.

The complex interactions that take place between wild and domestic animals, parasites (external: ticks, mosquitoes, tsetse flies; internal: worms and protozoa), micro-organisms and humans cause a wide range of diseases that, through complex mechanisms of transmission, end up in domestic animals (e.g., the fearsome Rabies and the tricky Toxoplasmosis, a scare for all pregnant cat-loving women).

Zoonotic diseases sicken 2.4 billion people, kill many of them and affect 1 in 7 livestock each year. Transmissions between farm animals and humans are generally through direct contact or food. Leptospirosis is one of the greatest threats, followed by rabies. Cysticercosis is transmitted to humans through contaminated pork, Brucellosis through milk (Grace 2012). This special group of diseases is often controllable through simple hygienic and food-safety measures, or by vaccination of animals or people. Only in very special cases do airborne *zoonosis*, like SARS and Bird/Swine flus, due to random mutations of their genetic makeup, manage to cross the species line and spread among humans, independently from the presence of animals.

Control of animal diseases, such as SARS in Asia and Foot and Mouth Disease (FMD) in UK has led to enormous economic losses (both on the order of $11.5 billion). The 2003 outbreak of SARS infected about 8,000 people in China but cost Asian countries between $30–50 billion, mostly due to economic repercussions from widespread public fear of the disease. The true cost of HPAI is still being evaluated. One estimate suggests that a human influenza pandemic today would cost roughly $2 trillion (IFAH 2012). With the globalization of milk and meat production, the association of livestock with threats to human well-being take on an urgent quality. This requires a multisectoral, multistakeholder, and multidimensional approach.

The Meat and Heat Debate

Agriculture releases substantial amounts of greenhouse gas emissions into the biosphere. Based on various reports, agriculture accounts, on average, for almost 40% of the global CO_2 equivalence.[3] Livestock has a relatively significant share in this: 65% of the total anthropogenic Nitrous Oxide (N_2O); 64% of the total anthropogenic ammonia (NH_3); 37% of the total anthropogenic methane (CH_4); 9% of the total anthropogenic carbon dioxide (CO_2). Roughly 17 billion domestic animals contribute 14–18% of the global greenhouse emission (Steinfeld 2006; Steinfield et al. 2008).

These emissions are all natural gases that have been part of the earth's atmosphere for eons. Methane is released by all processes of fermentation in absence of oxygen during the decomposition and digestion of natural fibers and unprocessed grains, carried out by bacteria. This happens in a variety of situations where anaerobic fermentation takes place. Methane is released in dumping sites, landfills, paddy rice cultivation, and in the digestive system of cows. When released as gas, methane remains in the atmosphere for 9–15 years and traps heat 21 times as effectively as CO_2. (Smith 2009) Nitrous oxide, which is formed mainly through the oxidation of ammonia and released by animal excreta, soil, and chemical fertilizers, is the most aggressive greenhouse gas. Nitrous oxide is 296 times as effective as CO_2 at trapping heat and remains in the atmosphere on average for 114 years.

There are differences among livestock species in greenhouse gas emissions. In general, red-meat production emits 2.5 times as much greenhouse gas as chicken production, simply because cattle are less efficient than chickens and they grow slower. To produce a Kg of beef requires up to 13 kg of grain plus forage. To produce 1 Kg of pork we may need 5.9 kg of grain, compared to 2.3 kilograms of grain to make every kilo of chicken. In terms of carbon footprint, eating a steak is equivalent of driving a 4x4 for 30 Km. It is claimed that the methane produced in a day by a dairy cow in large-scale farms could run a 2-liter engine for 1000 Km.[4] Approximately 83% of greenhouse gases come from the actual milk and meat production, of which 37% is CO_2, 26% N_2O due to fertilizer and manure, and 20% methane released from the cow. The rest comes from processing the food (MacKenzie 2008).

Water is an important input for livestock production. Water makes up over 98% of all molecules in the body and is necessary for regulation of body temperature, growth, reproduction, lactation, digestion, lubrication of joints, eyesight, and as a cleansing agent. The problem is that farm animals "eat" almost 100 times more water than they drink, to grow and produce. Livestock consume 32% of the global freshwater (Herero 2012). Most of the water is that used to produce animal feed, to grow grains and cultivated forages. To produce 1 Kg of grain, 96L of water is required, 2,000 liters, to grow 1 kg of rice, and up to 3000L to produce 1 kg of irrigated forage.[5] Although a majority of livestock feeding in developing countries depends upon crop residues and nonirrigated fodder, the preceding figures on water indicate significant dependence of livestock production on a scarce natural resource—water—especially in industrialized livestock rearing.

Lumping all livestock together in consideration of sustainability is a common but unproductive strategy. Constructive approaches to decreasing the environmental impact of intensive animal food production are obscured by a tendency of the present debate to portray a largely undifferentiated picture with an industrial production system bias. This perspective simplifies and misrepresents an extremely complex reality (see Watson, this volume). That reality ranges from highly sophisticated industry, to women milking and weaving the hairs of Yaks in the Himalaya, to landless women in Bangladesh, who, through microcredit, buy a goat to escape poverty. These differences matter. These are differences at the core of the mission of development co-operation, aimed at reducing hunger and defending the rights of the weakest and the most vulnerable.

Climate Change and the Livestock Catch 22

At its very simplest, the carbon story might be summarized in three short words: use less fuel. The matching nitrogen challenge is also clear: eat less meat. This is, in short, the message launched in September 2008 to already concerned politicians by a Nobel Prize-winning think tank, the UN's Intergovernmental Panel on Climate Change (IPCC).

This message apparently makes a lot of common sense. One recent study suggested that the average U.S. household's annual carbon food-print is 8.1 tons of equivalent CO_2. Half of this CO_2, 4.4 tons of CO_2 equivalence,[6] comes from what and how we eat. Red meat and dairy products are the most emission-intensive foods. Animal protein constitutes already one-third of the total protein intake. Americans consume 3 times more animal protein than needed; other rich countries have a similar profile. The increase of meat consumption foreseen in BRIC countries (Brazil, Russia, India, China) is a growing global threat to the climate. A sure-fire way of reducing CO_2 equivalence of our diet is to go vegetarian. After all, eliminating meat from our diets will also make us live longer. Overconsumption of animal protein and fats is one of the causes of obesity, which is known to be linked to chronic cardiovascular diseases (Smith 2009; Trivedi 2008).

Given the grave risks involved in climate change, policy questions for livestock become quite complex. Might either the feed or the animals be bred to be more climate-compliant? More radically, might animal-protein needs of humans be met without animals? Some research institutions led by the Netherlands suggest the production of *in-vitro* meat as the solution to animal natural digestive process. Meat would be cultivated from muscle stem cells from cows, pigs, and sheep. The cells are attached to either small edible spheres or a 3D scaffold and then cultured in a liquid nutrient broth until the clusters of muscle cells are large enough to harvest. The first "tube meat" to hit the market is likely to be burgers, sausages, chicken nuggets and other minced-meat products. In Europe, unsubsidized chicken costs around $2,400 a ton, whereas beef costs just over $4,700. Large-scale in-vitro meat production could be implemented now for around $4,500 a ton (Olsson 2008).

The organic label has become more globally popular, driven by consumer demand, social movements, and government policy decisions (Larsson, this volume). Organic has come to mean environmentally friendly and is considered by many people a way of lowering diet's carbon footprint. This is not necessarily true. Although organic grains in general have a much smaller carbon footprint, organic meat is not always a greener and a lower-carbon label. Organic milk, eggs, and meat are less environmentally friendly than commonly perceived by the public. Organic poultry, for example, requires 10% more energy than battery-farmed poultry; as the latter are raised in facilities where they can barely move, so more of their food energy is converted into protein (Trivedi 2008). Grazing cows may look happier from a human perspective, but a larger number of them are required to produce the same amount of food. Grain-fed dairy cows produce less CO_2 and methane than grass fed cow (Dijkman 2013). Wealthy consumers love their grass-fed beef, but there is an environmental cost.

Within this general pattern, significant qualifications are necessary. Regional differences in farming practices can make a big impact on the final CO_2 equivalence figures. Simply changing an animal's feed or feed practice can have a huge impact on its CO_2 equivalance footprint. Impacts cannot be generalized for different production systems; there are trade-offs. Even though intensive production is more efficient and has lower emissions, beef produced by a subsidized German farmer has a different dimension from beef produced by an Ethiopian Borana pastoralist, in terms of resource utilization and food systems. Similarly, the message of eating less meat has a different meaning for an average American than for the average Chinese. The portion of animal products in the diet of an average American is 39% (27% meat and 12% dairy products) versus a 19% of a Chinese (12% meat, 7% milk).

A positive aspect of the present debate over livestock is that it makes its paradox clear. Now, at the beginning of the twenty-first century, livestock is considered more as a threat than as a resource for furthering the global agenda for sustainable development that alleviates the worst consequences of poverty. The debate over livestock is well described as a classic catch-22 situation—a circular paradox that is difficult to solve. No matter how one thinks about developmental paths for livestock, there are always undesired results that can be foreseen. Development cooperation on a global scale is one means to address this dilemma, but livestock carries a number of political negatives. Some are concerned for the ethical treatment of animals: rearing them only for slaughter seems indefensible to many. Public concerns on food safety, animal welfare, and climate-changing emissions work against prioritizing research and development in the livestock sector. And yet, from the point of view of the most marginal and vulnerable, such concerns sound elitist and uninformed. The other side of the story concerns the welfare of some two billion people depending on livestock for livelihoods.

Message in the Bottle: Does Livestock Matter More?

The debate around "feeding the world" is a sensitive and sometimes emotional one; it is hard to make a credible argument that hunger is acceptable and inevitable (Korthals, this volume).

Paraphrasing the powerful image in James Martin's 2006 book, humankind at the beginning of the twenty-first century has now entered into a deep river canyon heading downstream on turbulent waters in multiple rafts toward a narrow bottleneck around 2050, before reaching calmer waters at the end of the century. The bigger the turbulences close to the narrow point of passage, the higher the risk is that the weakest rafters will not make it through. The way humanity will go through depends on decisions made today.

The objective of policy makers in development cooperation is to make the passage as smooth as possible and limit human and natural losses to a minimum. Finding suitable answers to deal with the livestock dilemma is a priority for this century. The goal is to ensure diverse food systems at global level with a two-pronged approach. The first is to support the transformation process of the almost two billion pastoralists and smallholder animal keepers to assure right to food and food-systems diversity (Pimbert 2008). The second is to continue to match supply with the demand of a growing urbanized, globally interlinked world population through intensive animal production, while ensuring minimum environmental damage and animal welfare.

Framing this more complex vision, however, confronts political challenges. Livestock is, in many discourses, becoming the stalking horse of the food crisis. The good and the bad of livestock are used ideologically, but not always factually or with nuance. There is an urgent need to have a nonideological, more informed, equitable, differentiated discussion about management of animal resources between North, East, and South. Farm animals can be seen both as a burden threatening the future of humanity or as an asset for helping ferry it toward a better future. As summarized in Table 20.1, livestock has, at

Table 20.1 Reviewing the pros and cons of Livestock sector

Livestock "*the burden*"	Livestock "*the answer*"
Use 33% of cropland for feed production	Support 2 billion people (600 million poor)
Emit 18% of the global greenhouse gases	Contribute 20–40% to agricultural GDP
Consume 32% of the global freshwater	Contribute 33% of world protein consumption
Eat 40% of the global grain production	Provide 17% of world calories (8% in Africa)

Source: Authors

the same time, a negative ecological footprint when farmed intensively, but a positive developmental footprint for alleviating hunger and poverty, when farmed in a greener way by the planet's poorest. It has not only an economic value of at least $1.4 trillion; it may be an invaluable resource for humanity to cope with the uncertainties of the climate change impact on global food security (Herrero 2012, Ficarelli 2009). We need to move to a new narrative for livestock (Dijkman 2013).

Popular food-systems thinker and writer Michael Pollan was asked what he would do if he could change just one thing about America's industrial food production. "I'd put animals back onto America's farms," he answered. The age-old practice of raising farm animals and growing crops together, he said, generates so many benefits, and on so many levels, that this to him was the single most important missing piece in transforming America's unhealthy and unsustainable industrialized food system into a healthy and sustainable (and less-industrialized) one (Pollan 2006).

This injunction is not without its critics in the world that Pollan imagines as our past heritage. The antilivestock arguments being made in reference to the world's poorest countries tend to focus on a different set of environmental concerns, citing rangeland degradation, and even widespread desertification, as evidence of the damage caused by growing pastoral and agropastoral communities keeping more cattle, sheep, and goats than their marginal lands can support; UNFAO labeled these concerns *Livestock's Long Shadow*. At the same time, environmental and other groups, fearing that livestock producers in China, India, Brazil, and other fast-developing countries are adopting the same industrial practices now under attack in rich countries, with the same predictable damage occurring to environmental, medical, and animal well-being in these emerging economies, are arguing for policies and regulations that keep livestock production systems in the emerging economies from going the way of factory farms in the industrialized world.

The two paths are not necessarily contradictory; we as a species live in radically different political economies. Whereas livestock began to disappear from farms in the world's industrialized countries starting in the 1960s, to be raised on ranches and feedlots and large-scale batteries and piggeries, livestock is still raised on hundreds of millions of farms throughout the developing world. One of the most important things donor agencies and policymakers could do to help Third World countries develop and sustain their agriculturally based economies is to support explicitly these ubiquitous "mixed" crop-and-livestock farming systems (on sustainable intensification, see Nelson and Coe, this volume).

Concluding Thoughts

Livestock livelihoods, a mainstay of small-scale farming in poor and developing countries, have become highly politicized in recent years. One result is a notable lack of focus on coherent solutions to knotty dilemmas.

With livestock foods offering high-quality nourishment and income opportunities for the poor, and with demand for livestock products skyrocketing in the developing world (levels of production are expected to double over the next 20 years, offering new pathways out of poverty for up to 1 billion people), and with livestock issues located at the intersection of much aid, development, environmental, and globalization issues in poor countries, one might expect high levels of funding, research, and development work on livestock-associated issues. That is not the case; livestock remain marginalized in terms of funding, research, and development work alike.

One observes a low policy and planning profile of agriculture overall and livestock in particular. As an implication, livestock production and marketing were not included in most developing-country poverty-reduction strategies and had to be added later to the Comprehensive African Agriculture Development Plan (CAADP) of the New Partnership for Africa's Development (NEPAD). A higher profile of bread and rice for the urban poor relative to livestock benefits for the rural poor reflects in part a weaker evidence base for the latter. Weak evidence links to weak advocacy.

It is also true that the ways forward lack not only consensus and clarity, but also feasibility. Developing countries are dominated by smallholder systems, especially in sub-Saharan Africa and South and Southeast Asia. This structural fact creates special policy challenges. First, parameters for measuring success and corresponding policy mechanisms are more complex (income, assets, productivity). Second, large numbers of smallholders are harder to organize and transaction costs for input supply, marketing and other activities are much higher. These factors have made investments in smallholder livestock improvement (as for some crops) more challenging; outcomes have worked well in only for a few systems (particularly dairy) in which smallholders are more competitive and easier to organize.

We end with the following thought: Livestock matters, and matters even more. It does matter to the large number of people who continue to remain dependent on animals for their livelihood and food, but it also matters to those who have the luxury of other options. When we look at livestock production through an environmental lens, we see threat, but one that may have solutions manageable with better science and policy, including better management of implications such as zoonotic diseases and threats to climate. And when we look through the livelihood lens, we recognize that ethical issues are seldom black and white. Whereas it may well be unethical to treat animals as commodities for slaughter, it is also unethical to deprive farming systems and their inhabitants of subsistence opportunities. We may end up with a stratified ethical conclusion: an ethic for the rich, who can afford better treatment of and reduction in consumption of animal protein, and an ethic for the poor, who have radically fewer and worse options.

Notes

1. Calculated from FAO food balance sheets: http://www.fao.org/economic/ess/ess-fs/fbs/en/
2. Calculations based on FAO food balance sheets: http://www.fao.org/economic/ess/ess-fs/fbs/en/
3. Equivalent CO_2 emissions, a measure that incorporates any other greenhouse gases produced alongside the CO) taking into account land use change (important) and fossil fuel use (less important).
4. Methane is produced in the guts of ruminant livestock because of methanogen bacteria and protozoa. The composition of the animal feed is a crucial factor in controlling the amounts of methane produced, but a sheep can produce about 30 liters of methane each day and a dairy cow up to 200.
5. Existing estimates of water used to produce forages vary from 01. to 03 Kg of forage per m3. of water. There is still a need to systematic evaluating water productivity of exiting forage and an animal feed.
6. Our diets account for up to twice as many greenhouse emissions as driving a vehicle consuming 9 liters per 100 kilometers for 19,000 km—a typical year's mileage.

References

Best, P. 2013. "Global pig production: Trends shaping the pork industry." Available online at: http://www.wattagnet.com/151623.html

Blench, R. 1999. Traditional Livestock Breeds: Geographical Distribution and Dynamics in Relation to the Ecology of West Africa." Working Paper 122 October Overseas Development Institute (ODI).

Catley, A. 2008. "The growing demand for livestock." *Id21 Insights 72*: 1–2. Available on line at: http://www.eldis.org/id21ext/publications/

Damodaran, H. 2012. "Amul's Gen-Next Farmers." *The Hindu Business Line*. Available online at: http://www.thehindubusinessline.com/opinion/columns/harish-damodaran/amuls-gennext-farmers/article4115993.ece

Delgado, C. et al. 2008. "Determinants and Implications of the Growing Scale of Livestock Farms in Four fast Growing Developing Countries." *IFPRI Research Report* 157.

Delagado, C, M. Rosengrant, H. Steinfield, S. Ehui, & C. Courbois. 1999. "Livestock to 2020: The Next Food Revolution." Washington DC: IFPRI. 2020 Brief No 61.

Dijkman, J. 2013. "People the Planet and Sustainable Livestock" Presented at ILRI. Nairobi, Kenya. Available on line at: http://www.slideshare.net/ILRI/ilri-talk

Evans, A. 2009. *The Feeding of the Nine Billion: Global Food Security for the 21st Century*. London: Royal Institute of International Affairs. Chatham House.

FAO. 2006. *Online Statistical Service*. Rome: FAO. Available online at: http://apps.fao.org". Food Production Index Graphic. Available online at: http://www.grida.no/graphicslib/detail/food-production-index_166a

FAO. 2007a. *The State of the World's Animal Genetic Resources for Food and Agriculture*. Rome: FAO.

FAO. 2007b. *Global Plan of Action for Animal Genetic Resources and the Interlaken Declaration*. Rome: FAO.

FAO. 2012a. *State of Food Insecurity in the World*. SOFI. FAO, Rome: SOFI, FAO. Available on line at: http://www.fao.org/publications/sofi/en/

FAO. 2012b. *FAO Statistical Year Book 2012*. Rome: FAO. Available on line at: http://www.fao.org/docrep/015/i2490e/i2490e00.htm

Ficarelli, P. P. 2009. "Livestock on the Line and other Cows' Stories." *Rural 21 Magazine* 43 (6): 30–31.

Grace, D. 2012. "Zoonoses: The Lethal Gifts of Livestock." *Livestock live talk*. Nairobi, Kenya: ILRI. http://www.slideshare.net/ILRI/zoonoses-the-lethal-gifts-of-livestock

Herrero, M. 2012. *Livestock and Global Change—Towards a Sustainable and Equitable Livestock Sector*. ILRI. Nairobi, Kenya: ILRI. Available on line at: http://www.slideshare.net/ILRI/livestock-livetalk

Herrero, M. and P. K. Thornton. 2009. "Mitigating Greenhouse Gas Emissions from Livestock Systems." Paper presented at Agriculture and Climate Change: An Agenda for Negotiation in Copenhagen. IFPRI, Washington DC. 2020 Vision. Focus 16. Brief 6, May.

IFAD. 2004. *Livestock Services and the Poor*. Rome: IFAD.

IFAH. 2012. *The cost of animal diseases*. Oxford Analytica. Report. International Federation for Animal Health, UK.

Kerven, C. (ed). 2003. *Prospects for Pastoralism in Kazakhstan and Turkmenistan- from State farms to Private Flocks*. London and New York: Routledge Curzon.

Kitali, A., E. Owen, N. Jayasuriya, & T. Smith. (eds.). 2005. *Livestock and Wealth Creation*. Nottingham, UK: Nottingham University Press.

MacKenzie, D. 2008. "What Price for More Food" *NewScientist Magazine* 2660: 28–33. www.newscientist.com

Martin, J. 2006. *The Meaning of the 21st Century*. London, UK: Transworld.

Mueller Thomas, Olson Kirk et al. 2008. 'In search of forage: predicting dynamic habitats of Mongolian gazelles using satellite-based estimates of vegetation productivity'. *Journal of Applied Ecology*. Volume 45, Issue 2, pages 649–658, April

NDDB. 2013. Annual report of national Dairy Development Board, Anand India. www.nddb.org

Nierenberg & Reynolds, 2012. "Disease and Drought Curb Meat Production and Consumption". Available on line at: http://vitalsigns.worldwatch.org/vs-trend/disease-and-drought-curb-meat-production-and-consumption

Olsson, A. 2008. "Grow Meat but off the Bone". NewScientist Magazine. 5th July Issue. Comment & Analysis. p. 18. www.newscientist.com

Patton, L. 1994. *Authority, Anxiety, and Canon*. Albany, NY: State University of New York Press.

Pimbert, M. 2008. *Towards Food Sovereignty: Reclaiming Autonomous Food Systems*. London: IIED.

Pollan, M. 2006. *The Omnivore's Dilemma: A Natural History of Four Meals*. London: Penguin.

Sachs, J. 2005. *The End of Poverty*. London: Penguin.

Smith, K. 2009. "Methane first, OK?" *NewScientist*, June 27: 24–25.

Smith, W. J. 2008. "Repositioning Livestock on the Development Agenda." ADG Annual Meeting. Available on line at: http://www.slideshare.net/coppldsecretariat/3-repositioning-livestock-on-the-global-donor-agenda-smith-wb

Smith, W. J. (2013). *Taking the Long Livestock View*. Nairobi, Kenya: ILRI. Available on line at: http://www.slideshare.net/ILRI/13-smith-presentationforglobalagendaforactionfinal22jan-16113353

Steinfeld, H., H. A. Mooney, L. E. Neville, P. Gerber, & R. Reid. 2008. "Livestock in a Changing Landscape". UNESCO/SCOPE/UNEP, Paris. Policy Brief Series. No.6.

Steinfeld, Henning. 2006. *Livestock long shadows*. Rome: FAO.

Tarawali, S. 2012. *Options for Enhancing Pastoral Systems*. Nairobi, Kenya: ILRI. Available on line at: http://www.slideshare.net/ILRI/options-for-enhancing-resilience-in-pastoral-systems

Tennigkeit, T. & A. Wilkes. 2008. "Carbon Finance in Rangeland." WISP/GEF/UNDP/IUCN report. Kunming, China: World Agroforestry Centre.

Torero, M. 2011. "Alternative Mechanisms to Reduce Food Price Volatility and Price Spikes." Science Review: SR21. Foresight Project on Global Food and Farming Futures. *Government Office for Science*.

Trivedi, B. 2008. "Dinner's Dirty Secrets." *NewScientist* 13: 28–32.

UNESCO. 2008. "Livestock in a Changing Landscape" April, Policy Brief No. 6.

USDA. 2008. "Composition of Foods Raw, Processed." Prepared Grid Arendal, UNEP USDA National Nutrient Database for Standard Reference, Release 20 USDA Feb.

Watt, 2010. Outlook projects pork production to grow steadily, Agricultural Outlook 2010–2019 report: Release Date: 15 June 2010.

World Bank. 2008. "Livestock Externalities, Public Investments Needs." ARD Report No. 44010-GLB, Washington, DC.

World Bank. 2012. "Urban Population Growth—Annual" DATA. Washington DC: World Bank. Available on line at: http://data.worldbank.org/indicator/SP.URB.GROW

Wroughton, L. 2012. "Global Food Prices Stable but Still High: World Bank." Washington, DC: Reuters. http://www.reuters.com/article/2012/11/30/us-worldbank-food-idUSBRE8AT00A20121130

CHAPTER 21

THE SOCIAL VISION OF THE ALTERNATIVE FOOD MOVEMENT

SIDDHARTHA SHOME

INTRODUCTION

THE alternative food movement is much more than just about food. It claims to promote a more sustainable, more environmentally friendly and more just socio-economic order. It is thus as much about politics as it is about food. As author Michael Pollan (2006) is fond of saying, eating is "a political act." The political acts that are promoted by the alternative food movement are inspired by a certain social vision and a certain ideology, as indeed all political acts are. This chapter seeks to explore and question the social vision and the ideological outlook that shape the metanarrative of the alternative food movement and define its value system. This exploration begins with a discussion of some ideas and thoughts of Wendell Berry, one of the chief architects of the alternative food movement's vision of American pastoralism. This is followed by a discussion of some of the views associated with Vandana Shiva, a prominent figure in the alternative food movement's vision of farmers and peasants in non-Western societies. This exploration then proceeds to a brief discussion of alternative food movement's environmental vision and contrasts this vision with that of two prominent American environmentalists. Finally, this exploration moves on to India, where the underlying ideology that shapes the alternative food movement has long found expression in the broader political discourse. The ideas of two prominent Indian leaders—one an exponent of this ideology and one who critiqued it—are presented.

Wendell Berry's Agrarian Ideal

A writer of rare genius, Wendell Berry (b. 1934) is not just a representative of the alternative food movement; he is also one of its founders. For more than forty years, Berry's ideas and have informed, influenced, and inspired this movement. In the introduction to *Bringing It to the Table*, a collection of Berry's essays, the author Michael Pollan, himself one of the stars of the alternative food movement, states,

> Americans today are having a national conversation about food and agriculture that it would have been impossible to imagine even a few short years ago. To many Americans it must sound like a brand-new conversation... But to read the essays in this anthology, many of them dating back to the 1970s and 1980s, is to realize just how little of what we are saying and hearing today Wendell Berry hasn't already said, bracingly, before.
>
> And in that "we" I most definitely, and somewhat abashedly, include myself. I challenge you to find an idea or insight in my own recent writings on food and farming that isn't prefigured (to put it charitably) in Berry's essays on agriculture.
>
> (Pollan 2009, x)

Even many of those who have never read Wendell Berry, or even heard of him, have directly or indirectly, intentionally or unknowingly, adopted some of his ideas. Referring to the White House organic kitchen garden and some of President Barack Obama's pronouncements, Michael Pollan comments, "I have no idea if Barack Obama has ever read Wendell Berry, but Berry's thinking had found its way to his lips" (Pollan 2009, x). An exploration of Wendell Berry's thinking thus provides useful insights into the underlying ideology and logic of the alternative food movement.

In moving poetry and eloquent prose, imbued with gentleness and grace, Wendell Berry has written about the goodness of a vanishing way of life in rural north-central Kentucky. His writing vividly celebrates the traditional way of farming as practiced around the time of his childhood. Berry writes of the balance that existed in the small self-sufficient rural community. He portrays that community as being in harmony with nature and with itself. He describes the hard work involved in farming, and lauds the joys and contentment that come from working the land. Sadly, says Berry, this near-perfect old world order is disappearing, replaced by mechanization, industrialization and urbanization. A profound sense of loss pervades Berry's writing, the "loss of local memory, local history, and local names" (Berry 2001, 138).

The agrarian order that Berry so lovingly and so eloquently eulogizes is not, however, without its dark sides. Consider, for instance, the fact that the farms that Berry so exalts are tobacco farms. Tobacco was a major—perhaps *the* major—crop on most of the farms that Berry writes about. As an integral part of the larger tobacco economy, these farmers were responsible—even if unintentionally—for millions of deaths. In so romanticizing tobacco farming, Berry romanticizes not only farming, but also tobacco. In spite of the overwhelming medical evidence, Berry is reluctant to condemn tobacco in unequivocal terms. "The tobacco controversy," says Berry, "distracts from the much greater danger that we are an addictive society; that our people are rushing from one expensive and dangerous fix to another, from drugs to war to useless merchandise to various commercial thrills, and that our corporate pushers are addicted to our addictions" (Berry 1993, 58). He even suggests that tobacco could serve a useful (if macabre) economic role: "The anti-smoking campaign, by its insistent reference to the expensiveness to government and society of death by smoking, has raised a question that it has not answered: What is the best and cheapest disease to die from and how can the best and cheapest disease best be promoted?" (Berry 2001, 145).

It should also be kept in mind that the pre–World War II socioeconomic order that Berry portrays as so much better than today's is in fact the socioeconomic order of the Jim Crow South. Not everybody agrees with Berry's assessment that the move from farm to factory, from rural to urban, from the agrarian South to the industrialized North, was an unmitigated disaster—least of all the people who did the moving. This phenomenon, much lamented by Berry and labeled "the unsettling of America," is seen in a very different light by the author Isabel Wilkerson, who has documented the migration of a large section of the southern population—blacks—from southern farms to northern cities. Wilkerson sees this great migration as a positive, even perhaps a necessary development:

> Over the course of six decades, some six million black southerners left the land of their forefathers and fanned out across the country.... The Great Migration would become a turning point in history. It would transform urban America and recast the social and political order of every city it touched. It would force the South to search its soul and finally to lay aside a feudal caste system....
>
> During this time, a good portion of all black Americans alive picked up and left the tobacco farms of Virginia, the rice plantations of South Carolina, cotton fields in east Texas and Mississippi, and the villages and backwoods of the remaining southern states—Alabama, Arkansas, Florida, Georgia, Kentucky, Louisiana, North Carolina, Tennessee, and by some measures, Oklahoma.
>
> (Wilkerson 2010, 9)

Nor does everybody share Berry's view that the mechanization of agriculture has been entirely negative. According to the historian Donald Holley, the mechanization of agriculture in the American South was closely associated with the desegregation of southern society:

> The First Great Emancipation freed the slaves. The Second Great Emancipation freed the Cotton South from the plantation system and its attendant evils—cheap labor, ignorance, and Jim Crow discrimination. These changes all derived in part from the development of the mechanical cotton picker, a dominant force for social and economic change in the South after World War II....
>
> The story of the cotton picker is more than the story of a machine. The mechanical cotton picker symbolizes how far modern agriculture has taken the Cotton South from the era of mules and tenants. The development of the mechanical cotton picker

> is part of a fascinating story of how the pre-World War II South of poverty and sharecroppers became the modern, urbanized South of the 1990s.
>
> (Holley 2000, xiv)

Wendell Berry's Basic Principles

Wendell Berry's work may be seen as dedicated to espousing certain basic principles, which have remained remarkably consistent over his more than forty years as a public intellectual. According to Berry, we must adopt these principles in order to reverse our present-day deviation from what he calls the "standard of nature" and return to the path of righteousness.

Local Is Best

A prominent theme in Berry's ideas is the goodness of the local: local food, local economy, local conventions, local loyalty, local community, local adaptations, and so on. We must think in terms of the local, says Berry, because only the local can be directly experienced and understood in its concrete particulars, while knowledge of the nonlocal must necessarily be abstract. Unfortunately, says Berry, people today are all too eager to disparage the local. Too many have been infected with a "characteristic disease of the twentieth century: the suspicion that they would be greatly improved if they were someplace else" (Berry 2004a, 49).

According to Kimberly Smith, the author of *Wendell Berry and the Agrarain Tradition: A Common Grace*, Berry's novels are centrally concerned with "how a place and a person can come to belong to one another—or, rather, how a person can come to belong to a place." According to Smith, Berry typically describes a place as representing a ritualistic union, a *marriage*, between people and nature (Smith 2004, 142). One's identification with a place, according to Berry, must be absolute and must submerge all nonlocal identities: "So long as we try to think of ourselves as African Americans or European Americans or Asian Americans, we will never settle anywhere. For an authentic community is made less in reference to who we are than to where we are (Berry 2002b, 180).

Berry also emphasizes community over individual identity: For Berry, "a part of [an individual's] properly realizable potential [lies] in its community, not in itself" (Berry2002c, 138). With individual identity suppressed, and with other identities superseded by a common place identity, Berry's vision leaves little room for diversity within local communities (though it does allow for diversity across communities).

Berry's notion of a sense of place and community has much in common with the German concept of *Heimat*, a word for which there is no real counterpart in the English language, but which may be taken to mean a native place to which one belongs by birth, by community, by culture, by work, and by other deep and enduring ties. For Berry, rural north-central Kentucky is his *Heimat*. During the Nazi era in Germany, this idea of *Heimat*, this sense of place, became the foundation of the the *Blut und Boden* (blood and soil) ideology, which celebrated the sense of place and glorified the local agrarian community. Jews were vilified in part because they were seen as a threat to the *Heimat*, defined more by their Jewishness than by any *Heimat* identity. This Nazi appropriation of the concept of *Heimat* shows the risks associated with an excessively acute sense of place. Glorification of the local necessarily carries with it a distrust of what is not local: food from afar, ideas from outside, and even outsiders themselves. If taken too far, the logic of Berry's sense of place, his glorification of the local, could, like the German notion of *Heimat*, lead to xenophobic tendencies.

We Need Cultural Solutions: Technological Fixes Won't Do

In Berry's view, we can never solve our social or environmental problems by means of scientific-technological solutions. Instead, workable solutions must take the form of local "culture-borne instructions" (Peters 2007a, 260). Trying to find scientific-technological solutions, is, according to Berry, like trying to "cure a disease by another disease." He addresses this search for a scientific-technological fix in reference to birth-control technology:

> What is horrifying is not only that we are relying so exclusively on a technology of birth control that is still experimental, but that we are using it casually, in utter cultural nakedness, unceremoniously without serious understanding, and as a substitute for cultural solutions—exactly as we now employ the technology of land use. And to promote these means without cultural and ecological insight, as merely a way to divorce sexuality from fertility, pleasure from responsibility—and to sell them that way for ulterior "moral" motives—is to try to cure a disease by another disease.... The technologists of fertility exercise the power of gods and the social function of priests without community ties or cultural responsibilities.
>
> (Berry 2002a, 130)

In Berry's view scientific knowledge and the technologies that depend on it are bound to cause more harm than good. This is partly because they are nonlocal (there is no north-central Kentucky science, for example, just as there is no German science or Jewish science). More importantly, it is because they rely on the human faculty of reason, which, according to Berry, is far too fallible for us to depend on. In the introduction to *Wendell Berry: Life and Work*, Jason Peters writes, "[Berry] makes bold to say that we will certainly use clean energy poorly, could we ever adopt it, because we are not good enough to know how to use energy well and not smart enough to know what it is for" (Peters 2007b, 8).

Berry is not inherently against complex techniques or methods or knowledge—just so long these are not based on reason. Once some technique or some knowledge has been distilled through generations and has become incorporated into the traditions and customs of a community, part of the community's "common sense" or "wisdom of centuries," it becomes acceptable to him. For Berry, knowledge achieves reliability not through reason but *by virtue of the abandonment of reason*. He addresses this in reference to certain farming techniques that he witnessed on his travels in Peru:

> They do as they have done, as their ancestors did before them. The methods are assuredly complex—this is an agriculture of extraordinary craftsmanship and ecological intelligence—but they were worked out over a long time, long ago; learned so well, one might say, that they are forgotten. It seems to me that this is probably the only kind of culture that works: though sufficiently complex, but submerged and embodied in traditional acts. It is at least as unconscious as it is conscious—and so is available to all levels of intelligence.... Not so with us. With us, it grows harder and harder even for intelligent people to behave intelligently, and the unintelligent are condemned to a stupidity probably unknown in traditional cultures.
>
> (Berry 1982a, 27)

In some ways, according to Jeremy Beer, Berry's ideas in this regard are very similar to Edmund Burke's famous defense of prejudice expounded in his 1790 *Reflections on the Revolution in France*. "We are afraid to put men to live and trade each on his own private stock of reason," wrote Burke. At its best, prejudice is the means by which the humble, especially, may be engaged in "a steady course of wisdom and virtue." Prejudice "does not leave a man hesitating in the moment of decision, skeptical, puzzled, and unresolved. Prejudice renders a man's virtue his habit" (Beer 2007, 223).

Wendell Berry's Ideology of Limits

Wendell Berry's principles are founded on a certain worldview, a certain ideological outlook. According to him, the fundamental problem that leads to all our other problems is that we human beings are simply too ambitious for our own good and for the good of nature. Our aspirations are too grand. Not only are they futile pursuits, they violate our natural limits and do not show sufficient respect for the mysteries of nature. Trying to go beyond the limits of place, community, tradition, and extant knowledge, is, says Berry, akin to assuming godly authority. "People are not gods," writes Berry. "They must not act like gods or assume godly authority. If they do, terrible retributions are in store. In this warning we have the root of the idea of *propriety*, of proper human purposes and ends" (Berry 1982b, 270). In Berry's view, our ultimate happiness lies in fully accepting and conforming to the limits that we are born into.

We have already seen Berry's antagonism toward science and technology. But there is one particular aspect of science that Berry finds extremely disturbing. Referring to eminent scientist E. O. Wilson's book *Consilience*, Berry observes,

> One of the deities or mythological prototypes...of modern science...is the pioneering navigator or land discoverer: Christopher Columbus or Daniel Boone. Mr. Wilson's book returns to this image again and again. He says that "Original discovery is everything." And he speaks of "new terrain," "the frontier," "the mother lode," and "virgin soil," "the growing edge" and "the cutting edge."...
>
> This figure of the heroic discoverer, so prominent in the mind of so eminent a scientist, dominates as well the languages of scientific journalism and propaganda. It defines, one guesses, the ambition or secret hope of most scientists, industrial technologists, and product developers: to go where nobody has previously gone, to do what nobody has ever done.
>
> (Berry 2001, 53)

This frontier spirit of science, this ambition to go beyond present-day limits of knowledge to make new discoveries and innovations, troubles Berry very deeply and contributes to his intense antagonism toward science. What is worse, says Berry, this sort of ambitious frontier spirit has spilled over from science to other fields, to the point of becoming pervasive in our society. This, according to Berry, has led to an unfortunate disregard for traditional social, cultural, geographical, and technological limits, and to a dangerous quest to continually keep expanding our horizons:

> Young people are being told, "You can be anything you want to be." Every student is given to understand that he or she is being prepared for "leadership." All of this is a lie. Original discovery is *not* everything. You don't, for instance, have to be an original discoverer in order to be a good science teacher. A high professional salary is not everything. You *can't* be everything you want to be; nobody can. Everybody *can't* be a leader; not everybody even wants to be.
>
> (Berry 2001, 55)

Berry grew up in the racially segregated South. In *The Hidden Wound* he explores his family's legacy of slave owning, and his own experience of living in a segregated society. He criticizes slavery and racism on many occasions. However there is one outcome of this system that appeals to Berry:

> [The white laborer] worked with the idea that his work would lead to ownership, or that at least, as a white man, the nigger work he was doing was unworthy of him; in neither case, because of his sense of racial superiority, did he find it necessary to come to emotional or philosophical terms with the work he was doing. Only the black man, the nigger to whom nigger work was appointed, for whom there was no escape, was able to face it as a present and continuing necessity, and to invent the means of enduring and living with it—and, if I understand the communal and emotional impetus of the work song, of building a culture, not beside or in spite of that necessity, but *upon* it to triumph over it. It seems to me that the black people developed the emotional resilience and equilibrium and the culture necessary to endure and even enjoy hard manual labor wholly aside from the dynamics of ambition.
>
> (Berry 1989, 81)

In other words, slavery imposed severe limits on black people, and these limits, according to Berry, served to extinguish any hint of ambition or any hope of reprieve, thereby creating the conditions necessary to produce what he describes as a positive outcome: a culture and an outlook that allowed black people to fully appreciate the beauty and joy of lifelong hard manual labor in the fields, uncontaminated by any sense of ambition. In *The Hidden Wound* Berry writes movingly of his memory of Nick, a black laborer on his grandfather's farm who, according to Berry, was possessed of considerable dignity "because there was a very conscious peace and faithfulness that he made between himself and his lot" (Berry 1989, 23). To Berry, Nick personifies something to aspire to:

> In these times one contemplates it with the same sense of hope with which one contemplates the sunrise or the coming of spring: the image of a man who has labored all his life and will labor to the end, who has no wealth, who owns little, who has no hope of changing, who will never "get somewhere" or "be somebody," and who is yet rich in pleasure, who takes pleasure in the use of his *mind*! Isn't this the very antithesis of the thing that is breaking us in pieces? Isn't there a great rare humane strength in this—this humble possibility that all our effort and aspiration is to deny?
>
> (Berry 1989, 75)

In Berry's portrayal, Nick stands as a moral exemplar because he was someone who (at least in Berry's telling) never rebelled, never even questioned the system, never had any ambition, never aspired for anything more, never longed for a different world, but found joy and beauty and grace, living and working as an farm laborer, entirely within the constraints and limits that the community and the locality had imposed on him. In Berry's view, the most outstanding quality that Nick possessed was that—unlike the Rev. Martin Luther King Jr.—he did not have a dream.

The Heroic Third World Peasant

The vision of American pastoralism with its ideology of limits and its deep suspicion of scientific and technological progress, as exemplified by Wendell Berry's writings, forms an important pillar in the ideology of the alternative food movement. Another important and mutually reinforcing pillar is the vision of heroic Third World peasants, who are portrayed as heroes of the planet, living joyous lives of bucolic peace and contentment, close to nature and to God—very different from the unhappy and unsustainable lives of those in the West.

One of the most prominent purveyors of this vision of heroic Third World peasants is the Indian environmentalist and food activist Vandana Shiva. Hailed for "placing women and ecology at the heart of the modern development discourse" (Right Livelihood Award 1993), the essence of Shiva's message is that human development and progress are fundamentally evil, particularly for those in the non-Western world.

Redemption for these people, according to Shiva, lies in embracing a premodern pretechnological way of life.

In her much acclaimed book *Staying Alive*, Shiva opens her attack on reason and science with a broadside against the Enlightenment. According to her, the spread of Enlightenment thinking has actually meant "the spread of darkness, the extinction of life and life-enhancing processes" (Shiva 1989, xiv) for people in the non-Western world. Shiva, a scientist by training, reserves special venom for science. "It is thus not just 'development' which is a source of violence to women and nature," she writes. "At a deeper level, scientific knowledge, on which the development process is based, is itself a source of violence" (Shiva 1989, 14).

The worldview promoted by Shiva is admiringly described by her supporters in the alternative food movement as "ecofeminism." Though the use of this label indicates a certain desire to claim the legacy of the feminist movement, its ideals are actually very different. For instance, one of the central goals of feminism is to enable women to have greater choice over how they live their lives. This is exemplified by the work of Margaret Sanger, a pioneering American feminist, who sought to make greater reproductive choice available to women and, as part of this endeavor, played a key role in the development of the contraceptive pill. Shiva's ecofeminism completely rejects Sanger's approach toward reproductive choice. In the book *Ecofeminism*, Shiva and her coauthor Maria Mies criticize "technical fixes" such as the contraceptive pill. Such "technical fixes," they claim, have only imposed on women "domination by pharmaceutical concerns, medical experts, the state, as well as by men who now expect women to be always available to them" (Mies and Shiva 1993, 221). In Shiva's ecofeminist worldview, the condition of peasant women in the non-Western world will be improved, not by giving them greater choice, but by reducing their dependence on modern entities such as corporations, the state, the scientific establishment, and so on, and by encouraging them to live their lives entirely according to the norms and practices of traditional societies, which are deemed to be close to women and to nature.

Peasant women in the non-Western world, claims Shiva, "expect nothing from 'development' or from the money economy." For Shiva, the ideal life is that of a peasant woman toiling away all her life in the fields, working harder than "men and farm animals, "invisibly with the earthworm" (Shiva 1989, 108–109) to sustain a subsistence-level existence. "Traditional economies," says Shiva, "are not advanced in the matter of non-vital needs satisfaction, but as far as the satisfaction of basic and vital needs are concerned, they are often what Marshall Sahlins has called 'the original affluent society' " (Shiva 1989, 12).

Shiva's portrayal of Third World peasants, particularly women, glorifies them and extols the supposed virtues of their way of life. But, ultimately, it also ends up dehumanizing them. Consider, for instance, that life expectancy in preindustrial societies is only about thirty years or less (Lomborg 2001, 50–51), compared to seventy years or more in the industrialized West ("List of Countries by Life Expectancy" 2013). Infant mortality in such societies is around 150 (or more) for every thousand live births (Lomborg 2001, 53), compared to 6.3 per thousand in the U.S. or 3.2 in Sweden (United Nations 2006, 88). When Shiva declares that traditional societies are better than modern technological societies at satisfying people's "basic and vital needs," she implies that these people do not desire to live long and do not wish to see their children survive past infancy. She implies that life itself is not a "basic and vital need" for these people.

Shiva glorifies traditional agricultural practices and criticizes any effort to introduce modern technological and commercial practices to farmers in India. She fails to recognize, however, that even after centuries of reliance on traditional farming techniques and the traditional socioeconomic order, India has never managed to eradicate devastating famines, some so severe that they led to cannibalism (Habib 1999, 113–116). Till as recently as the mid-1960s India's food situation was grim. Paul Ehrlich, in his celebrated 1968 book *The Population Bomb*, declared that there was "no hope" for food self-sufficiency in India (Ehrlich 1971, 147). Undaunted by such pessimism, however, a quiet revolution was already underway. Spearheaded by the American agronomist Norman Borlaug, new high-yielding varieties of seeds, along with other new technologies such as chemical fertilizers and pesticides and modern irrigation systems were introduced. These were eagerly embraced by Indian farmers and the result was a dramatic increase in India's food production—a phenomenon that came to be known as the Green Revolution. By 1974, not only was India self-sufficient in wheat, but it had become a net exporter. The specter of large-scale famine – ever present in India's long history – was finally banished. In spite of this success in boosting India's food production, however, Vandana Shiva has been fiercely critical of the Green Revolution, calling it a human and environmental disaster, without ever acknowledging its role in eradicating famine. It appears that Shiva does not consider freedom from famine a "basic and vital need" for people in India.

One of the features of the Third World peasant vision is that these people, being pure, innocent, and simpleminded, cannot be trusted to make choices by themselves for their own good. Hence a regime of prohibitions and restrictions needs to be imposed in order to shield them from the horrors of economic development and new technologies. This sentiment is evident in Shiva's strident calls for the force of law and the coercive power of the state to be used to deny Indian farmers access to agricultural biotechnology. Gail Omvedt, an American-born Indian scholar, takes a different view:

> Behind the appeal of the campaign [to ban genetically engineered seeds in India] is a distorted image of farmers . . . which depicts them romantically but demeaningly as backward, tradition-loving, innocent and helpless creatures carrying on with their occupation for love of the land and the soil, and as practitioners of a "way of life" rather than a toilsome income-earning occupation. . . .
>
> Farmers may love the land they work on. . . . But they are people who are trying to scratch out a living, who want a better life for their children and for whom farming is a source of income and not a very good income. They are familiar with hybrid seeds. . . . They buy them, try them out, and refuse to use them if they do not perform. . . . Farmers are economic actors and capable of making choices.
>
> (Omvedt 1998)

At the heart of the alternative food movement's vision of the heroic Third World peasant lies the simultaneous romanticization and dehumanization of farmers and peasants in the non-Western world. An example from popular culture serves to illustrate how this phenomenon works in practice. James Cameron's blockbuster 2009 movie *Avatar* is a story about progress and scientific and technological development plundering nature and bringing death and destruction to an indigenous people. In this movie, set in the year 2154, a space-faring multiplanetary corporation, driven by greed and armed with the latest technological tools, is seeking to mine a distant planet for a precious metal. The indigenous humanoid people of the planet, interested only in preserving their natural environment and their traditional way of life, oppose the corporation, refusing to succumb to the temptations of material prosperity and development.

Much like the portrayal of Third World peasants in the alternative food movement, the indigenous Na'vi people in *Avatar* are depicted as pure, innocent, authentic, and close to nature. They are also depicted as being utterly devoid of such uniquely human qualities as ambition, curiosity, or initiative. While space exploration is taken for granted by industrialized human beings, the Na'vi are depicted as being perfectly content in their small village. While humans are depicted as being intensely curious about the Na'vi, even mounting organized scientific efforts to learn more about them, the Na'vi demonstrate absolutely no curiosity (except of a certain romantic kind) about human beings. And eventually, it is not a Na'vi but an alien human being from the industrialized world who takes the initiative to organize the Na'vi into an effective fighting force.

The indigenous people in *Avatar* could well have been replaced by goats or cows, and (except for the boy-loves-girl romance) the storyline would hardly have needed any change. And this is also how many in the alternative food movement tend to view farmers and peasants in the non-Western world—in a romanticized but deeply dehumanizing manner. They are viewed almost as part of the flora and fauna, rather than as distinctly human beings.

Environmentalism and the Alternative Food Movement

If the vision of Western pastoralism and the vision of the heroic Third World peasant are two important pillars supporting the intellectual edifice of the alternative food movement, environmentalism is a third—and possibly even more important—pillar. For many, environmentalism has become virtually synonymous with the alternative food movement. The need to rescue nature is often presented as the raison d'etre for the alternative food movement. And the alternative food movement is often portrayed as indispensable for environmental sustainability.

This chapter is devoted to the social vision of the alternative food movement. An in-depth exploration of this movement's vision of nature is outside the scope of this chapter. However, given the central importance of the environmental justification in the alternative food movement narrative, this chapter questions whether the ideology of the alternative food movement is necessary—or indeed even useful—in order to address our environmental concerns. This is done by presenting the environmental visions of two prominent American environmentalists—visions that are radically different from that of the alternative food movement.

John Muir's Environmentalism

John Muir, the founder of the Sierra Club, has been described as "one of the patron saints of twentieth century American environmental activity" ("John Muir" 2013). Indeed, he can truly be regarded as one of the greatest environmentalists of the twentieth century. Yet Muir's environmentalism was very different from that of today's alternative food movement, and even hostile to it in some ways.

Muir's environmental vision was driven by the desire to preserve as much wilderness area as possible. He grew up on a small family farm in Wisconsin, but at the age of twenty-two he left the farm and headed to the University of Wisconsin, never to move back. In spite of his firsthand experience on a farm, Muir did not view low-tech small-scale agrarianism as environmental salvation. If anything, he viewed farms—whether small or large, hi-tech or low-tech—as essentially destructive to the wilderness. Muir's famous characterization of farm animals as "hoofed locusts" ("John Muir" 2013) is indicative of his intense antipathy toward agricultural settlements.

The stark contrast between Muir's environmentalism and the environmentalism of the alternative food movement can be seen in the very different way they view human land use: one is primarily concerned about *extent*, the other about *intensity*. For Wendell Berry, Vandana Shiva, Michael Pollan, and others in the alternative food movement, the primarily concern is about the intensity of human land use. Low-intensity land use in agricultural settlements represents, for them, the environmental ideal. They see the move from rural to urban—what Berry calls the "unsettling of America" as a human and environmental disaster because it means a change from low-intensity to high-intensity land use. For Muir, on the other hand, the primary concern was about the extent (i.e., the total area) of human land use. He wanted to preserve as much wilderness area as possible, and thus he wanted to limit the extent of human land use. He was not particularly concerned about intensity. If anything, the logic of Muir's environmentalism implies that increased intensity of human land use (such as increasing the per-acre output of farmland) is actually good for the environment because it means that more people can be supported per acre of nonwilderness land, thereby reducing the pressure to convert pristine wilderness areas into human use.

Rachel Carson's Environmentalism

With the possible exception of John Muir, Rachel Carson was likely the most important figure in twentieth-century American environmentalism. Carson's landmark 1962 book

Silent Spring had a major influence on the environmental movement, perhaps more than any other single piece of environmental writing before or since. *Silent Spring* documented some of the harmful effects of the excessive spraying of chemical pesticides, and it galvanized Americans into action. The celebration of the first Earth Day (1970), the passage of the Clean Air Act (1970) and the Clean Water Act (1972), and the setting up of the Environmental Protection Agency (EPA) can all be attributed, in part, to the influence of *Silent Spring*.

Carson's environmental vision was not as directly hostile toward the alternative food movement's vision as John Muir's was. Indeed, the first chapter of *Silent Spring*, "A Fable for Tomorrow," has a distinct fall-from-Eden quality to it, not unlike Wendell Berry's or Vandana Shiva's portrayal of a bucolic agrarian past rudely disrupted by scientific and technological progress. Because of this, Carson has often been appropriated by the alternative food movement. A more detailed reading of *Silent Spring*, however, shows how misleading that is.

Carson was a scientist, and much of *Silent Spring* is a scientific argument about the harmful effects of excessive chemical pesticide usage. The book is replete with scientific data, quotes from scientists, and scientific reasoning. The concluding chapter, "The Other Road," lays out Carson's vision of an environmentally friendly system of agricultural pest control—one that is radically different from that of the alternative food movement. What Carson wanted was more, not less, science, to be brought to bear on the problem of agricultural pest control. The entire concluding chapter of *Silent Spring* is an impassioned plea to adopt new biology based technologies to replace chemical pesticides. In a lecture, Carson remarked, "I criticize the present methods because they are based on a rather low level of scientific thinking. We really are capable of much greater sophistication in our solution of this problem" (quoted in Briggs 1987, 7).

Carson was not shy of science and technology driven projects to control agricultural pests, so long as they avoided excessive use of chemical pesticides. For instance, one project that she praised in *Silent Spring* involved irradiating huge numbers of insects:

> The project involved the weekly production of about 50 million [radiation sterilized] screw-worms in a specially constructed "fly factory," the use of 20 light airplanes to fly pre-arranged flight patterns, five to six hours daily, each plane carrying a thousand paper cartons, each carton containing 200 to 400 irradiated flies. . . .
>
> By the time the program was considered complete at the end of 17 months, 3 1/2 billion artificially reared, sterilized flies had been released over Florida and sections of Georgia and Alabama. . . . Thereafter no trace of the screw-worm could be discovered. Its extinction in the Southeast had been accomplished—a triumphant demonstration of the worth of scientific creativity, aided through basic research, persistence and determination.
>
> (Carson [1962] 2002, 281)

In addition, Carson also expressed praise for other such efforts:

> A truly extraordinary variety of alternatives to the chemical control of insects is available. Some are already in use and have achieved brilliant success. Others are in

> the stage of laboratory testing. Still others are little more than ideas in the minds of imaginative scientists, waiting for the opportunity to put them to the test. All have this in common: they are biological solutions, based on understanding of the living organisms they seek to control, and of the whole fabric of life to which these organisms belong. Specialists representing various areas of the vast field of biology are contributing—entomologists, pathologists, geneticists, physiologists, biochemists, ecologists—all pouring their knowledge and their creative inspirations into the formation of a new science of biotic controls.
>
> (Carson [1962] 2002, 278)

It even appears that Carson and her associates actively sought to dissociate themselves from the alternative food movement, which already existed then, though in a somewhat nascent form. Carson never endorsed the movement, either in *Silent Spring* or elsewhere. When *Silent Spring* was published, Marie Rodell, Carson's long-serving literary agent and valued friend, specifically instructed the publisher to make sure that no one placed ads in Rodale Inc. publications—then, as now, an important player in the alternative food movement (see Lear 1997, 415).

With its clarion call to develop new environmentally friendly biology-based technologies for controlling agricultural pests, it is not surprising that *Silent Spring* served as an inspiration for many pioneering scientists working in the fledgling field of agricultural biotechnology. In *Lords of the Harvest*, a book in which he traces the origins of genetically engineered crops, Daniel Charles highlights the views of a number of researchers in this regard:

> Pam Marrone, a researcher at Monsanto during the late 1980s [says] . . . "I remember having lunch with [then-CEO] Dick Mahoney and him saying, 'Because of parathion [a particularly hazardous chemical insecticide], I don't ever want to be in chemicals again. And that's why we're in biotechnology.' " . . .
>
> "During these years, all of us who went into biology were influenced by the wave of environmentalism," says Willy de Greef, who worked for Plant Genetic Systems in Belgium. . . . "The idea was reduce chemicals with biologicals or with genetics." Fred Perlak of Monsanto says . . . "We were all the children of the sixties and the seventies. We'd all read *Silent Spring*; we knew the connection between 2-4-D [a common herbicide] and 2-4-5-T, Agent Orange."
>
> (Charles 2002, 25)

In a complete repudiation of Rachel Carson's environmental vision, agricultural biotechnology is portrayed today by the alternative food movement as one of the greatest environmental evils.

The View from India

The alternative food movement is situated primarily in the industrialized West. The consequent lack of voices from the non-Western world does not, however, prevent this movement from trying to set the agenda for these societies on certain issues. Witness, for example, the intense lobbying carried out by some Western organizations seeking to bar farmers in India and Africa from gaining access to agricultural biotechnology.

How do people in these regions relate to such issues as development, sustainability, the use of science and technology, changing aspirations, and so on? The views of two prominent Indian thinkers might give us some useful insights.

Mahatma Gandhi

Mahatma Gandhi (1869–1948), the leader of the Indian independence movement, venerated as the "father of the nation," can be viewed from many different angles: Gandhi the nationalist; Gandhi the politician; Gandhi the prophet of nonviolence; and the Gandhi of *Hind Swaraj*, the repudiator of scientific and technological progress and "Western-style" industrial development. In *Hind Swaraj*, a short book that he wrote in 1909, Gandhi lays out a vision that is remarkably similar to the pretechnological pastoral vision of the alternative food movement, as the following quote regarding Western civilization demonstrates:

> [On Western civilization] Let us first consider what state of things is described by the word "civilization." ... Formerly, in Europe, people ploughed their lands mainly by manual labor. Now, one man can plough a vast tract by means of steam engines and can thus amass great wealth. This is called a sign of civilization. Formerly, only a few men wrote valuable books. Now, anybody writes and prints anything he likes and poisons people's minds.... This civilization takes note neither of morality nor of religion.... This civilization is irreligion.... This civilization is such that one has only to be patient and it will be self-destroyed.
>
> (Gandhi 1938, 29–30)

Gandhi had similar things to say regarding education:

> If we consider our civilization to be the highest, I have regretfully to say that much of the effort [for universal primary education for boys]... is of no use. .... To teach boys reading, writing and arithmetic is called primary education. A peasant earns his bread honestly. He has ordinary knowledge of the world. He knows fairly well how he should behave towards his parents, his wife, his children and his fellow villagers. He understands and observes the rules of morality. But he cannot write his own name. What do you propose to do by giving him knowledge of letters? Will you add an inch to his happiness? Do you wish to make him discontented with his cottage or his lot?
>
> (Gandhi 1938, 60)

In spite of Gandhi's iconic status in India, his *Hind Swaraj* worldview was never widely accepted. In 1945, Jawaharlal Nehru (who was to become independent India's first prime minister) wrote to Gandhi, saying, "it is many years since I read *Hind Swaraj*... but even when I read it twenty years ago it seemed to me completely unreal" (Rudolph and Rudolph 2006, 25).

Babasaheb Ambedkar

Among those that did not share Gandhi's *Hind Swaraj* worldview were the leaders of the downtrodden and the underprivileged, particularly those who represented the lower castes in India's hierarchical and hereditary caste system. One of the most important critiques of Gandhi's *Hind Swaraj* worldview came from Babasaheb Ambedkar, one of modern India's most important thinkers and leaders.

Bhimrao Ramji "Babasaheb" Ambedkar was born in 1891 to a family of untouchables, who were (and are) at the very bottom of India's caste system. With his father serving in the Army, young Bhimrao got a rare opportunity to acquire a modern education. He eventually earned doctorate degrees from Columbia University in the United States and from the London School of Economics in England, and he qualified as a barrister in London. Ambedkar went on to become an important political figure in India and an inspiring leader of the untouchables. Today, Ambedkar and his ideas are held in great esteem by the Dalit movement (former untouchables now call themselves "Dalits," which means "oppressed").

Ambedkar spent three years (1913–1916) at Columbia University in New York City—three years that played a crucial role in his intellectual development. He later recounted that it was at Columbia that he experienced social equality for the first time in his life, and that "the best friends I have had in my life were some of my classmates at Columbia and my great professors, John Dewey, James Shotwell, Edwin Seligman, and James Harvey Robinson" (quoted in Pritchett 2013). Especially influential was John Dewey, an intellectual giant of the American progressive era. Ambedkar, like Dewey, held that reason and science had the potential—for all people everywhere—to challenge unexamined tradition and prejudices by cultivating a collective, democratic "will to inquire, to examine, to discriminate, to draw conclusions only on the basis of evidence after taking pains to gather all available evidence" (quoted in Nanda 2003, 183). Ambedkar saw scientific and technological progress as fundamentally emancipatory for the oppressed, and the traditional rural socioeconomic order in India as fundamentally exploitative of the lower castes—a vision that was almost diametrically opposed to Gandhi's *Hind Swaraj* worldview.

A comparison of the words of Gandhi and Ambedkar demonstrates how much their views of "civilization" differed from one another. Gandhi expressed his view in *Hind Swaraj*:

> Civilization is that mode of conduct which points out to man the path of duty. Performance of duty and observance of morality are convertible terms. To observe morality is to attain mastery over our mind and our passions. So doing, we know ourselves. The Gujarati equivalent for civilization means "good conduct." If this definition be correct, then India . . . has nothing to learn from anybody else. . . . We notice that the mind is a restless bird; the more it gets the more it wants, and still remains unsatisfied. The more we indulge our passions the more unbridled they become. Our ancestors therefore set a limit to our indulgences. They saw that happiness was largely a mental condition. A man is not necessarily happy because he is rich or unhappy because he is poor. . . . . Millions will always remain poor. Observing all this,

> our ancestors dissuaded us from luxuries and pleasures. We have managed with the same kind of plough as existed thousands of years ago. We have retained the same kind of cottages that we had in former times and our indigenous education remains the same as before. We have had no system of life-corroding competition. Each followed his own occupation or trade and charged a regulation wage.
>
> (Gandhi 1938, 45)

Ambedkar, in contrast, provides a very different view:

> In Gandhism, the common man has no hope. It treats man as an animal and no more. It is true that man shares the constitution and functions of animals, nutritive, reproductive, etc. But these are not distinctively human functions. The distinctively human function is reason, the purpose of which is to enable man to observe, meditate, cogitate, study and discover the beauties of the Universe and enrich his life.... The conclusion that follows is that... the ultimate goal of man's existence is not reached unless and until he has fully cultivated his mind.... How then can a life of culture be made possible? It is not possible unless there is sufficient leisure.... The problem of all problems which human society has to face is how to provide leisure to every individual.... Leisure means the lessening of the toil and effort necessary for satisfying the physical wants of life.... Leisure is quite impossible unless some means are found whereby the toil required for producing goods necessary to satisfy human needs is lessened. What can lessen such toil? Only when machines take the place of man.... Machinery and modern civilization are thus indispensable for emancipating man from leading the life of a brute, and for providing him with leisure and making a life of culture possible.... A democratic society must assure a life of leisure and culture to each one of its citizens.... The slogan of a democratic society must be machinery, and more machinery, civilization and more civilization.
>
> (Ambedkar 2002, 158)

Questioning Development and Progress in the West

The alternative food movement is deeply suspicions of the entire paradigm of development and progress, which it sees as deeply flawed, a mark of human hubris and a futile and ultimately calamitous enterprise that violates nature's limits and is bound to invite nature's wrath. Going beyond the alternative food movement, this kind of thinking has had a major influence on the broader intellectual and political milieu in the industrialized West in recent years, and it has also problematized notions of development and progress, particularly for those who think of themselves as liberals and progressives.

Liberals and progressives in the West have long viewed development and scientific and technological progress as forces for good, essential for making available the practical means necessary to achieve their desired emancipatory goals. Convinced of the necessity and the desirability of progress, they were long suspicious of attempts to privilege traditional norms and practices as "natural" or "God ordained," viewing such efforts as conservative attempts to present socially unjust practices and traditional inequalities as unchangeable and therefore outside the purview of human questioning or improvement. This long cherished progressive outlook has in recent years been challenged by the very different social vision of the alternative food movement and allied ideological groups. Inevitably, this has given rise to a certain amount of tension in progressive thinking between emancipatory goals and the alternative food movement's desire to protect traditional norms and practices from the onslaught of progress and "Promethean science." A real world example from California serves to illustrate this tension.

In California, farm workers' unions and their allies have long sought to restrict "stoop labor," where farm workers work bent at the waist for hours at a time. Stoop labor is widely recognized one of the most painful forms of manual labor, which, according to the California Supreme Court, causes "abnormal degeneration of the spine, resulting in irreparable back injury and permanent disability" (Getz, Brown, and Shreck 2008). According to one study, 60 percent of all acute injuries suffered by farm workers were musculoskeletal injuries, with most affecting the lower back. In comparison, exposure to agrochemicals caused approximately 1 percent of serious injuries (Getz, Brown, and Shreck 2008). While some forms of stoop labor have been banned, the practice continues to this day in California, primarily in the form of hand weeding carried out by farm workers. A campaign by farm workers' advocates in California to reduce stoop labor culminated in the introduction in the California legislature of Senate Bill (SB) 534 in 2003, which sought to restrict hand weeding. Backed by farm workers and their unions, SB 534 ran into intense opposition from the organic farming sector. Organic groups denounced SB 534 as a bill "that Monsanto would have been proud to sponsor," which was designed to "get rid of hand weeding," and sent a message that you have to "spray everything . . . genetically modify everything . . . or move it out of California" (Getz, Brown, and Shreck 2008). Largely due to the opposition of organic farming groups, SB 534 failed to get the approval of the California legislature.

The political tussle over SB 534 demonstrates how the alternative food movement's goals of promoting traditional farming techniques, staying within "natural" limits and reducing our dependence on "Promethean science" can diverge sharply from the emancipatory goals of progressive political ideology.

References

Ambedkar, B. R. 2002. "Gandhism: The Doom of the Untouchables." In *The Essential Writings of B.R. Ambedkar*, edited by Valerian Rodrigues. New Delhi: Oxford University Press.

Beer, J. 2007. "Wendell Berry and the Traditionalist Critique of Meriticracy." In *Wendell Berry: Life and Work*, edited by Jason Peters, 212–229. Lexington: University Press of Kentucky.

Berry, W. 1982a. "An Agricultural Journey in Peru." In *The Gift of Good Land: Further Essays, Cultural and Agricultural*, 3–46. New York: North Point Press.

——. 1982b. "The Gift of Good Land." In *The Gift of Good Land: Further Essays, Cultural and Agricultural*. New York: North Point Press.
——. 1989. *The Hidden Wound*. New York: North Point Press.
——. 1993. "The Problem of Tobacco." In *Sex, Economy, Freedom, and Community: Eight Essays*. New York: Pantheon Books.
——. 2001. *Life is a Miracle: An Essay against Modern Superstition*. Washington, DC: Counterpoint.
——. 2002a. "The Body and the Earth." In *The Art of the Commonplace: Agrarian Essays of Wendell Berry*, edited by Norman Wirzba, 93–134. Washington, DC: Counterpoint.
——. 2002b. "Sex, Economy, Freedom, and Community." In *The Art of the Commonplace: Agrarian Essays of Wendell Berry*, edited by Norman Wirzba, 159–181. Washington, DC: Counterpoint.
——. 2002c. "Men and Women in Search of Common Ground." In *The Art of the Commonplace: Agrarian Essays of Wendell Berry*, edited by Norman Wirzba, 135–143. Washington, DC: Counterpoint.
——. 2004a. "Pray Without Ceasing." In *That Distant Land: The Collected Stories*, 38–76. Washington, DC: Shoemaker and Hoard.
——. 2004b. "The Wild Birds." in *That Distant Land: The Collected Stories*, 337–364. Washington, DC: Shoemaker and Hoard.
Briggs, S. A. 1987. "Rachel Carson: Her Vision and Her Legacy." In *Silent Spring Revisited*, edited by Gino Marco, Robert Hollingworth, and William Durham. Washingtion, DC: American Chemical Society.
Carson, R. (1962) 2002. *Silent Spring* New York: Mariner Books.
Charles, D. 2002. *Lords of the Harvest: Biotech, Big Money, and the Future of Food*. Cambridge, MA: Perseus.
Ehrlich, P. 1971. *The Population Bomb*. Cutchogue, NY: Buccaneer Books.
Gandhi, M. K. 1938. *Hind Swaraj*. English translation of original 1919 Gujarati edition. Ahmedabad: Navajivan Publishing House. http://tinyurl.com/GandhiHindSwaraj.
Getz, C., S. Brown, and A. Shreck. 2008. "Class Politics and Agricultural Exceptionalism in California's Organic Agriculture Movement." *Politics and Society* 36 (4): 478–507.
Habib, I. 1999. *The Agrarian System of Mughal India 1556–1707*. New Delhi: Oxford University Press.
Holley, D. 2000. *The Second Great Emancipation: The Mechanical Cotton Picker, Black Migration, and How They Shaped the Modern South*. Fayetteville: University of Arkansas Press.
"John Muir." 2013. *Wikipedia*. Accessed June 17. http://en.wikipedia.org/wiki/John_Muir.
Lear, L. 1997. *Rachel Carson: Witness for Nature*. New York: Houghton Mifflin Harcourt.
"List of Countries by Life Expectancy." 2013. *Wikipedia*. Accessed June 17. http://en.wikipedia.org/wiki/List_of_countries_by_life_expectancy.
Lomborg, B. 2001. *The Skeptical Environmentalist*. Cambridge: Cambridge University Press.
Mies, M., and V. Shiva. 1993. *Ecofeminism*. New York: St. Martin's.
Nanda, M. 2003. *Prophets Facing Backwards: Postmodern Critiques of Science and Hindu Nationalism in India*. New Brunswick, NJ: Rutgers University Press.
Omvedt, G. 1998. "Terminating Choice." *The Hindu*, December 14.
Peters, J. 2007a. "Education, Heresy, and the 'Deadly Disease of the World.'" In *Wendell Berry: Life and Work*, edited by J. Peters, 256–281. Lexington: University Press of Kentucky.

——. 2007b. "Introduction." In *Wendell Berry: Life and Work*, edited by J. Peters, 1–11. Lexington: University Press of Kentucky.

Pollan, M. 2006. *The Omnivore's Dilemma: A Natural History of Four Meals*. New York: Penguin.

——. 2009. Introduction to *Bringing it to the Table: On Farming and Food*, by W. Berry, ix–xvi. Berkeley, CA: Counterpoint.

Pritchett, F. 2013. "Dr. Ambedkar's Life—and Beyond: In the 1910s: Off to Columbia, and on to London." Accessed June 17. http://www.columbia.edu/itc/mealac/pritchett/00ambedkar/timeline/1910s.html.

The Right Livelihood Award. 1993. "Laureates: Vandana Shiva." http://www.rightlivelihood.org/v-shiva.html.

Rudolph, L. I., and S. H. Rudolph. 2006. *Postmodern Gandhi and Other Essays*. Chicago: University of Chicago Press.

Shiva, V. 1989. *Staying Alive: Women, Ecology and Development*. London: Zed Books.

Smith, K. 2003. *Wendell Berry and the Agrarian Tradition: A Common Grace*. Lawrence: University Press of Kansas.

United Nations 2006. *World Population Prospects: The 2006 Revision—Highlights*. New York: United Nations. http://www.un.org/esa/population/publications/wpp2006/WPP2006_Highlights_rev.pdf.

Wilkerson, I. 2010. *The Warmth of Other Suns: The Epic Story of America's Great Migration*. New York: Random House.

PART IV

FOOD VALUES: IDEAS, INTERESTS, AND CULTURE

CHAPTER 22

FOOD VALUES BEYOND NUTRITION

ANN GRODZINS GOLD

INTRODUCTION

This whole world is nothing but food!

(*Bṛhadāraṇyaka Upaniṣad*, Olivelle, transl. 1996:11)

Food, food, brahman is food: / only they eat / who know / they eat their god.

(*Taittiriya Upaniṣad*, Ramanujan, transl. 2009: 3)

Like the ancient Hindu seers, cultural anthropologists have an expansive understanding of food as a "many-splendored thing" (Counihan 1999: 6).[1] This chapter first invokes selected ways anthropologists portray food's links to wide realms of meaning. It then hastens to an ethnographic location in rural North India to examine three pervasive themes surrounding food in South Asian culture: solidarity, separation, and decline as a pervasive critique of modern tastelessness. Offering initially grounded examples of each theme, the essay moves to broader circles of meanings in practice and narrative. Thus deliberately tacking back and forth between spacious generalities and local specificities, this chapter employs a classical interpretive mode in cultural anthropology (Geertz 1973). In the context of a volume largely and properly focused on food materialities, the aim here is simply to evoke some less concrete, less quantifiable aspects of comestibles in human cultures that may be nonetheless relevant to understanding the interrelated workings of food, politics, and society.

BEYOND NUTRITION

To eat is a behavior that develops beyond its own ends, replacing, summing up, and signalizing other behaviors, and it is precisely for these reasons that it is a sign.

(Barthes 1997 [1961]: 25)

Cultural anthropologists are expressly interested in the ways that food, as Barthes (or more accurately his translator) puts it, "signalizes" other behaviors. Barthes, of course, was not himself an anthropologist, but his semiology, along with other linguistic and literary theories of meaning, had an enduring impact on anthropological analyses from the 1960s. We study food's "messages," the affects it carries, the ways its uses may organize many other aspects of human existence within diverse cultural worlds.[2] Such messages and affects are manifold; they may be obvious or subtle, banal or extraordinary, domestic or cosmological. Deeply linked to food in any given setting are myriad elements of behavior and emotion that would not necessarily have anything to do with caloric intake. Food meanings and metaphors can be bland as vanilla pudding or rich, mysterious, and complex as a Mexican mole. They may reach no deeper than pocketbooks, or they may suffuse hearts and souls.

The anthropology of food looks at all the ways food is more than food and its interpretative strategies are not limited to semiotics, but range through various notions of symbolism and representation; metaphor and synecdoche. Counihan (1999) writes about "bread as world" in Sardinia and tortillas "like life" in the San Luis Valley of Colorado (2009). Ohniko-Tierney addresses "rice as self" in Japan (1993). Food is cosmos and divinity. Food is identity, memory, and locality. Food is emotion, relationships, and sex, and is, needless to say, deeply intertwined with kinship ideals and gender roles. Food is gift, offering, rank, commerce, and usury. Food is agency and power.[3] Because there are very few humans who do not engage with food every day of their lives, there is simply no limit to contexts in which we can regard food as a substance on which, with which, and through which humans exist, whether its uses are festive or everyday, sacred or profane, benign or cruel. In many cultures, the dead do not cease to demand and consume food. Deliberate abstinence from food is a well-refined technology of power that has been deployed through history both to spiritual and political ends.

Textbooks on the anthropology of food may begin, as does Anderson's *Everyone Eats* (2005), with facts about nutrition, but they rapidly move on to a panoply of food-related topics including pleasure, medicine, religion and ethnicity. Others, such as the retrospective reader *Food and Culture* (Counihan and Van Esterik 1997), plunge head first into the vastness of food meanings, and then turn to organize these into collective aspects of food and eating, such as commensality, ethnicity and more individual aspects such as body image and fasting practices. Interestingly, in spite of their very different organizational modes, both these books, published in 2005 and 1997, respectively, conclude by focusing on hunger as a manifestation and consequence of inequities both national and global.

By making the link between food, culture, and endemic world hunger, such anthropological approaches lead readers to face what most residents of relatively prosperous nations know but normally refuse to contemplate on a regular basis: that some people are starving while others have more food than they need and even more than is good for their health. Still more disturbing is that there are structural reasons for this inequity that might be remedied if it were possible to implement a transnational food morality. Folk culture in many societies supports such morality, as the discussion of Indian food values, which follows, will exemplify. Market forces do not.[4]

Notoriously dependent on the kindness of strangers, anthropologists whose methodologies rely on intimacy and participation normally learn to eat as do the people with whom they live and who are the subjects of their studies. Thus, no ethnographer can fail to notice food, no matter what their research focus may be. Everyday processes of learning and consuming involve not just etiquette, taste, and cost, but often kinship, ritual practice, and kitchen skills however rudimentary.[5] My breakthrough moment came on a return visit in 1997 to a home where I had dined occasionally since 1979 and where I had recently resided for several months. While living in the heart of this household, I had never been invited to do more by way of food preparation than to join the very young children assigned to peel garlic, and I never volunteered to help in the kitchen due to an overly acute awareness of Hindu sensitivities absorbed more from books than observations.

As it happened, my arrival in the summer of 1997 coincided with preparations for a ritual celebrating the birth just a few days earlier of a new baby boy. Relatives from other villages had assembled, and the small household was in some turmoil—to which the arrival of my own family had certainly contributed. I was squatting uselessly near the open-air cooking hearth on the roof, where the household's senior female, Raji the paternal grandmother, was attending to the preparation of lapsi (a cracked wheat porridge sweetened with unrefined brown sugar). Abruptly she thrust the large spoon into my hand and ordered me to keep stirring the vigorously boiling pot, while she rushed downstairs to organize some other aspect of the busy day. Briefly alone, I stirred diligently with an amazed sense of responsibility and gratification. I knew this sweet dish entrusted to my inexperienced hands would be offered to the ancestral spirits. It must, therefore, be the case that Raji did not think of me as a polluted and incompetent barbarian. Although I had always touched her feet and received her blessing when arriving and departing, I never felt her true acceptance and my genuine incorporation, until this moment. With this personal recollection of cooking as kinship, we arrive in the North Indian village from which I draw my ethnographic sustenance.

Sketches from Rajasthan

> One main message of food, everywhere, is *solidarity*. Eating together means sharing and participating.... The other main message is *separation*. Food marks social class, ethnicity, and so on.
>
> (Anderson 2005, 125)

> ... food, in its temporal, spatial, corporeal, sensual, affective, discursive, and moral transactions with all kinds of others evokes a sense of place.
>
> (Janeja 2010, 2)

The examples that follow emerge from three decades of intermittent and varied research in rural north India where I have never specifically conducted fieldwork on food. I selected these examples in order to show some signal (and signalizing) uses of, and ideas about, food as it intersects with meanings and values within a particular social and cultural setting. Each of my small first-hand observations I easily locate in a large body of regional scholarship that corroborates and elaborates on the themes I seek to highlight. Thirty years ago Appadurai's (1981) explication of "gastro-politics" in India vividly demonstrated food's dual capacities—to construct intimacy and to sustain distance—and his observations remain pertinent today. To imbue food quality and usage with moral implications has ancient roots in South Asia, including some textual sources preceding the Common Era.[6]

The first example treats sharing of food: *solidarity*—the imperatives of hospitality as redistribution. Such imperatives are not only acted on in the everyday but, also, strongly affirmed in a plethora of moralizing tales that repeatedly portray greed and selfishness regarding food as being punished, whereas generosity is amply rewarded. The second sketch, separation, exemplifies the ways foods index social status and create invidious distinctions on which people may reflect from various positions in society. Here a semiotic of class, health, and modernity emerges from local evaluations and poetics of different grain foods. Third, I present a diffuse rural discourse on ecological and moral deteriorations: *decline* examines a critique of flavor or tastelessness in modern times, associated with transformations in agricultural practice as well as human relationships.

Solidarity

If I think back to my life in Ghatiyali, a North Indian village where I lived as an anthropologist for about 17 consecutive months in 1980–1981, returning for numerous briefer sojourns over what is now almost three decades, I am certain that the conversation I have had most often, with the most people, follows a thoroughly predictable pattern. As I walk past their open courtyard, someone calls out:

> O, Ainn-bai, have you eaten?
> Yes, I have eaten. [I learn to say this properly in an upbeat and cheerful way, not as if it were a monotonous convention, but rather a delightful affirmation.]
> Which vegetable did you eat today?
> I had spinach with tomatoes [or whatever the case may be].

At this juncture there are two alternatives. My interlocutor may say, "Good!" and the topic is closed; we speak of other matters or I continue on my way. However, far more often, especially if there is smoke rising from the cooking hearth in their home, the response is: "Come, eat some more!" This invitation is delivered with genuine fervor, and although the person offering it doubtless expects it to be declined, they will press me nonetheless: "Bread is cooking! Come and eat more."

Uttered at appropriate times of day, "Have you eaten?" often seemed to me to be more or less a meaningless interrogative greeting equivalent to "How are you?" or "How's it going?"[7] After all (this being a village), neighbors already knew when I ate, and likely even what vegetables had been purchased that day by the family with whom I resided. From my position of well-fed foreign advantage, I saw the perpetual offers of food as an almost bothersome aspect of traditional village hospitality. However, a reconsideration of this everyday exchange shows the ways food is used to express solidarity and enact morality.

In this drought-prone region, regular meals were not necessarily always enjoyed by one and all, year round; historically, the greeting, "have you eaten?" could be more than a convention of speech. Moreover, redistribution or an ideal sharing of food is an indication of cosmic well-being as well as a righteous (versus demonic) social order. The former unjust pre-1947 ruler of this area and his agents were consistently lambasted in local collective memories (evoked when I was gathering regional oral histories) for not opening their grain stores in time of famine, as virtuous kings charged with protection of the public ought to do (Gold and Gujar 2002).

Countless South Asian folktales condemn selfishness with regard to food. In the storyteller's world of divinities who walk on earth and test human kindness, simple, impulsive generosity with the most meager homely fare is rewarded with gold and jewels. One tale I recorded first in 1987, and again from three other tellers in 2007—the "Generous Potter and his Stingy Wife"—tells of a woman who refuses to continue making bread for two wandering holy persons after they outstay their welcome. Her husband admonishes her in these strong words:

> We have plenty of grain: this is Lord Shankar's own storehouse. Lord Shankar gives us all the wealth we possess, so for you to give a couple of pieces of bread, what trouble is that to you?

When the wife adamantly refuses to supply food to the lingering saints, her husband simply shares his own meager meal with them, willingly going hungry night after night. Ultimately the generous man is rewarded when the powerful holy persons turn his half of the pots in the kiln to pure gold, leaving his wife's clay (Gold 2012a). The definition of all food as belonging to "Lord Shankar's own storehouse," that is, as generically a blessing from God and *never* the sole result of individual effort, is a powerful charter for prescriptive sharing.

Another tale of simple-hearted largesse with simple fare is the story of Shakat, a woman's ritual tale with a narrative pattern known widely throughout North India. Here a guileless impoverished woman gives gruel and extraordinary hospitality freely to a deity in disguise. She is richly rewarded. When a better-off sister-in-law (or neighbor) sees the poor woman's boons and tries to replicate the exchange by offering the same meager food to the same deity, her reward is literal excrement (e.g.: Wadley 1986). The acquisitive woman's fault was double: first, this imitator gave poor food when she might have afforded better; second, she acted with crude expectations of profiting from her fundamentally hypocritical generosity. Shit was her just desserts.

Although stories such as these speak of rewards in this life, both generosity and stinginess with food have consequences after death as well in narrative traditions. A. K. Ramanujan concludes his lovely assemblage of South Asian food ideas, "Food for Thought," with a folktale from Karnataka about the imperative for food generosity, the moral of which is a reflection on such behavior's impact from birth to birth: "Because I gave you some food, I've been reborn now as a king's son. My wife refused to part with her food, and do you know where she is? She has been reborn in this very town as a pig" (2009, 25).

In the folktale "Heaven and Hell," which Kirin Narayan recorded from a living guru and tracked through many nations' folklore, the powerful moral is the necessity to feed others, to which there is no alternative but to suffer starvation. In this tale, hell is a place of starvation because its captives cannot bend their arms to feed themselves the delicacies they can see and smell. In heaven, with arms equally stiff, souls feed one another delectable morsels. Swamiji, the teacher on whom Narayan's book focuses, explicated the story's message: "The soul sits in the body of all creatures, and the body needs food. Give food. Do something for another soul. You will be serving and nourishing the soul" (1989, 203). The guru advises that the self is sustained through serving others; but, as in the tale of Shakat, one's motives cannot be (forgive the minor word play) self-serving,as is so beautifully embodied in the image of stiff arms.

To share food willingly out of pure and selfless love is a practice most highly valued in Hindu devotional traditions. These often emphasize that such love radically obliterates all concerns of ritual purity. The paradigmatic moment for this realization is the story—firmly attached in popular imagination to classical *Ramayana* tales, although textually apocryphal—in which Lord Rama accepts the berries offered by a poor tribal woman, named Shabari or Shavari. She has bitten each berry to make sure she gives God only the sweetest (Lutgendorf 2000). The power of Rama's recognition of Shabari's pure and purifying devotion, of his grace-giving consumption of her half-eaten offering, is rooted in Hindu notions of the ways saliva ordinarily generates pollution.

Separation

Generations of anthropologists have meticulously attended to the multitude of complex ways people in India give, accept, and refuse food in order to enact social and ritual hierarchies of caste and gender. Anthropologists, particularly in the 1950s–1980s, were fascinated by the rules of purity and pollution as they affected commensality, and by "Hindu transactions," which could serve not just to maintain a status quo but also to alter it through deliberate collective decisions about eating practices. Ethnographers extensively documented rankings negotiated via food.[8]

Village life affords countless opportunities to observe in action how rules of commensality, of purity and pollution, are both upheld and broken. Rather than offer further examples of a domain so well documented, I exemplify food's work of separation by turning to the words of a village poet. His verses show succinctly how producers and eaters understand delicate but deep distinctions of class that are embedded in consumption. These couplets offer a kind of "ethnosociology" (Marriott, ed. 1990).

In 1993 Ugma Mali, a middle-aged man of the gardening community, recited for me eight verses he himself had composed in the voices of different foods, mostly grains. In his oral compositions, grains speak of their own attributes. These are not idiosyncratic but, rather, poetic versions of common perceptions I heard expressed in many prosaic interviews. I offer three examples of Ugma's couplets, each highlighting the ways grain preparation and consumption index other elements of social status and life, condensing ideas about class, bodies, and work.

> Barley says: "My husk is hard, so pound me with the pestle to bare my head
> Grind me fine and sift me twice and my worth is twice all other grains."

Barley is hard to prepare; it is difficult to grind and requires double sifting. Its nutrition is double what other grains possess. The couplet's meaning is also double, I'm told. On the one hand the double effort required to prepare barley yields double nourishment; on the other hand, in modern times, as I was frequently advised, "no one" eats barley. This is partly because it is viewed as a low-class food, perhaps precisely because it gave people strength for hard labor. But the other reason that barley is no longer much consumed is because modern people lack the "digestive power" to benefit from its superior nutrients. This kind of causal circularity is indicative of the situation of village eaters in modern times.

Rajasthanis in this particular region think of corn bread—round, unleavened—as their most indigenous, down-home grain food. They staunchly argued against my assertion that corn was indigenous to my native land. This was inconceivable to Rajasthanis in the Banas Basin region. Cornbread is part of regional identity, and here is what Ugma Mali's corn claims:

> Corn says: "I wear a braid!
> Should you wish to relish me
> You must own a healthy buffalo."

This couplet is nostalgic for a flavorful and rich remembered diet, linked to more generalized health and eating pleasures ascribed to days gone by (possibly viewed through rose-tinted lenses). In this relished past, there were more dairy animals because there was more grazing land. Moreover, more dairy products were consumed in the village, rather than exported to town in exchange for cash as they are today. Most delectable in the winter, corn bread should be eaten warm with yogurt and a nice big lump of brown sugar—a highly satisfying meal (to which I may personally testify). The buffalo is necessary to provide the rich yogurt without which, people say, corn bread cannot be properly enjoyed. This couplet reflects an ideal for farmers who have prospered in traditional terms.

I always had to testify with extreme enthusiasm to my genuine passion for cornbread. People who happily consumed cornbread in their own diets made the false assumption that a foreigner such as myself would, by nature, prefer wheat. Once I actually convinced someone that I too genuinely enjoyed this thick country bread, they would discuss this predilection approvingly. Liking cornbread said something about who I was in relation to who they were. Although my wearing of locally made lakh bangles evoked similar commentary, people knew I might take them off in the United States; food consumed creates a more enduring self and bond.

Contrast the boasts of barley about nutrition; and of corn about pleasure, with the words of wheat, which are all about class:

> Wheat says: "My belly's grooved, and the great big merchant eats me."

In other words, wheat brags neither of its nutritional prowess, nor its tastiness, but rather of the social status of its eater: the proverbially fat shopkeeper who does no physical labor. Today almost everyone eats wheat, and the shift from cultivating barley and millet to wheat is emblematic in rural Rajasthan of both agricultural and social change. However, wheat itself is hardly a monolithic category; there are many varieties of wheat. The hybrid seeds promoted by government agents and requiring five waterings have seductive names like Golden Well-Being. These contrast with indigenous wheat—often just called local or red—that may be grown like barley on unirrigated land. Red wheat is treasured by the elderly for its special taste, texture, color, and healthful qualities; but it is less-often sown, and in ever-smaller amounts—only for home consumption, only in those rare households willing to sacrifice profit to nostalgia, as I will discuss in the next section.

In Ugma Mali's couplets, the three grains—barley, corn and wheat—signify multidimensional differences in class, in labor, in sense of self. A prosperous farmer might prefer corn bread, whereas a merchant would choose wheat, even if both eaters measured up equally according to their economic means. Poor day-laborers may well eat bread made of barley and, simultaneously, value the stamina it supplies while they remain sensitive to the lower-class identity they consume along with it. Such reflections on food and self, on the substances from which identities are made and altered, may be just as revealing of subtle social distinctions as a record of who eats at whose feasts.

Indian literature, questioning society's strictures, also plays brilliantly on themes of food, class, and gender. In Premchand's classic wrenching tale, the "Price of Milk" (1969), the orphaned son of an untouchable wet nurse to a landlord's child is driven by hunger to accept scorn along with leftovers, even though he is acutely aware that his own mother's milk nourished the healthy boy who now abuses him (1969). Premchand shows the ways that untouchability is malleable in the service of privilege. When the boy needed her milk to survive, an untouchable woman's feeding him, and her intimate proximity, carried no pollution, lowering neither his ritual nor his social status.

In a very different context and era, Gita Hariharan's much anthologized, "Remains of the Feast," portrays an educated granddaughter who complies with a dying widow's tragicomic demands for sweet and spicy foods denied her during long years of the ascetic regime rigidly prescribed for widows (1997). Both fictions in different ways deconstruct ideologies of separation imposed by rigid food rules to highlight hypocrisy and oppression on the one hand, and individual emotions and resistance on the other.[9]

Decline or the Tastelessness of Modernity[10]

During several research periods in India (1993, 1997, 2003) I recorded extensive open-ended interviews with farmers, herders, and artisans—most of them over 50—asking them to reflect on many aspects of changing times. One theme that frequently emerged was decline in food quality, a decline with multiple causalities, unanimously pronounced, and applied both to flavor and to nourishment. Many expressed a sincere preference for bread made with grains grown with organic manure and ground by hand. They regularly critiqued both the taste and healthfulness of new grain varieties grown with chemical fertilizer and ground in the power mill, yet these latter were their daily fare with few exceptions.

These interviews from the 1990s and early 2000s revealed the ways a shared assessment of decline in flavor and nutrition in everyday food was embedded in broader narratives of ecological and community deterioration. Thus, the loss of flavor resulting from transformed technologies and ongoing economic pressures meshes with many other aspects of the ways food bears meaning and emotion, and transacts the social order—both its moral solidarity and its hierarchical discriminations.

To demonstrate these pervasive ideas, I present here thoughtful reflections from a few persons who experienced, in their own lives and households, the pressures of expanded desire for cash and all it can purchase; not just things but also futures for children. They clearly posit trade-offs of flavor for money and associate these with other still-less-tangible shifts and losses. These speakers are unaware of how thoroughly the processes they identify and critique have already been discussed by social theorists addressing the "great transformation" from moral to market economies—a transformation that lies close to the core and heart of modernity experienced as conjoined material and moral change.[11] However, they are acutely and critically aware of a complex, intimate set of consequences affecting their everyday existence.

In one conversation from 2003, an educated farmer, Sohan Lal, speaks about why the need to increase crop production leading to cash trumps outright any inclination to grow foods that are less profitable but more flavorful, even for home consumption. His mother, Kesar, plaintively asserts her strong preference for indigenous wheat known as *deshi gehu* (local wheat), or *lal gehu* (red wheat). As noted in the previous section, indigenous wheat has just about vanished from this region. Although it requires far less water than modern wheat varieties, and might be life-saving in drought years, its yield is not profitable. Kesar says, "I would like to plant indigenous wheat, but he [Sohan Lal] doesn't let me plant it. He says [to me], 'who is even smelling this wheat?' [meaning there is no value to it, nobody bothers with it]."

A little embarrassed, her son, a school headmaster and a successful and knowledgeable agriculturalist, commented defensively, "Red wheat's production is very small." My colleague, Bhoju Ram Gujar, an old friend of the household, then provocatively addressed his fellow teacher, Sohan Lal: "She is thinking you should grow some to eat in your home." Sohan Lal's rebuttal resorted to a generalized position: "Today people pay more attention to earning money than they do to eating."

Bhoju continued to push or even needle Sohan Lal, as this three-way exchange followed:

Bhoju: If someone gave you some money would you sell the clothes you are wearing and the food you are eating?

Sohan Lal: Yes I can sell them, we might even sell our bread for money.

Bhoju [ADDRESSING KESAR]: It seems to me that in your family are two ways of thinking: old-time thought, which is to eat good things and local things. And new thought, like your son's. He thinks about earning money. Which do you like?

Kesar: Eat well, and don't worry about money. Who needs money? We need good food.

The divergence of viewpoints between mother and son is absolute.

We had other conversations with Sohan Lal in which he actually agreed fully that indigenous wheat tastes better and asserted that chemical fertilizers and hybrid crops with their demands for additional irrigation are dangerously depleting and damaging the land's two most vital natural resources—soil and water. In other words, Sohan Lal identified the very agricultural practices he embraced as unsustainable, and, in truth, agreed with his mother on everything except the necessary course of action. In his view, he has no choice but to pursue profit at the expense of all else. What drives him, however, is not amoral greed but a sense of responsibility to provide a younger generation opportunities that only money can buy—a classic double bind.

In 2009 in India, eggplant, commonly called *brinjal* in Indian English, became the center of stormy controversy due to a new genetically modified variety approved by the government for cultivation and consumption, an approval later retracted under pressure from opposing activists.[12] At the time of my 2003 research, eggplant was already a local food symbolic of changing times. As I read about the eggplant protests in December 2009, I developed retrospective understanding of eggplant's significance as a relished, filling, traditional, and humble vegetable.

During my winter 2003 research, talk about modern brinjal's lack of tastiness carried with it a subtle but perceptible moral evaluation. I had many conversations in January 2003 about two species of brinjal, one readily visible and one largely invisible. The latter scarce item is "*deshi*" brinjal, literally "of the land," implying local and indigenous. *Deshi* brinjals are whitish in color, and the vine on which they grow has annoying thorns on it, but everyone with whom I spoke asserted that this variety was the most delicious. Nonetheless, the widely prevalent species nowadays is called *disko*: it is small, shapely, perfectly purple, its stem free of unpleasant prickles, but people say it lacks in taste. *Disko* is not only easier to cultivate, but also sells better.

Barji Mali, a gardener woman, was among several who told us, "There used to be local brinjal (*deshi bangan*). We used to grow it, but now we have modern (*adhunik*) brinjal, called '*Disko*.' Now, *Disko* is available." Shambhu Nath, an educated villager in his 40s who has worked with me on and off over the years, immediately chimed in to emphasize a contrast in flavor: "The local brinjal was tasty, but it had prickles on it. It was really delicious, but the *Disko* has no flavor. Even today, the local is available in the market but it costs more than *Disko*." He then gave an elaborate recipe for what he said was the best way to cook deshi—stuffed with spices after roasting. Nostalgia for the tasty past is invested in the white variety that has shifted from staple to luxury, and it is now presumably cultivated by a few for sale to the well-to-do in town markets rather than village lanes.

This contrast between the pervasive, modern, shiny, purple, attractive *disko* and the indigenous variety—white, prickly, flavorful but no longer consumed—captures much about nostalgia for a past that people do not necessarily strive to reclaim. Pleasures such as the taste of white brinjal, roasted and spiced as Shambhu recalled it, are missed but deemed irretrievable. This seems to echo Sohan Lal's acknowledgement of the genuinely superior flavor of wheat he refuses to plant. There is additional symbolism in the *disko*/*deshi* contrast and the psychology of loss it evokes. Tasteless modernity is perfectly embodied in the shiny purple tasteless brinjal, named after an emblem of urban amorality—disco dancing.

Assessments of deterioration of flavor and morality have been documented elsewhere in India and the world. Other research finds farmers reflectively critical in their decisions to adapt agricultural technologies (Witcombe, Virk, and Farrington 1998); they are nostalgic for flavors of indigenous foods grown with organic fertilizer, even as they eagerly plant and profit from hybrid varieties grown with chemicals (Gupta 1998; Vasavi 1999; Wadley 1994). Greek anthropologist Seremetakis describes a discourse of "tastelessness" that is "common in discussions of modernity" (1996: 8).[13]

The discourse on modern tastelessness in Rajasthan is echoed in reverse by the kinds of exclamations I overhear complacent shoppers making in my hometown food coop over the unsurpassed flavor—to take a recent example—of organic grapes. Hang the cost! The difference is that poor and frugal Rajasthani farmers have had to give up their preferred flavors, whereas middle-class shoppers in Ithaca can afford to reclaim and savor the naturally delicious, and simultaneously experience the moral gratification of supporting environment and local workers.

Although several chapters in this volume treat activist and commercially successful alternative food movements, what I have encountered in Rajasthan is a discourse of awareness united with resignation: a world in which good flavors are knowingly sacrificed in the name of economic betterment. Such sacrifice constitutes the pursuit of tasteless profits. Moreover, the decline of flavor is deeply embedded in, and complexly interwoven with, other declines—a set of conditions that makes reversal inconceivable to many.

Although it does not speak of flavor, the following passage, elicited in oral history interviews, voices one of the clearest expressions I have recorded of a very common interwoven set of critiques of changing times. The speaker is Damodar Sharma Gujarati, a Brahmin, and one of the oldest men in the village when Bhoju Ram Gujar and I interviewed him in the 1990s:

> DAMODAR: The Kali Yuga [degenerate era] has come 100%. People used to be very happy and generous, but now they are misers. It used to be if I had grain and saw a hungry person I would give, and even if only women were home and one had no grain, she could borrow from another and clean it and grind it and make bread so no one could go to bed hungry.
>
> And there was so much power in the grain that when you boiled it, it spit [literally, it kicked] so no one could stand near the pot. But today there is no such spitting, no strength in the grain. . . . Just as the strength of grain is finished, so is people's love.
>
> BHOJU: O.k., people have changed because of selfishness, but there is no selfishness in grain, so what happened?
>
> DAMODAR: It is because we don't use goat dung and cow dung fertilizer any more. From urea more heat grows in the grain, and from this people also have greater heat. And that is why people have much more anger and egotism. People today get angry very quickly at everything.
>
> [Gold and Gujar 2002: 308–309]

Complex food themes emerge in Damodar's words. It is not merely the nutritional quality of food that has declined, but also, it would seem, the chemistry of the grains themselves, because they behave differently when boiled. It is not just an increase in human selfishness observed, but a causal link posed between the moral failures of modern times and the products of modern agricultural practice. In this passage, decline of "solidarity" or the morality of food sharing, discussed earlier in this chapter, is linked inextricably with specific agricultural technologies, on the one hand, and a food-based biochemical alternation of human nature, on the other.

Concluding Thoughts

The three themes highlighted in these sketches—solidarity, separation, and the conjoined decline of flavor and morality—intertwine in several ways. For example, Damodar Gujarati posits decline as undermining solidarity, when he claims that people no longer share the food that is no longer nourishing. Decline also undermines separation. In the 1990s I heard persons belonging to low-ranking, historically meat-eating communities voice, as a kind of black humor, the critique that nowadays Brahmins and Baniyas (priests and merchants),who traditionally would adhere to strict vegetarianism, were eating all the eggs and chickens, leaving none for them. Jamuni Regar, from one of the dalit or former untouchable communities, put it this way: "Nowadays, in our colony, all things are finished. Nowadays, Brahmins and Baniyas eat meat, all our chickens are finished because of that" (Gold and Gujar 2002: 102). That is, the poor folks who raise chickens can no longer afford to eat them—because, just like Sohan Lal, they care more about money than they do about relishing food. Ironically, when the keepers of chickens sell their animals to persons of superior wealth, the buyers lose their ritual superiority in the process. Brahmins and Baniyas ought to be pure vegetarians, and, therefore, these economic transactions are simultaneously a sign of degeneration of traditional Hindu hierarchies: not just chickens but "all things" are finished.

Down the road from Ghatiyali in the small market town of Jahazpur, a very differently framed reversal of eating habits has shaken up society: the majority of those who belong to the "butchers'" (Khatik) community have become vegetarian. Formerly traders in livestock, now produce-vendors and dealers in used goods, the Khatik have erected, in the heart of town, a glamorous temple dedicated to the vegetarian deity Vishnu. With a devotional solidarity at least partially grounded in food practices, they were able to overcome high-caste opposition to this enterprise. One of the leaders of the Khatik caste of former butchers described their shift of occupation, diet, religiosity and status over the last quarter-century as bringing many kinds of well being, including economic and social progress, to their expanding population (Gold n.d.). Many interviews that I conducted in 2010–2011 in Jahazpur found members of higher castes (priests and merchants alike) readily affirming Khatik progress, and attributing it to a variously proportioned combination of religious self-transformation and innovative, tireless entrepreneurship.

Changing eating habits are reported from other parts of India, signaling varieties of transformations; some manifest as increased attention to rules of food purity, some quite the opposite. In Bengal, according to Donner's ethnographic study, urban women may decide to embrace a "full" vegetarianism—non-fish-eating and, therefore, quite non-Bengali—for reasons having to do with identity, class, consumerism, sexuality and self-determination. Donner suggests that young wives deploy their adopted ascetic vegetarianism, "to make a stand, and create a space where their individuality has to be recognized by their affines." She argues further that, "this somatic truth is political insofar as it reconstitutes a gendered morality at a time when consumerist indulgence establishes a tight grip over middle class imaginations" (2008: 176). Janeja—who has also recently looked closely at food and society in Bengal and Bangladesh—points to different processes, namely to breeches of vegetarian identity in middle-class households where, as she vividly puts it, the refrigerator is "guilty of attacking boundaries" (2010: 80).[14]

Such disparate examples of the ways dietary habits interact with other social processes reveal food as predictably signalizing, even as they display evident unpredictability of just what messages are sent. I have barely skimmed the bubbling cauldron of non-nutritional food values in India, but these assembled examples do attest to the many ways that food—as it is cultivated, cooked, shared, begged, savored, or sold—is always more than food within any given cultural world documented by ethnography. Appadurai in 1981 argued that "South Asian civilization has invested perhaps more than any other in imbuing food with moral and cosmological meanings" (498). Although drawing on South Asian examples, as does Appadurai, this chapter claims that all cultures invest heavily in imbuing food with moral and cosmological meanings.

In her cogent contribution to a different handbook, Judith Farquhar states as anthropological principle that "links connecting food to everything else are irreducible, and should not be analytically dissolved" (2006, 147). The composition of that "everything else" includes power and politics. Dunn affirms this emphatically in the afterword to a recent collection of essays exploring food worlds in postsocialist Eastern Europe. Dunn stresses the ways food "jumps scale":

> ... food is the most important and frequently encountered material object that translates regulatory regimes and power relationships into lived experience. Thus food has the almost magical property of jumping scale: as it moves, it links the global economy and household economies, political bodies and the bodies of individuals, the world and the self. To study food, then, is to study power.
>
> (Dunn 2009, 208)

Here is how Ugma Mali of Ghatiyali, Rajasthan, interpreted the local proverb, "Grain is the seed of adornment." He told me, "We say this because grain is the source of life and health. If you are hungry you won't look good no matter how much jewelry you wear, but if you are healthy [that is, well fed] you look good, even without jewelry" (Gold 1998). This insight from a North Indian farmer returns us to the blunt knowledge that, although the world's abundant food lore is culturally constructed, to suffer pangs of hunger is a physical and visible plight. Food's capacity to "jump scale" means that the sight of a hungry person evokes knowledge that spans caloric and moral values. Narayan's Swamiji would insist that this plight demands recognition and action from other souls.

Notes

1. Many thanks to Jane Fajans, Ron Herring and Gloria Raheja for thoughtful readings and helpful suggestions.
2. See, of course, Lévi-Strauss's four-volume structuralist compendium, *Mythologiques*—especially the first volume (1983)—that finds food metaphors to encode the most primary understandings of human existence.
3. To sample works representative of these and related equations see Bender 2003; Caldwell 2009; Counihan 2004; Donner 2008; Flammang 2009; Hardiman 1996; Holtzman 2006; Janeja 2010; Khare, ed. 1992; Mankekar 2005; Nazarea 1998; Pellow 2007; Sutton 2001; Toomey 1994. Farquhar 2006 provides a most helpful survey.
4. Not all the anthropology of food points toward macro social-justice issues. Another recent reader (Watson and Caldwell 2005) takes a cultural studies approach, looking at local manifestations of global markets in foodstuffs and food brands: KFC in Beijing; Coca Cola in Trinidad; McDonalds in Moscow. It is about flow, image, and profit rather than need. Somewhat shockingly, it lumps together willful fasting and hapless starvation under the ethically neutral heading "absence of food."
5. See Stoller and Olkes 1986 for their influential, personal reflection on these matters, delightfully titled, "Bad Sauce, Good Ethnography."
6. Both the *Bhagavad Gita* (Miller 1986) and the *Law of Manu* (Doniger and Smith 1991) have a great deal to say on the ways that the "qualities of life" (*gunas*) are inherent in different kinds of foods that are appropriately consumed by different kinds of persons.
7. Variations on "have you eaten?" as a way of saying hello are not unique to Rajasthan, but, rather, are common in many parts of the world.
8. See especially Marriott 1976; Mayer 1970, Hanchett 1988 and Khare 1976 focus more broadly on ritual and domestic uses of food.
9. There is an abundance of fictional writings centered on food and its myriad meanings and uses in South Asia; see for example, Sharma 1997, 2009; Thieme and Raja 2009.
10. This section draws extensively on materials included in Gold 2009 and Gold 2012b, partially reworking them and without further reference to earlier renditions.
11. Much of this literature is centrally concerned with politics and economics, and I do not attempt to survey it. On Polyani's "great transformation" in a South Asian context see Herring 2001 as well as his introduction to this volume. For anthropological discussions of the ways cultural variables affect "moral confusion" resulting from impinging capitalist markets see Parry and Bloch, ed. 1989; Sahlins 2000. Scott 1977 based on research in Southeast Asia is the classic study of rural moral economy and its distributional requirements.
12. See Herring 2011 for many recent sources on this conflict and for a thorough and penetrating analysis of brinjal politics.
13. Reaction against just such tastelessness in affluent cultures would be movements like local food and terroir; see for example Trubek 2008; Weiss 2011; and several chapters in this volume.
14. See also Ghassem-Fachandi 2009 for the hardening of religious identities around food in tension-ridden Gujarat.

References

Anderson, E. N. 2005. *Everyone Eats: Understanding Food and Culture*. New York: New York University Press.

Appadurai, Arjun. 1981. "Gastro-politics in Hindu South Asia." *American Ethnologist* 8(3): 494–511.

Barthes, Roland. 1997 [1961]. "Toward a Psychosociology of Contemporary Food Consumption." In *Food and Culture: A Reader*, edited by Carole Counihan and Penn Van Esterik, 20–27. New York: Routledge.

Bender, Courtney. 2003. *Heaven's Kitchen: Living Religion at God's Love We Deliver*. Chicago: University of Chicago Press.

Caldwell, Melissa L., ed. 2009. *Food and Everyday Life in the Post-Socialist World*. Bloomington: Indiana University Press.

Counihan, Carole M. 1999. *The Anthropology of Food and Body*. New York: Routledge.

Counihan, Carole M. 2004. *Around the Tuscan Table: Food, Family, and Gender in Twentieth-Century Florence*. New York: Routledge.

Counihan, Carole M. 2009. *A Tortilla Is Like Life: Food and Culture in the San Luis Valley of Colorado*. Austin: University of Texas Press.

Counihan, Carole M. and Penny Van Esterik, eds. 1997. *Food and Culture: A Reader*. New York: Routledge.

Doniger, Wendy and Brian K. Smith. 1991. *The Laws of Manu: With an Introduction and Notes*. London, New York: Penguin Books.

Donner, Henrike. 2008. *Domestic Goddesses: Maternity, Globalization and Middle-Class Identity in Contemporary India*. Aldershot, England: Ashgate.

Dunn, Elizabeth Cullen. 2009. "Afterword. Turnips and Mangos: Power and the Edible State in Eastern Europe." In *Food and Everyday Life in the Post-Socialist World*, edited by M. L. Caldwell, 206–222. Bloomington: Indiana University Press.

Farquhar, Judith. 2006. "Food, Eating, and the Good Life." In *Handbook of Material Culture*, edited by Christopher Tilley et al., 145–160. London: Sage Publications.

Flammang, Janet A. 2009. *The Taste for Civilization: Food, Politic, and Civil Society*. Urbana: University of Illinois Press.

Geertz, Clifford. 1973. *The Interpretation of Culture*. New York: Basic Books.

Ghassem-Fachandi, Parvis. 2009. "The Hyperbolic Vegetarian: Notes on a Fragile Subject in Gujarat." In *Being There: The Fieldwork Encounter and the Making of Truth*, edited by John Borneman and Abdellah Hammoudi, 77–112. Berkeley: University of California Press.

Gold, Ann Grodzins. 1998. "Grains of Truth: Shifting Hierarchies of Food and Grace in Three Rajasthani Tales." *History of Religions* 38(2):150–171.

Gold, Ann Grodzins. 2009. "Tasteless Profits and Vexed Moralities: Assessments of the Present in Rural Rajasthan." *Journal of the Royal Anthropological Institute* 15:365–385.

Gold, Ann Grodzins. 2012a. "Awakening Generosity in Nath Tales from Rajasthan." In *Yogi Heroes and Poets: Histories and Legends of the Nāths*, edited by David Lorenzen and Adrian Muñoz, 91–108. Albany: State University of New York Press.

Gold, Ann Grodzins. 2012b. "Scenes of Rural Change." In *The Cambridge Companion to Modern Indian Culture*, edited by Vasudha Dalmia and Rashmi Sadana, 13–29. Cambridge: Cambridge University Press.

Gold, Ann Grodzins. n.d.. "Carving Place: Foundational Narratives from a North Indian Market Town." In *Place/No Place: Spatial Aspects of Urban Asian Religiosity*, edited by Joanne Waghorne. Unpublished manuscript.

Gold, Ann Grodzins and Bhoju Ram Gujar. 2002. *In the Time of Trees and Sorrows: Nature, Power, and Memory in Rajasthan*. Durham, NC: Duke University Press.

Gupta, Akhil. 1998. *Postcolonial Developments: Agriculture in the Making of Modern India*. Durham: Duke University Press.

Hanchett, Suzanne. 1988. *Coloured Rice: Symbolic Structure In Hindu Family Festivals*. Delhi: Hindustan Publishers.

Hardiman, David. 1996. *Feeding the Baniya: Peasants and Usurers in Western India*. Delhi: Oxford University Press.

Hariharan, Githa. 1997. "The Remains of the Feast." In *The Vintage Book of Indian Writing 1947–1997*, edited by Salman Rushdie and Elizabeth West, 422–429. New York: Vintage.

Herring, Ronald J. 2001. Contesting the "Great Transformation": Local Struggles with the Market in South India. In *Agrarian Studies: Synthetic Work at the Cutting Edge*, edited by J. C. Scott and N. Bhatt, 235–263. New Haven: Yale University Press.

Herring, Ronald J. 2011. "State Science and Its Discontents: Why India's Second Transgenic Crop Did Not Follow the Path of Bt Cotton." Presented to Association for Asian Studies, Honolulu, Hawaii, April 2.

Holtzman, Jon D. 2006. "Food and Memory." *Annual Review of Anthropology* 35:361–378.

Janeja, Manpreet K. 2010. *Transactions in Taste: The Collaborative Lives of Everyday Bengali Food*. London: Routledge.

Khare, R. S. 1976. *The Hindu Hearth and Home*. New Delhi: Vikas Publishing House.

Khare, R. S., ed. 1992. *The Eternal Food: Gastronomic Ideas and Experiences of Hindus and Buddhists*. Albany, NY: State University of New York.

Lévi-Strauss, Claude. 1983. *The Raw and the Cooked. Mythologiques*, vol. 1. Chicago: University of Chicago Press.

Lutgendorf, Philip. 2000. "Dining Out at Lake Pampa: The Shabari Episode in Multiple Ramayanas." In *Questioning Ramayanas: A South Asian Tradition*, edited by Paula Richman, 119–136. Oxford and New York: Oxford University Press.

Mankekar, Purnima. 2005. '"India Shopping:' Indian Grocery Stores and Transnational Configurations of Belonging." In *The Cultural Politics of Food and Eating: A Reader*, edited by James L. Watson and Melissa L. Caldwell, 197–214. Malden MA: Blackwell Publishing.

Marriott, McKim. 1976. "Hindu Transactions: Diversity Without Dualism." In *Transaction and Meaning: Directions in the Anthropology of Exchange and Symbolic Behavior*, edited by Bruce Kapferer, 109–142. Philadelphia: Institute for the Study of Human Issues.

Marriott, McKim, ed. 1990. *India Through Hindu Categories*. New Delhi: Sage Publications.

Mayer, Adrian C. 1970. *Caste and Kinship in Central India: A Village and its Region*. Berkeley, CA: University of California Press.

Miller, Barbara Stoller, transl. 1986. *The Bhagavad Gita: Krishna's Counsel in Time of War* New York: Columbia University Press.

Narayan, Kirin. 1989. *Storytellers, Saints, and Scoundrels: Folk Narrative in Hindu Religious Teaching*. Philadelphia: University of Pennsylvania Press.

Nazarea, Virginia D. 1998. *Cultural Memory and Biodiversity*. Tucson, AZ: University of Arizona Press.

Ohnuki-Tierney, Emiko. 1993. *Rice as Self: Japanese Identities Through Time*. Princeton, NJ: Princeton University Press.

Olivelle, Patrick, transl. 1996. *Upanisads*. New York: Oxford University Press.
Parry, J. and M. Bloch, eds. 1989. *Money and the Morality of Exchange*. Cambridge: Cambridge University Press.
Pellow, Deborah. 2007. "Attachment Sustains: The Glue of Prepared Food." In *Sustainability and Communities of Place*, edited by Carl A. Maida, 127–142. New York: Berghahn Books.
Premchand, M. 1969. "The Price of Milk." In *The World of Premchand: Selected Stories of Premchand*, translated by David Rubin, 175–185. Bloomington: Indiana University Press.
Ramanujan, A. K. 2009. "Food for Thought: Towards an Anthology of Hindu Food-images." In *The Table Is Laid: The Oxford Anthology of South Asian Food Writing*, edited by John Thieme and Ira Raja, 1–26. New Delhi: Oxford University Press.
Sahlins, M. 2000. *Culture in Practice: Selected Essays*. New York: Zone Books.
Scott, J. 1977. *The Moral Economy of the Peasant: Rebellion and Subsistence in Southeast Asia*. New Haven: Yale University Press.
Seremetakis, C. N. 1996. *The Senses Still: Perception and Memory as Material Culture in Modernity*. Chicago: University of Chicago Press.
Sharma, Bulbul. 1997. *The Anger of Aubergines: Stories of Women and Food*. New Delhi, India: Kali for Women.
Sharma, Bulbul. 2009. *Eating Women, Telling Tales*. New Delhi, India: Zubaan.
Stoller, Paul and Cheryl Olkes. 1986. Bad Sauce, Good Ethnography. *Cultural Anthropology* 1 (3): 336–352.
Sutton, David E. 2001 *Remembrance of Repasts: An Anthropology of Food and Memory*. New York: Berg Pub.
Thieme, John and Ira Raja. 2009. *The Table Is Laid: The Oxford Anthology of South Asian Food Writing*. New Delhi, India: Oxford University Press.
Toomey, Paul. 1994. *Food from the Mouth of Krishna: Feasts and Festivities in a North Indian Pilgrimage Centre* (Studies in Sociology and Social Anthropology). Delhi, India: Hindustan Publications.
Trubek, Amy B. 2008. *The Taste of Place*. Berkeley: University of California Press.
Vasavi, A. R. 1999. *Harbingers of Rain: Land and Life in South India*. Delhi, India: Oxford University Press.
Wadley, Susan S. 1986. "The Kathā of Śakaṭ." In *Another Harmony: New Essays on the Folklore of India*, edited by Stuart H. Blackburn and A.K. Ramanujan, 195–232. Berkeley: University of California Press.
Wadley, Susan S. 1994. *Struggling with Destiny in Karimpur, 1925–1984*. Berkeley: University of California Press.
Watson, James L., and Melissa L. Caldwell, eds. 2005. *The Cultural Politics of Food and Eating: A Reader*. Malden MA: Blackwell Publishing.
Weiss, Brad. 2011. "Making Pigs Local: Discerning the Sensory Character of Place." *Cultural Anthropology* 26(3): 438–461.
Witcombe, John, Daljit Virk, John Farrington, eds. 1998. *Seeds of Choice: Making the Most of New Varieties for Small Farmers*. London: Intermediate Technology Publications.

CHAPTER 23

CULTURAL POLITICS OF FOOD SAFETY

Genetically Modified Food in France, Japan, and the United States

KYOKO SATO

Introduction

The world's food supply has benefited tremendously from modern developments in agriculture, such as the steady introduction of new production technologies and the well-coordinated global systems of distribution. Conversely, these same characteristics that have enabled the abundance and quality of diverse and affordable food in industrialized countries have also presented new uncertainties and conflicts. The crisis of mad cow disease (bovine spongiform encephalopathy, or BSE), for example, revealed new challenges to global regulatory authorities in ensuring food safety, including the necessity of global cooperation and coordination in regulation and information management.

Genetically modified (GM) food—products made with modern biotechnology, especially genetic engineering or recombinant DNA (rDNA) technology—is a new global commodity that both challenges national authorities and reveals the persistent significance of the national. The global nature of the commodity is strikingly evident. Transnational corporations are prominent in development and production, and biotech seeds and food circulate globally. International rules have been worked out for coordinating trade, safety, and protection of biodiversity; opposition is notable for its presence in extensive transnational advocacy networks. Nevertheless, regulatory approaches and public responses to GM food exhibit striking national differences. In France and Japan, GM food has been ardently discussed in terms of risk since the late 1990s and cautiously addressed as a food-safety issue, subjected to mandatory safety evaluation and labeling, and avoided vigilantly by many consumers. In the United States, however, the safety of transgenic food has not garnered the same kind of policy response or far-reaching public attention. Genetically modified organisms (GMOs) have spread widely through American farmland and the American food supply since the mid-1990s, with little of the public outrage witnessed in other nations. Labeling is not required in national law, and despite a surge in state-level attempts in the 2010s to introduce mandatory labeling via ballot initiatives and bills, no state has yet established labeling requirements (as of July 2013).

These divergences in both policy and public responses are particularly intriguing because these countries shared liberal regulatory approaches and similar public uncertainty before GMOs entered food markets in the mid-1990s. Distinct national policy frameworks and public attitudes developed between the late 1990s and the early 2000s, and for the most part they remain intact.

From analysis of these divergent national trajectories, this chapter illustrates three important dynamics in the politics of food safety. First, how food safety became politicized differed across cases. The sequences, timing, and actors who mobilized the issue differed widely. Second, other aspects of the safety and desirability of genetic engineering in agriculture became intertwined with the politics of food safety. We cannot really understand food safety outcomes in isolation from the context in which other aspects—such as environmental concerns—were politicized. Third, the meaning of GM food itself in policy and public discourse—its salience and definition—mattered to divergence of national approaches to food safety. The boundaries between GM and non-GM food are not self-evident, but they are variable over time and across contexts (Sato 2007). As a result, labeling policy and practices becomes a contested site where specific boundaries are drawn and manifested (see Clough, this volume).

How GM food developed as a category—through eminently cultural *and* political processes—resonates with a distinctive tradition of anthropological inquiry: the same food—whether pork, dog meat, or rice—is often categorized in radically different ways across contexts (e.g., Douglas 1966; Harris 1985; Ohnuki-Tierney 1993). Without falling prey to the perils of cultural essentialism, we can still discern how each social collectivity develops its own ways of classifying a specific food item. Classification matters politically as well. In her comparative analysis of biotechnology regulation, Jasanoff (1995; 2005) notes that scientifically measurable characteristics of the final *product* have consistently been the basis for regulatory decisions in the product-oriented US framework, whereas the use of genetic engineering itself has served as a criterion for a special regulatory category in the UK's *process*-oriented approach. In contrast, German debates came down to the entire *programmatic* relationship between technology, society, and the state. Regulatory frameworks generate categories; biotechnology regulations have created not only new bio-legal entities, but also a series of administrative practices and technical instruments around such entities (Lezaun 2006). In the cases that follow, we analyze the politicization and institutionalization of food safety in each country by situating them in the development of "GM food" as a cultural category.

This framework offers an alternative to dominant approaches. The most common approaches explain differences in food-safety policy by looking at (a) political conflicts among actors with different material interest and resources (*political realism*); (b) different norms and values (*culturism*); (c) the different degrees to which the public understands the science of risk and safety (*public understanding of science*); and (d) specific events and historical contexts (*events*). It is common to find accounts that assume that food safety risks exist as scientifically objective facts and then seek to account for different responses using one or more of these approaches. Policymakers typically attribute consumer concerns to their ignorance, whereas the media often discuss national differences in culture (e.g., attitudes and values surrounding food, agriculture, and technology). Many scholarly works highlight political struggles among stakeholders, cultural differences (e.g., trust in authorities, attachment to traditional ways), events (e.g., food scandals like BSE), or a combination of these (see, e.g., Gaskell, Thompson, and Allum 2002; Bonny 2003; Vogel and Lynch 2001; Vogel 2003; Schurman and Munro 2009; Bernauer and Meins 2003; Maclachlan 2006). These factors all mattered to the cases at hand, but our emphasis is on chronicling how products of genetically engineered crops developed differently as a cultural category in different national settings. Furthermore, we seek to understand how this development affected *degrees* and *kinds* of significance attached to GM food's safety per se. This *cultural politics* approach sees the development of the category itself not as self-evident or universally agreed to, but as the result of dynamic processes, wherein various factors contributed, including those of the more common approaches mentioned above.[1] Rather than regarding culture to be static and deterministic, as in purely culturalist approaches, we seek to find out how such changeable cultural elements as boundaries, terms of debates, and symbolic meanings of GM food developed in different national contexts.

France

The French government long considered agricultural application of rDNA technology as a highly promising new area for the country's competitive edge in science, agriculture, and industry. Over a short period in the late 1990s, however, it became a major public issue that mobilized a variety of political actors, and the country's long-standing pro-GMO policy quickly turned into a decidedly cautious one. In this politicization of GM food, concerns about ecological risks preceded and facilitated the rise of food safety concerns and other issues. The first key opposition to GM food came from environmentalists, and the general policy reversal was first triggered by environmental risk concerns. At the same time, the heightened public awareness about food safety that followed a series of food crises like BSE also contributed to this initial politicization: environmentalists began to effectively highlight food safety and consumer choice as areas of contention, and consumer and farmer groups then became active in the opposition. This development helped raise the general public awareness of GM food rapidly, expanding the debates and the opposition. By the time alternative globalization activists joined the opposition, the issue of GM food encompassed wider debates about democratic decision processes, the future of European agriculture, and French identity and ways of life.

In sum, food safety concerns in France constituted only one aspect of this multifaceted, multivocal issue from the beginning. Various framings of GM food bolstered—rather than competed with—one another, together intensifying its stigma not only as a product, but also as a process of production and a societal program. This stigmatization, through which the already institutionalized category of GM food became more salient, significantly affected how French authorities pursued and further institutionalized stringent approaches in various aspects of GM food, including food safety assessment (Sato 2013).

From State Support to the First Opposition

Until the late 1990s, the French government maintained fairly hands-off and industry-friendly regulatory approaches to agricultural biotechnology. Furthermore, as a country with advanced molecular biology and a major agricultural exporter, France invested heavily in research and development in this field at public research institutes like the National Institute of the Agronomic Research (INRA). The Biomolecular Engineering Commission (Commission du Génie Biomoléculaire, or CGB), an expert committee created in 1986 under the Ministry of Agriculture, not only evaluated the risks of this new technology, but it also strove to ensure the growth and competitiveness of the domestic research and industry. In this favorable context, French researchers made considerable strides. For instance, in 1987, INRA researchers conducted two of the world's first field trials of GM plants. By the early 1990s, France had hosted more GMO field trials than any other country except for the United States (Kahn 1996). Concerns about biohazard and ecological risks were occasionally raised by Parliament members and environmentalists, but the government upheld the research- and industry-friendly policy paradigm (Kemph 2003). Meanwhile, much of the GMO regulatory framework was unified in the early 1990s at the European Community level to facilitate regional innovation and competitiveness in the field (Bradley 1998). With such domestic and European policy development, the idea that GMOs constitute a distinct category became further institutionalized in France. However, this was not necessarily a restrictive stance: though subject to unique regulatory requirements, products of biotechnology were also held to deserve special governmental backing and investment. Furthermore, the safety evaluation of a new GMO was nonbinding.

In the mid-1990s, France remained among the world's forerunners in development of biotechnology and leading hosts for field trials. It was environmentalists such as the Friends of the Earth, Greenpeace France, and Écoropa that began to inquire into GMOs' ecological implications and eventually became the first visible opposition force in France. Significantly, they capitalized on the general European climate of heightened awareness about food safety issues and the public skepticism toward the regulatory authorities that followed BSE and other regulatory crises (Vogel 2003; Schurman 2004). The shocking news that BSE had killed humans broke out in May 1996, only two months after the first EU approval of GM crops—American biotech giant Monsanto's herbicide-resistant soybeans. Quickly after this news, Écoropa announced an appeal for a moratorium on GMOs, with the support of well-established scientists. The arrival of bioengineered soybeans in Europe and the protests by environmentalists such as Greenpeace drew much media attention in France. The left-mainstream newspaper *Libération* reported on the impending arrival with a front-page headline, "Watch Out for Mad Soybeans."[2] This association between GM food and BSE continued to support opponents over the subsequent years.

The French government, however, maintained its promotional stance; it pushed for and achieved the EU authorization of the Swiss company Novartis's pest-resistant Bt176 corn despite opposition from most member states. In early February 1997, France approved the commercialization (i.e., import, sales, and consumption) of the maize, with an ambiguous labeling requirement based on an EU law for novel food that did not specify labeling criteria or methods.

Subsequent developments surrounding Bt176, both at the national and EU levels, revealed the unsettled nature of risks of GM food. While the commercial release was regulated at the EU level, cultivation of GMOs could be subjected to additional national rules. In mid-February, Prime Minister Alain Juppé announced the controversial decision not to authorize the domestic cultivation of Bt176, invoking the precautionary principle and dissemination risks.[3] The decision created a peculiar situation, highlighting ecological risks: Bt176 could be sold and consumed, but not grown, in France. This symbolically significant official decision was quickly followed in April by the European Parliament's resolution that expressed its nearly unanimous opposition against the commercialization and cultivation of Bt176 due to its potential risks to public health and the environment. Critical of the European Commission's stance, the resolution particularly emphasized the food safety aspect of the issue, explicitly connecting GM food with the "BSE crisis."

Later in the same year, the Juppé decision was overturned by his successor, Lionel Jospin. The Socialist Prime Minister announced the decision in November to authorize the cultivation of Bt176. At the same time, Jospin's administration showed their caution about ecological risks by deciding not to authorize the cultivation of GM beet and canola, crops more prone to cross-pollination with wild plants. The administration also presented forthcoming policy measures to address public concerns by increasing transparency, monitoring the ecological impact of authorized GMOs, and introducing labeling of food products containing traces of GMOs.

In 1998, GM food attracted increasing public attention as the opposition grew in scope and visibility. While environmentalists remained central, consumer and farmer groups also emerged at the forefront. Bt176's ecological risks were again highlighted in February when Greenpeace France and Écoropa lodged an appeal to the *Conseil d'Etat*, France's highest administrative court, against its cultivation authorization, arguing that the risk assessment was insufficient. Moreover, as the issues of food safety and consumer choice became increasingly more prominent in GM food debates, labeling and traceability became a key policy and consumer issue. The major retail chain Carrefour secured a GMO-free supply line and featured their non-GMO products in its in-store campaigns.

Meanwhile, direct action led by the farmer activist José Bové in January set in motion the gradual broadening of the GM food debate beyond risk issues (Heller 2002). He and two others from his Farmers' Confederation, France's second largest farmer union, were arrested in January after leading over a hundred farmers in tampering with Novartis's GM corn. This development not only drew much media attention to biotechnology food, but it also brought together various opposition activists. A joint campaign against GMOs was quickly launched by the Farmers' Confederation and several environmental and consumer organizations. At the trial in February, opposition leaders from some of these organizations testified to support the activists. The alternative globalization activist Vandana Shiva from India showed support in the audience. Bové argued that GM food symbolized the dominance of market concerns, and associated it with American hormone-treated beef, both imposed on European consumers and farmers by the World Trade Organization and multinational corporations.

At that point, the French government had a moderate stance, authorizing GMOs while introducing more cautious and less technocratic approaches. While particularly cautious about ecological risks of rDNA crops, the government was still invested in the future of this technology and sought to establish a practical framework that reconciled its promises and the public's risk concerns. In February 1998, in approving varieties of Bt176 corn for cultivation (the first European country to do so), the French government also announced launching a system to monitor the corn's environmental effects. A new advisory body consisted of not only scientific experts and government officials, but also representatives from opposition groups such as Greenpeace and the Farmers' Confederation. Furthermore, the government abstained from EU votes on authorizing three lines of GM corn on the basis of the lack of consumer acceptance and effective labeling regulations, rather than risk concerns (Marris et al. 2004).

At the time, public debates did not necessarily entail outright opposition to agricultural biotechnology as such. For instance, the highly publicized "Citizens' Conference," held in June at the National Assembly, produced a final report that was neither clearly pro- nor anti-GM food, with moderate recommendations. In this governmental attempt to be more inclusive, a panel of fourteen citizens faced scientific experts and civil society representatives—from Monsanto and Novartis to Greenpeace and the Farmers' Confederation—and debated GM food. The report discussed potential ecological and food safety risks and called for more open decision-making processes and consumer choice via labeling and traceability (Marris and Joly 1999).

Meanwhile, opposition intensified, highlighting issues of food safety and consumer choice. European anti-GMO activists began to effectively capitalize on the heightened public awareness of food safety, as well as the structural dependence of biotechnology firms on food processors and retailers, the industries particularly vulnerable to consumer perceptions (Schurman 2004; Schurman and Munro 2009). In France, Greenpeace France especially made its mark, with its direct actions in supermarkets and "black list" of products that contained GMOs. By late 1998 the idea that GMOs constituted a food safety issue became powerful enough to prompt Danon to decide not to use GMOs in their products for Europe; Nestle and Uniliver quickly followed.

In this context, the official French position on GMOs grew more cautious. In September 1998, the Conseil d'Etat made a controversial decision to suspend the authorization to cultivate Bt176 maize hybrids. Opposition groups lodged more such appeals against other authorizations, this time both for cultivation and commercialization. Regulatory procedures continued to grow more open. In particular, the CGB's dominance ended as the French Food Safety Agency (Agence Française de Sécurité Sanitaire des Aliments, or AFSSA) was launched in April 1999 and took over premarketing risk assessment of GM food. Established to respond to growing public concerns about general food safety, the new agency was independent from the Ministry of Agriculture in an attempt to separate risk assessment and management, and it was considered more transparent than the CGB. Labeling and traceability increasingly became more urgent policy issues, as the wide domestic consensus to demand a clear and reliable labeling system was unmet by ambiguous EU standards. In June the French government called for an EU-level suspension of further commercial authorizations of GMOs at the European Council of Ministers, following an earlier move by Greece. France demanded more stringent risk assessment procedures and more effective labeling and traceability rules as conditions to resume authorizations. This development led to a de facto moratorium. Thus, France had become one of the most vocal GMO opponents in Europe.

Stigma beyond Risk Issues

This dramatic policy reversal was followed by further expansion and visibility of the opposition movement, which more explicitly and successfully connected the issue of GM food with the critiques of globalization and neoliberalism, highly resonant in France at that time. Increasingly more stigmatized beyond risk issues, GM food in the French public discourses quickly became antithetical to French tradition and ways of life (Sato 2013).

The activist José Bové played a key role in this development, which had significant consequences for market practices and policy regarding GMOs. In August 1999, he and the Farmers' Confederation entered the media spotlight again by their direct action to dismantle a McDonald's franchise under construction in southern France. This was to protest the US government's decision to impose high duties on French products, which itself was in response to Europe's refusal to import US beef from cows treated with growth hormone. In his crusade against malbouffe (bad food), which included hormone-treated beef, fast food, and GM food, Bové became extremely popular in France.[4] Meanwhile, the ATTAC, a popular alternative globalization group close to Bové, joined the anti-GMO movement, while Bové joined antiglobalization protesters at the December WTO meeting in Seattle and became their global icon. Bové's popularity not only contributed to the new high level of public attention GM food received in France, but it also facilitated the association of GM food with McDonald's and hormone-treated beef. They all symbolized the global hegemony of market logic and its implications, such as standardization of distinct local culture and market dominance over democracy (Bodnar 2003). The issue of GM food was no longer merely about ecological risks and food safety, it now encompassed the larger issues of democratic decision-making, ethics, culture, and national identity. Eurobarometer surveys show that the public support for GM food in France declined from 54 percent of the decided public in 1996 to 35 percent in 1999 (Gaskel et al. 2006).

By 2000, GM food was stigmatized to such an extent that more food manufacturers and retailers began to eliminate GMOs from their products, and even from feed for their animal sources. France's largest feed supplier, Glon Sanders, launched GM-free feed, and Carrefour decided to stop the use of GMOs in the feed for their animals. In November 2000, when the Conseil d'Etat decided to end the suspension of Bt176, Novartis announced that it would not commercialize it due to the lack of consumer confidence. Direct actions to destroy field tests drew increasing public attention.

The French government's cautious and inclusive regulatory approaches became firmly institutionalized during this period, and they generally persist today. The highly politicized nature of the issue certainly contributed to the official turn to more vigilant approaches to food safety matters, as the safety of GMOs as food became established as a central area of policy concern, as seen with the key regulatory role of the AFSSA. Ecological risks of engineered crops also remained significant in public discourse. In May 2000, France became a signatory of the Cartagena Protocol on Biosafety, an international agreement adopted in January 2000 to protect biodiversity from possible negative effects of "living modified organisms," as did the European Union. France also played a pivotal role in maintaining the EU moratorium, demanding more reliable and precise labeling and traceability standards and more tests on the long-term safety of GM food. During the moratorium, the EU adopted increasingly restrictive regulatory provisions. Labeling and traceability at all stages became mandatory, with a threshold of 1 percent presence of GMOs. Following food safety scandals since the late 1990s—e.g., BSE, dioxins, contaminated Coca Cola, listeria—Europe incrementally revamped its food regulatory system, emphasizing traceability of food, transparency of decision-making, and incorporation of public concerns. With the establishment of the European Food Safety Authority, the risk assessment of GMOs became more centralized at the EU level.

In April 2004, the EU introduced a new stringent regulatory framework to resume GMO authorizations, ending its de facto moratorium, against which the United States, Argentina, and Canada had brought a high-profile case to the WTO in May 2003. The new framework accentuated the boundaries between GM and non-GM food, while consolidating some of the previously separate segments of regulatory procedure into a simpler one. It became possible for a developer to go through a single authorization procedure for cultivation, food, and feed (the "one key, one door" principle). Stricter labeling requirements covered not only products with traces of DNA and protein from genetic modification, but also those without such traces if GM material was used in their production. Labeling was exempt only for the accidental presence of GMOs below 0.9 percent.

GM food has remained highly contentious in France. According to the Eurobarometer, public support for it in France declined from 35 percent in 1999, to 30 percent in 2002, to 29 percent in 2005 (Gaskel et al. 2006). Organized direct actions to destroy field tests continued to flourish and gained considerable popularity, and a growing number of local communities—regions, departments, cities, and towns—declared themselves "GMO-free," even without legal authority to enforce it. R&D has diminished, and labels for GMOs have been hardly found in French food despite the strict criteria. In 2008 a biotechnology law was passed to create a new independent body, the High Council of Biotechnologies, to work with the French Food Safety Agency (AFSSA) and oversee not only environmental and public health aspects of GMOs, but also economic, social, and ethical ones. Only one type of GMO—MON810, Monsanto's pest-resistant corn—was cultivated on a small scale, but since 2008 the French government has banned its cultivation for concerns about uncertain ecological risks.

Summary

In France, the contentiousness of GM food politics was aided by, but not reducible to, the context of post-BSE consumer awareness. The environmental and ecological concerns, both in opposition movements and in government, initially politicized the issue of GM food in general, and this significantly facilitated, and was facilitated by, the rise of food safety aspects. In a short period between the late 1990s and early 2000s, concerns extended beyond scientific risk assessment to encompass larger societal questions such as democratic decision-making, globalization, and French culture and identity. As these multiple problem framings augmented each other, GM food became a highly salient issue, both in public discourses and policy debates.

Food safety—or consumption risks—constituted only one of the key issues surrounding GM food, albeit an important one. Larger issues of GMOs as a mode of production and as a societal program came to figure prominently, strengthening "GM food" as a salient category. Food safety concerns became merged with issues beyond scientific assessment of risk, such as democracy and national identity. The increasing general stigma and political salience contributed to an official turn to highly conservative approaches to consumption risks, as well as other aspects of agricultural biotechnology, including ecological risks and social consequences.

Japan

Japan also initially developed a liberal regulatory framework for agricultural biotechnology, coupled with active efforts to promote it as a key industrial domain. The government long maintained a position that approved GM crops should be treated the same way as conventional crops. In the late 1990s, as in France, this paradigm faced a considerable challenge from an emerging opposition. The central opposition actors in Japan were consumer groups, and the Japanese debate on GM food consistently focused on food safety. The opposition mobilized consumer concerns about safety, and effectively focused on labeling as a way to address consumption risk concerns, prompting the government to require more stringent safety assessment and labeling. This constituted an important—albeit limited—victory for the consumer movement in Japan, which had long addressed food safety as a top priority yet been excluded from policy processes (Maclachlan 2006). This success facilitated the politicization of other aspects of GM food. In the early 2000s, narratives that portrayed GM food as a threat to local agriculture and Japanese culture and identity emerged, particularly in the opposition against GM rice development and field trials. Ecological effects of biotech crops also garnered more public attention, and the government subsequently introduced stricter environmental regulation for cultivating them.

Successful politicization of consumption aspects of GMOs as products preceded and helped draw public attention to GM food as a category, and then to such production aspects as agriculture's significance to national and local culture and environmental risks. At the same time, the initial narrow focus on food safety and labeling affected the ways in which the general regulatory approaches were considerably more lenient than those of the EU or France. Consequently, despite high public awareness of the food safety issue, Japan continued to import—and consume—a significant amount of biotech crops from other countries.

From State Support to the First Opposition

In Japan, as in France, the regulatory framework for agricultural biotechnology was explicitly lenient and favorable to R&D and commerce for a long time (Fujihara 1997). In the 1980s the government began to invest heavily in the field, which it considered crucial for Japan's competitiveness in science and technology and for solving the country's low food self-sufficiency and dependence on imports (Yamaguchi and Suda 2010). The Ministry of Agriculture, Forestry and Fisheries (MAFF) gradually built an institutional setting conducive to public and private R&D and government-industry cooperation (Amagasa 2000, 2003).[5] From the late 1980s to the early 1990s, various crops developed by MAFF's research institutes, prefectural research centers, and private companies (e.g., chemical, beer, tobacco) moved from labs to greenhouses, then into the field. A pioneering opposition group, the DNA Issue Study Group, and the Environmental Agency raised concerns about ecological impact of field tests, but this did not result in much public or policy debate.

By the early 1990s, in preparation for the impending arrival of food made with rDNA technology, the government established a regulatory framework distinctly for it, from indoor experiments to field tests to safety as food. In 1994, under this framework, Japan quietly introduced its first GM food, two varieties of chymosin (an enzyme used in cheese-making) made by American and Dutch companies, and cheese made with them. On one level, this framework affirmed the category of GM food. On another, it was nonbinding and explicitly maintained that approved transgenic food was "the same" as the existing food. The latter idea was even more explicitly institutionalized in 1996 when the

Ministry of Health and Welfare (MHW) adopted the "substantial equivalence" principle. Officially articulated by the Organisation for Economic Co-operation and Development (OECD), this principle posits regulating the safety of GM food in the same way as conventional food if the former has the same chemical and nutritional compositions and usage as the latter.[6] In confirming the safety of seven products made by four foreign companies later in 1996, the ministry explicitly refused the idea of requiring labeling (Yasuda 1997). Meanwhile, both public and private R&D efforts intensified. By 1996 the majority of prefectural governments—longtime key players in developing seeds of major crops—had launched agricultural biotechnology research, and various GM crops (e.g., tomatoes, rice) were being developed throughout Japan (Nishimura 1997).

The first shipment of American GM crops entered Japan in September 1996, setting off widespread debates and an organized opposition mobilization of consumer groups on the basis of food safety concerns. These groups called for labeling as a way to avoid consumption risks. The progressive consumer group Consumer Union of Japan and the DNA Study Group launched the No! GMO Campaign, which quickly became an opposition leader in Japan. In December the Tokyo Assembly demanded that the government confirm the safety of GM food and promptly make labeling mandatory—a move subsequently followed by a number of local assemblies throughout Japan (Yasuda 1997).

Initially, the government took a firm stance against treating approved GMOs differently from conventional crops, but the rapidly growing opposition prompted it to reconsider labeling. As late as January 1997, Prime Minister Ryutaro Hashimoto pronounced labeling of "safe" approved GM food as gratuitous, even denying the necessity for the government to know how much entered Japan. However, by April the government received requests for mandatory labeling from about 140 local assemblies and 100 groups—including consumer cooperatives, consumer groups, environmentalists, and farmers.[7] Quickly, the MAFF and the House of Representatives each created a special panel for GM food labeling.

At the time, much debate about the safety of GM food occurred at the Diet (Japan's legislative body) and local assemblies. Some expressed their concerns for its effect on children via school lunch programs that the majority of grade schools have, while others invoked BSE in the United Kingdom and *E. coli* O157, which shocked Japan by killing school children and poisoning thousands in 1996. In 1997, nonetheless, GM food was still unproblematic for many Japanese. While some cautious food manufacturers began to avoid potentially contentious GMOs, most others remained passive and oblivious. R&D efforts continued in both public and private sectors.

It was during 1998 that GM food skeptics and opponents achieved consumer mobilization at an unprecedented scope, as official advisory panels deliberated on methods and criteria of labeling. The government pushed for voluntary labels, emphasizing the safety of *approved* GM food, Japan's high dependency on food imports, and the practical difficulty of requiring exporting countries to provide labeling. Conversely, consumers called for mandatory labels, specifically on the basis of food safety concerns: labeling would allow them to avoid GM food, whose consumption risks are uncertain. With the demand for mandatory labeling as a common denominator, a wide range of groups collaborated to collect petitions, including mainstream consumer co-ops—with an access to their millions of members—that were not opposed to GM food per se. More and more local assemblies officially demanded labeling of GM food, and voluntary "GM-free" labels by food manufacturers became common among the ubiquitous soy products. When the MAFF solicited public comments on the choice between mandatory and voluntary labeling in September, the majority of the 10,000-plus respondents—an atypically large number of comments—supported mandatory labeling (Wada 2000).

While playing a key role in this mobilization around labeling, the No! GMO Campaign also coordinated and led various types of actions to address other aspects of food safety and consumer choice. For instance, it urged consumers to boycott products of Kirin Brewery, which developed GM tomatoes—the first and then only approved domestic GM crop—in cooperation with the American firm Calgene. The campaign also started having food and feed products tested for traces of GMOs. In July 1999 it announced that three of six major domestic corn snack products tested positive for unapproved varieties of GM corn (Amagasa 2001).

The movement achieved a significant success in 2000, when the Ministry of Agriculture, Forestry and Fisheries (MAFF) and the Ministry of Health and Welfare (MHW) decided to revise two laws: the agriculture ministry revised one to introduce mandatory labeling, while the health ministry announced that voluntary safety assessments of GM food would become mandatory, effective April 2001. Despite their success in politicizing the issue of labeling, the campaign and consumer groups fell short in dictating the criteria for labeling requirements. While they explicitly demanded that labeling be required for any products that used GM or unsegregated crops, the government introduced more limited requirements: labeling was required only for food products in which "main ingredients" contained GMOs *and* modified DNAs or new protein were detectible.[8] This left many processed products with no traces (e.g., soy sauce, corn oil) exempt, even when they were made with American GM crops. The criteria allowed consumers to avoid food with novel, unfamiliar materials, such as traces of genetic modification, but it did not give them information on processes used in food production.

In October 2000 the No! GMO Campaign announced the discovery of traces of unapproved GMO in food, stirring public anxiety and further boosting the legitimacy of the opposition movement. The DNAs of StarLink corn, a type of Bt corn that had already been found in food products in the United States, were detected in a domestic cake mix. The corn was not approved either as feed or human food in Japan, although it was approved as animal feed in the United States. In this context, more and more food manufacturers began to actively exclude GM ingredients, label their products "non-GMO," and terminate their projects to develop biotech crops. Kagome Co., Ltd, a major food and beverage manufacturer, abandoned its GM tomatoes. Kirin Brewery gave up on commercializing their approved biotech tomatoes and declared that it would avoid starch from GM corn in its beer. Other beer makers, including Sapporo and Asahi, followed suit. Even food manufacturers that had not used GM material before started labeling their products "non-GMO."

Through these developments, food safety and labeling dominated and eclipsed such issues as ecological risks and ethical and cultural implications. Key opposition actors were consumer groups; environmental groups like Greenpeace Japan and the Friends of the Earth Japan, whose European counterparts played a key role in successful opposition to GM food in Europe, were not yet involved. Although many core opposition actors like the No! GMO Campaign were concerned about a wide range of issues, including ecological consequences, sustainability of agriculture, and corporate dominance, they highlighted consumption risks and labeling given the backdrop of high-profile scandals concerning food safety and government oversight, such as *E. coli* O157 poisonings. In particular, the demand for labeling powerfully unified diverse civil society groups with different stances toward GM food and led to the successful mobilization of consumers (Sato 2007). At the same time, however, the narrow problematization of GM food as an issue of consumption risks, coupled with the government concerns for the food supply, allowed more lenient regulatory requirements than EU or French ones. The government still considered GM food a great promise, and it sought to regulate consumption risks and labeling in a manner that would build consumer confidence in GM food, but without disrupting Japan's food supply or constraining domestic food distributors and biotech companies too much.

Beyond Food Safety and Labeling: GM Rice and the Cartagena Protocol

By 2000, most private projects to develop commercially viable GM crops had been suspended, but the Japanese government continued its push, and many public research facilities, national or prefectural, carried on their GM crop R&D projects, among which GM rice was the most prevalent (Kayukawa 2000). In late 2000, the No! GMO Campaign kicked off a campaign for GM rice, and three cooperative unions launched a network to oppose biotech rice. In addition to the political salience of both GM food and general food safety issues, the anti-GM rice movement also capitalized on the significance of rice as a symbol of national identity (see Ohnuki-Tierney 1993 for a look at rice and Japanese identity). Invoking rice as the most significant staple and a root of Japanese culture, and rice paddies as a site for traditional local practices and a unique ecosystem—in addition to food safety—the movement steadily gained public support. By April 2001 it collected more than 170,000 anti-GM rice petitions, and submitted them to the MAFF to call for a ban on the importation or production of biotech rice. Targeting the GM rice of Aichi Prefecture, developed in collaboration with Monsanto and the closest to commercialization in Japan at the time, the campaign held rallies in the Aichi capital, Nagoya, in 2002. After receiving 580,000 opposition petitions in November, Aichi announced in December that it would give up the commercialization of its GM rice. This opposition strategy that targeted specific research projects and test sites, often with local mobilization actions, spread and helped curb R&D efforts at the prefecture level.

Meanwhile, food safety drew further attention from Japanese consumers as they faced a series of high-profile food-related scandals, including the June 2000 food poisoning of 15,000 people, the StarLink scandal in October 2000, the first domestic case of BSE in September 2001, and the illegally high levels of pesticide residue found in vegetables from China from May 2002 on. Consequently, the government overhauled and restructured the food safety policy framework, creating the Food Safety Basic Law and establishing the Food Safety Commission in 2003. Set up under the Cabinet Office and headed by experts on a wide variety of food safety issues—such as toxicology, microbiology, and organic chemistry, as well as public health, consumer awareness and communication—the commission began to oversee an expert panel on GM food, which took over GM food safety assessment.

Ecological risks of GM food drew more attention in the early 2000s (Yamaguchi and Suda 2010). The Japanese government was initially against introducing additional regulation for the control of biosafety and did not sign the Cartagena Protocol when it was open for signature from May 2000 to June 2001. However, because of continuing public concerns, the government came to take the position that proper regulation in this area was necessary to gain acceptance of the technology. After months of interministerial deliberations, the government decided to accede to the protocol and adapt the domestic legal framework accordingly. In February 2004, the "Cartagena Law," overseen by the agricultural and environmental ministries, went into force.[9] The law is considerably more limited than its EU counterpart, in that it only applied to risks to Japan's wildlife, while the EU law covered not only undomesticated "nature" and agricultural crops, but also human health.

With these regulatory changes and widespread public resistance, most prefectural governments dropped or suspended their agri-biotech projects, including the development of GM rice. However, the national government's commitment to promote biotechnology and its agricultural application remained in place. By the end of 2004, active R&D of GM food crops in Japan was mostly carried out by public research organizations, such as MAFF institutes and regional agricultural centers. In particular, the government continued to invest in developing GM rice, invoking the centrality of rice for the country's food supply and culture.

Summary

In Japan, the initial visible opposition to GM food came from consumer groups, and food safety concerns consistently dominated public debates and opposition mobilization. Labeling as a means of dealing with uncertain consumption risks became a focal policy issue, uniting consumers, diverse opposition groups, and local communities throughout the country and propelling them to mobilize. This focus allowed the opposition to achieve an unprecedented scale of consumer mobilization and put GM food solidly on the regulatory policy agenda and in the spotlight in public discourses. Subsequently, the government rendered safety assessment and labeling compulsory.

Debates on labeling and food safety, together with ubiquitous non-GMO labels, kept the category of GM food politically salient and relevant. Concerns about protecting rice—and the culture and tradition surrounding it—emerged, slowing R&D efforts in rice. The government eventually acceded to the Cartagena Protocol, which it had earlier declined. Still, consumption risks remained the dominant concern, and this narrow focus contributed to the ways in which new regulatory approaches were considerably more lenient than those of the European Union or France.

The United States

The United States has consistently been a leader in modern biotechnology and its agricultural application. On the one hand, the government has long considered agricultural biotechnology as an essential industrial domain, and it has promoted it in various ways. On the other hand, the US policy on GM products, established in the mid-1980s, has significantly played down the use of genetic modification as a basis for a distinct regulatory category, and instead treated most GM food as equivalent to existing products. This general stance remains intact at the federal level, with minor revisions: no legislation has been created specifically for GMOs or GM food, and labeling has not been required. Under this regulatory framework, GMOs have steadily spread into the US food chain since 1994, without stirring up significant health-risk concerns among consumers. Despite the majority of corn and soybean products coming from rDNA crops and their pervasive use in processed food, the category of "GM food" does not officially exist—or matter to most Americans.

Although opposition has existed since the 1980s and raised a variety of concerns—ethical, ecological, and later food safety—it never reached the scope and contentiousness of its counterpart in France or Japan. It did not develop into a united movement or a larger voice to question the technology as presenting a unique set of risks, let alone representing non-risk problems. Still, opposition did succeed in preventing transgenic plants from qualifying as organic in the late 1990s, and it also incited policy debates about banning the cultivation of GM crops or requiring labeling on GM food at the county or state level in the 2000s and 2010s. A cultivation ban was achieved in some of these cases, and labeling became a significant political issue in some states.

Nonetheless, GM food as a category has never become as socially or politically relevant in the United States as it has in countries such as France or Japan. GMOs were widely diffused into American farms and food chains before concerns about food safety—or any other aspects for that matter—became substantial and visible enough to affect policy or the practices of mainstream food producers and distributors. Public awareness of GM food has been generally low despite pervasive consumption, and much opposition effort went into the boundary politics of establishing the distinctiveness of GM food—whether via organic standards or labeling requirements.

From Political Struggles to the "Coordinated Framework"

Initial regulatory approaches to GMOs in the United States—a birthplace of recombinant DNA technology and a perennial frontrunner in its agricultural application—were undoubtedly intended to encourage R&D, but not necessarily more so than the French or Japanese counterparts. Rather, the laissez-faire policy framework came out of early contestation and politicization of the technology as a conscious governmental attempt to establish a setting favorable to its development. In the late 1970s, a call for legislation to regulate rDNA technology emerged from the public, policymakers, and environmentalists, but a concerted campaign by researchers and industry representatives successfully prevented legislation, arguing that it would harm the competitiveness of US science and industry (Wright 1994). In the mid-1980s, on their part, critics of biotechnology managed to delay the first field trials with lawsuits and local protests after the government approved trials of the Ice-Minus, an engineered bacterium designed to protect crops from frost, in 1983. In this mobilization, the Foundation on Economic Trends, a group founded by author-activist Jeremy Rifkin, played a key role, challenging the government's evaluative criteria and decisions, especially in terms of ecological impact of field tests (Krimsky 1991). Criticizing biotechnology for changing humanity's relationship with the nature, Rifkin worked with diverse actors, including animal welfare, environmental, and religious organizations. Due to these efforts, it was not until 1987 that the California-based biotech firm Advanced Genetic Sciences and the University of California, Berkeley conducted the first field trials.

Alarmed by these developments, Ronald Reagan's administration sought to create a new regulatory framework that would facilitate domestic R&D efforts (Krimsky 1991). This subsequently resulted in a set of regulatory guidelines in 1986, known as the Coordinated Framework for Regulation of Biotechnology, which pieced together existing statutory authority of the three federal agencies. It explicitly stated that biotech products would be "reviewed by FDA, USDA, and EPA in essentially the same manner for safety and efficacy as products obtained by other techniques."[10] In other words, it denied the uniqueness of rDNA plants as a new and distinct regulatory category and institutionalized regulation based on measurable characteristics of the *product*, rather than the *process* whereby the plant's genome had been altered.

In the mid- to late 1980s, skeptics attempted to introduce more stringent regulation, but to no avail. Since 1987, the pro-agri-biotech United States Department of Agriculture (USDA) oversaw most field tests, and some members of Congress made legislative efforts to expand the Environmental Protection Agency's (EPA) authority, which was limited to the release of pesticidal agents. However, with no apparent problems arising from approved field trials, legislative efforts eventually died down (Sheingate 2006). Some opponents were fundamentally critical of biotechnology itself, but given the framework, they strategically targeted specific risk issues (Charles 2001). Groups like the Environmental Defense Fund, the Union of Concerned Scientists, and the Consumers Union began to critically examine the ecological and food safety risks of GMOs, but such efforts did not lead to visible public interest. Furthermore, a 1989

National Research Council report explicitly supported the Coordinated Framework's product-based approach, and the dominance of this scheme hampered the EPA's effort to introduce a more comprehensive, process-based approach (Jasanoff 1995).

As the prospects of commercially viable GM crops grew imminent in the early 1990s, the government maintained the Coordinated Framework, making adjustments that further strengthened its product-oriented approach and weakened the distinction between GM and conventional food. In particular, a 1992 Food and Drug Administration (FDA) policy statement was significant in establishing that, as a rule, GM crops would be given "generally recognized as safe (GRAS)" status and subject to no special rules or additional testing. The statement upheld the "substantial equivalence" doctrine posited by the Organisation for Economic Co-operation and Development (OECD) and maintained that GM food, as a category, did not present different or greater safety concerns than conventional food.[11] No labeling would be required unless GM food contained safety risks such as known allergens. Safety assessments were not mandatory: the responsibility of safety testing was left with the manufacturer of the product, who could consult with the FDA about the product on a voluntary basis. Prior to the statement, some within the FDA had called for a mandatory safety assessment of each new GM food product for possible novel toxins produced from genetic modification. However, under the heavy influence from a White House keen on economic competitiveness, the agency concluded that such procedures would be too costly and onerous for this promising new technology (Pelletier 2005, 2006; Pringle 2003; Kurt et al. 2001). This development prompted Rifkin to renew his efforts and launch the Pure Food Campaign, together with organic farmers, environmentalists, and consumer activists, to call for mandatory labeling of, and ultimately a moratorium on, all GM food.

GM products entered American food chains as the FDA began approving them in 1993, but not without contention. When the agency approved Monsanto's recombinant bovine growth hormone (rBGH), intended to increase milk production, opposition emerged for various reasons beyond its safety concerns, such as its effects on small farmers unlikely to benefit from it and on the welfare of dairy cows (Jassanoff 2005). Responding to a demand for labeling of rBGH milk, the FDA argued that labeling should be about special health risks, which it did not recognize in rBGH, and it even insisted that labels could mislead consumers to believe that there was any reason for concern. In the context of the product-oriented, risk-centered policy framework, advocates and opponents resorted to scientific evidence in debating whether rBGH was harmful for human and animal health or merited a distinction from BGH, but the FDA considered issues other than human consumption risks to be beyond its regulatory jurisdiction (Jassanoff 2005).

The first GM crop, Flavr Savr tomatoes—engineered to have a longer shelf life—was approved in May 1994 after three years of assessment that involved a public hearing and intense exchange between the FDA and the Californian developer Calgene, even though such an extensive review was not officially required (Pringle 2001; Martineau 2001). In 1994 and 1995, the FDA approved a number of GM crops, including corn, soybeans, potatoes, and canola, many of which contained pesticide and/or herbicide-resistant genes. While Flavr Savr failed on the market and disappeared, other crops entered the market rather quietly and spread quickly among American farms in 1996.

The government subsequently introduced changes in regulatory procedures that further blurred the boundaries between GM and conventional crops. In 1993 the USDA simplified the development and cultivation of GM crops by allowing them to be petitioned for a "deregulated" status. As a result, GM crops with plant pest risks no larger than conventional crops can be removed from the oversight for open commercial cultivation. In 1994 the EPA set up a division for biopesticides, which included pesticidal substances and genes that produce them in GM plants like Bt varieties, as well as naturally occurring biochemical substances and microorganisms. By lumping modified genes and proteins together with other biological pesticides, this move further undermined the idea that GM crops constituted a distinct regulatory category.

Unlike in Europe and Japan, the opposition did not flourish immediately after the market entry of GM crops in the United States, despite the pioneering efforts of such American organizations as the Union of Concerned Scientists, the Environmental Defense Fund, and the Foundation on Economic Trends, which strongly influenced opposition movements in Europe and elsewhere. The first consequential mobilization of the public regarding GM food came later, not as direct opposition, but as part of a broader struggle over national organic standards. In 1997 the USDA proposed allowing the use of genetic engineering—as well as irradiation and sewage sludge fertilizer—to be included in the definition of organic farming. This prompted an unprecedented mobilization by diverse groups, including the Organic Consumers Association, a spin-off of Rifkin's Pure Food Campaign, and the newly established Center for Food Safety, as well as the Environmental Defense Fund, the Union of Concerned Scientists, and the Consumers Union. During the four-month period from 1997 to 1998, the department received 275,000 public comments, an unparalleled volume, virtually all of which opposed the inclusion of the three controversial methods (Klein and Winickoff 2011).

This development was indicative of the intricacy with which various actors struggled and negotiated over the definitions and boundaries of organic, GM, and conventional food. The initial logic of the USDA, consistent with the *product* framing of the FDA, was that the *process* of genetic modification was not relevant to the organic standards. However, the proposed standards in fact entailed specifications on methods and facilities, amounting to much more than the composition or risks of the final product. The industry's acceptance of organic-labeled GM food therefore was inconsistent with its insistence on the product-based labeling, and behind this approach was its material interest in entering the lucrative, fast-growing organic market (Jasanoff 2005). For the USDA and the biotech industry, denying GM food the organic label would signal the same unacceptable message as requiring GM food labels would; namely, that the process of rDNA technology presents a distinct set of risks and other negative consequences in food production. Conversely, the opposition mobilized intensely to exclude GM food from the category of organic food, which was not simply about the use of synthetic pesticides, but also about a system of agriculture, philosophy on nature, and way of life. The struggle to protect the existing organic-conventional boundaries unified organic farmers and GM food opponents, and it resonated strongly with the wider public in a way that earlier attempts by the opposition failed to do. In May 1998 the USDA conceded to excluding GMOs—together with food made with irradiation and sewage sludge—from the organic category, acknowledging that the latter meant more than not using synthetic chemicals. USDA organic labels launched in October 2002. GM food, however, still did not constitute a meaningful and salient category for either policymakers or the American public.

Sustained Liberal Framework and Incremental Change

GM food attracted more US public attention than ever in 1999 and 2000. European opposition grew so strong in 1999 that it began to affect wider segments of the American food industry. The EU stopped authorizing new GMOs, while major European retail chains and food processors started eliminating GM soybean and corn ingredients from their products. As the media coverage of GM food markedly increased in the United States, Heinz and Gerber pledged to remove GM ingredients from their baby food, and the nation's leading grain processor, Archer Daniels Midland, shocked farmers by requesting that GM crops be segregated and announcing that it would reject GM corn varieties that Europeans had rejected. In addition, Frito-Lay told its corn suppliers not to grow Bt corn. GM crop vandalism—in university and corporate research facilities, as well as in test fields—spread from Europe to the United States (Charles 2001).

Furthermore, two high-profile episodes spurred domestic debates about risk. First, the ecological implications of GM crops drew much public attention with the May 1999 publication of a controversial study in *Nature*, in which Cornell University scientists reported on adverse effects of Bt corn pollen on monarch larvae in their experiment. With monarch butterflies as a powerful symbol, opposition groups ran a series of full-page ads in major newspapers across the country, discussing the risks GM crops posed to the environment and human health, as well as their moral implications. The EPA eventually demanded more data from Bt corn manufacturers. Then, in September 2000, the food safety aspects of GM food became further highlighted with the discovery of the DNA of an unapproved GM crop in packaged food. The Friends of the Earth announced that Kraft Foods' taco shells served at Taco Bell contained the DNA of StarLink corn, approved only as animal feed, not for human consumption (Charles 2001; Pringle 2001).

In this context, some political and administrative efforts were made in the late 1990s and early 2000s to institute stricter regulation of GM food. An important struggle took place over whether the boundaries between GM and non-GM food should be strengthened in regulatory policy. Members of Congress introduced a series of bills to make premarket safety assessment of GM food mandatory and to require labeling, while the FDA reviewed its approach to GM food labeling and proposed making premarket consultation mandatory. In the end, however, these developments did not lead to significant changes in the perception, production, or consumption of GM food, nor in policy regarding it. The biotechnology and food industries carried out intense campaigns against legislative efforts and other attempts to tighten regulatory requirements. The government maintained its risk-centered, product-oriented stance. Despite the strong public support for mandatory labeling expressed in over 50,000 written comments it received, the FDA concluded that there was no evidence of adverse health effects of GM food that would mandate labeling. The agency even warned that "GMO free" labels might be misleading because of the potential accidental presence of GM material, as well as the implication that the labeled food is superior to nonlabeled food.[12] The agency also dropped its proposal to require premarket consultation in 2003 (Miller and Conko 2004). Meanwhile, in 2001, the EPA clarified its position to regulate the pesticidal *properties* associated with the modified plant, rather than the plant itself.[13] For herbicide-resistant plants, the agency regulates the herbicide used with them, and coordinates with the USDA and FDA (McHughen and Smyth 2008). Such practices further underscore how the regulatory focus is on the characteristics of a product, not the process used in its production.

In the United States, much of "GM food" is still treated simply as "food." Genetic modification is considered one of many methods in food production and does not serve as a basis of a distinct social or regulatory category. Against this challenging backdrop, since the 2000s the opposition intensified their efforts to raise public awareness of GM food through campaigns at the county or state level. Some local opposition actions successfully achieved a ban on cultivation, but none of the state initiatives or bills led to labeling requirements yet (as of July 2013).[14] Americans continue to grow and consume GM food, mostly indifferent to its presence, risks, or meanings.

Summary

In the United States, the food safety aspects of products made with rDNA crops have not reached the level of contentiousness or public awareness that they have in France and Japan. One reason is that the very category of "GM food" has not become widely salient either socially or politically outside niche communities and movements. These understandings are consonant with a regulatory framework that has consistently rejected a systematic distinction between GM food and non-GM food. With policy focused on the *product's* certain characteristics—what the US regulators consider scientifically measurable, such as chemical composition, nutrients, and risks to human health and the environment—fundamental critiques of the technology made little headway, and evidence of specific risks failed to be established through mainstream science. Despite a few high-profile incidents that highlighted the issue of food safety and ecological risks, the general policy framework remained intact: labeling and food safety assessment did not become mandatory, nor did ecological risk assessment, for most GMOs other than those producing insecticidal proteins, regulated by the EPA. Social and political salience has thus remained consistent with the regulatory approach.

Conclusion

The food-safety aspect of genetic engineering of crops developed quite differently in three major industrial nations by the early 2000s. In France, environmentalists played a crucial role in politicizing GM food first; their mobilization, coupled with the post-BSE consumer climate of distrust in state authorities, helped raise the salience of risks to food safety. Debates over GM food subsequently expanded and intensified, as the category became increasingly stigmatized. This prompted the French government to take on more cautious regulatory approaches to food safety and labeling, as well as to ecological and even social implications—including French agriculture and ways of life.

In Japan, it was consumer groups that politicized GM food, beginning with demands for labeling on the basis of food-safety concerns. Their mobilization successfully resulted in new mandatory assessment and labeling, and it raised as well the general political salience of GM food, which facilitated the introduction of more stringent regulation of the ecological risks of biotech crops. However, Japan's dependence on food imports restrained policy change because of official concern with practical difficulties that could arise from stringent regulation. Consequently, a narrow focus on consumption risks in the debate allowed officials to institute regulatory approaches considerably less stringent than those of the EU and France.

In the United States, despite widespread prevalence of rDNA plants and food products, there was no highly politicized awareness of "GM food." Contestation over "GMOs" on ethical and ecological grounds did surface early on, but the political base of opposition was limited and the debate remained focused on risk, where mainstream science sided with supporters of the technology. Opposition never led to a powerful united movement comparable to its counterpart in France or Japan. Consequently, the US regulatory framework continued to reject the idea of GMOs as a distinct category, instituting a global rift around trade and science. The United States—like Argentina and other exporters of biotech crops—refused to sign the Cartagena Protocol, precisely because its regulatory policy denied the existence of the very category. Instead, a policy of "substantial equivalence" and insistence on "science-based policy" prevailed.

Comparison of these three cases illustrates how divergent patterns of food safety regulation cannot be reduced to political conflicts, cultural norms, scientific debates, or historical events only. Different configurations of these factors shaped shared understandings of GM food as a category: the construction of this category itself was political (Herring 2010), and so was denial of this category. Furthermore, development of meanings beyond food safety mattered greatly in determining outcomes. The Larsson shows how "organic" means different things to different political actors, and in the same way "biotech food" means different things to different actors. Attending to these multiple dimensions—rather than treating the politics of GM food as a fixed, uniform, and insulated domain—facilitates an understanding of national divergence in the food-safety dimension of regulating products of genetic engineering.

NOTES

1. This is similar to Hajer's (1996) approach ("cultural politics") to environmental politics, in that both problematize constructs and classifications as products of cultural and political processes. In both, culture is conceptualized to encompass not only enduring norms and values, but also changeable constructs, classifications, categories, and framing of an issue. Whereas Hajer addresses an entire discourse surrounding environmentalism, this chapter focuses more narrowly on the category of GM food.
2. "Alerte au Soja Fou," *Libération*, November 1, 1996.
3. For a detailed account of the "flip-flopping" of the French official position on Bt176, see Marris (2000).
4. For a further elaboration of Bové's fight against "bad food," see Bové and Dufour (2000).
5. Among most informative accounts of the early development of politics of biotechnology are those written by Keisuke Amagasa, a leading opposition activist and writer who started both the DNA Study Group and the No! GMO Campaign.
6. For "equivalent" GM crops, information on the inserted genes, added characteristics, and the original plants is required, rather than information on modified plants themselves.
7. Ryutaro Hashimoto, "Response to Councilor Kiyohiro Araki's Questions Regarding Labeling of Genetically Modified Food," House of Councilors, June 6, 1997.
8. Main ingredients are defined as the top three ingredients by weight and those exceeding five percent of the total weight.
9. The Environment Ministry had been upgraded from an agency in the January 2001 reorganization of the government.
10. Office of Science and Technology Policy, "Coordinated Framework for Regulation of Biotechnology," Federal Register 51: 23302. June 26, 1986.
11. Food and Drug Administration, "Statement of Policy: Foods Derived From New Plant Varieties," *Federal Register* 57: 22984. May 29, 1992.
12. Food and Drug Administration, "Guidance for Industry: Voluntary Labeling Indicating Whether Foods Have or Have Not Been Developed Using Bioengineering; Draft Guidance," January 2001. http://www.fda.gov/Food/GuidanceComplianceRegulatoryInformation/GuidanceDocuments/FoodLabelingNutrition/ucm059098.htm.
13. Environmental Protection Agency, "Plant-Incorporated Protectants; Final Rules and Proposed Rule," *Federal Register* 66: 37772. July 19, 2001.
14. In June 2013, Connecticut became the first state to pass a GMO labeling law, and this was quickly followed by Maine, although neither law would take effect unless several other states adopt similar legislation. As of July 2013, about two dozen states have GMO labeling bills pending or upcoming ballot initiatives.

REFERENCES

Amagasa, K. 2000. *Idenshi Kumikae Ine-hen*. Tokyo: Gendai Shokan.

——. 2001. "StarLink Jiken wo Ou: Shokuhin ni Hairikonda Kikenna Mishonin Kumikae Tomorokoshi," In *Idenshi Kumikae Ine no Shurai*, edited by the No! GMO Campaign. Tokyo: Ryokufu Shuppan.

——, ed. 2003. *Idenshi Kumikae Shokuhin no Hyoji to Kisei*. Tokyo: Commons.

Ansell, C., R. Maxwell, and D. Sicurelli. 2006. "Protesting Food: NGOs and Political Mobilization in Europe." In *What's the Beef?: The Contested Governance of European Food Safety*, edited by C. Ansell and D. Vogel, 97–122. Cambridge, MA: MIT Press.

Bernauer, T., and E. Meins. 2003. "Technological Revolution Meets Policy and the Market: Explaining Cross-National Differences in Agricultural Biotechnology Regulation." *European Journal of Political Research* 42:643–683.

Bodnar, J. 2003. "Roquefort vs Big Mac: Globalization and Its Others." *European Journal of Sociology* 44 (1): 133–144.

Bonny, S. 2003. "Why Are Most Europeans Opposed to GMOs?: Factors Explaining Rejection in France and Europe." *Electronic Journal of Biotechnology* 6 (1). http://www.ejbiotechnology.info/content/vol6/issue1/full/4/.

Bové, J., and F. Dufour. 2000. *Le Monde n'est pas une Marchandise: Des Paysans contre la Malbouffe*. Paris: La Decouverte.

Bradley, K. 1998. "The GMO-Committee on Transgenic Maize: Alien Corn, or the Transgenic Procedural Maize." In *EU Committees as Influential Policymakers*, edited by M. P. C. M. van Schendelen, Hampsire: Ashgate Publishing.

Charles, D. 2001. *Lords of the Harvest*. Cambridge, MA: Perseus.

Douglas, M. 1966. *Purity and Danger: An Analysis of the Concept of Pollution and Taboo*. Boston: Routledge & Kegan Paul.

Eichenwald, K., G. Kolata, and M. Peterson. 2001. "Biotechnology Food: From the Lab to a Debacle." *New York Times*, January 25.

Fujihara, K. 1997. *Idenshi Kumikae Shokuhin no Kensho*. Tokyo: Shinhyoron.

Gaskell, G., A. Allansdottir, N. Allum, C. Corchero, c. Fischler, J. Hampel, J. Jackson, et al. 2006. "Europeans and Biotechnology in 2005: Patterns and Trends—Eurobarometer 64.3: A Report to the European Commission's Directorate-General for Research." http://ec.europa.eu/research/press/2006/pdf/pr1906_eb_64_3_final_report-may2006_en.pdf.

Gaskell, G., P. Thompson, and N. Allum. 2002. "Worlds Apart? Public Opinion in Europe and the USA." In *Biotechnology: The Making of a Global Controversy*, edited by M. Bauer and G. Gaskell. Cambridge: Cambridge University Press.

Hajer, M. 1996. "Ecological Modernization as Cultural Politics." In *Risk, Environment and Modernity: Towards a New Ecology*, edited by S. Lash, B. Szerszynski, and B. Wynne. London: SAGE.

Harris, M. 1985. *Good to Eat: Riddles of Food and Cuisine*. New York: Simon and Schuster.

Heller, C. 2002. "From Scientific Risk to Paysan Savoir-Faire: Peasant Expertise in the French and Global Debate over GM Crops." *Science as Culture* 11 (1): 5–37.

Herring, R. J. 2010. "Framing the GMO: Epistemic Brokers, Authoritative Knowledge and Diffusion of Opposition to Biotechnology." In *The Diffusion of Social Movements*, edited by R. K. Givan, K. M. Roberts, and S, A. Soule.. New York: Cambridge University Press.

Jasanoff, S. 1995. "Product, Process or Program: Three Cultures and the Regulation of Biotechnology." In *Resistance to New Technology: Nuclear Power, Information Technology, Biotechnology*, edited by Martin Bauer. Cambridge: Cambridge University Press.

——. 2005. *Design on Nature*. Princeton, NJ: Princeton University Press.

Joly, P.-B., and C. Marris. 2001. "Agenda-Setting and Controversies: A Comparative Approach to the Case of GMOs in France and the United States." Paper prepared for the INSEAD Workshop on European and American Perspectives on Regulating Genetically Engineered Food, Fontainbleau, June 7–8.

Joly, P.-B., and S. Lemarié. 1998. "Industry Consolidation, Public Attitude and the Future of Plant Biotechnology in Europe." *AgBioForum* 1 (2): 85–90.

Kahn, A., ed. 1996. *Les Plantes Trangéniques en Agriculture: Dix Ans d'Expérience de la Commission du Génie Biomoléculaire*. Paris: John Libbey.

Kayukawa, J. 2000. "Nihonjin no Shushoku, Kome mo Idenshi Kumikae ni." In *Idenshi Kumikae Shokuhin no Soten*, edited by Rokufu Shuppan Henshubu.. Tokyo: Ryokufu Shuppan

Kemph, H. 2003. *La Guerre Secrete des OGM*. Paris: Editions du Seuil.

Klein, K., and D. Winickoff. 2011. "Organic Regulation across the Atlantic: Emergence, Divergence, Convergence." *Environmental Politics* 20 (2): 153–172.

Krimsky, S. 1991. *Biotechnics and Society: The Rise of Industrial Genetics*. New York: Praeger.

Lezaun, J. 2006. "Creating a New Object of Government: Making Genetically Modified Organisms Traceable." *Social Studies of Science* 36 (4): 499–531.

Maclachlan, P. 2006. "Global Trends vs. Local Traditions: Genetically Modified Foods and Contemporary Consumerism in the United States, Japan, and Britain." In *The Ambivalent Consumer: Questioning Consumption in East Asia and the West*, edited by Sheldon Garon and Patricia Maclachlan. Ithaca, NY: Cornell University Press.

Marris, C. 2000. "Swings and Roundabouts: French Public Policy on Agricultural GMOs 1996–1999." *Politeia* 60: 22–37..

Marris, C., S. Ronda, C. Bonneuil, and P.-B. Joly. 2004. *France: Battling with Expertise*. National report for the project, Precautionary Expertise for GM Crops. http://technology.open.ac.uk/cts/national/france%20national%20report%20PEG.pdf.

Marris, C., and P.-B. Joly. 1999. "Between Consensus and Citizens: Public Participation in Technological Decision-Making in France." *Science Studies* 12 (2): 3–32.

Martineau, B. 2001. *First Fruit: the Creation of the Flavr Savr Tomato and the Birth of Genetically Engineered Food*. New York: McGraw-Hill.

McHughen A., and S. Smyth. 2008. "US Regulatory System for Genetically Modified [Genetically Modified Organism (GMO), rDNA or Transgenic] Crop Cultivars." *Plant Biotechnology Journal* 6 (1): 2–12.

Miller, H., and G. Conko. 2004. *The Frankenfood Myth: How Protest and Politics Threaten the Biotech Revolution*. Westport, CT: Praeger.

Nishimura, K. 1997. "Nihon Seifu to Kigyo no Doko wo Yomu: Kisei Kanwa no Rekishi to Kanetsu Suru Kaihatsu Kyoso," In *Idenshi Kumikae Shokuhin no Kikensei*, edited by Rokufu Shuppan Henshubu. Tokyo: Ryokufu Shuppan.

Ohnuki-Tierney, E. 1993. *Rice as Self: Japanese Identities through Time*. Princeton, NJ: Princeton University Press.

Pelletier, D. 2005. "Science, Law and Politics in FDA's Genetically Engineered Foods Policy: FDA's 1992 Policy." *Nutrition Reviews* 63 (5): 171–181.

——. 2006. "FDA's Regulation of Genetically Engineered Foods: Scientific, Legal and Political Dimensions" *Food Policy* 31: 570–591.

Pringle, Peter. 2003. *Food, Inc.: Mendel to Monsanto—the Promises and Perils of the Biotech Harvest*. New York: Simon & Schuster.

Sato, K. 2007. *Meanings of Genetically Modified Food and Policy Change and Persistence: The Cases of France, Japan and the United States*. PhD diss., Princeton University.

Sato, K. 2013. "Genetically Modified Food in France: Symbolic Transformation and the Policy Paradigm Shift." *Theory and Society* 42: 477–507.

Schurman, R. 2004. "Fighting "Frankenfoods": Industry Opportunity Structures and the Efficacy of the Anti-Biotech Movement in Western Europe." *Social Problems* 51 (2): 243–268.

Schurman, R., and W. Munro. 2009. "Targeting Capital: A Cultural Economy Approach to Understanding the Efficacy of Two Anti-Genetic Engineering Movements." *American Journal of Sociology* 115 (1): 155–202.

Sheingate, A. 2006. "Promotion versus Precaution: The Evolution of Biotechnology Policy in the United States." *British Journal of Political Science* 36 (2): 243–268.

Vogel, D. 2003. "The Hare and the Tortoise Revisited: The New Politics of Consumer and Environmental Regulation in Europe." *British Journal of Political Science.* 33 (4) 557–581.

Vogel, D., and D. Lynch. 2001. "The Regulation of GMOs in Europe and the United States: A Case-Study of Contemporary European Regulatory Politics." A paper for a workshop on transatlantic differences in GMO regulation sponsored by the Council on Foreign Relations. http://www.cfr.org/genetically-modified-organisms/regulation-gmos-europe-united-states-case-study-contemporary-european-regulatory-politics/p8688.

Wada, M. 2000. "'Nosuisho Hyojian' ni Itaru KeiiL Shohisha Iin to Shite Sanka Shite," In *Idenshi Kumikae Shokuhin no Soten*, edited by Rokufu Shuppan Henshubu. Tokyo: Ryokufu Shuppan.

Wright, S. 1994. *Molecular Politics: Developing American and British Regulatory Policy for Genetic Engineering, 1972–1982*. Chicago: University of Chicago Press.

Yamaguchi, T., and F. Suda. 2010. "Changing Social Order and the Quest for Justification: GMO Controversies in Japan." *Science, Technology and Human Values* 35 (3): 382–407.

Yasuda, S. 1997. "Shohisha wa Do Subekika: Motomerareru Hyoji no Gimuka to Boikotto," In *Idenshi Kumikae Shokuhin no Kikensei*, edited by Rokufu Shuppan Henshubu. Tokyo: Ryokufu Shuppan.

CHAPTER 24

FOOD SAFETY

BRUCE M. CHASSY

Introduction: Food Safety

If one were to ask consumers what their expectations are about food safety, it is likely that 100 percent of them would respond that they expect the food they eat to be safe. An expert would immediately counter that achieving absolute food safety is impossible and that ensuring the safety of any food is a highly complex and technical challenge. A quick glance at the table of contents of a textbook of food science or food technology will reveal that food safety is indeed a complex and multifaceted subject (Vaclavik and Christian, 2007; Campbell-Platt, 2009). The raw ingredients of foods are usually produced on farms—an environment that is far from sterile and pathogen free. In developed countries, food ingredients are exposed to numerous hazards as they navigate from farms through a complex processing, manufacturing, warehousing, transportation and retailing system; the food systems of less developed countries may or may not be less complex; however, data show that they are also less safe.

Since a safe supply of food is an essential ingredient for a smoothly functioning society, most countries have elaborated food safety laws and regulations intended to ensure that the food that consumers purchase is *reasonably* safe; regional and local laws often supplement federal regulations. These laws and regulations often define the composition of products, set rules for safe food processing and packaging, specify safety systems and checks that must be in place, provide rules on record-keeping and traceability—important should food need to be recalled—and define standards or limits for microbial, chemical, and incidental contaminants and myriad other detailed requirements necessary to ensure safety, quality and wholesomeness. Since the system is not perfect,[1] provisions for adverse incident reporting and tracking, and incident investigation and mitigation, including food recalls, are an essential part of the food safety system.

Although most consumers are aware of food-borne illness as a result of widespread media coverage of food-borne disease outbreaks, there are many misconceptions about food safety. For instance, although awareness of food-borne outbreaks is high, some consumers purchase organic foods in the belief that they are safer than conventional food offerings. Recalling that organic food is often cultivated with composted manure, it should come as no surprise that at least 51 people died and over 3,000 were made ill as result of consumption of *E. coli*-contaminated organic sprouts across the EU in 2012.[2] As this is being written, a multistate outbreak of Hepatitis A has sickened 113 people who consumed an organic berry-pomegranate mixture. As a result of such misunderstandings, consumers often do not take proper steps to avoid eating contaminated foods and are frequently responsible for acquiring food-borne disease by malpractice in their own homes.[3] A quick scan of a food label provides a revealing insight into issues that manufacturers believe is of interest to consumers. Labels often declare that the product contains no MSG although scientific studies show that mono-sodium-glutamate, an amino acid that occurs naturally in food, is highly unlikely to cause an adverse reaction upon ingestion. In this regard, most consumers are unaware that a fresh tomato can have as much MSG as a Chinese meal and that food producers have replaced MSG with hydrolyzed vegetable protein (HVP) that contains as much MSG as was added when MSG was an ingredient that consumers would accept. The label would also probably indicate that the product contained nothing *artificial* and was all *natural*. These statements seem to imply that consumers should avoid human-made ingredients since their safety is suspect, and should instead consume only all natural products. Consumer belief in the superiority of things that are *natural* has been carefully nurtured by marketers, however, it does not hold up to scientific scrutiny. Human-made food ingredients are subjected to years of research and careful review by government regulators before they are approved for use in foods and thus represent the least hazardous and best-understood components of foods. In contrast, some of the most toxic substances known to science are natural products and the state of being *natural* does not inform a food-safety assessment in any meaningful way.

Another statement that may be found on food-product labels is that the product does or does not contain GM or GMO ingredients. In some countries a label declaration of this kind is required by law. At the present time, mandatory labeling is not required in the United States; however, mandatory labeling legislation has been introduced in the U.S. Senate and in numerous state legislatures. Connecticut has recently passed a somewhat limited mandatory GM labeling requirement; among the limitations are that the law does not take effect until 5 additional states pass similar legislation. One implication of mandatory GM food product labeling is that there is some difference in safety between conventional products and those that contain GM ingredients. This chapter examines the safety of GM or GMO foods that contain ingredients that have been isolated from plants produced using the tools of modern biotechnology. Many consumers have heard, and believe, claims about the dangers of consuming GM foods (Sato, this volume). A considerable number of consumers think that there exists significant doubt and an active scientific debate about foods produced using biotechnology. This chapter briefly outlines the factors that lead to the conclusions that GM crops, and the foods and feeds produced from them, are as safe as any other.

A Short History of Recombinant DNA [rDNA] in Food Crops

The roots of modern biotechnology can be traced to the first report of recombinant DNA (rDNA) having been transformed into a bacterium in 1973 (Chassy, 2007).[4] In little more than a decade, researchers succeeded in transferring genes isolated from a diversity of species into numerous plant, animal, and microbial species, which opened the way for production of transgenic organisms, and products derived from them, that promised to be useful in medicine, agriculture, and the food and chemical industries. Skeptics warned that moving genes across species barriers in the laboratory violated nature, was fraught with uncertainties, and likened rDNA technology to opening Pandora's Box. It was, however, the precautionary approach of the scientific community itself that led to the development of NIH rDNA guidelines in the United States; similar kinds of regulations for the safe handling of rDNA and rDNA-containing organisms were introduced in other countries. Over time, rDNA guidelines were considerably relaxed as it became clear with experience that rDNA posed no intrinsically novel risks.

In the early 1980s, transgenic herbicide-tolerant plants that had great potential utility for weed management in agriculture were developed. Insect resistant crops were developed in the same timeframe. Since it was now clear that transgenic plants could be developed and introduced into the marketplace, the U.S. Office of Science and Technology Policy (OSTP) requested the National Academy of Science (NAS) to consider the issue of the safety of transgenic crop plants and to make recommendations regarding the need for regulation of the safety of genetically engineered crops. The NAS and National Research Council (NRC) responded (NAS, 1987) that:

1. Transgenic crops pose no novel risks, on the principle that techniques of biotechnology are not inherently risky.
2. It is the safety of the product that is of concern and not the process used to produce it.
3. No new laws were needed to give government agencies the authority to ensure the safety of consumers, agriculture, and the environment since the risks were "the same in kind" as those presented by organisms bred using older conventional methods.

In spite of the science-based recommendation of the NAS that the mere fact that an organism has been genetically engineered should not be the reason for special regulatory review, the OSTP published the *Coordinated Framework for the Regulation of Biotechnology* (OSTP, 1986; Chassy et al., 2001), which empowered the U.S. EPA, U.S. FDA, and U.S. USDA to play defined roles in regulating crops produced using biotechnology. The regulation of food safety fell largely to FDA with EPA taking the lead role in plants containing pesticidal properties. The EU (Kuntz and Ricroch, 2012) chose to regulate bioengineered crops as well as to require that all products containing ingredients from transgenic organisms be labeled. Similar regulations were enacted in many countries, whereas a few choose to invoke outright bans of what they defined as GM plants, foods, feed and ingredients isolated from them (Chassy, 2008).

Over the last 20 years, transgenic crops have been widely planted around the globe and used to provide animal feed, chemicals, and food and food ingredients for humans.[5] The remarkably consistent and documented record of safety has confirmed the opinion of the U.S. NAS that there are no novel risks associated with crops produced using *in vitro* DNA methods. In fact, not a single incident of harm to humans or animals has been factually documented to have resulted from the consumption of transgenic crops. There have, however, been many anecdotal claims of harm caused by GM crops and a few peer-reviewed scientific papers have claimed results that point to potential dangers of GM crops. The media and World Wide Web abound with stories about the harms caused by, and the hypothetical dangers of, GM crops and animals. Many consumers are understandably concerned about GM safety, and, in the face of consumer concern as well as constant pressure from activist groups that oppose GM crops, governments in many countries have increased the regulatory scrutiny imposed on GM crops.

This chapter describes the scientific food-safety risk assessment of crops produced using biotechnology and details the rationale for the claim that crops produced using *in vitro* DNA-manipulation are no more or less risky than those produced by any other modality of plant breeding. It briefly reviews the kinds of changes in DNA and composition that occur as a result of conventional plant breeding and compares these with changes that are introduced by newer methodologies such as rDNA transgene insertion. The techniques of plant breeding continue to evolve and it is not clear that plant varieties produced by some newer methods of breeding will be considered to be GM plants. The challenge of deciding what is and what is not a GM food will be considered.

The scientific concepts and specific considerations of a food safety assessment of transgenic feeds and foods will be described (König et al., 2004; Chassy, 2007, Chassy, 2010). Three key issues (unintended effects of breeding, potential allergenicity, and risks associated with changes in composition) will be considered in detail. The value and power of animal feeding studies that are often used in the process of food safety assessment will be discussed. It is concluded that whole food animal-feeding studies are of little value and the use of animals in this manner is unethical. This leads to a discussion of the misuse of animal studies and what constitutes scientific misconduct.

The chapter will conclude that the risks presented by transgenic crops are no different than those presented by any other crop bearing a novel phenotype, that new crop varieties are almost without exception as safe as any other, and that crops produced by conventional breeding methods would be better candidates for premarket regulatory review than those produced using biotechnology. A focus on the safety of novel traits would prove more cost-efficient and scientifically justified. However, regulation of GM crops around the world is not science based, but rather driven by political and ideational factors that lump all rDNA plants together as especially worthy of surveillance and control on safety grounds. The time and money spent on regulation of GM crops has opportunity costs in terms of failure to regulate other food hazards that do real harm and cause real economic loss around the globe.

The Objective of All Breeding Is to Induce Mutations in DNA

The concept is so simple it seems almost unnecessary to state that breeding of new varieties of any organism requires that permanent changes (e.g., mutations) be introduced into the chromosomal DNA (genome). Historically, a variety of methods have been used to introduce DNA changes into crop plants (Chrispeels and Sadava, 2003). Presumably, the original farmers selected the seeds of edible wild plants and planted them in managed fields in the first attempts at agriculture (Hancock, 2012). The word *edible* is used with great caution here since many crop- plant ancestors are poisonous, as are a few of today's crops such as bitter cassava (*Manihot esculenta*). Most crops retain a battery of natural pesticides that are used by the plants for protection against pests and predators. The earliest plant breeders were ancient farmers who simply waited for natural variation of a crop that was originally a wild plant to create a spectrum of new phenotypes from which they selected the most desirable traits. Fortunately they did not have to wait long, since many crop plants display a high level of genomic fluidity, which is to say they have a high rate of spontaneous DNA mutation (Parrott, 2005; Weber et al., 2012). Farmers were able to select for plants that did not shatter (spread their seeds), which made harvesting easier, produced higher yields, displayed resistance to diseases, produced thinner husks and more rows of seeds, and a host of other important traits.

The process of plant domestication usually depended on a number important mutations that made the plant variety more attractive to ancient farmers and often less able to survive without human intervention (seed saving, planting, cultivation, fertilization, etc). This has been called the domestication syndrome. The resulting varieties do not exist in nature and very often do not recognizably resemble their original wild ancestors. By any reasonable criteria, almost all crop plants are not natural, do not occur in nature, and are highly genetically modified with respect to their *natural* wild ancestors (see McHughen, this volume).

Historically, different crop plants were developed in many different regions of the world. This occurred largely because the wild ancestors of various modern crops can only be found in one or a few restricted geographical areas. Tomatoes, potatoes, and maize originated in the Americas, rice from Asia, and wheat from the Middle East. Over the millennia, these crop plants were widely disseminated, but only in the past few centuries were most plant crops spread around the world. As a consequence of the era of European exploration, and more recently with the advent of modern shipping, the world's diet has been globalized. What the world eats has changed dramatically as a result (Chassy, 2010).

With the development of modern plant breeding over the last 200 years a number of methods were introduced that were intended to increase the rate of mutation and expand the spectrum of changes that were possible (Chrispeels and Sadava, 2003). Radiation and chemicals that could induce alterations in the genomic DNA sequence such as point mutations, frame shift mutations, duplications, insertions, and deletions were introduced (Parrott, 2005; Weber et al., 2012). Mutagenesis accelerated the production of improved varieties and allowed the creation of new varieties and species. Methods for making wide-crosses that allowed interspecific gene exchange between species that would not normally mate productively were also introduced.

It is worth noting that these and other methods used for breeding plants all depend on the production of unknown and uncharacterized changes in DNA. To restate the obvious, all plant breeding depends on *genetic modification*. Until recently, methods did not exist with which the nature of the mutations that lead to changes in phenotype could be assessed. Over the millennia, breeding has greatly increased the variety and productivity of crops as well as their resistance to various pests and diseases. Plant breeding also has proven to be quite safe, although a handful of examples of new varieties that produced adverse effects have been identified (Cellini et al., 2004). A potato variety that produced unacceptably high levels of toxic glycoalkaloids and a celery variety that produced high levels of toxic furanocoumarins are two examples.

Successful as traditional methods of plant breeding using passive selection, mutagenesis, and crossing have been, the methods suffer from a number of shortcomings and challenges. The methods are time consuming, labor intensive, and can be expensive over time as years of crossing, back-crossing, and selection may be required to introduce a new variety. Owing to the percentage of progeny that contain unintended and undesirable effects, or which lack desired phenotypes, tens of thousands of candidate plants may need to be cultured and evaluated (Cellini et al., 2004; König et al., 2004). Traditional breeding and breeding using biotechnology are alike in that they rely on crossing and selection to sort out unintended changes. Traditional breeders can spend many years searching for a sexually compatible plant that has a desired trait or on mutagenesis protocols designed to produce desired novel traits. Some targeted phenotypes have proven to be thus far impossible to achieve by conventional breeding methods, despite the introduction of sophisticated screening methods designed to accelerate the process and increase the chances of success (e.g., marker assisted selection, identification of quality trait loci, and various automated screening systems). The critical need for development of crops enabled to withstand the biotic and abiotic stresses that are being imposed by rapid climate change is a task to find which of the rapid, precise, and reliable breeding methods made available using modern biotechnology are well-suited (Newell McGloughlin, this volume).

Methods for the transformation of plants *in vitro* using rDNA emerged in the 1980s. These methods are, in principle, relatively simple (Chrispeels and Sadava, 2003). A target gene that encodes a desired trait is isolated. Any living organism can be used as a source since all living cells use DNA as their genetic code and the code is processed in exactly the same way in all organisms. Although most species may be sexually incompatible, there is no species barrier for genes. A small piece of DNA that encodes the selected gene is inserted by transformation into the target plant and transformed cells of that plant are regenerated into whole plants containing the desired gene. Additional DNA fragments may be combined with it to form an rDNA molecule. A means to select transformants is required for this scheme to succeed. Antibiotic resistance genes isolated from bacteria were originally used as markers for transformed cells, and became one element of political critiques of biotechnology. However, other methods have superseded the use of resistance genes or depend on their removal after selection thus ending polemics about the safety of antibiotic resistance genes in transgenic plants. It is, however, worth noting that risk assessors long ago concluded these genes were safe to use (Ramessar et al., 2007; Chassy, 2010). Candidate plants are then characterized and are eventually crossed with commercial varieties to produce transgenic varieties carrying the newly introduced trait. The *in vitro* rDNA techniques of modern biotechnology have been used to produce new varieties with traits that could not be achieved by conventional breeding. The process can also reduce the time required to develop a new variety. From a safety assessor's perspective, varieties produced in this manner are more amenable to safety assessment since the sequence and encoded genetic content of the inserted DNA is known *a priori.*

What's a GM Crop? A Revealing Truth and New Challenges

Most countries regulate what they have chosen to call GM or GMO plants, foods, and feeds. The exact legal definition of these terms, which differs from country to country, will have an impact on the regulation of new technologies whose products are appearing on regulators' desks or those that are under development. Differences in definition can result in a product being classified as a GMO in one country and not in others. For example, EU directives define a GMO as an "organism, with the exception of human beings, in which the genetic material has been altered in a way that does not occur naturally by mating and/or natural recombination." The intent of this definition obviously endorses all food that is *natural* and captures food that is changed in some way through human intervention. Since virtually all food would be classified GMO under this definition, the directives also exclude a number of categories including organisms produced through *in vitro* mutagenesis and even organisms into which genes isolated from unrelated organisms have been inserted. In the EU, a product that contains >1% by weight of a highly purified soybean oil isolated from GM soybeans, highly purified starch from GM corn, or highly purified sugar isolated from GM sugarcane or sugar beets, must be labeled as containing GM even though no trace of the GM plant, or inserted DNA and/or proteins, can be found in the highly purified products. Ironically, a cheese prepared with a transgenic bacterium, or wine or beer fermented with transgenic yeast, does not require a label indicating that it contains GM ingredients, although billions of live rDNA-containing organisms remain in the product. Nor is it required that chemicals produced by rDNA-containing GMO bacteria and yeasts be labeled. In the European Union, these transgenic organisms are considered to be only "processing aides."

A partial list of existing and potential new technologies and a brief explanation of each is presented in Table 24.1. It is instructive to look at the definition below of a GMO used by the World Health Organization of the UN (WHO) to determine if the technologies listed in Table 24.1 produce crop varieties that would be captured by this definition and therefore classified as GM:

> Genetically modified organisms (GMOs) can be defined as organisms in which the genetic material (DNA) has been altered in a way that does not occur naturally. The technology is often called "modern biotechnology" or "gene technology," sometimes also "recombinant DNA technology" or "genetic engineering." It allows selected individual genes to be transferred from one organism into another, also between non-related species.[6]

The definition would not capture small RNA methodology since no genes *per se* are transferred and no novel proteins are produced. Similarly, *in vitro* and *in vivo* mutagenesis would fall outside the definition for similar reasons. Modification of transcription factors[7] (TF) might fall under the definition if a TF from a different species is introduced. The definition appears to capture *cis*-genic methods although whether the genetic material has been altered is open to dispute since the genes inserted arise from the same specie; however, the definition literally excludes *transfer* of genes. Transient expression products would be excluded even if DNA were present in the specific method used since DNA is not transferred permanently into the genome (no gene transfer has occurred). Thus, it appears that at least one commonly accepted definition of GMO would fail to capture most of the technologies described in Table 24.1. A number of countries have chosen to define GMOs differently and as a consequence there is great potential for confusion in international trade. An international workshop was held in 2011 to consider the regulatory implications of diverse definitions of alternative and new gene technologies presented in Table 24.1 (Lusser and Davies, 2013).

It is important to note that mutagenesis, viral infections, and cross-breeding can produce the same kinds of DNA sequence and phenotypic changes as the technologies listed in Table 24.1 (Parrott, 2005; Weber et al., 2012). In fact, traditional breeders have, over the years, created a number of new varieties that are now known to involve changes in small RNAs, TFs, and nucleotide-level mutations (Parrott et al., 2010). This begs the question, "*Why are methods that produce the same result in a more exact and precise way than the older black-box methods of mutagenesis and crossing captured by a GMO definition that leads to rigorous safety assessment by regulators*?" One simple answer is that the definition seeks to regulate new varieties developed in a laboratory by means of *in vitro* DNA technologies that are viewed as *unnatural*—that is, they do not occur in nature.

Setting aside the fact that virtually none of our crop plants occur in nature in their present form and all are extensively genetically modified, the definition of GMO excludes products that could, in principle, be produced by other breeding methods and

Table 24.1 Alternative technologies for molecular plant breeding

Technology	Description	Comments
Small RNA (co-suppression, anti-sense, RNAi)	An RNA-dependent mechanism used primarily to suppress specific gene expression; occurs without the insertion of a gene that encodes a protein. DNA encoding specific RNA is inserted.	No novel protein is produced. Cross-infection immunity employed in traditional breeding operates by the same or similar mechanisms. Genetically engineered virus resistant crops have been approved.
In vivo mutagenesis	Reagents, enzymes, and nucleic acid templates are introduced into cells to bring about site-specific mutagenesis without the introduction of new DNA.	Although the method employs *in vitro* techniques no heterologous DNA is introduced. Identical DNA mutations could occur spontaneously.
In vitro mutagenesis	A gene is cloned from an organism and it is mutated *in vitro* by site-directed mutagenesis. The mutated gene is reintroduced into the parent organism by transformation and recombination.	Only mutated DNA isolated from the same organism is introduced. Identical DNA mutations could occur spontaneously. Can also be used to modify gene expression by mutating regulatory elements.
Modification of transcription factors	Transcription factors expression can be altered by manipulation of the TF promoter; alternative TFs can be introduced.	No new protein is produced or closely related proteins are produced. The level of protein expression is very low. Evidence shows that traditional breeding can modify or introduce novel TFs.
Cis-genic and intra-genic transformation	Genes from other varieties of the same species, or closely related sexually compatible species are introduced using *in vitro* transformation techniques. Allows introduction of iso-genes.	Genes are exchanged between varieties. Homologous DNA found in other varieties of the same species is introduced. Cross-breeding can produce the similar results.
Transient expression	Genes or gene products are introduced into the plant. Novel DNA is not inserted permanently into the genome. Genes can also be inserted and subsequently excised.	No novel DNA is present in edible parts of the organism. Novel characteristics typically depend on transient effects.
Grafting	Conventionally bred plants are grafted into transgenic rootstock. Useful for trees.	No novel DNA, protein, or metabolites need be present in the edible portions of the plant.

which would not be subject to the premarket safety assessment required of GM crops. Moreover, varieties produced using the methods listed in Table 24.1 would be difficult if not impossible to distinguish from those produced by spontaneous *natural* mutations and conventional breeding. All that could be established in a comparison of two varieties is that their genomic DNA sequences are different, and with some technologies no detectable differences in the genomic DNA sequence would be observed. It would, therefore, be impossible to determine the breeding process with which the varieties were developed. Clearly the "GMO" category has a high level of arbitrariness from a scientific point of view, and reflects political, economic, trade, and other considerations.

Food Safety of Transgenic Crops: A Point of Contention

Although each country may have differing laws, regulations, and agency roles associated with regulation of transgenic crops safety, food-safety assessors the world over have, for the most part, evolved a common view of the scientific principles upon which safety assessment should be based. A comprehensive rationale for the food safety assessment of transgenic organisms was published by *Codex Alimentarius* (2003, 2009). A number of good reviews that explain the safety assessment process in detail also have been published (see for example, König et al., 2004). The safety assessment process seeks to identify potential hazards, assess which hazards present real risks, and characterize the nature and extent of the identified risks. Responsibility for risk-management plans and risk communication is the responsibility of risk managers. Product approvals are informed by the scientific risk assessment; however, scientific risk assessors do not make approval decisions. The procedure for approval or disapproval of products is a complex political process that varies from country to country (Chassy, 2008).

The hazards associated with transgenic crops can be divided into two broad categories:

1. Hazards associated with the newly inserted material (usually DNA), expressed novel proteins, novel metabolites, and intended compositional changes.
2. Hazards associated with unintended changes that may have occurred as a result of the DNA insertion.

The approach to evaluating these two classes of hazards is, of necessity, fundamentally different since the nature of the newly introduced material and its products are known *a priori*, whereas unintended changes occur randomly as a *result* of the breeding process. Procedures have been developed to evaluate whether there are risks of adverse effects posed by the inserted DNA, any proteins encoded by the DNA, and any new metabolites or compositional changes that have been introduced. Experimental and *computer-based* procedures for evaluating the safety of the inserted material have been published and will not be described here in detail (König et al., 2004; Delaney et al., 2008). Suffice it to say that methods exist with which it is possible to determine if a protein will be digested in the stomach or denatured by food processing—both processes that could lead to loss of functional activity—or, by comparison, to databases if the protein bears any resemblance to known toxins or allegens. Composition studies, animal studies, and the evaluation of protein toxicity or allergenicity are discussed in subsequent sections.

Unintended changes occur in all types of plant breeding (Cellini et al., 2004; Parrott, 2005; Weber et al., 2012). Insertion of DNA into chromosomes can theoretically interrupt the function of genes, create new genes and/or pathways that encode novel products, activate cryptic pathways leading to the formation of potentially toxic or allergenic products, or through direct or indirect effects alter gene expression and cell composition. The challenge for the risk assessor is that none of these unforeseen changes can be anticipated. The strategy for identifying unintended effects is to screen carefully for new hazards, as, for example, a meaningful change in composition or phenotype of the crop plant. The ultimate challenge is to determine if any of the unknown changes that occurred in plant breeding has created a potentially harmful risk exposure. Changes *per se* are not dangerous.

Skeptics and critics have advocated a highly precautionary approach to GM crops approval. They argue, for example, that the inserted DNA may cause adverse effects such as the spread of antibiotic resistance genes or that the insertion of DNA elements into the human genome that could cause cancer, that the inserted proteins could be allergens, that alternative RNA splicing or unintended DNA fragment insertions could produce novel and potentially harmful proteins, and that new or cryptic pathways could be activated to produce toxic molecules (Latham et al., 2006; Smith, 2007; Dona and Arvanitoyannis, 2009). These are exactly the same hazards that can be found on the risk assessors' hazard scan. However, whereas skeptics worry about hypothetical hazards, risk assessors evaluate laboratory-derived data to determine which, if any, of the potential hazards have materialized in a newly formed transgenic variety creating a real risk of harm upon consumption.

Critics also argue that not enough safety research has been done and that we do not understand enough about the complex interactions and regulatory circuits that control living cells (Latham et al., 2006; Smith, 2007; Dona and Arvanitoyannis, 2009). What is typically not explained is why the same argument is not made against other modalities of breeding that have as a goal the production of changes in the DNA that will give rise to altered and/or novel phenotypes. Critics further assert, without providing direct evidence, that transgene insertion is unnatural in that it does not occur in nature and that it is fundamentally different than other modalities of breeding. However, horizontal gene-transfer between sexually incompatible species has been demonstrated to commonly occur in nature (Parrott, 2005).[8] The incorporation of heterologous genes in nature is mediated by the same systems that integrate transgenic DNA sequences in the laboratory. When breeders make crosses between species, heterologous genes are transferred and thousands of DNA insertions occur as whole chromosomes recombine (Chrispeels and Sadava, 2003). Genomic DNA sequencing has revealed evidence of numerous DNA insertions in many plant species. Insertions can be caused by DNA transposition mediated by transposition and insertion sequences, as well as by mutations that result in DNA duplications, inversions, and deletions (Weber et al., 2012).

A considerable body of genomic DNA sequence data has now been accumulated that demonstrates that conventional methods of breeding are likely to produce more changes in the genome DNA than do transgene insertions (Batista et al., 2008; Ricroch, Berge, and Kuntz 2011, Weber et al., 2012). It has been reported that mutagenesis can result in thousands of genomic mutations per cell, including point mutations, inversions, duplications, and deletions. During a single growing season, dozens of DNA transpositions can occur in a single crop plant. Varieties of the same crop may have genes that are present or absent in other members of the same species and the position of genes of the chromosomes of two varieties may differ markedly. On at least two occasions, the evolution of novel proteins has been observed in crop plants. These latter three observations can be explained by the extensive spontaneous random excision, relocation, and insertion of chromosomal DNA fragments in recombinational or transpositional events (Weber et al., 2012).

Critics of transgenic crops assert two reasons for special need for safety regulation. They argue first that all transgenic crops are fundamentally different from crops produced by other methods of breeding and, second, that the insertion of DNA coupled with the introduction of heterologous genes makes transgenic crop plants inherently more risky. Critics are reluctant to approve of any plant that is the result of the application of *in vitro* DNA methodology and focus their skepticism on *transgenic crops as a class*. In contrast, science-based risk assessment points toward the conclusion that genes move across species lines in nature, that genes have been transferred into new species as a result of plant breeding, and that both nature and breeding produce mutations and unintended effects in crop plants. Risk assessors coming from this understanding, therefore, focus on the individual new variety and ask if the newly introduced phenotype, or any unintended changes, will do unacceptable harm to consumers or the environment. Safety assessment then uses *case-by-case* evaluation and does not presume *a priori* that transgenic crops are either safe or unsafe. The standard by which new varieties are evaluated is comparative and seeks to ensure that there is a *reasonable certainty* that no harm will result if the food is consumed in the customary manner. Safety assessment does not conclude that new varieties are absolutely safe, since zero risk is impossible to establish. The assessment seeks to determine if new varieties are as safe as, or are safer than, other varieties of the same crop. This process is sometimes referred to as *comparative safety assessment*.

Composition as a Window on Intended and Unintended Effects: Substantial Equivalence

The cornerstone of comparative safety assessment is a comparison of the composition of a new variety with its parental variety as well as with other representative commonly cultivated varieties of the crop (König et al., 2004). Composition studies can be used to confirm if intended changes in composition have occurred, if new metabolites that were intended to be present are being produced, and if any unintended changes in composition have occurred (Cellini et al., 2004). The composition of each crop variety is different, each contributes different macro- and micronutrients to human and animal diets, and each can contain different toxicants, food allergens, antinutrients, and potentially beneficial phytochemicals (Chassy, 2010). As a consequence, a unique panel of constituents must be analyzed with each crop. Lists of key analytes have been compiled by expert panels and published by the OECD.[9] These expert consensus documents also provide detailed information about the crop; its cultivation; processing; and food, feed, and industrial uses, with particular emphasis on its importance in human nutrition. Compositional analysis is used to confirm that no potentially harmful changes such as losses in a key nutrient or increases in a known antinutrient have occurred.

A thorough knowledge of composition allows the risk assessor to evaluate nutritional value, and any potential toxic or allergenic effects. Nutrition, toxicological, and other studies documented in the literature describe the biological activity of each food constituent in detail. The effect of a food or feed on an organism can be computed and depends directly on the composition of the food or feed, how much is consumed, and how often it is consumed. If differences in composition are observed, it is also possible to evaluate any possible biological significance of the differences. Changes in composition are not *per se* harmful and, as is discussed later, differences in composition are often observed in a comparison of varieties of the same crop (Chassy et al., 2004).

Comparison of the composition of a new variety with other varieties is necessary to determine if changes in composition have occurred as a result of the breeding process. If differences in composition are observed, the significance of each difference must be evaluated through further study. This comparative process has been called the Substantial Equivalence (SE) paradigm. There has been much confusion, some perhaps deliberate, about the meaning of the SE process. It is often claimed that the evaluation proves that, when a product is concluded to be substantially equivalent, the new variety is safe. Critics of the paradigm argue that a new transgenic variety can never be identical to its conventional counterpart. There has been much polemical debate in the literature about this point, so it is important to be very clear about what SE is and is not. The framers of the paradigm noted that most components would be present in a new variety at concentrations very similar to those found in the parental variety and were thus likely to pose no new hazards. They asserted that since the two varieties being compared were substantially equivalent with respect to most components, safety assessors needed only to focus on the observed differences. The compositional comparison with which the SE paradigm begins is a jumping-off point, not a conclusion. The process identifies differences; since changes in composition are not *per se* risky, the biological and nutritional consequences of any observed differences must be evaluated further (Chassy et al., 2004; Chassy et al., 2008). It is, therefore, improper to assert that two plants are substantially equivalent. It is preferable to conclude that no biologically meaningful differences were identified through application of the SE paradigm.

Compositional analysis also provides a window into the presence of potentially adverse unintended effects and the presence of new and unintended novel metabolites. A major challenge in making such compositional comparisons is definition of the normal range of metabolites for each crop. It has been observed that macronutrients can vary by twofold or greater in different varieties of the same crop and micronutrients and other minor components may vary by as much as 100-fold or more (Harrigan et al., 2010; Harrigan and Chassy, 2012). Plant composition is highly variable (for further references see in Herman, Chassy, and Parrott 2009; Herman and Price, 2013; and Ricroch et al., 2011). To the question of how much difference in composition should trigger further investigation, it has been suggested that differences ranging from 3 percent to 20 percent in a component should be a trigger for further research. It is pointless to pick an arbitrary percentage difference since the biological significance of a difference is dependent on the role of that crop in the human diet, how much and how often it is consumed, and what percentage of the required intake of that nutrient is derived from that crop. A similar argument can be made with respect to antinutrients and toxicants; the potential harmfulness depends directly on dose and exposure and not on percent change. Risk assessors have established methods for making an analysis of the biological significance of differences in composition.

The concern has been expressed that transgene insertion could activate a cryptic biosynthetic pathway or in some other way lead to the production of a novel toxic compound. The unknown compound would not be analyzed since its presence could not be predicted. This is a possible but highly unlikely scenario for several reasons. The targeted compositional analysis that is applied to new transgenic varieties typically accounts for 85–99% of the biomass, thus only a small percentage of the crop mass could be present as a novel component. Based on the projected dietary consumption of the new variety the maximum dose and exposure to a novel metabolite can be calculated (Chassy et al., 2004). Such calculations reveal that a novel compound would need to be very highly toxic to have any adverse effect (Chassy et al. 2004). Moreover, it is difficult to imagine such a scenario since no novel toxic compound of this type has ever been identified in a crop plant either as a spontaneous occurrence or as a result of breeding, including transgene insertion. There is also no reason to believe that the chances of evolution of a toxic compound would be any greater in transgenic breeding than it would be in conventional breeding.

Some have expressed the concern that novel toxic molecules could spontaneously appear in transgenic crops. The production of novel toxic molecules requires the creation of new metabolic pathways for its biosynthesis. It is, however, very difficult for organisms to evolve novel biosynthetic pathways that are encoded by multiple genes. Evolving pathways using older mutagenic methods confronts the reality that great majority of mutations are cryptic or cause loss of function. Although novel single genes have appeared in crops, the spontaneous evolution of a novel multigene biosynthetic pathway has not been reported in any crop plant. Plant breeders have had difficulty evolving new pathways in order to produce desired metabolites, despite great effort. One motivation for using genetic engineering is that the technique allows the introduction of multiple genes, opening up the possibility of pathway engineering.

Recently, new analytical technologies called "-Omic" technologies have been developed Chassy, 2010). The principal omic technologies allow investigators to determine which specific genes are being expressed in an organism (transcriptomics); which proteins are present in cells, organs, or tissues (proteomics); or which metabolites are present (metabolomics). Although these methods have proven to be powerful research tools for comparison of cells or tissues, there are limitations. The methods are not standardized, there is no uniform methodology for reporting and analysis, and it is difficult to repeat and/or compare results from different laboratories. As of now, omic methods are very effective at measuring many analytes *poorly*, because analyte concentrations are not precisely, accurately, and reproducibly measured (Chassy, 2010; Harrigan and Chassy, 2012). It has been suggested that omic methods might enhance the safety assessment of GM foods by allowing assessors to compare the entire compositional profile, the proteins, and the levels of gene expression between a new variety and a parental strain. Yet it is clear that omictechnologies are not yet ready to apply to safety assessment; moreover no good case has been made that currently accepted methods of compositional analysis are inadequate.

Although omic profiling is not a useful technology for safety assessment, it can be a powerful tool for identifying differences between two or more samples. An analysis of 44 published comparisons of omic profiles obtained with conventional varieties and their transgenic counterparts revealed that transgenic crops profiles are more similar to those observed for the parental strain than are those collected for other cultivars of the same crop plant (Ricroch at al. 2011). The best explanation for this observation is that transgene insertion brings about fewer unintended changes in metabolomes, proteomes, and transcriptomes than does conventional breeding. This conclusion is consistent with an extensive published literature on compositional differences between transgenic and conventionally bred varieties of numerous crops, which confirms that transgene insertion has less impact on composition than do other modalities of plant breeding (Ricroch et al., 2011; Herman et al. 2009; Herman and Price, 2013). These observations provide strong support for the conclusion that fewer unintended changes are associated with transgenic breeding than with conventional breeding. This is perhaps why several recent publications have suggested that compositional analysis of transgenic crops is not scientifically justified unless there is a specific hypothesis to test, for example, when composition has been deliberately changed (Herman et al. 2009; Herman and Price, 2013).

Protein Safety, Food Allergy, and Allergens

Since modern biotechnology allows genes to be moved from almost any organism into crop plants, it is, in principle, possible that a gene(s) that encode toxin(s) or allergen(s) could be introduced into foods in which they would not normally occur. There are several means to avoid the introduction of toxin proteins or allergenic proteins. The first line of defense is to not insert genes isolated from plants known to produce toxins, antinutrients, or allergens. The level of precaution is raised if the inserted novel protein was isolated from a source that is not commonly eaten and with which there is very little *history of safe* use. Virtually all proteins are innocuous, but a few are known to cause harm to humans and animals (Delaney, et al., 2008). Most of these have been extensively studied. The sequences of these proteins have been deposited in databases and their structural features have been extensively analyzed. In recent years *comparative sequence* analysis has allowed the identification of common sequences, domains, and other structural features that are associated with harmful effects (Goodman, et al., 2008; Radauer, et al., 2008). For example, it is known that most plant allergens fall into one of two or three super-families of closely related proteins (Radauer, et al., 2008). For most allergens the exact sequence of amino acids, referred to as an epitope, that bind to specific receptors on immune cells has been identified. It is, therefore, possible to compare candidate proteins with databases of all known allergenic, toxins, or proteins with antinutrient activity. If no similarity to known harmful proteins is detected, it is highly unlikely that the protein will manifest harmful effects when consumed.

The digestibility of inserted proteins in simulated gastric fluid is also assessed since a protein that is extensively degraded in the stomach is unlikely to retain biological activity (Goodman et al., 2008; Goodman and Tetteh, 2011). The stability of the protein to feed and food processing steps to which the raw material is typically exposed is evaluated. Most, but not all, proteins can be thermally inactivated and many food-processing techniques expose foods to elevated temperatures. Toxins and antinutrients commonly found in beans, for example, are rendered harmless by cooking. One additional safety measure that can be taken to avoid the inclusion of potential allergens in transgenic crops is to use immune serum from allergy sufferers to test if the allergy-associated antibodies in their serum react with the newly inserted proteins. Note also that many food ingredients isolated from transgenic crops (i.e., soy and canola oils, starch, lecithin, emulsifiers, beet and cane sugar, HFCS, etc.) do not contain appreciable protein content and are thus unlikely to be manifest protein toxicity or evoke allergic reactions upon consumption.

Food allergy can be a life-threatening condition that forces the allergy sufferer to carefully avoid foods that contain the allergen to which they have become sensitized. This is often difficult since allergens can elicit a response in very small doses and can be intentionally included or inadvertently present in food products in which the consumer would not expect them to appear. Law requires packaged food products to be labeled with respect to allergen content; however, restaurants do not ordinarily label foods. Since about 5 percent of the population (3–4 percent of adults and 6–8 percent of children) may suffer from food allergies, and there is some evidence this number is increasing, there is understandable concern that new allergens should not be introduced into food products. The *comparartive sequence analysis* and laboratory evaluations described in the foregoing paragraphs are very effective at detecting and preventing the introduction of *known allergens* (Goodman and Tetteh, 2011).

What remains difficult is to predict if a protein with no history of safe use will become a *novel allergen*. Molecular-structure studies are beginning to lead to an ability to predict if a novel protein will be an allergen (Goodman, et al., 2008; Radauer, et al., 2008). There is, unfortunately, no validated and internationally accepted animal model system with which it is possible to predict if a protein will become an allergen; however, the search for a predictive animal model continues.

Critics of plant genetic engineering are particularly skeptical that novel allergens will not be introduced into crops. They often point to studies in which an allergen from Brazil nuts was introduced into soybeans as part of a project designed to raise the sulfur-containing amino acid content of soybeans as evidence of the dangers involved. Researchers screened the candidate soybean extracts with serum from Brazil-nut allergy-sensitive patients and observed a positive reaction (Nordlee et al., 1996). The protein allergen had not been previously identified, but the safety-assessment process detected its presence and the research was stopped in a very early stage. The experience proves that it is, in fact, possible to introduce allergens through genetic engineering and that it is also possible to effectively test for known or suspected allergens.

Critics also point to a study conducted by researchers in Australia who reported in 2005 that the production of a bean α-amylase in peas led to immune responses in a rat-model system that might signify that the protein would become an allergen (Prescott et al., 2005; Goodman et al., 2008). In spite of the fact that the rat-model system was not widely accepted in the scientific community, CSIRO[10] discontinued the research. In a recent publication, these, together with other investigators, were unable to confirm the previously reported results and observed no difference in immune response of rats between exposure to control or experimental peas (Lee et al., 2013).

Food allergy is a very important and emotional issue. There is an especially large amount of misinformation with regard to the potential for transgenic crops to cause allergy. Perhaps the worst of these is the claim that since the introduction of GM soybeans in 1996 the rate of food allergy has doubled (Smith, 2007). This is a classic example of a *post hoc* fallacy in which there is no causal connection demonstrated.

Rat Studies: What They Can and Can't Tell Us

> All chemicals are poisons; it is only the dose that makes that a thing is not a poison…
>
> —Paracelsus (1493–1541)

Toxicologists rely heavily on studies in animals to assess toxicity of chemical compounds. The 90-day chronic-toxicity animal study in which various fixed amounts of a compound to be tested are administered each day to determine a *dose-response curve* has become a standard for evaluating the maximum dose at which no adverse effects are observed (NOAEL), the lowest level at which adverse effects appear (LOAEL) and the level at which a compound becomes overtly toxic and/or lethal—often expressed as the level at which 50 percent of the animals die (LD_{50}). In practice, an important indicator of study quality is that as dose increases, the level and severity of any observed adverse effects increases. Using these studies, and taking into account differences between the test animals and humans as well as biological variation, toxicologists are able to estimate an acceptable daily intake (ADI), which is the level at which the compound may be safely consumed for a lifetime without adverse effect. This level is often set at 100- or 1000-fold higher than the LOAEL, which ensures a large margin of safety; note, however, that setting the level of desired safety is a political risk-management decision. These carefully designed studies are described in several internationally accepted protocols published by OECD, WHO, EPA and FDA.

The 90-day rat model study is sometimes used to evaluate potential toxicity of novel proteins that have been inserted into crop plants (Delaney et al., 2008). More commonly, a very high-level single dose can be used in an acute toxicity study. The underlying rationale is that toxic proteins are almost without exception acutely toxic, since they are either quickly digested or eliminated and are not absorbed as such. Proteins that have been incorporated into GM crops have been evaluated in an acute toxicity study and found to produce no harmful effects when fed at levels 1000- to more than one-million-fold higher than would normally be encountered in the diet. Some have been evaluated in 90-day chronic toxicity studies and found to be innocuous.

Whole food feeding studies (WFS) are also sometimes performed (Delaney et al. 2008, van Haver et al. 2008, Snell et al. 2012). These feeding studies are often performed using rats, and the design resembles the 90-day rat chronic-toxicity study described earlier. In WFS 10–30 percent, and sometimes even higher portions, of the test animal diets are composed of the transgenic crop being evaluated. Diets with a high percentage of a single ingredient are sometimes not palatable to animals, and it is often difficult to provide all necessary nutrients in a diet with exaggerated composition of one ingredient. Moreover, adverse effects are sometimes seen in animals fed large amounts of single food ingredients. A 42-day broiler study is also used in the same manner since it is both sensitive and rapid. These studies are particularly useful for evaluating nutritional value and feed performance; when similar studies are performed with production farm animals, they are called feed-performance studies.

Nonexperts generally believe that if a food contains potentially toxic components they could be detected by such feeding studies. At first glance, this seems to be a reasonable approach. Toxicologists have, however, determined that WFS lack power, have a number of other defects, and would be unable to detect novel toxicants present at the levels at which they would be likely to occur in transgenic crops—if such compounds occur at all since the generation of novel, and, therefore, not analyzed, toxic compounds in food and feed crops has never been observed. There are several recent papers, and another in press, that describe the deficiencies of whole food animal studies (Chassy et al., 2004; van Haver et al., 2008; Kuntz and Ricroch, 2012; Snell et al., 2012; Herman and Ekmay, 2013; Bartholomaeus et al., 2013).[11] This is not, however, a new conclusion.

The U.S. FDA concluded in 1980 that WFS lacked power, were fraught with confounders, and were not suitable for the evaluation of potentially toxic molecules produced in food through processes such as irradiation or thermal processing. The FDA concluded the preferred approach was direct analysis of the suspect compounds coupled with 90-day rat studies on pure compounds of interest to determine NOAEL, LOAEL, LD_{50}, and ADI. The reason for this can be found in simple arithmetic. It can be calculated that, based on the known toxicities and amounts that could be present, taken together with the amount consumed, the low levels of potentially toxic molecules present in the unanalyzed portion of foods or feeds derived from transgenic crops would not constitute a high enough dose to cause adverse effects in such studies. Even highly toxic molecules would most likely be present at levels below the level of toxicological concern. A more practical consideration for avoiding WFS is that these kinds of studies require considerable resources, are time consuming, are subject to significant biological variability unless large numbers of animals are used, and suffer from a number of other confounders. A serious ethical question arises from the use of so many animals in weak and pointless studies (on ethical questions in food generally, see Korthals, this volume).

In spite of the questionable merit of WFS, many WFS have been performed in a number of animal species testing various transgenic crops (van Haver et al. 2008: Snell et al., 2012, Bartholomaeus et al., 2013). Regulatory agencies in some jurisdictions require WFS to be conducted as a routine part of the premarket regulatory review. The U.S. FDA does not require WFS, and, in recent years, EFSA has stated that WFS are not a required part of the dossier for a new transgenic variety (van Haver et al, 2008).[12] Whole food studies also have been performed by independent researchers and reported in the peer-reviewed literature. The findings from these studies can be summarized fairly simply. Those studies that were carefully designed and conducted, and which followed widely accepted international guidelines, uniformly and without exception found no biologically significant differences between transgenic and nontransgenic counterparts (van Haver et al., 2008; Kuntz and Ricroch, 2012 Bartholomaeus et al., 2013). Results from those studies that did not follow internationally accepted protocols can be divided into a small group that observed one or more statistical differences between control and test groups in measured parameters, and a larger group that failed to observe any differences that could be attributed to the transgenic crop content of the feed.

A few researchers have made sensational claims about potential adverse effects associated with consumption of transgenic crops based on animal studies. These claims have been amplified and distorted by opponents of transgenic crops in an attempt to scare consumers and political decision makers. Among the first of these were Ewen and Pusztai (1999) who claimed that feeding GM potatoes to rats caused "cancerous and precancerous" changes in gastrointestinal epithelial cells. Critical analysis of the work by a Royal Society (UK) expert panel, among others, concluded that no meaningful scientific conclusion could be drawn from the work due to numerous flaws in the experimental design, conduct, and analysis (The Royal Society [UK], 1999). Others publications based on WFS with transgenic and conventional food and feed crops have reported a variety of differences between test and control animals such as differences in organ sizes, differences in overall weight, differences in the levels of enzymes, and morphological and histological differences in cells of specific tissue, and others.[13] A few general observations can be made about these studies: (a) the observations often differ from those reported in other similar published studies (which are often not cited by the study authors), (b) they do not follow internationally accepted protocols, (c) diets fed to the animals are not equivalent (food or feed not cultivated under equivalent controlled conditions, different varieties compared, no composition analysis reported, feed intake dissimilar between groups, etc.), (d) too few animals are studied and/or inappropriate statistical tests applied, and (e) researchers confuse normal biological variation with harmful effects. Widespread criticism by the scientific community and the subsequent publication of papers that point out the shortcomings of these papers leads this author—and likely many other scientists—to the conclusion that these studies should have been rejected by peer-reviewers and should not have been published (see for example commentary at: http://www.sciencemediacentre.org/expert-reaction-to-efsa-report-conclusion-that-seralini-study-conclusions-were-not-supported-by-data/ and http://www.efb-central.org/images/uploads/EFBStatement.pdf).

Media and Manipulation: An Illustrative Case Analysis

The previous section illustrated how flawed studies frequently influence both the media and the food consumer. One recent case demonstrates the politics of this phenomenon more clearly and raises the ethical question concretely. In September 2012, French microbiologist Gilles-Eric Séralini, who has vocally opposed transgenic crops and the herbicide Roundup™,[14] held a press conference for selected members of the press to announce the results of his latest study (Séralini et al., 2012). He claimed that consumption of GM herbicide-tolerant maize and Roundup™, caused tumors and premature deaths in rats. He presented color pictures of rats with grotesque tumors to emphasize his point. The electronic and print media quickly broadcast the findings as well as the grotesque photos and the news quickly spread around the globe. Professor Séralini also took the unusual step of requiring reporters to sign nondisclosure agreements before the press conference so that the reporters could not consult experts for fact checking prior to rushing to print the shocking results he reported. Séralini also used the occasion to announce the publication of his book *Tous cobayes*? (*Are we all guinea pigs?*); he provided a link to a YouTube video with the same title.

There can be little doubt that the orchestrated media event was part of a carefully laid plan to help discredit transgenic crops produced using modern biotechnology and the chemicals used with them. Séralini has a long history of opposition to them and has published a series of widely criticized papers on the harmful effects of transgenic crops and related agricultural chemicals such as Roundup™ (Doull et al., 2008; see also http://

academicsreview.org/reviewed-content/genetic-roulette/). He was well aware that the media would broadcast this exciting story and it that it would elevate fears of transgenic crops. He deliberately manipulated the media.

Numerous critiques by scientific societies, research institutes, regulatory bodies, and groups of scientists have pointed out the flaws in the Séralini study (see for example commentary at: http://www.sciencemediacentre.org/expert-reaction-to-efsa-report-conclusion-that-seralini-study-conclusions-were-not-supported-by-data/ and http://www.efb-central.org/images/uploads/EFBStatement.pdf). Several of these critiques have been published in the peer-reviewed literature; see for example a review by Arjó et al. (2013). The criticism of Séralini's study goes beyond a recitation of deficiencies such as too few animals in control groups, the inappropriate use of a strain of rats that is very tumor-prone, and the fact that there are no statistically significant differences in the results observed for test and control animals—a fact that Séralini himself freely admits. The criticism also points out that in his fervor to discredit modern biotechnology, Séralini may have committed scientific misconduct. He has refused to release the raw data on which his conclusions were based and he failed to cite other similar studies that did not support his conclusions.[15] In fact, he claimed no such studies had been previously performed, whereas a recent review that would have been available to the Séralini team presented a lengthy compendium of published similar long-term studies (Snell et al., 2012). Withholding data or selective citation is scientific misconduct. The mistreatment of animals described in the study violated animal welfare guidelines and is a violation of ethical practice.

The impact of the study was immediate and widespread as noted by Arjó et al. (2013):

> Within hours, the news had been blogged and tweeted more than 1.5 million times. Lurid photos of tumor-ridden rats appeared on websites and in newspapers around the world, while larger-than-life images of the rats were broadcast across the USA on the popular television show *Dr. Oz.* Activists destroyed a GM soybean consignment at the port of Lorient, France, in order to denounce the presence in the food chain of a product they considered to be toxic (Vargas 2012). The Russian Federation and Kazakhstan banned imports of the maize variety used in the study, Peru imposed a 10-year moratorium on GM crops (Bernhardt 2012) and Kenya banned all imports of GM food (Owino 2012).

The EU may repeat the Séralini studies to corroborate or disprove them. The EU also is considering requiring that long-term animal studies (WFS) be made mandatory in the premarket testing of all transgenic crops.

The peer-review process of vetting new science is not perfect. As noted in the preceding paragraphs, a few other flawed studies claiming harmful effects of transgenic crops have slipped through the peer-review process. Although the Committee on Publication Ethics (COPE) guidelines clearly require journals to retract flawed papers, and papers in which scientific misconduct or ethics violations have occurred, the *Journal of Food and Chemical Toxicology* (JSFT) has not retracted their acceptance of the Séralini paper.[16] Widespread protests of scientists in response to Séralini's flawed paper and unethical behavior have contributed to some journalists expressing their objection to being manipulated. The media often reacts to controversies by assuming that the truth lies somewhere between the extremes. The foregoing sections have outlined the basis of support for the assertion that GM crops are as safe as any other; there is no scientific basis to justify any middle ground.

Food Safety: What Really Matters?

There exists an international scientific consensus that bioengineered crops produced using modern biotechnology are as safe as, if not safer than, any other.[17] Virtually none of the world's crop plants exist as such in nature—none of them are natural; most have been extensively genetically modified. The term *GM crops* could probably best be applied to crops that were bred without the use of modern biotechnology since they are more likely to have suffered mutations, compositional changes, and other unintended effects than those produced using more exact modern *in vitro* molecular methods. Transgenic crops more closely resemble their parents than do crops produced by other methods. Extensive selection of phenotypes is also used to ensure that no unintended changes have occurred. Candidate transgenic varieties are subjected to a thorough premarket safety assessment that is not applied to crops developed using more random and more disruptive technologies. From a scientific risk-based perspective, as well as almost 20 years of use in world agriculture without incident, it can be concluded that placing transgenic crops in a class that is regulated while not regulating crops bred by other methods that have undergone similar changes or which possess similar phenotypes, is scientifically inappropriate if not overtly irrational. Food-safety regulators should, instead, be tasked with ensuring that the introduction of any novel phenotypes into food and feed crops will not pose any special risks or create harmful effects independently of the process used to develop the crop.

The closest approximation to the food-safety conclusions of the science discussed in this chapter is that in place in Canada. These regulations are directed at novel crops rather than GM crops. In spite of the Canada's expressed intention to regulate all novel phenotypes in a similar manner, the steps of a premarket safety assessment for a new transgenic variety are no different in Canada than they are in other countries, whereas non-GM crops receive only a cursory review. The cost of undue precaution regarding the safety of GM crops is high. It is generally believed that the direct cost of an approval for a new GM crop can exceed U.S.$100 million, though hard data to support this conclusion are lacking. Approvals can require as much as 5–10 years to complete. The indirect costs are even greater. Missed opportunities caused by not developing new GM crops or not adopting them is probably the greatest indirect cost. Another significant indirect cost is preoccupation with the risks associated with GM crops, which diverts resources and attention away from real food-safety risks. Consumers worry about GM-crops safety instead of food-safety risks that could actually do them harm.

The major risks in the food system are related to diet, chemical contaminants, and pathogens. About a billion people run the risk of not having enough food to eat and consequently suffer from malnutrition. This number is expected to grow as population and food prices rise unless reduction in poverty and enhancements in agricultural productivity can be achieved. WHO estimates that more than 15 million children die in the world each year because of malnutrition. In contrast, in many parts of the world hundreds of millions of consumers suffer from the adverse health effects of overnutrition and obesity (Sahn, this volume; Gaiha et al. this volume). There is also mounting evidence that a large percentage of the world's population does not consume a diet that ensures optimal health (Stein, this volume).

Food-borne and water-borne viral and microbial pathogens sicken hundreds of millions of people around the globe each year. WHO has estimated that more than 5 million deaths per year can be attributed to food-borne illness (Chassy 2010, and http://www.who.int/mediacentre/factsheets/fs237/en/). Controlling food-borne illness requires both improvements in technology and awareness. In the developed world, and increasingly in the less developed world, the food-safety chain has become very complex as it runs from the farm to the processor to the retailer to the consumer. A breach or failure at any point in the system can lead to a disease outbreak.

There are a number of other food-safety risks that can kill, injure, or make consumers ill. Naturally occurring compounds such as mycotoxins that are found in foods can cause cancer, illness, and death (Chassy 2010). Allergens pose a special hazard to sensitized consumers (Chassy 2010). Contaminants such as glass, metal particles, or environmental chemicals—sometimes called chance or indirect additives—are other potential hazards that must be controlled and are accordingly regulated (CFR 2002).

In summary, there are a number of material risks in the food and agricultural systems that could adversely affect the health of consumers; these have drawn the attention of producers and regulators, though administrative oversight remains problematic in many countries, as periodic outbreaks of food-related illnesses demonstrate. Opponents of modern DNA technology argue that transgenic crops fall into the category of special health-safety concerns, requiring special surveillance and regulation. The logic is based on the premise that plants bred with molecular techniques are inherently different from other plants in ways that mark them as unnatural. This chapter has briefly outlined the reasons that there exists a scientific consensus that transgenic crops are as safe as any other. Risk managers rank risks that cause illness, death, and economic loss and place priority for regulation, research, training, and communication to the public on those risks that do the most harm. By this criterion, a hierarchical ordering of food safety risks based on scientific risk assessment would place genetic engineering and transgenic crops in the category of least concern. Not a single death or illness has resulted from consumption of transgenic crops. Resources diverted to regulating transgenic crops would, therefore, almost certainly have higher returns if they were used to ensure the supply of safe food and sanitary water. This is particularly the case for resource-poor developing countries in which resources invested in costly regulation of transgenic crops draws down expenditures for other measures that could improve public health and economic productivity.

Notes

1. In the United States the "CDC estimates that each year roughly 1 in 6 Americans (or 48 million people) get sick, 128,000 are hospitalized, and 3,000 die of foodborne diseases." http://www.cdc.gov/foodborneburden/estimates-overview.html
2. http://www.efsa.europa.eu/en/press/news/120711.htm
3. http://www.cdc.gov/foodborneburden/attribution.html
4. Transgenic organisms contain DNA or genes isolated from other organisms transferred into them in a laboratory (*in vitro*) through a process called transformation. The technology is often referred to as recombinant DNA technology (rDNA) since the introduced fragment of DNA that encodes the selected genes must be recombined or inserted into the chromosome of the target organism. Transgenic organisms are also called genetically modified organisms (GMOs) or genetically modified (GM) plants, microbes and animals. The appellations GM and GMO are unfortunate misnomers since almost all domesticated crops and animals are extensively genetically modified– see *Safety of transgenic crops: A point of contention*. The term "transgenic" will be used here to denote an organism whose novel phenotype(s) is the result of application of *in vitro* DNA or RNA technology. As will be discussed in "*What's a GM Crop?: A Revealing Truth and New Challenges,*" not all transgenic or GM crops contain exogenous genes or DNA.
5. See http://www.isaaa.org (accessed March 15, 2013).
6. http://www.who.int/foodsafety/publications/biotech/20questions/en/ Accessed March 15, 2013).
7. Transcription factors (TFs) are proteins that bind to specific DNA sequences and in so doing either stimulate or repress the transcription of mRNA (messenger RNA) which leads to an increase or decrease in the expression of one or more gene or genes.
8. See also http://en.wikipedia.org/wiki/Horizontal_gene_transfer (accessed March 15, 2013)
9. http://www.oecd.org/env/ehs/biotrack/safetyassessmentoftransgenicorganismsoecdconsensusdocuments.htm (accessed March 15, 2013)
10. Commonwealth Scientific and Industrial Research Organisation. The Australian government's research branch.
11. See also http://agribiotech.info/details/Is%20This%20Study%20Believable%20V6%20final%2002%20print.pdf (accessed March 15, 2013).
12. The EFSA policy may soon change as is discussed in the following section.
13. See http://academicsreview.org/reviewed-content/genetic-roulette/ for an analysis of flawed WFS studies with various GM crops in several animal species.
14. TM Monsanto Corporation.
15. To his credit, it now appears that Séralini turned over his raw data to the Editor of JFCT.
16. On Nov. 19, 2013 Senior Editor Wallace Hayes made public a letter which was sent to Prof. Séralini which informed him that JFCT had retracted acceptance of the disputed paper. Editor Hayes' letter stated clearly that the sole reason for retraction was the use of too few animals which led to inconclusive results.
17. http://blogs.scientificamerican.com/guest-blog/2011/08/11/genetically-engineered-crops/

References

Arjó, G., M. Portero, C. Piñol, J. Viñas, X. Matias-Guiu, T. Capell, A. Bartholomaeus, W. Parrott, and P. Christou. 2013. "Plurality of opinion, scientific discourse and pseudoscience: An in-depth analysis of the Séralini et al. study claiming that RoundupTM Ready corn or the herbicide RoundupTM cause cancer in rats. Published online February 22, 2013. Transgenic Research.

Bartholomaeus, A., G. Bondy, W. Parrot and K. Walker 2013. The use of whole food animal studies in the safety assessment of genetically modified crops: limitations and recommendations. *Critical Reviews in Toxicology*. 43(S2): 1–24.

Batista, R., N. Saibo, T. Lourenço, and M. M. Oliveira. 2008. "Microarray Analyses Reveal That Plant Mutagenesis May Induce More Transcriptomic Changes Than Transgene Insertion." *Proceedings of the National Academy of Science USA* 4(105):3640–3645.

Campbell-Platt, G. (ed.). 2009. *Food Science and Technology*. Oxford, UK and Ames. IA: Wiley-Blackwell.

Cellini, F., A. Chesson, I. Colquhoun, A. Constable, H. V. Davies, K. H. Engel, A. M. Gatehouse, S. Karenlampi, E. J. Kok, J. J., Leguay, S. Lehesranta, H. P. Noteborn, J. Pedersen, and M. Smith. 2004. "Unintended Effects and Their Detection in Genetically Modified Crops. *Food Chemical Toxicity* 42(7): 1089–1125.

Chassy, B. 2008. "Global Regulations of Transgenic Crops in Molecular Genetic Approaches to Maize Improvement." In edited by Alan L. Kriz and Brian A. Larkins, pp. 106–124. Heidelberg: Springer-Verlag.

Chassy, B. 2010. "Can–Omics Inform a Food Safety Assessment?" *Regulatory Toxicology and Pharmacology* 58:S62–S70. doi:10.1016/j.yrtph.2010.05.009

Chassy, B. 2010. "Food Safety Risks and Consumer Health." *New Biotechnology* 27(5):534–544 doi:10.1016/j.nbt.2010.05.018

Chassy, B. M. 2007. "The History and Future of GMOs in Food and Agriculture." *Cereal Foods World* 52:169–173

Chassy, B., S. H. Abramson, A. Bridges, W. E. Dyer, M. A. Faust, S. K. Harlander, S. L. Hefle, I. C. Munro, and M. E. Rice. 2001. "Evaluation of the U.S. Regulatory Process for Crops Developed through Biotechnology." Council for Agricultural Science and Technology Issues Paper, October 2001, Washington, DC.

Chassy, B., M. Egnin, Y. Gao, K. Glenn, G. A. Kleter, P. Nestel, M. Newell-McGloughlin, R. H. Phipps, and R. Shillito. 2008. "Recent Developments in the Safety and Nutritional Assessment of Nutritionally Improved Foods and Feeds." *Comprehensive Reviews in Food Science and Food Safety* 7 (1), 50–113.

Chassy, B. M., J. J. Hlywka, G. A. Kleter, E. J. Kok, H. A. Kuiper, M. McGloughlin, I. C. Munro, R. H. Phipps, and J. E. Reid. 2004. "Nutritional and Safety Assessments of Foods and Feeds Nutritionally Improved through Biotechnology." *Comprehensive Reviews in Food Science and Food Safety* 3:35–104.

Chrispeels, M. J. and D. E. Sadava. 2003. "Plants, Genes, and Crop Biotechnology (2nd ed.). Sudbury, UK: Jones and Bartlett Publishers and the American Society of Plant Biologists.

Code of Federal Regulations, Title 21, Part 174.5 General Provisions Applicable to Indirect Food Additives, May 21, 2002.

Codex (Codex Alimentarius). 2003. "Principles for the Risk Analysis of Foods Derived from Modern Biotechnology." (CACGL 45–2003).

Codex (Codex Alimentarius). 2009. "GM Food Safety Assessment: Tools for Trainers."

Delaney, B., L. D. Astwood, H. Cunny, R. Eichen Conn, C. Herouet-Guicheney, S. MacIntosh, S. Meyer, L. Privalle, Y. Gao, and J. Mattson. 2008. *Food and Chemical Toxicology* 46: S71–S97. doi:10.1016/j.fct.2008.01.045.

Dona, A. and I. S. Arvanitoyannis. 2009. "Health Risks of Genetically Modified Foods." *Critical Reviews in Food Science and Nutrition* 49:164–175.

Doull J, D. Gaylor, H. A. Greim, D. P. Lovell, B. Lynch, and I. C. Munro. 2008. "Report of an Expert Panel on the Reanalysis by Séralini et al. (2007) of a 90-day Study Conducted by Monsanto in Support of the Safety of a Genetically Modified Corn Variety (MON 863)." *Food and Chemical Toxicology* 45:2073–2085.

Ewen, S. W., and A. Pusztai. 1999. "Effect of Diets Containing Genetically Modified Potatoes Expressing Galanthus nivalis Lectin on Rat Small Intestine." *Lancet* 354:1353–1354.

Goodman, R. E. S. Vieths, H. A. Sampson, D. Hill, M. Ebisawa, S. L. Taylor, and R. van Ree. 2008. "Allergenicity Assessment of Genetically Modified Crops: What Makes Sense?" *Nature Biotechnology* 26, 73–81.

Goodman, R. E., and A. O. Tetteh. 2011. "Suggested Improvements for the Allergenicity Assessment of Genetically Modified Plants Used in Foods." *Current Allergy and Asthma Reports* 11(4):317–324. doi: 10.1007/s11882-011-0195-6

Hancock, J. F. 2012. "History of Scientific Agriculture: Crop Plants." *eLS*. Published online August, 2012. doi: 10.1002/9780470015902.a0003099.pub2

Harrigan, G. G., Lundry, D., Drury, S., Berman, K., Riordan, S. G., Nemeth, M. A., Ridley, W. P. & Glenn, K. C. 2010. Natural variation in crop composition and the impact of transgenesis. *Nat Biotechnol*, 28, 402-4.

Harrigan, G. G. and B. M. Chassy. 2012. Challenges for Metabolomics as a Tool in Safety Assessments, Metabolomics, Dr Ute Roessner (Ed.), ISBN: 978-953-51-0046-1, InTech, Available from: http://www.intechopen.com/books/metabolomics/challenges-for-metabolomics-as-a-tool-in-safety-assessment

Herman, R., B. Chassy, and W. Parrott. 2009. "Compositional Assessment of Transgenic Crops Engineered with Input Traits: An Idea Whose Time Has Passed." *Trends in Biotechnology* 27:555–557.

Herman, R., and W. Price. 2013. "Unintended Compositional Changes in Genetically Modified (GM) Crops: 20 Years of Research." *Journal of Agriculture and Food Chemistry*. doi: 10.1021/jf400135r, Web publication date February 15, 2013. http://pubs.acs.org/doi/abs/10.1021/jf400135r (accessed March 13, 2013).

Herman, R., and R. Ekmay. 2014. "Do Whole-Food Animal Feeding Studies Have Any Value in the Safety Assessment of GM crops?" *Regulatory Toxicology and Pharmacology* 68(1): 171–174.

König, A., A. Cockburn, R. W. R. Crevel, E. Debruyne, R. Grafstroem, U. Hammerling, I. Kimber, I., Knudsen, H. A. Kuiper, A. A. C. M. Peijnenburg, A. H. Penninks, M. Poulsen, M., Schauzu, and J. M. Wal. 2004. "Assessment of the Safety of Foods Derived from Genetically Modified (GM) Crops." *Food and Chemical Toxicology* 42(7):1047–1088.

Kuntz, M. and A. E. Ricroch. "Is It Time to Adjust the Current Regulatory Risk Assessment for GM Food and Feed?" *ISB News Report*. Published on-line February 2012. http://www.isb.vt.edu/news/2012/Feb12.pdf (accessed March 15, 2013).

Latham, J. R., A. K. Wilson, and R. A. Steinbrecher. 2006. "The Mutational Consequences of Plant Transformation." *Journal of Biomedicine and Biotechnology* 2006:253–276.

Lee, R.-Y., D. Reiner, G., Dekan, A. E. Moore, T. J. V. Higgins, and M. M. Epstein. 2013. "Genetically Modified α-Amylase Inhibitor Peas Are Not Specifically Allergenic in Mice." PLoS ONE 8(1): e52972. doi:10.1371/journal.pone.0052972

Lusser, M., and H. Daves. 2013. "Comparative Regulatory Approaches for Groups of New Plant Breeding Techniques." *New Biotechnology* 30(5):437–446. doi: 10.1016/j.nbt.2013.02.004

NAS (National Academy of Sciences). 1987. *Introduction of Recombinant DNA-Engineered Organisms into the Environment: Key Issues*. Washington, DC: National Academy Press.

Nordlee, J. A., S. L. Taylor, J. A. Townsend, L. A. Thomas, and R. K. Bush. 1996. "Identification of a Brazil-Nut Allergen in Transgenic Soybeans." *New England Journal of Medicine*, 334:688–692.

OSTP (Office of Science and Technology Policy). 1986. "Coordinated Framework for Regulation of Biotechnology." 51 Fed. Reg. 23302.

Parrott, W. 2005. The Nature of Change: Towards Sensible Regulation of Transgenic Crops Based on Lessons from Plant Breeding, Biotechnology and Genomics. In *Proceedings of the 17th Meeting National Agricultural Biotechnology Council, Nashville, June 27–29*. pp. 209–220, NABC.

Parrott, W., B. Chassy, J. Ligon, L. Meyer, J. Petrick, J. Zhou, R. Herman, B. Delaney, and M. Levine. 2010. "Application of Food and Feed Safety Assessment Principles to Evaluate Transgenic Approaches to Gene Modulation in Crops." *Food and Chemical Toxicology* 8(7):1773–1790.

Prescott, V. E., P. M. Campbell, A. Moore, J. Mattes, M. E. Rothenberg, P. S. Foster, T. J. V. Higgins, and S. P. Hogan. 2005. "Transgenic Expression of Bean Alpha-Amylase Inhibitor in Peas Results in Altered Structure and Immunogenicity." *Journal of Agriculture and Food Chemistry* 53:9023–9030.

Radauer, C., M. Bublin, S. Wagner, A. Mari, and H. Breiteneder. 2008. "Allergens Are Distributed into Few Protein Families and Possess a Restricted Number of Biochemical Functions." *Journal of Allergy and Clinical Immunology* 121:847–852. doi: 10.1016/j.jaci.2008.01.025

Ramessar, K., A. Peremarti, S. Gómez-Galera, S. Naqvi, M. Moralejo, P. Muñoz, T. Capell, and P. Christou. 2007. "Biosafety and Risk Assessment Framework for Selectable Marker Genes in Transgenic Crop Plants: A Case of the Science Not Supporting the Politics." *Transgenic Research* 16: 261–280.

Ricroch, A. E., J. B. Berge, and M. Kuntz. 2011. "Evaluation of Genetically Engineered Crops Using Transcriptomic, Proteomic, and Metabolomic Profiling Techniques." *Plant Physiology* 155:1752–1761.

The Royal Society (UK). 1999. "Review of Data of Possible Toxicity of GM Potatoes." June 1999, Ref: 11/99. http://royalsociety.org/policy/publications/1999/toxicity-gm-potatoes/ (accessed June 22, 2013).

Séralini, G. E., E. Clair, R. Mesnage, S. Gress, N. Defarge, M. Malatesta, and D. Hennequin, and J. Spiroux de VendoÃ‹Â†mois. 2012. "Long-Term Toxicity of a Roundup Herbicide and a Roundup-Tolerant Genetically Modified Maize." *Food and Chemical Toxicology* 50:4221–4231.

Smith, J. 2007. *Genetic Roulette* (4th ed.) Fairfield, IA: Yes! Books!

Snell, C, A. Bernheim, J. B. Bergé, M. Kuntz, G. Pascal, A. Paris, and A. E. Ricroch. 2012. "Assessment of the Health Impact of GM Plant Diets in Long-Term and Multigenerational Animal Feeding Trials: A Literature Review." *Food and Chemical Toxicology* 50:1134–1148. doi: 10.1016/j.fct.2011.11.048

van Haver, E., G. Alink, S. Barlow, A. Cockburn, G. Flachowsky, I. Knudsen, H. Kuiper, D. P. Massin, G. Pascal, A. Peijnenburg, R. Phipps, A. Poting, M. Poulsen, W. Seinen, H. Spielmann, H. van Loveren, J. M. Wal, and A. Williams. 2008. "Safety and Nutritional

Assessment of GM Plants and Derived Food and Feed: The Role of Animal Feeding Trials." *Food and Chemical Toxicology* 46:S2–S70.

Vaclavik, V. A., and E. W. Christian. 2007. *Essentials of Food Science* (3rd ed.). New York: Springer.

Weber, N., C. Halpin, L. C. Hannah, J. M. Jez, J. Kough, and W. Parrott. 2012. "Crop Genome Plasticity and Its Relevance to Food and Feed Safety of Genetically Engineered Breeding Stacks." *Plant Physiology* 160:1842–1853.

CHAPTER 25

THE POLITICS OF FOOD LABELING AND CERTIFICATION

EMILY CLOUGH

INTRODUCTION

You are what you eat, the saying goes. The notion that one's food should not only taste good and meet one's dietary needs but should also reflect one's priorities, values, and identity is at the core of the politics of food labeling and certification. A rapidly proliferating array of labels cater to concerns about working conditions in developing countries, environmental sustainability, animal welfare, and health. In today's grocery stores, an environmentalist can purchase tomatoes grown without chemical pesticides, a socially conscious humanitarian can buy coffee grown by farmers guaranteed a minimum price and safe working conditions, and a health-concerned parent can select a cut of meat from animals that never ingested growth hormones. These so-called "ethical consumers" are able to identify these products because each carries a label that signifies that it has been certified to meet a particular set of standards. This act of buying food that is labeled as ethically sourced is sometimes called "voting with your dollar."[1]

From Fair Trade to Shade-Grown and from Organic to Rainforest Alliance certified products, food labeling and certification have become increasingly prevalent in the United States and other wealthy countries in recent decades. As the market for private food certification schemes has grown, it has shifted from the small niche market of idealists into the consciousness of mainstream consumers, becoming a source of controversy for pundits, academics, activists, and shoppers. Neither the proponents nor the critics of food labeling lack passion or conviction. It is understood, respectively, as a useful attempt to raise the standards of food production in the absence of strong state regulation, or as a marketing ploy by which firms capitalize on consumer demand for ethical products by "greenwashing" or "fairwashing" their public images. This chapter outlines these debates by highlighting some of the central claims made by proponents of food labeling as well as some key critiques, focusing particularly on Fair Trade and Organic certification standards; it also reviews existing research to evaluate positions in these debates.[2] The central question is: does food certification work?

Scholarly work on food certification and labeling is part of a broader literature on political consumerism, which understands the act of purchasing certain goods as a political act, in parallel to more conventional forms of political participation. Different strands of the literature, however, conceptualize political consumption variously as a substitute for and as a complement to more traditional forms of political involvement. On the one hand, politicized consumption may be seen as yet another form of political participation for people who already use formal public channels to express their political preferences.[3] On the other hand, market-based political action may be used as an alternative to formal public channels of political participation, particularly for marginalized or underrepresented groups. Scholars who emphasize both of these perspectives agree that the consumption of certain goods should be seen as a form of political action.

Despite the proliferation of certification programs in recent decades, the phenomenon of politicized consumption is not new. The history of ethical consumerism has roots in boycott strategies. In the 1790s, the British antislavery movement introduced a boycott against sugar produced by West Indian slaves, establishing the consumer boycott as what Tarrow calls a repertoire of contention (Sussman 1994, Tarrow 1994). Later social movements such as the civil rights movement and labor movements in the United States and the anti-apartheid movement in South Africa followed suit, using consumer boycotts to sanction companies that violated the movements' principles. Although much of this early consumer activism was in the form of punitive or negative boycotts, examples of what Boström and Klintman call "positive political consumerism" date back to the early nineteenth century. To protest the use of slave labor in producing consumer goods, the American "free produce" movement began opening retail stores in the 1830s that sold goods made with free labor (Faulkner 2007). Half a century later, in 1898, a labeling scheme called the White Label Campaign was organized by the National Consumers' League to distinguish products made in American factories that ensured improved working conditions (Boström and Klintman 2006). This approach—rewarding companies that engage in "good" practices as opposed to punishing companies that engage in "bad" practices—is mirrored in today's ethical labeling initiatives.

Today's certification and labeling schemes are aimed at remedying a litany of pressing problems in both the developed and the developing world, particularly in the areas of labor conditions, environmental sustainability, animal welfare, and health.

Labor conditions for farmers in developing countries are at the forefront of the concerns behind labels like Fair Trade, union-made, and GoodWeave. Small farmers are among the most economically vulnerable populations in the developing world. Half of the world's undernourished people, three-quarters of Africa's malnourished children, and the majority of people living in absolute poverty work on small farms (International Food Policy Research Institute IFPRI 2005). Child labor, though almost completely eradicated in the developed world, is still a reality in low-income countries. The most recent International Labour Organization (ILO) estimates indicate that 215 million children between the ages of 5 and 17 are working in some form of child labor. Of those children, 53 percent are engaged in work defined as hazardous, or "likely to harm [their] health, safety, and morals" (ILO 2011). The ILO lists agricultural work among the most hazardous sectors of employment, since farm workers are especially subject to toxin exposure, strenuous physical labor, and the use of dangerous equipment (see http://www.ilo.org/safework/areasofwork/hazardous-work/lang-en/index.htm). Labor-related certification schemes promise to remedy these conditions for their farmers.

In addition to labor issues, environmental problems take center stage in several food certification schemes. Concerns about the presence of pesticides, herbicides, and chemical fertilizers in farm runoff and their possible effects on local ecosystems motivate the ban of these chemicals in Organic standards (Trewavas 2001). Standards like Rainforest Alliance, Bird Friendly, and Demeter Biodynamic certification aim to curb agricultural practices resulting in deforestation, high levels of carbon emissions, the destruction of wildlife habitat, and reduced biodiversity (see http://www.rainforest-alliance.org/about or http://nationalzoo/scbi/migratorybirds/coffee/lover.cfm or http://demeter-usa.org/).

Animal welfare concerns drive demand for some types of ethically labeled food. Animals raised in confinement are often kept in crowded conditions, unable to move or express natural behaviors (Pew Commission on Industrial Farm Animal Production 2008). These practices also have implications for animal health, since high-density confinement can increase disease among livestock (Tilman et al. 2002). Physical alteration of animals is common in these conditions, including the removal of horns from cattle and beaks from poultry, typically without painkillers; 80 percent of eggs produced in the United States are produced under guidelines that recommend debeaking of poultry, a practice known to cause both short-term and chronic pain (Rodriguez 2011, Mench, Sumner, and Rosen-Molina 2011). The increasing publicity around these issues since the 1964 publication of Ruth Harrison's book, *Animal Machines*, has brought the issue of animal welfare to the attention of consumers (Mench et al. 2011). In a national telephone survey conducted in the United States, 49 percent of consumers agreed or strongly agreed with the statement, "I consider the well-being of farm animals when I make decisions about purchasing meat" (Lusk, Norwood, and Prickett 2007, p. 15). Labels like Certified Humane Raised and Handled, Free-Range poultry, Grass-Fed beef, Global Animal Partnership, and Animal Welfare Approved aim to address these concerns by guaranteeing conditions like outdoor access, freedom from close confinement, and protections from physical alteration without painkillers.

Finally, health concerns motivate the use of labels like Food Alliance and Organic certification. High levels of exposure to pesticides that are used in food production are known to cause birth defects, nerve damage, and cancer, and to pose particular health risks to children (EPA 2012). Increasingly, conventional agricultural land is being fertilized with biosolids or wastewater "sludge." Though biosolid-based fertilizers are known to contain pharmaceuticals, steroids, flame-retardants, heavy metals, hormones, and human pathogens, the health effects of using them to grow food are hotly debated

(Ferguson 2009). Hormones and antibiotics used in raising conventional food animals give rise to concerns about health hazards and the development of antibiotic-resistant strains of bacteria (Stephany 2001, Phillips et al. 2004). Although the government limits the amount of many of these additives in all U.S. food production, consumers can select from several certification standards to help them identify food that will further reduce their exposure. Although the American Medical Association, the National Academy of Sciences, and the World Health Organization have found no scientific basis for claims that genetically modified organisms (GMOs) pose risks to human health, scientists are only just beginning to document the longer-term effects of GMOs in laboratory feeding studies. Skeptical consumers concerned about as-yet unknown effects of the technology can avoid purchasing food bearing government-mandated GMO labels in the EU, and such labeling initiatives are under consideration in the United States (Domingo and Bordonaba 2011, Carter et al. 2012).

Often these certification initiatives operate at the intersection of the private sector, the civil society sector, and the state. To lend clarity, food standards programs can be usefully divided into categories along two cross-cutting dimensions (see Figure 25.1). The first dimension divides programs into voluntary standards (which firms may choose to opt into or out of) and government-mandated standards (to which firms are required by law to adhere). The second dimension divides standards into those set and enforced by the state and those set and enforced by non-state actors (including NGOs and the private sector).

Whether a standard is voluntary or mandatory reflects more than just the institutional arrangement for its enforcement. It provides a clue about where the issue in question falls along the contested dividing line between public and private in our collective political imagination. What is the appropriate role of the state in regulating private consumption decisions? When should the government intervene in the market? The answer has been, *it depends on the issue at stake*. We generally agree that states should govern on issues related to safety, and that states should not govern on issues purely related to personal conscience; we tend to disagree, however, about how particular issues fall

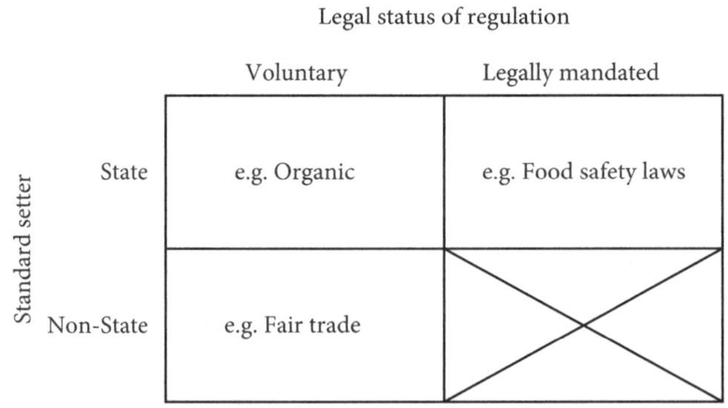

FIGURE 25.1 Food labeling schemes can be mandatory or voluntary in nature, and they can be monitored by state or non-state actors.

along that divide. The debates about regulation of GMO labeling capture this tension. Disputes about the science of GMOs' health impact has been central to the political battle over whether labeling should be mandatory in California, highlighting how the framing of these issues in terms of safety or personal preference is critical in determining whether regulation is state-mandated (Carter et al. 2012).

Moreover, all but the staunchest libertarians tend to agree that there are ethical issues beyond those of safety, often in the areas of social or environmental protection, that carry sufficient collective societal value to warrant state regulation. However, we disagree about *which* issues have that kind of societal value. The United States has universal laws prohibiting child labor, but this was not always the case. The idea that society has an interest in protecting *all* children from work hazards and freeing them to go to school, and that that interest is strong enough to warrant state interference in the market, is an idea that once lacked consensus in the U.S., and similar debates rage today on issues like environmental degradation, financial regulation, and wage standards. Given that players on all sides of these debates are invested in their preferred outcome, the framing of these issues is, to a large extent, the result of a political struggle between actors attempting to define the issues at stake in the language of safety, personal preference, and collective good.[4]

Although an extensive literature on state regulation addresses mandatory standards, this chapter summarizes a younger literature that focuses on voluntary standards. To illustrate the complexity of these voluntary initiatives, the chapter highlights one example of a voluntary certification standard run by private actors (the Fair Trade label) and one example of a voluntary certification standard run by the state (the Organic label) These programs, which rely on politicized consumption in the *private* sector to fuel regulation of the food production process, nevertheless have important implications for the *public* governance of labor markets, the environment, and human health. Private certification standards tend to arise when movements and—critically—markets demand production standards above and beyond the legal standards imposed by governments. Whether these private certification schemes complement government regulation or act as substitutes for the state is a question worth reflection, to which I will return at the end of this chapter.

Some proponents have lauded the voluntary nature of these certification schemes. Citizens and interest groups hold diverse views about how stringently labor and environmental practices should be regulated. Laws and regulatory policies passed by governments reflect a compromise among these views, which inevitably leaves some citizens' demand for higher standards unmet. One advantage of voluntary regulation is that those citizens who support stricter standards can choose to contribute resources toward that outcome, while those who prefer more lenient regulation are not coerced into doing so.[5] The same logic holds if these initiatives are understood as "self-taxing schemes" for conscientious consumers (Arnold, Plastina, and Ball 2006). These schemes can be seen as a private, voluntary parallel to public taxation, whether they take the form of voluntary redistribution of income from consumers in rich countries to poor farmers, or the form of funding for public goods like environmental preservation. In either case, the logic of self-taxation is that it allows each to contribute according to her preferences, accommodating pluralism of views toward redistribution better than a government policy that forces a single standard of contribution.

Other observers of voluntary schemes argue that, given the leniency of government policy, certification schemes can be useful alternatives to strict legal regulation (e.g., Henson and Murphy 2010). These commentators point to deficiencies in government regulation of environmental and health standards for agriculture, suggesting that powerful special interests—such as farm lobbies—influence government policy and prevent the state from setting appropriately protective legal standards. Even when relatively stringent labor laws exist formally "on the books," corruption, inefficient bureaucracies, and political calculations often limit government willingness and capacity to enforce them. Thus, supporters of certification standards claim that creating better channels of transparency and routing consumer dollars toward otherwise under-resourced, under-enforced safeguards will allow consumers to leverage the power of the market against poverty, environmental degradation, and health hazards when government resources or willingness falls short.

As voluntary standards have developed, they have expanded, commercialized, and become institutionalized, bringing in an increasingly diverse set of actors that span the private sector, civil society organizations, and the state. The Fair Trade industry was once the fair trade movement. It began in the civil society sector, led by churches, disaster-relief organizations, and solidarity groups that formed network-based trade channels with marginalized producers. Fair Trade began to enter mainstream markets in the late 1980s, and as the industry scaled, more commercial actors took the lead (Bacon 2005). The Organic industry was likewise once a network of social movements that coalesced into a transnational movement in the 1970s, laying the groundwork for commercially oriented actors to enter the market (see Larsson, this volume). Subsequently, the United States Department of Agriculture (USDA) took on the role of standardizing and overseeing organic certification standards.

Along with the growth and commercialization of these certification systems, tension has arisen over the question of how stringent these standards should be. There is a perceived trade-off between the strictness and scalability of standards, and stakeholders disagree about how to approach this choice (Gendron, Bisaillon, and Rance 2009, Auld 2011). On one side of the debate is a group we might call the "depth" advocates, who argue that lowering standards erodes the meaning and impact of the standard. On the other side of the debate is a group we might call the "breadth" advocates, who argue that making standards marginally less strict will make certification less daunting for significantly larger companies, thus appealing to a broader set of retailers and spreading standards further throughout the market.

The difference between these perspectives fundamentally boils down to how these advocates evaluate impact. Is the impact on environmental practices, labor conditions, and human health greater if a small number of companies follow very strict guidelines, or if many large companies make minor adjustments in their practices? This question remains at the center of debates on every labeling scheme visible enough to have gained a foothold in public discourse.[6] People in the food-labeling industry disagree vehemently about the best approach; one result has been the fragmentation and multiplication of standards as "depth" and "breadth" advocates go their separate ways. A microcosm of this debate can be seen in the 2011 split between Fair Trade USA and Fairtrade International over the former's decision to include plantation coffee in Fair-Trade certification standards rather than only small-holder coffee cooperatives, a move intended to make Fair-Trade coffee available to larger retailers and to reach more farmers (Fairtrade International [FLO] and Fair Trade USA 2011). The network of food labeling organizations and activists thus represent loose coalitions of actors who share basic goals but hold different views on how best to achieve them. Moreover, these ideologues are allied—often uncomfortably—with actors driven by profit motives rather than social or environmental goals. The result is a complex, multifold family of overlapping certification systems, characterized by both common ground and internal tensions.

Considerable debate exists concerning the question: *Do these food certification schemes do what they promise to do?* This question hinges on three critical issues, which will be considered in depth. First, is there enough consumer demand for ethically labeled products to fuel a market large enough to make a measurable impact? Second, assuming sufficient demand, do these ethical standards actually create intended positive outcomes for the producer, the consumer, or the farm—whether in the form of better labor conditions, increased protection of the environment, or the reduction of risks to human health? Third, do the certification agents credibly act as safeguards to the system?

This chapter will examine each of these questions in turn. Section II outlines the debates about the nature of consumer demand for ethically labeled food. Section III investigates the effects of labeling schemes for producers and the production process. Section IV interrogates the efficacy of certification agents (or "watchdogs"). Section V turns to implications of voluntary, market-based regulation schemes for state-mandated labor and environmental standards. Section VI concludes. This analysis suggests there is reason for cautious optimism that ethical labeling initiatives for food live up to their promises, albeit inconsistently and on a relatively small scale. Critically, however, the scope of their impact is constrained by limited consumer demand, label proliferation and fatigue, and structural barriers to transparency and accountability.

The Consumer

Theory

The ethical consumer represents the vital engine that drives demand for certified and labeled food. Without a critical mass of buyers willing to spend money on products that support social and environmental causes, the system falls apart.

Because almost all products that Americans purchase are produced far from the point of sale, until recently it has been impossible for consumers to observe the conditions under which their food is produced, and, therefore, difficult to act on their desires for value-consistent consumption. This lack of transparency has created an asymmetry of information between consumers and producers. Certification and labeling offer a solution to this form of market imperfection, providing information that allows consumers to distinguish among products and support a style of food production that reflects their values (Elliott and Freeman 2003, Brown 2006).

By establishing a channel of information connecting the consumer with the production process, labeled food also provides a sense of connectedness between consumers, their food, and the people and place from which it came (Dolan 2011). As Luetchford notes, "in ethical consumption the aim is to break down and demystify the distance between parties in the exchange and accentuate the relation between them." (Leutchford 2008, p. 3).

Finally, certification and labeling allow companies to "ethics-discriminate" (in a similar sense to premium-price discrimination) among customers to better tailor their offerings to more nuanced patterns of demand. While most shoppers prioritize price and quality over labor and environmental standards, some consumers care enough about the conditions under which their food is produced that they are willing to pay more. Certification and labeling allow firms to reduce deadweight loss by catering directly to that otherwise untapped demand. Thus, Kellogg has developed the Kashi brand, which uses certified organic and GMO-free ingredients in some of its cereals; PepsiCo has acquired Naked Juice, whose beverages are made with bananas certified by Rainforest Alliance; and Kraft has launched a line of certified Organic macaroni and cheese alongside its conventional product offerings (Strom 2012, http:www.nakedjuice.com/ourpurpose/ and http:www.kashi.com/ourcommitment). Food labeling allows companies to target consumers willing to pay for particular production standards. In theory, this is good for the farmer, the consumer, and the firm.

Different theories exist about what motivates consumers to buy ethically labeled food.[7] Understanding consumer motivations matters because the nature of those motivations determines how widespread and robust demand will be for ethically certified products, ultimately constraining the size and impact of the market.

One explanation for the decision to purchase ethically labeled food is that of altruism. An altruistic consumer would buy organic, fair trade food because she gleans personal satisfaction from the advancement of a cause she cares about ("pure altruism") or because the act of contributing to a cause makes her feel good about herself ("impure" or "warm glow altruism") (Andreoni 1989).

An alternative explanation is that consumers purchase ethically labeled food because their judgment is influenced by social norms. Norm-responsive consumers perceive that buying fair trade or organic food is the "appropriate" thing to do, since others in their reference group are doing it, too. Adherence to norms tends to be strongest when there are personal and contextual similarities between an individual and the group that embraces the given norm (Goldstein, Cialdini, and Griskevicius 2008). If a shopper is surrounded by other shoppers of a similar demographic and subculture who are buying ethically certified food, her own assessment of the value of that food (and the cause it supports) might be influenced positively and she may make the same choice out of adherence to a group norm.

A third (and related) explanation for ethical consumption is that consumers use labeled products for social signaling and status. What you buy can be understood as a signal for who you are and what social group you belong to (Bourdieu 1984). Purchasing certified food may be associated with highly valued qualities among some social groups. If someone living in Berkeley, Park Slope, or Cambridge wants to be seen by their peers as compassionate, selfless, or invested in environmental preservation, buying ethically labeled food may be a way of achieving social status, providing purchasing choices are observable (Holländer 1990). Ethical consumption, in this model, becomes a form of "conspicuous consumption."[8]

Finally, consumers may take certification labels as an indicator of the product's quality, whether in the form of taste or healthfulness. In a nationwide telephone survey, a 78 percent of respondents agreed or strongly agreed with the statement, "Animals raised under higher standards of care will produce safer and better tasting meat" (Lusk, Norwood, and Prickett 2007, p. 21). In an online survey conducted by Nielson in 2010, 76 percent of respondents reported that they purchase organic food because they believe it is healthier (http://blog.nielsen.com/nielsenwire/consumer/global-trends-in-healthy-eating/).

Since many purveyors of labeled food highlight the health and quality benefits of their products alongside the social, environmental and animal welfare benefits, it can be difficult in practice to categorize the consumption of a given labeled product neatly into Johnston and MacKendrick's typology of "political" consumption (motivated by collective goals) and "apolitical" consumption (motivated by individual goals) (see Johnson and MacKendrick, this volume).

Do these different sources of demand add up to a large, robust market for ethically labeled food? Proponents of ethically labeled foods suggest that certified products tap into widespread, latent consumer demand for food produced under good conditions, and that this demand is broad-based and robust enough to drive real change in labor conditions, the environment, and human health outcomes.

Critiques

Critics of labeling schemes present a more pessimistic view, raising several concerns about the nature of consumer demand for ethical food.

One common concern is that consumer demand is not sufficiently widespread to make a significant difference in outcomes like labor conditions or environmental degradation (e.g., Van der Zee 2007). Even if a handful of consumers are willing to pay a premium, critics argue that there are too few consumers of this kind to make these initiatives scalable and effective at a global level. The current size of the market reflects not only demand, but also the current level of supply for ethical goods. It is difficult to know which is the binding constraint, and, thus, to know exactly the extent of latent consumer demand for ethical goods, making it hard to settle this debate.

Another concern is that demand for ethically certified food is likely to be significantly constrained by income, limiting the scale of the market for labeled food. That is, lower-income consumers face budget constraints that may limit their ability to spend extra money on products that make ethical promises (Howard and Allen 2010). A related objection is that these initiatives are fundamentally classist in nature, excluding low-income consumers from this model of ethical action. Finally, the concern about income constraints on demand raises an additional alarm, which is that fluctuations in the economy will be reflected in fickleness of demand for labeled food; accordingly, in an economic downturn, sales of Fair-Trade and Organic groceries would fizzle (Cohen 2012, Hickman 2010).

A third concern centers on label proliferation and fatigue (Schuetze 2012, Harbaugh, Maxwell, and Roussillon 2011). Because there is no single governmental or nongovernmental body that oversees labeling standards, new certification standards are born every year, each designed by different agents and addressing a wide assortment of concerns. The number and variety of certification standard have grown in recent decades to the point that consumers may find it overwhelming and frustrating to sort through the various claims. In 2006, there were as many as 137 labels being marketed to socially conscious consumers that made claims ranging from "salmon-safe" to "ozone-friendly" (Alsever 2006). At the time this volume went to press, Ecolabel Index listed 432 ecolabels—ranging from "salmon-safe" to "bird-friendly"—across 246 countries and 25 industries" (www.ecolabelindex.com). Consumers, like voters, have limited time to investigate claims made by different labels, and this combined with the burgeoning of certification standards may have two consequences that limit the effectiveness of labeling schemes.

First, consumers may not be able to tell the difference between the claims made by different labels, creating an incentive for "greenwashing" or "fairwashing." The average consumer may glean basic information about a product from its label ("this is good for the environment"), but details about what is being guaranteed are often lost. Consumers may thus be unable to differentiate between rigorous and lax standards, and that disadvantages producers who subscribe to expensive, rigorous standards. The ill-informed nature of consumer demand for ethically labeled food may incentivize firms to adopt certification standards with few requirements, potentially creating a race-to-the-bottom dynamic.

Second, consumers may get fed up by the number of different labels and their lack of transparency, and disengage from ethical consumption entirely. Even the most conscientious, committed shopper could spend hours poring over the websites of standards providers without understanding the differences among similar-sounding certification rules. Well-meaning consumers may also discover that a favorite label carries fewer guarantees than its brand image would suggest; indeed, such an incident made the national news when consumers discovered that Kashi's "natural" cereals contained genetically modified ingredients (http://usatoday30.usatoday.com/money/industries/

food/story/2012-04-29/kashi-natural-claims/54616576/1). Under such conditions, critics worry that consumers will increasingly view food labels with suspicion and fatigue.

Together, these caveats raise doubts about whether consumers will wade through the plethora of standards they encounter in grocery stores and commit sufficient resources to ethical consumption to make a difference.

Research

To weigh in on these debates, it is helpful to turn to existing empirical research on the nature and extent of demand for ethically certified food. Research to date does little to disentangle the particular motivations of ethical shoppers, but it does support the existence of committed ethical consumers, though this group may be limited in size along demographic and income lines. The majority of the research has been survey based, but several recent experimental studies add richness to the literature.

Several surveys show that consumers report themselves to be willing to pay extra for products made under ethical conditions. In a survey of 808 respondents in Belgium, consumers reported that they would be willing to pay an average of 10 percent extra for Fair-Trade coffee. Those willing to pay the highest premium were more idealistic than others, less socially conventional, and tended to be aged between 31 and 44. Those who were willing to pay a somewhat lower premium were more idealistic than average but otherwise not significantly different from the average consumer in socio-demographic terms (De Pelsmacker et al. 2005). A U.S. survey conducted by the National Bureau of Economic Research found that roughly 80 percent of individuals claimed to be willing to pay a premium for an item if they were assured it was made under good working conditions (Elliott and Freeman 2003).

In another survey, a significant majority of respondents felt that if Americans are using products made by foreign workers, "this creates a moral imperative to ensure that they are not required to work in harsh or unsafe conditions." 76% of respondents from the same survey, 76 percent claimed they would be willing to pay $25 instead of $20 for a product if "an international organization... would check the conditions in a factory and, if acceptable, give them the right to label their products as not made in a sweatshop" (PIPA 2000, pp. 36–37). Blend and Ravensway conducted a household survey to gather data on intentions to purchase eco-labeled apples under varying conditions. Respondents reported that they would be willing to pay more for eco-labeled apples, though willingness declined as price premium increased (Blend and Ravensway 1999). Loureiro and Lotade conducted a willingness-to-pay survey of grocery shoppers, finding that they reported themselves as willing to pay a premium for Fair Trade, shade-grown, and Organic coffee (Loureiro and Lotade 2005). This growing body of evidence supports the idea that consumers express a willingness to pay extra for ethically labeled products.

The most critical drawback to self-reported survey data on people's willingness to buy ethically certified products is that it is subject to social desirability bias, or systematic error in data from self-reports because of a respondent's wish to project a favorable image (Fisher 1993, p. 303). Some surveys attempt to mitigate the effects of social desirability bias by using anonymous, mail-in surveys (e.g., De Pelsmacker et al. 2005). However, because social desirability bias comprises a self-deceptive aspect in addition to an other-deceptive aspect (Nederhoff 1985), there is reason to suspect that all self-reported data will overestimate consumer willingness to pay a premium on ethically certified food.

A small but growing number of empirical studies avoid problems of social desirability bias by measuring actual consumer purchasing behavior in response to the presence or absence of ethical labels on products in retail settings. The best of these studies are experimental, since their research design avoids the selection bias that often plagues observational studies. In a study of 150,000 eBay auctions that resemble "natural experiments," Elfenbein et al. found that auction participants were willing to pay 6 percent more for an identical product when it was advertised that the auction was for charity (Elfenbein et al. 2010). In a two-part field experiment of 26 stores of a major U.S. grocery chain, sales of coffee rose by 10 percent when a Fair Trade label was added, as consumers switched from unlabeled coffee (sales for unlabeled coffee dropped 9 percent when the labeled option appeared). This suggests that when consumers have a choice between labeled and unlabeled coffees that are otherwise identical and equally priced, consumers respond to the label. In the second part of the experiment, the addition of a price premium to two Fair-Trade-labeled coffees led to a 2 percent increase in sales in the case of the higher-end coffee and a 30 percent decrease in sales in the lower-end coffee, suggesting that some consumers are willing to pay a premium on Fair Trade labeled coffee, but that this willingness may be limited to higher-income shoppers (Hainmueller, Hiscox, and Sequeira 2011).[9]

Similar experiments on nonfood items support the idea that some types of consumers are willing to spend extra on ethically labeled products. In an experiment in a home goods store, sales of towels and candles rose by 10–20 percent when labels promising good labor standards were added (Hiscox and Smyth 2007). In an eBay experiment, consumers were willing to pay on average a 45 percent premium for Fair-Trade-labeled shirts over unlabeled shirts (Hainmueller et al. 2011). In an experiment in 111 Banana Republic factory outlet stores, the addition of labels conveying a fair-labor message increased sales of a high-priced women's clothing item by 14 percent, whereas labels had no significant effect on the sales of low-priced women's or men's[10] items (Hainmueller and Hiscox 2012a). In another experiment in 419 Banana Republic stores and 155 Gap Outlet stores, women proved willing to buy eco-labeled denim jeans sold in nonoutlet stores (sales increased by 8 percent in the presence of a label with an environmental message), but the labels had no effect on sales of men's jeans sold in nonoutlet stores or of women's jeans sold in outlet stores (Hainmueller and Hiscox 2012b).

While experimental studies offer the most rigorous tests of consumer demand for certified products to date, they, too, have limitations. The most important caveat concerns issues of generalizability. Demand for ethically certified products may be product specific. Additionally, none of the studies—even those conduct in outlet stores—effectively targeted low-income shoppers.

Existing evidence thus suggests that, while there is demand for ethically labeled products and this demand seems robust to modest price increases, it may be limited in scope to certain products, income groups, and demographics. In particular, these studies suggest that women and high-end shoppers may be the most willing to spend extra money to purchase products with ethical labels. The theoretical logic behind the observed income disparity seems fairly straightforward. The gender discrepancy is consistent with the general finding in the literature that women engage in politicized consumerism more frequently than men do. Scholars point out that this trend has historical roots: women tended to play a prominent role in early instances of political consumerism, including boycotts and food price strikes (Micheletti 2004). It is also consistent with the broader finding in the literature that women tend to act more altruistically than men in situations involving charitable giving or public goods investment (List 2004, Andreoni and Vesterlund 2001).

Finally, although price levels clearly impact consumer demand, there is also research that supports the idea that quality considerations are significant to the supply of ethically labeled food. In a small survey of natural foods stores, grocery stores, and cafes, Levi and Linton found that retailers offered Fair Trade certified products only if they perceived customer demand for it, but that customer requests for fair trade options were insufficient unless the retailer also perceived the product to be of high quality (Levi and Linton 2003). This research is consistent with the idea that an ethical claim, valued by the customer as it may be, is not enough to scale the market for labeled food; rather, ethical certification must be paired with quality.

The Production Process

Theory

No amount of consumer demand will make a difference unless ethical labeling initiatives create positive results on the ground for farmers and farms. At the other end of the supply chain from the ethical consumer is the production process being certified. Labeled food makes specific promises about how the purchase of that food will affect the people or place where it is produced. A key empirical question is whether and to what extent those promises are kept.

The promises are different in the case of each certification standard. With regard to the two labeling schemes considered in detail here, the Organic label promises that the food it certifies is not produced with any chemicals on the organics-prohibited list produced by the USDA. Additionally, proponents claim that organic food comes with health benefits and environmental payoffs for the farm and its surrounding ecosystem.

The Fair Trade label promises that workers are guaranteed a price minimum and are paid a social premium to be invested in local social programs, that food is grown in safe and healthy working conditions with no child labor, and that sustainable environmental practices are used. Each of the hundreds of existing food labels makes unique promises of this kind.

Critiques

Not all observers are convinced that ethical labeling initiatives are living up to their promises in terms of the impact they claim to have on the producers and the production process. Although many critiques of the purported impact of certification on farmers, farms, and food are specific to individual labeling initiatives, some critiques span all standards, particularly those that raise doubts about transparency and accountability, the use of price premiums, the tension between ethical and market imperatives, and the way in which standards might reinforce North-South power relations.

Perhaps the most common generalized doubt reflects skepticism about the extent to which labeling organizations are able to overcome logistical and structural barriers to ensuring transparency and consistent monitoring, and, therefore, to guarantee adherence to standards. Most food supply chains are not vertically integrated, but rather are characterized by aggregation and mixing of products, making an individual product difficult to trace from production to point-of-sale, particularly when supply chains span international borders. Given that most farms located in developing countries are only reachable by roads of dubious quality, arranging unannounced monitoring visits is costly and difficult. Many monitoring standards require only an annual visit, which is often known of in advance. As critics point out, this arrangement is insufficient to guard against violations throughout the rest of the year.

There is also debate about whether retailers capture too large a portion of the premium charged to consumers. Some point out that when retailers mark up ethically labeled food products, they may keep a large percentage of that margin for themselves, and the consumers are none the wiser (Downie 2007, Griffiths 2012). In one case, a retailer was criticized when it was found that 90 percent of the premium charged for a cup of Fair Trade coffee went to the retailer, whereas only 10 percent was passed along to farmers (Harford 2006). Rodrik voices skepticism about whether Fair-Trade farmers whose coffee is sold through Starbucks are seeing any improvement in their livelihoods or whether Starbucks is keeping the entire premium, using sympathetic consumers to make a profit (Rodrik 2007). Alsever criticized TransFair USA for using most of their revenue—$1.7 million of the $1.89 million they generated in licensing fees annually—on salaries, travel, conferences, and publications (Alsever 2006). The counter to such critiques, however, is that some portion of the premium must go to the retailer and the watchdog to cover costs associated with investing in a certified supply chain. Nevertheless, critics claim that certification organizations take too large a cut.

In the case of all standards, there tends to be a tension between the imperatives of the market and the social goals at the label's foundations (Luetchford 2011, Kennedy 2004). For example, for Fair Trade coffee traders to maintain high sales, the coffee must be of good quality. However, the poorest farmers tend not to produce the highest quality coffee. Indeed, the production of high quality food requires investments in better techniques, equipment, and inputs on the production end that is beyond the reach of many of the poor farmers who the label seeks to assist. The Fair Trade movement's core value of poverty eradication thus must be reconciled with the conflicting demands of the market, and this frequently means compromises, particularly as labels expand. Hardliners, or "depth" advocates, who seek higher standards lament the erosion of values from the early days of the movement, whereas commercially oriented or "breadth" advocates (who want standards to be more easily attainable and, therefore, widespread) are frustrated by what they perceive as the stubborn backwardness of the old guard purists.

For labeled food that is produced outside wealthy countries, another critique is that the rules are made in the United States and Western Europe and then implemented in developing countries, reflecting and reinforcing a power imbalance between the North and South in these certified supply chains. Vogel articulates what he sees as the danger of this approach: "To the extent that voluntary labor codes replace rather than complement state regulations, developing country governments are essentially ceding their sovereignty to the demands of western activists, who are the primary drivers and the main 'consumers' of labor codes. Many labor codes essentially empower NGOs, rather than developing country workers, and the two's priorities can often conflict" (Vogel 2008, p. 274). This line of argument emphasizes the inequitable nature of the historical power imbalances that have shaped the geopolitical context in which labeling schemes have emerged.

This chorus of critical voices calls into question the claims made by proponents of labeled food that systems of certification can create positive impact for farmers and the environment.

Research

Existing research is not thorough enough to assess all these claims and critiques empirically, but it can illuminate some issues surrounding the impact of food certification. As research on the impact of labeling standards tends to be standard-specific, I will focus here on empirical evidence about the effects of Organic and Fair Trade Certification.

The research on organic foods and indicators of human health is most thoroughly summarized in a meta-analysis by a team of research scientists at Stanford. The analysis (Smith-Spangler et al. 2012) reviews findings from 17 human studies and 223 studies of food, focusing on bacterial contamination, pesticide levels, human health biomarkers, and nutrition levels in organic versus conventional food, and yields mixed results.

The results suggest that, although organic food may not systematically reduce bacterial contamination, it may carry less antibiotic-resistant bacteria than conventional food. The Stanford team found no statistically significant difference in levels of pathogenic bacteria contamination overall, though a handful of studies documented differences: in one, organic food was found to carry a slightly higher risk of *E. coli* contamination; in another, organic food had 33 percent lower incidence of antibiotic-resistant bacteria; another found organic grains to carry a lower level of the fungal toxin deoxynivalenol.

Research on pesticides is somewhat more suggestive. Studies of food content found that organic produce had a 30 percent lower risk of pesticide contamination than conventional produce. Although there have been no adult studies, two studies of children found significantly lower urinary pesticide levels in those who followed an organic diet. Beyond pesticides, however, the reviewed human studies that examine health biomarkers and nutrient levels in the adults did not find differences between subjects on conventional and organic diets that were clinically meaningful.

In terms of nutrition, food studies in the Stanford analysis examining the vitamin and nutrient content of food found very few differences between organic and conventionally grown food. A few human and food studies found higher levels of beneficial fatty acids associated with organic food.

The general findings of the Stanford meta-analysis point to the cautious conclusion that organic food is likely to offer reduced levels of pesticides and reduced levels of antibiotic-resistant bacteria. The analysis suggests that there are few differences in levels of nutrition between organic and conventional food. The Stanford analysis did not include studies comparing the health of farm workers on organic and conventional farms; in a study of the health of 46 farmers in Mexico, researchers found that 20 percent of farm workers exposed to pesticides exhibited signs of acute poisoning (Payán-Rentieria et al. 2012).

The literature on the environmental impact of organic certification yields similarly mixed results, but points toward several possible benefits. One study on dairy production showed that organic dairy farms were at a lower risk for negative environmental response to fertilizers than conventional dairy farms. However, organic dairy farms also showed higher levels of methane emissions, suggesting that without also lowering emission of carbon dioxide and nitrous oxide they posed a higher risk of contributing to global warming. Moreover, organic farming reduced pesticide use but increased land use (De Boer 2003). Biao et al. find evidence that adherence to organic standards is associated with increased soil fertility, nutrient management, and biodiversity on farms (Biao et al. 2003). Nelson and Martin's (2013) mixed-methods studies of Organic-certified cocoa farms in Ecuador and tea estates in India link Organic certification with positive environmental outcomes (reforestation, conservation, and sustainable practices). However, attributing this outcome to Organic certification is difficult, both because there was some evidence that certified organizations may have been engaging in better practices prior to becoming certified and because most Organic-certified farmers studied were also Fair Trade- and/or Rainforest Alliance-certified.

Related literature on the effects of environmental labeling and certification for non-food production adds complexity to this empirical evidence. In a meta-analysis of nine Voluntary Environmental Programs (VEPs), researchers find that self-monitoring VEP participants performed *worse* with regard to emissions and waste management than nonparticipants, and third-party-monitored VEP participants performed *the same* as nonparticipants (Darnall and Sides 2008). Taken together, these results indicate that the environmental impact of organic farming is multidimensional and that it is not necessarily the case that "all good things go together."

A growing body of research investigates the impact of Fair Trade certification. While findings are mixed, they suggest possible benefits both in income and non-income areas. Because the empirical literature in this area is not yet as well developed as that on Organic certification, there are few conclusive answers, but the existing research warrants a review.

A number of studies document individual cases or small numbers of certified producers. These studies tend to show that Fair Trade-certified farmers are doing relatively well. In an evaluation of several cooperatives of cocoa farmers in Ecuador that sell cocoa through a Fair Trade NGO, farmers reported that Fair Trade brought them benefits, particularly in the area of price, fair weighing and grading, marketing skills, organizational development, and production techniques (Nelson and Galvez 2000). In his 2008 ethnographic study of Costa Rican coffee farmers, Luetchford finds Fair Trade certification to have a positive impact—the Fair Trade cooperative he studied marginally outperformed a noncertified plant—but the research design failed to control for significant differences between the two farms that might explain these results (Luetchford 2008).

Some research suggests that the impact of Fair Trade certification on farmer income may be limited for cases in which farmers sell only a small portion of their crop to Fair Trade buyers. It is not uncommon for farmers to sell to both the conventional and the specialty market, piecing together market demand to try to make a living. Luetchford's certified coffee growers, for example, sold just 2 percent of their coffee through "alternative" trade outlets (Luetchford 2008, p. 29). A study commissioned by the UK Department for International Development (DFID) found that Fair Trade coffee producers in Tanzania and cocoa producers in Ghana sold only a fraction of their product to Fair Trade markets (and, therefore, received a Fair Trade premium for only a portion of their products) (Jones, Bayley, Robins et al. 2000). Nelson and Martin (2013) find some evidence of the same phenomenon.

In these and similar cases, benefits seem to be more significant in the nonincome area. In a two-year study by the Center for Fair and Alternative Trade Studies on the effect of Fair Trade on Mexican and Central American farmers, the transfer of technical skills, improved marketing strategies, product diversification, and social benefits like clinics and schools outstripped the benefits of increased income (Glazer 2007). In the case of the Tanzanian coffee producers and the Ghanaian cocoa growers, the most important impact of Fair Trade appears to be in the area of capacity building, rather than income improvement (Jones, Bayley, Robins et al. 2000).

However, since these studies use small sample sizes, it would be inadvisable to draw firm conclusions about the general effects of Fair Trade labeling and certification from them. Although case studies can provide invaluable insights into the lives of Fair-Trade farmers and the mechanisms by which certification may impact their livelihoods, observations drawn from one or a few cases cannot be easily generalized to a whole population.

A growing number of large-*n* quantitative studies measure the effects of certification on farmers. In a series of studies focusing on Fair Trade-certified cocoa in Ghana and Ecuador and tea in Kenya and India, Nelson and Martin (2013) conducted both large-n surveys and qualitative research and found mixed results. The strongest indication of economic impact from these studies was increased market access, which was a consistent finding in all four country cases. Fair Trade certified farmers reported positive income effects in Ecuador and Kenya; often this effect seemed to result from increases in yield and/or quality. However, Fair Trade certification seems to have had no effect on income in Ghana or India. Non-economic benefits were also reported (e.g. social inclusion of women, community benefits like improved health and education, increased food security) but these benefits were not consistently present across cases. Importantly, many of the Fair Trade cooperatives that yielded these findings (those in Ecuador, Kenya, and India) were multi-certified, so Fair Trade's independent effect is uncertain in all but the Ghana results.

Other quantitative studies echo these cautiously positive results. Becchetti and Constantino's (2006) study of Kenyan farmers finds that farmers with Fair Trade certification have significantly higher price satisfaction[11] than non-Fair Trade certified farmers. A survey of 228 coffee farmers in Nicaragua showed that farmers participating in a certification scheme (including Fair Trade and Organic) are four times less likely than farmers selling only to conventional markets to perceive a risk of losing their land title due to low prices (Bacon 2005). In a 2006 survey of the effects of Fair Trade on 1200 coffee growers in Nicaragua, Peru, and Guatemala, findings suggest a correlation between participation in Fair Trade and improvements in life quality, health, education, material comforts, social participation, technical and social assistance, and sustainable agricultural practices (Arnould, Plastina, and Ball 2006).[12]

Even in the case of large-*n* quantitative studies, caution is warranted in drawing inferences about certification's causal impact on producers because of concerns about selection bias. Because studies on the effect of certification on producers have been mostly observational rather than experimental, there is strong reason to suspect that the population of farmers that selects into Fair Trade is not identical to the population of farmers that does not. Certification is voluntary and not costless, and farmers are unlikely to opt in if the expected costs outweigh the benefits. Since it is easier and less costly for farmers to become certified when they are already following certification standards, it is plausible that farmers who select into Fair Trade certification are already more or less following relatively good labor, financial, and environmental practices. Thus, any difference observed between certified and uncertified farmers may be picking up underlying differences in farmer type that existed prior to certification.

Indeed, in the view of one Fair Trade coffee cooperative manager, "involvement in Fair Trade is one *result* of development at the local and regional level. The modernizing process, the establishment of bureaucratic structures, the setting up of common agendas and networking have, he feels, opened up the possibility for expansion and progress and generated access to alternative trade" (Luetchford 2008, p. 28).

Another reason for caution is that researchers may not always be able to isolate the causal effects of certification from the results of other agricultural development programs. A farm or production facility that receives ethical certification often receives other kinds of benefits, interventions, or "treatments." In other words, agricultural development treatments often come in bundles. For example, a local development NGO might promote Fair Trade certification, distribute discounted organic fertilizer, train farmers on new techniques, and offer small loans for new farm equipment. Moreover, once a cooperative is established, farmers may more easily overcome collective action problems and more successfully improve production or market access. In these cases of bundled treatments, it is difficult to disentangle the effect of the certification from the effects of being organized into a cooperative or receiving capacity-building training.[13]

The best way around these issues is experimental research. Experimental studies of the effects of certification schemes on producers are on the horizon and offer the greatest potential for conclusive evidence on whether certification schemes actually help farmers.[14]

The Watchdog

The spread of third-party certification standards is unfolding alongside a parallel development: the spread of Corporate Social Responsibility (CSR) initiatives on the part of companies. Corporate Social Responsibility schemes often make claims similar to those of certification and labeling initiatives, from promoting safe and healthy working conditions to ensuring environmentally sustainable sourcing practices. They key difference is that CSR claims are made by the company selling the product, not by outside parties.[15]

There is a clear incentive for firms to make rosy claims about their sourcing practices without actually incurring the expenses of ameliorating hazardous working conditions, low wages, child labor, the use of toxic chemicals, high emissions, and poor treatment of animals in their production processes. Milton Friedman wrote in 1970, "I share Adam Smith's skepticism about the benefits that can be expected from 'those who affected to trade for the public good,'" (Friedman 1970) and the dangers of "greenwashing" and "fairwashing" are not lost on today's ethical consumers.

The advantage articulated by third-party certifiers is that, unlike companies with CSR initiatives, they are not motivated by profit and are in the position to act as watchdogs, providing accountability by certifying and monitoring production facilities and food supply chains from which they do not draw a profit. In other words, in the principal-agent problem that necessarily arises between a consumer and a standards provider—characterized as it is by an asymmetry of information—third-party certifiers are less susceptible than corporate standards providers to moral hazard (Deaton et al. 2010). Freeman argues that "some external labeling organization, private (*vide* Consumer Reports) or public, would be needed to assure the accuracy of labour conditions labels". (Freeman 1994, p. 83). Certification systems typically involve both a standard-setting body and certification agents. Standard-setting bodies are frequently nonprofit organizations, though this role is also sometimes played by the government. Fair Trade standards are set by nonprofit organizations, whereas Organic standards are set by the USDA. These standard-setting bodies then accredit and authorize certification agents. Certification agents are nonprofits, private companies, or government agents who visit farm sites, review production conditions, grant or deny certification for a given standard, and monitor compliance.

The central concern that critics (Griffiths 2012, Weitzman 2006) articulate about labeling organizations is that, although they lack the profit incentive that firms face, labeling organizations face incentives of their own that might undermine their objectivity, the quality of information they present to consumers, and the integrity of their standards enforcement.

One such incentive is the imperative of self-perpetuation. Organizations, once established, tend to develop a path-dependent inclination to remain in existence (Pierson 2000). For a standard-setting organization to remain in existence, it must maintain sufficient credibility in the eyes of the public so that its label is marketable to companies. This does not incentivize labeling organizations to publicize cases of system breakdown. If a certified farm is found to be violating standards, reporting violations to the public runs the risk of doing damage to the label's image if consumers view the problem to be endemic, and this could be detrimental to the labeling organization's future. Pritchett models a situation in which public-sector advocates with altruistic motives have the incentive to avoid rigorous investigation and evaluation of their pet programs in order to safeguard their budget for doing good in their chosen way (Pritchett 2002). The logic is similar here.

A related incentive is genuine concern on the part of third-party certifiers for the welfare of producers and environmental outcomes. This creates an added inducement to minimize publicity when violations are discovered, since damaged credibility could lead to decreased sales overall, ultimately hurting the social or environmental cause in question. It is easy to justify a lack of total transparency with the idea of protecting other farms from consumer backlash.

Together, these incentives run the risk of discouraging perfect transparency on the part of labeling organizations. After all, at present there is no watchdog to the watchdog (Follesdal 2004).[16] And although third-party certifiers are not selling products, they *are* effectively selling a brand (Granville 2009). In that sense they are both certifying products and marketing the concept of Fair Trade or Organic certification. At the front of its 2009/10 "Impact Report," Fair Trade USA quotes a worker from one of its certified farms: "Thank you to those who buy Fair Trade. By buying this fruit, you've made it possible for the dreams of families like mine to become a reality" (Fair Trade USA 2010). This kind of inspiring personal testimonial often stands in for a more rigorous measure of impact in public materials produced by third-party certification bodies. Critics suggest that labeling organizations tend to project an image of their impact that is unrealistic in order to sell their products, and worry about the potential of moral hazard on the part of labelers, particularly as competition between labels increases (Luetchford 2011, Canavari, Cantore, and Spadoni 2010).

Little research has been done to weigh in on these questions about the transparency, incentives, and performance of certifying watchdog organizations themselves. Existing literature does suggest that although consumers claim that they perceive third-party organizations to be most trustworthy, they still exhibit measurable trust in claims made by retailers or brands selling the products. In a survey of consumers conducted in the United States in 1990, 37 percent of respondents believed that "environmental groups" were the best source of unbiased information about the environment, whereas 8 percent believed the government was and 5 percent believed that product manufacturers were (Abt Associates 1994).

However, in Hiscox and Smyth's towel and candle study, consumers exhibited increased demand for products with ethical claims made by the retailer, not by a third-party certifier (Hiscox and Smyth 2007). Similarly, in Blend and Ravensway's household survey on consumer demand for eco-labeled apples, the comprehensiveness of the eco-claim and whether it was certified by the USDA or by the seller were both found to have insignificant impact on the consumer's willingness to pay a premium (Blend and Ravensway 1999). This evidence suggests that, while consumers trust third-party watchdogs best, they may not be good at distinguishing them from other kinds of claim verifiers. By extension, the lack of attentiveness to the rigor of the standard in these studies lends support to the concern that consumers may not discriminate between labelers with strong standards and those whose standards slip, removing the incentive for watchdogs to maintain perfect standards of integrity.

Little work has been done investigating the relative advantage of different types of third-party certification agents. How are the incentives and constraints faced by non-state labeling organizations different from those faced by state agencies? The USDA's long-run survival as an organization does not depend on the public image of organic standards since the fees from granting labels does not support their budget. Non-state third-party certifiers may be exempt from the politics constraining state agencies and may, therefore, exercise more independence in selecting standards, but conversely, government agencies may be exempt from the financial pressures to "sell" their standards that are faced by independent groups. Barring further examination of the constraints and resources available to state and non-state certification agents, and the implications of those differences for the standard-setting and enforcement process, it is difficult to settle debates over certification and watchdog effectiveness.

The State

Private certification systems occupy an interesting position relative to state regulation. By setting, monitoring, and enforcing standards of production, they act in parallel to legal regulation, providing standards in areas where state regulation is relatively weak. Is this relationship complementary? Or are there reasons to be concerned about voluntary systems acting as substitutes for legal standards?

In many ways, private labeling schemes seem complementary to legal regulation, filling in where the state is absent. In developing countries where myriad challenges, from a large informal sector to a corrupt bureaucracy, prevent functional social welfare states from being implemented, Fair Trade offers farmers a price floor and, therefore, a financial safety net. In light of the fact that the U.S. government has not banned the use of growth hormones and chemical fertilizers in conventional agriculture, Organic standards provide consumers with produce from certified farms free of these inputs, and decrease cropland, farm worker, and animal exposure to toxins. By this account, private certification of food coexists as a helpful supplement to state regulation.

Freeman's argument serves as a rejoinder: "... to the extent that consumers care about the existence of substandard conditions per se, regardless of whether they buy the goods so produced, legal enactment has an advantage" (Freeman 1994, p. 87). This points to a crucial difference between state-mandated regulation and regulation provided by market-based actors: Legal regulation at least purports to be universal to an entire set of citizens. The voluntary nature of private certification schemes means that consumers' demand for ethically produced food—and, therefore, the regulatory standards that go along with it—will reach only some producers. This should raise concerns about the equity and distribution of labor and environmental standards. Some but not all farmers will have access to financial safety nets. Only ecosystems in select areas will be protected. Consumers can buy organic food and avoid ingesting trace amounts of pesticides and hormones, but only those who can afford to pay for it.

Of course, it would be naïve to argue that the universalistic nature of government regulation translates into equitable distribution in any scenario. But in the case of legal regulation, laws and policies are supposed to apply to all citizens at least *de jure*, providing citizens with a formal entitlement to use as a basis for making demands on the state. In a market-based, voluntary version of a regulatory system, those outside the system have no recourse.

This lack of universalism in private regulatory systems does not necessarily present a fundamental difficulty as long as these systems truly work as a complement to legal regulation; in this case, they do not make things worse. But if private regulatory systems *compete with* or *crowd out* the role of universal state-mandated standards, there is cause for concern. If citizens, frustrated by the absence of functioning state regulation, become habituated to the idea of the private sector as the customary source of regulation, they may begin to shift their expectations toward private providers, introducing a risk that norms of state provision will begin to erode in the absence of citizen pressure. This could have long-term consequences for the distribution of regulation across the population.

Conclusion

Does ethically labeled food represent the answer to poor labor conditions for farmers, degradation of farmland ecosystems, and health risks posed by chemical agents in food? The evidence reviewed in this chapter suggests that it is part, but not all, of the answer.

Critics of these labeling schemes give us several important reasons to believe that private labeling of food does not represent a stand-alone answer. Demand for these products is likely to be limited by social norms and by income. Disagreements about how stringent standards should be will continue to drive the proliferation of labels, increasingly challenging consumers' already limited ability to distinguish between strong and weak standards. The logistical and structural challenges to effective monitoring of private standards by certification agents are likely to persist, making violations at the farm level difficult to detect and thus rendering perfect compliance elusive.

Our review of existing evidence points to five key issues as likely to affect the trajectory of labeling and certification schemes in the future.

First, all theories of consumer motivation suggest that social norms drive demand. The size of the market for ethical goods will be constrained by the extent to which proponents of labeling initiatives can recruit consumers beyond a narrow demographic, economic, and ideological base. The more broadly norms are spread, the more they are likely to affect individual consumers' decisions to buy ethically labeled goods.

Second, while we know little about how these norms are spread, new communities are unlikely to start conversations about food ethics if certification remains limited to a narrow set of products and retailers. Thus the extent of demand may be affected by the outcome of the depth-versus-breadth debate.

Third, if breadth strategies increase consumer demand and depth strategies deepen farmer impact, the debate between the two may be counterproductive because it suggests a false choice. Rather than choosing between a system of lenient standards that are accessible to a broad range of products and a system of strict standards that will likely remain a niche market, labels like LEED certification and the GlobalGAP program have developed unified certification systems with incremental standards that range from the baseline to the aspirational. If this type of tiered system of food certification is more broadly adopted across the ethical food market, giving merit points both for certification at high levels and for improvements at any level, it would likely moderate label proliferation and accommodate a range of companies by rewarding both excellence and improvement.

Fourth, our discussion of certification watchdogs suggests a pivotal role for journalists in determining whether standards remain credible. Similar to the role of independent media in safeguarding a democratic political system in which voters have limited information, journalists are in the position to step into the role of "watchdog to the watchdogs," helping consumers wade through the marketing materials of each standard-setting organization and flagging certifiers whose transparency clouds or whose standards slip.

Finally, although geographic dispersion of certified farms, poor transportation infrastructure, and complex supply-chain structures will continue to pose a challenge to transparency in international supply chains, traceability initiatives that have been dismissed as too complicated in the past will become increasingly within reach with the continued spread of mobile telecommunications technology. The impact of certification schemes on farmers and farms and the credibility of those schemes in the eyes of the public will, in part, depend on the ability of certification organizations to leverage rapidly evolving technology to continue to improve monitoring efforts.

Even if all these conditions are present, the impact of ethical labeling schemes will remain limited by their voluntary nature. As long as we think these schemes reflect issues of personal conscience or mere preferences on the part of consumers, their lack of universalism may raise few concerns. As we have noted, however, the dividing lines between issues of health and safety, issues of collective societal good, and issues of personal preference and conscience are dynamic, contested, and political. Insofar as these schemes protect values like food safety, worker safety, environmental protection, or the provision of basic income nets, the limited and unequal reach of voluntary standards might be viewed more critically. In this context, as a complement to state regulation, the system of voluntary certification and labeling of food may temporarily fill gaps left by the absence of strong state standards. Such systems can further provide test cases for how more stringent standards might work in practice and be used as a model for state regulation in the future. If citizens begin to accept voluntary, market-based standards as long-run substitutes for universal government-mandated regulation, however, these systems run the risk of institutionalizing inequalities in the distribution of labor, and environmental and health standards in the food system.

Notes

* I gratefully acknowledge the helpful comments and contributions of Evann Smith, Michael Hiscox, Shauna Shames, Laurel Eckhouse, Jim McKinsey, Elizabeth McKinsey, Tom Clough, and Ron Herring.

1. Although this phrase has been used more broadly in the economics literature to describe any purchase as a signal of consumer preferences, Johnston and MacKendrick (this volume) apply it specifically to the consumption of ethically labeled food, using the voting analogy to emphasize what they see as the political nature of the preferences expressed by that particular act of consumption.
2. Certified food is part of a broader phenomenon of ethically sourced products of all kinds, from denim jeans produced with environmentally safe dyes to Fair Trade basketballs and low-emissions chemicals. This chapter, though it is focused on ethically certified food, will draw insights and evidence from a broad literature on ethically labeled products more generally.
3. Goul Anderson and Tobiasen (2004)'s survey results are consistent with this perspective.
4. See Herring, this volume; text reflects Herring personal communication.
5. See, for example, the debate about whether GMO labeling should be voluntary or mandatory (e.g. Carter et al. 2012).
6. See, for example, the "Safeguard Organic Standards" campaign run by the Organic Consumers Association (http://www.organicconsumers.org/sos.cfm).
7. For an extensive outline of the literature on consumer motivation for ethical consumption, see Hainmueller, Hiscox, and Sequeira (2011).
8. See particularly Trigg's extension of the concept of conspicuous consumption (2001), which builds on Veblen ([1899] 1994) and Bourdieu (1984).
9. The author participated as a research assistant in this field experiment.
10. Note that this experiment does not constitute a test of gendered demand for ethical labeling since it does not include a high-priced men's item.

11. Price satisfaction is a subjective, self-reported measure of farmers' satisfaction with the price they receive for their products.
12. For a more detailed review of the literature, see Nelson and Pound (2009) and Nelson and Martin (2012).
13. For example, in Becchetti and Constantino's (2006) study of Kenyan farmers, the authors were unable to isolate the effects of individual certification standards because many of the farmers studied were Fair Trade certified, Organic certified, and members of a cooperative marketing organization.
14. New research is beginning to move in this direction (Nelson and Martin 2012; Hainmueller, Hiscox, and Tampe 2011).
15. Some firms use outside auditors to check compliance with their CSR policies in their sourcing sites. Timberland, for example, hired Verité, a nonprofit labor rights organization, to audit the facilities from which they buy their products.
16. ISEAL is beginning to play a role in attempting to define standards for what makes a certification system credible (see http://www.isealalliance.org/).

Bibliography

Abt Associates. 1994. "Determinants of Effectiveness for Environmental Certification and Labeling Programs." *Environmental Protection Agency.*

Alsever, J. 2006. "Fair Prices for Farmers: Simple Idea, Complex Reality." *The New York Times.*

Andreoni, J. 1989. "Giving with Impure Altruism: Applications to Charity and Ricardian Equivalence." *Journal of Political Economy* 97(6): 1447–1458.

Andreoni, J., & L. Vesterlund. 2001. "Which Is the Fair Sex? Gender Differences in Altruism." *Quarterly Journal of Economics*, (February): 293–312.

Arnould, E. J., A. Plastina, & D. Ball. 2006. "Market Disintermediation and Producer Value Capture: The Case of Fair Trade Coffee in Nicaragua, Peru and Guatemala." Working Paper. University of Illinois at Chicago Conference on Product and Market Development for Subsistence Marketplaces.

Auld, G. 2011. "Certification as Governance: Current Impacts and Future Prospects." In *The Politics of Fair Trade*, edited by M. Warrier, 68–86. London: Routledge.

Bacon, C. 2005. "Confronting the Coffee Crisis: Can Fair Trade, Organic, and Specialty Coffees Reduce Small-Scale Farmer Vulnerability in Northern Nicaragua?" *World Development*, 33(3): 497–511.

Becchetti, L., & M. Costantino, M. 2006. "The effects of Fair Trade on marginalised producers: an impact analysis on Kenyan farmers." Working Paper. Society for the Study of Economic Inequality (ECINEQ).

Biao, X., W. Xiaorong, D. Zhuhong, & Y. Yaping. 2003. "Critical Impact Assessment of Organic Agriculture." *Journal of Agricultural and Environmental Ethics* 16: 297–311.

Blend, J. R., & E. O. V. Ravenswaay. 1999. "Measuring Consumer Demand for Ecolabeled Apples." *American Journal of Agricultural Economics* 81(5): 1072–1077.

Boström, M., & Klintman, M. 2006. "State-centered versus Nonstate-driven Organic Food Standardization: A Comparison of the US and Sweden. *Agriculture and Human Values* 23(2): 163–180.

Bourdieu, P. (1984). *Distinction: A Social Critique of the Judgement of Taste*. Routledge & Kegan Paul Ltd.

Brown, D. K. 2006. "Consumer Product Labels, Child Labor and Educational Attainment." *Contributions to Economic Analysis & Policy* 5(1).

Canavari, M., N. Cantore, & R. Spadoni, R. 2010. "Role of Certification Bodies in the Organic Production System." In *Looking East, Looking West: Organic and Quality Food Marketing in Asia and Europe*, edited by R. Haas, M. Canavari, B. Slee, C. Tong, & B. Anurugsa, 85–102. Wageningen, Netherlands: Wageningen Academic Publishers.

Carter, C. A., G. P. Gruère, P. Mclaughlin, & M. Maclachlan. 2012. "California's Proposition 37: Effects of Mandatory Labeling of GM Food." *ARE Update (Giannini Foundation of Agricultural Economics)* 15(6): 3–8.

Cohen, R. 2012, September 6. "The Organic Fable." *The New York Times*. Accessed May 15, 2013. Available at http://www.nytimes.com/2012/09/07/opinion/roger-cohen-the-organic-fable.html?_r=0

Darnall, N., & S. Sides. 2008. "Assessing the Performance of Voluntary Environmental Programs: Does Certification Matter?" *Policy Studies Journal* 36(1): 95–117.

De Boer, I. J. M. 2003. "Environmental Impact Assessment of Conventional and Organic Milk Production." *Livestock Production Science* 80(1–2): 69–77.

Jones, Stephen, Brendan Bayley, Nick Robins et al. 2000. *Fair Trade: Overview, Impact, Challenges*. Accessed May 15, 2013. Available at http://portals.wi.wur.nl/files/docs/ppme/ACF3C8C.pdf.

De Pelsmacker, P., L. Driesen, & G. Rayp. 2005. "Do Consumers Care about Ethics? Willingness to Pay for Fair-Trade Coffee." *Journal of Consumer Affairs* 39(2): 363–385.

Deaton, J. B., L. Busch, W. J. Samuels, & P. B. Thompson. 2010. "A note on the economy of qualities: attributing production practices to agricultural practices." *Journal of Rural Social Sciences* 25(3): 99–110.

Dolan, C. S. 2011. "Branding Morality: The Case of Fairtrade." In M. Warrier (Ed.), *The Politics of Fair Trade*, edited by M. Warrier, 37–52. London: Routledge.

Domingo, J. L., & J. G. Bordonaba. 2011. "A Literature Review on the Safety Assessment of Genetically Modified Plants." *Environment International* 37: 734–42.

Downie, A. 2007, October 2. "Fair Trade in Bloom." *The New York Times*. Accessed April 15, 2013. Available at http://www.nytimes.com/2007/10/02/business/worldbusiness/02trade.html?pagewanted=all.

Elfenbein, D. W., & B. Mcmanus. 2010. "A Greater Price for a Greater Good? Evidence That Consumers Pay More for Charity-Linked Products." *American Economic Journal: Economic Policy* 2(May): 28–60.

Elliott, K. A., & R. B. Freeman. 2003. *Can Labor Standards Improve Under Globalization?* Washington, D.C.: Institute for International Economics.

EPA. 2012. "Pesticides and Food: Health Problems Pesticides May Pose." Accessed April 15, 2013. Available at http://www.epa.gov/opp00001/food/risks.htm

Fair Trade USA. 2010. *2009/2010 Impact Report: Fair Trade Certified Bananas*. Accessed May 15, 2013. Available at http://www.fairtradeusa.org/sites/default/files/Bananas_Impact_Report_2.pdf.

Fairtrade International, & Fair Trade USA. 2011. "Fair Trade USA Resigns Fairtrade International (FLO) Membership: Joint Statement." Accessed August 1, 2012. Available at http://www.fairtradeusa.org/press-room/press_release/fair-trade-usa-resigns-fairtrade-international-flo-membership.

Faulkner, C. 2007. "The Root of the Evil: Free Produce and Radical Antislavery, 1820–1860." *Journal of the Early Republic* 27(3): 377–405.

Ferguson, K. (2009, April 16). "Biosolids' and Human Health." *The New York Times Green: A Blog About Energy and the Environment*. New York. Accessed May 15, 2013. Available at http://green.blogs.nytimes.com/2009/04/16/biosolids-and-human-health/.

Fisher, R. J. 1993. Social Desirability Bias and the Validity of Indirect Questioning. *Journal of Consumer Research*, *20*(2), 303–315.

Føllesdal, A. 2004. Political Consumerism as Chance and Challenge. *Politics, Products, and Markets: Exploring Political Consumerism Past and Present* (pp. 3–20). New Brunswick, NJ: Transaction Publishers.

Freeman, R. B. 1994. A Hard-Headed Look at Labour Standards. In *International Labour Standards and Economic Interdependence*, edited by W. Sengenberger & D. Campbell, 79–92. Geneva: International Institute for Labour Studies.

Friedman, M. 1970, September 13. "The Social Responsibility of Business Is to Increase Its Profits." *The New York Times Magazine*, 32–33, 122–124.

Gendron, C., V. Bisaillon, & A. I. O. Rance. 2009. "The Institutionalization of Fair Trade: More Than Just a Degraded Form of Social Action." *Journal of Business Ethics* 86 (Supplement 1): 63–79.

Glazer, S. 2007. Fair Trade Labeling. *CQ Researcher* 17(19): 433–456.

Goldstein, N. J., R. B. Cialdini, & V. Griskevicius. 2008. "A Room with a Viewpoint: Using Social Norms to Motivate Environmental Conservation in Hotels." *Journal of Consumer Research* 35(3): 472–482.

Goul Anderson, J., & M. Tobiasen. 2004. "Who Are These Political Consumers Anyway? Survey Evidence from Denmark." In *Politics, Products, and Markets: Exploring Political Consumerism Past and Present*, edited by Michelle Micheletti, A. Follesdal, & D. Stolle, 203–222. New Brunswick, NJ: Transaction Press.

Granville, B. 2009. "Trust in Fairtrade: The 'Feel-Good' Effect." Working Paper. Centre for Globalization Research, Queen Mary University of London School of Business and Management.

Griffiths, P. 2012. "Ethical Objections to Fairtrade." *Journal of Business Ethics* 105(3): 357–373.

Hainmueller, J., M. J. Hiscox, and M. Tampe. 2011. *Sustainable Development for Cocoa Farmers in Ghana*. Accessed January 8, 2014. Available at http://www.theigc.org/sites/default/files/Cocoa_Ghana_paper_formatted.pdf.

Hainmueller, J., & M. J. Hiscox. 2012a. "The Socially Conscious Consumer? Field Experimental Tests of Consumer Support for Fair Labor Standards." Working Paper. Massachusetts Institute of Technology.

Hainmueller, J., & M. J. Hiscox. 2012b. "Buying Green? Field Experimental Tests of Consumer Support for Environmentalism." Working Paper. Massachusetts Institute of Technology.

Hainmueller, J., M. J. Hiscox, & S. Sequeira. 2011. "Consumer Demand for the Fair Trade Label: Evidence from a Field Experiment." Working Paper.

Harbaugh, R., J. W. Maxwell, & B. Roussillon. 2011. "Label Confusion: The Groucho Effect of Uncertain Standards." *Management Science* 57(9): 1512–1527.

Harford, T. 2006. *The Undercover Economist: Exposing Why the Rich Are Rich, the Poor Are Poor—and Why You Can Never Buy a Decent Used Car!* New York: Oxford University Press.

Henson, S., & J. Humphrey. 2010. "Understanding the complexities of private standards in global agri-food chains as they impact developing countries." *The Journal of Development Studies* 46(9): 1628–1646.

Hickman, M. 2010, February 22. Recession Affects Sales of Fairtrade Products. *The Independent*. Accessed May 15, 2013. Available at http://www.independent.co.uk/news/business/news/recession-affects-sales-of-fairtrade-products-1906827.html.

Hiscox, M. J., & N. F. B. Smyth. 2007. "Is There Consumer Demand for Improved Labor Standards? Evidence from Field Experiments in Social Product Labeling." Unpublished manuscript. Accessed April 15, 2013. Available at http://www.people.fas.harvard.edu/~hiscox/SocialLabeling.pdf.

Holländer, H. 1990. "A Social Exchange Approach to Voluntary Cooperation." *The American Economic Review* 80(5): 1157–1167.

Howard, P. H., & P. Allen. 2010. "Beyond Organic and Fair Trade? An Analysis of Ecolabel Preferences in the United States." *Rural Sociology* 75(2): 244–269.

International Food Policy Research Insititute (IFPRI). 2005. *The Future of Small Farms: Proceedings of a Research Workshop*. Washington, D.C. Accessed May 15, 2013. Available at http://www.ifpri.org/sites/default/files/publications/sfproc.pdf.

International Labour Organisation. 2011. *Children in Hazardous Work: What We Know; What We Need to Do*. Geneva: International Labour Organisation.

Kennedy, P. 2004. "Selling Virtue: Political and Economic Contradictions of Green/Ethical Marketing in the United Kingdom." In *Politics, Products, and Markets: Exploring Political Consumerism Past and Present*, edited by Michelle Micheletti, A. Follesdal, & D. Stolle, 21–44. New Brunswick, NJ: Transaction Publishers.

Levi, M., & A. Linton. 2003. "Fair Trade: A Cup at a Time?" *Politics & Society* 31(3): 407–432.

List, J. A. 2004. "Young, Selfish and Male: Field Evidence of Social Preferences." *The Economic Journal* 114(January): 121–149.

Loureiro, M. L., & J. Lotade. 2005. "Do Fair Trade and Eco-Labels in Coffee Wake Up the Consumer Conscience?" *Ecological Economics* 53(1): 129–138.

Luetchford, P. 2008. *Fair Trade and a Global Commodity: Coffee in Costa Rica*. London: Pluto Press.

Luetchford, P. 2011. "Falling Foul of Fair: The Politics of Supply Chains." In *The Politics of Fair Trade*, edited by M. Warrier, pp. 53–67. London: Routledge.

Lusk, J. L., F. B. Norwood, & R. W. Prickett. 2007. "Consumer Preferences for Farm Animal Welfare: Results of a Nationwide Telephone Survey." Working Paper. Department of Agricultural Economics, Oklahoma State University.

Mench, J. A., D. A. Sumner, D. A., & J. T. Rosen-Molina. 2011. "Sustainability of Egg Production in the United States—the Policy and Market Context." *Poultry Science* 90(1): 229–40.

Micheletti, Michele. 2004. "Why More Women?" In *Politics, Products, and Markets: Exploring Political Consumerism Past and Present*, edited by Michele Micheletti, A. Føllesdal, & D. Stolle, 245–264. New Brunswick, NJ: Transaction Publishers.

Nederhof, A. J. 1985. "Methods of Coping with Social Desirability Bias: A Review." *European Journal of Social Psychology* 15(3): 263–280.

Nelson, V. & A. Martin. 2012. "The Impact of Fairtrade: Evidence, Shaping Factors, and Future Pathways." *Food Chain* 2:1, 42–63.

Nelson, V. & B. Pound. 2009. *The Last Ten Years: A Comprehensive Review of the Literature on the Impact of Fairtrade*. Accessed January 8, 2014. Available at http://www.fairtrade.org.uk/includes/documents/cm_docs/2010/n/2_nri_full_literature_review_final_version.pdf

Nelson, V. & A. Martin. 2013. *Final Technical Report: Assessing the Poverty Impact of Sustainability Standards*. Accessed January 8, 2014. Available at http://www.nri.org/images/documents/project_websites/AssessingPovertyImpacts/AssessingThePovertyImpactOfSustainabilityStandards.pdf.

Nelson, V., & M. Galvez. 2000. *Social Impact of Ethical and Conventional Cocoa Trading on Forest-Dependent People in Ecuador*, 1–29. Natural Resource Institute, University of Greenwich.

Payán-Rentería, R., Garibay-Chávez, G., Rangel-Ascencio, R., Preciado-Martínez, V., Muñoz-Islas, L., Beltrán-Miranda, C., Mena-Munguía, S., et al. 2012. Effect of chronic pesticide exposure in farm workers of a Mexico community. *Archives of Environmental & Occupational Health* 67(1): 22–30.

Pew Commission on Industrial Farm Animal Production. (2008). *Putting Meat on the Table: Industrial Farm Animal Production in America*. 1–111.

Phillips, I., M. Casewell, T. Cox, B. De Groot, C. Friis, R. Jones, C. Nightingale, et al. 2004. "Does the Use of Antibiotics in Food Animals Pose a Risk to Human Health? A Critical Review of Published Data." *The Journal of Antimicrobial Chemotherapy* 53(1): 28–52.

Pierson, P. 2000. Increasing Returns, Path Dependence, and the Study of Politics. *The American Political Science Review* 94(2): 251–267.

Pritchett, L. 2002. "It Pays to be Ignorant: A Simple Political Economy of Rigorous Program Evaluation." *Policy Reform* 5(4): 251–269.

Program on International Policy Attitudes (PIPA). 2000. *Americans on Globalization: A Study of US Public Attitudes* (pp. 1–102).

Rodriguez, S. 2011. "The Morally Informed Consumer: Examining Animal Welfare Claims on Egg Labels." *Temple Journal of Science, Technology, & Environmental Law* 51: 53–81.

Rodrik, D. 2007. "Fair Trade: Savior or Ruse?" Dani Rodrik's weblog. Accessed July 29, 2012. Available at http://rodrik.typepad.com/dani_rodriks_weblog/2007/04/fair_trade_savi.html.

Schuetze, C. F. 2012, September 17. "What's In a Label? Not Necessarily Sustainability." *International Herald Tribune*.

Smith-Spangler, Crystal, Margaret Brandeau, Grace E. Hunter, et al. 2012. "Are Organic Foods Safer or Healthier Than Conventional Alternatives?" *Annals of Internal Medicine* 157: 348–366.

Stephany, R. W. 2001. Hormones in Meat: Different Approaches in the EU and in the USA. *APMIS, 109*(Supplement 103): S357–S364.

Strom, S. 2012, July 7. "Has 'Organic' Been Oversized?" *New York Times*.

Sussman, C. 1994. "Women and the Politics of Sugar, 1792." *Representations* 48(Fall): 48–69.

Tarrow, S. G. 1994. *Power in Movement: Social Movements and Contentious Politics*. New York: Cambridge University Press.

Tilman, D., K. G. Cassman, P. A. Matson, R. Naylor, & S. Polasky. 2002. "Agricultural Sustainability and Intensive Production Practices." *Nature* 418 (August 8): 671–677.

Trewavas, A. 2001. "Urban Myths of Organic Farming." *Nature* 410: 409–410.

Trigg, A. B. 2001. "Veblen, Bourdieu, and Conspicuous Consumption." *Journal of Economic Issues* 35(1): 99–115.

Van der Zee, B. 2007, May. "Could Do Better." *The Guardian*. Accessed April 15, 2013. Available at http://www.theguardian.com/environment/2007/may/10/ethicalliving.lifeandhealth.

Veblan, T. 1994. *The Theory of the Leisure Class. In The Collected Works of Thorstein Veblen*. Vol. 1. 1899. Reprint, London: Routledge, 1–404.

Vogel, D. 2008. "Private Global Business Regulation." *Annual Review of Political Science* 11(1): 261–282.

Weitzman, H. 2006, September 8. "The Bitter Cost of 'Fair Trade' Coffee." *Financial Times*, pp. 11–13.

CHAPTER 26

THE POLITICS OF GROCERY SHOPPING

Eating, Voting, and (Possibly) Transforming the Food System

JOSÉE JOHNSTON AND NORAH MACKENDRICK

Introduction

PEOPLE today are widely encouraged to "vote with their dollar" at the grocery store. The rhetoric of "voting with your dollar" is not only widely articulated within the popular press, but it is also a rallying cry for food activists. For example, the Canadian organization Local Food Plus (LFP) works to develop a local, sustainable food economy and encourages consumers to pledge to spend ten dollars a week on local foods. According to their "Buy To Vote" campaign,

> We don't have to solve all the world's problems at once. After all, Rome wasn't built in a day. But by shifting just $10 a week to local sustainable food, you can make a real difference by voting with your dollars for fare that is fair, healthier for communities and good food for tomorrow.
>
> (http://localfoodplus.ca/buy-to-vote)

Local Food Plus is not a lone voice in the food wilderness. Best-selling authors like Mark Bittman (2008) and Michael Pollan (2006) have urged thousands, if not millions, of consumers to reconsider their dietary choices in light of climate change, peak oil, and the various ills associated with a corporate-dominated industrial food system. Political eating discourse asks consumers in the affluent Global North to examine the origins of food, be skeptical of the claims made about food, and support commodity chains that are shorter and more transparent. Consumers are told that food becomes political when it is consumed in a conscious and deliberate way, and when you "vote with your dollar" to support initiatives that are green, clean, and socially just. The motivations are political, but the benefits are also framed as personal. For example, the cover of Mark Bittman's book *Food Matters* depicts a hybrid apple-globe graphic, with a label that reads, "Lose Weight, Heal the Planet."

As a strategy for transforming the global food system, consumer food politics[1] (hereafter referred to as "food politics") is promisingly popular, but far from straightforward. This chapter seeks to bring greater clarity to this topic by describing and assessing key debates about consumption and food system reform. The question of exactly how to empirically define when food choices become politicized is widely explored in the literature. Scholars suggest that politicized forms of food consumption involve the regular purchase of foods and/or modification of the diet with the deliberate purpose of contributing to the collective good (e.g., by improving environmental quality, contributing to social justice, or supporting local business; see Halkier 2008; Stolle and Hooghe 2004). Whether consumption can be considered a form of political action with transformative potential is up for debate (Johnston 2008; Gabriel and Lang 2006; Micheletti 2003). In this chapter, we aim to advance the debate concerning the transformative potential of food politics by drawing attention to the varied meanings given to consumption and consumerism by shoppers, and by providing a conceptual map, or typology, of these meanings. This typology helps move the debate beyond a simple dichotomy of the apolitical versus the political consumer. We document a range of political perspectives representing different ideas of how consumption may be harnessed to generate structural change in the food system. We see the greatest potential in citizenship perspectives that resist the commodification of food and food solutions, and we see politicized eating as only one way of addressing the inequalities and ecological degradation embedded in affluent North American diets. While market-based consumption strategies have some positive elements, including their popular appeal, we think it is important to challenge the idea that individual shopping strategies are a sufficient way to reform a highly inequitable food system dominated by corporate interests.

Taking different debates and critiques of food politics[2] into account, this chapter sets out three main goals: (1) provide a brief overview of the history and characteristics of consumer food politics, outlining key tensions between new consumer tastes, and market incorporation of consumer politics; (2) introduce a typology of consumer food politics to examine the varied meanings that consumers attach to food politics; and (3) discuss the strengths and limits of consumer-driven regulation of the food system.

A New Taste for Politics? A Brief Overview of Food Politics

The state is heavily involved in shaping the food system through various measures, such as subsidies to agricultural and corporate producers, the operation of regulatory bureaucracies that monitor agricultural production and establish health and safety standards for food commodities, and involvement in negotiating global trade agreements. While the state's role in the food system is highly significant, it is typically rendered invisible in everyday consumer interactions, particularly in an affluent North American context where markets play a dominant role in everyday food provisioning. In fact, as we argue below, contemporary food politics is more commonly associated with changing norms of personal consumption and food culture than with collective action directed at the state and regulatory reform.

Consumer food politics date back to the late nineteenth century, when consumer boycotts and cooperatives emerged to combat local monopolies that controlled grain milling and the price of food (Hilton 2003; Lang and Gabriel 2005, 41; Schudson 2007). In the latter half of the twentieth century, food emerged as central to the counterculture's critique of modern industrial life. Belasco (1989) documented the emerging food politics of the 1960s and 1970s, coining the term "countercuisine" to describe a movement that was heavily invested in exploring the political implications of food choices. The countercuisine was not a unified, monolithic movement, however, but instead operated from multiple vantage points such as food co-ops, the peace movement, and "back to the land" lifestyles. A common thread that united diverse culinary interests was a focus on unearthing the political implications of food choices. White bread was decried as a symbol of an industrial era of soulless convenience foods, while "brown rice became the icon of antimodernity," and a mechanism for standing (and eating) in solidarity with the world's oppressed peoples (27, 49).

Contemporary gourmet culture has taken up many of the themes of the 1960s and 1970s countercuisine, incorporating them into the contemporary valuation of authentic, exotic, and delicious foods (Johnston and Baumann 2010). Of course, not all dimensions of food politics are taken up with equal intensity, or by all "foodies." Some research (Johnston and Baumann 2007, 2010) suggests that environmental issues are most frequently incorporated into North American gourmet palates, with social justice and equity issues less commonly prioritized. While food politics has taken on increased importance, food quality, pleasure, and deliciousness frequently trump political commitments (Johnston and Baumann 2010, 127, 164). One self-described foodie explained this view: "Here's the thing, the ethical concerns are there. I have them, and they live in me as a kind of guilty conscience... but I'm too interested in my pleasure to actually impose them on myself" (Johnston and Baumann 2010, 168). In short, food politics has entered mainstream and gourmet food discourse in a significant way, even though not all people enact these politics in daily life, and even though there are numerous contradictions involved, particularly between sensual culinary pleasures and political commitments.

As food culture became more explicitly politicized, the study of consumers as political actors in late modern societies has expanded greatly since the early 1990s (see Micheletti 2003; Miller 1995; Sassatelli 2007; Slater 1997; Soper 2004; Szasz 2007; Zukin and Maguire 2004). While definitions of political consumerism abound, we draw on Micheletti's conceptualization of it as "the politics of products, which in a nutshell can be defined as power relations among people and choices about how resources should be used and allocated globally" (2003, x). This definition usefully draws attention to the critical power issues involved in food politics—which groups have power and resources and, which groups are marginalized. This point is particularly important in relation to global food resources and their maldistribution at a global scale (Paarlberg 2010). Moreover, food politics cannot be reduced to a specific practice or market mechanism, such as buying certified organic foods. Instead, food politics is better understood as a broad discourse that includes consumer imperatives to buy "green," local, fair-trade, and sustainable products in the service of health, social justice, and sustainability. Within that discourse, there are myriad tensions, contradictions, and questions (e.g., is it better to purchase local non-certified-organic foods or long-distance organic fare?), but there is also a unifying logic linking individual consumer change to improved ecological and social conditions.

Many scholars now recognize the importance of consumers as political actors, but there remains considerable debate about the political consequences and transformative potential of consumer-focused strategies for changing the food system. Rather than depicting this debate as involving two different, discrete camps of scholars, it is more useful to think about an active and continually emerging spectrum of arguments—particularly since some scholars highlight different ideas at different points of their writing, and certain arguments are more convincing in specific empirical contexts. At one pole of this spectrum, we find arguments depicting consumer politics as a legitimate form of political action, one that exists alongside—and might possibly encourage—other forms of political participation (Barnett et al. 2005; Lang and Gabriel 2005; Micheletti 2003; Micheletti, Føllesdal, and Stolle 2004; Neilson and Paxton 2010; Schor 2007). These perspectives identify the politicization of the private sphere of consumption and lifestyle (Giddens 1991; Stolle and Hooghe 2004; Stolle, Hooghe, and Micheletti 2005) especially among young people, the highly educated, and women (Tindall et al. 2003; Stolle et al. 2005; Neilson and Paxton 2010). They argue that citizens feel distanced from traditional public-sphere forms of political participation and distrust formal political institutions. Consumer choice is thought to afford individuals a sense of political agency, and allow them to align commodity choices with political preferences, morals, and values (Barnett et al. 2005; Connolly and Prothero 2008).

At the other pole of this spectrum, we find various perspectives that express skepticism about the transformative potential of consumer politics. These voices argue that consumer politics represents a form of neoliberalism that downloads responsibility to self-auditing individuals, leaving states and corporations less accountable for the public good (Power 1997; Rose 1999). In relation to food politics, researchers have identified fetishized consumer approaches to "local" and "organic" food projects, critiqued the class and racial biases of these consumption programs, cast doubt on the coherence of "citizen-consumers" acting in a corporate-dominated marketplace, and suggested the need for reflexive engagement with food politics (Dupuis and Goodman 2005; Guthman 2003; Hinrichs 2003; Johnston 2008; Maniates 2002; Moore 2006; Slocum 2004; Alkon and McCullen 2010). This literature problematizes consumption as a mechanism for political change, pointing to some of the contradictions between the imperatives of consumption and citizenship. Citizenship implies a commitment to broader social obligations, whereas—in a strict sense—consumers are obligated primarily to their personal preferences, tastes, and the size of their wallets (Jubas 2007). It is not that consumer interests can never be harnessed for a greater public good, but questions remain about where and when this mobilization actually takes place. Johnston's (2008) study of a "consumer-citizen hybrid," in the case of Whole Foods Market, suggests that in a corporate, profit-oriented context, individual self-interest is prioritized over citizenship-based objectives. While affluent food consumers undoubtedly have some agency in the marketplace (sending signals to firms about what foods are desirable, ethical, or objectionable), it is not clear whether consumers have sufficient agency to meaningfully shape the food system, especially in the absence of effective state intervention (Johnston 2008; Johnston, Biro, and MacKendrick 2009; Paarlberg 2010; Seyfang 2009). For example, Seyfang (2009) notes that individual consumer choices are bound within "infrastructures of provision"—that is, the institutional arrangements and social norms that constrain decision making—that cannot be transformed by individual consumer choices alone (p.16). In other words, the purchase of a local, organic apple at a grocery store may encourage a greater quantity and better quality of organic produce provided in the store, but this choice would have a negligible impact on the institutions of provision that shape food procurement—such as the mass producers and food distribution networks, or the grocery stores with large parking lots to accommodate shoppers who drive. Moreover, choice over one's food and the option to reflect on the sustainability and social justice implications of such a choice is a privilege that largely belongs to affluent consumers. Consumer politics therefore offers limited transformative potential for impoverished citizens who struggle to meet even basic food needs and have comparatively limited access to alternative markets.

Another set of questions raised at the more skeptical pole of the literature is the efficacy of conventional mass-markets for food system transformation. Rather than just ignore their critics, dominant market actors can quickly react and adapt to changing consumer values and countercultural movements (Frank 1997; Jaffe and Howard 2010; Turner 2006;), as evidenced by the introduction of new "sustainable" products and organic foods into mainstream shopping spaces like WalMart. Yet, in the case of organic food, this has not significantly moved the food system toward a state of sustainability, even though a greater volume of certified organic products has been made available through the corporatization and mass retailing of organics ("Big Organics") (Allen and Kovach 2000; Delind 2000; Guthman 2004). In the case of the seafood industry, a retailer-driven sustainability program has produced a confusing patchwork of sustainable and nonsustainable consumer options, with ambiguous outcomes for sustainable fisheries more generally (Konefal 2010). Moreover, messages from alternative agricultural initiatives (e.g., "eat local") that challenge the structure of the food system have proven to be easily incorporated into the marketing of corporate commodities (Johnston, Biro, and MacKendrick 2009), raising questions about the scale of corporate change required to achieve sustainability, and the extent to which consumers reflexively engage with food choices (Crossley 2004; Johnston and Szabo 2011).

Finally, at the margins of the debate about consumers and social change are two often overlooked variations of consumer politics that we wish to integrate into our discussion of food politics: voluntary simplicity (Elgin 1991; Etzioni 1998) and ecological citizenship (Dobson 2003; Wolf, Brown, and Conway 2009). In contrast to forms of consumer politics that focus on sourcing alternative commodities, these two approaches have a broader and more ambitious target: addressing consumerism and materialism as factors that discourage a sense of personal responsibility to the collective good and ecological commons. Voluntary simplicity results from dissatisfaction with mass consumption (Zavestoski 2002), and emphasizes noncommodity forms of meaning and fulfillment (Craig-Lees and Hill 2002; Etzioni 1998; Lorenzen 2012 Schor 1998). It involves demanding less consumption overall, rather than simply shifting consumption to a more sustainable basket of commodities (Shaw and Newholm 2002). Ecological citizenship confronts consumer culture in a similar way, but encapsulates a range of politicized lifestyle decisions and practices, including sustainable shopping, but also energy reduction in the home or the decision to use public transit over a personal vehicle. This form of consumer politics values justice, care, and compassion, and it emphasizes the citizen's responsibility to reduce one's environmental impact in both the public and private spheres (Dobson 2003; Seyfang 2005). So far, ecological citizenship has remained primarily a theoretical and normative concept (Dobson 2003), with only a few empirical studies of its application in everyday life (e.g., Kriflik 2006; Seyfang 2005; Wolf et al. 2009). Later in this chapter we identify the perspective of ecological citizenship as critical to the transformative potential of food politics (see also Seyfang 2005; 2009).

A Typology of Food Politics

As is clear from the previous discussion, we hope to avoid binary discussions of consumer politics, and join with others who view the discourse according to a typology reflecting a range of motivations—from the desire to save money through sustainable purchases or promote personal healthfulness, to the desire to reform social infrastructure in a way that transcends one's individual consumer desires (Seyfang 2009; Kriflik 2006). Applied to food politics, this approach recognizes that consumer motivations are complex, polysemic, and often competing (Holt 1997; Schudson 2007). Moral imperatives related to the environment and social justice can be crowded out by other considerations, such as thrift, convenience, and the desire to cultivate identity and a sense of belonging within one's social group (Seyfang 2009 15; Johnston and Szabo 2011; Johnston and Baumann 2010, 168–169).

Over the course of five separate research projects, involving interviews with over one hundred people, we have had the opportunity to examine the meanings that a diverse cross-section of consumers attach to their food choices (e.g., Johnston and Baumann 2010; Johnston and Szabo 2011). Looking at these interview data together, we are struck by the complex and polysemic nature of food politics, a realm where consumption is not only infused with political meaning but also reflects the individual's relationship to materialism and consumerism. Take, for example, two respondents from our studies, Trina and Phillippe—both of whom could be categorized as political food consumers. Trina is a 33-year-old public servant who does most of her shopping at a major grocery chain. She described the store in vivid terms, favorably mentioning the size of the cheese display and the range of food products available. She considers her grocery-shopping day a special treat that allows her to spend quality time with her husband. When the interviewer asked Trina what priorities influence her food shopping, she expressed specific political concerns about the food system, but despaired at the thought of reforming her shopping habits in ways that would limit choice and eliminate "interesting" foods. In the interview, she spoke about her discomfort about being implicated in a larger industrial food system that she finds deeply problematic:

> In the last twenty years we have so much genetic modification of our foods. If you go to India, the tomato is fresh and is going to get bad in a day and a half. Here, the tomato stays good for five days. Even the shape of our food, it's so perfect.... Being exposed in Canada to that perfection skews our perspective of what is real and what is not. We're totally capitalistic, consumeristic.... When I think about that, I'm indulging in that too. I'm contributing to that because I'm buying this food, I'm eating it, I'm preparing it...

Contrast her response to Phillippe, a 33-year-old professional in the financial sector who has chosen not to own a car, is strictly vegan, and runs his food shopping errands on his bike. Phillippe noted that his main priority with food shopping is the desire to lessen his environmental footprint. He ensures that none of the food products he buys for his family have plastic packaging, a difficult task that requires shopping at several different stores and a local farmers' market. He dislikes major grocery stores because they are "mechanistic and institutional" and prefers his neighborhood farmers' market and local health food store. His interview transcript demonstrates a strong desire to integrate environmental principles with everyday shopping practices:

> By far the most important issue [for me] is sustainability, and I shop for certain things at different stores depending on what they carry. I like the farmers' market because the food is local and usually is unpackaged. I guess I'm thinking about the environmental footprint of the product, but also the packaging. The next important thing is whether there's organic certification or a label, and the third is that it have only natural ingredients.... Cost and convenience are not really a consideration and we've decided to allocate a sizeable chunk of the household budget to food,... and I'll go out of my way if I need something and I don't want the plastic packaging.

To call Trina's and Phillippe's perspectives on food consumption "politicized" is accurate in a very basic way, but this obscures critical differences in how they articulate their approaches. Both interviews indicate that food choices are politicized, but Trina's interview displays an emphasis on replacing certain types of consumer products with alternatives, whereas Phillippe focused much less on substituting commodities, and more on his efforts to develop nonconventional patterns of eating and shopping that reduce consumption altogether. Whereas Trina emphasized how she enjoys shopping for food and describes it positively as a form of recreation, Phillippe conceptualized shopping as detrimental to his ecological footprint, and he spends considerable time and energy trying to meet basic needs by minimizing waste and consumption of disposable materials.

To put these different perspectives into context, in the following section we present a typology of food politics that maps out the complexity of consumer meanings. Our objective here is not to discover new types of consumers, but to capture, with greater clarity, some of the nuanced meanings of consumer politics, thereby improving our ability to understand the multiple manifestations of politicized food consumption. This typology is put forward as primarily empirical, rather than normative; our aim is to improve understanding of consumer motivations rather than cast judgment on "good" versus "bad" consumption choices. In addition, we want to emphasize that this typology presents ideal-types, and is not meant to represent a particular sample of consumers. Indeed, one consumer may articulate different aspects of the typology at different points in his or her lifetime, or even within a single interview. The consumer politics literature assumes that apolitical consumption is the dominant mode of consumption, although political forms of consumption represent an increasingly popular alternative (see, for example, Barnett et al 2005; Kriflik 2006; Shaw, Newholm, and Dickinson 2006). We deliberately avoid speculating on the relative distribution of consumers within these ideal types, because our studies had very specific recruitment criteria and prioritized recruitment of politically oriented consumers—the main focus of our discussion below. In short, this typology is intended to clarify the range of meanings involved in consumption politics, rather than measure the impact of these behaviors on the food system.

Figure 26.1 displays the dimensions of food politics along two separate axes, one to reflect politics (horizontal), the other consumerism (vertical). The politics dimension captures the extent to which people explicitly connect their consumer choices and food preferences to structural issues in the food system, such as social change, social justice, and sustainability. Here we draw on Stolle and Hooghe (2004, 280) who argue that political consumption is directed by motivations expressly linked to collective—rather

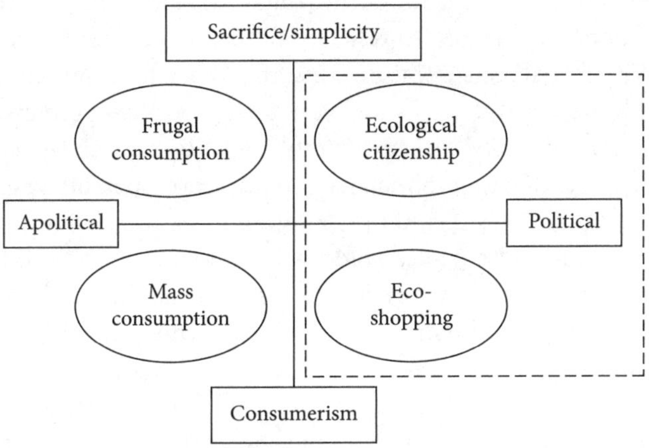

FIGURE 26.1 Typology of meanings embedded in consumer food politics.

than solely individual—goals, such as environmental improvement, equality, and social justice. Consumer perspectives falling closer to the political end of the spectrum, therefore, more consciously weigh political goals with purchasing decisions. Here we draw on much of the consumer politics literature described above, which suggests that political consumers are more likely to attribute political motivations to consumption activities. Perspectives that fall closer to the apolitical category are weighted more heavily toward individually scaled considerations (e.g., health, pleasure), and do not significantly incorporate collective goals into purchasing decisions. As such, a consumer account describing the purchasc of organic beef exclusively in terms of personal health benefits would be categorized as more "apolitical" than an account focused on how that same purchase contributed to food system sustainability.

The second, vertical dimension of the typology captures a range of meanings attached to the procurement of desired commodities, including food. For perspectives that fall closer to the consumerism end of the spectrum, the continual procurement of new and novel goods is a principal goal, and other, collective good considerations are secondary. Here consumption primarily takes on meanings already well examined within the sociological literature on consumption, including the desire to maximize pleasure and consumer choice, obtain value for money, achieve status, and mark one's location within a social group (Bourdieu 1984; Giddens 1991; Johnston 2008, 247–248). Consumer perspectives falling closer to the sacrifice/simplicity end have more in common with the voluntary simplicity perspective described earlier in the chapter; consumption itself is problematized and questioned, and there are deliberate efforts to forgo desired goods owing to a conscious desire to reduce consumption altogether. These sacrifices are not necessarily seen as hardships, but rather can be conceptualized positively by connecting reduced consumption with increased life satisfaction (Soper 2004).

The left-hand side of the quadrant is relatively apolitical, by which we mean that consumer politics, especially food choices, are not significantly framed as a way to ameliorate social and ecological problems in the food system, or to address power and resource inequities. Food choices and diets for both "frugal consumption" and "mass consumption" are not deliberately directed to reflect political objectives; instead, other priorities dominate. With frugal consumption, consumers seek to minimize consumption to minimize expenditures, and there is a relative disinterest in—perhaps even antipathy toward—accumulating new goods. Importantly, frugality is not always related to income constraints. Consumers that exemplified frugal consumption in our research were often from dual-income, middle-class, and upper-middle-class households. One example is Linda, a married, middle-class, 35-year-old teacher and mother of an infant. Linda does not enjoy cooking but is learning to prepare meals now that she is at home caring for her daughter. When asked about the most important priorities affecting her food choices, she explained that "price is a big concern.... And probably size... we buy in bulk a lot." Although Linda articulated concerns about pollution from pesticides at other points in her interview, she does not frame her shopping choices as politically motivated. Rather, maintaining a balanced food budget is the dominant priority: "Realistically I can't afford organic.... In an ideal world I would have much more time and money.... Plus I've read that some of the fruits, if you peel it, then that makes [enough of] a difference."

Mass consumption, in contrast, is a hegemonic mode of shopping where meaning is created through enjoyment of the process of accumulation, acquisition, and variety. This mode of shopping is highly normalized and has a "taken for granted" quality—even in retail settings that offer some promise of "shopping for change." The range of experiences in mass consumption can vary; sometimes shopping involves a search for low prices, and at other times it involves luxury goods or an experience that enhances feelings of social status. For example, Rob, a 31-year-old social worker, described Whole Foods Market positively as a "luxury food experience," and noted, "they call me sir—it's much more pleasing. You know, that extra special kind of attention." Similar to frugal consumption, mass consumption perspectives do not frame shopping as a political activity. Some food consumers we interviewed shopped consistently within this mode. Even when prompted about the political dimension of grocery shopping, or asked if they had any critiques of food system actors, these interviewees strictly limited their discussion about food shopping to concerns about nutrition, variety, price, and convenience.

Looking back at Trina and Phillippe, we see how they both conceptualize shopping as an extension of their politics, and therefore fit within the right-hand quadrant of the typology where we locate political food consumers. While both attach political meanings to commodity choices, we identify key differences in their perspectives on consumption: Trina's perspective fits within the eco-shopping category, whereas Phillippe's is best cast in the ecological citizenship category. Below, we draw on interview data from our various studies to expand on what we mean by these two categories, which we regard as the central contribution of this typology.

Eco-shopping

An "eco-shopping" perspective views political food shopping as an opportunity to replace conventional commodities with options that appear less harmful for people, animals, and the environment more generally. We use the prefix "eco" because the frame of environmental protection is the dominant theme of this mode of consumption, whereas labor and equity issues have a comparatively minor presence. This was clear in many of our interviews, where respondents primarily emphasized ecological concerns, with social justice concerns most often articulated in response to a specific follow-up question originating from the interviewer. For the eco-shopping ideal type, improvements in environmental conditions, reduction in waste, and elimination of labor injustices are possible through a form of commodity "substitutionism." In other words, consumption and attainment of more material goods are thought to be sustainable once they are incrementally shifted over to a more politicized basket of goods. Brenda, a 41-year-old health professional put it this way:

> I think doing one thing at a time [is the best way to make change]. Just making a decision, like "I'm not going to eat chicken anymore. I can eat everything else but I'm going to stay away from chicken." And then maybe the next step would be "I'm going to eat organic fruits or fruits that are grown by local farmers." . . . One thing at a time. It doesn't have to be everything.

Megan, a 31-year-old teacher living in a gentrifying neighborhood in Toronto, felt that sustainable lifestyles were already accessible where she lived. In this quotation, Megan presents an optimistic account of how consumer demand can shift the retail environment toward more progressive options:

> The fact that [the discount grocery store] now has a full aisle of organic products. Since we've lived here in the past two years, an organic bakery and organic butcher have moved in. So I think that shows that if you support those businesses then other businesses are going to open up.

Compared to the ecological citizenship ideal-type, shopping and consumption are relatively unproblematized in an eco-shopping perspective, and the experience of shopping for sustainable or green goods is characterized as a source of novelty and pleasure. Stores that offer exceptional choice and variety in sustainable commodities were often characterized as exciting places in interviews. For example, Megan described herself as someone who loves to shop for food, and she expressed excitement at visiting a new store where she could discover new products in the organic aisle: "If I'm at a different store . . . I will stop in the organics aisle and see what they have, just to check out if there's a new product or something different that we haven't tried before." In interviews with shoppers at Whole Foods, the most prominent theme articulated was the feeling of pleasure and enjoyment from the shopping experience, a theme that was particularly focused on the variety of commodities available (Johnston and Szabo 2011). Olivia, a 35-year-old real estate agent with two young children, saw a trip to Whole Foods as an accessible form of entertainment, given the busyness of working motherhood:

> I enjoy it. And, again that may go to my consumerism and the fact that I like to troll the aisles and look at the twenty different kinds of teas because that is my outlet right now. . . . My outlet right now is shopping. So walking down that aisle and looking at the packaging of the teas and the different varieties is my way of relaxing right now. Which is a sad commentary, but that is the truth. So I enjoy the selection there.

The eco-shopping perspective emphasizes the agency of consumer, and the potential of eco-shopping to produce change. This is not surprising, given that food politics discourse, as articulated within the marketplace, typically emphasizes the power of consumer demand and the ability to make change through market measures (Johnston 2008). Kerri, a project manager with an environmental group, described consumer agency as "very effective, actually, more so than the voting. Because it's all about consumer demand, right? If all these consumers are wanting all these green products then the companies are going to jump on board pretty quick." According to Marie, a business consultant, "consumers have a huge power in their wallets: It's . . . much more powerful . . . than people realize."

Even when an eco-shopping perspective was the dominant theme articulated in an interview, contradictions between beliefs, values and behaviors often surfaced. While the eco-shopping perspective does present political food shopping as "win-win," various interviewees described how they saw personal and political goals as contradictory, and they recounted how they sometimes had to sacrifice their politics while shopping. Audrey, a 27-year-old stay-at-home mother of two children, listed multiple environmental and social justice concerns that cross her mind when shopping for food, and motivate her to occasionally select organic and local foods from a farmers' market. However, she noted that most of the time she feels unable to resolve the contradiction between her beliefs and actions, and ultimately finds it necessary to prioritize her consumer interests:

> When I'm [shopping] I'm looking at the labels and ask, "Is it organic or not?" "What country did it come from? "Is this food that is seasonal or isn't it?" Although, you know, more often than not if I really feel that we need something or want something, I go ahead and get it anyway. So regardless of where it's coming from.... And lately I've been looking at the 100-mile diet.... That's really interesting. It's yet another thing that would be really interesting to try but I really can't commit myself to.

ECOLOGICAL CITIZENSHIP

An ecological citizenship perspective, as exemplified by quotes from Phillippe above, is comparatively more skeptical of consumption as a positive force for sustainability, and involves distancing oneself from the identities and lifestyles associated with consumerism. This perspective, not surprisingly, was the least commonly articulated perspective in our interviews with political consumers, and we can imagine this being a relatively minor perspective in the general population. When it was articulated in our interviews, this perspective focused less on the "right" things to buy, and more on the need to "give things up," reduce consumption, or redesign one's lifestyle to be more sustainable. As Jackie, a 25-year-old working in retail and sales, explained, "I think every choice I make is political. Not shopping is political. Not consuming is a huge and important act in and of itself." Karen, a 33-year-old freelance writer, described this same imperative as a sacrifice and illustrated this with an example of her experience trying to find crackers not packaged in plastic:

> It's funny, because somehow choosing one product over another may be a choice based on environmental reasons, but if you boycotted the product entirely then that would seem like more of a political act somehow... maybe it's because [there's] a sacrifice involved in making the decision. If you love crackers and you never, ever eat crackers [because of the plastic packaging] then somehow that's more of a personal sacrifice than just choosing [organic] whole-wheat crackers.

An ecological citizenship perspective also focuses on the importance of self-sufficiency, producing one's own food, locating local producers to shorten the commodity chain and make it more transparent, and avoiding large corporate food actors where transparency is seen as problematic. This perspective seeks to disconnect *consumption* from *consumerism* and the corporate commodification of food. Kaila, a 26-year-old consultant, put it this way:

> My reason for making a political statement through my consumer purchases is wanting to disengage from the way that food is a commodity... I believe in a community and I believe in a market where people know one another, and I don't think a consumer mentality applies in the same way to that kind of food system.

While Kaila critiqued the idea that "food is a commodity," she identified progressive possibilities in small-scale markets with social connections, like farmers' markets. An ecological citizenship perspective seeks to avoid or minimize commoditization, particularly on a large corporate scale, but need not reject all market projects. Ideal sites of consumption are typically located within realms where food is *relatively* decommodified and defetishized, particularly when compared to big-box supermarket shopping. Cara, a 35-year-old stay-at-home mother of three children, for example, explained this in terms of the importance of having a relationship to the people who produce her family's food. She drew on her experience raising three children to highlight this imperative:

> My eldest child once said to me, "Bacon comes from Whole Foods." And I [thought] "No, you can't think that!" So now it's very important to us to go to farmers' markets... [where] they can meet farmers [who will] talk about "oh, the chickens run over there." ... That's very important to me because [otherwise] you get too urban and you don't understand where [food] comes from, you don't respect it, and therefore you start to degrade it.

Similarly Kat, a 37-year-old social worker, discussed the importance of knowing where food comes from and being involved in growing it. Referring to a conventional grocery store in her neighborhood, she explained her distaste:

> It's a big corporation, and you just feel a bit more detached from that, even though they do say that they're providing more local food and stuff. I look at the stickers on the fruit [that say so] but I still don't always know.

Moreover, from an ecological citizenship perspective, sites for consumption that are disconnected from the corporate foodscape were viewed as opportunities for structural change. Self-sufficiency through growing one's own food, or forming farming or buying cooperatives, was frequently referenced as an opportunity for change, and as an opportunity to build community. Kat, for example, owns a share in a community-supported agriculture (CSA) operation, and every week she picks up her produce at a depot, allowing her to socialize with other shareholders. On the weekends she works in a community garden, and she hopes to take a leave from her paid employment to volunteer on an organic farm. She said this in reference to the food she eats:

> It is a very big part [of my life] actually. In fact, when I get together with friends it's always around food. That's how social gatherings happen and potlucks and it's a big part of my smaller community of friends.... My recreational activities [are] gardening, berry picking, growing food, learning how to grow food and do different

> things with food, cooking, canning. Actually, last summer I was determined to do the 100-mile diet.

In contrast to eco-shopping, an ecological citizenship perspective focuses on aligning everyday life activities and consumer choices, as much as is possible, with principles, values, and morals. When contradictions are identified, they are described as unacceptable, a source of guilt, or as inspiration to become more committed to one's principles. Put another way, the ecological citizenship perspective focuses less on "win-win" scenarios within the marketplace (e.g., accessing delicious food that is good for the planet and for the consumer), and more on problematizing and reforming one's consumption habits in relation to personal politics. For example, Chris, a 31-year-old working in education, described how he enjoyed shopping at Whole Foods, but he became increasingly concerned that the environmental claims that were made were not substantiated, especially their claim to sell naturally raised meat. He then made a point of writing a letter to the company, seeking greater clarification on their policies for animal husbandry, and ultimately made a choice to buy more of his meat from local butchers, which he perceived as being less convenient and more expensive, but more trustworthy.

Finally, because an ecological citizenship perspective is skeptical of the role of consumerism, this perspective is more critical of consumer-focused models of social change. In the words of Janet, a 33-year-old employee of a nonprofit group, as long as people "are just not willing to make a change in their life, they just [accept that] life is like this." Similarly, Julie, a 34-year-old human rights lawyer, critiqued the idea that simply giving consumers more information would necessarily change their behavior: "I just see social justice more about conduct and action as opposed to about knowledge, although it's somewhat informed through knowledge." Although Julie described enjoying the experience of shopping at Whole Foods, she also described how she and her husband tried to shop elsewhere because of their concerns about the company's problematic role in the food system.

In sum, we have presented a typology of consumer meaning and motivation that maps out the varied meanings behind food politics, and that moves beyond a simple characterization of political versus apolitical food consumers. We have identified two key quadrants of analysis: degrees of politicization, and degrees of critical engagement with consumerism. As noted above, our typology tries to acknowledge the complexity of consumer perspectives. Even though consumers may identify strongly with one particular perspective (e.g., Trina's and Phillipe's interview transcripts tended to exemplify the eco-shopping and ecological citizenship categories, respectively), consumers can manifest different perspectives in different instances, depending on their stage in the life course, their current economic situation, and the particular food they are purchasing (e.g., buying a birthday cake versus shopping for a staple food like milk). Our typology draws out the complexity in consumer food politics by identifying the varying salience of meanings in relation to consumerism and politicization.

Discussion: The Limits of Eco-shopping

Food politics not only reflects how commodity choices are politicized, but it also represents a particular way of problematizing consumption and consumerism. The paradigm of consumerism is being increasingly challenged by voices that highlight the ecological and social externalities of consumer capitalism. As a result, an eco-shopping perspective has arisen as the hegemonic mode of conceptualizing eco-social change through consumption. The eco-shopping quadrant of our typology is exemplified by consumer attempts to substitute foods perceived as harmful (e.g., non-certified-organic, industrially produced) with goods that have some sort of ecological credentials (e.g., organic, natural, local). Within an eco-shopping perspective, there is considerable optimism for a model of commodity substitutionism where existing consumer patterns are tweaked to incorporate less harmful commodities. Though some interviewees questioned the win-win scenarios of eco-shopping, they tended to do so alongside confessional accounts of conventional shopping practices (e.g., people who noted problems with big-box grocery stores, but also acknowledged that other factors ultimately influenced their decision to shop at these stores). An ecological citizenship perspective is more skeptical of consumerism as a model for social change, and critical of its role perpetuating ecological degradation and social injustices. Rather than smooth over potential tensions between consumerism and citizenship, ecological citizenship highlights contradictions and focuses on finding ways to realign personal consumption practices with political principles. Looking at food politics from this quadrant, multiple aspects of food commodity chains are problematized, and new, less corporate, and less commodified forms of producing and consuming food are envisioned and practiced.

As much as the eco-shopping model of commodity substitutionism has flourished in recent years, key elements of the corporate-industrial food system have not significantly changed. Corporate agribusiness has adapted rapidly to changing consumer preferences, such that "green," "fair trade" and "organic" goods now appear on the shelf alongside conventional commodities. The world's largest agri-food corporations now have organic brands and carry fair-trade varieties of chocolate, tea, and coffee, but even these commodities are distributed through complex and global commodity chains that are not transparent to the consumer. Boutique shops are now filled with luxury goods that "embrace the idea that being environmentally caring doesn't mean denying, abandoning or refusing the things we love, but rather designing, developing and using products in more informed, eco-friendly ways" (http://www.epistachio.com/ourMission.html). That consumption can be expanded and yet remain sustainable is congruent with the eco-shopping perspective, yet it contrasts with themes of decommodification and dematerialization emphasized by ecological citizenship perspectives.

While the eco-shopping standpoint has brought food politics to the fore in the public imagination, we identify three problematic tendencies with this perspective. In this way, we link the consumer meanings underlying food politics (mapped out in our typology) with our larger interest in food system transformation. First, commodity substitution is not necessarily organized around changing power relations within the food system or improving the transparency of commodity chains. Rather, the focus is on selecting the "right" commodity through small adjustments to existing shopping routines such that the general configuration of material accumulation remains fairly constant. In contrast, we see considerable value within an ecological citizenship perspective that confronts how food is commodified and produced, and that challenges a "win-win" perspective that smoothes over important contradictions that exist between maximizing individual consumer pleasures and securing sustainable and socially just collective outcomes.

Second, an important, albeit somewhat obvious, limitation of commodity substitutionism—one that too rarely surfaces in the consumer politics discourse—is that voting with one's dollar requires a certain level of purchasing power (Jubas 2007; Szasz 2008). Surprisingly, this critique is often minimized by those who focus on how the politics of the plate can make a difference. Those interested in the pursuit of delicious, green food often seem deeply unaware of the underlying class implications (Johnston and Baumann 2009, 2010).

Third, making the "correct" commodity choice is often a highly complex endeavor, especially given the sheer range of competing environmental sustainability and social justice concerns that factor into even the most mundane of purchases. In buying a package of coffee beans, for example, does one prioritize the packaging (and therefore waste), the company that produced the product (global corporation versus small start-up company), the particular Fair Trade or organic certification system used for that product, the store that sells it (major corporate chain versus a smaller, locally owned store), and, finally, whether one should even buy coffee as a basic "need"? The point of our chapter has been, in part, to question whether consumers should be expected to weigh such complex and competing concerns, especially since, in the last analysis, almost no product choice is completely "correct."

While the eco-shopping perspective has tremendous potential for tapping into and modifying existing consumer demand (e.g., converting conventional broccoli buyers into organic broccoli buyers), a fundamental weakness in this perspective is the reliance on individual consumer demand as the primary channel for structural reform of the agri-food system. Commodity substitutionism fits within a larger political-economic and ideological apparatus of consumerism, and it does not guarantee that consumption will be scaled down to promote sustainability and social justice, particularly on a global scale. We identify greater promise for reform from an ecological citizenship perspective, and even more concretely, through a normative ideal of food democracy. Food democracy advocates for greater decentralization and decommodification of the agri-food system, as well as cultivation of meaningful interactions between producers and consumers of food. Under this model, eaters of food are not just consumers but are *citizens* who have the opportunity and the responsibility to be involved in collective decisions about how food is produced and how a population feeds itself (Halweil 2005; Hassanein 2003). From this perspective, access to food is a basic right that does not depend on one's purchasing power and access to the market (Riches 1999). The food democracy ideal requires us not just to enjoy the incredible bounty our markets have to offer—the rows of organic melons, the pounds of fair-trade coffee, the deliciousness of locally grown apples—but to also question the outcome of our collective and accumulated consumption decisions.

Notes

1. We acknowledge that food politics includes a wide range of issues, in addition to the consumption end of commodity chains. Debates also extend to agricultural production, including debates on agricultural subsidies and international trade agreements. Our usage of the term "politics" is not restricted to the formal political realm (e.g., regulatory decisions, voting, and elected representation), but also includes the desire to transform existing power relations and hierarchical patterns of authority. This usage draws from historical-materialist, feminist, and post-structuralist insights. From historical-materialist perspectives, power is evidenced not in individual action, but through a capacity to make change and transform material structures, and, conversely, through the absence of change—"securing the continuity of social relations rather than producing radical change." (Jessop 2001, 8; Harvey 1996, 54–55). From feminist and post-structuralist perspectives, "private" consumption acts of social reproduction, usually considered in opposition to the formal political realm, have important connections to economies and governance. From here, we see that consumption decisions are embedded in power relations, and we are encouraged to study the interconnections between social reproduction and public structures of political authority and ownership (e.g., Katz 2003).
2. There are many terms that can be used to describe the contemporary "politics of the plate," including ethical consumption, conscientious consumption, alternative consumption, critical consumption, and political consumption. Bracketing debates about the various pros and cons of varied terminologies, we use the terms "food politics" and "political food consumers" to focus attention on the question of consumer politics we raise here.

References

Alkon, A., and C. McCullen. 2010. "Whiteness and Farmers Markets: Performances, Perpetuations... Contestations?" *Antipode* 43 (4): 937–959.

Allen, P., and M. Kovach. 2000. "The Capitalist Composition of Organic: The Potential of Markets in Fulfilling the Promise of Organic Agriculture." *Agriculture and Human Values* 17:221–232.

Barnett, C., P. Cloke, N. Clarke, and A. Malpass. 2005. "Consuming Ethics: Articulating the Subjects and Spaces of Ethical Consumption." *Antipode* 37:23–45.

Belasco, W. J. 1989. *Appetite for Change: How the Counterculture Took on the Food Industry, 1966–1988*. New York: Pantheon.

Bittman, M. 2008. *Food Matters: A Guide to Conscious Eating with More than 75 Recipes*. Toronto: Simon & Shuster.

Bourdieu, P. 1984. *Distinction: A Social Critique of the Judgement of Taste*. Cambridge, MA: Harvard University Press.

Connolly, J., and A. Prothero. 2008. "Green Consumption." *Journal of Consumer Culture* 8:117–145.
Craig-Lees, M., and C. Hill. 2002. "Understanding Voluntary Simplifiers." *Psychology and Marketing* 19:187–210.
Crossley, N. 2004. "Fat Is a Sociological Issue." *Social Theory and Health* 2:222–253.
DeLind, L. B. 2000. "Transforming Organic Agriculture into Industrial Organic Products: Reconsidering National Organic Standards." *Human Organization* 59:198–208.
Dobson, A. 2003. *Citizenship and the Environment*. New York: Oxford University Press.
DuPuis, E. M., and D. Goodman. 2005. "Should We Go "Home" To Eat?: Toward a Reflexive Politics of Localism." *Journal of Rural Studies* 21:359–371.
Elgin, D. 1981. *Voluntary Simplicity*. New York: William Morrow.
Etzioni, A. 1998. "Voluntary Simplicity Characterization, Select Psychological Implications, and Societal Consequences." *Journal of Economic Psychology* 19:619–643.
Frank, T. 1997. *The Conquest of Cool: Business Culture, Counterculture, and the Rise of Hip Consumerism*. Chicago: University of Chicago Press.
Gabriel, Y., and T. Lang. 2006. *The Unmanageable Consumer*. 2nd ed. London: SAGE.
Giddens, A. 1991. *Modernity and Self-Identity: Self and Society in the Late Modern Age.* Cambridge, UK: Polity Press.
Guthman, J. 2003. " Fast Food/Organic Food: Reflexive Tastes and the Making of 'Yuppie Chow.' " *Social and Cultural Geography* 4:45–58.
——. 2004. *Agrarian Dreams: The Paradox of Organic Farming in California.* Berkeley: University of California Press.
Halkier, B., and L. Holm. 2008. "Food Consumption and Political Agency: On Concerns and Practices among Danish Consumers." *International Journal of Consumer Studies* 32:667–674.
Halweil, B. 2005. "The Rise of Food Democracy." *UN Chronicle* 42:71–73.
Harvey, D. 1996. *Justice, Nature, and the Geography of Difference*. Malden, MA: Blackwell.
Hassanein, N. 2003. "Practicing Food Democracy: A Pragmatic Politics of Rransformation." *Journal of Rural Studies* 19:77–86.
Hilton, M. 2003. *Consumerism in Twentieth-Century Britain: The Search for a Historical Movement*. New York: Cambridge University Press.
Hinrichs, C. C. 2003. "The Practice and Politics of Food System Localization." *Journal of Rural Studies* 19:33–45.
Holt. 1997. "Poststructuralist Lifestyle Analysis: Conceptualizing the Social Patterning of Consumption in Postmodernity." *Journal of Consumer Research* 23 (4):326–350.
Jaffee, D., and P. Howard. 2010. "Corporate Cooptation of Organic and Fair Trade Standards." *Agriculture and Human Values* 27: 387–399.
Jessop, B. 2001. "Developments in Marxist Theory." In *The Blackwell Companion to Political Sociology*, edited by K. Nash and A. Scott, 7–16. Malden, MA: Blackwell.
Johnston, J. 2008. "The Citizen-Consumer Hybrid: Ideological Tensions and the Case of Whole Foods Market." *Theory and Society* 37:229–270.
Johnston, J., and S. Baumann. 2007. "Democracy versus Distinction: A Study of Omnivorousness in Gourmet Food Writing." *American Journal of Sociology* 113 (1): 165–204.
——. 2009. "Tension in the Kitchen: Explicit and Implicit Politics in the Gourmet Foodscape." *Sociologica* 1. http://www.sociologica.mulino.it/doi/10.2383/29565.
——. 2010. *Foodies: Democracy and Distinction in the Gourmet Foodscape*. New York: Routledge.
Johnston, J., A. Biro, and N. A. MacKendrick. 2009. "Lost in the Supermarket: The Corporate-Organic Foodscape and the Struggle for Food Democracy." *Antipode* 41:509–532.

Johnston, J. and M. Szabo. 2011. "Reflexivity and the Whole Foods Market Consumer: The Lived Experience of Shopping for Change." *Agriculture and Human Values* 28 (3): 303–319.

Jubas, K. 2007. "Conceptual Con/Fusion in Democratic Societies: Understandings and limitations of Consumer-Citizenship." *Journal of Consumer Culture* 7:231–254.

Katz, C., S. Aronowitz, H. Gautney, and C. W. Barrow. 2003. *Implicating Empire: Globalization and Resistance in the 21st Century World Order.* New York: Basic Books.

Konefal, Jason. 2010. "The Marriage of Big Green and Big Food: A Case Study of Sustainable Seafood." Presentation at 2010 ASFS/ASHVS/SAFN Conference, Bloomington, Indiana, June 3, 2010.

Kriflik, L. 2006. "Consumer Citizenship: Acting to Minimise Environmental Health Risks Related to the Food System." *Appetite* 46:270–279.

Lang, T., and Y. Gabriel. 2005. "A Brief History of Consumer Activism." In *The Ethical Consumer*, edited by R. Harrison, T. Newholm, and D. Shaw, 39–52. Thousand Oaks, CA: SAGE.

Lorenzen, J. A. 2012. "Going Green: The Process of Lifestyle Change." *Sociological Forum* 27:94–116.

Maniates, M. 2002. "Individualization: Plant a Tree, Buy a Bike, Save the World?" In *Confronting Consumption*, edited by T. Princen, K. Conca, and M. Maniates, 43–66. Cambridge, MA: MIT Press.

Micheletti, M. 2003. *Political Virtue and Shopping: Individuals, Consumerism, and Collective Action*. New York: Palgrave Macmillan.

Micheletti, M., A. Føllesdal, and D. Stolle. 2004. *Politics, Products, and Markets: Exploring Political Consumerism Past and Present*. New Brunswick, NJ: Transaction.

Miller, D. 1995. "Consumption as the Vanguard of History: A Polemic Way of Introduction." In *Acknowledging Consumption: A Review of New Studies*, edited by D. Miller, 1–57. New York: Routledge.

Moore, O. 2006. "Understanding Post-organic Fresh Fruit and Vegetable Consumers at Participatory Farmers' Markets in Ireland: Reflexivity, Trust, and Social Movement." *International Journal of Consumer Studies* 30:416–426.

Neilson, L. A., and P. Paxton. 2010. "Social Capital and Political Consumerism: A Multilevel Analysis." *Social problems* 57:5–24.

Paarlberg, R. 2010. "Attention Whole Foods Shoppers." *Foreign Policy*, May/June. http://www.foreignpolicy.com/articles/2010/04/26/attention_whole_foods_shoppers.

Pollan, M. 2006. *The Omnivore's Dilemma: A Natural History of Four Meals*. New York: Penguin.

Power, M. 1997. *The audit society: Rituals of verification.* Oxford, UK: Oxford University Press.

Rose, Nikolas. 1999. *Powers of freedom: Reframing political thought.* Cambridge, UK: Cambridge University Press.

Riches, G. (1999). Advancing the Human Right to Food in Canada: Social Policy and the Politics of Hunger, Welfare, and Food Security. *Agriculture and Human Values* 16: 203–211.

Sassatelli, R. 2007. *Consumer Culture: History, Theory and Politics*. London: SAGE.

Schor, J. 1998. *The Overspent American: Upscaling, Downshifting, and the New Consumer.* New York: Basic Books.

——. 2007. "In Defense of Consumer Critique: Revisiting the Consumption Debates of the Twentieth Century." *Annals of the American Academy of Political and Social Science* 611:16–30.

Schudson, M. 2007. "Citizens, Consumers, and the Good Society." *Annals of the American Academy of Political and Social Science* 611:236–249.

Seyfang, G. 2005. "Shopping for Sustainability: Can Sustainable Consumption Promote Ecological Citizenship?" *Environmental Politics* 14:290–306.

——. 2009. *The New Economics of Sustainable Consumption: Seeds of Change.* New York: Palgrave Macmillan.

Shaw, D., and T. Newholm. 2002. "Voluntary Simplicity and the Ethics of Consumption." *Psychology and Marketing* 19:167–185.

Shaw, D., T. Newholm, and R. Dickinson. 2006. *"Consumption as Voting: An Exploration of Consumer Empowerment."* In "Consumer Empowerment," special issue, *European Journal of Marketing* 40: 1049–1067.

Slater, D. 1997. *Consumer culture and modernity.* Oxford: Polity Press.

Slocum, R. 2004. "Consumer Citizens and the Cities for Climate Protection Campaign." *Environment and Planning A* 36:763–782.

Soper, K. 2004. "Rethinking the 'Good Life': The Consumer as Citizen." *Capitalism, Nature, Socialism* 15:111–116.

Stolle, D., and M. Hooghe. 2004. "Consumers as Political Participants? Shifts in Political Action Repertoires in Western Societies." In *Politics, Products, and Markets: Exploring Political Consumerism Past and Present*, edited by M. Micheletti, A. Føllesdal, and D. Stolle. New Brunswick, NJ: Transaction.

Stolle, D., M. Hooghe, and M. Micheletti. 2005. "Politics in the Supermarket: Political Consumerism as a Form of Political Participation." *International Political Science Review* 26:245–269.

Szasz, A. 2007. *Shopping Our Way to Safety: How We Changed from Protecting the Environment to Protecting Ourselves.* Minneapolis: University of Minnesota Press.

Tindall, D. B., S. Davies, and C. Mauboules. 2003. "Activism and Conservation Behavior in an Environmental Movement: The Contradictory Effects of Gender." *Society & Natural Resources* 16:909–932.

Turner, F. 2006. *From Counterculture to Cyber Culture: Stewart Brand, the Whole Earth Network, and the Rise of Digital Utopianism.* Chicago: University of Chicago Press.

Wolf, J., K. Brown, and D. Conway. 2009. "Ecological Citizenship and Climate Change: Perceptions and Practice." *Environmental Politics* 18:503.

Zavestoski, S. 2002. "The Social-Psychological Bases of Anti-consumption Attitudes." *Psychology and Marketing* 19:149–165.

Zukin, S., and J. S. Maguire. 2004. "Consumers and Consumption." *Annual Review of Sociology* 30:173–197.

CHAPTER 27

THE POLITICAL ECONOMY OF REGULATION OF BIOTECHNOLOGY IN AGRICULTURE

GREGORY D. GRAFF, GAL HOCHMAN, AND DAVID ZILBERMAN

Introduction: Technical Change and Schumpeter's "Creative Destruction"

Genetically modified (GM) crop varieties are effectively banned throughout Europe and in many developing countries, and the direct use of genetically modified crops as food for human consumption is limited to just a handful of niche agricultural products, such as papaya, squash, and sweet corn, in just a few countries (Bennett et al. forthcoming). This state of affairs has persisted for more than a decade despite the high adoption rate of the technology by farmers in the United States, Canada, Argentina, Brazil, and other countries where it has been approved, and despite a preponderance of evidence of positive impacts, such as increasing yields and decreasing pesticide use, and despite the consensus among major scientific bodies that food from GM crops is at least as safe as food from crops developed using other breeding technologies (Newell-McGlouglin, this volume). The GM varieties have, thus far, been widely adopted to produce cotton fiber in North and South America; in some Asian countries, most notably India and China; and in some African countries. The GM varieties are also widely grown for animal feed and biofuel in North and South America. Restrictions on the cultivation and use of GM crops products in Europe and other countries around the world are thus, clearly, not a result of agronomic limitations or a lack of market value of the technology; rather, such restrictions are the outcomes of public decision-making processes reflecting the interplay of sometimes conflicting economic interests of different groups within society.

The arguments in this chapter build upon the political-economy literature and, in particular, its applications to agricultural and environmental policy. First, we review the main findings of this literature in Section 1. We follow this with a simple conceptual voting model in Section 2, to illustrate how political choices regarding GM crops can be understood to have evolved over time, shaped by the evolving influences of various interest groups together with availability of new information. This analysis suggests that understanding policy outcomes requires careful identification of the salient interest groups affecting biotechnology policies, their benefits and losses that result from those policies, and their respective political weights and influence. Section 3 then reviews the major findings of the agricultural economics literature regarding the distributional impacts of the adoption of GM crops within the agricultural economy, which provides a starting point for us to then consider how the introduction of GM crop varieties affects the economic welfare of other groups within society as well. We then present, in Section 4, our political-economic analysis of the formation and evolution of agricultural biotechnology policies in Europe, considering the salient interest groups affecting and affected by biotech policies. Analysis includes not only consumers, farmers, and environmental interest groups, but also industrial sectors—differentiating, in particular, the interests of the seed and agrochemical businesses—and emphasizes the importance of differences in the alignment of interests in some cases from country-specific perceptions.

We conclude that, in Europe and other countries where agricultural biotechnologies continue to be heavily restricted or banned outright, these policy outcomes are rational results of the vulnerabilities of the underlying economic welfare of the major interest groups to the introduction of this disruptive technology. The innovations of agricultural biotechnology have unleashed a wave of "creative destruction" (Schumpeter 1934). The political system responds to demands to protect the interests of some groups with capital stocks at risk of destruction in the face of technological innovation, but also to those interest groups positioning themselves to capture the benefits of its creativity. The distribution of these groups varies across countries, and also over time as new information becomes available. The result is a highly complex equilibrium with path-dependent effects in regulatory institutions and rules.

Literature on the Political Economy of Regulatory Policies

The "Classic" Political-Economy Literature

Economists have long understood that economic choices are determined by political systems as well as by markets; a large body of literature assesses how collective or public choices affect economic outcomes. This literature distinguishes between two public choice mechanisms: one involving voters and the other involving regulators or bureaucrats (Romer and Rosenthal, 1979). The median voter model (Downs, 1957) can be used to analyze the behavior of different categories of voters, including presidential, legislative, local elections, or referenda. Similarly, a number of theories have been advanced by economists and political scientists to explain the behavior of regulators and the shape and strength of the policies they make (see Rausser, Swinnen and Zusman 2012). Such theories take into account the influence that groups of regulated economic agents have on regulators and have promulgated popular concepts, such as the "capture theory" (Posner, 1974). More sophisticated models have been designed to accommodate multiple features of political systems (Becker, 1983; Grossman and Helpman, 2001). There is a large body of literature that empirically evaluates alternative theories of political economy. Anderson, Rausser, and Swinnen (2013) document the major evolution of agricultural policies around the world since the 1950s and their implications on the welfare of various groups in the economy. They interpret these changes in light of the findings of the various political-economic frameworks. Most of these frameworks reduce to policymakers or a regulator who weighs the influence of the range of politically salient groups within the economy, i.e., groups that have managed to solve their internal collective action problems and are well-enough informed with respect to their likely costs or benefits arising from the regulations in question. A few scholars have developed political-economic models in a dynamic setting to explain long-run survival and growth of groups (Acemoglu, Johnson, and Robinson, 2005).

Literature on the Politics of Agricultural Biotechnology Policies

The types of policies that impact the innovation and adoption of new agricultural technologies, like agricultural biotechnology, include public research investments, intellectual property policies, trade policies, and a range of environmental, biosafety, food-safety, and product-labeling requirements (Paarlberg, 2001). Prakash and Kollman (2003) argue that internal domestic politics in North America and in Europe caused agricultural biotechnology policies to diverge. In Europe, slow progress of member states in agreeing upon and implementing coordinated regulations was the direct cause of the halting of new product approvals in 1998. Some have argued that government regulators, particularly in the United States, were too closely aligned with the regulated industry, as individuals rotated between industry and government, thus putting the interests of companies like Monsanto before those of the public (Newell and Glover, 2003; Seelye, 2001). Meanwhile, others have contended that regulators, particularly in Europe, capitulated to the tactics of political activists and thus reflect the agendas of organizations, such as Greenpeace or Friends of the Earth, more than they do the actual welfare of farmers or working class consumers (Byrne, 2006; Gilland, 2006; Miller and Conko, 2004).

The European situation prompted more sophisticated analyses by economists motivated by questions of whether or not these policies are trade distorting (Lapan and Moschini, 2004; Sheldon, 2004) and, indeed, certain European policies toward the import of GM crop products resulted in a formal World Trade Organization (WTO) dispute, which Europe lost (WTO, 2003). Bernauer (2003) attributes the set of restrictive European policies to the mobilization of mass opinion among consumer and environmental interests, which prevailed over the more concentrated industry and agricultural producer interests. This is an exception to the typical political-economic observation of concentrated interests prevailing over diffused interests. Consumer and environmental activist groups instead rallied and served those diffused interests by providing extensive input to the media, educating the public, influencing markets, and effectively driving a wedge between agricultural industry interests in biotechnology and the interests of food manufacturers and grocery retailers (Sato, this volume). Thus, it is argued that the policy situation in Europe influenced domestic policies within Europe's trade partners as they similarly struggled with broad public and consumer concerns over the safety and efficacy of the technology. Falkner (2006) describes this process as the transformation of the European Union from a laggard to a leader in the international politics of biotechnology regulation, arguing that its international influence has stemmed from the shift in Europe's internal politics.

But questions have been raised about these interpretations. Graff and Zilberman (2007) and Graff, Hochman, and Zilberman (2009) broach the question directly about whether European policies toward agricultural biotechnology might reflect underlying strategic interests of the European chemical industry and farm interests, which were then capitalized on by political environmental groups. These groups significantly influenced the European consumer opinions.

A Basic Voting Model with an Evolution of Perceived Benefits

This chapter develops a general framework of collective choice based on voting behavior that is relevant for many contexts and illustrates how voting outcomes are determined by the influence asserted by those interest groups affected by the proposed policy. Later, with this framework in mind, we will attempt to identify the key interest groups affecting the biotechnology debate and policy outcomes in Europe, with implications for analysis of developing countries, where European law, markets, and social-movement organizations have played an important role in regulation of biotechnology.

The starting point of this exercise is the median voter model popularized by Downs (1957). The voters may be individual voters as in California Propositions 37, representatives in a parliamentary system as in the U.S. Senate or the European Parliament, or even backers of competing power centers within an organization such as the Chinese

Communist Party. In all cases, what "votes" are cast is affected by information provided by the various competing groups; yet, this information is always weighted by the credibility of the groups in the eyes of the voters.

The Model

We assume a political system in which there are N voters indexed by i, ranging from 1 to N. There are M interest groups, indexed by $j = 1$ to M. A proposition is put to a vote at time t. Let b_{ij}^t be the perceived net benefit to group j from the proposition passing at time t. Also, assume that each voter assigns a weight for how much he or she actually cares about the well-being of each interest group, and let W_{ij} denote that weight given by individual i to the net benefit of group j. For simplicity, assume that the voter aggregates the weighted net benefits to the groups in determining his or her overall assessment of the proposition. Thus, $B_i^t = j = 1 * Mw_{ij}b_{ij}^t$ is the *perceived net social benefit* according to voter i from the passing of the proposition. We can consider a straightforward voting system where a voter will vote for the proposition if the net social benefit is perceived to be positive, $B_i^t \geq 0$, and will vote against it otherwise. Let V_i^t denote the current vote of voter i at period t, designated to equal 1 when the voter is supporting the proposition and 0 otherwise. Thus,

$$V_i^t = 1 \; if \; B_i^t \geq 0$$

$$V_i^t = 0 \; if \; B_i^t < 0.$$

Now, let us assess the outcome of a voting system wherein a proposition passes simply by obtaining a majority of votes. Let the final result of the vote be denoted by $R^t = \frac{\sum_{i=1}^{N} B_i^t}{N}$, or simply the fraction of the voters who support the proposition: It passes if the final result is greater than one-half or $R^t \geq 0.5$. If we rank the voters at time t in a decreasing order of the their perceived net benefit from the proposition, we can identify the median voter at time t as the individual $i = i_m^t$ located at the middle of this lineup of voters.[1] A sufficient mathematical condition for the proposition to pass with a simple majority vote is that the net benefit perceived by that median voter be positive, that is, $B_{i_m^t}^t = \sum_{j=1}^{M} w_{i_m^t j} b_{i_m^t j}^t > 0$. In this case, the benefits perceived—adjusted by the weights assigned—by the median voter (or, to generalize, by the median group of voters) will determine the outcome of the vote.

This basic model can be used to determine outcomes in other public-choice situations. If we allow "horse trading," such that voters are able to trade their votes with other voters, as is the case in parliamentary systems, then voters who strongly support the proposition may compensate others for changing their vote. If there are zero transaction costs and voters have full information about other voters' preferences, then the system of trading among voters will produce an outcome that will maximize the aggregate perceived net benefit of all voters. Namely, the proposition will pass if aggregate perceived net benefits are positive, that is, $\sum_{i=1}^{N} B_i^t = \sum_{i=1}^{N} \sum_{j=1}^{M} w_{ij} b_{ij}^t > 0$.[2] When voters can engage in side payments, the final outcome depends on the net benefits from the proposition across the board. Voters who strongly support the passing of the proposition may be ready to compensate opponents in order to obtain their vote. One example is when the French government erected restrictions on GM crops in order to mute environmental resistance to nuclear power (Stratfor, 2011).

The literature on bureaucratic decision making (Rausser, Swinnen, and Zusman, 2011) suggests that their decisions reflect the weighted sum of perceived net benefits of interest groups, which is consistent with the framework presented here. However, it is important to emphasize the evolutionary nature of political decision making, because perceived net benefits change over time. Thus, b_{ij}^t, which is the perceived net benefit to group *j* of individual *i* at time *t*, is a stock variable and is modified by NI^t, which is the new information made available during time period *t*. Thus, the total stock of information available in period *t* is the sum of the stock of information in period *t-1* plus the additional information made available in time period *t*, and the equation of motion is $b_{ij}^t = b_{ij}^{t-1} + \Delta b\left(NI^t\right)$. Changes in perception of benefits from the technology resulting from new information will affect voting patterns over time.

Proposition 37 in California is a good example of how perceptions and voting behavior can evolve over time. The proposition, if passed, would have required labeling of GM contents in all food products sold in California. Results from early polls (May 2012) showed initial support as high as 80 percent for the proposition, yet, in the end, it was defeated in November 2012 with only 46% of the voters supporting it. Zilberman et al. (2014) documents the evolution of the debate. The large early support for the proposition stemmed from the conception that GM crops were bad for health and the pubic had the right to full information. Opponents of the proposition pointed out that a voluntary labeling system already exists. For example, companies may choose to verify and label a product as "GM-free"; this option, in combination with organic food standards, effectively serves as a regulated "GM-free" labeling system. Opponents also presented results of studies from major national academies of science of various countries, finding that genetically modified GM foods are at least as safe as conventional foods. The publicity of such information lent to a reduction in support for the proposition. More decisively, the proposition was ultimately defeated when, during the final stages of the campaign, estimates were published of the increase in food prices for consumers likely to result from the costs of labeling all food products. In the end, it seems that voters gave the price effect a greater weight than other considerations. Once that information was introduced to the public and was considered reliable by the public, their voting preferences changed.

Applications and Extensions of the Basic Voting Model

The policy regime in place within a country can be considered the cumulative outcome of many "votes" by different groups over a series of different policy decisions. The European community, for example, is made up of many countries, and the perceptions and political considerations in each of these countries regarding agricultural uses of biotechnology are different. Kurzer and Cooper (2007) demonstrate how the current European stand on strict restrictions on GM crops was the result of political choices at the national level that contradicted and dominated policies that were proposed by the European Commission. Just, Alston, and Zilberman (2006) document how decisions about regulation and use of GM crops are made by multiple agencies, including regulators and legislative bodies at national and regional levels, as well as direct voting. Our framework suggests that, in all cases, decisions reflect a weighted sum of the benefits of the proposed policy as perceived by the various constituent interest groups. However, preferences change over time, and the weights of different interest groups vary across location and institutions, as new information is constantly being introduced. Thus, a good understanding of controversial policies requires precise identification of the relevant interest groups, reliable estimates of their net benefits from the policy, and their credibility and weight with the actual voters. The United States has 50 different states, each of whose voting procedures are different, but we consistently observe that the United States, Canada, and Latin America have, for more than a decade, held a more positive disposition toward agricultural biotechnology than Europe (Gaskell et al., 1999). Each voter in the European parliament or in European member states' national parliaments place different weights on the net benefits of interest groups in considering alternative biotechnology policies. It is the alignment of those benefits filtered through the political weighting that determines the European policy regime.

The Impacts of Agricultural Biotechnology Innovations on Different Interest Groups

In reviewing empirical studies of the political economy of environmental policies, Oates and Portney (2003, p. 337) pose the challenge that, "In any particular application... the identification and characterization of the relevant interest groups is an essential and challenging part of the analysis." In taking up the challenge of Oates and Portney (2003) to identify the key interest groups affecting the policy debate and policy outcomes in agricultural biotechnology, we turn first to the existing quantitative economic studies assessing the distributional impacts of commercially adopted agricultural biotechnologies. We then broaden the analysis to consider the extent and mechanisms by which the full range of interest groups are likely affected.

Empirical Welfare Analysis Estimates of Agricultural Biotechnology Innovations on a Core Set of Primary Interest Groups

There is a vast literature on the distributional impacts of commercially adopted agricultural biotechnologies (see National Research Council (NRC), 2010; Brooks and Barfoot, 2013; Bennett et al., 2013), which provides an essential starting point for our political-economic analysis. Virtually all of the uses of recombinant DNA technology in crop agriculture have been for controlling insect and weed pests even though several different uses of the technology have been explored.

Economists have estimated the economic impacts of these pest-control traits. Qaim and Zilberman (2003) modeled GM varieties with pest-control genetic traits, demonstrating that they may reduce cost when they replace costly alternatives and may increase yields when alternatives do not exist or are less effective. The GM varieties are adopted by farmers when they are likely to be more profitable than alternatives, given prevailing prices of inputs and outputs.

Table 27.1 (adapted from NRC, 2010) overviews estimates from 15 studies of the distribution of economic benefits from the adoption of pest-control traits in cotton, soybeans, and corn, primarily in the United States, between 1996 and 2004. The results suggest significant overall economic gains due to the technology—in some crops more than a billion dollars annually. Yet, the shares of these benefits that accrue to different groups vary across countries and time.

The companies that innovate and sell the technology are estimated to capture from 6 to 68 percent, with an average of 33 percent, of the total economic value generated by these new crop technologies. Thus, even though companies like Monsanto, Pioneer-DuPont, and Syngenta own patents and charge farmers royalty fees for use of the technology, they are only able to capture a minority portion of the total economic value they helped to create.

The farmers' share of total economic benefit generated by the technology varies widely across these studies, ranging between 4 and 77 percent, with the average being around 30 percent. The relative share of total benefits estimated to go to domestic consumers, largely in the form of lower prices, again, varies widely, from 4 to 53 percent, with the average being 22 percent. Finally, the share of total economic value created by the technology going to consumers in the rest of the world, due largely to the technology lowering global commodity prices, varies from 4 to 28 percent, with an average of 18 percent. The absolute values of the total annual benefits have likely increased since adoption levels and overall food prices have both increased in the intervening 10 years since these studies were conducted.

Aggregate global analysis by Brookes and Barfoot (2013) suggests that, in 2011, total benefit to farmers globally from growing GM crops was U.S.$19.8 billion, divided equally between yield gains and cost savings. Fifty-one percent of these farm benefits

Table 27.1 Distribution of total economic benefits from adoption of genetically engineered crops

Year(s)		Total benefits (millions)	Share of total benefits (%) to… U.S. Farmers (%)	Innovators (%)	U.S. consumers (%)	Rest-of-world net benefit
Bacillus thuringiensis (Bt) cotton						
1996		$134	43	47	6	-
1996		$240	59	26	9	6%
1997		$190	43	44	7	6%
1998		$213	46	43	7	4%
1996–1998		$131–$164	5–6	46	33	18%
1996–1999		$16 – $46	100[a]	-	-	-
1997		$210	29	35	14	22%
Herbicide-tolerant cotton						
1997		$232	4	6	57	33%
Herbicide-tolerant soybeans						
1997	(LE[a])	$1,1000	77	10	4	9%
	(HE[b])	$437	29	18	17	28%
1997		$310	20	68	5	6%
1997		$206	16d	49	35	NAe
1999		$804	20	45	10	26%
2001		$1,230	13d	34	53	NAe
Bt maize						
2004		$836	22	15	63	-

[a] LE = low elasticity; assumes a U.S. soybean supply elasticity of 0.22.

[b] HE = high elasticity; assumes a U.S. soybean supply elasticity of 0.92.

Sources: NRC 2010

went to farmers in developing countries. They also estimate that the innovating companies gained around 20 percent of the total global benefits created (about U.S.$4 billion). Brookes and Barfoot (2011) suggest that the adoption of GM crops has increased the output of those crops significantly, but they do not assess the impact on commodity prices.

Barrows, Sexton, and Zilberman (2013) estimate output effects of GM crop technology, including the resulting price effects. In particular, they suggest that global output of corn increased between 3 and 19 percent, output of cotton increased by up to 55 percent, and output of soybeans increased between 12 and 42 percent. They estimate that the decline in the commodity price of corn due to biotechnology was 13 percent, the decline in the commodity price of cotton was 33 percent, and the decline in the commodity price of soybeans 38 percent. This drastic reduction in prices significantly affected consumers of corn, cotton, and soybeans, including other producers in the value chain for whom these commodities represent major input costs. Yet, for final consumers, since the cost of raw inputs make only a small contribution to the final retail price of food, these reductions in the commodity prices of corn, cotton, and soybeans have a relatively small impact—around a 3 or 4 percent reduction—on retail food costs to consumers in the United States.[3] However, the reduction in commodity prices due to biotechnology arguably has a much larger relative impact on consumers in developing countries, in part due to the fact that a much larger share of household budgets go toward food consumption.

Sexton and Zilberman (2011) argue that, had rest of the world adopted available GM corn and soybean traits, the price effect would have been much greater than it was under the partial adoption—largely taking place by North and South American farmers—and much of the commodity price hikes that have occurred since 2008 would have been less severe. Furthermore, if Bacillus thuringiensis (Bt) and Roundup Ready varieties of wheat and rice had been adopted, the yield effects would have been of a similar order of magnitude as was experienced in corn, cotton, and soybeans, and much of the global rise in commodity prices would have been avoided altogether.

Considering the Impacts of Agricultural Biotechnologies Across the Full Range of Relevant Interest Groups

Following the challenge recognized by Oates and Portney (2003) that identifying and characterizing the relevant interest groups is essential to fully understand the alignment of forces that give shape to a policy outcome, we began our analysis with the typical welfare analyses reviewed in the previous section. These analyses provide a general sense of the economic impacts of agricultural biotechnologies, at least on the primary groups involved, such as the innovating companies, farmers growing GM crops, and consumers of the products that result from GM crop commodities. But it may be necessary to identify and characterize other groups external to these market relationships or to distinguish particular subsets within consumers, farmers, or input suppliers, which have decidedly different interests when it comes to agricultural biotechnologies. For example, in a developing country, we might differentiate between export-oriented commercial farmers and domestic subsistence farmers. Thus, we proceed by considering the full list of affected groups likely to share common interests. Our goal is to achieve a disaggregation into groups that share common welfare impacts in order to highlight vertical as well as horizontal interactions as well as the key political consortia involved in policy negotiations for agricultural biotechnology.

Consumers

Consumers' attitudes toward an agricultural commodity reflect the economic benefit (utility) they derive from the use of that commodity or derivative products made using that commodity, which largely considers perceptions about intangible product characteristics. Such intangible characteristics include the characteristic of "genetic modification" use of recombinant DNA technology to produce the genetic characteristics of the crop variety. Consumers may also consider the fact that the technology was provided by a large multinational corporation and thus have a negative attitude toward the product for that reason as well.

The welfare analyses reviewed in Table 27.1 reveal that consumers in the United States benefit only marginally from the price reductions resulting from the increased productivity due to GM crops. For example, the largest single-point estimate of consumer benefit, revealed by Qaim and Traxler (2005), indicates that U.S. consumers received 53 percent of the U.S.$1.23 billion in total benefits (or U.S. $652 million) from the herbicide-tolerance trait in soybeans. Although this is a large value in total, for each of the 300 million U.S. consumers, it comes down to just US$ 2.17 per person. Several scholars have pointed out that, because consumers do not perceive this small amount as a real benefit, they are, thus, not inclined to actively support policies favoring the introduction of crop biotechnology, especially when accompanied by other perceptions that there may also be risks associated with the technology (Paarlberg, 2001; among others). Indeed, under such conditions it appears quite reasonable for average food consumers to remain "rationally ignorant"—in the political sense proposed by Stigler (1971)—of the benefits that they derive from agricultural biotechnology and to be unmotivated to mount any significant collective action regarding policies relative to this issue. Instead, consumers exercise their influence individually and largely out of their default position of "rational ignorance" when making purchasing decisions in the marketplace and on rare occasions when voting, such as in California's Proposition 37.

The results in Table 27.1 present earlier estimates on consumer welfare in the adoption of GM technology, ending with results for 2001. As the rate of adoption increased, the impact on supply increased as well, resulting in the substantial impact on the prices of soybeans and corn reported earlier. However, the large reductions in the prices of commodities translate to much lower reductions in the price of the final goods bought by consumers in developed countries.[4] The impact on food prices in developing countries, where the degree of processing is lower, is likely to be higher.

The literature on the demand for food suggests that consumers' behavior choices are strongly affected by food prices in the market. However, the relatively low price effect of genetically modified organisms (GMO) on the retail prices of food products in developed countries and the complex and nontransparent linkages between the price of food and the use of GMO globally may explain why the price effect of GMO did not motivate consumers to support them politically. At the same time, there is a large body of literature that documents consumers' willingness to pay to avoid GM products for health risks and other reasons (see Lusk and Coble, 2005). However, consumers' willingness to pay varies significantly depending on how the framing of the issue changes with the introduction of new information (Kiesel, McCluskey, and Villas-Boas, 2011).

Based upon these considerations, we can (at least stylistically) identify three basic subgroups of consumers based on their willingness to pay. (1) **Price-sensitive consumers** are those who care significantly more about price than about intangible product attributes, like GM, and will always make purchases based on lowest price. In welfare terms, these are the consumers who benefit the most from the introduction of crop biotechnology, gaining from the lower prices and not losing anything in terms of perceived product quality. It is often presumed that the bulk of U.S. consumers are of this sort, essentially unaffected by the "GM" attribute of products they purchase. Such consumers are always hurt by a restriction on crop biotechnologies.

(2) A middle group of **attribute-price comparing consumers** are those consumers who perceive the intangible attribute of genetic modification as lower-quality or less-desirable but view that as a trade-off for the lower price offered. They will buy products with the less favorable intangible attributes when offered at a sufficiently lower price, but will avoid GM if the cost is sufficiently low. Clearly, there are enough consumers of this sort for food manufacturers and retailers to find it worthwhile to advertise and promote products as GMO free in mainstream markets. It is reasonable to assume that the majority of European consumers are of this type. Many of this type of consumer will, on average, be hurt by a restriction of crop biotechnologies: whenever the difference in price is greater than the difference in their willingness to pay.

(3) **Attribute-sensitive consumers** are those consumers who care significantly more about the intangible attributes of a product than they do about the price and are willing to pay for products with a favorable profile of intangible attributes almost regardless of price (see Johnston and MacKendrick, this volume; Clough, this volume). In an ironical twist, these consumers may actually gain in welfare terms by the introduction of GM products, because such products will free resources to produce specialized products. Such consumers make up a small percentage of the U.S. population and typically choose to shop at specialized outlets and markets and are likely to be well-to-do. It is often assumed that many more European consumers are of this category than U.S. consumers; however, that is an empirical question that is difficult to test.

These heterogeneous subpopulations of consumers are differently affected and are thus likely to weigh in quite differently on various public-policy proposals for regulating agricultural biotechnologies.

Retailers

A retailer's profits are highly dependent upon the reputation of its brand, which is a function of consumers' perceptions. Accounts from the retail sector in Europe clearly indicate the strong effect that consumers' attitudes toward biotech foods clearly have had on retailers' policy positions (Kane, 2001). Thus, although retailers are in most cases agnostic about the methods by which the products they sell are produced, they do care about how those products are perceived and valued by consumers (Sato, this volume).

Since the major food retailers tend to be fairly large chains—such as Walmart or Kroger in the United States and Carrefour in Europe—their decisions can strongly influence the production decisions of food manufacturers and agricultural suppliers up the value chain. These large private-sector actors can dictate product standards. Price-sensitive producers may seek to stop adoption of a technology if they are worried that major domestic retailers or foreign export markets decide not to purchase products that use that technology. For example, potato growers effectively ended the development of GM Bt potatoes in the United States and eventually across the globe in response to the decision in 1999 by McDonalds Corporation to not purchase GM potatoes (Kaniewski and Thomas 2004).

Farmers

Farmers' attitudes toward any agricultural technology, including crop varieties with genetically engineered traits, reflect the net present value of the economic benefits they expect to realize as a result of the technology's impact on their own farm operations' costs (both monetary and "nonpecuniary" costs) and revenues. Costs can be directly affected by adopting the technology. Revenues are a result of the operation's yields, which, again, can be affected by adopting the technology, and the prices they are able to garner, which are affected by other farmers adopting the technology as well as public policies toward the technology. We disaggregate agricultural producers into the subgroups that may be affected differently by the regulation of agricultural biotechnologies.

1. **Early adopting farmers.** The literature (Feder, Just, and Zilberman, 1985) suggests that early adopters are the ones that can afford, have much to gain from, and have access to the technology. Initial adopters gain from cost saving and yield effects of the GM technology, and in the early period do not suffer much from price reduction associated with large volume of adoption. They are likely to be supporters of the technology.
2. **Late-adopting or nonadopting farmers in markets where GM crops have already been introduced.** Although early adopters of the technology profit, at least temporarily, due to the lower costs and higher yields they enjoy, late or nonadopters may suffer losses. The increased output from adoption of yield-increasing technologies expands supply and puts downward pressure on prices. Late and nonadopters are squeezed between falling market prices for their output and the higher costs of continuing to use the older technology, a phenomenon known as "Cochrane's Treadmill" (Cochrane, 1993).

3. **Farmers in markets where GM crops have not been introduced.** Profitability in markets where GM varieties have not been introduced, such as in Europe, become threatened by competition from lower priced GM imports. It is, therefore, logical for farmers in such a position to oppose approval of GM varieties if there is a prospect for maintaining some product differentiation and continuing to sell the conventional product at the previous, higher price.
4. **Livestock operations.** Because feed grain is such a significant share of the input costs of livestock operations, beef, pork, poultry, dairy, and even aquaculture, producers all benefit from the introduction of price-reducing GM varieties in feed-grain crops. Even in Europe, livestock and dairy groups have managed to maintain imports of GM soybeans from the United States, Brazil, and Argentina in order to be able to continue feeding their flocks and herds at a competitive cost.
5. **Organic operations.** Organic operators have opposed the introduction of GM crops as part of their overall philosophy aiming to maintain "natural products" Yet, they may have benefited significantly from the introduction of GM products. This is due to the enhanced product differentiation between mainstream or conventional GM products and organic products. The presence of GM products in the market place is a significant quality contrast that increased demand for and enabled organic producers to charge higher prices. Introduction of GM products that increase farm productivity may also increase resource availability.

Organic farmers would have been most threatened if GM crops were originially designated as organic, as was initially contemplated under the proposed U.S. Department of Agriculture (USDA) organics standards in the 1990s. In particular, Bt-based biopesticides had long been utilized in organic growing operations. If genetically engineered Bt crops had been designated as organic, their rapid spread would have undermined the product differentiation essential to the profitability of organic producers. The political outcry that arose from the organic farming community during the federal comment period for the proposed USDA organics standards overturned the proposed designation of "plant-incorporated biopesticides" as organic.

Agricultural Input Providers

Agricultural input suppliers are one of the primary interest groups that can benefit from the introduction of GM crop varieties.

1. **Large innovating GM seed suppliers.** Table 27.1 shows that the innovative companies that create and then sell or license GM crop varieties have benefited substantially. They are estimated to have captured a quarter to a third of the total benefits created by the technology. These innovators consist today of just a handful of companies: Monsanto, Pioneer Hi-Bred, Dow AgroSciences, Bayer CropSciences, Syngenta, and BASF. Even within this small set of companies, Monsanto tends to dominate, in

terms of technological innovation and in terms of benefit capture, at least when it comes to genetic traits.

Although these large companies certainly advocate for a working regulatory pathway to admit GM crops onto the market, it is not necessarily within their interests to have too much of a *laissez-faire* regulatory environment. This is because, of course, the introduction of a new GM crop variety by one company invariably represents a competing product for the other companies. Thus, the regulatory-policy process effectively becomes an arena of competition among these companies. Moreover, these companies also have competing pest-control products in their chemical businesses and GM crops can compete with those products as well.

There is a further incentive for these companies to advocate for a stricter regulatory regime. The resulting high costs of regulatory compliance are an investment that these large corporations are willing to make. In particular, these high costs erect a barrier to entry by smaller competitors. Obtaining approvals from a stringent regulatory process can represent a kind of sanctioned market exclusivity.

2. **Small innovating agbiotech start-up companies**. Smaller innovators, however, are largely intimidated by high regulatory compliance costs and would, in general, benefit from being able to introduce GM crop varieties to market at a lower cost. As a result of the high entry costs, most of the smaller agricultural biotech companies active today are engaged in commercialization partnerships with one of the large innovating companies.

3. **Competing input suppliers.** Competing inputs include both conventional seed varieties as well as chemical inputs, such as insecticides, fungicides, and herbicides. Producers and distributors of competing inputs include multinationals, such as Bayer or BASF, that produce patent-protected and branded products as well as national companies in developing countries that produce generic pest-control products.

Preliminary analysis shows that, when it comes to pesticide companies, their losses from the introduction of genetic-modification technologies have been quite substantial. Comparisons between the global markets of 1991 and 2001 show four crucial trends over the decade. First, sales in chemicals were basically flat over the decade, indicating that this is a mature technology with conditions forcing an intense struggle for any kind of growth by the firms in the industry. Second, chemical sales by U.S. firms did actually grow (from 25 to 30 percent of the global market), whereas chemical sales by European firms dropped (from 55 to 47 percent of the global market), likely driven by the tie-in of some herbicides with the complementary genetic tolerance, especially the popular package of glyphosate with glyphosate-tolerant soybeans. Third, growth in genetics far outstripped growth in chemicals, providing virtually all the expansion in the crop protection market. Fourth and finally, European firms made a disproportionately small contribution to these rapidly growing biotech sales, given their initial market share in the industry, and in particular relative to U.S. firms. (Graff and Zilberman, 2007).

Environmentalists (versus the environment)

Finally, in addition to the impact on farming profits and consumer prices, Brookes and Barfoot (2011), NRC (2010), and Barrows, Sexton, and Zilberman (2013) suggest that the adoption of genetic pest control has significantly impacted the environment. By increasing yields (output per acre), GM crops tend to reduce the size of the land footprint required for agricultural production because of the yield effect, and thus tend to reduce habitat conversion as well as the greenhouse gas emissions due to land-use changes (e.g., deforestation and land clearing) and soil cultivation. The herbicide-tolerance trait has been associated with a switch by farmers to low- and no-tillage soil cultivation practices, greatly reducing soil erosion and increasing soil organic carbon sequestration and moisture retention (NRC, 2010). Genetic pest-control technologies also reduce, to a degree, the application of toxic chemicals that contaminate watersheds and harm wildlife (NRC, 2010). There is also a reduction in toxicity of pesticide residues in foods and a reduction in on-farm risk to farm workers (Hossain et al., 2004).

However, although there is documented evidence of the actual benefit of GM crops to the environment, the perception is that genetic modification is bad for the environment due to unknown and unspecified risks, including gene flow, impact on nontarget organisms, and the emergence of resistance among invasive pests and weeds. Avoidance of unknown risks is the basic logic of the precautionary principle.

Finally, there needs to be a distinction between the interests of the environment and the interests of environmentalists. The social welfare derived from environmental goods and services of natural resources can be conceptualized and sometimes quantified, and is shared at different levels by members of society. Environmental activist organizations or environmental nongovernmental organizations (NGO) consist of both people who care about environmental issues as well as environmental groups that have their own bureaucracy that needs to be supported. Their welfare as organizations is distinct from environmental welfare *per se*. The survival and thriving of an activist organization—and thus the political economy of activism—relies on their ability as an organization to capture sufficient resources, such as donations or grants, to perpetuate the activities of the organization (see Byrne, 2006 for a suggestive analysis of activist groups' financing). Success can be manifested in size of budget and staff, rents diverted to supporters of the organization, as well as building a reputation or "brand" among those portions of the public who have sufficient concern about environmental issues to make donations.

Environmental organizations succeed and fail in very real ways, often as a function of the policy position they advocate and their ability to influence policy outcomes (Collingwood, 2006). Revenues for such groups are sustained by being viewed by potential donors and grant makers as effective in at least two ways: (1) collecting and sharing information that may be more complete or more objective than official government or industry accounts (a "watchdog" or "informant" function) and (2) representing the donors' interests in the policy process and ultimately changing policy to serve those donors' interests (an "advocate" or "representative" function).

In policy areas like agricultural biotechnology, where uncertainty causes anxiety levels to be high and unfamiliarity causes information levels to be low, incentives exist for activist organizations to provide information, or even misinformation, that accentuates this anxiety and undermines trust in the information provided by others. Yet, complete resolution of a policy issue tends to have an unfavorable effect on donations to activist organizations as well as their political relevance. Thus, those organizations that tend to persist are those that periodically achieve high-profile but partial "wins" in the policy arena, enough so that the organizations can claim credit and legitimacy for making progress but not so much as to assuage donors that their underlying problems have been fully resolved. Furthermore, the success and survival of these organizations depends upon information revelations and policy actions being reliably communicated to an often highly dispersed donor base.

Mark Lynas (2013) suggests that objection to GM crops became a major program emphasis of several environmental groups, which made them attractive to certain donors. Those groups may then persist with this nominal position regarding biotechnology and the environment even when new evidence does not support it. Thus, the political-economic analysis must recognize this distinction and the potential for objective tensions between the interests of the environment, *per se*, and the interests of environmentalists.

The media

There appears to be a natural symbiosis between activist organizations and the media. Analyses indicate that economic interests of the media mirror those of successful activist organizations' strategies, as revenues to media are enhanced by repeating familiar stories, perpetuating stereotypes, playing on public anxieties, and emphasizing bad news over good news (Curtis et al., 2008; Gaskell et al., 1999; McClusky and Swinnen 2011). The media can be considered as having an influence over policy decisions, but there is not necessarily a direct impact on its welfare resulting from the outcome. The media does play an essential role in the public debate, and gains from reporting the news generated in the course of the public controversy regardless of how it gets settled in the end. If anything, like environmental groups, the media tend to benefit from the perpetuation of controversy rather than resolution.

Applying a Dynamic Version of the Framework to Explain the Political Economy of Agricultural Biotechnology Regulations in Europe

We adapt the voting model developed in the second section to explain the factors leading to the practical ban of GM in Europe. This model suggests that "voters" (citizens, representative, regulators, rulers) consider the impacts of proposed policies on the perceived welfare of various groups, and assign weights to these perceived welfare levels in making their choices. Policymaking is evolving, and decision makers update the assessment of impacts of policy proposals based on new information that may be obtained by exchange and dialogue between the interest groups. (For a more detailed technical version of this dynamic model, see Hochman, Graff, and Zilberman, 2012.) What results is a process in which each of the various groups seeks, in the public debate, to shape the voters' perceptions in a direction that generally serves its own interests (Herring, 2008). In Europe, there has been a vibrant process of environmentalists and industry aiming to inform and shift public opinions about GM (e.g., Gaskell et al., 2005).

Applying the Model to Explain the European Policy Regime

We now apply this dynamic voting framework to analyze the regulatory regime of GM crop agriculture as it unfolded in Europe in the 1990s. Specifically, we consider whether differences between U.S. regulations and European regulations primarily reflect differences in consumer preferences, as many contemporary accounts argue or imply (see, for example, Bernauer, 2003; Sheldon, 2004). We look in detail first at the interests of agricultural inputs producers and then at the interests of farmers and of consumers. We then consider the respective political weights and interactions among these various groups as they have influenced European regulators.

As a starting point, we consider differences in the innovative capacities of the U.S. and European agricultural input industries. Patent data on agricultural biotechnology and agricultural chemical technologies indicate broad national differences in innovative capacity (Graff and Zilberman, 2007). In agricultural biotechnology, American inventors, in both academia and in industry, have been far more prolific in the quantity and the quality of patents granted to them than have European inventors (Graff and Zilberman, 2007). One metric used to rank the quality or value of a patent is the number of citations that it receives from other patents. Analysis shows that the agricultural biotechnology patents granted to U.S. inventors since 1980 have historically garnered roughly 10 times more patent citations than the agricultural biotechnology patents granted to European inventors since 1980, and that the imbalance was particularly striking in the early foundational developments in the 1980s and early 1990s before there was much public awareness of the technology (Graff and Zilberman, 2007). By comparison, agrochemical patents granted to U.S. inventors have historically garnered a similar number of citations compared to the agrochemical patents granted to European inventors.

In summary, American companies enjoyed an innovative comparative advantage in agricultural biotechnology innovation when European companies enjoyed a comparative advantage in agricultural chemical innovation. European (and particularly the German) chemical industry has long been the globally dominant innovator and supplier of agricultural chemicals. For example, in 2001, global sales of agricultural biotechnology or genetic crop-protection products experienced annual growth of

13 percent. Yet, to break that out by nationality of the major companies, sales of genetics by major U.S. companies, at $3.8 billion, made up the bulk of the agbiotech side of the crop-protection market and were the portion that experienced such high growth. Sales of genetics by major European companies, at $1.1 billion, were much smaller and had grown by just 2 percent from the previous year. In contrast, in 2001, sales of agrochemical pest-control products declined globally by 7.4 percent, whereas the sales of the dominant European companies declined 2.9 percent (Phillips McDougall, 2002).

Taken together, it becomes clear that the U.S. pest-control industry has a comparative innovative advantage in a new technology that is gaining market share, and the incumbent European industry has a comparative innovative advantage in an older technology where market share is being displaced. To the extent that this is an accurate description, we would expect the ascendant biobased U.S. industry to advocate for regulations that would help it to maintain its newfound comparative advantage, in particular against its larger but slower rivals in the European chemicals sector. Similarly, we would expect the major European chemical firms to favor a regulatory regime that would, at the very least, slow the rate at which they are losing market share to biotechnology, if not halt those losses altogether.

Next, let us consider European farmers and GM crops. It would be expected that, all else being equal, some European farmers would prefer to plant GM varieties because of their cost-saving characteristics. However, supporting the ban on biotech crops is presumed to have helped a large proportion of European farmers in other ways, primarily as a nontariff barrier to trade that protects prices for domestic producers. European farmers may also support more stringent regulations on biotech crops as they create an opportunity for systematic price differentiation of their commodity outputs, allowing them to collect an additional price premium while maintaining existing production practices of growing conventional crops. Furthermore, since a large proportion of European farmers are at least partially supported under the crop subsidy programs of the Common Agricultural Policy (CAP), any policy that tends to support farm incomes through other means was likely to be favored politically for alleviating some of the budget demands of the CAP.

The relationship between European consumers and GM foods may simply be interpreted as one of straightforward rejection—a case in which the benefits of biotech for consumers simply do not outweigh the costs and risks. It is estimated that European consumers pay 3 to 5 billion euros more per year in food costs as a result of the ban on biotech agricultural products (Anderson and Jackson, 2004). This indicates the extent to which European consumers' perceived welfare diverges from a typical economic welfare analysis of their consumer surplus. Such a divergence can result from two instances. First, food consumers are arguably less well organized as an interest group than are the European agrochemical industry or European farmers and, following Stigler (1971), some of the excess cost may be a result of more concentrated interests prevailing against the less concentrated in the policy process. Consumers as individuals may each be paying a few euros more per year on food, but the cost to organize an opposition to the prevailing policy might cost individuals more than it would save. Thus, inaction on this issue may be the rational response. Second, there is also likely some extent to which there is a premium that European consumers are willing to pay to reduce the risk to which they perceive themselves to be exposed. These perceptions and the relative risk aversion of European consumers have reasonable groundings. Yet, we must be clear that they largely derive from the public debate that has been informed by other groups who have their own interests in the matter, including activists, industry, and farmers, as well as being shaped by the public's recent experience with regulators' inefficacy at mitigating food-related risks like bovine spongiform encephalopathy and foot-and-mouth disease. It has been widely noted that European consumers have less confidence in their food safety regulators and, conversely, that environmental activists and Green political parties enjoy greater credibility in Europe than they do in the United States.

However, the dynamics of how the perceptions of European consumers developed over time are far more complex and nuanced than conventional accounts often suggest. European activist organizations have utilized the issue of food biotechnology to engage in a contest with European regulators for legitimacy according to the logic of how such organizations survive and advance. Changes in media coverage in Europe were largely driven by the campaigns of activist organizations pursuing such a strategy. Analysis of early media coverage of biotech foods in the U.S. and Europe (Gaskell et al. 1999) indicates that the volume and content of press accounts were roughly comparable through about 1990. Thereafter, the quantity of coverage increased in the European press relative to the United States. New narratives emerged in the European public debate encompassing two major themes. One maintained that biotech crops do not serve consumer interests, ignoring the effect that a cost-reducing agricultural technology tends to have in reducing consumer food prices, where welfare impact on developed economies, especially in Europe, is very small in contrast to developing economies where consumers might spend more than 50 percent of their income on food consumption (Paarlberg, 2008). The other theme has been to hold up GM technology as a symbol of the negative effects of globalization, characterizing it as an "American" technology that is antigreen and pitted, in some sense, against a European way of life.

In conclusion, the ban of biotech food in Europe does not appear to be simply a crisis of consumer acceptance but rather a convergence of the influence of several distinct economic interest groups within Europe, each with self-interests in slowing or stopping the introduction of biotechnologies into European and global markets. To summarize, we argue that U.S. academic scientists and companies since the 1970s held a relative advantage in biotech innovation that, by the mid-1990s, began to threaten the market dominance of European corporations in agricultural pest-control markets. The interests of the European chemical industry concurred with the interests of other groups that stood to gain from restricting biotechnology, and European chemical corporations did not need to be proactive in their opposition. First, since any new technology of this sort requires a new regulatory regime to be implemented, all the incumbent industry needed to do was to abstain from advocating for the implementation of a new policy. Without an effective champion, policy formation stalled. Second, given that activist groups were already highly motivated for their own reasons, all the incumbent industry needed to do to achieve a desired result was to abstain from intervening and to leave the activists unchallenged in forming the public's opinions and risk perceptions of biotechnology. The convergence of these multiple interests then had a significant influence on the decisions of European regulators, effectively allowing the approval of new biotech crops to come to a halt in 1998, withholding certain forms of patent protection from biotech crops, underfunding public research in plant biotechnology, and introducing labeling requirements that impose supply chain costs and further stigmatize the technology in the eyes of consumers.

Conclusion

Agbiotechnology is a disruptive innovation; it has triggered a cycle of "creative destruction" in agriculture and related sectors. It has also modified the perceived relationship between humans and nature, triggering suspicion and fear. Both "creative destruction" and fear evoked political forces, causing the future of the technology, to a large extent, to be determined in the political arena. Political responses reflected of the impact of the anticipated changes caused by the technology on different groups in different countries. Economists tend to analyze how technologies affect different sectors, but differences of impact on various groups within sectors resulted in different regulation across countries. The "creative destruction" enabled by agricultural biotechnology was apparent in the agricultural input sector. Although small start-ups and large life-science companies, like Monsanto, which tend to be American, stood to gain from the technology, producers of chemical pesticides, many of which are European, faced potential losses. Although U.S. corn and soybean farmers anticipated growing demand and could benefit from the increased supply and reduced costs associated with the technology, European producers felt threatened by expanded global supply associated with the technology; they were content with regulation that would allow them to operate in a segregated market. Environmental groups by nature stand for conservation and are suspicious of change, especially of a technology that may perpetuate both monoculture and the expansion of agribusiness. Consumers were caught in the middle, receiving conflicting information from supporters and opponents of the technology. Consumers in developing countries did not experience any immediate gain from the technology, but learned of potential risks of adoption.

The outcome in different countries reflects responses of different groups to the technology and how they expressed themselves in the political arena. These responses were conditioned by historical period. Most of the intellectual property behind the technologies was owned by American companies, and there was originally relative trust in the U.S. government food-safety regulations that allowed the technology to be accepted. When the technology was introduced in Europe, trust in government food regulation was at its lowest level, in part because failures in official regulation and science illustrated by mad-cow disease. Both farmers and industry were not likely to gain much from biotechnology. The credibility of environmental groups, strength of the emergent green movement in Europe, and the fact that the technology was American in a period when America refused to sign the Kyoto Protocol, did not make for favorable acceptance of the GMO. These factors contributed to a practical ban on agricultural biotechnology in 1998.

Different starting points in Europe and the United States thus resulted in different paths of regulation of agricultural biotechnology. Historical divergences driven by interests of powerful players have been important in path-dependent ways, and have influenced interests of other countries in a global trading system. Nevertheless, our analysis illustrates how new information may change perception of interests, and thus political behavior. As knowledge about biotechnology changes, different groups update their perceptions and sometimes convince others to change their preferences. Efforts to modify regulation of GMOs in both the European Union and the United States are continuous; global mobilization likewise points in different directions in different nations at different times. Agricultural biotechnology is little used in Africa, but intensely used in Latin America (Paarlberg 2008). As the technology evolves, and economic situations change, the fate of the technology may change, driven by a fluctuating mix of objective conditions and subjective preferences. Continuous increases in food prices and scarcity, breakthrough innovations and applications that make the technology more beneficial to humans, or increased utilization of the technology in Asia, may lead Europe to relax its restrictive regulations, for example. Reciprocally, a major catastrophe in the United States, or development of plant-breeding technologies that can increase productivity and environmental sustainability without relying on genetic engineering may lead to new restrictions on the technology in its historically strongest base. Though these dynamics are in principle unpredictable, it is clear from the analysis of this chapter that both interests and information require careful examination for a robust understanding of biotechnology's spatial and temporal diffusion.

Notes

1. If N is an odd number, there is one median voter (the voter ordered at the middle spot). If N is an even number, there are two voters in the middle of the order. In this case we will define for our purposes the median voter as the (N/2)+1 voter.
2. In this case we have a transition from a voting equilibrium to a maximization of voters' aggregate net benefit (Just, Hueth, and Schmitz, 2008).
3. Sexton and Zilberman (2011) find that the price reduction because of GM is, more or less, of the same order of magnitude as the commodity price increase in corn and soybean because of growing demand for production of biofuels. Consumers in the US suffered only a 3% increase in the price of food because of biofuel, which suggests that the price reduction because of GM is, again, around 3%-4%.
4. This can be inferred from an approximately 30 to 40 percent increase in the price of grains because of biofuel, which resulted in a 2 to 3 percent increase in the price of food to consumers (Hochman et al., 2011).

References

Acemoglu, D., S. Johnson, and J. A. Robinson. 2005. "Institutions as a Fundamental Cause of Long-Run Growth." In *Handbook of Economic Growth*, edited by Phillip, Aghion, and Durlauf, Amsterdam: Elsevier. Bd. 1A, 385–472.

Anderson, K., and Jackson, L. A. 2004, August 1–3. Standards, trade and protection: The case of GMOs. Paper presented at the Annual Meetings of the American Agricultural Economics Association, Denver, CO.

Anderson, K., G. Rausser, and J. Swinnen. 2013. "Political Economy of Public Policies: Insights from Distortions to Agricultural and Food Markets." *Journal of Economic Literature* 51 (2): 423–477.

Barrows, G., S. Sexton, and D. Zilberman. "Agricultural Biotechnology: The Promise and Prospects." Department of Agricultural and Resource Economics, University of California at Berkeley. Working Paper, 2013.

Becker, G. S. 1983. "A Theory of Competition Among Pressure Groups for Political Influence." *The Quarterly Journal of Economics* 98(3): 371–400.

Bennett, A. B., C. Chi-Ham, G. Barrows, S. Sexton, and D. Zilberman. 2013. "Agricultural Biotechnology: Economics, Environment, Ethics and the Future." *Annual Review of Environment and Resources*, 249–279.

Bernauer, T. 2003. *Genes, Trade, and Regulation: The Seeds of Conflict in Food Biotechnology.* Princeton, NJ: Princeton University Press.

Brookes, G., and P. Barfoot. 2011."Global Impact of Biotech Crops: Environmental Effects 1996–2009." *GM Crops* 2(1): 34–49.

Brookes, G., and P. Barfoot. 2013."The Global Income and Production Effects of Genetically Modified (GM) Crops 1996–2011." *GM Crops and Food: Biotechnology in Agriculture and the Food Chain* 4(1): 74–83.

Byrne, P. 1993. "Deconstructing the Agricultural Biotechnology Protest Industry." In *Let Them Eat Precaution*, edited by J. Entine. Washington, DC: American Enterprise Institute, 2006.

Cochrane, W. W. 1993. *The Development of American Agriculture: A Historical Analysis.* Minneapolis, MN: University of Minnesota Press.

Collingwood, V. 2006. Non-governmental organisations, power and legitimacy in international society. *Review of International Studies* 32(3): 439.

Curtis, K. R., McCluskey, J. J., & Swinnen, J. F. M. 2008. Differences in global risk perceptions of biotechnology and the political economy of the media. *International Journal of Global Environmental Issues*, 8(1&2): 77–89.

Downs, A. 1957. *An Economic Theory of Democracy.* New York: Harper.

Falkner, R. 2006. *The European Union as a* "Green Normative Power"? *EU Leadership in International Biotechnology Regulation* (Harvard University Center for European Studies Working Paper Series #140). Cambridge, MA: Harvard University.

Feder, Gershon, Richard E. Just, and David Zilberman. 1985. "Adoption of agricultural innovations in developing countries: A survey." Economic development and cultural change, 255–298.

Gaskell, G., M. W. Bauer, J. Durant, N. C. Allum. 1999. "Worlds Apart? The Reception of Genetically Modified Foods in Europe and the US" *Science*, 285 (July): 384–387.

Gaskell, George, Toby Ten Eyck, Jonathan Jackson, and Giuseppe Veltri. 2005. "Imagining nanotechnology: Cultural support for technological innovation in Europe and the United States." *Public Understanding of Science* 14(1): 81–90.

Gilland, T. 2006."Trade War or Culture War? The GM Debate in Britain and the European Union." In *Let Them Eat Precaution*, edited by J. Entine. Washington, DC: American Enterprise Institute.

Graff, G. D., G. Hochman, and D. Zilberman. 2009. "The Political Economy of Agricultural Biotechnology Policies." *AgBioForum* 12(1): 34–46.

Graff, G. D., and D. Zilberman. 2007. "The Political Economy of Intellectual Property: Reexamining European Policy on Plant Biotechnology." In *Agricultural Biotechnology and Intellectual Property: Seeds of Change*, edited by J. Kesan, pp. 244–265. Wallingford, UK: CAB International.

Graff, G. D., D. Zilberman, and A. Bennett. 2009. "The Contraction of Agbiotech Product Quality Innovation." *Nature Biotechnology* 27(8): 702–704.

Grossman, G. M., and E. Helpman. 2001. *Special Interest Politics*. Cambridge, MA: The MIT Press.

Herring, R. 2008. "Opposition to Transgenic Technologies: Ideology, Interests, and Collective Action Frames." *Nature Reviews Genetics* 9: 458–463.

Hochman, G., G. D. Graff, and D. Zilberman. 2012. "The Political Economy of Controversial Technologies," Paper presented at the Agricultural and Applied Economics Association Annual Meeting, August 13, 2012.

Hochman, G., D. Rajagopal, G. Timilsina, and D. Zilberman. 2011. "The Role of Inventory Adjustments in Quantifying Factors Causing Food Price Inflation." World Bank Policy Research Working Paper Series.

Hossain, F., C. E. Pray, Y. Lu, J. Huang, C. Fan, and R. Hu. 2004. "GM Cotton and Farmer's Health in China: An Econometric Analysis of the Relationship between Pesticide Poisoning and GM Cotton Use in China." *International Journal of Occupational and Environmental Health* 10(3): 307–314.

Just, R. E., D. L. Hueth, and A. Schmitz, eds. 2008. *Applied Welfare Economics*. UK: Edward Elgar Publishing Ltd.

Just, R. E., J. M. Alston, and D. Zilberman, eds. 2006. *Regulating Agricultural Biotechnology: Economics and Policy*. Amsterdam: Springer.

Kane, M. 2001. GMO regulations: Food safety or trade barrier? In G.C. Nelson (Ed.), *Genetically Modified Organisms in Agriculture: Economics and Politics*. San Diego, CA: Academic Press.

Kaniewski, W. K., and P. E. Thomas. 2004. "The Potato Story." *AgBioForum*, 7(1&2): 41–46.

Kiesel, K., J. J. McCluskey, and S. B. Villas-Boas. 2011. "Nutritional Labeling and Consumer Choices." *Annual Review of Resource Economics* 3(1): 141–158.

Kurzer, P., and A. Cooper. 2007. "Consumer Activism, EU Institutions and Global Markets: The Struggle over Biotech Foods." *Journal of Public Policy* 27(2): 103.

Lapan, H. E., and G. Moschini. 2004. "Innovation and Trade with Endogenous Market Failure: The Case of Genetically Modified Products." *American Journal of Agricultural Economics* 86: 634–648.

Lomborg, B. 2001. *The Skeptical Environmentalist: Measuring the Real State of the World*. Cambridge, UK: Cambridge University Press.

Lusk, J. L., and K. H. Coble. 2005. "Risk Perceptions, Risk Preference, and Acceptance of Risky Food." *American Journal of Agricultural Economics* 87 (2): 393–405.

Lynas, Mark. 2013. http://www.marklynas.org/2013/04/time-to-call-out-the-anti-gmo-conspiracy-theory/

McCluskey, Jill, and Johan Swinnen. 2011. "The Media and Food-Risk Perceptions." *EMBO Reports* 12(7): 624–629.

McDougall, Phillips. 2002. "Agrochemical and Seed Company Sales: The Crop Protection Sector." *AgriFutura* 29(March): 1–4.
Miller, H. I., and G. Conko. 2004. *The Frankenfood Myth: How Protest and Politics Threaten the Biotech Revolution*. Westport, CT: Praeger Publishers.
Newell, P., and D. Glover. 2003. *Business and Biotechnology: Regulation and the Politics of Influence* (IDS Working Paper 192). Brighton, UK: Institute of Development Studies, University of Sussex.
NRC. 2010. *Impact of Genetically Engineered Crops on Farm Sustainability in the U.S. National Research Council*, Washington, DC: National Academies Press.
Oates, W. E., and P. R. Portney. 2003. "The Political Economy of Environmental Policy." *Handbook of Environmental Economics* 1: 325–354.
Paarlberg, R. L. 2001. "Shrinking International Markets for GM Crops." *AgBioView* 22: 1–5.
Paarlberg, Robert. 2008. *Starved for Science: How Biotechnology Is Being Kept Out of Africa*. Cambridge, MA: Harvard University Press.
Posner, R. A. 1974. "Theories of Economic Regulation." *Bell Journal of Economics* 5(2): 335–358.
Prakash, A., and K. L. Kollman. 2003. "Biopolitics in the EU and the US: A Race to the Bottom or Convergence to the Top?" *International Studies Quarterly* 47(4): 617–641.
Qaim, Matin, and Greg Traxler. 2005. "Roundup Ready soybeans in Argentina: farm level and aggregate welfare effects." *Agricultural Economics* 32, (1): 73–86.
Qaim, M., and D. Zilberman. 2003. "Yield Effects of Genetically Modified Crops in Developing Countries." *Science* 299(5608): 900–902.
Rausser, G. C., J. Swinnen, and P. Zusman. 2012. *Political Power and Economic Policy: Theory, Analysis, and Empirical Applications*. New York: Cambridge University Press.
Romer, T., and H. Rosenthal. 1979. "Bureaucrats versus Voters: On the Political Economy of Resource Allocation by Direct Democracy." *The Quarterly Journal of Economics* 93(4): 563–587.
Schumpeter, J. A. 1934. *The Theory of Economic Development: An Inquiry into Profits, Capital, Credit, Interest, and the Business Cycle*, translated by Redvers Opie. Cambridge, MA: Harvard University Press.
Schumpeter, J. A. 1942. *Capitalism, Socialism, and Democracy*. New York: Harper and Brothers.
Seelye, K.Q. 2001, May 12. Bush is choosing industry insiders to fill several environmental positions, *New York Times*.
Sexton, S., and D. Zilberman. 2011. "How Agricultural Biotechnology Boosts Food Supply and Accommodates Biofuels." National Bureau of Economic Research, Working Paper 16699.
Sheldon, I. 2004. "Europe's Regulation of Agricultural Biotechnology: Precaution or Trade Distortion?" *Journal of Agricultural and Food Industrial Organization* 2(2): 1–28.
Stratfor. 2011. "France: The Potential for a Europe-wide Anti-fracking Movement." http://www.stratfor.com.
Stigler, George J. 1971. "The theory of economic regulation." *The Bell Journal of Economics And Management Science* 2: 3–21.
WTO. 2003. *European Community—Measures Affecting the Approval and Marketing of Biotech Products*—Request for Consultations by the United States. World Trade Organization.
Zilberman, D., S. Kaplan, E. Kim, and G. Waterfield. 2014. "Lessons from the California Labeling Proposition on the State of Crop Biotechnology." Chapter 38 in *Handbook on Agriculture, Biotechnology and Development*, Stuart J., Smyth, Peter W.B, Phillips and David Castle, eds. London: Edward Elgar, 538–549.

CHAPTER 28

CO-EXISTENCE IN THE FIELDS? GM, ORGANIC, AND CONVENTIONAL FOOD CROPS

JANICE E. THIES

> Freedom is not merely the opportunity to do as one pleases; neither is it merely the opportunity to choose between set alternatives. Freedom is, first of all, the chance to formulate the available choices, to argue over them—and then, the opportunity to choose.
>
> C. Wright Mills

THE GLOBAL RIFT OVER TRANSGENIC CROPS

IT was Halloween 2008. The community screening of *Bullshit* (the movie) (Holmquist and Khardalian 2005) at the Cornell University Cinema had just ended. My colleague leading the discussion, Ron Herring, welcomed questions from the audience, sparse though they were. *Bullshit*, a Swedish film directed by PeÅ Holmquist and Suzanne Khardalian (2005), chronicles the accomplishments of Vandana Shiva, an Indian activist, on a range of issues, including her fight against a patent on neem, her battle with Coca Cola, Inc. over water use and water rights for Indian villagers, her attempt to block food distribution in Mexico because some of the products contained GM (genetically modified) maize, and her equanimity with regard to receiving the "Bullshit Award for Sustaining World Poverty."[1] The award was bestowed on behalf of Indian farmers by Barun Shankar Mitra of the Liberty Institute, New Delhi, for Shiva's work in fighting the approval and commercial use of GM seeds, particularly Bt[2] cotton and Bt eggplant in India. Shiva's response was to treat the award as an honor. In

India, she said, "bullshit" is an important cooking fuel source, gathered by women and shaped into pats, with each woman's handprint duly pressed into the pat and left to dry—quite an honor. Although a wide range social issues were highlighted in the documentary, our audience homed in on the issue of GM crops to begin the discussion period.

The first question from the audience was about *gene flow,*[3] specifically, about the presence of transgenes[4] that had been detected in maize landraces in Oaxaca, Mexico, by Quist and Chapela (2001), an occurrence the questioner referred to as "genetic pollution." As the "science" half of the team, I took the question. I began to describe recent work undertaken by Ortiz et al. (2005) in which they were unable to substantiate the findings of Quist and Chapela (2001). Before I could elaborate any further, I was suddenly being called a "handmaiden of the industry." Ron and I were called "criminals" and a woman from the audience stood up and said she was "ashamed to be on the same faculty" with us and stormed out. I sat there stunned. What had just happened and why?

I had observed this level of animosity toward Cornell researchers once before. Oddly, in the same venue after the screening of Deborah Kerns Garcia's film, *The Future of Food* (2004), a film critical of both transgenic technology and the biotechnology industry. The film was followed by a panel discussion during which Garcia, Ignacio Chapela, and a few of the Cornell faculty fielded questions from the audience, which packed the theater. Here, too, Cornell researchers were accused of being in bed with the biotech industry, Monsanto Corporation and its ilk. Transgenic crops, said members of the audience, were destroying soil ecology, contaminating the food supply, and, along with the biotech industry, conducting a massive experiment on the American people. This was more than just a "town-gown" conflict.

As a scientist, I thought I was used to controversy. We debate among ourselves constantly, but these arguments focus on aspects of the science. Personal accusations are not typically a part of these debates. But, here, in these public venues, there was no such decorum. It was shocking to me and difficult to engage with; robust research data were not welcome here. My colleague, Ron Herring, was like a duck in water, letting it all shed right off of him. "Oh, this happens all the time," he said, "it's political." No wonder scientists don't enjoy engaging in these discussions, I thought, these are personal attacks that normally do not belong in scientific discourse. It was then that I realized this had nothing to do with scientific discourse; instead, this was politicized social discourse on a highly contentious technology. How had such an enormous rift developed between those who choose to use GM (genetically modified) technologies and those who passionately oppose their use? This rift has its roots in the shift from an agrarian-based rural development model of agriculture to the *agri-industrial paradigm* (Levidow and Boschert, 2008), where policy has—in the main—supported a consumptive, technology-driven approach to food production, favoring factory farming and its associated economies of scale, and one that has marginalized those choosing alternative agricultural approaches.

Farming Systems

Farming is a way of life. Those working the land vary in their relationship to it and in the means they choose to manage it. Farmers (land managers) make daily decisions on what inputs they will use on their farmland, decisions based strongly on their worldview or "lifeworld" (Shurman and Munro 2010). *Organic* farmers rely on inputs largely derived from the environment, e.g., manures, crop residues, and composts, to maintain soil fertility and "natural"[5] products and processes for pest control. *Conventional* farmers invest in synthetic fertilizers, pesticides, and other industrial technologies to ensure crop nutrition and to control pests for high yields. While no single model of conventional farm management prevails, this term refers to farms that tend to embrace the agri-industrial paradigm of production. These practices involve the broad-scale use of products emerging from the chemical industry.

The bulk of farmland in industrialized nations is managed conventionally. The total US farmland under crop production in 2008 was 844 million acres; of this, only 0.57% (4.8 million acres) was certified organic. Total US acreage for livestock and pasture land was 473 million acres, with certified organic farms representing 0.46%.[6]

The advent of transgenic crops has created a new designation, that of *GM agriculture*, which has provoked a whole new set of contentions. Transgenic crops are those that have been developed using gene splicing technology, also known as genetic engineering. Here, the DNA comprising a gene of interest is taken from the genome of one organism, or synthesized in the laboratory, and introduced into the genome of another. The introduced gene is then expressed in the receiving organism. For example, the soil bacterium *Bacillus thuringiensis* (Bt) produces a crystal protein that is toxic to specific classes of insects. The gene that codes for this protein has been cloned into the maize (*Zea mays*) plant genome enabling the maize plant to produce the insecticidal protein in its own tissues. An organism, in this case the maize plant, that receives a gene from another species is called *transgenic*. If the introduced gene is from the same species, the resulting organism is called *cisgenic*.

GM agriculture is, by and large, based on the same agri-industrial paradigm as conventional agriculture (Levidow and Boschert 2008). However, the advent of GM agriculture could lead to four basic agroecologies: GM conventional, non-GM conventional, organic, and GM organic. There are many variations on these basic approaches to production, including conservation agriculture, no or low-tillage systems, biodynamic systems, and other variations on organic agriculture, termed alternative farming systems.[7] The use of some transgenic crops, particularly insect resistant (Bt) crops, may prove to be the more sustainable of these agricultural paradigms, as their use has been shown to decrease the use of chemical insecticides (Brookes and Barfoot 2010). GM organic is not considered an option in the United States because the US organic industry disallows the use of GM crops in certified organic agriculture.[8] The ability to retain the integrity of each production approach in the face of the new challenges presented by GM agriculture is the central theme of this chapter.

The Industrialization of Agriculture: Postwar Applications for War-Time Chemicals

The health and environmental safety of the use of synthetic chemicals in conventional agriculture began to be questioned in the 1950s as many new control products, born out of chemical research programs during World War II, made their way to the marketplace. Prior to World War I, nearly all farming was what is now referred to as *organic agriculture*. The Haber-Bosch process[9] was developed in Germany to convert atmospheric nitrogen (N_2) into ammonia (NH_3) and then into nitrate (NO_3), which was used subsequently to make bombs and other explosive devices. The details of the Haber-Bosch process were stolen by the French near the end of the war and passed on to their allies. Natural supplies of mineral nitrogen (N) were becoming more and more difficult to procure; thus, a logical peace time application of the Haber-Bosch process was to make ammonia- and nitrate-based fertilizers. Likewise, mustard gas and other neurotoxins and defoliants developed during wartime also found their way into postwar agriculture as pesticides. Thus, the age of synthetic, chemical-based agriculture was born. Oddly, this form of agriculture is known today as *conventional agriculture*, one in which synthetic pesticides (including herbicides), fertilizers, and other industrial inputs are used to promote high yields, even though the negative effects of chemical use on humans and the environment are now well known.

"DDT is good for me" was a prominent slogan aimed at manipulating public sentiment. Evidence began mounting in the 1940s and 1950s that these chemicals were having devastating effects on human and environmental health (Rosner and Markowitz 2013). The issue broke out into the open with the publication of Rachel Carson's book *Silent Spring* (1963),[10] which documented ten years of research into the biosafety of these products. Chemical companies responded vociferously and resisted attempts to ban their products, insisting that they were safe until proven otherwise. Even labeling products as toxins and potential carcinogens (cancer-causing substances) was fought with fervor by the chemical industry. The publication of *Silent Spring* is often cited as the beginning of the environmental movement in the United States, which ultimately led to the formation of the Environmental Protection Agency (EPA). Carson biographer Mark Hamilton Lytle (2007) wrote that Carson "quite self-consciously decided to write a book calling into question the paradigm of scientific progress that defined postwar American culture." In the final chapter of *Silent Spring*, Carson anticipated the advent of crop biotechnology by suggesting that the need for chemical insecticides could be circumvented by advances in plant breeding that would yield pest-resistant crops.

Over the next decade, research would document that most of these chemicals were highly toxic and some were also carcinogenic and thus needed to be more tightly regulated or banned.[11] As an early "whistle-blower," Carson was roundly criticized.

White-Stevens, then a biochemist at American Cyanamid, stated: "If man were to follow the teachings of Miss Carson, we would return to the Dark Ages, and the insects and diseases and vermin would once again inherit the earth."[12] In a letter to Dwight D. Eisenhower, former secretary of agriculture Ezra Taft Benson reportedly concluded that because she was unmarried, despite being physically attractive, she was "probably a Communist."[13] These comments mimic those surrounding the global debate on the use of transgenic crops today, including personal attacks on those not embracing the agri-industrial model of agriculture, which is the dominant paradigm that drives current US agricultural policy.

In the 1960s, the United States Department of Agriculture (USDA) was responsible for both regulating pesticides and promoting the welfare of the agriculture industry, making for a clear conflict of interest. In response, the EPA was established in 1970 during the Nixon administration. Its mission was to address the environmental issues arising from industry, agriculture, and pest control programs. Much of the regulatory framework that strictly controls the use of synthetic inputs to agricultural systems was developed by the EPA under the Federal Insecticide, Fungicide, and Rodenticide Act.[14] A significant early outcome was the ban on the use of DDT for insect control in 1972. Several chemicals, including methyl bromide and atrazine, have been banned widely across the globe. However, in the United States, farmers continue to use these chemicals under a special exemption issued by the EPA. Methyl bromide is a fumigant that is used to control insects, termites, rodents, weeds, nematodes, and soil-borne diseases. Methyl bromide is also a powerful ozone depleting compound that was slated to be banned in the United States by 2005. However, this date has been pushed forward repeatedly as farmers insist that no viable alternatives exist, particularly for control of nematodes and soil-borne fungal and bacterial pathogens.

As evidence and awareness of the hazards resulting from pesticide use continued to mount, rejection of their use by some farmers followed. Those choosing not to use synthetic inputs began organizing under the banner of organic agriculture (see Larsson, this volume, for the rise of the transnational organic movement), a practice in which the use of fertilizers, pesticides, and other synthetic inputs are not permitted. The history of agriculture in the United States shows that those who have chosen not to adopt these technologies have been increasingly marginalized by the inability to compete with the high yields obtained by adopters. Higher yields on conventional farms led to sharply decreased commodity prices and a downward economic spiral ensued. The mantra became "Get Big or Get Out" (Krebs 1992; Hauter 2012). In addition to economies of scale, it is important to note that large US corporate farms have also benefited because they have largely not been held accountable for the environmental costs associated with this form of production (referred to by economists as "externalities"); rather, the US taxpayer has, or, in the absence of paying the costs, the environment has paid the price. In contrast, an explicit goal of the organic farming movement is to maintain and enhance the environment on the farm and its surrounding areas, where farmers bear the costs associated with environmental protection themselves.[15] Co-existence[16] between neighboring farms became increasingly strained as evidence mounted that synthetic inputs used on conventional farms were finding their way onto organic farms, predominantly as run-off and spray drift, thereby contaminating both the land and the crops of organic farmers.

Co-existence in the Age of Synthetic Chemical Inputs

When the US National Organic Program (NOP) standards[17] were conceived, a very pragmatic approach was taken. Organic certification would be based on adherence to prescribed practices rather than on any battery of tests on the grains or produce sold. Thus, no extensive surveillance or testing systems were mandated in the USDA-NOP rules. Instead, third-party testing has become available as an option for farmers.[18] Part of the reasoning for this "practice standard" was that most synthetic chemical inputs were expected to dissipate or break down in the environment over time. Those that did not, such as DDT, were banned or became highly restricted. The reasoning that synthetic chemicals would eventually dissipate was used to develop the requirements farmers need to follow to obtain organic certification when first stopping conventional practices. Three years of strict adherence to the organic standards is now required before a transitioning farm can be certified organic.[19] With this liberal policy, as Larsson (this volume) notes, both the USDA-NOP and the International Federation of Organic Agriculture Movements (IFOAM) have drifted from their purist roots. It is remarkable that such compromises, however uneasy, were achieved at all considering the widely documented damage done by fertilizers and pesticides to the environment.[20] Many insecticides are also highly toxic to humans and wildlife;[21] evidence of their harm is undeniable (e.g., Goulson 2013; Hayes 2005; Rosner and Markowitz 2013). Yet, organic farmers were forced to accept that use of agricultural chemicals is the dominant farming paradigm in most countries, and while continued activism to curtail their use altogether goes on unabated, their presence in the environment was a fact they could not change; they could only manage their own land and behavior.

The uneasy relationship between conventional and organic farmers is constantly simmering and bursts into public consciousness in the news media with articles entitled "Organic Farming Alone Can't Feed The World, Say Researchers"[22] or "Yet Again, Organic Ag Proves Just as Productive as Chemical Ag."[23] Reliance on synthetic inputs by conventional farmers is justified most frequently by the need to intensify crop production to feed a growing population. The organic agriculture movement is often criticized as being "unable" to meet this increasing demand[24] and that hunger and famine will be the inevitable result. The organic movement counters that chemical inputs are destroying soil health and water and air quality, and that an alternative paradigm is needed urgently in order to sustain agricultural productivity now and in the future (Rosset and Altieri 1997).

Extent of Adoption of GM Crops by Industrialized and Poor Countries

The year 2013 marked the eighteenth year of commercial cultivation of transgenic crops.[25] That year, transgenic crops were grown on 175 million hectares (ha) worldwide, which represented a one hundred-fold increase in land area planted over 1996, which was the first year transgenic crops were grown commercially. James (2013) reports that 18 million farmers grew transgenic crops in 2013, of which 90% were smallholder, resource-poor farmers. These crops were grown in twenty-seven countries, of which only eight were industrialized nations. Herbicide tolerant (HT) crops made up approximately 55%, insect resistant (IR) crops made up about 18%, and stacked traits (HT+IR) comprised 27% of global plantings. In addition, 2,000 farmers planted the first transgenic drought tolerant maize on 50,000 ha of land in the United States. The average adoption rate for all transgenic crops in the United States exceeded 90%. India and China had Bt cotton adoption rates of 95% and 90%, respectively. In Canada, the adoption rate for GM canola was 96%. In the European Union (EU), five countries (Spain, Portugal, Romania, Slovakia, and the Czech Republic) grew Bt maize (MON810), 94% of which was grown in Spain (an adoption rate of 31%). James (2013) cites onerous regulation (EU coexistence policy, CEC, 2003) as restricting expansion of transgenic crop cultivation in Romania, Slovakia, and the Czech Republic. The adoption rates reported reveal the fastest adoption rate of any crop technology to date, far exceeding the rates tested in an EU-Joint Research Centre study (Bock et al., 2002), where co-existence was already deemed "virtually impossible" if the threshold for adventitious presence[26] of GM in non-GM seed, grain, or food were to be set at 0.1% (the analytical detection limit). With high global adoption rates and the inability to control adventitious presence, the potential for adverse economic impacts on GM non-adopters and the potential for "precluding producer and consumer choice" are high.

New Challenges to Co-existence Posed by GM Crops

Coexistence between conventional and organic farmers with regard to chemical pesticides has been possible in most cases because these chemicals are expected to ultimately dissipate in the environment—with some notable exceptions (Rosner and Markowitz 2013). With transgenic crops, a new set of issues has come to the fore. These issues are based on (1) the ability of GM seeds to reproduce and multiply in the environment, thus amplifying their presence over time and space, and (2) the ability of GM crops to cross-pollinate with compatible non-GM crops, a process called *gene-flow*—the passing

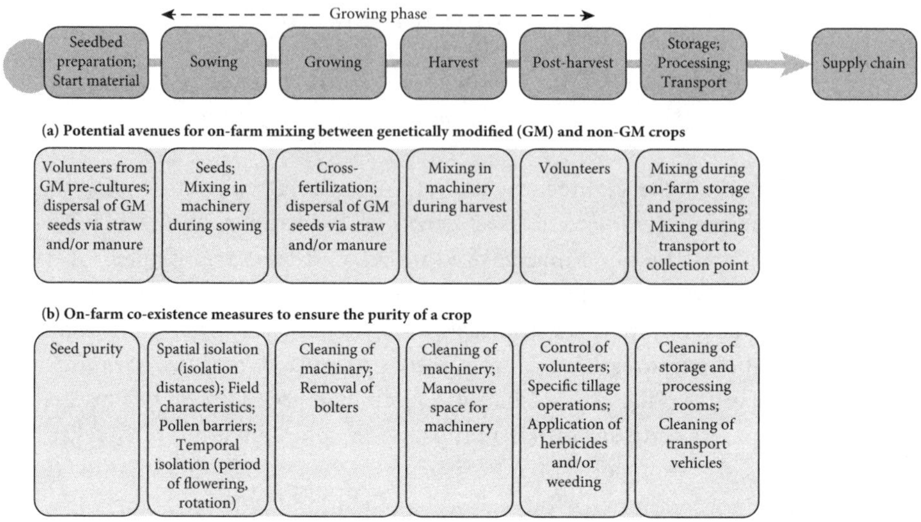

FIGURE 28.1 Potential avenues for on-farm adventitious mixing between genetically modified (GM) and non-GM seeds (a), and proposed on-farm co-existence measures aimed at ensuring the purity of a crop during the production process (b) (Devos et al. 2009).

on of transgenes to viable offspring through cross-pollination. GM seeds cannot be distinguished readily from non-GM seeds visually; molecular tests are needed to detect them. It is therefore not possible for producers to confirm the presence of GM crops on their land or monitor/manage their spread, except through costly genetic testing. Several issues arise from the reproductive properties of GM crops that present new risks to organic producers not encountered with the use of synthetic agrichemicals. For example, non-GM farmers are vulnerable to inadvertently committing a "patent violation" by having rogue transgenic offspring appearing in their fields. This can happen if non-GM plants are cross-pollinated with their GM counterparts and the resulting seed is saved and planted in the following year. This can also happen if seeds produced from a GM crop fall to the ground and are left to germinate and grow as *volunteers* in field plots planted with non-GM seed in the following seasons. Seeds produced by these volunteer GM plants could then become commingled with non-GM seed during harvest, which may result in a positive test for the presence of the GM seed in an ostensibly GM-free seed shipment. A positive test for the presence of GM seed directly affects the ability of organic (or non-GM) farmers to obtain a premium price for their seeds.

Fukuda-Parr (2007) suggested that three major areas of risk underlie the global debate over the use of transgenic crops in agriculture: (1) ecological and human health risks, (2) socio-economic risks and, (3) cultural risks of foreclosing consumer and public choice. A substantial literature covering the ecological and human health risks strongly supports the safety of the transgenic crops currently approved for commercial use (e.g., Thies and Devare 2007), with a few, highly publicized exceptions, such as Séralini et al. (2012), a study whose validity is strongly disputed in mainstream science, and one in which the findings were eventually retracted by the journal that had published it (http://

www.gmwatch.org/files/Letter_AWHayes_GES.pdf). Potential human and animal health risks are not discussed here. Rather, the focus is on potential economic risks, risks that may preclude the ability of stakeholders to exercise their freedom of choice and potential means to mitigate those risks.

Avenues by which GM seeds could become commingled with non-GM seeds on farm and possible mitigation strategies are summarized in Figure 28.1 (Devos et al. 2007).

Seed Purity

Certified organic and non-GM seed producers are most concerned with preventing cross pollination from GM crops that could compromise their ability to maintain *seed purity* and the underlying biodiversity of their seed stocks. Fruition Seeds[27] is a small company in northern New York State. They grow and select organic seeds specifically adapted for use in northern climates. I attended a "seed walk" on their farm recently that was held to commemorate their formal entry into the organic seed industry. While they introduced themselves, the farm's partners spoke about their personal reasons for undertaking this enterprise. Among their aims are the preservation of diversity in heritage seed lines and selecting and propagating seeds best adapted to the climate in the northeastern United States, which for each of them is linked to the preservation of a sense of community. Each partner expressed his/her deeply held belief in the sanctity of the overarching ecological system in which their business was embedded, their recognition of the tendency of conventional cropping systems to reduce genetic diversity by monocropping "elite" lines of various crops, and their acknowledgment of the urgent need to preserve existing seed diversity for sustaining human and ecosystem health into the future.

Like other organic seed producers, Fruition Seeds faces many challenges. High on the list is *seed purity*. How can they keep their seed pure in the face of potential gene flow from neighboring farms? They thresh and package their own seed, so they have not yet had to contend with the inadvertent presence of GM seed in the rest of the supply chain or *traceability* issues. They have made a conscious choice not to grow maize. They knew they would be vulnerable to gene flow from neighboring farms and did not want to accept the risk and the attendant testing that is now part and parcel of organic certification and product identity. In the face of ever-increasing use of transgenic crops by the majority of conventional farmers and the increasing number of crops that have now been engineered, co-existence strategies are needed to protect Fruition Seeds and other providers of certified organic seed from the possibility of gene flow and ensure they are able to maintain the genetic purity of their germplasm, which is fundamental to their economic survival.

Gene Flow to Neighboring Farms

Agriculture is an open system. As such, gene flow between compatible crop species and their wild relatives is common and, between plants capable of hybridizing, inevitable if grown within the crop's pollen dispersal range and if the two crops share the same flowering time.[28] Despite attempts at physical containment,[29] it is generally accepted that complete containment of pollen in male fertile lines is impossible. Therefore, genes will move. How far and how fast will be determined by prevailing weather patterns and conditions at the time pollen is shed, the method of pollen dispersal (for example, wind or insects), the amount of pollen produced and its longevity, the distance between the donor and compatible recipient, and whether the crop out-crosses or is self-pollinated.[30]

Gene exchange is the essence of the evolution of diversity and adaptation for living organisms, a natural and ongoing process across millennia. The literature is considerable on natural rates of gene flow between compatible plant species; however, the potential for and extent of gene flow from transgenic to non-transgenic crops or to compatible wild relatives is just beginning to be understood as are the potential ecological consequences of these processes.

Gene flow from transgenic crops to non-GM counterparts has been confirmed in (1) canola, an outcrossing, insect-pollinated species (e.g., Beckie et al. 2003; Damgaard and Kjellsson 2005); (2) traditional landraces of maize in Mexico (Quist and Chapela 2001); (3) weedy rice (red rice or shatter cane) from GM rice (Lu 2004); (4) non-GM maize (Palaudelmas et al. 2009) (5) wild relatives of cotton (Wegier et al. 2011); (6) wild, weedy relatives of sugar beet (Cureton et al. 2006; Fenart et al. 2009); and, most recently, (7) non-GM wheat in Oregon. In the latter example, authorized GM wheat was grown in test plots but was never released commercially (Ledford 2013). The source of the transgenes introgressed into formerly non-GM wheat is under investigation.[31] Only genetic testing can confirm whether or not introgression (genetic admixing) has occurred.

Humans as Vectors

Gene flow and adventitious presence are strongly affected by one vector in particular: humans. "Stealth seeds" are those seeds that find their way to the field, without the benefit of any regulatory knowledge or approval, by the actions of people (Herring 2007). The spread of unauthorized GM seed can be rapid when the advantages, as perceived by farmers, of having the transgenic seed outweigh the potential consequences of planting it. Under this scenario, it becomes impossible to know the real adoption rate of some GM crops or their spread within the farming community. It also becomes impossible to keep them segregated from sexually compatible, non-GM crops (Herring 2013). Herring (2007) describes the increasing presence of Bt cotton in Indian farmer's fields that occurred prior to government approval of widespread planting. To slow down the emergence of bollworms resistant to the Bt protein produced by the cotton plant, regulators and seed producers mandate planting 10% of the field area to a non-transgenic variety. In the "stealth seeds" scenario, no such precautionary steps were taken. Close study of this situation may help researchers better understand the potential for bollworm resistance development and the extent of any gene flow from Bt cotton into non-transgenic local varieties.

Another highly publicized example of human-facilitated gene flow was reported by Quist and Chapela (2001), who found that DNA from transgenic Bt maize had introgressed into traditional maize landraces in Mexico. They used a polymerase chain reaction protocol to detect the presence of the 35S promoter (p-35S) from the cauliflower mosaic virus (CMV), a common element in transgenic constructs. They obtained a positive PCR signal in five of the seven pooled maize seed samples they tested. Maize seed imported from the United States as food, which was not approved for planting, was the likely source of the transgenic maize detected by Quist and Chapela (2001). Their results led to a six-year de facto moratorium on the planting of transgenic crops in Mexico. The results of Quist and Chapela (2001) were challenged by the findings of Ortiz-Garcia et al. (2005). Ortiz-Garcia et al. (2005) sampled maize seeds from 870 plants in 125 fields in eighteen locations in Oaxaca, Mexico, in 2003 and 2004. They tested 153,746 seeds for the presence of the 35 S promoter of the CMV and the nopaline synthase gene from *Agrobacterium tumefaciens*; one or both of these transgenic elements are present in all commercial varieties of transgenic maize. They detected no transgenic sequences in any of the samples tested. While not contesting the report of Quist and Chapela (2001), they suggested that the negative results they obtained were likely a result of reduced GM maize imports and education of local farmers.

Unauthorized herbicide tolerant wheat was found recently in non-GM wheat fields in Oregon.[32] It has been difficult and time-consuming to determine where (which industry test plots) the rogue GM wheat came from, which is still unknown. The industry proposed that anti-GM activists (human vector) might be responsible in that seed could have been purposefully put into the field to stir up the gene flow issue. Until the source is identified, we will not know if it was a human vector or other events that led to both its presence and its discovery.

Gene flow from GM to non-GM crops can have cultural and biodiversity implications. Conventional breeding has already led to wholesale replacement of landraces with elite line monocultures, thereby reducing biodiversity. Such a result is no more, nor less, a concern with transgenic crops. Other expressed concerns are: (1) could transgenic traits, such as drought or pest resistance, lead to an expansion in the niche of transgenic crops that might lead to reduced biodiversity in the surrounding areas? (2) could the widespread adoption of stress-tolerant plants, for example, increase pressure on fragile, marginal lands, thus potentially destroying valuable natural ecosystems? (3) could transgenes confer increased plant fitness that might enhance the invasiveness of weedy species? and (4) could plants carrying transgenic traits have other, unintended effects on non-target species or trophic interactions? The answers to all these pressing questions will depend on the nature of the gene involved and on the biology and ecology of the recipient, and they may be case specific. Research is underway, but the answers are not well known as yet (Newell-McGloughlin, this volume). The need for research to enhance the potential for co-existence between GM and non-GM farmers was identified during a USDA Risk Assessment Stakeholder Workshop in 2003. Research needs that were cited included: (1) identifying factors controlling the rate of flow and fate of genes in wild populations as well as the spatial dimensions; (2) developing means to detect transgenes in wild populations; (3) understanding the consequences of gene flow, such as fitness effects, impacts on plant community structure, and variations in these for different constructs; (4) developing biological containment strategies and evaluating their stability, such as auto-suicidal mechanisms, tissue-specific excision, gene silencing, and chloroplast transformation; (5) new means of physical confinement, such as trap-crop border rows, (6) means to mitigate effects and slow the spread or limit expression of the transgenes, and (7) longer-term monitoring. Information obtained from these research efforts are needed to develop robust coexistence policies. In the EU, CoXtra was initiated to address many of these issues in efforts to develop and support a robust co-existence policy for the European Union.[33]

Adventitious Presence

A key aspect of co-existence is the ability of organic and non-GM practitioners to preserve the genetic identity of their seed and produce along the commodity chain (identity preservation). Even without hybridization (gene flow), adventitious presence of GM in non-GM seed stocks can readily occur. Adventitious presence refers to the presence of any unwanted material that becomes mixed with seeds at any point along the commodity chain (e.g., weed seeds, stones, insect parts, and the like). Farmers and food processors accept a low level of adventitious material as unavoidable. But the adventitious presence of GM seed presents serious challenges for producers and processors—especially for the organic food industry—who want to ensure they retain their price premium and that they provide GM-free foods to their customers.

On farms, GM and non-GM seed can be commingled during sowing, crop production, harvesting, post-harvest handling, and storage (Figure 28.1, Devos et al. 2007). If a GM farmer also grows non-GM crops on the land and uses the same equipment for planting and harvesting and the same storage facilities for both types of seeds, commingling of GM and non-GM seed can occur. Unintentional movement of GM seed between farms can also occur if machinery is shared and the machinery is not properly cleaned between operations. Residual seed in storage areas, vehicles used to transport seed, and seed at processing plants can all contribute to the adventitious presence of GM in non-GM seed and products. Thus, at many points along the commodity chain, organic and non-GM seed could become mixed with GM seed and lead to a positive test for the presence of the GM seed.

The extent of the problem of keeping GM seeds separate from organically grown and non-GMO seeds[34] was not fully realized until the US “Starlink” maize incident of 2000 (Schurman and Kelso 2003). “Starlink” was a maize hybrid genetically modified to be resistant to lepidopteron pests, specifically the European corn borer. It contained the *cry9C* gene, a gene that codes for an insecticidal protein that is derived from the soil bacterium, *Bacillus thuringiensis* (Bt). The resulting protein produced has insecticidal activity against the Lepidoptera. “Starlink” had been approved by the EPA for use as animal feed only.[35] The EPA and other regulatory agencies were confident that animal feed could be completely segregated from maize intended for human consumption, until evidence emerged that taco shells had tested positive for the presence of the genetic modification unique to "Starlink" maize. This highly publicized incident succeeded in pouring gas on the smoldering anti-biotech campaign in the United States, which now had proof that unapproved GM grain could be found in the US food supply. US public consciousness was finally raised to the notion that GM crops existed, that they were in a wide variety of food products on grocery store shelves, and that segregating them from non-GM and organic crops was, potentially, not possible. Thus, the US anti-biotech movement gained considerable momentum, and their activities have continued to reverberate up and down the US commodity supply chain (Shurman and Kelso 2003).

Managing Co-existence

In the EU, organic produce and products that contain greater than 0.9% transgenic material must be labeled as containing GMOs (CEC 2001), according to the EU Coexistence Policy.[36] Should this occur, organic and non-GM farmers would lose the premium price they would otherwise have received for their products. Member states vary in how liability is assigned in such cases. In 2011, a suit for damages was brought by a German beekeeper, whose honey had been rejected at the point of sale because it contained traces of GM pollen. The European Court of Justice ruled that honey containing traces of GM pollen, although unintentional, "must always be regarded as food produced from a GMO."[37]

In the United States, there is no co-existence policy, no mandatory labeling, and no clear means to assign liability if adventitious presence is detected. Instead, US organic and non-GM growers must monitor the supply chain themselves and take necessary precautions to prevent inadvertent commingling of their products with those containing GM.

In light of gene flow and adventitious presence, it is clear that GM seeds cannot be completely segregated from non-GM seeds using standard operating procedures in the field, during transport or during processing. Increasing public pressure in the EU prompted the European Commission Joint Research Centre (Bock et al. 2002) to test coexistence scenarios for three crops, namely oilseed rape (OSR), maize for animal feed, and potato for human consumption. Each of these crops varies in its potential for gene flow. Oilseed rape is an outcrossing species that is also bee pollinated, which represents the most likely of the three crops to present a gene flow problem for non-GM farmers in a given region. Maize is intermediate in gene flow risk; maize pollen is much heavier and does not travel as far so gene flow is likely to be manageable through use of appropriate isolation distances. The potato, which is propagated vegetatively, would present the lowest gene flow risk. Risk scenarios were evaluated by computer simulations and expert opinion. The scenarios considered several variations in the allowable limit for GM content in non-GM plant material: 0.1%, which represents the limit of detection for the presence of GM in plant material; 0.3%, which represents the threshold for GM presence in seed supplies; and 0.9%, the legal limit set in the EU for adventitious GM presence in a sample that automatically triggers labeling of all end products sold. The EU study objectives were to (1) "identify sources and estimate levels of adventitious presence of GM crops in non-GM crops at the farm level," (2) "identify and assess changes of farming practices that could reduce adventitious presence of GM crops in non-GM crops below policy-relevant thresholds," and (3) "estimate the costs of relevant changes in farming practices, costs of monitoring systems and cost of potential insurance systems to cover possible financial losses due to adventitious presence of GM crops in non-GM crops."[38] Models were run given either a 10% or a 50% adoption of GM crops in the study area. Results indicated that a 0.3% threshold (for seed production) and a 0.9% threshold (for food/feed labeling) might "technically be possible" but would be economically challenging. No scenario was tested that led to no adventitious presence at all.[39] For GM potato, no significant changes in farming practices would be needed and estimated costs of segregation were low, so co-existence could be a reality without additional effort. Maize occupied an intermediate position; increased costs and some changes in farming practices would be required to ensure co-existence and some types of intensive operations presented more difficulties for co-existence than others. Note that in the EU, MON810 maize is the only GM crop approved for commercial use. Ninety-four percent of all transgenic maize grown in the EU in 2013 was grown in Spain, where it represented only 31% of total maize plantings.

Based on these results and continuing public pressure, coexistence guidelines were enacted in the EU in 2006.[40] The European Coexistence Bureau (ECoB) was tasked with developing "Best practice documents for coexistence of genetically modified crops with conventional and organic farming" for maize (Czarnak-Kłos and Rodrígues-Cerezo 2010) and for "Coexistence of genetically modified maize and honey production" (Rizov and Cerezo 2013).

In the United States, the costs associated with implementing traceability landed squarely on non-GM crop producers and processors. Stakeholder response was swift. Why should those choosing not to use GM technologies have to bear the costs associated with assuring the purity of their products? One reason put forward as to why organic farmers should bear the cost of implementing co-existence measures is that they receive a price premium for their crops. This premium results from the value processors and consumers place on having access to foods grown without synthetic chemicals or GM seeds. The price premium is an acknowledgment of the additional cost and effort involved in production, particularly when they face the potential of losing their organic certification should either gene flow or adventitious presence be detected on their farms or in the produce sold. They already bear the costs of identity preservation. In truth, the real premiums and profits go to the GM seed producers, who benefit greatly from the patents they hold and associated restrictions they place on the use of GM seed (e.g., payment of technology fees, no seed saving). Hence, the cost of controlling gene flow and adventitious presence in the EU is now borne largely by those promulgating and benefiting from the use of GM seeds, which was also defensible under the "newcomer principle" (Devos et al. 2009). In the United States, the "chips fall" quite differently. The prevailing sentiment of US lawmakers is that those farmers adopting the new technologies should not be unduly burdened with regulation, as they, too, have the "right to choose." Yet, for large, public cross-contamination disputes, such as the "Starlink" corn debacle and the ProdiGene vaccine fiasco,[41] technology providers have been held accountable for damages sustained.

Co-existence Policy—the European Union versus the United States

Key issues that coexistence policies are aimed to address revolve around ensuring and preserving non-GM crop genetic identity and seed purity, traceability along the commodity chain, labeling to enable and ensure consumer choice, and determining liability and compensation in cases where economic harm has been alleged (CEC 2001).

Government regulations aimed at protecting the ability of non-GM and organic producers to produce GM-free crops, and protect them from the adventitious presence of GM crops along the commodity supply chain, are not in place in the United States currently. Threats to the organic "brand" by GM contamination are perceived as so acute that the organic industry has taken it upon itself to police its own practices and supply chains, at its own expense.[42] In fact, the industry would prefer that the government simply stay out of it.[43]

In contrast, the European Union (EU) has made significant progress in grappling with co-existence issues—not without considerable and continuing controversy (Levidow and Boschert 2008). Consumers in the EU had already been sensitized to GM crops as a "manifestation of American imperialist science" and were having none of it. Anti-biotech activists pressured the EU into a de facto moratorium on planting GM crops, even in violation of WTO rules.[44] In response, the EU spent 81 million euros on intensive, replicated research trials to examine the environmental effects of GM crops in a range of agro-ecologies (Firbank et al. 2003). These farm-scale trials found that the herbicide tolerant crops tested could inadvertently reduce populations of song birds due to the efficient control of weed species, whose seeds are a major food source for these hedge-row dwelling bird species (Chamberlain et al 2007). No other risks to wildlife or ecosystem integrity were identified. Despite these findings, public sentiment demanded a more measured approach, which has resulted in a series of policy statements and reviews that aim to enable co-existence between farmers choosing to use GM maize and organic producers. Likewise, the Swiss national research program on "Benefits and Risks of the Deliberate Release of Genetically Modified Plants" (NRP 59) studied the environmental, economic, and social impacts of GM crops in field trials over a five-year period. They concluded that plant biotechnology did not pose risks to human health or the environment and that increased use of GM crops could add significant value to the Swiss economy.[45]

Attention has since turned to how non-GM and organic production systems may be able to "peacefully" co-exist—side by side—with production of GM crops. The EU Commission (Article 43, Regulation 1829/2003) recognized there were indeed several significant barriers to co-existence. Rigorous, ongoing research in the EU is focused on resolving these barriers and has made good progress in negotiating mechanisms to enable co-existence that address each barrier.[46] Yet, this has not been without considerable "compromise" on the part of non-GM advocates. As Levidow and Boschert (2008) stated, the European "co-existence" policy sought to avoid or manage political-economic conflict over agbiotech.

In contrast, the USDA has only recently begun to consider a similar process.[47] In 2013, Secretary of Agriculture Tom Vilsak reached out to the farming community in an open letter aimed at initiating a dialogue on the issues of co-existence so that these might be addressed openly.[48] Vilsack commented that "I see my job as not dictating the answer or not even indicating what I think the answer ought to be. I see my job as putting people in the room" to find a solution among themselves.[49] In response to Secretary Vilsak's open letter, the Agriculture Committee of the US House of Representatives made it clear that they would not support such co-existence measures, especially if they increased the financial burden on those growing GM crops.[50] Clearly, the organic industry is on its own in dealing with the issue and many in this industry prefer it that way.[51]

The EU co-existence policy (European Commission 2013) addresses *ex ante* preventative measures aimed at preventing cross-pollination of GM and non-GM crops and reducing adventitious presence; and *ex post* liability actions, should *ex ante* measures fail. The Co-Xtra program was subsequently established under the European Commission's Framework Research Programme. "Conducted by 52 partners in 18 countries, the Co-Extra project developed cost-effective and reliable tools for the co-existence and traceability of GM, conventional and organic crops. The design of such tools must consider gene flow management, costs and methods of segregating GM and non-GM products, GMO sampling and detection, and liability and compensation."[52]

MNCs Reject GM in Some Product Lines

With regard to consumer sentiment, activism has led several multinational corporations (MNCs) to reject the use of GM ingredients in their products, particularly those bound for European markets.[53] Actions taken by MNCs have profound effects on the commodity supply chain. For example, McDonald's is the world's largest purchaser of potatoes, among other crops. Their quest for global uniformity in products sold has led to massive monocultures of nearly genetically identical non-GM potatoes. Threats to biodiversity, soil health, and water quality would be just as acute in these cropping systems as those that include GM crops. Neither of these systems is well buffered from unanticipated shocks, such as drought, disease, or pestilence. Thus vulnerability is high, as seen with corn crops in the US Midwest that experienced severe drought in 2010–2012. The threat to biodiversity posed by GM crops is far more nuanced. The US regulatory system examines each successful transgenic "event"[54] in terms of biosafety. The approved "event" is then hybridized with a wide variety of genotypes that have already been selected for their performance in the range of conditions in which the seeds will be sown, and this germplasm represents hundreds of varieties. In non-GM conventional agriculture catering to MNCs, the genetic diversity is, by comparison, significantly reduced. The aim is uniformity, which is achieved largely by limiting genetic diversity. In this light, the argument that rejection of GM crops by some multinationals protects biodiversity is simply not valid.

Blocking/Managing Gene Flow and Adventitious Presence

There are two major approaches to managing gene flow: use of spatial and/or temporal separation and genetic engineering. The first approach involves preventing cross-pollination by use of spatial or temporal isolation in the field. Spatial isolation is achieved through the use of specific isolation distances and use of buffer zones where trap crops are planted to act as a pollen barrier. Temporal isolation takes advantage of differences in flowering time between different crop cultivars (Devos et al. 2009). Both approaches require that neighbors meet and agree on how to contain the GM crop to enable non-GM producers to also thrive. Other important means to prevent adventitious presence is to thoroughly clean all equipment that might have been used for processing GM seeds, including planting and harvesting equipment, vehicles used to transport seeds, seed storage facilities, and any location where commingling could occur in processing plants that produce both GM and non-GM products.

The second and more controversial approaches to restricting gene flow employ genetic engineering to biologically "contain" the transgenes by (1) reducing or eliminating pollen shed; (2) eliminating transgene presence and/or expression in pollen by transforming organelles (i.e., plastids in plants) whose DNA is not contained in pollen, thus preventing the transfer of transgenes during pollination (transplastomic plants); (3) use of sterile male lines (cytoplasmic male sterility) and (4) cross-incompatibility. Publicly funded research organizations in the United States have undertaken work using these classic approaches, along with genetic engineering approaches to "biocontainment" to reduce the potential for gene flow from GM to non-GM crops. The latter are referred to as genetic use restriction technologies (GURT), the most notorious of which has been dubbed the "terminator" technology by anti-GM activists. While a working model was developed jointly by Delta Pine Land and the USDA and purchased subsequently by Monsanto Corporation, the technology was never proven in field trials or commercialized. Despite this, activists continue to rail against a "terminator" technology that does not exist outside the laboratory.

The Transcontainer Project

The Transcontainer Project (2002–2006), funded by the European Commission, supported nine research institutions in eight European countries, along with several companies and one government agency. The aim of the project was to develop biological containment strategies for GM crops. None of the strategies developed was to be tested in the field, only in laboratories and greenhouses. The purpose of the project was ostensibly to promote co-existence of GM and non-GM agriculture in Europe by finding biological means to decrease the potential for gene flow from GM crops and thus simplify existing rules for coexistence. Part of the project was to assess the potential economic impact and enhance consumer understanding and acceptance of the biocontainment approach. The research undertaken focused on chloroplast transformation in sugar beet and oilseed rape, controlling flowering in sugar beet and forage crops, and controlling plant fertility in oilseed rape, forage crops, tomato, and eggplant. Chloroplasts, contained in plant cells, have their own DNA that can potentially be transformed via genetic engineering. An advantage of targeting chloroplasts for transformation is that they are not contained in pollen and thus would not be transferred to a cross-pollinated plant, in essence, biologically "containing" the GM trait. Work on controlling flowering focused on crops that are grown for their vegetative parts. By inhibiting flowering, the spread of pollen could be contained. The Transcontainer Project used two approaches to repress flowering, one based on the CETS gene family and one based on MADS-box genes. Most projects that focused on fertility control concentrated on male sterility-based transgene containment systems; but, one project that aimed to develop a transgene containment system in oilseed rape was based on "recoverable block of function" (RBF). This latter approach is quite reminiscent of what the anti-biotech movement had dubbed the "terminator." Similar to the "terminator," the RBF would be a genetic use restriction technology (GURT) that would function by blocking germination of GM seeds. The RBF would have one gene construct that would cause the seed to fail to germinate and another that would allow recovery of germination by using an environmental or chemical trigger. This approach would not actually address the gene flow issue because the pollen would still be fertile and could still cross with non-GM compatible plants on neighboring properties. Farmers using the RBF would have to "restore fertility" of the seeds each year by activating the patented engineered trait. The claim was that this system would facilitate co-existence by limiting the potential spread of transgenes to wild relatives—any seed produced in such a cross-pollination event would not germinate, it would be essentially sterile. This technology was subsequently dubbed "Zombie Technology" by anti-biotech activists.

Part of the Transcontainer Project involved a community consultation and communication program, in which project personnel interviewed anti-GM activists, GM farmers, organic farmers, scientists, lobbyists, and regulators. The attitudes of each group toward the Transcontainer Project and GM crops in general were explored in these interviews (AGRAPEN 2009). Anti-GM activists considered genetic engineering to be a "misappropriation of nature" and that money invested in biotech instead of in sustainable agricultural solutions was "obscene." Organic farmers expressed their commitment to maintaining healthy soil, air, water, and food, and they did not think it necessary to use GM technologies, which they felt were inconsistent with sustainability. Scientists in general thought their work was making an important contribution to feeding an ever-growing world population as did GM farmers. GM farmers who had adopted Bt maize reported that they could reliably control the European corn borer, leading to increased yield with significantly less insecticide use and thus better environmental outcomes.

Pharming: Emergent Issues of Co-existence

In 2002, APHIS approved the field testing of pharmaceutical-producing plants at thirty-four sites comprising 130 acres; most test sites were less than five acres. In 2003, APHIS changed the regulations to improve confinement of these transgenic crops, much in keeping with the EU co-existence policy for GM maize. Changes made included increasing the perimeter fallow zone from 25 to 50 feet to ensure that test plants were not inadvertently commingled with those to be used for food or feed; restricting planting of food or feed crops in the following season to reduce the possibility of volunteer plants being inadvertently harvested with the following crop; and requiring the use of dedicated planting and harvesting machinery and storage facilities for the regulated crop. Additional conditions for field testing maize engineered to produce pharmaceuticals were established, which included an isolation distance of one mile for open-pollinated maize and a half-mile for controlled pollination field tests. This increased stringency stemmed from the failure of ProdiGene to correctly follow existing regulations when they field tested maize designed to produce a pig vaccine. In one trial, nearby crops may have been pollinated by the vaccine-producing transgenic crop, leading to an order for complete destruction of nearby crops and payment by the firms for all damages to local farmers.[55] Public and regulatory concern over potential environmental consequences of plant-made pharmaceuticals or plant-made industrial proteins and the current inability to contain the flow of transgenes in field situations may prevent biotechnology firms from further pursuing deregulation of these crops. The very real concern of gene-flow requires that these crops be tightly contained and monitored and thus not be widely disseminated to farmers. Since gene flow from crops to wild populations is not only likely but also inevitable, possible risks and consequences require considerably more research.

Conclusions

Perversely, the rise of the global anti-GM movement has taken considerable heat off the chemical industries with regard to the use and safety of pesticides and other synthetic inputs that are now highly regulated. Many activists now focus their energy on GM crops, putting pesticides and their associated, proven health and environmental hazards somewhat on the back burner. Many pesticides are highly toxic and do kill thousands of people annually, primarily in poor countries. Some chemicals used to control pests are deadly neurotoxins and/or carcinogens, whereas the vast majority of published research indicates that the transgenic crops currently commercialized are neither toxic nor carcinogenic. Indeed, growing evidence suggests that the use of GM crops may lead to improvements in environmental health, especially where decreases in insecticide use have been documented.

The GM crop debate has also affected relationships between scientists in sometimes pitting them against each other (Waltz 2009). As a result, the independence of non-industry researchers has come into question. Every report published that has suggested a potential negative impact of GM crops is subject to intense scrutiny and often receives a scathing critique—in essence, protecting the position of the MNCs and undermining public trust in science.

Two key arguments against the use of GM crops are corporate control of the food supply and patents on particular gene constructs, termed "patents on life." Two GM crops that do not conform to these characterizations are the virus-resistant papaya and golden rice.

The papaya industry in Hawaii was nearly devastated by the papaya ring spot virus (PRSV), thought to have been introduced to the Hawaiian Islands in the 1930s. Carol and Dennis Gonsalves developed a transgenic papaya resistant to PRSV at Cornell University that enabled the resurrection of the Hawaiian papaya industry.[56] The virus-resistant papaya was developed by a public institution and is openly available for use by farmers, who can replant if they desire; nevertheless, this technology has been as vociferously attacked and criticized as those developed by multinational companies. A clear advantage of the use of the PRSV-resistant papaya is that it has enabled organic papaya to once again be grown in Hawaii. The virus-resistant papaya is planted as a border "trap" crop completely surrounding non-transgenic papaya trees, thus protecting them from possible attack by aphids, which are the vector by which the virus is spread from tree to tree. The VR-papaya literally saved the Hawaiian papaya industry and has enabled organic papaya production rather than threatened it. Golden rice, which is able to make a substantial contribution to alleviating vitamin A deficiency and is also available to poor farmers without technology fees if farm profits do not exceed USD$10,000, is likewise vilified. Proponents characterize the fight against use of golden rice as a "crime against humanity."

Opposition often rests on individual beliefs, not on science-based evidence. And to support particular beliefs, scientific evidence is purposefully misconstrued or outright lies are perpetrated, as in the case of the "terminator" technology. This technology has never been commercialized and is not in use anywhere in the world. Despite this verifiable fact, even well-informed individuals believe it is being used and continue to perpetuate the lie. In the face of this type of resistance and misinformation, there will never be sufficient evidence of "no harm" that will convince detractors.

So why do those in the anti-GM movement appear so "uncompromising" and vitriolic? It may be that the deck, especially in the United States, appears stacked against them; and many perceive no avenue by which their freedom of choice and economic security can be assured. The US regulatory system clearly embraces the technocentric, agri-industrial paradigm of production and does not seem disposed to develop robust coexistence measures to protect organic and non-GM producers from either the gene flow or the adventitious presence that potentially endangers their industries. Yet, the US organic industry prefers the government stay out of it and allow the third-party system implemented by the Non-GMO Project to work.[57]

Many of the issues presented here will only magnify with many of the GM products now in the pipeline, including plants that produce pharmaceuticals or industrial products and transgenic animals and fish. Given our obvious inability to prevent either gene flow or adventitious presence in the commodity supply chain, we might reconsider—as a global society—whether crops that produce products with mammalian activity should be used in open agricultural systems. While currently commercialized GM crops do not present specific biosafety hazards, each new venture that delves deeper into the genetic engineering of new traits will need rigorous oversight, backed by solid research. How this research will affect farming is, of course, a question of politics, not of science.

Notes

1. http://www.libertyindia.org/events/bullshit_award_28august2002.htm. Accessed 7/7/14.
2. *Bacillus thuringiensis* (Bt) is a soil bacterium that produces an insecticidal protein specific to certain classes of insects; some target the Lepidoptera, some target the Coleoptera, and others target the Diptera. The gene has been introduced into the genome of several commodity crops, herein also called GM or transgenic crops.
3. http://en.wikipedia.org/wiki/Gene_flow. Accessed 7/7/14.
4. Genes that are transferred from one species to another by genetic engineering.
5. Although organic farmers use *natural* products, this does not imply they are "safe." Many of these products can also be highly toxic to humans and wildlife, yet they are not as tightly regulated as synthetic pesticides.
6. http://www.nal.usda.gov/afsic/pubs/organicstats.shtml. Accessed 7/7/14.
7. http://afsic.nal.usda.gov/. Accessed 7/7/14.
8. http://www.ams.usda.gov/AMSv1.0/getfile?dDocName=STELPRDC5096493&acct=nopgeninfo.

9. For a history of the development of industrial nitrogen fixation, see Thomas Hagar, *The Alchemy of Air* (New York: Harmony Books, 2008).
10. With chapters first appearing in magazine articles in 1962.
11. http://www.rachelcarsoncouncil.org/index.php?page=pesticides-chemicals-alternatives provides a current list of harmful chemicals used in agriculture and possible alternatives.
12. http://en.wikipedia.org/wiki/Rachel_Carson#CITEREFLear1997.
13. Ibid.
14. FIFRA, 1972.
15. http://www.nal.usda.gov/afsic/pubs/ofp/ofp.shtml.
16. Co-existence refers to the ability of farmers to make an informed choice between alternative farming systems.
17. http://www.ams.usda.gov/AMSv1.0/nop.
18. http://www.nongmoproject.org/.
19. NOP §205.202 http://www.ecfr.gov/cgi-bin/text-idx?SID=dc448c85b26f64c7f169745b3f2d0955&node=7:3.1.1.9.32.3.354.3&rgn=div8.
20. http://en.wikipedia.org/wiki/Dead_zone_%28ecology%29.
21. http://epa.gov/ncct/toxrefdb/.
22. http://www.ibtimes.co.uk/articles/334535/20120428/organic-farming-alone-t-feed-world-researchers.htm.
23. http://www.motherjones.com/tom-philpott/2011/11/organic-ag-more-productive.
24. http://www.nass.usda.gov/Newsroom/2010/02_03_2010.asp.
25. James, Clive. ISAAA, 2013 http://www.isaaa.org/resources/publications/briefs/46/default.asp.
26. The unintentional and incidental commingling of trace amounts of one type of seed, grain, or food product with another.
27. www.fruitionseeds.com.
28. John Innes Center http://www.jic.ac.uk/corporate/about/publications/gm-debate/gene-flow.htm.
29. http://www.fas.org/biosecurity/education/dualuse-agriculture/2.-agricultural-biotechnology/prodigene-incident.html.
30. John Innes Center http://www.jic.ac.uk/corporate/about/publications/gm-debate/gene-flow.htm.
31. http://www.npr.org/blogs/thesalt/2013/05/30/187103955/gmo-wheat-found-in-oregon-field-howd-it-get-there.
32. http://www.npr.org/blogs/thesalt/2013/05/30/187103955/gmo-wheat-found-in-oregon-field-howd-it-get-there.
33. http://www.coextra.eu/research_themes/.
34. Non-GMO refers to seeds, farms, and farmers that do not use transgenic seeds on their farms, but otherwise farm conventionally. See the Non-GMO Project http://www.nongmoproject.org/.
35. http://www.fas.org/biosecurity/education/dualuse-agriculture/2.-agricultural-biotechnology/starlink-corn.html.
36. http://ecob.jrc.ec.europa.eu/documents/COM_2006_104final.pdf.
37. www.euractiv.com/cap/court-ruling-challenges-eu-laws-news-507332.
38. Bock et al. 2002. "Scenarios for Coexistence of Genetically Modified, Conventional and Organic Crops in European Agriculture."
39. Ibid.

40. http://ecob.jrc.ec.europa.eu/documents/COM_2006_104final.pdf.
41. http://www.fas.org/biosecurity/education/dualuse-agriculture/2.-agricultural-biotechnology/prodigene-incident.html.
42. http://www.nongmoproject.org/.
43. http://www.non-gmoreport.com/articles/jan07/organic_gm_coexistence.php.
44. http://www.activistpost.com/2014/02/19-eu-states-reject-gmo-corn-council.html.
45. http://www.gmo-safety.eu/news/1424.plant-biotechnology-swiss.html.
46. http://www.coextra.eu/.
47. http://www.usda.gov/documents/ac21_report-enhancing-coexistence.pdf.
48. http://www.usda.gov/wps/portal/usda/usdahome?contentid=2010/12/0674.xml.
49. http://www.agri-pulse.com/Vilsack_on_Organic_and_GMOs_04062011H.asp.
50. Vilsack's GMO "Co-Existence" Plan Opposed by Lawmakers, 2011. http://www.agweb.com/article/vilsacks_gmo_co-existence_plan_opposed_by_lawmakers/.
51. Quote from the non-GMO project newsletter.
52. http://www.coextra.eu/introduction/.
53. http://www.progress.org/gene45.htm. "Major U.S. Companies Drop Genetically Engineered Foods in Europe, Citing Consumer Fears Survey Says Kellogg, Coke, Pepsi, Kraft, Heinz, Others Add to Growing List of Companies Going GE-Free—But Not in U.S."
54. A successful "event" is the transformation of the plant genome by the "construct" carrying the GM trait. The gene coding for the trait of interest is accompanied by a promoter gene, other gene markers for selection, and identification and sequences needed for a successful transformation.
55. http://www.fas.org/biosecurity/education/dualuse-agriculture/2.-agricultural-biotechnology/prodigene-incident.html.
56. http://www.apsnet.org/publications/apsnetfeatures/Pages/PapayaHawaiianRainbow.aspx.
57. http://www.nongmoproject.org/.

References

AGRAPEN. 2009. *The Transcontainer Project*. Video ©AGRAPEN. http://www.youtube.com/user/TransContainer

Beckie, H. J., S. I. Warwick, H. Nair, and G. Seguin-Swartz. 2003. "Gene Flow in Commercial Fields of Herbicide-Resistant Canola (*Brassica napus*)." *Ecological Applications* 13:1276–1294.

Bock, A.-K., K. Lheureux, M. Libeau-Dulos, H. Nilsagård, and E. Rodriguez-Cerezo. 2002. "Scenarios for co-existence of genetically modified, conventional and organic crops in European agriculture." IPTS-JRC Report EUR 20394EN ftp://ftp.jrc.es/pub/EURdoc/eur20394en.pdf

Brookes, G., and P. Barfoot. 2010. "Global Impact of Biotech Crops: Environmental Effects, 1996-2008." *AgBioForum* 13:76-94.

Central European Convention (CEC). 2003. *Commission Recommendation of 23 July on Guidelines for the Development of National Strategies and Best Practices to Ensure Coexistence of GM Crops with Conventional and Organic Farming*. Orahovica, Croatia: Central European Convention.

Chamberlain, D., S. N. Freeman, and J. A. Vickery. 2007. "The Effects of GMHT Crops on Bird Abundance in Arable Fields in the UK." *Agriculture, Ecosystems & Environment* 118:350–356.

Commission of the European Communities (CEC). 2001. *Commission of the European Communities, Proposal for a Regulation concerning the Traceability and Labelling of GMOs and Traceability of Food and Feed Produced from GMOs*. COM (2001) 1821 final. Brussels: Commission of the European Communities.

Cureton, A. N., H. J. Newbury, A. F. Raybould, and B. V. Ford-Lloyd. 2006. “Genetic Structure and Gene Flow in Wild Beet Populations: The Potential Influence of Habitat on Transgene Spread and Risk Assessment.” *Journal of Applied Ecology* 43:1203–1212.

Czarnak-Kłos, M., and E. Rodrígues-Cerezo. 2010. *Best Practice Documents for Coexistence of Genetically Modified Crops with Conventional and Organic Farming. Booklet 1. Maize Crop Production*. EUR 24509 EN. European Coexistence Bureau (ECoB), European Commission Joint Research Centre, Institute for Prospective Technological Studies, Spain. http://ecob.jrc.ec.europa.eu/documents/Maize.pdf. Accessed 7/7/2014.

Damgaard, C., and G. Kjellsson. 2005. “Gene Flow of Oilseed Rape (Brassica napus) According to Isolation Distance and Buffer Zone.” *Agriculture, Ecosystems and Environment* 108:291–301.

Devos, Y., M. Demont, K. Dillen, D. Reheul, M. Kaiser, and O. Sanvido. 2009. “Coexistence of Genetically Modified (GM) and Non-GM Crops in the European Union: A Review.” *Agronomy for Sustainable Development* 29:11–30.

European Coexistence Bureau (ECoB). 2010. *Best Practice Documents: Maize Crop Production*. Scientific and Technical Report No. 24509. Luxembourg: Publication Office of the European Union.

European Commission, Agricultural and Rural Development. 2013. *Coexistence of Genetically Modified Crops with Conventional and Organic Agriculture* [updated 2013 July]. Brussels. Available from http://ec.europa.eu/agriculture/gmo/coexistence/index_en.htm [Accessed 26 July, 2014].

Fenart, S., F. Austerlitz, J. Cuguen, and J.-F. Arnaud. 2009. “Long Distance Pollen-Mediated Gene Flow at a Landscape Level: The Weed Beet as a Case Study.” *Molecular Ecology* 16:3801–3813.

Firbank, L. G., M. S. Heard, I. P. Woiwod, C. Hawes, A. J. Haughton, G. T. Champion, R. J. Scott, M. O. Hill, A. M. Dewar, G. R. Squire, M. J. May, D. R. Brooks, D. A. Bohan, R. E. Daniels, J. L. Osborne, D. B. Roy, H. I. J. Black, P. Rothery, and J. N. Perry. 2003. “An Introduction to the Farm-Scale Evaluations of Genetically Modified Herbicide Tolerant Crops.” *Journal of Applied Ecology* 40:2–16.

Goulson, D. 2013. “An Overview of the Environmental Risks Posed by Neonicotinoid Insecticides.” *Journal of Applied Ecology* 50:977–987.

Hagar, T. *The Alchemy of Air. 2008*. New York: Harmony Books.

Hauter, W. 2012. *Foodopoly*. New York: The New Press.

Hayes, T. B. 2005. “Welcome to the Revolution-Integrative Biology and Assessing the Impact of Endocrine Disruptors on Environmental and Public Health.” *Integrative and Comparative Biology* 45:321–329.

Herring, R. J. 2007. “Stealth Seeds: Biosafety, Bioproperty, Biopolitics.” *Journal of Development Studies* 43 (1): 130–157.

Herring, R. J. 2013. “Re-constructing Facts in Bt Cotton.” *Economic and Political Weekly* 48 (33): 63–66.

Holmquist, P., and S. Khardalian. 2005. *Bullshit: A Film*. HB PeÅ Holmquist Film, New York: Cinema Guild, ©2006.

James, C. 2013. *Global Status of Commercialized Biotech/GM Crops: 2013*. ISAAA Brief No. 46. Ithaca, NY: International Service for the Acquisition of Agric-Biotech Applications.

Accessed May 31, 2014. http://www.isaaa.org/resources.publications/briefs/46/default.asp

Krebs, A. V. 1992. *The Corporate Reapers: The Book of Agribusiness*. Washington, DC: Essential Books.

Ledford, H. 2013. "Hunt for Mystery GM Wheat Hots Up." *Nature* 499:262–263. Accessed 7/7/14. http://www.nature.com/news/hunt-for-mystery-gm-wheat-hots-up-1.13392

Levidow, L., and K. Boschert. 2008. "Coexistence or Contradiction? GM Crops versus Alternative Agricultures in Europe." *Geoforum* 39:174–190.

Lu, B.-R. 2004. "Gene Flow from Cultivated Rice: Ecological Consequences." Accessed 7/7/14. http://www.isb.vt.edu/articles/may0402.htm

Lytle, M. 2007. *The Gentle Subversive: Rachel Carson, Silent Spring and the Rise of the Environmental Movement*. Oxford: Oxford University Press.

Mills, C. W. 1959 [1976]. *The Sociological Imagination*, p. 176. Oxford University Press, NY.

Ortiz-García, S., E. Ezcurra, B. Schoel, F. Acevedo, J. Soberón, and A. A. Snow. 2005. "Absence of Detectable Transgenes in Local Landraces of Maize in Oaxaca, Mexico (2003–2004)." *Proceedings of the National Academy of Sciences, USA*, 102:12338–12343.

Palaudelmàs, M., G. Peñas, E. Melé, J. Serra, J. Salvia, M. Pla, A. Nadal, and J. Messeguer. 2009. "Effect of Volunteers on Maize Gene Flow." *Transgenic Research* 18:583–594.

Quist, D., and I. H. Chapela. 2001. "Transgenic DNA Introgressed into Traditional Maize Landraces in Oaxaca, Mexico." *Nature* 414:541–543.

Rizov, I., and E. Rodríguez-Cerezo. 2013. *Best Practice Documents for Coexistence of Genetically Modified Crops with Conventional and Organic Farming. Booklet 3. Coexistence of GM Maize and Honey Production.* European Coexistence Bureau (JRC IPTS Report EUR 26041 EN). Seville, Spain: European Commission, JRC, IPTS.

Rosner, D., and G. Markowitz. 2013. "Persistent Pollutants: A Brief History of the Discovery of the Widespread Toxicity of Chlorinated Hydrocarbons." *Environmental Research* 120:126–133.

Rosset, P. M., and M. A. Altieri. 1997. "Agroecology versus Input Substitution: A Fundamental Contradiction of Sustainable Agriculture." *Society & Natural Resources: An International Journal* 10(3):283-295.

Schurman, R. A., and D. D. Kelso. 2003. *Engineering Trouble: Biotechnology and Its Discontents*. Berkeley: University of California Press.

Schurman, R. A., and W. A. Munro. 2010. *Fighting for the Future of Food: Activists versus Agribusiness in the Struggle over Biotechnology*. Minneapolis: University of Minnesota Press.

Séralini, G.-E., E. Clair, R. Mesnage, S. Gress, N. Defarge, M. Malatesta, D. Hennequin, and J. Spiroux de Vendômois. 2012. "Long-Term Toxicity of a Roundup Herbicide and a Roundup-Tolerant Genetically Modified Maize." *Food and Chemical Toxicology* 50:4221–4231.

Thies, J. E., and M. H. Devare. 2007. "An Ecological Assessment of Transgenic Crops." In *Transgenics and the Poor: Biotechnology in Development Studies*, edited by R. Herring, 97–129. New York: Routledge.

Waltz, E. 2009. "Battlefield." *Nature* 461:27–32.

Wegier, A., A. Piñeyro-Nelson, J. Alarcón, A. Gálvez-Mariscal, E. R. Álvarez-Buylla, and D. Piñero. 2011. "Recent Long-distance Transgene Flow into Wild Populations Conforms to Historical Patterns of Gene Flow in Cotton (Gossypium hirsutum) at its Centre of Origin." *Molecular Ecology* 20:4182–4194.

PART V

GLOBAL MEETS LOCAL: CONTESTATIONS, MOVEMENTS, AND EXPERTISE

CHAPTER 29

GLOBAL MOVEMENTS FOR FOOD JUSTICE

M. JAHI CHAPPELL

Introduction

The surge in interest in food systems of the past decades, and the concurrent rise of food movements, should come as no surprise given recent trends in the global food system.[1] A number of factors have contributed to the rise of these movements, including the following:

- food system consolidation
- diminishing proportions of the food dollar arriving in farmers' hands
- neoliberalization of the food system and withdrawal of state support for agriculture
- persistent and widespread hunger
- 25–50 percent of produced food ending up as waste
- homogenization of diets
- the continuing plight of the world's hungry and poor—with smallholder farmers ironically making up over half of the hungry in the world[2]

These factors offer more than sufficient grounds for the rise of food movements contesting the direction and nature of these trends.

These movements are fighting for the reinsertion of "defensible values" into the food system; namely, the reprioritization of human rights, aesthetics, sustainability, and equity. They claim that the neoliberal aspirations of minimal state involvement, nominally free markets, and the extension of private property regimes have led to market concentration and excessively large and powerful corporations. Further, this has come at the cost of increasing inequality and the continued neglect of less powerful populations and important nonmarket values (Holt-Giménez et al. 2009; Gold, this volume).

For example, the Slow Food movement emphasizes the importance of the aesthetic and cultural quality of food, affirming the right of all people to have nutritional, enjoyable, and sustainable food. Slow Food also emphasizes artisanal food production, although movement members and leadership have increasingly recognized the limits of this emphasis with regards to issues of equity and justice (Viertel 2011). The International Federation of Organic Agriculture Movements (IFOAM) is another prominent actor, largely concerned with supporting the evolution of national and international organic food markets (Geier 2007; Larsson,this volume). The fair trade movement seeks to provide producers with a greater portion of the "consumer dollar" spent on end products.[3] This represents an attempt to build alternatives to current trade regimes by explicitly integrating values of equity and fairness into the market—values that free markets are admittedly ill equipped to provide (Daly 2007; Gold, this volume).

In contrast to the above moments, which hinge on the direct involvement of local or global economic elites as supposedly ethical consumers, the Farmer to Farmer movement (Movimiento Campesino a Campesino, or MCAC) is organized by and focused on small, mostly poor farmers in Latin America. MCAC has existed for over thirty years and claims to have several hundred thousand farmer-promoters: small farmers trained in an empowerment-based pedagogy who travel to other villages and other countries to directly train other small farmers. Using this peer-to-peer knowledge network, MCAC seeks to empower promoters and farmers, and to build autonomy and sustainable livelihoods based on agroecological methods and a culture of experimentation (Holt-Giménez 2006).

Beyond these prominent, organized transnational actors, recent years have seen numerous other examples of food movements, including national and subnational movements for agrarian reform (Herring 2003; Ondetti 2008), and government agri-environment schemes seeking to integrate the cultural, environmental, and economic functions of agriculture (i.e., multifunctional agriculture: Buttel 2007; Otte et al. 2007). There has also been growing public and government interest in community-supported agriculture (CSA), farmers' markets, and urban agriculture (USDA 2006, Brown and Miller 2008, Mogk et al. 2012). This period has also seen the spread and innovation of food policy councils (Harper et al. 2009; Maluf 2010), as well as acclaimed documentaries and books challenging the values existing (or lacking) in the current food system (e.g., *The Omnivore's Dilemma*, by Michael Pollan; *Fast Food Nation*, by Eric Schlosser; *Stuffed and Starved*, by Raj Patel; *Food, Inc.*, by Karl Weber; *Le Monde selon Monsanto*, by Marie-Monique Robin; and *King Corn*, by Lee Roy Stewart).

Analyzing these phenomena brings into question the degree to which any of them may be considered "transnational movements." Tarrow (1998), for example, developed a typology of four types of transnational collective action: cross-border diffusion, political exchange, transnational issue networks, and true transnational social movements (p. 237).[4] Under his typology, most of the above examples would fail to meet the criteria for transnational social movements *per se*. True transnational social movements are defined as exhibiting transnational interactions sustained over time, and a continuous, high degree of integration between transnational actors and indigenous social networks.

Using these criteria, the only two true transnational social movements discussed thus far would be Fair Trade and MCAC. However, there is one more important movement meeting these criteria that has yet to be mentioned: *La Vía Campesina* (LVC), or the International Peasant Farmers' movement.

Although Fair Trade, MCAC and LVC are all worthy of scholarly consideration, LVC is unique in the breadth of its goals and reach. Neither MCAC, which extends through Central America, Mexico, and the Caribbean, nor Fair Trade, with member farmers in an estimated sixty countries, can match the sixty-nine countries with LVC member organizations. Further, MCAC has focused on farmer-to-farmer education and has no infrastructure for lobbying or mobilization, and the values addressed by Fair Trade are limited by its focus on consumer sovereignty (Fridell 2007, Johnson and MacKendrick, this volume). LVC's combination of sustained transnational interactions and mobilization, an ambitious agenda, and global reach make it unique even among true transnational food movements. For these and other reasons, this piece focuses on LVC. To a large extent, LVC may be seen as an axis around which other contemporary movements for defensible values in food systems turn. It has shaped debate and conceptual terrains at the international level (e.g., within the FAO, World Bank, and WTO) with varying levels of success (Desmarais 2007; Borras 2008). "Its member organisations have even helped topple national governments... or defended them," (Martínez-Torres and Rosset 2010, 151).

In this chapter, I will examine La Vía Campesina as a social movement and its advocacy of "defensible values." Specifically, I will describe its fight for *normatively defensible values*—for a food system reflecting ideals of ethics and justice—and its quest to build and maintain *defensible lifespaces* for small farmers in terms of socioeconomic, ecological, and political autonomy. Lastly, I will examine how their aims and tactics align with current scholarship on the issues of sustainability and autonomy.

Defining La Vía Campesina and Defensible Values

La Vía Campesina and the Global Peasantry

Around 40 percent of the world population directly depends on agriculture for livelihood. Further, nearly 90 percent of these people work on small farms (i.e., under two hectares in size), occupying around 60 percent of the world's arable land (IAASTD 2009, 8). Thus, "smallholder farming... remains the most common form of organization in agriculture, even in industrial countries" (World Bank 2007, 91).

In the nearly twenty years since its inception, LVC has worked consciously to adopt and promote an umbrella "peasant identity" that includes most of these estimated 404 million small farms, intentionally conflating family farmers, subsistence farmers, sharecroppers, agricultural wage laborers, and the landless (Naranjo 2012, 232). They have sought to "[Build] Unity within Diversity" through direct, open discussion and deliberation on "issues of gender, race, class, culture, and North/South relations" (Desmarais 2007, 27). Founded in 1993 by farm leaders from every continent but Australia, LVC is currently composed of 148 peasant organizations in sixty-nine countries (Desmarais 2007; La Vía Campesina 2008). Through its member organizations, LVC claims to represent the interests of at least 200 million farmers and has been argued to be the largest, and one of the most important, social movements in the world (Chomsky 2003; Hardt and Negri 2004; Perfecto et al. 2009). However, as Rosset and Martínez-Torres (2005) argue, social movements' constituents "often cannot be precisely identified... Movement participants may never recognize themselves as such" (4). Peasants, in their own day-to-day struggles within their own communities or countries, may not recognize these struggles as part of a transnational social movement—"yet that does not mean that they are not part of it" (4).

A key to understanding LVC, "the international peasants' movement," is understanding how it defines "peasant." In English, "peasant" tends to connote not just low social status but often backwardness and a lack of sophistication. In Spanish, however, the roughly equivalent word *campesino* does not necessarily carry the same negative overtones. For LVC and their allies, campesinos, or peasants, are characterized most by what they *do*, and the context they do it in:

> A peasant is a man or woman of the land, who has a direct and special relationship with the land and nature through the production of food and/or other agricultural products. Peasants work the land themselves, rely above all on family labour and other small-scale forms of organizing labour. Peasants are traditionally embedded in their local communities and they take care of local landscapes and of agro-ecological systems. The term peasant can apply to any person engaged in agriculture, cattle?raising, pastoralism, handicrafts?related to agriculture or a related occupation in a rural area. This includes Indigenous people working on the land. The term peasant also applies to landless [rural persons].
>
> (La Vía Campesina 2009, 6–7)

Van der Ploeg (2008) further qualifies that for peasants, "[p]roduction is oriented toward the market as well as toward the reproduction of the farm unit and the family," (1). These definitions bridge the artificially rigid separation some scholars have placed between peasants, who farm for their own subsistence, and entrepreneurial farmers, who farm for profit: small-scale producers around the world have long engaged in varying degrees of cash cropping and long-distance trade alongside local provisioning (Edelman 2005; van der Ploeg 2008).[5] This is not to say that notable wealth and class disparities do not exist within the class of peasant farmers (Naranjo 2012, 232–235). But condensing all of these groups into the term "peasant" allows LVC to include millions of farmers in the "Minority World" (the industrialized countries/Global North; see Alam 2008), who may be "far more peasant than most of us know or want to admit" (van der Ploeg 2008, xiv), and many of whom are members of LVC.[6]

How can LVC include *all* of these people, in their economic, cultural, and political variation, under the rubric of "peasant"? Clearly, as a movement, LVC cannot genuinely claim to have sustained integration between its international networks and the social networks of every family farmer, subsistence farmer, sharecropper, agricultural laborer, and landless person in the world (i.e., meet both of Tarrow's requirements for a true transnational movement). An inclusive view of membership, such as Rosset and Martínez-Torres's statement that peasants may be part of the international peasants' movement without even recognizing it, rather refers to LVC's development of what Hardt and Negri (2004, 66) call "new subjectivities": "Who we are, how we view the world, [and] how we interact with each other."[7] LVC defines peasant identity as resisting and opposing empire, in the sense of the term used by van der Ploeg (2008) and Hardt and Negri (2004):

> The state and the market... flow together and converge within Empire. In this respect, Empire emerges as the mutual co-penetration, interchange and symbiosis of state and markets... the rationale and justification of any activity no longer rest with that activity... but are, instead, linked to, and therefore dependent on, their (assumed) contribution to the profitability and expansion of Empire... tight cycles of planning and control are enforced.
>
> (van der Ploeg 2008, 252)

LVC's vision of who peasants *are* and what they want, in contrast, is rooted

> in the complex and diverse realities of peasant agriculture... using our local knowledge, ingenuity, and ability to innovate. We are talking about relatively small farms managed by peasant families and communities... with diversified production and the integration of crops, trees and livestock. In this type of agriculture, there is less or no need for external inputs, as everything can be produced on the farm itself.
>
> (La Vía Campesina 2010, 2–3)

This "somewhat stylized dichotomy" appears to define out entrepreneurial medium-scale farmers who maintain both peasant and agribusiness identities (Rosset and Martínez-Torres 2012, 5). However, it may be viewed tactically as a way of creating a clear alternative pole to maintain activist identity and mobilization (cf. Ondetti's outline of "activist strategy" theory; Ondetti 2008, 31).

Encapsulating LVC's overall perspective and approach is the term *food sovereignty*, or "the rights of local peoples to determine their own agricultural and food policy, organize production and consumption to meet local needs, and secure access to land, water, and seed" (Wittman 2010). Originated by LVC at the World Food Summit in 1996, food sovereignty was conceived of as a distinct alternative to the more apolitical term *food security*. Since its formulation, food sovereignty has served as both an aspiration and a rallying cry. Its rapid growth as a concept in international and academic discussions is an indication of LVC's reach and the strength of its approach (Patel 2009, Wittman et al. 2010, De Schutter 2012).

After decades of protests and participation in international forums, LVC has recently secured a further victory for its vision of peasant identity and food sovereignty. In September 2012, the United Nations Human Rights Council adopted a resolution to prepare a draft declaration "on the rights of peasants and other people working in rural areas" (UNHRC 2012). The language used by the council parallels LVC's *Declaration of Peasant Rights—Men and Women* (La Vía Campesina 2009). The definitions and compromises created in the years to come over the UN's possible declaration will shed further light on the effectiveness of LVC's strategy, and the merits of their particular definition of peasant identity.

Defensible Values

As previously established, defensible values may be thought of as normative (i.e., moral and ethical) defensible values, and as the practical value of *defensible lifespaces/defensibility* (i.e., being able to define and defend normative values through socioeconomic autonomy and well-functioning communal and political spaces). Both types of defensible values can be seen emerging from LVC's internal and external discourse throughout its evolution (e.g., Desmarais 2007, 67–69, 72–73). And while the term *food sovereignty* directly signals a relationship to the "autonomy" elements of defensibility, it is clear from their rhetoric that LVC also intends for the term to encompass a discrete set of moral and ethical values.

The *Declaration of the Rights of Peasants—Women and Men*, for example, directly reveals the centrality of both types of defensible values. Its preamble includes statements of how "The policies of neoliberalism worsen the violations of Peasants' Rights" and "The struggle of the Peasants to uphold and protect their Rights." The Declaration proper begins with the statement "Women peasants and men peasants have equal rights," giving gender equality primacy of place after only their definition of the peasant identity itself. (This is also evident in that the declaration is "*of the Rights of* Peasants—*Women and Men*.") It goes on to recapitulate basic human rights outlined under international convention and law, rights related to conservation and biodiversity, and rights that can be classified as allowing the maintenance of defensible agricultural lifespaces (e.g., rights to seeds and traditional knowledge, the means of agricultural production, and to actively participate in food system policy design and implementation). For our purposes, these groups of rights might be restated as the *right to self-determination* of a peasant lifestyle and identity; the *right of peasants to have rights*; and the *fundamental importance of gender equality*. LVC sees these as key to the *defensibility* of sustainable, secure, and autonomous lifespaces. Taken together, these values represent LVC's demand for food sovereignty.

In casting its demands as food sovereignty, LVC seeks changes in social institutions, at all levels: food sovereignty implies participatory citizenship seeking to overcome differences in class, culture, and roles within the peasant movement and within the societies they are part of.

Normatively Defensible Values

The values endorsed by LVC draw on international human rights treaties, and specifically on the rights enumerated around food—in other words, rights nearly universally agreed upon, at least in name. One-hundred and sixty countries are party to the International Covenant on Economic, Social, and Cultural Rights, which begins with:

> All peoples have the right of self-determination. By virtue of that right they freely determine their political status and freely pursue their economic, social and cultural development; . . . The States Parties to the present Covenant . . . shall promote the realization of the right of self-determination, and shall respect that right.

This Covenant commits signatories to the recognition of self-determination, one of the fundamental normative values supported by LVC. Yet dominant contemporary food systems do not provide for the type of self-determination envisioned by LVC. LVC and many of the groups mentioned in the introduction—Slow Food, MCAC, Fair Trade—largely agree that current international market structures fail to allow or promote self-determination, and have often pushed reforms directly inimical to it. Neoliberal approaches such as structural adjustment policies and preferences for international trade subordinate national sovereignty and regional self-determination to international market forces (Rosset 2006, Desmarais 2007, 45–73; IAASTD 2009, 45–46, 85).

In line with the idea of self-determination, LVC and its allies have asserted that food sovereignty cannot be simply approached as a concept or academic definition, but must arise "from a collective, participatory process that is popular and progressive . . . constantly enriched through various agrarian debates and political discussions" (Stédile and de Carvalho 2011, 25). They advocate participatory political processes as a way to negotiate differing and conflicting values, both within the movement itself and within society more broadly. Representation is achieved through a horizontal process of consultation and discussion; LVC leaders are meant to be strictly accountable to and to represent the interests of their members through well-defined constituencies within regional and local peasant organizations (Desmarais 2007, 28).[8] Through this approach, LVC aims to reflect the self-determination it calls for in broader society.

In demanding self-determination and other rights for peasants, LVC fundamentally demands the "right to have rights over food," (Patel 2009, 663)—a demand to political systems at all levels to recognize and actively support defensible values. "For rights to mean anything at all, they need a guarantor, responsible for implementing a concomitant system of duties and obligations" (668). Yet Patel's analysis also asserts that food sovereignty's radical and inherently contestable character undermines the very notion of rights' guarantor, as its formulators reject the idea that states have paramount authority. If the states that have signed documents like the ICESCR do not have paramount authority, who then may serve as a guarantor?

LVC, in its conception of food sovereignty, is perhaps most clear on who or what will *not* serve as guarantor. Food sovereignty is founded in a rejection of the sovereignty of supposed *free markets*, and the concomitant collusion of states (i.e., empire).[9] This collusion within empire represents a form of top-down control that LVC sees as taking autonomy away from peasants and civil society more generally. Yet the rights-based ideas underlying food sovereignty, like all rights, depend crucially on a social agent (e.g., the state) to protect them. This tension is resolved, in part, by realizing that food sovereignty opposes governance decisions made without a participatory democratic process and not necessarily to all centralized action by the state.[10] But beyond a call for participatory governance, LVC uses rights-based rhetoric as a "platform for strategic action"—a conceptual base for mobilization and identity-building (Patel 2007, 89). In specifying who the guarantors of rights should *not* be rather than who they are, LVC argues for a "sustainable and widespread process of democracy that can provide political direction to the appropriate level of government required to see implementation [of food rights] through to completion" (Patel 2007, 91).[11]

The third normatively defensible value central to LVC is gender equality. Women still experience significant repression and discrimination around the world, including (perhaps especially) in agricultural systems (Dwyer and Bruce 1988; Patel 2007; Agarwal, this volume). While gender equality has not always enjoyed its fundamental status in LVC's agenda—and the degree to which LVC is currently living up to its nominally foundational importance is debated—the rights of women has been repeatedly affirmed as an ongoing core issue (Desmarais 2007; Martínez-Torres and Rosset 2010). The process that brought it to the fore has in fact been key in cementing deliberative processes as a healthy practice within the movement: gender equality became one of its central identifying platforms only as a result of work by women and allies within the participatory structures of LVC. Nevertheless, some constituent groups and allies have consistently voiced concern that gender issues are not high enough on the agenda, and that representation (especially at the national, rather than international, level) continues to be a problem. Although there has not been a systematic study of women's power within LVC as compared to other movements or organizations, one possible resolution to this seeming contradiction (the prominence of gender on LVC's agenda, yet its persistent appearance as a leading concern by internal and external actors) may be that LVC has accomplished significant, and possibly unique, progress on the issue, but that the distance to gender parity is far enough that a level of dissatisfaction is also reasonable. Lacking further evidence, however, this remains conjecture.

This contradiction notwithstanding, the process that saw a group within LVC raising gender to be a central issue represents perhaps a key element of LVC, and sets it apart from many predecessor movements. LVC is able to reformulate and address issues and internal contradictions more readily than a group of its size and diversity might be expected to. This perhaps reflects a novel, dynamic structure that embraces adaptive management alongside deep democracy. The decisions at the international level, in its secretariat, nominally come from the wishes agreed upon democratically by each national and regional representative. Although they admit continuing difficulties in accomplishing this (Rosset and Martínez-Torres 2005; 13–16, A1.33; Desmarais 2007, 136–144), they appear to be pursuing the challenge of Hardt and Negri's (2004, 68) *Multitude*: "The challenge of the multitude is the challenge of democracy... that is, the rule of everyone by everyone." The multitude seeks to balance the necessity of unity as a voice for political change with the imperative to avoid homogenization and capitulation of differences in the cause of such unity. The tensions and actions around gender within LVC both result from and reflect the values of self-determination and the right to have rights. Determining what exactly these mean in the area of gender calls on the very processes of participatory democracy that food sovereignty seeks to propagate.

Autonomy, Democracy and a Defensible Lifespace

LVC is a proponent of *defensible lifespaces* (after Friedmann 1992, in Desmarais 2007, 67–68). Concisely stated, a defensible lifespace is a physical and social space enabling a family to make a living and to exert a degree of autonomy over their own conditions. Autonomy here is not meant in the narrow sense of being completely self-provisioning (a common misapprehension of the demands of the localization and peasant movements), but rather is related to the ability to influence and change material conditions and social structures. In practical terms, this implies the ability to make a dignified and sustainable living as a peasant—as opposed to, for instance, escaping poverty by leaving one's community to make a go of it in the city. Defensibility would mean that, rather than the ability to *leave* poor rural circumstances, peasants and peasant communities have the ability to *change* the sociocultural and physical infrastructures creating and maintaining endemic hardships.[12]

Unconstrained international trade places the control necessary for this physically and socioculturally outside the reach of individual communities—the loci of control of local prices and supply are moved from within a community, region, or country into the hands of the supposed "invisible hand." Alternatively, the loci of control lies beyond this force: the formulation of empire elaborates on how cycles of planning and control, the ability to enter and exit the market, what a farmer produces and how, all become constrained within empire, forming a "visible hand" (van der Ploeg 2008, 252; cf. Araghi 2008's "visible foot"). The "hands" of the market, visible or invisible, move sites of control away from individual communities and into the stock exchanges and boardrooms of the Minority World. Any given community must now push to enact change in a marketplace influenced by millions of their compatriots around the world, besides the (from the point of view of the Majority World[13] farmer) completely unaccountable decisions of executives and foreign governments[14]—though this is a continuing, not new, trend (Davis 2002; McMichael 2009). The results are food products tailored for their suitability for mass and elite markets, rather than to the desires or needs of individual communities;

food systems and agriculture influenced not by the civic conversation Patel referred to, but rather characterized by food products' durability and consistency. Under the continuous influence of "imperial" socioeconomic powers, food markets are increasingly supplied by a very small range of crops and animals, forming raw materials for a wide array of "fabricated flavors" (Weis 2007, 16). This corresponds to huge amounts of food waste due to pesky crops or animals that do not come out perfectly each time, no matter how much their genetic stock is narrowed, and perfectly edible food that is thrown away because it does not meet cosmetic standards (van der Ploeg 2008; Stuart 2009). Thus a system is created where nonproductive energy must be spent disposing of usable but "off-spec" food, while energy is simultaneously spent to increase control and return to industrial specifications. This additionally decreases the sustainability of the food system, as control and uniformity of a heterogeneous world requires significant and continuously growing inputs of energy (Tainter 1988), and is in opposition to the idiosyncrasy, variety, and thus adaptability and stability of peasant farming systems (Di Falco and Perrings 2003; Edelman 2005; Jarvis et al. 2011). Social traditions, diversity, and culture are also lost, as "subsistence customs and traditional social relations [are replaced] with contracts, the market, and uniform laws" (Scott 1976, 189, in Edelman 2005).

LVC and the ideals of food sovereignty seek to ground decisions about food and agriculture in institutions at lower socioeconomic and biophysical scales (e.g., national, regional, and local). In this, they attempt to restore communities' ability to guarantee values and rights, to preserve cultural diversity, and to acknowledge and support the vital role of small farmers in preserving genetic and cultural diversity and producing much of the world's food (Jarvis et al. 2008; Martínez-Torres and Rosset 2010).

The commonly raised counterpoint to these positions is that the peasant lifestyle is losing its defensibility because of its inefficiency. One might in fact argue that defensibility is an indulgence—surely not every sector or way of life can demand the ability to keep existing. The lifespace defensibility of, say, criminals or quacks is of little moment and actively undesirable to society. In fact, one might reasonably hope that ways of life taking more from society than they give back will lack the power to demand defensibility and subsidization.

The demand of LVC and related movements is quite distinct from such a case against inefficiency or undesirability for several reasons:

1. Despite decades, if not centuries, of assuming peasant agriculture is backwards and inefficient, numerous researchers have found peasant agriculture to be more efficient in terms of its use of energy, land, and other resources, compared to industrial, "high modern" agriculture, and to generally better support long-term sustainability of the environment and its components (e.g., Altieri and Toledo 2011; Chappell and LaValle 2011; Lin et al. 2011).
2. Peasant agriculture generates a significant amount of value, including cultural, aesthetic, and spiritual aspects that are not reflected in industrial agriculture (Duncan 1996; Pretty 2002; Gold, this volume). Peasants also produce a disproportionately large amount of the food produced in many societies (e.g., Rosset et al. 2011: 181).

Further, inherent in the concept of food sovereignty is a call for open, democratic discussions of values. True food sovereignty would generate processes involving the citizens and communities of any given area capable of determining the priorities and shape of the food system:

> [Food sovereignty takes direct aim at] a one-size-fits-all approach to agriculture, as opposed to the context specific results generated by democratic deliberation. By leaving the venues of subnational engagement open... La Vía Campesina calls for new political spaces to be filled with argument... a call for people to figure out for themselves what they want the right to food to mean in their communities, bearing in mind the community's needs, climate, geography, food preferences, social mix, and history... *We will know if the promise of food sovereignty has been realized when we see explicit discussions of gender politics and food production.*
>
> (Patel 2007: 91; emphasis added)

There is no reason that such discussions could not also involve debate over the value of peasant identity and peasants' rights to a given society; negotiating between peasants' rights and priorities and those of other citizens will be a delicate and interesting process. Another difficult element—the right venues and scales for these democratic discussions—may find its solution in a useful tautology implied by food sovereignty: decisions and food systems should be localized as far as is possible and effective, but no further.[15] LVC's multiscale and polycentric democratic traditions will also help them in navigating this difficulty, if the democratic processes they seek do become as commonplace as they hope.

LVC's priorities around participatory democracy also align with several converging bodies of academic literature. Researchers of collective action and common property management have pointed out that local communities and civil society—not formally of "the market" or "the state"—can create and maintain socially and ecologically sustainable resource use regimes (Ostrom 1990; Poteete et al. 2010). Localization and autonomy is also supported by current research on the potential of participatory and deliberative democratic forms (Prugh et al. 2000; Herbick and Isham 2010), and the possible social and environmental benefits of localized systems (Feenstra 1997; Pretty 2001; De Young and Princen 2012; though localization is not without critique: Tregear 2011). All of these literatures point to the possibility of new sovereignties and subjectivites. In this, Hardt and Negri's (2004) conceptualization of *multitude* is useful, as its crucial distinction from previous democratic forms is that it does not require the sacrifice of *singularities*. That is, diverse peoples are able to work together, negotiate, and lobby for societal changes and restructuring, without giving up their distinctiveness (cf. Note 18). Rather, they work together pragmatically on the areas of agreement. This tension between unity and uniqueness, compromise without complete capitulation of differing values, is seen throughout LVC, and it was recently witnessed in the form of the "Occupy" movement (Razsa and Kurnik 2012). The full potential of the multitude, as a concept and a mode of action, remains to be seen, but there are empirical and theoretical reasons to be optimistic based in the literatures above. From the MCAC, the LVC member organization

MST (The Landless Rural Workers' Movement), and the Mexican Zapatista resistance, to *panchayat* reforms in India, habitat conservation planning and neighborhood governance councils in the United States, and participatory budgeting in Brazil, alternative democratic forms exist and are being recognized both within scholarly and civic circles (Fung and Wright 2003).

Beyond LVC's commitment to local and national constituent autonomy, it has innovated or revived useful democratic "technologies," including collective and rotating leadership (Martínez-Torres and Rosset 2010), and the creation and maintenance of cultural, spiritual, and collegial ties, especially the ceremony of the *mística* (Issa 2007; Martínez-Torres and Rosset 2010). Further, in order to address concerns that the group had too "Latin American" a focus, the international secretariat was moved to Indonesia, with the Indonesian Henry Saraigh elected as General Coordinator.[16] Personal conversations with LVC members during the COP15 summit in Copenhagen in December 2009 indicated that the secretariat would next be moving to Africa in order to strengthen LVC's roots and presence there, but this does not appear to have been confirmed in public documentation.

Defending Defensible Lifespaces

Autonomy, sovereignty, and a participatory democracy have been explored as important components of defending a defensible lifespace—LVC maintains that extending sovereignty and autonomy to consumers and small-scale food producers would go far toward providing such a lifespace to the global peasantry. But aside from the broad political structures, there are several further, specific ways that LVC advocates for defensibility—in this case, in the form of livelihood security. Some of these approaches are briefly outlined here.

Agroecology and agroecological methods are key components of LVC's ideals and conceptual platform, and they are closely tied to normative values as well as defensibility. In particular, agroecology's focus on regenerative, self-maintaining ecological processes decreases peasants' reliance on outside inputs and increases their autonomy. Research has also found that small-scale farming and agroecology can increase a community's internal social connections and farming's contribution to the local economy (Goldschmidt 1978; Lockeretz 1989; Lyson et al. 2001). Normatively, many agroecologists value and support the preservation of the cultural and spiritual values of agriculture (Pretty 2002) and seek to improve the percentage of the "food dollar" captured by farmers rather than intermediaries, food system monopolies, and monopsonies (Jaffee 2007; Holt-Giménez et al. 2009). The biodiversity underlying agroecological methods may also serve to buffer against climatic shocks like drought and hurricanes, which are likely to increase in frequency with continuing global climate change (Holt-Giménez 2002; Philpott et al. 2008), and to buffer farm families from price and production fluctuations and other unplanned exigencies (Di Falco and Perrings 2003; Méndez et al. 2010). Further discussion of agroecology's range of biodiversity- and knowledge-based practices, social and ecological goals, and ability to support peasants' income, yields, and livelihoods can be found in Uphoff, and in Nelson and Coe (both in this volume), and in several other recent works (e.g., Kloppenburg 2010; Jarvis et al. 2011; Pautasso et al. 2012; Rosset and Martínez-Torres 2012).[17] Pertinent to LVC's values, agroecology can also improve socioeconomic conditions for women, though it is likely that these gains are tied to a tendency within agroecology to acknowledge the importance of gender, and thus specific efforts to address gender within agroecological improvement programs (Bezner-Kerr 2008; De Schutter 2011; Rosset et al. 2011).

Alongside LVC's support of agroecology, its opposition to genetically engineered (GE) crops has been a defining issue. Its committed rejection of GE crops reflects both the experiences and perceptions of many (though not all) of its members regarding the dangers of modern industrial agricultural developments (Holt-Giménez 2006; Desmarais 2007, 40–45). It also emerges from the experience many farmers have had with centuries of enclosure and appropriation of physical and intellectual goods (Kloppenburg 2004; Weis 2007; Kloppenburg 2010), and the long-term, ongoing patterns of international imperial/hegemonic consolidation of control over agriculture and food systems.[18]

In its opposition to GE crops, as well as its staunch criticisms of international trade institutions like the World Trade Organization (WTO) and World Bank, LVC has maintained what Martinez-Torres and Rosset (2010, 158–159) characterize as "collective defiance" (*sensu* Piven and Cloward 1977), giving grist to Piven and Cloward's finding, "in general, that poor peoples' organizations are most effective at achieving their demands when they are most confrontational, and least effective when they take more conciliatory positions and invest their energies in dialogue." Although LVC's stance of nonengagement with actors such as the WTO and World Bank has been criticized by some who believe the organization could accomplish more with a more cooperative stance, Doimo's classic (1995) work on Brazilian post-1970 social movements reinforces Piven and Cloward's claim. Doimo found what she called a "double-ethos" in Brazilian social movements. The first was an "expressive-disruptive" ethos, "through which movements manifest their moral values or ethico-political appeals, and which simultaneously tend to delegitimize public authority and establish intergroup frontiers" (69).[19] This ethos aligns with LVC's use of food rights as both a mobilization tool and a critical platform. Doimo, like Piven and Cloward, found this ethos to be an important element in successful movements, though she noted that at some point movements tended to switch to an alternative "cooperative-integrative" ethos, to "seek to acquire higher levels of social integration in terms of access to goods and services" (69). Thus far, LVC seems both comfortable and effective in its "disruptive" stance. The group remains concerned with the possibilities and threat of co-optation from cooperation and integration, and sensitive to how cooperation and integration may neutralize the most pointed criticisms of activist groups and movements. Instead, with delegitimization of imperial structures and sociocultural disruption and reorganization still on its agenda, it seems likely that LVC will maintain its tactics of nonengagement. LVC seeks to maintain the autonomy and defensibility of the movement itself, and it sees these oppositional stances as still useful and philosophically important—while at the same time recognizing that member organizations may need to act differently within their own national and regional contexts (Rosset and Martínez-Torres 2005, A1.31; Desmarais 2007, 135–160).

Lastly, LVC's emphasis on *gender equality* itself plays into the building of a defensible lifespace. Although it is clear that LVC does not approach gender from an instrumentalist standpoint—that is, it does not appear to support gender equality *because* it is connected with lower household malnutrition (e.g., Smith and Haddad 2000)—it is nevertheless the case that interventions increasing the status of women are connected to a number of positive developments, including increased agricultural productivity. Gender equality clearly advances the goals of autonomy, defensible and sustainable livelihoods, and democracy alongside the inherent normative value of such equality itself (Agarwal, this volume).

Conclusion

Essentially, movements like La Vía Campesina may, at base, be seen as movements for fulfilling the promises of democracy. Not just democracy in the form of nominal representation, electoral, or procedural rights, but the fulfillment of human dignities and rights. Further, defensible values as articulated by these movements rest on an implicit understanding that there is no democracy without *capabilities* (*sensu* Sen 1992), and that such capabilities must be guaranteed by a strong civil society in ongoing discourse, and perhaps tension, with the state.

The parallel tensions within the movement and outside of it—conflicting identities, issues of representation, countries or regions without member groups, and heterogeneity within members at subnational levels—have not been extensively dealt with here. Borras et al. (2008) note several important and surprising "silences in the literature" of transnational agrarian movements, including a lack of analyses of their internal dynamics, and of the true dynamics of interconnectivity between international, national, and local levels of existing movements (10–12). They also note that the contentious question of representation is underanalyzed by movement leaders, activists, and academics. Instead, to make the complexities manageable, "a great many important details tend to be taken for granted or missed in the analysis and discourse that [transnational agrarian movements] produce" (17). Class, race, and restrictive or prescriptive notions of identity make it difficult to truly represent a large and diverse class such as "peasants," much less the rural poor more broadly. While it is of course in any movement's interest to claim as broad a representation as possible, most transnational agrarian movements lack any large presence in many areas of the world, "notably Russia, Central Asia, the Middle East and North Africa region, and most especially China" (14)—areas that host much of the world's rural poor. Further, the constituency that LVC seeks and claims to represent, by its very nature, means that many of LVC's member organizations will be something of ciphers to the academic world: a movement seeking to represent the world's rural poor is simultaneously a movement of people and places lacking easy access to the rest of the world, lacking a large endemic academic class, and lacking significant outside attention and resources. The ability to check LVC's claims of representation, or to examine the extent to which its peasant identity speaks to the world's one billion-plus peasants is simply not (yet) there.

Nevertheless, an important distinction for LVC as a movement is its acknowledgement and endorsement of the principle that people must have power to set their own agendas, and this power must be reflected through all different strata of society—peasant to consumer, retailer to producer, man to woman. The movement's construction of a peasant identity should be taken to be as much aspirational and tactical as representative—seeking to build an inclusive identity that invites a multitude of singularities. The rejection of organizations like the World Bank and WTO, of imperial structures and transnational corporations, is a rejection of these organizations' democratic unrepresentativeness and unresponsiveness. LVC and likeminded movements observe that free-market structures and ideology have not provided democratic leveling and horizontal participation; those with little or no money have little or no vote in the marketplace. In demanding recognition of the small farmers' fundamental support of the human race, LVC advocates for deep democracy. Better connections between differing people and identities and a true discussion of priorities and vision may not, in the end, lead to a universal embrace of LVC's specific goals and vision. Yet LVC's desire for a truly sovereign, autonomous world where participatory democratic discussion and deliberation takes place is possibly its most valuable and defensible contribution—one that implies it will continue to be a touchstone within transnational food movements. In this support for an active and engaged citizenship, LVC may also help create the sociopolitical spaces necessary to realize the goals of other movements, such as Fair Trade, and advance the promises of ecological and agrarian citizenship (Johnson and MacKendrick, this volume; Wittman, 2010). The extent to which LVC (and other transnational movements) may be willing and able to compromise on their values within the kind of democratic processes they seek remains to be fully tested.

Notes

1. This chapter benefitted greatly from comments by Maywa Montenegro, Jessica Zemaitis, Jude Wait, Jamie Stepniak, James Moore, and Ron Herring. Any errors likely stem from failing to heed their advice, and are mine alone.
2. See, e.g., Holt-Giménez et al. (2009), IAASTD (2009), Lang and Heasman (2004) and FAO (2012) for information on these trends.
3. Jaffee (2007) provides an excellent overview of the Fair Trade movement. See also Johnston and MacKendrick (this volume) for more on consumer-based attempts to integrate ethics and conscience into food systems.
4. Tarrow's work in this area is foundational; interested readers might additionally seek out Tarrow (2005) and Tarrow (2011).
5. The number of peasants making significant portions of their income from nonfarm employment or remittances from family members is, however, large and growing.

6. Approximately one-fifth of LVC's member organizations hail from Europe, the United States, Canada, or Japan.
7. Although only acknowledged in passing here, it is clearly in the interest and "nature" of any movement to "claim to represent more than they represent" (R. Herring, *pers. comm.*). An excellent overview of the tensions between identity, representation, and reality in transnational agrarian movements is given in Borras et al. (2008).
8. Further explanations of LVC's internal processes and structures can be found in Desmarais (2007, 27–33, 135–189).
9. Panitch (1994) has observed that free markets in fact represent the transformation of the state to protect the interests of capital, not (as is commonly perceived) the retreat of states from regulation. See also Pinder (2011).
10. Many of the measures called for by LVC in fact imply and necessitate state involvement. Thanks to M. Montenegro for pointing this out. Elaboration on the conceptual tensions here can be found in Patel (2009).
11. Similarly, Johnston and MacKendrick (this volume) "identify greater promise for reform" from a citizen-based, democratic approach than from one based in so-called "consumer sovereignty." Their conception of ecological citizenship echoes Wittman's agrarian citizenship, a model seeking to "reconnect agriculture, society, and environment through systems of mutual obligation" (Wittman 2010, 91).
12. Gender is a particularly important element here, as rural women's labor often goes uncompensated, undercounted, or gets overlooked, while their political rights are underemphasized (Bruce and Dwyer 1988, Agarwal, this volume).
13. As before, this refelcts Alam's (2008) nomenclature of the Minority (Global North) and Majority (Global South) Worlds.
14. "Corporate power is now so great within and between national borders that it is redefining what is meant by a "market"... corporate policy is becoming more fully engaged in public policy to further its own interests, thus raising questions about accountability," (Lang and Heasman 2004, 127).
15. This intentionally echoes Einstein's oft-paraphrased comment: "The supreme goal of all theory is to make the irreducible basic elements as simple and as few as possible without having to surrender the adequate representation of a single datum of experience" (Einstein 1934, 165).
16. "It is remarkable in today's world that a movement can be coordinated by a Muslim, and incorporate Christians, Hindus, Buddhists and members of many other religions, together with radical Marxist and social democratic atheists, all scarcely without raising an eyebrow internally. The mística plays a key role in making this possible" (Martínez-Torres and Rosset 2010).
17. Although seeds have not been extensively discussed here, LVC has declared that "sustainability is completely impossible if the right of the peoples to recover, defend, reproduce, exchange, improve and grow their own seed is not recognized" (La Vía Campesina 2001).
18. Relatedly, Rangnekar (2002) found evidence of increasingly rapid planned obsolescence in commercial wheat varieties in the UK, creating pressure to buy new, patented seeds on a more and more frequent basis.
19. Translated from Portuguese by the author (MJC).

References

Agarwal, B. 2015. "Food Security, Productivity, and Gender Inequality." In *Oxford Handbook of Food, Politics and Society*, edited by R. Herring. Oxford: Oxford University Press.

Alam, S. 2008. "Majority World: Challenging the West's Rhetoric of Democracy." *Amerasia Journal* 34:87–98.

Altieri, M. A., and V. M. Toledo. 2011. "The Agroecological Revolution in Latin America: Rescuing Nature, Ensuring Food Sovereignty and Empowering Peasants." *Journal of Peasant Studies* 38:587–612.

Araghi, F. 2008. "The Invisible Hand and the Visible Foot: Peasants, Dispossession and Globalization." In *Peasants and Globalisation: Political Economy, Rural Transformation and the Agrarian Question*, edited by Haroon Akram-Lodhi and C. Kay, 111–147. London: Routledge.

Bezner-Kerr, R. 2008. "Gender and Agrarian Inequality at the Local Scale." In *Agricultural Systems: Agroecology and Rural Innovation for Development*, edited by S. S. Snapp and B. Pound, 281–308. Burlington, MA: Elsevier.

Borras, S. M., Jr. 2008. "La Vía Campesina and Its Global Campaign for Agrarian Reform." *Journal of Agrarian Change* 8:258–289.

Borras, S. M., Jr., M. Edelman, and C. Kay. 2008. "Transnational Agrarian Movements: Origins and Politics, Campaigns and Impact." In *Transnational Agrarian Movements: Confronting Globalization*, edited by S. M. Borras Jr., M. Edelman, and C. Kay, 1–36. West Sussex, UK: Wiley-Blackwell.

Brown, C., and S. Miller. 2008. "The Impacts of Local Markets: A Review of Research on Farmers Markets and Community Supported Agriculture (CSA)." *American Journal of Agricultural Economics* 90:1298–1302.

Bruce, J., and D. H. Dwyer. 1988. "Introduction." *In A Home Divided: Women and Income in the Third World*, edited by J. Bruce and D. H. Dwyer, 1–19. Stanford, CA: Stanford University Press.

Buttel, F. 2007. "Envisioning the Future Development of Farming in the USA: Agroecology between Extinction and Multifunctionality." In *The Many Meanings and Potential of Agroecology Research and Teaching*, 1–14. Madison: University of Wisconsin-Madison.

Chappell, M. J., and L. A. LaValle. 2011. "Food Security and Biodiversity: Can We Have Both? An Agroecological Analysis." *Agriculture and Human Values* 28:3–26.

Chomsky, N. 2003. "Confronting the Empire." Speech delivered at the III World Social Forum, February 2, 2003, Porto Alegre, Brazil. www.chomsky.info.

Daly, H. E. 2007. "Ecological Economics: The Concept of Scale and Its Relation to Allocation, Distribution, and Uneconomic Growth." In *Ecological Economics and Sustainable Development: Selected Essays of Herman Daly*, 82–103. Cheltenham, UK: Edward Elgar.

Davis, M. 2002. *Late Victorian Holocausts: El Niño Famines and the Making of the Third World.* London and New York: Verso.

De Schutter, O. 2011. *Agroecology and the Right to Food: Report Submitted by the Special Rapporteur on the Right to Food.* New York: United Nations Human Rights Council.

De Schutter, O. 2012. "CFS Round-Up: Shaping a Coherent Global Governance of Food Security." http://www.srfood.org/index.php/en/component/content/article/1-latest-news/2533-cfs-round-up-shaping-a-coherent-global-governance-of-food-security.

Desmarais, A. A. 2007. *La Vía Campesina: Globalization and the Power of Peasants.* London and Ann Arbor, MI: Pluto Press.

De Young, R., and T. Princen, eds. 2012. *The Localization Reader: Adapting to the Coming Downshift.* Cambridge, MA: MIT Press.

Di Falco, S., and C. Perrings. 2003. "Crop Genetic Diversity, Productivity, and Stability of Agroecosystems: A Theoretical and Empirical Investigation." *Scottish Journal of Political Economy* 50:207–216.

Doimo, A. M. 1995. *A Vez e a Voz do Popular: Movimentos sociais e participação política no Brasil pós-70*. Rio de Janeiro: Relume-Dumará/Associação Nacional de Pós-Graduação em Ciências Socias.

Duncan, C. A. M. 1996. *The Centrality of Agriculture: Between Humankind and the Rest of Nature*. Montreal: McGill-Queen's University Press.

Dwyer, D. H. and J. Bruce. 1988. *A Home Divided: Women and Income in the Third World*. Stanford, CA: Stanford University Press.

Edelman, M. 2005. "Bringing the Moral Economy Back In...to the Study of 21st-Century Transnational Peasant Movements." *American Anthropologist* 107:331–345.

Einstein, A. 1934. "On the Method of Theoretical Physics." *Philosophy of Science* 1:163–169.

Feenstra, G. W. 1997. "Local Food Systems and Sustainable Communities." *American Journal of Alternative Agriculture* 12:28–36.

FAO (Food and Agriculture Organization of the United Nations). 2012. *The State of Food Insecurity in the World 2012: Economic Growth is Necessary but Not Sufficient to Accelerate Reduction of Hunger and Malnutrition*. Rome: FAO.

Fridell, G. 2007. "Fair-Trade Coffee and Commodity Fetishism: The Limits of Market-Driven Social Justice." *Historical Materialism* 15:79–104.

Friedmann, J. 1992. *Empowerment: The Politics of Alternative Development*. Cambridge, MA: Blackwell.

Fung, A., and E. O. Wright, eds. 2003. *Deepening Democracy: Institutional Innovations in Empowered Participatory Governance*. London: Verso.

Geier, B. 2007. "IFOAM and the History of the International Organic Movement." *In Organic Farming: An International History*, edited by W. Lockeretz, 175–186. Wallingford, UK: CAB International.

Gold, A. G. 2012. "Food Values Beyond Nutrition. " In *The Oxford Handbook of Food, Politics and Society*, edited by R. J. Herring. Oxford: Oxford University Press.

Goldschmidt, W. 1978. *As You Sow: Three Studies in the Social Consequences of Agribusiness*. New York: Allenheld, Osmun.

Hardt, M., and A. Negri. 2004. *Multitude: War and Democracy in the Age of Empire*. New York: Penguin.

Harper, A., A. Shattuck, E. Holt-Giménez, A. Alkon, and F. Lambrick. 2009. *Food Policy Councils: Lessons Learned*. Oakland, CA: FoodFirst Institute for Food and Development Policy. https://www.foodfirst.org/sites/www.foodfirst.org/files/pdf/Food_Policy_Councils_Report_full_final.pdf.

Herbick, M., and J. Isham. 2010. "The Promise of Deliberative Democracy." *Solutions* 1:25–27.

Herring, R. J. 2003. "Beyond the Political Impossibility Theorem of Agrarian Reform." In *Changing Paths: International Development and the New Politics of Inclusion*, edited by P. P. Houtzager and M. P. Moore, 58–87. Ann Arbor: University of Michigan Press.

Holt-Giménez, E. 2002. "Measuring Farmers' Agroecological Resistance after Hurricane Mitch in Nicaragua: A Case Study in Participatory, Sustainable Land Management Impact Monitoring." *Agriculture Ecosystems & Environment* 93:87–105.

—— 2006. *Campesino A Campesino: Voices from Latin America's Farmer to Farmer Movement for Sustainable Agriculture*. Oakland, CA: Food First.

Holt-Giménez, E., R. C. Patel, and A. Shattuck. 2009. *Food Rebellions: Crisis and the Hunger for Justice*. Cape Town: Pambazuka Press; Oakland, CA: Food First Books; Boston, MA: Grassroots International/.

IAASTD (International Assessment of Agricultural Knowledge Science and Technology for Development). 2009. *Agriculture At a Crossroads: International Assessment of Agricultural*

Knowledge, Science and Technology for Development (Global Report). Washington, DC: Island Press.

Issa, D. 2007. "Praxis of Empowerment: Mistica and Mobilization in Brazil's Landless Rural Workers' Movement." *Latin American Perspectives* 34:124–138.

Jaffee, D. 2007. *Brewing Justice: Fair Trade Coffee, Sustainability, and Survival*. Berkeley: University of California Press.

Jarvis, D. I., A. H. D. Brown, P. H. Cuong, L. Collado-Panduro, L. Latournerie-Moreno, S. Gyawali, T. Tanto, et al. 2008. "A Global Perspective of the Richness and Evenness of Traditional Crop-Variety Diversity Maintained by Farming Communities." *Proceedings of the National Academy of Sciences* 105:5326–5331.

Jarvis, D., T. Hodgkin, B. Sthapit, C Fadda, and I. Lopez-Noriega. 2011. "An Heuristic Framework for Identifying Multiple Ways of Supporting the Conservation and Use of Traditional Crop Varieties within the Agricultural Production System." *Critical Reviews in Plant Sciences* 30:125–176.

Johnson, J., and N. MacKendrick. 2012. "The Politics of Grocery Shopping: Eating, Voting, and (Possibly) Transforming the Food System." In *The Oxford Handbook of Food, Politics and Society*, edited by R. J. Herring. Oxford: Oxford University Press.

Kloppenburg, J. 2004. *First the Seed: The Political Economy of Plant Biotechnology*. 2nd. ed. Madison: University of Wisconsin Press.

Kloppenburg, J. 2010. "Seed Sovereignty: The Promise of Open Source Biology." In *Food Sovereignty: Reconnecting Food, Nature and Community*, edited by H. K. Wittman, A. A. Desmarais, and N. Wiebe, 152–167. Halifax, NS: Fernwood.

La Vía Campesina. 2001. "The Position of Vía Campesina on Biodiversity, Biosafety and Genetic Resources." *Development* 44:47–51.

——. 2008. *Our Members*. Jakarta, Indonesia: La Vía Campesina. ViaCampesina.org.

——. 2009. *Declaration of Rights of Peasants—Women and Men*. Seoul: International Coordinating Committee of La Vía Campesina.

——. 2010. *Sustainable Peasant and Family Farm Agriculture Can Feed the World*. Jakarta, Indonesia: La Vía Campesina.

Lang, T., and M. Heasman. 2004. *Food Wars: The Global Battle for Mouths, Minds and Markets*. New York: Earthscan.

Larsson, T. 2012. "The Rise of the Organic Foods Movement as a Transnational Phenomenon." In *The Oxford Handbook of Food Politics*, edited by R. J. Herring. Oxford: Oxford University Press.

Lin, B. B., M. J. Chappell, J. Vandermeer, G. Smith, E. Quintero, R Bezner-Kerr, D. M. Griffith, et al. 2011. "Effects of Industrial Agriculture on Global Warming and the Mitigation Potential of Small-Scale Agro-ecological Farms." *CAB Reviews: Perspectives in Agriculture, Veterinary Science, Nutrition, and Natural Resources* 6:1–18.

Lockeretz, W. 1989. "Comparative Local Economic Benefits of Conventional and Alternative Cropping Systems." *American Journal of Alternative Agriculture* 4:75–83.

Lyson, T. A., R. J. Torres, and R. Welsh. 2001. "Scale of Agricultural Production, Civic Engagement, and Community Welfare." *Social Forces* 80:311–327.

Maluf, R. S. 2010. "Construção do SISAN, mobilização e participação social." In *Fome Zero: Uma história brasileira*. Vol. 2, edited by A. V. Aranha, B. Lazarini, L. Schwarz, and M. Carvalho, 14–26. Brasília: Ministério do Desenvolvimento Social e Combate à Fome.

Martínez-Torres, M. E., and P. M. Rosset. 2010. "La Vía Campesina: The Birth and Evolution of a Transnational Social Movement." *Journal of Peasant Studies* 37:149–175.

McMichael, P. 2009. "A Food Regime Analysis of the 'World Food Crisis.'" *Agriculture and Human Values* 26:281–295.

Méndez, V. E., C. M. Bacon, M. Olson, K. S. Morris, and A. Shattuck. 2010. "Agrobiodiversity and Shade Coffee Smallholder Livelihoods: A Review and Synthesis of Ten Years of Research in Central America." *Professional Geographer* 62:357–376.

Mogk, J. E., S. Kwiatkowski, and M. J. Weindorf. 2012. "Promoting Urban Agriculture as an Alternative Land Use for Vacant Properties in the City of Detroit: Benefits, Problems and Proposals for a Regulatory Framework for Successful Land Use Integration." *The Wayne Law Review* 56:1521–1580.

Naranjo, S. 2012. "Enabling Food Sovereignty and a Prosperous Future for Peasants by Understanding the Factors that Marginalise Peasants and Lead to Poverty and Hunger." *Agriculture and Human Values* 29:231–246.

Nelson, R. and R. Coe. 2012. "Agroecological Intensification of Smallholder Farming." In *The Oxford Handbook of Food, Politics and Society*, edited by R. J. Herring. Oxford: Oxford University Press.

Ondetti, G. A. 2008. *Land, Protest, and Politics: The Landless Movement and the Struggle for Agrarian Reform in Brazil.* University Park: Pennsylvania State University Press.

Ostrom, E. 1990. *Governing the Commons: The Evolution of Institutions for Collective Action.* Cambridge: Cambridge University Press.

Otte, A., D. Simmering, and V. Wolters. 2007. "Biodiversity at the Landscape Level: Recent Concepts and Perspectives for Multifunctional Land Use." *Landscape Ecology* 22:639–642.

Panitch, L. 1994. "Globalisation and the State." *Socialist Register* 30:60–93.

Patel, R. C. 2007. "Transgressing Rights: La Vía Campesina's Call for Food Sovereignty." *Feminist Economics* 13:87–93.

——. 2009. "What Does Food Sovereignty Look Like?" *Journal of Peasant Studies* 36:663–673.

Pautasso, M., G. Aistara, A. Barnaud, S. Caillon, P. Clouvel, O. T. Coomes, M. Delêtre, et al. 2012. "Seed Exchange Networks for Agrobiodiversity Conservation: A Review." *Agronomy for Sustainable Development* 33:1–25.

Perfecto, I., J. H. Vandermeer, and A. L. Wright. 2009. *Nature's Matrix: Linking Agriculture, Conservation and Food Sovereignty.* London: Earthscan.

Philpott, S. M., B. B. Lin, S. Jha, and S. J. Brines. 2008. "A Multi-scale Assessment of Hurricane Impacts on Agricultural Landscapes Based on Land Use and Topographic Features." *Agriculture, Ecosystems & Environment* 128:12–20.

Pinder, S. O. 2011. "The Nation State in the Era of Globalizaiton: Some Challenges." *International Journal of Humanities and Social Science* 1:139–148.

Piven, F. F., and R. A. Cloward. 1977. *Poor People's Movements: Why They Succeed, How They Fail.* New York: Random House.

Poteete, A. R., M. A. Janssen, and E. Ostrom. 2010. *Working Together: Collective Action, the Commons, and Multiple Methods in Practice.* Princeton, NJ: Princeton University Press.

Pretty, J. N. 2001. "Some Benefits and Drawbacks of Local Food Systems." Briefing Note for TVU/Sustain AgriFood Network, November 2, 2001. http://www.sustainweb.org/pdf/afn_m1_p2.pdf.

——. 2002. *Agri-Culture: Reconnecting People, Land, and Nature.* London: Earthscan.

Prugh, T., R. Costanza, and H. E. Daly. 2000. *The Local Politics of Global Sustainability.* Washington, DC: Island Press.

Rangnekar, D. 2002. "R&D Appropriability and Planned Obsolescence: Empirical Evidence from Wheat Breeding in the UK (1960–1995)." *Industrial and Corporate Change* 11:1011–1029.

Razsa, M., and A. Kurnik. 2012. "The Occupy Movement in Žižek's Hometown: Direct Democracy and a Politics of Becoming." *American Ethnologist* 39:238–258.

Rosset, P. 2006. *Food is Different: Why We Must Get the WTO Out of Agriculture.* London: Zed.

Rosset, P. M., B. Machin Sosa, A. M. Roque Jaime, and D. R. Avila Lozano. 2011. "The Campesino-to-Campesino Agroecology Movement of ANAP in Cuba: Social Process Methodology in the Construction of Sustainable Peasant Agriculture and Food Sovereignty." *Journal of Peasant Studies* 38:161–191.

Rosset, P. M., and M. E. Martínez-Torres. 2005. *Participatory Evaluation of La Vía Campesina.* Oslo, Norway: Norad—Norwegian Agency for Development Cooperation.

Rosset, P. M., and M. E. Martínez-Torres. 2012. "Rural Social Movements and Agroecology: Context, Theory, and Process." *Ecology and Society* 17:1–12.

Scott, J. C. 1976. *The Moral Economy of the Peasant: Rebellion and Subsistence in Southeast Asia.* New Haven, CT: Yale University Press.

Sen, A. 1992. *Inequality Reexamined.* Cambridge, MA: Harvard University Press; New York: Russell Sage Foundation.

Smith, L. C., and L. Haddad. 2000. *Explaining Child Malnutrition in Developing Countries: A Cross-Country Analysis.* Washington, DC: International Food Policy Research Institute.

Stédile, J. P., and H. M. de Carvalho. 2011. "People Need Food Sovereignty." In *Food Movements Unite!*, edited by E. Holt-Giménez, 21–34. Oakland, CA: Food First Books.

Stuart, T. 2009. *Waste: Uncovering the Global Food Scandal.* New York: W. W. Norton.

Tainter, J. 1988. *The Collapse of Complex Societies.* Cambridge: Cambridge University Press.

Tarrow, S. G. 1998. "Fishnets, Internets, and Catnets: Globalization and Transnational Collective Action." In *Challenging Authority: The Historical Study of Contentious Politics*, edited by M. P. Hanagan, L. P. Moch, and W. te Brake, 228–244. Minneapolis: University of Minnesota Press.

——. 2005. *The New Transnational Activism.* New York: Cambridge University Press.

——. 2011. *Power in Movement: Social Movements and Contentious Politics.* Cambridge: Cambridge University Press.

Tregear, A. 2011. "Progressing Knowledge in Alternative and Local Food Networks: Critical Reflections and a Research Agenda." *Journal of Rural Studies* 27:419–430.

UNHRC (United Nations Human Rights Council). 2012. *Promotion of the Human Rights of Peasants and Other People Working in Rural Areas.* A/HRC/21/L.23. Geneva: United Nations Human Rights Council.

USDA (United States Department of Agriculture). 2006. *Farmers Market Growth.* Washington, DC: Agriculture Marketing Service of the United States Department of Agriculture.

Uphoff, N. 2012. *Alternative Paths to Food Security.* In *The Oxford Handbook of Food, Politics and Society*, edited by R. J. Herring. Oxford: Oxford University Press.

van der Ploeg, J. D. 2008. *The New Peasantries: Struggles for Autonomy and Sustainability in an Era of Empire and Globalization.* London: Earthscan.

Viertel, J. 2011. "Beyond Voting with Your Fork: From Enlightened Eating to Movement Building." In *Food Movements Unite!*, edited by E. Holt-Giménez, 137–148. Oakland, CA: Food First Books.

Weis, A. J. 2007. *The Global Food Economy: The Battle for the Future of Farming.* London: Zed.

Wittman, H. K. 2010. "Reconnecting Agriculture and the Environment: Food Sovereignty and the Agrarian Basis of Ecological Citizenship." In *Food Sovereignty: Reconnecting Food,*

Nature and Community, edited by H. K. Wittman, A. A. Desmarais, and N. Wiebe, 91–105. Halifax, NS: Fernwood.

Wittman, H. K., A. A. Desmarais, and N. Wiebe, eds. 2010. *Food Sovereignty: Reconnecting Food, Nature and Community*. Halifax, NS: Fernwood.

World Bank. 2007. *World Development Report 2008: Agriculture for Development*. Washington, DC: World Bank.

CHAPTER 30

THE RISE OF THE ORGANIC FOODS MOVEMENT AS A TRANSNATIONAL PHENOMENON

TOMAS LARSSON

INTRODUCTION

ONCE largely considered the preserve of eccentrics and ideologues on the fringes of both right and left, the establishment of an organic garden at the White House by the First Lady of the United States, Michelle Obama, shortly after her husband's inauguration, signalled the arrival of the organic foods movement into the social and political mainstream (Beam 2009). Tellingly, the comedy news program *The Daily Show with Jon Stewart* proceeded to make fun not of the organic-gardener-in-chief but rather of the critic from the American Council on Science and Health who claimed that the presidential patch should come with a warning label, as the promotion of organic foods would cause starvation, obesity, and cancer.[1] The tables have turned, and it's now those who deny the health and environmental benefits of organic foods who are considered "kooks."

In another part of the world, in a society beset with problems rather different from those of the United States, organic farming is also enjoying a mini boom. In Thailand's Isaan region, Buddhist monks are promoting organic cultivation methods among farmers because these are regarded as being in tune with the *Dhamma* (Parnwell and Seeger 2008, p. 114). In addition to the religious sanction of *kaset insii*, the organic message was further amplified by the enigmatic Thai monarch's Buddhism-inspired "self-sufficiency" doctrine of economic development and nongovernmental organizations (NGOs) such as the Earth Net Foundation (*Muunithi Saaiyai Phaendin*), as well as by foreign aid programs supporting the development of the country's organic foods sector (Delegation of the European Commission to Thailand 2006; GTZ 2009; UNDP 2008; Ellis et al. 2006).

These two brief examples are highlighted to illustrate how the rise of the organic foods movement as a global phenomenon has come to involve a wide range of actors with a variety of interests and intentions and with access to a diverse set of organizational and institutional resources.

In organizational terms, the birth of the organic foods movement as a transnational phenomenon can be dated rather precisely. On November 5, 1972, national organizations from France (*Nature et Progrès*), the United Kingdom (Soil Association), Sweden (*Biodynamiska Föreningen*), South Africa (Soil Association of South Africa), and the United States (Rodale Press) met in Versailles to found the International Federation of Organic Agriculture Movements (IFOAM). Since then, the umbrella organization has grown to encompass more than 750 member organizations from 116 countries.[2] Through its involvement in "organic" standard setting, accreditation, and certification, IFOAM has, since the 1980s, been a driving force in the development of a transnational regulatory regime governing the organic sector, and it is recognized by the International Organization for Standardization as an official standard-setting body (Coleman and Reed 2007).

In parallel with the expansion of this organic agriculture network, the market for organic foods has grown dramatically. According to one recent survey, the land area under organically managed crops has topped 30 million hectares, with the greatest areas found in Oceania, with 42 percent of the worldwide total, and in Europe, with 24 percent of the total (Willer, Yussefi-Menzler, and Sorensen 2008, p. 28). The fast-growing market for organic products was estimated to be valued at more than $38 billion in 2006, double its value six years earlier. On a per capita basis, consumption of organic foods is greatest in Switzerland, Denmark, Sweden, and Austria (Willer et al., 2008, p. 54). Although the overwhelming majority of organic food products are consumed in Europe and North America, the rapid expansion of market demand and support activities by aid organizations has led to the diffusion of export-oriented organic foods production to developing countries. Developing countries already account for more than a quarter of the land area under organic management. In absolute terms, China and Argentina have the largest organic land areas among the developing countries, but, in relative terms, tiny Timor-Leste has emerged as a leader in the developing world, with organic land accounting for 7 percent of all agricultural land, a level comparable to that of Sweden (Willer et al. 2008, pp. 29, 40).

"Organic Foods" as a Mobilizing Frame

How can we account for the readily apparent success of "organic" as a mobilizing frame for a social movement concerned with what we eat? A fundamental strength of the "organic" frame lies in its ability to bring together principled issue groups with agents pursuing more narrowly defined economic interests. Thus, the organic frame is embraced by, for instance, contemporary followers of Rudolf Steiner's spiritual philosophy, as well as by what would appear to be close to their antithesis in what Pollan (2001) calls the "organic-industrial complex." An odd "coalition" between family farmers seeking to create and sustain "alternative" forms of community and profit-seeking multinational corporations has been made possible, in part, by the fact that "organic" foods are defined not by the characteristic of the final products (such as their nutritional values and wholesomeness) but rather by their production, which follows a set of technical standards that, frequently, have been defined by state authorities in ways that do not fully express core "organic" values. Although the hypothetical organic Twinkie that was the focus of concerned debate in the 1990s appears to never have made it to market and organic Coca-Cola remains a fictional product (Mensvoort 2008), organic "junk foods" such as chipotle barbecue potato chips and chocolate fudge brownie ice cream fill supermarket shelves.[3]

In addition, "organic foods" displays a considerable "frame-bridging capacity" (Tarrow 2002, p. 243), such that the designation has been found useful by actors pushing a range of different agendas and issues. Whereas "organic foods" was initially almost exclusively concerned with methods for cultivating the soil, it has since come to extend to entirely new areas of food production, principally relating to dairy and meat. The organic frame was extended to these areas in response, in part, to rising concerns with the welfare of animals in these industries.[4] Some countries have also incorporated fish into the organic frame by embracing the idea that aquaculture—seen as a potential solution to global overfishing—can also be done in accordance with "organic" principles.[5] In addition, "organic" has been extended to incorporate the collection of "wild" foods, such as berries, mushrooms, nuts, and honey. The organic frame has also been made relevant for social-justice issues such as "fair trade," women's rights, the empowerment of indigenous peoples, and "food sovereignty." Likewise, the real or imagined dangers of new technological developments, such as the utilization of transgenic organisms in food production, provided an opportunity to present "organic foods" as the safer alternative. More recently, a bridge has been built between "organic foods" and the threat of global warming, with organic agriculture touted as a means by which climate change can be mitigated (Kotschi and Müller-Sämann 2004). Organic foods are proffered as a potential solution not only to local environmental problems, but to planetary-scale challenges as well.

The wide range of issues that "organic" is assumed to be able to address is indicated by the U.S.-based Organic Consumers Association declaration, on its webpage, which states that it is "campaigning for health, justice, sustainability, peace and democracy."[6] In all these cases, "organic foods" serves as a bridge between extrinsic and intrinsic values that have become increasingly central to modern individuals, as they seek to develop and live by an ethic that balances care for personal health and for the natural and social environment in its local and global dimensions. Because of the remarkable ability of organic food ideologues and marketers to link organic foods to narratives of the multiple ways in which organic foods production and consumption improves ourselves and our world, it would be a mistake to conceive of the organic foods movement as a single-issue movement.

The frame-bridging capacity of "organic" is evident also in its embrace by political parties with disparate ideological profiles and political agendas. Historically, organic foods production appealed mainly to parties and groups at polar opposite ends of the left–right ideological spectrum. In the 1930s, organic farming found broad support from the European far right, including the Nazi regime in Germany.[7] Since the 1960s, in contrast, organic food has found a new home in the countercultural New Left (Guthman 2004). Reflecting these historical political affinities, it is not entirely surprising that the organic foods movement today finds allies in both far-right parties such as the British National Party and the Alliance for the Future of Austria (*Bündnis Zukunft Österreich*) and extreme-left parties such as Denmark's Red-Green Alliance (*Enhedslisten*). However, green parties are even more closely aligned with the organic movement, and these have generally been in a better position to influence government policy, directly or indirectly. The British Green Party wants to provide free organic meals in schools and convert at least "10 percent of UK food production to organic every five years" (Green Party 2010, pp. 22, 39). To reduce the difference in price between organic food and conventionally produced food products, the Swedish green party proposes, among other things, to make organic food exempt from value-added taxation and to raise taxes on synthetic fertilizers and pesticides (Miljöpartiet de gröna 2005). At the level of the European Parliament, the European Greens have declared that "[t]he future of agriculture lies in organic farming and fair trade" (European Green Party 2009). Even though the organic movement may have closer affinities with some political parties than others, organic farming is nevertheless finding support, to a greater or lesser extent, throughout the party-political arena in Europe. The organic foods movement has transcended its early ideological origins and become part of the political mainstream.

The cooptation of organic farming by religious movements offers another striking illustration of its frame-bridging capacity. The example of Buddhism in Thailand has already been noted. In India, Meera Nanda observes that, "organic agriculture and other small-is-beautiful movements are being recoded into a [Hindu] religious idiom which serves as the mobilizing ideology for the peasantry" (Nanda 2005, p. 157; see also Nanda 2003). At the consuming end of the commodity chain, it is noteworthy that it is now possible to find certified organic foods products that are simultaneously certified as kosher or halal. The religious diversity thus evidenced is yet another indication of the ability of the organic frame to bridge significant identity divides.

The growth of the organic foods movement has also been facilitated by its ability to generate and then capitalize on scientific, and hence authoritative, knowledge about the benefits and potentialities related to soil ecology, pests and diseases, weed management, nutrition, food quality, and the like that are associated with food production based on "organic" methods. Much of this research has been conducted by researchers associated with "movement" institutes, such as the Rodale Institute in Pennsylvania (established in 1947), the Research Institute of Organic Agriculture (*Forschungsinstitut für biologischen Landbau*) in Switzerland (established in 1973), and the Louis Bolk Institute in the Netherlands (established in 1976). IFOAM organized the first international scientific conference on organic agriculture in 1977. Today, much of the research on organic agriculture is conducted at "ordinary" universities and research institutes (which are not otherwise a part of the organic movement) and receives considerable funding from governments (Stinner 2007). The International Society of Organic Agriculture Research (ISOFAR) was founded in 2003, with the aim of promoting and supporting "research in all areas of organic agriculture, as it is defined by the global consensus of organic agriculture movements and documented in the IFOAM Basic Standards for Organic Production and Processing."[8] There is also the International Organic Food Quality and Health Research Association, founded in 2004, which promotes research into the effects of organic foods on human health.[9] These networks of scientists have played a central role in developing the transnational dimensions of the organic movement.

The "organic" frame was not the first frame applied to the development of an "alternative" approach to agriculture. The biodynamic agriculture movement inspired by Rudolf Steiner had introduced a standard and a certification scheme (using the brand "Demeter," after the Greek goddess of the harvest) already by the late 1920s (Vogt 2007, p. 22). Yet, according to Demeter International, only 145,000 hectares of agricultural land are managed according to biodynamic principles, a miniscule area in comparison with the 30 million hectares claimed to be under organic management.[10] Why, in spite of its head start, has the biodynamic movement not been able to expand further? On this, we may of course only speculate, but one possible answer is that "biodynamic," in comparison with "organic," has an inferior frame-bridging capacity because of its firm grounding in a mystical worldview influenced by Hinduism, homeopathy, and astrology (Purdue 2000).

We may ask the same question about the way in which previously dominant approaches to "alternative agriculture" in developing countries have come to be eclipsed by "organic." That question is addressed by Peter Vandergeest (2009) in a study of alternative agriculture in Thailand. An important part of his explanation is that organic farming has had a superior ability to speak to multiple audiences and appeal to a diverse set of actors. In Thailand, the earliest approaches to "alternative" agriculture—such as "natural farming" and "integrated farming"—were explicitly framed as anticommercial and antistate. Their development thus depended, largely, on the (gradually waning) enthusiasm of NGO activists and the Western aid agencies that funded their projects. In contrast, "organic" has won the support not only of a myriad of local rural development–oriented NGOs and community groups, but also of domestic commercial interests and the Thai state. Historically mutually suspicious social groups and organizations have thus been able to collaborate and cooperate within the "organic" frame in ways that would be almost unthinkable for many of the rival approaches to alternative agriculture. Other "alternative" models of food production such as "integrated farming" or system of rice intensification (SRI), which may be highly relevant in an Asian context, have been eclipsed because they, unlike "organic," do not have readily available equivalents in other developed or developing regions. Not only are they therefore less familiar to globally dominant food producers and consumers, they also have more limited transnational movement support.

This discussion of organic foods as a mobilizing frame has implications for how we conceptualize the organic foods movement. First, it suggests that it is difficult to conceive of the organic foods movement as a single movement. There are, strictly speaking, several organic foods movements, and organic foods is incorporated into the agenda of a variety of much broader movements that have ultimate goals and ambitions that go far beyond questions of how food is produced.

Second, these "organic foods" movements do not conform to common understandings of transnational social movements, which according to Tarrow's definition are distinguished, in part, by their engagement in "sustained contentious interaction with powerholders in at least one state other than their own, or against an international institution, or a multinational economic actor" (2001, p. 11). Such contention hardly characterizes the behavior of most organic farmers or consumers of organic foods, who are not necessarily engaged in contentious politics even with regards to powerholders in their own state (Tovey 1997, 2002). An exception to the rule might be found in a social movement that has an affinity with the organic movement, namely the anti-GMO (genetically modified organism) movement—but here the rallying cry is for "GMO-free" (or GM-free) rather than for "organic" foods. Although the latter is by definitional fiat GMO-free, so is much "conventionally" produced food as well. The organic foods movement was but one of many social movements that joined in the surprisingly successful fight against biotech, in which the repertoire of contention included tactics such as "bio-sabotage" (Schurman 2004; Schurman and Munro 2009).

At the associational level, the organic movement is engaged in intensive interaction with powerholders in governments, international institutions, and multinational corporations, but this interaction is highly routinized. The rise of the organic foods movement as a transnational phenomenon has taken the primary form of institutionalization as an international NGO that is concerned with "enacting, codifying, modifying, and propagating world-cultural structures and principles" (Boli and Thomas 1999, p. 19).

What began as local or, at most, national organic foods movements have also nurtured the growth of what we might call a transnational "epistemic community" that, thanks to specialized scientific knowledge and expertise, is in a powerful position to influence policy decisions relating to the organic field (Adler 1992; Haas 1992).

A central conflict within the organic movement is to be found in the perceived tension between the "alternative" visions of its pioneers and the extensive incorporation of organic foods into the "conventional" industrialized and globalized market economy—and its institutionalization in the attendant regulatory frameworks—that has taken place in the course of the past three decades (Guthman 2004; Buck, Getz, and Guthman 1997; Noe 2006). Farmers who convert from conventional to organic agriculture today are not necessarily part of any "movement" at all, if this is understood to involve an ideological commitment to a more or less clearly defined set of "organic" values (Sligh and Cierpka 2007), rather than to the rational exploitation of profit opportunities in a niche market, the attractiveness of which is, in part, a function of government subsidies that have created organic "rent havens." At the other end of the commodity chain, consumers of organic foods do not necessarily self-identify as members of any organic movement. This is particularly true of all those who consume organic foods as a consequence of public procurement policies that ensure that organic products account for a rapidly growing share of the food served in kindergartens, schools, hospitals, and other public services. Such nonmovement producers and consumers of organic foods may be considered products of the movement's successful institutionalization.

The theoretical significance of this is that, although the market for organic foods ultimately rests on an interpretive frame, its recent expansion—both in terms of area under cultivation and food consumption—is to a large extent driven by material incentives. But these, in turn, are to a considerable extent dependent on government policies that directly or indirectly provide financial support for the production and consumption of organic foods. As such, the organic foods market—and by extension the movement as such—is vulnerable to shifts in public policy.[11] But as long as the frame itself remains secure, disconfirming evidence about the economic and developmental benefits of organic farming—such as studies showing that organic coffee farmers in Nicaragua have lost ground, in terms of poverty, relative to conventional farmers (Beuchelt and Zeller 2011) or that Norwegian farmers "drop out" from organic certification schemes because of unsatisfactory economic returns and the burdens associated with "red tape" (Flaten et al. 2010)—are likely to be met by demands for increased and better targeted public subsidization rather than a withdrawal of public support.[12]

The "organic" frame as such is mainly vulnerable to evidence that undermines belief in the positive externalities, in terms of the environment and public health, on which its public policy appeal rests. There is still doubt whether organic foods are really better for our health (Dangour et al. 2009). There is also doubt whether organic foods production, on a larger scale, would be compatible with the environmental ideals embraced by the movement itself (Paarlberg 2010). As the phenomenon of organic foods production has become more widespread, it has also become the object of more critical attention. Can the movement live up to all its promises, whether explicit or implicit?

Institutional Opportunities

The rise of the organic foods movement as a transnational phenomenon has been made possible, to no small degree, by a proliferation of institutional opportunities over the past few decades (Tarrow 2002, pp. 241–242).

First, a series of international environmental events have provided important mobilizing opportunities for the organic foods movement. The United Nations (UN) Conference on the Human Environment, held in Stockholm in 1972; the UN Conference on Environment and Development, in Rio de Janeiro in 1992; and the World Summit on Sustainable Development, in Johannesburg in 2002 are major events that have developed the concept of "sustainability" and turned "sustainable agriculture" into an explicit political commitment of the international community. It is no coincidence that IFOAM was formed within months of the Stockholm conference. International organizations also sponsor annual events such as the Food and Agriculture Organization (FAO)'s "World Food Day" (16 October) and the UN Environment Program (UNEP)'s "World Environment Day" (5 June), which provide recurring mobilizational focal points for the organic foods movement.

Second, initiatives by state allies have contributed to the growth of the organic foods movement in a number of ways. Most important, states have provided heavy direct and indirect subsidies to farmers for converting from conventional to organic methods of food production. Denmark was a pioneer in this regard. In 1987, the minority center-right government headed by conservative Prime Minister Poul Schlüter passed a landmark Act on Organic Farming (the first of its kind), which has provided financial subsidies for conversion to organic farming, research and development, certification, and more. The law also created an Organic Farming Council, today known as the Organic Food Council (*Det Økologiske Fødevareråd*), in which representatives of environmental and organic movements, farmers, consumers, industry, and government agencies have cooperated in the development of governance mechanisms in support of the country's organic foods sector.[13] In essence, the Danish state has approached the organic foods industry as one would expect when a "developmental state" identifies a strategically important "infant industry," utilizing a variety of supply-side and demand-side policy instruments to spur the industry's growth and development (Daugbjerg and Halpin 2010).

Over the past 30 years or so, it is probably safe to say that it is the European Union (EU) that has provided the greatest institutional opportunities for the transnationalization of the organic foods movement. Since 1993, EU legislation establishing "a legally enforceable and officially recognized common standard for organic crop production, certification and labelling" has facilitated the emergence not only of an EU-wide common market in organic foods, but also a global market (Padel and Lampkin 2007, p. 97). Once EU law provided a definition of organic agriculture, it became possible for the EU to provide financial support to organic agriculture within the framework of the Common Agricultural Policy (CAP). EU grants for agri-environmental and rural development schemes have provided a significant support for the conversion of land from conventional to organic foods production and for marketing and processing of organic foods. In addition, the EU has also supported the development of transnational research projects focusing on various aspects of organic food and farming through schemes known as CORE-Organics I and II.[14] European commitment to the promotion of organic food is further evidenced by the development of and publication, in 2004, of a European Action Plan for Organic Food and Farming (http://www.orgap.org).[15] Finally, it might be noted that the enlargement of the EU has provided a powerful impetus for the development of organic farming in the post-communist states of Central and Eastern Europe (Stracansky 2010). At the European level, policy development and implementation involves extensive consultation with so-called stakeholders. As recognized stakeholders, representatives of the organic foods movement have been able to exercise considerable influence over the development of EU policy relating to organic food and farming. The organic foods movement has successfully portrayed itself not only as a repository of professional expertise, but also, and more significantly, as "owners of the ideas of organic agriculture" (IFOAM EU Group 2006, p. 5). Because of the latter, the credibility and legitimacy of government regulation of the organic field—particularly as this relates to standards and certification—is critically dependent on official initiatives receiving the blessing of the movement.

Clearly, the European polity has functioned as a "coral reef," to use Tarrow's metaphor (2001, pp. 15–16; 2002, p. 242), that has provided ample institutional opportunities for the development of transnational dimensions of the organic foods movement. To a somewhat lesser extent, but more global in scope, this is true also of UN institutions such as FAO, the UN Conference on Trade and Development (UNCTAD), the World Trade Organization (WTO), and the World Health Organization (WHO). These organizations work closely with IFOAM in developing standards and also in promoting organic agriculture, not the least in developing countries.

The UN agencies have also helped legitimate further action to promote organic foods production. A particularly significant UN-led initiative is known as the International Assessment of Agricultural Knowledge, Science and Technology for Development (IAASTD). Initiated by the World Bank and co-sponsored by a wide range of UN agencies, the IAASTD process brought together representatives of governments, civil society (including IFOAM), and scientists to make an international assessment of the role of agricultural science and technology in "reducing hunger and poverty, improving rural livelihoods, and facilitating equitable, environmentally, socially and economically sustainable development." The drafting and editing of the report provided a focal point for civil society activism (Scoones 2009), and the final report, presented in 2008, has, with its endorsement of organic agriculture, helped shift the debate on agricultural policy in ways welcomed by organic food advocates (McIntyre et al. 2009; IAASTD Watch 2008).

The Organic Foods Movement as a Model

The rise of the organic foods movement to a position of power and influence in world politics may partly be explained by the efficacy of the organic frame and by the plethora of institutional opportunities offered by states and international organization. However, *how* the movement has been organized and operated at the transnational level has also helped legitimate the transnational dimension in relation to both its own members and to external stakeholders (states, corporations, international organizations, and other INGOs). It is a telling indicator that the organic foods movement has come to serve as a model for other social movements seeking to develop a transnational element to their own work on issues relating to social and environmental "sustainability." Notably, IFOAM served as an organizational "blueprint" when the Forest Stewardship Council (FSC) was founded in 1993, and it furthermore "provided the institutional model for certification as the primary policy instrument used by the FSC and later also by a variety of other transnational rule-making organizations" (Dingwerth and Pattberg 2009, p. 723).[16] In addition, key organizational features pioneered by IFOAM were subsequently adopted by other prominent international NGOs (INGOs) concerned with global sustainability. These include a parliamentary-style governing body and an organizational culture that emphasizes democratic norms and processes (transparency, accountability, participation, etc.) (Dingwerth and Pattberg 2009). A recent assessment of the "accountability capabilities" of powerful global organizations identified IFOAM as the most accountable among the INGOs (Lloyd, Warren, and Hammer 2008).

The transnational organic foods movement thus derives its legitimacy, in no small part, from its embrace of "democratic" practices of two different kinds: first, by giving producers and consumers a choice about whether to make or buy "organic"; and second, by operating internal democratic procedures that give members effective voice in the continuous evolution of the meaning of "organic" and the methods used for certification.[17] Of course, this does not mean that IFOAM in particular or the organic foods movement in general are immune from criticism. One notable area of concern is in regards to the difficulties that producers from poor countries face in influencing the formulation of organic standards, as well as in complying with them (Hatanaka 2010; Vandergeest 2007). Smallholders in tropical countries are particularly disadvantaged by the expensive and bureaucratic certification regime that has been developed over the past few decades, primarily with the conditions of Western Europe in mind (Raynolds 2004).

Conclusion

The transnational organic foods movement is today one of the most well-established of a new crop of civil society organizations and networks that seek to discipline and "civilize" states, corporations, and individuals wherever on the planet they happen to be located (Bowden and Seabrooke 2006). However successful it has been in the past, a new global context poses fresh challenges.

Whereas "organic" in the past few decades was fortuitously positioned, as a matter of definition, as the diametrical opposite of agricultural models that relied on the heavy use of synthetic pesticides and transgenic seeds, "organic" as it is currently understood has a much more ambivalent relationship to the issues on which IFOAM's most recent advocacy campaigns are focused: climate change, biodiversity, and food security. If the political salience and urgency of these issues continue to grow in the years ahead, the organic foods movement may face a growing credibility problem. Although organic agriculture may very well have advantages over "conventional" agricultural methods in terms of carbon footprints, biodiversity, and impact on the world's most metabolically vulnerable populations, as IFOAM asserts, it is not necessarily so. Whether it does is highly contingent on the context. The movement's positioning of organic as an answer, if not *the* answer, to these global ills is rendered particularly vulnerable because certified organic standards do not (as yet) differentiate between organic farming operations that, all things considered, have net beneficial effects on climate change, biodiversity, and food security, and those that do not.[18]

Moreover, any current advantages associated with organic farming techniques may prove unsustainable in the longer term as organic's ideologically less constrained "Other" (i.e., conventional farming) evolves in response to the changing political, commercial, and ecological context. In so doing, it is able to draw on a wider repertoire of agricultural models and techniques—conventional, organic, no-till, integrated pest management, SRI, conventional and genetic plant breeding, and more.[19] In the long run, so-called conventional farmers are likely to be better positioned than their organic colleagues to harvest the private benefits of combining organic farming methods with transgenic technology while in the process generating larger positive externalities. The classic example is no-till farming, which typically is done with herbicide-tolerant transgenic seeds. In this light, it is difficult to see how the organic foods movement's dominant frame—positing a binary between organic and conventional—can be maintained as increasingly sophisticated and pragmatic consumers, producers, and regulators search for answers to new questions. The transnational organic foods movement is vulnerable to shifts in the standards by which environmental impacts are measured.

However, efforts to adapt to these shifting priorities and standards will exacerbate tensions within the coalition of diverse interests and organizations that shelter under the transnational movement's umbrella. For example, while IFOAM has put the issue on the top of its advocacy agenda, many organic farmers remain, like some in New Zealand, "among the most adamant climate change sceptics" (Campbell and Rosin 2011). There may thus be less of an elective affinity between the environmental sensibilities of organic farming and other environmental concerns than is often assumed. In a similar vein, the temptation to follow the cue of the "global justice" movement and adopt its communitarian and anticapitalist answers to the question of "how to feed every person on the planet whilst safeguarding its future" (Reed 2010, p. 148) must be tempered by the realization that doing so would exclude the supporters of organic foods in the transnational "social movements for global capitalism" (Sklair 1997), most notably the large retailers. Managing these conflicting external pressures and internal demands is the challenge that the organizations that make up the transnational organic foods movement now face.

Notes

1. The segment can be viewed at http://www.thedailyshow.com/watch/thu-may-14-2009/little-crop-of-horrors. This public reaction can be contrasted with that experienced by Prince Charles, who was regarded as a loony eccentric who "talked to his plants" when he began promoting organic foods in the early 1990s (Shnayerson 2007).
2. On the history of IFOAM, see Geier (2007).
3. This is part and parcel of the broader trend toward so-called conventionalization that has been observed in the organic foods industry. See, for instance, Buck et al. (1997) and Howard (2009).
4. For dairy, it was also the consequence of a negative consumer reaction to the introduction of Monsanto's genetically engineered recombinant bovine growth hormone (rBGH) in the early 1990s (DuPuis 2000).

5. This view was initially rejected in the United States (Mansfield 2004; Eilperin and Black 2008).
6. http://www.organicconsumers.org/
7. On the relationship between fascist movements and ideas about organic farming, see, for example, Brüggemeier et al. (2005), Biehl and Staudenmaier (1995), Conford (2001), and Moore-Colyer (2004).
8. http://www.isofar.org/about/documents/isofar-statutes-2006.pdf
9. http://www.organicfqh.org/about_fqh/index.html
10. Demeter International was founded in 1997 by 16 national biodynamic agriculture associations (http://www.demeter.net/). It has established a liaison office in Brussels in order to lobby the EU.
11. Indeed, uncertainty about the future direction of public policy may be one important factor that is holding farmers back from converting from conventional to organic methods of farming (Kuminoff and Wossink 2010).
12. Such support can be justified if the price premium attached to organic food products is insufficient to compensate not only for the costs associated with the conversion from conventional to organic, but also for lower land and labor productivity of organic farms relative to conventional farms and the higher transaction costs associated with certified-organic farming.
13. By the late 1980s, Denmark had developed an unusually active and entrepreneurial "grassroots" environmental movement, and, in national-level politics, a consensual approach that emphasized market-based approaches to solving environmental challenges had been established. The organic foods initiative was thus just one of many similar "green" initiatives that, today, have helped establish Denmark as a leader in the field of organic agriculture and wind-power technology. However, the success of the environmental movement has also engendered a backlash in the form of environmental skepticism (Jamison 2004).
14. Details on these transnational research projects can be found at http://coreorganic.org.
15. In addition, many individual EU member states have developed national "action plans" to support the development of organic foods production.
16. These include, most notably, the two remaining founding members of the International Social and Environmental Accreditation and Labelling (ISEAL) Alliance (established in 1999): the Fairtrade Labelling Organizations International (1997) and the Marine Stewardship Council (1997).
17. IFOAM has three different levels of affiliation (member, associate, supporter). Full voting rights at the general assembly are given to members only. To become a member, an organization or corporation must qualify as "predominantly organic."
18. The Climate, Community & Biodiversity Alliance has launched a certification scheme that attempts to address some of these issues. The Alliance is backed by leading NGOs, such as CARE, the Wildlife Conservation Society, and the Rainforest Alliance, and is funded by companies such as BP, Hyundai, and Weyerhaeuser.
19. On the combination of organic farming with genetic engineering, see Ronald and Adamchak (2008).

Bibliography

Adler, Emanuel. 1992. "The Emergence of Cooperation: National Epistemic Communities and the International Evolution of the Idea of Nuclear Arms Control." International Organization 46(1): 101–145.

Beam, Christopher. 2009. "Organic Panic: Michelle Obama's Garden and Its Discontents." Slate, 4 June.

Beuchelt, Tina D., and Manfred Zeller. 2011. "Profits and Poverty: Certification's Troubled Link for Nicaragua's Organic and Fairtrade Coffee Producers." Ecological Economics **70**(7): 1316–1324.

Biehl, Janet, and Peter Staudenmaier. 1995. *Ecofascism: Lessons from the German Experience.* Edinburgh: AK Press.

Boli, John, and George M. Thomas. 1999. "INGOs and the Organization of World Culture." In *Constructing World Culture: International Nongovernmental Organizations Since 1875*, edited by J. Boli and G. M. Thomas. Stanford: Stanford University Press.

Bowden, Brett, and Leonard Seabrooke, eds. 2006. *Global Standards of Market Civilization.* London: Routledge.

Brüggemeier, Franz-Josef, Mark Cioc, and Thomas Zeller, eds. 2005. *How Green Were the Nazis? Nature, Environment, and Nation in the Third Reich.* Athens: Ohio University Press.

Buck, Daniel, Christina Getz, and Julie Guthman. 1997. "From Farm to Table: The Organic Vegetable Commodity Chain of Northern California." Sociologia Ruralis **37**(1): 3–20.

Campbell, Hugh, and Christopher Rosin. 2011. "After the 'Organic Industrial Complex': An Ontological Expedition Through Commercial Organic Agriculture in New Zealand." Journal of Rural Studies *27(4): 350–361.*

Coleman, William D., and Austina J. Reed. 2007. "Legalization, Transnationalism and Organic Agriculture." In *Law and Legalization in Transnational Relations*, edited by C. Brütsch and D. Lehmkuhl. London: Routledge.

Conford, Philip. 2001. *The Origins of the Organic Movement.* Edinburgh: Floris.

Dangour, Alan D., Sakhi K. Dodhia, Arabella Hayter, Elizabeth Allen, Karen Lock, and Ricardo Uauy. 2009. "Nutritional Quality of Organic Foods: A Systematic Review." American Journal of Clinical Nutrition **90**(3): 680–685.

Daugbjerg, Carsten, and Darren Halpin. 2010. "Generating Policy Capacity in Emerging Green Industries: The Development of Organic Farming in Denmark and Australia." Journal of Environmental Policy and Planning **12**(2): 141–157.

Delegation of the European Commission to Thailand. 2006. "*Thai organic exports receive boost*" 30 August. http://www.deltha.cec.eu.int/en/news_2006/Organic%20exports_EN.htm.

Dingwerth, Klaus, and Philipp Pattberg. 2009. "World Politics and Organizational Fields: The Case of Transnational Sustainability Governance." European Journal of International Relations **15**(4): 704–744.

DuPuis, E. Melanie. 2000. "Not in My Body: rBGH and the Rise of Organic Milk." Agriculture and Human Values **17**(3): 285–295.

Eilperin, Juliet, and Jane Black. 2008. "USDA Panel Approves First Rules For Labeling Farmed Fish 'Organic.'" Washington Post, 20 November.

Ellis, Wyn, Vitoon Panyakul, Daniel Vildozo, and Alexander Kasterine. 2006. *Strengthening the Export Capacity of Thailand's Organic Agriculture.* Geneva: International Trade Centre.

European Green Party. 2009. "A Green New Deal for Europe: Manifesto for the European Election Campaign 2009." http://europeangreens.eu/euroarchive/fileadmin/logos/pdf/manifesto_EUROPEAN_GREENS.pdf

Flaten, Ola, Gudbrand Lien, Matthias Koesling, and Anne-Kristin Løes. 2010. "Norwegian Farmers Ceasing Certified Organic Production: Characteristics and Reasons." Journal of Environmental Management **91**(12): 2717–2726.

Geier, Bernward. 2007. "IFOAM and the History of the International Organic Movement." In *Organic Farming: An International History*, edited by W. Lockeretz. Wallingford: CAB International.

Green Party. 2010. *Fair Is Worth Fighting For: Green Party General Election Manifesto 2010*. London: Green Party of England and Wales.

GTZ. 2009. "GTZ and Thai Organic Trade Association Join Hands to Expand Thai Organic Exports." http://www.thai-german-cooperation.info/news-events/news/gtz-and-thai-organic-trade-association-join-hands-to-expand-thai-organic-exports.html

Guthman, Julie. 2004. *Agrarian Dreams: The Paradox of Organic Farming in California*. Berkeley: University of California Press.

Haas, Peter M. 1992. "Epistemic Communities and International Policy Coordination." International Organization **46**(1): 1–35.

Hatanaka, Maki. 2010. "Certification, Partnership, and Morality in an Organic Shrimp Network: Rethinking Transnational Alternative Agrifood Networks." World Development **38**(5): 706–716.

Howard, Philip H. 2009. "Consolidation in the North American Organic Food Processing Sector, 1997 to 2007." International Journal of Sociology of Agriculture and Food **16**(1): 13–30.

IAASTD Watch. 2008. "A New Era of Agriculture Begins Today. International Agriculture Assessment Calls for Immediate Radical Changes." http://www.agassessment.org/docs/Civil_Society_Statement_on_IAASTD-28Apr08.pdf

IFOAM EU Group. 2006. *Stakeholder Involvement and Transparency in the EU Regulation for Organic Food and Farming*. Brussels: IFOAM EU Group.

Jamison, Andrew. 2004. "Learning from Lomborg: Or Where Do Anti-Environmentalists Come From?" Science as Culture **13**(2): 173–195.

Kotschi, Johannes, and Karl Müller-Sämann. 2004. *The Role of Organic Agriculture in Mitigating Climate Change: A Scoping Study*. Bonn: IFOAM.

Kuminoff, Nicolai V., and Ada Wossink. 2010. "Why Isn't More US Farmland Organic?" Journal of Agricultural Economics **61**(2): 240–258.

Lloyd, Robert, Shana Warren, and Michael Hammer. 2008. *2008 Global Accountability Report*. London: One World Trust.

Mansfield, Becky. 2004. "Organic Views of Nature: The Debate Over Organic Certification for Aquatic Animals." Sociologia Ruralis **44**(2): 216–232.

McIntyre, Beverly D, Hans R. Herren, Judy Wakhungu, and Robert T. Watson, eds. 2009. *Agriculture at a Crossroads: Synthesis Report*. Washington DC: IAASTD and Island Press.

Mensvoort, Koert van. 2008. "Organic Coca-Cola." 29 December. http://www.nextnature.net/2008/12/i-want-my-organic-coke/

Miljöpartiet de gröna. 2005. "Partiprogram." http://www.mp.se/files/82000-82099/file_82014.pdf

Moore-Colyer, Richard. 2004. "Towards 'Mother Earth': Jorian Jenks, Organicism, the Right and the British Union of Fascists." Journal of Contemporary History **39**(3): 353–371.

Nanda, Meera. 2003. *Prophets Facing Backward: Postmodern Critiques of Science and Hindu Nationalism in India*. New Brunswick: Rutgers University Press.

——. 2005. "Response to my critics." Social Epistemology **19**(1): 147–191.

Noe, Egon. 2006. "The Paradox of Diffusion of Organic Farming: A Case Study in Denmark." In *Sociological Perspectives of Organic Agriculture: From Pioneer to Policy*, edited by G. Holt and M. Reed. Wallingford: CAB International.

Paarlberg, Robert. 2010. "Attention Whole Foods Shoppers." Foreign Policy 179 (May/June): 80–85.

Padel, Susanne, and Nicolas Lampkin. 2007. "The Development of Governmental Support for Organic Farming in Europe." In *Organic Farming: An International History*, edited by W. Lockeretz. Wallingford: CAB International.

Parnwell, Michael, and Martin Seeger. 2008. "The Relocalization of Buddhism in Thailand." Journal of Buddhist Ethics **15**: 79–176.

Pollan, Michael. 2001. "Behind the Organic-Industrial Complex." New York Times Magazine, 13 May.

Purdue, Derrick A. 2000. "Backyard Biodiversity: Seed Tribes in the West of England." Science as Culture **9**(2): 141–166.

Raynolds, Laura T. 2004. "The Globalization of Organic Agro-Food Networks." World Development **32**(5): 725–743.

Reed, Matthew. 2010. *Rebels for the Soil: The Rise of the Global Organic Food and Farming Movement*. London: Earthscan.

Ronald, Pamela C., and Raoul W. Adamchak. 2008. *Tomorrow's Table: Organic Farming, Genetics, and the Future of Food*. New York: Oxford University Press.

Schurman, Rachel. 2004. "Fighting 'Frankenfoods': Industry Opportunity Structures and the Efficacy of the Anti-Biotech Movement In Western Europe." Social Problems **51**(2): 243–268.

Schurman, Rachel, and William Munro. 2009. "Targeting Capital: A Cultural Economy Approach to Understanding the Efficacy of Two Anti-Genetic Engineering Movements." American Journal of Sociology **115**(1): 155–202.

Scoones, Ian. 2009. "The Politics of Global Assessments: The Case of the International Assessment of Agricultural Knowledge, Science and Technology for Development (IAASTD)." Journal of Peasant Studies **36**(3): 547–571.

Shnayerson, Michael. 2007. "A Funny Thing Happened on the Way to the Throne." Vanity Fair, May. http://www.vanityfair.com/politics/features/2007/05/princecharles200705

Sklair, Leslie. 1997. "Social Movements for Global Capitalism: The Transnational Capitalist Class in Action." Review of International Political Economy **4**(3): 514–538.

Sligh, Michael, and Thomas Cierpka. 2007. "Organic Values." In *Organic Farming: An International History*, edited by W. Lockeretz. Wallingford: CAB International.

Stinner, Deborah H. 2007. "Science of Organic Farming." In *Organic Farming: An International History*, edited by W. Lockeretz. Wallingford: CAB International.

Stracansky, Pavol. 2010. "Organic Farming Blossoms." IPSnews.net, 1 April.

Tarrow, Sidney. 2001. "Transnational Politics: Contention and Institutions in International Politics." Annual Review of Political Science **4**(1): 1–20.

——. 2002. "From Lumping to Splitting: Specifying Globalization and Resistance." In *Globalization and Resistance: Transnational Dimensions of Social Movements*, edited by J. G. Smith and H. Johnston. New York: Rowman & Littlefield.

Tovey, Hilary. 1997. "Food, Environmentalism and Rural Sociology: On the Organic Farming Movement in Ireland." Sociologia Ruralis **37**(1): 21–37.

——. 2002. "Alternative Agriculture Movements and Rural Development Cosmologies." International Journal of Sociology of Agriculture and Food **10**(1): 1–11.

UNDP. 2008. "Project Brief: THA-06-19 Promotion of organic rice." http://www.undp.or.th/resources/documents/tha-06-19_002.pdf

Vandergeest, Peter. 2007. "Certification and Communities: Alternatives for Regulating the Environmental and Social Impacts of Shrimp Farming." World Development **35**(7): 1152–1171.

——. 2009. "Opening the Green Box: How Organic Became the Standard for Alternative Agriculture in Thailand." Paper presented at the Berkeley Workshop on Environmental Politics, April 17.

Vogt, Gunter. 2007. "Origins of Organic Farming." In *Organic Farming: An International History*, edited by W. Lockeretz. Wallingford: CAB International.

Willer, Helga, Minou Yussefi-Menzler, and Neil Sorensen, eds. 2008. *The World of Organic Agriculture: Statistics and Emerging Trends 2008*. Bonn: IFOAM and FiBL.

CHAPTER 31

THE DIALECTIC OF PRO-POOR PAPAYA

SARAH DAVIDSON EVANEGA AND MARK LYNAS

Introduction

ALTHOUGH according to some analyses genetic engineering is the "fastest-adopted crop technology in recent history" (James 2014), it can equally be argued that the use of molecular techniques of recombining DNA for crop breeding has failed to achieve even a fraction of the potential for which its early developers hoped. Large-scale adoption has so far been limited to just four crops: corn, soy, canola, and cotton, and, among them, just two traits—herbicide-tolerance and insect-resistance.

Major world commodity crops such as wheat and rice have so far been entirely locked out of the biotech revolution, while applications in fruit-growing and horticulture are noteworthy only by their scarcity. Some early innovations, such as the Flavr-Savr tomato and NewLeaf potato, have been dropped altogether, despite their promised benefits to farmers and others in the food sector. Other horticultural crops, such as squash and sweet pepper, remain at very low levels of adoption in only one or two countries, while others, such as bio-fortified and disease-resistant potatoes, bananas, beans, and others, remain in the development pipeline even after many years of research work (efforts are ongoing by the African Agricultural Technology Foundation, the Agricultural Biotechnology Support Project II, and other projects worldwide).

A partial exception that proves the rule is the focus of this chapter. The development and rapid adoption of genetically engineered virus-resistant papaya in Hawaii, followed by its subsequent political rejection when introduced into Thailand, illustrate both the reasons for rapid adoption of plants of unique utility to growers and the political obstacles that have slowed adoption of biotech crops. This case study of a little-known genetically modified horticultural crop is of sufficiently small scale that we can detail obstacles to adoption in Thailand in ways that illuminate the global biotechnology controversy more broadly (see McHughen; Newell-McGloughlin; Harriss and Stewart, this volume).

The papaya case study is of particular interest because this innovation represents a rare example of public-sector biotechnology aimed at supporting resource-poor farmers growing a relatively small-scale crop and, therefore, stands in contrast to genetically engineered (GE) applications developed by multinational seed companies and primarily utilized by large-scale farmers producing for world markets. The experience of GE papaya may also be helpful in disentangling the threads of opposition to biotechnology: widely held concerns about the patenting of seeds and the rights of farmers obviously did not apply in this case. The chapter will conclude with implications for projecting the future of projects developed in the public sector and focused on smallholder farmers. Virus resistance is a trait that is not available through other than molecular techniques, unlike the more common applications such as herbicide tolerance; bioproperty is not contested. In this sense, the papaya case parallels contestation around bio-fortification (see Stein, this volume). "Golden Rice," for example, addresses a micronutrient deficiency in a major food crop in which no breeding alternatives for beta-carotene enrichment exist. Like Golden Rice, papaya is a public-sector project using techniques with no known alternatives. Despite these characteristics, genetically engineered papaya faced political resistance similar to that confronting bulk commodities in which the desired trait could be produced by other techniques and carrying property claims of major life-science corporations such as Monsanto.

Papaya as a Food Crop

Papaya is a minor crop by the standards of world trade, but as a fruit predominantly produced and consumed in the developing world it is nevertheless an important and highly nutritious food source for many consumers in poorer countries. Papaya is consumed as a fresh fruit, as a raw green "vegetable" in salads, and as a cooked "vegetable." It is grown in the developing world both on a commercial scale as well as by small-scale farmers for home or local consumption. It is close to an ideal crop for small-scale subsistence growers because it can be easily grown from seed and requires few inputs. Moreover, the first mature fruits can generally be harvested a mere nine months after seed sowing, and the fruit is produced continuously year-round. As a tropical herbaceous plant, papaya trees can reach 12 feet tall in a single year of growth (Gonsalves 1998).

Papaya is a valuable source of micronutrients for impoverished people with diets dominated by rice or other nutrient-poor caloric sources. It is high in vitamin C and rich in pro-vitamin A carotenoids, both of which indirectly facilitate iron uptake. A 100-gram serving of ripe papaya (a quarter or less of a single fruit) provides 133 percent of the recommended daily intake (RDI) of vitamin C for an adult and 33 percent of the RDI for vitamin A (Duxbury 2003). Thus, although it receives little attention from development experts concerned with food security, papaya already helps alleviate two of the "big three" micronutrient deficiencies that plague undernourished people globally (iron, vitamin A, and iodine) and clearly holds considerable promise for further diversifying the diet of the rural poor in tropical countries.

In Thailand papaya has special culinary and cultural importance. It is the primary ingredient in *som tam* (green papaya salad), which is consumed daily by ordinary Thai people—especially rural people working in the paddy fields where a shared bowl of *som tam* complements the sticky rice staple. More than 90 percent of papaya consumed in Thailand is grown in Thailand, much of that at the household scale in backyard gardens or peripheral areas around rice paddy fields (Davidson 2008).

Papaya Ringspot Virus

Papaya ringspot virus (PRSV) belongs to the genus *Potyvirus*, and it has a single-stranded RNA genome encapsidated by the genome-encoded coat protein (CP) (Tripathi et al. 2008). PRSV is a vector-borne pathogen, mainly transmitted by aphids. Symptoms of infection typically include characteristic ringspot symptoms on the fruits of infected trees as well as chlorosis on leaves and the stunting of affected plants.

Although first reported in 1945, PRSV may have been observed as early as 1937 on the island of Oahu in Hawaii. Initially a relatively mild pathogen, PRSV evolved a more virulent strain in the 1950s, virtually wiping out the papaya industry in Oahu by the late 1960s. Around this time the virus was first detected in Brazil, the world's largest papaya producer, and it gradually forced the entire papaya industry to relocate inland away from the initial growing areas around São Paolo and Rio de Janeiro to more pristine uninfected areas in the remoter west of the country (Gonsalves 1998). In Taiwan, PRSV had spread throughout the entire island by the late 1970s, devastating the production industry. It was discovered in 1991 in Queensland, Australia, the center of papaya production in that country, and it is now considered a worldwide problem with no producer country being free of the virus.

Various mitigation strategies have been attempted in different regions with varying degrees of effectiveness. In Taiwan, for example, the destructiveness of PRSV has forced farmers to grow papaya as an annual crop, with trees removed immediately after the harvest of the first mature fruit, by which time they will usually have become infected. In Taiwan some farmers have also adopted the expensive strategy of growing papaya under protective nets to exclude aphids until first fruit production. In Brazil, a vastly larger country, the key growing areas have continually shifted to try to keep one step ahead of the spread of the virus. However, this has raised shipping costs and lowered the quality of the fruit, which is fragile and easily damaged during transportation (Gonsalves 1998).

Development of Transgenic Virus-resistant Papaya

Given the devastating effects of PRSV on papaya productivity and its increasingly global spread, scientists began more than forty years ago to investigate the potential for developing resistant papaya varieties. Early attempts focused on the possibility of "cross protection," whereby plants would be deliberately infected with a mild strain of the virus to protect against later infection by a more virulent strain—a process analogous to vaccination with live but weakened virus in humans. These attempts met with only mixed results, however: The milder strains of PRSV still produced symptoms of infection, marking the fruit and making farmers reluctant to deploy it. It also failed to confer total protection against virulent PRSV when deployed in the field in both Taiwan and Thailand from 1985 onward (Gonsalves 1998).

Coincidentally, at around this time, the science of molecular biology began to yield new tools for transforming plants and other organisms, including the use of recombinant DNA technology, which offered the potential to move genes between unrelated organisms. Simultaneous advances in understanding of the mechanisms whereby plant viruses parasitize their hosts led to the proposal in 1985—by John Sanford at Cornell University and Stephen Johnston, then at Duke University—of "pathogen-derived resistance" (PDR), namely that resistance to a pathogen could be conferred by introducing a gene from that pathogen into the host (Sanford and Johnston 1985).

Sanford and Johnston recognized that this mechanism already exists in nature in the phenomenon of cross protection (discussed above). The challenge would therefore be to refine the technique by introducing the necessary genes without the need to infect the plant (or other organism) with a related virus, and to do so reliably with the genes being heritable as necessary. Later this phenomenon of pathogen-derived resistance was identified as resulting from "RNA interference" (RNAi), a process by which RNA molecules inhibit gene expression. The two scientists who identified RNAi and coined the term (Andrew Fire and Craig Mello) shared the 2006 Nobel Prize in Physiology or Medicine for their 1998 *Nature* publication identifying RNAi in the nematode worm *C. elegans* (Fire et al. 1998).

A plant virus is a relatively simple structure composed primarily of its hereditary material (either RNA or DNA), which is typically housed in a protein structure termed a "coat protein." Even back in 1985, Sanford and Johnston had proposed that one of the ways resistance could be derived might be from utilizing the viral genetic sequences involved in producing this coat protein. Just a year later, a separate team showed that transgenic tobacco expressing the coat protein gene of tobacco mosaic virus did indeed exhibit resistance to infection by the virus (Abel 1986). This appeared to be pathogen-derived resistance in action; in the case of tobacco the genes were introduced by the newly discovered method of using *Agrobacterium tumefaciens* to insert viral DNA into the genome of the target plant.

In the same year (1986), plant virologist Dennis Gonsalves at Cornell University began a project to use pathogen-derived resistance against viruses that affect fruits and vegetables—principally papaya, but also cucumber, watermelon, and squash. Gonsalves's work was given additional real-world relevance by the anticipated likelihood that papaya ringspot virus would island-hop in Hawaii to affect the main papaya-growing Puna district on the Big Island. Given the sensitivities that would eventually arise around utilizing the new transgenic technology in an important food crop, an attractive aspect of the PDR approach is that no actual protein is expressed by the plant—the mere introduction of viral DNA into the genome of the papaya plant is enough to shut down viral replication and thereby prevent infection by the virus.

Gonsalves and his team utilized the newly invented "gene gun" (rather than *Agrobacterium*) to introduce the virus coat protein genes into papaya, together with new techniques for tissue-culturing transformed plants. The first papaya varieties to be genetically engineered in this way were the Hawaiian red-fleshed "Sunset," which was subsequently crossed to the consumer-preferred and Big Island–adapted yellow fleshed "Kapoho" variety. The resulting transgenic lines demonstrated extremely robust resistance to Hawaiian strains of PRSV. By the end of 1992, the Cornell team began to conduct field trials of one of the new papaya varieties at Waimanalo on Oahu island, where PRSV was first discovered many decades earlier. Giving particular urgency to the project, PRSV was indeed discovered in the main papaya-growing Puna region of Hawaii in the same year, and the virus began to spread rapidly. Despite an eradication program involving the destruction of thousands of infected papaya trees, within five years the entire growing region was severely affected and the industry under threat of destruction.

Introduction of Virus-resistant Transgenic Papaya in Hawaii

In 1995 a large-scale field trial of new transgenic yellow-fleshed F1 hybrid "Rainbow" papaya variety was begun in Puna, Hawaii—resistant papayas were planted in a virus-infested area, with non-transgenic varieties surrounding the test site as controls. The reported results were striking: while the susceptible papaya varieties withered under the pressure of virus infection, the transgenic variety demonstrated near-total resistance, even when physically inoculated with the virus. Yields of the resistant "Rainbow" variety were more than 2,200kg/ha (more than three times the industry average), as compared to negligible 56 kg/ha for susceptible "Sunset" variety after full infection (Ferreira et al. 2002). Because the trial was undertaken in the primary papaya-growing region, local farmers were able to visit and see evidence of the success of transgenic papaya at first hand in the field.

Meanwhile, Hawaii's papaya industry was suffering a crisis, and full-scale collapse threatened: by 1998 commercial production had fallen to about half the 1992 level, and what fruits were harvested all came from PRSV-infected fields. Three of the five papaya packing houses had closed in Puna by 1998, and the two remaining facilities had ceased to operate full-time. However, the process to deregulate transgenic papaya for full-scale production had already begun: Approval was obtained from the USDA-Animal Plant Health Inspection Service (APHIS) in 1996, and from the Environmental Protection Agency in 1997, along with the necessary consultation with the federal Food and Drug Administration (Fuchs and Gonsalves 2007).

With official clearance obtained, transgenic papaya seeds were distributed free to growers via the Papaya Administrative Committee in Hawaii under a lottery system based on need and the severity of PRSV infection on farms. Because of the severity of the crisis, most farmers planted their transgenic seeds soon after they received them—within a year, by 1999, visibly healthy fields of papaya trees were commonplace. Today about 70 percent of the papaya-growing area in Puna, Hawaii, is transgenic, and GE papaya fruits can be purchased by consumers throughout the United States, Canada, and, to a limited extent, Japan.

To date no breakdown of resistance to the virus has been reported, even with rapid and widespread deployment. The commercial release of transgenic papaya has also had the wider benefit of assisting non-transgenic papaya recovery by dramatically reducing the overall prevalence of the virus—an example of the so-called halo effect of some pest and disease-resistant GE crops. Transgenic papaya has also had the environmental benefit of allowing papaya production to be focused on existing virus-infected land, reducing the pressure to clear highly biodiverse forested land in a constant quest to avoid the virus (Fuchs and Gonsalves 2007).

The introduction of transgenic papaya into Hawaii is particularly relevant for study because the transformed cultivars were not developed by private companies for commercial gain but in the public sector by teams based at academic institutions (principally Cornell University) in response to perceived need in a small-scale farming sector. Papaya growers on Hawaii are primarily of Filipino ethnic background, and the industry mainly consists of small, family-oriented growers—many of whom supplement their incomes by holding off-farm second jobs (Fuchs and Gonsalves 2007). Thanks to this rapid and carefully targeted deployment of biotechnology, a family-farm industry continues today in Hawaii when it otherwise might have been wiped out by a virulent agricultural disease.

Papaya Transformed for Virus-resistance in Thailand

As detailed earlier, papaya ringspot virus is not a problem confined to Hawaii. In Thailand the papaya ringspot virus was first observed in 1975, and in following years it became an increasingly serious threat to production. An eradication program launched by the Thai Department of Agriculture focused on the immediate eradication of infected trees, but this strategy met with limited success due to the reluctance of villagers to destroy any papaya trees even with minimal fruit-bearing potential (Thitiprasert 2003). Because of the burden of disease, average yield from papaya cultivation fell significantly from the 1980s to the 1990s, while the price per kilogram more than doubled nationwide (Napasintuwong 2009). Papaya area under cultivation and overall tonnage produced continued to fall by 50 percent between 1997 and 2006. Given the importance of papaya both in Thai culture and in the nutritional well-being of ordinary Thai people, PRSV had by this time been identified by the Thai authorities as an agricultural threat of national importance.

There was obvious potential, therefore, for the approach using transgenic pathogen-derived resistance in papaya developed for Hawaii to be also applied in Thailand. Thailand also seemed a promising location because the country had already established a reputation as a leader in biotechnology: from 1992 to 2000, forty genetically engineered crops were approved for study in Thailand, and the Thai government had invested heavily in building national capacity for biotechnology from the 1980s onward (Sriwatanapongse et al. 2007). Thailand also had expert personnel directly concerned with the protection and promotion of papaya cultivation. One of these, the government plant virologist Vilai Prasartsee, had worked since the 1970s at the Khon Kaen Plant Material and Technical Service Center in Khon Kaen, Thailand, a facility located in one of Thailand's most important agricultural areas.

Prasartsee was charged with finding a means to control the papaya ringspot virus in Thailand. With this objective in mind, she forged a collaboration with Dennis Gonsalves at Cornell University as early as 1981, at first employing non-transgenic approaches to control the virus, though with little success. When Gonsalves's group finally began to make headway back in Hawaii by applying a transgenic PDR approach to virus control, Prasartsee and her team moved quickly to replicate the approach for Thailand. The effort would be more complex than simply importing Hawaiian transgenic papaya seeds, however: The sweet, yellow-fleshed, palm-sized Hawaiian varieties are neither adapted to Thai growing conditions nor acceptable to Thai consumers, who look for large zucchini-shaped varieties bred for *som tam*.

The Thai researchers therefore had to separately transform their own locally grown Thai papaya varieties with the coat protein gene isolated from Thai strains of the virus. This work began in 1995, when, with modest funds from the Thai Ministry of Agriculture and Cooperatives and the United States Agency for International development (USAID), Prasartsee arranged for two of her colleagues to go to the Gonsalves laboratory at Cornell University with the aim of creating a transgenic, virus-resistant papaya. The researchers took with them isolates of PRSV from Thailand and their own papaya material to transform. Just two years later, they had successfully transformed two Thai-preferred papaya varieties and returned home with the new transgenic plants.

The new virus-resistant papaya could not be released straight away, however, because of the need to demonstrate safety and lack of environmental harm for a transgenic plant to satisfy the regulatory process. Tests showed that the virus resistance trait was passed down at least three generations of the plant with enduring 97 to 100 percent effectiveness. Extensive multiyear health and biosafety tests failed to find any negative effects on human health or the environment (Sakuanrungsirikul et al. 2004). Nor were any negative effects identified on pollinators or on beneficial insects or predatory mites, and no differences were observed in soil microbes around GE or non-GE plants.

Allergenicity risks were also assessed and came up negative. The feeding behaviors of rats were studied and found to be equivalent between rats fed GE and those fed non-GE papaya. The nutritional profiles of GE and non-GE papaya were assessed and also found to be equivalent (Sakuanrungsirikul et al. 2004). The issue of gene flow was also judged to be of minimal concern: Most cultivated papaya plants are self-pollinated, and even in the worst case of outcrossing the result would be other papaya acquiring virus resistance; not necessarily a negative outcome for farmers. Moreover, it was argued that in Thailand no risk to wild relatives should exist, as *Carica papaya*'s closest related genus, *Vasconcellea*, has its center of origin in the Andes, far away from the fields of Thai farmers.

Greenpeace Challenges Deployment

The greatest challenge facing those charged with introducing virus-resistant transgenic into Thailand, however, turned out to be not a technical but a political one. Greenpeace, the multinational nongovernmental organization (NGO) based in the Netherlands, had established a Southeast Asia office in 2000 in Bangkok. This Southeast Asia group took an early decision to drop the wider Greenpeace campaign for forest protection and focus instead on an anti-GMO campaign, an effort that was identified as having a higher chance of success for the newly established organization (Davidson 2008). Prasartsee's newly transformed virus-resistant papaya was identified as a campaigning target given that it would represent the first GE crop proposed to be grown in the country.

On 27 July 2004 Greenpeace activists dressed in white-hooded personal protection suits, goggles, and respiratory masks traveled to Khon Kaen research station and used a ladder to climb over the barbed wire fence that surrounded Prasartsee's experimental GE papaya field trial. Having already alerted local and national television and print media, photographers recorded powerful and emotive images of gloved hands transferring genetically modified plant material into hazardous waste bins. Other activists held large yellow banners that read, in both Thai and English, "Stop GMO Field Trials."

Greenpeace's strategy involved more than a direct action approach aimed at symbolically uprooting GE papaya crops in order to raise attention to its concerns. The organization simultaneously released news that transgenic papaya seeds had already been removed from the Khon Kaen station and they were in unregulated use by Thai farmers. This revelation established a clear media and political narrative for the issue as concerning the unexpected and uncontrolled "contamination" of GE materials becoming widespread in Thailand's environment. The Greenpeace allegation seriously embarrassed the Thai government and, in particular, the Ministry of Agriculture, as it presented an undeniable failure of regulation. The ministry and the researchers therefore had little opportunity to defend the transgenic papaya on its own merits as the political scandal widened.

It is important to acknowledge that Greenpeace was almost certainly correct in its assertion that transgenic papaya seeds had left the research station prematurely and were being cultivated by farmers. Although to date it is still not established beyond doubt what happened, the most likely explanation is that field laborers hired by the research station took papaya seeds from the site and distributed them. Indeed, villagers interviewed later openly admitted receiving papaya seeds from relatives who worked at the station (Davidson 2008). An obvious incentive existed for them to do this: The virus-resistant papaya looked healthy and appeared even to the casual observer to deliver a much more productive crop than the virus-affected plants farmers were used to growing.

The 2004 situation in Thailand can therefore be viewed as an example of the unregulated spread of GE "stealth seeds," biotech seeds carrying highly desired traits coming into use by farmers long before being assessed or approved by regulators. In India, for example, GE pest-resistant Bt cotton seeds were in wide circulation years before transgenic cotton was deregulated by the Indian government in 2002, while in Brazil unapproved GE soy was similarly smuggled across the border from Argentina by farmers eager to utilize its herbicide tolerance trait for better weed control (Herring 2007; Herring 2013). There are many more examples: as a biologically self-replicating technology, transgenic seeds are clearly difficult to control, especially in polities with little regulatory capacity and border protections.

Greenpeace took the opportunity of the failure of regulation of a genetically engineered crop in Thailand to put strong pressure on the Thai government. A "feature story" published on its international website on the day of the direct action began as follows: "We warned the Thai government over a year ago not to play with genetically engineered (GE) papaya but they didn't listen. Now they have left the whole country's papaya crop wide open to contamination," it asserted (Greenpeace 2004). Greenpeace's GE campaigner in Southeast Asia, Varoonvarn Svangsopakul, was quoted in the same piece as saying: "This is potentially one of the worst cases of genetic contamination of a major food crop in Asia as this station is one of the largest suppliers of papaya seeds in the country. This is the hard evidence we needed to prove that GE contamination has broken in Thailand."

Greenpeace was therefore able to portray its 27 July 2004 action as a last-resort measure to protect the public from the Thai government's failure to properly control the use of potentially dangerous technology. From the outset the issue was discussed by the activists, the media, and policymakers as one of how "contamination" could be contained before it escalated even further out of control in the countryside. In addition, Greenpeace was careful to present itself as taking the side of Thai farmers. As Jiragorn Gajaseni, executive director of Greenpeace Southeast Asia, stated at the time: "All farmers who have purchased papaya seeds from the research station have a right to know whether GE papaya trees are growing on their land and whether their families are already eating GE papaya. Farmers [are] a victim of the environmental crime committed by the Department of Agriculture" (Greenpeace International 2004).

Impact on Thai Agriculture and Biotechnology

In retrospect, the interests of Thai farmers were certainly not as readily evident as represented by Greenpeace, however. Although the "contamination" issue led to uncertainty and confusion among producers, the eventual outcome of the saga was an undeniable restriction of farmers' choice over whether or not to adopt the GE approach to virus-resistance in papaya that had long been successfully deployed in Hawaii. Farmers who were known to have purchased seed from the research station had their farms visited and checked for transgenic papaya by government staff mandated to carry out village sweeps to eradicate any trees suspected to be virus-resistant.

Anecdotal but widespread reports told of negative impacts on farmers' livelihoods resulting from these actions. One instance, of farmer Mae Somkhuan from Khon Kaen province, is detailed in an earlier paper by one of the current authors (Davidson 2008). Mae stated that she was visited by Greenpeace activists, who removed sacks of her papaya after informing her that it could "contaminate" other trees. Rumors spread around the village that her papaya could cause sterility, early death, or cancer, and Mae was socially ostracized and left in near-bankruptcy after having invested heavily in a large loan to finance her smallholder papaya business. Many other smallholder farmers may have faced similar challenges, although this has not been documented systematically.

The wider impact of the scandal was to transform the political climate of Thailand from one that was cautiously supportive of agricultural biotechnology to one of outright hostility. The minister of agriculture—formerly a supporter of the virus-resistant papaya project—ordered that Prasartsee's field trial be eradicated and the project suspended. Workers cut down all the plant material in the 1.8-hectare plot and buried it in pits dug onsite. Greenpeace kept up political pressure by stating that these workers had worn "no protection" in destroying the GE papaya plots, again implying that they were dealing with bio-hazardous material (Greenpeace Southeast Asia 2006).

Greenpeace also successfully recruited other key stakeholders to take up its campaign banner. For example, the chairman of the Thai National Human Rights Commission told the *Bangkok Post* at a press conference in September 2004 that "it is likely contamination has occurred" in more than ten provinces and emphasized that "the danger of genetic engineering technology...could cause grave damage to the country's agricultural sector and biological resources." Prasartsee, instead of being celebrated for saving Thailand's papaya industry as she might have anticipated, was left facing disciplinary charges for "alleged negligence involving the leakage of GM papaya seeds from the station," as the *Bangkok Post* put it (Samabuddhi 2004).

Victory for the anti-GE campaigners was finally cemented when the prime minister, backed by a cabinet decision, ordered the destruction of all GE field trials in the country two months after the initial Greenpeace action (Waltz 2009). The combined effect of Greenpeace's direct action and "contamination" revelations, the ensuing scandal, and the resulting passage of prohibitive legislation was to bring all agricultural biotechnology in Thailand to a virtual standstill—a situation that persists more or less unchanged to this day.

It is important to emphasize that not only transgenic papaya was affected by the new more hostile political climate ushered in by the papaya scandal. Earlier GE crops trialed in Thailand had included chili and tomato resistant to viral diseases, yard-long bean and cotton resistant to insect pests, and rice resistant to ragged stunt virus and tolerant to saline conditions (Attathom and Navarro 2011). Following the cabinet and prime minister's ban, none of these projects could be continued or restarted, and to date all projects are either dormant or have been abandoned. Moreover, although twelve GE crop events received earlier official approval in Thailand (all for herbicide-tolerance and insect-resistance traits in maize and soybean), none are in commercial cultivation (ISAAA).

Although Greenpeace's campaign clearly had enormous impact, it did not arise in a vacuum—GE field trials had long been controversial, with NGO-led protests over Bt cotton field trials leading to an earlier suspension of field trials in 2001. In addition, the political instability that enveloped Thailand following the September 2006 coup against the Thaksin government made it impossible to resolve the situation clearly, with several changes of government and ongoing deadlock between monarchist protesters and pro-Thaksin government supporters on the streets of Bangkok.

When specific ministers did try to move forward, anti-GE campaigners remobilized to stop them: the post-coup agriculture minister Thira Sutabutra was ready to submit a proposal to cabinet in August 2007 to lift the GE ban but held back after Greenpeace protesters dressed as "zombie fruits" and wearing alien eyeballs dumped 10 metric tons of papaya (labeled "GMO?") outside the Agriculture Ministry (Davidson 2008). Embarrassingly for Greenpeace, all papayas were quickly scooped up and carried away by street crowds and workers in the ministry.

It is notable also that the pro- and anti-GE forces in Thailand do not divide along party lines in what is a very politically polarized country: instead, the anti-GE campaign has united a coalition of civil society NGOs, led informally on occasion by Greenpeace in a so-far successful campaign to prevent GE innovations from being tested or adopted in Thailand.

Conclusions

To return to some themes highlighted in the introduction to this chapter, we now consider what the virus-resistant papaya case study suggests in terms of reasons for the slow uptake of biotechnology outside the realm of a small number of large-scale commodity crops. What lessons might be learned for understanding and predicting the future of non-commercial projects designed primarily for use in comparatively less-industrialized countries? Though concerns that relatively poor countries and farmers cannot benefit from agricultural biotechnology because of patents and control by multinational life-science corporations, the politically powerful property issue proves to be more variable than common accounts suggest (Cohen 2005; Lybbert 2003). Some disaggregation of the lumped together term "GMOs" is illustrated by papaya. In the case of PRSV-resistant papaya in Thailand, property rights should not ostensibly have raised opposition from anti-GE activists on the specific grounds of multinational corporations being the sole beneficiaries, because the papaya was developed by a nonprofit-making international consortium of public-sector scientists; the seeds were distributed for free in Hawaii and would have been in Thailand as well had protests not succeeded.

Similarly, concerns about non-replicable and patent-protected seeds reducing the rights of farmers are shown in this case to be misplaced, as in the case of "Golden Rice." The virus-resistance trait in papaya was fully heritable and any patents were registered and held in the public interest by universities and research institutes. Furthermore, public fears about human health dangers of genetically engineered foods were addressed by multiyear safety trials published in the peer-reviewed academic literature, as has been the case with other GE crops (Chassy, this volume). Finally, the proven success of transgenic papaya in Hawaii could also have provided real-world evidence reassuring Thai farmers and consumers concerned about the prospects of GE papaya.

The issue of segregated international markets might, however, have raised some concerns requiring careful consideration. Specifically, Thailand is a major trader in agricultural commodities; export markets might be negatively affected by the presence of unauthorized transgenes in papaya. However, economic impacts would likely have been manageable given that the vast majority of Thai-produced papaya is consumed domestically; moreover, the smallholder papaya-growing sector produces exclusively for local consumption. The potential for cross-pollination from GE papaya, another frequently raised concern by opponents, was studied and found to be limited. Papaya is mostly self-pollinating; moreover, the impact of even a worst-case outcrossing of transgenic papaya would merely have been to spread virus resistance more widely, protecting more trees from disease and premature death. It is not clear why this outcome would necessarily represent a genuine environmental threat such as those, like deforestation and climate change, on which Greenpeace typically focuses its campaigns.

These factors raise the intriguing possibility that it may have been precisely because the GE papaya could not be opposed on the basis of many of the most common anti-GE arguments that it generated such a strong outpouring of activist opposition in Thailand. A safe transgenic crop delivering obvious consumer benefits, produced in the public sector for the use of small farmers in a developing country, might therefore be seen as more threatening to activist groups than GE applications with a more explicitly commercial focus, such as tolerance to proprietary herbicides. The stakes would have been particularly high with the new Greenpeace Southeast Asia office looking to mount a successful first major campaign after establishing itself in a rapidly emerging and economically important region.

The case of PRSV-resistant papaya in Thailand therefore illustrates the potential fate of any transgenic crop perceived as a "gateway GMO" and therefore prioritized for opposition by activists. Related arguments have been made about other non-commercial GE crops developed with ostensibly humanitarian objectives, such as vitamin A-enriched Golden Rice, which has been similarly criticized by activists as a "Trojan horse" for the entrance of biotech corporations (Pringle 2003: chap. 2). Moreover, had Thailand successfully gone ahead with transgenic papaya, governments and scientific agencies in neighboring Asian countries might have been emboldened by a GE success story to move forward faster with their own agricultural biotechnology programs. Thus the "gateway GMO" crop might have been regional or global as well as national in impact.

As an alternative outcome, a failure to deploy transgenic papaya could have a chilling effect on biotechnology throughout the entire region, especially given the ban applied to all GE field trials and applications in Thailand triggered by the protests. This impact would also encourage activists to expand their campaigns elsewhere, and indeed Greenpeace campaigners have since opposed Golden Rice in Bangladesh, China, and the Philippines, and they have carried out a direct action attack on a Bt *talong* (eggplant) field trial in the Philippines in February 2011 (Greenpeace International 2013; Greenpeace Philippines 2011; ISAAA 2011). Genetically engineered eggplant, like papaya, is the product of international cooperation in which technology fees and patent claims are foregone by the developers and farmers are exempt from any additional charges (Kolady and Lesser 2008).

One of the most salient lessons from the Thailand case is how the political and media debate played out. Once Greenpeace had successfully framed the media and political narrative of GE papaya as being primarily about "contamination," its activists had established a battlefield on which the agricultural scientists had little chance of winning public support. The idea of "contamination" evokes visceral fears about pollution and loss of purity in food, always an emotive and controversial issue for obvious reasons. Once placed on the defensive, the scientists were unable to make a clear case for why virus-resistant papaya was needed, safe, or useful in Thailand. The lesson here is clear: unless those charged with developing transgenic crop varieties demonstrate that they can control deployment of the technology in accordance with established regulatory procedures, opposition has an important political tool. The irony is that the "terminator technology" so effectively used in mobilizing anti-biotechnology forces in the early 2000s would prevent the gene flow now considered "pollution." Yet it was political opposition to the "terminator" that—along with doubts about efficacy—prevented it from being deployed in any crop, popular media accounts notwithstanding.

Another clear lesson is that activists are better at politics than are scientists. Although their case might well have been hopeless, in retrospect it is also clear that the Thai scientists failed to mount a coordinated rearguard campaign to defend their work. They did not succeed in mobilizing farmers, the intended direct beneficiaries, into a vocal constituency supporting the introduction of virus-resistant papaya. Nor did consumers apparently express any enthusiasm about the prospect of being able to eat virus-free, cheaper, domestically produced papaya. Media access and savvy also prove to be important in GM politics. Media coverage was minimal in advance of the introduction, enabling Greenpeace to establish a political debate that reflected its own perspective as the dominant narrative; there is a first-mover advantage in politics as in business. The case also illustrates a common phenomenon in the sociology of science communications: Failure to put credible and useful information into the public domain in terms resonant with popular understandings of agriculture and science prevalent in mass publics can diminish public acceptance of new technologies. Transparency is limited by the isolation and technical difficulty of much scientific work, contributing to a failure to mobilize potentially supportive stakeholder constituencies to participate in a more inclusive and science-based debate. But scientists in any event do not typically see political advocacy as their job or comparative advantage.

New technologies, especially those producing food, face an uphill struggle for many reasons, as the long European debates have shown (Bonny 2003; Tait 2001). Even when a biotech crop appears to have become widely accepted and established, as has been the case in Hawaii with transgenic papaya, successes are not irrevocable and progress can be unexpectedly reversed. In 2013 in Hawaii a widespread and polarizing public debate took place about whether multinational companies developing transgenic seeds should be targeted with new restrictive local legislation. The spillover of this debate has also negatively affected public perceptions of the long-established GE virus-resistant papaya. Orchards were damaged or destroyed by vandalism and vocal demands made for the whole industry to be eradicated and replaced with virus-susceptible organic crops (Harmon 2014). Despite having operated apparently successfully and with little challenge for nearly two decades, Hawaii's papaya growers now face the very real prospect of losing the disease-resistance technology on which they have come to depend.

The case also has lessons for understanding the political obstacles to increased adoption of transgenic crops. Opposition of anti-GE activists is deep-seated and persistent; it has proved resistant to contrary factual information or ameliorative policy measures to address specific objections, such as seed patenting or corporate ownership. In this sense, anti-GE activists mirror those opposing technological applications in other sectors, such as the vaccination of children or the use of anti-retroviral drugs to combat HIV/AIDS (Lewandowsky et al. 2013). The widespread Internet-based dissemination of demonstrably false conspiracy theories on GE is further supportive of this conclusion and suggests that tackling specific fears with only scientifically derived factual information may not have much impact and may even be counterproductive.

Risks and benefits of GE crops will remain a highly contested area for many years to come. As a consequence, concerns about real risks not targeted by political mobilization remain unaddressed. Through this skewing of political practice, well-established potential benefits are foregone: in Thailand, transgenic virus-resistant papaya seeds remain locked in a refrigerator, while ring-spot virus continues to damage conventional papaya production (Waltz 2009). In Hawaii, Denis Gonsalves has been forced out of retirement in order to defend his virus-resistant transgenic papaya against activist demands that all GMOs in Hawaii should be eliminated by law.

Any long-term outcome of this debate remains by its nature unpredictable. It is clear that activist efforts against GE crops that have been developed outside the main commercial commodity sectors, where the presence of multinational corporate firms is significant, have been—at least in the case of transgenic papaya in Thailand—instrumental in preventing their deployment. The Thai case reinforces a general conclusion of comparative studies: It is the politically controversial nature of GE crop development that has so far done most to limit its deployment rather than any limitations inherent in the technology itself or its failure to produce tangible benefits (Herring 2008).

References

Abel, P. P., R. S. Nelson, B. De, N. Hoffmann, S. G. Rogers, R. T. Fraley, and R. N. Beachy. 1986. "Delay of Disease Development in Transgenic Plants That Express the Tobacco Mosaic Virus Coat Protein Gene." *Science* 232: 738–743.

Attathom, S., and M. Navarro. 2011. "Information Tug-of-War: Saga of Biotech Papaya." In *Communication Challenges and Convergence in Crop Biotechnology*, edited by R. Hautea and M. Navarro, 156–179. Ithaca, NY|Los Baños, Philippines: International Service for the Acquisition of Agri-biotech Applications (ISAAA)|SEAMEO Southeast Asian Regional Center for Graduate Study and Research in Agriculture (SEARCA), and Ithaca, NY|Los Baños, Philippines: International Service for the Acquisition of Agri-biotech Applications (ISAAA)|SEAMEO Southeast Asian Regional Center for Graduate Study and Research in Agriculture (SEARCA).

Bonny, S. 2003. "Why Are Most Europeans Opposed to GMOs? Factors Explaining Rejection in France and Europe." *Electronic Journal of Biotechnology* 6(1): 50–71.

Cohen, J. I. 2005. "Poorer Nations Turn to Publicly Developed GM Crops." *Nature Biotechnology* 23(1): 27–33.

Davidson, S. N. 2008. Forbidden Fruit: Transgenic Papaya in Thailand. *Plant Physiology* 147: 487–493.

Duxbury, J. M. 2003. "Food Systems Approached to Nutrition and Health: The Role of Transgenic Papaya." *Virus Resistant Transgenic Papaya in Hawaii: A Case Study for Technology Transfer to Lesser Developed Countries, Hilo, Hawaii, October 22–24, 2003: Proceeedings*. Paris: Organisation for Economic Co-operation and Development.

Ferreira, S. A., K. Y. Pitz, R. Manshardt, F. Zee, M. Fitch, and D. Gonsalves. 2002. "Virus Coat Protein Transgenic Papaya Provides Practical Control of Papaya Ringspot Virus in Hawaii." *Plant Disease* 86: 101–105.

Fire, A., S. Q. Xu, M. K. Montgomery, S. A. Kostas, S. E. Driver, and C. C. Mello. 1998. "Potent and Specific Genetic Interference by Double-Stranded RNA in Caenorhabditis elegans." *Nature* 391: 806–811.

Fuchs, M., and D. Gonsalves. 2007. "Safety of Virus-Resistant Transgenic Plants Two Decades after Their Introduction: Lessons from Realistic Field Risk Assessment Studies." *Annual Review of Phytopathology* 45: 173–202.

Gonsalves, D. 1998. "Control of Papaya Ringspot Virus in Papaya: A Case Study." *Annual Review of Phytopathology* 36: 415–437.

Greenpeace International. 2004. "GE Papaya Scandal in Thailand." July 27. Accessed January 31, 2014. http://www.greenpeace.org/international/en/news/features/ge-papaya-scandal-in-thailand/.

Greenpeace International. 2013. "Golden" Rice. Accessed March 11, 2014. http://www.greenpeace.org/international/en/campaigns/agriculture/problem/genetic-engineering/Greenpeace-and-Golden-Rice/.

Greenpeace Philippines. 2011. "Greenpeace Moves to Decontaminate Bt Eggplant Field Trial Site in the Philippines." Accessed March 11, 2014. http://www.greenpeace.org/seasia/ph/multimedia/slideshows/Greenpeace-moves-to-decontaminate-Bt-eggplant-field-trial-site-in-the-Philippines/

Greenpeace Southeast Asia. 2006. Illegal GE Seeds Found in Packages Sold by Department of Agriculture. Accessed January 31, 2014. http://www.greenpeace.org/international/Global/international/planet-2/report/2006/6/GEpapayaThailand.pdf.

Harmon, A. 2014. "A Lonely Quest for Facts on Genetically Modified Crops." *New York Times*, January 4.

Herring, R. 2007. "Stealth Seeds: Biosafety, Bioproperty, Biopolitics." *Journal of Development Studies* 43 (1): 130–157.

Herring, R. 2008. "Opposition to Transgenic Technologies: Ideology, Interests, and Collective Action Frames." *Nature Reviews Genetics* 9 (6): 458–463.

Herring, R. 2013. "Re-constructing Facts in Bt Cotton: Why Skepticism Fails." *Economic and Political Weekly* 48 (18): 33.

ISAAA. Undated. "GM Crop Events Approved in Thailand." Accessed January 31, 2014. http://www.isaaa.org/GMapprovaldatabase/approvedeventsin/default.asp?CountryID=TH (accessed 31 Jan 2014)

ISAAA. 2011. "NAST President and University Chancellor Condemn Attack on Bt Eggplant Field Trial." Crop Biotech Update, February 18. Accessed March 11, 2014. http://www.isaaa.org/kc/cropbiotechupdate/article/default.asp?ID=7391.

James, C. 2014. "Brief 46: Global Status of Commercialized Biotech/GM Crops: 2013." ISAAA.

Kolady, D. E., and W. Lesser. 2008. "Potential Welfare Benefits from the Public-Private Partnerships: A Case of Genetically Engineered Eggplant in India." *Journal of Food, Agriculture and Environment* 6 (3–4): 333–340.

Lewandowsky, S., G. E. Gignac, and K. Oberauer. 2013. "The Role of Conspiracist Ideation and Worldviews in Predicting Rejection of Science." *PLoS ONE* 8 (10): e75637. [doi: 10.1371/journal.pone.0075637]

Lybbert, T. J. 2003. "Humanitarian Use Technology Transfer: Issues and Approaches." *Journal of Food, Agriculture & Environment* 1 (3–4): 95–99.

Napasintuwong, O., and G. Traxler. 2009. "Ex-ante Impact Assessment of GM Papaya Adoption in Thailand." *AgBioForum* 12: 209–217.

Pringle, P. 2003. *Food Inc.: Mendel to Monsanto: The Promises and Perils of the Biotech Harvest*. New York: Simon & Schuster.

Sakuanrungsirikul, S., V. Prasartsee, N. Sarindu, S. Chaikiatiyos, R. Siriyan, M. Sriwatanakul, P. Lekananon, C. Kitprasert, P. Kosiyachinda, G. Fermin, and D. Gonsalves. 2004. "Update on the Development of Virus Resistant Papaya: Virus-Resistant Transgenic Papaya for People in Rural Communities of Thailand." *Food and Nutrition Bulletin* 26 (4): 422–426.

Samabuddhi, K. 2004. "Somsak Says GM Papaya Has Spread." *Bangkok Post*, September 15.

Sanford, J. C., and S. A. Johnston. 1985. "The Concept of Parasite-Derived Resistance—Deriving Resistance Genes from the Parasites Own Genome." *Journal of Theoretical Biology* 113: 395–405.

Sriwatanapongse, S., N. Iamsupasit, S. Attathom, O. Napasintuwong, and G. Traxler. 2007. "The Study of Agricultural Benefits in Thailand." Bangkok: Biotechnology Alliance Association.

Tait, J. 2001. "More Faust than Frankenstein: The European Debate about the Precautionary Principle and Risk Regulation for Genetically Modified Crops." *Journal of Risk Research* 4 (2): 175–189.

Thitiprasert, W. 2003. "Status of Policy and Regulation on Transgenic Plants in Thailand." *Virus Resistant Transgenic Papaya in Hawaii: A Case Study for Technology Trransfer to Lesser Developed Countries, Hilo, Hawaii, October 22–24, 2003: Proceedings*. Paris: Organisation for Economic Co-operation and Development.

Tripathi, S., J. Y. Suzuki, S. A. Ferreira, and D. Gonsalves. 2008. "Papaya Ringspot Virus-P: Characteristics, Pathogenicity, Sequence Variability and Control." *Molecular Plant Pathology* 9: 269–280.

Waltz, E. 2009. "Hungry for GM Crops." *Scientific American Worldview*, May 2009. Accessed February 11, 2014. http://www.saworldview.com/wv/archive/2009/hungry-for-gm-crops/

CHAPTER 32

THINKING THE AFRICAN FOOD CRISIS

The Sahel Forty Years On

MICHAEL J. WATTS

Introduction

> In 1948 the first Director-General of the FAO, Sir John Boyd Orr, resigned from the organization, famously complaining that "when people ask for bread, we give them pamphlets." ... With pamphlets now replaced by satellite images and integrated information systems, the criticism remains hauntingly pertinent.
>
> Rupert Alcock, *Speaking Food*, 2009

A long time ago—in the early 1970s to be precise—I was resident in Sahelian West Africa during the great drought-famine. Subsequently I wrote a book, *Silent Violence* (Watts 1983), about famines and food crises in that part of the world, specifically the dryland savannas of northern Nigeria near the Niger border. It remains an open question whether the political-economic conditions, the life chances, and the vulnerabilities to climatic volatility confronting the farming households among whom I lived—and who now confront the dark clouds of global climate change—have substantially improved since that time. Situating northern Nigeria on a larger Sahelian canvas extending from Senegal to the Horn of Africa, a reasonable person might conclude that the deep problems of poverty and food insecurity among peasant and pastoral forms of livelihood have been remarkably resistant to human intervention across the Sudano-Sahelian region. My intention in this chapter is to reflect upon the enduring character of the Sahelian crisis—what Lauren Berlant (2007) referring to rather different circumstances calls "slow death"—and what it might suggest about the operations of, and prospects for, African agro-food systems, on a continent upon which the crashing waves of land grabs, climate change, resource scrambles, and the next phase of the GMO-charged Green Revolution are apparently already breaking.

There are four sections to the chapter. The first examines empirically the dimensions of the current Sahelian food crisis in the context of the wider landscape of African, and indeed global, hunger. The second reviews theoretical and conceptual scholarship—in large part triggered by the African famines of the 1970s and 1980s—addressing the causation and dynamics of famine and starvation. The third section provides a detailed case study of the continuing crisis of food insecurity and agrarian stagnation by returning to, and updating, a village study I conducted between 1976 and 1978 in Katsina, northern Nigeria. Finally, I reflect upon how the Sahel and the West African savannas have provided a sort of crucible within which theories and practices of food security have been forged, and indeed how these regions remain an important laboratory for the manufacture of contemporary thinking about dryland development in a region now confronting the grave challenges of global climate change.

Sahel Redux

There are close to one billion people in the world who go to bed hungry each night.[1] In historical terms, it is of course quite true that the proportion of the global population who are undernourished has fallen since the late 1960s—according to the United Nations World Food Program, hunger prevalence fell from 33 percent in 1969–1971 to 16 percent in 2011 (FAO 2011). FAO's latest 2012 report, armed with a new computational methodology, claims that undernourishment since 1990 has fallen even further than was previously believed (FAO 2012). In practice, a disproportionately large share of this impressive decline is accounted for by the explosive performance of the East Asia growth machine and its remarkable success in reducing poverty and improving well-being. Most of the progress in reducing hunger in any case was achieved prior to 2007. In short, the stark fact remains that 15 percent of the world's population remains malnourished; the figure for sub-Saharan Africa is 26 percent. Low-income states, in fact, have seen an overall setback in terms of the number of hungry people, from 827 million in 1990–1992 to 906 million in 2010. Indeed, the complete picture of hunger in the Global South is incomplete because there is as yet no full accounting of the recent price hikes and economic recession in many parts of the globe.

Historically speaking, hunger has proven to be exceptionally durable. The world, as the *Economist* (February 18, 2012, 62) recently put it, has not been terribly good at fighting hunger. Since the 1960s, the global hunger headcount has remained largely unmoved, at roughly 0.9 billion. To compound this sense of failure, another billion are undernourished in the sense of micronutrient deficiency, and a further billion are malnourished because they eat too much and are obese. A report by Save the Children titled *A Life Free from Hunger* (2012) claims that malnutrition alone accounts for 2.6 million deaths each year—one-third of the global total. One in four of the world's children are stunted, and global progress on reducing malnutrition has been pitifully slow for the last twenty years, falling at an average rate of only 0.65 percentage points per year since

1990. The report concludes that if current trends continue, an extra 11.7 million children will be stunted in sub-Saharan Africa in 2025 (compared to 2010), and the lives of more than 450 million children globally will be affected by stunting in the next 15 years (Save the Children 2012, xiii). In January 2008, *The Lancet*—one of the most respected medical journals in the world—published a five-part series on the irreversible effects of early childhood malnutrition (cited in Bread for the World 2010). When all is said and done, it is a damning record on virtually every front.

As I write in late 2012, the UN is calling for a massive food-aid mobilization in view of a looming subsistence crisis in the Sahel; according to the World Food Program, over 8 million people, in the wake of the poor 2011 rains, will require "life-saving food assistance" (World Food Program 2012). The World Food Program notes that while the earlier food crises of 2005 and 2010 were severe in Chad and Niger, the looming current crisis is affecting a broad swathe of countries across the region. Output is down by at least a third, food prices are considerably higher than in 2010, and many households have not recovered from the food shortage and high prices of the previous year. Here is the assessment of the Sahel forty years after I first saw famine refugee camps and terrible hardship in the region:

> The 2009-10 food crisis highlighted a host of long term policy failures, including adapting to climate change and controlling volatile prices of food in the markets…linked to state fragility and governance, and the ineffectiveness of aid. The 2010 crisis made visible the deep structural food and nutrition security problems that have persisted for decades. Most strikingly, the severe food deficit situation of households, combined with structural factors such as gender inequality and poor access to healthcare, have been generating catastrophic rates of child under-nutrition in the Sahelian zone of Chad for many years.
>
> (Gubbels 2011, 41)

The structural hunger problem is now located on a yet bleaker landscape. The Sahel has emerged as a new front in the prosecution of a counterinsurgency against radical Islam. The donor community's Sahelian "success story"—namely Mali—has recently descended into civil war. The Sahel is also one of the regions in which, according to the Intergovernmental Panel on Climate Change (2007), the deadweight of global warming is about to fall. In some quarters—Christian Parenti (2011) from the left, US Department of Defense (2011) on the right—this new conjuncture of violence, poverty, and climate change defines the coming apocalypse—the "tropic of chaos," as Parenti calls it. The awful reality is that one can plausibly claim that large swaths of Africa suffer from something close to "permanent famine," due to serial crises that have become the new normal. It is a life of what Paul Farmer (2003) calls "extreme suffering."

To see durability in the world hunger picture is not to infer that nothing has changed over the last fifty years in the West African Sahel, or for that matter in the circumstances in which the poor across the African continent and the Global South find themselves as net buyers or sellers of food. The dynamics of food provisioning *have* changed, and the centrality of grain markets, and their operations, in the lives of the poor has deepened.

Take, for example, the enduring question of the price of bread and John Stuart Mill's observation, long ago, that "men might as well be imprisoned, as excluded from the means of earning their bread." Real and nominal prices of staple foods have actually declined steadily since the global food crisis of the early 1970s, and they remained relatively low and stable between 1990 and 2006. Prices surged higher between late 2006 and mid-2008, driven by the financial crises and the biofuel boom, and again in 2010–2011.

According to the UNDP (2012, 41), however, these two price hikes had different causes and consequences. The 2010–2011 price hikes were led by maize, wheat, oil, and sugar, whereas the price of rice, an import for many sub-Saharan African countries, spiked in 2007–2008. Rice was less affected in the later episode because of good harvests in Asia, the main global supplier. A second difference is that the pass-through of global prices to local African markets, strong in 2007–2008, was weaker in 2010–2011, and on the surface, the poverty impacts of the price spikes appear to have been more limited in 2010–2011 than in 2007–2008.

Nonetheless the effects on poverty in both instances were dramatic. Rising prices in 2007–2008 may have led to a short-term surge of 105 million more extremely poor people. An updated analysis suggests that the comparable price rise in the second half of 2010 led to 44 million more poor people (UNDP 2012, 41). Between 2005 and 2009, the world's hungry probably grew from roughly 850,000 to slightly over 1 million. Price volatility and the turbulence of global food markets reverberated across the globe among the rural and urban poor, with catastrophic consequences for food-insecure households. Food prices had fallen sharply by mid-2008, but, ominously,, prices began a sharp ascent once again two years later, and through 2011 they were running at levels in excess of the high point of prices in 2008. What is new, in other words, is not the return of the Malthusian specter (demographic growth) or the challenges of low agricultural productivity—both of which are real. Rather, what is on offer is a reconfiguration of the landscape of global food provisioning and a coupling—what Ghosh (2012) calls an "unnatural coupling"—of food, fuel, and global finance.

Sahelian and Other Famines

I wish to inquire / Into the whereabouts of the dead.

W. G. Sebald, *Across the Land and the Water*, 2011

Nowhere has the acute stubbornness of hunger revealed itself with more drama than in sub-Saharan Africa (FAO 2011, 2012). Almost a quarter of a billion Africans suffer from hunger and malnutrition, moderate and severe stunting stands at 38 percent, and the number of undernourished exploded from 170 million in 1990 to 223 million in 2006–2008 (the proportion of undernourished stalled, only shifting from 26 percent to

23 percent over the period 2000–2012. Nobody seriously expects that the Millennium Development Goal (MDG) of halving the number of hungry people between 1990 and 2015 will be met in Africa—or indeed globally. The new UNDP (2012) human development report on Africa, devoted entirely to food security, paints a stark picture:

> Sub-Saharan Africa is plagued by intolerable levels of malnutrition. Left unchanged, this could result in irreversible mental and physical disabilities in this and future generations. Chronic malnutrition, measured by the share of preschool children who are stunted, is estimated to have fallen only 2 percentage points (from 43 percent to 41%) between 1990 and 2010 and is projected to fall just 1 percentage point over the next decade. For children who are underweight, a measure that also captures acute malnutrition, the picture is similarly grim. For both measures the absolute number of malnourished children has risen over the past two decades and is expected to continue to rise to 2020. The situation is particularly worrisome in East and West Africa, home to three of every four of the continent's malnourished children in 2010. All African sub-regions now have a higher prevalence of stunting than do Asia and South America. (19)

More than one-third of all climatological disasters affect sub-Saharan Africa, and agricultural productivity, according to UNDP data, has remained essentially unchanged since 1960. The gendered nature of the food security question— that is to say the stark differentials between men and women as regards access to land, mortality and morbidity rates, or nutritional status —is especially bleak. UNDP (2012) identified three sources of instability in African food systems: weather variability, food price volatility, and violent conflict. Recent hikes in food prices sparked demonstrations and riots in Burkina Faso, Cameroon, Cote d'Ivoire, Guinea, Mozambique, Senegal, and Uganda, with thousands taking to the streets. Studies show a positive long-term correlation between international food prices and antigovernment protests and civil conflict in low-income countries. They also identify three emerging threats— environmental degradation, climate change, and demographic pressures—that will increasingly disturb food systems and fray the link between food security and human development.

Globally, the incidence of famine—and famine mortalities—has seemingly declined since the 1960s,[2] leading some, like Cormac O'Grada in *Famine: A Short History* (2009), to refer to contemporary food crises as "small-scale famines." Yet Africa remains a striking outlier. In 2011 some 10 million people were drawn into the clutches of the terrible food crisis in Somalia, Kenya, and Ethiopia.

To speak of famines—writ small or large[3]—as discrete or hermetically sealed events characterized by mass mortality and starvation is open to question. Famines and food crises are social processes, and complex processes at that. There is now a substantial corpus of work on food crises, much of it focused on Africa and the semi-arid zones. One line of engagement, stimulating a substantial amount of debate, is derived, not unexpectedly, from Amartya Sen's (1980) work on entitlements. Sen and his collaborator Jean Drèze, in their important book *Hunger and Public Action* (Drèze and Sen 1989), address the poverty-hunger equation primarily in economic terms through forms of command over food (see also Drèze and Sen 1990). Famine and hunger are defined by entitlement collapse and expressed through the socially circumscribed distribution of entitlements over basic necessities. Although entitlement-based theories of vulnerability have the great merit of highlighting the specific social, economic, and institutional relations between food and people (in contradistinction to an emphasis on supply-side dynamics), and why some social classes are affected by hunger and others hardly touched, there remains a question of what sort of explanation (if any) entitlements actually provide (Watts and Bohle 1993; Watts 1991, 2000).

While Drèze and Sen see entitlements, in a wide sense, as embracing not only food intake (biology) but also access to health care and education (the social environment)—that is to say, the broader domain of well-being and advantage—they have less to say about the political economy of what they call "capability" and the "totality of rights" that secure basic needs. Firstly, entitlement as commodity bundle provides a "conjunctural" analysis, highlighting the immediate, triggering or proximate mechanisms (price movements, speculation, drought) that precipitate a shift in entitlements. It has much less to say about the long-term structural and historical processes by which specific patterns of entitlements and property rights come to be distributed or shift temporally—in other words, political economy. In failing to elaborate structural and often contradictory political, economic, and social determinants that mark the onset of the famine process, entitlement misses an important opportunity to link crisis theory with the longer-term processes that allocate and deprive households and individuals of assets and endowments.

Secondly, the entitlement approach also fails to take into account the central dimensions of famine consequence and recovery. It explains neither what transpires in the wake of mass starvation nor the lineaments linking a single famine to earlier or later crises. In this sense, entitlement—especially when read in a narrow legal or market sense—runs the grave danger of neglecting historical processes and, to invoke Gramsci, the situations and conjunctures producing such calamitous outcomes. Lastly, entitlements have often been construed much too narrowly, and this narrowness of vision constrains the variety of social domains in which claims over food and security can be exercised, as well as the social processes that shape individual entitlements. Concerns with gender, generation and age, and caste and ethnicity, for example, have received less attention than occupational status, property, and the market[4].

In my view, entitlements have to be radically extended not simply in a social or class sense, but also politically and structurally. In other words, an analysis of famine and hunger based on entitlements must account for the particular distribution of entitlements and how they are reproduced in specific circumstances; the larger canvas of rights by which entitlements are defined, fought over, contested, and won and lost (i.e., empowerment or enfranchisement); and the structural properties (what I have called "crisis proneness") of the political economy that precipitates entitlement crises. To encompass these questions, entitlements would need to be deposited in what Sen (1980, 180) himself calls, but does not explore, the mode of production. My own work (Watts 1983; Watts 2001) explored how climatic variability, food price volatility, and food availability were shaped not simply by inter-household inequalities, but also by the operations of the grain, labor, and land markets that collectively could both impoverish and enrich differing classes of peasants during periods of food scarcity and famine itself (see Davis 2001).

Another body of work has an even more restrictive economic account in that it limits the purview of famine to the functioning of markets (see Ravallion 1987). More precisely, famine in this view is seen as a function of imperfect markets that are weak, unintegrated, and possibly driven by speculative or hoarding behavior. Collectively, these market pathologies drive up food prices beyond the capacity (of some) to buy. The International Food and Policy Research Institute's (IFPRI) synthetic work on African famines is a case in point (von Braun et al 1998). Famine is largely seen in technocratic terms—a function of institutional, organizational, and policy failures—which is to say, famine is a poverty problem rooted in poor economic performance and failed or weak states. Policy failures are never construed as political or military, both of which are simply seen as derivative of, and secondary to, low productivity of the poor and an anodyne sense of "policy failure." Yet, paradoxically, much of the famine corpus of the last two decades necessarily focused on Africa, where it was glaringly clear that famines could *only* be understood in relation to politics, civil wars, militarism, and Cold War conflict.

The politics of famine point to the third strand of research, which starts from the presumption that famines are crises of political accountability, both national and international (de Waal 1989, 2009; Keen 1994; Kenally 2011; Davis 2001). In this accounting, famines are "complex emergencies"—humanitarian crises linked to large-scale violent conflict—in which violence is the handmaiden of food distribution. Compelling analyses of the food crises in Sudan and the Horn of Africa raise the prospect of what Devereux (2007) calls "new famines." Starvation reflects not simply the absence of a political contract—the notion that crises are deterred by anti-famine contracts between rulers and ruled—but also of the failures by humanitarian agencies and international governments to shape how and whether food relief—the central requirement in alleviating failed entitlements—is effective (Clapp 2011).

Food and food aid are, and have been, regularly deployed as weapons—but the larger point is that food entitlements and food delivery are themselves political. Some of the most compelling work on famine of late extends politics beyond the boundaries of African civil war and conflict and locates the crises of accountability within the vortices of state power. Mukerjee's (2010) analysis of Churchill's secret war on India, Frank Dikotter (2011) and Yang Jisheng's (2012) extraordinary accounting of the internal political struggles surrounding the Great Leap Forward and the devastating Chinese famine (1958–1962), and not least Lizzie Collingham's (2011) brilliant examination of the global reverberations of the Second World War, which resulted in the starvation of over 20 million people (including, of course, the Great Bengal Famine) are outstanding exemplars of the genre. Each of these studies can perhaps be best seen bookends to the remarkable—and devastating—picture painted by Mike Davis of the great forcing house of starvation produced by the intersection of two global processes: telekinetic activity in the world's climate cells through the El Niño Southern Oscilliation (ENSO), and the late nineteenth-century imperialism that Hanna Arendt (1948) called the political emancipation of the bourgeoisie. The violence of primitive accumulation (draped in the ideology of late Victorian capitalism) running headlong into global climate perturbation took the lives of some 60 million people.

One of the signal lessons to have been learned from the serial failures to improve food security and life chances in the arid lands of West Africa is that the boundary lines between mass starvation and the *longue duree* of permanent hunger and undernourishment are porous and flimsy. Existentially, what we are witnessing is something close to slow death, a death by attrition: "The phrase *slow death* refers to the physical wearing out of a population and the deterioration of people in that population that is very nearly a defining condition of their experience and historical existence" (Berlant 2007, 754; see Nally 2011). Put somewhat differently, what I have called "silent violence," which conveys the permanency and normalization of hunger, is in fact the necessary ether from which famines and mass starvation draw their ignition and fuel. At the same time, this violence represents the radical reduction of human existence down to what Agamben (1998) calls "bare life." Famine and hunger are inextricably intertwined, the deepest expressions of what Davis (2001) properly called the "war over the right to existence."

The Dynamics of Food Insecurity: A Nigerian Story (1976–2012)

My book *Silent Violence* was written against the backdrop of, and in some measure as a direct response to, the great Sahelian famine that struck West Africa and the Horn of Africa between 1969 and 1974. Over half a million people perished, perhaps many more. In its wake came devastating famines in Bangladesh, Mozambique, Sudan, Korea, and Uganda. In 1976 I arrived in northern Nigeria to conduct a village study in Kaita, a Hausa community near Katsina town[5] (Figure 32.1), a region located at the southern perimeter of the Sahelian savannas. The goal was to study a set of paradoxes; namely, why was hunger and starvation not accompanied by absolute scarcity (there was always food in the market), why were those who perished typically those who grew food, and why would farmers sensitive to the vagaries of rainfall in a drought-prone and high-risk environment resign themselves to starvation in the face of drought?

Silent Violence argued that Hausa peasants possessed a sophisticated grasp of local agroecology, but these practices—in relation to, say, rainfall variability—were shaped by their class position. The commercialization of land, grain, and labor—and the coercive operations of these markets in the face of unequal asset distribution—produced particular social patterns of vulnerability to drought and food insecurity rooted in the relations of production. At the same time, local protection systems rooted in the moral economy of the community were rapidly eroding, exposing peasants to the vicissitudes of the market. These findings have, in a sense, become the starting point for the study of food security across the Sahel, though conventional wisdom held otherwise in the 1970s. In an excellent report on the Sahel, Gubbels (2011, 16) argues that the rural economy

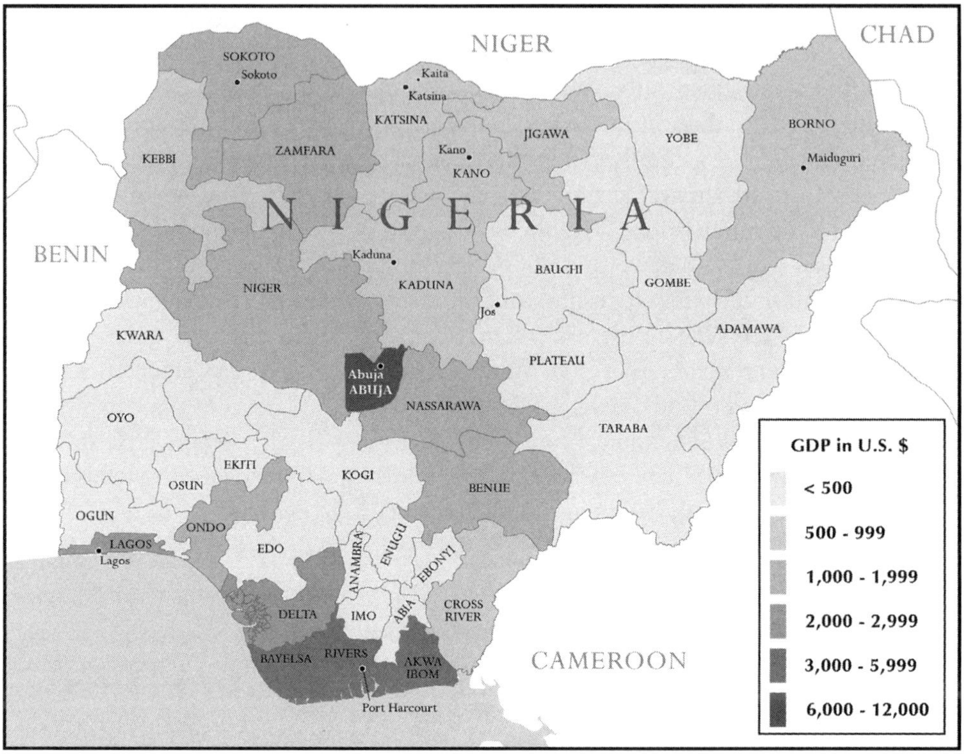

FIGURE 32.1 Nigeria: GDP per capita by State and location of Kaita Village in Katsina State.

in the Sahel has become highly commodified, that food security for the poor is highly market-dependent, and that food security and livelihood security are all but indistinguishable. As he shows, the vulnerability of households to food insecurity in Niger is highly variable even within the same communities. There is growing inequality in the distribution of productive assets. In particular, wealthier households (one quarter of the population) generate 9 to 15 times the amount of revenue compared to poorer households, and they possess 50 percent of the cultivated land and over two-thirds of livestock assets (15).

Since the 1970s —and in spite of the insertion of vast oil wealth[6]—northern Nigerian agriculture seems to have changed little; indeed, the picture appears frighteningly, and instantly, recognizable (Mortimore 2010). Land scarcity, endemic poverty, the annual round of preharvest food scarcity, food price volatility, periodic bouts of asset liquidation as farmers desperately purchase grains, harvest fluctuations, declining food output, and stagnant yields—all these woes were located on the larger canvas of a deepening commercialization of the food sector. The area harvested in Katsina State between 1990 and 2000 reveals a secular decline for almost all staple foodstuffs; yields over the same period did not budge—except for cowpeas maize, which fell dramatically, and cotton, which increased. Significantly average annual staple prices revealed a slow downward trend over the same period, suggesting—something to which I shall shortly turn—that cross-border trade and massive imports were compensating for the slump in domestic output (Ayodele Ariyo, Voh, and Ahmed 2001). Since 2003 the staple food price index has risen inexorably from 100 in January 2003 to 260 in January 2011. As if to drive home the sense of a food system on the brink, lurching from one bout of vulnerability to the next, the Katsina State government was compelled to release grains for sale at a 50 percent discount in February 2012 in the face of unsustainably high local prices and aimed at "alleviating the suffering of the people" (Olaniyan 2008). In some respects it all seems the same, but worse.

None of this should imply a regional economy locked into the prison-house of rural stagnation and decay. The last three decades and more have witnessed an extraordinary transformation—or rather a raft of transformations— in rural and urban livelihoods in Nigeria, and across the Sahel. This period has seen extraordinary rates of urbanization, Islamization, and deepening rural commercialization—the effects (always local and specific) of the neoliberal reforms from the mid-1980s and the waves of oil revenues cascading through the economic and political system. What Katsina and Kaita village have to show for all of this oil wealth is precious little. The Nigerian Bureau of Statistics estimates that the poverty rate for the northwest zone (including Katsina State) grew from 52 percent in 1985 to 71 percent two decades later (the comparable figure in the so-called South-South region for 2005 was 35 percent). Nearly three-quarters of northerners currently live on less than $200 a year, far below any poverty line (*Economist*, January 14, 2012, 44). In Katsina State the poverty head count grew from 54.7 percent to 60.9 percent between 2004 and 2010. After four decades of oil development, the social and human development indices for the state remain shockingly low even by Nigerian standards. Among a population of 6.4 million, 1.83 million have never attended school; 68.3 percent reside in mud or thatch dwellings; almost half obtain water from lakes, streams, and unprotected wells; and nearly two-thirds are without electricity (Federal Government of Nigeria 2009).

A gloss of rural conditions in the state can be gleaned from a baseline study of farmers in three Katsina local government areas (LGAs) in 2004, conducted by UN International Fund for Agricultural Development (IFAD 2004). It reveals an utterly miserable profile of rural poverty in the state. Two-thirds of the sample never attended school, 0.4 percent had higher education, and about 90 percent of the respondents had never taken the *hadj* (an indication of economic well-being). 91.7 percent owned a wood/mud-thatched roof, while only 0.2 percent owned a modern cement and block/brick zinc roof. The survey revealed that 71.4 percent acquired water from a well, while 2.3 percent got water from rain water, and 90 percent used firewood as fuel. Household income derived from the previous season's crop sales revealed that about 67.4 percent of the respondents received N15,000 (US$115) or less. Over 81 percent of the respondents held less than one hectare of land, and 61.8 percent of households purchased food (14 percent daily, 35 percent weekly). Three-quarters of respondents indicated a food shortage coped with by borrowing money (27.5 percent), borrowing food (23.5 percent), and selling assets (20.3 percent) (IFAD 2009, 30). A subsequent USAID survey in March–April 2007 in Bulungudi, Zango LGA, to the east of Kaita, sketched a similar pattern. Almost 40 percent of the households were poor (less than two hectares), 80 percent of staples were purchased, and 65 percent of household income was derived from casual work and remittances (USAID 2007). In effect, then, almost half the rural population were semi-proletarians.

Katsina is certainly not the poorest state in the federation, but incontestably it is part of a vast northern region—a Muslim bloc comparable in size and complexity to Egypt, Turkey, and large parts of the Middle East— now mired in abject poverty. As Lubeck (2010) has shown, across the Sharia states, malnutrition is almost twice the national average; the human poverty index is 45.88, compared to 27.8 in the non-Sharia states; female literacy in the north is 17 percent compared to 69 percent in the south; the percentage of married women using contraception is 3.4 percent in the Sharia states, compared to 14 percent nationally; and, not least, total fertility rates in the north are over 7 per woman, making for a massive youth bulge (the comparable figure in the Niger delta is 4.7). Overall, the picture is one of economic descent and declining per capita income coupled with radically declining health and education standards, but also of a crisis of legitimacy for the institutions of secular national development, and for northern ruling classes facing growing hostility from millions of *talakawa* (commoners). The northern poor occupy a world of material, political, and spiritual insecurity (Last 2005).

These enduring weaknesses of northern Nigeria's agro-food provisioning system, it turns out, is rooted in the political economy of oil. Urban-based construction drawing labor out of agriculture, the inflationary effects of the oil boom, and disinvestment from agriculture by political classes only concerned to capture oil rents trough contracting, public office, and graft triggered the downward spiral in rural livelihoods. Oil wealth did permit the state the capability to fall back on the global marketplace. Since the mid-1990s, the Nigerian food import bill has grown to assume truly gargantuan proportions. In 1994, Nigerian food imports amounted to 0.67 million metric tons (US$0.75 billion); by 2001 it was almost 7 million metric tons (US$ 2 billion). More recently (2008–2011), food imports have been running at between 9 and 11 percent of merchandise imports, costing over $3 billion annually. In August 2011 the minister of agriculture solemnly announced that Nigeria was one of the largest food importers in the world. The food import bill of Nigeria in 2007–2010 was a staggering N98 trillion (almost $8 billion). In 2010 alone, Nigeria spent 635 billion naira on the import of wheat, N356 billion on importation of rice, and N217 billion on sugar imports—all commodities cultivated in Nigeria, and for which the country purportedly possesses a comparative advantage.

The persistence of food insecurity in the north is rooted in the commodification of foodstuffs and patterns of rural inter-household inequality (social differentiation), especially patterns of landholding, livestock and other assets, access to inputs, and household self-sufficiency in staples (whether households are grain deficit or surplus). As *Silent Violence* shows, a significant proportion of households were already in grain deficit by 1976. In Matlon's (1977) study, roughly concurrent with my own in a grain surplus region of southern Kano State, indicates that high grain prices constituted serious threats to the 20 percent of households that were grain-deficit producers. After structural adjustment in the mid-1980s, the impact of rises in production and reproduction costs compounded the vulnerability of grain-deficit families. Rising prices of agricultural inputs and food compelled households to shift to off-farm occupations, especially wage labor, at the same time that the use of fertilizers and the planting of the hybrid varieties introduced in the earlier period decreased substantially. Mustapha and Meagher (2000) estimate in their rural Kano study that the proportion of grain-deficit families increased by almost 20 percent among small farmers (and by almost as much among medium farmers) between 1989 and 1993. New research that makes effective use of an earlier survey by Chris Udry of Yale University compares agrarian change over a twenty-year period (1988–2008) among four communities near Zaria (in Kaduna State), and is suggestive in this regard (Dillon and Quilones 2010; Dillon and Quilones 2011). The increase in total land cultivated is consistent across villages, but landless households increased by 40 percent. Land holdings decreased by almost three hectares over the twenty-year period, while the number of plots cultivated by households also decreased. Plot sizes and total land cultivated decreased, but access tolowland, *fadama* plots remained constant across households between the two survey years. Land rentals—almost nonexistent in 1988—are now widespread. Fallowing had in effect disappeared entirely, and farmers widely endorsed the view that soil fertility is declining. Crop values per hectare increased, but income effects were radically shaped by stark class differences. In sum, the class map of rural communities had changed, and was changing, dramatically, despite the picture of "economic recession."

This is a specifically Nigerian story, of course, in which oil wealth makes it a special case. But the deepening commodification of land, labor, crops, and animals is the hallmark of the region as a whole. Unlike other parts of the continent, where purported land grabs have shaped these agrarian dynamics (Thaler, this volume), the West African Sahel has largely avoided these most direct forms of primitive accumulation. The connection between food prices and speculative activity in global food markets (especially as investors withdrew from other instruments in 2008) is another story, one that certainly is transforming the face of food provisioning. But to the extent the Sahel remains a diverse peasant-based economy, the question of the prospects of smallholder agriculture in the face of hard but uncertain effects of global climate change—the challenges of adaptation, as the conventional wisdom has it—remains at the heart of the Sahel's future. It is here that a historical perspective—the perspective of old age in my case—has much to offer.

Governing Food and Famine: The Sahelian Laboratory

In the 1970s the arid and drought-prone drylands of West Africa were what Tilley (2010) calls an "African laboratory." The period between the late 1960s and the early 1980s was a long decade of economic and political turbulence driven by the oil boom and bust, by financial liberalization and the launching of structural adjustment programs, and the massive human ecological crisis triggered by the drought-famines that extended across the Sahel. At base, this was a crisis of the agrarian and pastoral economies—peasants and herders for the most part—who occupied the great swaths of the semiarid savannas, which is to say the ecological heart of the continent. The great drought-famines of the 1970s were framed by two important events: the first was the UN Conference on the Human Environment held in Stockholm in 1972, and the second was the release of the Club of Rome's report *Limits to Growth* (Meadows et al. 1972) in the same year. Both were foundational to the rise of a sort of "international environmentalism" addressing what was later to be understood as the challenges of "sustainable development." Both were fundamentally shaped by a robust Malthusianism. For the Club of Rome, founded as a global think tank in 1968 by an Italian industrialist and a Scottish international scientific civil servant (Aurelio Peccei and Alexander King, respectively), the oil crisis was a harbinger of a larger structural problem of resource scarcity, population pressure, and ecological degradation. Methodologically, the Club outsourced its study to the MIT Systems Dynamics Group, a team made up of seventeen researchers from a wide range of disciplines and countries, led by Dennis Meadows. They assembled vast quantities of data from around the world to feed into the model, focusing on five main variables: investment, population, pollution, natural resources, and food. Calibrated to examine the interactions among these variables and the trends in the system as a whole over the next ten, twenty, and fifty years, assuming extant growth rates, their scenarios predicted various sorts of system collapse or system unsustainability.

Peter Taylor (1999) has referred to the prevailing *Limits to Growth* discourse as "neo-Malthusian environmentalism," and he interestingly made use of, as a historian of science and an ecologist, the influential studies conducted by the Systems Dynamics team at MIT on agropastoral systems in the West African Sahel conducted in the wake of the 1970s crisis. By 1973 the semiarid Sahel region had experienced five years of drought and developing crisis. Many pastoralists (livestock herders) and farmers were in refugee camps, their herds decimated and their crops having failed again. Prevailing analysis at the time focused not only on famine relief but on the causes of the crisis and on prospects for the region's future, a view that heralded drought and famine as a forerunner of future demographically driven scarcity and shortage (through human increases and related settlement into increasingly marginal and overexploited environments, and animal overstocking on open ranges). MIT developed a capacious menu of factors and mathematical relationships, all converted into a systems analysis anchored in (and confirmatory of) the "tragedy of the commons" (Picardi et al. 1974). Garrett Hardin (1968), after all, had raised the specter of the "lifeboat ethic" as the cost associated with the implacable logic of overpopulation, overgrazing, resource scarcity, and inadequate property rights displayed in the Club of Rome report. It was, in sum, a Malthusian dystopia. The commons stood as a metaphor for the old anti-scarcity system, which, as Malthus and others predicted in the early nineteenth century, would compound the problem of food security, improvement, and growth. Soil degradation and eventual desertification could be avoided only if all the pastoralists replaced their individual self-interest (and outdated forms of communal property) with "long-term preservation of the resource base as their first priority," perhaps requiring them to enter ranching schemes that privatized or strictly supervised access to pasture.

The environmental and related agrarian crisis of the 1970s proved to be a veritable laboratory for economic ideas. Ecology, food, and climate fed into arguably one of *the* founding documents in the rise and consolidation of neoliberal development and the rise of the Washington Consensus, namely, the Berg Report (named after Michigan economist Elliot Berg), released as *Accelerated Development in Sub-Saharan Africa* by the World Bank in 1981. At the core of Africa's crisis was "domestic policy" and a poor export performance in basic commodities in which the continent had a comparative advantage. Distorted markets and state marketing boards became the conceptual front lines in a ferocious assault on the African state, a critique backed up with the prescriptive heavy artillery of structural adjustment and stabilization. The solutions to the environment-development crisis resided in a technical fix (bringing the Green Revolution and irrigation, and improved transportation, to the continent), and in exploiting export markets by releasing peasant innovativeness from the yoke of the state. The African peasant emerged, in this account at least, as one part indigenous ecologist and one rational economic agent. But climate, environment, and populations needed to be managed, and improvement, market forces, and property rights were modalities to be deployed. It was the vision of John Stuart Mill and Adam Smith, confirmed by the raft of market studies conducted in the wake of the famine by, perhaps appropriately, Elliot Berg and his associates at the University of Michigan, who confirmed that markets were efficient and "non-monopolistic" but required investments in transportation and credit to realize their potential (Berg 1977). Africa, if overpopulated and crippled by state corruption and poor weather, was at least inhabited by some form of *Homo economicus*.

Eventually, the neo-Malthusian model and the incomplete or distorted market (neoclassical) account were increasingly questioned by a new wave of social science research rooted in careful ethnographic and local studies of human ecological dynamics and the intersection of social and ecological relations of production among rural producers, which in a statistical sense represented the majority of Africans (Richards 1985). The challenges came from several fronts, several of which I have already gestured to. Amartya Sen's pivotal book *Poverty and Famines* decisively broke the purportedly causal connection between drought and famine. Food crises and starvation bore no necessary relation to absolute food decline, and the effects of drought were typically mediated by farming practice and the market (in the latter case compounded by the deleterious effects of price increases and entitlement declines). Second, a body of work operating under the sign of peasant studies saw African communities as less composed of self-interested individuals (*contra* Hardin) than enmeshed in processes of commodification and social relations of production that rendered significant proportions of the rural populace vulnerable to all manner of ecological events even in "normal" times. The effects of climate and of ecological conditions were, in other words, experienced differentially in relation to class, asset holding, and the operations of the market.

The sense in which indigenous knowledge and vernacular peasant practice could be captured and deployed was sharply constrained by the social relations of production in farming communities. The adaptive capacity much praised by geographers, anthropologists, and rural sociologists could be, and often was, undercut, eroded, or lost by the operations of the market. This was the heart of James Scott's (1976) influential book on the moral economy of the peasantry after all—and this was the heart of what I tried to argue in *Silent Violence*. This realization had direct implications for who was vulnerable, how ecological processes were experienced, and, in turn, how people and land might recover. Finally, there was a turn toward discursive analysis, led by the likes of Melissa Leach, Jeremy Swift, and others, to point to what they called dominant models or narratives of environmental crisis that reflected particular readings or constructions of local African conditions (Fairhead and Leach, 1996). By the 1980s and into the 1990s, these intellectual developments—partly rooted in the field of political ecology, partly in ecological science and science studies, and partly in anthropological critiques of development—represented a fundamental challenge to the legitimacy and standing of the conventional narratives of Africa's environmental conditions, its actors, and its agents. Curiously, however, what has emerged from this critique is a new laboratory of ideas, this time shaped by the intersection of neoliberalism and the new science of resiliency that has taken on notions of peasant vulnerability, local adaptive capability, and empowerment and woven them into an all-encompassing field theory of stabilization, protection, and human security. Virtually the entire development industry addressing global climate change now rests on building resilient peasant households and resilient communities.

Securing Sahelian Futures: Building Resilience through Social Risk Management

The West African Sahel, according to the Intergovernmental Panel on Climate Change (2007), will be potentially devastated by the transformation of rainfall dynamics due to continued global warming. The threat of rainfall reduction and increased variability in heavily populated rain-fed agricultural regions has produced a wide-ranging policy debate over strategies for climate adaptation (Schipper and Burton 2009) and "drought proofing." At the same time, climate is now seen to be simply one dimension of a wider set of security problems; indeed, environmental security (encompassing food, water, energy, pasture, and so on) provides a powerful policy discourse designed to help assist in how rural communities across the Sahel, confronting drought and resource scarcity, can adapt and avoid conflict (Mason and Muller 2008). Gone is the language of overpopulation, incomplete markets, poor transportation, and local management deficits; gone, too, is any lingering sense of state welfare. In its place is a model of security to be achieved by supporting local adaptive capacity in the face of vulnerability, managing risk socially, and above all by building resiliency (WRI 2008; Gubbels 2011; UNDP 2012; Adger 2006; Folke, Oslo and Norberg 2005).

The very uncertainty of the effects of global climate change (global climate change models are robust on system dynamics but weak on regional and local predictions) is antithetical to the sort of predictive modeling exercises practiced by the Club of Rome. The securitization of the environment not only embraces threats to food, agrarian, pastoral and water systems but now encompasses the likelihood of conflict and violence around access to scarce resources (Dalby 2009; US Department of Defense 2011). Implicit in the science behind the current global climate change debate is a worldview somewhat at odds with the Dawinian orthodoxy of evolutionary gradualism (Boal 2009). Climate could, and has, changed (historically), but for human occupation and livelihood this represents a deep historical time—the very *longue duree*. What is on offer now is something unimaginable until relatively recently: abrupt, radical, and life-threatening shifts framed in the language of uncertainty, unpredictability, and contingency. It is an emergent science of planetary disaster demanding an urgent public response—political, policy, civic, and business—of an equal magnitude and gravity.

Global warming encompasses, and has direct consequences for, two of the most fundamental human provisioning systems, food and energy, but to these one can add war, conflict and militarism, critical infrastructures, and systemic financial risk, all of which are now seen to be inseparably and organically linked in a complex of networks of teleconnected effects (OECD 2003). This worldview mobilizes and enrolls powerful actors around the threat of massive, catastrophic risks and uncertainties. Central to this vision is a construal of the nature of biological life itself, drawing especially upon the molecular and digital sciences—complexity, networks, and information are its avatars—which shape the nature of what is to be governed and how. If life is constituted through complex and continual adaptation and emergence, it rests upon a sense of radical uncertainty in which danger and security form an unstable present, what Dillon and Reid (2009, 85) call a life "continuously becoming dangerous." Ash Amin (2012, 138) sees this as "the condition of calamity," or catastrophism:

> The recurrence, spread, severity and mutability of the world's natural and social hazards are considered as symptomatic of this state (of permanent risk), and its latent conditions are understood to be too volatile or random and non-linear to permit accurate prediction and evasive action. In the apocalyptic imaginary, hazard and risk erupt as unanticipated emergencies, disarming in every manifestation and in every way.

In this account each threat is potentially catastrophic and the disaster is imminent or at least foreseeable, the near future is prioritized (preemption, precaution, and preparation are its key deployments), and the calamity is a crisis of security requiring securitization (Anderson 2010; Guyer 2009; Floyd 2010).

Against this backdrop, the old models of Sahelian development have been replaced with new modalities that can render the uncertainties of global climate change thinkable and something that can be prepared for and remediated. It is at this point that culture—especially institutions, many of which are indigenous or hybrids of local custom and the modern—meets up with the so-called resiliency school and theories of "complex adaptive systems" (Adger, Lorenzoni, and O'Brien 2009). Its function is to incorporate social and economic systems in an overarching complex science of "socio-ecological resilience" rooted in civil society (the community looms very large here). The scope and scale (and institutionalization) of resiliency thinking is now vast, encompassing most fields of expertise that address security in the broadest sense (from the IMF to Homeland Security). Here are excerpts from two reports on food security in Africa and the Sahel:

> Resilience can be thought of as the opposite of vulnerability. Resilient food systems can withstand political, economic, social and environmental shocks. Resilience makes individuals, households and communities less vulnerable... it helps them withstand multiple stresses—occurring with varying frequency, predictability and intensity—and break free of persistent poverty and accelerate human development.
>
> (UNDP 2012, 99)

> Both analytically and pragmatically, resilience is becoming a more useful focus than vulnerability. Vulnerability refers to the inability of people to avoid, cope with or recover from the harmful impacts of hazards that disrupt their lives and that are beyond their immediate control. Vulnerability is a deficit concept.... Resilience, on the other hand... requires enabling people to discover how their livelihood/food access system might be made more resilient to shocks, and how to renew or reorganize their system, should such shocks occur. This requires developing an understanding of where resilience resides in the system, and when and how it can be lost or gained, which means identifying the points in the household food system where interventions can increase the resilience to future hazards.
>
> (Gubbels 2011, 144)

Resiliency is now a vast academic and policy industry—among policymakers, activists, consultants, and the donor community—that encompasses vast swaths of the social, economic, and political landscape (Davidson 2010; Adger 2006). Local knowledge and practice, notions of vulnerability and exposure—in other words, the critical responses to the neo-Malthusian approach to Sahelian problems of the 1970s—have been grafted onto a new turbocharged systems theory, derived in particular from the work of the ecologist C. S. Holling and his associates, who have been brought together in a highly influential think tank called the Stockholm Resilience Center (Holling 1986, 2001). Sahelian communities can now be fine-tuned—paradoxically building on their traditional strengths (e.g., the social capital of village communities) yet supplemented by the expertise of development and state practitioners.

Holling extended his view of resiliency by suggesting that all living systems evolved through disequilibrium, that instability was the source of creativity. Crisis tendencies were thus constitutive of complex adaptive systems. Indeed, resiliency is now so central to the notion of environmentally sustainable development—the cornerstone of the major multilateral development and international environmental NGOs—that the complex adaptive systems framework (including the sorts of measures of standardization and accounting for assessing ecosystem resilience) has been taken up by the likes of the World Bank and UN HABITAT in such diverse arenas as sustainable urbanism, ecosystem services, and climate adaptation and mitigation (Lentzos and Rose 2009). Resiliency, in short, is the form of governmentality appropriate to *any* form of perturbation and uncertainty: dealing with extreme weather events in not merely analogous to coping with recurrent financial shocks. By integrating prior work on vulnerability and poverty, with current concerns with participation and empowerment at the community level, resiliency provides a powerful systematic, interdisciplinary, and pragmatic approach. As Béné et al. (2012, 11) put it: "The concept of resilience is thus becoming a form of integrating discourse that rallies an increasing number of people, institutions, and organisations under its banner, as it creates communication bridges and platforms between disciplines and communities of practices, and offers common grounds on which dialogue can then be initiated between organisations, departments or ministries which had so far very little, or no history of collaboration."

The notion of adaptive capacity and resilient institutions through community organization does, of course, rest on a substantial body of research demonstrating how rural communities in Africa (and elsewhere) adapt to climate change through mobility, storage, diversification, communal pooling, and exchange by drawing on social networks and their access to resources. Yet what is on offer instead is a bland and bloodless shopping list of "conditions" for adaptive governance, including "policy will," "coordination of stakeholders," "science," "common goals," and "creativity," all held together by social risk management. How, for example, resiliency will be built—to take the conclusions of the recent Sahel report (Gubbels 2011)—from and within state fragility and conflict, corruption, class power, land and asset inequality, and asymmetric state capabilities is entirely unclear. Perhaps most drastic is the failure of resiliency theory to propose an account of power and human agency. What is on offer is a particular view of individuals—peasant, pastoralist, woman—as autonomous agents who have the power to negotiate their own lives with the unproblematic arena of "the community." Power, self-determination, and democracy fit very uneasily with the dynamics of living systems drawn from "non-equilibrium ecosystems" (Duit et al 2010).

At the time that Holling was laying out his first ideas (and in the midst of the Sahelian famine in Africa as it happened), Friedrich Hayek delivered his Nobel Prize speech, which, as M. Cooper and J. Walker (2011) brilliantly show, has an elective affinity with Holling's ideas. Hayek was moving toward his mature theorization of capitalism as an exemplar of the biological sciences: the extended market order is "perfectly natural...like biological phenomena, evolved in the course of natural selection" (Hayek 1988, cited in Cooper and Walker 2011). In the resiliency paradigm, ecosystem-based enterprises, rooted in community resource management, will entail local-state and private-civic partnerships and enterprise networking. Markets in ecosystem services, and delegation of responsibility to communities and households as self-organizing productive units, will constitute the basis for survival in biophysical, political, economic, and financial worlds defined by turbulence, risk, and unpredictability. Some will be resilient, but others will be too resilient or not resilient enough.

Resiliency is the calculative metric for a brave new world of turbulent capitalism, the global economic order, and a new ecology of rule. The Sahel's "bottom billion" provides a laboratory in which the poor will be tested as the impacts of change manifest. Resiliency has become a litmus test of the right to survive in the global order of things (Cooper 2010; O'Malley 2010). Resiliency is an apparatus of security that will determine the process of "letting die." Africa, once again, is the testing ground for a vision of security and care in which life is nothing more than permanent readiness and flexible adaptiveness. As such, it is a deeply Hayekian project—an expression of the neoliberal thought collective—in which the idea of a spontaneous market order has become, ironically, a form of sustainable development. Building resilient peasants and resilient communities in the West African Sahel turns on an amalgam of institutions and practices geared toward individuals armed with improved and upgraded traditional knowledge and institutions but rooted, as Dillon (2008) says, in a distinctive moral and behavioral economy of existence. The challenges of adapting to the radical uncertainties and perturbations of global climate change produce a vision of *Homo economicus* for the new millennium; the African peasant, as Foucault (2008, 241) noted, becomes "an entrepreneur of himself," a hedge-fund manager for his own impoverished life.

Notes

1. Two-thirds of the hungry live in just seven countries (Bangladesh, China, Democratic Republic of the Congo, Ethiopia, India, Indonesia, and Pakistan), and over 40 percent live in China and India alone (see The World Food Program, *Global Hunger Declining but Still Unacceptably High*, Rome: FAO, September 2010. http://www.fao.org/docrep/012/al390e/al390e00.pdf.)
2. Devereux (2000, 7) estimates that famine mortalities increased every decade beginning in the 1930s to peak in the 1960s; they fell sharply thereafter, with a small upward trend during the 1990s. He estimates that over 70 million people died from famine during the 20th century.
3. This immediately, of course, raises the thorny question of how precisely one defines famine. Famines are less aberrant events than extensions of the normal; behaviorally, many famine victims do not regard excess mortality as the defining quality of famine, since many famine mortalities are a function of disease rather than absolute food scarcity (see de Waal 1989 and Nally 2011). Some famines are ordinary, some are catastrophic and deadly. As Devereux points out, "mass starvation is one possible outcome of the famine process" (2000:4).
4. Only relatively recently have entitlement analyses begun to link different levels of investigation, focusing, for example, on household entitlements and their links to the state, regions vis-a-vis nations, and national entitlements in relation to global food security; see Devereux (1993) and Platteau (1991).
5. In 1976, Kaita was located in North-Central State; it became part of the new Katsina State in 1996.
6. Oil revenues after 1970 came to dominate the Nigerian economy, constituting 85 percent of state revenues, 98 percent of export earnings, and close to 40 percent of GDP. Between

1970 and 2012, Nigerian oil wealth was over three-quarters of a trillion dollars (US). Nigerian became an archetypical "petro-state."

References

Adger, N. 2006. "Vulnerability." *Global Environmental Change* 16:268–281.

Adger, N., I. Lorenzoni, and K. O'Brien, eds. 2009. *Adapting to Climate Change*. Cambridge: Cambridge University Press.

Agamben, G. 1998. *Homo Sacer: Sovereign Power and Bare Life*. Stanford, CA: Stanford University Press.

Alcock, R. 2009. "Speaking Food." Working Paper 07–09. Briston, UK: University of Bristol, Department of Politics.

Amin, A. 2012. *Land of Strangers*. London: Polity.

Anderson, B. 2010. "Preemption, Precaution, Preparedness." *Progress in Human Geography*, 34 (6): 777–798.

Arendt, H. 1948. *Imperialism*. New York: Harcourt.

Ayodele Ariyo, J., J. Voh and B. Ahmed. 2001. "Long Term Change and Food Provisioning in the Kano Region 1960–2000." Working Paper 34. Crewkerne, UK: Drylands Research.

Berg, E. 1977. *Marketing, Food, Policy and Storage of Grains in the Sahel*. Vol. 2. Ann Arbor: Center for Research on Economic Development, University of Michigan.

Berlant, L. 2007. "Slow Death." *Critical Inquiry* 33 (Summer): 754–777.

Béné, C., R. Godfrey Wood, A. Newsham, and M. Davies. 2012. "Resilience: New Utopia or New Tyranny?" IDS Working Paper 405. Brighton: University of Sussex, Institute for Development Studies.

Boal, I. 2009. *Globe, Capital, Climate*. Berkeley, CA: RETORT.

Bread for the World. 2010. *Our Common Interest*. Washington, DC: Bread for the World.

Clapp, J. 2011. *Hunger in the Balance: The New Politics of International Food Aid*. Ithaca, NY: Cornell University Press.

Collingham, L. 2011. *The Taste of War*. London: Allen Lane.

Cooper, M. 2010. "Turbulent Worlds: Financial Markets and Environmental Crisis." *Theory, Culture & Society* 27 (2–3): 167–190.

Dalby, S. 2009. *Security and Environmental Change*. London: Polity.

Davis, M. 2001. *Late Victorian Holocausts*. London: Verso.

Davidson, D. J. 2010. "The Applicability of the Concept of Resilience to Social systems: Some Sources of Optimism and Nagging Doubts." *Society & Natural Resources* 23 (12): 1135–1149.

Devereux, S. 1993. *Theories of Famine*. London: Harvester Wheatsheaf.

Devereux, S. 2007. "Introduction: From 'Old Famines' to 'New Famines.'" In *The New Famines*, edited by S. Devereux. London: Routledge.

de Waal, A. 1989. *Famines That Kill: Darfur, Sudan 1984–1985*. Oxford, Clarendon Press.

de Waal, A. 2009. *Famine Crimes: Politics and the Disaster relief Industry in Africa*. Bloomington: Indiana University Press.

Dikotter, F. 2011. *Mao's Great Famine*. New York: Walker.

Dillon, A., and E. Quinones. 2011. "Gender Differentiated Asset Dynamics in Northern Nigeria." ESA Working Paper 11-06. Rome: Food and Agricultural Organization of the United Nations, Agricultural Economics Division.

Dillon, A., and E. Quinones. 2010. "Asset Dynamics in Northern Nigeria." IFPRI Discussion Paper 01049. Washington, DC: International Food Policy Research Institute (IFPRI).
Dillon, M. 2008. "Underwriting Security" *Security Dialogue* 39 (2–3): 309–332.
Dillon, M., and J. Reid. 2009. *The Liberal Way of War*. London: Routledge.
Drèze J., and A. Sen. 1989. *Hunger and Public Action*. Oxford: Oxford University Press.
Drèze J., and A. Sen, eds. 1990. *The Political Economy of Hunger*. 3 volumes. Oxford: Oxford University Press.
Duit, A., V. Galaz, and K. Eckerberg. 2010. "Governance, Complexity, and Resilience." *Global Environmental Change* 20 (3): 363–368.
Fairhead, J., and M. Leach. 1996. *Misreading the African Landscape: Society and Ecology in a Forest-Savanna Mosaic*. Cambridge: Cambridge University Press.
FAO (Food and Agricultural Organization of the United Nations). 2011. *The State of Food Insecurity* 2011. Rome: FAO.
FAO (Food and Agricultural Organization of the United Nations). 2012. *The State of Food Insecurity* 2012. Rome: FAO.
Farmer, Paul. 2003. *Pathologies of Power: Health, Human Rights and the New War on the Poor*. Berkeley: University of California Press.
Federal Government of Nigeria, National Bureau of Statistics. 2009. *Social Statistics in Nigeria*. Abuja: Federal Government of Nigeria.
Floyd, R. 2010. *Security and Environment*. Cambridge: Cambridge University Press.
Folke, K. Hahn, P. Oslo, and J. Norberg. 2005. "Adaptive Governance of Socio-Ecological Systems." *Annual Review of Environment and Resources* 30:441–473.
Foucault, M. 2008. *The Birth of Biopolitics*. London: Palgrave.
Ghosh, J. 2010. "The Unnatural Coupling: Food and Global Finance." *Journal of Agrarian Change* 10 (1): 72–86.
Gubbels, Peter. 2011. *Escaping the Hunger Cycle: Pathways to Resilience in the Sahel*. Washington, DC: Sahel Working Group, Groundswell International. http://community.eldis.org/sahelworkinggroup/.5a337e1b/.5a338083.
Gunderson, L., and C. S. Holling, eds. 2002. *Panarchy: Understanding Transformations in Human and Natural Systems*. Washington, DC: Island Press.
Guyer, J. 2009. "Prophecy and the Near Future." *American Ethnologist* 34 (3): 409–421
Hardin, G. 1968. "The Tragedy of the Commons." *Science* 162:1243–1248.
Hayek, F. 1988. *The Fatal Conceit: The Errors of Socialism*. London: Routledge.
Hills, J. and A. Sen, eds. *Social Security in Developing Countries*. Oxford: Clarendon Press.
Holling, C. S. 1973. "Resilience and Stability of Ecological Systems." *Annual Review of Ecology and Systematics* 4:1–23.
Holling, C. S., ed. 1978. *Adaptive Environmental Assessment and Management*. London: Wiley.
Holling, C. S. 1986. "Resilience of Ecosystems: Local Surprise and Global Change." In *Sustainable Development of the Biosphere*, edited by W. C. Clark and R. E. Munn, 292–317. Cambridge: Cambridge University Press.
Holling, C. S. 2001. "Understanding the Complexity of Economic, Ecological and Social Systems." *Ecosystems*, (4) 390–405.
IFAD (International Fund for Agricultural Development). 2004. *Country Programme Evaluation: Federal Republic of Nigeria*. Rome: IFAD, Office of Evaluation. http://www.ifad.org/evaluation/public_html/eksyst/doc/country/pa/nigeria/.
IFAD (International Fund for Agricultural Development). 2009. *Kano State Household Baseline Survey*. Dakar, Senegal: IFAD Africa. http://www.fidafrique.net/article936.html.

Intergovernmental Panel on Climate Change. 2007. *IPCC Fourth Assessment Report: Climate Change* 2007. Geneva: Intergovernmental Panel on Climate Change.
Jisheng, Y. 2012. *Tombstone*. New York: Farrar and Strauss.
Keen, D. 1994. *The Benefits of Famine: A Political Economy of Famine and Relief in Southwestern Sudan, 1983–1989*. Princeton, NJ: Princeton University Press.
Kenally, T. 2011. *Three Famines: Starvation and Politics*. New York: Perseus.
Last, M. 2005 Toward a political history of youth in Muslim northern Nigeria 1750–2000, in J. Abbink and Ivan Kessel (eds)., Vanguard or Vandals. Boston: Brill.
Leach, M., and R. Mearns. 1996. *The Lie of the Land: Challenging Received Wisdom on the African Environment*. Portsmouth, NH: Heinemann.
Lentzos, F., and N. Rose. 2009. "Governing Insecurity." *Economy and Society* 38 (2): 230–254.
Lubeck, Paul. 2010. "Nigeria: Mapping the Shari'a Movement." Working Paper. Santa Cruz, CA: UC Santa Cruz: Center for Global, International and Regional Studies.
Mason, S., and A. Muller. 2008. *Linking Environment and Conflict Prevention*. Zurich: Center for Security Studies (CSS).
Matlon, P. 1977. "The Size, Distribution, Structure, and Determinants of Personal Income among Farmers in the North of Nigeria." PhD diss., Cornell University.
Meadows, D. H., D. L. Meadows, J. Randers, and W. Behrens W. 1972. *The Limits to Growth: A Report on the Predicament of Mankind*. London: Earth Island.
Mortimore, M. 2000. "Profile of Rainfall Change and Variability in the Kano-Maradi Region, 1960–2000." Working Paper 25. Crewkerne, UK: Drylands Research.
Mukerjee, M. 2010. *Churchill's Secret War: The British Empire and the Ravaging of India during the Second World War*. New York: Basic Books.
Nally, D. 2008. " 'That Coming Storm': The Irish Poor Law, Colonial Biopolitics, and the Great Famine." *Annals of the Association of American Geographers* 98 (3): 714–741.
Nally, D.. 2011. *Human Encumbrances*. Notre Dame, IN: University of Notre Dame Press.
Obioha, E. 2009. "Climate Variability, Environmental Change and the Food Nexus in Nigeria." *Journal of Human Ecology* 26 (2): 107–121.
OECD (Organisation for Economic Co-operation and Development). 2003. Emerging Risks in the 21st Century. Paris: OECD. http://www.oecd.org/dataoecd/20/23/37944611.pdf.
O'Grada, C. 2009. *Famine: A Short History*. Princeton, NJ: Princeton University Press.
O'Malley, P. 2010. "Resilient Subjects." *Economy and Society* 39 (4): 488–509.
Parenti, C. 2011. *Tropic of Chaos: Climate Change and the New Geography of Violence*. New York: Nation Books.
Picardi, A. C. 1974. "A Systems Analysis of Pastoralism in the West African Sahel." Appendix to *A Framework for Evaluating Long-Term Strategies for the Development of the Sahel-Sudan Region*, edited by W. W. Seifert and N. Kamran. Cambridge, MA: MIT, Center for Policy Alternatives.
Platteau, J.-P. 1991. "Traditional Systems of Social Security and Hunger Insurance: Past Achievements and Modern Challenges." In *Social Security in Developing Countries*, edited by E. Ahmad, J. Drèze, J. Hills, and A. Sen. Oxford: Oxford University Press.
Ravallion, M. 1987. *Markets and Famines*. Oxford: Oxford University Press.
Richards, P. 1985. *Indigenous Agricultural Revolution: Ecology and Food Production in West Africa*. London: Unwin.
Sahel and West Africa Club. 2006. *Food Security and Cross Border Trade in the Kano-Katsina-Maradi Corridor: Joint Mission Report*. Paris: Sahel and West Africa Club/ OECD. http://www.oecd.org/swac/events/38490617.pdf.

Save the Children. 2012. *A Life Free from Hunger: Tackling Child Malnutrition*. London: Save the Children.
Scott, J. 1976. *The Moral Economy of the Peasantry*. New Haven, CT: Yale University Press.
Sen, A. 1980. *Poverty and Famines*. Oxford: Oxford University Press.
Taylor, P. 1999. "What Can Agents Do? In *Advances in Human Ecology*. Vol. 8, edited by L. Fresse, 125–156. Greenwich, CT: JAI Press.
Tilley, H. 2010. *Africa as a Living Laboratory: Empire, Development, and the Problem of Scientific Knowledge, 1860–1960*. Chicago: University of Chicago Press.
USAID (United States Agency for International Development). 2007. *Preliminary Livelihood Zoning: Northern Nigeria.*, Washington DC: USAID. http://pdf.usaid.gov/pdf_docs/PNADL380.pdf.
UNDP (United Nations Development Program). 2009. *Human Development Report: Nigeria*. Abuja: UNDP.
UNDP (United Nations Development Program). 2012. *African Human Development Report 2012: Toward a Food Secure Future*. New York: UNDP.
US Department of Defense. 2011. *Trends and Implications of Climate Change for National and International Security*. Washington, DC: US Department of Defense. (http://www.acq.osd.mil/dsb/reports/ADA552760.pdf).
Von Braun, J., J. T. Teklu, and P. Webb. 1998. *Famine in Africa: Causes, Responses and Prevention*. Baltimore: Johns Hopkins University Press.
Walker J., and M. Cooper. 2011. "Genealogies of Resilience." *Security Dialogue* 42 (2): 143–160.
Watts, M. 1983. *Silent Violence*. Berkeley: University of California Press.
Watts, M. 1991. "Entitlement or Empowerment?: Famine and Starvation in Africa." *Review of African Political Economy* 51:9–26.
Watts, M. 2000. "The Great Tablecloth." In *The Oxford Handbook of Economic Geography*, edited by G. L. Clark, M. S. Gertler, and M. P. Feldmann, 195–215. Oxford: Oxford University Press.
Watts, M. 2001. "Black Acts." *New Left Review* 9:125–140.
Watts, M. and H.-G. Bohle. 1993. "The Space of Vulnerability: A Realist Theory of Famine and Hunger." *Progress in Human Geography* 17 (1): 43–67.
World Food Program. 2012. *The Sahel Crisis*. http://www.wfp.org/crisis/sahel.
WRI (World Resources Institute). 2008. *Roots of Resilience*. Washington, DC: World Resources Institute.

CHAPTER 33

TRANSFORMATION OF THE AGRIFOOD INDUSTRY IN DEVELOPING COUNTRIES

THOMAS REARDON AND C. PETER TIMMER

INTRODUCTION

THE agrifood industry has been transforming rapidly over the past three decades in developing countries. What took a century in the United States and Western Europe has been accomplished in several decades in many countries, often in ways contrary to expectations. In retail, for example, a "supermarket revolution" contradicted both broadly shared self-perceptions in developing countries, as well as the pre-1990 retail literature—where often one read that "traditional food culture," dense cities, low opportunity cost of labor, and "habit of frequent shopping" militated against modern retail. Both market forces and government policy have shaped transformations of the sector; foreign direct investment provides the main vector of effects on agrifood globalization. These transformations have potential to affect farmers via increased incomes and modernized technologies, and consumers via cheaper and safer food. On the other hand, modernized agrifood industry segments (wholesale/logistics, processors, retailers) are broadly competitive with—and apparently, over the longer term, broadly destructive of—their counterparts in the traditional sector. Consolidation within these segments, and synergies across them, have emerged far faster than in currently wealthier countries, with still poorly understood consequences for the units that matter for welfare analysis—consuming households and small farms. This chapter analyzes the sector from its wholesale and logistics operations, which connect to farmers, through processing to retail establishments, which connect to consumers.

By transformation we mean changes in structure and in behavior. Structural changes include consolidation and multinationalization; changes in behavior include the organization and institutions and technologies of procurement, processing, and distribution by firms. The drivers of this transformation include government actions through policies/regulations and investments in both infrastructure and in the segments themselves, and private sector actions in both institutions and investment activities. There have also been important concomitant actions by NGOs, donors, and farmer associations.

The most recent comprehensive reviews of comparative trends in the transformation of agrifood systems in developing regions were by Reardon and Timmer (2007), focused mainly on retail transformation, and Wilkinson (2004) and Gehlhar and Regmi (2005), focused mainly on changes in processing sector trade, product composition, institutions, and foreign direct investment (FDI). There has been no comprehensive review in the 2000s on the wholesale sector. There have also been several region-specific reviews of retail and processing, such as Laffan, 2001, for Asia. These earlier reviews have left several gaps.

First, the reviews tended to focus on one segment or other, but did not explore in depth the relations of transformation among the segments—wholesaling, processing, and retailing. We will show that "symbioses" among the modernizing segments were important.

Second, the earlier cross-region reviews were mainly based on data from the mid-1990s and before. Much has happened both in the transformation itself and in the research literature on it in the past half decade. As we will show, there was a major crescendo in the industry—a full take-off of supermarkets—in countries like India and Vietnam and a continuation of extremely rapid growth in China; in Latin America and parts of Asia the wholesale/logistics sector experienced a wave of modernization, with the processing sector leaping forward in regional multinationalization. Moreover, procurement systems for fresh produce started to transform, with an emergence of direct sourcing.

Third, in particular in the past half decade, a new set of development strategies has developed—partnered by governments, agrifood industry, and civil society. These strategies seek to increase linkages among agrifood industry segments and to small farmers by cutting transaction costs and increasing economies of agglomeration.

These three gaps in the literature are important because they include the channels by which the transformation has been accelerated, extended, and, potentially, made more inclusive. This review focuses on these gaps by updating the analysis on the transformation of the three basic segments of the agrifood industry and by evaluating the impact of the transformations now underway. The chapter is organized around the three segments, in parallel to the sequence of overall phases of transformation.

We proceed as follows. The second section briefly provides a new framework of "drivers" of transformation of the industry and its procurement systems/supply chains that are shared across the segments—procurement, processing, and distribution—as well as a general sketch of the three geographical waves of transformation that apply to all segments.

The third section discusses the bimodal paths of transformation of the wholesale/logistics sector. This was both the earliest sector to be transformed, with government actions driving transformation from the 1960s to the 1980s, and the latest, with private sector investment and modernization of wholesale/logistics in the late 1990s and especially the 2000s.

The fourth section discusses the paths of transformation of food processing, which also had an early partial transformation with government-driven changes such as parastatals from the 1960s on, then entered a modernization phase with liberalization mainly in the late 1980s and into the 1990s.

The fifth section discusses the paths of retail transformation. There is an important, but little appreciated, initial transformation via government cum cooperative action, such as fair price shops and cooperative and state retail chains (little discussed in the retail or development literature), before the 1990s, often for food security reasons, then the rise of modern-private retail in the 1990s and 2000s.

The sixth section begins with a discussion of the "symbioses" among the three transformed agrifood industry segments, emphasizing ways in which they reinforce each other and enter preferred supplier relations with each other. This sets the stage for discussing emerging impacts of the previously mentioned transformations on small and medium enterprises (SMEs) and farmers, focusing on recent evidence and noting gaps in current knowledge.

The seventh section discusses a new set of policy/program drivers is emerging in the form of programs to develop linkages that encourage a faster, more integrated, and more inclusive growth path for these transformations over the next decade. It is far too early to tell if these new programs will be successful, especially in keeping small farmers in food supply chains or promoting their welfare.

Determinants and General Diffusion Path of Transformation

There have been two "broad phases" of agrifood industry transformation over the past 50 years: "preliberalization/preglobalization" (mainly 1960s–mid-1980s) and "liberalization/ globalization" (mainly mid-1980s to now) (Reardon and Timmer, 2007). Contained within those two stages are the successive transformations of the three segments of the agrifood industry. The timing of the transformation of each segment is approximate, because it differs by region and country: (a) transformation of *wholesaling*, in two waves, with a public-sector-driven stage mainly in the 1960s-1990s, and a private-sector-driven stage, mainly in the 2000s; (b) transformation of *processing*, with a colonial and public-sector phase mainly up through the 1970s, and then a private-sector stage mainly in the 1980s to now; (c) and then the transformation of *retailing*, with a small public-sector stage in the 1960s-1980s, then a private sector stage mainly in the 1990s–2000s.

Roughly shared over segments is a set of mutually conditioning determinants of transformation, with the specifics of the determinants differing somewhat by segment.

First, there was a set of demand-side factors that determined demand for processed foods and transaction-cost saving in retail shopping. Important among these were income growth and emergence of middle classes (Ravallion 2010), urbanization,[1] and women entering the outside-home labor force. The ability of consumers to use modern retail in turn was enabled by the diffusion of refrigerators and vehicles, as well as better infrastructure. Urbanization and income growth also gave impetus to growth of wholesale markets (from fragmented, dispersed origins).

Second, there were two sets of policy interventions partially driving transformation.

On the one hand, there were public investments in wholesale markets, logistics platforms, processing parastatals, and state retail chains. These operated mainly in the 1960s–1980s (but some continued beyond that) and involved: (a) heavy investment by governments in public wholesale markets, first for grains, and then for produce, meat, and fish; (b) heavy investment by governments in parastatals that had wholesale (procurement) arms, as well as capacity for processing/milling and distribution to the population, sometimes via state retail chains such as the Fair Price Shops in India, the state grain stores in China, and so on. This development also gave rise to public certification of or operation of slaughterhouses.

These interventions were driven by both context and perceptions: (a) the recurrence of food-security crises was perceived to be linked to distribution constraints; (b) rapid urbanization, laying open an increasingly large urban population to food-supply constraints and vicissitudes, and required the efficient delivery of volumes, much larger than in the past, of food to urban areas; (c) rapid rise in incomes (in the first and second wave countries) gave rise to—based on Bennett's Law—rapid increase in demand for meat, fish, fruits and vegetables, and dairy; (d) perception that supply chains from rural areas were fragmented and traditional (with what would later be termed "high transaction costs"), rife with exploitation and speculation from avaricious middlemen, and that urban markets were poorly served by a smattering of truck markets and small grain markets.

Third, there was a set of supply-side factors grouped around investment into the segments. The surplus for this investment came first from colonial enterprises (for the export oriented agrifood industrial enclaves and plantations) and the state (in investment in public wholesale markets, and parastatal processing and retail) and later from state-owned enterprises (SOEs) in the modern sector, investment by private domestic conglomerates, and foreign direct investment (FDI). The latter is, in turn, a function of relative saturation in sending countries (South Korean retailers into China, Thai processors into Vietnam, UK retailers into Asia) combined with the attraction of the investment sites, itself a function of the aforementioned two sets of factors.

Fourth, there was a set of supply-side factors grouped around production- and procurement-system modernization by modern-sector firms in the three segments, which created efficiency gains that further increased their competitiveness *vis a vis* traditional firms. These included investment in scale of production to reap economies of scale and scope in processing, marketing, and procurement, and in procurement-system modernization such as use of distribution centers and warehouse networks, supply-chain coordination via explicit and implicit contracts (Key and Runsten 1999, Dries et al. 2009) and "private standards" (Reardon et al. 1999, Farina, Marino, & Guedes 2000, Reardon and Farina, 2001, Henson and Reardon 2005, Fulponi 2007, Swinnen 2007), and use of modern firms to coordinate intermediation, such as "dedicated wholesalers" (Farina and Machado 1999, Reardon and Berdegue 2002) and modern logistics firms (Reardon and Berdegue 2002, Han, Trienkens, and Omta 2009), themselves elements of a transformed wholesale/logistics sector.

The diffusion of a system of modern procurement, similar for modern processors and retailers, is a function of several elements (Reardon et al. 2003): (a) the ability of the traditional wholesale system to meet procurement officer objectives without the chain having to resort to costly investments in an alternative system; this varies considerably over countries, for example, strong in China (Wanget al. 2009) and weak in Indonesia (Natawidjaja et al. 2007) or India (Minten, Reardon, and Sutradhar 2010, Fafchamps, Vargas Hill, and Minten 2008); (b) the need to reduce costs of procurement by saving on inputs, in this case purchased product costs and transaction costs with suppliers; this need was driven by competition on costs and price-sensitivity of target consumers; (c) the need for consistent quality either of inputs (to produce quality outputs, or to produce commodity outputs at lower cost, by having consistent quality inputs to reduce processing costs, as in dairy in Brazil and Argentina (Farina, 2002; Farina et al. 2005); (d) the financial and managerial capacity of the company to make these investments, favoring larger companies.

Given the heterogeneity of distribution of these conditioners of transformation—over products, over firms, over countries, over regions, over time—one expects unevenness in the diffusion of transformation. This unevenness was observed in a relatively homogeneous environment such as in retail in the United States over decades (Kinsey 2004), hence, is even more likely over the extreme economic heterogeneity of developing countries. Still, there is some regularity and timing of "waves" of diffusion, which occurred geographically (over countries and within countries, over income classes, and over products), for all three agrifood industry segments.

The *first wave* tended to be the countries that started their post-WWII growth spurt earlier, urbanized and started industrializing somewhat earlier—in particular, the larger South American countries, East Asia outside China, South Africa, and north-central Europe. The start of processing transformation occurred with FDI liberalization and the start of privatization in the mid-1980s to early 1990s, and retail transformation "took off" from the early 1990s.

The *second wave* tended to be the countries that had their growth and urbanization spurts later and/or had strong internal pressure to limit FDI; these limits were often more for retail FDI than processing FDI. Hence one found that in Mexico, Central America, Southeast Asia, and southern Central Europe processing transformation took off in the 1980s but retail transformation did not start until the mid- to late 1990s.

The *third wave* tended to be countries that had their growth and urbanization spurts mainly in the 1990s/2000s, and/or had lagged liberalization into the 1990s. This was the case of Russia, China, India, and Vietnam, among others. Processing transformation then occurred somewhat before retail, with the latter mainly in the late 1990s and into the 2000s. As we show in the following section, the retail revolution only took off in earnest in the mid-2000s in India and Vietnam, and then grew rapidly. In India, although FDI liberalization in retail has not yet occurred, the sales of modern retail's leading food-selling chains leapt from $200 million in 2001 to 5 billion in 2009 (Reardon, Gulati, and Minten 2010)—mainly driven by domestic conglomerates, themselves creatures of the economic boom. This also happened in Russia and South Korea. There was also, as a lagged part of the third wave, a relatively weak emergence of processing and retail transformation in a few countries in East/Southern Africa.

There were some striking anomalies in the waves, however, and, in particular, in the third wave. For example, India had as early a public-sector transformation of the three segments as any first-wave country, and kept this public-sector apparatus to the present, not only intact but enlarged—whereas transition countries such as China, Russia, and Vietnam had already moved to privatizing state processing and retailing in the 1990s.

Finally, diffusion of the transformation (in all three segments) tended to occur earliest in more urban and later in more rural areas, and earliest and fastest in processed, then semi-processed, and then fresh products.

The Two-stage Transformation of the Wholesale/Logistics Segment

Public-Sector Induced Transformation of the Wholesale Sector

The "regulated" or state wholesale markets were substantial investments by cities or provinces, and were put in place in waves mainly from the 1960s on, starting with main cities, then secondary cities, and so on. A typical pattern was a hub-and-spokes model, with a set of primary wholesale markets in big cities and then "feeder" or secondary wholesale markets in smaller cities and rural areas, such as one finds in Brazil, China, Indonesia, Mexico, and India. The large markets are huge: today Delhi's Azadpur market moves 4 million tons of fresh produce per year; Beijing's Xinfadi, 8 million tons; the markets in Mexico City and Sao Paulo are each much larger yet. The growth of public markets was spectacular. For example, China's wholesale market volume increased 11,000 percent from 1990 to 2000 (Huang et al. 2007; Ahmadi-Esfahani and Locke, 1998), and India's regulated wholesale markets went from 450 regulated (formal) wholesale markets in 1948 to 5,500 wholesale markets in 2008 (Reardon et al. 2010). A similar rapid growth had occurred in the first- and second-wave countries in the 1960s–1970s.

The massive investments in public wholesale markets partially transformed this segment—substantially "de-fragmenting" and integrating markets, by providing "economies of agglomeration" and channeling wholesale from field brokers into a network of covered markets with *in situ* wholesalers, and thus also altering both technology and organization. By imposing regulations, public investments changed institutions, at least for the portion that passed through regulated markets.

There is emerging evidence that the public-sector "wholesale market" segment, after being established and proliferating, is consolidating (shown in studies from Indonesia (Natawidjaja et al. 2007), Mexico (Echánove and Reardon 2006), South Africa (China; Huang et al. 2007), Peru (Escobal and Agreda 1997), and India (Minten, Randrianarison, and Swinnen 2009), and even privatizing (for Brazil; Farina and Machado 1999) and multinationalizing (for example, with Paris's Rungis market investing in Chinese wholesale markets in joint partnerships in 2008 www.rungisinternational.com, and Sydney's in India's, see Reardon et al. 2010).

On the one hand, there is some interwholesale market concentration, such as in South Africa (Louw et al. 2007) where the share of the main market has risen over time. Moreover, within wholesale markets there has tended to be consolidation over wholesalers. Some of this was driven by differential capitalization that allowed some to grow larger and larger based on economies of scale in transport and warehousing (for Mexico, Echánove and Reardon 2006, and Peru, Escobal and Agreda, 1997), and regulations limiting the number of licensed wholesalers (as in India, Minten, Vandeplas, et al. 2010, or Turkey, Koç et al. 2007), and some has been due to the decline of the traditional clients of the smaller wholesalers (such as the small shops) in the 1990s on with the rise of supermarkets and competition off-market from "dedicated wholesalers" discussed next. There is also emerging evidence (such as from Indonesia and China) that wholesalers based in wholesale markets increasingly buy directly from farmers and compete down the share of the rural or field brokers.

Second Stage: Liberalization and the Rise of Modern Private Wholesale/Logistics

Building from the initial base of public-sector driven transformation of the wholesale sector, emerging in the 1990s and 2000s (again, depending on the "wave") is a second stage of transformation—this time mainly private-sector driven. This transformation has several dimensions.

First, in the 1990s–2000s, there were reactions against wholesaling regulations—with charges that although those regulations were originally designed to quell speculation and mercantile oligopoly, they had eventually created anticompetitive forces and a cadre of entrenched commission agents who proceeded to earn oligopolistic margins. There were few formal tests of this hypothesis, but the perception became strong among two sets of lobbying groups—the farmers, and the private sector logistics, processors, and retailers who wanted to buy direct from farmers and bypass the mandated wholesale markets. Eventually, in some countries, such as Brazil (Farina and Machado 1999) and South Africa (Louw et al. 2007) in the late 1990s, and half the states in India after 2003 (Reardon et al. 2010—in Turkey the debate is still engaged; Koç et al. 2007), the regulations were relaxed.

This liberalization opened the door to progressive "dis-intermediation"—such as contract farming by processors and collection centers by supermarkets. It is argued by various researchers (e.g., Farina and Machado in Brazil, Echánove and Reardon in Mexico, Louw et al. in South Africa) that dis-intermediation combined with the decline of traditional clients has led to a decline in volumes of wholesale markets, such as 25 percent over the 1990s in Sao Paolo, 30 percent over the first half of the 2000s in Mexico City.

Second, the counterpart of dis-intermediation has been the rise in the 1990s and 2000s of various "off-market" actors specialized in meeting the sourcing requirements of modern processors and supermarkets. These include the following.

The first of the modern actors are the "dedicated wholesalers" (such as Hortifruti in Central America, first associated with the Costa Rican multinational retailer CSU, then global retailer Ahold, then Walmart; or Bimandiri working with Carrefour in Indonesia). These wholesalers are dedicated to either one company or a segment (such as modern retail, processing, or HORECA (hotels, restaurants, catering) or exports), tend to be specialized in a category, and handle procurement relations suppliers. They add value (relative to the simple spot market of the traditional wholesale segment) by managing the relation, collecting, sorting, grading, packing or processing, and delivering of commodities.

The second of these are modern logistics companies. Commonly they undertake a variety of logistics tasks—wholesaling (intermediation), warehouse management, information and communication technology (ICT) system integration into retail and distribution systems of companies, cold chain development, and packaging. They may also forward integrate into retail management of specific divisions (such as Radhakrishna Foodland in India becoming an external "channel captain" managing fresh produce for second-tier India supermarket chains, Reardon et al. 2010).

FDI has been an important driver of the rise of these firms, spurred by liberalization of FDI as part of general liberalization in the 1990s and 2000s. In China and India, this occurred in the 2000s, and was immediately followed by a rush of foreign companies investing. For example, Snowman is a Japanese company in India that has become, in a few years, one of the leading logistics companies in South Asia. Some (such as Penske and TNT) "followed" global retailers and processors in their spread into developing countries (Reardon, Henson, and Berdegué 2007)—known as "follow sourcing." For a food company, this creates a shortcut to the time waiting for local logistics capacity to build and adapt to their needs, and quickly puts in place state-of-the-art techniques that also give them an advantage over local firms using only traditional wholesalers and truckers. In some cases, a large retailer seeks a multinational logistics company that can integrate its operations over a whole region, as in Central Europe (see Dries, Reardon, and Swinnen 2004), and also set up an export platform from that country back to the host region, such as Western Europe.

There has also been important domestic investment in this sector, sometimes from transport company roots (such as CONCOR in India for the rail segment), maritime company roots (such as Adani in India), and hotel roots—in short, companies that had some transport functions that then were extended into logistics for modern agrifood companies. Some were conglomerates that had food operations and saw the unmet demand for modern logistics and added logistics; in India, Pantaloon (the leading retailer) started a major logistics company (see Reardon et al. 2010 for India cases).

A third element of the modernizing wholesale sector is the "cash&carry" chain. This is in direct competition with the traditional wholesalers and stockist networks, supplying traditional retail and traditional HORECA (hotel, restaurant, and catering sector). Global chains operating in this segment include Metro, Walmart (Sam's Club), Makro, and others. But domestic retailers also tend to open (or start as) cash&carries, as they are operating in markets still dominated by small shops. The cash&carries use bulk buying and supply-chain efficiencies to lower costs, and then add services like bundling, delivery, and retail consulting, to compete with traditional wholesalers. Often the cash&carries start as wholesale chains and transition into part retail. In some cases, global retailers enter as cash&carries when retail FDI restrictions are still in place, as Walmart did in 2008 in India (as a cash&carry and as a "back-end" or procurement partner with Bharti, a domestic conglomerate operating a retail chain), and Tesco did in 2009 in India with Tata (in a similar arrangement to Walmart's). The cash&carry format is often politically advantageous because it is focused on serving the small retailers who form the opposition to the large retailers.

The Two-stage Transformation of Agrifood Processing

Key Stylized Facts and Trends as Background

Processed foods are from cereals and pulses (dried peas, beans, and lentils), tubers, fish, meat, dairy/eggs, edible oils, and condiments. These are either minimally (semi-) processed or fully processed. They are sold both packaged (bagged, boxed, wrapped, bottled) and nonpackaged (like loose flour). The processed food sector has grown quickly in the past several decades, overlain with a "westernization" of diets, with a shift to rice and wheat (Senauer, Sahn, and Alderman 1986), and to processed meats and dairy (Pingali 2006). These trends are driven by increases in income, urbanization, women increasing their participation in labor markets outside the home and wanting to save time cooking, improvements in packaging and processing technologies, and eventually, by diversification of the variety of processed foods, abetted by modern retail (Gehlhlar and Regmi 2005).

This rise is correlated both with rising incomes in a country over time, and over countries: using the "packaged food" subset of processed food, the share of packaged food in food expenditures is roughly 7 percent in low, 30 percent in lower-middle, and 45 percent in upper-middle income countries; total packaged food sales are growing at only 2–3 percent annually in developed countries, versus 13 percent, 28 percent, and 7 percent in low, lower- middle, and upper-middle income developing countries, much faster than GDP growth rates (Gehlhar and Regmi 2005; Wilkinson and Rocha 2009).

The composition of the food processing sector also changes with income: the share of grains in processed food sector value-added is about 20 percent in lower income, and drops to 15 percent in upper- and lower-middle income countries; the share of dairy climbs from 7 percent to 10–13 percent over the three sets of countries; the rest is the share of processed meats, fish, fruits, vegetables, fats, and baked goods/noodles (Wilkinson and Rocha 2009).

Finally, the great majority of processed food output and growth has occurred domestically within developing countries, rather than in international trade networks. Although processed food trade grew quickly up to the mid 1990s, it has stagnated in the 15 years after that; at present only 10 percent of global processed food output is traded (Gehlhar and Regmi 2005). In general, little of the food produced or consumed is imported or exported: about 3 percent of produce, 4 percent of meat, and 10 percent of grain output or consumption of developing countries is exported or imported (Reardon and Timmer 2007).

First Stage of Transformation of Food Processing—Driven Mainly by the Public Sector

As with wholesale, governments' effects on processing transformation came via direct action and policy.

Although the topic has been important in urban food security debates for decades, the government's direct role in inducing food-processing transformation has been limited in most countries, even in its heyday in the 1960s/1970s. It was mainly confined to grain sold to urban markets. In that period, the urban population share and the marketed share of grain were lower than today. The local small-scale (and thus not parastatal) share of grain processing was higher. And the parallel market (not via parastatals) was often larger than the government channels. There was then rapid privatization of grain parastatals in most countries in the late 1980s or 1990s. Only a few countries' governments still have substantial food processing operations into the 2000s. For example, in Asia, it is only India that maintains a substantial presence via its grain parastatal (see Bharat and Ramaswami, this volume), which procures only 20 percent of India's grain output (and 40 percent of the market). The numbers are far lower in other Asian countries (Rashid, Cummings, and Gulati 2007), and lower yet in other regions.

Nevertheless, state policies had other effects. Policies cheapening credit increased the scale of plant in some countries (such as in rice processing in Indonesia, Timmer 1974); regulations concerning hygiene and construction of slaughterhouses increased the scale and formalized livestock slaughter. In many countries (such as Peru) import licenses were granted to a limited number of large feed mills and dairy firms to import yellow corn, powdered milk, and so on, and, thus, *de facto* consolidated part of processing (for

Peru, Lajo Lazo, 1983). However, sometimes regulation resisted transformation: for example, India "reserved" most of food processing for small enterprises until 1998 (Bhavani, Gulati, and Roy 2006).

Second Stage of Transformation of Food Processing in Developing Countries—Driven by Private-sector Investment

The late 1980s through today has seen rapid growth in the food-processing sector noted earlier, combined with rapid consolidation; multinationalization; and technological, institutional, and organizational change. There are several salient points.

1. *The Initial Impetus for Transformation in the Second Stage: Privatization and Liberalization and the First Round of Consequences*

In many countries, with structural adjustment in the 1980s and 1990s, state grain mills and slaughterhouses were privatized or eliminated, and import licenses disbanded. This led to two contrary lines of consequences.

On the one hand, especially in the 1990s, the demise of public-sector operations and delicensing of processing, and diversifying products for growing urban and rural markets and encouraged by market deregulation led to proliferation of small and medium scale enterprise (SME) grain mills and dairy, meat, fish, and produce processing competing for the newly opened space. Examples of such proliferation were observed in diverse settings, from dairy and wheat and horticultural product processing SMEs in Brazil (Farina 2002, 1997) to maize and vegetable and fruit processing in Africa (Broutin and Bricas 2006, Jaffee 1995, Jayne and Jones 1997, Traub and Jayne 2008; and Rubey 1995). This flowering of SMEs was indeed a goal of liberalization.

On the other hand, privatization led not only to domestic private-sector bids, but also, due to widespread liberalization of processing FDI, an avalanche of FDI. The latter came first mainly from Western Europe and the United States (with global firms like Nestle, Kraft, Danone, seeking less saturated markets with higher profit rates, Gehlhar and Regmi 2005), then Japan, and eventually from regional multinationals such as Mexico's Bimbo into Central America, Thailand's CP into China and other Southeast Asian countries (last year CP created the largest shrimp processing firm in the world in Indonesia), Philippine's San Miguel into Vietnam and Del Monte Asia (Philippines).

The consequence was that foreign firms form a major share of the large processing sector in a number of first and second wave countries by the 2000s, although that process appears to be just starting in third-wave countries like China and India in the 2000s. The consolidation this produced is often striking. For example, by the early 2000s, Nestle alone had a market share in Latin America for key packaged foods (specifically, confections, soups, pet food, baby food, dairy, and baked goods) of 61 percent, and 26 percent in Eastern Europe; in Brazil that share was 83 percent, in Philippines 37 percent, and so on. Unilever had similar dominance: its market share in a set of key packaged goods was

38 percent in Poland, 43 percent in Argentina, 37 percent in Indonesia, 47 percent in South Africa, and so on (Bolling and Gehlhar 2005). However, the country composition of the FDI senders may change over time, indicating the importance of rising regional multinationals in "south-south FDI" (Wilkinson and Rocha 2009, Reardon, Henson, et al. 2007).

Moreover, the FDI acquired large outmoded grain mills and dairies and slaughterhouses and refurbished and relaunched them as modern, larger operations. For example, Smithfield's (the leading pork processor in the world) acquired Romanian ex-state slaughterhouses at a tenth of the cost of such processing facilities in the United States in the 2000s (Sharpe, 2006). In the late 1980s, in two years, Parmalat bought 24 SME Brazilian dairy firms as part of a much larger and longer acquisition spree, itself much smaller than that of rival Nestle, that moved the two foreign firms from minor players in Brazilian dairy in 1990 to the majority of the sector by 2000—a sector that had itself grown 10-fold over just that period. This same story played itself out in many countries in various sectors—such as for dairy in Argentina and Central and Eastern Europe in that same period (Farina et al. 2005; Hartmann and Wandel 1999).

Contrary to conventional wisdom, the role of product trade in the globalization of the food-processing sector was small, because the share of imports is small, and those imports have grown little after the early mid 1990s. The flip side of this is that outgoing FDI in food processing from developed-country firms is much more important than processed-food exports from developed countries by those firms; for example, U.S. processed-food firms produce five times more in foreign countries than they export to foreign countries (Gehlhar and Regmi, 2005). Many reasons (like transport costs and tariffs) make FDI more attractive than export. *Agrifood globalization's main vector of effects is FDI.* As with the other segments, the diffusion path of that FDI was correlated with the waves.

2. *Consolidation in the Processing Segment into the 1990s and 2000s*

There has been rapid consolidation in developing-country food processing (Rama and Wilkinson 2008), again, in the sequence roughly of three waves. The drivers of this consolidation are as follows.

First, there is evidence that even in the SME subsegment, there has been gradual consolidation, with micro-enterprises of 1–2 persons giving way (growing into or being out-competed by) SMEs of 5 and more persons. This was noted in India by Bhalla (1997), showing how, over several decades, rural food-processing SMEs had shifted gradually from villages to rural towns along highway corridors, with an increase in average size. Similarly, in Latin America, the average size of food-processing SMEs (and other rural nonfarm firms) has increased over several decades, with wage-labor share rising (Reardon, Berdegué and Escobar 2001). This may have been due to the rise of secondary and tertiary towns and cities in the 1970s–1980s and the "de-protection" of rural economies by improvements in infrastructure and increased competition with processing firms in urban areas (as suggested by Taylor in Mexico), and large-scale factories sending their cheaper goods into rural areas, out-competing traditional micro-enterprises, as with tortillas in Mexico (Rello and Saavedra 2007), or cassava *gari* in Cote d'Ivoire—and indeed with packaged biscuits in the United States in the 1880s (Levenstein 1988). The emerging penetration of rural towns by modern retail, selling branded processed foods at a discount, may accelerate this competition (Reardon, Stamoulis, and Pingali 2007).

Second, in some cases, such as India, the processing sector was "reserved" to SMEs, to protect employment. In 1998, as part of overall liberalization, the sector was "de-reserved," and a flood of investment quickly increased the concentration indices and deepened capital (Bhavani et al. 2006).

Third, regulations affecting the segment appeared to accelerate the pressures on SMEs. For example, rezoning of cities to reduce congestion, application of business registration laws to increase municipal revenues, and application of food-safety and hygiene regulations to food businesses have been important examples imposing special burdens on small firms who lacked the investment surplus and access to bank loans to shift location, register their firm, and adopt all the measures (such as hygiene facilities and cement floors) needed to conform to new laws. This has occurred in food service in Brazil, and poultry and egg companies in Vietnam with avian flu regulations. There is mounting evidence that consumers are drawn to supermarkets as a result of food safety concerns about small processors and traditional markets (for Thailand, see Posri and Chadbunchachai, 2006). After the recent food-safety crises, the Chinese government is launching a food-safety regulatory initiative that it expects to bankrupt half the food processing SMEs. This would even pale with the massive impact such a food law had in the United States in 1908 on food SMEs through the 1910s, such as with the exit of 90 percent of dairy SMEs in the main eastern cities just in the 1910s (Levenstein 1988.)

Fourth, while the "pie" of the sector was increasing rapidly, the massive investments by domestic and foreign firms, creating or enlarging large-scale processors, has resulted in out-competing many small firms. There are several reasons for this.

1. Large firms have the bargaining power and monitoring and "resource provision contract" capacity to enforce coordination of their supply chains (such as via contracts and private standards). They can increase the quality and consistency of their intermediate inputs from farmers, driving down costs, controlling for plant size. A striking example of this is in the Brazilian dairy industry, where private standards enforced in coordinated supply chains reduced sediment and bacteria in milk, reducing processing costs for the large firms.
2. Large firms can borrow more cheaply than small, and foreign firms more cheaply than domestic (such as in Mexico, see Shwedel 2003).
3. In many categories of processing, larger plants have economies of scale. Moreover, a critical mass of output is needed to defend a brand, and the brand provides a competitive attribute over nonbranded product, especially where credence goods like food safety are involved. To these can be added economies of scope, as more lines can be added and thus the company can create a "one stop shop" for retailers to source the diversity they require.

4. Large processing firms (like large retail chains) have greater capacity to put in place more efficient marketing systems; large processors put in place distribution centers and logistics fleets.

Moreover, innovation on the input side, such as vegetable seeds that allow harvest at a single time rather than staggered over the season, or greater shelf life, allow large-scale plants to fill capacity and source threshold volumes. Multinational seed companies help drive this innovation, in symbiosis with large processing companies.

Finally, there has emerged a "symbiosis" between large-scale processors and supermarket chains. The latter drive down consumer prices and extend the market, as discussed next.

The Two-stage Transformation of Food Retail in Developing Countries

First Stage of Transformation of Food Retail—Driven Mainly by the Public Sector

Many developing-country governments have actively worked to develop modern retail—regardless of whether they termed their efforts so. There are three types of public sector cum cooperative retail that flourished mainly in the 1970s/1980s, and then were dismantled or privatized, although some continued into the 1990s/2000s and "morphed" into competitors with modern private chains. These included the following.

First, governments developed "food security focused" state retail chains dedicated to the subsidized distribution mainly of staples. Examples of these include the Fair Price Shops in India, the Grain Stores in China, the SAM stores in Mexico. These were generally in forward-integration from grain parastatals. In most countries, these retail chains were privatized or dismantled along with the processing parastatals in the early 1990s. Some survived into the liberalization era, such as in India, where the Fair Price Shops form about 15 percent of urban food staples retail, and have about $600 million of sales, ranking them among the leading chains (Reardon et al. 2010; Gaiha et al, this volume).

Second, closely related to the aforementioned were chain stores in forward-integration from state-supported or state-subsidized cooperatives. This was common in Central and Eastern Europe and India, among other countries. The most common was in dairy, but it was also done in meat and other processed goods (Dries et al. 2004). In many cases these were dismantled or privatized when traditional state cooperatives declined in the 1990s. Although this was induced by SAPs (Structural Adjustment Programs) and strong competition from the rise of private modern retail in developing countries, it paralleled the rise and then decline by the 1950s of coop store chains in the United Kingdom and the United States. Some have survived into the liberalization era: an example is the

Mother Dairy chain in India—started in the 1970s and developing by the late 2000s into a dairy kiosk chain with $200 million in sales in Delhi alone (Reardon et al. 2010).

Third, in some countries there are state-owned enterprises (SOE) that made a transition from a staples stores or coop chains to SOE supermarkets. Such is the case of the number-2 chains in Vietnam (Saigon Coop) and China (Lianhua, with $10 billion in sales in 2009) today (calculated from data from www.planetretail.net). They were modernized and capitalized and re-launched to compete in this segment. This indicated the importance of retail as a modernization mechanism in the transition countries. Some of these have been privatized.

In sum, the sheer size and the early incidence of the state and cooperative cum state sectors in initiating retail transformation has been neglected in the literature but has been significant and continues in some countries today as a significant impetus to modernization.

Second Stage of Transformation of Food Retail in the 1990s-2000s—Driven Mainly by the Private Sector

1. *The Rapid Rise of Supermarkets*

The retail sector in many developing countries has been transformed—consolidated and multinationalized—in a "supermarket revolution," starting in the early 1990s and continuing to present. This was firmly predicted to be impossible by the retail literature in the 1980s and before. Its surprising takeoff in the 1990s is documented by a body of literature emerging mainly in the 2000s (e.g., Reardon et al. 2003, Traill, 2006).

In broad strokes, the diffusion of modern food retail has rolled out in three waves over countries: (1) the first wave, with take-off in the early 1990s, was in East Asia (outside Japan and China), South America, South Africa, and Central Europe; the share of modern retail in food retail went from roughly 5–10 percent in 1990 to some 50–60 percent by the late 1990s; (2) the second wave, in the mid-late 1990s, was in Southeast Asia (outside transition countries like Vietnam), and Central America and Mexico; the share reached some 20–50 percent by the late 1990s; (3) the third wave, in the late 1990s and 2000s, has been mainly in China, Vietnam, India, and Russia. The share climbed to some 5–20 percent by end 2000s, in a rapid rise. In Africa outside South Africa, mainly in Eastern/Southern Africa, modern retail is just starting in some countries.

There has been a steep crescendo in modern retail growth in the third-wave countries in the 2000s. For example, using raw data from the leading retail data source, Planet Retail, we calculated leading modern retail sales (for chains selling food) growth rates in representative Asian countries in the three waves. The rates of growth vary over the "waves" as one would expect: the East Asian "first-wave" countries (South Korea and Taiwan) indeed show slower modern-retail sales growth rates (a compound growth rate of 11.2 percent over the 8 years from 2001 to 2009), the second wave (Indonesia, Malaysia, Philippines, Thailand) in the middle (a compound growth rate of 17.9 percent annually), and the third wave (China, India, Vietnam) the highest (40.9 percent compound growth rate), as expected due to the most recent starters advancing fastest and the earliest relatively saturated.[2] These rates can be compared to approximately 5 percent annual growth in real GDP over 2000–2008 in the first- and second-wave countries, and 7.5–10 percent in the third-wave countries. Even at these rapid GDP growth rates, modern retail sales grew 2–3 times as fast in the first- and second-wave countries, and 4–5 times as fast in the third-wave countries. This implies that modern retail's share of the retail pie continues to expand.

Inside a country, typically the diffusion has rolled out in the following two sets of paths: (1) from large cities to small cities and finally into rural towns in adapted formats, and from upper to middle to poorer classes; (2) from processed foods to semiprocessed foods to fresh produce.[3] These paths are essentially the same as occurred "historically" (in the twentieth century) in developed countries.

2. *The Determinants of the Accelerated Transformation*

The accelerated penetration of retail clashes both with broadly shared self-perceptions in developing countries, as well as the pre-1990 retail literature (where often one heard that somehow the "traditional food culture," dense cities, low opportunity cost of labor, and "habit of frequent shopping" militated against modern retail). Why did it occur so quickly? Several factors explain it.

First, beside the growth in the demand-side drivers (such as urbanization) being much faster than had been the case in developed countries as they experienced retail transformation, there was, as with processing, an influx of investment from both domestic sources and an avalanche of FDI. Retail FDI liberalization occurred in the first- and second-wave countries mainly in the 1990s and in most (but not India) of the main third-wave countries in the 2000s—recently culminating for example in full liberalization with World Trade Organization (WTO) accession by China in 2004 and Vietnam in 2009. The upshot is that multinationalization has accompanied the rise of the modern retail sector and its consolidation: the share of foreign firms in the top 6 firms in Latin America is the ratio 4.5/6 (whereas, in most countries, the top chain is foreign), versus about the ratio 3/6 for the "third-wave" countries in Asia and Russia (based on www.planetretail.net data).

Yet competitive domestic investment has also been important. On the one hand, the crucial role that massive investments by conglomerates (their presence or size or both generated by the economic boom of the past two decades) in the past four years have played in the spectacular rise of modern retail in India is striking—even with multi-brand retail FDI still not allowed. Private domestic investment also created major regional multinationals—such as South Korea's Lotte investing in China, Vietnam, Indonesia; and Hong Kong's Dairy Farm investing in India, China, and Southeast Asia.

On the other hand, SOE chains continue to be an important investment driver in the second stage in particular in the "transition" countries. The share of SOEs and public private partnerships (PPP), or joint ventures between state and private firms) is also about a third ($30.5 billion of sales) of the leading 47 chains in China; in Vietnam,

$700 million of the $2 billion of the leading 15 chains (based on www.planetretail.net data). Instead of combating and regulating heavily supermarkets as the United States did for the first 30 years, egged on by small retail lobby forces (Reardon and Hopkins 2006), the third-wave countries (except India) are actually promoting supermarkets as a modernization strategy.

Second, using supply-chain efficiencies, modern retailers can charge lower prices for processed and semiprocessed foods (a dominant share of their sales as they are a dominant share of overall food purchases) than can traditional retailers. (For a review of 10 countries' evidence, see Minten and Reardon 2008, and Minten et al. 2010 for India, for rice, wheat flour, and mustard oil, and Gorton, Sauer, and Supatpongkul 2009 for vegetables in Thailand.) These efficiencies, in turn, derive from modernization of their procurement systems, moving gradually from traditional spot wholesale market and stockist networks to using direct sourcing and dedicated wholesalers, distribution centers, private standards, and modern logistics. The procurement modernization tends to occur earliest and fastest in correlation with the "waves," with the efficiency of local wholesale markets, with the size of the chain and its capacity to make these investments, with processed and semiprocessed products much earlier than for fresh produce (the latter being about 10–15 percent of the sales of supermarkets, as of the diets in developing countries), and with the degree of development of modern logistics and agribusiness companies to act as partners. Modernization provides a cost advantage to the large businesses and an acceleration of consolidation inside the modern retail segment, even at early stages.

Third, the retail literature on developing countries of the 1950s–1980s held a rigid and limited view of the format and socioeconomic targeting of supermarkets: that of a "big box" (large format only), focused on imports and processed products, targeted at the high-income niche consumers with cars and refrigerators, in big cities, and interested in "western" images. To that image was counterposed the characteristics of the mass of consumers (many in dense cities, without cars, or in towns, many with limited incomes, most shopping frequently near their homes). From that contradiction was derived the prediction that modern retail could not "take off."

But modern food retail spread beyond the upper-income niche, and beyond even the middle class, into the food markets of the poor, and into small cities and rural towns. That spread was accomplished both by lowering prices *and by adapting formats and marketing strategies.*

On the one hand, from an initial march from small to large supermarkets (usually stand-alone but sometimes in malls), modern food retail bifurcated into hypermarkets on one hand, and a welter of "small formats" on the other—from pushcart chains in India, to "hard discount" stores in Argentina and South Africa and China, to "neighborhood stores" in India, Mexico, and Thailand, to "fresh produce store chains" in India, South Africa, and Indonesia, to the familiar convenience stores in most countries. This allowed penetration of dense urban spaces (allowing frequent visits close to home), scale to suit small towns, rapid rollout where real-estate markets are tight, a means of targeting and adapting to a variety of consumer types, a means of franchising (and thus co-opting small retailers), and a means of getting under regulations limiting store sizes.

On the other hand, the penetration of rural towns and poor areas in cities is facilitated by the small formats, cheap pricing, and flexible inventories. The latter becomes most innovative when modern retail sets up "one-stop shopping" for rural consumers. For example, "rural business hubs" in India are combinations of small supermarkets and farm input stores with joint venture banks and even health units in rural areas, such as Choupal Saagar or Hariyali Kisaan Bazaar (Gulati, Minten, and Reardon 2008, Bell et al. 2007). In China, the government has started chains of rural supermarkets. These forays appear to be driven by increasing rural incomes, the dearth of services available locally, and the recognition that modern retail brings cheaper staple foodstuffs and nonfood goods (Chakravarty et al. 2007).

Impacts on SMEs and Farmers

In developing countries, millions of the poor are employed in small and medium enterprises (SME) in all three agrifood industry segments, and on farms. The transformation of the agrifood industry has myriad effects, realized and potential, on SMEs and small farms. The research on these is only emerging, but already suggests some broad lines.

Modern agrifood companies have a *direct* impact only on SMEs in wholesale/logistics, processing, and retailing—from which they may directly source or with which they directly compete—and fresh produce growers, from which the companies may source. Thus, we treat those two groups below. Here we do not consider *indirect* effects, such as how the relation between a supermarket and large processor in turn affects the farmers supplying the latter.

Impacts on Traditional-sector SMEs in Processing, Wholesaling, and Retail

First, modernized agrifood industry segments (wholesale/logistics, processors, retailers) are broadly competitive with—and apparently, over the longer term, broadly destructive of—their counterparts in the traditional sector. The modern company brings economies of scale and supply-chain sourcing efficiencies to bear on the production/service-rendering and input sourcing side. On the marketing side, the company arms itself with adaptive flexibility of form to mimic small outlets and units, variety of output to adapt to differing tastes over classes and localities, branding to win consumers, credit programs for suppliers and consumers, and advertising.

Nevertheless, the traditional enterprise has some advantages it uses to resist or avoid competition from the modern segments. As it is in the informal sector, it saves the costs of taxes and registrations (although it may pay bribes to police) and largely avoids costs of meeting regulations on food standards. It uses its own family labor flexibly, and intensively should target quality production and extra services. It often forms long-standing social networks and sometimes credit relations with clients and suppliers. Its small size allows it to fit into nooks and crannies and shift its locations. But from the steady march of the modern segments, of course at very different paces in different countries and products and segments, one can infer that these advantages are not decisive or permanent.

Second, there is evidence emerging that the three modern agrifood industry segments are in a mutually reinforcing "symbiosis." The following explains this critical point.

Large processors reduce transaction costs for modern retailers by facilitating dis-intermediation, delivering to the DCs or stores of the retailers (for Argentina and Brazil examples, see Farina et al. 2005, for Poland, Milczarek-Andrzejewska et al. 2008). They adapt packaging and variety to the needs of the retailers. Their inventory systems reduce chances of retail stock-out. Their national headquarters can negotiate deals with the retail headquarters, and if both are multinational, they can do so globally.

In turn, modern retailers facilitate market size and scope development for large processors. Supermarkets tend to carry a limited set of brands per product category, and these tend to be mainly from medium and large processors, and a smattering of small company brands for noncommodity products. Retail chains provide large shelf space (compared to traditional retailers) in which to multiply the diversity of the processors products (Dries and Reardon 2005), cold chain and shelves, advertising, and promotions. Modern retailers develop markets for processed products because they tend to sell them cheaper than traditional stores once procurement systems are modernized (Minten and Reardon, 2008). These advantages of modern retail to the large processor are offset partially by competition from retailers' private label products, slotting fees and other charges, and—if the chain is large—strong bargaining power from large-volume purchases.

Finally, large processors and supermarket chains provide the initial key markets for modern wholesalers (the "dedicated wholesalers" noted earlier) and modern logistics firms.[4] These firms are competing with traditional wholesalers to serve the modern retailers and processors—and do so by offering often superior services of transport (with modern cross-docking and refrigerated vehicles), warehousing management, and services not usually found in traditional distribution segments such as operating packing houses, packaging, ICT systems, and cold chains, and managing contract farming, merchandise inventory, and international networks. Multinational processors and retailers sometimes ask global or regional logistics firms serving them in developed markets to "follow source" into the new developing markets. For example, Carrefour brought Penske into Brazil, and major Taiwanese and Japanese retailers bring their home logistics firms into China.

It appears that these developing symbioses among modern segments lead to gradual displacement of traditional retailers, wholesalers, and processors as suppliers to the modern segments. For example, selecting the perspective of retail's sourcing, one finds ample case-study evidence of supermarkets shifting from sourcing from stockists and wholesalers and SMEs to preferred supplier direct relationships with large dairies in Poland, Brazil, Argentina, Zambia, Russia, with large flour and rice millers in India, with large meat packers in Central America, and so on. Just emerging is the evidence of supermarkets moving to dedicated wholesalers to dis-intermediate from traditional wholesale markets in fresh produce—with emerging cases as recently as the early to mid-2000s in the first-/second-wave countries like Mexico, Indonesia, and Brazil.

Impacts on Farmers

The direct impact on farmers of modernization across the three segments is a complex subject. Assessment would require a review of contract farming of a wide variety of products by processors, and direct sourcing of produce by supermarkets and their dedicated agents. A recent review (Reardon et al. 2009) finds that effects differ depending on a variety of conditioners, such as: (a) if companies have access to medium and large farmers and have an option to eschew small farmers if they want; (b) if farms are mainly small, the distribution over farms of nonland assets such as irrigation and education or training (such as in Guatemala, see Hernandez et al. 2007); (c) if factor markets function well or there are idiosyncratic market failures constraining small-farmer access to credit and inputs. In the latter case, companies may resort to "resource-providing contracts" (Austin 1981) that have been found to be common in export agriculture or domestic markets, in which a processor is sourcing from small farmers.[5]

Given that supermarkets in developing countries have so recently started to sell produce and even more recently to source produce in ways other than through the use of wholesale markets, the literature on impacts is only emerging. It is somewhat more established for contract farming with processors.

In terms of participation (inclusion versus exclusion of small farmers), studies show mixed results. Supermarkets and processors are found to source from large and medium farms where available. (Studies on the latter relationships tend to be case studies given the small samples.) Where large and medium farms have better options (such as export) or are judged to have too much bargaining power, and companies or NGOs are willing to resolve idiosyncratic market constraints of small farmers, or where only small farmers are available, companies source from small farmers. Evidence tends to point to their sourcing from small farmers with more nonland assets or "threshold investments" requisite for consistent and quality supply, such as irrigation, road access, education.[6]

In terms of impact on incomes, many studies report from moderate to substantial gains in incomes comparing participants in modern supply chains versus traditional arrangements, either between treatment and control groups, or before and after. But there are relatively few studies that control fully for the asset and liquidity situations of farmers so as to isolate the effect of the relation with modern channels per se. This relationship is somewhat difficult in a cross-section; it is ideal (but rare) to have a panel data set to test. An example of the latter is Michelson (2010) showing strong impacts on net income of farmers supplying Walmart in Nicaragua relative to traditional markets.

Some studies (such as Maertens and Swinnen 2008) show indirect effects, on off-farm employment in agro-industries.

Emerging Innovative Strategies to Facilitate Linkages Among Agrifood Sectors and with Small Farmers

The transformation of the agrifood sector in developing countries is having a rapid and profound impact on the structure, conduct, and performance of the sector. Consolidation within each of the three subsectors and synergies across them have emerged far faster than earlier experiences in developed countries, with still poorly understood consequences for the units that matter for welfare analysis, that is, consuming households and small farms.

A number of policies and programs condition the speed and nature of the transformation, as discussed in previous sections. In order to condition the impacts of this transformation on farmers, there is a welter of innovative development strategies emerging in the 2000s. We conclude the paper by focusing on these innovations.

Governments, donors, NGOs, and the private sector are putting in place a variety of partnerships and programs to increase economies of agglomeration among agrifood industry segments and reduction of the costs of transaction of their linkages with farmers. These strategies include: (a) *corridors* combining highways and other government-supplied infrastructure, agrifood companies, and linkages with farmers, such as the new Beira Corridor starting in Mozambique to stretch to Angola, or the new corridor to stretch from the Mekong Delta to Southern China; (b) "hubs" or "platforms" or "parks" in which various companies and services cluster and include links with farmers, such export platforms, new "mega food parks" or "integrated agrifood parks," private rural business hubs, and modern terminal markets that cluster sellers; (c) "diamond linkages" involving partnerships over the three segments of the agrifood industry, plus a farmer cooperative, plus an input company, all supported by state-provided services. A prime example is Carrefour, aided by the dedicated-wholesaler Bimandiri, and input and credit provider Syngenta, with specialized extension from the government, working with a melon-farmers association in Indonesia for sales in Indonesia and to Carrefour stores in the region.

These approaches tend to cluster companies and add the state and NGOs to provide the missing services (such as output procurement, processing/packing/cooling, technical assistance, credit, insurance) and products (inputs and equipment of requisite quality) required for small farmers to compete. Moreover, there tends to be a "hub-and-spoke" model with collection centers or depots to which farmers deliver. This approach is designed to meet the input and service needs of farmers, reduce transaction costs by putting retailers and processors into rural areas, but provide the missing infrastructure and service base for the companies, who, in turn, make concomitant investment in packing plants and logistics facilities.

The general concept of the new approach is reminiscent of the "integrated rural development programs" of the 1970s/1980s, and the "processing export platforms" of the 1990s.[7] An important difference is that the integrated programs were usually government investments in particular areas, and the earlier platforms tended to be focused only on exports. The integrated programs ended up in large measure failing due to coordination and management problems—and perhaps because there was not often an explicit and established link to dynamic sources of market demand and/or the requisite steps were not taken to meet the market requirements. This new wave of private-public hubs and parks may meet the challenges bequeathed by these earlier programs and serve as dynamic links for small farmers. It is early on in the new approach to evaluate their functioning and impacts.

Notes

1. The urbanization rates in these countries were extraordinary: whereas 40 percent of the U.S. population was in cities in 1900 and 75 percent nine decades later, by 1990—that same shift of shares occurred, for example, in South Korea in the two decades up to 1990 and in Brazil the three decades up to 1990 (Henderson 2002).
2. The calculations are based on sales data for leading chains from www.planetretail.net
3. For example, in "third-wave" China, Goldman and Vanhonacker (2006) found that modern retailers already have a retail market share of 79 percent in packaged and processed goods, 55 percent in baked goods, 46 percent in meat, 37 percent in fruit, 35 percent in poultry, 33 percent in fish, and 22 percent in vegetables in large cities. Compare that to the more advanced ("first-wave") case of Hong Kong, which may represent the average Asian consumer sometime in the medium-term future. Hong Kong supermarkets have a 59 percent share in fruit retail and a 55 percent share in vegetables (thus, a share similar to supermarket penetration of produce retail in Brazil), 52 percent in meat, 39 percent in poultry, and 33 percent in fish (Coca-Cola Retailing Research Council Asia 2005). See Ho (2005) on modern retail penetration of rice retail in Hong Kong.
4. For cases of partnering between modern logistics firms and modern processors or retail chains, see, for example, Han et al. 2009 for pork processing in China, and horticulture products in India (Reardon et al. 2010).
5. See Key and Runsten (1999), and Schejtman (1998), in general, and Bivings and Runsten (1992) for Mexico and von Braun et al. (1989) for Guatemala and Minten et al. 2009 for Madagascar for vegetables, Gow and Swinnen (1998) for Slovakia for sugar, Dries and Swinnen (2004) for Poland for dairy; there are a number of other examples.
6. See Hernandez et al. (2007) for Guatemala, with similar results in Indonesia, Nicaragua, China, Mexico, Mozambique. Studies on the latter tend to be econometric studies; however many tend to be cross-section (given limited access to panel data) and sometimes to not adequately establish causality because asset observations were not lagged. The cited studies do not suffer from the latter.
7. For an example of many, see Cling, Razafindrakoto, and Franc (2005), for Madagascar.

References

Ahmadi-Esfahani, F. Z. and C. G. Locke. 1998. "Wholesale Food Markets with 'Chinese Characteristics.'" *Food Policy* 23(1): 89–103.

Austin J. E. 1981. *Agroindustrial Project Analysis*. Baltimore: Johns Hopkins University Press.

Bell, D. E., N. Sanghavi, V. Fuller, M. Shelman. 2007. *Hariyali Kisaan Bazaar: A Rural Business Initiative*, Case N2-508-012, November 15, Cambridge, MA: Harvard Business School.

Bhalla, S. 1997. *The Rise and Fall of Workforce Diversification Processes in Rural India: A Regional and Sectoral Analysis*. Centre for Economic Studies and Planning, DSA Working Paper. New Delhi: Jawaharlal Nehru University.

Bhavani T. A, A. Gulati, D. Roy. 2006. "Structure of the Indian Food Processing Industry: Have Reforms Made a Difference?" Paper presented at the Workshop "From Plate to Plough: Agricultural Diversification and its Implications for the Smallholders," New Delhi, September 20–21.

Bivings L, D. Runsten. 1992. *Potential Competitiveness of the Mexican Processed Vegetable and Strawberry Markets*. Report to the Ministry of Agriculture, Fisheries, and Food, British Columbia.

Bolling, C. and M. Gehlhar. 2005. "Global Food Manufacturing Reorients to Meet New Demands." In *New Directions in Global Food Markets*, edited by M. Gehlhar and A. Regmi, chapter 5. Agricultural Information Bulletin no 794. Washington, D.C.: USDA, Economic Research Service.

Broutin, C. and N. Bricas. 2006. *Agroalimentaire et lutte contre la pauvreté en Afrique subsaharienne: Le rôle des micro et petites enterprises*. Paris: Éditions du Gret _ collection Études et travaux.

Chakravarty K, V. Sridhar, P. Bhardwaj, and N. Bhattacharjee. 2007. *Rural Retailing—The Next Phase in Retailing*. Report, New Delhi: Confederation of Indian Industry—YES BANK Knowledge Report.

Cling, J-P., M. Razafindrakoto, and O. R. Franc. 2005. "Export Processing Zones in Madagascar: A Success Story under Threat?" *World Development* 33(5): 785–803.

Coca-Cola Retailing Research Council Asia. 2005. *The Fresh Imperative: Creating Excellence in Asian Fresh Food Retailing*. Study by Accenture, commissioned by Coca-Cola Retailing Research Council.

Dries, L., E. Germenji, N. Noev, and J. F. M. Swinnen. 2009. "Farmers, Vertical Coordination, and the Restructuring of Dairy Supply Chains in Central and Eastern Europe," *World Development* 37(11): 1742–1758.

Dries, L. and T. Reardon. 2005. *Central and Eastern Europe: Impact of Food Retail Investments on the Food Chain*. London: FAO Investment Center—EBRD Cooperation Program, Report Series no. 6, February.

Dries, L., T. Reardon, and J. Swinnen. 2004. "The Rapid Rise of Supermarkets in Central and Eastern Europe: Implications for the Agrifood Sector and Rural Development," *Development Policy Review* 22(5), September: 525–556.

Dries, L. and J. Swinnen. 2004. "Foreign Direct Investment, Vertical Integration and Local Suppliers: Evidence from the Polish Dairy Sector." *World Development* 32(9): 1525–1544.

Echánove, F. and T. Reardon. 2006. *Wholesale Markets, Horticulture Products, and Supermarkets in Mexico*. Staff Paper 2006–17, April, East Lansing: Michigan State University.

Escobal, J. and V. Agreda. 1997. *Analisis de la competitividad y la eficiencia en el Mercado mayorista de productos agropecuarios en Lima*. Lima: GRADE, July.

Fafchamps, M., R. Vargas Hill, and B. Minten. 2008. "Quality Control in Nonstaple Food Markets: Evidence from India," *Agricultural Economics* 38(3), May: 251–266.

Farina, EMMQ. 2002. Consolidation, Multinationalization, and Competition in Brazil: Impacts on Horticulture and Dairy Product Systems. *Development Policy Review* 20 (4): 441–457.

Farina, E. M. M. Q. (ed.). 1997. *Estudos de Caso em Agribusiness, Focalizando as Seguintes Empresas: Moinho Pacifico, Illycaffe, Cocamar, Sadia, Iochpe-Maxion, Norpac.* Sao Paulo: Pioneira.

Farina, E. M. M. Q., M. K. Marino, and T. M. Guedes. 2000. "Nestle-Sococo: Private Certification in Quality Management." Case study presented at the Maple Leaf Conference, Chicago.

Farina, E. M. M. Q., G. E. Gutman, P. J. Lavarello, R. Nunes, T. Reardon. 2005. "Private and Public Milk Standards in Argentina and Brazil." *Food Policy* 30(3): 302–315.

Farina, E. M. M. Q. and E. L. Machado. 1999. "Government Regulation and Business Strategies in the Brazilian Fresh Fruit and Vegetable Market," Paper presented at the II Workshop Brasileiro de Gestão de Sistemas Agroalimentares, organized by PENSA/FEA/USP, Ribeirão Preto.

Fulponi, L. 2007. "The Globalization of Private Standards and the Agri-Food System." In *Global Supply Chains Standards and the Poor: How the Globalization of Food System and the Standards Affects Rural Development and Poverty*, edited by J. Swinnen. Oxford, UK: CABInternational.

Gehlhar, M. and A. Regmi (eds.). 2005. *New Directions in Global Food Markets.* Agricultural Information Bulletin no 794. Washington, D.C.: USDA, Economic Research Service.

Goldman A, W. Vanhonacker. 2006. "The Food Retail System in China: Strategic Dilemmas and Lessons for Retail Internationalization/Modernization." Paper presented at the Globalizing Retail Conference, University of Surrey, Guildford, UK.

Gorton M, J. Sauer, and P. Supatpongkul. 2009. "Investigating Thai Shopping Behavior: Wet-Markets, Supermarkets and the 'Big Middle.'" Paper presented at the International Association of Agricultural Economists Conference, Beijing, August 16–22.

Gow H. R. and J. F. M. Swinnen. 1998. "Up- and Downstream Restructuring, Foreign Direct Investment, and Hold-Up Problems in Agricultural Transition." *European Review of Agricultural Economics* 25(3):331–350.

Gulati A, B. Minten, and T. Reardon. 2008. *Open-Source Intermediaries in Agricultural Markets in India.* Report, IFPRI New Delhi Office to the Bill and Melinda Gates Foundation. June.

Han, J., J. H. Trienekens, and S. W. F. Omta. 2009. "Integrated Information and Logistics Management, Quality Management and Firm Performance of Pork Processing Industry in China." *British Food Journal* 111(1): 9–25.

Hartmann, M. and J. Wandel (eds.) 1999. *Food Processing and Distribution in Transition Countries: Problems and Perspectives.* Kiel: Wissenschafsverlag Vauk Kiel KG.

Henderson V. 2002. "Urbanization in Developing Countries." *The World Bank Research Observer* 17(1): 89–112.

Henson, S. and T. Reardon. 2005. "Private Agri-Food Standards: Implications for Food Policy and the Agri-Food System." *Food Policy* 30(3), June: 241–253.

Hernández, R., T. Reardon, and J. A. Berdegué. 2007. "Supermarkets, Wholesalers, and Tomato Growers in Guatemala." *Agricultural Economics* 36(3): 281–290.

Ho, S. C. 2005. "Evolution versus tradition in marketing systems: The Hong Kong food-retailing experience." *Journal of Public Policy and Marketing* 24(1): 90–99.

Huang J, Dong X, Wu Y, Zhi H, Nui X, Huang Z, Rozelle S. 2007. *Regoverning Markets: The China Meso-level Study*. Report, Beijing: Center for Chinese Agricultural Policy, Chinese Academy of Sciences, July.

Jaffee, S. 1995. "Transaction Costs, Risk, and the Organization of Private Sector Food Commodity Systems." In *Marketing Africa's High-Value Foods: Comparative Experiences of an Emergent Private Sector*, edited by S. Jaffee and J. Morton. Dubuque, IA: Kendall/Hunt Publishing Company.

Jayne, T. S. and S. Jones. 1997. Food marketing and pricing policy in eastern and southern Africa: a survey. *World Development* 25(9):1505–1527.

Key, N. and D. Runsten. 1999. Contract Farming, Smallholders, and Rural Development in Latin America: The Organization of Agroprocessing Firms and the Scale of Outgrower Production. *World Development* 27 (February): 381–401.

Kinsey, J. 2004. Supply Chain Innovations in the U.S. Retail Sector. Presentation at the International Conference Supermarkets and Agricultural Development in China: Opportunities and Challenges. Shanghai, May 24–25.

Koç, A. A., J.-M. Codron, Y. Tekelioğlu, S. Lemeilleur, S. Tozanli, S. Aksoy, A. C. Bignebat, R. Demirer, and N. Mencet. 2007. *Component 1 Regoverning Market Programme: Restructuring of Agrifood Chains in Turkey, Turkey National and Local Meso Study (Modules 1 and 2 of C1) Report*. Antalya: Akdeniz University, Department of Economics. November.

Laffan, J. 2001. *Agrifood Multinational Corporations in Asia, Volume 1 of Subsistence to Supermarkets II: agrifood globalization and Asia*. Department of Foreign Affairs and Trade, Australia.

Lajo-Lazo, M. 1983. *Situación de la agroindustria y la alimentación*. Lima, Peru: Universidad La Catolica Press.

Levenstein, H. 1988. *Revolution at the Table*. New York: Oxford University Press.

Louw, A., D. Chikazunga, D. Jordaan, and E. Bienabe. 2007. *Restructuring Food Markets in South Africa: Dynamics in Context of the Tomato Sub Sector*. Meso Report for the Regoverning Markets Program. University of Pretoria. May.

Maertens, M., and J. F. M. Swinnen. 2009. Trade, Standards, and Poverty: Evidence from Senegal. *World Development* 37 (1): 161–178.

Michelson, H. 2010. "The Determinants and Impacts of Farmers' Supplying to Supermarkets in Nicaragua," AMA CRSP Working Paper, Cornell University.

Milczarek-Andrzejewska, D., A. Malak-Rawlikowska, J. Fałkowski, and Wilkin J. 2008. "Restructuring Process at Farm Level: Evidence from Dairy Sector in Poland," Micro Report Module 3 of Component 1, Regoverning Market Program, IIED, London.

Minten B., and T. Reardon. 2008. "Food Prices, Quality and Quality's Pricing in Supermarkets versus Traditional Markets in Developing Countries." *Review of Agricultural Economics* 30(3): 480–490.

Minten B, T. Reardon, and R. Sutradhar. 2010. *Food Prices and Modern Retail: The Case of Delhi*. Report, IFPRI New Delhi Office.

Minten, B., L. Randrianarison, and J. F. M. Swinnen. 2009. "Global Retail Chains and Poor Farmers: Evidence from Madagascar," *World Development* 37(11):1728–1741.

Minten, B., A. Vandeplas, Y. Ghorpade, and J. Swinnen. 2010. "Horticulture Wholesale Trade and Governance in India: Evidence from Uttarakhand." *Journal of South Asian Development* 5(1): 113–136.

Natawidjaja, R., T. Reardon, and S. Shetty, with T. I. Noor, T. Perdana, E. Rasmikayati, S. Bachri, and R. Hernandez. 2007. *Horticultural Producers and Supermarket Development in Indonesia*. UNPAD/MSU/World Bank. World Bank Report no. 38543, published by the World Bank/Indonesia, July.

Pingali, P. 2006. "Westernization of Asian diets and the transformation of food systems: Implications for research and policy." *Food Policy* 32: 281–298.

Posri W, S. Chadbunchachai. 2006. "Consumer Attitudes towards and Willingness to Pay for Pesticide Residue Limit Compliant "Safe" Vegetables in Northeast Thailand." *Journal of International Food and Agribusiness Marketing* 19(1):81–101.

Rama, R., and J. Wilkinson. 2008. "Foreign Direct Investment and Agri-Food Value Chains in Developing Countries: A Review of the Main Issues." In *Commodity Market Review 2007–8*, pp. 51–67. Rome: FAO, Trade and Markets Division.

Rashid, S., R. Cummings, and A. Gulati. 2007. "Grain Marketing Parastatals in Asia: Results from Six Case Studies," *World Development* 35(11):1872–1888.

Ravallion, M. 2010. "The Developing World's Bulging (but Vulnerable) Middle Class," *World Development* 38(4): 445–454.

Reardon, T., C. Barrett, J. Berdegué and J. Swinnen. 2009. "Agrifood Industry Transformation and Small Farmers in Developing Countries," *World Development* 37(11):1717–1727.

Reardon, T. and J. A. Berdegué. 2002. "The Rapid Rise of Supermarkets in Latin America: Challenges and Opportunities for Development." *Development Policy Review* 20(4): 317–334.

Reardon, T., J. Berdegué, and G. Escobar. 2001."Rural Nonfarm Employment and Incomes in Latin America: Overview of Issues, Patterns, and Determinants." *World Development* 29 (3), March. 395–409.

Reardon, T., J-M. Codron, L. Busch, J. Bingen, and C. Harris. 1999. Global Change in Agrifood Grades and Standards: Agribusiness Strategic Responses in Developing Countries. *International Food and Agribusiness Management Review* 2(3): 195–205.

Reardon, T., and E. M. Farina. 2001. "The Rise of Private Food Quality and Safety Standards: Illustrations from Brazil." International Food and Agribusiness Management Review 4(4): 413–421.

Reardon T., A. Gulati, and B. Minten. 2010. *The Transformation of Food Retail in India and Its Impact Downstream and Upstream in the Food System*. Report, IFPRI New Delhi Office and Michigan State University.

Reardon, T., S. Henson, and J. Berdegué. 2007. "'Proactive Fast-Tracking" Diffusion of Supermarkets in Developing Countries: Implications for Market Institutions and Trade." *Journal of Economic Geography* 7(4):1–33.

Reardon, T. and R. Hopkins. 2006. "The Supermarket Revolution in Developing Countries: Policies to Address Emerging Tensions among Supermarkets, Suppliers, and Traditional Retailers." *European Journal of Development Research* 18(4):522–545.

Reardon, T., K. Stamoulis, and P. Pingali. 2007. "Rural Nonfarm Employment in Developing Countries in an Era of Globalization." *Agricultural Economics* 37(s1):173–183.

Reardon, T. and C. P. Timmer. 2007. "Transformation of Markets for Agricultural Output in Developing Countries Since 1950: How Has Thinking Changed?" In *Handbook of Agricultural Economics, 3: Agricultural Development: Farmers, Farm Production and Farm Markets*, edited by R. E. Evenson, and P. Pingali, chapter 55, pp. 2808–2855. Amsterdam: Elsevier Press.

Reardon T, C. P. Timmer, C. B. Barrett, and J. A. Berdegue. 2003. "The Rise of Supermarkets in Africa, Asia, and Latin America." *American Journal of Agricultural Economics* 85(5): 1140–1146.

Rello, F. and F. Saavedra. 2007. *Implicaciones estructurales de la liberalización en la agricultura y el desarrollo rural*. El caso de México, Report to RuralStruc Project, mimeo, World Bank.
Rubey, L. 1995. "The Impact of Policy Reform on Small-Scale Agribusiness: A Case Study of Maize Processing in Zimbabwe." *African Rural and Urban Studies* 2(2–3):93–119.
Schejtman, A. 1998. "Agroindustria y pequeña agricultura: experiencias y opciones de transformación." In *Agroindustria y pequeña agricultura: vínculos, potencialidades y oportunidades comerciales*, edited by CEPAL. Serie Libros de la CEPAL, N° 46 (LC/G.2007-P), Santiago de Chile, Comisión Económica para América Latina y el Caribe (CEPAL).
Senauer, B., D. Sahn, and H. Alderman. 1986. "The Effect of the Value of Time on Food Consumption Patterns in Developing Countries: Evidence from Sri Lanka." *American Journal of Agricultural Economics* 68(4):920–927.
Sharpe, R. 2006. "Smithfield International Operations." PowerPoint presentation to the Department of Agricultural Economics, Michigan State University, East Lansing, November 2.
Shwedel, K. 2003. Sector agroalimentario en México. Presentation at the Seminar, Conglomerados y Empresas Transnacionales. Economic Commission for Latin America and the Caribbean (CEPAL), 26–27 November, Santiago, Chile.
Swinnen, J. (ed.) 2007. *Global Supply Chains, Standards and the Poor*. Wallingford: CABI Publishing.
Timmer, C. P. 1974. "A Model of Rice Marketing Margins in Indonesia." *Food Research Institute Studies* XIII(2):145–167.
Traill, W. B. 2006. "The Rapid Rise of Supermarkets?" *Development Policy Review* 24(2): 163–174.
Traub, L. N. and T. S. Jayne. 2008. "The Effects of Price Deregulation on Maize Marketing Margins in South Africa." *Food Policy* 33(3): 224–236.
Von Braun, J., D. Hotchkiss, and M. Immink. 1989. *Non-traditional Export Crops in Guatemala: Effects on Production, Income, and Nutrition*. Research Report 73, Washington: IFPRI.
Wang H., X. Dong, S. Rozelle, J. Huang, and T. Reardon. 2009. "Producing and Procuring Horticultural Crops with Chinese Characteristics: The Case of Northern China." *World Development* 37(11):1791–1801.
Wilkinson J. 2004. "The Food Processing Industry, Globalization, and Developing Countries." *Electronic Journal of Agricultural and Development Economics*—e-JADE, FAO, 1(2): 184–201.
Wilkinson, J., and R. Rocha. 2009. "Agro-industry Trends, Patterns and Development Impacts." In *Agro-industries for Development*, edited by C. A. da Silva, D. Baker, A.W. Shepherd, C. Jenane, and S. Miranda-da-Cruz, pp. 46–92. FAO/UNIDO/IFAD, New York: CAB International.

CHAPTER 34

THE TWENTY-FIRST CENTURY AGRICULTURAL LAND RUSH

GREGORY THALER

Introduction

In Mali in late 2010, the 2,000 inhabitants of the farming village of Soumouni learned that their land had been sold to Libya. Their houses would be leveled and they would all have to leave. The rice, beef, and other agricultural products grown on their land would be shipped back to Libya to feed Libyans. Across the 100,000 hectares leased by the Libyans, perhaps 20,000 farmers would be affected, and those who protested said they had been beaten and jailed, but they were "ready to die to keep their land" (MacFarquhar 2010). Several months later, the fate of the Libyan project seemed uncertain as Libya succumbed to the wave of unrest sweeping across the Arab world—unrest that many have attributed at least in part to rising global food prices (Cha 2011, Arezki and Bruckner 2011).

Two years earlier, in November 2008, the South Korean company Daewoo Logistics announced that it had negotiated a 99-year lease for 3.2 million hectares of farmland in Madagascar, or about half of all the country's arable land. Daewoo planned to use three-quarters of the land to grow corn in an effort to reduce by half South Korea's reliance on corn imports from the United States and South America. The other quarter of the land would be used for palm oil production for biofuel. News of the deal sparked protests in Madagascar and inflamed sentiment against Malagasy president Marc Ravalomanana, who incidentally is also the owner of Tiko, Madagascar's largest food conglomerate. Popular anger over the deal helped solidify support for Antananarivo mayor Andry Rajoelina, who in March 2009 succeeded in toppling Ravalomanana and seizing power in a coup. One of Rajoelina's first acts on coming to power was to cancel the Daewoo land deal, underlining the critical role the deal had played in bringing down Ravalomanana's government (Walt 2008; BBC 2009; Keesing's Worldwide 2009).

Food prices spur riots and topple regimes in North Africa, while land deals invite revolt in Mali and Madagascar. The global food system is teetering; its attempts at balance are visible in nodes of violent urban protest and rural land use change, dispossession, and resistance. As many as thirty countries experienced food riots during the 2007–2008 food crisis (Patel and McMichael 2009, 9). In its aftermath, observers have noticed a rapid acceleration in large-scale land acquisitions, of which the Malagasy and Malian projects are examples, in a process that activists have labeled a "global land grab." In the characterization of GRAIN, an international NGO:

> On the one hand, "food insecure" governments that rely on imports to feed their people are snatching up vast areas of farmland abroad for their own offshore food production. On the other hand, food corporations and private investors, hungry for profits in the midst of the deepening financial crisis, see investment in foreign farmland as an important new source of revenue. As a result, fertile agricultural land is becoming increasingly privatised and concentrated. If left unchecked, this global land grab could spell the end of small-scale farming, and rural livelihoods, in numerous places around the world.
>
> (GRAIN 2008, 1)

As this quotation indicates, the examples of "food security land grabbing" from Mali and Madagascar are just one face of the phenomenon of large-scale land acquisition. In fact, private-sector land transfers (or "investment land grabbing") are estimated to involve much greater areas than government-led deals (Anseeuw et al. 2012; Cotula 2011).[1] Additionally, as in the case of the Madagascar deal for food and biofuel production, land acquisitions are aimed not just at the production of food crops, but also at "flex crops" that may be used for food or biofuels (e.g., soybean, sugarcane, oil palm), and nonfood crops (e.g., rubber, jatropha).[2] Land grabbing thus involves a variety of public and private actors with distinct economic and political interests in different forms of agricultural production.

Developing a more complete picture of the magnitude and character of land grabbing worldwide is an extremely difficult endeavor: empirical data on land deals are critically scarce, in part because the details of many transactions are never made public. As a result, scholarly treatments of land grabbing have remained limited in scope or preliminary in their ability to generalize. Currently, efforts are underway to compile more comprehensive data on land deals,[3] and case study material is contributing to a more contextualized understanding of the phenomenon.[4] At a basic level, however, it seems clear that the acceleration in large-scale land acquisitions by both public and private sector actors is indicative of a fundamental shift in actors' understandings of the global food system and, more generally, of the global political economy.

A Political Economy Approach

Given the nascent state of knowledge in this area, the purpose of this chapter is to situate the global land grab in its historical context and to explore some of the contours of the land grab phenomenon, especially in the dimension of the global political economy. Due to the intimate interconnections among various actors and processes—foreign and domestic capital, investment and food security land grabbing, agrofuel and agri-food production—Borras and Franco (2010b) advocate focusing on the "nature and terms of agrarian change" in the context of the "emerging global agro food-energy complex," as opposed to focusing on the transnational character or nationality of home and host countries for land deals (2010b, 21). Borras and Franco's approach is useful in its attention to systemic developments in the global economy that drive land acquisitions through a variety of different concrete processes, but it elides the political geography of agrarian change. The identities of home and host country actors are key to the global structures of power and circuits of capital through which an "agro food-energy complex" is emerging. Consequently, the empirical and theoretical issues associated with land grabbing as seen from the standpoint of the global political economy, which comprehends the symbiotic relations of power and wealth, are integral to a complete understanding of agrarian change. This chapter therefore seeks to present a political economy approach to land grabbing sensitive to the (trans)national identities of the actors involved.[5]

The chapter begins by exploring what is "new" about the twenty-first century land rush. The first section describes the magnitude of the phenomenon, and the following section situates it in a historical context of political-economic change and crisis. The basic contention is that in response to the perceived instability of the global political economy, land grabbing represents an effort to reconstruct a stable political-economic order, both on the part of investment capital seeking to relaunch accumulation in the wake of the financial crisis and on the part of political actors and companies seeking to secure stable supplies of food and energy necessary for economic and social functioning. The next sections look at land grab investors and hosts, considering private sector and state investors followed by an examination of host countries. These sections present an analytical framework for understanding the geography of the land grab through the interrelated variables of land availability, the structural position of a country in the global economy, and a country's domestic institutional structure. Finally, a section is devoted to sketching the main theoretical positions in the debate over land deals, and to exploring their linkages to different political positions on what is to be done with regard to large-scale land transactions. The conclusion offers a general view through a political economy lens on the theoretical and practical implications of the land grab phenomenon.

What's New about the Land Grab?

The wake of the 2007–2008 food crisis has been characterized by a sharp increase in international land transactions, as well as a trend toward more rapid expansion of the global agricultural area. Compared to an average expansion of global agricultural land of less than 4 million hectares per year prior to 2008, the World Bank has predicted the opening of at least 6 million hectares of agricultural land annually through 2030, a more than 50 percent increase (World Bank 2010, vi, 11). Meanwhile, an analysis of the Land Matrix database, the most comprehensive record of land deals since the year 2000, finds a surge in the number of land acquisitions after 2005, accompanying rising commodity prices, with a peak following the global food crisis in 2009. Although reported land deals have declined somewhat since 2009, possibly as a result of the financial crisis and critical media coverage of land grabbing, the reporting of deals with signed contracts continues to occur at a level significantly higher than at the beginning of the decade, suggesting an enduring increase in the number of international land transactions (Anseeuw et al. 2012, 6). Even deals that are not fully implemented may impact local livelihoods as expectations of foreign demand spur land grabbing by local elites, or as investors restrict access to an area and then fail to use the land productively (World Bank 2010, 48–49). Furthermore, the rapid overall expansion of agricultural land and the acceleration of land transactions is accompanied by a shift in the locus of production: the UN Food and Agriculture Organization (FAO) predicts that even without accounting for biofuels and forest plantations, there will be a decrease of 27 million hectares of agricultural land in developed countries and an increase of 74 million hectares in developing countries from 2010 to 2030 (World Bank 2010, 11).[6]

In qualitative terms, these land deals may appear not as a fundamental break with the past, but rather as an acceleration of historicaltrends. De Schutter (2011) notes a rising trend of foreign direct investment (FDI) in agriculture prior to the 2007–2008 food crisis, as well as the prior existence of practices of offshore agricultural production for food security by countries like Japan and China (251).[7] However, the sheer magnitude of reported deals[8] and the significant projected increase in agricultural expansion approach a quantity-quality threshold, signaling fundamental changes in the organization of the agricultural food-feed-fuel complex and in the perspectives of states and investors regarding agricultural production. These changes in actor perceptions and the evolving public and private sector interactions driving agricultural land deals emerge from the conjuncture of financial, food, and ecological crises that rocked the global system at the end of the 2000s.

Change and Crisis in the Global Political Economy

The conditions for interlinked financial, food, and ecological crises developed over the 1990s and early 2000s to reach the point where combined weather and financial shocks in 2006–2007 pushed the global economy into a critical state. Among the salient background processes were (1) financialization in the global economy and speculation in commodity markets, (2) declining investment and low productivity growth in food production, and (3) climate change and climate policy responses, especially (4) the expansion of biofuels production.

Financialization is the process through which financial transactions come to represent an ever-larger share of economic activity and increasingly come to determine production and circulation in the real economy. In the United States, the financial service industry's share of corporate profits rose from 10 percent in the early 1980s to 40 percent in 2007 (Quiggin 2010, 46). Already in the early 2000s, prior to the subprime mortgage collapse, financial investors had begun to use commodities indexes to balance against stocks and other securities. These indexes included oil and minerals as well as agricultural commodities, and so rising oil prices (driven substantially by speculation; see Dugan and Pleven 2011) began to drive up agricultural prices not just through rising costs of production, but also through the packaging of derivatives. The gross market value of commodity derivatives rose by a factor of 25 between June 2003 and June 2008 to reach $2.13 trillion, far outpacing the growth in commodity production or the need for derivatives to hedge risk (Moberg 2011; Basu and Gavin 2011). Thus, external to the dynamics of food production itself, the conditions for food price volatility were sharpened through financial speculation in commodities markets.

Declining investment and low productivity growth in food production, meanwhile, contributed internally to the fragility of the food system. Timmer (2010) identifies an agricultural investment cycle where high food prices are met with policies supporting increased production and lower prices, but subsequent low prices discourage investment in research and infrastructure to the point where the growth in the food supply falls behind the growth in demand, setting the stage for renewed crisis. Rising commodity prices in the late 2000s followed a period of low food prices during the 1980s and 1990s, during which publicly funded agricultural research and development declined and productivity growth slowed (Timmer 2010; Trostle 2008). Rapid growth in demand (due in part to growing populations and changing diets) outpaced growth in supply, leading to declining global stock-to-use ratios for grains and oilseeds, which in 2007 sank to their lowest level since 1970 (Trostle 2008). Reduced stocks and increased demand made the food system less resilient in the face of the economic and environmental shocks that helped catalyze the 2007–2008 food price surge.

Climate change places additional pressure directly on food production. Rising temperatures, in particular, may be responsible for significant reductions in maize and wheat production since 1980, contributing to a net increase in commodity prices on the order of 5 percent (Lobell et al. 2011). A more substantial effect of climate change on the food system in the near term, however, has resulted from the promotion of biofuels as a climate change mitigation strategy. Here, high oil prices and concerns about the climatic effects of carbon emissions from fossil fuels were funneled by agribusiness lobbies into policies supporting the development of agricultural crops as "biofuels." While the contribution of biofuels to reducing emissions is dubious (Pimentel and Burgess, this volume; Kanter 2011), impacts of biofuel production on the food system are substantial.

Expansion of biofuels production strains food crop markets while increasing demand for agricultural land. In some cases, biofuel production removes acreage from food crop production and increases demand for fuel crops that are also important food and feed crops, such as corn and soy (Headey and Fan 2008; Mitchell 2008). Corn ethanol production, in particular, has been singled out as a primary driver of rising food prices during the late 2000s (Lagi et al. 2011). Biofuels substitute for fossil fuels, so biofuel markets respond directly to changes in oil prices. The expansion of biofuel production thus combines with the financialization of commodities markets to link food prices ever more closely to the vicissitudes of the energy market (Timmer 2010, 6), in addition to increasing demand pressure on food crops and land.

These background processes of financialization and speculation, declining investment and low productivity growth in agriculture, climate change, and the expansion of biofuels production contributed to the increasing interconnectedness of the financial system, the food system, and the global climate such that a combination of weather and financial shocks in 2006–2007 pushed the food system into full-blown crisis. Poor weather conditions during this period resulted in a shortfall in the wheat supply.[9] Coinciding with the collapse of the US housing bubble, which created an investment vacuum driving capital into commodities and other markets, the wheat shortfall triggered speculative investment that began to drive wheat prices quickly upward in May 2007, followed later in the year by corn prices under additional pressure from biofuel production.[10] India experienced a poor wheat harvest in 2007, similar to other parts of the world, and the high world wheat prices made it costly to make up the shortfall with imports. As a result, India decided to retain a larger share of its rice production for domestic consumption through the imposition of export restrictions. Other rice-exporting countries began to discuss restrictions as well, and importing countries, finding themselves in a vulnerable position, quickly moved to increase domestic stockpiles, contributing to a surge in demand that sent rice prices skyrocketing. While grain prices later declined from their 2007–2008 peak, they have remained extremely volatile, spiking again in 2010–2011, when the FAO Food Price Index reached its highest level ever (FAO 2011).[11]

The 2007–2008 food crisis thus emerged in articulation with financial and climate crises as the concrete manifestations of longer-term trends in the global political economy. Taken together, these trends are representative of a fundamental shift such that "cheap food" and "cheap energy," the foundational inputs of the post–World War II economic order, can no longer be guaranteed (Araghi 2009; Moore 2010). The 2007–2008 food crisis was a critical event that altered actors' perceptions of their structural context, exposing the instability of the global food system and heralding a new era of substantially higher and more volatile food prices.[12] Changing perceptions of structural conditions led actors to update their preferences regarding the organization of agricultural production and trade, leading to a new wave of foreign land acquisition that brought together investors seeking profits and governments seeking secure food and energy supplies. The land rush was therefore triggered by the food crisis as one proximate cause, but more generally it is indicative of the punctuated evolution of actor perceptions of the changing structure of the political economy.[13] In sum, as a response to perceived instability, the land grab is an effort to reconstruct a stable political-economic order, both on the part of investment capital seeking to renew accumulation in the aftermath of the financial crisis, and on the part of political actors and companies seeking to stabilize the provisioning of food and energy necessary for economic and social functioning.

What is the geography of these land transactions? Who are the investors, and who are the host countries? The spatial configuration of land grabbing can be conceived as a function of the dynamic interaction between first-order or "local" phenomena, third-order or "systemic" phenomena, and second-order or "state-level" phenomena that mediate between the global system and the local context. At the local level, biophysical and domestic sociopolitical determinants of land "availability" are key determinants of land deals. At the systemic level, the structural position of a country in the global political economy is a primary concern. At the state level, domestic institutional structures play a critical role in determining the nature of land transactions. The following sections deploy this analytical framework of land availability, structural position, and domestic institutions in order to explore the geographies of the land grab, first from the side of investors, and then from the side of the host countries.

Who Are the Land Grabbers?

Private investors are often more prominent than foreign governments in the current wave of land transactions, and domestic capital may in many cases be more important than foreign actors. At the same time, a focus on identifying home countries seeking out foreign agricultural land is critical to understanding the geography of emerging global transformations in production and circulation. This section discusses first the role of private sector actors, then the role of governments and private-public linkages in the rush for foreign farmland.

Private-sector actors seeking land generally take the form of either private companies or investment funds, with private companies representing the most active category of investor overall (Anseeuw et al. 2012, 24). The involvement of investment funds in land acquisition is related to the expectation of long-term price increases for land and agricultural products, as well as to the desire to use land to diversify investment portfolios and hedge against inflation (Cotula 2012, 666). While the growing presence of investment funds in land markets is indicative of financialization in agriculture, the resurgent preference of private companies for direct control over land and the agricultural production process reflects a basic transformation in the logic of agricultural value chains. In the postcolonial period, the agricultural sector has been characterized by the dissociation of capital from primary production and a concentration of capital in processing and distribution.[14] The movement of agro-industrial capital into production responds to a shifting calculus of the ownership of productive assets versus value chain coordination (Cotula 2012, 665). Where the 2007–2008 food crisis signals increased supply insecurity and price volatility for agricultural commodities, private companies are moving to stabilize their supply chains and profit from rising land and commodity prices.

The line between private- and public-sector actors in land deals is frequently blurred, however, and the public sector often provides crucial support to investors in private land deals. Cotula (2011) highlights government funds providing services such as subsidies, loans, guarantees, and insurance to companies engaged in agricultural FDI, as well as informational, technical, and diplomatic support from government agencies and government-to-government investment treaties facilitating private-sector land investment. The involvement of a national government in foreign land acquisitions, and the public or private modalities it employs to realize these investments, can be understood as a function of land availability, the structural position of the country in the global economy, and the country's domestic institutional structure. Land availability determines the need for foreign farmland, structural position determines whether the state has sufficient resources to become involved in offshore land deals, and the domestic institutional structure determines the modalities of state involvement.

The origin countries for land deal investments include emerging market countries such as China, South Korea, and India; North African countries (e.g., Libya, Egypt) and members of the Gulf Cooperation Council (GCC) (UAE, Bahrain, Saudi Arabia, Oman, Qatar, Kuwait); and the industrialized countries of the Global North such as the United States, EU member states, and Japan (GRAIN 2008; UNCTAD 2009; Daniel and Mittal 2009; Anseeuw et al. 2012).

Land availability is a function of both biophysical (hydrological, pedological) supply and sociopolitical (demographic, dietary, industrial) demand.[15] The United States and European Union have abundant land and water resources and heavily subsidized agriculture, obviating the need for foreign food security investments. As a result, US and EU foreign land investments are primarily carried out by private companies (Anseeuw et al. 2012), often producing fuel and flex crops to take advantage of biofuel mandates in their home countries. On the biophysical side, the presence of a number of North African and Middle Eastern states on the list of investor countries is supportive of the observation that the land grab is also a water grab (Brown 2009; Vidal 2010; see also Woodhouse 2012). Where domestic water scarcity limits the productive potential of large-scale agriculture, acquisition of farmland abroad responds to food scarcity while conserving domestic water resources—at the same time that water use by offshore operations may well conflict with the water needs of the local population in the host country. On the sociopolitical side, emerging market countries and the North African and Gulf states, many of which already suffer from biophysical constraints to agriculture, are characterized by growing populations and expanding industry, leading to increased demand for agricultural commodities. At the same time, many of these societies are currently undergoing a dietary transition toward increased caloric intake and increased consumption of meat and milk (Delgado 2003), implying a massive surge in the demand for staple grains as both food for people and feed for livestock.[16] Land scarcity in these countries is thus partly a product of biophysical conditions, but it is also a product of demographic and industrial growth and shifting consumption patterns.

For land-scarce countries, their structural position in the global economy determines whether the state becomes involved in foreign land acquisition. A variety of market strategies, such as futures contracts and grain reserves, are available and already employed by land-scarce, food-importing countries to hedge against commodities markets. However, in the context of distorted and volatile markets exposed by the 2007–2008 food crisis, countries have an incentive to seek direct home control of agricultural supply chains to insure the security of their food supply. The governments actually involved in offshore land deals generally represent land-scarce middle- and high-income countries, according with the popular depiction of land-grabbing countries as "capital-rich, natural resource-poor" (e.g., Robertson and Pinstrup-Andersen 2010, 271).[17] The involvement of these countries in the land rush is indicative at a general level of their deep integration into the circuits of global capital, the petrostates as suppliers of energy and the newly industrialized countries as suppliers of skilled and unskilled labor in manufacturing and services. Hence these governments have an urgent and fundamental interest in stabilizing the global political economy on which they depend, and land grabbing represents one project toward that end.

The domestic institutional structure of home country governments helps determine the modalities of state involvement in foreign land transactions. Domestic structure can be difficult to characterize,[18] and home countries directly involved in land purchases range from the former "neopatrimonial" Qaddafi regime in Libya to "cohesive-capitalist" Japan (cf. Kohli 2004). Nonetheless, it appears that states that have somewhat less highly coordinated economies, such as India, are involved in land deals more indirectly through support of corporate-led investment,[19] whereas states with more highly coordinated or authoritarian economies, such as China and the Gulf countries, are more likely to engage in direct acquisitions of land through state-owned enterprises or sovereign wealth funds (cf. Cotula 2011, 9) (Fig. 34.1).

Who Are the Hosts?

The necessary complement to an understanding of the identity of home countries in the land grab phenomenon is an understanding of the identity of the host countries. If the land grab is a political-economic project to expand and stabilize the agro-industrial food-feed-fuel complex in the interests of accumulation and systemic socioeconomic function, what determines the geography of that expansion? Why are some countries more likely than others to be involved in large-scale land transfers

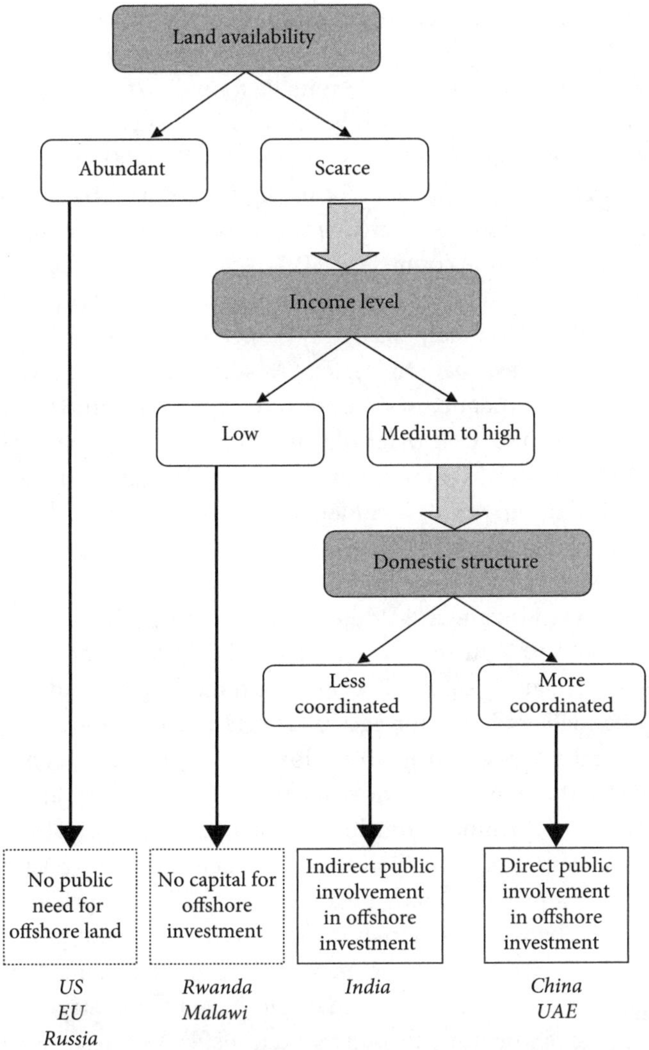

FIGURE. 34.1 Who are the land grabbers? Determinants of public sector offshore farmland investment

to foreign investors and governments? As with the question of home countries, land availability, structural position in the global economy, and domestic institutional structure are likely to be key variables in determining which countries are the sites of large-scale land transactions.

With regard to land availability, host countries generally have higher ratios of arable land per capita and water resources per capita than home countries, and higher levels of land availability may also be associated with lower social demands on agricultural resources (e.g., through less meat-intensive diets). The World Bank (2010), in its report on large-scale farmland acquisition, sought to identify the "potential supply of land suitable for rainfed cultivation" by country, considering, inter alia, potential output for five major crops of the food-feed-fuel complex (wheat, maize, soybean, sugarcane, oil palm), current land use, population density, and infrastructure access. The report found the largest areas of land potentially suitable for cultivation in Africa, followed by Latin America, with more than half of global availability (224 million out of 446 million hectares) concentrated in seven countries: Sudan, Brazil, Australia, Russia, Argentina, Mozambique, and Democratic Republic of the Congo (World Bank 2010, 56; see also Deininger 2011).[20] As would be expected from these statistics, foreign investors have indeed sought land in all these countries (GRAIN 2011), and Africa has been particularly prominent as a site of land transactions. Though the overall proportion of African deals may be inflated due to media bias, fully 62 percent of the agricultural land deals in the Land Matrix database were in Africa (Anseeuw et al. 2012). UNCTAD (2009, 122) also highlights the abundance of water resources in host countries relative to home countries, though per capita fresh water resources range widely—in the Gulf States, for example, from 49 cubic meters (m3) in UAE to 399 m3 in Oman; and in host countries from 366 m3 in Pakistan and 813 m3 in Sudan to 29,000 m3 in Brazil.[21]

Complementing biophysical and social conditions of land availability, the structural position of a country in the global economy bears on whether or not land is likely to be transferred to foreign investors. Middle-income, semi-peripheral countries such as Brazil and Argentina and high-income countries like Australia are likely to be attractive in principle to foreign investors seeking large tracts of farmland, due to their large areas of land potentially suitable for agriculture. However, these countries also have more developed and politically organized domestic agricultural complexes, and the overall economies in these countries are less critically dependent on agriculture than the economies of most low-income countries. Low-income, peripheral countries, meanwhile, tend to have less capital-intensive, less market-oriented agricultural sectors,[22] but at the same time a proportionally greater dependence on agriculture for employment and foreign exchange. Under these circumstances, countries with more highly capitalized domestic agricultural sectors may see foreign involvement in land deals as a threat to national resource sovereignty and domestic agro-industry, while low-income countries may see the opportunity through land transfers to earn foreign exchange and develop domestic infrastructure and technological capabilities. Land abundance is therefore mediated by the structural position of a country in the global economy, with low-income countries with less capital-intensive agricultural sectors more likely to be hosts to offshore farmland investments (cf. Anseeuw et al. 2012, 10). As an example, Indonesia (a lower-middle-income country) in 2010 changed its regulations to allow foreign participation in staple food crop production, permitting foreign ownership of up to 49 percent in staple crop plantations (Government of Indonesia 2010), while Brazil (a higher-middle-income country) since 2010 has sought to impose more stringent legal limits on the acquisition of farmland by foreigners (Government of Brazil 2010).

Domestic institutional factors interact with land availability and structural position to help determine host country participation in land deals. Data on land deals indicate that the most-targeted host countries for large-scale farmland acquisition tend to have weaker rural land tenure security, raising concerns for the respect of the rights of local populations affected by land transfers (World Bank 2010, 37; Anseeuw et al. 2012, 10–11). In general, part of the justification for large-scale farmland transactions rests on the claim that there are large areas of "potentially available," "marginal," or "reserve" agricultural land that can accommodate the large-scale expansion of cultivation. (World Bank calculations of "land availability" are one example of this perspective.) As Borras and Franco (2010a, 516) note, "accepting the notion of reserve agricultural land necessarily consigns existing local land-based social relations and practices that are diverse and distinct to being vestiges of the past.... They simply do not 'fit' the economic development grid,... they are not the beneficiaries of the 'responsible agricultural investment' that is envisioned." The likely outcome is "dispossession in the name of transforming "marginal" land into economically productive spaces." They give the example of a land deal in the Philippines where 1.4 million hectares of "marginal" lands were promised to China. The lands were considered marginal because they were officially catalogued as public, but they were in fact inhabited by communities practicing a variety of land-based livelihood strategies (517). Indeed, data from the Land Matrix indicate that nearly half of all land acquisitions target areas with existing agricultural activities, especially cropping mosaics that often are associated with smallholder land use (Anseeuw et al. 2012, 17–18).

In countries where state recognition of rural land rights is weak, investors may be able to obtain large tracts of land through host country governments without engaging the local population.[23] These processes of dispossession and displacement of local populations may be compounded by corruption in host country institutions as domestic business and political elites seek to benefit from foreign investment. The receptivity and attractiveness of host countries for investors may likewise be affected by the existence of investment treaties and trade agreements that limit the conditions host countries may impose on new investment (De Schutter 2011, 266), and by active host country measures to attract investors, such as elimination of short-term property taxes and reduction of export tariffs (Robertson and Pinstrup-Andersen 2010), or allowing for greater foreign participation in staple crop production (as in the case of Indonesia). This domestic institutional context, and especially the conditions of rural land tenure, affects the social construction of land availability and is constituted in interaction with a country's structural position in the global economy. Taken together, these factors represent important determinants of host country participation in large-scale farmland transactions (Fig. 34.2).

Institutional Positions and Political Responses

The previous sections have attempted to situate the land grab in historical context and to provide a framework for understanding the geography of foreign farmland acquisitions. This section turns to an exploration of the current academic and political approaches

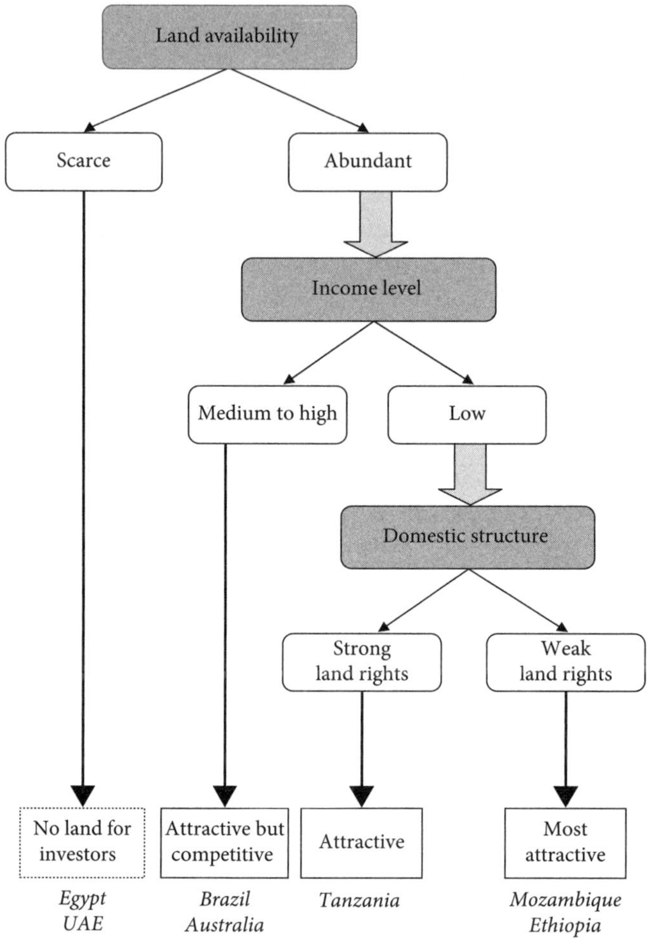

FIGURE. 34.2 Who are the hosts? Determinants of host country attractiveness for international farmland investment

to land grabbing, which illustrate how scholars, activists, politicians, and others are attempting to come to grips with the twenty-first century land rush.

At present, theoretical approaches in academic and political discussions of land grabbing gravitate into two main perspectives. The liberal perspective is founded on a belief in the virtually unlimited potential of market capitalism to generate well-being. From this perspective, the 2007–2008 food and financial crises were a contingent moment of instability in the global economy. The wave of large-scale farmland acquisition in response to this instability is seen as the linear continuation of the expansion of capitalist agriculture toward rationalized global production. Large-scale land deals for agro-industrial production are part of a natural unfolding of economic logic, and the most important practical issue is not whether such expansion should occur, but rather how it can be "managed" to accord with some normative standards—of equity, justice, or sustainability, for example. The liberal perspective is common within many governments, in major development organizations such as the World Bank, and among academics (e.g., Timmer 2010; Robertson and Pinstrup-Andersen 2010; World Bank 2010).

An alternative perspective emphasizes, inter alia, historical contingency in the construction of the political economy and the cyclical nature of capitalist growth and transformation. This perspective holds that alternatives to large-scale agro-industrial expansion are real and viable. The land grab is seen as deepening the contradictions of the agro-industrial food system, and thus is ultimately self-defeating. The practical issue for this perspective is how to discourage land grabbing and encourage alternative models of agricultural production. Actors adopting this alternative perspective include a number of scholars and activist organizations (Araghi 2009; De Schutter 2011; Borras and Franco 2010a; McCarthy et al. 2011; La Vía Campesina 2011b; McMichael 2012).

These two perspectives inform distinct political responses to the land grab phenomenon. The main political response from the liberal position, which views large-scale agro-industrial expansion as inevitable, has been to propose a "Code of Conduct" for land deals to ensure that land transactions conform to general principles of justice and sustainability (von Braun and Meinzen-Dick 2009; Deininger 2011).[24] International organizations—FAO, IFAD, UNCTAD, and the World Bank—have developed a set of "Principles for Responsible Agricultural Investment" (RAI) as a contribution toward a code of conduct. These principles, and the advocacy for a code of conduct generally, are premised on engaging "multiple stakeholders" to manage the perceived "risks" of large-scale land transactions in order to achieve "win-win" solutions for development (Borras and Franco 2010a, 510). They have been presented in various international fora, and are a part of the ongoing debate in the UN system regarding a global political response to the new wave of land investment (De Schutter 2011, 254–255).

Actors taking an alternative perspective tend to oppose large-scale agro-industrial expansion at the expense of smallholders, and they have argued that the RAI principles, by reframing the risks of land grabbing (violence, dispossession, ecological degradation, food insecurity) as manageable side effects of an "essentially beneficial cure" (Borras and Franco 2010a, 512), serve to legitimize land deals that should be unacceptable in principle (De Schutter 2011, 254). They argue to the contrary that the current pattern of large-scale agricultural investment is supportive neither of food security nor of social justice.[25]

One alternative to the code-of-conduct approach comes from advocates of a "rights-based" response to land grabbing that centers on the "right to food" (see Kotwal and Ramaswami, this volume), enshrined as an international legal human right in the Universal Declaration of Human Rights (Article 25.1) and the International Covenant on Economic, Social and Cultural Rights (Article 11). Some actors also extrapolate from the right to food a basic "right to land" (Borras 2008, 265). The rights-based approach has institutional backing in land-grabbing debates through the office of the UN Special Rapporteur on the Right to Food, Olivier De Schutter. De Schutter has put forward a set of "Minimum Human Rights Principles Applicable to Large-Scale Land Acquisitions or Leases" that mandates the prioritization of the long-term needs and human rights of local communities in the context of any land deal. According to De Schutter,

> the human right to food would be violated if people depending on land for their livelihoods, including pastoralists, were cut off from access to land, without suitable alternatives; if local incomes were insufficient to compensate for the price effects resulting from the shift towards the production of food for exports; or if the revenues of local smallholders were to fall following the arrival on domestic markets of cheaply priced food, produced on the more competitive large-scale plantations developed thanks to the arrival of the investor.
>
> (2009, para. 4)

Since he argues that in the majority of cases, large-scale land acquisitions and leases will result in these rights violations, De Schutter (2011, 250) uses the rights-based framework to argue for an "alternative program for agricultural investment" to support smallholder agriculture. Outlines of this program include public goods provision to improve productivity and market access, institutional developments such as cooperatives or contract farming (properly managed) to increase farmer revenue, and equitable access to land through land reform coupled with comprehensive rural development policies (262–263).

Dovetailing with the rights-based approach is the "food sovereignty" approach of activist organizations led by La Vía Campesina. A global network of peasant movements, La Vía Campesina has called for rejection of the RAI principles, the suspension of all large-scale land transactions, and redirection of investment toward food sovereignty—understood as "the right of peoples to healthy and culturally appropriate food produced through sustainable methods and their right to define their own food and agriculture systems" (Via Campesina 2011c). In addition to supporting local resistance to land deals (e.g., through a "Global Alliance against Land-Grabbing" [La Vía Campesina 2011a]), actors taking a human rights or food sovereignty orientation toward land grabbing have sought to establish their position at the international level through the "Voluntary Guidelines on the Responsible Governance of Tenure of Land, Fisheries and Forests in the Context of National Food Security," developed through the FAO's Committee on World Food Security. These guidelines, which received input from governments and international organizations as well as independent experts and civil-society organizations (De Schutter 2011, 255), were substantially influenced by a human rights perspective, and their adoption in May 2012 provides a further tool for those seeking practical political action in response to the rising trend of large-scale farmland transactions.

Conclusion

This chapter has sought to develop a political economy perspective on the current wave of large-scale farmland acquisitions—the "global land grab"—and to review the main theoretical and political positions that have emerged around this phenomenon. The discussion has also highlighted a number of the potential implications of the land grab for the future of the global system. This concluding section revisits the question of implications to underscore the main debates about the nature and effects of the land grab.

The recognition that many land deals are announced but never completed, and that actual new farmland development often falls short of its planned extent, might tempt us to conclude that the land rush is more apparent than real. However, available empirical work confirms that the areas of land changing hands are substantial, significant increases in agricultural expansion are projected, and perceptions of the importance of land and the nature of food security in the global economy have been fundamentally altered. As production from these new land investments comes on line in the future, the broader impacts of land grabbing on the food system will become more apparent. Immediate impacts are already substantial, however, with billions of dollars in investment, millions of hectares changing hands, and tens of thousands of people displaced.[26]

On a more fundamental level, the land grab may prove symptomatic of a systemic crisis of the global political economy, with this wave of farmland acquisition establishing the foundations for a new cycle of accumulation, or deepening the contradictions of the present crisis toward the disintegration of global capitalism as a socio-ecological system (Araghi 2009; Moore 2010; McMichael 2012). The real historical significance of structural changes in the global political economy, manifested in the coincident crises of finance, food, and ecology, and acknowledged in changing actor perceptions and actions including the rush for land, suggests that the implications of the land grab will be durable and systemic.

Understood as a project to stabilize the global political economy, the twenty-first century land rush is effectively a synecdoche for the contemporary agrarian question. Can large-scale farmland acquisitions enhance global food security? Will they undermine food sovereignty? Does land grabbing generate a productive surplus, or only a redistributive surplus through expropriation? Can large-scale agro-industrial expansion stabilize the conditions of production for the global economy, even launching a new wave of growth? Does the land grab spell the end of the global peasantry? These questions force a recognition of the agrarian question, crystallized in the current land rush, as fundamental to our present conjuncture and key to the future of the global political economy and global ecology.

Notes

1. The terms of these acquisitions vary widely, from short- or long-term leases to freehold sales. For a review, see HLPE 2011.
2. The "land grab" framing has been further extended to consider nonagricultural land deals, such as for mineral extraction or nature conservation (e.g., Zoomers 2011), as part of a general phenomenon of "new enclosures" (White et al. 2012). This chapter maintains a focus on land acquisitions for agriculture, which represent over 80 percent of the deals catalogued in the Land Matrix, the most comprehensive available database on international land transactions since 2000 (Anseeuw et al. 2012).
3. The best available global data on land deals come from the Land Matrix database, compiled by the International Land Coalition (ILC) and partner organizations. The public database,

released in beta version in 2012, documents 924 deals since the year 2000, involvingmore than 48 million hectares of land (http://landportal.info/landmatrix). GRAIN also continues its efforts to provide more comprehensive aggregate data on land grabbing (GRAIN 2011).

4. A notable effort is the Oakland Institute's Africa country reports in their Understanding Land Investment Deals in Africa series (http://www.oaklandinstitute.org/publications).
5. A focus on state actors alone is clearly insufficient for understanding the land grab phenomenon, particularly when global political-economic processes are increasingly transnational in character, while local actors are highly differentiated in their political and economic relations. Given the prominence of national governments in international land deals, however, and the continued relevance of the state in the space connecting local and global processes, maintaining some focus on country-level phenomena remains important and illuminating.
6. The World Bank considers all low- and middle-income countries (i.e., those having a GNI per capita of US$12,275 or less) to be "developing countries," and high-income countries are considered "developed" countries. Developed countries under this definition include, inter alia, most EU member states; the United States, Canada, Australia, and New Zealand; Japan and South Korea; and the members of the Gulf Cooperation Council (Bahrain, Kuwait, Oman, Qatar, Saudi Arabia, and the United Arab Emirates).
7. The UNCTAD *World Investment Report 2009* discusses similar examples of efforts at establishing offshore production by the Gulf States and Korea in the 1960s and 1970s.
8. The Land Matrix records over 1,200 reported agricultural land deals since the year 2000, covering more than 83 million hectares in developing countries, an area more than twice the size of Germany. Production was reported to have started on projects covering over 20 million hectares, an area roughly the size of the United Kingdom (Anseeuw et al. 2012, 4).
9. The chronology in this paragraph is based on Timmer (2010).
10. Major grains are mutually substitutable for many purposes, and their market prices generally correlate.
11. Where 2002–2004 food prices are weighted to 100, the Food Price Index for February 2011 averaged 238.
12. In a typical retelling, Borras and Franco (2010b) describe national governments of food importing countries as "shocked" by the food price crisis and "rushing" to find land and labor to produce food for themselves (4 fn. 6). UNCTAD suggests that the new wave of offshore food security land investments may be more successful than such investments were in the past, in part because "many home countries see the latest changes in the global agricultural industry as a sea change from the past, with high prices, shortages, and volatility in food crops persisting into the future" (UNCTAD 2009, 161–162).
13. On this view of the interaction between structural change and critical events in history, compare Sewell 2005.
14. Corporations involved in banana production in Central America, for example, have moved away from plantation production toward purchasing bananas from smallholders and providing technical assistance. The tea industry in Kenya and the tobacco industry globally provide similar examples of a transition away from direct corporate ownership of land and control of production toward a model of decentralized production coupled with centralized processing and distribution (UNCTAD 2009, 105).

15. In a similar vein, energy scarcity is a function both of a country's natural energy endowments and that country's overall energy demand and policy. Oil price shocks and the volatility of international markets have similarly led import-dependent countries to seek self-sufficiency or guaranteed supplies from abroad. One need look no further than American energy policy—from domestic oil shale development to military commitments in the Middle East—for an example.
16. Japan is not a newly industrialized country, but it is in the later stages of a nutrition transition toward a diet higher in fats and animal protein (e.g., Drewnowski and Popkin 1997).
17. Land-scarce low-income countries (e.g., Rwanda) do not have the capital resources to develop offshore agricultural production.
18. For a review of the domestic structure literature see Evangelista 1997.
19. GRAIN reports that India's Ministry of External Affairs targeted Burma, Australia, and Africa as sites for Indian agribusiness firms to develop food crops for export back to India (GRAIN 2008, Annex).
20. It is important to note, however, that in many cases investors seek not uncultivated, potentially available land, but land that is already under cultivation—irrigated and with good access to markets (Mittal 2011, Anseeuw et al. 2012). Under these circumstances a land deal may result in the displacement of local inhabitants. These land grabs are less a function of land availability than they are of domestic institutional characteristics, such as tenure insecurity and corruption, that facilitate dispossession and displacement.
21. These are figures for the year 2008. World Bank calculations of land suitability focused on rainfed cultivation, while measures of water resources per capita also bear on irrigation potential.
22. Indeed, developing country agriculture has been systematically undermined by the cheap food regime of subsidy-driven US and EU agriculture (Weis 2007), and by the developmentalist bias of Southern elites who in many cases exploit agriculture to benefit an urban-industrial "modernization" perspective on socioeconomic development (see Bates 1984).
23. Dispossession and displacement of local populations for large-scale agricultural investment points toward questions of violence and the physical security of people and investments in land deals. There is an apparent paradox to investments that seek food security in insecure places, and land acquisitions that ignore local land rights may be rendered less economical by local opposition and resistance. A powerful example of the potential for militarization of land investment comes from Pakistan, which has promised a 100,000-person security force to protect agricultural investors and their investments (Kugelman 2009, 3). A full exploration of the security issues associated with land grabbing is beyond the scope of this chapter. I will limit myself here to observing that the security issues associated with offshore agricultural production are not novel, but in a context of systemic crisis in the global political economy, they may well become more intense, and they are intimately related to changes in the global security regime, such as the militarization of accumulation (Robinson 2010) and the privatization of security (Mandel 2002; Avant 2005). The toppling of the Malagasy government and the contribution of food insecurity to the Arab revolts are extreme examples of the kind of upheaval potentially associated with land grabbing in host and home countries at the present conjuncture.
24. This code-of-conduct approach is analogous to approaches to "sustainability" or "corporate social responsibility" as voluntary multi-stakeholder processes that have emerged in other sectors of the global economy (e.g., rainforest-friendly coffee, fair trade handicrafts,

or corporate "social investment" funds) as the retreat of state regulation under neoliberalism has externalized corporate oversight to the sphere of domestic and international civil society.

25. Comprehensive critiques of the code of conduct approach and expositions of a rights-based framework are Borras and Franco 2010a and De Schutter 2011.
26. The Land Matrix database includes only forty cases with information on displacements (in other cases whether displacement has occurred is unknown), but of those forty deals, twenty-five are reported to have led to evictions of at least 1,000 people, with ten of those cases involving evictions of over 10,000 people (Anseeuw et al. 2012, 41).

References

Anseeuw, W., M. Boche, T. Breu, M. Giger, J. Lay, P. Messerli, and K. Nolte. 2012. *Transnational Land Deals for Agriculture in the Global South: Analytical Report Based on the Land Matrix Database*. Bern: CDE; Montpellier: CIRAD; Hamburg: GIGA. http://www.oxfam.de/sites/www.oxfam.de/files/20120427_report_land_matrix.pdf.

Araghi, F. 2009. "Accumulation by Displacement: Global Enclosures, Food Crisis, and the Ecological Contradictions of Capitalism." *Review* 32 (1): 113–146.

Arezki, R., and M. Bruckner. 2011. "Food Prices and Political Instability." IMF Working Paper WP/11/62. Washington, DC: International Monetary Fund.

Avant, D. D. 2005. *The Market for Force: The Consequences of Privatizing Security*. New York: Cambridge University Press.

Basu, P., and W. T. Gavin. 2011. "What Explains the Growth in Commodity Derivatives?" *Federal Reserve Bank of St. Louis Review* 93 (1): 37–48.

Bates, R. H. 1984. *Markets and States in Tropical Africa: The Political Basis of Agricultural Policies*. Berkeley: University of California Press.

BBC. 2009. "Madagascar Leader Axes Land Deal." 19 March. http://news.bbc.co.uk/2/hi/africa/7952628.stm.

Borras, S. M., Jr. 2008. "La Vía Campesina and Its Global Campaign for Agrarian Reform." *Journal of Agrarian Change* 8 (2–3): 258–289.

Borras, S. M., Jr., and J. Franco. 2010a. "From Threat to Opportunity? Problems with the Idea of a "Code of Conduct" for Land-Grabbing." *Yale Human Rights and Development Law Journal* 13 (2): 507–523.

——. 2010b. "Towards a Broader View of the Politics of Global Land Grab: Rethinking Land Issues, Reframing Resistance." ICAS Working Paper Series No. 001. The Hague: Initiatives in Critical Agrarian Studies. http://www.tni.org/sites/www.tni.org/files/Borras%20Franco%20Politics%20of%20Land%20Grab%20v3.pdf.

Brown, L. R. 2009. "Could Food Shortages Bring Down Civilization?" *Scientific American* 300 (5): 50–57.

Cha, A. E. 2011. "Spike in Global Food Prices Contributes to Tunisian Violence." *Washington Post*, January 14. http://voices.washingtonpost.com/political-economy/2011/01/spike_in_global_food_prices_tr.html.

Cotula, L. 2011. *The Outlook on Farmland Acquisitions*. Commercial Pressures on Land Series. Rome: International Land Coalition. http://www.landcoalition.org/sites/default/files/publication/899/IIED_fatmland_web_11.03.11.pdf.

——. 2012. "The International Political Economy of the Global Land Rush: A Critical Appraisal of Trends, Scale, Geography and Drivers." *Journal of Peasant Studies* 39 (3–4): 649–680.

Daniel, S., and A. Mittal. 2009. *The Great Land Grab: Rush for the World's Farmland Threatens Food Security for the Poor*. Oakland, CA: The Oakland Institute. http://www.oaklandinstitute.org/great-land-grab-rush-world%E2%80%99s-farmland-threatens-food-security-poor.

Deininger, K. 2011. "Challenges Posed by the New Wave of Farmland Investment." *Journal of Peasant Studies* 38 (2): 217–247.

Delgado, C. L. 2003. "Rising Consumption of Meat and Milk in Developing Countries Has Created a New Food Revolution." *Journal of Nutrition* 133:3907S-3910S.

De Schutter, Olivier. 2009. "Large-Scale Land Acquisitions and Leases: A Set of Minimum Principles and Measures to Address the Human Rights Challenge." Addendum to Report of the Special Rapporteur on the Right to Food, Olivier De Schutter. UN Human Rights Council, 13th Session. A/HRC/13/33/Add.2.

——. 2011. "How Not to Think of Land-Grabbing: Three Critiques of Large-Scale Investments in Farmland." *Journal of Peasant Studies* 38 (2): 249–279.

Drewnowski, A., and B. M. Popkin. 1997. "The Nutrition Transition: New Trends in the Global Diet." *Nutrition Reviews* 55 (2): 31–43.

Dugan, I. J., and L. Pleven. 2011. "As Oil Spiked, Many Traded—Corporations, Foreign Funds Appear On List of Investors During Oil's Peak." *Wall Street Journal*, August 18, C1.

Evangelista, M. 1997. "Domestic Structure and International Change." In *New Thinking in International Relations Theory*, edited by M. W. Doyle and G. J. Ikenberry. Boulder, CO: Westview Press.

FAO (Food and Agricultural Organization of the United Nations). 2011. FAO Food Price Index. Rome: FAO. http://www.fao.org/worldfoodsituation/wfs-home/foodpricesindex/en/.

——. 2012. *Voluntary Guidelines on the Responsible Governance of Tenure of Land, Fisheries and Forests in the Context of National Food Security*. Rome: Committee on World Food Security, FAO.

Government of Brazil. 2010. *Parecer CGU/AGU No. 01/2008 approved and published in Diário Oficial da União on 23 August 2010* (Parecer No. LA-01). http://www.in.gov.br/imprensa/visualiza/index.jsp?jornal=1&pagina=1&data=23/08/2010.

Government of Indonesia. 2010. Presidential Regulation (Perpres) No. 36 of 2010. http://www.bkpm.go.id/file_uploaded/PPres-36-2010.pdf.

GRAIN. 2008. "Seized!: The 2008 Land Grab for Food and Financial Security." Issue brief, September 20. Barcelona: GRAIN. http://www.grain.org/article/entries/93-seized-the-2008-landgrab-for-food-and-financial-security

GRAIN. 2011. "New Data Sets on Land Grabbing." December 14.Barcelona: GRAIN. http://www.grain.org/es/bulletin_board/entries/4429-new-data-sets-on-land-grabbing.

Headey, D., and S. Fan. 2008. "Anatomy of a Crisis: The Causes and Consequences of Surging Food Prices." *Agricultural Economics* 39 (Suppl.): 375–391.

HLPE (High Level Panel of Experts on Food Security and Nutrition). 2011. *Land Tenure and International Investments in Agriculture*.. HLPE Report. Rome: Committee on World Food Security.

Kanter, J. 2011. "Questioning Europe's Math on Biofuels." *New York Times*, September 25. http://www.nytimes.com/2011/09/26/business/global/questioning-europes-math-on-biofuels.html.

Keesing's Worldwide. 2009. "Madagascar: Seizure of Power." Keesing's World News Archive, April 28. http://www.keesings.com/breaking_history/africa/madagascar_seizure_of_power_pub._april_28,_2009/madagascar_seizure_of_power_-_full_text. http://www.keesings.com/breaking_history/africa/madagascar_seizure_of_power_pub._april_28,_2009/madagascar_seizure_of_power_-_full_text

Kohli, A. 2004. *State-Directed Development: Political Power and Industrialization in the Global Periphery*. New York: Cambridge University Press.
Kugelman, M. 2009. "Introduction." In *Land Grab? The Race for the World's Farmland*, edited by Michael Kugelman and Susan L. Levenstein, 1–23. Washington, DC: Woodrow Wilson International Center for Scholars. http://www.wilsoncenter.org/sites/default/files/ASIA_090629_Land%20Grab_rpt.pdf.
Lagi, M., Y. Bar-Yam, K. Z. Bertrand, and Y. Bar-Yam. 2011. "The Food Crises: A Quantitative Model of Food Prices Including Speculators and Ethanol Conversion." arXiv:1109.4859, September 21, 2011. Cambridge, MA: New England Complex Systems Institute. http://necsi.edu/research/social/foodprices.html.
La Vía Campesina. 2011a. "Conference Declaration: Stop Land-Grabbing Now!" Declaration of the Nyeleni Conference (Mali), November 17–19, 2011. http://viacampesina.org/en/index.php/main-issues-mainmenu-27/agrarian-reform-mainmenu-36/1127-stop-land-grabbing-now
——. 2011b. "It's Time to Outlaw Land Grabbing, Not to Make It 'Responsible'!" Press Release, April 17, 2011. http://viacampesina.org/en/index.php?option=com_content&view=article&id=1076:its-time-to-outlaw-land-grabbing-not-to-make-it-qresponsibleq&catid=23:agrarian-reform&Itemid=36.
——. 2011c. "What is La Vía Campesina?" http://viacampesina.org/en/index.php?option=com_content&view=category&layout=blog&id=27&Itemid=44. Accessed 30 December 2011.
Lobell, D. B., W. Schlenker, and J. Costa-Roberts. 2011. "Climate Trends and Global Crop Production since 1980." *Science* 333:616–620.
MacFarquhar, N. 2010. "African Farmers Displaced as Investors Move In." *New York Times*, December 21. http://www.nytimes.com/2010/12/22/world/africa/22mali.html.
Mandel, R. 2002. *Armies without States: The Privatization of Security*. Boulder, CO: Lynne Rienner.
McCarthy, J., S. Afiff, and J. Vel. 2011. *A Land Grab Scenario for Indonesia? Diverse Trajectories and Virtual Land Grabs in the Outer Islands*. Paper presented at the International Conference on Global Land Grabbing,April 6–8, 2011, at the Institute of Development Studies, University of Sussex. http://www.future-agricultures.org/index.php?option=com_docman&task=cat_view&gid=1552&Itemid=971.
McMichael, P. 2012. "The Land Grab and Corporate Food Regime Restructuring." *Journal of Peasant Studies* 39 (3–4): 681–701.
Mitchell, D. 2008. "A Note on Rising Food Prices." Policy Research Working Paper 4682. Rome: World Bank, Development Prospects Group.
Mittal, A. 2011. "Understanding Land Investment Deals in Africa." Presentation, October 19, at Cornell University, Ithaca, NY.
Moberg, D. 2011. "Diet Hard: With a Vengeance." *In These Times*, March 24.http://www.inthesetimes.com/article/7112.
Moore, J. W. 2010. "The End of the Road? Agricultural Revolutions in the Capitalist World-Ecology, 1450–2010." *Journal of Agrarian Change* 10 (3): 389–413.
Patel, R., and P. McMichael. 2009. "A Political Economy of the Food Riot." *Review* 32 (1): 9–35.
Quiggin, J. 2010. *Zombie Economics: How Dead Ideas Still Walk among Us*. Princeton, NJ: Princeton University Press.
Robertson, B., and P. Pinstrup-Andersen. 2010. "Global Land Acquisition: Neo-colonialism or Development Opportunity?" *Food Security* 2 (3): 271–283.
Robinson, W. I. 2010. "The Crisis of Global Capitalism: Cyclical, Structural, or Systemic?" In *The Great Credit Crash*, edited by M. Konings. London: Verso: 289–312.

Sewell, W. H., Jr. 2005. *Logics of History: Social Theory and Social Transformation.* Chicago: University of Chicago Press.

Timmer, C. P. 2010. "Reflections on Food Crises Past." *Food Policy* 35:1–11.

Trostle, R. 2008. *Global Agricultural Supply and Demand: Factors Contributing to the Recent Increase in Food Commodity Prices.* Outlook Report WRS-0801. Washington, DC: Economic Research Service, USDA.

UNCTAD (United Nations Conference on Trade and Development). 2009. *World Investment Report 2009: Transnational Corporations, Agricultural Production and Development.* New York: United Nations. http://unctad.org/en/docs/wir2009_en.pdf.

Vidal, J. 2010. "How Food and Water Are Driving a 21st-Century African Land Grab." *The Observer*, March 7. http://www.guardian.co.uk/environment/2010/mar/07/food-water-africa-land-grab.

von Braun, J., and R. Meinzen-Dick. 2009. "'Land Grabbing' by Foreign Investors in Developing Countries: Risks and Opportunities." IFPRI Policy Brief 13. Washington, DC: International Food Policy Research Institute. http://www.ifpri.org/sites/default/files/publications/bp013all.pdf.

Walt, V. 2008. "The Breadbasket of South Korea: Madagascar." *Time*, November 23. http://www.time.com/time/world/article/0,8599,1861145,00.html.

Weis, T. 2007. *The Global Food Economy: The Battle for the Future of Farming.* New York: Zed Books.

White, B., S. M. Borras Jr., R. Hall, I. Scoones, and W. Wolford. 2012. "The New Enclosures: Critical Perspectives on Corporate Land Deals." *Journal of Peasant Studies* 39 (3–4): 619–647.

Woodhouse, P. 2012. "New Investment, Old Challenges: Land Deals and the Water Constraint in African Agriculture." *Journal of Peasant Studies* 39 (3–4): 777–794.

World Bank. 2010. "Rising Global Interest in Farmland: Can It Yield Sustainable and Equitable Benefits?" 7 September 2010. Washington, DC: World Bank.

Zoomers, A. 2011. "Introduction: Rushing for Land: Equitable and Sustainable Development in Africa, Asia and Latin America." *Development* 54 (1): 12–20.

CHAPTER 35

AGRICULTURAL FUTURES

The Politics of Knowledge

IAN SCOONES

Introduction

Global assessments have become central to international debates on a range of key policy issues.[1] The International Assessment of Agricultural Knowledge, Science and Technology for Development (IAASTD) is one of many, following in the wake of the International Panel on Climate Change (IPCC), the Millennium Ecosystem Assessment (MA), and the Millennium Project's Millennium Development Goal (MDG) task forces, among others. The IPCC even won the Nobel Peace Prize in 2007, the first assessment to do so.[2] All of these efforts attempt to combine "expert assessment" with processes of "stakeholder consultation" in what are presented as global, participatory assessments on key issues of major international importance. Such assessments contribute to a new landscape of governance in the international arena, offering the potential for links between the local and the global and presenting new ways of articulating citizen engagement with global processes of decision making and policy. In many respects such assessments respond to the critiques of the top-down, Northern-dominated expert assessments of the past and make attempts to be both more inclusive and more participatory in their design and process, offering new opportunities for mobilization and the articulation of alternative knowledge in the global policy domain. But how far do they meet these objectives? Do they genuinely allow alternative voices to be heard? Do they create a new mode of engagement in global arenas? How are local and global processes articulated? And what are the power relations involved, creating what processes of mediation, inclusion, and exclusion?

Taking the case of the IAASTD, this chapter explores these issues through a focus on the underlying knowledge politics of a global process. Four intersecting questions at the heart of contemporary democratic theory and practice are posed: How do processes of knowledge framing occur? How do different practices and methodologies get deployed in cross-cultural, global processes" How is "representation" constructed and legitimized? How, as a result, do collective understandings of global issues emerge? Drawing on a detailed analysis of the IAASTD process between 2003 and 2008, the chapter argues that, in such assessments, the politics of knowledge need to be made more explicit, and that negotiations around politics and values must be placed center stage. The black-boxing of uncertainty, or the eclipsing of more fundamental clashes over interpretation and meaning, must be avoided for processes of participation and engagement in global assessments to become more meaningful, democratic, and accountable. Following Mouffe (2005), the chapter offers a critique of simplistic forms of deliberative democratic practice, and argues that there is a need to "bring politics back in."

The International Assessment of Agricultural Knowledge, Science and Technology (IAASTD)

The overall purpose of the IAASTD, which concluded with a final plenary session in Johannesburg in April 2008, was "to assess agricultural knowledge, science and technology in order to use it more effectively to reduce hunger and poverty, improve rural livelihoods, and facilitate equitable, environmentally, socially and economically sustainable development."[3] No one could argue with that goal of course. But how was this ambitious aim to be realized?

The IAASTD was announced during 2002, and it was initiated on five continents in early 2003 with a series of consultation meetings. Since then five regional reports and one global report (IAASTD 2009) have been produced, all contributing to a synthesis and summaries for decision makers for each continental report and the global report. A total of 400 authors were recruited to write the reports, and an overall framework was hammered out in a series of meetings,[4] a process overseen by a complex governance structure (Scoones 2008).

The IAASTD received very substantial financial backing from a wide range of bilateral donors, UN organizations, and the World Bank, with a total budget of more than US$15m.[5] With agriculture and technology once again rising in importance in the development agenda, many agencies saw this as an excellent opportunity to map out a way forward. A combination of a multi-stakeholder and an intergovernmental UN process proved appealing, as this offered the combination of inclusion and dialogue, including civil society and private business actors as well as formal decision making and buy-in by nation-states. Was this perhaps the model for the future—picking the best of the IPCC and the MA and combining them in an approach to global decision making that was at once scientifically sound, politically legitimate, and participatory?

A number of unique attributes are highlighted by Robert Watson, the director, including: an advisory structure that encompasses governmental representatives as well as civil society; the "inclusion of hundreds of experts from all relevant stakeholder groups"; an "intellectually consistent framework"; a global, multi-scale, and long-term approach, resulting in "plausible scenarios" to 2050; the "integration of local and institutional knowledge"; and a multi-thematic approach, encompassing nutrition, livelihoods, and human health, linking science and technology issues to policies and institutions.[6] A multi-stakeholder process involving everyone from grassroots groups to scientists and representatives of large corporations, with the final product being signed by national governments, the IAASTD constitutes a, to date, unparalleled approach. As such, the IAASTD provides fascinating insights into processes of participation and global engagement and the implications that these developments have for the contestation of global knowledge and the construction of global citizenship (Leach and Scoones 2005).

The IAASTD, as with the other global assessments, is seen by its proponents as a brave attempt at engaging a diverse group of stakeholders on a key topic with major global ramifications. In this regard it marks a major departure from previous models of global expert decision making, where attempts at dialogue and debate were largely absent and processes were open only to an exclusive expert elite.

In this way, the IAASTD is in harmony with a central theme of the more optimistic strands of the literature on globalization and civil society. These suggest that, with the opening up of opportunities for engagement at the global level and the increasing connections between local-level actors and issues and those in global arenas, the opportunities for participation and influence increases through a "global civil society" (Archibugi 2008; Edwards and Gaventa 2001; Keane 2003). With this opening up, processes become more complex and require increasingly sophisticated forms of mobilization by activists and movements in order to engage (Tarrow 1994). But the net result is a pluralization of knowledge and claims and inputs into cosmopolitan global contexts, which, it is argued, results ultimately in a more democratic and accountable system of governance and policymaking (Held and McGrew 2002; Heater 2002).

The IAASTD could be seen as one avenue for such new styles of engagement, knowledge production, and claim making; and, indeed, the rhetoric associated with it suggests that this is, in part, the wider aim. A vision of cosmopolitan diversity and democratic decision making is portrayed, governed by rules and procedures allowing rational decisions and objective science to prevail.

A closer look at the processes and practices of the IAASTD, however, reveals some major limits to such a vision. In particular, it highlights, following Fischer (2000), the important contemporary tensions between professional expertise and democratic governance, and that, as Jasanoff and Martello argue, with the reassertion of local knowledge claims in global environmental processes, "the construction of both the local and the global crucially depends on the production of knowledge and its interactions with power" (2004, 5). Tracing these knowledge-power interactions is thus central to any understanding of local-global engagements. The aim has been to go beyond the well-rehearsed rhetoric of participation, inclusion, and citizen engagement and ask: What has been the practice, experience, and underlying politics of the IAASTD? The next section looks at the particular interaction between diverse sources of expertise and the way this politics of knowledge constructs notions of citizenship.

Experts and Citizens

The assessment process witnessed the engagement of diverse forms of expertise beyond the "usual suspects" of accredited scientists and government representatives, and they included nongovernmental organizations (NGOs), farmers' groups, consumer organizations, and others. What has this revealed about the relationships between experts and citizens, and how have diverse forms of citizenship been practiced in such local to global engagements?

In international assessment processes of this sort much of the hard work comes in the review and editing process. Here the minutiae of textual differences are discussed and a particular wording and pitch is required. A (perhaps) apocryphal story suggested that the US government had employed a thousand people in the US Department of Agriculture and USAID to go over the final documents with a fine-tooth comb, picking up sections, paragraphs, and even words, which their negotiators would dispute in the final sessions before approval was granted any text. To be effective, this required hard work and the learning of new negotiation skills by NGO/CSO participants. As one complained: "Our work is unrecognizable in the final version. The odd bit here and there, but often not the meaning."[7] Another countered: "this is part of the re-shuffling of understanding that is the positive outcome of multi-stakeholder dialogues and efforts to create something new together."[8] The internal dynamics of author groups was critical along with the capacity for effective, inclusive facilitation.

But to what degree does this sort of slow, highly political negotiation process allow for the "injecting" of alternative, grassroots perspectives from farmers themselves? How does "the local" get represented in "the global"? And what kinds of knowledge politics emerge? In discussions with a variety of participants in the assessment, a number of themes were raised.[9] Everyone recognized that, because of the way the IAASTD was organized, "real" farmers and their organizations did not really get a look in—whether at the early consultation stages in the regions or subsequently. Some regarded this as a fundamental design flaw of the whole process, undermining the legitimacy of the effort as a whole; others saw it as probably a necessary consequence of convening such a process, but one that allowed space for representation by NGOs and other CSOs. For some this mediation role was not a problem: These were people who worked on the ground in different locations and so could reflect the concerns of farmers. Others saw the processes of intermediation and translation as problematic as well as the claims made by NGOs to "represent" others. Some industry and government participants, for example, claimed that GM crops were a concern to (Northern) NGOs but not to farmers from the Global South.[10]

Participants also reflected on their own positions—both as experts and as citizens from particular places, and how their origins, ethnicity, gender, and experience were intimately bound up with their contributions as experts. As one African author, a middle-class university lecturer in Zimbabwe who was trained in the UK but who came originally from a rural home in a farming area, observed: "Yes I am an economist, but I am also from Africa, and I am a woman. I have lived in these places, and experienced the life of farming in a dryland setting."[11] Of course, much politically correct talk is associated with the IAASTD about Southern perspectives and involvement, but, in practice, the Southerners who get a look-in are sometimes as elite—in their lifestyles, outlooks, and influences—as many of their Northern counterparts. Does living behind razor wire in a smart suburb of Harare or Nairobi provide special access and insights? Or is this just another of many different "lived citizenships" that are rather selectively added to the mix? Thus, in people's own experiences of the IAASTD a multiplication of identities, types of affiliation, and forms of solidarity are apparent. A fragmented and contingent notion of citizenship is realized through such experiences—constituting the wider political action that this implies (Leach and Scoones 2006).

The professed aim of the IAASTD was to involve a more diverse group of expertise than would be usual in a conventional approach, and a very conscious effort was made to be inclusive; however, in the end, it was deliberation on the basis of scientific evidence that would be the key. Thus, an interesting contradiction occurred in the simultaneous talk of engagement and involvement of diverse, multi-stakeholder perspectives and its confrontation with the ideal of consensus and an appeal to a universalized objectivity of science and expertise: the ultimate global vision. Often this tension was not addressed and led to some underlying challenges such that knowledge politics and power relations failed to be confronted, resulting in some major fudges. Yet, in a more pragmatic tone, one participant commented:

> Perhaps for the first time, different constituencies had to wrestle with the evidence and experiences that inform a point of view. These could no longer be dismissed as simply differing ideologies or power gradients. We *all* had to put our trust in the IAASTD principles. The hard part was getting all contributors to be accountable to them.[12]

Confronting Controversy: GM Crops

But what happened when people disagreed—on science, on values, and on politics? Perhaps inevitably the biggest controversy that dogged the IAASTD process was that surrounding GM (genetically modified and, specifically, transgenic) crops. When the assessment was proposed in 2002, this issue engendered a raging debate, particularly in Europe and across NGO and civil society groups around the world (Scoones 2002). While some from mainstream scientific institutions and biotechnology corporations dismissed this uproar as a diversion, one that was not based on "sound" understandings of science and one that resulted in the undermining of poverty reduction and development by withdrawing new scientific and technological opportunities, it was a debate that would not go away.

Many in the NGO community feared that the IAASTD was simply going to serve as a front for the backers of GM crops and that the enlistment of NGOs and civil society groups under an umbrella of participation and consultation was going to provide an illegitimate justification for recommending GM crops be central to future agricultural R and D strategies globally. Given the keen interest of some important industry players, as well as some major GM advocates within the CGIAR system for example, this fear was, given the timing, probably justified. For example, the pro-biotech, industry-funded website run by the ISAAA argued that the IAASTD would provide a scientific assessment of biotech crops and so perhaps "proof" of their utility.[13]

Following the report of the steering committee and the subsequent first plenary session in Nairobi,[14] alongside the thirty government representatives, six members of NGO/civil society groups had accepted invitations to serve on the Bureau of the assessment (including Greenpeace International, the Pesticide Action Network, and Practical Action), and so they were central to the overall governance. But so had representatives from "industry" (including Syngenta, Unilever), "consumers" (including the Center for Science in the Public Interest and Consumers International), "producers" (including International Federation of Agricultural Producers and the International Federation of Organic Agriculture Movements) and "institutions" (including the Third World Academy of Sciences, the World Conservation Union (IUCN), the CGIAR, and CAB International). This group of thirty to sixty government and thirty non-government organizations was not an easy group to convene, let alone one in which agreement on anything could be easily reached. A co-chair of the assessment reflected:

> This was a difficult time. No one trusted anyone else. X kept walking out. It was very disruptive, and we could not make much progress for a while. We had to be patient. The GM issue was a diversion. We had to get down to the real issues.[15]

While the GM debate continued to be discussed, and while it remained often the "elephant in the room," the overall framework and approach of the assessment cast the debate much wider. Indeed, by framing the overall debate in relation to broader questions of agricultural knowledge, science, and technology (AKST) within a loose framework that looked fundamentally at outcomes relating to poverty reduction and environmental management, it was possible for a much larger—some would say poorly focused—discussion to take place. This was framed not in terms of whether GM crops are somehow "good" or "bad" but in terms of what combination of technologies make sense given the diverse future requirements of the needs of different peoples in different parts of the world. Thus, the overall framing, and the decentralized process, managed at times to get away from the narrow perspective of the GM debate, which dominated discussion at that time by either firmly pro- or anti-camps. Debates centered on whether new GM crops met the exacting IAASTD goals on the basis of well-documented evidence. The challenge, of course, was that much talk of new biotechnology application in agriculture, by both the science establishment and the corporates alike, is one of prospect and promise. The evidence from the field remains weak, limited, and contradictory (Glover 2010). The argument presented is that "if only companies are given the freedom to operate, then all sorts of panaceas for the world's ills will be unleashed." This claim is countered by the argument that current evidence does not stand up to scrutiny and a highly precautionary stance must be applied to future options. Wider questions of corporate control, intellectual property, and biosafety were also introduced as arguments against a simple endorsement of GM crops. A stalemate therefore quickly emerged, with fundamentally different framings competing with each other.

The sense among Bureau members interviewed was that the GM issue was not the one to confront; yet, it persisted through the writing and reviewing process with attempts by different groups to insert elements of their positions. The final global synthesis report ended up quite equivocal, and this is reflected in the summary, which states:

> A problem-oriented approach to biotechnology R&D would focus investment on local priorities identified through participatory and transparent processes, and favor multifunctional solutions to local problems. These processes require new kinds of support for the public to critically engage in assessments of the technical, social, political, cultural, gender, legal, environmental and economic impacts of modern biotechnology.[16]

Interpretations of this final outcome differ (inevitably). Some view this as a fudge, a failure to address the issues; while others view this is a sensible way forward, one that settles an unhelpful debate and moves on. Certainly the private sector company representatives involved in GM technology found it unacceptable. They angrily abandoned the process in late 2007 before the conclusion, provoking a storm of controversy and leading to much frustration among certain writing teams, who had been subject to foot-dragging delays over many months.[17] A representative of CropLife International, a biotech industry umbrella body, indicated that this decision was prompted by "the inability of its members to get industry perspectives reflected in the draft reports."[18] In a clearly heart-felt opinion piece written for the *New Scientist*, Syngenta scientist Deborah Keith explained why she, along with other industry representatives, walked out:

> Despite our active participation, the draft IAASTD report does not adequately represent the contributions of plant science to sustainable agriculture.... The decision was not taken lightly, given our commitment to agricultural development and sustainability. But there was blatant disregard for the benefits of existing technologies, and for technology's potential to support agriculture's efforts to meet future crop needs. I think this was in part because the differences between various participants' perceptions about these technologies, and the scientific facts, were not maintained and highlighted. Sadly, social science seems to have taken the place of scientific analysis.[19]

Of course this sort of naive appeal to a particular set of "scientific facts" and a dismissal of what she calls "social science" has been typical of many interventions by the biotechnology industry over time, but the impasse that this created, with the industry lobby unable to countenance a compromise framed by interests other than their own, proved a big, and late, stumbling block, allowing certain governments to pull back from the process and back their industry lobbies.

Although approved by fifty-seven countries, the final document remained unsigned by the United States, Canada, and Australia, with the United Kingdom, in the end, signing up.[20] Objections are contained in the annexes of the agreed documents. The Canadian government resorted to a similar argument about "objectivity" in complaining that "there remain a number of assertions and observations that require more substantial, balanced and objective analysis."[21] Many in the NGO community believe that the real reason for the reluctance of certain countries to sign up was because of the pro-GM position of key governments and their unwillingness to back a document that, if not explicitly anti-GM, is certainly not enthusiastically in favor.[22] This is apparent, for example, in the US objection noted in the Annex to the Global Summary for Decision Makers: "the USA does not believe that there is sufficient balance in reflecting the use/range of new technologies, including modern biotechnology in Key Findings 10 and 11."[23]

Despite the failure of some governments to sign up, the conclusion of the final plenary session and the majority agreement of the final document by governments from across the world gave rise to exuberant celebrations by the NGO grouping whose members had worked so hard to influence the process. The press releases highlighting particular passages of the final document emphasized how "the old paradigm of industrial, energy-intensive and toxic agriculture is a concept of the past. The key message of the report is that small-scale farmers and agro-ecological methods provide the way forward."[24] In numerous press interviews, YouTube clips, and podcasts, Watson himself has argued that "business as usual is not an option."[25]

But did this change of tune and the promotion of a integrative, holistic vision really mean that local voices were finally being heard in the international arena? Was this the genuine success of an inclusive, deliberative process? Or, rather, was this another type of selective, global expertise getting the upper hand—through hard work, diligent campaigning, and the deployment of alternative forms of elite expertise? In the next section, the way expertise is constructed and negotiated in a "global" context is discussed along with the implications this process has for participation, accountability, and wider governance of international processes.

The Politics of Knowledge in Global Assessments

So what does the IAASTD experience suggest for wider debates about democracy and participation in global arenas?

The IAASTD reports, as we have seen, like many others of a similar ilk, represent the bringing together of diverse types of knowledge as largely unproblematic. The emphasis is on neutrality and objectivity. For example, the guidelines state that "assessment reports should be neutral with respect to policy, and deal objectively with scientific, technical and socio-economic factors."[26] But these assumptions are difficult to uphold under closer scrutiny. Further questions inevitably arise: Whose expertise counts? How are cultural and institutional commitments brought into supposedly neutral expert statements and review processes? What overt and tacit routines legitimate and validate collective knowledge? What happens to other forms of knowledge and expertise—with different epistemological and ontological bases? These processes played out in different ways in different parts of, and at different moments in, the assessment. Sometimes the knowledge encounters were productive and fruitful, challenging participants to reflect on assumptions and to include otherwise neglected perspectives. At other times, such engagements were less productive, being dominated by particular perspectives and interests.

While the explicit, formal design of the assessment was rather blind to the questions of knowledge politics, in practice in the author groups, the review process, and the wider discussion around the assessment intense reflection on knowledge, its validity, and the nature of expertise took place. As in the case of GM crops, contests over knowledge claims and the framing of issues have been very important. The end result allowed a plural set of perspectives to emerge despite attempts by powerful interests to constrain the debates. This shows, at one level, a sensitivity of the process to such issues. But this was not explicitly part of the formal design, and a key lesson has been that such issues of knowledge framing need to be more centrally and explicitly considered from the start.

A key feature of such assessments is that they are in some way "representative," investing as they do in large-scale—and very expensive—consultations. The IAASTD website makes great plays of the diversity of actors involved, and the Secretariat includes a number of Southern researchers, activists, and others. Clearly, simple forms of representation—direct or indirect—are impossible at a global level. But how do global processes of this sort gain legitimacy for what they do and how are representatives and representation constructed by the organization itself, its sponsors, and the actors involved?

As discussed above, the formal process allows for representation by different groups according to strict quotas, with nongovernment and government, NGO and business all carefully balanced numerically on the Bureau, for example. As an intergovernmental process, representation is also via states, with 110 countries involved and thirty government representatives from all regions on the Bureau. And in the public review process, the web commentary facility allows anyone with access to the Internet to have their say. This means representation, and ways to influence the process, can happen via multiple routes. The NGO/civil society grouping, for example, has been very active in mobilizing participants, engaging in debate, and tracking the process through a dedicated website. Equally, the US government invested substantial resources in the review process, persistently trying to get its view across and objecting to alternative framings.

The NGO/civil society grouping is seen by the conveners of the assessment as a key route through which voices of poorer farmers across the Global South can have a say, thus bringing wider legitimacy to the process and its outcomes. But this is an awkward intermediary, bridging position. Some NGO groups argue that, despite the fact that they have no formal mandate to represent "poor farmers," this is a legitimate role, one based on solid experience and dialogue with people in the field. Yet this position clearly comes with much baggage. It is far from neutral. Indeed, there is a clear line on many issues, linked to some high-profile, strategic campaigning, something that critics see as more reflective of a middle-class, left-leaning, European/North American position than the legitimate voice of the masses. In the context of the IAASTD, whether on issues concerning GM crops or industrial agriculture, some NGO groupings have been voluble and consistent in their positions, something not necessarily reflecting the diverse and often conflicting views of poorer farmers across the world.

A key challenge for democratic theory in an era of globalization is how collective perspectives, values, and outcomes are negotiated across diverse cultural and institutional settings at an international level. Global assessments, such as the IAASTD, claim to do this through a process of expert assessment supported by stakeholder consultations. But how collective is the "collective vision" that is exemplified in the final report? What have been the processes of exclusion, dissent, and controversy that lie behind an expert-approved "consensus"? What are the unwritten codes and practices that shape formal choices and decisions reflected in the final report? How have perspectives from particular places, including those drawing on more experiential knowledge, interacted with global ones situated in particular centers of power?

As we have seen, the final global report, as well as the summary for decision makers, has been at pains to include a diversity of views (IAASTD 2009). For some this is a "lowest common denominator consensus—a 24 hour wonder";[27] for others it is the result of effective inclusion, a process in which controversies have been dealt with and compromise sought. Three styles of knowledge politics were ongoing simultaneously in the IAASTD (Jasanoff 2005): "the view from nowhere," dominated by "objective," universalized facts and statistics, competed with "the view from somewhere," based on particular, located experiences and case studies, and this competition was mediated in turn by "the view from everywhere" that tried to incorporate, combine, and generate consensus through a complex representative stakeholder process defined by governance structure and the writing and review procedures. Each of these styles of knowledge politics acts to include and exclude, creating winners and losers in the process. Those able to move between such approaches—arguing their case on the basis of formalized data at the same time as drawing legitimacy from particular settings and experiences—were those most able to make the case that theirs was the consensual "view from everywhere."

The complexity and intensity of the process added to the processes of exclusion too. Only those with the time and resources—and endless patience and attention to detail—were able to engage effectively to the end. While opportunities arose for linking those in expert mediating roles with broader communities, this was often in practice limited. As one African author explained: "There is no money to do consultations. We are based here and try to reflect the situation, but we cannot go out and have discussions with farmers. We must look at the literature and find our way."[28] Indeed, it was often the practical difficulties of communicating and discussing under intensive deadlines that proved to be the major constraint. One African author put it as follows: "The time is too tight. The chapter draft comes, we have to revise it, and then we must go to the next meeting. My email was down for weeks here at the university so we are very behind on our chapter."[29]

The elaborate governance structure and procedural arrangements for the preparation of the reports created a particular style of knowledge making. This was centered on the principles of inclusion and deliberation but within severely circumscribed limits. Again, such formality excluded some. A set of institutionalized routines allowed for the involvement of different interest groups or "stakeholders"; each had particular representation on the decision-making body of the Bureau and each was supposed to have equivalent input into the expert-led report production and review process, garnering a procedural accountability and so, it was hoped, trust and confidence in the authority and legitimacy of the process. This structured form of representation thus aimed at global coverage, covering all bases and creating a comprehensive, all-encompassing approach to knowledge making on a global scale.

But these formal arrangements were of course also complemented by more informal interactions and processes of alliance building and lobbying. As discussed in relation to the NGO/civil society grouping (and no doubt replicated among governments and private-sector "interest groups"), much maneuvering took place to gain access and influence. Peer-to-peer relationships within the Africa writing group too allowed for more personal connections to be made and for informal networks to arise through the process, which transcended often the "interest group" categorization of the governance structure to create forms of association around the regional, African position vis à vis the "global" perspective.

This vision of multiple voices being heard in an open deliberative forum at the global level is certainly the ideal to which many aspire. In this sense, the IAASTD is seen as a potential for the realization of a global deliberative democratic institution, that numerous theorists and commentators have argued for (Dryzek 2002). A key argument of the IAASTD is that, through engaging multiple stakeholders in an open debate about the future, an institutional form will develop, resulting in more robust frameworks for policy decision making. This is an argument put forward by many involved in debates about institutional transformation, particularly when dealing with scientific debate and public controversy (Miller 2007).

The ideal is to create a "reflexive institution" that is inclusive and deliberative and allows multiple, culturally embedded versions to be discussed and a collective vision to be produced. It allows contrasting framings to be debated and different political and value positions to be acknowledged. It also does not bury uncertainty, controversy, or dissent; rather it makes these explicit in interrogating alternative options (Voss and Kemp 2006). This is a tough call, especially for disciplinary and professional orientations built on particular forms of certainty and expertise and where ambiguity is threatening and where it is unheard of to admit ignorance.

Beyond the conceptual discussion of principles, discussion of what a "reflexive institution" actually looks like is often vague, and certainly it is so at a global level. In many respects the IAASTD is seen by its proponents as an attempt to create a reflexive institution, although they do not use this language. Many of the key design principles are there—inclusivity, openness, plurality of knowledge, and a commitment to democratic processes. But there have been notable limitations. These center on two issues. The first involves the challenges of confronting uncertainty and controversy and the expectation that these will be resolved by rational, objective, scientific debate among expert peers. The second—and related—is the obscuring of very real struggles over knowledge, politics, and values in an attempt to construct the "view from everywhere" by seeing this primarily in terms of representation of different interest groups. These two gaps, I would argue, have at times created a lack of reflexivity in the process—a lack of ability to reflect on positions, framings, and politics, which sometimes has resulted in an inability to deal with the really tough issues and choices confronting the future of science and technology.

CONCLUSION

The key lessons from this case study are that the politics of knowledge must be made more explicit and that negotiations around politics and values must be put center stage. In addition, we must avoid black-boxing issues of uncertainty or more fundamental clashes over interpretation and meaning. And, finally, we must seek ways by which processes of participation and engagement can become more meaningful, democratic, and accountable.

These are, of course, major challenges at the center of debates about democratic theory, and they constitute the core of the concerns of this book. As Chantal Mouffe (2005) argues in a critique of the recent arguments for deliberative forms of democratic practice, a need exists to "bring politics back in." In a withering attack on those who believe "partisan conflicts are a thing of the past and consensus can now be obtained through dialogue" and the assumption that "thanks to globalization and the universalization of liberal democracy, we can expect a cosmopolitan future," Mouffe challenges this "post-political" position:

> Such an approach is profoundly mistaken and that, instead of contributing to the "democratization of democracy," it is at the origin of many of the problems that democratic institutions are currently facing. Notions such as "partisan-free democracy," "good governance," "global civil society," "cosmopolitan sovereignty," "absolute democracy,"—to quote only a few of the currently fashionable notions—all partake of a common anti-political vision which refuses to acknowledge the antagonistic dimension constitutive of "the political." Their aim is the establishment of a world "beyond left and right," "beyond hegemony," "beyond sovereignty," and "beyond antagonism." Such a longing reveals a complete lack of understanding of what is at

> stake in democratic politics and of the dynamics of constitution of political identities and, as we shall see, it contributes to exacerbating the antagonistic potential existing in society. (2005, 1–2)

It is this absence of an explicit attention to the political that has been perhaps the Achilles' heel of the IAASTD. The formal assessment process did not confront controversy head-on, even if the micro processes in author groups and review interactions certainly did. No procedures or mechanisms appeared to exist to either surface or deal with such debates and divergent views. A lack of recognition of antagonistic politics—over knowledge, identity, and the construction of futures—means that the cosmopolitan, deliberative ideal that the IAASTD presents as its model, suppresses, diverts, and bottles up such tensions; or, at least, it relegates them to off-the-record debates within text-writing and reviewing groups rather than making such issues central and explicit. How can this be addressed?

On a practical level, a key lesson for the IAASTD—and similar assessment processes—is the urgent need to inject some systematic reflexivity into the process, one that involves all parties. This requirement is an explicit way of meeting the challenge of Mouffe and others of ensuring that politics are central. As she argues:

> ... the belief in the possibility of a universal, rational consensus has put democratic thinking on the wrong track. Instead of trying to design the institutions which, through supposedly "impartial" procedures would reconcile conflicting interests and values, the task for democratic theorists and politicians should be to envisage the creation of a vibrant "agonistic" public sphere of contestation where different hegemonic political projects can be confronted.
>
> (Mouffe 2005, 3)

In focusing on the concept of "reflexive institutions" and the governance processes they require, this chapter highlights the challenge of finding ways that design elements can be introduced into the procedures and practices of assessments such as the IAASTD in ways that allow this type of explicit confrontation of politics, perspectives, values, and interests. While the design of the process, its governance, and institutional form can be criticized for lack of reflexivity, the behind-the-scenes negotiations over framings, values, and politics have, as we have seen, been heated and continuous. However, a key starting point is to make the framing of assumptions around diverse positions and knowledge claims more explicit: placing them front-stage, not just backstage. This of course does not mean that the examination of scientific issues should not take place; instead, such reflexivity hopefully results in increased rigor, avoiding the dangers of a false, fudged "consensus." I would argue that opening up both the inputs and outputs of the assessment process, including an acceptance that consensus and agreement may not be appropriate or desirable, can result in more effective, rigorous and more widely accepted outcomes (Stirling 2005). The IAASTD has been an ambitious attempt to create a forum for cross-stakeholder dialogue of a critical issue at the global level. It has inevitably been fraught and flawed, but there have been some important lessons learned, some of which have been highlighted by this chapter. The challenge for the future—as new, different issues emerge that require similar global responses—will be to develop new designs and processes that allow for even more effective, inclusive reflexive governance that build firmly on these lessons.

Notes

1. This chapter derives from earlier work on this subject (see: Scoones 2008; Scoones 2009; Scoones 2010), and was put together in 2011–12. The research was produced as part of the Citizenship, Participation and Accountability Development Research Centre based at the Institute of Development Studies, University of Sussex. I would like to thank colleagues in the "local-global" working group, together with Jan Aart Scholte, for feedback on earlier versions of this chapter, and to Stephen Biggs, John Gaventa, Marcia Ishii-Eiteman, Janice Jiggins, Beverly McIntyre, Erik Millstone, Marcelo Saguier, and Rajesh Tandon who provided detailed comments. I would also particularly like to thank the many people who were involved in the IAASTD process in different capacities who took time to discuss with me.
2. The Nobel Peace Prize 2007. Accessed July 2011. http://nobelprize.org/nobel_prizes/peace/laureates/2007/index.html.
3. What Is the International Assessment of Agricultural Knowledge, Science & Technology, IAASTD? Accessed July 2011. http://www.agassessment-watch.org/docs/IAASTD_on_three_pages.pdf.
4. Meetings of global authors were held in Turkey (November 2005), Bangkok (May 2006), Costa Rica (November 2006), and Cape Town (June 2007). Africa report meetings were held in Nairobi (January 2006), Dakar (June 2006), Addis Ababa (November 2006), and Cape Town (June 2007).
5. The formal hosts are the Food and Agriculture Organization, GEF (Global Environment Facility), United Nations Development Programme, United Nations Environment Programme, United Nations Educational, Scientific and Cultural Organization, the World Bank, and the World Health Organization. The UK Department for International Development is a significant backer of the assessment.
6. See www.agassessment.org. Accessed July 2011.
7. Interview, Zimbabwe, 2007.
8. Personal communication, August 2008.
9. See the thoughtful commentary on the fraught knowledge politics at play by IAASTD insider Janice Jiggins (Jiggins 2008).
10. In making such claims, of course, these commentators were offering an unreflective, alternative intermediary position, suggesting that their views were "better" representations of developing world farmers than those of NGOs.
11. Interview, Zimbabwe, 2006.
12. Personal communication, August 2008.
13. IAASTD to conduct agri-biotech assessment, April 7, 2006, CropBiotech Update, http://www.isaaa.org/kc.
14. Final Report of the Steering Committee for the Consultative Process on Agricultural Science and Technology (August 12, 2003). Accessed August 2011. http://www.

agassessment-watch.org/docs/final_report.pdf; Nairobi Plenary, minutes, August–September 2004; http://www.agassessment-watch.org/nairobi_minutes.html.

15. Interview, Sussex, September 2007.
16. http://www.agassessment.org/docs/SR_Exec_Sum_210408_Final.pdf (page 15).
17. See: "Monsanto and Syngenta withdraw from the assessment" (January 17, 2008) http://knowledge.cta.int/en/dossiers/cta_and_s_t/developments/iaastd_monsanto_syngenta_withdraw_from_the_assessment (accessed July 2011) (although actually Monsanto were not involved directly). See also: Anonymous (2008), "Deserting the Hungry?" *Nature* 451: 223–224; Anonymous (2008), "Off the Rails," *Nature Biotechnology* 26: 247; and E. Stokstad (2008), "Dueling Visions for a Hungry World," *Science* 319: 1474–1476. See also a commentary on the media response to IAASTD at http://www.bioscienceresource.org/commentaries/documents/BSRcommentary10.pdf.
18. *Nature*, January 17, 2008.
19. Deborah Keith, "Why I Had to Walk Out of Farming Talks," Opinion, *New Scientist* 2650, May 4, 2008.
20. http://www.publications.parliament.uk/pa/cm200708/cmhansrd/cm080609/wmstext/80609m0001.htm#column_6WS. Accessed August 2011.
21. http://www.agassessment.org/docs/Global_SDM_050508_FINAL.pdf. Accessed August 2011.
22. Phone interview, United Kingdom, 2008.
23. http://www.agassessment.org/docs/Global_SDM_050508_FINAL.pdf (annex, note 2). Accessed August 2011.
24. See NGO press release (April 15, 2008): http://www.agassessment-watch.org/docs/Civil%20Society%20Statement%20on%20IAASTD.pdf and that by Greenpeace (http://www.agassessment-watch.org/docs/greenpeace__15_april.pdf). Accessed July 2011.
25. See for example: http://www.youtube.com/watch?v=B-0B4Z-7A4s; http://www.guardian.co.uk/environment/audio/2008/apr/15/vidal.food.shortage?popup=true; http://www.guardian.co.uk/environment/2008/apr/15/food.unitednations1. Accessed August 2011.
26. Page 7, Annex 3, Principles and Procedures Governing an Intergovernmental Assessment on Agricultural Science and Technology, In: Final report of the Steering Committee, 12 August 2003.
27. Interview, Austria, April 2008.
28. Interview, university researcher, Zimbabwe, 2007.
29. Interview, university researcher, Zimbabwe, 2007.

References

Archibugi, D. 2008. *The Global Commonwealth of Citizens: Toward Cosmopolitan Democracy.* Princeton, NJ: Princeton University Press.

Dryzek, J. 2002. *Deliberative Democracy and beyond: Deliberative Democracy*. Oxford: Oxford University Press.

Edwards, M., and J. Gaventa, eds. 2001. *Citizen Global Action.* Boulder, CO: Lynne Rienner.

Fischer, F. 2000. *Citizens, Experts and the Environment: The Politics of Local Knowledge.* Durham, NC: Duke University Press.

Glover, D. 2010. "Exploring the Resilience of Bt Cotton's "Pro-Poor Success Story." *Development and Change* 41 (6): 955–981.

Heater, D. 2002. *World Citizenship: Cosmopolitan Thinking and Its Opponents.* London: Continuum.

Held, D., and A. McGrew, eds. 2002. *Governing Globalisation: Power, Authority and Global Governance.* Cambridge, UK: Polity Press.

IAASTD (International Assessment of Agricultural Knowledge, Science and Technology for Development). 2009. *Agriculture at a Crossroads: The Global Report International Assessment of Agricultural Knowledge, Science, and Technology.* Washington, DC: Island Press.

Jasanoff, S. 2005. *Designs on Nature: Science and Democracy in Europe and the US.* Princeton, NJ: Princeton University Press.

Jasanoff, S., and M. Martello. 2004. "Introduction: Globalization and Environmental Politics." In *Earthly Politics: Local and Global in Environmental Governance,* edited by S. Jasanoff and M. Martello, 1–30. Cambridge, MA: MIT Press.

Jiggins, J. 2008. "Bridging Gulfs to Feed the World." *New Scientist,* no. 2650, April 5, 16–17.

Keane, J. 2003. *Global Civil Society?* Cambridge, UK: Cambridge University Press.

Leach, M., and I. Scoones. 2005. "Science and Citizenship in a Global Context." In *Science and Citizens: Globalisation and the Challenge of Engagement,* edited by M. Leach, I. Scoones, and B. Wynne, 15–40. London: Zed Press.

Leach, M., and I. Scoones. 2006. "Mobilising Citizens: Social Movements and the Politics of Knowledge." *IDS Working Paper* No. 276. Brighton, UK: Institute of Development Studies.

Miller, C. 2007. "Democratization, International Knowledge Institutions and Global Governance," *Governance* 20 (2): 325–357.

Mouffe, C. 2005. *On the Political.* London: Routledge.

Scoones, I. 2002. "Can Agricultural Biotechnology Be Pro-poor? A Sceptical Look at the Emerging 'Consensus.'" *IDS Bulletin* 33 (4): 114–119.

Scoones, I. 2008. "Global Engagements with Global Assessments: The Case of the International Assessment of Agricultural Knowledge, Science and Technology for Development (IAASTD)." *IDS Working Paper* No. 313. Brighton, UK: Institute of Development Studies.

Scoones, I. 2009. "The Politics of Global Assessments: The Case of the International Assessment of Agricultural Knowledge, Science and Technology for Development (IAASTD)." *Journal of Peasant Studies* 36 (3): 547–557.

Scoones, I. 2010. The Politics of Global Assessments: The Case of the International Assessment of Agricultural Knowledge, Science and Technology for Development (IAASTD)." In *Globalizing Citizens: New Dynamics of Inclusion and Exclusion,* edited by J. Gaventa and R. Tandon, 96–118. London: Zed Press.

Stirling, A. 2005. "Opening Up or Closing Down? Analysis, Participation and Power in the Social Appraisal of Technology." In *Science and Citizens: Globalisation and the Challenge of Engagement,* edited by M. Leach, I. Scoones, and B. Wynne, 218–231. London: Zed Press.

Tarrow, S. 1994. *Power in Movement.* Cambridge, UK: Cambridge University Press.

Voss, J., and R. Kemp, eds. 2006. *Sustainability and Reflexive Governance.* Cheltenham, UK: Edward Elgar.

Index